10.20.M

WHO WERE THE FASCISTS

WHO WERE THE FASCISTS

Social Roots
of European Fascism

Edited by
STEIN UGELVIK LARSEN
BERNT HAGTVET
JAN PETTER MYKLEBUST

with the assistance of
GERHARD BOTZ
STEPHEN FISCHER-GALATI
REINHARD KÜHNL
PETER H. MERKL
STANLEY G. PAYNE

UNIVERSITETSFORLAGET

BERGEN – OSLO – TROMSØ

© UNIVERSITETSFORLAGET 1980
ISBN 82–00–05331–8

Cover design by Olaf G. Hexum

Distribution offices:

NORWAY
Universitetsforlaget
Postboks 2977, Tøyen
Oslo 6

UNITED KINGDOM
Global Book Resources Ltd.
37 Queen Street
Henley on Thames
Oxon RG9 1AJ

UNITED STATES and CANADA
Columbia University Press
136 South Broadway
Irvington-on-Hudson
New York 10533

Printed in Norway by
Reklametrykk A.s, Bergen

CONTENTS

PREFACE 9
PART 1. ON THE THEORETICAL STUDY OF COMPARATIVE FASCISM
Reinhard Kühnl   Introduction 12
Stanley G. Payne   The Concept of Fascism 14
Bernt Hagtvet and
Reinhard Kühnl   Contemporary Approaches to Fascism:
                      A Survey of Paradigms......................... 26
Stanislav Andreski   Fascists as Moderates.......................... 52
Alan S. Milward   Towards a Political Economy of Fascism 56
Bernt Hagtvet   The Theory of Mass Society and the Collapse of the
                      Weimar Republic: A Re-Examination 66
Reinhard Kühnl   Pre-Conditions for the Rise and Victory of Fascism
                      in Germany 118
Bernt Hagtvet and
Stein Rokkan   The Conditions of Fascist Victory 131
Juan J. Linz   Political Space and Fascism as a Late-Comer 153

PART 2. VARIETIES OF FASCISM IN AUSTRIA
Gerhard Botz   Introduction 192
Gerhard Botz   The Changing Patterns of Social Support for Austrian
                      National Socialism (1918–1945).................. 202
Bruce F. Pauley   Nazis and Heimwehr Fascists: The Struggle for Supre-
                      macy in Austria, 1918–1938 226
John Haag   Marginal Men and the Dream of the Reich: Eight
                      Austrian National-Catholic Intellectuals, 1918–1938 239
John Rath and
Carolyn W. Schum   The Dollfuss-Schuschnigg Regime: Fascist or
                      Authoritarian? 249

PART 3. THE FASCIST CORE COUNTRIES: GERMANY AND ITALY
Peter H. Merkl   Introduction 258
Peter H. Merkl   The Nazis of the Abel Collection: Why They Joined
                      the NSDAP 268
Nico Passchier   The Electoral Geography of the Nazi Landslide.... 283
Friedrich Zipfel   Gestapo and the SD: A Sociographic Profile of The
                      Organizers of Terror 301
Renzo de Felice   Italian Fascism and the Middle Classes 312
Joseph Baglieri   Italian Fascism and the Crisis of Liberal Hegemony:
                      1901–1922 318
David D. Roberts   Petty Bourgeois Fascism in Italy: Form and Content 337

PART 4. FASCISM IN EASTERN EUROPE

Stephen Fischer-Galati Introduction 350
Jerzy W. Borejsza East European Perceptions of Italian Fascism 354
Yeshayahu Jelínek Clergy and Fascism: The Hlinka Party in Slovakia and the Croatian Ustasha Movement 367
Zeev Barbu Psycho-Historical and Sociological Perspectives on the Iron Guard, the Fascist Movement of Romania . 379
Miklós Lackó The Social Roots of Hungarian Fascism: The Arrow Cross 395
György Ránki The Fascist Vote in Budapest in 1939 401

PART 5. THE DIFFUSION OF FASCISM IN SOUTHERN AND WESTERN EUROPE

Stanley G. Payne Introduction 418
Stanley G. Payne Social Composition and Regional Strength of the Spanish Falange 423
Philippe C. Schmitter The Social Origins, Economic Bases and Political Imperatives of Authoritarian Rule in Portugal 435
Beat Glaus The National Front in Switzerland 467
Zeev Sternhell Strands of French Fascism 479
Luc Schepens Fascists and Nationalists in Belgium, 1919–1940 ... 501
Daniéle Wallef The Composition of Christus Rex 517
Herman van der
Wusten and
Ronald E. Smit Dynamics of the Dutch National Socialist Movement (the NSB): 1931–1935 524
John D. Brewer The British Union of Fascists: Some Tentative Conclusions on its Membership 542
Maurice Manning The Irish Experience: The Blueshirts 557
Yannis Andricopoulos The Power Base of Greek Authoritarianism 568

PART 6. FASCISM AND NATIONAL SOCIALISM IN THE NORDIC COUNTRIES

Stein Ugelvik Larsen Introduction 586
Stein Ugelvik Larsen The Social Foundations of Norwegian Fascism 1933–1945: An Analysis of Membership Data 595
Jan Petter Myklebust
and Bernt Hagtvet Regional Contrasts in the Membership Base of the Nasjonal Samling 621
Hans Hendriksen Agrarian Fascism in Eastern and Western Norway: A Comparison 651
Sten Sparre Nilson Who Voted for Quisling? 657
Hans-Dietrich Loock Support for Nasjonal Samling in the Thirties 667
Risto Alapuro Mass Support for Fascism in Finland 678
Reijo E. Heinonen From People's Movement to Minor Party: The People's Patriotic Movement (IKL) in Finland 1932–1944 687

Henning Poulsen and
Malene Djursaa   Social Bases of Nazism in Denmark: The DNSAP . . 702
Bernt Hagtvet   On the Fringe: Swedish Fascism 1920–45 715
Asgeir Gudmundsson Nazism in Iceland 743

PART 7. COMPARING FASCIST MOVEMENTS

Peter H. Merkl 752

LIST OF CONTRIBUTORS 784

NAME AND SUBJECT INDEX 789

Preface

The last twenty years have witnessed a profound resurgence of interest in fascism, both as a political phenomenon, an economic system and as a set of cultural beliefs and values. This interest, cross-national in focus and inter-disciplinary in method, has produced a vast literature, ranging from biographies of fascist leaders, traditional historical narrative accounts and detailed electoral studies to discussions of fascist ideology and more ambitious attempts at theory-building across single cases. A corollary of this scholarly concern has been a growing debate on the concept of fascism itself: was it a generic phenomenon produced by a deep crisis within Western civilization, or can it more properly be understood as a national response to specific problems arising out of and comprehensible only in the context of national historical trajectories?

To these questions, this volume is devoted. Our purpose is to present a comparative overview of European fascism focusing on the socio-economic background and the collective and individual motivations behind the various fascist movements.

The frontiers of research differ considerably from country to country. Hence the contributions to this volume vary both in terms of scope, empirical grounding and comprehensiveness. These variations become particularly glaring when comparing the material available on the larger fascist movements with research on the peripheral ones. In this book we have made an attempt to redress this imbalance by deliberately devoting more space to the lesser-known fascist parties. There is of course no argument that fascism in Germany and Italy was far more important than similar movements on the European fringe. But one leading idea behind this work is that not all fascist movements were sheer imitations. Most warrant study on their own terms. They all help to shed light on a complex phenomenon from new angles. The fascist impulse spread throughout Europe and was filtered through the political cultures of a dozen countries. What became specifically national in each movement, and what retained the character of borrowings from the ideological centres is in itself worth studying.

Specifically, we want to draw attention to the following questions:

1. What is the best way to test various theories of fascism? How far can a strict sociological analysis take us in building a theory on the pre-conditions of fascist success in Europe? Which questions remain unanswered after a quantitative analysis of this kind has been completed?

2. Our aim is to construct a theory of fascism which is explicitly comparative. To what extent can comparative sociological analysis be brought to bear on the controversial issue of «generic» fascism? What are the common features of the fascist impulse in Europe? Do these form a coherent pattern sufficiently general to warrant a concept of «generic» fascism? What precisely is the role of membership studies and electoral analyses for elucidating this question?

3. On a more practical level: What should the standards be for getting access to archives and organizing the vast material now available on the fascist movements in the interwar period? Would it be possible, either through UNESCO or other international scholarly networks, to work out procedures in this field? In our work, systematic comparisons across countries have been made more difficult by the existence of numerous classification methods. Without some common agreement on what constitutes a category, cross-national research is in constant danger of being rendered meaningless.

4. How should international co-operation between scholars in this field be organized? Should there be more institutionalized means of information exchange, a clearing central of some kind, more systematic attempts to publish abstracts of new work, or even a journal solely devoted to studies of fascism? We want to raise these questions in the scholarly community and express the hope that this book will show the value of international co-operation in this field. The annual output of books now clearly exceeds what one single individual can digest in reasonable time. With more reference work, including summaries, duplication of efforts could be diminished and inspire further collective endeavors. We hope this book will accelerate further development along these lines.

The book in its present form is an outgrowth of the proceedings at a conference on comparative European fascism, held in Bergen, Norway from June 19 to 21, 1974. The conference was called to make a survey of the state of research on the social bases of fascist movements in Europe and facilitate communication among scholars. In editing the book we have aimed at comprehensiveness to make it useful as a text-book for courses both in history and the social sciences. Since the papers presented at the conference did not cover all the countries we wished to analyze, nor were sufficiently broad in scope, we decided to solicit original contributions from other scholars in the field. This explains the delay in preparing the entire manuscript for publication. We are most grateful to our assistant editors Gerhard Botz, Stephen Fischer-Galati, Reinhard Kühnl, Peter H. Merkl and Stanley G. Payne for their efforts to organize their sub-sections.

The reader will find as many as five articles on Norway. This is in part due to the availability of data on Norwegian fascism, information which hitherto has been largely inaccessible to English-speaking readers. But this predominance of Scandinavian work also reflects the book's origin as part of the research on the NS conducted at the University of Bergen.

The book has been edited in a team, but Bernt Hagtvet assumed a major responsibility for creating order and terminological coherence out of a series of disparate contributions. In this work he sought the advice and encouragement of the fellows and students of Nuffield College, Oxford, during the academic year 1975/76, to whom we are greatly indebted. Derek Urwin and Francis Castles, of the University of Bergen and the Open University, UK, respectively, also gave generous help in commenting on drafts presented to them. Esther Nilsen and Aslaug Aaseth undertook the laborious work of typing the many corrected versions. Our editors at Universitetsforlaget Knut Lie, and Janikke Mietle have given us constant support throughout the production of the book. Their care and professional guidance have helped produce a better book. We would like to express our gratitude to them all.

Finally, we should also like to record our gratitude to UNESCO for a grant under the Participation Programme which helped defray the cost of the conference. The University of Bergen provided facilities and financial support for which we are also grateful.

Bergen, May 1980

Stein Ugelvik Larsen   *Bernt Hagtvet*   *Jan Petter Myklebust*

PART 1

ON THE THEORETICAL STUDY OF COMPARATIVE FASCISM

Reinhard Kühnl — Introduction

Stanley G. Payne — The Concept of Fascism

Bernt Hagtvet and
Reinhard Kühnl — Contemporary Approaches to Fascism:
A Survey of Paradigms

Stanislav Andreski — Fascists as Moderates

Alan S. Milward — Towards a Political Economy of Fascism

Bernt Hagtvet — The Theory of Mass Society and the Collapse of the
Weimar Republic: A Re-Examination

Reinhard Kühnl — Pre-Conditions for the Rise and Victory of Fascism
in Germany

Bernt Hagtvet and
Stein Rokkan — The Conditions of Fascist Victory

Juan J. Linz — Political Space and Fascism as a Late-Comer

Introduction

REINHARD KÜHNL

In this section several perspectives are employed to review European fascism:

– To provide perspectives on the body of literature on fascism from both sides of the Atlantic, we have included two survey articles. From their different vantage points, Stanley G. Payne, Reinhard Kühnl and Bernt Hagtvet give overviews of the state of research on fascism, assessing the value of the most common approaches in the study of fascism;

– Stanislav Andreski takes issue with the common assumption that fascism was an extremism of the center. Instead he offers the thesis that in both theory and practice the various fascist movements, rather than being extremist, occupied at least on some important points, a *middle* ground between the extreme positions of the Left and the Right;

– Alan S. Milward expresses some doubts upon the thesis that we can understand the actual working of fascist regimes by reference to the economic interests of the clientele which were originally drawn to fascism. He sees in the restrictions imposed on large-scale private enterprise an argument against the hypothesis which makes fascism essentially a continuation of capitalist dominance;.

– Bernt Hagtvet focuses on the downfall of the Weimar Republic to question the validity of mass theory as a method to explain Nazi mobilization. Testing the writings of Arendt, Lederer, Neumann and Kornhauser against the historical record, he assesses the utility of mass theory in analysing strains upon regimes;

– Reinhard Kühnl sees the demise of Weimar democracy as the result of the interplay between structural weaknesses in the German polity (for example a strong tradition of authoritarian deference, the absence of a decisive democratic breakthrough) and conjunctural incidents (defeat in World War I, inflationary crises, and the legacy of defeat in the scramble for overseas territories);

– Stein Rokkan and Bernt Hagtvet try to untangle the preconditions for fascist successes in Western Europe by building a geo-political model using macro-historical variables linked to the peripheralization in the world economy since 1500 of those territories that were later to succumb to fascist rule. This long-term view is combined with a consideration of the timing of national unification and territorial consolidation to explain why Italy and Germany exhibited the typical «accumulation of crises syndrome»: the simultaneous occurrence of several developmental crises that severely limited the time and capability of the political system to adapt;

– Juan J. Linz elaborates his concept of political space to explain the room for manoeuvre available to a latecomer such as fascism. Only by employing the most uncommon and cruel political methods could the fascists penetrate the party system space of Europe which had been filled through earlier political mobilization arising from the State/civil society/capitalist reproduction relationship, industrialization and

12

democratization. Linz also contributes a list of seven factors which may explain the failure and success of fascist movements in Europe.

In their scope and methodological diversity, these essays convey an impression of vitality. The variety of methods is well suited to the phenomenon itself: its elusiveness and complexity still make fascism a subject of controversy. However, one common theme deserves to be emphasized. In all of these contributions it is hard to say which profession prevails: the inter-disciplinary approach is evident. Hopefully, this indicates a trend which will continue to gain momentum in the years to come.

The Concept of Fascism

STANLEY G. PAYNE

Ever since the March on Rome, political analysts and historians have tried to formulate an interpretation capable of explaining the phenomenon of European fascism. As the only genuinely novel or original form of radicalism emerging from World War I, and one that seemed to involve multiple ambiguities if not outright contradictions, fascism did not readily lend itself to monocausal explanation or a simple unified theory. For more than half a century the debate has gone on, and there is still no general consensus regarding an explanatory concept.[1]

The principal theoretical concepts of fascism have been directed primarily either toward a definition of the underlying nature of this species of politics, its overall significance, or more commonly, the principal sources or causes that gave it life. For convenience's sake, they may be summarized in nine categories:

1. A violent, dictatorial agent of bourgeois capitalism.
2. The product of a cultural or moral breakdown.
3. The result of neurotic or pathological psychosocial impulses.
4. The product of the rise of amorphous masses.
5. The consequence of a certain stage of economic growth, or historical sequence of national development.
6. A typical manifestation of twentieth-century totalitarianism.
7. A struggle against «modernization».
8. The expression of a unique radicalism of the middle classes.
9. The denial that such a thing as «generic fascism» ever existed due to the extreme differences between putatively fascist movements, and hence denial of the possibility of a general concept of «fascism».

Each of these theories or concepts will be briefly considered in turn. Before doing so, however, it should be pointed out that very few who attempt to develop a causal theory or explanatory concept of fascism make a serious effort at empirical definition of what they mean by the term, that is, to exactly which parties, movements or forces they refer. Aside from general references to the NSDAP and PNF (normally both together, without much effort to distinguish between the two), it is more often than not merely assumed that the identity of «fascists» is understood, and all manner of right authoritarian and anti-leftist forces are frequently thrown into a general conceptual grab-bag under this label. Hence the very lack of an empirical definition of what is meant by fascism, and precisely the groups to which the term is thought to refer, has been a major obstacle to conceptual clarification of the phenomenon.

Fascism as a Violent, Dictatorial Agent of Bourgeois Capitalism

The notion that fascism was primarily to be understood as the agent of «capitalism», «finance capital», the «bourgeoisie», or some combination thereof, is one of the oldest, most standard and widely diffused interpretations. It was formulated to some extent even before the March on Rome, and began to be given general currency – though referring primarily only to Italy – as early as 1923 in the formulations of the Hungarian Communist Gyula Sas[2] and the German Clara Zetkin[3]. This became the standard communist and Third International interpretation of fascism, and was also adopted by some non-communists as well. Leading exponents of the concept were R. Palme Dutt[4] and Daniel Guérin[5], though some serious qualifications were introduced into the original Marxist interpretation by Franz Borkenau[6]. Leading recent exponents of the Marxist concept of fascism are Reinhard Kühnl[7], Nicos Poulantzas[8], Boris Lopukhov[9], Alexander Galkin[10], and Mihaly Vajda[11].

Among the leading critics of the Marxist theory are Henry A. Turner, Jr.[12], A. James Gregor[13], Renzo de Felice[14], and Tim Mason[15]. Their data indicate that the main support of big business in Germany and Italy, for example, went to the right-wing DNVP and ANI, respectively, and they argue that once in power Hitler and also Mussolini moved increasingly to control and subordinate capitalist interests. The latter point has to some extent been incorporated into the variants of the Marxist concept of fascism as formulated by Galkin and Vajda.

In general, those who follow the Marxist concept of fascism do not distinguish – or reject the significance of any possible distinction – between the core fascist groups and forces of more conservative right authoritarianism.

Fascism as the Product of a Cultural or Moral Breakdown

Historians of culture in Germany and Italy, led by such figures as Benedetto Croce[16] and Friedrich Meinecke[17], have seen the general phenomenon of European fascism as the product of cultural fragmentation and moral relativism in European ideas from the late nineteenth century on. In this view, the crisis of World War I and its aftermath, producing intense economic dislocation, social conflict and cultural anomie, resulted in a kind of spiritual collapse that permitted new forms of radical nationalism to flourish. One of the most cogent statements of this approach will be found in a study by Peter Drucker.[18]

The weakness of the «cultural or moral crisis» approach alone is that it only tries to explain what conditions permitted fascist movements to develop, without accounting for their specific ideas, forms or goals. Quite a different approach has been taken by A. James Gregor in his *The Ideology of Fascism* (New York, 1969), which argues that Italian fascism developed a coherent ideology that was not the product of a nihilistic cultural collapse but rather the consequence of specific new cultural, political and sociological ideas stemming from Western and Central Europe in the late nineteenth and early twentieth centuries.

Fascism as the Result of Neurotic or Pathological Psychosocial Impulses

There are three principal, though considerably different, statements of this concept. One of the best-known is Erich Fromm's *Escape from Freedom* (New York, 1941, 1965), which contended that fascism should be seen as the product of decaying central European middle-class society, but differed from the standard Marxist approach by laying the main emphasis not on direct economic factors but on feelings of isolation, impotence, anomie and frustration among middle-class people.

15

A more extreme Freudian approach may be found in Wilhelm Reich's *The Mass Psychology of Fascism* (New York, 1930, 1946, 1970), which propounded a psychosexual explanation of the origins and nature of fascism. Reich's interpretation viewed fascism as a matter of sexual repression and sadomasochistic compensatory and aggressive impulses, and as the natural consequence of a «bourgeois society» grounded on sexual repression.

A different but somewhat related approach may be found in the work of Theodor Adorno, et al., entitled *The Authoritarian Personality* (New York, 1950). The implication of this study was that fascism could be understood as the prime expression of certain «authoritarian personality» traits that tended toward rigidity, repression and dictatorship, and might be most commonly expected among the interwar central European middle classes.

The weakness of this approach to the understanding of fascism is the essentially speculative nature of the concepts of Fromm and Reich, and the peculiarly reductionist nature of the latter's sexual ideas, which cannot be rendered methodologically applicable to the main dimensions of the problem. The «authoritarian personality» inventory is more empirical and specific, but subsequent data collection has not been able to substantiate clearly any assumptions about middle-class or central European personality traits in this regard.

Fascism as the Product of the Rise of Amorphous Masses

Another concept of fascism considers it to be the product of unique qualitative changes in European society, as the traditional class structure gives way to large, undifferentiated and atomized populations – the «masses» of urban, industrial society. This idea was first advanced by José Ortega y Gasset[19], and in varying ways has been reformulated by Emil Lederer[20], Talcott Parsons[21] and Hannah Arendt[22], and perhaps most cogently by William Kornhauser[23]. This approach emphasizes the irrational, anti-intellectual and «visceral» nature of the fascist appeal to «mass man», and thus to some extent may be thought to complement the «cultural crisis» concept.

This approach tends, however, to obfuscate the extent to which practical ideological content and cogent appeals to tangible interests figured in the programs and practice of the fascist movements, as well as the extent to which many of their supporters were still identified and definable as members of structured social or institutional sectors.

Fascism as the Consequence of a Certain Stage of Economic Growth, or Historical Phases of National Development

All four of the preceding approaches to understanding and categorizing fascism were «classical concepts», formulated originally in the 1920s and early 1930s, and couched in terms of fundamental interests or impulses of European society or its economic structure. A different approach emerged twenty years after the defeat of Nazi Germany, and was influenced by general ideas about the structural and political imperatives of economic modernization and the recent experiences of newly emerging «Third World» countries.

The stages of growth or development concept held that the process of modernization and industrialization frequently tended to produce severe internal conflict as the balance of power shifted between or threatened various social and economic groups.

16

Those who lean toward this approach differ from the standard Marxists in that they do not reduce the conflict to a capital versus labor approach, but define it more broadly in terms of a large range of social/structural forces and do not suppose that fascism is merely the agent of «monopoly capital» as a primary force.

Two of the leading exponents of this approach are A. F. K. Organski and Ludovico Garruccio. Organski[24] has suggested that the potential for fascism arises at the point at which the industrial sector of the economy first begins to equal in size and labor force that of the primary sector, creating the potential for severe social conflicts that serve to elicit aggressive nationalism and authoritarian government. The trouble with this concept is that its author has never refined it sufficiently to make it uniquely applicable to Italy and other countries undergoing a «fascist» experience, and as such it cannot apply to Germany (nor does its author attempt so to apply it). Most countries passing through that stage of growth have never known anything that could be called fascism.

Perhaps the most serious effort to understand fascism in terms of broad comparative patterns of development and modernization is Ludovico Garruccio's *L'Industrializzazione tra nazionalismo e rivoluzione* (Bologna, 1969). It suggests that what is known as fascism was the central European variant of a common period of crisis, normally issuing into authoritarian government, that accompanies the effort of modern nations (or empires, in the case of Russia) to establish their identity and power on a modern basis, overcome internal conflict and complete their economic or social modernization. This concept is extremely suggestive, and may help to explain the relationship of fascism to communism and to Third World development dictatorships, but fails to identify or explain the unique historical features of European fascism.

Fascism as a Typical Manifestation of Twentieth-Century Totalitarianism

In the immediate aftermath of World War II, when the specter of a Europe dominated by Hitlerian Nazism was replaced by that of one dominated by Stalinist Communism, a new line of interpretation developed among some Western political theorists which suggested that fascism, and particularly German National Socialism, did not constitute a unique category or genus, but was merely one typical manifestation of the much broader and more sinister phenomenon of twentieth-century totalitarianism, which would endure long after the specific fascist movements had expired.[25] This concept momentarily enjoyed considerable vogue in certain Western countries during the 1950s, but soon drew increasing criticism. Hannah Arendt, author of one of the leading books on the historical origins of totalitarianism, excepted Mussolini's Italy from the whole category of totalitarian systems, and that undercut the concept of generic fascism as «totalitarianism». In a major article, Wolfgang Sauer[26] drew attention to common features of national socialism with fascist movements and the differences from communist ones, casting doubt on the common identity of generic totalitarianism. Western theorists have in general encountered increasing difficulty in defining totalitarianism, and some have doubted its existence as a continuous, comparable category.[27]

Fascism as the Resistance to Modernization

The concept that fascism is to be understood above all as an expression of resistance to «modernization» or «transcendence» has become especially popular in Western countries during the past twenty years, and has been given varying formulation by

17

such diverse theorists and historians as Ernst Nolte, Wolfgang Sauer, Henry A. Turner, Jr., Barrington Moore, Jr., and Alan Cassels. What the proponents of this approach have in common is the emphasis on a definition of fascist movements as opponents of urbanization, industrialization, liberal education, rationalist materialism, individualism, social differentiation and pluralist autonomy, and international cooperation or peace. Though the concept of modernization is rarely defined as such, the preceding inventory of referential phenomena seems to be what these analysts have in mind, and it is of course intimately bound up with Western liberal democracy. Nolte, in his classic *Three Faces of Fascism* (Munich, 1963; New York, 1966), argues that fascism was, among other things, opposed to international peace and modern «transcendence», a philosophical term that seems to be related to the concept of modernization in the social sciences. For Wolfgang Sauer, fascism was the political movement of the «losers» in the modernization process. Henry A. Turner, Jr., largely agrees with them, postulating that fascism was the product of the forces that oppose all those phenomena associated with modernization.[28] Barrington Moore believes that fascism was the product of a modernization process controlled by martial, rural élites.[29] Alan Cassels offers, however, a major qualification to the anti-modernist thesis by his concept of «two faces of fascism», suggesting that in some underdeveloped countries fascism was a modernizing force but turned against the modernization process in countries like Germany that were already industrialized.[30]

Some of the major critics of the concept of fascism as mere reaction and antimodernism are A. James Gregor, Karl D. Bracher and Renzo de Felice. Gregor has documented the appeal of the Italian movement for the construction of a new industrial Italy, its stress on technological futurism and productivism, the expansion of Italian industrialization and ecological *ridimensionamento*.[31] De Felice makes the same points, and goes beyond to stress the similarity of some of the concepts of Italian fascists and Jacobins, the roots of the Italian movement in eighteenth-century ideals and its faith in education in building the new Italy.[32] Karl D. Bracher extends Cassels' concept of the ambivalence of some fascist movements to National Socialism as well, stressing the latter's originality and unique revolutionary qualities.[33]

More categorical is the interpretation of Eugen Weber, which finds in various forms of national socialism the characteristic revolution of the twentieth century, and considers some varieties of fascism to be as revolutionary as communist movements. Weber emphasizes that some fascist movements mobilized large numbers of peasants and workers; in more backward countries they filled the role of a revolutionary lower-class movement for drastic socio-economic change.[34]

Fascism as a Unique Radicalism of the Middle Classes

At least two leading scholars have viewed fascism as a unique form of radicalism developed by and expressing the autonomous interests of the middle classes, as distinct from upper-class élites and worker movements. Seymour M. Lipset has presented an interpretation of fascism as an independent force quite apart from aristocratic élite reaction or proletarian radicalism, representing unique new twentieth-century forces.[35] Renzo de Felice employs much the same concept with regard to the social and cultural definition of Italian fascism as the vehicle of new radical middle-class élites distinct from the old liberal upper-middle class forces or new proletarian Socialists.[36]

18

Denial of the Coherence of any Concept of Generic Fascism

The debate about the definition, origins, causes, meaning and significance of fascism has now gone on for more than half a century, and is no nearer resolution than ever. Indeed, it may be that the passage of time, rather than providing definitive answers, simply provides the perspective for more questions. Further research, rather than producing agreement, provides evidence for new theories and the continuation of old debates. Thus considerable doubt has been cast on the classic concepts of fascism as sufficient grounds for understanding in and of themselves, but no consensus has been reached regarding their substitution.

It may be noted that very little attention was paid by the formulators of the classic concepts to the question of empirical definition and taxonomy of fascist movements themselves, even to the extent of defining exactly what characteristics made a move-ment «fascist» and exactly which political forces were understood to be «fascist» and which were not. Nearly all the theorists of fascism have as a minimum referred to both Italian fascism and German National Socialism as part of the same generic category, but even that identity has become increasingly a subject of dispute.

In recent years a number of leading scholars in various Western countries have adopted an extreme nominalist position and denied the very existence of a common political species or category of «fascism» that could embrace a variety of movements in diverse countries in terms of common qualities or characteristics. Renzo de Felice finds Italian fascism and German National Socialism fundamentally distinct, incapable of belonging to a common species. Karl D. Bracher takes much the same position, and like De Felice, points out other extreme differences in more widely scattered putative-ly fascist movements. Henry A. Turner, Jr., also suggests that the label is a red herring, and proposes that such movements be re-classified with regard to their relationship to the fundamental question of modernization. The analysis of fascism has thus come full circle, from a variety of monocausal explanations to the denial that the generic phenomenon even existed.

The Need for a Criterial Definition of Generic Fascism

The only attempt at a comprehensive description of the full range of European fascist movements remains Ernst Nolte's *Die Krise des liberalen Systems und die faschis-tischen Bewegungen* (Munich, 1968). In it Nolte recognized the need for some sort of «fascist minimum», a set of criteria that could set standards according to which a given political movement might be objectively recognized and defined as fascist, or not. He suggested six points of criteria:

> Anti-Communism
> Anti-Liberalism
> Anti-Conservatism
> Leadership Principle
> Party-Army
> Aim of Totalitarianism

This criterial description represented a significant advance in clarity over preceding informal and off-hand suggestions that other writers made merely in passing. None-theless, it seems to me inadequate in the following respects:a) While it recognizes the distinctive fascist negations, it fails to deal fully with characteristic goals and program (if indeed such existed) or to define what at the time seemed most striking about fascists – their particular style and choreography; b) The reference to fascist anti-conservatism, while essentially correct, tends to blur the fact that fascists always had to rely at least momentarily on rightist allies to come to power; c) Though all fascistic parties tended toward strong personal leadership, it may be misleading to impute to them the predominantly German character of the *Führerprinzip;* d) Most fascist parties sought, but never achieved, a genuine «party-army»; e) The goal of totalitarianism is an ambiguous formulation, difficult to define or apply; f) The distinctively fascist form of nationalism and political radicalism cannot be understood without reference to the ultimate goal of some form of imperialism or at least a drastic realignment of the nation's status and power relations in the world.

Given the difficulty in arriving at a common definition of the putatively fascist movements, it is always possible that the extreme nominalists and skeptics could be right, and that a true «fascist minimum» did not exist. Against such skepticism, we have the relative agreement of the majority of contemporary observers in the 1930s that a new form and style of politics had emerged in the radical new nationalist movements of Europe customarily called fascist, a position generally adopted by the majority of scholars and analysts since. But what were the basic common qualities generally referred to by this label? We are still left with the problem of an adequate description.

A Possible Typological Description of Generic Fascism

It seems possible, at least hypothetically, to achieve this goal through a typological description of the principal features held in common by the movements we refer to as fascist – thus establishing justification for our use of the generic concept – while at the same time taking into account valid arguments by critics of the generic concept through recognition that such a common description does not by any means exhaust the inventory of major characteristics or goals of individual movements. It would only define the minimal characteristics that they had in common as distinct from other types, though specific fascist groups sometimes had other beliefs, characteristics and goals of major importance to them that did not contradict the common features of generic fascism but were simply added to them or went beyond them.

If an analogy were made for morphological purposes, fascism would then be understood to constitute a certain political species, one of about half a dozen that compose the broader genus of modern revolutionary mass movements. In order to arrive at a criterial definition applicable to the species, it then seems appropriate to follow a suggestion made by Juan J. Linz and identify a) the fascist negations, b) common points of ideology and goals, and c) special common features of style and organization.

A. The Fascist Negations:

Anti-liberalism
Anti-communism
Anti-conservatism, but of a more qualified nature, with a degree of willingness to compromise at least temporarily, with rightist groups and principles.

B. Ideology and Goals:

Creation of a new nationalist authoritarian state not merely based on traditional principles or models.

20

Organization of some new kind of regulated, multi-class integrated national economic structure capable to some extent of transforming social relations, whether called national syndicalist, national socialist or national corporatist.

The goal of empire or a revolution in the nation's relationship with other powers.

Specific espousal of an idealist, voluntarist creed, normally involving the attempt to realize a new form of modern, self-determined secular culture.

C. Style and Organization:

Emphasis on esthetic structure of meetings, symbols and political choreography, stressing romantic and/or mystical aspects.

Attempted mass mobilization with militarization of political relationships and style, and with the goal of a mass party militia.

Positive evaluation of – not merely willingness to use – violence.

Extreme stress on the masculine principle and male dominance, while espousing an organic view of society.

Exaltation of youth above all other phases of life, emphasizing the conflict of generations, though within a framework of national unity.

Specific tendency toward an authoritarian, charismatic, personal leadership style of command, whether or not to some degree elective.

Space precludes full discussion of the components of this inventory, but it can perhaps serve as a guideline to explain in most cases what serious scholars refer to as fascist movements, while recognizing that it can be used as an analytical tool only as a relatively integrated whole. There is no implication that every single characteristic in the inventory was unique to fascist movements, for most individual facets might be discovered to have existed individually or partially within a number of other radical groups. The uniqueness of fascism as a political species was rather that only fascist-type movements shared each of these characteristics (if in varying degrees) jointly and simultaneously: the suggested typology will be of use in identifying a specific movement as fascist only if the group in question exhibits not merely most but all or almost all of the qualities described.

The Varieties of Fascism

As explained, identification of a typology is not intended to imply that within the species of fascism all groups were fundamentally about the same and did not differ greatly among themselves with regard to further national characteristics, beliefs, values and goals above and beyond those minimal features which they all held in common. Much confusion has resulted from the assumption that if fascism is to be identifiable as a generic phenomenon it must somehow be regarded as a uniform type bearing essentially homogeneous traits, whereas in fact it was a broad species that included widely varying subtypes or subspecies.

Among the subspecies or «varieties of fascism», in Eugen Weber's telling phrase, a minimum of six may be identified:

1. Paradigmatic Italian fascism, pluralistic, diverse and not easily definable in simple terms. Forms to some extent derivative appeared in France, England, Belgium, Hungary, Austria, Romania and possibly even Brazil.

2. German National Socialism, a distinct and remarkably fanatical movement, and the only one of the entire species to achieve a total dictatorship and so to begin to develop its own system. Somewhat parallel or derivative movements emerged in

Scandinavia, the Low Countries, the Baltic states and Hungary, and more superficially in several satellite states during the war.

3. Spanish Falangism. Though to some extent derivative from the Italian form, it became a kind of Catholic and culturally more traditionalist type that was more marginal to the species.

4. The Romanian Legionary or Iron Guard movement, a mystical, kenotic form of semi-religious fascism that represented the only notable movement of this kind in an Orthodox country and was also marginal to the species.

5. Szalasi's «Hungarist» or Arrow Cross movement, somewhat distinct from either the Hungarian national socialists or Hungarian proponents of a more moderate and pragmatic Italian-style movement, momentarily perhaps the second most popular fascist movement in Europe.

6. Abortive undeveloped fascisms attempted through bureaucratic means by right-wing authoritarian regimes, mainly in Eastern Europe during the 1930s. None of these efforts, however, produced fully formed and complete fascist organizations.

The Need to Distinguish Between Fascist Movements and Fascist Regimes

Much of the confusion about defining a typology of fascism has stemmed from the failure to distinguish between fascist movements and regimes. Nearly all fascist parties failed to develop beyond the movement stage, and even in Italy the fascist party never assumed full power over the government and all the institutions of the country. Hence in the case even of Mussolini one cannot speak of a total party regime system as in Nazi Germany or Communist Russia.

In the absence of examples other than Nazi Germany of situations in which fascist-type parties came to full power or totally dominated regimes, it must be recognized that we are speaking of certain generic tendencies in the form of movements, but not of systems. This also says much about the limitations of the appeal and strength of fascism, even in the supposed «fascist era», and underlines the fact that the historic significance of the whole phenomenon was primarily bound up with Hitlerism and not with generic fascism.

The Distinction Between Fascism and Right Authoritarianism

Much of the confusion surrounding the identification and definition of generic fascism has lain in the failure to distinguish clearly between fascist movements and the nonfascist (or sometimes protofascist) authoritarian right. During the period of World War I and after there emerged a new cluster of conservative authoritarian forces in European politics that rejected moderate nineteenth century conservatism and simple old-fashioned traditional reaction in favor of a more modern, technically proficient kind of new authoritarian system that spurned both leftist revolution and fascist radicalism. The new right authoritarian groups have often been confused with fascists because both were authoritarian and nationalist and up to a point were opposed to many of the same things (leftists and liberals). Moreover, circumstantial alliances were made between fascists and new rightists in a number of countries, especially in Germany, Italy and Spain, but also elsewhere. Nonetheless, the fact that communists and liberals are both opposed to fascism and rightism and have sometimes formed circumstantial alliances in a number of countries since 1935 has not generally led most analysts to the false conclusion that communism and liberalism are the same thing.

Similarly, the distinction between fascism and right authoritarianism should be clearly understood for purposes of analysis, taxonomy and conceptualization.

The basic differences might be synthesized as follows:

a) The new authoritarian right was anticonservative only in the very limited sense of a qualified opposition to the more moderate, parliamentary forms of conservatism.

b) The new right advocated authoritarian government, but hesitated to embrace radical and novel forms of dictatorship and normally relied either on monarchism or Catholic neocorporatism, or some combination thereof.

c) In philosophy and ideology, the right was grounded on a combination of rationalism and also religion, and normally rejected the secularist irrationalism, vitalism and neoidealism of the fascists.

d) The new right was based on traditional élites rather than new formations of déclassé radicals, and aimed their tactics more at manipulation of the existing system than toward political conquest from the streets.

e) The new right never projected the same goals of mass political mobilization.

f) Whereas the fascists aimed at changes in social status and relations, the new right explicitly intended to maintain and affirm the existing social hierarchy, if anything increasing the degree of dominance of established groups.

g) The new right tried to rely a great deal on the army and was willing to accept praetorian rule, rejecting the fascist principle of militia and mass party militarization.

Limitations of space make it impossible to expand this inventory and illustrate it in detail, but this will serve at least to introduce the nature of the problem.

Some Ingredients of a More Empirical and Comprehensive Concept of Fascism

It has been said that the chief weakness of the classic interpretations of fascism has been their tendency toward a kind of theoretical monocausality and reductionism. A more adequate concept of the phenomenon must be able to take into account a wide variety of factors, and interpret the problem in terms of its particular historical setting or environment. «Finance capital» can never explain fascism, since the overwhelming majority of the political expressions of finance capital from the nineteenth century to the present have had nothing to do with generic fascism. That a «cultural crisis» existed in Europe during the early twentieth century is beyond dispute, but the formulators of the «cultural crisis» theory have neither given us an accurate definition of the fascist culture produced in this atmosphere nor a fully viable explanation of why such a cultural ambience should necessarily result in significant fascist movements in some countries but not in others.

After the works by Gregor, Jaeckel[37] and Hildebrand[38] the oft-repeated assumption that fascist movements lacked recognizable ideologies or a kind of cultural Weltanschauung of their own seems increasingly doubtful. A more empirically valid concept of fascism in the future must thus take into account the background and development of the new ideas of fascist culture and ideology in the period 1910–40 with the same rigor and precision being demonstrated in the study of social mobilization and class support.

Clearer analysis is required of the political, social, economic, and national/historical variables involved in those countries where the fascists achieved significant mobilization (e.g., 15 per cent or more of the vote), compared with similar factors in other European countries where this support did not exist. A more exact definition of the unique structural and cultural problems of South and Central European countries in the 1920s and 30s, and their relationship to fascist strength (or its absence), may serve to elucidate to what extent facism was merely a conjunctural historical phenomenon or whether it is likely to be paralleled or approximated by new forces in the future, whether in Western countries or the new polities of the Third World.

NOTES

[1] There are two useful anthologies that have collected statements of some of the leading interpretations: Ernst Nolte, ed., *Theorien über den Faschismus* (Cologne, 1967), and Renzo de Felice, ed., *Il fascismo: Le interpretazioni dei contemporanei e degli storici* (Bari, 1970). The latter is more thorough and complete, and contains more extensive analysis. The most incisive critique of the standard interpretations is A. James Gregor, *Interpretations of Fascism* (Morristown, N.J., 1974). Gilbert Allardyce, *The Place of Fascism in European History* (Englewood Cliffs, N.J., 1972), presents a briefer anthology. See also H. A. Turner, Jr., *Reappraisals of Fascism* (New York, 1975).

[2] Gyula Sas, *Der Faschismus in Italien* (Hamburg, 1923), reprinted in De Felice, 68–80, and in the same vein, German Sandomirsky, *Fashizm* (Moscow-Leningrad, 1923), 2 vols.

[3] Clara Zetkin, «Der Kampf gegen den Faschismus», in the *Protocols* of the 1923 Comintern Conference, reprinted in Nolte, 88–111.

[4] Rajani Palme Dutt, *Fascism and Social Revolution* (London, 1934).

[5] Daniel Guérin, *Fascisme et Grand Capital* (Paris, 1936).

[6] Franz Borkenau, «Zur Soziologie des Faschismus», *Archiv für Sozialwissenschaft und Sozialpolitik,* 68 : 5 (Feb., 1933), reprinted in Nolte, 156–81.

[7] Reinhard Kühnl, *Formen bürgerlicher Herrschaft: Liberalismus-Faschismus* (Hamburg, 1971).

[8] Nicos Poulantzas, *Fascisme et dictature* (Paris, 1970).

[9] Boris Lopukhov, *Fashizm i rabochoe dvizhenie v Italii (1919–29)* (Moscow, 1968).

[10] Alexander Galkin, «Capitalist Society and Fascism», *Social Sciences: USSR Academy of Sciences* (1970), 2: 128–38.

[11] Mihaly Vajda, «The Rise of Fascism in Italy and Germany», *Telos* (1972), 12: 3–26.

[12] H. A. Turner, Jr., «Big Business and the Rise of Hitler», *American Historical Review,* 75: 1 (1969), 56–70.

[13] Gregor, *Interpretations of Fascism,* 128–70.

[14] Particularly in the four volumes to date of De Felice's monumental *Mussolini* (Turin, 1965–74), and in his *Intervista sul fascismo* (Bari, 1975), edited by Michael Ledeen.

[15] Tim Mason, «The Primacy of Politics», in S. J. Woolf, ed., *The Nature of Fascism* (London, 1968), 165–95.

[16] References to and evaluation of various of Croce's writings on fascism will be found in Gregor, *Interpretations,* 29–32.

[17] Selections from Meinecke, Hans Kohn and Gerhard Ritter in this vein are presented and discussed in De Felice, *Il Fascismo,* 391–437.

[18] Peter Drucker, *The End of Economic Man* (New York, 1939, 1969).

[19] José Ortega y Gasset, *The Revolt of the Masses* (New York, 1932).

[20] Emil Lederer, *The State of the Masses* (New York, 1940).

[21] Talcott Parsons, «Some Sociological Aspects of the Fascist Movements», in his *Essays in Sociological Theory* (rev. ed., New York, 1949).

[22] Hannah Arendt, *The Origins of Totalitarianism* (New York, 1951).

[23] William Kornhauser, *The Politics of Mass Society* (New York, 1959).

[24] A. F. K. Organski, *The Stages of Political Development* (New York, 1965), and «Fascism and Modernization», in Woolf, *The Nature of Fascism, op.cit.*

[25] The key statement of this approach is Carl J. Friedrich and Zbigniew Brzezinski, *Totalitarian Dictatorship and Autocracy* (New York, 1956). Also Carl J. Friedrich, ed., *Totalitarianism* (New York, 1954).

[26] Wolfgang Sauer, «National Socialism: Totalitarianism or Fascism?», *American Historical Review*, 73: 2 (1967), 404–22.

[27] Cf. Herbert Spiro, «Totalitarianism», *International Encyclopedia of the Social Sciences* (New York, 1968), vol. 16.

[28] Henry A. Turner, Jr., «Fascism and Modernization», *World Politics*, 24: 4 (1972), 547–64, reprinted in Turner's *Reappraisals of Fascism*.

[29] Barrington Moore, Jr., *Social Origins of Dictatorship and Democracy* (Boston, 1966).

[30] Alan Cassels, «Janus: The Two Faces of Fascism», *Canadian Historical Papers 1969*, 166–84, and Cassels' book, *Fascism* (New York, 1974).

[31] Especially in Gregor's article, «Fascism and Modernization: Some Addenda», *World Politics*, 26: 3 (April, 1974), 370–84.

[32] In volumes two to four of De Felice's *Mussolini*, but especially in the *Intervista sul fascismo*. English ed. *Fascism. An Informal Introduction to its Theory and Practice*, New Jersey, 1977.

[33] Particularly in two of Bracher's recent essays in his *Zeitgeschichtliche Kontroversen um Faschismus Totalitarismus Demokratie* (Munich, 1976).

[34] Eugen Weber, *Varieties of Fascism* (New York, 1964) and «Revolution? Counter-Revolution? What Revolution?», *Journal of Contemporary History*, 9: 2 (April, 1974), 33–48.

[35] «Fascism – Left, Right and Center», Chapter 5 of Lipset's *Political Man* (New York, 1960).

[36] See the references in n. 32.

[37] Eberhard Jaeckel, *Hitler's Weltanschauung* (Middletown, Conn., 1972).

[38] Klaus Hildebrand, *The Foreign Policy of the Third Reich* (Berkeley-Los Angeles, 1974), and also Norman Rich, *Hitler's War Aims* (New York, 1974), 2 vols.

Contemporary Approaches to Fascism:
A Survey of Paradigms

BERNT HAGTVET AND REINHARD KÜHNL

Fascism in its variety of national manifestations produced human degradation on such a vast scale and was, as a form of tyranny, so unprecedented that scholars have been somewhat at a loss in coming to grips with it ever since. The reasons for this are many and intertwined. The sheer novelty of the phenomenon[1], the savagery of the fascists towards their enemies, the dynamism, aestheticism and ideological eclecticism of the fascist parties and their conscious appeal across class lines – all these make fascism a movement that defies simple historico-political categorization. Fascism has often been described as an embodiment of a «metapolitical mind»[2]: it was an appeal to rage and resentment that ran deeper and was more sinister than ordinary interest defense. As a result, few historical phenomena have generated so much heated argument and given rise to such a range of explanations. And although we know infinitely more about the workings of fascist movements now than in 1945, there is still no evidence of a foreseeable consensus on the essential characteristics of fascism, and even less agreement on the place of fascism within a broader theory of politics in the 20th century.

Confronted with this theoretical discord, scholarship on fascism faces a two-fold task: First, to process the enormous amount of historical data now available in such a way as *to capture the phenomenon in all its dimensions* – political, cultural, economic, psychological, aesthetic and social. Such a program does not, of course, exclude attempts to differentiate between various historical determinants and assign causal priority to some dimensions over others. Rather, it means that in order to comprehend the phenomenon fully, the fallacy of reductionism and mono-causality should be avoided. Fascism was an elusive movement, often contradictory and unpredictable because of the explicitly ideological and practical opportunism of the leadership. Fascism displayed a curious autonomy of the leadership in relation to the masses who flocked to the movement in its initial phases. The result is perplexing for the political sociologist, for it reveals the limitations of a strictly sociological approach to fascism. Tracing the social origins of members and voters of fascist parties can only be the beginning. The main theoretical challenge is to delineate the essential character of fascism *over time*. This implies a sensitivity not only to the social bases of the movements, but also to their *functions* and their *telos*. Only through such a multilevel approach can there be any hope to explain the opportunism of most fascist movements: their tactical compromises and their shift of alliance partners.

In pursuing this level of analysis problem in the study of fascism a few distinctions should be kept in mind. First, in order to pin down the changes in the class character of fascism, it will be necessary to untangle in detail the social support of the movements *before and after their seizure of power*. Break or continuity, shifting patterns of regional distribution of support – these are the questions which should guide research

26

efforts. Second, the *social functions* of fascist movements, their actual behavior once in control, may or may not be in accord with the aspirations of their initial supporters. And, third, an analysis of the functions of a movement may not bring us far in understanding the *goals* pursued by the party élite. The instrumental view of ideology in fascism was paralleled by a conscious espousal of the doctrine of «primacy of politics»[3]: the ruthless subjugation of the previous autonomy of the economic, cultural and social spheres from political considerations.

This autonomy of the leadership touches a crucial problem in studies of fascism: the role of ideology. Are ideological pronouncements to be given any causal weight at all, or should they primarily be seen as rationalizations, the expression of the twisted minds of the leadership or of the interests of outside groups using the fascist apparatus of violence to bolster their grip on state power? Fascism can be analyzed on all these levels: in terms of its mass base, its political and social effect on social groups, its ruling techniques, and its long-term goals. Knowledge on one level may have limited value for understanding the working of fascism at another, and even less for comprehending the phenomenon as a whole. Unless distinctions of this kind are made, scholarship on fascism is not likely to go beyond single countries or movements.

The second requirement of a theory of fascism is that it should remain *open enough to accommodate national variations while maintaining a minimum of conceptual unity*. Its scope should be cross-national, its method comparative. The need for a cross-national comparative approach to our mind is evident: Only the most nominalistically inclined would deny that the inter-war period saw the emergence of a new brand of dictatorship, related to, yet distinct from earlier autocracies. The fascist parties shared a common contempt for parliamentary democracy. They were violently anti-labor and embraced a particularly aggressive brand of nationalism which in some, but not in all cases, fused with extreme racialism to make for an expansionist foreign policy. Verbally anti-capitalist, the fascists were nevertheless willing to enter into close alliance with the holders of economic power. Some were committed to a kind of ideologically founded «utopian anti-modernism»[4], i.e., a notion of pre-industrial community reminiscent of a state of nature before modernization produced fragmentation and de-mythologized the world. Fascists preached submission to authority yet built their initial power base on mass mobilization directed against existing authority. This deliberate strategy of inciting the masses for direct political involvement on the symbolic level is probably the most characteristic feature of fascist dictatorships, which on the whole set them apart from autocracies of a more traditional or restorative kind. Although the debate on the concept of «generic» fascism continues unabated, a theory of fascism should be able to separate the specifically fascist components in anti-democratic movements from features that are part of a broader tradition of political authoritarianism.

1. Theories of Fascism: The Search for a Typology

Whether explicitly or implicitly, most attempts of constructing typologies of approaches to fascism revolve around *fascism's autonomy in relation to capitalism,* or more broadly, processes of modernization. Theories which assert that fascism is «produced» or «determined» in one way or another by the course of capitalist development are contrasted with theories which hold that fascism showed a marked autonomy in relation to the economic system, or at least cannot be reduced to a mere representation of the economy in the political sphere. This view argues that fascist regimes were able substantially to alter the economic infrastructure and the relations of production. It denies that an identification of the social interests behind fascist movements yields much insight into the essential nature of the phenomenon. The first view is usually labelled the «heteronomic», the second the «autonomic» theory of fascism. This division is arguably the most basic in the entire literature of fascism[5]. The most representative of the first category of theories is the one advanced by the Third International in the thirties which saw fascism as an agent of powerful economic interests. The view that fascism was the expression of the bent-up frustrations of the middle class is an example of the second.

Ernst Nolte, on the other hand, has attempted to apply more *political* criteria for his six-fold classification[6]: *Christian* theories see fascism as the moral disease of Europe and the result of man's revolt against God in secularized society. *Conservative* interpretations focus on the revolt of the masses and the concomitant breakdown of traditional morality in the wake of rapid socio-economic change. Their solution is a return to the stability of the period before mass democracy. *Liberals,* seeing in fascism the very denial of freedom, use the concept of totalitarianism to grasp the essence of fascist movements. *Nationalists* vary in their opinions: some argue that fascism was the culmination of national aspirations, whereas others regard it as an aberration and share with the conservatives a longing for the stability of pre-mobilization Europe. *Marxists* differ widely in their views, to which we shall return, but share a common reference point in interpreting fascism as the last convulsion of a moribund economic system, a desperate crisis solution involving the suspension of parliamentary democracy in an effort to uphold the rights of private property. Nolte ends his scheme by outlining his own theory which claims that fascism was epochal in nature and limited to a specific period in European history, the two decades between the wars. To Nolte, fascism was a supra-national and meta-political force.

Writing the history of fascism today inevitably means writing the history of scholarship on fascism[7]. From its very inception fascism provoked analysis. A typology of the existing body of literature could also be organized along *chronological* lines. Leaving principles of organization aside, we would like to survey the main strands of theorizing in the field. Here we shall confine ourselves to a mapping of the intellectual landscape, giving in footnote form bibliographical references to the most representative works. In subsequent sections we shall single out a few of these traditions for analytic discussion.

We would suggest that the body of literature on fascism can be divided into the following sub-fields:

1. Fascism as the product of a «daemonic» *Führer* personality. This mode of analysis gained widespread popularity after World War II and is prominent in the interpretations of scholars like Golo Mann, Meinecke, Tellenbach and Fabry. It is also part of the implicit message of quite a few of the most recent biographies of Hitler, most notably in Fest[8].

2. Fascism as the result of Europe's *moral disease,* an interpretation propounded among others by Croce, Ritter, Hans Kohn and the Catholic tradition[9].

3. Fascism as a product of a particular *developmental sequence* confined to Germany and Italy, both peripheralized within the European economy, both suffering the impact of an accumulation of «developmental crises». This tradition has assumed many forms, from the earlier theories of a German road to Nazism (Vermeil, McGo-

28

vern, Viereck)[10] to later attempts to view fascism within the context of national history (Lukács, Bracher[11]).

4. Marxist theories: Fascism as a *product of capitalist society* and as an expression of anti-proletarian hysteria. Fascism can be seen as «the power of finance capital itself» (Dimitrov)[12], or as the result of *class equilibrium* and the formation of a relatively independent state executive which determines the way in which the economic domination of society by the bourgeoisie should be organized (Bonapartism)[13]. There is also a growing literature on fascism as *a partner* in alliance with the traditional Right. This interpretation avoids the sterile economism of the agent theory and can be found in a variety of forms[14].

5. Fascism as a manifestation of *totalitarianism*, which holds that there is an essential similarity between communist and fascist dictatorships[15].

6. Fascism as a «revolt against transcendence»: Ernst Nolte's phenomenological approach which exercised an important influence on scholarship on fascism in the 1960's and generated the renewed interest in the phenomenon[16].

7. Fascism as the outgrowth of the *social structure*. This theory can be sub-divided into two groups: a. Sociological theories which portray fascism as an independent movement of the frustrated *middle class*[17], and b. *psychosocial theories* which focus on the impact of the economic infrastructure[18] on the authoritarian character structure of individual members of fascist parties.

8. Fascism as a particular stage in broader processes of *modernization* (Moore, Dahrendorf, Schoenbaum, Turner, Organski)[19].

9. Fascism as an *aesthetic* aberration[20].

10. Fascism as the product of a pathological *cultural tradition*[21].

11. Fascism as the expression of a specifically European syndrome of *counter-revolution*[22].

In presenting this survey, we have made no attempt to discuss the literature on its merits, but in the subsequent sections we have singled out 6 traditions which to our minds have proved most promising in building a unified theory of fascism. What follows is a discussion of their ability to furnish material for a comparative and testable theory of fascism based on the two requirements outlined in the introduction.

2. The Middle Class Thesis Today

As is argued in several contributions to this volume, the middle classes were clearly over-represented among the supporters of fascist movements. This is an old observation. As early as 1923, the Italian historian Luigi Salvatorelli wrote of Italian fascism: «Fascism represents the class struggle of the petty bourgeoisie, which is placed between big business and the proletariat like a third man between two fighters»[23]. The sociologist Theodor Geiger noted that this was also true of German National Socialism in 1932, when he looked at the social stratification of the German people[24]. In 1960, S. M. Lipset expanded this sociological analysis into a broader theory of fascism as the «extremism of the center»[25].

Geiger and Lipset and other theorists of the middle class attempt to explain the predominance of the middle strata among the voters and members of fascist parties by reference to broader processes of rationalization and anomie in industrial society, and, more specifically, to the precarious socio-economic position of the middle class and the outlook generated by that position: «The force of socialism had grown to menacing proportions on the left, while from the right came the frightening pressure of

29

the large industrial concerns». – «The growing economic distress of the propertied middle class was sufficient mental preparation for a petty bourgeois radicalism»[26]. The concentration of capital and the connected phenomena of the dispossession and proletarianization of small businessmen have in fact gone on steadily in all capitalist countries since the beginnings of industrialization, and are necessarily linked with the capitalist principle of competition.

But not only the small concerns in trade, handicraft and farming protested at the «levelling tendencies of the class society»[27], the aversion was shared by the lower and middle salaried employees (and officials) who aspired to being «middle class» and wanted to distance themselves from the working masses.

Theories of the middle class see in this position of the two «middle classes» – the small retailers and the salaried employees – the basis for their susceptibility to fascist ideology. The precariousness of their social existence triggered off their yearning for a pre-industrial, pre-capitalist society characterized by agriculture and small business-es, their opposition to both the labor movement and big business by which they felt threatened, their desire for the «strong state» which, they hoped, would secure their threatened position in society, and their identification with the whole, with the nation which, they trusted, would provide security and self-esteem[28]. We are thus dealing with those strata that mainly supported parties of the centre (and moderate right) before their turn to fascism. Lipset draws on electoral statistics to support this thesis: «As the relative position of the middle class declined . . ., its 'liberal' ideology – the support of individual rights against large-scale power – changed from that of a revolutionary class to that of a reactionary class»[29].

Lipset's interpretation can be challenged on several points. First, there is a problem about his use of the term 'liberal' to denote the people who left the middle parties to vote Nazi[30]. In the German context the word 'liberal' as it is used by Anglo-Americans clearly fails to grasp the socially conservative nature of these parties. The ideology of the German *Mittelstand* was openly anti-Semitic, oriented towards the introduction of market-regulating devices like guilds and state control of larger business corporations, and it was clearly hierarchical and nationalistic. The political sentiments in this sector of the German population were as much a part of a rightist populist tradition as of any 'liberal' persuasion. This view is supported by the shifts in the German electorate in the Weimar period. The desertion from the liberal and middle sector interest parties – between 1928 and 1933 these parties lost 80 per cent of their voters to the Nazis – started earlier and was not as unmediated and direct as Lipset seems to suggest. The Nazi upsurge was the end-result of a gradual shift to the Right among *Mittelstand* voters starting as early as 1924[31]. The DNVP and smaller regional and sectional in-terest parties became the prime beneficiaries of this rightward trend before, in 1930, as a last resort, the broad middle class strata turned to the NSDAP. Given the autho-ritarian predispositions of the *Mittelstand* and the middle parties, it is difficult to con-struct any political kinship between 'liberalism' and Nazism. Rather, Nazism accord-ing to this view must be seen as a more plebeian and vulgar form of traditional authoritarian German conservatism.

Even more damaging to Lipset's theory is his failure to distinguish between diffe-rent levels of his analysis of fascism. To determine the social roots of fascism is insufficient as an analysis of the entire phenomenon, especially the political perfor-mance and socio-economic functions of the fascist movements once they had acquired power. As we have pointed out, the contradictions between the mass base of fascist movements and the fascist élites illustrate the limits of a strictly sociological appro-ach.

The middle class theory refuses to analyze this contradiction. In effect, the theory overlooks the complicity of landowners and industrial élites in bringing fascism to power and avoids the question of the functionality of fascism altogether. In power fascism pursued aims which were partly at odds with the aspirations that originally drove the middle class into its ranks. It subjected classical capitalist prerogatives like profit maximization and investment to political control, but it did not touch private property rights as such. On the whole, the petty bourgeoisie gained relatively little from fascism. The rank and file provided legitimation to a regime which soon departed from its promised goals. By concentrating on the social base Lipset is able to present fascism as an extremist middle response located somewhere between the two poles of socialism and conservatism. He convincingly shows how the ideology of 'national concentration' can be traced to the precarious position of the middle classes in industrial society. But by blurring over the political direction and the interests served by the fascist regimes in power, he fails to grasp the symbiosis of capitalism and fascism and its unity in crushing the left. Any political analysis which does not include this vital political function of fascist regimes is bound to be insufficient.

An even more fundamental challenge to the middle class theory has been launched by Richard Hamilton[32]. Reanalyzing the voting returns from Hamburg and Berlin and several other cities he casts doubts about the entire middle class theory. He found that the highest levels of support for the Nazis came from the upper and upper middle class districts in the cities. Excluding the working class and Jewish minorities in the well-to-do district of Hamburg, he indicates for instance that roughly two thirds of the upper and upper middle classes cast their votes for Hitler in the July 1932 election. He argues that the oft-repeated middle class theory is largely unsupported and in need of thorough revision.

3. Psychological Theories: End or Revival of a Tradition?

The deep-rooted, stored-up frustrations let loose by fascist movements, the sadism of fascist thugs and Nazi extermination squads and the apparently abnormal conduct and personality of many fascist leaders have given rise to a wide variety of psychological explanations. They can roughly be divided into two main categories: 1. theories trying to explain the susceptibility of the *masses* to fascist propaganda, including theories linking this behavior to underlying socio-economic conditions; and 2. theories about the pathological character structure of *individual* fascists. We shall concentrate on the former.

Fascism clearly appealed to resentments that were more sinister than ordinary interest aggregation. Subordination to authority, mass hysteria, degradation of the enemy beyond any limit justified by his presumed danger and a pervasive irrationalism were prominent features of the fascist movements. The first attempts to account for the irrationalism and aggressiveness of the fascist movements were undertaken by Wilhelm Reich and Erich Fromm[33]. In their view, the thinking and behavior of social strata can only be made comprehensible by reference to social position and the immediate social environment, that is, through an analysis of the socio-economic determinants shaping the individual's psychological make-up. Both attempt to bring together Sigmund Freud's psychoanalysis and Karl Marx' social theory in a new critical social psychology. Younger scholars have also taken up this approach[34].

Reich defines his psychology as «an investigation of the 'subjective factor in history', of the character structure of man in a given epoch and of the ideological structure of society that shapes it»[35]. Psychology's task is «to discover the means and mechanisms by way of which social existence is transformed into psychic structure and, with that, into ideology»[36], or put another way, «to clarify in detail the mental consequences in the individual of the system of production, that is, the formation of ideologies 'in men's heads'. Psychoanalytical interpretation of the psychology of the socialized human being introduces a series of connecting links between the two poles of society's economic basis and its ideological superstructure, whose causal connection has been generally explained by the materialistic interpretation of history»[37]. Reich examines the officials who are «subordinate to the top» but «representative of . . . . authority» to the bottom, and who are characterized by «a complete identification with state power»[38], and the company employees who, living in a similarly intermediate position, identify with the firms for which they work and keep «looking to the top», appearing representative to the outside world even when their financial position is poor[39]. The same characteristics of «looking to the top» pre-dominate among small proprietors in trade and handicrafts, who once had a secure position in the ranks of the bourgeoisie and whose outlook continues to be moulded by this past. Compensation for economic decline has to be sought in the moral sphere, and from this source flows their receptivity to the ideology of honor, duty, loyalty, authority and patriotism. Reich gives special emphasis to the role of the authoritarian father in the way children are brought up, as «the foremost and most essential source of reproduction in every kind of reactionary thinking»[40]. In Reich's view, religion and the church have the same effect. Of particular significance in this respect is the suppression of sexual impulses and needs. For these structural reasons the middle strata have been in particular pre-disposed to follow «a party whose leadership was objectively as well as subjectively in diametrical opposition to the interests of the working masses»[41].

Fromm is also concerned to clarify «the role which psychological factors play as active forces in the social process; and this eventually leads to the problem of the interaction of psychological, economic and ideological factors in the social process»[42]. In proceeding with this task, however, he follows a different path from Reich. He attempts to depict the origins and development of bourgeois society by analyzing the way in which the competitive struggle characteristic of capitalism has given rise to fear and isolation and, in consequence, to an authoritarian or sado-masochistic potential. In the twentieth century, amid the circumstances of monopoly capitalism and increased social and economic pressure upon the middle classes, this potential was brought to the fore in a mass movement of fear and protest, in the guise of fascism. «We see that when a certain class is threatened by new economic tendencies it reacts to this threat psychologically and ideologically . , . In other words, social conditions influence ideological phenomena through the medium of character; character, on the other hand, is not the result of a passive adaptation to social conditions but of a dynamic adaptation on the basis of elements that either are biologically inherent in human nature or have become inherent as the result of historical evolution»[43].

There can be no doubt that these theories of fascism merit close scrutiny. Why did large sections of the middle classes show an often blind trust and fanatical devotion to a party whose ideology was primitive and irrational, and whose policies proved not only brutal and terroristic, but also quite at odds with the interests of its own followers?

Despite the plethora of books on psycho-history in recent years, the application of social psychology to history is still in its infancy. With the exception of the psycho-

32

historical tradition, psychology as applied to fascism has so far tended to interpret historical events either as the arbitrary product of leader-personalities who are equipped with certain mental qualities, or as the necessary product of the human psyche which is irremediably determined by nature. Under this heading we must also place all those theories which take as their starting-point man's innate aggressiveness. These theories are unable to explain why mass-based aggressive behavior is an intermittent, and not a constant, occurrence in history[44].

Essentially the same conclusions are reached by theories which interpret man's mental structure as the mechanical product of his environment, which, in these accounts, appears as a force external and hostile to man, more or less a force of nature. In both cases, man stands abstracted and apart from his environment, and either man determines his environment uni-laterally, or the environment determines man. What is required, however, is to see the relationship between man and society as one of mutual interaction. A given social environment, with all its systems of values, its patterns of behavior, beliefs and structural determinants is just as much the product of human activity (that of past generations) as every new generation, every social group and every individual is initially determined by this existing framework.

Reich recognizes this problem of reciprocity with the external world when he attempts to explain how social existence is transformed into consciousness in the human mind, and how the resulting consciousness in turn has an effect upon social and political development[45]. Psychoanalysis as a means of explaining collective behavior is built on a speculative basis and thus defies strict empirical verification. There is a problem inherent in any attempt to explain mass behavior drawn from individual clinical experience. The idea of a biologically determined structure of impulses is abandoned in Reich's and Fromm's theories in favor of the idea of a mental structure that can, within limits, be altered by social and historical influences. The limits of this alterability remain unspecified, however, as do the connections between societal development and the structure of personality. Even in the work of Reich and Fromm there is a tendency to use the analysis of capitalism to trace the roots of the fascist personality rather than the origins of fascism itself. On the whole, psychological theories suffer from the same limitation as all theories which confine themselves to a consideration of the social bases of fascism and the personality structure of its leaders and followers without including in their analysis a discussion of the social function of fascist movements, its ultimate aims and its entire form of dominance.

4. Theories of Totalitarianism: A Critique

Among the least attractive additions to the political vocabulary of the twentieth century, the term totalitarianism is likely to remain the most controversial. Its basic contention is that the fascist and communist dictatorships represent historically a novel form of government. Taken together they form an antithesis to Western democratic systems. Both in form and substance, it is argued, Stalinism and fascism show a vital structural similarity.

In Friedrich's and Brzezinski's original version from 1956[46] the point was not to explain the origins of totalitarianism as a form of government, as was the explicit aim of Hannah Arendt, but to present a 'general descriptive theory'. As part of this theory they named six 'decisive essential traits' which were seen to be common to all totalitarian dictatorships and constitutive of their form. In their attempt to delineate

33

the model, the concept of totalitarianism was constructed as a syndrome of inter-related features:

1. An elaborate ideology, i.e. an officially prescribed doctrine with explicit views of all existential and philosophical aspects of life, including the origins and final ends of the human race.
2. A single mass party, led by a dictator, hierarchically organized and monolithic.
3. Terroristic police control, which not only supports but also supervises the party.
4. Monopoly control over communications.
5. A near-complete control over the armed forces.
6. A centralized bureaucratic control of the economy. There is no organizational pluralism.

The authors admit that the list may not be exhaustive, and reserve the right to add other items to the syndrome[47]. In Friedrich's latest version[48] there is an attempt to break down the syndrome into three, plus one with three variants. The 'generally accepted set of facts' in this version include:

1. A totalist ideology.
2. A single party committed to this ideology and usually led by one man.
3. A secret police.
4. Three kinds of monopoly control:
   a. Mass communications
   b. Operational weapons
   c. All organizations of a centrally planned economy.

While conceding that the need for simplicity might reduce the six essential characteristics to three plus control of communications, the intermediary network and the economy, Friedrich has remained firm in his insistence that totalitarianism denotes a modern form of dictatorship; 'historically unique' and *'sui generis'*. Its value in scholarly discourse was defended. In the 1965 edition of «Totalitarian Dictatorship and Autocracy» Friedrich stuck to his six points but admitted that although the Nazi and Soviet systems «are basically alike» this means that they are «not wholly alike» (p. 7, italics in the original). He also made allowance for the changing nature of Soviet totalitarianism and pointed to the different historical preconditions which shaped the national forms of Nazism and communism. Nevertheless, the Soviet regime still warranted classification as «totalitarian» because violence was still being used on ideological grounds against dissidents.

The literature on totalitarianism is now enormous. The criticism against the original totalitarianism thesis can be summarized in the following points:

1. The theory is weak on *conceptual* grounds. It is not put in a form that facilitates comparison with other forms of non-democratic politics, in particular the modernizing variants. The totalitarianism thesis suffers from a «unitotalitarian bias» that serves insufficiently to distinguish the regimes it purports to distinguish from others[49]. This is all the more serious since the whole argument of Friedrich's work is to demonstrate the distinctiveness of the Nazi, Fascist and Soviet regimes. The charge that the totalitarianism thesis is too miscellaneous can be traced to the decision to define totalitarianism as a cluster of characteristics rather than concentrating on a teleological or essentialist approach. There is no explicit connotative definition, and the denotative inclusion of the Italian fascist regime produces an elastic and indiscriminate conception of totalitarianism that is of limited value in systematic political comparison.

34

2. A second basic deficiency in the totalitarianism approach lies in its confining itself to the *form* and *method* of rule at the expense of analyzing its *purpose* and *content*. All theories of totalitarianism thus assume that similarities in the exercise of power in communist and fascist states are more characteristic of their essential nature than far more crucial differences in socio-economic structure and ideological goals. Despite Friedrich's 1965 revision, the theory remains fundamentally a-historical and hence tends to become an abstracted typology which mistakes appearances of similarity for an essential identity. Admittedly, Friedrich himself recognizes that fascist and communist dictatorships differ in their intentions and in the aims they set for themselves, that fascist movements «offered themselves to a fear-ridden middle class as bulwarks against Communism»[50] (and to the upper classes, it should be added, whose acquiescence was pivotal in assuring victory). But he regards this distinction as inessential. At any rate, this observation does not induce him to alter his theory substantially.

This very point touches on a crucial debate in the history of scholarship on fascism. It has often been pointed out that any analysis which ignores the relations of production and the resulting social structure is of limited value. The Nazis introduced a 'command economy' which restricted the exercise of market forces, but it is wrong to claim that they achieved «the central direction and domination of the entire economy» and the «bureaucratic co-ordination of all previously independent elements of the economy»[51]. There were significant differences in the autonomy of various sectors in the economy under fascist rule. The organizations for the wage earners were indeed crushed, removing any independent interest articulation. But big business and banking retained not only a large measure of autonomy, but also a position of significant power in the political and economic system which allowed them to foster their own interests at the expense of those of other classes and strata. The institution of private ownership was hardly touched as such[52]. Indeed, by replacing a weak and vacillating parliamentary state by the new *Führerstaat,* private ownership was reinforced. Despite all talk of Hitler's 'social' revolution, the Nazi period did not produce any redistribution of property or remove any barrier to social advancement except as inevitable by-products in the process of economic mobilization for war. The Nazi 'revolution' was aimed at the elimination of the rights of the liberal state. This undermining of liberal rights included the violation of traditional liberal rights of property. Obviously, the attack on liberal capitalism and its replacement by an economy geared to war is of a different order than the communist attack on private ownership and the market economy. Fascism stood for hierarchy, and the strengthening of existing social relationships. Communism sought a fundamental re-structuring of society.

3. The assertion that fascist and communist *ideology* is essentially the same is expanded in several totalitarian theories. But it is wrong to assert, as Friedrich does, that fascist (and communist) ideology proclaim «the ultimate condition of mankind, a paradise on earth», «the dream of the classless society»[53]. On the contrary, fascist ideology proclaims the natural necessity of dominance and subordination, the eternal struggle for existence between peoples and races, the brutal life principle that might is right. It is no less wrong to maintain that both fascism and communism put «faith in the place of reason and magical incantation . . . in the place of healthy common sense»[54]. Here again, fascist irrationalism and voluntarism are diametrically opposed to communism. In his attempt to show the ideological convergence between fascism and communism, Friedrich even supports his assertions with incomplete quotations from Marx[55].

4. As a theory tradition, the totalitarianism thesis restricts itself to *describe* some of the characteristics of the fascist system without *explaining* it.

Friedrich names only two general pre-conditions of «totalitarian dictatorships»: «modern technology» and «mass democracy»[56]. As far as modern technology is concerned, it is in fact the pre-requisite of any effective system of government in the modern era – even parliamentary – and so cannot be specifically linked to fascism. As for «mass democracy», fascism should be understood as a counter-movement, a radical attempt to stop the movement towards democracy that began with the French Revolution of 1789, to «rub out» the year 1789, as the Nazis proclaimed. And in fact fascist dictatorship means the extinction of all those rights which the popular masses have struggled to acquire since the French Revolution, and should thus be characterized as counter-revolutionary and reactionary in the original sense of the words. By contrast, theories of totalitarianism imply that the intervention of the masses in the process of history and the democratization of state and society were themselves the cause of fascism, and that «totalitarian dictatorship» is not a reaction against this process, but a completion of it. The historical explanation of fascism provided by theories of totalitarianism is thus too general, and partly wrong.

5. In addition to these criticisms, three arguments have been advanced in favor of abandoning the concept altogether: it was (and is) a cold war term, which improperly masks the essential differences between Stalin and Hitler and served to bolster the restorative forces after World War II, who, by equating fascism with communism, could convert the anti-fascist struggle into an anti-communist crusade[57]. Secondly, the term totalitarianism was useful in the past in that it pointed to the specifically modern flavor of totalitarianism as distinct from previous autocracies. With the post-Stalin changes in the Soviet Union it is outmoded and useless in political discourse, too much tainted as a slogan for political expediency[58]. Thirdly, the totalitarianism thesis has been attacked for its analysis of a polity in terms of the relationship between those who rule and those who are ruled. Treated as distinct categories, this is out of date and overlooks modern conditions in which the individual's liberty is not so much threatened by the state as by private elements within the nation which are outside public control, private monopolies in the economy and social forces which transcend liberal theory's dualistic cleavage between abstract public and private spheres. These are powerful arguments. In the light of this criticism, scholars have attempted either to redefine the term or abandon it altogether[59]. To our minds, neither of the revisionist schools have been entirely successful. The basic failing of the totalitarianism thesis is that it confines itself to a description of external characteristics of total systems without providing a causal analysis and without due regard to their specificity. Its heuristic value is now very limited[60].

5. Fascist Dictatorship as a Form of Social Alliance or Coalition

As regards the emergence of fascist dictatorships, a large number of non-Marxist scholars now agree with their Marxist counterparts that the fascist parties were nowhere able to seize power on their own, but required the support of the upper classes in order to do so[61]. The bourgeoisie's fear of communism and their desire for a state both internally and externally strong are cited as particularly potent reasons for this support. This constellation of forces in the establishment of fascist dictatorships provokes the conclusion that an essential element of the fascist system was a compromise between the fascist party and the traditional socio-political and economic élites. Studies of fascist policies and of the structure of fascist rule appear to lend empirical support to this thesis.

There is relative unanimity about two aspects of this compromise: 1. the workers' movement was crushed and so removed from the political battle-field, which served the interests of the upper classes as well as the wishes of the middle class fascist masses; 2. after the fascist militias had, with the aid of the state, completed the suppression of the working class, they were no longer needed, and became a danger to the new system of dominance because they gave voice to the plebeian and anti-capitalist elements in fascism. They were therefore stripped of their power and their leaders were murdered. This was the decisive precondition for the suppression of all petty-bourgeois anti-capitalist and middle class aspirations that had any influence within the fascist party; and so the middle strata were also removed from the political battle-field[62].

The only remaining groups with any political influence were, on the one hand, the traditional circles of the élite in big business, the armed forces and the higher civil service, and, on the other, the leading factions in the fascist party, who controlled a widely ramified system of mass organizations and who had taken over the running of the instruments of state. The fascist system is seen to have been founded upon a compromise between these forces. In the Italian context, Seton-Watson talks of a «division of power» and «dyarchie»[63], Arno Klönne of a «coalition of interests» and a «division of power»; in the German context[64], Schweitzer of several «pillars» of dominance (party, big business, military)[65], Kühnl of an «alliance»[66], Sohn-Rethel of an alliance of necessity: «The two partners are chained together in a relationship of mutual dependency»[67]. S. J. Woolf regards the contradiction between the revolutionary aims of fascist movements and the conservative policies of fascist regimes, their compromise with established élites, as a general (if not universal) characteristic of fascism[68].

This alliance theory appears plausible and is of considerable heuristic value in coming to grips with the contradictory nature of fascist movements. Its explanatory potential is increased, however, if the theory is put on the following form: Who managed to promote what interests to what extent by what means? Are there continuities over time? What specific interests continued to be represented by the fascist party once its anti-capitalist and middle class adherents had been suppressed? Since there are no permanent traces of middle class interests in the policies of fascist regimes, many writers talk of the irrational quality of fascist policies. A connection is seen between «the irrational tendency towards self-destruction» and the «ultimate failure to cope with reality . . . . [characteristic of] fascist dictatorships» on the one hand, and the growth of the middle strata as an «autonomous political force» under fascism on the other[69].

Another view of the specific interests of the fascist party in the system of dominance is the description of this system as a dictatorship of the fascist leadership clique. Thus H. A. Winkler talks of the absolute dominance of a clique controlled by no social power-grouping and of «the primacy of politics embodied by this group»[70], while I. Fetscher speaks of the «dominance of a radical minority . . . made up of the de-classed petty bourgeois, the lumpenproletariat and the half-educated»[71]. We learn little from such descriptions about the content of fascist policies, however, and the latter can clearly not be explained merely by alluding to the power- and career-interests of the fascist leaders.

The various alliance theories differ widely in their conceptions of the form of alliance found in fascist systems. The basic questions remain unsolved. The argument continues as to whether big business interests (Kühnl) or the fascist leadership clique (Winkler) played the predominant role under fascist dictatorship; whether we should speak of the «primacy of politics», that is, of the state (Mason) or of the «primacy of the economy» (Czichon)[72]. Controversy also surrounds the question of whether big business played an active and determining part in the shaping of fascist policies (Kühnl), or whether the fascist state represented the interests of big business objectively without conceding genuine political influence to it[73], or whether indeed fascist dictatorship, in Germany at least, falls into two phases, the first of which was founded upon a compromise («partial fascism») and the second upon the pre-dominance of the party leadership («full fascism»), as is claimed by Schweitzer and Petzina.

6. Fascism and Modernization

In its different forms the modernization theory represents a profound attempt to understand fascism[74]. The influence of the theory in academic discussions of fascism has grown significantly in the last decade. Proof of this influence can be seen in the diffusion of modernization themes in new branches of scholarship. In its refined form, the theory of fascism as a stage in broader modernization processes claims to explain not only individual aspects of fascism (its social base, ideology, or its form of domination), but indeed the total phenomenon of the genesis and structure of fascism, and the historical status of fascism in the development of modern industrial society. Its theoretical foundation is derived from the theory of industrial society which by Rostow is given an explicit anti-communist form: it is presented as the «alternative to the Marxist theory of development»[75].

The basic tenet of this theory is that mankind's history has developed through various stages (Rostow distinguishes 5, Organski 4) which have as their central distinctive feature the differing levels of development of science and technology. The highest stage to date is the consumer society, an advanced phase of industrial society. By contrast, the way a society is organized and its patterns of ownership are considered inessential; thus socialism is seen not as an alternative to capitalism but, since it has until now taken root mainly in less developed countries, merely as an outdated form along the road to the modern industrial society. In this interpretation, the future of mankind is represented by the society with the highest level of industrial, technological and scientific development, by the «capitalism of wastefulness» (Organski), by «mass consumption» – in specific terms, by the USA.

If this theory is applied to fascism, the central question is how to define the connection between the processes of industrialization and modernization, and fascism. The usefulness of the theory can be demonstrated through the example of the American social historian, Barrington Moore[76]. By a comparison of the ways in which Britain, France, the USA, India and Japan have developed since feudalism, Moore attempts to arrive at a typology of patterns of development which can explain the establishment of stable democratic regimes. His central hypothesis is that the specific conditions of feudalism in individual countries largely determined their subsequent development. As long ago as the feudal period, the essential pre-conditions had been created for the later establishment in a country of either a capitalist democracy or a fascist dictatorship or a communist peasant's revolution.

38

Focussing primarily on Japan and Germany (and only tangentially on Italy), Moore argues that the victory of fascism depends on the power base of the landed upper classes and their political ability to «maintain intact the pre-existing peasant society», as in Japan, and introduce only as many changes as are necessary «to ensure that the peasants generate a sufficient surplus»; or they succeed in securely anchoring serfdom, by means of which the peasants are tied to the land – as for example in Prussia (p. 433). Both variations demand a strong state apparatus of suppression, monarchic and bureaucratic in character, which also holds the urban bourgeoisie in dependence; their ideologies contain élitist, authoritarian and militarist elements. When these «labor-repressive agrarian systems» are brought into difficulties by «competition from more technically advanced (systems) in other countries» – for example, by the export of grain from the USA after the end of the American Civil War – they respond to this challenge by a further strengthening of their authoritarian and reactionary defense mechanisms. At the same time, however, a «conservative modernization» through a «revolution from above» is introduced, which is intended to make possible the transition to a modern industrial state while retaining «as much of the original social structure as (possible)». Often this results in «a rough working coalition between influential sections of the landed upper classes and the emerging commercial and manufacturing interests» which are «too weak and dependent» to take power themselves (p. 435 ff.). Growing internal contradictions and increasing activity by the organized masses finally drive the ruling class to the fascist solution: «Fascism was an attempt to make reaction and conservatism popular and plebeian . . .» (p. 447) which could be seen in an inchoate form in the German Empire at the end of the 19th century. This explains the specifically fascist mixture of ideological elements of hierarchy, discipline and obedience on the one hand and plebeian anti-capitalism on the other. Although this ideology was well-suited to win mass support among those groups threatened by capitalism (farmers, small traders and artisans), the war-time economy of the fascist systems was necessarily founded upon industry.

Since Moore clearly distinguishes between those who provide mass support for a movement or a system and those who profit from it, that is, between social basis and social function, he is able to state that German and Japanese fascism was characterized by «repression at home and expansion abroad. In both cases, the main social basis for this program was a coalition between the commercial-industrial élite (who started from a weak position) and the traditional ruling classes in the countryside, directed against the peasants and the industrial workers» (p. 305) the so-called «iron-rye» coalition. And of Italy: «Essentially fascism protected big agriculture and big industry at the expense of the agricultural laborer, small peasant, and consumer» (p. 452).

With this broadly based comparative examination, backed up by extensive empirical material, Moore has undoubtedly brought to light essential differences between the development of the monarchic-reactionary, later fascist systems on the one hand, and of the bourgeois democracies on the other. How far he has solved the causal problem by so doing, and what exact connection exists between the conditions and characteristics he adduces, would of course have to be examined separately.

Moore is well aware that the agrarian conditions he analyzes were «not the only cause» (p. 433) of this differentiation, that he is isolating one factor among many. This occasionally leads to a false evaluation of fascism as a whole, and a more thoroughgoing critique would take this as its point of departure. The rough outlines of such a critique are sketched below.

It is without doubt true, and has been convincingly demonstrated by Moore, that the survival of feudal, monarchic-authoritarian traditions in some countries helped to prepare the ground for fascist ideology and to this extent favored the ascent and triumph of fascism. But within the ruling classes it was not primarily the large feudal land-owners who paved the way for the establishment of a fascist system, but the dominant sections of business and banking; and it was also not the large landowners who profited most from fascism, but big business. This is demonstrated particularly clearly by the example of Germany (and applies less forcefully to Japan and Italy also). At the end of the nineteenth century the grand bourgeoisie had become the determining element within the ruling class of the German Empire, even if considerable executive powers still remained in the hands of the feudal monarchic stratum. The imperialist and colonialist policy of the Empire can only be understood by reference to business interests, not to the interests of the large land-owners, and this insight is supported by the fact that the bourgeois democracies followed a similar policy. We reach the same conclusion if we analyze the war-aims of German imperialism, which were largely identical in the two world wars. Whether the concept under consideration be that of the central African colonial empire, the expansion to the South-East or the conquest of Russian territory with the Donets Basin and the petroleum of the Caucasus – in each case the basic aim was the conquest of new sources of raw materials for industry, new markets and capital-productive areas, in other words, capitalist interests. Ideological elements such as Social Darwinism and racism which prepare for and accompany this imperialist policy can also only be understood in this context, and not by reference to large agrarian interests.

If we proceed from the assumption that the main function of fascism was to crush the workers' movement at home and to set the imperialist war in train abroad, it becomes quite clear that business interests were primarily at work, and not those of the large land-owners. Indeed, after 1933 the influence of the large agrarian concerns was progressively reduced, despite some social concessions, while representatives of industry and banking were included in all executive areas of the fascist system (the level of their representation varying according to specific function). The fact that German imperialism turned to fascism whilst imperialism in the Western democracies did not, has to be explained by reference to the special circumstances of Germany, particularly its late participation in industrialization and thus in the dividing-up of the world, which led to the tension between a powerful expansionist potential at the end of the nineteenth century and the severely limited possibilities for real expansion (this late participation is of course linked to its strong feudal traditions).

It follows that the possibility of the emergence of fascism is by no means precluded if feudal power groupings lose their influence and a capitalist system is definitively established, and only if we bear this in mind can we understand a remark that Moore makes quite without preamble. He states that, in respect of the rejection of fundamental structural reforms in the interests of the working masses, «since the Second World War, Western democracy has begun to display more and more of the same traits» as the reactionary systems of the nineteenth century in those countries where fascism was later to triumph (p. 442).

No other theory of modernization achieves the same breadth of investigative horizon or the same level of theoretical consideration as Moore's writings. It is chiefly the connection between the fascist movements and the interests of the upper classes – which Moore always has in mind – that is often overlooked. Thus, borrowing from the middle class theories, fascist movements are for example often seen one-sidedly as a mere rebellion against industrial and capitalist development, as the irrational «anti-modernism»[77] of groups and strata who adhered to a pre-industrial mentality. Little consideration is given to the fact that fascism also represented an organized attempt by the upper classes «to make reaction and conservatism popular and plebeian» (as Moore states).

Moreover, fascist dictatorship promoted the exact opposite of «anti-modernist» policies. It drew support from the large industrial and banking concerns and quickly shattered the pre-capitalist illusions about social estates of its adherents, and it also greatly reduced the vestiges of feudalism – particularly in Germany. This is often seen as a thrust towards modernization, a social revolution and thus a trail-blazer for modern democracy. According to Dahrendorf, «the brutal break with tradition and the thrust into modernity (was) the characteristic feature of the social revolution of National Socialism»[78]. In so doing, it created «the foundations of liberal modernity» (p. 442). Schoenbaum speaks of a «revolution» and of an «overthrow of the class structure»[79], Turner of «modernization»[80], and Sauer of a «social revolution» which destroyed the «basis of traditional resistance to modernity and liberality» and thereby opened the way for «democratic self-determination» after Hitler[81]. Hitler thus becomes a progressive figure who «propelled both Germany and large parts of the world into the twentieth century»[82].

This interpretation invites refutation on the following grounds:

1. Industrialization and technology cannot serve as the highest criteria for judgment and for categorization as «progressive», because they are only means to an end, and not an end in themselves. Their true purpose is the improvement of living conditions, the development of human abilities and the better fulfilment of human needs. If this is taken as the yardstick for judgment, information about the level of technology, science and productivity tell us little if no examination is made of the distribution of wealth, educational opportunities – in a word, social conditions.

2. There is also no validity in the assertion that fascism improved the pre-conditions necessary for the establishment of a democratic state and society, and was in this sense progressive. In the first place, fascist dictatorship used the methods of terror to achieve the long-lasting suppression of democratic forces and ideas; it physically exterminated many of the leading advocates of democracy and firmly embedded fascist ideology at all levels of the population through the state monopoly of propaganda and information. The task of establishing a democratic state and society after the collapse of fascism was made all the more difficult by this. In the second place, there is empirical evidence to refute the assertion that the way in which fascist dictatorship changed the structure of society was tantamount to a social revolution: The gulf between the rulers and the working population widened still further, both in respect of social differences (wealth, income) and in respect of the system of dominance (the destruction of all popular rights to co-determination in political, economic and industrial life). In contradiction of this modernization thesis, Arthur Schweitzer is right to stress «that the pretended revolution (was) no more or less than a version of counter-revolution»[83]. The real destruction of democracy and pluralism was accompanied by powerful propaganda about a «folk community» and some purely external concessions, propaganda which the state monopoly of information made sure was disseminated to the subject population. The display in National Socialism of the trappings of democracy was, as Schweitzer argues, «a typical case of ideological deception»[84].

7. The State of Marxist Theories

Marxist theories share with theories of industrial society and modernization the aspiration to provide a scientific explanation of the history of mankind, its inner impulsive forces, its direction and shifting patterns of conflict[85]. In the case of fascism, Marxist theories take as their common vantage point the explanation of political forms by reference to underlying economic contradictions. The various aspects of this relationship between the economy and fascism receive differing emphasis in Marxist scholarship, but there is general agreement that special attention should be paid to the following aspects:

1. Capitalism implies the power of the owners of capital to control the means of production. This leaves considerable political and propagandistic power in the hands of the big capital-owners, and produces a varying, but never insignificant, degree of impotence and disorientation among the mass of wage-earners and the independent middle classes.

2. For reasons of its internal regularity, capitalism evolved to the stage of imperialism and so produced those ideological elements which served to guarantee mass support for imperialist policies. Fascism merely developed these elements to their logical extremes.

3. Capitalism brought about a progressive proletarianization of the independent middle classes and so created – in conjunction with an authoritarian pre-disposition that had been implanted by socialization, the ruling ideology and everyday experience – the social potential which provided a basis for the fascist movements.

4. Capitalism led to severe economic crises which unleashed this potential, and allowed fascist parties to grow into mass movements in some countries.

5. The economic crises shook the political and ideological stability of the capitalist system and led to the emergence of anti-capitalist forces and trends, against which, in some countries, the ruling class was able to defend itself only by overthrowing governmental legality and parliamentarism. The defense took the form of a fascist dictatorship.

6. This political course necessitated the financial and political support of the fascist movement by relevant sections of the ruling class, and their intensive co-operation with the fascist leadership after the fascist state had been set up.

7. A state organized on the lines of parliamentary legality, which gave a strong workers' movement the continuing opportunity to make its influence felt, could not provide the basis for the armed conquest of new imperialist spheres in competition with powerful enemies. This demanded a form of state which was capable of concentrating all economic, political, military and psychological resources to this end, and which could ruthlessly crush all opposition forces. Only fascism could do this.

Even this brief outline makes it clear that, in examining the connections between capitalism and fascism, we are dealing with a highly complex, primarily structural problem, and not primarily with the personal links between the wealthier representatives of big business and the leaders of the fascist party. This is but one aspect of the problem, and by no means fundamental.

The explanatory value of Marxist theories propounded to date lies in two areas above all: firstly, they give theoretical weight to the relationship between the capitalist system as a whole and focus explicitly on the creation of the social pre-conditions for the genesis and emergence of fascist movements; and secondly, they do much to illuminate the part played by leading sections of business in the establishment of fascist dictatorships, and in the implementation of their policies[86]. The emphasis lies on the investigation of the social causes and the social function of fascism. The problems and weaknesses of these theories are chiefly the following:

1. There is as yet no fully satisfactory explanation of why, and under what conditions, certain sections of the population support fascism, and what mental and social processes are involved. This lack has to do with the fact that, although the basic elements of Marxist psychology have been defined[87], their integration into a system is not yet far enough advanced for it to be applied to socio-historical processes like fascism. The belief that the behavior of the masses can simply be explained as the result of conscious manipulation by the ruling class is often encountered in older Marxist writings. This is unsatisfactory, however, and has largely been abandoned.

2. No clear exposition has been made of the conditions that must prevail for the ruling class to support the establishment of a fascist dictatorship. The thesis of «preventive counter-revolution» assumes that this occurs only when the survival of the capitalist system is threatened (by a severe economic crisis and the emergence of anti-capitalist and revolutionary forces)[88]. An antithetical argument claims that, even in the event of a «threat to only a few of its main political interests», big business moves to abolish parliamentary democracy and to set up a fascist dictatorship; this could for example be the case if the government's ability to act is inhibited by the extreme fragmentation of bourgeois parties, or if the aims of an expansionist policy cannot otherwise be achieved[89];

3. The relationship between the facist leadership and state, on the one hand, and big business, on the other, has been examined in a great number of empirical investigations, particularly in the German context; but as yet this relationship has not been researched well enough to allow a precise theoretical definition to be made. The definition of the fascist state as the agent, the instrument, or the executive organ of big business which may often be found in theories elaborated in the past, is undoubtedly too rough in its approach. On the other hand, the empirical investigations which have now been published, undermine the Bonapartist theory propounded by Otto Bauer and August Thalheimer[90], which mechanically separates the political power of the fascist leadership from the economic dominance of the capital-owners, and accords the fascist state – at least temporarily – a position completely independent of the ruling economic interests. Nor does a consideration of state intervention in the economy offer any conclusive evidence of the precise relationship between economy and politics in fascism, because such intervention was called for by the large industrial and banking concerns themselves, and its effects were largely determined by them. The theory of an «alliance» or «compromise» between various forces (the fascist party, big business, the military, the higher civil service) does no more to provide an adequate explanation unless, as we have pointed out, it is clearly indicated what the relationship between the alliance parties was, and who achieved what degree of influence.

More recent Marxist theories emphasize that the fascist state uses its power to maintain capitalism and serves the economic interests of big business, at the expense of wage-earners and the middle classes. However, they define the position of the state as one of «relative independence» of big business in the formulation of its aims and in the strategy of their achievement; the precise meaning in individual cases of the phrase «relative independence» (which has links with the writings of Friedrich Engels)[91] is as yet inadequately explained, and can be explained only by further empirical studies.

4. There are considerable differences of opinion on the question of the distinction

between fascist systems and other kinds of terroristic and reactionary systems. Argument also surrounds the issue of whether the mass movement is properly a criterion for the definition of fascism, or whether any system that promotes the interests of big business by terroristic methods and outlaws all other interests and organizations should be called fascist[92]. In this respect, empirical comparisons need to be made of the political systems in Spain (1936–78), Portugal (until 1974), Greece (1967–73), Chile (from 1973), which did not emerge from a mass movement or enjoy mass support, but were maintained solely or mainly by a state apparatus of suppression. Likewise, the differences between the Italian and German experiences should be further explored. The analytical theories of the state are also in need of further refinement and elaboration.

NOTES

Sections 3, 5 and 6 are translated from German by Paul Bristow.

[1] Cf. the bewilderment expressed by an early observer: «Not a single prophet, during more than a century of prophecies . . . ever imagined anything like fascism. There was in the lap of the future, communism and syndicalism and what not: there was anarchism . . . war, peace, deluge, Pan-Germanism, Pan-Slavism; . . . there was no fascism. It came as a surprise to all . . .» G. A. Borgese, «The Intellectual Origins of Fascism», *Social Research*, I (Nov. 1934) pp. 475–76, quoted from H. Stuart Hughes, *The Sea Change. The Migration of Social Thought* (New York 1975) p. 70.

[2] Cf. Peter Viereck, *Metapolitics: From the Romantics to Hitler* (New York 1941).

[3] The expression is brought into current usage by T. W. Mason. See his early formulation in «Der Primat der Politik. Politik und Wirtschaft im Nationalsozialismus», in *Das Argument* 41, 1966, pp. 473–94, and the English version «The Primacy of Politics and Economics in National Socialist Germany» in S. J. Woolf (ed.), *The Nature of Fascism* (London 1968), pp. 165–195.

[4] Cf. Henry Ashby Turner, Jr. «Fascism and Modernization» in *World Politics*, 24, 1972, pp. 547–564. For a rejoinder, with material from Italy, see A. James Gregor, «Fascism and Modernization: Some Addenda», *ibid.* 26, 1974, pp. 370–84.

[5] A good discussion is provided by Axel Kuhn, *Das faschistische Herrschaftssystem und die moderne Gesellschaft* (Hamburg 1973) and Martin Kitchen, *Fascism* (London 1976), especially ch. 8.

[6] Ernst Nolte, «Vierzig Jahre Theorien über den Faschismus» in the author's *Theorien über den Faschismus,* pp. 15–75 (Cologne 1970) and his *Three Faces of Fascism* (paperback ed.) p. 38 ff (New York 1969).

[7] Broad surveys of the state of research on fascism is provided by W. Laqueur in his edited collection of articles *Fascism: A Reader's Guide* (London 1976); Helga Grebing, *Aktuelle Theorien über Faschismus und Konservatismus. Eine Kritik* (Stuttgart 1974); Renzo de Felice, *Interpretations of Fascism* (Cambridge, Mass. 1977); G. Schulz, *Faschismus – Nationalsozialismus. Versionen und theoretische Kontroversen 1922–1972* (Berlin 1974); A. James Gregor, *Interpretations of Fascism* (Morristown, N. J. 1974); R. Saage, *Faschismustheorien. Eine Einführung* (Munich 1976); W. Wipperman, *Faschismustheorien* (Darmstadt 1976); H. U. Thamer & W. Wipperman, *Faschistische und Neo-faschistische Bewegungen* (Darmstadt 1977). A useful survey is also M. Weissbecker, *Entteufelung der braunen Barbarei. Zu einigen neueren Tendenzen in der Geschichtschreibung der BRD über Faschismus und faschistische Führer* (Frankfurt a.M. 1975); E. Hanisch, «Literaturbericht. Neuere Faschismustheorien», in *Zeitgeschichte,* 1 1973, pp. 19–23 and J. Sigmann, «Fascismes et National-Socialisme», *Annales* 24, 1969, pp. 195–233.

For the positions taken by the New Left in the 1960's, see *Das Argument. Berliner Hefte für Probleme der Gesellschaft,* issues dealing with *Faschismustheorien* I–VI, 1964–70.

In addition to his broader surveys, Ernst Nolte provides a short discussion of recent literature, «Der Faschismus als Problem in der wissenschaftlichen Literatur der jüngsten Vergangenheit» in *Der Nationalsozialismus* (Munich 1973) pp. 197–208, reprinted in H. A. Turner, Jr. (ed.) *Reappraisals of Fascism* (New York 1975), pp. 26–43.

Kühnl's work is printed in «Probleme der Interpretation des deutschen Faschismus», in *Das Argument*, 1970, no. 58; «Der deutsche Faschismus», in *Neue Politische Literatur*, 1970, no. 1; «Tendenzen der Faschismusforschung», in *Frankfurter Hefte* 1970, no. 6; *Formen bürgerlicher Herrschaft* (Reinbek 1971); «Der deutsche Faschismus in der neueren Forschung», in *Das Argument* 1973, no. 78; «Probleme einer Theorie über den deutschen Faschismus» in *Jahrbuch des Instituts für deutsche Geschichte*, University of Tel Aviv, vol. 3, 1974 (reprinted and slightly abridged in «New German Critique», no. 4, Winter 1975); «Probleme einer Theorie über den internationalen Faschismus», Part 1 in *Politische Vierteljahresschrift*, 1970, no. 2–3, part 2 in *ibid.*, 1975, no. 1. See also Kühnl, *Faschismustheorien. Texte zur Faschismusdiskussion 2. Ein Leitfaden* (Reinbek 1979).

[8] Golo Mann, preface to E. Calic, *Ohne Maske. Hitler-Breiting Geheimgespräche 1931* (Frankfurt 1968) pp. 5 and 8, and his address to the 29th German Historical Convention, 1972: «Ohne Geschichte leben?», printed in *Die Zeit*, 41/1972. The personalistic interpretation of history looms large in these writings: Hitler became dictator because «he wanted to». For other interpretations in this tradition, see G. Tellenbach, *Die deutsche Not als Schuld und Schicksal* (Stuttgart 1947), Ph. W. Fabry, *Mutmassungen über Hitler* (Düsseldorf 1968) and F. Meinecke, *Die deutsche Katastrophe* (Wiesbaden 1946) (English edition *The German Catastrophe*, Cambridge, Mass. 1950).

The literature on the leadership problem in fascism is steadily growing. A balanced analysis of Hitler, with a review of recent scholarship is provided by Karl D. Bracher, «The Role of Hitler: Perspectives of Interpretation», in W. Laqueur, *Fascism: A Reader's Guide* (London 1976) pp. 211–229. See also R. Kühnl, *Faschismustheorien. Texte zur Faschismusdiskussion 2. Ein Leitfaden* (Hamburg 1979) pp. 47–69 which surveys the German literature. The psychohistorical approach to Hitler has been reviewed by Hans W. Gatzke, «Hitler and Psychohistory», in *American Historical Review*, 78, no. 2 1973, pp. 394–401. See also L. Papeleux, «Psychanalyse d'Hitler», in *Revue d'histoire de la deuxieme guerre mondiale* 24/96 (October 1974) pp. 105–108. The production of books on Hitler seems to be a most thriving industry. A sample of recent offerings: Robert G. L. Waite, *The Psychopatic God Adolf Hitler* (New York 1977); *Hitler Close-Up* by H. Hoffmann and Henry Picker (London 1974); Horst von Maltlitz, *The Evolution of Hitler's Germany; The Ideology, the Personality, the Movement* (New York 1974); Rudolf Binion, *Hitler Among the Germans* (Elsevier 1976); John Toland, *Adolf Hitler* (New York 1977); *Hitler: Legend, Myth and Reality* by Werner Maser (New York 1974); J. P. Stern, *Hitler. The Führer and the People* (London 1975); R. Payne, *The Life and Death of Adolf Hitler* (New York 1973) and of course J. Fest, *Hitler* (New York 1974).

[9] A survey of this tradition is given by Renzo de Felice, *Interpretations of Fascism* (Cambridge, Mass. 1977) pp. 14–30. De Felice makes Meinecke, Gerhard Ritter's *Die Dämonie der Macht* (Munich-Stuttgart 1947), Croce's *Scritti e discorsi politici 1943–47* (Bari 1963), Golo Mann's *The History of Germany since 1789* (New York 1968), Hans Kohn, *The Twentieth Century: The Challenge to the West and Its Response* (New York 1949) and in part the works of the Catholic writers Jacques Maritain and A. Del Noce, the basis for this interpretation.

[10] Edmond Vermeil, *Doctrinaires de la Revolution Allemande 1919–1938* (Paris 1939); W. Montgomery McGovern, *From Luther to Hitler: The History of Fascist-Nazi Political Philosophy* (New York 1941), and P. Viereck, *op. cit.*

[11] G. Lukács, *Die Zerstörung der Vernunft* (Neuwied 1962), K. D. Bracher, *The German Dictatorship* (New York 1970). Bracher denies that there is such a phenomenon as 'generic' fascism: German National Socialism was specifically German and can only be viewed within the context of German history. This rejection of any general concept of fascism is shared by Henry Ashby Turner, Jr. who in his collection of articles *Reappraisals of Fascism* (New York 1975) writes that «. . . it seems unwise to continue with studies of fascism that start with the assumption that there must have been such a generic phenomenon» . . . «It seems more appropriate to

consider carefully whether some or even all of the movements and regimes alleged to have been fascist may not be classified more meaningfully in some other way». (p. 133, *passim.*)

The 'accumulation of crises' syndrome which forms the basis of the developmental approach to the study of national unification sequences and the subsequent instability of regimes was first brought into common usage in L. Binder *et al. Crises and Sequences in Political Development* (Princeton, N.J. 1971). For a more recent elaboration, see the contributions by C. Tilly and S. Rokkan in Tilly (ed.) *The Formation of National States in Western Europe* (Princeton, N.J. 1975) especially pp. 66–73 and pp. 562–600. The question of the timing of national unification has been suggestively discussed by Helmut Plessner, *Die verspätete Nation* (Stuttgart 1959). See also Kühnl, *op. cit.* pp. 69–89 and the contribution by Stein Rokkan and Bernt Hagtvet in this volume. The entire problem of continuity in German history has spawned an enormous literature. A guide can be found in W. Wipperman, *Faschismustheorien* (Darmstadt 1976) pp. 104–122, and in W. Sauer, «Das Problem des deutschen Nationalstaates», in H.–U. Wehler, *Moderne deutsche Sozialgeschichte* (Cologne, Berlin 1966) pp. 407–436. For similarities in foreign policy, see the discussion by A. Hillgruber, *Kontinuität oder Diskontinuität in der deutschen Aussenpolitik von Bismarck bis Hitler* (Düsseldorf 1969). For discussions of late nation-building and regime instability in the Italian case, see Adrian Lyttelton's «Introduction», pp. 1–15 in his *The Seizure of Power. Fascism in Italy 1919–1929* (London 1973) and C. Seton-Watson's magistral work, *Italy from Liberalism to Fascism 1870–1925* (London 1967). An extensive discussion is also found in K. Priester, *Der italienische Faschismus. Ökonomische und Ideologische Grundlagen* (Cologne 1972). See also the survey of recent scholarship by A. Lyttelton, «Italian Fascism», in Laqueur (ed.) *Fascism, op. cit.* pp. 125–151. The major Italian interpretations are examined by De Felice, *op. cit.* pp. 107–190.

[12] For an analysis of the Comintern 'agent theory', see M. Kitchen, *op. cit.* pp. 1–15 and Wipperman, *op. cit.* pp. 11–37. See also De Felice, *op. cit.* pp. 40–51. For contemporary discussions of the relationship between heavy industry and fascism, see K. Gossweiler, R. Kühnl, R. Opitz, *Faschismus: Enstehung und Verhinderung. Texte zur Demokratisierung* (Frankfurt a.M. 1972); D. Stegmann, «Zum Verhältnis von Grossindustrie und Nationalsozialismus 1930–33» in *Archiv für Sozialgeschichte,* 1973, 13, pp. 399–482; K. Gossweiler, *Faschismus und antifaschistischer Kampf: Texte zur Demokratisierung* (Frankfurt a.M. 1978). See also Gossweiler's *Grossbanken, Industriemonopole, Staat. Ökonomie und Politik in staatsmonopolistischen Kapitalismus in Deutschland 1914–1932* (Berlin 1971) and A. Kuhn, «Die Unterredung zwischen Hitler und Papen im Hause des Barons von Scröder», in *Geschichte in Wissenschaft und Unterricht,* 24, 1973, pp. 709–22. Further bibliographical information can be found in R. Kühnl, *Faschismustheorien, op. cit.* pp. 231–41. Henry A. Turner, Jr. has presented a different opinion on the relationship between industry and fascism. See his *Faschismus und Kapitalismus in Deutschland* (Göttingen 1972) and his more recent contributions, «Das Verhältnis des Grossunternehmertums zur NSDAP», in Hans Mommsen *et al.* (ed.) *Industrielles System und Politische Entwicklung in der Weimarer Republik* (Düsseldorf 1974). See also his response to Axel Kuhn and Dirk Stegmann: «Grossunternehmertum und Nationalsozialismus 1930–33» in *Historische Zeitschrift,* vol. 221 (August 1975), pp. 18–68. For the debate up to 1970, see the balanced view by Eike Hennig, «Industrie und Faschismus. Anmerkungen zur sowjetischen Interpretation», in *Neue Politische Literatur,* 1970, pp. 432–449.

[13] For a review of the entire Bonapartism thesis, see M. Kitchen, «August Thalheimer's Theory of Fascism», *Journal of the History of Ideas,* vol. 34, no. 1, 1974, pp. 67–79, Kühnl, *Faschismustheorien, op. cit.* pp. 192–213. For further bibliographical guide to the classical literature, see Wipperman, *op.cit.* pp. 42–49. For an up to date discussion of scholarship on National Socialism, see Hans Mommsen, «National Socialism: Continuity and Change» in Laqueur, *op. cit.* pp. 179–210.

[14] Variants of the partner theory are discussed in section 5 in this essay. For a contemporary analysis, see «Faschismus als Bündnis» in R. Kühnl, *Faschismustheorien, op. cit.* pp. 167–192 with extensive bibliographical references.

[15] The most recent comprehensive analysis of the concept of totalitarianism is provided by Juan J. Linz, «Totalitarian and Authoritarian Regimes» in Fred I. Greenstein and Nelson W.

Polsby (eds.) *Handbook of Political Science,* vol. 3. «Macropolitical Theory» pp. 175–413 (Reading, Mass. 1975). The German scene is surveyed in B. Seidel & S. Jenkner, *Wege der Totalitarismusforschung* (Darmstadt 1968), W. Schlangen, *Theorie und Ideologie des Totalitarismus* (Dissertation, Bonn 1972); M. Greiffenhagen, R. Kühnl, J. B. Müller, *Totalitarismus. Zur Problematik eines politischen Begriffs* (Munich 1972); K. Hildebrand, «Stufen der Totalitarismusforschung», in *Politische Vierteljahresschrift,* 9, 1968, pp. 397–422; M. Greiffenhagen, «Der Totalitarismusbegriff in der Regimenlehre», in *Politische Vierteljahresschrift,* 9, 1968, 372–396 and P. C. Ludz, «Offene Fragen in der Totalitarismusforschung», *Politische Vierteljahresschrift,* 1961, no. 2, pp. 319–47. A lucid review of the current state of the debate is given by M. Kitchen, «The Theory of Totalitarianism» in his *Fascism* (London 1976) pp. 25–35.

[16] The reader's attention is directed to three earlier reviews of Nolte: C. J. Friedrich, «Fascism versus Totalitarianism: Ernst Nolte's Views Reexamined», *Central European History,* vol. 4, no. 3, September 1971, pp. 271–284 and K. Epstein, «A New Study of Fascism», in World Politics, vol. 26, January 1964, no. 2, pp. 302–321, reprinted in Turner, (ed.) *Reappraisals . . . op. cit.* and M. Kitchen. «Ernst Nolte and the Phenomenology of Fascism», in *Science and Society,* Vol. 38, No. 2. (1974), pp. 130–149.

[17] For a more extensive discussion, see section 2 in this essay. The most updated discussion of the middle class theory is found in W. Scieder (ed.) *Faschismus als Soziale Bewegung* (Hamburg 1976) which includes material on Italian Fascism. The book contains good bibliographical references.

[18] See section 3 in this essay and ch. 2 in Kitchen, *Fascism, op. cit.* for further bibliographical references.

[19] See section 6 in this essay. The positions in the modernization literature can be found in the following works: C. E. Black, *The Dynamics of Modernization* (New York 1966); S. N. Eisenstadt, *Modernization: Protest and Change* (Englewood Cliffs, N.J. 1966); David Apter, *The Politics of Modernization* (Chicago 1965). For a recent summary of the debate: E. Hennig, *Bürgerliche Gesellschaft und Faschismus in Deutschland* (Frankfurt a.M. 1977) and Kühnl, *Faschismustheorien, op. cit.* pp. 152–67.

[20] For a most interesting attempt to analyze the aesthetic underpinnings of German politics, showing the continuities between Nazi taste and the «national aesthetics» of Germany, tracing the component of primordial, pagan religiosity in the German reaction to the dehumanizing aspect of industrialization: G. L. Mosse, *The Nationalization of the Masses* (New York 1977). An earlier work is R. Winegarten, «The Temptations of Cultural Fascism» in H. A. Turner, Jr., *Reappraisals, op cit.,* pp. 215–231.

[21] Cf. F. Stern, *The Politics of Cultural Despair* (New York 1967) and *ibid. The Failure of Illiberalism* (New York 1972), and G. L. Mosse, *The Crisis of German Ideology* (New York 1967).

[22] A. J. Mayer, *The Dynamics of Counter-revolution* (New York 1967).

[23] L. Salvatorelli, *Nazionalfascismo,* (Turin 1923) reprinted in E. Nolte (ed.), *Theorien über den Faschismus:* here p. 131.

[24] Th. Geiger, *Die soziale Schichtung des deutschen Volkes,* (Stuttgart 1932) the chapter on «Die Mittelstände im Zeichen des Nationalsozialismus» is reprinted in: Th. Geiger, *«Arbeiten zur Soziologie»,* (Neuwied and Berlin 1962); the references that follow are to this later edition. Similar observations about the middle classes are to be found in: E. Lederer & J. Marschak, *Der neue Mittelstand,* (Tübingen 1926), E. Grünberg, *Der Mittelstand in der kapitalistischen Gesellschaft,* (Leipzig 1932). For a more recent examination, cf. H.A.Winkler, *Mittelstand, Demokratie und Nationalsozialismus* (Cologne 1972).

[25] S. M. Lipset, «'Fascism' – Left, Right and Center» in *Political Man: The Social Bases of Politics.* (New York 1960).

[26] Geiger, pp. 350 & 349.

[27] Geiger, p. 351.

[28] An early important work on the moral predispositions of the lower middle class is S. Ranulf, *Moral Indignation and Middle Class Psychology (*Copenhagen 1938). See also De Felice's discussion, *op. cit.* pp. 87–99.

[29] Lipset, p. 136.

[30] Cf. H. A. Winkler, «Extremismus der Mitte?» in *Vierteljahreshefte für Zeitgeschichte* (20), 1972, pp. 175–191.

[31] *Ibid.* p. 176–77.

[32] R. Hamilton, «The Bases for National Socialism: The Electoral Support for Hitler 1924–32», mimeo. Department of Sociology, McGill University, Montreal, Canada, forthcoming. See also B. Hagtvet's essay on mass theory in this volume, note 64.

[33] W. Reich, *Die Massenpsychologie des Faschismus* (Copenhagen 1933); published in English as *The Mass Psychology of Fascism* by Souvenir Press (London 1972), references are to this later edition. E. Fromm, *The Fear of Freedom* (London 1942). See also Kitchen, *op. cit.* pp. 12–25.

[34] Cf. for example the essay by K. Horn in: R. Kühnl (ed.), *Texte zur Faschismusdiskussion* I, (Reinbek bei Hamburg 1974) and a recent attempt in psycho-history: P. Loewenberg. «The Psycho-Historical Roots of the Nazi Youth Cohort», in *Am. Historical Review*, 76, 5 (December 1971), pp. 1457–1503.

[35] Reich, p. 16.

[36] W. Reich, *Charakteranalyse* (Cologne 1970), published in English as *Character Analysis* by Vision Press (London 1969), the quotation is from p. (xxii) of the latter edition.

[37] W. Reich, *Dialektischer Materialismus und Psychoanalyse*, in: Bernfeld *et al.*, *Psychoanalyse und Marxismus*, (Frankfurt a.M. 1970), p. 176.

[38] Reich, *Mass Psychology*, pp. 46 & 47.

[39] *Ibid*, pp. 46–48.

[40] *Ibid*, p. 60.

[41] *Ibid*, p. 40.

[42] Fromm, *The Fear of Freedom*, p. 4.

[43] *Ibid*, pp. 252–253.

[44] Not only do these theories divert attention from the real social causes of aggressive behavior and from the social groups who profit from war and the politics of force, but they also deny mankind any hope of securing a peaceful future by a rational ordering of social relationships.

[45] The following works could provide a general methodological basis for such an interpretation: K. Holzkamp, *Sinnliche Erkenntnis – Historischer Ursprung und gesellschaftliche Funktion der Wahrnehmung*, (Frankfurt 1973) A. N. Leontiew, *Probleme der Entwicklung des Psychischen*, (Frankfurt 1973).

[46] C. J. Friedrich and Z. K. Brzezinski, *Totalitarian Dictatorship and Autocracy* (Cambridge, Mass. 1956).

[47] *Ibid*, p. 10.

[48] C. J. Friedrich, «The Evolving Theory and Practice of Totalitarian Regimes», in C. J. Friedrich, M. Curtis and B. R. Barber, *Totalitarianism in Perspective* (New York 1969), p. 126. See also the extensive discussion by Robert Orr, «Reflections on Totalitarianism, Leading to Reflections on Two Ways of Theorizing», in *Political Studies*, vol. 21 no. 4, pp. 481–89.

[49] This is the main point in R. Burrowes' incisive critique, «Totalitarianism: The Revised Standard Version», in *World Politics* (1969) pp. 272–294.

[50] Friedrich, 1965 edition, p. 19.

[51] Friedrich, *ibid*, p. 20.

[52] Cf. Kitchen, *op. cit.*, p. 31 *passim*.

[53] Friedrich, p. 19 & 22.

[54] *Ibid*, p. 54.

[55] Marx does not call religion «opium for the people» («Opium für das Volk» – Friedrich, German Edition p. 22), which would mean that the rulers consciously use this instrument to anaesthetize the people, but «the opium of the people» («das Opium des Volkes»), in other words an aid with which the people consoles itself for life's hardships: «Religion is the sigh of the oppressed creature, the conscience of a heartless world, as it is the spirit of spiritless conditions. It is the opium of the people». (K. Marx, «Zur Kritik der Hegelschen Rechtsphilosophie»,

Marx-Engels-Werke, vol. 1. p. 378). Friedrich's other comments on Marxist theory (cf. especially p. 24 *passim.*) are consistently based on misinterpretations.

⁵⁶ Friedrich, p. 23.

⁵⁷ Cf. B. R. Barber & J. J. Spiro, «The Concept of 'Totalitarianism' as the Foundation of American Counter-Ideology in the Cold War», paper, Am. Pol. Sci. Association Meeting, 1967.

⁵⁸ L. Schapiro, *Totalitarianism* (London 1972) discusses this, p. 105 ff. As early as 1961, P. G. Ludz made the same point, «Totalitarismus der Totalität» in *Soziale Welt,* 1961, no. 1, pp. 129–145.

⁵⁹ B. R. Barber, «Conceptual Foundations of Totalitarianism» especially pp. 33–34 in Friedrich *et al. Totalitarianism in Perspective, op. cit.* For attempts to modify the concept, see Robert Tucker, «The Dictator and Totalitarianism», *World Politics,* 17, July 1965, pp. 555–583 and *ibid.* «Toward a Comparative Politics of Movement Regimes», In *The Am.Pol. Science Review,* 60, (June 1961) pp. 281–89.

⁶⁰ Cf. also M. Jänicke, *Totalitäre Herrschaft – Anatomie eines politischen Begriffes* (Berlin 1971).

⁶¹ This has been convincingly demonstrated in the case of Italy by Angelo Tasca and C. Seton-Watson, for example, and in the German context by Stegmann, Broszat and others: A. Tasca, *Nascita e avvento del fascismo – L'Italia dal 1918 al 1922,* (Paris 1938), (new German-language edition entitled *Glauben, Gehorchen, Kämpfen,* Vienna 1969), C. Seton-Watson, *Italy from Liberalism to Fascism, 1870–1925,* (London 1967); D. Stegmann «Zum Verhältnis von Grossindustrie und National-sozialismus, 1930–1933», in *Archiv für Sozialgeschichte,* 13, 1973; M. Broszat, *Der Staat Hitlers. Grundlegung und Entwicklung seiner inneren Verfassung,* (Munich 1969). The ideological preparation for this alliance in Germany is discussed in: W. Struve, *Elites against Democracy. Leadership Ideals in Bourgeois Political Thought in Germany, 1890–1933* (Princeton, N.J. 1973); K. Sontheimer, *Antidemokratisches Denken in der Weimarer Republik,* (Munich 1962), and, as a general thesis, in: W. Scieder, «Faschismus und kein Ende?» in *Neue Politische Literatur,* 1970, no. 2, pp. 166–187.

⁶²Cf. A. Schweitzer, *op. cit.;* Ch. Bloch, *Die SA und die Krise des NS-Regimes 1934,* (Frankfurt 1970); H. Lebowics, *Social Conservatism and the Middle Classes 1914–1933,* (Princeton, N.J. 1969). Lebowics observes that the decision to abandon petty bourgeois socialism in favor of the pact with the haute bourgeoisie had been taken before 1933 in Germany.

⁶³ Seton-Watson, *op. cit.* pp. 700 & 702.

⁶⁴ A. Klönne, «Was heisst Faschismus», in *Werkhefte,* 1969, No. 10, p. 279.

⁶⁵ Schweitzer, *op. cit.* Schweitzer's thesis is taken up by D. Petzina, *Autarkiepolitik im Dritten Reich. Der national-sozialistsche Vierjahresplan,* (Stuttgart 1968) and by Tim Mason, «Der Primat der Politik», in: *Das Argument,* No. 41.

⁶⁶ Cf. *Former bürgerlicher Herrschaft. Liberalismus und Faschismus,* (Reinbek bei Hamburg 1971).

⁶⁷ A. Sohn-Rethel, *Ökonomie und Klassenstruktur des deutschen Faschismus.* (Frankfurt 1973), p. 198.

⁶⁸ S. J. Woolf (ed.), *European Fascism,* London 1968, see introduction. The idea of polyarchy is also fundamental to M. Greiffenhagen's approach, in: M. Greiffenhagen, R. Kühnl, J. B. Müller, *Totalitarismus, op. cit.* (Munich 1972); D. Schoenbaum, *Die braune Revolution. Eine Sozialgeschichte des Dritten Reiches,* (Cologne and Berlin 1968). English edition: *Hitler's Social Revolution* (New York 1967); K. D. Bracher, W. Sauer, G. Schulz, *Die nationalsozialistische Machtergreifung,* (Cologne & Opladen 1962); H. Mommsen, *Beamtentum im Dritten Reich* (Stuttgart 1966); M. Broszat, *op. cit.;* W. Sauer, «National Socialism: Totalitarianism or Fascism?» in: *The American Historical Review,* 73, 1967, No. 2, pp. 404–424. The idea that, in looking at fascism, we are dealing with a somehow fragmented power structure probably derives from E. Fraenkel, *The Dual State* (New York, London, Toronto, 1941); and F. Neumann, *Behemoth* (New York, London, Toronto, 1942).

⁶⁹ B. Blanke, «Thesen zur Faschismus-Diskussion» in: *Sozialistische Politik,* October 1969, no. 3, pp. 55 & 62; N. Kadritzke, «Faschismus als gesellschaftliche Realität und als unrealistischer Kampfbegriff», in: *Probleme des Klassenkampfes,* 1973, H. 8/9, p. 172 *et seq.*

[70] H. A. Winkler, *op. cit.* p. 161 & *passim.*

[71] I. Fetscher, «Faschismus und Nationalsozialismus. Zur Kritik des sowjet-marxistischen Faschismusbegriffs», in: *Politische Vierteljahresschrift,* 1962, no. 1, p. 62.

[72] On this controversy, cf. *Das Argument, 47.*

[73] Cf. E. Hennig, *Thesen zur deutschen Sozial- und Wirtschaftspolitik 1933 bis 1938,* (Frankfurt 1973).

[74] For an overview, see for example J. P. Nettl & R. Robertson, «International Systems and the Modernization of Societies», (New York 1968). For a more recent approach, see W. L. Goldfrank «Fascism and World Economy», in B. H. Koplan (ed.) *Social Changes in the Capitalist World Economy* (London 1978), pp. 75–117.

[75] Cf. W. W. Rostow, *The Stages of Growth. A Non-Communist Manifesto* (Cambridge, Engl. 1960).

[76] Barrington Moore Jr., *Social Origins of Dictatorship and Democracy,* (London 1967), and his most recent book, which fills the gap on Germany left open in *Social Origins: Injustice, The Social Bases for Obedience and Revolt* (London 1978).

[77] Cf. for example S. N. Eisenstadt, *Modernization: Protest and Change,* (Englewood Cliffs 1966), and H. A. Turner, Jr., «Fascism and Modernization», *op. cit.*

[78] R. Dahrendorf, *Gesellschaft und Demokratie in Deutschland* (Munich 1965), p. 432.

[79] Schoenbaum, *op. cit.,* p. 333.

[80] H. A. Turner, *op. cit.,* p. 126.

[81] W. Sauer, «National Socialism» *op. cit.* p. 418.

[82] J. C. Fest, *Hitler,* (London 1974) p. 759. The first writer to apply the modernization thesis to fascism was surely Franz Borkenau, «Zur Soziologie des Faschismus», in: *Archiv für Sozialwissenschaft und Sozialpolitik,* 1933, No. 68; reprinted in: E. Nolte (ed.), *op. cit.,* p. 156 *et seq.* Eugen Weber also calls fascism not conservative but revolutionary, although he justifies this description differently, by claiming that fascism was supported by workers and peasants as well, and that its dynamism appeared in the glorification and application of strength which, as social energy, made history. *(Varieties of Fascism. Doctrines of Revolution in the 20th Century* (London & New York 1964) esp. p. 34).

[83] A. Schweitzer, *op. cit.* p. 137.

[84] *Ibid.* p. 141.

[85] For a general treatment of the Marxist theory of man and history, cf. W. Hollitscher, *Der Mensch im Weltbild der Wissenschaft,* (Vienna 1969); B. G. Ananjew, *Der Mensch als Gegenstand der Erkenntnis,* (Berlin 1974); E. Engelberg (ed.), *Probleme der marxistischen Geschichtswissenschaft,* (Cologne 1972).

[86] As regards the role of big business in the establishment and running of the fascist dictatorship in Germany, see notes 12 and 90. A recent appraisal of the question of financial backing is provided by J. and S. Pool, *Who Financed Hitler? The Secret Funding of Hitler's Rise to Power 1919–1933* (New York 1979).

[87] Cf. Petrowski et al., *Allgemeine Psychologie,* (Cologne 1974); S. L. Rubinstein, *Sein und Bewusstsein,* 7th. (ed. Berlin 1973); Autorenkollektiv, Wissenschaft Psychologie, *Materialistische Wissenschaft der Psychologie* (Cologne 1975); L. Seve, *Marxismus und Theorie der Persönlichkeit,* (Frankfurt 1972); I. S. Kehn, *Soziologie der Persönlichkeit,* (Cologne 1971); B. A. Cagin, *Der subjektive Faktor,* (Cologne 1974).

[88] For an early expression of these ideas, cf. A. Tasca, *op. cit.;* A. Rosenberg «Der Faschismus als Massenbewegung», Karlsbad 1934 (reprinted in abridged form in: W. Abendroth (ed.), *Faschismus und Kapitalismus* (Frankfurt 1967)). Similar views of this question are held by R. Kühnl, see especially *Formen bürgerlicher, op. cit;* M. Clemenz, *Gesellschaftliche Ursprünge des Faschismus* (Frankfurt 1972) and W. Alff, *Der Begriff Faschismus und andere Aufsätze zur Zeitgeschichte* (Frankfurt 1971).

[89] Thus R. Opitz, *op. cit.*

[90] Examples of empirical investigations written up to the 1940's may be found in: Th. Pirker (ed.), *Komintern und Faschismus 1920–1940,* (Stuttgart 1965); and in the collection edited by Abendroth (see note 88). The more recent Marxist discussion has been documented by R. Kühnl

(ed), *Texte zur Faschismusdiskussion, op. cit.;* and important essays may also be found in: *Das Argument,* 41, 47, 58, 78 & 87. For the results of East German research, which plays a leading role in the discussion of fascism in the Socialist countries, cf. esp.: E. Paterna *et al., Deutschland 1933–1939, op. cit.;* W. Bleyer *et al., Deutschland 1939–1945, op. cit.;* M. Weissbecker, «Nationalsozialistische Deutsche Arbeiterpartei», in: *Die bürgerlichen Parteien in Deutschland,* vol. II (Leipzig 1970); M. Weissbecker, «Wesen und Erscheinungsformen des gegenwärtigen Faschismus», in: Institut für Internationale Politik und Wirtschaft, *Berichte* 1975, no. 8; D. Eichholtz & W. Schumann (ed.), *Anatomie des Krieges. Neue Dokumente über die Rolle des deutschen Monopolkapitals bei der Vorbereitung und Durchführung des zweiten Weltkrieges* (Berlin 1969); G. Hass & W. Schumann (ed.), *Anatomie der Aggression. Neue Dokumente zu den Kriegszielen des faschistischen deutschen Imperialismus im zweiten Weltkrieg* (Berlin 1972); K. Gossweiler, *Grossbanken, Industriemonopole, Staat, op. cit.;* W. Schumann *et al., Deutschland im zweiten Weltkrieg,* 4 vols., (Cologne 1975–1977); W. Schumann & L. Nestler (ed.) *Weltherrschaft im Visier. Dokumente zu den Europa- und Weltherrschaftsplänen des deutschen Imperialismus von der Jahrhundertwende bis Mai 1945,* (Berlin 1975). – The Bauer and Thalheimer texts are reprinted in the collections edited by Abendroth and Kühnl (see above); cf. as well the controversy between Mason, Czichon, Gossweiler and Eichholtz, in: *Das Argument,* 47.

[91] According to Engels, the state power «has to follow the movement of production by and large, but it can also react, by virtue of the relative independence it possesses which, once transferred, is gradually developed further . . . It is the mutual interaction of two uneven forces». (Letter from Engels to Konrad Schmidt, *Marx-Engels-Werke,* vol. 37, p. 490).

[92] The concept of fascism is expanded by some writers to such an extent that it includes the present bourgeois-democratic systems, thus losing any specificity and any explanatory value. Cf. for example A. Glucksmann *et al.,* «*Alter Faschismus – Neue Demokratie*», (Berlin 1972).

Fascists as Moderates

STANISLAV ANDRESKI

Reification is perhaps the most common pitfall in reasoning about social processes. In speaking of *high* and *low* status, *rigid* customs, breakdowns, explosions, growths, or the Right and the Left, people often implicitly assume that the attributes of the spatial relations from which these terms have been derived – such as linearity, additivity and transitivity – also characterize the cumulative results of multiplex human interactions to which they are metaphorically applied. This is the case with the term 'extremist', although is should be clear to every thinking person that this is a meaningless label without a specification of the continuum to which it is supposed to refer, as nothing can be extreme full stop. Consequently, the 'extremists' must be extreme in some respects (though neither necessarily nor possibly in all), and the question is: which quality (or dimension if you like) are we referring to? The seemingly obvious answer is that the fascists represent the extreme right and their most determined opponents the extreme left; but this merely replaces one reification by another, as 'right' and 'left' are also spatial metaphors, the precise meaning of which is almost never made clear.

The thesis of the present article is that in many important respects the fascists were moderates rather than extremists; and that this was one main reason why many people who were not especially attracted to violence supported them at one stage or another. The fascists' posture as purveyors of middle-of-the-road remedies for the ills of capitalism also accounts for the well-known fact that, by and large, the fascist movements attracted proportionally most support from the socio-economic categories situated in the *middle* of the ladder of wealth and status. In his *Political Man* S. M. Lipset describes fascism as 'the extremism of the centre'; to which I would like to add that with equal validity it could be interpreted as 'centrism of the extremists'.

Before developing this thesis I must pause for a few clarifications. Firstly, I must make clear what I mean by fascism because the meaning of this label has been stretched so much that it has become a blanket word of abuse. I prefer to confine the denotation of this word to movements and régimes which imitated Mussolini's ideology, the organisation of his party and state, and his method of striving for power by setting up a militarised political party. I exclude many other forms of authoritarian rule such as purely military or bureaucratic dictatorships (e.g., the Greek under Papadopoulos) or the racist political systems in South Africa or Rhodesia which can be labelled a *Herrenvolk* democracy, to use the apt term coined by Heribert Adam. The second point is the nature of the dimensions in respect of which the fascists can be characterized as extremists, which also raises the question of what was the opposite extreme and who exemplified it most closely. I suggest that as the essential characteristic of fascism we can take the militarisation of society from outside the normal armed forces. This is something entirely different from militocracy – the rule by professional soldiers – which need not (and usually does not) lead to a militarization of society. Fascism involved the importation into as many provinces of social life as possible of the military patterns of organization, of the military values and the military paraphernalia. The first of these three features figures almost as prominently in the communist states but the second is much less conspicuous while the third is hardly present at all. The fascists score highly (and can therefore be called extremists) in respect of intolerance of dissent, pervasiveness of repression, aggressive nationalism and imperialism; but none of these tendencies has been their monopoly, and a number of non-fascist parties or regimes have surpassed them in these directions. On any of the five continua the opposite is exemplified not by what is conventionally called 'the other extreme', or 'the extreme Left' but by pacifist liberals (in John Stuart Mill's sense of the latter word).

In contrast to extremism on these matters the fascist idea of the corporate state offered a half-way house between *laissez-faire* capitalism – then very much in existence and supported by all the conservative parties, but visibly grinding to a standstill – and the Marxist programme of expropriation, collectivism and central planning. Indeed, the fascist policies foreshadowed most of the fundamental features of the economic system of Western European countries today: the radical extension of governmental control over the economy without a wholesale expropriation of the capitalists but with a good dose of nationalization, price control, incomes policy, managed currency, massive state investment, attempts at central over-all planning (less effectual than the fascist because of the weakness of authority). With its love of *'Gleichschaltung'* (making alike) its zeal for expanding bureaucratic controls and personnel, the British Labour Party's economic policies are even closer to the fascists' than is the case with its continental counterparts, with the crucial difference that the over-riding power of the independent labour unions makes central planning impossible.

If we interpret the conventional labels Right and Left as referring to the preferences for independent private business versus collectivism, then in the alignment of the political parties in most countries of Europe the fascists appeared in the centre of the continuum, with the conservatives and liberals at one end and the communists and revolutionary socialists at the other. The German National Socialist Labour Party (which never called itself fascist, despite its leader's recognition of Mussolini as the source of his initial inspiration, and whose members didn't attach the label of «fascists» to themselves either) should be placed on this continuum to the left of the British Labour Party of the same period, most of whose members at that time simply wanted some reforms which would help the poorer classes, and were not particularly keen on central planning. When the *laissez-faire* system was visibly tottering the painless Keynesian remedies were not yet known, the conservatives had no idea what to do, and among the older parties only the Marxists had a coherent programme of action, but one which scared all who had something (even if very little) to lose from a general expropriation, the fascist half-way house strongly appealed to large sections of the intermediate layers.

The other possible way of making sense out of the metaphorical labels the Right and the Left is to take them as referring to the attitudes to the established privileged classes, or more broadly (but which comes down to much the same) as indicating an approval or disapproval of the existing pattern of inequality of wealth and other privileges, with the Right being in favour of preserving or accentuating them while the Left wants to level them. In this respect too the fascists appeared as moderates who seemed to offer a half-way house between the conservative defenders of all the ramparts of privilege and the communist and socialist levellers, by appealing to national solidarity, and proposing to reconcile the classes and to attenuate the inequalities without going to extremes. True, they promised more than they achieved in this direction. Nonetheless, the conventional Marxist picture of the fascists as the guard dogs of capitalism contains as much falsehood as truth, the proportions varying from case to case. This picture fits the Italian prototype much better than the Nazis, who did much more levelling which was felt as such by the Germans, even though it affected status barriers more than the distribution of wealth. New channels of social ascent were opened to people from non-privileged classes – in the party, the public administration and even the army (where Hitler broke the Junkers' monopoly of the top posts) and a massive re-shuffling in social positions took place. All this was an essential part of the design to bring the feelings of national solidarity to the point of effervescence to prepare the nation for war. Although the old Prussian tradition undoubtedly helped, the amazing performance of the German army in World War II (in which it had no rival in quality, while in World War I it was not much better than the French) seems to have been connected with Hitler's success in weakening class barriers in Germany. Obversely, the extraordinarily poor performance of the Italian army (by far the worst in World War II) was connected with Mussolini's lack of appeal to the poorer classes and his stronger leanings towards the old aristocracy and the capitalists. Hitler was much more of a revolutionary and a leveller than Mussolini.

A belief that a hierarchic ordering of society is not only inevitable but also desirable need not entail approval of the present or previous membership of the privileged layer. In respect of their programme to renovate this membership, the fascists also appeared as moderates, proposing to dislodge only a part of the dominant class. In practice again the Nazis carried out a more thorough renovation of this kind than did the followers of Mussolini.

The fascist and semi-fascist movements in Eastern Europe exhibited particularly strong populist and anti-capitalist tendencies. The latter can be accounted for by the fact that in Poland, Hungary, and Romania the capitalists were mostly either Jews, ethnic Germans, or foreigners. The populist streak can be explained on the following grounds: in Italy, Austria, Germany, and further west, democracy gave so much power to the poorer classes that in time of economic crisis the wealthy and even moderately privileged felt threatened: some of them welcomed the idea of replacing the dangerous contraption of general elections (and perhaps forestalling a mass uprising) by a dictator whom they hoped to domesticate. Further east (with the exception of Czechoslovakia) dictatorships provided ample protection from popular unrest for the privileged classes. So the fascist and semi-fascist movements were mostly fuelled by the discontent of the intermediate layers; and, far from protecting the holders of wealth and power, were in fact attacking them. The fascists' attempts to set up replicas of Mussolini's and Hitler's militia were suppressed. This constellation of forces probably accounts for the fact that no fully fascist regime came into existence in this part of the world.

In Eastern Europe, moreover, there was no need for an antiparliamentary rhetoric. Even more: the Polish National Party which in the thirties acquired a fascist youth movement – which in turn begat an independent and most purely fascist Radically National Camp (ONR) – began as a body oriented entirely towards parliamentary politics, bearing initially the name of National Democracy. But even after they had adopted the fascist salute, its spokesmen harangued against Pilsudski and his heirs for abolishing democracy, and continued to call for free elections.

To move to the other end of Europe: Franco's regime should be classed as semi-fascist rather than fascist; which implies no judgment of value because until 1943 it was far more ferocious than Mussolini's. In terms of numbers of victims Franco was in the same league with Hitler and Stalin rather than Mussolini whose political prisoners numbered only a few thousand, less in fact than the number Novotny held in Czechoslovakia. Franco's system even in its hey-day should be described as clerico-bureaucratic military dictatorship – reactionary in the correct sense that it succeeded in reversing the trends and restoring the essential features of the *ancien régime*. It came into existence through a military uprising and its main props were the army, the police, the Church, the bureaucrats and the wealthy property owners, with the Falange playing only a small part. It is interesting, from the viewpoint of the present thesis, that among the pillars of the regime it was this small fascist party which showed most concern for the non-privileged classes and for the effect of the extremely unequal distribution of wealth. Employing the usual hackneyed metaphors, we can say that even in this case the fascists stood to the left of the conservatives and the clericalists. Even less amenable to pigeon-holing is the case of Peron who (in his first and the only important reign) combined assorted items of the fascist ideology and institutional arrangements with stridently populist policies. This dictator, an admirer and avowed disciple of Mussolini, liberated the industrial workers from intimidation by their employers, set up unions, substantially raised the wages and organised welfare services, and (especially through Evita) engaged in extravagant flattery of the masses, while humiliating many members of the established upper class. I would not however classify Peron as a fascist because he had no militarised mass party. He was overthrown by the old military élite when they felt threatened by his attempts to set up such a party. Peronism is a very interesting phenomenon because it exhibited a conjunction of features which did not go together in other parts of the world. From the viewpoint of the conventional dichotomy, it could with equal justification be assigned to the Right or the Left or the middle-of-the-road, which shows how misleading these labels can be.

Towards a Political Economy of Fascism

ALAN S. MILWARD

Until recently the National Socialist German Workers Party was the only fascist party about whose membership and support historians and political scientists had collected sufficient evidence to enable any meaningful statements to be made. The papers in this volume show how this situation is changing. Hitherto the concept of a pan-European, and even perhaps universal, set of political ideas identified as fascism has rested on attempts to show the resemblances in the intellectual assumptions and the similarities in political attitude amongst the membership, and especially amongst the leadership, of the parties in question. But it is now becoming possible to make comparisons between the social composition of the membership of these parties. In spite of the national differences which emerge and in spite of the importance of local and regional issues in persuading electors to vote fascist, the overall picture which emerges is that there are in fact sufficient similarities in the social bases of the parties in question to add a further justification for considering as one the movements labelled as fascist.

In spite of the early connections between the intellectual ideas of fascism and those of the anarcho-syndicalist wings of certain social revolutionary parties it proved subsequently very difficult for fascist parties to recruit support from the ranks of organised labour. One other group seems to have remained equally aloof: political parties organised with a specifically Roman Catholic outlook. The common social basis of fascist parties was that of a new political alliance between a fairly homogenous group of rural voters and a much less homogenous group of urban voters who were either middle-class or had middle-class attributes. The first group was made up of small landowners, sharecroppers and occasionally larger landowners. The second group was made up, in widely-varying proportions, of shopkeepers, shop-workers, bureaucrats and officials (if they were permitted by the law to join), professional people, students, handicraft workers and unemployed officers of the armed forces.

Greater refinement of statistical method and a greater accumulation of evidence may show this to be too simple a generalisation. But it does have the immediate advantage of providing a hypothesis which might steer research away from the rarefied atmosphere of the intellectual origins of fascism towards the more concrete facts of the history of fascist movements. The more numerous and influential a fascist movement, the more difficult it became for it to be guided solely by the early revolutionary ideology, both because this had little applicability to many of the real problems which the movements faced, (especially if they obtained power), and also because the social basis of the movements expanded in so unforeseen a way. Until the moment when, for example, electoral success in rural areas led, both in Italy and Germany, to a sudden acquisition of political power, neither of the fascist parties in those countries could be said to have designed an agricultural programme; their political outlook was almost exclusively urban.

How far does the study of what fascist parties in power actually did bear out this evidence on their social composition? To what extent did they pursue socio-economic

56

policies in favour of the groups from which, the evidence suggests, they drew their main support? These questions are the more important because the most consistent and frequently-encountered hypothesis on the political economy of fascism is still that which sees the fascist state as the defender of the major capital interests. According to this interpretation the first priority of fascist economic policy would have been a set of actions whose purpose would fall somewhere between 'saving the capitalist system' and 'furthering the purposes of monopoly capitalism'. Such economic priorities would certainly not be easy to reconcile with economic policies designed to satisfy the particular interests of the rural and urban supporters of the movements. Their support was given to fascist parties because they felt themselves threatened by the pace of economic change, by the forces of organized labour and organized capital. A vote for a fascist party was frequently an attempt to stop the apparently inexorable economic changes associated with the capitalist economy, an attempt to find a resting place in a restless sea of social change. What does fascist economic policy tell us about the political pressures on and the political nature of fascist parties? Is it now possible on the foundation of this new evidence about the support for and composition of fascist movements to construct a working hypothesis on the political economy of fascism?

Fascism, Organized Labour and the Agricultural Sector

Given the failure of fascist movements to achieve any substantial power base among industrial workers, it is not surprising that they felt themselves freer to pursue a policy which was very unfavourable to organized labour. The political power of organized labour was systematically weakened by the absorption of separate labour unions into one all-embracing party-controlled organization. Once formed, an organization like the German Labour Front was certainly not free of the anti-capitalist attitudes of the early fascist manifestoes, and as far as the material comforts of working life was concerned it continued to press successfully for changes. But the paternalistic and politically subservient attitudes of the fascist labour unions did not serve so well as collective bargaining as an instrument for increasing the real incomes of workers in employment. The qualification is important because policies of national recovery in Germany and Italy sustained the level of employment above its level in the liberal democracies and in so doing sustained a higher level of income. Actual incomes received in Germany were probably higher than the available figures because of the illegal competition for skilled labour by German entrepreneurs after 1936. Even so in a period of successful economic reflation and of intensive rearmament the increase in real earnings of German workmen between 1933 and 1939 remains remarkably low. Real weekly wages, for an increased working week, rose at an annual average of less than three per cent, in a period when the annual average rate of growth of National Income was more than eight per cent.[1] The imperfect information on real wages in Italy suggests also that they fell between 1934 and 1939 during a period of growing National Income.

It was not only wage controls and the destruction of union bargaining power which were responsible for this but also the high level of food prices. Agricultural price supports in both countries and the comparatively high prices paid in Germany for food imports from south-eastern Europe eroded the gain in wage rates after 1933. The available evidence fully supports the view that fascist economic policy both in Germany and Italy was as extraordinarily favourable towards the agricultural sector as it was unfavourable to industrial labour. Both in direct subsidies and in indirect financial

57

benefits agriculture was one of the main beneficiaries of the public purse in both countries. Direct subsidies usually were for the purpose of specific improvements. New equipment, better seed, local agricultural competitions were all subsidised in this way. More expensive was the creation of new farms. In Italy this took the form of the extension of the cultivable area, chiefly by the drainage of marsh land. The total expenditure in land reclamation there between 1921–22 and July 1936 was almost three times that of the period between 1870 and 1921.[2] In Germany the creation of new farms had a specifically ideological basis. The new units were small peasant farms between 7.5 and 10 hectares whose tenures were virtually inalienable. The indirect financial benefits came through the protection against low international primary product prices and through tax benefits. The value of food imports into Germany in 1935–38 was only thirty per cent that of 1925–28 and in most years after 1932 Italian wheat imports were only 25 per cent of their level in 1925–28.[3] Part of the income gain to the farming community was also eroded by higher prices for fodder. Nevertheless the increase in the earnings of self-employed farmers in Germany between 1933 and 1938 was over three times the increase in weekly wage rates over the same period.[4] In Italy the annual mean percentage rate of growth of capital in the agricultural sector between 1920 and 1939 seems to have been higher than in the preceding and following periods.[5] It was not only in propaganda that the fascist regimes held up to admiration the image of a stable wholesome and pure peasant rurality; they actually sought by legislation to make this utopian vision a reality. The new inalienable farm units in Germany were created to be 'independent of the market and the general economic situation'.[6] Marriage loans made available to agricultural labourers could be eventually written off if the labourer stayed on the land. In Italy legislation in the growth years 1928 and 1929 specifically forbade migration from the countryside. Of course policies of this kind could not work. More than that, given the economic trends they were a positive handicap. But the utopian vision of a prosperous and stable rural society which had influenced rural voters to vote for a political creed evolved in an urban intellectual milieu was incorporated into the making of fascist economic policy and added its weight to the other influences suggesting a redistribution of economic rewards towards landowners.

Fascism, Big Business and the Expectations of the Urban Middle Class

So far, so good. But it is much less possible to show that similarly tangible economic rewards accrued to the urban middle-class supporters of fascist movements. The range of psychological satisfactions they were offered, unambiguous symbols of their status, incorporation into a fixed and assured hierarchy, had their own importance.[7] So of course did the brake applied to the improvements in real incomes and social status of the groups below them. But early legislation in Germany against department stores or to protect handworkers' associations had less economic effect than similar government intervention in the agricultural sector. And the winds of economic and social change let loose by other aspects of government policy blew all the more keenly. The number of small firms in Germany in the 1930s fell faster than in the previous decade. The list of benefits accruing to the urban middle-class supporters of fascist movements seems very small. This is the major weakness in attempts to elaborate a hypothesis of the political economy of fascism which would be in harmony with the present findings of research into the social bases of the movement.

Indeed, the most common hypothesis on the political economy of fascist movements has been that which identifies fascism as a stage in imperialism and sees fascist governments as an instrument of 'big business'.[8] The evidence that major capital interests conspired to bring fascist parties to power or that they gave their financial and moral support more to fascist parties than to other non-socialist parties does not stand up to objective historical examination. The last year of the National Socialist government and the episode of the Republic of Salo show how separate were the ultimate economic social and political goals of fascism from those of the business world. None of this, however, contradicts a thesis such as that of Reinhard Kühnl which suggests that the major capital interests were prepared to help fascist parties to power if they felt the alternative outcome of the political situation would be more threatening to their own interests. But here, of course, it is necessary to ask how serious the threat of a revolution from 'the left' actually was in Italy and in Germany. Neither does the historical evidence on the suspicions and disagreements over long-term social objectives between major capital interests and fascist parties in Germany and Italy preclude temporary alliances in the common interest. The evidence published by Eichholtz, Schumann, Radandt and others does not substantiate the claim that German commercial policy and foreign policy were dictated by the interests of the German business world.[9] But it does show that some less scrupulous companies such as the Deutsche Bank, I. G. Farben and Carl Zeiss with particular interests in the parts of Europe where the foreign policy of the government led to an increase in German political influence, were ready to take advantage of the German government's own unscrupulousness to further their own interests. I. G. Farben, for example, sought successfully to suppress the manufacture of certain organic chemical products in south-eastern Europe and also to re-establish the German domination over the French organic chemicals industry as it had existed before the Versailles Treaty.[10] The Mansfeld copper works and Vereinigte Aluminiumwerke were able to acquire possession of new sources of raw materials.[11] The Deutsche Bank sometimes extended its capital interests in central and south-eastern Europe by bringing pressures from the Reich government to bear during negotiations.

In fact the control exercised by the central government in Italy and Germany over capital investment and the domination of investment by public treasury spending on costly programmes of rearmament and import substitution would have made it unlikely that major capital interests could in either country have conspired to pursue a course of action unsympathetic to government policy. But what made this completely out of the question was the party control exercised over the business world by its integration into the administrative machinery of the corporate state. Rearmament and import-substitution brought to the forefront in both countries a restricted group of armament, steel and chemical manufactures with easy access to government contracts. The personnel of I. G. Farben played a decisive role in staffing the Four Year Plan Office in Germany and in making official decisions about the industry which the company itself dominated.[12] Given the nature of government's economic objectives there was little place for small businesses and less for the estates of handworkers; rearmament contracts went to the largest producers. But this by no means meant that these powerful groups of business interests dominated the political machinery of the state. What in fact must have worried the business world was the loss of the capacity to make independent decisions. The decision to build the Salzgitter steel works to use high-cost low-ferrous content domestic iron ore was inspired and carried through by the government against the wishes of important groups in the German steel industry.

When the invasion of Ethiopia and the sanctions imposed by the League of Nations brought about a rapid deterioration in Italy's already dangerous foreign trading situation, the Italian government did not compromise with the opposition of capital interests.[13] Guarnieri's opinion that in Italy the limits of government intervention were 'suggesting a few names for the various boards of directors' is blatantly false.[14]

The committee structure of the corporate state was designed to increase the control of government over the business world. Trade and exchange controls, import licensing and control of the capital market all strengthened the central government's position.[15] Although therefore the process of *Gleichschaltung* in the Nazi state could still leave an organization like the *Fachgruppe Werkzeuge* with virtually the same personnel as its predecessor in the liberal state, The Machine Tool Manufacturers' Association, the ultimate control of the *Wirtschaftsgruppe Maschinen* and, beyond that, of the responsible minister or plenipotentiary was not merely a constitutional nicety. With the creation of a Ministry of Armaments in Germany in 1940 the two ministers were able gradually to turn the manufacturers' committees of the corporate state into full-time organs of state administration.

The relationship between fascist governments and major capital interests remained suspicious and ambivalent. There is still of course a lot to be discovered about events in this area in Italy. But there government control was ultimately as inescapable as in Germany. The assets of the firms in whose capital IRI had a controlling interest eventually were more than 17 per cent of total capital investment, and the technological importance of these firms for the economy was often particularly high. What is most striking about these relationships, however, is that both for the governments at the time and for historians subsequently a correct definition and understanding of them has seemed almost the central problem in defining the political economy of fascism. What happened to the political influence of small businesses, of handicraft organizations, of the fearful employees in the service sector of the economy upon fascist movements once those movements were in power? Attempts to legislate against department stores, higher profits and capital gains taxes, attempts to translate into specific action party manifestoes distinguishing between 'creative' capital and other less useful forms, all faded quickly into the background only to emerge once more in defeat in the policies of men like Sauckel and Farinacci.[16]

This is the fundamental objection to constructing a hypothesis of the political economy of fascism solely on the foundation that international comparisons of fascist parties do show great similarity in the social bases of membership and support. One of the major social groups joining and supporting fascist parties everywhere in Europe and particularly in Germany and Italy appears to have exercised very little influence on the economic policies of the two fascist parties that did seize power without the support of an occupying army. By contrast economic policy distorted the trend of economic development and income distribution in both countries in favour of the other main body of support for the party, the rural voters.

Are we to assume that, faced with the task of carrying out a policy of employment-creation and rearmament, fascist governments abandoned what amounted to half their support and drew closer to those major capital interests whose support was so essential to implement these policies? Schweitzer argues strongly that this is what happened and puts the date of this change of allegiance in Germany at 1936.[17] The continuity of National Socialist economic policy after the seizure of power, however, is more marked than its discontinuity. It is true that the more specifically fascist rural reforms, that creating the *Reichserbhöfe* for example, and the few attempts to translate parts of Feder's original manifesto into political action are confined to the first two years of rule. But even in the first year of office, although investment in social overhead capital was the main force in employment-creation, military expenditure still rose to 18 per cent of all public expenditure. When to this is added the cost of the agricultural support programmes, the implications of such policies in so discouraging an international environment are, in retrospect, not hard to see. They led to a trading deficit of 700 million Reichsmarks by autumn 1934 which resulted in a much tighter set of exchange trade controls and in the redirection of German trade through the New Plan. Within less than two years the Four Year Plan would be pouring public monies with even greater profligacy into costly import-substitution programmes. Furthermore the trend of Italian economic policy in the early years of the regime was towards maintaining full links with the multilateral payments system. Attempts at implementing parts of the fascist manifesto came later rather than earlier and were one of the causes of the movement towards autarky and insulation against world prices.

Fascist Economic Policy, the Preparation for War and the Imperatives of Ideology

It would be a convenient but not very convincing way out of this dilemma to draw a clear distinction between the support for and economic policy of fascist movements and fascist governments. Short of making this distinction, how may we construct a more satisfactory hypothesis of the political economy of fascism? To do so it is first necessary to recognize that although small fascist sects were indeed only turned into powerful political movements in those few countries where conditions were such that they could attract wider electoral support, the economic policies of fascist governments were *less* determined by the nature of political support and by the pressure of economic events than were the policies of liberal parliamentary parties. They were more determined by prior ideological assumptions about the nature of economic activity. A vote for a fascist party was an important step in the process of conversion to the new sensibility and set of mental attitudes which, if the fascist revolution were ultimately to be successful, it would be necessary to instil in a majority of the population. It was not seen as a bargaining counter but as act of faith. Because the real facts of economic life in the inter-war period differed considerably from the fascist interpretation of them, this act of faith was even more a renunciation of economic rationality and a desperate double commitment. Firstly it was a commitment to accepting, whatever the international economic situation, the absolute priority of the political will to refashion the nation and the continent. Secondly it was a commitment to force economic facts as far as possible to fit the pattern required by this prior commitment to remaking political society.

The instrument by which political society would be remade was war. The agricultural policy of the fascist governments is as well explained by the desire for a strategic self-sufficiency in food supply to avoid the dangers of blockade and dependence on foreign suppliers for food as by an attempt to shelter small rural landowners from the force of economic change, although the ideological importance of a stable and wholesome rurality for the fascist world of the future was certainly more than rhetorical. In this future war the urban white-collar supporters had a less glamorous function to fulfil.

By forcibly incorporating the labour movement into the machinery of the fascist state the fascist governments wanted at least to prevent a recurrence of the 'stab-in-

61

the-back' of 1918, even if the conversion of their members into loyal brothers in the new society could not be immediately hoped for.[18]

In any valid hypothesis on the political economy of fascism the central importance of war would have to be incorporated. There were obviously in fascist ideology no reasons for eschewing war as an instrument of national policy. But more than this war came to be seen as an instrument in forging the new society, as a positive and beneficial policy. In war the selfish liberal vices were suppressed and the more heroic and less egotistical aspects of fascist man brought to the forefront. 'Fascism', wrote Mussolini, 'the more it considers and observes the future and the development of humanity, quite apart from political considerations of the moment, believes neither in the possibility nor the utility of perpetual peace'.[19] One of the main reasons why economic growth in the inter-war period was more associated with fascist regimes than the parliamentary democracies was because of the profligate spending of treasury funds on military purposes, in Germany after 1936 over 40 per cent a year. The growth of G.N.P. had no implicit connection with welfare. It was associated with quite different purposes, the exaltation of the nation and the ability to pursue an independent policy.

This attitude to warfare was only one of the inescapable historical and ideological inheritances of fascist movements and governments. These inheritances would have to be incorporated into any satisfactory hypothesis on the political economy of fascism and would have to receive equal weight with the established historical evidence about who paid for and who voted for fascist parties. They were just as important in framing policy as the immediate and short-run political and economic pressures. Although economic policy might make significant temporary deviations to meet immediate and unforeseen contingencies in its longer-term objectives, it remained not only subordinate to but also an integral part of the ideological and political ambitions of the fascist movement.

In the first place the original revolutionary (or counter-revolutionary) ideology of fascism would have to be incorporated into any satisfactory definition of the political economy of fascism. This ideology was the possession of very small groups in all European societies. It saw the Enlightenment, the French Revolution and the evolution of the 'materialist' creeds of liberalism, socialism, communism and democracy not as an aspect of human progress but as deep wounds inflicted on human society. Only in a fascist society could man again be restored to his original wholeness and a true social harmony be born out of a disputatious and greedy society. This healing process must begin with the small surviving uncorrupted élite which preserved an instinctual human awareness more truly democratic than a pencilled cross on a ballot paper, an awareness interpreted and translated into action in the personality and will of the leader, himself the embodiment of the instinctual will to action.

The economic importance of these concepts in the administration of the fascist state has often been shown. They were one of the things responsible for the competing and disjointed nature of the executive organs in spite of the outwardly monolithic appearance of the centralized state. Each branch of the economic administration competed in the formulation and execution of economic policy with every other branch. No systematic process of arriving at rational economic solutions in committee was possible. Indeed economic rationality was not, given the nature of the fascist creed, a highly-valued quality. It is the way in which one economic policy and organ of administration was encouraged by 'the leadership-principle' to vie with another that makes us describe the fascist economic administration as 'inefficient'. But the significance of the early ideology for economic life was much deeper. This may be seen from the history of the war years in Germany. When, after 1941, with the abandonment of the *Blitzkrieg* economy it became necessary to rationalize and unify the structure of the economic administration for the purpose of winning the war, this unification and rationalization never embraced the SS. The SS was seen as the new fascist society coming to birth in the débris of the old and the persistence of this idea explains why, at the peak of the war effort, the SS was allowed to use large labour resources at absurdly low levels of productivity in such enterprises as the German Earth and Stone Works and in concentration camps.[20]

In the second place this ideology, although élitist, was for an age of mass participation in political life. Its early development was in anarchist and syndicalist groups. In Spain Ledesma actually called his organization 'national syndicalism'. Although the ambitions of a 'working-class' fascism were never fulfilled, the 'socialist' concepts in fascism were always present. Once again this can be seen most clearly in the last years in Germany and in the Republic of Salo in Italy. Liberated from the constraints of existence in a more complicated political world, both regimes reverted to denunciations of 'plutocrats' and 'international capital' and took up again some of the economic positions of the original fascist and national socialist manifestoes.

In the third place, the importance of the nation was overwhelming. The common elements in the national historical experience of Italy and Germany have often been stressed as explanations for the coming to power of fascist governments in these two countries, and in particular the late and imperfect achievement of national unification. It was this which encouraged the intellectual alliance between the deeply-held sentiments of nationalism and the more rarefied and revolutionary ideas of fascism. This marriage was achieved in Italy by the events of World War I. In Germany, where political conditions were very different, it needed the social instability of the hyperinflation and also of the depression of 1929–33 to cause voters to select the NSDAP out of all the other parties whose intention was to overturn the Versailles settlement. The offspring of this alliance was a nationalism with a much deeper popular appeal. Fascist economic policy was couched in such terms as to appear to offer the individual some chance of useful action and combination against the apparently overwhelming power of big business and of big labour organizations. It did indeed, in Turner's phrase, promise 'an anti-modernist Utopia'. But in making that promise it seemed to offer to the fearful a possibility of genuine participation in formulating a new path of economic policy, of arresting the seemingly inexorable forces of social change in the capitalist economy, of feeling once again a sense of human worth and capacity beyond that of a mere economic unit. That the promise was for the most part spurious mattered neither to supporters nor to government. As a part of the new nation the individual could assert his individuality against impersonal forces face to face with which he had previously felt quite powerless.

In the fourth place, the alliance of this fascist ideology with nationalism produced a new and virulent conception of racial purity. The fascist élite was an élite of the blood and for economic life this also had a profound significance. The worst threat to the healing of society came from the polluting presence of people of an alien blood. Such ideas were obviously much more useful as vote-winners in Germany than in Italy where the population was racially remarkably homogenous. But although their practical usefulness often determined the extent to which they were used, their fundamental importance for the political economy of fascism can not be doubted. German economic policy in Poland and the Soviet Union can only be understood by accepting the integralness of these racial considerations in fascist ideology. Auschwitz was as much the logical outcome of fascist economic ideas as the blast furnaces of Salzgitter. When in 1944 labour was becoming a scarce economic factor in the battle for survival in Germany economic resources were *increasingly* allocated to furthering the planned extermination of the Jewish race.

A historically acceptable hypothesis of the political economy of fascism would first of all have to attribute to these four inescapable aspects the economic weight which, in reality, they merit. Starting from such a basis it would then be possible to assess more justly and to understand more exactly why the convincing evidence which we now have on the similarity of social groups from which fascist movements drew support was not more exactly expressed in the economic policy of fascist governments. The need to meet the economic demands of these groups was only one restricted aspect in formulating economic policy. And since economic policy itself by the nature of fascist thought was never a first consideration in determining important decisions, the ideological framework within which economic decisions were made often had even more weight than the practical questions of satisfying the economic wishes of those groups which supported the regime.

NOTES

[1] D. Petzina, *Grundriss der deutschen Wirtschaftsgeschichte 1918 bis 1945,* in Institut für Zeitgeschichte, *Deutsche Geschichte seit dem Ersten Weltkrieg,* vol. 2, (Stuttgart, 1973), p. 757.

[2] W G. Welk, *Fascist Economic Policy,* (Cambridge, Mass.), 1938, p. 192.

[3] *Statistisches Jahrbuch für das Deutsche Reich; Annuario statistico Italiano.*

[4] Petzina, *op. cit.*

[5] G. Fuà, *Formazione, distribuzione e impiego del reddito dal 1861; sintesi statistica,* (Istituto nazionale per lo studio della congiuntura, Rome, 1972.)

[6] D. Schoenbaum, *Hitler's Social Revolution: Class and Status in Nazi Germany 1933–1939,* (New York, 1966), p. 157 (1967 edition).

[7] Schoenbaum, *op. cit.;* H. Mommsen, *Beamtentum im Dritten Reich.* Schriftenreihe der Vierteljahrshefte für Zeitgeschichte, no. 13, (Stuttgart, 1966).

[8] Among the numerous examples may be cited, D. Eichholtz, *Geschichte der deutschen Kriegswirtschaft 1939–1945,* vol. 1, 1939–1941, (Berlin, 1969); K. Gossweiler, *Grossbanken, Industriemonopole, Staat. Ökonomie und Politik des staatsmonopolistischen Kapitalismus in Deutschland, 1914–1932,* (Berlin, 1971); E. Czichon, *Wer verhalf Hitler zur Macht?* (Cologne, 1967); D. Guérin, *Sur le fascisme; fascisme et grand capital,* (Paris, 1936, 1965); E. Rossi, *Padroni del vapore e fascismo,* (Bari, 1955).

[9] D. Eichholtz, *op. cit.;* D. Eichholtz and W. Schumann, *Anatomie des Krieges: neue Dokumente über die Rolle des deutschen Monopolkapitals bei der Vorbereitung und Durchführung des zweiten Weltkrieges,* (Berlin, 1969); H. Radandt, 'Die I. G. Farbenindustrie und Südosteuropa 1938 bis zum Ende des zweiten Weltkrieges', in *Jahrbuch für Wirtschaftsgeschichte,* no. 1, 1967; W. Schumann, 'Das Kriegsprogramm des Zeiss-Konzerns' in *Zeitschrift für Geschichtswissenschaft,* 1963.

[10] A. S. Milward, *The New Order and the French Economy* (Oxford, 1970), p. 101 ff.

[11] H. Radandt, *Kriegsverbrecherkonzern Mansfeld, Die Rolle des Mansfeld-Konzernes bei der Vorbereitung und während des zweiten Weltkrieges* (Berlin, 1957); A. S. Milward, *The Fascist Economy in Norway,* (Oxford, 1972), p. 86.

[12] D. Petzina, *Autarkiepolitik im Dritten Reich,* Schriftenreihe der Vierteljahrshefte für Zeitgeschichte, no. 16, (Stuttgart, 1968), p. 123.

[13] R. Sarti, *Fascism and the Industrial Leadership in Italy, 1919–1940,* (Berkeley, 1971).

[14] F. Guarneri, *Battaglie economiche tra le due grandi guerre,* (Milan, 1953), vol. 1, p. 317.

[15] The best study is J. S. Geer. *Der Markt der geschlossenen Nachfrage,* (Berlin, 1961).

[16] A. S. Milward, 'French Labour and the German Economy, 1942–1945: An Essay in the Nature of the Fascist New Order' in *Economic History Review,* XXIII, no. 2, 1970. On the Republic of Salo see F. W. Deakin, *The Last Days of Mussolini,* (London, 1962).

[17] A. Schweitzer, *Big Business in the Third Reich* (Bloomington, 1964).

[18] T. W. Mason, *Arbeiterklasse und Volksgemeinschaft: Dokumente und Materialien zur deutschen Arbeitspolitik 1936–39,* (Opladen, 1975).

[19] Quoted by Welk, *op. cit.,* p. 190.

[20] E. Georg, *Die wirtschaftlichen Unternehmungen der SS,* Schriftenreihe der Vierteljahrshefte für Zeitgeschichte, no. 7, (Stuttgart, 1963); J. Billig, *Les camps de concentration dans l'économie du Reich hitlérien* (Paris, 1973).

65

The Theory of Mass Society and the Collapse of the Weimar Republic: A Re-Examination

BERNT HAGTVET

> *The totalitarian movements aim at and succeed in organizing masses – not classes.*
>
> *Hannah Arendt*

Prefatory Remarks

Close to half a century after its demise, the fate of the Weimar Republic still conveys a sense of contemporary relevance. Not only its vulnerability, its instability, but also its cultural and intellectual vitality amid a sense of impending doom speak to the crisis-conscious political sensibilities of the late 70's. In art, literature and thought Weimar left a legacy of modernity, energy and experimentation. This outburst of creativity outlasted the end of the Republic and was transplanted to America in one of the most impressive intellectual migrations hitherto witnessed.[1] But in politics the Republic came to symbolize modern society's capacity for self-destruction. The excitement of the Weimar cultural renaissance yielded to fear, fanaticism and a particularly rigid form of group selfishness which proved impossible to contain within the democratic structures set up in 1919. What began as a reluctant but promising experiment in parliamentary government in a semi-absolutist setting, ended in the grimmest throwback to political primitivism in the 20th century.

The causes of Weimar's failure have fascinated scholars ever since. With the benefit of hindsight it is easy to see that some of the problems of the Republic were self-inflicted, the result of sheer incompetence or human cowardice in confronting the regime's enemies. Others can be blamed on foreign powers or Germany's Imperial past, a heritage of doubtful value to the troubled Republic. What makes the Weimar period so complex is the extraordinary *range* of problems it had to face: a very narrow democratic potential at home, an increasingly disloyal opposition, feelings of national humiliation, a deeply segmented society and a paralyzed parliament – and underlying all these, a crisis-ridden economy which further reduced the room for manoeuvre and intensified the resentments of a volatile electorate turning to extremes in its search for solutions.

The disintegration of constitutional democracy in Germany can be approached in two related yet analytically distinct ways: 1. as the outcome of specifically German problems, comprehensible only within the context of German history.[2] Or, 2. as an example of dangers potentially afflicting any democratic regime. In the second case the Weimar period becomes a testing ground for more general theories of regime viability and the social and economic requisites of democracy.[3] These two approaches are, of course, not mutually exclusive. Both require an unusual sensitivity to the *level of analysis* problem in historical explanation, and, ideally, a theory capable of separating the *purely conjunctural* from the underlying *structural* determinants in the disintegration sequence. In the Weimar case this problem is particularly acute. How is one to estimate the relative weight of the legacy of the Imperial period – prolonged *Junker* dominance, a political culture more attuned to the *Obriegkeitsstaat* than to parliamentary democracy, a party system basically geared to a pre-industrial social formation – as against critical conjunctures such as the military defeat in 1918, the Versailles treaty, the recurring inflationary spirals and the agrarian depression? How to assess the force of personalities, including the obvious co-responsibility of Hindenburg in bringing about the fall of the Republic? How to integrate in a comprehensive theory the impact of constitutional arrangements like article 48 which enabled Brüning to rule by decree for so long and facilitated Hitler's usurpation of power later? To build a theory aimed at integrating all these perspectives would clearly exceed the scope of this paper.[4] Instead of attempting such a total explanation, I shall focus on just a few critical issues in the contemporary debate on Weimar's weaknesses as a democratic system.

This essay has a threefold purpose:

1. To discuss the view held in common by all mass theorists that the *instability of the Weimar Republic was fundamentally of a socio-structural kind*, and that the upsurge in support for the NSDAP both at the polls and at the membership level was due to a widespread sense of *social isolation* in the German population both within primary groups and with respect to central authority.

2. To examine *whether Weimar society can meaningfully be described as a 'mass society'*, i.e. a society characterized by a weak or non-existent network of intermediary associations, widespread atrophy within this intermediary structure, evaporation of kinship bonds, accelerating centralization of power, growing distance between élite and citizenry and increasing restlessness, egotism and emotionalism leading to mass 'availability' and a yearning for security in the form of «the great simplifier».

3. To highlight the *interplay between two different but related modes of social analysis* in the study of breakdowns in democratic regimes: 1. *mass theory* with its core concepts of 'atomization', 'fragmentation' and 'marginality', and 2. traditional *social class* analysis. I shall discuss the utility and limitations of each approach, using data on the success of the NSDAP in varying groups and their organizational attachments as an empirical test.

In summary, I shall argue the following points:

1. Contrary to the claims of mass theory, Weimar can in no meaningful sociological sense be portrayed as «massified». The basic premise of earlier mass theory – that National Socialism attracted the socially uprooted from all classes – is rejected.

Social blocs in voting patterns persisted throughout the Weimar period – hence atomization cannot mean, as Hannah Arendt claimed, «the fall of protective class walls».

2. The crucial issue in the analysis of the downfall of the Weimar Republic is *not* paucity of intermediary bonds, nor lack of organizational resources, nor diminished access to executive and legislative power. Weimar society was segmented. It was the prototype of a «centrifugal democracy», and lacked integration across class and religious cleavages. Each group pursued its own interests with increasing vehemence. The failure of the intermediary network to articulate, aggregate and *integrate* diverse and conflicting claims and the *erosion of parliament* as a bargaining arena with adjudicative capacities can be traced to historical factors. Paramount in this historical dimension is the *inflexibility of the German party system:* its incapacity to reflect more adequately changes in the social structure. This lack of adjustment which showed itself in a tenacious identification with the parties' primary clienteles, led to a perpetu-

ation of outmoded conflict fronts and restricted the integrative capacities of the parties. The fixation on conflict dimensions which had been instrumental in structuring the party system in the early phases of mass politics in Germany also made the parties increasingly incapable of performing any *conflict mediation*. The effectiveness of parliament was also limited by the prevailing anti-democratic political culture which did not recognize the parliamentary form of government as legitimate.[5] The legitimacy of the Weimar system, already impaired by the circumstances of its inception, was further weakened by the party fragmentation which, in turn, in a vicious spiral of cause and effect, reduced governmental effectiveness, a factor which again reduced the survival chances of the regime.

3. The apparent ease with which the Nazis were able to whip up support in the final years of the Republic was due to their ingenuity in turning the intermediary network to their own purposes through infiltration and propaganda. This raises the question of the *theoretical* status of the intermediary bonds in mass theory: did the organizations restrain or channel, even intensify, anti-regime resentments? It is maintained that the failure of mass theory to grasp the role of organizations as *agents* and *legitimizers* of anti-democratic unrest derives from a confusion about the exact nature of the organizational mediation and a mechanistic concept of social isolation.

The discussion will proceed as follows in four parts:

The first will provide a short survey of the historical roots of modern mass theory. The object will be to show the prominence of this mode of reasoning in Western thinking about the genesis of social unrest and political instability. The next section (2) will provide brief summaries and a discussion of the views of four selected modern mass theorists, Hannah Arendt, Emil Lederer, Sigmund Neumann and William Kornhauser. These writers will first be subjected to criticism within their own frame of reference. Since each of these writers published their work at different times, their access to research on the downfall of the Republic varied. Nonetheless the body of literature generated by these writers forms a whole, representative of the main trends in contemporary mass theorizing. The next section (3) will be a confrontation of mass theory with the wealth of material now available on the process leading to the end of parliamentary rule. The discussion will concentrate on a few critical issues with an immediate bearing on the validity of the theory: 3.1, on the segmentation of Weimar society; 3.2, on the social characteristics of the Nazi following on different levels: at the polls, among previous non-voters and the unemployed, and within the ranks of the party itself. Following the comparison of the tenets of mass theory with the conclusions which can be drawn from this material, there will be an examination of the role of social cohesiveness and external interest representation in the middle class (3.5); a discussion of internal cohesion and external bonds of the peasantry (3.6); an analysis of the theoretical status of internal cohesion and the intermediary network in increasing the susceptibility to mass appeals (3.7); and finally an assessment of the question whether associations have a restraining or a channelling effect on anti-democratic sentiment (3.8). By way of conclusion, the last section (4) will provide a discussion of alternative ways of explaining the sudden rise in Nazi voting (4.1) and a note on the concept of social isolation as used in mass theory (4.2).

1. The Tradition of Mass Theorizing

Close to twenty years after its appearance, William Kornhauser's *The Politics of Mass Society* (1959) remains one of the most comprehensive statements of the genesis and functions of modern authoritarian movements. The nomenclature of the book – concepts like 'mass', 'mass society', 'atomization', 'alienation' and the more colorful phrases used by other representatives of the mass theory tradition, such as «the lonely crowd», «mass man» and his «fear of freedom» – has become part of popular discourse. These concepts came into vogue as convenient catch-words crystallizing various ills in contemporary society: rootlessness, feelings of impotence and meaninglessness, impersonal human relations, lack of control because of size and complexity, etc. Peter Drucker expressed this *Zeitgeist* rather well when, as early as 1939, he wrote:

> «The function of the individual in society has become entirely irrational and senseless. Man is isolated within a tremendous machine, the purpose and meaning of which he does not accept and cannot translate into terms of his experience. Society ceases to be a community of individuals bound together by a common purpose, and becomes a chaotic hubbub of purposeless isolated monads.»[6]

This interpretation of industrial society found its way into a host of sociological and psychological studies in the fifties and early sixties,[7] and was even echoed in philosophical form in the post-war existential wave. Thus mass theory became a constitutive part of a mood, a general *Kulturkritik*. It was intermittently directed against modernity, vaguely conceived, or more specifically, against industrialism and the levelling tendencies following in its wake. In this latter form mass theory developed important affinities with influential Marxist critiques of modern capitalism and its culture.[8]

The influence of mass theory clearly reflected a widespread feeling of malaise in Western industrial civilization and a fear of the long-term effects of increased popular participation in political life. As a representative of the latter, mass theory is a blend of diverse yet related components, dating as far back as Aristotle's warning in book V of the *Politics* of the affinity between mob rule (rule of the *demos*) and tyranny.[9] The concept of *mass* can thus be regarded an important unit-idea in Western social thought intimately related to the concept of *community*.[10] Aristotle's observations were to occupy a variety of writers after him, most notably the romantic spokesmen of the ancien régime, de Maistre, Gentz and de Bonald among them, united in defense of the political realm against the unruly populace. In its latter-day manifestations, the concept of mass is inherited from this reaction against the French Revolution, but warnings against the onslaught of the masses were voiced again and again by such diverse writers as Jakob Burckhardt and Nietzsche in the 19th century and by Spengler and Ortega y Gasset in the 20th. When Ortega in 1930 spoke of «hyperdemocracy» and the dangers of the «accession of masses to complete social power»,[11] he only reiterated ancient fears made more imminent by the advent of mass politics and universal suffrage. In this way, mass theorizing provided the sociological underpinnings of the aristocratic critique of democracy and became an indispensable part of that broader theory of totalitarianism in which mass conditions are seen as necessarily preceding the establishment of a totalitarian regime.[12] In its more specifically sociological tenets, it can be viewed as an extension of the *Gemeinschaft-Gesellschaft* theme expounded by Tönnies and Weber. As an intellectual tradition it is also related to the literature on *anomie* and *alienation* originating from Marx and Durkheim.[13] As to the presumed stabilizing effects of the intermediary associations and the mutual protection provided by the *pouvoirs intermédiaires* to rulers and subjects alike, de Tocqueville is the main inspiration. In fact, contemporary mass theory, in particular Kornhauser's version, is primarily an updating and systematization of de Tocqueville's insights. By emphasizing the integrative functions of social norms, mass theory has affinities with modern structural-functionalism. Another source is Gustave LeBon. He pointed to the formation of crowds in *l'ére de foules,* as he termed his age, to their formlessness, irrationality, and gullibility. Possessing no reasoning power of its own, the crowd is credulous and subject to collective hallucination. It is prone to exaggeration and acts on images presented to it. In the crowd the individual loses his individuality and becomes submerged in the trans-personal «mass soul».[14] Exactly the same applies to the individual in mass society: alienated, deprived of the supportive contacts provided by social bonds and established hierarchies, he is thrown out in the open, an easy target for irrationalist appeals.

In its contemporary form mass theory may appear antiquated and too flavored by the traumas of World War II. Yet it goes to the core of the theory of requisites of viable parliamentary democracy and as such belongs very much to the contemporary intellectual landscape. It is not to be forgotten that mass theory has certain important merits. Its hallmark lies in its attempt to combine two dimensions not frequently found in social science theory construction: the *historical* and the *predictive.* It remains the most general theory of political extremism trying to incorporate actual historical cases. By pinpointing systemic factors such as paucity of social bonds and isolation of groups, and by highlighting conditions which are likely to give rise to these structural weaknesses, mass theory has identified a series of vulnerable areas where anti-democratic mobilization efforts can find support. Developments in these potential «crisis areas» can then be used to predict the performance of democratic regimes, or form parts of a more general theory of stability in democracies. As such mass theory is closely related to theories of pluralism, and it prefigured the literature on cross-cutting cleavages, including the theory of multiple membership affiliations as tension-reducing devices in ethnically and socially segmented societies.[15]

An analysis of the structural weaknesses of Weimar society cannot grasp the whole period in its full complexity. What an analysis of social structure can do, however, is to cast light on the medium through which the various disintegrative forces worked. Analyzing social structure in this context means to elucidate the whole life situation of different strata. It includes tracing each group's position in relation to the economy, not only its horizontal and vertical social affiliations. It also includes exposing the cultural and perceptual grids which determine each group's self-interpretation and affect its political behavior. Only thus can an attempt be made to understand the differences in response to economic and social distress: why one set of proposed solutions to Weimar's crises was so uncritically embraced by some groups and so determinedly rejected by others.

2. The Tenets of Mass Theory

Implicit in all mass theorizing are three assumptions which will provide the groundwork for the subsequent discussion:

1. All such theories exhibit notions about the *nature of the masses:* whether atomization primarily affected *individuals,* or whether it meant the *isolation of social groups as a whole.*
2. They all formulate assumptions about the *causes for atomization.*
3. They imply a time-table, setting forth notions of the *timing* of the crucial waves of «massification».

The first question is the most important. Obviously there is no clear-cut distinction between isolation of individuals and groups, but rather a continuum. The distinction is of some theoretical significance, however. Those who insist that atomization is a phenomenon primarily affecting groups stress their *external isolation,* i.e. the weakening or withering away of bonds between the groups and between the groups and the state or both. To Kornhauser it is this gradual erosion of the intermediate affiliations which constitutes the main threat to the stability of parliamentary rule. Lack of internal cohesion may explain differences in receptivity to mass appeal but becomes dangerous only in combination with external isolation in regard to the rulers. This first category also concerns the question of the recruitment to the Nazi movement: was it uniform throughout, or did certain segments recruit disproportionately to its ranks? Mass theory as a theoretical system hinges to a great extent on this question.

The second point, about causes for atomization, does not in a strict sense pertain to our analysis of the theoretical status of atomization, but it reveals nonetheless important differences between our four theorists. Kornhauser, for instance, makes it clear that economic stress in itself will have negligible impact on the stability of a regime unless it produces sharp social dislocations. In other words, to him the influence of economic change is *indirect.* This is a difference we will have occasion to return to.

As to the timing of «massification», the observation that the Nazis suppressed all expression of organized interests outside their own ranks in their sweeping *Gleichschaltung* moves after the take-over reduces, of course, the value of mass theory as a theory about preconditions of extremism.[16] Central to the totalitarianism thesis as found in both Arendt and Neumann is the *creation* of masses and the need to keep this process in perpetual motion. In the present analysis we shall leave aside this question of the *ruling technique* once in power and concentrate on the question whether the existence of masses prior to the seizure of power proved contributory to the Nazi victory.

Fig. 1 summarizes the positions taken by the four mass theorists under consideration on the nature of the masses, the locus of support for the Nazis, the causes for atomization and the timing of massification.

2.1 Hannah Arendt

Of the four writers under consideration Hannah Arendt is the most deductively inclined and also the most general. In a strict sense, because of her dialectical way of reasoning, her concepts defy sociological categorization; putting them into causal schemes sometimes seems to do violence to her intricate argument and her richly spun prose. A further complicating factor is the outline of her work: the section on totalitarianism is but the third part of a more comprehensive study tracing the origins of anti-Semitism and imperialism and their conncetion with the rise of totalitarianism.[17] In her highly original conception she sees totalitarianism as the end-result of two interconnected processes: on the one hand, the decline of the nation-state, with its stable legal and territorial structures in favor of «endless» imperialist ventures overseas or, in the case of Europe, in the form of diverse «pan» movements; and, on the other, a complementary tendency for individuals to identify themselves not as citizens or members of a class but as representatives of a particular race or ethnic group. As such her work encompasses both political science and history but transcends both. It is a profound attempt to make intelligible how totalitarianism could come about by tracing back into European history the elements which facilitated its growth. In reply to

Fig. 1. *Traditions of Mass Analysis: A Theoretical Overview 1940–1959*

	Type of Isolation and Role of Intermediate Bonds	Cause of Atomization	Timing of Atomization	Nature and Locus of Nazi Mass Support
Hannah Arendt	Atomization leading to loneliness of the *individual*; no contention of group isolation: no discussion of intermediate associations.	Destruction of the nation-state in favor of imperialism; fall of protective class roles as a result of the loss of the cementing influence of nationalism; complementary tendency to identify with race instead of class resulting in a sense of superfluity abetted by unemployment and population growth.	Two-stage theory: mass atomization both facilitated the Nazi seizure of power and provided the base for continued fascist domination.	Undifferentiated concept of mass. Nazi *membership* consisting of apathetic, people «outside» interest organizations.
Emil Lederer	Atomization leading to loneliness of the *individual*; no contention of group isolation; discussion of intermediate associations does take place, but no theoretical significance is given to them.		Prime emphasis on massification *after* accession of power. No discussion of mass conditions as precipitating factors of susceptibility to Nazism.	A short chapter on the «new» middle classes. No unified theoretical elaboration on support. Close to Arendt's undifferentiated concept of mass.
Sigmund Neumann	Same as above.	Depression leading to unemployment; inflation undermining the economic security of the middle classes leading to irrational reaction in the amorphous middle sector, compounded by survival of an anti-democratic political culture from the Imperial period; the working class saved from becoming amorphous by its dense network of organizations. (Neumann)	Two-stage theory like the one argued by Hannah Arendt.	Theory of «crisis strata» vulnerable to Nazism: the «new» middle class, the unemployed, youth military veterans. Proletariat basically immune. Catholics also resistent. In both cases the network of organizations and the development of a cultural and political «sub culture» the main cause.
William Kornhauser	Atomization in a strict sense viewed as an individual phenomenon. Individual atomization does not give rise to mass movements, however. Only when isolation insulates *groups* from wider social contact and integration does atomization become a threat to stability. Structural-functionalist view of stabilizing effects of incorporation and the restraining effects of social bonds.	Major discontinuities in social processes, including political authority, caused by rapid industrialization and urbanization, producing discontinuities in *community* which in turn trigger atomization.	Two-stage theory as above. Emphasis, however, on the difference between factors encouraging mass movements once they have achieved control and factors encouraging mass movements at the outset. After the mass movement has secured its power base, the élite insulates itself; population open to conscious manipulation.	Differentiated concept of mass. In the case of Nazism, old middle class more susceptible than new. *Marginality* crucial: marginal business, unattached intellectuals, unemployed.

criticism on this point she has made clear that she does not regard *The Origins of Totalitarianism* as a history of totalitarian dictatorship but rather as an analysis of the elements that 'crystallized' into it.[18] Nonetheless, despite this attempt to soften criticism of her use of causal links, this remains the basic problem of the book. Her book should now be evaluated again in light of recent scholarship on the Nazi movement. In a way this is unfair since the book now is close to thirty years old, yet it is necessary because if it can be shown that her assumptions about National Socialism, or more broadly, totalitarianism, are untenable, such a conclusion will have repercussions for her general political philosophy as developed in her later books.

To Hannah Arendt the process of atomization primarily affects individuals.[19] The Nazis recruited mainly from the previously unpolitical, the apathetic, the «mass of apparently indifferent people whom all other parties had given up as too apathetic or too stupid for their attention».[20] This atomized, unorganized mass of people who had nothing in common except their loneliness, came from *all* parties.[21] Their passions had hitherto been contained by the educational and restraining influence of belonging to a class.[22] On this point Arendt is explicit: it was the downfall of the protective class barriers which set the stage for the formation of the European «mass man». It was his lack of normal social relationships which created his «crowd psychology». This dissolution of class bonds was accompanied by the breakdown of the party system: the parties ceased to attract support from the younger generation in particular, and lost the silent approval of the unorganized, who suddenly went wherever there was an opportunity to voice their new violent opposition.[23]

Her theory of the advent of National Socialism can be illustrated as in Fig. 2.

Fig. 2. *Hannah Arendt's Theory of the Rise of Mass Movements*

| Breakdown of the traditional class system | → | Atomization of the individual as the result of being deprived of normal social relationships | → | «Masses» | → | Loss of tacit support for the traditional parties from the previously unorganized; the young turning Nazi; general susceptibility to mass appeal |

Arrows indicate causal relationships.

Although this scheme provides answers to the question about the nature of atomization (where she deviates considerably from William Kornhauser), her theory is largely unsatisfactory about the causes for atomization and also about the timing of the processes of massification. In the first place, is the «breakdown of classes» the *prime* cause for the atomization of the individual? Or is this class fluidity only an intermediate link between more deep-rooted factors and Nazism? On this point Hannah Arendt offers little beyond vague generalities like the following statement, which at the same time conveys the flavor of her argument in relation to historical interpretation:

«Loneliness, the common ground for terror, the essence of totalitarian government, and for ideology and logicality, the preparation of its executioners and victims, is closely connected with uprootedness and superfluousness which have been the curse of modern masses since the beginning of the industrial revolution and have become acute with the rise of imperialism at the end of the last century and the breakdown of political institutions and social traditions in our own time.»[24]

By bringing in the notion of superfluousness Hannah Arendt anticipated themes which would occupy historians and political scientists at a much later stage. For her, the concept is associated with a cluster of negatively laden terms: rootlessness, stateless-ness, homelessness, and loneliness. But despite its central place in her argument it remains devoid of precise empirical content. Who were most vulnerable to becoming superfluous? Apart from a reference to superfluousness as the concomitant of mass unemployment and of population growth during the last 150 years,[25] there is no systematic effort to isolate structural causes for this phenomenon: the precarious economic existence of the middle classes, and their growing panic in face of creeping obsolescence as they saw themselves pinched in between growing industrial concentration and rationalization in the economy on the one hand, and organized labor, tightly organized and intent on using that power, on the other. The causes of unemployment are never spelt out. Arendt's level of reasoning is in a curious sense meta-historical. Her analysis focuses on an essential problem inherent in all mass theorizing: What exactly is the *theoretical status* of mass atomization? Mass atomization may supplement the understanding of fascism by showing how the general crisis syndrome of alienation and political powerlessness increased the receptivity of the German population to propaganda. But both the downfall of class loyalties and fragmentation are *effects* of social and economic dislocation, not its cause. Both phenomena certainly intensified and widened existing grievances, but caution should be displayed in giving them independent status in a theory of explanation.

Similar weaknesses are discernible in the concept of mass itself. Where exactly did the uprooted masses come from? The term 'masses' applies, according to Arendt, «only where we deal with people who either because of sheer numbers, or indifference, or a combination of both, cannot be integrated into any organization based on common interest, into political parties or municipal governments or professional organizations or trade unions. Potentially they exist in every country and form the majority of those large number of neutral, politically indifferent people who never join a party and hardly ever go to the polls».[26] It was the «slumbering majorities *behind all parties*» who were transformed into «one great unorganized and structureless mass of furious individuals».[27] (Italics mine.) These claims have generated a whole body of literature which will be dealt with extensively in the third section of this study.

2.2 Emil Lederer and Sigmund Neumann

Emil Lederer and Sigmund Neumann agree with Arendt that atomization primarily affects individuals, and that the institutionalization of masses and the transformation of society into a crowd represent the essence of fascist domination. Lederer and Neumann vary, however, in their sensitivity to variations of atomization between groups in society and to the timing of the process of fragmentation. As for the causes of atomization, they are both more explicitly historical and concrete in isolating both long-term and immediate causes.

Whereas Lederer emphasizes the swiftness with which the old and strong organizations were destroyed after a few weeks of Nazi rule[28], Neumann takes pains to argue that the masses were both antecedent to and the result of National Socialism.[29] In this sense he adheres to the same two-stage theory as that expounded by Hannah Arendt. Mob psychology was the result of the disintegration of society and became in turn the basis for the rise of the one-party state, «the state of the masses» in Lederer's words.

Whereas for Neumann massification is an intervening variable between a series of circumstances on the one hand and National Socialism on the other, i.e. an intensifying factor, for Lederer the relationship between historical determinants on the one hand and one-party rule on the other is less mediated through massification. In Lederer's view, massification is more of a conscious creation of Nazi rule and a prerequisite for its continuance.

Of greater importance for any coherent theory of mass society is their disagreement over the sociological locus of Nazi support. To Emil Lederer National Socialism was not a manifestation of class struggle, but the «destruction of society at large».[30] He echoes Hannah Arendt's a-sociological approach, though he points out, with Neumann, that the unemployed were particularly prone to Nazi sympathies because of their insecurity. Lederer is also sensitive to the precarious situation of the new middle class; the negative unity of the white-collar workers in private and public service and in the technical and teaching professions, their abhorrence at the thought of being mistaken for proletarians, their lack of any firm root in the economic system, which made them as vulnerable to market fluctuations as the workers, their romantic image of society and their dispersion, throughout the economy.[31] They represented the «social dynamite» in a time of universal crisis. Strangely, however, Lederer does not extend these observations to German society as a whole. There are only scattered remarks about the general scepticism among workers regarding communism which compared favorably with the lack of political understanding on the part of the aristocrats, the industrial millionaires, the officers of the army and ministers in the church who supported fascism.[32] Lederer, then, though attempting to differentiate between different kinds of masses, ultimately becomes a victim of his own theoretical perspective. Like Arendt, he is blinded by the apparently demonic emergence of masses threatening civilized life in all its manifestations.

More emphatically than either Arendt or Lederer, Neumann is aware of the differentiated nature of the masses who supported Nazism. He repeatedly maintains that although the urban proletariat historically meant the beginning of the «new masses», the proletariat as a group was saved from the threat of amorphous existence by its class consciousness, its shared plight in industrial society and by the network of organizations which penetrated the working class and gave it cultural and economic shelter.[33] As Günther Roth has done after him,[34] Neumann underscores the identity-building and cohesive character of the Marxian ideology in providing a unified worldview which placed the proletarian in the position of standard-bearer for the future society. In Imperial Germany the workers had been 'negatively integrated' into society; they formed a sub-culture, isolated from the rest of society. This continued basically unchanged in the Weimar period, despite the workers' newly won access to executive organs. Devoid of all the social ties which had made them socially and psychologically secure in the countryside, the migrant laborers in the cities could easily have fallen prey to mass appeal. But the socializing experiences of factory life disciplined, matured and rationalized the proletariat. Its insurance schemes, its pleas for collective bargaining, its dream of a planned society and economic democracy and its own organization of communal life – all these were the responses of rational masses, according to Neumann. This newly awakened class consciousness had tremendous effects on the morale of the proletariat in face of growing societal disintegration and made them largely immune to National Socialism. Instead of developing a general mass theory, like Arendt, and to a less extent Lederer, Neumann sets the stage for Kornhauser's theory seventeen years later by pointing out the «crisis strata» of society: a shifting new middle class, the *Angestellten,* the rootless unemployed, the warlike militia, in Wolfgang Sauer's phrase the «military desperadoes».[35] Negatively united, not fitting in the scheme of rationality developed in the 19th century, they were the first and most sensitive targets for emotional appeals.

Supplementing Lederer's analysis of the social insecurity of the middle classes, Neumann points to their growing awareness of being a group between big capital and organized labor, to their anti-plutocratic, but also anti-proletarian sentiments and their yearnings for a return to the social forms of the pre-industrial handicraft society of small independent artisans in which everyone knew his station in life and its duties. The social level of the group sank, chances for advancement declined, and jobs for salaried employees no longer required the special training which could give rise to the differences in wages on the basis of education and responsibility which the middle classes had hitherto taken for granted. Mechanization made white-collar work as monotonous as workers' factory routines. Both wages and social security were brought down to proletarian levels. Inflation hit savings and swelled the number of job holders who had previously been independent small capitalists. Depression brought the menace of unemployment. «The tragedy of the white-collar class», Neumann wrote in 1942, «was that its whole existence had become a borrowed life – and so dangerously unreal: Its romanticism, its passion, its irrationalism – genuine though they were – did not grow out of superabundance of strength but resulted from «collective escapism» . . .«Such an escapist attitude found its crystallization within the new middle class, yet it came to include ever wider circles of a society in turmoil» . . »[36]

2.3 William Kornhauser

With William Kornhauser, mass theory is developed into a general theory of the social requisites of pluralist democracy. What distinguishes his version of mass theory from the tenets of the three preceding writers is 1) his insistence on atomization as primarily a *group* phenomenon: isolation of social groups from wider social contact; 2) his emphasis on the stabilizing effects of social, cross-cutting, intermediary associations which insulate both élites and non-élites from direct and conflict-prone contact, and 3) his elaboration of the social bases of mass movements, (in which he includes communism), where he exhibits some slight differences in emphasis from his predecessors.

In a strict sense, atomization primarily affects individuals in Kornhauser's theory too. But while individual isolation and loneliness of the sort which may even occur within the family can give rise to personal deviance (crime, psychic disorders), atomization at the individual level does not pose a threat to societal stability before it affects groups as social aggregates. In this respect, there is a marked and important theoretical difference between Kornhauser's version of mass theory and that of his forerunners. As he states:

«Mass society is a situation in which an aggregate of individuals are related to one another only by way of their relation to a common authority, especially the state. That is, individuals are not directly related to one another in a variety of independent groups. A population in this condition is not insulated in any way from the ruling group, nor yet from elements within itself. For insulation requires a multiplicity of independent and often conflicting forms of associations, each of which is strong enough to ward off threats to the autonomy of the individual . . .»[37]

And in the tradition of de Tocqueville:

«Mass society lacks intermediate relations, but it is not to be conceived merely as the absence of social relations. The central feature of primary groups in mass society is not so much their internal weaknesses as it is their external *isolation* from the larger society. The isolation of primary groups means that by themselves they cannot provide the basis for participation in the larger society . . .»[38] (Italics in original.)

It follows that in societies of this kind the state must perform a series of functions that the citizens are either unwilling to perform in voluntarily established associations or have left to the state to undertake. This in turn results in centralization of national communication and decision-making. To the extent that people participate in the larger society, they do so through the state or other inclusive nationwide structures. National organizations that are centralized at the expense of smaller forms of associations contribute to creating amorphous masses.[39]

As to the timing of the processes of fragmentation, Kornhauser, more systematically than his forerunners, takes care to distinguish between factors which encourage the development of totalitarian movements in democracies and factors which sustain them once they have seized power. The two are not necessarily the same. Mass society, on the one hand, requires both accessible élites and available non-élites. This means that the population can easily select and replace people «in high positions with special responsibility», which is Kornhauser's definition of «élite».[40] Élites are accessible and non-élites available as a result of a paucity of independent groups for mutual protection. It follows that in the absence of social autonomy at all levels of society, «large numbers of people are pushed and pulled towards activist modes of intervention in vital centers of society; and mass-oriented leaders have the opportunity to mobilize their activism for the capture of power».[41] Totalitarian society, on the other hand, requires an inaccessible élite and an available population if it is to prolong its own existence as a system with control from above. The élite is closed in the sense that succession is secured by the incumbents through co-option, by virtue of their monopoly of the means of coercion and persuasion.[42] Concerning the timing of atomization, Kornhauser's view fits into a two-stage theory. He maintains that mass theory, in order to be useful as an explanation of the transformation of democratic societies into totalitarian ones, *necessarily* presupposes accessible élites.[43] He complements this assertion by stating that the non-élites must be readily available for mobilization by the élites. These are the preconditions for the rise of the one-party state. While arguing that National Socialism, like all mass movements, drew support from all classes, he concedes that it recruited disproportionately from the *Mittelstand*.[44] Surprisingly, however, he disagrees with both Neumann and Lederer in isolating the *old* middle classes of small shopkeepers, artisans, peasants and unattached intellectuals as more vulnerable to mass appeal than the new middle class of *Angestellte*, white-collar workers.[45] Given this emphasis on social integration, it is no surprise to find that he portrays the *unemployed* as a prime source of mass support, though he differentiates between wage-earners who became communist when they were thrown out of work and employed wage-earners who stayed socialist as long as they remained employed.[46] Unemployed white-collar workers turned Nazi more frequently than employed white-collar employees. He also states that in the absence of effective communication and organic bonds inside the trade unions and between different sections of the trade union movement, which was a result of growing bureaucratization on the part of the leadership, membership in the socialist unions declined, and both communists and

Nazis increased their working-class support.[47] Since Kornhauser's theory is more empirically specific and richer than those previously discussed, my critical remarks on his theory will follow after the presentation of the empirical material.

3. The Empirical Validity of Mass Theory

We shall now turn to an examination of the specific claims of mass theory to determine whether it can stand up to a closer scrutiny of social conditions in Germany prior to the Nazi victory in 1933. A first set of questions will focus on Weimar society as a whole: was it atomized? If so, in what sense? What are the units of analysis – isolation of individuals as a result of loss of support previously provided by family bonds, community norms of organizational ties? Or does it make more sense to speak of a division of German society into mutually hostile groups, isolated both vertically in relation to the state and horizontally in relation to other groups? To what extent did this isolation, if found, also imply defense against pressures from below? A third case is also conceivable: that Germany suffered from extreme *Verzuilung,* to use the Dutch expression, but that even within the strictly segmented «pillars» of each social group there was widespread perceived atomization. The possible configurations are legion and the distinctions difficult to draw, but without answers to these questions the validity of the theory remains open to question.

A second set of questions relates to the sources of Nazi support. Did the Nazis draw their support disproportionately from the most uprooted and alienated segments of German society? What part, if any, can be attributed to weakening of social bonds within the strata supporting the Nazis? Were these groups cut off from representation in central decision-making bodies, and if so, what explanatory power does this lack of organizational mediation carry in explaining their support for the NSDAP? These questions will be discussed in the sections dealing with the social bases of Nazi strength.

3.1 Weimar Society: Segmentation from Above

If atomization is taken to mean a thin or non-existent layer of intermediary associations which leaves large parts of the population without support or means of voicing their grievances, Weimar society was far from atomized. On the contrary, it seems well established that each class in Weimar Germany was densely permeated by its own network of intermediary organizations.[48] Far from suffering from a lack of intra-class links, it had a dense network of intermediate relations *within* class segments but few links *across* class boundaries. In his micro-study of «Thalburg», W. S. Allen reports that in 1930 there were no fewer than 161 separate clubs, an average of about one for every sixty persons in the town. Altogether there were twenty-one sports clubs, forty-seven with an economic or occupational background, twenty-three religious or charitable societies, twenty-five veterans' or patriotic associations and forty-five special interests and hobbies' groups.[49] But with hardly an exception, Allen contends, they followed the town's class lines. The claim is strongly borne out that the many clubs and societies cemented individual citizens together, and that prior to the Nazi seizure of power, Thalburg would have been an amorphous society without this close organizational network. The only obstacle to the total integration of social life in the town before 1933 was the distinct class cleavage permeating every sphere of activity – a factor which under the impact of steadily declining economic conditions was to become crucial in polarizing the community.

The phenomenon of organizations in German public life is not new. As early as 1910 Max Weber remarked that joining together was as typical of Germany as of the United States. He said that in a city of 30,000 inhabitants he had found «approximately 300 different associations or one per hundred inhabitant and one per 20 heads of a family».[50] They did not restrict themselves to purely charitable or social purposes. Each class or group in Germany rallied behind its own political party and its own set of interest organizations. Lepsius has shown that the stability of the German party system from Bismarck to the depression was due to its links with these enduring, tightly integrated but closed subcultures.[51] These organizations reached deep into their clienteles and were geared in all their activities to specific strata and their interests. During the Weimar Republic these organizations managed to formalize their influence on the executive, on parliament and on the bureaucracy to such an extent that it makes good sense to describe the resulting system as institutionally segmented at the highest level: the institutionalization of interest representation and influence was even given the form of judicial recognition in areas like law-making and economic policy and accepted as part of the normal workings of government.[52] In the 1920's, for example, the German business community depended on a high degree of organizational unity to achieve its objectives. Not only did the businessmen and the industrialist have access to all the bourgeois parties through influential contacts, they also gravitated towards compact, close-knit *Spitzenverbände* which could coordinate their political activities. The most important of these powerful umbrella organizations were the National Federation of German Industry *(Reichsverband der deutschen Industrie)* and the Confederation of German Employer's Associations *(Vereinigung deutscher Arbeitgeberverbände)*. The degree of organization for furthering the collective interests of German business vis-à-vis the state and other social groups was higher than among the workers, and even the agricultural producers.[53] A similar dense pattern of interest representation between social groups and the government is found among other occupational strata in Germany, to which we shall return in more detail in sections 3.5 and 3.6.

3.2 The Nazi Following on the Electoral Level

If German society was atomized, sudden shifts in party allegiance might be expected. Rootlessness breeds gullibility, and gullibility increases the capacity of the masses to be manipulated and led into new movements. More important than mere shifts in party allegiance are fluctuations between the main blocs in the German electorate. Did the German pattern of voting *en bloc* along class lines collapse in the final years before the Nazi seizure of power? Who lost in the struggle for votes from 1928 to 1932 when the NSDAP leapt from 2.6 to 37.3 per cent of the vote and the conservative and *Mittelstand* parties declined from 41 to 11 per cent? After more than 40 years of debate, the consensus is growing that the Nazi electoral upsurge came disproportionately from the liberal and conservative parties and that there was a close correlation between Nazi voting and white-collar groups, artisans, retailers, in short the petty bourgeoisie.[54]

What is remarkable and damaging to any undifferentiated concept of mass is the striking ability of the working-class and Catholic segments of the German voting population to persist in their class and confessional loyalties in the face of growing economic disintegration. Taking the socialist vote first, the noticeable feature is that the lowest ebb did not occur in the post-depression period but in May 1924, in the period following the Ruhr invasion, when the appeal from the Deutsch-Nationale Volkspartei was most likely to strike chords of nationalism in the working-class population. Apart from that, the figures show remarkable stability:

Table 1. *Total SPD and KPD Vote as a Percentage of all Votes Cast in the General Election of the Years 1924–32*[55]

May 1924	1928	1930	July 1932	November 1932
33.1	40.4	37.6	35.9	37.3

Within the working-class, however, there was a fairly steady drift leftwards, towards the KPD:

Table 2. *Percentage of all Votes Cast*

	1928	1930	July 1932	November 1932
SPD	29.8	24.5	21.6	20.4
KPD	10.6	13.1	14.3	16.9

The trend towards support for the KPD came in those regions most heavily affected by industrial unemployment. Contemporary commentators like the French analyst René Pinon noted that the struggle for the cities, at least for the mainly Protestant ones, was not between the Nazis and the Left, but between the SPD and the KPD.[56] A glance of the ten most industrialized electoral districts (Wahlkreise) makes clear what little inroads the NSDAP actually made into the total left vote. In table 3 material is presented to substantiate this claim. As can be seen, between 1928 and 1930 there was a slight falling off in the left vote, but thereafter it remained steady, showing its strength again in November 1932.

Table 3. *Left Vote (KPD plus SPD) as Percentage of all Votes Cast*

Wahlkreise	1928	1930	July 1932	November 1932
Berlin	63.6	61.0	61.3	60.9
Potsdam II	48.1	45.6	46.6	46.0
Potsdam I	51.7	48.7	46.8	47.1
Magdeburg East	50.2	47.2	43.1	44.4
Düsseldorf West	41.4	39.7	38.5	39.8
Düsseldorf	31.9	29.3	30.0	32.1
Dresden	49.4	47.1	45.4	46.5
Leipzig	53.1	52.1	51.8	52.9
Chemnitz	49.7	46.8	42.0	43.7
Hamburg	53.6	50.0	49.4	50.5

Similarly, the Catholic vote, as might be expected, remained remarkably stable throughout the whole Weimar period. These figures confirm Neumann's observations about the role of the church in the everyday lives of its members, even if they were not actual communicants, a role the Lutheran churches had long ceased to play. It is noteworthy that this electoral stability held up even in the extraordinary circumstances of the election of March 1933, when terror and threats made a mockery of the secrecy and integrity of the act of voting. The total Catholic vote – the added vote of the *Zentrum* party and the Bavarian People's Party – is shown in table 4.

Table 4. *Catholic Vote as Percentage of all Votes Cast*

1928	1930	1932 (I)	1932 (II)
15.2	14.8	15.7	15.0

Furthermore, the great Centre party strongholds in the Rhineland, Bavaria, Baden and Württemberg along with the region of Southern Silesia, remained absolutely solid throughout the Weimar period.

3.3 The NSDAP, the Unemployed and the Previous Non-Voters

On the basis of misleading correlations between the rise in unemployment and the rise of the Nazi vote, early mass theorists were led to believe that the NSDAP must have attracted a substantial proportion of the jobless. A close analysis of the electoral statistics must lead us to dismiss that notion, however. Contemporary analysts noticed that the Nazi gains were most spectacular in those areas where there was little industrial unemployment, i.e. rural areas. Though the Nazi gains in the crucial election in 1930 were impressive – the party leaped from 2.6 per cent to 18.3 in two years – Werner Stephan in an article from 1932 could show that the greatest strength of the NSDAP lay in those areas of Germany which were agricultural and Protestant.[57] His views are confirmed if we look at the ten electoral provinces which registered the highest Nazi vote in 1930 and which maintained the highest average Nazi vote for the period 1930–1933. Except for two of these *Wahlkreise* (Chemnitz-Zwickau and Pfalz), they were all largely agricultural and protestant.

Table 5. *Wahlkreise with Highest Average Nazi Percentage of the Votes, 1930–33*[58]

Schleswig-Holstein	44.0
Pomerania	42.9
East Hannover	41.8
East Prussia	41.5
Frankfurt	41.4
Liegnitz	41.2
Chemnitz-Zwickau	41.0
South Hannover	39.9
Pfalz	38.9
Breslau	30.6

Summarizing the literature on the relative urban and rural strength of the NSDAP, Lipset states that «the various interpretations of Nazism as the product of the growth of anomie and rootlessness of modern urban industrial society» are sharply challenged.[59] The remarkable stability of the working-class parties also lends credence to the view that the unemployed on the whole stayed in their original social blocs, and that the shifts that took place could not have been significant: the unemployed workers went predominantly to the KPD, the unemployed employee became mostly a Nazi supporter.

In a detailed study of Berlin and Hamburg, Richard Hamilton has looked closely at the assertion that the Nazis found a fertile recruiting ground among the urban jobless. In Hamburg he found that the district most heavily affected by unemployment actually showed a level of support for the NSDAP significantly *below* the average vote for the Nazis in other working-class districts. In the most depressed working-class areas of Hamburg only one in five voters cast their vote for the Nazis, whereas in Hamburg's less crisis-ridden working-class district the ratio was one in four. The workers who came to support the Nazi party seem to have been those who had previously voted for a liberal or a conservative party.

In the case of Berlin Hamilton doubts that it was the unemployed workers who turned to National Socialism. Here evidence suggests that it was the previous supporters of the DNVP, the DDP and the DVP who shifted to the Nazis, not the people out of work. In the majority of the city's working class districts the vote for the NSDAP from 1924 to 1932 was consistently below average for all the city's electoral districts, and the more «proletarian», the smaller was the Nazi vote, even at the height of the depression. [60]

Before comparing these conclusions with the claims of mass theory, it is imperative to determine whether, as Hannah Arendt asserts, the NSDAP got its support from the *apathetic,* the *previous non-voters,* the «masses» outside any organized political activity. This question has produced a whole literature on its own. Two traditions have crystallized: Bendix, writing in 1956, questioned the whole approach of class analysis as applied to National Socialism, arguing that the previous non-voters provided Hitler with his greatest accretions of strength in the September 1930 elections, and that, consequently, an inference can be made that the appeal of the NSDAP was not, at least initially, to any one class but to the disaffected and apolitical of all strata.[61] S. M. Lipset, on the other hand, dismisses as statistically insignificant the overall increase in voting participation, but asserts that new voters figured importantly in the Nazi rise from 1930 to 1933, though not in the early increase from 1928 to 1930.[62] Bendix' position has been taken up anew by Karl O'Lessker who, using a more precise correlation technique, argues that new voters figured heavily in the Nazi vote in *both* periods.[63] In a reanalysis of O'Lessker's data Allan Schnaiberg finds that from 1928 to 1930 the Nazis did *not* gain more of their votes from among new voters than other parties did.[64]

The bare facts are clear: From 1928 to the July election in 1932 there was an increase in the number of eligible voters from 41.2 million to 44.2 million. In the same period there was an increase in turnout from 75.6 per cent in 1928 to 84.1 per cent in 1932 (1). The NSDAP added 13 million votes to its strength in these years. The total increase in valid votes was approximately 6 million, of which about 2 million can be traced to increase in turnout. These figures in themselves indicate that the accretions to the strength of the Nazis could not have come purely from the previous non-voters or from the newly enfranchised. Using fluctuation in percentage points, not absolute numbers, as the basic for his analysis, Kaltefleiter concludes that in the period 1928–32, the NSDAP was the only party to profit disproportionately from higher turnout. This does not mean, however, that the higher turnout benefited the Nazis only; rather, it means that among the voters who did not vote in 1928 but participated in 1932, the Nazi share was larger than the proportion of votes cast in favor of other parties in that election. Naturally, there is no way of knowing whether these additions to the Nazi vote came from previous non-voters or from young persons who had been previously ineligible.[65]

To draw any firm conclusions from this debate is relatively difficult since it involves different uses and interpretations of the same data on the basis of divergent methodological presuppositions. A strong case can be made in favor of Lipset's formulation by pointing to the fact that the increase in turnout was uniform – indeed, it was higher in the cities, where the Nazi gains were less dramatic, than in the rural areas – and all parties appear to have benefited. Thus the balance in class voting was not fundamentally altered. All parties merely reached deeper into their potential support, the Nazis as a bourgeois party deeper into the middle-classes. If non-voters supported the NSDAP almost exclusively, then we should expect the percentage of the total left and the total Catholic vote to decline much more significantly than it actually did. The conclusion, therefore, must be that the relationship between the turnout and the Nazi vote was an extrinsic and a coincidental one. Even if we do not accept Lipset's assertion that there was, in fact, a *negative* rank order correlation between turnout and the Nazi vote, it is difficult to deny the proposition of McKibbin, Loomis and Beegle[66] and Pollock[67] that the correlation is at least no more positive for the National Socialists than for any other party. As such, Lipset's conclusion must stand. More recently, however, even his position has come under heavy and sophisticated attack. W. P. Shively, in his article «Party Identification, Party Choice and Voting Stability: The Weimar Case» argues that all previous arguments in favor of Lipset's theses that the Nazi party drew disproportionate support from new voters between 1930 and 1933 have been based on some form of ecological correlation or regression, relating changes in the Nazi vote, by district, to changes in voting turnout. It is possible, he argues, that the recurring biases of estimation produced by the repetition of this pattern may have given a result which is replicable but spurious. Using complementary designs analysis over time, he concludes that during its periods of growth, from 1928 until 1932, «the Nazi party did not draw unusual support from among previous non-voters. The 1933 election may have been an exception, but the likelihood remains that the Nazi party essentially was not a party of new voters».[68]

3.4 The NSDAP: Its Membership and Leaders

The sociological characteristic of being a movement of the middle class and the petty bourgeoisie extends also to the party *membership* and its *élite*. Contrary to its original designation – Hitler had often expressed the wish to make the NSDAP into a «working-class party»[69] – worker's representation in the cadres and in the membership remained low. As early as in the fall of 1923, according to Kater, only 9.5 per cent of all Nazis in Gemany could be termed «proletarians».[70] The party records at this early stage show an overrepresentation of artisans *(Handwerker)*, who constituted 1/5 of the membership, then follow shopkeepers *(Kaufleute)*, salaried employees and peasants *(Landwirte)*.[71] The social composition of the Nazi membership has been subjected to thorough statistical scrutiny by Wolfgang Schäfer, who on the basis of the party records from 1930 found that the working-class was heavily under-represented in the Nazi ranks. His figures are (in parentheses the group as a percentage of the total population): Workers 28 (45.9); salaried employees 25.6 (12.0); independents 20.7 (9.0); civil servants *(Beamten)* 8.3 (5.1) and peasants 14.0 (10.6).[72] Two studies on Nazi regional strength, one on Lower Saxony, the other on Bavaria,[73] show the same pattern of a high proportion of typical *Mittelstand* groups, peasants, artisans, shopkeepers, small businessmen and white-collar workers. Doblin and Pohly, using 717 Nazi members in the *Reichstag* of 1938 as their sample, confirm this conclusion on the élite level. The group of manual workers in the Nazi Reichstag amounted to 11.4 per cent versus 53.6 per cent in the population at large according to the census classification. As expected, the participation of salaried people was exceedingly high (51.4 versus 19.5 per cent),[74] owing mainly to the large quota of business employees and civil servants, including elementary, secondary and university teachers. Neumann is proven right in his emphasis on the military and the war generation as strongholds of support for the Nazis. In the Doblin-Pohly group at least 164 of the 717 members joined military organizations such as *Wehrwolf, Freikorps-Epp* and the like; almost two-thirds of the group were war veterans.[75] Kornhauser is supported in his contention that marginal academics played a pivotal role in the Nazi leadership; 165 of the 717 had actually entered universities, but the number of failures was remarkably high: only between 84 and 97 got their degree, an unusual case in the German educational system.[76] Lerner, in his study based on the *Führerlexikon* which was published in 1934, concludes that the Nazi élite was first of all totally *male,* «marginal», both geographically (a disproportionate number came from border areas) and in comparison with the élite it replaced. The male character of the party is confirmed in the official party statistics. While women played an important role as Nazi voters, only 5 per cent of the membership was female, but women were underrepresented in other parties as well. Party figures also confirm the high proportion of farmers in the party.[77] It also had a young élite (in 1938 the average age in the Nazi élite was eight years below that of the preceding non-Nazi leadership and five years below that of the German population as a whole). Moreover, Lerner shows the extent to which the members of the Nazi élite led «unstable» lives: few had regular jobs and many established families late.[78] The striking age pattern of the party is confirmed on the regional level in Lower Saxony and Bavaria.[79]

Altogether these figures amount to a confirmation of the contemporary political diagnosis of Herman Rauschning. As early as 1938 he noted that «National Socialism has made the petty-bourgeois the backbone of the movement».[80] Certain important conclusions pertaining to mass theory follow:

First, the depression had virtually no effect on the class/religious pattern of German voting. Those who had traditionally voted for the Centre, including the Bavarian People's Party, continued to do so. Similarly, those who had cast their vote for the left remained unaffected by the Nazi appeal. As a bloc the middle-class vote was not fundamentally affected either. But *within* the already established blocs of class voting profound changes took place. On the right, the NSDAP virtually wiped out the liberal and conservative parties and heavily damaged the regional ones at the same time. The *Deutsch-Nationale Volkspartei* (DNVP) was reduced to a traditional conservative party. On the left, the swing towards the KPD has already been noted. As a result, if by atomization is meant the loosening of class loyalties, as reflected in shifts *between* the class blocs, then Weimar society was *not* atomized. A strong case has been made for the conclusion that previous non-voters, the supposedly most apathetic and unorganizable section of the population, did *not* flock in significant numbers to the Nazi movement. Likewise, a case has been made that the supposedly most uprooted segment of the population, the unemployed, did not become Nazi at least in the industrial sector. Regional contrasts are significant here, for there can be no doubt that marginality and uprootedness did play a role for certain groups in the countryside, especially young unemployed workers and employees in middle-sized firms outside the cities.

In the latter case their affiliation with the Nazi party is not surprising. Workers in these firms in the private sector did not regard themselves in a psycho-social sense as belonging to the working class. Common to these groups was their lack of organizational ties to the working-class proper. As a result the social protection offered by these ties did not extend to them. On the question of the role of unemployment in driving people into the ranks of the NSDAP, Broszat has estimated that of the approximately 270,000 workers who joined the party before 1933, between 120,000 and 150,000 were unemployed.[81] In Bavaria the number of unemployed in the party tripled between 1930 and 1933, although very few of these new entrants rose to leadership positions.[82] The party thus remained thoroughly bourgeois in character. Noakes, in discussing electoral returns in Lower Saxony, concludes that a large proportion of the support for the NSDAP in the election in 1930 came from people who because of previous apathy, ineligibility or alienation had not voted before. In 1930 the Nazis won 458,298 more votes than in 1928. The combined loss of the bourgeois parties in the province, i.e. excluding the SPD, was 214,887, of which a few may be assumed to have gone to the Centre. Thus over half of the increase in the Nazi vote came from voters who had either transferred their loyalties from other parties, had previously been ineligible or had not voted before.[83] With regard to the unemployed, it is safe to assume that their social existence was in a state of fluidity. But there is no way to prove the assertion that atomization also drove the *new* voters as a whole to the polls. Their previous absence may have been for quite different reasons, including ineligibility, and they may even have voted as a result of mobilization efforts by interest organizations. By way of conclusion it seems safe to assert that atomization cannot account directly for the massive swing of the vote in favor of the Nazis from 1928 to 1932. The distribution of the vote between areas most severely hit by unemployment, i.e. cities, and rural areas, and the resistance of the working-class wards most affected by lack of jobs, is in itself a refutation of such a proposition.

This result undermines the sociological foundation of Hannah Arendt's totalitarianism thesis and destroys any undifferentiated concept of mass. In a broad sense we are instead dealing with the reaction of *particular* groups to political and economic dislocation. The remedy lies in understanding the reasons behind their sense of frustration and the causes for their activism, not in restructuring interaction rules on the level of representation. The demonstration that class identities persisted in voting has rendered Arendt's notion of the breakdown of the protective class barriers useless as an analytical tool. Instead considerable support has been accumulated in favor of the role of the theory of «crisis strata» expounded by Sigmund Neumann. Whereas his insistence on the role of the military caste in the rise of anti-democratic movements has been borne out, he errs like his fellow theorists in his assumption that the unemployed were particularly vulnerable to the Nazi appeal.

Hence we are again left with the question of the exact theoretical status of social cohesion in bringing about receptivity to 'mass appeal'. After analyzing the diverse claims about the social roots of Nazism, we are now in a position to rephrase this question and narrow it down to the *Mittelstand* of small producers and retailers and the growing segment of white-collar *Angestellte:* were these segments characterized by conditions of massification? If so, can the *lack* of internal social cohesiveness and the paucity of associations reaching out towards the state and society at large explain the willingness of these middle classes to react favorably to the Nazis? Ultimately, this is the question upon which the reliability of mass theory as a general theory of stability in democracy rests.

3.5 Internal Cohesion and the External Bonds of the Old and New Mittelstand

The section of the German population which can be subsumed under the broad category of *Mittelstand* was employed in a variety of enterprises. According to an occupational census conducted in 1925, approximately 48 per cent of the German population belonged to an intermediary stratum located between the industrial working class on the one hand and the powerful class of industrial entrepreneurs, financiers and large landowners on the other.[84] In 1925 there were at least 5 million small economic undertakings: more than 2 million in agriculture, more than 1 million in retailing and handicraft production, 250,000 in catering and almost 100,000 in transport. To give an indication of the crucial importance of this segment in German society, it can be estimated that the *Mittelstand* in the sense of people belonging to the enterprises cited above comprised a labor force at least twice as numerous as the employees in large-scale industry. In 1926 between 12 and 13 per cent of the entire population was employed in crafts subsumed under the category *Handwerk* (handicraft industries).[85] Significantly, the number of retired people and rentiers also rose, from 3.8 million in 1925 to 5.8 million in 1933 (8.9 per cent of the total population).[86]

Allen's findings in «Thalburg» are representative for the *Mittelstand* as a whole. Overall the tendency to organize was strong. In the *Handwerk* membership in guilds increased from 477,402 in 1907 to 936,498 in 1926.[87] Nowhere was the tendency to organize tightly along strict 'estate' lines stronger than among the artisans. Although internally segmented, the middle sector remained highly organized within the boundaries set by craft distinctions. By adding together the membership figures for the three main white-collar unions, the *Gewerkschaft der Angestellten* (socialist), the national-liberal Hirsch-Dunker unions and the racist-national *Deutschnationaler Handlungsgehilfenverband (DHV)*, founded in 1893, Schoenbaum estimates that fully 87.1 per cent of the white-collar labor force belonged to economic interest organizations.[88] Using employment figures from 1932 and union membership data from the same year, Jürgen Kocka concludes that 43 per cent of the *Angestellten* were unionized as against 32 per cent of the workers.[89] In cross-national perspective even this latter figure is rather remarkable: *the German white-collar unions reached even deeper into their clientele than did the socialist trade unions, which with their long traditions of organization, were generally regarded as the strongest organized working class in Europe.* Like the working class subculture, the middle class unions and the guilds promoted a distinct way of life by founding their own organizations encompassing cultural and social activities as well. Thus they tried to preserve the distinctions between petty bourgeois and proletarian lifestyles. These distinctions had less and less basis in income differentials but were for that very reason guarded more zealously than before.

So ingrained was the inclination to belong to an interest organization among employees that membership figures showed an upward trend even during the depression years (1929–33). In the same period the strength of the trade unions declined. (See tables 6 and 7.) It is symptomatic of the political rightward trend in the 1920's and early 30's that the *Afa* association *(Allgemeine freie Angestelltenbund)* which was rather left-wing and affiliated with the newly established German trade unions federation (DGB), had 690,000 members in 1920 and at that time was larger than the right-wing *Gesamtverband Deutscher Angestelltenwerkschaften* (Gedag) which had 463,000. It was also larger than the *Gewerkschaftsbund der Angestellten* (GdA) with 300,000 members, a *mittelständisch,* nationalist and anti-socialist association. The DHV was a sub-group under the umbrella of the Gedag. By 1930, however, the Gedag held a commanding position while the left-inclining Afa-Bund had lost almost 30 per cent of its members, probably in part due to the introduction by the DHV of a comprehensive insurance scheme which made membership more attractive.[90] The cautious shift to the left among the middle class discernible after World War I, which found expression in limited co-operation between workers' unions and employees' unions, had thus been reversed. It is indicative of the peripheral role of organizing affiliations as an independent variable in explaining political behavior that whilst membership declined in the trade unions, the working class as a whole remained immune to the Nazi appeal.

As for the *external* bonds between the middle class and the political system, it is significant that in 1926, 1,591 members of the DHV *alone* (note again that the DHV was merely a sub-division of the larger Gedag) were elected to promote the interests of their association and its membership in the *Land* parliaments. At the end of 1931, 1,088 DHV parliamentarians were elected, 10 to the *Reichstag,* 25 to *Land* assemblies and 1,053 to different local and provincial councils. In fact, the DHV relied on an elaborate network of liaisons *(Querverbindungen)* which permeated *all* the bourgeois parties, but towards the end of the Republic, by 1931, the largest contingent of DHV representatives was affiliated with the NSDAP.[91]

Table 6. *Membership Figures in the Three Biggest German Employees' Organizations – in 1000's*

	1920	1922	1925	1927	1929	1930
Afa	690	658	428	396	453	480
Gedag	463	460	411	460	558	592
GdA	300	302	313	290	375	385
	1,453	1,420	1,152	1,146	1,386	1,457

Membership Figures in Per Cent

	1920	1922	1925	1927	1929	1930
Afa	47.5	46.3	37.2	34.6	32.7	32.9
Gedag	31.8	32.4	35.6	40.1	40.2	40.6
GdA	20.7	21.3	27.2	25.3	27.1	26.5
	100.0	100.0	100.0	100.0	100.0	100.0

Source: F. W. Fisher, *Die Angestellten und ihre Bewegung ung Ideologie* (Staatswissenschaftliche Dissertation, Heidelberg 1931), p. 44, 46. Ref. in Kocka, «Zur Problematik . . .», op.cit., p. 799.

Table 7. *Trade-Union Membership (1,000)*

	Germany	U.K.	U.S.A.
1920	9,193	8,346	5,034
1929	5,740	4,858	3,567
1931	5,177	4,624	3,526
1933	—	4,392	2,857

Source: S. Pollard, «The Trade Unions and the Depression 1929–33», in Mommsen et al.: *Industrielles System und Politische Entwicklung in der Weimarer Republik* (Düsseldorf 1974), p. 240.

Table 8 shows that artisan representation in the German parliament increased dramatically throughout the Weimar period only to drop in the July elections in 1932. These figures make it rather difficult to speak of a weakening of the intermediary bonds between the *Mittelstand* and the legislature, either in the form of access to central authority or in terms of membership strength. It may be argued that the representation was not impressive at the outset, though it should be remembered that the people here elected were nominated by their organizations and then subsequently elected by the parties. Because of constant organizational pressure outside parliament, the actual influence of artisans' interests in policy decisions far exceeded the actual number of representatives in the national assembly proper.

Table 8. *Representation of the Handwerk in the German Parliament*

Legislative periods	Total number of delegates	Number of artisan representatives	Percentage of artisan representatives
National Assembly	421	7	1.66
1920–24	469	12	2.56
May 1924	472	13	2.75
1924–28	495	19	3.83
1928–30	491	19	3.87
1930–32	576	23	4.00
July 1932	608	*16	2.63

* of whom 10 belonged to the NSDAP.
Source: *Deutsche Allgemeine Handwerks-Zeitung 37 (1932) no. 41.* Quoted from H.A. Winkler, *op.cit.* Anhange II, p. 299.

The issue of the organizational density among the *Mittelstand* is in a strict sense not yet settled, for we have only taken into account the most articulate and best organized groups in the middle sector. The NSDAP may still have recruited disproportionately from people who were too scattered or who had too few common interests to form coherent social units. The free professions may have been such a group – doctors, academics at the universities and lawyers both inside and outside the civil service. Schoolteachers pose another problem as they were partly organized within the white-collar organizations, and partly outside. Their nationalist sentiments are well known. The older parts of the population, those dependent on incomes from capital funds or pensions, were also loosely organized, as were several technical professions, engineers and technicians in industry among them. There can be little doubt that marginality did play some part in determining the political behavior of these groups, but most of the Germans who became members of the Nazi party did not do so in the manner specified by mass theory.[92] It is difficult to see what role socio-psychic needs resulting from atomization could have played in increasing Nazi support. But mass theorists may still argue that sociological data pointing towards a dense criss-crossing of affiliations within the social blocs most vulnerable to Nazi recruitment reveals nothing about the *quality* of such participation. In other words, despite a high degree of organization, these bonds may not have provided much social and psychological gratification. The organizations could have been mere 'shells' with a top-heavy administrative apparatus and little contact downwards. One complicating factor here is the generation gap. The Nazi movement attracted the young; the organizations were run mainly by older people. This may account for some of the lack of intergrative capacity in the intermediary network but cannot explain the whole Nazi appeal. We shall return to this argument in section 3.8.

3.6 *Internal Cohesion and External Bonds of the Peasantry*

Efforts to organize the German peasantry started early: the first organization with specific interest goals emerged in 1885 under the name of *Deutsche Bauernbund.* Propelled into action by Caprivi's relaxation of the tariffs, the Junkers presided over the establishment of the *Bund der Landwirte* in 1893, which was soon to become the most powerful of the farmer's organizations east of the Elbe and in the Protestant regions in the west and south, and which was thoroughly dominated by big landowner interests. From 1893 to 1913 its membership rose from 162,000 to 330,000.[93] In 1920/21 the *Bund* was replaced by the *Reichslandbund* which in March 1929 became the mainspring of the Green Front, a super-pressure group which co-ordinated agrarian interest articulation and consisted of the *Deutsche Bauernschaft* (formerly *Bauernbund*) which drew its strongest support from small and medium-sized farms in the northwest, from mid-Germany and from Bavaria, the *Vereinigung der christlichen-deutschen Bauernvereine,* and the *Deutsche Landwirtschaft,* the central organization for all chambers of agriculture. In spite of bitter internal disagreements over policy, and the short life of the Green Front, the farmers exercised a powerful influence especially in the final years of the Republic, when their organizations interfered directly in the affairs of the executive.[94]

In 1927 the *Reichslandbund* with its central bureaucracy, its periodicals and numerous sub-organizations commanded a following of 1.7 million fully-fledged members owning land. In all it had 5.6 million members, making it a most formidable organization in the anti-parliamentary front.[95] In East Prussia, 94 per cent of the big landowners owning more than 100 *ha* land were organized in the *Landwirtschaftsbund Ostpreussen,* 49 per cent of those owning between 5 and 10 *ha,* and 59 per cent of all farmers owning more than 5 hectares of land altogether. If the percentage calculation is based on the number of farms actually tilled by the proprietors themselves, 63 per cent of them were organized – a rather remarkable figure given the geographic distances in the region.[96] Both with regard to organizational access to the executive and to the number of channels available for expressing demands, the German peasantry was most advantageously situated.

As for the internal conditions in the villages close to the land, the long-established homogeneity and the sense of community of the German village makes it difficult to use atomization as an explanation for the Nazi inroads into the rural population. It cannot, at any rate, be used as the sole factor, not even in the geographically remote and marginal areas in Northern Germany. Rudolf Heberle, in his study of Schleswig-Holstein, takes pains to emphasize that «a large part, if not the majority» of the rural population living in the areas recruiting heavily to the Nazis belonged to «comparatively homogenous communities with a strong sense of solidarity».[97] This judgement is echoed in T. A. Tilton's more recent study of the continuities of right-wing alignment in the Schleswig-Holstein region: the Nazis' most conspicuous success came in the regions with the greatest communal cohesion.[98] In other words, it was not the people with the fewest social ties who were most receptive to mass appeals, as Kornhauser asserts, but those most thoroughly integrated. This applies to their secondary attachments as well. Heberle is able to show that the Nazi vote was not only associated with farming as such but with type of soil, size of farm and socio-economic position, and type of labor (wage-earner vs. self-employed). Similarly, the voting behavior of the self-employed differed from that of wage-earners. There was a very clear positive correlation with support for Nazism in the former case, but a strikingly negative one in the latter.[99] Districts with the particular sandy or 'sour' type of soil called *geest,* which is particularly prevalent along the Baltic coast, were far more inclined to vote in favor of the NSDAP than were more fertile 'marsh' areas.[100] C. P. Loomis and J. A. Beegle have found the same pattern in those farming districts of Germany similar to the *geest* landscapes of Schleswig-Holstein[101]. These differences in voting behavior between the self-employed and the wage-earners suggest a conflict not primarily attributable to atomization. Rather, it indicates a more traditional class-based interest conflict. Furthermore, among the farmers, the size of the farm was crucial in determining party allegiance.[102] It is doubtful, indeed, whether atomization in the farmer communities and variations in the external interest representation can explain these divergent reactions to the economic crises. The fact is that the crisis, as in many other European countries, increased agricultural indebtness to the point of forcing whole communities into foreclosures. In the *geest* areas market fluctuations were massive. Traditionally, income was earned principally from the sale of fattened cattle and pigs, but it was exactly these products which had so disastrously been affected by the fall in prices in 1930, the crucial year of increased Nazi support. Given the fact that these areas were at the same time the most primitive in farming techniques and that by 1930 land values were the lowest in the *Reich,*[103] some kind of political upheaval was to be expected. But, crucial to our analysis of mass theory, the *form* of this rebellion was more dependent on these material conditions than on atomization in the countryside. The secondary organizations did not mysteriously collapse. They were not lacking in membership strength or organizational resources. But they were unable to alleviate the plight of the depressed areas. The farmers tried a series of political forms, from working inside the existing parliamentary parties to forming regionalist parties and vigilante *Schicksalsgemeinschaften* like the *Landvolk* movement.[104] Only after their failure to wrest more concessions from the government had became obvious did the farmers turn to the Nazis. This time sequence is crucial for an assessment of mass theory: it suggests that political action on the part of the crisis-stricken farmers was not the result of restless masses being driven to despair because of a lack of *voice,* or because of a weakening of group loyalties or the withering away of the intermediary associations. Joining the NSDAP was a conscious political decision, the result of having seen previous political activity lead nowhere. The Nazis showed both by their language and political tactics that they could put more muscle behind their promises than the traditional parties. Contrary to what mass theory maintains, the secondary attachments did not prevent Nazi incursions. A pertinent case in point which illustrates this general trend outside the Schleswig-Holstein region is the fate of the *Reichslandbund*. Through Darré's *Agrarpolitischer Apparat*, the branch of the NSDAP responsible for political propaganda among the farmers, the Nazis infiltrated the RLB easily in the end-phase of the Republic. Through the RLB it then disseminated its own views to the membership, gaining legitimacy for Nazi agricultural policies by presenting them through the established organizational channels and at the same time, though skilful electioneering at the local level, replacing hesitant or hostile elected officers with loyal ones. Instead of proving an obstacle to Nazism in the countryside, the RLB and other agricultural organizations became convenient conveyor-belts for Nazi propaganda reaching deep into the rural population. In this way the intermediate groups facilitated the rise of Nazism.[105] Likewise, in Schleswig-Holstein, the farmers' transfer to Nazism was a *collective* action: when the rural producers joined the Nazi party, they did so as members of precisely the same intermediary network which, in theory, is presumed to establish social defense against extremism.[106] The plurality of independent groups, which in Kornhauser's words «support liberty» and at the same time authority,[107] in reality performed exactly the opposite function.

It should be added that the farmers were receptive to the Nazi appeal because the ground had been prepared. Those who called for a rational approach to the crisis, advocating reform in economic policies and pressing for agriculture's adjustment to changing market conditions, were drowned in nationalist, and anti-Marxist prejudice. The conspiratorial *völkisch* flavor of Nazi propaganda was well attuned to the peasants' political inclinations. The Nazis never tired of blaming the crisis on the manipulations of international Jewry, the bankers and the socialists. The sense of urgency among the farmers was also intensified by their awareness of being politically isolated. Contrary to what happened in Scandinavia,[108] there were no readily available alliance partners for the small farmers, except the *Junkers* under whose dominance they had been since the formation of the *Bund der Landwirte*.[109] Any formal political contact with the Left was made impossible by the farmers' fear that the SPD would take away their property, a fear which was not without foundation in view of the SPD's crude adoption of the Marxist dogmas of accelerated concentration and the ultimate doom of smallscale agriculture.[110]

3.7 The Theoretical Status of Social Cohesion in Explaining the Rise of Anti-Democratic Movements

Both the number of associations *within* the old and the new *Mittelstand*, including the farmers, and the active pursuit of middle class interests through the proliferation of *Interessenverbände* in close contact with the political system as a whole cast doubt on the notions of the German petite bourgeois as a desolate, atomized individual and of his social class as an isolated social unit. We shall return to the concept of weakened intermediate social relationships in the next section, but the conclusion warranted by our data so far is that neither internal fragmentation nor external social isolation can be viewed as *prime* causes for increased support for the Nazis by the middle sector. Lack of attachments irrespective of level can have no *independent* status in a scheme of linkages explaining the success of Nazism in the Weimar period. The persistence of class alignments in voting and the increase in membership in the white-collar interest organizations during the last years of the Republic suggest that atomization in any form may not even have served as an intermediate, intensifying or accelerative link between socio-economic strain and susceptibility to the Nazis, except in the case of certain minor groups, as previously discussed.[111]

In the case of William Kornhauser there are particular problems. He is generally correct in his estimation of the social basis of Nazism, in his emphasis, for instance, on unattached intellectuals, marginal small businessmen and artisans, though his point on marginality as a factor in determining which industries gave contributions to Hitler seems somewhat far-fetched and dated.[112] Likewise, he seems to underestimate the sociological specificity of the Nazi movement, basing his data mostly on Gerth and arguing, as outlined before, that Nazism attracted uprooted elements from all classes.

Even more serious is his difficulty in devising a criterion to determine which *direction* mass affiliation will take. Since, in his own words, «differences in receptivity to mass symbols and leaders are due primarily to the strength of social ties, and not to the influence of class, or any other social status, by itself»,[113] the dilemma is this: With the KPD termed a 'mass movement' in Kornhauser's theory, and with concepts like 'class' or 'class interest' treated as marginal in his analysis or at best derivative, what can account for differences in receptivity to mass appeal?[114] Intensity of atomization? If so, at what point does deep and widespread atomization make people turn Nazi or communist? Unable to use class interests and perceptions of group advantage as decisive influences in determining political choice, Kornhauser overlooks the element of *conscious intentionality* which clearly must have played a role in swinging so many voters to the left in the economically depressed end-phase of the republic. Similarly, the fact that so many among the petite bourgeoisie became ardent Nazi supporters and not ordinary conservatives must be accounted for by their realization that Hugenberg was less likely to look after their small-scale crafts than his clients' industrial combines. Hitler was closer to the petty bourgeois in origin, style and promises. With the exception of Sigmund Neumann, there is a tendency in all mass theory to derive political behavior from purely structural conditions. Thus both Arendt and Kornhauser betray distinctly reductionist tendencies, under-estimating the role of political conflict *per se* in moulding political allegiances, and unwittingly employing a mechanistic view of the development of political consciousness. After all, the Nazi party emerged as the archetypical counter-revolutionary party, as self-professed 'anti-Marxists' with the avowed aim of crushing the workers' associations.

There is another flaw in Kornhauser's theory of mass society: its repetition of the underlying tenet of nineteenth century liberalism that there is a natural harmony of interests in society which provides the common ground for the preservation of the social and political system. In mass theory, sharp social conflicts are indicative of disruptions primarily in the *form* of social arrangements.[115] For Kornhauser, therefore, there is no room for appreciating that the substance of politics, the *contents* of conflicts, may be such as to make the resolution of conflicts impossible within the existing pluralist form of order. This is a prominent characteristic of Kornhauser's version of mass theory: deprivation is always *mediated* through the intermediate structure, and threatens stability only when this secondary structure is seriously weakened. Thus when he and other mass theorists consider strains and deprivations, they view the sources of strain as part of the wider processes of industrialization and urbanization. Processes of this kind may give rise to mass movements *not primarily because they cause deprivation but above all because they weaken the system of attachment between élites and non-élites.*[116] One is led to assume, therefore, that in Kornhauser's theory the intermediate structure and the proliferation of attachments it engenders are the *prime* determinants of success or failure of extremist movements. This point is theoretically significant. That the occurrence of political disruptions may be a symptom of rational interest articulation arising out of injustices and real deprivations and *not* the result of weakened social ties *per se* seems to be a possibility under-estimated in Kornhauser's theory. His inclinations may therefore have led him to concentrate on secondary phenomena. At the same time, it is clear that a strong intermediate network of attachments, besides ascertaining the loyalty of the citizen to the state and providing a check on the élites may also serve to disseminate ideas of legitimation from the top to the governed. Kornhauser's theory therefore becomes not only a theory of stability in democracy, but also a plea for the essential preservation of the *status quo*. Indeed, Kornhauser is quite explicit on this point.

Secondly, Kornhauser's theory is flawed by the absence of any distinction between *different* élites, and by the lack of appreciation of competing interests existing *within* the élite. Kornhauser's concept of an 'élite' – «people who by virtue of their social position have special responsibility for standards in a given social context» (p. 51) – is too broad to take internal divisions within the ruling segments into account. For instance, in the Weimar case, did the inaccessibility and self-recruitment of *economic* élites contribute more to the downfall of parliamentary democracy than the penetrability of the *political* élite? Given the rather dismal record of the German business community as a bastion of anti-democratic, partially pro-monarchist sentiments, greater accessibility from below might actually have contributed to a strengthening of the commitment to democratic procedures in the closing years of the Republic (besides, of course, rendering more difficult the atmosphere of camaraderie between government and business which laid the foundation for the *Osthilfe* and *Gelsenkirchener* scandals which were pivotal in bringing down the Brüning government). Thus it should not be taken for granted, as Kornhauser seems to do, that shielding the élite in itself is a guarantee of adherence to democratic values. His theory is also ill-equipped to deal with the kind of conspiratorial bargaining between the economic and political élites which contributed to Hitler's victory. In spite of the current debate on the extent to which German big business actually financed Hitler's campaigns,[117] a pertinent point to make in this connection is that the German business élite was divided. After the November 1932 elections, a group of businessmen and bankers, at the instigation of the circle of friends around Hitler's adviser Wilhelm Keppler, petitioned Hindenburg to transfer the reins of government to the «leader of the largest national group».[118] This group consisted of Thyssen, Schacht, Schröder, Reinhart, Eichorn, Helfferich and other leading bankers and businessmen. Others were more restrained in their support for Hitler; the business leadership overwhelmingly supported the conservative parties.[119] Nevertheless, it was the support of von Papen by the business community which enabled him to strike a bargain with Hitler at the meeting between Hitler and himself in the home of the Cologne banker Schroeder on January 4, 1933.[120] We are here confronted with bargains at the highest levels whose anti-democratic character was not the result of élite accessibility by the masses. Rather, what led the industrialists into their complicity in destroying the Republic was their inaccessibility as a group, their self-recruitment and their zealous pursuit of class interests.

3.8 The Intermediary Network: Agents of Mobilization or a Restraint on Mass Behavior?

As we have pointed out, the underlying tenet of Kornhauser's theory is that the intermediary structure between the primary and secondary levels of society exerts a restraining influence on group behavior. The organizational network between «the élite» and the «non-élite» serves as a protection in both directions: it staves off undue interference – direct and unmediated pressure – from below, and acts as a buffer against arbitrary rule from above. What constitutes a major deficiency in the theory, is the failure to see that in themselves the *pouvoirs intermédiaires* which were so important for de Tocqueville's conception of stability in feudal Europe and for his critique of mass democracies, may equally serve as agents of mobilization. They may also give opportunities to channel, even to bestow a flavor of legitimacy on, all sorts of fringe beliefs. As already shown in the case of the peasantry, the artisans and the white-collar workers, it was precisely this process of making fringe sentiments more respectable and more widespread through the organizational network which characterized the last years of the Weimar Republic. Thus the DHV actively promoted the Nazi cause within its membership and further facilitated the expression of Nazi views in public life. Far from containing mass behavior, the DHV, through its very proximity to Nazi ideology, prepared the ground for a further acceptance of the Nazi creed. This was particularly the case in the critical years 1929 and 1930, when the NSDAP first showed its strength at the polls.[121]

In summary, the question of whether anti-republican and anti-democratic beliefs would have lingered on only as an under-current, is not resolved by the strength or weakness of the intermediate structure *per se*. In this sense the intermediary bonds are «neutral»: they respond to, rather than create, resentments. The strength and weakness of the intermediary organizations *qua* intermediaries may therefore at best have secondary consequences in aggravating or intensifying, in addition to channelling and making respectable, existing grievances which have their origins elsewhere. If frustration is strong enough, organizational channels of expression will be established anyway, either inside or outside the existing network. The organizations, in particular their leaders, may even find it opportune to encourage what have hitherto been fringe beliefs as a means to organizational survival, thus accelerating the process of governmental collapse by strengthening the anti-democratic forces. In short, as Maurice Pinard has argued,[122] the existence or non-existence of a strong intermediary structure can never be a *sufficient* explanation for the appearance of mass movements. It is doubtful whether it is even a *necessary* condition in a theory of extremist politics.

When contacts between economic interest organizations and parties broke down in the Weimar Republic, thus creating the isolation between 'élite' and 'non-élite' which Kornhauser discusses, the reason was usually no more mysterious than policy disagreements. A good case in point is the increasingly tenuous link between the German Peoples Party (DVP) and the DHV, the white-collar interest organization. In response to severe setbacks at the polls from 1928 onwards, the DVP leadership sought to enter into closer alliances with the DNVP in an effort to consolidate the bourgeois bloc. These moves alienated the white-collar reform-minded wing of the party around men like Thiel and Glatzel, who saw in the party's swing to the right the danger of a complete elimination of all social programs which interfered with the process of capital accumulation. The final break came in June 1932 and was symptomatic of a more general malaise in the political system towards the end of the

Republic. The DVP, like the DNVP and the DDP, had been created to accommodate and reconcile divergent and frequently antagonistic social interests under one ideological umbrella. Under the pressure of deep economic distress, these fragile alliances began to falter and dissolve into warring groups.[123] Organized interests were the main solvent in this process: they intensified the process of segmentation and made it irrevocable. The process was so thorough that it reached a point when it was no longer possible to reconcile the interests of the groups who had once made up the base of the middle parties. We have demonstrated the dense criss-crossing of farmers' pressure organizations, but the remarkable fact remains that despite the common danger of a structural crisis in the German agriculture there was little *political* cohesion between these organizations. Even within the Green Front there was little joint action among the socially and ideologically similar despite its access to federal authority. Not even massive external pressure from outside could force these sub-communities to merge with other, like-minded interests.

This is the crux of the matter. Weimar's paralysis was not caused by a withering away of intermediary bonds, but by their increasing tenacity.[124] Far from becoming available to manipulating élites because of loosened ties, the German population remained firmly anchored in their cohesive social blocs which interacted strongly with the political system. So pervasive was this tendency towards organization that building such organizations became an end in itself. There was, in fact, «a ritualization of sub-cultural loyalty symbols» to the point of making organization a fetish.[125] With zealous rigidity these social blocs felt themselves to be competing defensively against each other. Along with this process of sub-community identification went an increasing recognition that group chauvinism had replaced commitment to the national community as a whole. The success of the Nazis must be seen as a response to this rigid stratification. The NSDAP became a political force through being identified as the prime *integration* party. To the extent that there was any consistent appeal in the Nazi propaganda at all, it was the appeal for a *Volksgemeinschaft*. The corollary needed hardly to be spelt out: only through a dissolution of the divisive party system and the leadership of a mythical *Führer* beyond all temporal loyalties could the national paralysis be transcended.

Not surprisingly, this appeal for a strengthening of the nation found a particularly fertile ground among the middle classes. Whereas the working class and the Catholic segment largely managed to «immunize» their adherents against Nazi intrusion,[126] the bourgeois, Protestant middle did not. The instability and the ultimate doom of the Republic was essentially due to liberalism's failure to keep the loyalty of its primary groups and incorporate its clientele into the fabric of 20th century industrial society. To be able to evaluate Kornhauser's concept of social isolation properly, the underlying causes for this failure, which also go a long way towards explaining vulnerability of the middle sector, must be examined in more detail:

A persistent theme in the body of literature on the origins of the German party system from the *Reichsgründung* onwards is its impotence in providing integration across entrenched socio-political alignments. German politics in the Hohenzollern period was already stratified and segmented along the cleavage lines adumbrated by Lipset and Rokkan, i.e. worker-employer; confession (Catholic minority/secular state); agrarian/industrial, and region.[127] The party system lacked crucial integrative capacities because it remained focalized on regional attachments and social groups which were already politically mobilized at the time of Bismarck. The parties continued to protect the autonomy of their primary groups rather than linking them to a broader national political community. Under the impact of increasing social mobility and differentiation, the primary social blocs whose essentially pre-political *Weltanschauung* the parties expressed, slowly disintegrated. Instead of adapting themselves to the structural transformation which German society had undergone since the early 20th century, the parties resisted becoming tools of representation along more functional lines. As a result, they also proved incapable of *mediating* interests across sub-cultures. Through this inflexibility, cleavages and party alternatives which had been current in Germany around 1870 gained a life of their own and were «frozen». By the 1890's this conflict structure, as mirrored in the party system, had lost most of its relevance. By World War I it was hopelessly out of date.

Manifestations of the stagnation of German liberalism can be detected at the very outset of mass politics. From 1871 to 1887 the parties representing the German middle class added to their vote in proportion to the demographic growth of the population. But from 1886 onwards the liberal parties lost their ability to attract new voters in proportion to the increased number of eligible participants. Shortly after the war, the liberals scored slightly above their 1912 level, but in 1924 again started to lose votes.[128] The Republic saw the disintegration of the middle into a host of sector and protest parties such as the *Wirtschaftspartei des deutschen Mittelstandes* and the *Christlich-National Bauern und Landvolkpartei*, to name only two.[129] It was particularly the decline of the «old Middle classes» and the concomitant emergence of the 'new' white-collar middle class which produced the highly unstable situation in the Republic. No established bourgeois party managed to respond to these dislocations adequately. The result was that the «old» middle class organized new political parties along class or vocational lines, whereas the «new» middle class relied more on interest representation through its white-collar unions. But this group remained politically under-represented throughout the Weimar period. For both of these groups the consequence was the same: a growing sense of despair born of political impotence.

In analyzing the causes for this breakdown of intermediate interest integration, we have already touched on the most important: the social and economic *diversification* of the middle sector. Owing to the impact of industrialization and the accompanying processes of urbanization, economic concentration and secularization of the German social structure, the middle class had lost its homogenous social character. In the Republic, its interests had grown so diverse that it proved impossible to reconcile them within one single party.[130] The failure in the last months of 1918 to form a single bourgeois *Sammelpartei* and the ensuing split between the DDP and DVP was the most prominent sign of this fragmentation of the middle. As subsequent events were to show, this division within the middle class camp put the *Mittelstand* at a distinct disadvantage in comparison with the political cohesiveness both of the industrial proletariat and of the entrepreneurial class.

There are other reasons as well for this lack of integrative capacity. In Imperial Germany, because the executive was shielded from the legislature by the semi-absolutist constitution, power in parliament was not immediately translated into increased political leverage. Hence the party leaders were neither compelled nor expected to build alliances beyond their immediate core groups, whether in parliament or outside. This tendency was reinforced by Bismarck's skilful technique of *divide et impera* in his dealing with the parliamentary factions and by his victimization of large sectors of the population as 'Reich enemies'. Their best defense was to close their ranks and intensify their efforts at sub-cultural autonomy. This suspicion of compromise and integration, understandable in view of political experience, created a style which survived essentially unchanged even through the *Burgfrieden* years to the Republic.

More important, acceptance of the parties as tools of interest articulation *as well as* vehicles for integration was made more difficult by the widespread intellectual style of thought which argued that there was a distinctly German road to modernity which could avoid the pitfalls of Western-style liberalism. Interest representation and parliamentary mediation was on the whole antithetical to this concept. In fact, a whole «mandarinate» of official ideologues persistently attacked the entire idea of interest representation as an un-German form of government.[131] Similar themes were endemic in the tracts of the *völkisch* theorists whose mystically bound Germanic community transcended any need for mechanistic integration. Thus distrust of democracy was in the air and formed a formidable intellectual barrier to democratization. Instead, according to the *völkisch* tradition, there ought to be co-operation between social units in an estate-like form of society *(berufständische Ordnung)*. In a spirit of welfare-oriented paternalism, virtue and competence should be exercised by a well-educated élite, not represented by a group of impersonal parliamentary bureaucrats. Social conflicts should be solved by appeals to the public good rather than fought out in elections or settled by super-imposed compromises. Integration should come as the result of commitment to the national community, and not as a consequence of the pursuit of particular interests. The state should have ultimate moral and political authority over and above the autonomous forces of society.[132] This organic view, although by no means fascist or totalitarian, struck responsive chords in the German bourgeoisie fatigued by democracy, a form of government which only seemed to institutionalize division. In more vulgar forms it percolated down to the petty bourgeoisie and the peasantry, and proved an appropriate ideological weapon with which to combat the ascendancy of the working class.

When we speak of a «weakening» of the intermediary network in the Republic, it should be pointed out that there are indications of a communication gap between the educated part of the bourgeois political élite and the rank and file. The liberal party leaderships consisted primarily of members of a professional class who derived their incomes mainly from government service, or from services performed on behalf of government, business or private individuals. Tending to view politics from a predominantly ideological point of view, they devoted too little attention to the more immediate social and economic interests of the spectrum of groups making up the ordinary membership of the parties.[133] These discrepancies in style and conceptions of politics added to rank and file feelings of powerlessness and fuelled the frantic search for more interest-specific representation, a process which of course was accelerated by the depression.

This detailed analysis of the workings of the intermediary network in the Weimar Republic has been necessary because it affects the core of mass theory. Whether Kornhauser can be said to have identified an essential aspect of Weimar society depends in large measure on the meaning he attaches to the words denoting a «disappearance» or a «weakening» of the intermediate social relationships. In which sense did Weimar «lack» intermediate social relationships, as Kornhauser contends? The intermediary associations of course did not vanish, in the sense that the administrative apparatus of each organization ceased to function, thus leaving the field open for un-mediated confrontation between the élite and the non-élite – Kornhauser's most dreaded future prospect. In this sense, Weimar society did not «lack» intermediary social relations. But as pointed out, there was no political cohesion within this

97

intermediary stratum of society. The intermediary structure was left powerless but well-structured, partly because of the internal splits among groups that 'normally' should have been able to work out a common interests platform, partly because the crisis imposed strict limits on the resources available to alleviate the plight of the most crisis-stricken layers of the population. To make matters worse, most of the grievances of the *Mittelstand* were of the regressive, backward-looking anti-capitalist kind and represented such an all-out attack on modern industrial society that no party, with the significant exception of the Nazis, could even consider redressing them in full. The extremity of the *Mittelstand* demands seriously limited the *Koalitionsfähigkeit* of the political system.

A close comparison between Kornhauser's interpretation of Weimar society and the evidence suggested in this essay indicates that Kornhauser is correct on one important point: there was little communication between sub-communities. Kornhauser defines a mass society to be «a situation in which an aggregate of individuals are related to one another only by way of their relation to a common authority, especially the state» (p. 32). Political communication between Germany's communities very often assumed this form.

But what are the implications of this observation? Social isolation can be located on two distinct levels: 1. between the state and the organizations, and 2. between the organizations and their clientele. In the first instance, the population is assumed to be well incorporated in organizations, and their concerns are communicated to the state. But the process yields little of importance to the members. In this context, isolation means primarily political impotence. In the second case, there is a failure on the part of the organizations to reach into their clienteles. Because of the atomized social existence of aggregates of people, the organizations are of diminishing relevance to their lives, and are increasingly unable to provide support in any form. This latter interpretation approximates to the classical mass theorizing of Arendt and Lederer, since it focuses on unfulfilled socio-psychic needs of the individual as the prime variable in understanding why organizations fade away from the political horizon of the community.[134]

Our analysis has not supported the first interpretation. There was ample contact between the political system and the intermediary stratum, but few benefits flowing. As for the second interpretation, we have suggested that there might have been a gap in communication between élite and rank and file. A weakening in this sense assumes the population to be well incorporated, but unable to channel its interests *inside* its own organizations. It can lead to an extreme form of rupture between organizational hierarchy and rank and file: *exit* from the organization. This intra-organizational «weakening» could conceivably be taken to support the notion that the organizations had become «empty shells», run by faceless bureaucrats, unable to provide any meaning or gratification to the individual. Irrespective of the number of affiliations recorded by statistical methods on the individual level, and irrespective of the actual increase in membership within the middle class group, there was «hidden» massification, so this version of mass theory might argue.

This line of reasoning could rescue Hannah Arendt's concept of 'mass man' by denying that dense patterns of membership implied anything about the *quality* of participation. It is difficult to see, however, how such a position could be defended. First, is it likely that there could have been such a wide discrepancy between what the numbers of membership suggest about social cohesion, and subjectively perceived estrangement? Second, one should remember that the political behavior of the middle class – its transfer of loyalties to the Nazis, its fierce illiberalism and high-pitched nationalism – cannot be taken as an indication of atomization in itself. There is an important empirical and conceptual difference between paucity of bonds and volatile political activism: the latter can well come into existence without the former. Activism of the kind channelled by the Nazis can flow from a sense of despair even in the least atomized communities provided the resentments run deep enough and are filtered through an appropriately conspiratorial and authoritarian political philosophy.

In any case, such a rehabilitation of the traditional concept of mass would only rescue parts of mass theory. For Kornhauser, individual atomization may give rise to individual deviance (crime, suicide, etc.), but the stability of regimes is only threatened when the intermediary network is threatened. We have rejected the first possible interpretation of his notion of «weakened intermediary network»; the second makes a few concessions to the impact of the élite/non élite communication gap. But this communication gap, if it made any difference at all, is not enough to warrant the use of words like «lack» or «absence» to describe conditions in the intermediary stratum. Kornhauser's own emphasis on the stabilizing influence of the intermediary influence prevents him from taking refuge in a resuscitated psychological atomization theory. If he wishes to defend his focus on the intermediary structure, he is compelled to accept one or other of these interpretations of the notion of «weakening» within the intermediate network: either 1. 'inability to effect improvements because of Germany's segmented class divisions and the lack of integrative capacities flowing from this rigidity'; or 2. 'exit from existing organizations due to individual, psychological atomization'. If Kornhauser maintains the latter, which is his original description of Weimar society, he is factually wrong. If he retains the description of Weimar as psychologically massified but agrees that «weakness» must mean «lack of integration», he undermines the very core of his own theory: the explanatory power assigned to the protective and stabilizing functions of the intermediary network. To talk of lack of integration means that the organizations failed to provide durable links to other strata and hence failed to resolve interest clashes; but it is implied that they remained intact and functioned well as representatives for their sector interests. There are important divergencies between Kornhauser's concept of «weakening» as «breakdown», and the alternative way of interpreting this weakness: to interpret it as an absence of adequate integration because of unsurmountable class barriers. We will focus on these class barriers in the next section.

4. National Socialism as an Outgrowth of Intensified Class Animosities

Central to all mass theory, with the exception of Sigmund Neumann, is the assertion that ordinary sociological concepts like 'class' and 'class interests' do not suffice to explain the peculiar extremism of mass movements; they are useful only in «normal» times.[135] Alternatively, it can be argued that the extremism of the Nazis was directly derivative, not from a softening of class cleavages, but from a situation where ordinary class divisions were perceived to be deeper and more threatening than before. The success of the Nazis can then be understood as a result of middle class fear and the Nazis' skill in manipulating this anxiety.

Two traditions are discernible on this point. Arthur Rosenberg has argued that there are «invisible and numerous transitional stages» between the middle classes and the proletariat, and that to posit a sharp distinction between these two layers as an explanation for the rise of Nazism is to blow «sociological soap bubbles».[136] W. S. Allen, on the other hand, gives evidence in his meticulous study of Thalburg that the middle class in this town was not decisively affected by the economic crises, and that it was class polarization, rather than any growing irrelevance of class divisions, which accounted for the militancy with which the middle class embraced National Socialism in the town:

> «. . . the most important factor in the victory of Nazism was the active division of the town along class lines. Though there was cohesion in Thalburg before the Nazis began their campaign leading to the seizure of power, the cohesion existed within the middle class or the working class and did not extend to the town as a whole. The victory of Nazism can be explained to a large extent by the desire on the part of Thalburg's middle class to suppress the lower class and especially its political representative, the Social Democratic party.»[137]

Any discussion of this complex aspect of pre-1933 Nazi history must take care to distinguish between *perceptions* of economic inequalities and these *inequalities themselves* as they can be described statistically. Strictly speaking, there are three ways of exploring the fate of the commercial middle classes during the depression: first, by looking at the total *turnover* of sales; secondly, by analyzing changes in the *size of firms* over time, and thirdly, by tracing fluctuations in the *number employed* in *mittelständische* occupations. Statistical evidence shows that turnover was related both to types of goods and to ability to re-invest: firms producing durable goods like furniture, textile wares and electrical equipment for which there was a «flexible» demand, and the building trade fared generally worse than firms in trades based on more «stable» demands like food. Taking 1925 as a base year (= 100), turnover in the baking industry, for example, fell from 110.2 per cent in 1930 to 104.3 per cent in 1931 and 94.7 per cent in 1932. Corresponding figures for the saddlers were 81.7, 60.3, and 44.6. Shoemakers, painters, tailors, watch-makers and enterprises in crafts covering wood and metal manufactures are to be found in between these two extremes. On average, sales in the *Handwerk* declined by 50 per cent between 1928 and 1932. In the retailing business, turnover declined from 36.3 billion Marks in 1928 to 23.1 billion Marks in 1932. It should be noted, however, that the overall proportion of handicraft trade, retailing and restaurant business increased in relation to the national turnover from 28.0 per cent in 1928 to 29.2 in 1931.[138]

As for the size of firms the evidence suggests that the image of the middle classes as strongholds of misery must be substantially modified. The proportion of firms with less than five employees to the total of commercial enterprises increased from 86.8 per cent in 1925 to 91.9 in 1933, although this rise may have been caused by an increase in unemployment in bigger firms, thus swelling the ranks of those with less than five employees. In the category «industry and handicraft» in the counting of professions and enterprises in 1925, the proportion of one-man firms rose from 40.5 per cent to 53.1 in 1933. Between 1925 and 1933 the category «employment in the public sector and in private service businesses» showed an increase (to 19 per cent) as did the share of «independents» of the total number of employed (from 16.2 to 20.0 per cent).[139] As already pointed out, these increases were paralleled by a rise in the number of «independents without professions», rentiers and retired.

In discussing these figures, Winkler takes pain to emphasize that the middle-sized firms had suffered losses equal to those of the larger firms. The increase in the proportion of middle-sized firms can be accounted for by adding the number of larger firms sinking down into the bracket below. Nevertheless, between 1925 and 1933, the share of employees in firms with up to five workers in the «industry and handicraft» category had increased from 22.4 to 33.9 per cent. In the category «commerce and communications» the increase was negligible, from 48.5 to 48.8 per cent.[140]

This detailed analysis of the plight of the *Mittelstand* has been necessary for several reasons. First, the image of the middle sector on its death-bed must be substantially modified. During the depression a contemporary commentator expressed the view that «the large firms had suffered to an exceptional degree, and that the small and medium-sized, less capital intensive enterprises are better able to adapt to the business cycles».[141] There is no denying that the crisis critically impaired the existence of several branches of *Mittelstand* crafts. By the end of the 20's, for example, it was impossible to distinguish the artisans and the independent businessmen from the industrial proletariat on the criterion of income.[142] The question must nonetheless be asked whether the middle sector was more severely affected by the downturn than other groups. Because firms and home were so often inextricably linked, the repercussions of the crisis were probably felt more immediately at a directly personal level among the middle classes than among large-scale entrepreneurs. On the other hand, less than 1 per cent of one-man retail shops went bankrupt in 1932.[143] In terms of wages the handicraft sector was severely hit, however: in 1932 hourly wages declined dramatically, to 33.5 per cent of what was normal in 1928.[144] On the whole, the conclusion seems warranted that small retailing and handicraft businesses were substantially worse affected than industry; no doubt conditions were much worse than the *Mittelstand*, with its accustomed position in the Reich, would have wished it to be. But the figures presented give an interesting perspective of the *Mittelstand* «panic» the sociologist Th. Geiger spoke of. Geiger himself was one of the more optimistic. In 1932 he dismissed any talk of the impending doom of the middle classes, conceding only that small shopkeepers had to guard against overcapacity.[145] To the extent that the middle class had found new tasks to perform and new services to offer alongside the industrial sector, they had also found a new sense of security and dignity, he asserted. New opportunities offered themselves in crafts requiring individual skill, particularly in the mending and repair trade on the local level. In these trades competition from industrial capitalism had been successfully fought off. Schumpeter, echoing Geiger, argued that the handicrafts were not all a sinking ship. He argued that there was room for subsidiary and individualized skills of the kind the *Mittelstand* could offer, and that in fact the vehement anti-capitalism of these classes could be abandoned and an era of co-operation with industry launched.[146] The *Institut für Konjunkturforschung* concluded in 1933 that the depression was not primarily a structural crisis of the middle sector but rather a problem affecting the economy as a whole.[147] Although its share of the population had declined, the *Mittelstand* had succeeded in consolidating its commercial position in several sectors. If it had shown more flexibility in catering for needs which organized capitalism could not satisfy, it need not have feared extinction. But instead the artisans and the handicraftsmen viewed themselves as the main victims of industrialization, and regarded the need to adapt themselves as indicative of a decline in social morality.[148] It should be pointed out that lack of capital certainly made such accommodative behavior difficult, particularly after World War I. It was precisely this lack of appreciation of the situation and its inherent possibilities and the refusal to accommodate to changed market conditions which constituted the main core of the retrograde *Mittelstand* ideology in the Weimar Republic. The «panic» in the middle classes cannot, therefore, be viewed solely as a straightforward reaction to the prevailing material conditions. What made the middle sector act like the anti-systemic 'social dynamite' so crucial for the downfall of the Republic, was its ideology of social protectionism. The longing for a privileged position vis-à-vis the working class, the denial of legitimacy to political opponents, the emphasis on obedience and stable authority patterns and a largely preindustrial notion of commerce and social hierarchy – these were the ideological end-products of the artificial protection afforded to the middle class in Imperial Germany by an autocratic state anxious to preserve this *Stände* consciousness as a shield against democratization and prevent the intrusion of working class beliefs into the lower middle classes.[149]

In the heated climate of the concluding years of the Republic economic fears mingled with political anguish, in turn touching off fears about diminished social distance between workers and the petty bourgeoisie. During the depression years, because of trade union strength, the workers were able to gain a more favorable position in the labor market than had been the case before.[150] Their improved position was particularly strong relative to the salaried employees, who, due to technological rationalization and a culturally conditioned unwillingness to use the strike weapon in bargaining, found their services less irreplaceable and their bargaining position weakened. As a result, the workers were sometimes more effective in negotiating better contracts, or at least in staving off attempts to cut back wages and pensions. In this sense the middle class had reason to fear that proportionally they would fare worse than the classes below, and that, therefore, the distinction which they had guarded so zealously between themselves and the working classes would gradually be diminished. This decreased *economic* distance may have triggered off fears of diminished *social* distance. In Thalburg, the burghers felt that as unemployment hit larger segments within the working class, the *political* distance between them and the workers would increase and generate a trend towards revolutionism in the working class. Allen speaks of the burghers in Thalburg becoming «desperate through fear and obsession with the effects of the depression, especially the sight of the unemployed».[151] In summarizing the position of the Nazi party in Lower Saxony, Noakes extends Allen's findings to this region:

> «With its vicious attacks on the 'Marxists', the NSDAP actively took the lead in the class conflict at local level, a conflict which was being intensified by the depression. With this tactic the NSDAP won over a large number of the middle class who no longer felt capable of mastering the situation and feared the coming of Bolshevism. The NSDAP thus established in effect another united Bourgeois Front, but with the difference that this time the old establishment had had to give up control to the petty bourgeoisie, as represented by the local leadership of the NSDAP.»[152]

Instead of galvanizing the SPD, the depression weakened its potential to resist effectively. The social democrats, who along with the Centre and the DDP were the only party wholeheartedly behind the democratic Republic, found themselves in an awkward position. They had to defend the established order against the Right, the very same order which inflicted so much economic misery and working class suffering. Wanting to reform the economic base of the state, they were compelled to defend its bourgeois political institutions. Allen shows how the Nazi strategy of «coup d'etat by instalments» avoided the one decisive situation in which the SPD *Reichsbanner* could have been forced to respond. In spite of this evident paralysis of the working class, the burghers reacted with violent nationalism. Using the word «paranoid» to describe middle-class reaction to workers, Allen writes that «the actions and beliefs of the Thalburgers during the last years of the Weimar Republic were the same as if World

War I had never ended. It was in this sort of atmosphere that the SPD might seem treasonable and the Nazis reasonable».[153]

4.1 Conclusion: On the Inadequacy of the Mass Concept of 'Social Isolation'

The reason why Kornhauser never transcends the limitations of making the intermediary structure *qua intermediaries* the pivotal element in his theory, is the mechanistic meaning he attributes to the concept of 'social isolation'. In Kornhauser's conception of mass theory, 'social isolation' is primarily taken to mean simply the absence of formal associations between the individual and his social group on the one hand, and between his group and the wider society, including the state, on the other. The concept of isolation may also mean, however, increasing superfluity within the economy. Superfluity in this sense has an objective base in the fact that in the course of industrialization, cartellization and technological development render certain classes obsolete. Their services and tasks become superfluous as needs change and competition is stiffened; their labor is gradually replaced by machinery, their status threatened. Subjectively these dislocations are likely to cause feelings of bitterness, frustration and revolt. When Kornhauser speaks of «an economic explanation of the rise of mass movements» (p. 163) he seems to mean a theory which purports to explain the support for mass movements as the result of «frustration of economic interests». This can be an example of a very narrow use of the word «economic interests». It does not suffice to explain middle class support for Nazism in Germany by reference to the severity of depression as such. Decreased income, inflation, evaporation of funds for investment, and insolvency are serious enough, and would place severe strain on existing loyalties in any country. The crisis is also crucial in explaining the working-class presence in the NSDAP. But the middle classes in other countries fared equally badly, sometimes worse, without going to extremes in the way that the German middle class did.

Frustration of economic interest can hardly be over-estimated in any explanation of the rise of Nazism, but to understand such a ferocious political response to the crisis it will be necessary to add to this concept a broader understanding of the nature of the threat felt by the *Mittelstand*. The concept of interest should include not only protection of economic interests, but more generally protection of the distinctiveness of the group as such, its life-style, its morals and outlook on the world, its distance from other groups, its self-respect, its cultural traditions, – in short, its whole social existence. The *form* this political response took depended to a crucial extent on these cultural and ideological factors. Maintaining income differentials was but one short-term aspect of this social defense, but it was the fear of superfluity on a long term basis which fuelled the drift towards Nazism. During Bismarck's rule, this *grande peur* had found expression in a desperate fight against early industrial capitalism, symbolized in industry's demand for *Gewerbefreiheit* (unrestricted freedom of trade). After 1918 the conjunctural threat of economic and social decline had aggravated the internal divisions of the *Mittelstand* and made it increasingly susceptible to xenophobic and metapolitical demands. Nazism was the extreme, but logical extension of beliefs found in embryonic form from the very onset of industrialization.

Thus a case can be made that it was not primarily fear of actual *revolution* which drove the lower middle class into the kind of atavistic millenarism which the NSDAP epitomized. Rather, it was its fear of the *evolutionary* trends in the modern economy.[154] In this sense, the middle class was truly 'anti-modernist'.[155] The spectre of revolution seemed more and more distant after the post-war insurrectionary mood had ebbed in the early twenties. The most visible sign of the precarious position of the *Mittelstand* and its future prospects was nevertheless the ascendancy of the working class in political life. Behind the lower middle class dream of a 'Volk' community where class divisions had been eradicated, there lurked a belief that National Socialism was the only force which could effectively contain the workers, halt or modify the process of concentration in the economy and protect the social distance the *Kleinbürgertum* cherished so much. The depression deepened this longing for the ways of the Hohenzollern *Obriegkeitsstaat*, but without significantly atomizing the social existence of the middle class, nor isolating it organizationally from the rest of society any more than in the Imperial period. If the middle class did not get a hearing through its increasingly formalized pressure channels, its diminishing societal weight and reduced political bargaining power was to blame, not the lack of an intermediate structure.

Contrary to the claims of mass theory, it was *the high level of participation in secondary associations under conditions of superimposed segmentation which made for the rapid mobilization of people into the Nazi movement*. In Germany, due to the absence of any thoroughgoing democratic revolution, agrarian protest and middle class unrest did not apeal to democratic ideals against established rulers. On the contrary, because capitalism was never forced to make itself legitimate through democracy in Germany, agrarian and lower middle class rebellions almost immediately revealed their anti-democratic and authoritarian potential. And yet, the notion of the middle class as the prime instigating force behind Nazism does not go to the heart of the matter. The NSDAP soon departed from its social base. The chain stores were not broken up. Except for certain symbolic concessions there was no significant attempt to bolster the *Mittelstand* in the Third Reich. The general economic recovery certainly benefited the small retailer and the small producer, but they were given no preferential treatment outside the realm of political symbolism.[156]

How much of the ideologically founded anti-modernism would have been resurrected if Germany had not developed a war economy, will always be subject to speculation. But regardless of the social base of the movement, the result of the Nazi seizure of power – its undisputed political function – was to destroy the organizations of the working class. Through this destruction it protected the essentials of the existing power structure and stabilized an economic system in crisis. By the same token, the ascent of Hitler to the Chancellorship would have been impossible without the complicity of the ruling conservative élites. As a whole, National Socialism harked back to the vulgar conservatism of the Imperial era. Despite its professed aim of a «primacy of politics», and its relative autonomy from both the electorate on whose shoulders it climbed to power, and from its upper-class collaborators within the economic and political establishment,[157] Nazism can be viewed as but another plebeian and extreme form of the traditional Right. In its failure to grasp these historical processes and make them into an integral part of its theory, mass theory reveals its most critical shortcomings.

NOTES

This paper has greatly benefited from discussions with friends and colleagues in Oxford and at Yale, in particular Michael J. Clark, Peter E. Koppstein, Tim W. Mason, Jeremy C. Mitchell and Peter G. J. Pulzer. I would like to express my gratitude to these readers without holding them

104

responsible for the way I have used their comments. Thanks are also due to Professor Henry Ashby Turner, Jr. of Yale University for his initial encouragement of this study, and to the Warden, Fellows and students of Nuffield College, Oxford, for providing a congenial environment for its completion during the academic year 1975–76. Professor Jürgen W. Falter gave me valuable advice on German electoral statistics. I am also indebted to Halvard Grude Forfang, Mette Kleive and Jan Petter Myklebust for assistance and encouragement at various stages in Norway and at Yale.

[1] For assessments of this cultural diffusion, see the extensive bibliographic references in Peter Gay, *Weimar Culture: The Outsider as Insider* (New York, 1968); L. Fermi, *Illustrious Immigrants: The Intellectual Migration from Europe 1930–41* (Chicago 1968); H. S. Hughes, *The Sea Change: The Migration of Social Thought 1930–65* (New York 1975); D. Fleming & B. Bailyn (eds.), *The Intellectual Migration: Europe and America, 1930–1960* (Cambridge, Mass. 1969); *The Legacy of the German Refugee Intellectuals* (special issue of the review *Salmagundi* fall 1969–1970); and H. Pross, *Die deutsche Akademische Emigration nach den Vereinigten Staaten 1933–1941* (Berlin 1955).

[2] In West-Germany to-day, this tradition is most prominently represented by Karl Dietrich Bracher.

[3] For more recent attempts to formulate a general theory of breakdowns in parliamentary regimes using the collapse of Weimar and the Second Spanish Republic as cases, see Juan J. Linz, «The Breakdown of Democratic Politics», in J. J. Linz & A. Stepan (eds.), *The Breakdown of Democratic Regimes: The European and Latin American Experience* (Baltimore 1978) and M. Rainer Lepsius' article in the same volume, «From Centrifugal Party Democracy to Presidential Government and National Socialist Take-Over: Germany». Further theoretical refinement is found in Linz' article «Crisis, Breakdown and Re-equilibration of Competitive Democracies», *mimeo*, Department of Sociology, Yale University, New Haven, USA, 1969. V. Rittberger's extensive discussion of the Weimar case «Revolution and Pseudo-Democratization: The Formation of the Weimar Republic», in G. A. Almond et al. (eds.), *Crisis, Choice and Change* (Boston 1973) belongs to the same tradition.

[4] Clues to a more comprehensive treatment of the Weimar years can be sought in one of the narrative accounts of the period, most notably Erich Eyck's two-volume narrative, *A History of the Weimar Republic* (New York 1967); Th. Eschenburg et al., *The Road to Dictatorship: Germany 1918–1933* (London 1970); H. Heiber, *Die Republik von Weimar* (Munich 1966); K. Buchheim, *Die Weimarer Republik. Das Deutsche Reich Ohne Kaiser* (London 1968); J. W. Hiden, *The Weimar Republic* (London 1974); H. Holborn (ed.), *From Republic to Reich* (New York 1972); R. Kühnl & G. Hardach, *Die Zerstörung der Weimarer Republik* (Cologne 1977); E. Mathias & A. J. Nicholls (eds.), *German Democracy and the Triumph of Hitler* (London 1971) and G. Jasper, *Von Weimar zu Hitler* (Cologne & Berlin 1968).

[5] On the tradition of authoritarian and anti-liberal sentiment not only within the German élite but also in the German population, see the studies by Fritz Stern, *The Failure of Illiberalism* (New York 1972); Ralf Dahrendorf, *Society and Democracy in Germany* (New York 1967); Kurt Sontheimer, *Antidemokratisches Denken in der Weimarer Republik* (Munich 1962); K. D. Bracher, *Die Auflösung der Weimarer Republik* (Villingen in Schwarzwald 1971); G. Schulz, *Zwischen Demokratie und Diktatur. Verfassungspolitik und Reichsreform in der Weimarer Republik* (Berlin 1963) and W. Conze, «Die politischen Entscheidungen in Deutschland 1929–1933», in W. Conze und H. Raupach (eds.), *Staats und Wirtschaftskrise des deutschen Reiches* (Stuttgart 1967).

[6] Peter F. Drucker, *The End of Economic Man* (London 1939), p. 53.

[7] In addition to the four writers under consideration, the literature on mass theory is voluminous. In a broad sense Erich Fromm's *Escape from Freedom* (first published New York 1941) introduced the modern versions of mass theorizing. Similar themes can be found in Karl Mannheim's *Man and Society in An Age of Reconstruction* (London 1940) and in *The Quest for Community* by Robert Nisbet (New York 1963). An early statement was Ph. Selznick, «Institutional Vulnerability in Mass Society», in *Am. Journal of Sociology*, 56 (January 1951), no. 4, pp. 320–331, later to be expanded in his *The Organizational Weapon* (Glencoe, Ill. 1960). A discussi-

on which prefigured later mass theorizing is G. DeGré, «Freedom and Social Structure», in *American Sociological Review,* vol. 11, no. 5 (October 1946), pp. 529–536. Talcott Parsons, in his «Some Sociological Aspects of the Fascist Movements», in *Essays in Sociological Theory* (Rev. ed. N.Y. 1949), and Erich Hoffer in a more popular vein in *The True Believer* (N.Y. 1951) both evoked themes found in mass theory by their emphasis on disruptions of communal life and 'anomie' as precursors for extremism. J. Talmon's *The Rise of Totalitarian Democracy* (Boston 1952) also belongs to the classical statements of mass theorizing. A summary of the contemporary state of the field is N. Babchuk & J. N. Edwards, «Voluntary Associations and the Integration Hypothesis», in *Sociological Inquiry* 35 (number 2, 1965), pp. 149–162 and E. N. Walter, «'Mass Society'. The late Stages of an Idea», *Social Research* 31, (Winter 1964), pp. 390–410.

A specific application of mass theory to the realm of culture and mass cultural consumption flourished in the late fifties and early sixties. See B. Rosenberg & D. Manning White (eds.), *Mass Culture* (Glencoe, Ill. 1957); Edward Shils, «Mass Society and its Culture», *Daedalus* 89, (Spring 1960), pp. 288–314 and Harold L. Wilensky, «Mass Society and Mass Culture: Interdependence and Independence», in *Am. Sociological Review,* vol. 29, no. 2 (April 1964), pp. 173–197. See also Daniel Bell, «America as a Mass Society: A Critique», in *The End of Ideology* (Glencoe, Ill. 1960).

A critical evaluation of the images of mass theory as applied to Western society is given in Edward Shils, «The Theory of Mass Society», in *Diogenes,* 39, pp. 45–66. For a review of the entire tradition, see the secondary works by Cesare Mannucci, *La società di massa* (Milan, 1967); H. Stuart Hughes, *The Sea Change, op.cit.,* ch. 4; A. J. Gregor, *The Interpretations of Fascism* (Morristown, N. J. 1974), ch. 4 and M. Jay, *The Dialectical Imagination* (Boston 1973), especially pp. 143–219. A scathing and somewhat unfair critique is George Lichtheim, «Is There a Sociologist in the House?», in *Collected Essays* (N.Y. 1973), pp. 134–150. Gregor's book contains also an analysis – and a rejection – of mass analysis as a tool for understanding the rise of Fascism in Italy.

Mass theory is also explicitly used in the works by David Riesman and C. Wright Mills. While these two authors have described modern society as «mass-like», they tend to underscore the trend towards conformity and passivity rather than political extremism as the more likely outcome of mass conditions. The two most recent works on the subject are S. Halebsky, *Mass Society and Political Conflict* (Cambridge 1976) and S. Giner, *Mass Society* (London 1976).

For an application of modes of reasoning reminiscent of mass theory to the history of the Weimar Republic, see Gerhard Ritter, «The Historical Foundations of the Rise of National Socialism», in the collection of essays entitled *The Third Reich,* pp. 381–416, edited by Maurice Baumont et al. (London 1955).

[8] Cf. H. Marcuse, *One-Dimensional Man* (Boston 1964) and Th. W. Adorno, *Minima Moralia: Reflexionen aus dem beschädigten Leben* (Frankfurt 1951). Adorno never used the term 'mass society' because of the connotations the term conveyed. Instead he spoke of the *verwaltete Welt,* the administered world of technological domination in which culture was but an extension of the machine civilization large-scale industry had created.

Marcuse's concept of one-dimensionality, though far more explicit in its critique of the economic relationships underlying the vulgarization and commercialization of mass culture, resembles mass theory, broadly conceived, in that it focuses on the uniformity and conformist pressures of American society, its ideological ignorance and political apathy and its lack of real alternatives.

[9] *The Politics of Aristotle.* Edited and translated by Ernest Barker (N.Y. 1962). Book V, «Causes of Revolution and Constitutional Change», pp. 203–235.

[10] For a stimulating discussion of the concept of «unit-idea», see A. Lovejoy, *The Great Chain of Being* (Cambridge, Mass, 1936) pp. 3–23, and on the concept of «community», see Robert Nisbet, *The Sociological Tradition* (London 1967), pp. 47–107 and his *The Quest for Community* (New York 1963).

[11] J. Ortega y Gasset, *The Revolt of the Masses* (N.Y. 1932), pp. 11 and 13.

[12] For a critique of the political uses of the totalitarianism thesis, see H. Spiro and B. Barber, «The Concept of 'Totalitarianism' as the Foundation of American Counter Ideology in the Cold

War», prepared for delivery at the Annual Meeting of the American Political Science Association, Chicago, September 1965. For an extensive critique of the totalitarianism theory see also R. Burrows, «Totalitarianism: The Revised Standard Version», in *World Politics,* XXI (1969), pp. 272–294, and Klaus Hildebrand, «Stufen der Totalitarianismus-Forschung», in *Politische Vierteljahresschrift* (September 1968), pp. 397–422. M. Kitchen, *Fascism,* ch. 3 (London 1976) gives a good updating of the discussion. For rejoinders, see Friedrich, Curtis and Barber, *Totalitarianism in Perspective: Three Views* (New York 1969), and L. Schapiro, *Totalitarianism* (London 1972). The current state of research is admirably summed up by Juan J. Linz in his article, «Authoritarian and Totalitarian Regimes», in F. Greenstein & N. Polsby (eds.) *Handbook of Political Science* (Reading, Mass. 1975) vol. 3. The German scene is discussed in B. Seidel & S. Jenkner (eds.) *Wege der Totalitarismus-Forschung* (Darmstadt 1968).

[13] A good discussion is provided by Anthony Giddens, *Capitalism and Modern Social Theory: An Analysis of the Writings of Marx, Durkheim and Max Weber* (Cambridge, 1971).

[14] Gustave LeBon, *La Psychologie des Foules* (Paris 1895), English ed. *The Crowd* (London 1896). A concrete application of LeBon's theory is his *La Révolution Française et la Psychologie des Révolutions* (Paris 1912). For an incisive critique of LeBon and a contemporary re-evaluation, see Franz Neumann, «Anxiety and Politics», in *The Democratic and the Authoritarian State* (N.Y. 1957), pp. 270–301 and Robert A. Nye, *The Origins of Crowd Psychology: Gustave LeBon and the Crisis of Mass Democracy in the Third Republic* (London 1975).

[15] David Truman, *The Governmental Process* (New York 1953) is the most cogent and early expression of this tradition. A. Lijphart's *Democracy in Plural Societies* (New Haven & London 1977) gives an overview of the literature on segmented pluralism.

[16] A good discussion of the deliberate regimentation of the organizations *after* 1933 is R. M. Lepsius, «The Collapse of an Intermediary Power Structure: Germany 1933–34», in *The International Journal of Contemporary Sociology,* IX, 1967, pp. 289–301.

[17] A summary is found in M. Canovan, *The Political Thought of Hannah Arendt* (New York 1974).

[18] 'A Reply' to Eric Voegelin's review of the *Origins of Totalitarianism,* in *Review of Politics,* vol. 15, January 1953, p. 84.

[19] *Origins of Totalitarianism* (New Edition, New York 1966), p. 315.

[20] *Ibid.,* p. 311.

[21] Cf. the following statement, *ibid.,* p. 315:
«The fall of the protective class wall transformed the slumbering majorities *behind all parties* into one great unorganized, structureless mass of furious individuals who had nothing in common except their vague apprehension that the hopes of party members were doomed, that, consequently, the most respected, articulate and representative members of the community were fools and that all the powers that be were not so much evil as they were equally stupid and fraudulent . . .» (Italics mine).

[22] Cf. the note above and the following:
The truth is that the masses grew out of the fragments of a highly atomized society whose competitive structure and concomitant loneliness of the individual had been held in check only through membership in a class . . .
Ibid., p. 317.

[23] *Ibid.,* p. 315.

[24] *Ibid.,* p. 475.

[25] *Ibid.,* p. 311.

[26] *Ibid.,* p. 311.

[27] *Ibid.,* p. 315.

[28] Emil Lederer, *State of the Masses* (New York, 1940), p. 107.

[29] Neumann, Sigmund, *Permanent Revolution* (New York 1942), p. 115.

[30] Lederer, *op. cit.,* p. 50. See also his and Jacob Marschak's *The New Middle Class* (New York 1937), translated by S. Ellison from «Die neue Mittelstand» in *Grundrisse der Sozialökonomik,* IX, Abteilung I, Tübingen 1926.

[31] Lederer, *op. cit.,* p. 52.

[32] *Ibid.*, p. 84.

[33] For an elaboration of this point, see Neumann, *op. cit.*, pp. 101–106.

[34] Günther Roth, *The Social Democrats in Imperial Germany* (Totowa, N.J. 1963), particularly pp. 159–193 (VII) and 193–212 (VIII).

[35] Wolfgang Sauer, «National Socialism: Totalitarianism or Fascism?», in *American Historical Review*, LXIII (1967), pp. 404–424, p. 411 especially.

[36] Neumann, *op. cit.*, p. 100. For a contemporary conceptualization and analysis, see A. J. Mayer, «The Lower Middle Class as Historical Problem», in *Journal of Modern History*, 47 (September 1975), pp. 1109–36.

[37] William Kornhauser, *The Politics of Mass Society* (Glencoe: The Free Press 1959), p. 32.

[38] *Ibid.*, p. 74.

[39] *Ibid.*, p. 94.

[40] *Ibid.*, p. 51.

[41] *Ibid.*, p. 41.

[42] *Ibid.*, p. 41.

[43] *Ibid.*, p. 37.

[44] *Ibid.*, p. 179.

[45] *Ibid.*, p. 211.

[46] *Ibid.*, p. 162.

[47] *Ibid.*, p. 97.

[48] A. Oberschall, *Social Conflict and Social Movements* (Englewood-Cliffs 1973), pp. 108–113.

[49] W. S. Allen, *The Nazi Seizure of Power: The Experience of a Single German Town* (Chicago 1965), p. 16.

[50] Max Weber, *Gesammelte Aufsätze zur Soziologie und Sozialpolitik* (Tübingen 1924), pp. 441–442.

[51] M. R. Lepsius, *Extremer Nationalismus: Strukturbedingungen der nationalsozialistischen Machtergreifung* (Stuttgart 1966), pp. 378–382, the same author's «Parteiensystem und Sozialstruktur: Zum Problem der Demokratisierung der deutschen Gesellschaft», in W. Abel *et al.* (eds.), *Wirtschaft, Geschichte und Wirtschaftsgeschichte. Festschrift zum 65. Geburtstag von Friedrich Lütge* (Stuttgart 1966), pp. 371–393 and his contribution to the Linz-Stepan volume *Breakdown of Democratic Politics . . ., op. cit.* For a broader treatment, see also S. Neumann, *Die Parteien der Weimarer Republik* (Stuttgart 1932, rev. ed. 1965).

[52] For an incisive analysis, see C. Böhret, «Institutionaliserte Einflusswege der Verbände in der Weimarer Republik», in H. J. Varain, *Interesseverbände in Deutschland* (Cologne 1973).

[53] L. E. Jones, ««The Dying Middle»: Weimar Germany and the Fragmentation of Bourgeois Politics», in *Central European History*, vol. V, no. 1, 1972, p. 28 and V. Rittberger, «Revolution and Pseudo-Democratization» . . . in Almond *et al., op. cit.*, p. 377. On organizational strength within the business community, see also R. A. Brady, «Policies of National Manufacturing *Spitzenverbände*», in *Political Science Quarterly*, LXI (1941), pp. 199–225 and G. D. Feldman, «The Social and Economic Policies of German Big Business, 1918–1929», in *American Historical Review*, LXXV (1969), pp. 47–55.

[54] The basic source for this contention is Samuel A. Pratt, «The Social Basis of Nazism and Communism in Urban Germany. A Correlational Study of the July 31, 1932 Reichstag Election in Germany». M. A. Thesis (Microfilm) Michigan State College, East Lancing, Mich. 1948, especially p. 117. Using a sample of 193 German cities, Pratt found that the correlation between what he calls «upper-class» and NSDAP support in the 1932 election was +.23 in cities between 25 and 50 000 inhabitants, +.58 in cities between 50 000 and 100 000 and +.33 in urban areas with more than 100 000 citizens. His concept «upper middle class» refers to salaried employees *(Angestellte)* and civil servants *(Beamte)*. For the category of «lower middle classes» which refers to *Angestellten* and *Beamten* in lower positions, not the «old» middle class, the numbers are +.25, +.57 and +.27. Lipset, on the other hand, has shown that the trend is clearly recognizable also with regard to the artisans. Among the parties which lost most heavily was the *Wirtschaftspartei* which represented primarily small businessmen who were self-employed and artisans. In percen-

tage, its portion of the total vote went down from 4.5 in 1928 to 0.3 in 1932. In other words, the NSDAP emptied the old liberal-conservative parties. See Seymour Martin Lipset, *Political Man* (New York: Doubleday Anchor edition 1963), p. 138, basing his assertion on K. D. Bracher, *Die Auflösung der Weimarer Republik* (Stuttgart and Düsseldorf 1954), p. 94. For the social composition of the *Wirtschaftspartei*, see Martin Schumacher, *Mittelstandsfront und Republik 1919–1933: Die Wirtschaftspartei – Reichspartei des deutschen Mittelstandes 1919–1933* (Düsseldorf 1972). The most recent analysis of the social bases of National Socialism, Thomas Childers, «The Social Bases of the National Socialist Vote», in *Journal of Contemporary History*, 1976, pp. 17–42 emphasizes the discontinuities in the sociographic profiles of NSDAP supporters in the 1920's and 30's.

The propensity towards Nazism is confirmed with respect to the Protestant peasantry and the artisans in the North German countryside. See R. Heberle, *Landbevölkerung und Nationalsozialismus: Eine soziologische Untersuchung der politischen Willensbildung in Schleswig-Holstein 1918–1932* (Stuttgart 1963). Heberle's figures are: (Numbers express the percentage correlation between the different social groups and the proportion of NSDAP votes) peasantry and forestry workers: +28.6; industry and *Handwerk* +.52.4; industry and *Handwerk* plus trade and service +45.2; peasants, artisans, industrial managers and employees in the service sector together: (without the *Rentner*, persons living of income from shares and interests) +52.4. See page 109. As Rudolf Küstermeier has demonstrated, this «Wanderung nach rechts» of broad middle and upper-middle class segments started as early as 1920. Rudolf Küstermeier, *Die Mittelschichten und ihr politischer Weg* (Potsdam 1933), p. 39. For additional evidence of the class specific voting behavior of the German electorate, see E. A. Roloff, «Wer wählte Hitler», in *Politische Studien*, 15 (1964), June-May Hefte 153, pp. 293–301, and A. Schoun-Wiehl, *Faschismus und Gesellschaftsstruktur* (Frankfurt 1970), pp. 52f. Extensive references to contemporary discussions on the political behavior of the lower middle class is found in J. Kocka, «Zur Problematik der deutschen Angestellten 1914–1933», in H. Mommsen et al., *Industrielles System und Politische Entwicklung in der Weimarer Republik* (Düsseldorf 1974), p. 798, n. 10; A. Weber, *Soziale Merkmale der NSDAP Wähler. Eine Zusammenfassung bisherigen empirischer Untersuchungen* (diss. Freiburg 1969), and R. Kühnl (ed.), *Der deutsche Faschismus in Quellen und Dokumenten* (Cologne 1973), p. 96ff.

The discussion is far from closed, however. In a sharp challenge to the lower middle class thesis, Richard Hamilton argues that while the lower middle class theories all presuppose a close link between the upper class and the DNVP, this presupposition may prove more tenuous than expected. The supporters of the DNVP, he asserts, are better described in terms of region, religion and rural/small town setting than in terms of class. Probably the party comprised larger sections further «down» into the social structure than previously assumed: small farmers and even workers (much of the German National strength in Berlin was found in working-class districts). Generally speaking, the upper and upper middle classes rallied mostly behind the DVP, the right liberals, or at least their loyalties were divided between the DNVP and the DVP. As a result, to equate the DNVP with the upper class and the DDP and the DVP with the middle class is an oversimplification. The class bases of these parties were different from region to region and varied between town and country. The disappearance of the 'middle class parties', the DDP and the DVP, may accordingly reveal more about upper and middle class propensities than about those of the lower middle class, the frequently accused recruiting ground for the National Socialists. In meticulous local studies of Berlin and Hamburg, Hamilton finds support for the thesis that the above average support for the Nazis in the crucial July 1932 election came *first of all in the upper and upper middle class districts*. The voting record of the lower middle class areas is «undistinguishable» and do not show any disproportionate support for the NSDAP. The familiar pattern of below average voting support for the Nazis in working class areas is borne out again. Against the Pratt thesis, Hamilton argues that by lumping together three white-collar categories, a series of classification problems are created which cast doubt on the division of the middle class into an «upper» and a «lower» segment. The data in the Pratt thesis can only serve as a basis for comparing the voting tendencies of the «old» vs. the «new» middle classes. They do not permit any equation of persons of independent means with «the upper», or of salaried personnel with the «lower» segments. The correlations for both the «old» and the «new» middle classes were positively related to Nazism. But given the difficulties of the measures, Hamilton says that the most appropriate conclusion would be that the results in the Pratt thesis provide no conclusive evidence as to the difference in support for the Nazis between the «lower middle» and the «upper middle classes». The differences in correlation figures are too small. Richard Hamilton, «The Bases for National Socialism: The Electoral Support for Hitler 1924–32», chapters 1, 4 and 5, *Mimeo,* Department of Sociology, McGill University, Montreal. I am grateful for permission to quote from his forthcoming book.

Hamilton's painstaking research undercuts the conventional wisdom in the literature on patterns of Nazi voting. But in essence what he has done is to replace the traditional argument that the social specificity of Nazi support may be identified with the lower middle classes with the view that this specificity must be extended to include higher echelons of society. To my mind he has not undermined either the argument that the Nazi following was on the whole socially specific, or that the Nazi party recruited disproportionately from certain population groups. He has shifted the focus higher up in the German social structure and retained what is most important in our context, namely the view that the working class, including the unemployed workers, remained on the whole immune throughout.

[55] Unless otherwise stated I take all these figures from A. Milatz, *Wähler und Wahlen in der Weimarer Republik* (Bonn 1965). For specific discussion, see also his chapter «Das Ende der parteien im Spiegel der Wahlen 1930 bis 1933», in E. Matthias and R. Morsey (eds.), *Das Ende der Parteien* (Düsseldorf 1960), and R. I. McKibbin, «The Myth of the Unemployed: Who Did Vote for the Nazis?», in *Australian Journal of Politics and History,* XV, 1969, no. 2, pp. 25. See also Weber and Kühnl, *ibid.*

[56] R. Pinon, in *Revue des deux Mondes* (October 1930), pp. 711–712. The first one to demonstrate that the greatest Nazi strength lay in those areas of the country which were agricultural and Protestant was the German political scientist Werner Stephan. See his «Grenzen des nationalsozialistischen Vormarsches: Eine Analyse der Wahlsiffern der Reichstagswahl 1930», in *Zeitschrift für Politik,* XXI, 1932.

[57] W. Stephan, *ibid.*

[58] These averages have been calculated by J. K. Pollock in «An Areal Study of the German Electorate 1930–1933», in *Am. Pol. Science Review,* XXXVIII (February 1944), p. 90.

[59] Lipset, *op. cit.,* p. 144.

[60] R. Hamilton, «The Social Bases of National Socialism», *mimeo,* forthcoming. See note 54.

[61] Reinhard Bendix, «Social Stratification and Political Power», in Bendix and Lipset (eds.), *Class, Status and Power* (1st edition Glencoe, Ill., 1953). That essay has been omitted from the last edition of the book, however (1966), and in a 1959 article by Bendix and Lipset the following statement sums up Bendix' position: «Lipset has convinced Bendix that the shift of non-voters to the Nazis occurred only in 1933, whereas in the preceding elections middle-class extremists predominated among Nazi supporters». «On the Social Structure of Western Societies: Some Reflections on Comparative Analysis», in *Berkeley Journal of Sociology,* V. (Fall 1959), p. 12.

[62] Lipset, *op. cit.,* pp. 148–152.

[63] Karl O'Lessker, «Who Voted for Hitler? A New Look at the Class Basis of Nazism», in *American Journal of Sociology,* 74 (1968–69), July, pp. 63–69.

[64] Allan Schnaiberg, «A Critique of Karl O'Lessker's 'Who Voted for Hitler?', in *American Journal of Sociology,* 74 (May 1969), pp. 732–735.

[65] W. Kaltefleiter, *Wirtschaft und Politik in Deutschland* (Cologne and Opladen 1968), pp. 37–39.

[66] Loomis and Beegle, «The Spread of Nazism in Rural Areas», in *American Sociological Review,* XI (1946), p. 733.

[67] J. K. Pollock, *op. cit.,* pp. 93–94.

[68] W. Phillips Shively, «Party Identification, Party Choice and Voting Stability: The Weimar Case», in *American Political Science Review,* vol. LXVI, no. 4 (December 1972), p. 1216. Jürgen W. Falter's most recent discussion of the positions in the debate on Weimar elections, «Wer verhalf der NSDAP zum Sieg», in *Das Parlament,* February 1979, was unavailable at the time of writing.

110

[69] See Th. Geiger, *Die soziale Schichtung des deutschen Volkes* (Stuttgart 1932). D. O. Orlow, *The History of the Nazi Party* (Pittsburgh, Pa. 1969), p. 19 and Max H. Kele, *Nazis and Workers: National Socialist Appeals to German Labor 1919–1933* (Chapel Hill 1972).

[70] M. H. Kater, «Zur Soziographie der frühen NSDAP», *Vierteljahresheft für Zeitgeschichte*, 19, 1971 (April), p. 149. For additional evidence, see H. Gerth, «The Nazi party: Its Leadership and Composition», in *American Journal of Sociology* (Vol. XLV), 1940, pp. 517–541, where he estimates that the party was composed of 58 per cent white collar employees, and that the manual workers were underrepresented by 14.8 per cent in comparison with the total number of people gainfully employed.

[71] Kater, *op. cit.*, p. 138. In a more recent study, Kater takes his case further and states that in 1932, even the «obere Mittelstand» in which he includes leading industrialists, white-collar workers *(Angestellte)* in superior positions, and higher civil servants as well as academics, was overrepresented in the NSDAP in relation to its share of the gainfully employed population. See his «Sozialer Wandel in der NSDAP im Zuge der nationalsozialistischen Machtergreifung», in W. Scieder (ed.), *Faschismus und sozial Bewegung: Deutschland und Italien in Vergleich* (Hamburg 1976), p. 25ff.

[72] Wolfgang Schäfer, *NSDAP. Entwicklung und Struktur der Staatspartei des Dritten Reiches* (Marburg/Lahn 1957), p. 17.

[73] J. Noakes, *The Nazi Party in Lower Saxony* (Oxford 1971), p. 141 and G. Pridham, *Hitler's Rise to Power: The Nazi Movement in Bavaria 1923–33* (London 1973), p. 186.

[74] E. M. Doblin and C. Pohly, «The Social Composition of the Nazi Leadership», in *American Journal of Sociology*, LI, no. 1, (July 1945), p. 48.

[75] *Ibid.*, p. 46.

[76] *Ibid.*, p. 46.

[77] Martin Broszat, *Der Staat Hitlers* (Munich 1969), p. 49 and 50. Broszat confirms the findings referred to above, citing the *Parteistatistik* in support p. 51. See also the discussion in Reinhard Kühnl's contribution to this volume and the Freiburg dissertation of A. Weber on the social characteristics of the NSDAP voter, (see note 54).

[78] D. Lerner et al., *The Nazi Elite* (Stanford 1951).

[79] Noakes, *op. cit.*, p. 60 and Pridham, *op. cit.*, p. 205.

[80] H. Rauschnig, *Der Revolution des Nihilismus* (Zürich 1938), p. 62.

[81] Broszat, *op. cit.*, p. 52. This estimate is highly controversial. See Broszat's footnote on p. 52 for the basis on which it is arrived at.

[82] Pridham, *op. cit.*, p. 188.

[83] Noakes, *op. cit.*, p. 153.

[84] Geiger, *op. cit.*, pp. 72–76.

[85] H. A. Winkler, *Mittelstand, Demokratie und Nationalsozialismus* (Cologne 1972), p. 30. For a summary of his whole argument with a direct bearing on the organizational density of the German middle class, see his «From Social Protectionism to National Socialism: The German Small-Business Movement in Comparative Perspective», in *Journal of Modern History*, 48 (March 1976), pp. 1–18.

[86] *Ibid.*, p. 32.

[87] *Ibid.*, p. 30.

[88] H. Speier, «The Salaried Employees in German Society», *mimeo*, Columbia University Department of Social Sciences and WPA, N.Y. 1939, pp. 97–99, quoted from Schoenbaum, *Hitler's Social Revolution* (New York 1966), p. 8.

[89] Jürgen Kocka, «Zur Problematik der deutschen Angestellten», in Mommsen et al., *Industrielles System und Politische Entwicklung in der Weimarer Republik* (Düsseldorf 1974), p. 803.

[90] Jürgen Kocka, «The First World War and the 'Mittelstand': German Artisans and White-Collar Workers», in *Journal of Contemporary History*, vol. 8, no. 1 (January 1973), p. 123.

[91] Iris Hamel, *Völkischer Verband und Nationale Gewerkschaft* (Frankfurt 1967), pp. 190–191.

[92] For a discussion of marginality, see H. Dickie Clarke, *The Marginal Situation* (London 1956).

111

[93] H. J. Puhle, *Agrarische Interessenpolitik und preussischer Konservatismus in Whilhelmini-schen Reich (1893–1914)* (Hannover 1966), p. 309.

[94] Werner T. Angress, «The Political Role of the Peasantry in the Weimar Republic», in *The Review of Politics*, vol. 21 (July 1959), no. 3, p. 543, and D. Gessner, «Agrarian Protectionism in the Weimar Republic», in *Journal of Contemporary History*, vol. 12, no. 4 (October 1977), pp. 759–778, and the same author's *Agrarverbände in der Weimarer Republik* (Düsseldorf 1977), and *Agrardepression, Agrarideologie und Konservative Politik in der Weimarer Republik* (Wiesbaden 1977). See also, J. E. Farquharson, *The Plough and the Swastika. The NSDAP and Agriculture in Germany 1928–1945* (London 1977).

[95] C. Schulz, «Über Entstehung und Formen von Interessengruppen in Deutschland seit Beginn der Industrialisierung», in Varain, *op. cit.*, p. 42.

[96] D. Hertz-Eichenrode, *Politik und Landwirtschaft in Ostpreussen 1919–30* (Cologne/Opladen 1969), p. 75.

[97] R. Heberle, *From Democracy to Nazism* (New York 1970, first published 1945), p. 122.

[98] T. A. Tilton, *Nazism, Neo-Nazism and the Peasantry* (Bloomington & London 1975), p. 67.

[99] Heberle gives the following figures: (Page 109).

Correlation between self-employed and the Nazi and Socialist vote in July 1932.

Occupation	NSDAP	Socialist
Agriculture and Forestry	28.6	÷ 42.9
Agricultural Industry and Commerce	52.4	÷ 65.5
Industry and Commerce	45.2	÷ 56.0
Other Occupations	52.4	÷ 60.6

The correlations are almost reversed when the voters are *wage earners* in the same occupation category (Page 111)

Occupation	NSDAP	Socialist
Agriculture and Forestry	÷ 29.8	40.5
Agricultural Industry and Commerce	÷ 51.2	64.3
Industry and Commerce	÷ 29.8	46.4
Other Occupations	÷ 34.5	46.4

[100] Heberle, *Landbevölkerung, op. cit.*, p. 16.

[101] Loomis and Beegle, «The Spread of Nazism in Rural Areas», in *American Soc. Review*, XI (1946), pp. 726–728.

[102] The correlation between the Nazi vote and electoral districts where the average farm size was both *below* 2 hectares and *above* 100 hectares was distinctly negative. The Nazi rural vote was likely to come from areas where the average farm size was 2–20 hectares. The reason is obvious: these were the holdings of the farm proprietors, i.e. farms worked by one man and his family, ordinarily without agricultural laborers. (See Loomis and Beegle, *op. cit.*, pp.730–731.) Farms under 2 hectares were usually worked by wage-earning laborers who tended to vote socialist. Farms above 100 hectares employed considerable numbers of laborers who were not Nazi, while the owners themselves, because farming was more secure, continued to vote for the DNVP, the *Deutschnationale Volkspartei*, the traditional conservative party.

For an interesting parallel, see Stein Rokkan's description of farm size in the *Østland* region in Norway in comparison with the *Sørland-Vestland* region. He argues that farm size and conditions of relative equality in the communities had similar importance in deciding the socialist vote in these two provinces. See Rokkan, «Geography, Religion, Social Class: Cross-Cutting Cleavages in Norwegian Politics», in Rokkan and Lipset, *Party Systems and Voter Alignments* (New York 1967).

[103] McKibbin, *op. cit.*, p. 34.

[104] Besides Heberle's work, the best analysis of the political behavior of the Schleswig-Holstein farmers is G. Stoltenberg, *Politische Strömungen im schleswig-holsteinischen Landvolk 1918–1933* (Düsseldorf 1962). Se also Tilton, *op. cit.*, especially pp. 60–72.

[105] See H. Gies, «NSDAP und landwirtschaftliche Organisation in der Endphase der Weimarer Republik», in *Vierteljahrshefte für Zeitgeschichte* XV (1967), pp. 341–376. In English in H. A. Turner, Jr. (ed.), *Nazism and the Third Reich* (N.Y. 1972), pp. 45–89. For a discussion of similar tactics in relation to the various *Mittelstand* organizations, see Winkler, *Mittelstand . . .*, *op. cit.*, p. 170. Ch. 8 in this book provides an analysis of the virtual pre-1933 *Gleichshaltung* of the intermediary *Mittelstand* network by the Nazis through grassroot pressure.

[106] Tilton, *op. cit.*, pp. 70–71.

[107] Kornhauser, *op. cit.*, p. 136.

[108] The farmer-worker relations in Scandinavia are extensively discussed in Sten Sparre Nilson, Jan Petter Myklebust and Bernt Hagtvet's contributions to this volume.

[109] See E. David, *Der Bund der Landwirte als Machtinstrument des ostelbischen Junkertums 1893–1920* (Dissertation, Halle 1967); H.-J. Puhle, *op. cit.;* U. Lindig, *Der Einfluss des Bundes der Landwirte auf die Politik des Wilhelminischen Zeitalter 1893–1914 unter besondere Berücksichtung der preussischen Verhältnisse* (Dissertation, Hamburg 1953), and D. Gessner, «Agrarian Protectionism . . .» *op. cit.* See also H. Beyer, «Die Agrarkrise und das Ende der Weimarer Republik», *Zeitschrift für Agrargeschichte und Agrarsoziologie,* 13 (1965), p. 62ff.

[110] The classical study of German agriculture and the SPD's unwillingness to focus serious attention on the rural population is, A. Gerschenkron, *Bread and Democracy in Germany* (Los Angeles 1943), see especially pp. 28–33. See also H. G. Lehmann, *Die Agrarfrage in Theorie und Praxis der deutschen und internationalen Sozialdemokratie. Von Marxismus zum Revisionismus und Bolschewismus* (Tübingen 1970), especially pp. 113–278.

[111] It would be a misrepresentation of Kornhauser to assert that he pays no attention to economic factors in determining political, especially mass behavior. He portrays mass analysis as a more *general* theory (p. 163) applicable to «all cases where widespread extremist mass movements develop» *(ibid.).* Such movements, he maintains, are generated for instance in «the early phase of industrialization, during periods of rapid population changes, in times of severe military defeat, as well as during acute and prolonged economic crises» *(ibid.).* Frustration of economic interest is hardly such a general factor, he writes, nor is it likely to create that specific psychological climate peculiar to mass movements: alienation and suggestibility. On page 211 Kornhauser mentions the loss of social ties as an *additional* factor to considerations of «poorer market conditions». Manfred Clemenz in his study *Gesellschaftliche Ursprünge des Faschismus* (Frankfurt 1972) attacks Kornhauser's concept of social strain, accusing him of reducing materially founded power structures into subjectively experienced states of mind (p. 30), and (rightly, to my mind), for failing to explain why society is subject to a sudden centralization process leading to its massification (p. 241). For his entire argument, see pp. 26–58 and 240–245.

[112] Kornhauser, *op. cit.*, pp. 201–202. Within heavy industry, support for Hitler came from the steel industry, which can scarcely be called 'marginal'. For further references, see note 117.

[113] Kornhauser, *op. cit.*, p. 237.

[114] W. Kaltefleiter, *op. cit.*, discusses the probabilities of right vs. left political alignments in the Weimar elections. He shows that the agrarian protest vote went to the Nazis wherever it was not 'immunized' by a Catholic organization. The urban and industrial protest shifted to the NSDAP where the labor unions were weak and where industry was of moderate size. In large-scale industry where the trade unions were strong, the protest vote was retained within the socialist camp, some moving leftwards. See also R. M. Lepsius, *Extremer Nationalismus, op. cit.*, and the same author's «From Centrifugal Party System to Presidential Government and

113

National Socialist Take-Over: Germany», in Stepan & Linz, *op. cit.*, ch. 4 «The Economic Situation».

[115] For a discussion, see Joseph R. Gusfield, «Mass Society and Extremist Politics», in *American Sociological Review*, XXVII (1962), pp. 19–30.

[116] Kornhauser, *op. cit.*, pp. 119–174, especially pp. 162–167.

[117] The main issues are found in G. W. Hallgarten, *Hitler, Reichswehr und Industrie* (Frankfurt A.M. 1955); Eberhard Czichon, *Wer verhalf Hitler zum Macht?* (Cologne 1967) and in Henry Ashby Turner, jr., «Big Business and the Rise of Hitler», in *American Historical Review*, vol. 75 (October 1969), pp. 56–70. (Also published in his *Faschismus und Kapitalismus in Deutschland* (Göttingen 1972) and the same author's «Zur Verhältnis des Grossunternehmertums zur NSDAP», pp. 919–932 in Mommsen *et al.*, *op. cit.* A survey of the current state of research is found in U. Hörster-Phillips, «Grosskapital, Weimarer Republik und Faschismus», in R. Kühnl and G. Hardach (eds.), *Die Zerstörung der Weimarer Republik* (Cologne 1977), pp. 38–142, and in Clemenz, *op. cit.*, pp. 40–53, esp. pp. 49–51. See also note 12 in B. Hagtvet's and R. Kühnl's article in this volume.

The actual financing of Hitler's party by industrialists is to my mind a side-issue. Much more important is the contribution made to the fall of Weimar by the industrial élite through its persistent anti-republicanism and its deep-rooted reluctance to allow free interplay between organized labor and employers. The historical record of the German haute bourgeoisie is complex. There were industrialists who were strongly in favor of the Republic (Otto Wolff, the Klöckner family and others). But on the whole it is fair to conclude that the fragile democracy in Germany was more affected by the recurrent attempts of the industrial élite to weaken the elected parliament in favor of a strong executive unhampered by popular controls and by attempts to subordinate workers than by payments to the NSDAP, which apparently never received more than other bourgeois parties. The willingness of some industrialists to be accomplices in the Nazi seizure of power is but an illustration of a prominent aspect of Weimar history: Some industrialists still lived in the world of the *Obrigkeitstaat*. In their attempt to locate power in a bureaucratic élite, they showed that their political horizon had not transcended the Imperial era. The political leadership within the industrial bourgeoisie had never learnt to fight for parliamentary majorities, or had played down the importance of parliament altogether. Such a necessity would probably, in H. A. Winkler's judgment, have led to compromises with the lower middle class and restricted the struggle with the working class to the parliamentary arena. «Dieser Erfahrung ungewohnt, liess sich das deutsche Bürgertum durch autoritäre Wunschbilder daran hindern, soziale Konflikte als solche zu erkennen und austragen». For an excellent analysis of corporatist ideas among the *Handwerk* and the anti-democratic sentiments of the industrial bourgeoisie, see his «Unternehmerverbände zwischen Ständeideologie und Nationalsozialismus», in Heinz J. Varain (ed.), *Interessenverbände in Deutschland* (Cologne 1973), pp. 228–258, esp. p. 247.

[118] See Czichon, *op. cit.*, p. 70.

[119] Turner, *op. cit.*, p. 59 and 66.

[120] For a discussion of this meeting, see Manfred Clemenz, *Gesellschaftliche Ursprünge des Faschismus* (Frankfurt 1972), p. 52; G. W. Hallgarten, «Adolf Hitler and German Heavy Industry», in *Journal of Economic History* XII (1952), pp. 222–246, especially p. 224, and Turner, *op. cit.*, p. 67.

[121] Jürgen Kocka, «Zur Problematik . . .», *op. cit.*, pp. 800–801. See also I. Hamel, *op. cit.*, pp. 225, 228ff, 232, 237, 238–261, especially p. 243 and 251. For further discussion on the consensus between the NSDAP and the DHV and their mutual contacts, see the memoir by Albert Krebs, *Tendenzen und Gestalten der NSDAP* (Stuttgart 1959), (English edition, *The Infancy of Nazism*, ed. by W. S. Allen, New York 1976). Chapter 1 gives a vivid description of the process of infiltration by the Nazis aimed at turning the DHV to their own political purposes.

[122] Maurice Pinard, «Mass Society and Political Movements: A New Formulation», in *American Journal of Sociology*, (July 1968), pp. 682–690.

A pertinent case that illustrates that the links between the individual and the state may serve as useful agencies of manipulation and control from *above*, is Vidkun Quisling's attempt to regiment the Norwegian population during World War II. Keenly aware of the potential importance of the organizations for the success of his policy of *Nyordning*, Quisling's party tried to take over a series of Norwegian interest organizations, particularly in the field of education, and use them to reach deep into the population. Through offers of preferential treatment to those who stayed, he hoped to implement his complete restructuring of Norwegian society and split the anti-Nazi front. As it turned out, however, although incumbent elected officers were replaced by Quisling's collaborationists, the results were the abandonment of the existing organizations and the creation of new ones, or going underground or withdrawing into passivity. It is diffucult to see in what sense the strength or weakness of the intermediate structure *per se* protected the Norwegian population. Rather it was resistance and political acumen *within* the organizations which proved decisive. The failure of Quisling must be sought in a straightforward political contempt for this treachery and in the remarkable discipline which grew out of that disdain. Those were the primary reasons; the organizational network proved merely to be important as arenas in which the struggle was carried out. The standard work on this struggle is Thomas Chr. Wyller, *Nyordning og motstand* (Re-organization and Resistance) (Oslo 1958).

[123] L. E. Jones, «The Crisis of White-Collar Interest Politics: DHV and DVP in the World Economic Crisis», in Mommsen et al., *op. cit.*, pp. 811–823.

[124] As convincingly argued by W. S. Allen, «The Appeal of Fascism and the Problem of National Disintegration», in H. A. Turner, jr. (ed.), *Reappraisals of Fascism* (New York 1975), pp. 44–69, esp. pp. 56, 60.

[125] M. Reiner Lepsius, «Parteiensystem und Sozialstruktur . . .», *op. cit.*, pp. 388–389, and H. A. Winkler, «Pluralismus oder Protektionismus. Verfassungspolitische Probleme des Verbandswesens im deutschen Kaiserreich» (Institute of European History, Mainz, published in Wiesbaden 1972).

[126] On the mechanism of «immunization» of tightly-knit «political churches», see W. D. Burnham, «Political Immunization and Political Confessionalism: The United States and Weimar Germany», in *Journal of Interdisciplinary History*, vol. III (1972), pp. 1–30.

[127] See S. M. Lipset & Stein Rokkan, *Party Systems and Voter Alignments* (New York 1967), «Introduction», pp. 1–64. See also the extensive discussion by Derek Urwin, «Germany: Continuity and Change in Electoral Politics», pp. 109–171, in R. Rose, *Electoral Behavior: A Comparative Handbook* (New York 1974).

[128] For the full story, M. Rainer Lepsius' work is the best source, in particular his «Parteiensystem und Sozialstruktur», *op. cit.* especially pp. 379–380, and Heino Kaack, *Geschichte und Struktur des deutschen Parteiensystems* (Opladen 1971), particularly pp. 61, 69ff.

[129] L. E. Jones surveys the whole process admirably in his essay, «The Dying Middle: Weimar Germany and the Fragmentation of Bourgeois Politics», *op. cit.*, in particular pp. 35, *passim.*

[130] *Ibid.*

[131] W. S. Allen, «The Appeal of Fascism», *op. cit.*, p. 52; Leonard Krieger, *The German Idea of Freedom* (Boston 1967) and Fritz Ringer, *The Decline of the German Mandarins, 1890–1933* (Cambridge, Mass. 1969). On the diffusion of *völkish* ideas among educators, see G. L. Mosse, *The Crisis of German Ideology* (New York 1967), ch. 8, pp. 149–170, and on German political culture in general, F. Stern, *The Failure of Illiberalism* (N.Y. 1972) and his *The Politics of Cultural Despair* (N. Y. 1967). A good analysis is also to be found in H. Lebovics, *Social Conservatism and the Middle Class in Germany 1914–1933* (Princeton 1969).

[132] Cf. Lepsius, «From Centrifugal Party Democracy to . . .» in Linz & Stepan, *op. cit.*, ch. 1. So pervasive and persistent was this ideology that Ralf Dahrendorf in his *Society and Democracy in Germany* (N.Y. 1967) devotes considerable energy to tracing the roots of this yearning for harmony and reconciliation and showing its intellectual vacuity.

[133] It is difficult to assess the impact of this socially imbalanced recruitment to the liberal political class, but Jones in his discussion of the fragmentation of the middle (see note 129) makes a point of Th. Heuss' apparent inability to grasp the underlying social and economic issues swaying people to become Nazi supporters. See Th. Heuss, *Hitlers Weg. Eine historisch-politische Studie über den Nationalsozialismus* (Stuttgart, Berlin and Leipzig 1932) and Jones, *op. cit.*, p. 32.

[134] Doubts can even be expressed as to whether intermediary associations are important as reference groups at all, even in close-knit communities. On this problem, see D. Holden, «Associations as Reference Groups: An Approach to the Problem», in *Rural Sociology*, 30 (1965), pp. 63–74. Referring to this work, Maurice Pinard writes:

«. . . a large number of organizations do not actually represent reference points for their members, even in small communities. In this regard, a pluralist society with a proliferation of autonomous intermediate groupings could be relatively little more restraining than a mass society. It would seem, in fact, that if restraining effects are to be ascribed to the intermediate structure, primary groups and the social networks of small communities, rather than most associations and organizations, are the groupings to be considered, since they are more likely to act as reference points.»

M. Pinard, *The Rise of a Third Party. A Study in Crisis Politics* (Englewood-Cliffs, N.J. 1971), p. 184. For a discussion, see the M. A. Thesis by Jan Ole Rød, «Massesamfunnsteori og nazisme» (The Theory of Mass Society and Nazism), Inst. of Pol. Science, University of Oslo 1977, p. 28.

[135] Kornhauser, *op. cit.*, p. 15.

[136] Rosenberg in Abendroth et al. (eds.), *Faschismus und Kapitalismus* (Frankfurt 1968), p. 107.

[137] W. S. Allen, *The Nazi Seizure of Power, op. cit.*, p. 276. Likewise, the Norwegian historian Hans Fredrik Dahl argues that the Nazi upsurge must be seen as a reaction to polarization of class distinctions, in other words to a situation where ordinary class barriers were regarded as deeper and sharper than before. H. F. Dahl, *Hva er fascisme?* (What is Fascism) (Oslo 1972).

[138] Winkler, *Mittelstand, op. cit.*, p. 33.

[139] *Ibid.*, p. 32.

[140] *Ibid.*, p. 33.

[141] Käthe Gabel, «Die Entwicklungstendenzen des gewerblichen Klein- und Mittelbetriebes», in *Soziale Praxis*, 42 (1934), p. 283, quoted from Winkler, *op. cit.*, p. 34.

[142] E. Grünberg, *Der Mittelstand in der kapitalistischen Gesellschaft. Eine ökonomische und soziologische Untersuchung* (Leipzig 1932), p. 165.

On the impact of rationalization upon the German artisans, see J. Dethloff, «Das Handwerk in der kapitalistischen Gesellschaft», in *Strukturwandlungen in der deutschen Volkswirtschaft*, ed. B. Harms (Berlin 1929), II, pp. 3–41. For a statistical analysis of the economic decline of the independent middle class in the period after World War I, see L. D. Pesl, «Mittelstandsfragen», in *Grundriss der Sozialökonomik* (Tübingen 1926–27), IX: I, pp. 79–119, and Jones, *op. cit.*, p. 25.

[143] Winkler, *op. cit.*, p. 34.

[144] *Ibid.*

[145] Geiger, *Die Soziale Schichtung . . ., op. cit.*, p. 87.

[146] Joseph A. Schumpeter, «Das Soziale Antlitz des deutschen Reiches», in *Aufsätze zur Soziologie* (Tübingen 1953), p. 221, quoted from Winkler, *op. cit.*, p. 37.

[147] Winkler, *op. cit.*, p. 38.

[148] For an extensive discussion of state intervention for political purposes in the Hohenzollern period, see H. A. Winkler (ed.), *Organisierter Kapitalismus, Voraussetzungen und Anfänge*. The proceedings from the 29th Convention of German historians (Kritische Studien zur Geschichtswissenschaft, vol. 9, Göttingen 1974).

[149] Winkler, *Mittelstand . . ., p. 50.

[150] Jürgen Kocka, «The First World War and the German 'Mittelstand'», *op. cit.*, pp. 101–123. Kocka writes that between the end of World War I and the Nazi victory the differential between wages and salaries continued to shrink, though not as rapidly as during the war and the 1923 inflation. «The money income of workers (average annual values) rose by two thirds in the 15 years between 1913 and 1928, while that of employees rose only about one-third» (page 121).

[151] Allen, *op. cit.*, p. 276.

116

[152] Noakes, *op. cit.*, p. 136.

[153] Allen, *op. cit.*, p. 276.

[154] H. A. Winkler, «Extremismus der Mitte? Sozial-geschichtlicher Aspekte der nationalsozialistischen Machtergreifung», in *Vierteljahreshefte für Zeitgeschichte*, 20 (1972), pp. 175–191.

[155] In a similar vein P. C. J. Pulzer in his book *The Rise of Political Anti-Semitism in Germany and Austria* (New York 1964) argues that German industrialization was so fast that large sections of the German population, particularly the peasantry and the artisan classes, found their lives profoundly disrupted. Unable to adjust themselves to the changes in the economy and society as fast as these changes were taking place, they became highly susceptible to a demagogic variety of poltitics in which the Jew was the principal scapegoat. A similar argument has been advanced with respect to Norway by Edvard Bull d.e., the difference being, however, that in Norway it was the working-class that supposedly was disrupted and radicalized through rapid industrialization. For a critical review of the Bull hypothesis and a discussion of industrialization as a disrupting force, see W. M. Lafferty, *Economic Development and the Response of Labor in Scandinavia* (Oslo 1971). For an interesting attempt to understand fascism as a response to broad processes of modernization, see H. A. Turner, jr., «Fascism and Modernization», in *World Politics,* vol. XXIV (July 1972), no. 4, pp. 547–564, and subsequent rejoinders by A. J. McGregor and H. A. Turner, jr. in the same journal. See also A. F. K. Organski, *The Stages of Political Development* (N.Y. 1965).

[156] Franz Neumann shows for instance that the number of handicraft enterprises fell from 1.734.000 in 1934 to 1.471.000 in 1949. Franz Neumann, *Behemoth* (New York 1963), p. 283. This is confirmed by Schoenbaum, *Hitler's Social Revolution* (New York 1967), p. 127, 132, 143. For a more general discussion of the economic policies of the NSDAP, see H. F. Dahl, *Hva er fascisme?* (Oslo 1972), pp. 110 ff.

[157] For a critical and very suggestive discussion of this 'autonomy' of National Socialism, see T. H. Mason, «The Primacy of Politics – Politics and Economics in National Socialist Germany», in S. J. Woolf (ed.), *The Nature of Fascism* (New York 1969), pp. 165–196.

Pre-Conditions for the Rise and Victory of Fascism in Germany

REINHARD KÜHNL

Methodological Problems

A satisfactory, and thorough analysis of German fascism cannot be achieved by a mere presentation of political events in their chronological order. To give adequate explanations for the rise of fascism in Germany, the conditions conducive to its ultimate victory must be scrutinized. This means that not only the NSDAP itself has to be subjected to analysis, but also the political and social forces which contributed to or impeded its growth. Accordingly, the first question to ask is this: What was the NSDAP? Which social groups were drawn to it as voters, as members, or as party functionaries? Under what conditions and for what reasons were these groups attracted to the Nazi party?

Historical events have shown – in Germany and elsewhere – that fascist movements are unable to seize power on their own, even in cases where they are supported by wide segments of society. It is thus significant that the NSDAP did not reach power at the peak of its electoral strength after the election in July 1932 when it received 37.3 per cent of the votes. Importantly, its ultimate victory occurred after the November elections the very year when its support at the polls had declined to 33.1 per cent. The party thus seemed already in a process of decline. Conversely, the fascists in Italy gained power without having experienced any electoral breakthrough; there the party had even a relatively small rank and file. It is clear that fascist movements can only acquire power under conditions of alliance; they have to be supported by significant sections of industry, banks, landed aristocracy, the military and the central state apparatus. Hence, secondly, we have to ask which groups of the ruling classes supported the NSDAP in its ascendancy either by blocking or suppressing anti-fascist forces, by tacit or overt political agreements, by lending ideological support, or by direct aid, financially or by putting other material resources (such as printing facilities, housing and transport) at their disposal. Under what conditions and for what reasons did they do that?

The development of fascist movements cannot be fully understood unless the strategies and choices of the anti-fascist forces are taken into account. For this reason we have to ask a third set of questions: Which were the forces that could put up the strongest resistance to fascist intrusion into the political system? Why in so many cases were they unable to prevent the fascists from seizing power?

Fascism proved successful in many European countries, though not in all. In the countries where no fascist victory was achieved there nevertheless existed conditions which are commonly regarded as necessary though not sufficient causes for the ultimate victory of fascism: economic crisis with a high rate of unemployment, social decline of the middle sector etc. This prompts a fourth question: What specific conditions distinguished Germany from other capitalist industrial nations in this period?

A theory explaining the rise of fascism in Germany in this way has to examine at least these four sets of questions. So far no completely satisfactory answer has been given. In the following, some very short theses will be developed. A full-fledged theory of fascism would require a discussion of the fascist system of power, its structure and social function. The attitude of the upper classes towards fascism cannot be understood unless the actual results of the policies of the party in power are analyzed and the nature of the fascist power structure is fully comprehended. Some discussion of this topic is therefore indispensable.

The Social Composition of the NSDAP

The NSDAP claimed to be a true «popular» movement aiming at the mobilization and representation of all social strata. Empirical research has shown, however, that this claim has no root in historical reality: certain social groups predominated both inside the party and at the polls, whereas others refused their support.

The first fascist wave emerged immediately after the end of World War I. In 1922 this led to the victory of fascism in Italy, and in 1923 to the rebellion of the German National Socialists. Immediately after the boom in 1924, fascism in Germany subsided. In these years the fascist movements were largely composed of social groups which had been socially and intellectually uprooted by their war experiences and by the post-war upheavals. They were unable to get a firm footing in post-war bourgeois life and comprised a mixture of officers who, finding no position in the small armies during the period of peace, looked for possibilities to preserve their martial way of life and military style of thinking. They were also young men deeply impressed by their experiences in the trenches, men now looking for exciting and adventurous comradeship, despising parliamentary democracy as commonplace and tedious. «And as those former combatants have no perspectives for the future, they again turn ...to the past», as Tasca expressed it. [1] Dislocated persons who found in the fascist parties a movement which could give them opportunities for self-assertion swelled the ranks. From these fringe groups the future élite of the fascist parties were drawn. Their military outlook and authoritarian ways determined the militaristic organizational structure of the parties. They also formed the core of the new combatant teams, which through direct terrorism frightened their political enemies into submission.

Had German fascism, however, consisted merely of persons or social groups which could not adjust to the peace period, it would not have been able to achieve such importance. If it had not succeeded in expanding from this initial base, it would have been confined to the immediate post-war period. It could only become a stable political factor because the social development of capitalism produced a social basis for it. This potential could be mobilized by ingenious propaganda.

Economic competition had intensified since the advent of industrialization. In the course of the concentration of capital, huge cartels and monopolies were established which more or less subordinated or completely ruined smaller business firms. Since the second half of the 19th century, the percentage of autonomous entrepreneurs in the developed industrial countries had been continually decreasing. As late as in 1882, 25.6 per cent of the population lived as autonomous employers in the German Reich; in 1907 this proportion had dropped to 18.8 per cent.[2] Owners of small property in commerce, industry and agriculture saw their basis of income tottering and looked to be rescued. On the one hand, they felt themselves threatened by big corporations in trade and industry and thus became sensitive to anti-monopolistic slogans. On the other hand, they energetically kept the working-class at a distance. In relation to it they stressed their status as owners, and claimed to represent the middle-class, feverishly trying to protect their privileges and style of life against the wage-earners.

As long as the general socio-economic situation remained stable, this potential dissatisfaction could be exploited by the traditional bourgeois parties. The comparatively small crises before World War I had already caused a considerable increase in anti- Semitic and nationalist tendencies. Social conservative groups, like the *Christliche Soziale Arbeiterpartei* of the court chaplain Adolf Stöcker, a party which achieved some regional success as early as 1890, combined nationalist, anti-Semitic, anti-liberal, anti-socialist and anti-monopolistic elements, creating that kind of demagogic ideology which fascism developed to perfection. The same is true of the *Action Française,* which exerted considerable influence particularly in circles of the academic French bourgeoisie even prior to the outbreak of World War I, as well as of the *Christlich-Soziale Partei* of Karl Lueger, who was elected mayor of Vienna in 1897.

After 1918, the situation of the middle-classes had clearly deteriorated in several respects. This was especially the case in Germany and Austria, as also in Italy. Overcome by nationalist war ecstasy, these classes had transferred parts of their savings to the government as war loans which proved to have been lost after the War. The inflation in the following years, which may be characterized as a gigantic redistribution of the wealth of the nation in favour of powerful capital, took the rest of their savings from the middle-classes.[3]

In addition, disappointment with the defeat in 1918 in Germany and Austria stood in sharp contrast to the traditional aspiration for national greatness and to imperialist phantasies that envisaged the German Reich as a continental block stretching from Eastern France to the Ukraine. Similar tendencies could also be found in Italy which, though formally a victor, hardly succeeded in realizing any of her far-reaching imperialist claims. On the other hand, the socialist movement reaching its climax after the end of the War: the victory of the revolution in Russia, the proclamation of the Soviet republics in Hungary and Bavaria, the factory occupations in Italy and powerful strike movements in nearly every European country seemed to announce the socialist revolution.

To this provocation the middle classes reacted variously. One section continued to rely on the bourgeois parties, while others in increasing numbers turned to right-wing groups demanding violent suppression of the worker's movements which rapidly increased in strength after 1918. Considerable segments of the lower middle class at first drew quite different conclusions, however. They joined the socialist movement, which promised a complete transformation of the capitalist system. Immediately after the revolution in 1918, the social-democrats and the left-liberals, their coalition partners, won widespread support at the polls. The disappointment of the electorate came to the surface, however, as early as 1920. Only when the left proved incapable of carrying out a fundamental reform of German society did the lower middle class tend to look for new affiliations.[4]

The dominating ideologies which had assumed more and more fierce nationalist, racial and imperialist forms since the end of the 19th century, reaching a climax in the propaganda during the years of war 1914–18, had not failed to make an impact on the working class. Nonetheless, this social class proved to be the most powerful bulwark against fascist propaganda. Only certain marginal groups proved to be susceptible to the fascist appeal: farm labourers, young unemployed workers, workers within middle-range businesses in the countryside; i.e. mainly those groups which were neither organized in trade unions nor in socialist parties. Until 1930, only 8.5 per cent of the members of the NSDAP belonged to the working class.[5] A far more important part was played by those groups of the so-called «new middle-class» and the «free occupations», that is the small and middle-range white-collar workers and officials, the doctors and barristers and academic youth. The number of white-collar workers had been rapidly increasing in the industrialized Western nations since the turn of the century. In 1882 there were only 300,000 white-collar workers in the German Reich; in 1925 their number had risen to 3,5 million.[6] But their social and economic plight grew worse and worse with the steady process of capital concentration. Whereas the white-collar worker in small business firms in the 19th century had still performed duties which put him in the category of management, and had fulfilled delegated functions of the employers, he was more and more relegated to a mere subordinate role within the administrations of the big corporations. He performed neither intellectual nor executive functions; his work and often also his income gradually became indistinguishable from the work and income of the workers. This displacement was precisely the reason why a great many white-collar workers, particularly those recruited from the autonomous middle-classes, clung to their specific self-consciousness in relation to the working class. Many white-collar workers continued to regard themselves as representatives of the management, in the same way that many officials felt themselves to be supporters of state sovereignty.

In sum, as Martin Broszat has pointed out, «white-collar workers, artisans, shop-keepers, employees in state and municipal administration (Beamte) and the free professions counted in percentages almost twice as much within the NSDAP as compared with the entire working population». The lower middle-class character of the party emerged more clearly among the voters than among its members. «The fact that the overwhelming majority of the small peasants and cottagers . . . . . voted for the NSDAP in 1932, can, for example, be considered as having been proved. The same is true for millions of white-collar workers, rentiers, pensioners, small merchants, tradesmen, who all from an economic point of view lived mostly on a proletarian level but felt themselves to belong to the middle-class.»[7]

This statement corresponds to the results of the most thorough analysis of the social characteristics of the NSDAP-voters so far, carried out by Alexander Weber.[8]

After the outbreak of the world wide economic crisis in 1929 it turned out that there was a powerful fascist potential in Germany. Whereas the NSDAP had obtained a mere 2.6 per cent of the votes in the Reichstag election in 1928, its share rose to 18.3 per cent in 1930 and to 37.3 per cent in July 1932. At the same time the parties which hitherto had been supported by the middle classes were to a large extent decimated. The middle-range bourgeois parties broke down completely, as can be seen from the following figures: the *Deutsche Demokratische Partei* down from 4.8 per cent to 1 per cent; the *Deutsche Volkspartei* from 4.5 per cent to 0.4 per cent and the right-wing *Deutschnationale Volkspartei* lost more than half of its votes and declined from 14.2 per cent to 5.9 per cent. The crisis mobilized masses of people mainly in the small towns and in the countryside and from amongst the middle classes that had hitherto kept out of politics: turnout rose from 75.6 per cent to 84.1 per cent. Despite this enormous increase in voting participation, the Catholic parties the *Zentrum* and the *Bayerische Volkspartei* remained rather stable with a share hovering around 15 per cent. The bloc of the left also remained rather stable. Although capable of raising the number of its voters by about 1 million, its share of the total number of votes cast sank, due to the higher turnout, from 40.4 per cent to 36 per cent. (In this case the crisis had the effect of bolstering the Communist party at the expense of the SPD, the Social Democrats.)

The Support by Sections of the Upper Classes

The deep economic depression in the capitalist countries, leading to mass unemployment and rapid processes of social degeneration in the middle classes, also revealed a high potential for dissatisfaction with the existing political and social order and brought anti-capitalist tendencies into the open.

The interests of the upper classes naturally led to attempts to take advantage of the dissatisfaction of the masses and direct their frustration into channels that did not threaten their privileges and the social system in which they felt secure. Precisely this double function as perceived by the upper classes was consciously exploited by the NSDAP: on the one hand the Nazi party articulated the animosity and the anti-capitalist sentiments of the masses by attacking «the system» and by proclaiming a radical fight against what they perceived to be its prime attributes: parliamentarism and the party state, Weimar democracy, liberalism and capitalism. On the other hand, fascism was relatively harmless to the existing power system for several reasons: First, because it did not attack the institution of private property and the social order which had private property rights as its base, limiting itself instead to certain symptoms caused by the exercise of these rights and on the whole defending private property resolutely; and secondly because fascism veiled the connection between capitalism and the depression and instead directed the anger of the masses towards minorities within the national boundaries and toward foreign peoples. Finally, the energy released by the crisis could even be activated in defence of the capitalist system: by portraying communism as the true enemy of the people and the cause of all evil, and by using the fascist movement as a terrorizing instrument for the destruction of labour organizations.

Hence the gap between the ideology of the fascist followers and the objective functions of the fascist movement was large. While the masses supporting fascism primarily believed it to be an attack on «the system» and an attempt to destroy not only bourgeois democracy as a form of state, but also capitalism as a state of society threatening the middle-classes, they served to secure the capitalist system and to destroy its true enemy: the left. After the *Machtergreifung,* when the real function of fascism became evident, conflicts were bound to result from this contradiction.[9]

When it is asserted that upper class support was necessary to enable the Nazis to seize power, more is implied than partial funding of fascist organizations by some industrialists. Upper class complicity in the Nazi victory comprises a weakness on the part of the established institutions to defend democracy in face of fascist subversion. In the two «core» fascist countries, Italy and Germany, the spinelessness of officialdom and the liberal political class assumed a variety of forms, like the toleration and passivity of the police in the face of growing fascist violence (as in Italy and Germany); the failure of the judicial system to prosecute vigilants of the SA and other combatant organizations and its attempts to conceal or treat leniently the actions and attempted coups of fascists (as in Italy and Germany); the provision of weapons to the fascist movements by the military (as in Italy) or the benevolent toleration of the bourgeois press towards fascism and its adherents and towards their acts of violence (as in Italy and Germany); the readiness of the church and the monarchy to enter into alliances with fascism (as in Italy); and above all, the realization by big capital, the most influential upper-class stratum tacitly or overtly (or both) to support fascism, that parliamentary democracy no longer served its purpose and that hence a fascist system had to be instituted.[10]

Just this phase occurred in Germany in the autumn of 1932. In November 1932 an influential minority of industrialists, bankers and landed artistocrats in a written paper demanded from Reichspräsident Hindenburg the nomination of Hitler as Reichskanzler.[11] Up to that time only parts of heavy industry and landed artistocracy wanted the Nazi party to form the government. These parts of the upper classes were particularly hit by the economic crisis and therefore determined to try an extremely reactionary and imperialist policy. Most representatives of big capital, led by the modern chemical and electric industries, agreed to the abolition of parliamentary democracy, but believed a presidential dictatorship to be sufficient. This situation changed in November 1932. The elections showed a considerable loss for the NSDAP and a further gain for the KPD. Now the majority of the industrialists, the financiers and the landed aristocrats came to the conclusion that a Hitler government was necessary.[12] In this government, formed on January 30th, 1933, representatives of the *Deutschnationalen* (DNVP) and the state administration were also represented. The Hitler-Hugenberg government which was only the final results of a coalition which began in 1929 between the «moderate» and «extreme» right, clearly demonstrates that the success of the Nazi party was based on an alliance between the fascist mass movement and parts of the upper classes. Further illustrations of the character of this alliance are the meeting between Hitler and the leaders of the Reichswehr on February 3rd, that is, four days after the *Machtergreifung*, and the meeting, two-and-a-half weeks later, between Hitler and representatives of the most powerful corporations, at which he sought to present his governmental intentions and to solidify the alliance, and he succeeded in doing so.

From a sociological point of view, the military was closely related to the landed aristocracy. What it expected from fascism is easy to recognize. The military forms of organization and the military-like conduct exhibited by the fascists was bound to arouse the approval of the military. Fascism proclaimed the soldier to be the general human prototype and thus raised his prestige in public. The military also hoped from the fascist system a general strengthening of the desire for military preparedness, a new esteem for martial virtues and a central place for the armed forces within the political power system. Not only did the desire for prestige and power play a role, but very concrete material interests did so too. The military expected a firm policy of rearmament, a generous expansion of the army and thus excellent opportunities for advancement within the military hierarchy. These hopes were not disappointed. In the light of the social origins of the officers and their concepts of authority and hierarchy, it is immediately comprehensible that the military sympathized with the destruction of the labour parties and the trade unions which they had always considered as elements dangerous to the state.

During Hitler's conference with the military on February 3rd, 1933, he made his intentions unmistakably clear, including his plan for the imperialist war. In the minutes the following aims are recorded:«. . . The complete extirpation of Marxism. Preparing the ground for acceptance of the thought among youth and the whole population that only battle can save us and that everything had to be subordinated to this goal . . . Re-education of youth and use of every means to strengthen the will to self-defense. Capital punishment for betrayal of country and people. Strictest authoritarian national government. Liquidation of the cancerous sore of democracy . . . How ought political power, when seized, to be used?. . . Perhaps struggling to get new export openings, perhaps – which could certainly be better – occupation of further *Lebensraum* to the east and its ruthless Germanization. ...». The generals were very much in sympathy with these perspectives.[13]

The middle and high officials in the judicial system[14] and the academics at the universities and *Gymnasien* (secondary or grammar schools)[15] had loyally served the authoritarian monarchy in Germany prior to 1918, a regime which in return protected their privileges. Only reluctantly did they agree with the dull Republic in which, in their opinion, trade unions and labour parties were too powerfully represented. In their view, fascism seemed to be able to restore domestic tranquillity and to reassert the powerful position of the Reich in foreign relations. The Weimar Republic was duly required for this naively conceived tolerance.

The churches also considered fascism to be a partner against the common enemy on the left: socialism, liberalism, rationalism, and atheism. Both the churches (the Catholic more so than the Protestant) and fascism had irrationalism as their common ideological base. They also converged on reactionary conceptions of morality, sexuality and family life as well as on the authoritarian and hierarchical principle of organization. Accordingly, important conditions for a political understanding were present.

The churches did not directly support the rise of fascism in Germany, but by according legitimacy to this new regime they contributed eminently to its stabilization once in power.[16] As they were rather complex, the interests of the diverse personnel in the top economic positions cannot be summed up in a short formula. But at least five components can be discerned as relevant for their decision to collaborate with the fascist forces. Above all, fascism could establish a strong executive which would be able to control the economic process and overcome the economic crisis. It was evident that, contrary to the theory of the «free market economy», the market mechanism was no longer capable of regulating the workings of the economy and keeping it going at acceptable growth rates, as in the earlier phases of capitalist development. Due to the alarming rate of unemployment, the stability of the system as a whole was in jeopardy. One crisis solution, the replacement of parliamentary democracy by authoritarianism in the form of a presidential dictatorship in 1930, was not sufficient. Even this regime, which reduced but did not abolish the power of parties and of the legislature, showed itself too weak to master the crisis and stabilize the capitalist system.

The fascist state apparatus thus had to secure the political means for regulating the economy and intervening in the sphere of private property. In order to stabilize private enterprise on the whole, the state had to be capable of restricting it in particular cases. Furthermore the fascist state had to gain a certain autonomy and freedom of decision in opposition to the powerful economic groups.

Fascism not only expected to overcome the economic crisis, but also to overcome it in a certain way. It was important to thrust the costs of the crisis and of crisis management on to the broad masses and to achieve an optimal profit for the big corporations. The immense fiscal spendings with which the fascist state apparatus created jobs and again set the economy in motion, were not primarily applied to social investments and improvements in the infra-structure of society (schools, hospitals, housing, parks, streets, and dams), but to the rearmament industry. In this sphere, because production is not to be seriously hampered by lack of money on the part of the consumers and the uncertainties of the market, profits are at a maximum and secured in the long run by state guarantees.

The rearmament policy corresponded to the mentality of followers of fascism and to the aims of its élite cadres, for it strengthened the role of the military within society and the military power of the state in foreign relations. As the rearmament drive also corresponded to the interests of the military, the most important controllers of the fascist power system converged at this level: the fascist party, the most powerful economic groups and the military.

The economic power groups also expected the preservation of their interests by a fascist power system in the field of foreign policy. German and Italian imperialism in particular came off badly during the partitioning of the world at the end of the 19th century, and neither nation had been able to improve its position in World War I. Fascism could finally have rendered possible a determined policy of expansion and satisfied the imperialist desires of great capital. On this matter, the interests of the large concerns concurred again with the aims of the fascist government and the hopes of the fascist rank and file. In his speech of January 27th, 1932, Hitler had already pointed out to the leading industrialists the connection between fascist *Herrenrasse* ideologies and imperialist interests in the economy.[17]

These aims – rearmament, the raising of profits, and imperialist expansion, – could not be realized within the framework of bourgeois democracy. As long as there were trade unions and labour parties, as long as there was the possibility of public and radical criticism, and as long as there were free elections, these goals would trigger strong resistance. The fascist state thus had to be freed from democratic obstacles and the obligations normal in a constitutional state. The left had to be destroyed. Bourgeois democracy had to be replaced by a dictatorship which could make the necessary decisions without any hindrance.

Considering the interests of the entrepreneurs and industrialists, it is easily comprehensible that they had no objections to the abolition of democracy. They could realize their aims much better – as the German monarchy before 1914 had shown – if parties, unions and parliament did not exist or were without political influence. The direct way, via the political descision-making apparatus, government and bureaucracy, promised better results and greater predictability. In this fashion the influence of parties and parliament, which were at least partly exposed to the influences of the lower classes, was by-passed. These influences were sufferable as long as economic growth left room for granting concessions to wage-earners without endangering profits. With the economic crisis, this free play decreased. Democracy became a principal obstacle to the realization of profits and to the necessary reinvestment – to say nothing of its inability to neutralize the threatening dissatisfaction of the masses.

On February 20th, 1933 Hitler, then Chancellor, once again outlined his program for the impending destruction of democracy before an audience of influential industrialists. The industrial representatives were then glad to place the necessary monetary means for the approaching election campaign at the disposal of the NSDAP.[18]

The destruction of all democratic organizations not only offered the advantage of a policy of armament and imperialist expansion for the entrepreneurs, but also the restoration of their authority in the factories. In Germany as in Italiy, the autonomous representative organizations of the wage-earners – factory councils and unions – were dissolved. The entrepreneurs again became «Herr im eigenen Hause», the workers and white-collar workers again became subordinates unable to defend themselves.

Thus fascism not only guaranteed the entrepreneurs the elimination of all dangers presented by the revolutionary working class movement, it also annihilated all gains and rights secured by the reformist working class movement in their one-hundred-year fight: free organizations of wage-earners, the right to bargain, and co-determination in question of wages and hours.

The Weaknesses of the Left

The likelihood of a fascist success did not depend solely on the problem of how severely the socio-economic crisis affected the masses, of the nature of their political and ideological traditions or how the ruling class behaved . Such a supposition would smack of fatalistic determinism: fascism seen as a «natural» event which happens inevitably under certain conditions – conditions that make resistance to it senseless. In fact, fascism was a product of power constellations in which the working-class organization also played an essential rôle.

The fascists were successful because until 1933 the left was unable to work out common policies against the NSDAP. We cannot go into detail here why Communists and Social Democrats fought each other as vehemently as they did their common enemy. Only with the establishment of the fascist dictatorship in 1933 did the turning-point come. Fascist terror affected Social Democrats and Communists alike and painfully brought home to them the need to unite at least against fascism. However the common front came too late seriously to endanger the Nazi grip on power once consolidated. Fortunately, the left in other countries learnt some lessons from the German debacle. When, in February 1934, the fascist groups in Paris made their (badly prepared) attempt to overthrow the French parliament, Socialists and Communists united to form a common-front resistance which finally repulsed the fascist offensive and in 1936 resulted in a popular front government.

Particular Conditions in Germany

Now the question arises why fascism was particularly strong in Germany. Three factors should be emphasized in explaining the success of the NSDAP:

1. Compared with the Western industrial states, Germany had followed a special course of development leading to a stable and long-pervasive authoritarian monarchy.[19] Due to the long habituation to authoritarian ways of thinking and conduct and the lack of liberal and democratic traditions, the German bourgeoisie was more susceptible to authoritarian and fascist ideologies than its English, French and Belgian counterparts.

2. The German *Reich* finally lost World War I, which it had started, hoping for a European super-power position. The nationalistically conditioned masses saw themselves disappointed and cheated. After the left had proved its inability to make fundamental changes in 1918–19 and parliamentary democracy had been unable to guarantee social security, they turned to the movement which promised revenge for this defeat, the NSDAP. In the agitation of the National Socialists revanchism, anti-communism and anti-Semitism, were the principal points of attraction. The English and French people did not suffer from such a collective national frustration.

3. The impact of the great economic crisis had been more widely felt by the middle and working classes in Germany than in the other capitalist industrial countries in Europe. The German *Reich* was weakened economically by the war and by reparati-

ons and losses of territory. The German middle classes had lost their financial reserves through war-loans and inflation so that the depression immediately threatened their social and economic position. Other industrial nations could respond to the economic upheavals by further exploiting their colonies. But in 1918 Germany had lost its colonial possessions, which were not very important anyhow. Thus to maintain profits, German capital was forced to intensify the exploitation of the wage-earners in its own country.

In terms of industrial growth and colonial aspirations, Italy and Germany had essential features in common. Both countries were united rather late, and both had entered the industrial revolution at a later stage than Britain and France and for these reasons came off badly during the early scramble for colonies. After 1870, however, the German *Reich* had risen so rapidly that at the turn of the century it had taken the top position among the European industrial nations. The belated but rapid growth of the economy and population in Germany is shown by the following tables.

	Population (in millions)[20]		
	Germany	England	France
1870	41	31	37
1910	65	45	40

	Percentage of world industrial production[21]		
	Germany	England	France
1870	13	32	10
1913	16	14	6

When Germany entered the imperialist arena, the other powers had already established their colonial empires. The colonial possessions in 1914 were distributed as follows:[22]

	area (million km²)	population (million)
Germany	2,9	12,3
France	10,6	55,5
England	33,5	393,5

As German capital was prevented from investing in the African, Asian and Australian colonies, it had to exploit the more problematic possibilities of occupying positions in formally autonomous countries in America and Europe:

	Capital investments in billion Mark before 1914		
Invested in	England	France	Germany
America	37	4	10
Asia	11	1	4
Africa	10	7	2
Australia	8	0	1
Europe	4	23	18
Total sum	70	35	35

Before 1914, the economic strength of German capitalism was extremely disproportional to its expansionist possibilities as compared with the other industrial countries. From this disproportion resulted the demand of German imperialism for sources of raw material, cheap labour and favourable investment possibilities similar to those England, France and Belgium possessed in their colonies, and the demand for a redistribution of the world.

During World War I the German Reich tried to bring about a redistribution of the world by military power. Its war aims included extensive annexations reaching from the Eastern French regions to the west of Russia which could have resulted in the hegemony of Germany in Europe and a position of global supremacy in connection with the middle-African colonial empire.[23] This attempt failed, but it did not weaken German imperialism to the extent that it gave up its aims completely. After having quelled the socialist revolution in 1918–19 and after having consolidated their forces during the subsequent period, imperialist interests began to organize a new attempt at military expansion.[24]

After 1918 the parliamentary party-state was no longer adequate for a determined imperialist policy. The colonial imperialism of the period before 1914 could still be realized by means of parliamentary democracy in the Western countries: the labour parties had no decisive influence (parts of them, particularly in Britain, even supported colonial expansion), and the upper classes still held power tightly in their hands. After 1918, however, power had shifted. Although socialist attempts at revolution during the years 1918 – 1923 could be quelled in all European countries, the labour parties and unions preserved a very important political influence. That is true for the countries discussed here – Italy and Germany – as well as for other capitalist countries in Europe. As a result of the workers' experience in World War I, any attempt to launch a new policy of imperialist expansion was likely to meet with stiff resistance.

The imperialist interests – if they wanted to stick to their aims – had no other possibility than to eliminate these organizations. This aim was an essential reason for union with National Socialism, for this party not only promised the complete destruction of labour organizations, but was also able to apply new suggestive techniques for a total mobilization of all resources, manpower as well as material, for the imperialist war. This expansionist program, proclaimed by Hitler since 1925, included conquest of greater parts of Western Russia besides the states of East and South-East Europe and thus conformed widely to the war aims of German imperialism for World War I.

The upper classes in the Western countries had evidently no reason to unite with fascism from such considerations. The powers which had divided the world in the 19th century tended to preserve their possessions against the competitors who had come too late. They fought World War I for the preservation of the status quo. On the whole this aim was achieved.

The different behaviour of the upper classes in Germany and Italy, as compared with élites in other Western industrial countries, might also have been the result of different political and intellectual traditions apart form their concrete interests.

In Germany up to 1918 the upper classes had been accustomed to a form of state which gave the entrepreneurs the possibility of keeping their workers in a position of subservience, safeguarding their interests at the level of political decision-making, politically suppressing the labour organizations, as happened at the time of the *Sozialistengesetze* from 1878 to 1890. After 1918 it was still beyond their conceptual framework, their set of beliefs, to respect the interests of the unions, even to accept their existence as legitimate partners, and to consider changing the social structure by means of parliamentary democracy. When the labour movement seemed uncontrollable and the economy crisis-ridden, National Socialism presented itself to the propertied upper classes as the most convenient opportunity to stem the tide of further democratization, a vehicle for a possible return to the stable authority patterns of the Imperial era. It was also a means whereby to cast off the impediments to German re-armament imposed by Versailles and enable Germany once again to fight for supremacy in Europe.

NOTES

[1] A. Tasca, *Glauben, gehorchen, kämpfen. Aufstieg des Faschismus*, Europa Verlag, Wien-Frankfurt-Zürich 1969, p. 124.

[2] H. Steiner, *Soziale Strukturveränderungen im modernen Kapitalismus*, Dietz Verlag, Berlin 1967, p. 12; Steiner compiles the statistical data of the social structure of Germany from 1882 – 1965.

[3] The small shopkeeper and craftsman, who had saved some ten thousand marks, now in fact was expropriated: on February 10th, 1923 one pound of bread cost 2200 marks. The big owners of the means of production were able to produce extremely cheaply (they paid money that was undergoing rapid depreciation as a result of inflation to their workers in return for their production of real goods). As a result, they were able to expand even further by buying the small bankrupt enterprises and now held a favourable position on new export markets because of low domestic costs.

[4] From Jan. 1919 to June 1920 the Social Democrats (SPD) and the left liberals (DDP) lost a remarkable proportion of their vote to the right: the German National People's Party (DNVP) and the right wing liberals (DVP) gained large support. The SPD declined from 37.9 to 21.6 per cent, the DDP from 18.6 to 8.3 per cent. The DNVP increased from 10.3 to 14.9 per cent and the DVP from 4.4 to 13.9 per cent.

[5] A. Tyrell, *Führer befiehl . . . Selbstzeugnisse aus der «Kampfzeit» der NSDAP*, Droste Verlag, Düsseldorf 1969, p. 379.

[6] W. Abendroth, *Antagonistische Gesellschaft und politische Demokratie*, Luchterhand Verlag, Neuwied-Berlin 1967, p. 26.

[7] M. Broszat, *Der Staat Hitlers*, Deutscher Taschenbuch Verlag, München 1969, p. 50 and 52.

[8] A. Weber, *Soziale Merkmale der NSDAP-Wähler*, Diss. Freiburg 1969; see also: H.A. Winkler, «Mittelstandsbewegung oder Volkspartei? Zur sozialen Basis der NSDAP»; M. H. Kater, «Sozialer Wandel in der NSDAP im Zuge der nationalsozialistischen Machtergreifung» (papers at the *Historikertag* in West Germany in 1974).

[9] A considerable part of the followers of the NSDAP expected anti-monopolist measures and a kind of middle-class-socialism, which they called «Stände-Staat». In the summer of 1934 the most influential groups of this movement, the leading groups of the SA, were murdered by the

129

Hitler government. In 1935 the organizations of the *Mittelstand* were deprived of their influence and incorporated into the industrial organizations dominated by big capital. (See A. Schweitzer, *Big Business in the Third Reich*, Indiana University Press, Bloomington 1964; Ch.Bloch, *Die SA und die Krise des NS-Regimes 1934*, Suhrkamp-Verlag, Frankfurt 1970).

[10] The controversy over the relationship between politics and economics both before and after the seizure of power is dealt with in the following publications: *Das Argument* 41 and 47 (articles by Mason, Czichon, Eichholtz/Gossweiler); in Gossweiler, Kühnl, Opitz, *Faschismus: Entstehung und Verhinderung*, Röderberg Verlag Frankfurt/Main 1972; in Kühnl (Ed.) *Texte zur Faschismusdiskussion I: Positionen und Kontroversen*, Rowohlt Verlag, Reinbek b. Hamburg 1974 (in particular the articles by Opitz and Schäfer). A good survey of the process of fascist intrusion into German society is D. Stegman, «Zum Verhältnis von Grossindustrie und Nationalsozialismus 1930–33. Ein Beitrag zur Geschichte der sogenannten Machtergreifung» in *Archiv für Sozialgeschichte* 13, 1975; pp. 399–483. In my opinion fascism is not to be understood as a mere tool of capital, but as a spontaneously developed mass movement representing an autonomous factor in politics. Big capital did not merely stand to profit from fascist policies. Industrial and financial interests also actively influenced the policy of the fascist government in Germany in the field of social and economic policy as well as in matters relating to war aims. As a result, fascism can neither be described as an illustration of «the primacy of politics» nor as a reflection of the economy. The relationship between the fascist leadership and big capital should rather be defined as an alliance between two partners in need of each other.

[11] Text in: Internationales Militärtribunal, vol. XXXIII, p. 531 ff, published in: R. Kühnl (Ed.), *Der deutsche Faschismus in Quellen und Dokumenten*, Pahl Rugenstein Verlag, Cologne 1975, Dok. Nr. 90, p. 160–162.

[12] See Dok. Nr. 91a and 96, in: R. Kühnl. *Der deutsche Faschismus*, p. 163–164 and 172–174.

[13] Text in: *Vierteljahreshefte für Zeitgeschichte* 2 (1954), p. 434–435.

[14] Cf. with respect to German fascism: H. Mommsen, *Beamtentum im Dritten Reich*, Deutsche Verlagsanstalt, Stuttgart 1966; I. Staff, *Justiz im Dritten Reich*, Fischer Bücherei, Frankfurt/Main- Hamburg 1964; H.and E. Hannover, *Politische Justiz 1918–1933*, Fischer Bücherei, Frankfurt/Main 1966.

[15] Concerning the attitude of the academic teachers cf. H.P. Sleuel, *Deutschlands Bekenner, Professoren zwischen Kaiserreich und Diktatur*, Sherz Verlag, Bern-Munich-Vienna 1968.

[16] Documents in: R. Kühnl, *Der deutsche Faschismus*, Dok. Nr. 113–121, p. 210–226.

[17] The speech is published in: M. Domarus (Ed.), *Hitler. Reden und Proklamationen 1932–1945*, vol. I, Domarus Verlag, Würzburg 1962.

[18] Internationales Militärtribunal, vol. XXXV, p. 42 ff.

[19] The causes, forms and results of this peculiar German development are discussed in: R. Kühnl, *Formen bürgerlicher Herrschaft. Liberalismus und Faschismus*, Rowohlt Verlag, Reinbek b. Hamburg 1971, p. 64 ff.; G. Lukács, *Die Zerstörung der Vernunft*, Luchterhand Verlag, Neuwied 1961: H. Plessner, *Die verspätete Nation*, Kohlhammer Verlag, Stuttgart 1959; K. D. Bracher, *Die deutsche Diktatur*, Verlag Kiepenheuer und Witsch, Cologne 1969; B. Moore, *Social Origins of Dictatorship and Democracy*, The Penguin Press, Harmondsworth 1967.

[20] *Sachwörterbuch der Geschichte Deutschlands und der deutschen Arbeiterbewegung*, Dietz Verlag, Berlin 1969, vol I, p 807.

[21] ibid. p. 811.

[22] ibid. p. 947.

[23] As to this complex cf. F. Fischer. *Griff nach der Weltmacht. Die Kriegszielpolitik der kaiserlichen Deutschland 1914/18*, Droste Verlag, Düsseldorf 1964.

[24] Already in 1925 Gustav Stresemann, Minister of Foreign Affairs, wrote in a letter to Wilhelm von Hohenzollern: «The third big task is to change the Eastern border, to win back Danzig, the Polish corridor and to change the border in upper Silesia». The German Peoples Party (DVP), to which Stresemann belonged, had very close relations to big capital. (The letter is published in: G. Stresemann, *Vermächtnis. Der Nachlass in drei Bänden*, ed. by H. Bernhard, vol. II, Berlin 1932, p. 553–555.) See also the documents in: R.Kühnl, *Der deutsche Faschismus*, op. cit. p. 57–72.

The Conditions of Fascist Victory:

Towards a Geoeconomic-Geopolitical Model for the Explanation of Violent Breakdowns of Competitive Mass Politics

BERNT HAGTVET AND STEIN ROKKAN

The Problem

Scholars have diverged in their definitions and their interpretations of fascism ever since the March on Rome. The divergencies increased dramatically after Hitler's *Machtergreifung* in 1933 and the Dollfuss coup in 1934: what did these ideologies, these movements, these strategies have in common? was there a core concept of fascism and how could this essence be identified in the welter of complex interactions in each concrete development?

However difficult this search for conceptual communalities, there was, by the time of the final confrontation during World War II, not much doubt about the actual alignment of cases:

Five of the countries of Western Europe had succumbed to movements of this general type and been turned into plebiscitarian one-party dictatorships.

However divergent their national trajectories, these five countries, Italy, Germany. Austria, Spain and Portugal had succumbed to similar fates.

1. They had all experienced a number of *competitive elections* under broadening suffrage criteria and had passed through a shorter or longer period of *rapid mobilization* of new strata of the territorial population under mass parties and parallel movements and agencies:

2. They had all run into a series of *constitutional crises* in the management of these waves of competitive mobilization, and had finally succumbed to a movement determined to put an end to such pluralistic tolerance and to introduce *monolithic control* of mass politics:

3. Finally, these monolithic movements had all reached their positions of dominance through extensive use of *extra-legal violence* against political opponents and had maintained their power through ruthless mobilization against internal no less than external enemies.

Other countries in Western Europe had been through similar phases of development: extensions of the suffrage, phases of competitive mass mobilization, sequences of crises in the management of the strains generated by such competitive pressures. *But they had not succumbed to monolithic control under one mass movement.* Some of the countries came near to the breaking point: England during the Irish crisis just before World War I, Finland during the first couple of decades after Independence, France in 1934. But of the seventeen countries within what we would today call Western Europe, only five fell prey to a monolithic movement dedicated to the overthrow of the pluralist system of multi-party competition.

We exclude from this reckoning the whole of Eastern Europe. In none of these countries do we find anything approaching the step-by-step sequence that led up to the fascist victories in the five Western cases. What we find here are at best brief and erratic periods of competitive politics preceding the onset of military-authoritarian rule and, after World War II, the victory of monolithic parties exerting strict control over all sources of pluralism. The one exception is Czechoslovakia. Here we find an impressive series of regularly organized competitive elections after Independence, but no endogenously generated victory of monolithic forces: National Socialism was imposed from outside, through military occupation.

There were obviously movements of fascist-National Socialist inspiration all across Eastern as well as Western Europe and they are certainly all worth detailed scrutiny. Our concern in this analysis, however, is not with the proliferation of movements or ideologies of this type, but with the *conditions for their success within systems of competitive politics* with the characteristics of the national coalition structure which made it possible for such movements to seize central power and to establish effective monolithic control. This leaves us with the five Western cases: Germany and Italy, Austria, Spain and Portugal.

To avoid misunderstanding: we do not claim that the *régimes* established in each of these five cases were «fascist». There were indeed important differences in the structure and the contents of the victorious ideologies and these were clearly reflected in the institutions built up and the practices followed by the victors. Our analysis concentrates on the one feature these five cases have in common: the sequence leading from a series of competitive elections under multi-party systems to the victory of a monolithic alliance and the abolition of rights of pluralist opposition. This is the sequence we find in our five cases[1] and not in the other twelve. How can we account for these differences in the outcomes of the mobilization processes between these five and the others? How can we identify the prerequisites for success and the conditions leading to failure in the struggle to maintain competitive pluralism under full-suffrage mobilization?

We propose to start our search for answers by reviewing some possible leads generated from a general model of democratization processes in Europe. This model was originally constructed in an attempt to offer a parsimonious set of explanations of the well-documented *sequences of suffrage extensions and party alignments* in Western Europe.[2] The model has gone through a number of stages of recasting and has still to be worked out in detail component by component, but it has proved useful as an engine for the generation of hypotheses for testing through comparisons by pairs of countries.[3] So far, the model has never been explicitly used to generate hypotheses about the constellations of conditions making for successes or failures in the maintenance of pluralist competition in the later phases of democratization: this would be an extension beyond its original purpose but we see interesting possibilities in this direction and would like to explore these in this paper.

We have been encouraged in this endeavor through a quirk of inductive «serendipity»: the five cases of failure to maintain competitive mobilization occur in the cells for «late centre formation» «frustrated imperialism» or «arrested nation-building» in the «conceptual map of Europe» generated by the model.

The Model

The model spans the entire history of state formation, nation-building and mass politics in Western Europe: it represents an attempt to identify the crucial variables in the long and complex process that led up to the current constellations of territories, economies and political alignment systems.

The essential message of the model is simple enough:

you cannot explain the marked variations in the structuring of mass politics in Western Europe without going far back in history, without analyzing the differences in the initial conditions and the early processes of territorial organization, of state building, and of resource combination.

In practice this means going back to the High Middle Ages, to an analysis of the decisive differences in the conditions of centre formation and territorial control. These constellations of conditions set the stage for the further steps of development: the fragmentation of the Holy Roman Empire, the build-up of strong dynastic states at the edges of that territory, the violent upsurge of the capitalist economy, and the establishment of Western empires across the oceans.

The model does not cover the whole of Europe: to keep it within manageable bounds it concentrates on the Europe of the *Celtic*, the *Latin* and the *Germanic* peoples. There is some fuzziness on the Eastern marches: most of the accounting schemes include Finland because of the heavy dominance of the Swedes until 1809 but excludes Estonia, Hungary and the Slavic states established after 1918.

The model starts out from a simple classification of sources of variation at this take-off stage: it identifies as a crucial *economic* variable the strength of the city network and the concomitant flow of long-distance trade, it identifies as a *territorial* variable par excellence the military-administrative strength of dynastic centres, and it suggests an equally important *cultural* variable, the ethnic-linguistic homogeneity of the populations controlled from given centres.

The model proceeds to a corresponding specification of variables for the next stage of development: the consolidation of territorial states and the restructuring of the geo-economy during the troubled decades of internecine conflict from 1500 to 1648.

The model does not specify the same broad range of variables for the period of consolidation from the Treaty of Westphalia to the French Revolution: for this stage of development the model retains only one source of variation, the strength of representative institutions during the reign of Absolutism.

This complex set of *Precondition Variables* offer a spring-board for the analysis of a set of *Intervening Process Variables* in the model: these are the variables posited as essential in any systematic account of the *generation of cleavage fronts* during the century and a half after the French Revolution. This was again a period of great political turmoil: the French Revolution set the stage for a wide variety of efforts of centralization, territorial consolidation, national self-assertion; and the Industrial Revolution brought about even greater contrasts between the economically advanced core territories and the stagnant provinces and peripheries. The interaction of these parallel Revolutions generated complex variations in cleavage structures and these in their turn produced marked differences in the style and the structure of the emerging politics of mass mobilization across Western Europe.

This complex set of *Intervening Process Variables* finally offer a spring-board for the analysis of the *Explicanda,* the variations in political response structures. Here again the model specifies two stages and three sectors of variation. At the first stage,

133

questions are asked about the *structuring of political alternatives:* what sorts of options were set for the emerging mass citizenries and how stable, how vulnerable did these structures turn out to be? At the final stage questions are asked about the *decisive dimensions of mass alignments* in each territorial system: what is the weight of ethnic-religious-cultural commitments, what difference can be found between ascending and stagnant classes and strata, between the old and the new middle class, between the peasantry and the industrial working class?

The schematic structure of the model is given in Fig. 1. Each of the variables retained are indicated in simple keyword style: full explication would take us far beyond the confines of this one paper.

The variables listed in the scheme can be used to characterize units at different levels of complexity. Reading the scheme *en aval,* to use the term so dear to the *Annales* school, you can use the variables as *direct* attributes of historical regions, *pays, Landschaften,* or as *contextual* attributes of the larger units they are integrated into (example: Alsace can be characterized directly as located within the «dorsal spine» on var. I:T, but contextually as integrated into the centralizing *French* system during the 17th–18th century, var. II:T.) Using the scheme *en amont,* upstream, you

Fig 1. *THE PRIMARY ELEMENTS OF THE MODEL*

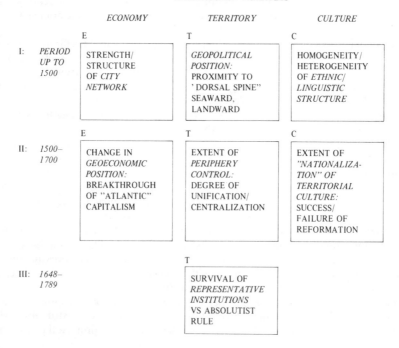

PRECONDITION VARIABLES

		ECONOMY	TERRITORY	CULTURE
		E	T	C
I:	PERIOD UP TO 1500	STRENGTH/ STRUCTURE OF *CITY* NETWORK	GEOPOLITICAL POSITION: PROXIMITY TO 'DORSAL SPINE" SEAWARD, LANDWARD	HOMOGENEITY/ HETEROGENEITY OF *ETHNIC/ LINGUISTIC STRUCTURE*
		E	T	C
II:	1500– 1700	CHANGE IN *GEOECONOMIC POSITION:* BREAKTHROUGH OF "ATLANTIC" CAPITALISM	EXTENT OF PERIPHERY CONTROL: DEGREE OF UNIFICATION/ CENTRALIZATION	EXTENT OF "NATIONALIZA- TION" OF TERRITORIAL CULTURE: SUCCESS/ FAILURE OF REFORMATION
			T	
III:	1648– 1789		SURVIVAL OF REPRESENTATIVE INSTITUTIONS VS ABSOLUTIST RULE	

INTERVENING PROCESS VARIABLES:
INTERACTION OF
"NATIONAL" WITH " INDUSTRIAL" REVOLUTION
1789–1920s

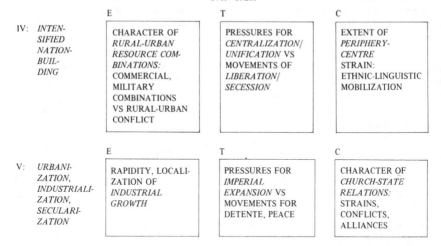

		E	T	C
IV:	*INTEN-SIFIED NATION-BUIL-DING*	CHARACTER OF *RURAL-URBAN RESOURCE COM-BINATIONS:* COMMERCIAL, MILITARY COMBINATIONS VS RURAL-URBAN CONFLICT	PRESSURES FOR *CENTRALIZATION/ UNIFICATION* VS MOVEMENTS OF *LIBERATION/ SECESSION*	EXTENT OF *PERIPHERY-CENTRE* STRAIN: ETHNIC-LINGUISTIC MOBILIZATION

		E	T	C
V:	*URBANI-ZATION, INDUSTRIALI-ZATION, SECULARI-ZATION*	RAPIDITY, LOCALI-ZATION OF *INDUSTRIAL GROWTH*	PRESSURES FOR *IMPERIAL EXPANSION* VS MOVEMENTS FOR DETENTE, PEACE	CHARACTER OF *CHURCH-STATE RELATIONS:* STRAINS, CONFLICTS, ALLIANCES

EXPLICANDA:
VARIATIONS IN POLITICAL RESPONSE STRUCTURES
1848–1950s

		Rights: extension	*System alternatives*	*Party alternatives*
VI:	*THE STRUCTU-RING OF ALTERNA-TIVES*	SEQUENCING OF STEPS TOWARDS *UNIVERSALIZATION OF POLITICAL RIGHTS*	FREQUENCY/ INTENSITY OF *CRISES OF TRANSITION.* EXTENT OF VIOLENT DISRUPTIONS	SEQUENCING OF STEPS IN FORMATION OF *SYSTEM OF PARTY ALTERNATIVES*

		R	S	P
VII:	*CONSEQUENT MASS ALIGNMENTS*	CLASS/CULTURE CONDITIONING OF LEVELS/TYPES OF *PARTICIPATION*	CLASS/CULTURE CONDITIONING OF *ATTITUDES TO SYSTEM:* ACCEPTANCE VS REJECTION	CLASS/CULTURE CONDITIONING OF *PARTY CHOICE*

start off with the territorial units established after, say, 1945, and characterize these either *directly* or through aggregations of the *values for their constituent units* (e.g. France may be administratively highly centralized but not ethnically/linguistically homogeneous (var. IV:C) because of the incorporation of such diverse territories as Britanny, Flanders, Lorraine, Alsace, Savoie and Nice, Occitania and the Basque region). In the accounting schemes cited below you will normally find that we follow the *en amont* procedure, but in one case we find it essential to divide a globe territorial

135

unit into two sets of constituent ones: the Northern vs. the Southern provinces of France.

The model seeks to balance contextual totality against systematic parsimony. No single explanatory or intervening variable can be linked up with a dependent variable in isolation from the context: whether across systems or across stages. And no variable can justify its position in the scheme simply because it helps to describe the conditions in one particular system at one particular stage: to qualify for inclusion in the analysis a variable must specify a necessary or a sufficient condition for a patent difference in later-stage outcomes between at least two distinct systems. So far, only parts of the model have been subjected to detailed testing against such criteria. The bulk of the efforts thus far have concentrated on the link-ups between «Cleavage Generation» variables (rows IV and V in Fig. 1.) and variables for the «Structuring of Political Alternatives» (row VI), particularly the steps in the extension of suffrage rights and the genealogies of party systems. An attempt has also been made at a systematization of the links between the Precondition Variables and the Intervening Process Variables: these links have been expressed in a «topological typology» of territories, in what has been called a «conceptual map of Europe»[4]. But very little has been done to link up variables across the entire range of stages in the model: this joint paper in fact represents a first serious effort in this direction.[5]

To make it possible to assess the potentialities of the model we shall first review quickly some of the simpler accounting schemes generated through the concatenations of several variables over time and then proceed to the discussion of conditions making for fascist victories.

A «Conceptual Map» of Europe

Three of the Precondition Variables combine to produce a *conceptual map of Europe*. This is a schematized system of co-ordinates generated through the combination of one territorial, one economic and one cultural variable in the model:

I:T Geopolitical position
I:E Strength/structure of city network
II:C Outcome of Reformation.

Variables *I:T* and *I:E* combine to produce a five-step *West-East* typology.[6] Variable *II:C* divides the Europe of the Celtic, Latin and Germanic peoples into three slices from *South to North*. This gives the two-dimensional map set out in Fig. 2.

This effort of schematization represents an attempt to come to grips with the «great paradox of European development»: the fact that the strongest and the most durable systems emerged at the periphery of the old Empire; the heartlands, the Italian and German territories, remained fragmented and dispersed until the nineteenth century.

To quote from an early presentation of the «map»:

To reach some understanding of this paradox we have to reason in several steps:

1. The heartland of the old Western Empire was studded with cities in a broad trade route belt stretching from the Mediterranean to the east as well as west of the Alps northward to the Rhine and the Danube;
2. This «city belt» was at the same time the stronghold of the Roman Catholic Church; this territory had a high density of cathedrals, monasteries, and ecclesiastical principalities;

Fig 2. A «CONCEPTUAL MAP» OF 16TH–18TH CENTURY WESTERN EUROPE*

THE «STATE-ECONOMY» DIMENSION: WEST-EAST AXIS

Territorial centres / City networks	Weak Weak *Seaward peripheries*	Strong Strong *Seaward empire-nations*	Weak Strong *City-state Europe*			Strong Weak *Landward empire-nations*		Strong Weak *Landward buffers*
Conditions of consolidation	Distant from city belt	Close to city belt	Integrated into larger system	Consocia-tional formation	Fragmented until 19th cent.	Close to city belt	Distant from city belt	
Protestant state Church	Iceland — Norway ↓ Scotland Wales — *England*	*Denmark*				*Sweden* *Prussia*	Finland	
Mixed territories				*Netherlands* *Switzerland*	Hanse Germany Rhineland	Bohemia		Baltic territories
National Catholic Church	Ireland Brittany	*France*	«Lotharingia» Burgundy Arclatum			*Bavaria* — Poland →	Poland	
Counter-Reformation		*Spain* *Portugal*	Belgium ↑ Catalonia		Italy	*Austria* — Hungary →	Hungary	

THE «STATE-CULTURE» DIMENSION: SOUTH-NORTH AXIS

* Arrows indicate changes in geopolitical position. Territories *underlined* were sovereign powers 1648–1789.

3. The very density of established centres within this territory made it difficult to single out any one as superior to all others; there was no geography-given core area for the development of a strong territorial system;
4. The resurrection of the Holy Roman Empire under the leadership of the four German tribes did not help to unify the territory; the emperors were prey to shifting electoral alliances; many of them were mere figureheads and the best and the strongest of them expended their energies in quarrels with the Pope and with the Italian cities;
5. By contrast, it proved much easier to develop effective core areas at the edges of the city-studded territories of the old Empire; in these regions, centres could be built up under less competition and could achieve command of the resources in peripheral areas too far from the cities in the central trade belt;
6. The earliest successes in such efforts of system-building at the edges of the old Empire came in the west and in the north, in France, in England, in Scandinavia, later also in Spain; in all these cases the dynasties in the core areas were able to command resources from peripheral territories largely beyond the reach of the cities of the central trade belt;
7. The second wave of successful centre-building took place on the landward side: first the Habsburgs, with their core area in Austria; then the eastern march of the German Empire; next the Swedes; and finally, and decisively, the Prussians;
8. The fragmented middle belt of cities and petty states was the scene of endless onslaughts, counter-moves and efforts of reorganization during the long centuries from Charlemagne to Bismarck: firstly, the French monarchs gradually took over the old Lotharingien-Burgundian buffer zone from Provence to Flanders and incorporated such typical trade cities as Avignon, Aix, and Lyons; secondly, the key cities to the north of the Alps managed to establish a defense league against all comers and gradually built up the Swiss confederation; similar leagues were established along the Rhine and across the Baltic and the North Sea but never managed to establish themselves as sovereign territorial formations; thirdly, the Habsburgs made a number of encroachments both on the west and on the east of the belt and for some time controlled the crucial territories at the mouth of the Rhine triggering the next successful effort of consociational confederation, the United Netherlands; finally in the wake of the French Revolution, Napoleon moved across the middle belt both north and south of the Alps and set in motion a series of efforts of unification which ended with the successes of the Prussians and the Piedmontese in 1870.[7]

A remarkably similar classification of the territories of Western Europe has been proposed by the French geographers Juillard and Nonn.[8] They distinguish between three main types of urban networks and consequently three types of regional structure: the first they call the *modèle rhénan*, the second the *modèle parisien* (three subtypes) and the third they call the *modèle périphérique* (two subtypes). In Map I we have outlined our proposed classification of territories in Europe which is very much in line with the Juillard – Nonn-models. The *modèle rhénan* corresponds to our city belt: Juillard and Nonn place this along the Rhine and in the English Midlands. The *modèle parisien* corresponds to the seaward or the landward centre formations in our conceptual map: Paris, London and Madrid, Munich and Vienna. There is a difference in the classification of Italy, however. Juillard and Nonn consider this a polycephalic constellation of three *Parisien* models: Milan, Rome and Naples. This, of course, is a

The Conceptual Map of the 'State — Economy Dimension' in Western Europe 16 — 17 th century

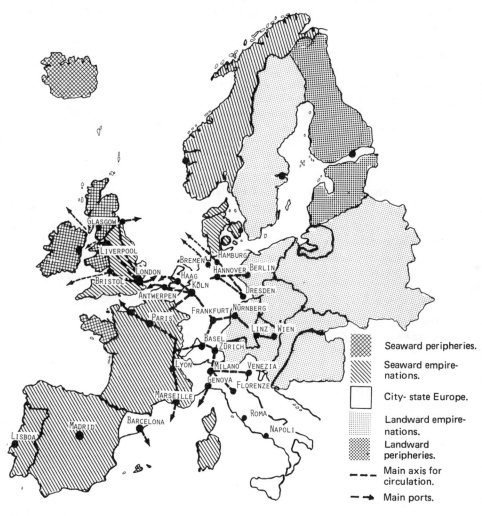

Seaward peripheries.

Seaward empire-nations.

City- state Europe.

Landward empire-nations.

Landward peripheries.

- - - Main axis for circulation.

— ➤ Main ports.

Note:

This map has been drawn with reference to Stein Rokkan's article: "Nation Building. A review of Models and Approaches" in *Current Sociology,* 19, 1971 p 7—38.
The axis of economic/communicational circulation is more or less directly adapted from "The Juillard — Nonn Classification of West European Centre Structures."

Mr. Jonny Pedersen has outlined the map and assisted the editors in preparing it for the volume.

matter of cut-off points in the definition of network structures: what is important is that Italy contains at least three major centres within the same territory. The *modèle périphérique* finally covers the rest of Western Europe: these territories are either regions dominated by externally oriented centres (Dublin-Belfast, Glasgow-Edinburgh, Hamburg-Bremen, Bilbao-Catalonia) or simply backward regions with only weak centres.

The Juillard–Nonn scheme is essentially based on 20th century statistics for the central cities and their regions: for this very reason it is remarkable how close a fit we find with our own historical classification of territories.

Whatever the precise delimitations of each cell in the map, this «typological-topological» scheme has proved useful in our efforts to sort out the preconditions for a broader range of variations across Western Europe at later stages of political development.

Applications to Concrete Tasks of Explanation: Examples

Let us first review the simplest schemes of explanation within this over-all model and then proceed to the discussion of the possibilities of combining this essentially geopolitical scheme with the geo-economic dimensions pinpointed by Wallerstein.

Variations in Sequences of Suffrage Extension

The simplest scheme is probably the one proposed for the explanation of variations in the sequences of *steps toward universal suffrage:*[9]

Fig. 3. *AN ACCOUNTING SCHEME FOR VARIATIONS IN THE PROCESSES LEADING TO UNIVERSAL SUFFRAGE*

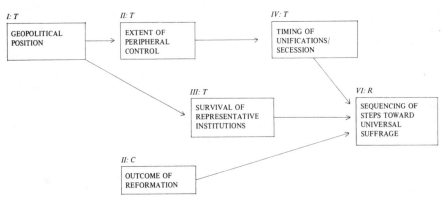

140

The values of the six variables in this scheme were linked up in these combinations:

Stage I	Stage II		Stage III	Stage IV	Stage V
Geopolitical position	Periphery control	Outcome of Reformation	Representative Institutions	Unification/ Secession	Sequencing of steps
Distant from central city belt	*Extensive*	*Protestant domination*	*Minor* interruptions only	*Early unif.*	*Slow:* G. Britain Sweden
—»—	*Extensive*	—»—	—»—	*Late secession*	*Sudden:* Finland
—»—	*Middling*	—»—	*Absolutist rule*	*Earlier secession*	*Slower:* Norway
—»—	—»—	—»—	—»—	*Late secession*	*Slower:* Iceland
Close up to or in city belt	*Minor*	—»—	*Repr. rule*	*Early unif.*	*Slow:* Netherlands
—»—	—»—	—»—	—»—	*Same, but threat of secession*	*Sudden:* Switzerland
—»—	*Middling*	—»—	*Absolutist rule*	*Early unif.*	*Sudden:* Denmark
—»—	*Extensive*	—»—	—»—	*Late unif.*	*Sudden:* Prussia
—»—	—»—	*Nat. Catholicism*	—»—	*Early unif.*	*Sudden:* France
	(any values)	*Counter-Reformation dominant*	—»—	(any value)	*Slow:* Austria Belgium Italy Spain

One message stands out clearly: a long history of continuous centre-building favors a slow, step-by-step, sequence of suffrage extensions. Systems passing abruptly from absolutism to representative rule also tended to pass quickly to maximal suffrage, at least for men: Denmark, Prussia, France. Threats of territorial secession also tended to trigger rapid increase in suffrage: Switzerland after the *Sonderbundkrieg*, Norway in the 1890s, Finland in 1906. By contrast, the countries marked by strong Counter-Reformation traditions generally tended to go through longer series of steps toward full manhood suffrage: Austria, Spain, Belgium, Italy. Rapid democratization was clearly a strategy of national unification against entrenched particularisms, whether social, linguistic or religious. Where the nation-building alliances had had early successes (England, Sweden) there was little need to use this strategy. Where the Catholic Church was particularly well-entrenched, it proved able to slow down the process of democratization and mass mobilization, at least for some time.

Variations in Party Systems

The explanation of variations in the *contents* of mass politics calls for a very different structure of linkage: the focus changes from territoriality to functionality, from external to internal generation of cleavage fronts.

The simplest scheme for the explanation of variations in *party systems* would have to link up at least five conditioning variables with the most distinctive components of the structures of electoral alternatives[10]:

The full combinatorics of this scheme are too complex to warrant presentation in this context. A few simple tables will help to bring out the gist of the scheme.

Fig. 4. *AN ACCOUNTING SCHEME FOR VARIATIONS IN THE STRUCTURE OF PARTY SYSTEMS UNDER FULL SUFFRAGE*

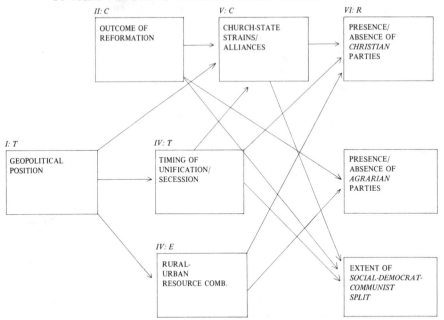

Let us first review the combinations of variables generating differences in the conditions for the emergence of *Christian* party fronts in the competitive pressures for mass mobilization. Conditions for the success of this type of political entrepreneurship differ markedly between the Protestant North and the Catholic South of Western Europe:

Fig 5. *THE «CONCEPTUAL MAP» OF VARIATIONS IN THE MASS POLITICIZATION OF CHURCH-SECT-STATE CONFLICTS*

II:C: *Outcome of reformation*	I:T: Geopolitical position				
	Seaward periphe-ries	Seaward Empire-nations	City Belt	Landward empire-nations	Landward periphe-ries
– Protestant domination, few Catholics					
IV:T: Timing, of unification/ secession		*Denmark:*		*Sweden:*	
– early		Broad Liberal front: recently minor Christian party		Liberals split over prohibition: minor Christian party	

	I:T: Geopolitical position				
II:C: *Outcome of reformation*	Seaward peripheries	Seaward Empire-nations	City Belt	Landward empire-nations	Landward peripheries
– Protestant domination – late	*Iceland:* Broad Agrarian front, *no* Chr. party	*Norway:* Broad Liberal front: split in 1920s. *Significant Christian Party*			*Finland:* Christian movement aggregated within *Nationalist* front
– Significant Catholic minority	*Ulster:* significant Catholic party	*Rest of U.K.:* Christian movements aggregated within *Liberal* front	*Netherlands:* significant Calvinist and Cath. parties. *Rhinel., Germany, Switz.:* Imp. Catholic parties	*Prussia:* Broad Conservative front; *no* Chr. party	
– Catholic domination *V:C: Church-state relations* – Alliance 19th cent.	*Ireland: Church* interests aggr. within *Nationalist* fronts		*Belgium: Strong* Catholic party	*Austria: Strong* Catholic party	
– *Conflict*		*France, Spain:* Church interests defended within *Right* fronts	*German Reich, Italy: Strong* Catholic parties		

The table tells us that the conditions for the emergence of distinctively Christian parties are *most* favorable in the territories of the *city belt*, whether religiously mixed or predominantly Catholic. Such parties are *least* likely to occur in the peripheral territories last to achieve full independence: Iceland, Ireland, Finland. The table also brings out a difference among the long-established Catholic empire-nations at the edges of the city belt: no distinctive Christian parties in the countries where the Church-State conflict was intense and protracted (France, Spain), strong Christian parties wherever there were closer links between Church and State.

A very similar scheme can be established for the identification of the conditions for the emergence of distinctive *Agrarian* parties:

Fig. 6. *THE «CONCEPTUAL MAP» OF VARIATIONS IN THE MASS POLITICI-
ZATION OF RURAL-URBAN CONFLICTS*

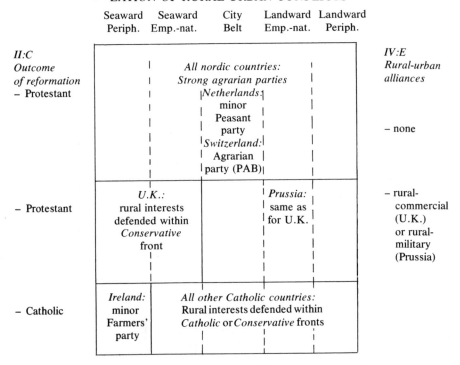

Three of the five key dimensions turn out to discriminate significantly in a parallel scheme proposed for the explanation of variations in the severity of *splits within the working class party fronts* in Western Europe:

144

Fig. 7. A «CONCEPTUAL MAP» OF THE CASES OF DEEP COMMUNIST-
SOCIALIST SPLIT

	Seaward Periph.	Seaward Emp.-nat.	City Belt	Landward Emp.-nat.	Landward Periph.
Prot. IV:T *Timing of unif./ secession* – Early					
– Late	*Iceland:* deep split	*Norway:* split early 1920s	*Reich-Prussia:* deep split during Weimar Rep. ↑		*Finland:* deep split
Cath. V:C: *Church state rel.* – Alliance					
– Conflict		*France, Spain:* deep splits	*Reich-Prussia:* deep split during Weimar Rep. ↓ *Italy:* deep split		

The message is simple: in Protestant Europe the *latest nation-states* to be unified or to secede were most vulnerable to severe splits within the working class; in Catholic Europe the same was the case in the territories which had experienced *the sharpest conflict over Church-State relations*. In both cases there was a clearcut syndrome: difficulties of élite integration in an early phase of nation-building made for strains within the working class leadership and set the stage for deeper Communist-Social Democrat splits than elsewhere in Europe.

The Use of the Model in the Explanation of Fascist Victories

Having given these examples of the basic style of reasoning in this topological-typological effort of systematization we shall now proceed to broaden the range of the «explanatory potential» of the model by adding further dimensions.

The initial accounting scheme generated by the model focused on variations that had largely manifested themselves in each country *by the end of World War I*: variables VI:R and VI:P in Fig. 1.

Can the same basic of variables be used in accounting for the contrasting developments within Europe during the late 'twenties and the 'thirties? Are they of any use in identifying the conditions that made for *victories or defeat for the nationalist-fascist monolithic party fronts* that emerged during this period?

Let us go back to the conceptual maps set out in full detail in Fig. 2. One conclusion is clear: our five cases fall into several distinctive cells of the map; they do not form one single cluster. They do share one basic set of characteristics, however:

they are either located *inside* the central belt of cities from the Mediterranean across the Alps to the North Sea and the Baltic or their territories were historically *closely linked* to this belt, whether on the seaward side as in the cases of Spain and Portugal, or on the landward, as in the cases of Prussia-Austria. But these chosen characterizations suffer from a considerable margin of imprecision: there were other territories within as well as close to the city belt and these did *not* succumb to monolithic movements of the fascist type. To identify a distinctive configuration for the five, to develop an adequate accounting scheme, we have to incorporate *further variables*.

Three variables appear crucial in the further specification of conditions for violent breakdowns in the process of mass democratization.

The first of these was not explicitly spelled out in the original model: it is implicit, however, in the ordering of the basic variable *I:T: Geopolitical Position*. We shall call this component the *Strength of the Imperial Heritage*. The early history of Europe can be telescoped into three successive failures of internally generated empire-building: the fall of Rome, the fragmentation and ultimate disintegration of the Empire of Charlemagne and its German successors, the failure of the Habsburgs to achieve control of Europe from their strongholds in the two corner territories, Austria and the Iberian peninsula. These successive failures left bitter memories of past glory in four territories: in a fragmented Italy, in the vast German congeries of petty princedoms and free cities, in Austria, in Spain and in Portugal.

What made these failures of empire an even greater source of pent-up aggression was the *subsequent peripheralization within the emerging geoeconomics of capitalism*. This is our variable *II:E*: the central variable in Immanuel Wallerstein's pathbreaking reinterpretation of European history since 1492. The opening up of new territories across the Oceans and the rapid expansion of trade set the stage for a gigantic struggle between South and North in Europe: the Habsburgs tried desperately to establish a new great Empire across the dorsal spine of Europe, but to not avail. The Middle Ages had left too strong a heritage of multi-centred diversity: the city-studded belt from Northern Italy to the North Sea, the empire-nations on the seaward and later the landward edges. The decisive fight was fought out between the Habsburgs and France: this ended with bankruptcy and the stalemate treaty of Cateau-Cambrésis in 1559. In the next round, the hegemony moved to the Northwest: Atlantic capitalism established its core territories in the Netherlands and in England and the old strongholds of imperial power in Europe were reduced to what Wallerstein calls «semi-peripheries». The final *dénouement* came with the Treaty of Westphalia and the subsequent division of the Habsburg territories: Austria and Spain were left each in their corner and could no longer hope to achieve mastery in Europe. Portugal, for 62 years a territory under Spain, retained her overseas empire but her influence in European affairs was severely reduced. In the central belt, Germany and Italy were left fragmented and stagnant: both territories strongly marked by imperial traditions, both of them culturally unified through remarkably vigorous standard languages, both of them characterized by dispersed networks of cities and princedoms dominated by patriciates embittered by centuries of stagnation.

The fates of Austria, Spain and Portugal were largely sealed during this stage of geoeconomic restructuring from 1500 to 1789. The trajectories of Germany and Italy were decisively changed in the wake of the French Revolution and the short-lived spurt of empire-building that ended at Waterloo. The Napoleonic wars set the stage for a massive upsurge of nationalism in the two territories and the subsequent spread of the Industrial Revolution increased the pressures for joint action against the hegemo-

146

nic core of world capitalism. The massive movements of territorial unification were triggered through the interaction of the two Revolutions: the National and the Industrial. In fact, the one Revolution fed on the other. The dynamic sectors of the bourgeoisie saw great opportunities in the new industrial technologies but they could only defend themselves against competition from the advanced economies through alliances with unified territorial powers. In addition, the traditionalist elements of the bourgeoisie, the artisans and the family-sized merchant firms, tended to rally to the nationalist fronts simply in the hope that unification would protect them against the worst ravages of rapid industrialization. The representatives of the bourgeois corporations proved unable to solve these problems of national unity against foreign economic pressures at the Frankfurter Parlament in 1848. The next step was an alliance with a stronger territorial power to the east: this was Bismarck's great achievement. He extended the alliance already established in Prussia between the territorial administration and the landowners to a broader alliance with large chunks of the bourgeoisie of Western and Southern Germany: this alliance built up the power of the *Reich* and made it a real threat to the dominant capitalist powers England, France and later the United States. A parallel development took place in Italy. The heartland of the Roman Empire was again unified but there was an important difference in the direction of integration: in Germany, the decisive movement of integration originated in the rural East, in the militarized periphery; in Italy the final decisions were taken in the urban North and the movement spread southward into a stagnant periphery.

Our five cases clearly differ in a number of important variables but they still share three decisive characteristics:

First, the *imperial heritage;*

secondly, the *geoeconomic peripheralization* brought about by the two great waves of capitalist advance, first the restructuring of trade flows in the sixteenth century, secondly the lags in the spread of industrial technology in the nineteenth;

and thirdly, the successive attempts to *reestablish their position in the international system through deliberate military-industrial alliances.*

The *first* of these characteristics can be generated through a combination of two successive territorial variables: *I:T* and *II:T* in Fig. 1.

The *second* characteristic represents a value of variable *II:E Change in Geoeconomic Positions* but this is again linked to the much later variable *V:E Rapidity, Localization of Industrial Growth.*

And the *third* characteristic finally represents one of the possible resource combinations listed under variable *IV:E* in Fig. 1.

However similar in these three variables, the five cases clearly differ in their territory-building histories: *early centre-building* but arrested national integration in Austria and in Spain, early nation-building but *frustrated empire-building* in the case of Portugal, *late centre-building* within culturally highly homogeneous territories in Germany and in Italy.

Let us now go back to the «conceptual map» to pin down these additional sources of differentiation: see Fig. 8.

The recast map brings out the crucial contrasts in territorial fates: the Northwestern geoeconomic core against the peripheralized territories to the South and to the East; the early histories of consolidation in the four corners and, remarkably, at two transition areas in the city belt, the Netherlands and Switzerland; the much later consolidation or secession of the units within the rest of the city belt.

Perhaps the most intriguing of all the comparisons suggested by these juxtaposi-

Fig. 8.   *GEOECONOMICS, GEOPOLITICS AND TERRITORIAL*
CONSOLIDATION: A RECASTING OF THE CONCEPTUAL MAP
FOR WESTERN EUROPE

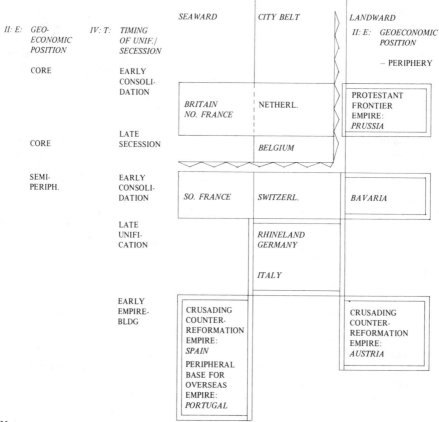

Note:

The territories marked by *double* frames are those that made up the five key cases of violent breakdowns of competitive mass politics. The territories marked by *wavy* frames are those of the "capitalist core" from the 17th century onwards.

tions is the one between *France* and our five of fascist victory cases. France was built up through continuous accretion of territories in all directions from the initial core. This congeries of differently structured units was kept together against heavy odds: the constant threats of «exit» at the borders[11] could only be contained through the build-up of a highly centralized military-bureaucratic machinery, but even this heavy machinery could not move towards full unification of institutional structures during the *ancien régime*. What proved even more important was the extreme unevenness of economic developments: the Northwest was part of the early core of capitalist expansion while the West and the South was increasingly peripheralized. Immanuel Wallerstein, in a fascinating flight of historical imagination, suggests that Northwest France might have lead the world industrially if it had not been for the heavy burden of military-administrative control of the South.[12]The *ancien régime* had left a heritage of great territorial diversity: the Great Revolution and the paroxysm of expansion under Napoleon represented a great leap forward in the building of central institutions and in the unification of national culture but left the territorial élites deeply divided over constitutional fundamentals. France was to oscillate for a century and a half between complex corporate bargaining and centralizing plebiscitarianism. In one sense the *coup d'état* of Louis Napoleon on 2 December, 1851 represents the first case of a successful break with competitive politics under mass suffrage: to this extent Karl Marx's analysis of the social basis of Napoleon's victory in *Der achtzehnte Brumaire* offers a paradigm for the comparative study of the twentieth century fascist victories.[13] But there were important differences: France had experienced one or two elections under universal suffrage before the coup but there had been no time to build up nation-wide mass organizations for electoral competition. What turned out to be crucial was the long period of nation-building at the mass level from 1875 to 1914: France was unified not only through conscription, obligatory schooling and massive migration but even more through the development of nation-wide party fronts.[14]

What distinguished the five twentieth-century cases was the step-by-step-sequence: extensive suffrage, competitive mass parties, crisis, *Machtergreifung* by a monolithic movement. The 1848–1851 sequence in France was simply too short: there was mass mobilization under universal manhood suffrage but there was no tradition of organized electoral competition, no party system to break up. If France had succumbed to fascism in 1934 the parallel with Germany and Italy would have been only too obvious: a long period of multiparty elections under the Third Republic and then the violent overthrow of party competition by a monolithic movement. But France did not succumb to internal disruption: the process of nation-building, at the mass as well as the élite levels, had gone far enough to prevent an effective coalition with the radical right.

The analysis of the French case is important in several perspectives. In the «typological-topological» scheme France represents a nodal area: half-way between the inland city belt and the advancing ocean-based empires to the West, half-way between the nation-building Protestantism of the North and the cross-territorial Church of Rome to the South. In Wallerstein's «map» of Europe, the North of France maintained a position within the core of the emerging world economy, while the South was part of the peripheralized Mediterranean area. This position at the «cross-roads» helps to account for the two Napoleons and for the long series of constitutional crises in the era of mass politics: it also helps to account for the extraordinary viability of the Third Republic and the resistance against the attempts at fascist take-over.[15]

Concluding Note

Generalizing beyond Wallerstein's initial design, we might conclude, at least for the period up to 1939, that the chances for the *survival* of competitive multiparty politics was greatest within the capitalist *core* of the world economy, that the likelihood of *fascist-type* victories was greatest in the *semi-peripheralized* territories of earlier city-studded empires – and that the probability of *communist-type* victories was greatest in the much more markedly *peripheral* areas of earlier empires of the «agrarian bureaucracy» type, empires with poorly developed commercial-industrial bourgeoisies. This formulation comes very close to Barrington Moore's in his great work on *The Social Origins of Dictatorship and Democracy:* again an attempt to identify in the early configurations of state-building alliances the preconditions for the defeat or victory of totalitarian mass movements at a much later stage in the history of each system. The structure of Wallerstein's analysis differs fundamentally from Moore's but it still leads to a very similar classification of long-term trajectories.

This reinforces us in our belief that progress *can* be made towards some higher level of systematization – if not strict formalization – of the basic dimensions of macro-history. We are the first to concede the inadequacies of the current efforts of systematization, yet we venture to believe that this step-by-step process of confrontation, recasting and retesting of models will eventually help us forwards toward the construction of a unified theory of socio-cultural, economic and political change, at least for the territories of Europe once under the domination of the Roman Empire or the Church of Rome. What is important is that these efforts of schematization and of systematization be taken seriously by work-a-day historians and data-handling social scientists: that efforts be made to broaden the empirical bases for the testing and the questioning of the implications of the models, not only *within* particular territories but *across*. If our discussions of alternative schemes of interpretation should also have consequences at this level of concrete historical analysis we shall not have worked in vain.

NOTES

[1] We are well aware that there are important differences between the five countries in the character of the sequences leading up to the victory of the monolithic alliances. *Portugal* is clearly a marginal case in this classification. Stanley Payne has established the following comparative table of sequences for Italy, Spain and Portugal:

Phase	Italy	Spain	Portugal
Elitist doctrinaire liberalism	1860–1876	1843–1881	1833–1857
Two-party *trasformista* liberalism	1876–1898	1881–1899	1857–1906
Pre-mass politics reformism	1899–1915	1899–1923	1910–1917
Authoritarian interlude	1915–1918	1923–1931	1917–1918
Compulsive mass politics	1919–1922	1931–1936	1919–1926

But Payne comments that the last category «does not fully fit Portugal, which *never really knew a phase of genuine mass politics.*» (our italics), see «Spanish Fascism in Comparative Perspective» pp. 142–169 in H.A. Turner, Jr. *Reappraisals of Fascism.* (New York: Watts, 1975). We still feel justified in including Portugal with the other four: even though the level of mass mobilization was low, there was a sequence leading from competitive electoral politics to the victory of a monolithic movement.

[2] S.M. Lipset & S. Rokkan, «Introduction», *Party Systems and Voter Alignments* (New York: Free Press 1967), S. Rokkan *Clitzens, Elections, Parties* (Oslo: Univ.forl. 1970), Ch. 3.

[3] S. Rokkan, «The Growth and Structuring of Mass Politics in W. Europe», *Scand.Pol.Stud.* 5, 1970: 65–83, «Entries, Voices, Exits», *Soc.Sci.Info.* 13 (1), 1974: 39–53.

[4] See Stein Rokkan «Dimensions of State Formation and Nation-Building» pp. 562–600 in C. Tilly *ed. The Formation of National States in Western Europe.* (Princeton: Princeton Univ. Press 1975) and «Cities, States, Nations» pp. 73–86 in S.N. Eisenstadt & S. Rokkan *(eds.) Building States and Nations* vol. I (Beverly Hills: Sage, 1973).

[5] A first, cryptic formulation was made in «Entries, Voices, Exits» *op.cit.*: this was expanded a bit further in notes prepared for meetings of the Association Française de Science Politique in June, 1974 and in December, 1976: «Macro-histoire et analyse comparative des processus de développement politique» and «Une famille de modèles pour l'histoire comparée de l'Europe Occidentale».

[6] This West-East gradient is of course a central dimension both in Wallerstein's and in Anderson's analysis: see I. Wallerstein. *The Modern World-System* (New York: Academic Press, 1974) Ch. 2 and 6, Perry Anderson *Passages from Antiquity to Feudalism* (London: NLB 1974) pp. 1–3 and 213–264 and *Lineages of the Absolutist State* (London: NLB 1974) pp. 195–235 and pp. 430–431. The West-East array in the «conceptual map» combines two different dimensions, however, and establishes a *typology* of conditions for politico-economic development: a city-studded belt with only minimal *Flächenstaat* elements in the middle, in the west a set of seaward empires-turned-nation-states with extensive peripheries as well as strong commercial cities, in the East similar expanses of periphery waiting to be mastered but much weaker city networks. Jürgen Habermas, commenting on an earlier version of the «conceptual map», has brought out with great clarity the double significance of the city belt for the territorial fates of Germany and Italy: the cities played a crucial role in the *initial development* of capitalism but could not compete with the *Flächenstaaten,* the territorial nation-states, at the stage of the *generalization (Durchsetzung)* of capitalist modes of production, *Zur Rekonstruktion des Historischen Materialismus* (Frankfurt a/M: Suhrkamp, 1976) p. 258. This contrast between city belt and territorial nation-state clearly needs further differentiation in the light of Wallerstein's analysis. The contrast between the two first core territories of the new Atlantic-Indian Ocean geoeconomy, *Portugal* and the *United Provinces,* can clearly be analyzed within the combinatorics of the conceptual map: both were able to exploit their position at the edge of the Atlantic but the Dutch core territory was closer to the North Sea Rhine-Italy trade routes and could benefit from the multiplier effects across this dense network of well-established cities. The Netherlands was in its turn handicapped in the contest with other core territories with larger peripheries: England and later the United States.

[7] Stein Rokkan, «Cities, States. . .» *op. cit.* p. 81.

[8] E. Juillard and H. Nonn, *Espaces et régions en Europe occidentale* (Paris: Eds du GNRS, 1976).

[9] For a detailed discussion of the sources of variation, see Stein Rokkan, *Citizens, Elections, Parties, op. cit.,* pp. 79–87.

[10] For a detailed discussion, see *Citizens, Elections, Parties, op. cit.,* pp. 96–138.

[11] For a further development of this theme see S. E. Finer, «State-Building, State Boundaries and Border Control». *Soc.Sci.Info.* 13 (4/5) 1974, 79–126.

[12] Wallerstein *op.cit.* p. 296.
The North-South, East-West gradients within France have fascinated scholars at least since the Revolution. The early collection of thematic maps by Adolphe d'Angeville, *Essai sur la statistique de la population française.* Paris 1836. Reprinted with an introduction by E. Le Roy Ladurie, (Paris: Mouton, 1969) called attention to the important dividing line from St. Malo to Geneva: the economically advanced regions to the north of this line, the backward regions to the south and west. François Furet and Jacques Ozouf have recently added another perspective on these regional contrasts: they have analyzed in great detail data on the spread of *literacy* since the 16th century and have concluded that the most marked contrast opposes the *Northeast* and the *West* (a triangle running roughly from the Spanish border on the Atlantic, northward to Brittany and eastward toward Valence on the Rhône), see *Lire et écrire. L'alphabétisation des français de Calvin à Jules Ferry* (Paris: Eds de Minuit, 1977), esp. vol. 1, concluding chapter.

[13] For an example of the use of Marx's *Brumaire* analysis in current theorizing about fascism, see Axel Kuhn, *Das faschistische Herrschaftssystem und die moderne Gesellschaft* (Hamburg: Hoffmann u. Campe, 1973), Kap. III A.2 «Das Vorbild: Die Bonapartismus-theorie von Karl Marx». pp. 102–113.

[14] For a fresh reinterpretation of this late phase of nation-building see Eugen Weber *Peasants into Frenchmen* (Stanford: Stanford University Press, 1976).

[15] For a detailed analysis of the French-German differences in levels of economic organization and their consequences for the vulnerability to fascist take-over see Charles S. Maier *Recasting Bourgeois Europe* (Princeton: Princeton Univ. Press 1975), especially Ch. 8 : «The Radical Socialist constituency avoided fascism in the 1930's for the same reason that it had endured economic confusion in the 1920's: *the continuing viability of economically archaic modes.* French democracy was to remain buffered by the society's *proverbial reluctance to organize»* (p. 511, our italics).

Political Space and Fascism as a Late-Comer:

Conditions Conducive to the Success or Failure of Fascism as a Mass Movement in Inter-War Europe

JUAN J. LINZ

Introduction: The Integralist Character of Fascism and the Availability of Political Space

In the years between the two world wars, fascist movements and groupuscules sprang up all over the world. Other parties, particularly government-created single parties, assumed fascist characteristics. In some sense one can speak of the era of fascism, but at the same time only a few of those movements gained broad popular support and only the Italian fascists and the German National Socialists were able to take power on their own. Any comparative analysis of «Why fascism?» has to keep in mind the difference between movements which grew out of the particular historico-sociological conditions of a few societies and those small groups which tried to imitate Italian fascism and National Socialism, and which were quickly condemned to failure due to the absence of favorable conditions and capable leadership.[1] In many respects the question presents parallels with any effort to account for the very different success of communist parties in that same period, with the difference that fascism in the thirties was already polycentric while Moscow, except for some small dissident groups, represented the only pole of attraction for communists. In addition, despite the affinities between parties and the undercover subsidies they received, the ultra-nationalism essential to the fascist ideology constituted an obstacle to the emergence of an overtly international fascist movement led from Rome or Berlin. Furthermore, the ideological ambiguities of fascism as an anti-movement and its incorporation of a variety of ideological strands into what it wanted to be a new synthesis, made it possible for many of its competitors to include fascist ideas, symbols, and organization patterns into their own political appeal and thus compete successfully for the same potential clientele or ingratiate themselves with the *Duce* or the *Führer*. Neither polemicists nor scholars have always been able or willing to distinguish the genuine product from the imitations. Both conservatives eager to protect the status quo and leftists seeing in fascism a means of capitalist class rule, the last defense of capitalism in conditions of extreme decay, basically had the same view. Thus there is little difference between Palme Dutt[2] when he wrote that «only two paths are therefore open to present society, the alternative of fascism or communism» and the formulation by a fascisticized conservative like Calvo Sotelo when he maintained that

> Fascism here and elsewhere is not an original postulate but an anti-thesis, not an action, but a reaction. In England where there is no communism, there is scarcely any fascism. In Spain where communism is a reality . . . fascism, not as a specific organized force which is least significant – but as an uncoerced indefinable sentiment of national defense, which many do not know how to define or organize, will continue to grow until the social danger disappears.[3]

On the other hand, both fascists and scholars are aware of the basic differences between imitators and the true movements, particularly the contrast with the single parties created from above in the authoritarian regimes of Eastern and Southern Europe. A memorandum prepared for Mussolini in August 1929 conveys, as many similar texts, this difference:

> The Fascist Revolution was passion, struggle, and blood. It had within itself three elements, without which it is almost impossible to bring about the miracle of infusing a new way of life in a people: victory in war, a *condottiero,* a myth. De Rivera's noble movement in Spain was undoubtedly something more than a mere ministerial crisis, but it was certainly much less than a revolution. There was no victorious war. The myth was painfully absent, as has been demonstrated by the pitiable party which was completely devoid of soul and vitality. The *condottiero* has proven to be a little more than an intelligent and energetic gentleman. His followers are neither numerous nor enthusiastic, and he tends to hold them back rather than to encourage them. [His proposed constitution is an] artificial compilation, a mosaic of timid imitations and of uncertain intentions, halfway between Fascist and democratic-electoral principles.[4]

Attempting to answer the question why fascism arose and became victorious on the basis of either of the two images reflected in the texts just quoted, will inevitably lead to different answers. To some extent the disagreements on the definition and significance of fascism hinge on this point. The first perspective with its emphasis on the conservative and anti-revolutionary character of fascism is more likely to focus on the function performed by fascist movements of destroying organized labor and defending private property, the alliances they made in the process of *Machtergreifung* and the conservative policies pursued by fascists in power. From this perspective the ideology and social appeal of the founding groups of fascist parties, particularly some of the less successful ones, the left wing dissidents in the movements, and the historical social conditions in which they emerged, tend to be neglected. It also obscures the more positive aspects of fascist regimes that contributed to their stability and appeal.

Is there any interpretation which could account for these contradictory dimensions in the political phenomenon we call fascism? In our view there is such a possibility if we take into account three factors: 1. That fascism was a late-comer on the political scene at a point when in most European societies a large part of the population had already identified itself with a variety of ideological positions and very often had been integrated into parties, interest groups and mass organizations impenetrable to the fascist appeal; 2. that the basic themes of fascist ideology, particularly the integral nationalism, the ideal of overcoming under a new leadership the internal cleavages in a society based on class, religion and partisanship by advocating common goals, would integrate into a new synthesis the best of the positions it rejected,[5] enabled such catch-all movements to attract a heterogeneous following and make inroads into a variety of social strata with varying success depending on the particular historical, social and political constellation in each country; and 3. that the success of Mussolini and particularly Hitler in taking power and the policies they pursued had a decisive impact on the fate of the fascist parties founded in the thirties. These late-comers found a more hostile environment on the part of liberal democratic authorities,[6] in some cases a greater willingness of socialist parties to work with other political forces in sustaining democratic regimes and in opposing the fascists, and often less sympathy on the part of true conservatives who at that time had grown more aware of the threat those potential allies against the left represented to their own positions in society. In other cases, reactionary and conservative forces felt that they could protect their

154

interests through authoritarian solutions with the support of the armed forces and the bureaucracy as well as the monarchy without resorting to the always risky popular mobilization by fascist movements. It is no accident, even when it might seem paradoxical, that some of the fascist movements with broad popular appeal should have been outlawed and persecuted by authoritarian regimes which at the same time were in many respects imitating fascism. The fate of the Iron Guard, the Arrow Cross, the Brazilian Integralists under Vargas, the Wabse in Estonia[7], the Perkonkrust in Latvia[8] and even the tiny group of national syndicalists in Salazar's Portugal, is significant in this respect. Obviously, those authoritarian rulers, as Franco did with even more success, attempted frequently to co-opt the fascists into their political system. Paradoxically, genuine fascist mass movements could only grow in the context of a liberal, democratic society committed to and recognizing their right to proselytize, regimes which until the middle thirties found it difficult to restrict the fascist's activities.[9]

Obstacles to the Success of a Late-Comer: Why Many or Few Fascists?

It is the late-comer character of fascism, late-latecomer in some cases, that in our view account not only for the very different success of movements with similar ideologies and for the very different social bases of support gained by groups whose initial nucleus of activists, ideological position, style and programmatic appeal were quite similar. As mentioned, in our view it is the ambivalent character of movements based on the rejection of existing political alternatives, combined with efforts to integrate these alternatives into a new synthesis, itself in part explained by this late appearance, which also accounts for the success of fascist movements among quite different strata in dissimilar societies. The fascists were often unable to gain support among strata to which they wanted to direct their appeal, while sometimes to their surprise and even their discomfort they found it in other quarters.[10] However, their ideal of national integration made it difficult to reject support from wherever it came and tended to make them catch-all parties, although their voluntarism and political élitism allowed them to believe that ultimately they could control their followers and prevent their supporters from using them for their own purposes.

Because of this late-comer character it is impossible to understand the success or failure of fascist parties without looking closely at the social bases of their competitors. Their success among the working class was certainly a function of the degree to which the socialist, anarcho-syndicalist and communist movements and trade unions had organized the working class and penetrated sectors of the peasantry and the new middle classes.[11] The solidity of the farmers' parties with their professional and cooperative organizations in northern and Baltic Europe and of the peasant parties in eastern and Balkan Europe was another obstacle in their way.[12] Major competitors with a similar classless integrative appeal were the Catholic and Christian social parties with their extensive network of functional groups and the organization of the Catholic sub-community. It is no accident that in the Catholic countries where inter-class parties had emerged in the course of the *Kulturkampf* against liberalism, specifically in the *Zentrum* in Germany and similar parties in Belgium, the Netherlands, Luxembourg, Switzerland, Lithuania and even Austria, the fascists could find their electorate and functional organizations largely impenetrable despite many ideological affinities, such as their anti-communism, their anti-liberalism, their hostility to masonry, and their advocacy of corporativist institutions to overcome the class conflict.[13] Moreover, it is typical that they were more successful among Protestants,[14] particularly the more secularized sectors of the bourgeoisie, with a notable exception of countries where nationalism could be fused with religion like Romania, Slovakia and Croatia. Until after World War I the non-expedit had prevented the effective independent political organization of Italian Catholics and the Popolari into a new party competing with the fascists in northern Italy. This accounts both for the availability of an electorate there and a lesser capacity to resist fascism than shown by the *Zentrum* when the Church pursuing its own interests, was ready to accommodate with a party coming close to power.[15] The case of Spain in the thirties shows clearly how a Catholic party and the emerging fascists competed for much of the same social groups, and how the success of one pre-empted that of the other. The CEDA *(Confederación Española de Derechas Autónomas)* led by Gil Robles was at least until the spring of 1936 able to mobilize the same strata against the left and a bourgeois republic that in other societies made up the mass support for fascism. Spanish political Catholicism did not succeed in doing so without assimilating, particularly in its youth organization, some of the ideological themes, theoretical bases and style of its competitors.[16]

The relative strength of a variety of modern, well-organized class movements for workers and peasants as well as the strength of the religious sub-cultures, the Catholic, and in the Netherlands the Protestant, limited the political space to which fascist late-comers could successfully direct their appeal.

Paradoxically, economic and social development and with it the persistence of traditional clientist politics was another obstacle to the success of a modern mass movement. Let us not forget that except in Apulia, where organized class conflict had reached unique intensity, right until the March on Rome fascism remained weak in southern and island Italy as it did even in the anti-Catholic rural and provincial Spain and in the less developed Balkan countries, although there authoritarian rule was probably an even more important obstacle than clientelism.[17] It could be argued that in the more traditional societies fascism was premature. Without the more or less successful articulation (and even failure) of the positions and forces it wanted to attack and destroy, fascism could not rise.

Why Fascism in the First Place? Conditions Conducive to the Emergence of an Initial Fascist Core Group

The factors just discussed can help to explain the relative success of fascist parties in gaining mass membership and broad electoral support. They are, however, inadequate to account for the early or late appearance of a fascist *activist core,* for the relative originality or purely imitative character of the different movements, or for the appeal and quality of the initial nucleus. They help us to answer the question of why many or few fascists, but not why fascism or no fascism.

To answer this second question we have to turn to the specific historico-political constellation of each country in the inter-war years and to some extent to the cultural and ideological heritage of the pre-war years on which fascists could base their appeal.

It is important – and would avoid many misunderstandings and useless debates – to keep very distinct several questions that tend to get confused when people ask: who were the fascists? As in the case of other parties but probably more so in the case of fascists, we have to divide that question into a series of questions: who were the *founders* of fascist movements and the members of the initial activist nucleus?[18] Who were the new *recruits* in the early days of the movement when the chances of reaching power were still dim? Where did the *mass membership* in the case of the Italian fascist and particularly of the NSDAP in the early thirties come from? Finally, who *voted* for the fascist parties, particularly in the few countries in which they obtained a large electoral support?[19] Those questions cannot be answered in any case by data we might have on the membership of the parties once they gained power. Unfortunately the data available for different movements do not always deal with the same questions and therefore lead to unwarranted comparisons. The dual character of many fascist parties of being at the same time membership parties and militant organizations of a para-military character obliges us to ask: to what extent did the membership of the party and the squads differ? Only in the case of the NSDAP, the SA and the SS do we have some data bearing on this important question.[20]

Independently of explaining why some fascist movements were able to gain a significant membership and electoral support, we have to account for the fact that in some countries even the initial nucleus of founders and activists was insignificant or small, appeared late on the scene, and from the beginning was more a result of imitation and diffusion than a genuine response to the particular social strains of their society. Certainly, Swedish, Danish or Czech fascism, even the Norwegian *Nasjonal Samling* and the British Union of Fascists (BUF), irrespective of their limited support, were fundamentally different from Italian fascism, German National Socialism and the Iron Guard in what we might call political creativity and initial appeal of the founding nucleus of activists. Let us emphasize that the difference in the early appearance of the movement and its originality is not necessarily a function of the intellectual and even human quality of the founders; in fact, some of the movements which failed in attracting a sufficiently significant core following were led by some of the most intelligent and in some cases personally attractive leaders. In this respect we only have to think of Sir Oswald Mosley, Ramiro Ledesma Ramos, José Antonio Primo de Rivera and some of the French leaders like Drieu la Rochelle and even Doriot. These men compare favorably with the men who participated in the Beer Hall *Putsch* and followed Hitler to rule Germany. It is the historico-social context and the ideological pre-dispositions that account for the decisive initial success. In fact one might be tempted to explain the emergence of original fascist movements of some strength in terms of unique national factors. Certainly, many of the early explanations, particularly by Italian contemporaries, of the appearance of fascism were formulated in terms of the historical political backwardness of Italy, the legacies of the unification process and the national political style. Italian fascism was interpreted as a specifical-ly Italian phenomenon.[21] Those who reject the category of fascism as meaningful for politico-sociological analysis and emphasize the uniqueness of National Socialism also tend to see Hitler's movement as a result of distinctive characteristics of German history, (the *verspätete Nation* syndrome), of distinctively German cultural tradi-tions, particularly the reaction to modernity in the late 19th century, if not of German national character. We would not deny that, in accounting for the distinctive traits of each national fascist movement, those national factors should be taken into account, but we would also argue that the appearance and initial strength of the more original rather than imitative movements has to be explained by a limited number of factors present in certain societies. This does not mean that those factors will have an equal weight in each case nor that all of them are present simultaneously.

Among those factors we would list the following:

1. The impact of World War I on the societies and the generation that participated in the war, particularly in the defeated nations and in those that felt cheated in the fruits of victory. (Italy in particular).

2. The presence of revolution attempts by radical leftists, particularly communists, and the presence of maximalist rather than social reformist Marxist parties.

3. The heightened sense of nationalism, particularly when the boundaries of the nation did not coincide with those of the state and when the country was perceived as not occupying its proper place in the competition between states and nations.

4. Unresolved cultural conflicts within the state, particularly ethnic minority conflicts and more specifically in a number of countries the problems pertaining to the place of the Jews in the society.

Significantly, the four problems just mentioned in a number of cases tend to overlap either in fact or in the perception of significant segments in the population. In addition, not only did the fascists attempt to respond to those problems, but other parties also. Clearly, some of the factors mentioned are strongly related to the initial split between democratic socialists and communists and the initial strength of the latter.

The War and its Aftermath

Without any doubt, the impact of war on European society in the late 1910's and early 20's was the single most important factor in provoking the crisis of liberal and emerging democratic societies in the early decades of the 20th century.[22] Defeat and national humiliation is even a more significant factor. It is no accident that the most important protofascist political movement in Europe, the *Action Française,* and the radical nationalism mixed with the anti-Semitism of Drumont and Barrés also arose after the defeat of France in the Franco-Prussian War. Even Bolivian fascism was not unrelated to the impact of the Chaco War on that country.[23]

The evidence is quite clear. Among six neutrals in World War I we find no strong movement, either in membership or electoral appeal, and three practically insignificant parties. Among the eight countries which emerged victorious after the war, four have no significant movements, although in two cases, Czechoslovakia and Yugoslavia, this statement is true only of the state-building nationalities: the Czechs and the Serbs. In the other two, the United Kingdom and France, in spite of relatively capable leadership and (in the case of France) of some other favorable factors, fascist movements emerged late and with limited strength. It could be argued that in Poland, Yugoslavia and Portugal, authoritarian solutions to the political crisis prevented the rise of true fascist movements. In none of the new successor states except for Slovak and Croat nationalism did the initial nucleus seem to have any strength. However, among the victors we find two countries with genuine original and powerful movements: Italy and Romania. In both cases, particularly in Italy, the impact of the War lies at the origins of fascism, despite Italy's formal membership in the victorious camp.[24] Among the six defeated countries, fascism did not become a major political factor in three, the Soviet Union[25] Turkey and Bulgaria.[26] In our view, the national authoritarian single party regime created by Atatürk in Turkey cannot be considered fascist, but certainly many fascist intellectuals perceived a fundamental affinity between their national revolutions and Kemalism, while criticizing the persistence of liberal democratic ideological commitments in that regime.[27] Despite their anti-communism, the sense of common destiny of the defeated and their shared hostility to the victorious pluto-democracies of the West made fascists see the Soviet Union, particularly Stalinism, as another variant of the national integrative authoritarian revolutions.[28] The one case which is more difficult to explain is Bulgaria. In that country a number of fascist groups appeared without success in spite of defeat, the existence of irredentism, the presence of a nationalist minority threat in Macedonia and an early and strong communist movement. The establishment of authoritarian, monarchical military rule after the defeat of populist peasant rule under Stambolisky pre-empted and later prevented the emergence of an appealing fascist movement. The same authoritarian rule curtailed but could not prevent an interesting and successful «left» fascist party – the Arrow Cross – in Hungary, a country in which a failed communist revolution and strong anti-Semitism also were favorable factors. Let us not forget that in the 1939 semi-free election, fascist groups in opposition to the government party managed to win 25 per cent of the votes. Austria in the twenties produced its own type of fascism in the *Heimwehren,* and in the thirties authoritarian rule incorporating native fascism faced the growing appeal of National Socialism. It was in Germany, the new great democracy born in defeat, where fascism emerged as a mass party. Several countries were neither victors nor defeated in the war, but emerged as a result of it and had to struggle for their independence in its aftermath: Finland, the three Baltic republics and Greece (which was defeated in its struggle with Turkey). Among those five, in two, Finland and Estonia, semi-fascist movements gained widespread support despite the limited political ability of their leadership.[29] Only Greece with its unstable politics, the conflicts between monarchy and republicanism, the persistence of clientelistic, personalistic parties and prolonged periods of military rule did not produce a significant fascist party. However, a number of the other factors we have emphasized were not present there.

On the other hand fascism was a late late-comer and unsuccessful in all the neutrals in the war: Sweden, Denmark, Norway, the Netherlands, Spain, to which we could add Portugal, whose participation in the war had been limited (even when contributing to the crisis of the republic). For a variety of reasons the war waged by Spain in Morocco did not have the effects on the population, and only a delayed impact on the army officer corps, that World War I had on the belligerents. No nationalistic veterans movement, no student nationalism, no chauvinistic bourgeoisie emerged from that war. On the other hand the defeat inflicted on Spain by the United States in 1898 created a climate of crisis of parliamentary institutions which unleashed an intellectual response of somewhat proto-fascist character with which the fascists of the thirties attempted to link up.

The Threat of Revolution, Defeated Revolutions and the Rise of Fascism

The division in the socialist movement between reformists, orthodox Marxists and revolutionaries on the one hand, and pacifists, internationalists, and those more ready to integrate into a democratic nation-state on the other, always latent in the early decades of the century, came into the open in the countries participating in the war. The Russian Revolution brought those conflicts to a head, and the social and economic crises provoked by the war in some countries seemed to open the door to revolutionary attempts, particularly in Hungary, Germany, Finland and the Baltic countries.[30] The post-war crisis and the initial rejection of interventionism reinforced the maximalist tendencies in Italian socialism manifest in the Red domination in the Po Valley and the occupation of factories – all factors in the birth of Italian fascism. In many cases the radical rhetoric was not followed by action and the revolutionary attempts were defeated or fizzled out. In others like Finland, they led to a bitter civil war. All of them frightened the bourgeoisie and were perceived as threats to national interests in a time of crisis, particularly in Germany where the *Dolchstosslegende* served as an alibi for the defeated army and conservative forces. The contrast between the class solidarity experienced in the trenches and the sacrifices of the generation fighting the war, particularly those who volunteered for service on the one hand, and the persistence of social fragmentation[31] on the other, proved to be a cultural shock for those returning home. The efforts to re-establish order and authority of governments by relying on the co-operation of armed civilians gave birth to nationalist bourgeois para-military organizations out of which some of the initial cadres of fascism would be recruited. Intense anti-communism and counter-revolutionary activism as well as the latent and not-so-latent sympathies of broad bourgeois strata for such groups were born in that context. The impotence of the liberal democratic state when faced with the mobilized working class in a time of economic and political crisis contributed to the deep hatred against that state. At the same time, particularly in the case of Italy, representatives and agents of that state, frustrated by their own impotence, would sympathize with and support the fascists who promised to repulse that threat. The counter-revolutionary component in fascism is combined with non-economically motivated resentments. The interventionist Mussolini turned against his socialist comrades, founding the *Fascio* in Milan with a nationalist but still revolutionary program.

The evidence is clear that wherever a communist or soviet type revolutionary attempt was made and wherever the socialist parties embraced a maximalist ideology rather than a social democratic one, fascism in one or another version was more likely to emerge. In some cases a non-fascist authoritarian alternative imposed by the army pre-empted the rise of fascist movements, as exemplified by the Primo de Rivera dictatorship which emerged in response to anarcho-syndicalist activism in Catalonia.[32]

In the countries where in the inter-war years the social democratic parties enjoyed disproportionately greater strength than the communists, the fascists were unable to gain any significant mass support and were generally late late-comers by imitation rather than responses to a national predicament. Only in those countries where the socialists supported revolutionary or pseudo-revolutionary attempts and turned to a maximalist ideology or rhetoric did they contribute to the fear that mobilized support for the fascists, particularly after the danger had subsided. This was true even where the socialists were «lambs in wolves' clothing», to use the expression of the Austro-Marxist leader Victor Adler[33]. Typically the formation of socialist para-military organizations, or workers' guards, aroused deep hostility and served as justification for the formation of much more effective citizens or «white» guards which became parts of the fascist organizations and movements.

On the other hand, fascist movements gained significant support where the communists enjoyed considerable support and were relatively strong by comparison with the socialists. That was the case not only in Germany, but also in Finland, Estonia, and Romania where socialists were relatively insignificant, the communists controlling the small segment of mobilized voters. There is one clear deviant case, France, where in the thirties the communists were relatively strong compared to the socialists, but where the fascist wave did not crest. Even among the smaller stable democracies, the difference in fascist strength between Belgium and the Netherlands might not be unrelated to the different position of the communists and socialists in the elections in the thirties. In Czechoslovakia, the extraordinary strength of the communists in Slovakia with 13.0 per cent of the vote compared to 11.4 per cent for the socialists, contrasting with 9.0 per cent and 18.0 per cent in Bohemia and 8.6 and 13.3 in Moravia in the 1935 elections would help to account for the fascist undercurrent within Slovak Catholic nationalism. Among the Scandinavian countries, Norway stands out because of the affiliation of the Labour Party with the Third International in the early twenties and its persistent radicalism, at least on the programmatic level, until the early thirties. While the *Nasjonal Samling* never became a major party, it remained the strongest Scandinavian fascist movement. There are obviously countries like Bulgaria and Greece in which the communists were ahead of the socialists but where no fascist movement appeared. However, in both countries, authoritarian regimes defeated the left and at the same time pre-empted the opportunity for a genuine fascist party.

Conditions for Extreme Nationalism and Fascism

If there is one characteristic of fascism on which all analysts agree it is the central place of nationalism in its ideology, particularly the type of nationalism that goes as far as placing loyalty to the nation ahead of loyalty to the state. It has been the merit of Hannah Arendt to emphasize the importance of pan-nationalisms in the emergence of what she considers totalitarian tendencies in politics.[34] Italian fascism was born out of the interventionist nationalism and the Fiume expediton of D'Annunzio, where young activists were ready to disobey the state for the sake of Italian nationalists' interests, thus providing the movement with many of its symbols, its rhetoric, and its cadres.[35] Nationalism also furnished the context in which the ambivalence of young officers toward the authority of their superiors was born. The border struggles between nationalities in Austria, Germany, and in Eastern Europe created the personal loyalties and patterns of violent politics that would nourish fascist movements. Irredentism and border nationalism would be one of the main themes and supports of fascism in Italy, Germany, Hungary, Finland and the Baltic. Even in a country with settled and undisputed borders like Norway, the NS tried to capitalize on a nascent expansionist national fervor, connected with the dispute over the sovereignty over Greenland. Although some sections among the Agrarians seemed susceptible, on the whole the endeavor failed. World War I and the Wilsonian support for the principle of nationalities created new states and aroused the sentiments of nationalities unable to gain statehood. The victors, except the Italians who felt that their national aspirations had been betrayed at the peace conference, had no reason to feel that heightened sense of nationalism to the same extent. In fact, their power position was guaranteed by the alliance with the victorious Western democracies. Italy's situation could therefore serve as a political model for the Czechs as well.[36] Confronted with social, economic and ethnic minority problems their governments sometimes chose the path of authoritarian rule. Neither in the cases of Czechoslovakia, Poland or Yugoslavia nor among the Czechs, Poles and Serbs did significant fascist movements make their appearance. However, in the thirties those nationalities unable to achieve statehood, like the Slovaks and the Croats and to some extent the Flemings, would exhibit a nationalism more vulnerable to the fascist appeal partly because they could hope for support from the victims of Versailles. There are obviously exceptions to this generalization such as the peripheral nationalist groups in Spain, (except in the thirties) the separatist semi-fascist *Estat Català* movement, and Macedonian nationalism which, confronted with authoritarian rulers, opted for traditional terrorist tactics rather than an impossi-

161

ble mass mobilization. Similarly the historical situation did not allow Ukrainian nationalism to become fascisticized until the 1940's.[37]

Fascism seized upon a theme first developed by Corradini in Italy, the inequality of nations, particularly as it showed itself in the distribution of colonial spoils. This doctrine lead to an emphasis on class conflict between the poor and the rich nations rather than between classes within a nation. The proletarian nations (the agrarian dependent nations) were contraposed to the rich, advanced industrial countries which to a large extent were the U.K. and France, two democracies which could be labelled pluto-democracies. This was a theme to become even more prominent in the thinking of the Spanish fascist Ramiro Ledesma Ramos in his attempt to explain the economic backwardness and political crisis of modern Spain. Internal unity, the overcoming of class conflicts and a new national mobilization were to be the themes of these nationalists in their efforts to improve the nation's position in the conflict between states. Western democracy was perceived as an enemy on two counts: as the holder of economic power and defender of the status quo, and as a political system weakening the country internally in the Darwinian struggle between nations.

William S. Allen[38] has rightly linked the appeal of fascism with the problem of national disintegration in the case of the two late-comers to national statehood, Italy and Germany, and contrasted these trajectories with the Western and Northern European early- established states, a theme developed upon a broad historical canvas in the essay by Stein Rokkan and Bernt Hagtvet in this volume The early and stable statehood of Portugal, France, the United Kingdom, Sweden, Denmark, Norway, Switzerland, Spain, the Netherlands, and to a lesser extent Belgium, goes far to explain the relative weakness of the appeal to nationalism in its most extreme forms as a means to integrate the nation.[39] In the case of the United Kingdom, France, the Netherlands, Portugal and even Belgium we have to add the fact that compared to the proletarian nations and late-comers they were to one degree or another satisfied colonial powers. Marxists have linked the material and psychological benefits of imperialism with the weakness of radical working class consciousness. In the same way we could link the lack of susceptibility to fascism in what the Italians have called the humanistic bourgeoisie, to satisfaction with the imperial mission of their nation. The support for that mission in France, bringing French civilization to the colonies, was shared by leftist democrats there. Among these early states, only Spain offered some ground for a fascist nationalism in response to the loss of empire, the discrimination in the colonial penetration of Africa and the disintegrative tendencies of peripheral nationalisms. The fact that in the 19th century, liberal governments had granted extensive mining rights to British and French companies and the major role played by foreign investors in Spanish capitalist development offered Spanish fascists another theme for their nationalism and for their hostility to the plutocratic democracies. All those issues were present in the ideological formulations of Spanish fascism, but other factors in the political history of 20th century Spain channelled the discontent of potential fascist strata in other directions. In fact, I would argue that the intellectual elaboration of a fascist program in Spain was highly articulated and consistent compared with those in other countries. Neutrality in World War I and the lack of popular involvement in the Moroccan wars, however, deprived the fascists of the crisis strata which could form their initial nucleus before 1936 at a time when the threat of a proletarian revolution and the political failures of Catholic conservatism and bourgeois liberal reformism became apparent, at least to the youthful generation.

More perplexing is the absence of fascist responses in the nationalist peripheries of

Western states, particularly Spain, and to some extent the United Kingdom. Perhaps if Ireland had not achieved independence in 1922, if the Catholic cultural integration had not been so strong, if one party had not been so ready to incorporate ideological themes akin to fascism and to absorb the nucleus of activists ready to initiate a fascist movement, Ireland would have provided fertile ground for fascism. If we add the absence of a proletarian Marxist revolutionary ferment we can account for its failure. It could even be argued that the IRA linking with pre-independence traditions of nationalist struggle was a functional alternative.[40] In the case of the Basque country, the linkage of nationalism with Catholic clericalism and the convergence with the struggle against a left-bourgeois secularizing republic in 1931 channelled nationalism into a Christian democratic party, the PNV (Partido Nacionalista Vasco), [41] rather than into fascism. If the peripheral nationalisms in France and the U.K., so evident today, had been awakened in the twenties and thirties, there is little doubt that they would have assumed fascist forms. In fact, the limited expressions of the peasant populist semi-fascist protest of a Dorgeres found their strongest echo in Brittany.

Anti-Semitism and fascism are two distinct phenomena which, however, have a strong tendency to overlap. The Nazi success provokes an anti-fascist coalition in which Jews take an active part. Therefore, only with the victory of Nazism do anti-Semitism and fascism tend to fuse.[42] Let us emphasize that there were anti-Semitic parties in the late 19th century in Germany, Austria[43] and in the Balkan countries[44] which were not fascist, that anti-Semitism is strongly advocated by non-fascist parties as well and that a number of fascist parties, including the Italian, initially rejected anti-Semitism.[45] However, the special position of Jews in some Central and Eastern European societies was one factor in the emergence of fascist movements, particularly in Romania,[46] Hungary and Slovakia as well as in Austria, and on a more ideological than social structural level in Germany. Both in real social structural terms and in symbolic terms, anti-Semitism becomes central to the problem of national, cultural and social integration and as such to the emergence of fascism.

Cultural Crisis and Ideological Heritage

The last factor in our list headed «Why fascism?» is the most difficult to define. We find it in many of the non-Marxist interpretations of fascism. It is also the least comparable one for a wider range of countries. It is what we might call the cultural crisis factor, sometimes also described as reactions to modernity, as anti-urbanism, as romanticization of pre-capitalist society,[47] and in more psychological terms as search for community and escape from freedom. This factor is crucial in the appeal of fascism to intellectuals and pseudo-intellectuals, to students and the humanistic bourgeoisie, but also in facilitating a sense of affinity in other non-fascist sectors of society to the emerging movements.[48] It constitutes a decisive factor in the climate of opinion in which fascism can begin to grow. Intellectual historians have made important contributions to the analysis of this factor as a direct or indirect antecedent of fascism, particularly in Germany and in France. The often neglected work by Robert Michels[49] on the complex relationships between nationalism and social revolutionary thought in Italy is in the same line as is the debate on the relationship between the Risorgimento and fascism. Without an analysis of the intellectual and aesthetic responses to modernity, the language, the style, and even some forms of the social organization of fascist movements would be difficult to understand. It is no accident that in France, where many of the factors we have discussed were unfavorable to its emergence, the cultural

163

crisis was at the roots of some of the most interesting fascist groups and the flourishing of literary fascism.[50]

It is this cultural factor which allows us to establish a link between secularization and fascism. As long as the hostile response to modern society and the concomitant rejection of liberalism and democratization remain embedded in traditional religious forms, and reactionary or conservative politics is linked with the defense of the position of the church, there is little room for the emergence of a fascist intelligentsia. Fascism offered a secularized semi- or pseudo-traditional but not conservative ideology of national integration, aimed at overcoming the religious cleavages.[51] Only when religion, nationalism, anti-Semitism, and the rejection of cosmopolitan cultural dependency became fused (as in Romania) can a strong non-secularist and distinctively fascist movement appear in full force.

Obviously, other political movements in competition with the fascists have often seized upon the same themes of cultural crisis, particularly the populist and peasantist movements growing out of a *narodnik* tradition in Balkan Europe. In Western Europe the dominant position of the Roman Catholic Church and the symbol of Vaticanism as an obstacle to a new secular national integration and cultural creativity allowed intellectuals reflecting that same sense of crisis to support the laicist left. In this respect, the birth of Spanish fascism in the same milieu that gave its support to Azaña's secularist national bourgeois revolution is symptomatic.[52]

Cultural malaise, search for roots in the past, a romanticizing of the people by urban intellectuals, particularly the peasant and the artisan as genuine bearers of culture in contrast to cosmopolitan, foreign, academic, bourgeois culture, and the rejection of modernist, international culture, sometimes rightly or wrongly identified with the Jews, provided fertile ground for anti-Western responses. The dominant position of Western capitalist democracies in the Europe of the twenties, their commitment to the Versailles *status quo* and their control of the League of Nations, allowed fascists to blend cultural protest with anti-liberalism, hostility towards Western forms of democracy, a particular type of anti-capitalism, anti-Semitism, in quite a few cases anti-clericalism if not anti-Chatholicism, and even pagan anti-Christianity. In some Catholic countries that same rejection of cultural dependency, particularly on France and the cultural/political myth derived from the French revolution, led to forms of national Catholicism on the fringes of fascism. To some extent, the ideological roots of native Austrian fascism, of *Açāo Integralista Brasileira* (Brazilian Integralism), and of the *Acción Española* fit into this pattern. Just as nowadays certain forms of Third World hostility towards Western democracy are not reluctant to link intellectually with ideological protest in the West, these groups often derived their inspiration from the proto-fascist intellectual protest of the *Action Française*.

Let us stress that this last variable is less important in explaining the appeal of fascism to a broader social base than are the other factors, but it is not irrelevant in accounting for the generational revolt in Italy, the attractiveness of fascism to students, and the different ideological creativity of the various movements.

In the case of Nazism the coarseness of its ideological formulation and the personality of Hitler explain that the party as such had little appeal to intellectuals and that students played relatively less important roles in the early growth of the movement than in other countries. The rich intellectual and ideological ferment both outside of the dominant parties of the Weimar coalition and in opposition to it created a cultural milieu that predisposed many Germans to the sloganized versions of those ideas formulated by the NSDAP.[53] Many of those who in the myriad of politico-intellectual groupuscules on the extreme right and on the right of the extreme left contributed to the alienation from Weimar, would end in opposition or flee into internal migration under the Third Reich.[54] The impact of intellectual criticism on the social order is always difficult to judge, but certainly in modern societies with large numbers of educated people alert to the latest fads, it cannot be ignored. In this context George Mosse[55] rightly underlines the role of middle brow culture in contrast to the more academic and «classical» Weimar culture in explaining the readiness of the German *bien pensant* bourgeoisie to co-opt and/or trust the Nazis despite their reservations about the Nazi leaders and their more unsavory actions. It was that climate reinforced by a bourgeois local press, that made the electoral landslide possible and later facilitated the transfer of power to the Nazis. The cultural ghettos in which Marxist and Catholic intellectual life developed, indirectly limited the expansive capacity of the parties with which they identified.

The Crisis of the State, and the Loss of the Monopoly of Violence

One dimension in the rise of fascism that has received relatively little attention though it was already emphasized in the early analysis by Luigi Salvatorelli[56] in his insightful *Nazionalfascismo,* is the concomitance of fascism with a crisis of the state. Fascist movements have as one essential characteristic the exaltation and deliberate use of organized political violence. They therefore challenge the monopoly of force by the state and its agents. Certainly left-wing revolutionaries, particularly the anarchists, had also romanticized and used violence, but they claimed to challenge not only the state but the existing social order as such. The novelty of fascism was to turn to violence presumably to defend the social order and/or the nation against its presumed internal and external enemies. That had been and is the function (maybe the most important one) of the state, of its gendarmes and armed forces. Fascism, therefore, was a profoundly subversive movement even though it claimed to be conservative rather than socially revolutionary. Fascists were right when they claimed that there was no alternative between open or latent civil war or their taking over the state.[57] Unfortunately, a large part of the political class, particularly in Italy, did not understand this novel phenomenon.

Fascism, therefore, was not possible without a crisis of the authority of the state, a crisis of its monopoly of force for political purposes and the commitment to defend that monopoly. That crisis occurred only in some European societies due to unique historical circumstances. In this respect the tolerance of the Italian state in relation to persistent mob pressure to force intervention in the war, the ambivalence of Italian governments toward the insubordination of the military supporting the D'Annunzian adventure in Fiume until Giolitti cut it short, and the unwillingness or incapacity to stop fascist violence in North Central Italy were steps in this abdication on the part of the state, making the transfer of power after the March on Rome possible if not inevitable. Perhaps the consciousness of the state and its authority was less developed among Italians, as Salvatorelli suggests. Perhaps the still recent memory of the creation of the state by political activists in the *Risorgimento,* in contrast to more established Western European states with a long monarchical tradition, accounts for this tolerance of patriotic activism.[58] In Germany, the fall of the monarchy and the readiness of sectors of the army officer corps, civil servants, and academics to distinguish the state as a permanent, almost mythical entity, from the Weimar regime and the governments in power created the fundamental crisis of legitimacy. This crisis was accentuated by the fateful decision of the victors to limit the size of the armed forces and to fully professionalize the small army by forbidding regular conscription. The fact that even democratic governments required the cooperation of privately organized citizen guards to defeat revolutionary attempts and to control border areas made possible the emergence of ideological para-military units whose members would often find their way into the Nazi movement. All the ambivalences of the Black *Reichswehr* and the illegal rearmament contributed to undermine state monopoly of force. The crisis of authority of the state in the case of Austria had some similar roots to which one has to add the lack of commitment to a separate statehood imposed by the victors. While in Western Europe the armed forces and the defense of the territory were the result of the existence of the state, in the borderlands of the old Czarist empire, the volunteer armed units, sometimes with foreign support, simultaneously created the state and fought the revolutionary threats linked with the Bolshevik revolution. It is not surprising that in Finland and the Baltic countries the veterans of those struggles would years later reappear in fascist movements and other authoritarian responses to the crisis of the state in multi-national, economically weak, and politically fragmented democracies.[59] The state, its constitution, parliaments, and parties had for them often less legitimacy than the men who had fought for independence and created the state and also less legitimacy than the civil or white guards formed in the immediate post-war period. In addition, states whose boundaries had been defined by the victors and whose territory did not correspond with the boundaries of the nationalities, leaving irredentista and hostile minorities, did not command the same legitimacy as the nation-states of Western and Northern Europe.[60]

The weakness of the state, therefore, enabled armed citizens to take over functions of the state or attempt to create a state with the boundaries they felt it should have. This «legitimacy vacuum» contributes to explain the emergence of a new and violent style of politics ranging from the private party army, through the romantic violence of a confraternity like the Iron Guard, to the conspiratorial terrorist group like the Ustashi.

A Multi-factor Analysis

The different saliency of each of the four factors and their variants here discussed accounts for the importance and size of the different activist nuclei founding and following fascist organizations in the early stages, and also for the ideological differences within the fascist syndrome.[61] They also account for the relative importance of the membership parties, the student organizations, and particularly the para-military squads. To give one example, the war, interventionism, nationalism, class integration, and cultural protest constituted the basis of urban Milanese fascism. Border nationalism in Venezia Giulia, where the border struggle with Yugoslavia reinforced the squadristi element, is another example. The hatred of landowners and wealthier peasants of the Red domination of the Po Valley countryside and against the peasant trade unions sponsored by the *Popolari* gave impetus to agrarian fascism, as it did in Toscana and Apulia. Within a single movement the four factors discussed in previous pages contributed to the fascist wave which brought Mussolini to power. Significantly, given the Italian context, anti-Semitism at this time did not play a role. On the other hand, some of the themes we have discussed played perhaps a greater role in a movement soon to fuse with fascism, one with a pre-war history, the *Associazione*

Nazionalista.[62] In this case as in those of other successful fascist movements, the climate created by factors mentioned extended to broader segments of the society, particularly the right and interventionist sectors of conservative liberalism. There is no space to illustrate with examples from other countries how some of the variables involved converged in the birth of fascist nuclei and contributed to their relative strength. Such an analysis would, we maintain, support our emphasis on a multi- rather than a mono-causal analysis of why fascism arose, across countries, within countries and over time. It explains also why authors studying particular movements or periods in the history of fascism should give different weight to the various factors. In our view the relative importance of each of them can account for the initial appeal and character of fascist groups or their absence before the inevitable diffusion of successful models led to the mushrooming of fascist groups without vitality and roots in the socio-historical traditions of each individual country.

The Conditions for Fascist Success or Failure

Once a comparative analysis provides answers to the question why fascist parties or movements did or did not make their appearence in a particular country and period, the question of their broader bases of support requires a somewhat different answer. As we have emphasized, all these movements were late-comers on the political scene. Therefore a large part of the political space was pre-empted by parties, movements, and organizations or sub-cultures which isolated their members from the fascist appeal. As a result, the question is to some extent narrowed down to this: under what circumstances can the fascist activist nucleus extend its influence, gain members for the party and the para-military organizations and in some cases voters within the political space open to their appeal?

To the factors already discussed when answering the question «Why fascism?» we have to add three others of a structural and conjunctural character.

1. The extent of social and economic change taking place as a consequence of the war and in succeeding years. The literature dealing with the rise of Nazism has paid particular attention to shifts in the German class structure, specifically the growth of the new middle classes, a topic that occupied the attention of German sociologists; to the downward mobility of certain social groups, particularly of former army officers; to changes in the rigid status structure inherited from Wilhelminian Germany; and to the impact of economic processes of capitalist concentration and new forms of commercialization on *Handwerk* enterprises, small business and shopkeepers. The best of those sociological analyses emphasize the ideological self-consciousness of those strata inherited from the status system of a society that had not yet become fully bourgeois when confronted with a working class which had acquired a new self-consciousness on its own. In the case of Italy, studies of agrarian fascism have noted the great changes in the number of peasant owners after the war, many of them recruited from former share tenants (the *mezzadros),* and their economic and social conflicts with a sizable agricultural proletariat and poor peasantry once allied with them, but now demanding employment and wages. It was in this stratum that the large agrarians in the Po Valley, the Emilia and the Romagna could find their supporters.[63] Less attention has been paid to the sudden and large increase in the number of those with higher education unlikely to find employment opportunities congruent with their aspirations.[64] The changes in social structure in Romania and Hungary which might be

related to the upsurge in Iron Guard and Arrow Cross support have not yet been studied systematically, nor have similar changes in the Baltic area. What is even more wanting is any systematic comparison in these respects of social change in Germany and Austria with that in France, the United Kingdom and Northern Europe.

No one would question that the Great Depression in Germany, Austria, Czechoslovakia and to a lesser extent in other countries contributed to a process of political radicalization and that the appeal of both communism and fascism can be linked with the economic crisis in this period. Only in the case of Germany has Kaltefleiter[65] analyzed the process in some detail, but no comparable studies exist for other countries. It would be interesting to have a more systematic analysis of the relationship between the economic situation and fascist membership growth in Northern Italy in the period 1919–1922. The impact of the depression on the German minority in Czechoslovakia and its shift from the various idelogical camps it had affiliated with before Henlein's *Sudetendeutsche Partei* would repay an ecological analysis.[66] The impact of agrarian crisis, indebtedness to mortgage holders and tax collectors and the consequent foreclosures have been noted in Germany and Norway but not studied in cases like Romania. Undoubtedly, those who became fascist or voted for fascist parties as a result of economic crises responded to factors different from those leading to the emergence of the initial activist nucleus. More difficult to analyze, but certainly important in the German case, is the impact of inflation and particularly the succession under the Weimar Republic of inflation and depression. Recent studies of the linkages between political behavior and business cycles have shown the impact of inflation to be at least as important if not more than post-war recessions.

The comparison of the consequences of the depression in different advanced societies, however, shows that without the presence of other factors facilitating the link between the economic crisis and fascist ideology the political consequences were quite different.[67] Certainly the depression had grave social consequences in the United States without leading the small fascist and semi-fascist movements to major success.[68]

2. Crises, corruption and instability of parliamentary government. We should not ignore the failures of democratic leadership and the crisis of parliamentary institutions as a factor in the rise of fascism. It is obviously not always easy to distinguish cause and effect, but whatever contribution fascism makes to the crisis of democratic regimes, their crisis is also an independent factor in the rise of fascism. Ideological rigidities, the interference of interest groups in the political process, low quality of party leadership, and in a number of cases the corruption of politicians, became one more factor in the rise of fascism. We only have to think of how effective the fascists were in exploiting the Stavisky affair in France, the *straperlo* in Spain and some cases of corruption in Belgium. The traditional corruption of Balkan politics, particularly in Romania, was one of the main themes of the anti-system parties, particularly the Iron Guard, as it was of the peasantist parties in opposition. Unfortunately, we have no survey data on the attitude of the population toward parliament, parties and leaders and the loss of confidence in them. We have, however, one clear indicator of the crisis of the parliamentary regime: the instability of government. Ignoring for a moment the question of the cause and effect relationship, we see that the upsurge of fascism is closely related to government instability even when we consider only the period just before the cresting of the fascist wave.

3. A factor generally ignored in the literature on the rise of the fascist wave is the political and institutional context. Only the role of different electoral systems in

slowing down or facilitating the fascist flood has been widely discussed.[69] Much less attention has been paid to the *timing* of the elections. There can be little doubt that the fact that the last British election before the war took place in 1931 prevented Mosley from gathering a protest vote. Likewise the formation of the PPF after the 1936 general election in France certainly diminished its prospects of mobilizing broad support.

One variable that has been almost totally neglected in accounting for why some fascist movements failed to gain a mass basis in countries where for other reasons we would have expected them to do so, is the lack of freedom for their agitation if not the outright repression of their movements as well as the dishonest electoral practices favoring government parties. The authoritarian regimes in a number of Eastern European countries not only served some of the social and economic interests that otherwise might have supported fascism (especially if the Marxist left had been given opportunity to expose and challenge their privileges); they also perceived fascist movements as a threat to their rule. The limited progress of Bulgarian fascist groups, the radical sectarian character of Croat Ustasha terrorism and the limits imposed upon Baltic fascisms by authoritarian regimes, all come to mind in this context.[70] Let us not forget that Codreanu was one of the few founders of the fascist movement who died violently before the end of World War II under the guns of government agents; that among the few fascist founders going to jail in those years we find Szalasi under the Horthy regime and Sirk in Estonia under the presidential authoritarianism of Päts; that Rolão Preto, the founder of the Portuguese national syndicalists, had to choose exile; and that the most important and interesting Latin American fascist party, *Integralismo*, was outlawed by the Estado Novo of Vargas and its leader exiled in 1939.[71] Fascism could only grow in liberal democratic societies, but only a few of them presented favorable conditions for its growth, while a number of countries where fascist success could be expected were ruled by authoritarian regimes hostile to any form of political participation and mobilization, including one by the fascists.

Internal Problems of Fascist Movements

One obstacle in the formation of modern mass parties, as fascism generally intended to become, is factional fragmentation. Personalistic and clientelistic leadership was no obstacle to the relative unity of loosely structured liberal and conservative parties and even for radical democratic bourgeois parties. While socialist parties often suffered from ideological divisions between an independent left and a reformist majority in addition to the communist split, the trade unions often provided a strong integrating basis. The influence of the church, the often corporative character of membership and to some extent the antipathy to personalistic charismatic type of leadership allowed Christian parties to retain their unity. In contrast, fascist parties, particularly those founded late, encountered great difficulties in unifying and maintaining their unity. Paradoxically, parties whose ideological commitment was to unity were unable to fuse a variety of groups that had sprung up independently and followed different leaders. While fascist parties in their statutes and even practice initially allowed for the election of leaders, very soon a *Führerprinzip* became essential. In quite a few cases this represented a serious difficulty for the collaboration and ultimate fusion of fascist groupuscules. In the case of Spain for example, the fusion of the Falange and the National Syndicalists required the creation of the Triumvirate whose instability led to the single leadership of José Antonio Primo de Rivera and ultimately to the withdrawal of Ramiro Ledesma Ramos from the party. In a number of cases the conflicts, even violent ones, between fascists were as great as those with their other antagonists. Particularly in France the plurality of fascist movements has to be taken into account in explaining the ultimate weakness of the fascist appeal. The leadership principle and the concepts of personal loyalty linked with it, combined with the lack of an institutionalized social basis, the heterogeneity of the following and the polycentric attraction of Rome and Berlin, as well as ideological differences in groups where intellectuals played a major role, all contributed to the ultimate weakness of fascism in many countries. They also explain the hasty drive for power, sometimes the willingness to engage in coalitions in contradiction to the commitment to ideological purity, and the incapacity to build a mass organization. In this respect, Nazism under the leadership of Hitler was an exception, as in so many other respects.

Economic Development and the Rise of Fascism

This is not the place to review and take issue with the many varieties of Marxist interpretations of the rise of fascism. It should be obvious that our multi-causal analysis excludes a purely Marxist analysis, but also that in a number of cases variables noted by Marxist scholars can account, not so much for the rise of the fascist founding nuclei as for its greater or lesser mass appeal and the circumstances bringing the movements closer to power. Although the question of the function performed by fascist movements in power, the *a cui bono* question, lies outside the scope of this essay, we do not want to ignore the injunction of Max Horkheimer that whoever does not want to speak of capitalism should also remain silent on fascism.

Unfortunately, the debate has been mostly centered on the role of business in the breakdown of the Weimar Republic, the conditions for the success of the Nazi Party, Hitler's coming to power, and the Nazi policies after the *Machtergreifung*. With few exceptions little effort has been devoted to systematically comparing the economic systems of Europe in the inter-war years in relationship to the rise of fascism. A lack of conceptual clarity in many of the Marxist analyses makes it difficult to proceed to such an analysis. To establish a relationship between capitalism and the rise of fascism we would have to characterize certain countries as capitalist or at least as more or less capitalist. Another alternative would be to distinguish types of capitalism and inquire whether some of them are more closely linked to the rise of fascism than others. In the literature we seldom find such an analysis. In addition, the analysis becomes murky because so many of the authors use the term fascism in a way that covers a wide range of political phenomena. In fact, it tends to be identified with any anti-democratic movement and regime when it is not – with a convoluted logic like the communist theory of social fascism – extended to democracies and parties like the social democrats. Even assuming that all anti-democratic movements and regimes aiming at the suppression of socialist and communist labor movements perform the same function, and that therefore the movements we have narrowly defined as fascist are only variants of the same genus, that is, functional alternatives in the pursuit of the same policies, the question would still remain why there are alternative roads to the same goal. Why turn to fascism to defeat labor rather than to military-bureaucratic dictatorship? The answer would require the specification of additional variables. If we would wish to retain an economic interpretation this specification would have to make reference to the organization of productive forces or social-structural characteristics derived from the economic infrastructure. In this line of analysis we find those who emphasize the role of the petty bourgeoisie and its fears of being caught between organized labor and a dynamic and politically powerful big business. Ignoring for the moment the loose use of the term petit bourgeoisie, if we want to stay within a Marxist framework, we still would have to account for the pressures to which this stratum is subject in terms of its location in the economic structure. That is, we would have to explain the variations from country to country in the pressure of organized labor by reference to the level of economic development, the occupational structure, or the type of capitalism in each country. Ideally, we would need to know more about how different middle classes are affected in different societies by socio-economic change and how this provides the leadership and mass basis for fascist movements. After all, the capitalists would be neither capable or not interested in supporting fascist movements for their own purposes unless they would not have a good chance of recruiting a following. To stay in a Marxist framework, that chance would have to be explained in terms of the socio-economic structure. Even assuming that a Marxist interpretation would be valid for the case of Germany and/or Italy, a comparative analysis would lead us to expect similar consequences in countries where the same factors were present, while their absence would account in turn for the absence of fascist movements. In the literature we find no analysis attempting to use the variables developed in Marxist theories in this way. Only if we were to argue that the only fascist movements were the PNF and the NSDAP would the test of the Marxist theories not require such a comparative analysis. But no Marxist would accept such a narrow interpretation of his theories and agree that the economic structural variables were unique to those countries.[72]

In the space allotted to us we obviously cannot explore in depth the co-variation between the success or failure of fascist movements and the economic and social structure of European countries. However, a look at the occupational structure about 1930[73] suggests that it would be very difficult to account for the strength of fascist movements exclusively in terms of economic structure. Among industrial countries we find at least five with weak and derivative movements and three or four in which original, native fascist organizations emerged and represented some threat to democracy. However, due to the timing of elections only in Belgium and the Netherlands is there any indication of their mass appeal, while in the United Kingdom and France the significance of the fascist movements is measured more by the quality of their leadership and the public impact of their presence than by their numerical strength. Among twelve industrial countries, i.e., those with less than 1/3 of the population dependent on agriculture, fascism in one form or another can be considered successful only in Germany and Austria. Outside of those two countries it is only in France and Czechoslovakia (and there only in agrarian Slovakia) that fascism or other authoritarian tendencies represented a real threat. Certainly the industrial countries we have mentioned, Scandinavia, Belgium and the Netherlands would be on one's list of most advanced capitalist countries and make it difficult to establish a link between capitalism and the rise of fascism or even the alternative authoritarian political responses as predicted by the most vulgar Marxist theories of fascism.[74] In fact, even if we consider the mobilization of the working class in trade unions and their support for leftist parties questioning the capitalist system, the link would be difficult to establish since, after all, Czechoslovakia and France were countries in which the communists gained considerable electoral support.

When we turn to the semi-industrial countries, the Marxist thesis counting as fascist all anti-democratic political tendencies including authoritarian regimes finds considerable support. Only two of the countries in that category, Ireland and Finland, managed to save their democratic institutions, and of these two, Finland was very close to a breakdown and barely retained parliamentary institutions by limiting the freedom of the communists. In Italy the fascists gained power, and in Spain and to some degree in Hungary they participated in power, while in Estonia and Latvia successful fascist movements were defeated in the struggle for power by authoritarian solutions to the inter-war crisis. In four other countries, Portugal, Greece, Poland, and Lithuania no significant fascist movements were able to emerge, power coming into the hands of authoritarian regimes with more or less pseudo-fascist characteristics. It would be difficult to find any common characteristic of a social- economic character among the countries where fascist movements acquired some importance and countries where they failed. Certainly the development in these countries gives some support to Borkenau's thesis about fascism as a developmental dictatorship and his emphasis on the accumulation of social tensions resulting from the early phases of industrialization and the premature diffusion of a labor movement whose demands cannot be satisfied.[75] This line of argument could be reinforced if we look at the score for the three most agrarian societies, Romania, Yugoslavia and Bulgaria. All three had periods of authoritarian rule that destroyed incipient and weak democracies or a radical peasantist regime (as in the case of Bulgaria). Only in Romania could a popular fascist movement acquire a personality of its own and considerable mass appeal. Looking at that list of semi-industrial and agrarian societies, we discover that fascist movements might have been somewhat stronger in countries with a more stratified rural society and a larger number of large holdings than in those where landowning peasants constituted a larger proportion of the rural population. But even that generalization does not hold very well since both Latvia and Estonia (after the agrarian reforms) were countries with a large proportion of peasant owners. On the other hand, while peasant owners were very numerous in Portugal, large holdings in the south gave the country a social configuration more like that of Spain or Hungary.

Since so much of the analysis of the social basis of fascism focuses on the role of the salaried middle classes we might look at the proportion of salaried employees in the gainfully occupied population. By definition that proportion is higher in the industrial than in the semi-industrial or agrarian countries. The proportion of salaried employees was disproportionately high in Germany, where it made up 20 per cent of the labor force. In Italy (10 per cent) it was below that of most industrial countries. In quite a large number of countries with a high proportion of white collar employees fascism made very little headway. Nor does the proportion of employers and independent workers belonging to the old small business and artisan middle classes and the class of independent farmers provide any clue. Their number is high in the peasant countries of Eastern and Balkan Europe, too, and variations within them do not account for variations in fascist strength. In the industrial countries where a large proportion of the self-employed would belong to the small and medium business sector, the variations do not seem to show any clear pattern of relationship with the success of fascist movements.

Our analysis does not exclude that other characteristics of the economic system, of the type of capitalist development and of international economic relationships would account for the reaction to the economic crises in the twenties and the thirties, nor that the explanations in socio-economic terms of fascist movements among certain social strata within their particular societies would not be valid. It only confirms our impression that mono-causal economic interpretation seems inadequate. Nor is it, we may add, wholly satisfactory to explain the varying strength of communism or anarcho-syndicalism among labor or the maximalist tendencies within socialist parties in this way. Since we consider the character of the left to be one contributing factor to the fascist response, it is not easy to link the economic structure with the rise of fascism through that intervening variable either. Our comparative digression indirectly strengthens our emphasis on a multi-causal analysis which would include more strictly political and cultural historical factors. We feel that our appro-ach, emphasizing the political space occupied and the character of fascism as a late-comer, better explains the success of fascist movements amongst various strata in the population and the diverse social composition of their following, than do theories based solely on differences in social structure from country to country.

Proto-fascism: Would Fascism Have Been Possible Without World War I?

Because we have emphasized World War I, and particularly the defeat or disap-pointments following in the wake of the armistice as one of the conditions for the emergence of sizeable nuclei and the availability of a generation of men and women for the new and violent style of politics, it is tempting to ask what would have happened if there had been no World War. Would there have been no fascism? Our answer must be a qualified no. There would have been political movements and parties, at least in some countries, with many of the characteristics of fascism, but it seems doubtful if the complex phenomenon that was Italian fascism would have been possible.[76] Without Italian fascism, it is difficult to conceive the broader ideological appeal of fascism in the Europe of the inter-war years. It also seems doubtful that a movement of the scope of Nazism could have arisen in Germany, even though political tendencies with similar characteristics would undoubtedly have appeared, either in a democratized German empire or in a subsequent democratic republic. It is fairly clear that populist, anti-democratic, anti-liberal, anti-western, anti-Semitic mass movements and terro-rist groups with the characteristics we find in the Union of the Russian People before the war and later in the Iron Guard would have surfaced.

There is no comparative study of the movements and ideologies that we might call proto- or pre-fascist before World War I. A number of studies have traced fascism back to movements like the *Action Française*,[77] the *Associazione Nazionalista Italiana*,[78] the anti-Semitic parties in Germany and Austria, the *Alldeutscher Verband* and pan-Germanism as well as the *Deutsche Arbeiterpartei*[79] (in 1918 to become the NSDAP), the Union of the Russian People (URP) and similar groups in Czarist Russia.[80] Those movements and parties were obviously very different. The intellectually sophisticated *Action Française* seems far removed from the populism of the Black Hundreds, and historians might legitimately question the usefulness of a comparison of pre- and proto-fascist political manifestations in this way. Scholars have hesitated in their discussion of such movements and their ideologies.[81] They locate them in the broad spectrum of what might be called the Right, but at the same time feel that they are fundamentally different from the conservative Right holding power in many countries in that period, that is, the conservative Establishment, aristocratic, bourgeois or bureaucratic Right, linked with the traditional institutions of Crown, Church and Army. As a result of this taxonomical and substantive uneasiness we find expressions like the New Right, Radical or Revolutionary Right, Populist Right, Plebiscitarian Right, etc. These phenomena are not easy to define, the differences are evident and sometimes the boundaries are fuzzy, but there can be little doubt that the leadership of these movements, their social bases, their style, their forms of action and their ideological themes are different from traditional conservatism while they share some of the same hostilities against the heirs of the French Revolution and the emerging, still internationalist, labor movement as the conservatives. The problem becomes even more complicated because sectors of the Establishment have links with these forces, tolerate them, or attempt to manipulate them and sometimes go as far as incorporating into their own program some of their themes. These are patterns we will encounter again later in the case of fascism. The boundaries between pure reaction, moderate conservatism, clerical conservatism and the new revolutionary conservatism with proto-fascist characteristics are far from clearly drawn. Moreover, the political manifestations at the interstices of the basic social and political cleavage-lines emerging in the second half (and particularly in the last quarter) of the 19th century differ greatly from country to country.

For this reason it is not easy to define this elusive phenomenon. A better understanding of its historical and social roots seems essential, however, for identifying some structural problems to which fascism would be a response and to delineate the ideological heritage out of which fascism grew or with which it could link in the struggle for power.

These movements, which we hesitantly might call proto-fascist, emerge in a period in which the *ancien régime* for a variety of reasons is in crisis. The new liberal democratic and social forces find it difficult to assert themselves in the multi-national empires threatened by conflicts of modern nationalism and in societies confronted with the demands of modern imperialism. The traditional legitimacy of crown, church and the bureaucratic military state is increasingly questioned, but the new forms of democratic, liberal, legal, and rational legitimacy are far from being generally accepted. Proto-fascist politics attempts a contradictory synthesis of tradition with modernity, attacking many of the values of the Establishment and at the same time rejecting its modern challengers. In this respect it shows a homology with fascism, which also attempted to question the traditional and bourgeois capitalist order while rejecting democratic reformist, socialist and even Christian-social challenges to it. Like fascism, these proto-fascist movements are ultra-nationalist in the sense of putting loyalty to a mystical nation or «*Volk*», sometimes understood in racist or pseudo-religious terms, ahead of loyalty to a state which could not be identified fully with the nation. All these movements attempt in one way or another to escape from the distinction between rulers and ruled, between a political class and the people. They share an antipathy, scorn or hatred against those in power, be it a transnational aristocracy, the court, the Junkers, the bureaucracy, notables in politics, parliamentarians, a wealthy bourgeoisie, the ecclesiastical establishment or even a politically influential academic and intellectual élite. They are fundamentally anti-élitist but at the same time argue for the need for a new élite. In one way or another they are hostile to the emerging class-conscious working class, particularly to the extent that it questions the nationalistic identification in the name of internationalist socialism. Ideologically they grope for new forms of social integration, beyond those based on submission to the authority of the state, strong enough to overcome the interest conflicts within society, to face adequately actual or imagined threats coming from other societies, and to be successful in the Darwinian struggle between political units in the era of imperialism. The leadership of these movements does not on the whole come from the Establishment, even if déclassés or marginal elements of it sometimes

174

join them. Neither does it come from the emerging organizations of the underprivileged, but from a variety of groups with an ambiguous status both in the traditional and the emerging industrial capitalist society: intellectuals and journalists rather than established academics, middle-level educators and school teachers, minor civil servants and priests, independent artisans, small land-owners and businessmen and very often students. In contrast to the old Establishment, they are conscious of the need in a democratic era to mobilize the common man, often seizing upon grievances of particular groups like peasants, artisans, small businessmen, lower civil servants and in some cases of workers. Their demagogy is directed to the defense of interests threatened by socio-economic change and the competition between ethnic and national groups. It is very often directed against Jews who have benefited from legal equality and growing opportunities in education and business. These movements rise in defense of traditional values, religious and cultural, that in their view are ineffectively defended or even betrayed by the ruling élites and threatened by new socio-economic forces linked with the Industrial Revolution and modern capitalism as well as by the emergence of new self-conscious nationalities challenging their position in the state. The renewed strength of a transnational, «ultramontane» (as it was called in the German culture area), Catholic Church after 1870, sometimes leads them to forms of anti-clericalism and religio-political nationalism. There is in these movements a fundamental anti-modern and anti-international streak which we will find again in fascism. There is also a basic ambiguity in their relation to the modern state and in its ways of conducting international relations in a world of states rather than of nations and an awareness that the established authorities and institutions cannot and sometimes do not want to mobilize the people for collective enterprises which constitute the national dream. The defeat of the state in war or in international diplomacy or its lack of interest in imperial expansion becomes a stimulus for the ultra-nationalist efforts at national integration. We have only to think of the impact of the Italian defeat at Adowa in 1896, the Russo-Turkish War and the defeat by Japan, the impact of the language settlement by Badeni in Austria, and obviously the defeat of France in the Franco-Prussian War in the emergence of these movements.

These proto-fascist movements were an expression of the political, socio-economic, cultural and religious crisis of European societies, particularly of some of the multi-national empires and the newly unified Germany and Italy. They found little parallel in the established nation-states of Western and Northern Europe and similar tendencies were more successfully absorbed by the political system of the United Kingdom. They had their high point in the last decade of the 19th century and persisted with ups and downs until World War I to re-emerge strengthened after the war. Inept leadership and a basic lack of sympathy on the part of the Establishment very often weakened them, but they left a heritage that would be articulated more successfully or co-opted by some of the fascist movements. An analysis of proto-fascism has to be included in any serious study of the origins of fascist movements. Proto-fascisms share with their successors the rejection of parliamentary and electoral politics as the main arena of political discourse, the emphasis on mass mobilization through membership and public demonstrations of strength, the appeal to all sectors of the population rather than to distinct socio-economic groups, and the bid to create affiliated interest groups or penetrate existing organizations. In this respect proto-fascisms are a modern political manifestation. They shared with the fascists a passion for violence, but only World War I would provide mass politics with effective armed para-military groups. Even in the aesthetics of such movements we find some affinities with fascism, but only after World War I would the fascist style become one of the great political innovations.

In summary, the late 19th century saw the emergence of a confused and contradictory undercurrent in politics that the established structures might have condoned, but basically looked upon with suspicion and might have had success only in a few societies or been absorbed by left radical political structures. World War I allowed those undercurrents to emerge with force and acquire a certain degree of respectability and power. In this context the unique constellation of factors that made Italian fascism possible cannot be over-emphasized: its fusion with the *Associazione Nazionalista* and with its more respectable leadership and the incorporation of a variety of intellectual and ideological elements dating back to the pre-war period. Without the war, however, it is doubtful whether the Giolittian project would have been so fully defeated, and without that defeat and Mussolini in power, there probably would have been no era of fascism as Nolte has described it.

On the other hand, without the *völkisch*, anti-Semitic movements, the racial imperialism, and the pan-Germanism in the Germanic center of Europe, that era would have had a very different character.[82] Fascism would still have been a powerful anti-democratic, anti-liberal nationalist and anti-proletarian attempt at social integration, but its effects would never have been so tragic. Without such *völkisch* undercurrents it is also doubtful whether the defeat of the fascist ideological alternative would ever have been so total.

The Diffusion of Fascism

Our analysis has focused on the conditions favorable to the emergence of a genuine fascist nucleus rooted in a particular society and the limits of its appeal to a broader electorate. We have still to account for the patterns of diffusion of fascism outside of the centers of its success. It was always difficult to conceive of fascism as an international movement since extreme nationalism was essential to its appeal and national interests could easily be perceived to conflict with those of the major fascist powers. Until the *Anschluss* the existence of two poles of attraction with somewhat different ideological emphases and their competition for influence allowed the minor parties to choose their international reference point and the connection most compatible with their national interest. To put it in contemporary terminology, the polycentrism of fascism facilitated its diffusion.[83] A hindrance to the diffusion of fascism was the fact that only in a few cases did it have links with the pre-World War I traditions and organizations. This was in clear contrast to the communist movement which emerged from the splits within the pre-war socialist movement and could in part draw on its political and organizational experience. Proto-fascist movements and parties never acquired a cohesion comparable to the fascist parties, nor attain such organizational strength and stable constituency. Fascists sometimes grew out of them, but less through splits than by a generational revolt. In addition, the proto-fascist movements had no international links like the socialists reinforcing their appeal.

Nor did the fascists find a supporting basis in a transnational institution like the Catholic Church and the intellectual networks linked with it, such as the Christian Democratic parties would find. In view of all this, the appearance of minor fascist parties poses a problem. Even though there is evidence, as in Borejsza's article in this volume, of direct or indirect support coming from Rome or Berlin after the founding of such parties, the initiative was local. In a number of cases the founders had spent periods is one or another capacity – mainly as students – in countries where fascism was on the rise, but this explanation would not hold for the political evolution of men like Mosley, Doriot, Quisling or Degrelle. It is worth noticing that these and other founders of fascist movements abandoned a potentially successful career in other parties to drift toward fascism.

The history of minor parties tells us a lot about the dynamics of the diffusion of political models in modern times. One crucial fact was undoubtedly the perception these men (and many others at the time) had of the achievements of fascism in power.[84] Mistakenly, political leaders in the thirties could see fascism as the wave of the future. In addition, they could in some countries see collaboration or accommodation with successful powers on the basis of ideological affinity as one way to pursue the national interest. In a paradoxical way, national fascism was seen as a way to avoid the international conflict looming on the horizon. Another factor was the limited space provided by a well structured modern party system for dissident and ambitious leaders. This limitation contrasted clearly with the less disciplined parties and more personalistic and clientilistic politics in the nineteenth century. A dissident from his party like Mosley, Degrelle, Doriot, and Quisling could see a chance to create his own following in the structured and ideological politics of the thirties only by identifying with the new transnational ideological stream, hoping to adapt it to the national context. Paradoxically, however, in the case of fascism this transnational appeal became the undoing of such leaders. The case of Mosley's BUF in contrast to his New Party is paradigmatic.

In a strange way a more selective incorporation of fascist ideas by other parties rejecting any identification or connection with fascism as a whole was often more successful politically. The penetration of fascist ideas and appeals into other movements would deserve a serious study. In quite a few cases, other similar movements took away the ground from the emerging genuine fascist movements. In this context we only have to think of the Baltic and certain Balkan countries or even of the Iberian peninsula. The functions that fascism could perform in the socio-political system of societies in crisis as underlined in a Marxist analysis could be performed without invoking many of the other distinctive characteristics of fascism. Particularly the organizational forms and the para-military structure could not be transferred to societies where the social bases for such organizations were not favorable. On the other side, the fascist style, the rhetorical and aesthetic dimensions, the shirts, the songs, the rituals that made it so appealing to a minority of the inter-war generations, particularly the students, did not find the same echo in many societies.[85] This suggests that an explanation of both the success and the failure of fascism requires greater attention to what we might call the dramatic and aesthetic aspects of the movement.

In our view the appeal of genuine fascism has to be explained on the basis of a three-dimensional definition of the phenomenon in terms of its ideology, its style and its new forms of political action and organization. Only where all three could find an echo in the society were there genuine movements. It is the loss of appeal and viability of at least two of those dimensions after the defeat of the Axis that accounts, together with many other factors, for the lack of vitality of neo-fascism after World War II. In this context the policies of democratic governments in the later thirties limiting the public manifestation of fascism, probably helped to weaken its appeal and even more its destructive impact on the social and political fabric of their societies.

The Marxist interpretation, which in our view is insufficient in accounting for the emergence and success of fascist parties, is nevertheless fruitful in pointing to the need to analyze functional alternatives to fascism in societies in crisis. Behind the confusion of labelling other movements and regimes fascist lies a valid insight.[86] The Estados Novos of Salazar or Vargas were not the result of a fascist movement taking power, but they would also be difficult to understand without reference to the era of fascism. On the other side, it would be important for the comparative study of politics in this period to analyze more thoroughly the implications of the absence or weakness of the fascist component in authoritarian regimes. There can be little doubt that the penetration into society, the degree of social integration achieved, the difficulties in articulating new oppositional stances, the degree of institutionalization and stability achieved in Italy and particularly in Nazi Germany have no parallel in other rightist regimes around the world. The defeat of fascism has deprived post-war anti-democratic political systems of all claim to any genuine ideological appeal and legitimacy beyond their borders. To account for that appeal we cannot ignore the actual or apparent achievements of fascist regimes, their new conception of «a welfare with soul» (others would say public relations), and the degree of consensus they achieved for a few years, won the admiration even from those who rejected them. To examine these achievements is a distasteful yet necessary task for scholars, and so far unaccomplished. In this context, even the comparison of Franco's Spain and Salazar's Portugal could shed light on what distinctive contribution even a weak fascist movement could make to what otherwise might have been a purely conservative traditional bureaucratic military regime. In the context of anti-democratic authoritarian solutions in semi-developed countries with a capitalist economy, the modernizing component of fascism, the leftist ideological themes, the effort of social mobilization, the idea of national integration on secular basis, the populism[87], and the creation of channels of mobility through the party and its organizations, which might to some extent be discounted in a broader structural analysis, might in that case turn out to be significant. Indirectly, such a comparison provides us with some clues for an answer to the questions «why fascism?» and «why fascists?»[88] It would also reduce to its proper limits what is valid in Marxist and neo-Marxist interpretations of fascism in power.

NOTES

Some of the themes of this paper are developed further in my essay: «Some Notes Toward a Comparative Study of Fascism in Sociological Historical Perspective» in Walter Laqueur, ed. *Fascism: A Reader's Guide,* (London: Wildwood House, 1976). There, and in the chapters on the various fascist movements in this volume the reader will find empirical data on the social characteristics of the founders of the fascist parties (compared to the leadership of Christian Democratic, Socialist and Communist parties), the membership and the electorate. That essay also provides bibliographic references supporting our argument, here reduced to a minimum for brevity's sake.

[1] It should be emphasized that this essay does not deal with fascist regimes and their successes or failures, but the conditions conducive to the emergence, varying strength, and success of fascist movements. Renzo de Felice in *Intervista sul fascismo a cura di Michael A. Ledeen,* (Bari: Laterza, 1975) has rightly underlined the need to distinguish the movement from the regime in the case of Italian fascism, and the same can be said about other fascisms. It could also be argued, however, that without a fascist movement it is difficult to conceive a fascist regime in the sense in which he uses the term and we would use it. Without a strong movement before the take-over of power it is difficult to see how a regime that pretends to be fascist could develop some of its distinctive characteristics, particularly its stress on the need to mobilize the popula-

tion, its emphasis on ideology, its view on the transformation of man through action, its policy of subverting the established hierarchies of society and replacing them by political cadres created through the movement, etc. Only Italian fascism, National Socialism, and perhaps the Iron Guard were movements capable of creating fascist regimes. Only the first two succeeded in doing so. In the course of the Civil War and in its immediate aftermath, the Falangists believed that they could establish a fascist regime in Spain. But even if Franco, despite his displaying the trappings of fascism, had not preferred from the beginning an authoritarian regime with quite different characteristics, it is unlikely that a movement so weak in its roots in the society and in the country's politico-cultural traditon as the Falangists could have succeeded. Even assuming that Franco were more sincere in his commitment to the fascist model, in itself a doubtful assumption, it is unlikely that he would have understood the essence of the fascist phenomenon. Likewise, it is improbable that the surviving fascist leaders could ever have found support to displace him and their other allies in the Civil War. They would probably have shared the same fate as the Iron Guard in the hands of Antonescu. Another question we cannot explore here is whether in a more favorable international context than the one created by the German Nazi hegemony in Europe and the war, the fascist movements, suppressed or co-opted by authoritarian regimes, would have resurfaced and installed fascist regimes in those countries where they represented a politically significant force. Had the more strictly fascist elements within the Italian and German regimes (if they had lasted) outlived Mussolini and Hitler, it might even be debated whether they would have had the vitality to carry on the ideas of the movement. This is a question beyond the scope of this essay.

[2] R. Palme Dutt, *Fascism and Social Revolution* (New York: International Publishers, 1934).

[3] Calvo Sotelo in parliament on May 5, 1936, quoted by Stanley G. Payne, *The Spanish Revolution. A Study of the Social and Political Tensions that Culminated in the Civil War in Spain,* (New York, Norton, 1970), pp. 196–197. In *Claridad,* the mouthpiece of the maximalist socialists, Araquistain reached the same conclusion: «The historical dilemma is fascism or socialism, and only violence will decide the issue», maintaining that since what passed for «fascism» in Spain was weak, socialism would win. *Claridad,* February 13, 1936 (p. 194).

[4] Summer of 1929 report prepared by the ministry of Foreign Affairs for Mussolini, quoted by John F. Coverdale, *Italian Intervention in the Spanish Civil War* (Princeton, New Jersey: Princeton University Press, 1975), p. 36.

See also the report of Italian Ambassador Guariglia in 1933 on his policy toward Spanish fascism: «We have to help them . . to overcome their purely Catholic, monarchist and even reactionary prejudices. We must aid them to avoid taking up the ideology of the *Action Française,* and to forget primoderiverismo. Military pronunciamientos . . must be avoided. Propaganda among the agricultural and laboring masses is essential. . . adopt the modern ideal of unanimous collaboration of all classes, united by the single superior principle of the authority of the state,» quoted by Coverdale, *op.cit.,* p. 47–48. On the ambivalent relation of Spanish fascism to the right, the tensions within it, its search for a popular base, see Javier Jímenez Campo, *El Fascismo en la crisis de la segunda república española,* Madrid, Centro de Investigaciones Sociológicas, 1979.

[5] The author has developed the ideological themes involved in a definition of fascism as both an anti-movement and a new synthesis movement in the chapter in W. Laqueur, *op.cit.* There the appeal to the anti-themes and the distinctive themes and style to different bases of support in the disorganized societies of post-war Europe is analyzed in great detail.

[6] See Karl Loewenstein, «Legislative Control of Political Extremism in European Democracies», *Columbia Law Review,* 38, No. 4, April 1938, pp. 591–622, No. 5, May 1938, pp. 725–774 for an excellent review of those efforts.

[7] Tönu Parming, *The Collapse of Liberal Democracy and the Rise of Authoritarianism in Estonia,* [Beverly Hills: Sage (Contemporary Political Sociology Series), 1975], see pp. 39–41 44–46, 55–56.

[8] A good example of a national fascist movement with no foreign identification whose leader would end in the resistance and a Gestapo concentration camp was the Latvian *Perkonkrusts* suppressed by a fascistiziced regime created by the peasant party leader Ulmanis, see Jürgen von

Hehn, *Lettland zwischen Demokratie und Diktatur,* (Munich: Isar Verlag, 1957 (Jahrbücher für die Geschichte Osteuropas)).

[9] Significantly, Wilhelm Alff, *Der Begriff Faschismus und andere Aufsätze zur Zeitgeschichte* (Frankfurt am Main: Suhrkampf, 1973), p. 50, in his definition of fascism, writes: «The growing success of the organized proletariat under conditions of relatively developed democracy, that is, freedom for social forces on the left and their mobilization, is a condition for the emergence of fascism.» The same point is made by Eugen Weber, «The right. An Introduction» in Hans Rogger and E. Weber, (eds.), *The European Right. A Historical Profile,* (Berkeley: University of California Press, 1965) who rightly notes: «The state provides the great revolutionary force before the age of mass democracy. But it is hard to define it as of the Right or the Left, as in a truly authoritarian system such categories have little relevance. They only become significant when freedom of thought and speech creates the opportunity for political action and debate». (p. 16–17).

[10] This was true for the urban campaign of the Nazis in 1928 and the unexpected success among farmers, described by Orlow. See Dietrich Orlow, *The History of the Nazi Party: 1919–1933,* (Pittsburgh: University of Pittsburgh Press) 1969, Chap. 4, «The Failure of the Urban Plan», pp. 76–127. Another example is the lack of success of the Spanish followers of Ledesma Ramos penetrating the syndicalist trade union masses of the CNT (in spite of solidarity, demonstrations with one of their strikes and adoption of the colors of the anarchosyndicalist flag, etc.).

[11] In this context the inability of the SPD to appeal to the German peasantry and the belated revision of its agrarian program, in contrast to the readiness of Scandinavian labor parties to work with the peasant parties in response to the depression acquires special importance. This has been rightly emphasized by Sten S. Nilson, «Wahlsoziologische Probleme des Nationalsozialismus», *Zeitschrift für die gesamte Staatswissenschaft,* Vol. 110, 1954, p. 279ff. To some extent the question of fascism among white collar employees in Germany can be reversed by asking: why did the Socialists fail in appealing to them, followed by the question why a social group, feeling politically homeless, should have chosen fascism. More generally on the relations between the SPD and the German peasantry, see A. Gerschenkron, *Bread and Democracy in Germany* (Los Angeles: University of California Press 1943).

[12] The upsurge of the Iron Guard is in part a result of the crisis of the Peasant party. In Poland the fact that the Peasant party under the leadership of Vitos was in opposition to the emerging authoritarian regime might have pre-empted political space from any populist fascist movement.

[13] Chapters in this book provide ample evidence of this barrier encountered by fascists, even in those cases like Belgium where Rex emerged out of the Catholic political subculture. We have shown in Laqueur, *op. cit.* table 14, p. 83, the weakness of the Italian fascists in areas of *Populari* strength.

[14] It is noteworthy that the most successful of the Baltic fascist movements was in Protestant Estonia while in Lithuania no significant fascist mass movement arose. There the Catholic party would be supporting the establishment of an authoritarian corporativist regime.

[15] The PPI vote in 1921 was 21.2%. In 1924 (with Mussolini in power) it had been reduced to 9.1%, a loss of 57.1%, while the *Zentrum* in July 1932 obtained 12.5% of the vote, only to find itself reduced in March 1933 (with Hitler already in power) to 11.2%, a loss of 10.4%.

[16] This dimension of the CEDA *(Confederación Española de Derechas Autónomas)* and particularly the JAP *(Juventud de Acción Popular)* led to their stigmatization as «fascist» by the left, a label that «justified» the tragic October 1934 revolution to prevent its entry into the government. Contemporary historians like Paul Preston, *The Spanish Right under the Second Republic: An Analysis,* (Occasional Publications, No. 3, University of Reading, School of Contemporary European Studies, 1971) and «The 'Moderate' Right and the Undermining of the Second Republic in Spain 1931 – 1933,» in *European Studies Review,* 3,4, 1973; and Richard A.H. Robinson, *The Origins of Franco's Spain: The Right, the Republic and Revolution, 1931–1936,* (Pittsburgh: University of Pittsburgh Press, 1970), continue the debate, marshalling the inevitably contradictory and ambiguous evidence. The question is homologous to that of assigning weight to communistoid and other antidemocratic tendencies in the ideology (and sometimes political actions) of socialist parties that rejected social democracy and competed successfully with the communists. Who would deny that in comparison with the German or

180

Czech social democrats during those years the anti-Marxist SPÖ with its stance reduced the space of the KPÖ by presenting itself in «wolf's clothing». Likewise, the «bolshevization» (to use their own term) of the PSOE under the leadership of Largo Caballero in Spain left little room for the PCE, although no one would call those parties communist. Ultimately, for those socialists the alternatives were not democracy or fascism but socialism or fascism, as for the right they were fascism or socialism. The work by Norbert Leser, *Zwischen Reformismus und Bolschevismus, Der Austromarxismus in Theorie und Praxis* (Vienna, Europa, 1968) is the best analysis of those ideological and practical ambiguities in the Austrian case.

[17] The affiliation rate per thousand males over age 21 to the PNF on April 30, 1921 (given by De Felice, *op.cit.*, pp. 8–11) south of Rome was 5.0%, in Sicily and Sardinia 5.3%, while north of Rome it was 11.0%. These were regions certainly with more clientelistic politics.

[18] On this point see my preliminary analysis of the biographical data of the founders and top leaders of fascist parties compared to communists, socialists and demo-Christians, in W. Laqueur, *op.cit.*

[19] For data on the electoral strength of fascist parties, see table in Juan J. Linz, *ibid*, table 15, pp. 89–91.

[20] On this point see some of the contributions in this volume and Peter H. Merkl, *Political Violence under the Swastika: 581 Early Nazis*, (Princeton, New Jersey: Princeton University Press, 1975). Unfortunately, there is no similar study comparing *squadristi* and members of the PNF not ready to fight in the streets of Italy.

[21] There is an extensive bibliography on this theme quoted in my essay in Laqueur, (ed.), *op.cit.* Renzo de Felice, *Intervista sul fascismo a cura di Michael A. Ledeen*, (Bari: Laterza, 1975), also tends to see fascism as an Italian phenomenon and to question the usefulness of a broader category. Paradoxically, in the introdction to the Nazi review of European fascist and national socialist movements by Werner Haas, *Europa will leben. Die nationalen Erneuerungsbewegungen in Wort und Bild* (Berlin, Batschari, 1936), the opposite thesis is stated, that fascism could have a more universal appeal and that the «exclusivity» of the *völkisch* National Socialism and its racism limited that possibility.

[22] On the involvement of different states and nationalities in World War I and the magnitude of the conflict, see Lewis F. Richardson, *Statistics of Deadly Quarrels* (Pittsburgh: Boxwood, 1960), pp. 32–35.

[23] Typically, in the speech accepting the leadership of the Falange Socialista Boliviana, Oscar Unzaga de la Vega said, after mentioning his brother's death in the war: «Our generation found itself facing its destiny. It was the pain of the war that made us into men, the pain of the war that armed our spirit and our hand to fight for the Fatherland . . *the moral pain of the defeated fatherland.*» in *Conozca Falange Socialista Boliviana*, (La Paz: Editorial Universitaria, 1972), p. 139.

[24] Although Italy was among the victors the circumstances under which intervention took place, the widespread opposition to the venture which was not launched in response to aggression, the inequities in the draft of the rural population, the defeat at Caporetto, the later efforts of psychological mobilization and the expectations of social change, the hostility of the working class and its parties to the returning officers, etc. account for the different reactions from those in other countries. See: Giovanni Sabbatucci, *I combattenti nel primo dopoguerra* (Bari: Laterza, 1974). The war and defeat at Caporetto forced a rethinking of the problems of national integration. The disappointment to nationalist aspirations in the Adriatic at the peace conference lead to the «victory without wings» idea and the paramilitary efforts in that area which fostered the rise of fascism.

[25] The non-existence of a fascist movement in Russia despite its defeat in the war and despite the loss of much of its Western border territories is explained by the victory of the Soviets; but as Wilhelm Alff, *Der Begriff Faschismus und andere Aufsätze zur Zeitgeschichte, op.cit.* notes, a liberal-republican regime would have provided fertile ground for a fascist movement linking with pan-slavist anti-Western populism.

[26] It is significant that the Rodna Zaschtita «home guard» with a fascist program was founded in 1923 in opposition to the Stambuliski radical peasant regime. Like other parties it appealed for the revision of the peace treaties and took an anti-Semitic stand. Both this party and the

Nationale Zadruga Faczisti founded in 1931, as all others, were dissolved in 1934 following the consolidation of authoritarian rule.

[27] The writings of Ramiro Ledesma Ramos,¿*Fascismo en España? Discurso a las juventudes de España* (Esplugues de Llobregat, Ariel 1968), first published in 1935, p. 42 and of Michael Manoilescu, *El Partido Unico* [Zaragoza; Biblioteca de Estudios Sociales, 1938 (Spanish translation of the work of the Romanian politician)], pp. 151–160 are examples among others.

[28] See for example, Ramiro Ledesma Ramos, *Ibid.*, p. 62, 288–291; Reinhard Kühnl, *Die nationalsozialistische Linke 1925–1930*, (Meisenheim am Glan: Anton Hain, 1966), pp. 38, 118–26 and the Italian articles quoted in footnote 36 in James Gregor «On understanding Fascism: A Review of some Contemporary Literature», *American Political Science Review*, Vol. 67, No. 4, 1973, pp. 1332–1347.

[29] Risto Alapuro and Erik Allardt, «Crisis and Re-equilibration: The Lapua Movement in Finland,» in Juan J. Linz and Alfred Stepan (eds.) *The Breakdown of Democratic Regimes.* (Baltimore: Johns Hopkins University Press, 1978, pp. 122–141).

[30] One aspect of the birth of the extreme right groups (and indirectly of the climate in which Nazism grew) that cannot be ignored is the influx into Germany of Baltic intellectuals and those who had formed their anti-Bolshevism and revolutionary nationalism in the border conflicts with the Soviet Union.

[31] This theme is well documented for Germany in Peter Merkl, *Political Violence under the Swastika, op. cit.* The new consciousness and political demands derived from it among Italian *combattenti* can be found in Giovanni Sabbatucci, *I combattenti nel primo dopoguerra*, (Bari:Laterza 1974). See also Michael A. Ledeen, «The War as a Style of Life,» in Stephen Ward, ed. *The War Generation: Veterans of the First World War.* (New York: Kennikat, 1975).

[32] However, social revolutionary radicalism is no sufficient explanation, as Nolte has noted in reference to Spain. Neither the continuous and violent conflict between employers, syndicalists and anarchists in Catalonia nor the semi-revolutionary general strike organized by the socialists, nor the «trienio bolchevique» in the Andalusian countryside, gave rise to a fascist or fascist type movement, but to gunmen for hire, repression by the authorities and ultimately to the army's pronunciamiento.

[33] Victor Adler in letter to Edward Bernstein, (London) March 17, 1899, quoted in Victor Adler, *Briefwechsel mit August Bebel, gesammelt und erläutert von Friedrich Adler*, Vienna, 1954, p. 298.

[34] Hannah Arendt, *The Origins of Totalitarianism* (Cleveland: Meridian Books, 1958), chap. 3, pp. 222–266. There can be little doubt about the impact of pan-Germanism on the early NSDAP and Hitler, and the rejection by Hitler of the Habsburg state and later Austria, as states. The same desire to escape the boundaries of the state can be found in Szalazi's ideas of a Carpatho-Danubian Great Fatherland, or The United Lands and the March of Hungary in which the national minorities would have their autonomy. Van Severen likewise, aimed at founding a Dietschland, a state where the Dutch-speaking areas would be reunited, spelling the doom of Belgium as a state, later to become a *Dietsch Rijk* including the Benelux countries. Spanish fascists and fascisticized rightists discovered the Hispanidad as a broader cultural and even economic community opposed to dollar diplomacy dominated pan-Americanism. These pan-tendencies broke in a sense with the state as a basic focus of loyalty putting the nation and sometimes the race first, often with a strong imperialist component.

[35] The politics of the «war generation» is probably more complex than is generally assumed, see Stephen R. Ward, *The War Generation*, (op.cit.) with chapters on Great Britain, the U.S., France, Italy and Germany. On Italy in addition to the chapter by Michael A. Ward, *op.cit.*, see the excellent monographs by Giovanni Sabbatucci, *I combattenti nel primo dopoguerra, op.cit.* and Fernando Cordova, *Arditi e Legionarii Dannunziani*, (Padova: Marsilio, 1969), which show the divisions among the veterans' organizations in relation to their political action and the limits of support of the fascists among them, particularly in their competition with D'Annunzio.

[36] On Czech fascism, see the essay by A. Gejanova (pp. 67–91) and Tomas Pasak (pp. 92–111) in *Fašismus a Europa (Fascism and Europe).* An International Symposium, Prague, Institute of History, Czechoslovak Academy of Sciences, 1969 and Bela Vago, *The Shadow of*

the Swastika, The Rise of Fascism and Anti-Semitism in the Danube Basin, 1936–1939 (London: Institute of Jewish Affairs, Saxon House, 1975), pp. 75–78. In the 1935 elections the Czech fascists could only gain 167,000 votes among 8,231,412 (six of 300 deputies) but Henlein's party became the country's largest with 1,249,000 votes and Hlinka's Slovak People's party, 564,273.

[37] John A. Armstrong, «Collaborationism in World War II: The Integral Nationalist Variant in Eastern Europe», *Journal of Modern History*, 3, September 1968, pp. 396–410.

[38] This theme is excellently developed by William Sheridan Allen, «The Appeal of Fascism and the Problem of National Disintegration» in Henry A. Turner, jr., *Reappraisals of Fascism* (New York: Franklin Watts, 1975), pp. 44–68.

[39] It might be noted that with the exception of Italy fascism was most successful in countries without a monarchy, or where a monarchy had been overthrown or discredited (like in Romania). Among the monarchies in 1930 (the United Kingdom, the three in Scandinavia, Belgium, the Netherlands) none had a major fascist movement. The Spanish Conquista de Estado was founded days before the proclamation of the Republic. But in ex-monarchies like Germany and Austria with democratic freedoms, fascism acquired considerable strength. Even in Italy fascism was initially a-monarchical and penetrated in areas where republicanism was a tradition, while its pro-monarchical competitor, the *Associazione Nazionalista*, had its main strength in the regions that even after World War II would support the monarchy. The argument could be advanced that the monarchy as a focus of legitimacy above parties satisfied some of the emotional needs for symbolic national unity. Jean Stengers, «Belgium» in Hans Rogger and Eugen Weber, *The European Right, op.cit.*, p. 133, notes how the prestige of King Albert I «silenced more than one voice that would otherwise have appealed for a «strongman»». Even in Greece the polarization of the conflict between monarchy and Republic probably absorbed political passions that in another context might have been channeled into fascism.

[40] See the chapter by Maurice Manning in this volume for further details.

[41] The PNV had its own scouts, guards (mendigoitzales) that in another context would have been a militia. The Basques knew, however, that given the hostility of Castilian Spanish nationalism to their aspirations, their hopes lay ultimately in the democratic republic. The competition between a Spanish and a Basque fascism would have been to their disadvantage.

[42] The relationship between anti-Semitism and fascism deserves more systematic study. Anti-Semitism had considerable appeal before fascism, was part of movements we might call proto-fascist like the *Action Française* and those in Czarist Russia. It was also present in parties and movements competing with the fascists. Certainly in countries where Jews represented more than one percent of the population, anti-Semitism was one of the program points. In Poland (9.5% of the population) and Lithuania (9.4%) anti-Semitism was so widespread that it did not lead to distinctive anti-Semitic parties ot fascist movements, as it did in Hungary (5.6%), Latvia (4.1%), Romania (3.6%), Slovakia (3.4%). However, the initial saliency of the issue in the NSDAP cannot be explained by the number of Jews in Germany (0.3%, 4% in the highest city), nor can its importance in France be derived from the numerical strength of the Jews (0.3%), particularly if we consider that in the Netherlands the Jews numbered 1.6% and 8% (highest city), respectively.

[43] Peter G.J. Pulzer, *The Rise of Political Anti-Semitism in Germany and Austria* (New York; John Wiley, 1964), with annotated bibliography.

[44] Bela Vago and George L. Mosse, eds., *Jews and Non-Jews in Eastern Europe 1918–1945* (New York; John Wiley, 1974). «The Attitude towards the Jews as a Criterion of the Left-Right Concept», p. 21–49, questions the stereotype of the nationalist and anti-Jewish Right and the non-natonalist, non anti-Jewish, or somewhat pro-Jewish left, as schematic and over-simplified. See also p. 34–38 on the oversimplification of the Jewish link with the socialist and communist left, in Romania Jews must have given their votes to the Liberal Party, the peasant's party and the bourgeois parties.

[45] In fact, anti-Semitism was one of the divisive issues among fascists at the Montreux conference organized under Italian auspices by the *Comitati d'azione per l'Universalità di Roma* in December 1934, at which, significantly, no representatives from Nazi Germany were present. At that meeting Ion Mota of the Iron Guard raised the issue and spokesmen of fascist groups in

Greece, Italy, Portugal, Austria and the Netherlands rejected any attempt to make a general statement about the Jews. The final compromise statement said that each nation had to judge what was best for itself and that«the question cannot be dealt with in a universal campaign of hate against the Jews». Jews should be condemned, the statement continued, when they engage in nefarious activities, fail to contribute to the development of the nation, or remain a kind of State within the State. The commission created at Montreux condemned «any materialistic concept which exalts the exclusive domination of one race over others.» The ultimate crisis of those fumbling attempts to establish a fascist international is not unrelated to the saliency of this issue concomitant with the rise of Hitler's power and the formation of the Axis. See Michael Arthur Ledeen, *Universal Fascism: The Theory and Practice of the Fascist International, 1928–1936* (New York: Howard Fertig, 1970), Chapters 4 and 5.

[46] Stephen Fischer-Galati, «Fascism, Communism, and the Jewish Question in Romania,» in Bela Vago and George L. Mosse, eds. *Jews and Non-Jews . . . op.cit.,* p. 157–175.

[47] The topic has attracted considerable attention in the case of Nazism but we still have no comparative analysis of the attitude toward different social strata and the image of society of *all* fascist movements, since too often scholars generalize from one to others. The agrarian romanticism, the appeal to artisan values, and so on, might rather reflect national cultural patterns (shared by other parties) than be distinctively fascist. It is rather the explicit rejection of a mythification of the proletariat and the stereotyping of a certain type of bourgeois that is common to fascism. It is congruent with its idea of integration of all classes that the fascist should reject the two classes that created the conflict in society, antagonized other sectors and were politically most self-conscious. Agreement on the anti-themes was greater than on the themes underlined in the attempted new synthesis of fascism. On German ideological and partisan responses to the process of transition to modernity and industrial society which the NSDAP capitalized on, see Heinrich August Winkler, *Mittelstand, Demokratie und Nationalsozialismus. Die politische Entwicklung von Handwerk und Kleinhandel in der Weimarer Republik.* (Cologne: Kiepenheuer und Witsch, 1972), mainly pp. 157–182, and Klaus Bergmann, *Agrarromantik und Grosstadt-feindlichkeit* (Meisenheim am Glan: Anton Hain, 1970). These German traditions have led Henry A. Turner, Jr. to include anti-modernism in the fascist syndrome, «Fascism and Modernization», *World Politics,* 24, 4. July 1972, pp. 547–564, a position vigorously debated by James Gregor «Fascism and Modernization: Some Addenda» *World Politics,* 26. April 1974, pp. 370–384.

[48] Alastair Hamilton, *The Appeal of Fascism. A Study of Intellectuals and Fascism. 1919 – 1945* (New York: Avon, 1971), covers Italy, Germany, France and England. It would be interesting to compose a collective portrait of intellectuals who identified with fascism in one or another degree and compare it with those affiliated to or fellow-travelling with communism and those rejecting both temptations in the course of the inter-war years.

[49] Robert Michels, *Sozialismus und Faschismus in Italien* (Munich: Meyer and Jessen, 1925).

[50] French literary-cultural fascism has been the object of a number of excellent studies, see Tarmo Kunnes, *Drieu La Rochelle, Celine. Brasillach et la tentation fasciste* (Paris: Les Septs Coleurs, 1972) Paul Sérant, *Le Romantisme fasciste. Etude sur l'oeuvre politique de quelques écrivains français* (Paris: Pasquelle, 1959). For the intellectual climate of the time, see also Jean-Louis Loubet del Bayle, *Les non-conformistes des années 30. Une tentative de renouvellement de la pensée politique française* (Paris: Seuil, 1969), which shows that intellectuals responded differently to that crisis.

[51] The anti-clericalism we find in almost all fascist movements, except in those where the national identity could only be defined in religious terms and where the enemy was a secularized bourgeoisie as in Romania, is a constant that is easy to understand because of the desire of the fascist movements to effect a nationalist revolutionary integration of society. Anti-clericalism was especially pronounced in countries where clericalism and anti-clericalism had divided the nation and where integration, particularly of the working class on the basis of a Catholic corporativist conception, was doomed to failure. In addition it should not be forgotten that the Vatican was an international force suspect to extreme nationalists. However, the basic supra-nationality of the Catholic church was not in itself an impediment to including religion as part of the national heritage to be exalted. In its positivist, a-religious manipulation of religious traditi-

ons the *Action Française* provided an antecedent and exercised a competing influence over a number of fascist movements.

52 The classic formulation of Azaña that the Church owed more to Spain than Spain to the Church certainly would not have been displeasing to some Spanish fascists. Significantly, the Falangists had nothing but hate for Gil Robles, the leader of the «vaticanist» party competing with them for the same social basis, and a love/hate relation with Azaña.

53 Edgar Jung, one of the intellectuals of the conservative revolution two years before he was murdered by the Nazis, in a text quoted by Kurt Sontheimer, *Antidemokratisches Denken in der Weimarer Republik,* (Munich: Nymphenburger Verlagshandlung, 1968), p. 285, describes very well how spiritual assumptions for the German *völkisch* revolution were created outside of National Socialism. Jung mentions the contributions of intellectuals like himself to the Nazi success, particularly among the «gebildete» strata, his admiration for the victorious *Gauleiter* and *Sturmführer,* but gives also a critique of the «arrivisme» of the upcoming Nazis that allowed them to look down on their intellectual precursors.

54 One of the best «maps» of the myriad of groups of the extreme right and extreme left of the extreme right can be found in Jean Pierre Faye, *Theorie du récit, introduction aux langages totalitaires* (also published as *Langages totalitaires),* (Paris: Hermann, 1972). The fertile ideological ground for such movements probably had no parallel in any other country.

55 George L. Mosse, *The Crisis of German Ideology, Intellectual Origins of the Third Reich* (New York: Grosset & Dunlap, 1964).

56 Luigi Salvatorelli, *Nazionalfascismo* (Torino: Piero Gobetti, 1923), pp. 51–55.

57 On this point see the revealing statements of Salandra in a letter: «As you know I am, like you, both admiring and worried about fascism. Six years of weak and absent government, on occasion treacherous, have led one to put the hopes of saving the country in a force armed and organized outside the powers of the State. This is a profoundly anarchic phenomenon in the strict sense of the word,» (August 15, 1922), R. de Felice *Mussolini il fascista. I La conquista del potere 1921–1925.* (Torino: Einaudi, 1966), p. 286. And Mussolini's comment to a fellow fascist C. Rossi: «If there were a government in Italy deserving of that name today, it should without further delay send its agents and carabinieri (national police) to seal and occupy our offices. An organization armed with both cadres and a *Regolamento* (disciplinary code for its members) is inconceivable in a State with its Army and its police intact. Therefore there is no normally functioning state in Italy. The state, then, being *hors de combat,* our assumption of power becomes inevitable if the history of Italy is not to be a *pochade* (an unfinished draft)», *op.cit.* p. 317. This process initiated a drift toward a transfer of initiative to those challenging the existing state in the hope of restoring the monopoly of coercion in a state controlled by fascists, i.e. the very same people who had contributed so much to subvert its authority.

58 Another example would be the irregular war in East Karelia in opposition to government policy after the settlement between the Finnish state and the Soviets.

59 Significantly, the members and particularly the officers of the Czech legion who fought in Russia (and who had not gone over, as some did, to communism) were successfully integrated into the democratic state, perhaps because leaders of the «Castle» establishment made a point of creating an institute – Monument of the National Resistance – devoted to its history. See Peter Burian: «Demokratie und Parlamentarismus in der Ersten Tschechoslowakischen Republik», in Hans-Erich Volkmann, ed., *Die Krise des Parlamentarismus in Ostmitteleuropa zwischen den beiden Weltkriegen* (Marburg/Lahn: J.G. Herder-Institut, 1967), pp. 85–132, see pp. 110–113. For a discussion of the role of the legacy of the Civil War in determining the perceptions of the Lapua rank and file, see Risto Alapuro's contribution to this book.

60 Let us note that in Eastern Europe nationality conflicts also contributed to strengthen communism, as R.V. Burks in his *The Dynamics of Communism in Eastern Europe* (Princeton, N.J.: Princeton University Press, 1961) has shown in the case of the Magyars in Slovakia, the Ruthenes in Czechoslovakia, the Belorussians and the Ukrainians in Poland, the Macedonians in Bulgaria and Yugoslavia, while often socio-economic variables have little explanatory power.

61 The rejection of a monocausal explanation and the emphasis on the differential impact of different factors would seem to lead to abandonment of a generic category of fascism. This is,

however, not so. In our review, it is the conjunction and combination of those factors which account for a phenomenon that despite its diverse national manifestations had fundamental common characteristics and whose supporters and leaders felt a basic affinity across the borders, an affinity which persisted, even in spite of conflicts derived from different nationalist commitments. To deny this basic similarity between the inter-war fascists would even force us to say that the different movements within a single country and even the different tendencies rooted in different sectors of society within the same movement could not be considered fascist.

[62] A comparison of the social characteristics of the leadership and membership of the *Associazione Nazionalista* and the *Fasci* would be extremely interesting. The relative strength of the *Nazionalisti* and their Sempre-Pronti blue shirts in the south and the late penetration of the fascists below Rome would require explanation. One factor must have been the initial attiude of both movements toward the monarchy and church, but also the different social characteristics of their initial leadership.

[63] See the chapter by Joseph Baglieri in this volume for references.

[64] Marzio Barbagli, *Disoccupazione intellectuale e sistema scolastico in Italia 1859–1973* (Bologna: Il Mulino, 1974) provides data on the rapid expansion of education and gives references to the ongoing debate about the *spostati*. The results of this rapid expansion could often lead to disillusioned political radicalization, which as Gramsci noted, could turn either right or left. One problem with the relationship between the intellectual «proletariat» and the rise of fascism in Italy is that this «proletariat» was more numerous in the South where fascism was weak. This indicates that in the absence of other factors this layer is *per se* not a powerful explanation.

[65] Werner Kaltefleiter, *Wirtschaft und Politik in Deutschland. Konjunktur als Bestimmungsfaktor des Parteiensystems* (Cologne: Westdeutscher Verlag, 1968) and R.I. McKibbin, «The Myth of the Unemployed: Who did Vote for the Nazis? *The Australian Journal of Politics and History,* August 1969, XV, 2, pp. 25–69. For further references, see Bernt Hagtvet's discussion of the literature on the social bases of the NSDAP in his analysis of mass theory in this collection.

[66] Heinrich Dennecke, *Wirtschaftliche Depression und politischer Radikalismus,* (Munich, Olzog, 1970), analyses the impact of the depression on political stability in Austria. Bennecke also notes how the massive shift of Sudeten German voters from the socialist and Catholic German parties to the nazified *Sudetendeutsche Partei* was not only due to heightened nationalism and the appeal of a powerful German led by Hitler, but to the particularly strong impact of the depression on their economic condition.

[67] However, the impact of the depression can only account for the success of an ongoing movement but not for the rise of fascism. A look at the comparative statistics shows that while the German unemployment rate of 43.8% in 1932 had no equal anywhere, the rate of 34.3% in 1931 and 22.7 in 1930 was approached in other industrial countries without a rise of fascism: 31.7% in Denmark in 1932, 32.7% in the Netherlands in 1936 (with already 25.3% in 1932, sustained at more than 25% over five years); 33.4% in Norway in 1933, 23.3% in Sweden in 1933 and 22.1% in the U.K. in 1932.

Certainly, the Lower U.K. and Belgian peak figures (18.9% in 1934) help to account for the limited success of the BUF and the Rex, but the higher figures in other countries suggest that neither the fascist nor communist wave in Germany can be explained satisfactorily by the crisis of capitalism in general. (Data from Walter Galenson and Arnold Zellner, «International Comparison of Unemployment Rates,» in: National Bureau of Economic Research, *The Measurement and Behavior of Unemployment* (Princeton N.J., Princeton University Press, 1957).

[68] It might surprise the reader that the relatively rich and brilliantly analyzed data on American rightist anti-democratic movements found in Seymour M. Lipset and Earl Raab, *The Politics of Unreason, Right-Wing Extremism in America, 1790–1970.* (New York; Harper & Row, 1970), particularly in chapter 5: «The 1930s Extremism of the Depression», pp. 150–208 and chapter 6, «The 1950s McCarthyism», pp. 209–247, should not be incorporated into our analysis. In spite of the affinities of some of those movements in the thirties and the underlying sentiments of the opinion support for the Senator from Wisconsin, it seems very dubious whether they would fit our multidimensional definition of fascism. It would require an article: «Why fascist tendencies, but no fascism in America» to justify our decision. Certainly, the nativist

leaders had much in common with the German Nazis, but only a few like the Silver Shirts attempted to organize movements with the style of the European fascists.

[69] The question of the relationship between the rise of fascism and electoral systems has been the object of prolonged and intense polemic since F.A. Hermens in his *Democracy or Anarchy?* (Notre Dame, Ind.: Notre Dame University Press, 1941) launched his blistering attack on the destructive implications of proportional representation. Maurice Duverger with his classic work on *Political Parties* (New York: John Wiley, 1963), Anthony Downs' *Economic Theory of Democracy* (New York: Harper & Row, 1957), and the numerous writings of Giovanni Sartori and the polemics surrounding them, have continued this debate. The most important monograph is Douglas W. Rae, *The Political Consequences of Electoral Laws* (New Haven: Yale U.P., 1971). The case of Weimar has been analyzed in great detail by the monograph of Hans Fenske, *Wahlrecht und Parteiensystem. Ein Beitrag zur Deutschen Parteiengeschichte* (Frankfurt a.M.: Athenäum, 1972). The theoretical refinements and the empirical analysis of difficult cases make it questionable to put all the blame on P.R. since a majority system can lead to equally destructive consequences in a polarized society with large extremist minorities. Much depends on the point in the crystallization of the party system at which one or another electoral system is introduced.

[70] On the authoritarian regimes established by leaders of «democratic» parties out to suppress growing fascist parties in Baltic countries, see Tönu Parming, *The Collapse of Liberal Democracy and the Rise of Authoritarianism in Estonia* [Beverly Hills, Calif., Sage (Contemporary Political Sociology. 06-010) 1975]; Jürgen von Hehn, *Lettland zwischen Demokratie und Diktatur, op.cit.;* and Georg von Rauch, «Zur Krise des Parlamentarismus in Estland und Lettland in der 30er Jahren», in Hans-Erich Volkmann, ed., *Die Krise des Parlamentarismus in Ostmitteleuropa zwischen den beiden Weltkriegen* (Marburg/Lahn: J.G. Herder Institut, 1967), pp. 135–155.

[71] See, Hélgio Trindade, *Integralismo. O fascismo brasileiro na década de 30*, (São Paulo: Difusao Européia di Livro, 1974). See also J. Chasin, *O Integralismo de Plínio Salgado. Forma de regressividade no capitalismo hiper-tardio*, São Paulo, Editora Ciencias Humanas, 1978, and Jarbas Medeiros, *Ideologia Autoritaria no Brasil, 1930–1945*. Rio de Janeiro, Fundação Getulio Vargas, 1978. Integralismo was the most important Latin-American (unless we consider Peronismo fascist) and non-European fascist movement. There are some variables, like the impact of World War I, that are inapplicable in accounting for its emergence, but certainly others are quite relevant: the rebellion of Prestes (1925–1927) and the existence of an active communist party; the danger to national unity derived from regional secessionist efforts, and a cultural crisis. The short-lived existence of the movement is reflected in this brief chronology: October 1930 Plinio Salgado returns from Europe; October 1932: the Manifesto Integralista and the founding of the A.I.B. (the same month that Mosley founds the BUF and Degrelle launches Rex); April 1933: interdiction by the Vargas government of the militia, August 1933: interdiction of the use of the green shirt; November 1937: Constitution of the Estado Novo proclaimed by Vargas; December 1937: dissolution of AIB, and May 1938: integralist *Putsch;* May 1939 exile of Plinio Salgado.

[72] Wolfgang Wippermann, *Faschismustheorien,* (Darmstadt; Wissenschaftliche Buchgesellschaft, 1972), reviews critically the past and contemporary discussion, providing bibliographic references, pp. 1–55. See also A. James Gregor, *Interpretations of Fascism* (Morristown, New Jersey: General Learning Press, 1974), chapter 5, «Fascism as the Consequence of Class Struggle», pp. 129–170.

[73] The data on occupation about 1930, in Dudley Kirk, *Europe's Population in the Interwar Years*. (Geneva: League of Nations, 1946), tables 13 and 14, pp. 200 and 203.

[74] Palmiro Togliatti, «A proposito del fascismo,» reprinted in C. Casucci, ed. *Il Fascismo* (Bologne: Il Mulino, 1961). With its ideas about the «weakest link» in the capitalist world, this offers an interesting alternative to the «last stage of capitalism» thesis.

[75] The link between fascism and economic development was first formulated in the «productivist» theories in the idelogy of Italian Fascists, as A. James Gregor has emphasized. It is also prominent in Ledesma Ramos. It became central in Franz Borkenau, «Zur Soziologie des Faschismus», first published in 1933 and reprinted in Ernst Nolte, (ed). *Theorien über den Faschismus* (Cologne: Kiepenheuer u. Witsch, 1967), pp. 156-181.

Mary Mattossian, «Ideologies of Delayed Industrialization: Some Tensions and Ambiguities», in John H. Kautsky, ed. *Political Change in Underdeveloped Countries, Nationalism and*

Communism, (New York, Wiley, 1962, pp. 252–64), Ludovico Garruccio, *L'industrializzazione nazionalismo e rivoluzione,* (Bologna: Il Mulino, 1969).

A.F.K. Organski, *The Stages of Political Development* (New York: Knopf, 1965) and «Fascism and Modernization», in S.J. Woolf, ed., *The Nature of Fascism* and Henry A. Turner jr., «Fascism and Modernization» in *World Politics,* 24, 1972, pp. 547–564. A. James Gregor, *Italian Fascism and Developmental Dictatorship,* Princeton, N.J., 1979.

[76] See Roland Sarti, «Fascist Modernization in Italy: Traditional or Revolutionary,» *American Historical Review,* 75, 4. April 1970, pp. 1029–1045, and note 74.

[77] Eugen Weber, *Action Française. Royalism and Reaction in Twentieth-Century France,* (Stanford: Stanford University Press, 1962) and Ernst Nolte, *Three Faces of Fascism. Action Française, Italian Fascism, National Socialism* (New York: Mentor, 1969), Eugen Weber notes that the *Action Française,* (and the same could be said about the *Associazione Nazionalista Italiana* and the *Alldeutscher Verband*) was never a party (as defined by Max Weber or Carl Friedrich): an organization to secure for its leaders control of the government. Rather it was a movement purporting to «affect power and influence society, but only indirectly in the role, not of executive, but of teacher» (*op.cit.* p. 529). This contrasts with the single-minded and exclusivist drive to power displayed by fascist movements. In this context see also Zeev Sternhell, *Maurice Barrés et le Nationalisme Français,* (Paris, Colin 1972), and Robert Soucy, *Fascism in France. The Case of Maurice Barrés* (Berkeley: University of California Press, 1972).

[78] Wilhelm Alff «Die Associazione Nazionalista Italiana von 1910», in W. Alff, *Der Begriff Faschismus und andere Aufsätze zur Zeitgeschichte, op.cit.,* pp. 51–95. Franco Gaeta, Il *Nazionalismo italiano* (Naples: Edizione Scientifiche Italiane, 1965). R. Molinelli, *Per una storia del nazionalismo italiano* (Urbino: Argalia, 1966), Carlo Vallauri, *Le radici del corporativismo* (Rome: Bulzoni, 1971) pp. 51–90, 123–143. Paolo Ungari, *Alfredo Rocco el'ideologia giuridica del fascismo* (Brescia: Morcalliana, 1963). Alexander J. DeGrand, *The Italian Nationalist Association and the Rise of Fascism in Italy,* Lincoln, University of Nebraska Press, 1978.

[79] Let us not forget that the first party which called itself National Socialist German Workers' Party (1918) was the successor of a *Deutsche Arbeiterpartei* founded 1904 in Bohemia as the result of the ethnic competition between German and Czech workers and internal migration patterns. See: Andrew Whiteside, *Austrian National Socialism before 1918* (The Hague: Martinus Nijhoff, 1962). The announcement of the party clearly stated the conflict between the Social Democratic vision of the class conflict and the realities of class conflict in a multi-ethnic society when it stated:

1. The German Workers' Party seeks the liberation of the working classes of the German people from their present state of economic, political and cultural oppression.
2. The German Workers' Party is convinced that the worker can achieve full credit for his labor and intelligence only . . . . within the natural boundaries of his *Volkstum.* We reject international organization because it levels the condition of advanced *(fortgeschritten)* workers down to that of the backward *(niedrigen)* and bars the German worker in Austria from all economic progress.
3. The German Workers' Party affirms the proposition that an improvement of economic and social conditions is only attainable by trade-union *(berufsgenossenschaftliche)* organization . . . . We are no narrow class party. We represent the interests of all honest productive labor . . . We are a liberal *(freiheitlich)* national party that opposes all feudal, clerical and capitalistic privileges and all foreign influence. The proper valuation of work and skill in state and society is our goal. The economic and political organization of the German workers as a means of achieving this end is the purpose of the German Workers' Party.

[80] On the Russian pre-revolutionary movements, see Hans Rogger, «Was there a Russian Fascism? The Union of the Russian People» in Henry A. Turner jr., ed. *Reappraisals of Fascism* (New York: Franklin Watts, 1975), pp. 170–198. Let us not forget that Lenin conceived the Italian Fascists as an equivalent to «Black Hundredism».

[81] A serious comparative study of parties and movements that cannot be considered fascist *strictu sensu* but which were influenced in various ways by fascism would be of great interest, as would research on the ideology, organization, leaders and membership of official state-created single parties. Central to such a study would be a clearer definition of the difference between

188

genuine fascist movements and those influenced by them. It is my opinion that a blind analysis of representative materials, such as programs, speeches, propaganda leaflets etc. would with relatively high reliability reveal the difference. The same would show up in an analysis of the style of those movements, using their songs and symbols, photographs from films of their rallies, etc. Likewise, a systematic comparison of the social characteristics of their leaders, particularly the experiences typical of their age-group would disclose a similar pattern.

[82] A better understanding of the activist nuclei of the early NSDAP would require a greater knowledge of the social bases and linkages of the anti-Semitic and *völkisch* groups, see for example the monograph by Uwe Lohalm, *Völkischer Radikalismus. Die Geschichte des Deutschvölkischen Schutz-und Trutz-Bundes 1919–1923* (Hamburg, Leibniz, 1970), particularly pp. 88–121 on membership, local organizations, leadership, finances, occupational background, age, regional strength, and the relationship with the NSDAP and the contribution to the Nazi élite, pp. 283–330. Without such groups and their predecessors at the end of the Whilhelminian period like the *Alldeutsche Verband,* the *Reichshammerbund* and the anti-Semitic parties, it would be difficult to understand the distinctive characteristics of Nazism vis-à-vis other fascisms and its capacity to penetrate German society. In a sense Nazism could build on an undercurrent in German political life, and in this respect was less a late-comer than other fascist parties, except in France where conservative-radical anti-republicanism had a tradition since the Dreyfus Affair.

[83] On the polycentrism of fascism, see Renzo de Felice, *Mussolini il duce. Gli anni del consenso 1929–1936* (Torino: Einaudi, 1974), p. 593. For a report reflecting that dualism in poles of attraction, see Ministero Affari Esteri, Appunti sui movimenti fascišti esteri, in *op. cit.,* p. 587–596.

[84] A phenomenon that might deserve some analysis is the critical stance taken by a number of fascists toward the Italian Fascist regime. Ramiro Ledesma Ramos, ending his *¿ Fascismo en España? (op.cit.)* wrote: «What there was of fascism in the old JONS has been taken over by Primo de Rivera . .» And: «the red shirt of Garibaldi might fit Ramiro Ledesma and his comrades better than the black shirt of Mussolini.» (p. 205). Similarly Otto Strasser in his polemic with Hitler would attribute the betrayal of the national socialist ideal to the influence of Italian Fascism, ultimately to the Latin influence. Left fascists, aware of the compromises Mussolini had made with the Establishment, with institutions like the monarchy and/or the Church and his failure to incorporate the working classes, started questioning «fascism» to reaffirm their commitments.

[85] The «style» element in fascism cannot be over-estimated and still deserves more systematic and comparative study. An important contribution to this problem is: George L. Mosse, *The Nationalization of the Masses, Political Symbolism and Mass Movements in Germany from the Napoleonic Wars through the Third Reich* (New York: Howard Fertig, 1975).

[86] One of the best analyses of the differences between official «single» parties and the mobilizational fascist parties is Andrew C. Janos, «The One-Party State and Social Mobilization: Eastern Europe between the Wars,» in Samuel Huntington and Clement H. Moore (eds.), *Authoritarian Politics in Modern Society. The Dynamics of Established One-Party Systems,* (New York: Basic Books, 1970), pp. 204–236.

[87] The inconsistency between the radical program of early fascism and the realities of fascism in power explains the paradox that when exposed to the ideology some sectors of the younger generation more often than the depoliticized sectors of society evolved toward a variety of opposition stances, first within and later outside the system. See Gino Germani, «Political Socialization of Youth in Fascist Regimes: Italy and Spain,» in Samuel P. Huntington and Clement Moore, (eds.) *Authoritarian Politics in Modern Society op.cit.,* pp. 339–379, see pp. 357–359 and 362–365, and Juan J. Linz «Opposition in and under an Authoritarian Regime: The Case of Spain», in Robert A. Dahl, *Regimes and Oppositions,* (New Haven: Yale University Press, 1972), pp. 171–259, see pp. 197–199; José M. Maravall, «Political Socialization and Political Dissent. (Spanish Radical Students, 1955–1970), *Sociology,* January 1976, and «Students and Politics in Contemporary Spain» in *Government and Opposition,* April 1976.

[88] See Renzo de Felice, *Mussolini il duce. Gli anni del consenso 1929–1936* (Torino: Einaudi, 1974), pp. 537–596.

PART 2

VARIETIES OF FASCISM IN AUSTRIA

Gerhard Botz   Introduction

Gerhard Botz   The Changing Patterns of Social Support for Austrian National Socialism (1918–1945)

Bruce F. Pauley   Nazis and Heimwehr Fascists: The Struggle for Supremacy in Austria, 1918–1938

John Haag   Marginal Men and the Dream of the *Reich:* Eight Austrian National-Catholic Intellectuals, 1918–1938

John Rath and
Carolyn W. Schum   The Dollfuss-Schuschnigg Regime: Fascist or Authoritarian?

Introduction

GERHARD BOTZ

Unlike the various fascist forces in Italy, Spain, Germany and Finland, those in Austria were only partially united in one single movement. In this respect Austria very much resembles countries which are linguistically, ethnically or confessionally heterogeneous such as Belgium, Switzerland, Czechoslovakia and Yugoslavia. In these countries extremist right-wing movements and fascist organizations were unable to obtain a monopolistic position within the whole nation – and if they did, they succeeded only through foreign intervention. In order to delineate the reasons why Austrian fascism never became fully unified, an analysis must be made of the historical origins of the domestic political system in the First Republic and the impact of the international situation on Austria in the inter-war period.

In the last decades of the 19th century the great social and national pressures in the Habsburg Empire led to a split in the bourgeois middle-class and to the formation of two political mass configurations on the right. On the left, the newly created workers' movement found political expression in a strong Social Democratic party, particularly in Vienna and in the industrial areas of Wiener Neustadt, St. Pölten, Steyr and in Upper Styria.[1] Since then Austrian domestic politics has not been generally determined by this two-class society pattern but by three distinct politico-social subsystems. Each of the three subsystems was based on specific social groups, each providing a voice for different interests in a more or less tightly interwoven organizational network, and each embracing expressive ideological styles of propaganda. Following the Austrian historian Adam Wandruszka, they will here be called the Socialist (or Marxist), the Catholic Conservative and the German National *Lager* (camps or segments).[2] As the fascist movement's forerunners are found only in the two bourgeois segments, the Socialist *Lager* will not be considered in this context.

Above all, in the Catholic Conservative *Lager* the followers of Karl Lueger and the Christian Social Party were concentrated in the urban lower middle classes who found themselves threatened by big enterprises in distribution and production, and among the rural farming population. Apart from attempts to work out social policies directed at the working class and the salaried employees, the Christian Social Party catered especially for the interests of the commercial urban middle class and property-owning farmers. Among the issues seized upon were protective measures against competition from large-scale capitalist ventures, intervention against socialist consumer cooperatives, special tax privileges for its clientele and easier access to credit – in short, a series of supportive provisions in the tradition of social protectionism undertaken by the state to bolster the middle class and shield it from the vicissitudes of the market. In addition, the party advocated the establishment of agricultural co-operative purchasing societies, colleges of agriculture and business schools, and also turned itself into an ardent spokesman for landlord and rentier interests. Even more unifying were loyalty towards the Roman Catholic Church and support for the Habsburg monarchy, the two main pillars in the ideology of the Catholic Conservative *Lager*.

192

The higher echelons of the urban middle class groups on the other hand, especially the civil servants and the mounting numbers of white-collar professionals, were more concerned with the predominance of German influence in the multinational empire.

In both the objective and the subjective sense, the growth of national identity and self-consciousness among the Slavic population in the Danube monarchy posed as great a threat to the social status of the urban middle class as the first victories of organized labor. Along with some sections of the rural population who were better off than the farmers supporting the Christian Social Party, these urban strata had seceded from the Catholic Church. This exodus made it even easier for them to join the ranks of Georg von Schönerer[3] and a number of independent German national parties which gradually and in varying degrees opted for anti-clericalism.

The national and anti-clerical parties comprising the German National *Lager* never obtained organizational uniformity, however, as did the other two segments. This fragmentation persisted even after 1920 when the major proportion of the urban German national splinter parties merged into the Greater German People's Party *(Grossdeutsche Volkspartei)*, whereas the Peasant's League *(Landbund)* and the Austrian National Socialists remained organizationally independent as before. These political parties, along with numerous cultural and interest groups, formed the German National *Lager*. In contrast to Western Europe, anti-clerical movements in Austria have been only loosely connected with liberalism and democracy, traditions only poorly established there as in many other areas of middle and Eastern Europe. This weakness of democratic sentiment can in turn be traced to the different outcome and the later timing of the industrial and political revolutions in Austria as compared with the rest of Europe.

In spite of World War I and the resultant political and social upheavals in the First Republic all three segments proved extremely stable. Even after the interruption by National Socialist rule (1938–1945), the domestic political structure of the Second Republic remained much the same as in the years between the wars. Even the fascist movements of the twenties and early thirties, which at their peak made only limited inroads into the socialist camp, only partly succeeded in overcoming the political and subcultural border lines between the two bourgeois segments.[4] Significantly, the Anschluss question and thereby the question of Austrian national independence which loomed large as an issue after 1918, deepened the socially and economically based conflict between anti- and pro-clericals.

This conflict was further aggravated in the First Republic through the overlapping of German and Italian spheres of influence. Austria occupied a key position for the two great powers to the west and south of her in their struggle for economic and military penetration in South-Eastern Europe. External tensions, both in the form of financial pressure and outside propaganda, played an important part in Austrian internal affairs between 1918 and 1938.[5]

For all these reasons, apart from the more general causes of fascism which are intentionally neglected here as they will be discussed by other writers in this book, the specific types of fascist movements in Austria developed within the Catholic-Conservative and German national camps. This segmental split is also the main reason why fascism remained factionalized in Austria, and as such finally managed to gain power or to participate in power only through the support of Italy (1933–1938) and Germany (1938–1945). We are here concerned with the National Socialists, who in 1932 and 1933 were joined by the Styrian Home Guard *(Steirischer Heimatschutz)* on

193

the one hand, and the *Heimwehr* in the rest of Austria and the Front Veterans' Association on the other. These two brands of fascism will be called «National» fascism and *Heimwehr* fascism respectively. In a schematic manner, the organizational and ideological relationships between the different strands of Austrian fascism and their genesis, can be presented in the following way. (See table «Genealogy of Fascism in Austria».)

The differences in domestic aims between the two movements were not too great; they were rather in degree than in kind. Both movements wanted fascism, the first a fascism similar to the German model, the other a fascism similar to the Italian variant. Both wanted to abolish democracy, destroy the labor organizations and establish, by means of violence, their one-party-system.

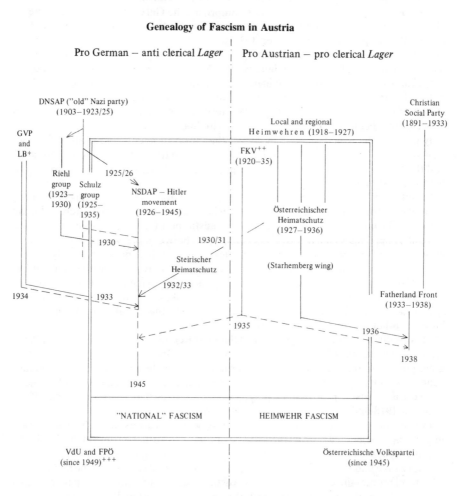

Genealogy of Fascism in Austria

Pro German — anti clerical *Lager*   Pro Austrian — pro clerical *Lager*

DNSAP ("old" Nazi party) (1903–1923/25)

Christian Social Party (1891–1933)

Local and regional Heimwehren (1918–1927)

GVP and LB+

FKV++ (1920–35)

Riehl group (1923–1930)   Schulz group (1925–1935)   1925/26

NSDAP – Hitler movement (1926–1945)

Österreichischer Heimatschutz (1927–1936)

1930   1930/31

Steirischer Heimatschutz

(Starhemberg wing)

1932/33

1934   1933

Fatherland Front (1933–1938)

1935   1936

1938

1945

"NATIONAL" FASCISM   HEIMWEHR FASCISM

VdU and FPÖ (since 1949)+++

Österreichische Volkspartei (since 1945)

+   *Grossdeutsche Volkspartei* (GVP) and *Landbund* (LB).

++   *Frontkämpfervereinigung* (Front Veterans' Association).

+++ *Verband der Unabhängigen* (1949–55) and *Freiheitliche Partei Österreichs* (since 1955).

194

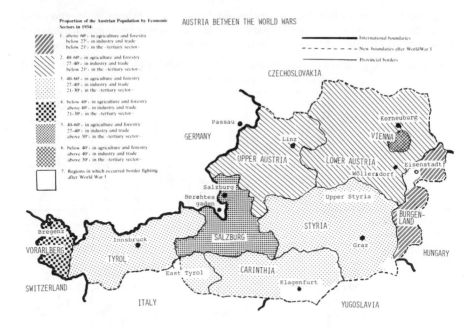

Proportion of the Austrian Population by Economic
Sectors in 1934:

1. above 60% in agriculture and forestry
   below 27% in industry and trade
   below 21% in the -tertiary sector-

2. 40-60% in agriculture and forestry
   27-40% in industry and trade
   below 21% in the -tertiary sector-

3. 40-60% in agriculture and forestry
   27-40% in industry and trade
   21-30% in the -tertiary sector-

4. below 40% in agriculture and forestry
   above 40% in industry and trade
   21-30% in the -tertiary sector-

5. 40-60% in agriculture and forestry
   27-40% in industry and trade
   above 30% in the -tertiary sector-

6. below 40% in agriculture and forestry
   above 40% in industry and trade
   above 30% in the -tertiary sector-

7. Regions in which occurred border fighting
   after World War I

International boundaries
New boundaries after WorldWar I
Provincial borders

The two groups were split over their foreign policy aims, however. The «National» fascists aimed at an Anschluss with Germany; the *Heimwehr* fascists wanted to preserve the independence of Austria from Germany and would have preferred a political connection between Austria and Hungary and the restoration of the Habsburgs. The degree of anti-Semitism was another distinctive mark. While the pro-clerical *Heimwehr* fascists were moderate anti-Semites, the Nazis, and to a less degree the Styrian Home Guard, propagated a radical and racially motivated anti-Semitism. This was matched, in the first case, with a distinct Catholic conservative attitude, in the other case by a pseudo-revolutionary and anti-clerical attitude, although both types of fascist movements were rarely found in their pure form.

Geographically, the former was stronger in the western and northern parts of Austria, the latter had its strongholds in the southern provinces, where border problems in 1918 to 1920 had played a great role and national minority problems remained sources of friction. «National» fascism also had its strongholds in the province of Salzburg and in Vienna. As shown on the map of Austria, both kinds of fascism succeeded mostly in provinces which had reached a relatively high level of industrialization (more than 27 per cent of the population belonging to industry and trades, less than 60 per cent to agriculture and forestry). In the main areas of both kinds of fascism a medium or strong proportion of the population belonged to the «tertiary sector» (more than 21 per cent). This was the case in Tyrol, Salzburg, Carinthia, Styria and Vienna. The only exception was Vorarlberg, a predominantly Catholic conservative province in which fascism never really gained a foothold.

From a sociological point of view the pro-Italian wing can be characterized as *aristocratic middle class and rural,* the pro-German wing more as *lower middle class and urban.*[6] The following table shows the social profile of the adherents of the *Heimwehr* and National Socialism, both in their élite strata and their militant cadres.

195

Care should be taken, however, to distinguish between candidates for election and other leading groups. Candidates for parliamentary elections are not representative of leading groups in their entirety within fascist movements.

Social Origins of Candidates and «Militants» in the Austrian Heimwehr and National Socialist Movement (in per cent)

	landed proprietors (and «Grossbauern»)	farmers	non-agrarian self-employed	free professions	students	public servants	employees	workers	others	total
CANDIDATES for parliamentary elections in *Lower and Upper Austria* in 1930										
NSDAP (n=88) .	2	2	7	6	–	48	17	14	4	100
Heimatblock (n=98)	9	24	19	6	–	17	6	15	4	100
MILITANTS* in whole of *Austria* (1923 – 1933)										
National Socialists (n = 167)	–	–	8	2	9	9	26	36	10	100
Catholic-Conservatives (and Heimwehr) (n=42)	–	2	19	2	–	10	7	56	4	100
for comparison: «Marxists» (n=66)	–	–	2	–	–	11	5	82	–	100

* «Militants» are here defined as follows: Broadly members in all three segments who were so involved in propagating the political views of their respective segments that they were willing to devote a substantial part of their time to manifest political activity, turning up for *streetfighting* or joining *demonstrations*. In police records, court records (Gerichtsakten) and newspaper articles these people show up as 1. either *victims* of political violence (killed or wounded) 2. perpetrators of acts of violence or 3. as *witnesses* to such acts.

Source: *Ergebnisse der Wahl in den Nationalrat am 9. November 1930 in Oberösterreich* (Linz 1930); *Ergebnisse der Nationalratswahl vom 9. November 1930 in Niederösterreich* (Vienna 1930), Gerhard Botz: *Gewalt in der Politik. Attentate, Zusammenstösse, Putschversuche, Unruhen in Österreich 1918 – 1934* (Munich 1976), p. 243.

Therefore caution must be displayed in drawing inferences from this sample to the social basis of the *Heimwehr* and the NSDAP members as a whole. The fact is that the urban population and the lower classes in general were affected by unemployment and economic crises stronger than other social classes and appeared in a surprisingly high proportion among the «militants». But that says little about the nucleus which instigated the movements and filled the leadership positions. Landed proprietors and large-scale farmers («Grossbauern»), farmers and non-agrarian self-employed played a much greater part in the Catholic-Conservative *Lager* and in the *Heimwehr* than among the National Socialists. Students and employees in private enterprises on the other hand were more strongly over-represented in the Nazi organizations than among Catholic-Conservatives and *Heimwehr* men.

The first contribution in this section discusses the historical development of these two forms of Austrian fascism and their influence on each other. Bruce F. Pauley adds to this a survey of the social origins of the Heimwehr members, the «Front Veterans» and the National Socialists. My own contribution concentrates on Austrian National Socialism and is an attempt to investigate the change over time in the social background of leaders, party members and voters at different stages in the development of the NSDAP from 1919 until the seizure of power. John Haag gives a general summary of eight case studies dealing with the important role of leading «National Catholic» intellectuals in weakening the resistance of the Catholic Conservative segment to fascism and the concomitant National Socialist undermining of Austrian anti-Nazism in the second half of the thirties.

So far in this introduction we have only been talking about the two types of fascist movements, Heimwehr and «National», before their ascent to power. There is still a third political phenomenon which is quite often labelled fascist, i.e. «Clerical fascism».[7] This term refers to the so-called «Christian Corporative State» of Dollfuss and Schuschnigg, which has posed problems of classification for a long time. Threatened from the outside by Italy and Germany and from the inside by the growing menace of National Socialism, the coalition government which had gained power through parliamentary means in 1932, became a victim of its own preoccupation with the anti-socialist ideology of the Catholic petty bourgeoisie and embarked upon establishing a regime which came not far from the full-blown fascist dictatorships of Hitler and Mussolini. The coalition which in the beginning consisted of the Christian Social Party, the Peasant's League and the *Heimwehr,* never rivalled the German or even the Italian fascists in totalitarian efficiency, however. Finally these parties ended up forming the backbone of a dictatorial regime with fascist leanings.[8]

In the last contribution to this section, R. John Rath and Carolyn W. Schum apply some modern theories of fascism to the Austrian case. They investigate in detail which elements of the «Christian Corporative State» corresponded to a fascist model, and which were rather expressions of a traditionalist dictatorship, and also to what extent political power affected the different sectors of society.

As a result of the incorporation of Austria into the German *Reich* in March 1938, a discussion of the complete fascist system of power established in Austria after the invasion of Hitler's troops would be superfluous since it no longer reflected indigenous Austrian social forces. The name «Austro-fascism»[9], therefore, refers to three different fascist or pseudo-fascist phenomena on two different levels of definition and at different points in time: on the level of *fascist (mass-)movements,* to National Socialism and to Heimwehr fascism; on the level of *fascist systems,* to the authoritarian Dollfuss-Schuschnigg «Corporative State» (1933–1938), a regime which fused strong conservative and fascist elements.[10]

The fragmented nature of Austrian fascism confronts the scholar with a series of methodological problems which will not be discussed further here. While not allowing any concept of a homogeneous Austrian fascism, Austria is an interesting case for comparative historical and sociological analyses. Comparisons on the basis of the Austrian experience can proceed on two levels: in their focus they can either be *intra-national* or *inter-national*.

In the first case, using the nation as a basis for comparisons, the domestic political system can be regarded a constant, i.e. all fascist forces had to operate within the same politico-juridical framework. What explains the varying numerical strength of the different fascist movements and their divergent sources of recruitment are variables like levels of economic development, degree of monopolization in the economy and sensitivity to international market fluctuations, unemployment, rate of inflation, prevailing confessional traditions and political cultural center-periphery tensions, existence of border conflicts or linguistic or ethnic conflict, etc. To give an example: If, as in Austria, fascism assumed two forms – one pseudo-revolutionary and middle class, the other conservative and aristocratic – intranational comparisons like the ones carried out in countries like Austria could tell more about the relationship between these types of fascist movements on the one hand and urban-rural-cleavages or confessional alignments on the other. Such comparisons will be more useful in explicating the precise determinants in the total social environment making for adherence to the one fascist movement or the other than comparisons of fascist parties across different countries. An intra-national comparison of fascist movements like the one possible in Austria can also yield valuable insight into the effects of foreign political influence on fascist movements.[11]

In my view, the crucial factor in accounting for the existence of two fascist movements in Austria and their different clientele is membership in either the German National or the Catholic Conservative *Lager*. Segmental affiliations predisposed towards either of the two movements, because *Lager* connections were simply a shorthand expression of a cluster of inter-related social characteristics: socio-economic status, religious belief and place of residence. From this follows the general proposition argued in this introduction that the *Heimwehr* was the fascist movement of the Catholic segment: it was predominantly rural, traditionalist and aristocratic. National Socialism on the other hand was gravitated to by the urban petty bourgeoisie: it was anti-Catholic and *mittelständisch* and tended to find support in urban, industrial and Protestant regions in the country. The absence of a clearly defined *Verzuiling* structure, to use the standard Dutch phrase, in Germany and Italy is part of the reason why the German Nazis and Italian fascism succeeded in overcoming regional, social and ideological splits rather early and more successfully than Austrian fascism which remained segmentally divided until forced to merge by the invader.

In *inter-national* comparisons, the divergent political systems in a broad sense, not just the economic and social structure inside one nation, must be included in the list of variables. Comparisons, therefore, become considerably more complex, having to account for the inter-action between social and economic structure on the one hand and the political system on the other.

One suitable area of inter-national comparisons of a more limited kind would be analyses of the fascist movements in Germany, Austria and the *Sudeten* areas of Czechoslovakia. Here the cultural traditions are rather similar, yet different enough to enable the scholar to assess the relative weight of cultural traditions and historical legacies as opposed to socio-economic conditions in explaining the form and strength of the various fascist movements in the region. So far no comparative project of this kind has been undertaken.

In comparison with other countries, sociological and social historical research into Austrian fascism has not yet made more than a start. Our knowledge of the social and political origins of the fascist party members, its voters and leading groups has only been marginally extended beyond the level reached by Austro-Marxists such as Otto Bauer[12], Karl Renner[13] and Robert Danneberg[14] as early as the beginning of the thirties out of the need to fight fascism. Some of their studies, and the later well-known study of the social and psychological effects of prolonged unemployment in the small industrial village of Marienthal[15], represented the beginning of empirical social research in Austria. If allowed to carry on, this research could have given valuable information on fascism in Austria but it was interrupted by the Dollfuss dictatorship and the German occupation.[16]

Only recently has research on fascism in Austria gained new momentum[17] and transcended the mere description of details. Research on Austrian fascism is now conducted at several universities and independent institutes. Since the early sixties the Institute of Contemporary History at the University of Vienna under the direction of Professor Ludwig Jedlicka has presented an assortment of valuable material particularly on biographical and organizational aspects of Austrian fascism and on foreign policy.[18] The Ludwig-Boltzmann-Institute of Labor History and the Institute of Modern and Contemporary History under the supervision of Professor Karl R. Stadler at the University of Linz are doing research on the socialist movement and on fascism by combining political and social history, using in part social-scientific methods.[19] The Institute of Ecclesiastical Contemporary History at Salzburg headed by Professor Erika Weinzierl, in close cooperation with the Historical Institute of the University of Salzburg, analyses problems of the ideology of Austrian fascism, particularly in the context of the Catholic Church and anti-Semitism.[20] Since being appointed to the newly founded chair of Contemporary History at the University of Klagenfurt, Professor Norbert Schausberger has been leading research into the economic history of Austria during the period of fascism.[21] The «Dokumentationsarchiv des österreichischen Widerstands» (The Document Archive on Austrian Resistance) in Vienna which is in possession of a great number of valuable sources on our subject is concerned with studies on the Austrian resistance under the «Corporative State» and the Third *Reich*. With very few exceptions,[22] sociologists and political scientists in Austria have not concerned themselves with fascism.[23]

NOTES

[1] Alfred Diamant, «The Group Basis of Austrian Politics», in: *Journal of Central European Affairs*, vol. 18, no. 2 (Denver, 1958), pp. 134–155.

[2] Adam Wandruszka, «Österreichs politische Struktur», in: *Geschichte der Republik Österreich*, ed. by Heinrich Benedikt (Vienna, 1954), p. 291; cf. also Klaus Berchtold, *Österreichische Parteiprogramme 1868–1966* (Vienna, 1967), p. 12.

[3] For a discussion of Schönerer's movement, see A. G. Whiteside, *The Socialism of Fools* (Berkeley & Los Angeles, 1976).

[4] Karl R. Stadler, «Austria», in: *European Fascism*, ed. by S. J. Woolf (London, 1968), pp. 88–110.

[5] See Ludwig Jedlicka, «Österreich 1932–1936. Innen- und aussenpolitische Probleme», in: *Religion, Wissenschaft, Kultur*, vol. 16–21 (Vienna, 1970); Ludwig Jedlicka, «Aufteilungs- und Einmarschpläne um Österreich, 1919–1934», in: *Festschrift Franz Loidl*, vol. 1 (Vienna, 1970).

[6] Otto Bauer, «Um die Demokratie», in: *Der Kampf*, vol. 26, no. 7 (Vienna, 1933), pp.

269–276; Johann Hirsch, «Zur Soziologie des Austrofaschismus», in: *ibid.*, vol. 22, no. 5, pp. 222–227.

[7] Charles A. Gulick, *Austria from Habsburg to Hitler* (Berkeley, 1948), vol. 1, pp. 1, 7 *seq.* and vol. 2, *passim;* cf. also my paper «Faschismus und Lohnabhängige in Österreich (1918–1939)», presented in the 10th «Linz Conference of the Historians of the Labour Movement» in 1974.

[8] See R. John Rath, «Authoritarian Austria», in: *Native Fascism in the Successor States, 1918–1945* (Santa Barbara, 1971), pp. 24–43 and Ludwig Jedlicka, «Das autoritäre System in Österreich», in: *Aus Politik und Zeitgeschichte. Beilage zu «Das Parlament»* (Bonn, July, 25 1970), pp. 3–15. Cf. also Stanley Payne's classification of fascist and conservative dictatorships in the introduction to the section on Southwestern Europe in this volume.

[9] Generally on the discussion of concepts of Austrian fascism see Grete Klingenstein, «Bemerkungen zum Problem des Faschismus in Österreich», in: *Österreich in Geschichte und Literatur,* vol. 14, no. 1 (Graz, 1970), pp. 1–13.

[10] See the article of R. John Rath in this book; see also Reinhard Kühnl, *Formen bürgerlicher Herrschaft. Liberalismus – Faschismus* (Reinbek, 1971), p.157 and my essay «Die historische Erscheinungsform des Faschismus» in: *Beiträge zur historischen Sozialkunde,* vol. 4, no. 3, (Vienna, 1974), pp. 56–62.

[11] On this point, see for instance the article by Juan J. Linz in *Comparing Nations,* ed. by Richard Merrit and Stein Rokkan (New Haven, 1966), pp. 268 seqq.

[12] Otto Bauer, *Zwischen Zwei Weltkriegen. Die Krise der Weltwirtschaft, der Demokratie und des Sozialismus* (Bratislava 1936); Otto Bauer, «Der Faschismus», in: *Der sozialistische Kampf – La lutte socialiste,* (Paris, vol. 1938), pp. 75–83.

[13] Karl Renner, *Wandlungen der modernen Gesellschaft. – Nachgelassene Werke,* vol. 3 (Vienna, 1953).

[14] Robert Danneberg, *Die Wiener Wahlen 1930 und 1932. Statistische Betrachtungen* (Vienna, 1932); see also: *Der Kampf,* vol. 25 (Vienna, 1932).

[15] Marie Jahoda, Paul F. Lazarsfeld and Hans Zeisel, *Die Arbeitslosen von Marienthal* (1st ed., Leipzig, 1932, 2nd ed. Allensbach, 1960).

[16] *Soziologie, Forschung in Österreich,* ed. by Leopold Rosenmayr and Sigurd Höllinger (Vienna, 1969), pp. 3 seq. and 43–46.

[17] The increasing interest in international fascism in the sixties produced some valuable publications which also deal with Austrian fascism. As important steps of the research process one has to mention the books by Seymour Martin Lipset, Ernst Nolte and Francis L. Carsten, the first issue of the Journal of Contemporary History (See above all Ludwig Jedlicka's article «The Austrian Heimwehr» in: *Journal of Contemporary History,* vol. 1, no. 1 (1966), pp. 127–144), the international conferences on fascism in Seattle, Washington, in 1966, at the University of Reading, England, in 1967, and at the Czechoslovak Academy of Sciences in Prague, in 1969, proceedings from which are printed in: *Native Fascism in the Successor States, 1918–1945,* ed. by Peter F. Sugar (Santa Barbara, Calif., 1971) (articles «The Background of Austrian Fascism» by Fritz Fellner and «Authoritarian Austria» by R. John Rath); *European Fascism,* ed. by S. J. Woolf (London, 1968) (article «Austria» by Karl R. Stadler); *Fascism and Europe,* ed. by the Institute of History, Czechoslovak Academy of Sciences, vol. 2 (Prague 1970) (article «Faschismus und Nationalsozialismus in Österreich bis 1945» by Gerhard Jagschitz.)

[18] See for instance the numerous articles by Ludwig Jedlicka, recently re-edited in his book: *Vom alten zum neuen Österreich. Fallstudien zur österreichischen Zeitgeschichte 1900–1975* (St. Pölten, 1975), the articles by Gerhard Jagschitz cited in this introduction and the other contributions to the Austrian section of this book (especially his newly published book: *Der Putsch. Die Nationalsozialisten 1934 in Österreich* (Graz, 1976)), and the numerous doctoral dissertations coming out of Jedlicka's institute, e.g. the ones by Rudolf Brandstötter, «Dr. Walter Riehl und die Geschichte der nationalsozialistischen Bewegung in Österreich» (unpublished thesis, Vienna, 1969), Josef Hofmann, *Der Pfrimer-Putsch. Der steirische Heimwehrprozess des Jahres 1931* (Vienna, 1965), Peter Huemer, *Sektionschef Robert Hecht und die Zerstörung der Demokratie in Österreich* (Vienna, 1975), Ingeborg Messerer, *«Die Frontkämpfervereinigung Deutsch-Österreichs»* (unpublished thesis, Vienna 1963), Wolfgang Rosar, *Deutsche*

Gemeinschaft. Seyss-Inquart und der Anschluss (Vienna, 1971), Franz Schweiger, *«Geschichte der niederösterreichischen Heimwehr von 1928–1930 mit besonderer Berücksichtigung des sogenannten Korneuburger Eides»* (unpublished thesis, Vienna, 1964), and Anton Staudinger, «Bemühungen Carl Vaugoins um Suprematie der Christlichsozialen Partei in Österreich (1930–33)», in: *Mitteilungen des Österreichischen Staatsarchivs,* vol. 23 (1970), pp. 297–376.

[19] See for instance Karl R. Stadler, *Österreich 1938–1945 im Spiegel der NS-Akten* (Vienna, 1966); Karl R. Stadler, *Austria* (London, 1972); Hans Hautmann and Rudolf Kropf, *Die österreichische Arbeiterbewegung vom Vormärz bis 1945* (Vienna, 1974); Robert Schwarz, *«Sozialismus der Propaganda. Das Werben des «Völkischen Beobachters» um die österreichische Arbeiterschaft 1938/39* (Vienna, 1975) and some of my own publications, cited in the following section of this anthology.

[20] See for instance Erika Weinzierl, *Zu wenig Gerechte. Österreicher und Judenverfolgung 1938–1945* (Graz, 1969); Erika Weinzierl, «Österreichs Katholiken und der Nationalsozialismus», in: *Wort und Wahrheit,* vol. 18 (1963) and vol. 20 (1965); Rudolf G. Ardelt, *Zwischen Demokratie und Faschismus. Deutschnationales Gedankengut in Österreich 1919–1930* (Salzburg, 1972); Ernst Hanisch, «Neuere Faschismustheorien», in: *Zeitgeschichte,* vol. 1, no. 1 (1973).

[21] See Norbert Schausberger, *Rüstung in Österreich 1938–1945,* (Vienna, 1970); Norbert Schausberger, *Griff nach Österreich* (unprinted manuscript, Klagenfurt, 1974).

[22] Anton Pelinka, *Stand oder Klasse. Die christliche Arbeiterbewegung Österreichs 1933 bis 1938* (Vienna, 1972).

[23] For further bibliographical details see the introductory statements of R. John Rath in his article and the note on sources in Bruce F. Pauley's article in this anthology. For other recent publications of non-Austrian historians, see for instance Clifton Earl Edmondson, *The Heimwehr and Austrian Politics, 1918–1934* (diss., Duke Univ. 1966); John J. Haag, *Othmar Spann and the Politics of «Totality»: Corporatism in Theory and Practice* (diss., Rice University 1969); Reinhard Kondert, *The Rise and Early History of the Heimwehr Movement* (diss., Rice Univ. 1971); Bruce F. Pauley, *Hahnenschwanz und Hakenkreuz. Steirischer Heimatschutz und österreichisher Nationalsozialismus 1918–1934* (Vienna, 1972).

Since this introduction has been finished in 1975, a number of excellent articles and books on this topic has been published, for instance Francis L. Carsten, *Fascist Movements in Austria. From Schönerer to Hitler* (London, 1977; 2nd German ed.: Munich, 1979); Radomir Luža, *Austro-German Relations in the Anschluss Era* (Princeton, 1975; German ed.: Vienna, 1977); C. Earl Edmondson, *The «Heimwehr» and Austrian Politics 1918–1936* (Athens, Georgia, 1978), Willibald Holzer, «Faschismus in Österreich 1918–1938», in: *Austriaca,* no. spécial 1 (1978), pp. 69–170. See also: Evan B. Bukey, «The Nazi Party in Linz, Austria, 1919–1939: A Sociolocigal Perspective», in: *German Studies Review,* vol. 1, no. 3 (1978), pp. 302–326; Bruce F. Pauley, «From Splinter Party to Mass Movement: The Austrian Nazi Breakthrough», in *ibid.,* vol. 2, no. 1 (1979), pp. 7–29; Bruce F. Pauley, «Fascism and the *Führerprinzip:* The Austrian Example», in: *Central European History,* vol. 12, no. 3 (1979), pp. 272–296. One has also to notify that Prof. Ludwig Jedlicka died in 1977, and Prof. Weinzierl has taken Jedlicka's chair.

The Changing Patterns of Social Support for Austrian National Socialism (1918–1945)

GERHARD BOTZ

The Pre-fascist Phase (1918–1921)

Austrian National Socialism, which found its prime organizational expression in the German National Socialist Workers' Party *(Deutsche Nationalsozialistische Arbeiterpartei – DNSAP)*, was in the First Austrian Republic an inheritance from the Habsburg monarchy. The DNSAP, or rather its predecessor the German Workers' Party *(Deutsche Arbeiterpartei – DAP)*, founded in 1903, had its social and organizational backbone in the pan-German trade unions of workers in trade and industry, miners, railwaymen and shop assistants in North Bohemia and in other German-speaking industrial areas in old Austria, particularly in areas of close economic and national competition (usually with Czech workers). In terms of social position, the leaders of these parties hardly differed from the majority of leaders in the Social Democratic workers' movement. The DAP, which in the *Reichsrat* elections of 1911 received 26,670 votes and thus only managed to gain a fraction of the Austrian Social Democratic Workers' Party's* share, included in their party program a number of democratic demands and also calls for social reforms and restrictions on monopolistic trends in the economy. It also tried to attract voters by appeals to German national and anti-Semitic sentiments. In the range of parties in the Danube Monarchy the DAP, which since May 1918 called itself DNSAP, can therefore be placed fairly near the German national right wing of the Social Democrats, the Engelbert Pernerstorfer wing.[1] Yet it cannot be called fascist, if «fascist» is taken to mean a combination of national and pseudo-socialist demands coupled with anti-democratic attitudes, the acceptance of the *Führer* principle, worship of violence and close connections with a vigilant paramilitary militia.

When, in 1918, the new state frontiers separated the DNSAP from their main area of support in the «Sudeten» lands in the Czechoslovak republic, its party organization was substantially weakened. Until the parliamentary elections on February 16, 1919, the party did not even manage to present its own lists of candidates in most constituencies.[2] As a result, in eight constituencies the DNSAP was supported by only 23,334 voters (0.78 per cent), an insignificant number in view of the almost 3 million valid votes cast. However, in Vienna-Northeast (districts 2, 20 and 21), which was the constituency of the party leader Dr. Walter Riehl, a lawyer, it obtained more than 4 per cent; in Salzburg, where another active member of the party leadership, Rudolf Jung, an engineer, was first candidate under the old name DAP, it even obtained 7.14 per cent (or 7,382 votes). Above all, the DNSAP (DAP) was then, as later on, a party of the small and medium-sized towns.[3] The parliamentary elections in 1920 show that the

---

Sozialdemokratische Arbeiterpartei Österreichs, the forerunner to the contemporary SPÖ, *(Sozialistische Partei Österreichs)*, the Austrian Social Democratic Party.

DNSAP was predominantly a male party. A thousand votes were cast by men compared with only 815 votes cast by women.[4]

These election results provide ground for suspecting that only in their traditional centres did the DNSAP succeed in obtaining the support of a very small proportion of the industrial employees and workers. Its appeal to employees in public service, railwaymen and commercial employees met with most success in the small and medium-sized towns in the rural Alpine areas.

The list of candidates for the 1919 election gives some clues to the professions to which the leading officials belonged, and to the social groups to which the DNSAP directed its primary appeal. Of the candidates, about one seventh were women, a relatively high proportion compared to that of women candidates in the Social Democratic party, and one to be accounted for by the newly-won female vote. The left column of table 1 shows that more than half of the candidates were in the lower echelons of the public service; 21 per cent were civil servants proper, that is, working in the state bureaucracy; 14 per cent railwaymen and 7 per cent teachers. (The proportion of holders of public offices and regional and local government officials was, however, relatively low (8 per cent altogether)). Approximately 11 per cent were workers.

13 per cent were employees in trade, commerce and industry. 3 per cent were self-employed in these branches and 3 per cent were self-employed farmers. Another 9 per cent were members of the free professions, such as lawyers and writers. The medical profession was not represented among the candidates. Thus, 21 per cent originated from the propertied middle class.

Also, to judge from the results of various elections, no shift seems to have occurred in social composition of the DNSAP in the two succeeding years. Apart from local set-backs the party succeeded first in the region of Salzburg. There it obtained two seats. It also won a seat in Vienna – Lower Austria, as well as a larger number of seats in local councils. In the parliamentary elections on October 17, 1920, the DNSAP stood for election in nearly all constituencies but obtained only 34,000 votes.[5]

The Early Fascist Wave (1922–1925)

It proved decisive for the development of Austrian National Socialism that the DNSAP already at the end of 1919 decided to contact foreign national socialists, particularly the Germans. These contacts continued in the form of intensive co-operation. Between 1920 and 1922 the two parties arranged four «inter-state» meetings. To the extent Hitler became dominant in German National Socialism, German influence on the Austrian development also increased. At a party conference in Salzburg in August, 1923, the Hitler line won the majority. This caused the former Austrian party chairman, Riehl, to resign and led to a deepening of the signs of splits which were to surface in full the following years.

In October, 1922, the Austrian chancellor Ignaz Seipel (1922–1924 and 1926–1929) and representatives of the British, French, Italian and Czechoslovak governments signed the Geneva protocol to bolster the Austrian finances, which were badly disturbed by the years of inflation (1921/22). The Geneva Protocol succeeded in restoring the state's finances, but at the same time led to mass redundancies among civil servants and to a rapid increase in unemployment.[6] The discontent of the middle

Table 1. *Percentwise Social Composition of the Nazi Leadership by Occupation in Austria (1919 – 1938)**

	Candidates for the parliamentary elections 1919 (n = 71)		Members of the provincial diets and the «Bundes-rat» 1932 (n = 31)		Members**of the «Grossdeutscher Reichstag» 1938 (n = 73)	
Self-employed	12		16		12	
Of these, farmers		3		6		5
Professionals	9		13		11	
Public servants	51		45		38	
Of these,						
railway men		14		13		3
teachers...................		7		6		10
military		1		6		8
Employees	13		16		25	
Of these,						
higher empl.				10		19
Workers	11		10		14	
Others***	4		–		–	
Sum	100		100		100	

* Horizontal comparison possible only with great reservations.
** Occupation trained for (actual occupation at the time of the «election» was not considered).
*** People of private means and housewives.

Sources: Beiträge zur Statistik der Republik Österreich, no. 2 (Vienna 1920), pp. 12 seqq.; *Land und Gemeinde,* vol. 1 no. 1 (Linz 1932); cf. also: *Ergebnisse der Wahl in den oberösterreichischen Landtag am 19. April 1931* (Linz 1931), pp. 4–12; *Der Grossdeutsche Reichstag, IV. Wahlperiode* (Berlin 1938).

class, pauperized by inflation in the years 1921/22, was probably the main cause behind the rapid advancement of the Nazi movement, and it triggered important changes in the party's goals, organization and membership stock. After 1922 Austrian National Socialism, particularly its Hitler wing, must be called fascist in the sense specified above.[7] By the middle of 1923, a Nazi newspaper reported that the Nazi party had now 34,000 enrolled members in 118 local groups.[8] The paramilitary *Ordnertruppe,* founded in the previous year and organized with German assistance, had 9,800 members. The circulation of the party newspaper, the daily *Deutsche Arbeiterpresse,* increased its circulation within one year from 4,000 to 22,000 and a number of new Nazi weeklies were founded.[9]

In the ferment of domestic politics in the years 1922/23, National Socialism seems to have received a push from petty bourgeois and semi-proletarian elements. Above all there was an influx of pupils and apprentices threatened by unemployment and of students. Many non-commissioned officers in the armed forces tried to find employment after being discharged and when unsuccessful entered vocational schools and universities. The failure rate of these people was high; hence they experienced defeat twice in their lives and became the bitterest fighters for fascism. Teachers, school organizations and the German Athletes' Association *(Deutscher Turnerbund)* played a crucial role in winning youth for National Socialism. Alongside former officers and petty officers who had been rejected by the republican army, these very groups recruited the most active members of early fascism. According to the Austrian Marxist Otto Bauer, in some respects Austrian Nazism can be considered to be the result of three closely inter-related social processes: 1. the establishment of a fascist militia made up of *déclassé* war veterans, 2. the rebellion of the pauperized petty bourgeoisie, and 3. the counter-revolutionary efforts of big business.[10]

In this period[11] very close personal, organizational and ideological ties existed between National Socialism and other fascist or right-wing radical groups, particularly in the Catholic Conservative *Lager*. This organizational and ideological convergence found its foremost expression in the monarchist *Ostara* band and the *Frontkämpfervereinigung* (Frontline Veterans' Association). Quite a few members of the latter organization were also enrolled in the *Ordnertruppe,* the predecessor of the SA. Even National Socialist leaders, such as the Vienna Gauleiter Alfred Eduard Frauenfeld (1931–1933), came from these groups.

In accordance with the Munich *Putsch* tactics, the party refused to take part in the parliamentary elections on October 21, 1923. Because regional interpretations of elections in the twenties are missing altogether and also because no party card indexes from that period have been preserved, statements on the social composition of the Nazi party membership are not possible. With due reservations, some evidence on the social composition of the paramilitary formations of the three Austrian social segments, the German National, the Socialist, and the Catholic-Conservative (including the pro-Austrian wing of the *Heimwehr)*[12] can be presented. The data analyzed in tables 2, 3 and 4 derive from personal statements by National Socialists who were either killed or injured in armed conflicts with political opponents or appear in official inquiries as perpetrators or witnesses.[13] Mainly members of the paramilitary formations, but also some simple party members are included in these tables. Both categories of supporters of the various political groups are called «militants» in this paper.

(A cautionary note is appropriate here: From a strictly methodological point of view, the numbers on which the following inferences are based, are too small to warrant valid conclusions. They are not the result of random sampling techniques, but represent nevertheless the only available information on the membership of these Nazi organizations. More recent research by G. Jagschitz on the prisoners of Wöllersdorf (see note 42) and by Ernst Hanisch on the early DNSAP chapter in Salzburg (work in progress in the Department of History, University of Salzburg) tends to confirm the figures in these tables.)

The average age of the Nazi «militants», who are to be considered as the armed branch of the entire German National *Lager,* was (between 1923 and 1933) approximately 23 years. A comparison with the «militants» of both other *Lager* (see table 2) reveals the significant rôle played by the young in National Socialism already in the early twenties.

Table 2. *Average Age of «Militants»* of all Political Lager*

	Socialists (n = 41)	Catholic-Conservatives (and Heimwehr) (n = 29)	National Socialists (n = 134)
1923–27	34,7	28,0	22,7
1928–33	26,5	24,4	23,4
1923–33	27,7	27,2	23,1

* Participants in political acts of violence as perpetrators, casualties and witnesses.

Between 1923 and 1927, on average the militant members of the working class *Lager* were 12 years older and the Catholic Conservatives 5 years older than the National Socialists. Between 1928 and 1933 this difference diminished to 3 years and 1 year respectively.

Table 3 presents the social background of Nazi «militants» by occupation in the early fascist phase (1923–1925) and in the period of breakthrough to a mass movement (1929–1933). A comparison of the two social profiles is rendered difficult by the fact that for the period 1923–25 practically the only data available are from Vienna.

Table 3. *Social Structure of Nazi «Militants»* and of Wöllersdorf Prisoners (1923–1934) in per cent*

	Self-employed of these: farmers	Professionals	Students	Public servants	Employees	Workers' total of these: unskilled workers	Pupils, apprentices	Others	Sum
1923–1925 (mainly in Vienna) (n = 73)	5 —	–	14	8	32	33 / 1	4	4	100
1929–1932 in whole of Austria (n=34) ...	12 —	6	3	12	26	35 / 6	6	–	100
1933 in whole of Austria (n=60) ...	8 —	2	7	10	18	42 / 7	13	–	100
May 1934** Wöllersdorf prisoners (n=301) ..	11 / 3	3	7	7	24	47 / 27	–	1	100

* Participants in political acts of violence as perpetrators, casualties and witnesses.
** Calculated from: Gerhard Jagschitz, «Die Anhaltelager in Österreich», in: R. Neck & L. Jedlicka (eds.) *Vom Justizpalast zum Heldenplatz* (Vienna 1975), pp. 150 *seq.*

Between 1923 and 1925, the Nazi «militants» in Vienna were made up of approximately one third manual workers and one third employees in private enterprises. 8 per cent were civil servants, 18 per cent students, pupils or apprentices and only 5 per cent self-employed tradesmen. In comparison with males eligible to vote in Vienna (in 1923)[14], the workers were not represented in due proportion to their strength in the population as a whole.

Employees in the private sector and students were heavily overrepresented (by two and ten times respectively), and the civil servants and the self-employed underrepresented (by two and three times respectively).

From these facts it can be concluded that the lower social strata were more strongly represented in all three political *Lager* on the level of «militants» than in the segments as a whole. Comparing the armed militia with the rest of the «militants», table 4 shows that the lower classes tended to predominate in these armed formations, and that their proportion was higher there than among the «militants» as a whole. This applies to each of the three Austrian segments. The upper strata restricted themselves almost exclusively to the leading positions, which were usually taken by private employees and local council workers among the Social Democrats. Among the Catholic-Conservatives and *Heimwehr* as well as among the National Socialists these positions tended to be occupied by small tradesmen and their sons. The unemployed appear in the available sources at around 10 per cent, which approximately corresponds to the total national unemployment rate in this period.[15]

Table 4. *Social Origins of Nazi «Militants»: Members of the NSDAP, the SA and the SS by Occupation in Austria (1923–1933) in per cent*

	Self-employed	Professionals	Students	Public servants	Employees	of these: in commerce	Workers	of these: unskilled w.	Pupils, apprentices	Others	Sum
All Nazi «Militants» (n=167)	8	2	9	9	26	13	36	4	8	2	100
of these: Nazis* (n = 49)	16	5	7	9	14	5	34	5	15	–	100
SA-men** (n=37)	3	–	5	10	29	14	44	3	6	3	100
SS-men*** (n=23)	–	–	4	18	39	26	39	9	–	–	100

* National Socialists without detailed specification (party members).
** *Ordnertruppe, Vaterländischer Schutzbund*, SA.
*** From 1932 on.

National Socialism and the Völkisch Trade Unions

It is important to mention that the pan-German *(völkisch)* trade unions had a special place in *early* National Socialism in Austria. The *völkisch* unions, independent of political parties but part of the German National *Lager,* were united in the *Deutscher Gewerkschaftsbund für Österreich* (German Trade Union Federation in Austria); in fact, many of its branches were in such close relationship to (the anti-Hitler wing of) National Socialism that the National Socialists listed them in their yearbook of 1925 and 1926 as National Socialist organizations, which implied a kind of official recognition. After a steep rise in membership, as early as 1923, the *völkisch* trade unions together had more than 45,000 members (according to other, less reliable, sources even 53,000), reaching their maximum of 51,247 members in 1928. Membership figures then fluctuated between 47,000 and 49,000.[16] Thus they included approximately only 5 per cent of the total number of trade union members of all political persuasions. It should be mentioned that because of their organizational independence the development of membership of the *völkisch* trade unions was hardly affected by the considerable increase in membership within the National Socialist party itself. The strength of these unions remained more or less at the same level irrespective of the surges in Nazi party membership.

Within the small *völkisch* trade unions, the railwaymen had a clear majority. The German Transport Union *(Deutsche Verkehrsgewerkschaft),* which had a membership of 23,000 to 24,000, permanently made up 45 per cent of the membership of the pan-German trade unions. In the elections for the *Personalvertretung* (a kind of shop stewards body in the public service) of the Austrian State Railways in 1923, 1926 and 1931, approximately 16 to 18 per cent of the votes went to the pan-German trade unions (77 per cent, 78 per cent and 75 per cent respectively went to the Social Democrats).[17] In these elections, the German Transport Union achieved its greatest success (1923: 52 per cent, 1926: 55 per cent and 1931: 47 per cent) among people in central administrative positions in the state railways, where the percentage of high-ranking and intermediate level civil servants was especially high. A little weaker, but still stronger than average, were the *völkisch* unions among the intermediate civil servants at the railway stations (1923: 26 per cent, 1926 and 1931: 23 per cent). They were well below average (1923: 6.9 up to 11.9 per cent) in all branches where the major proportion of railwaymen consisted of qualified workers and temporary workers. Those positions remained the stronghold of the Social Democratic trade unions. Nevertheless it is remarkable that while the *völkisch* share of votes showed a marked increase in these branches, especially between 1923 and 1931, there was stagnation or decrease in support for the *völkisch* unions among the higher or intermediate service categories in the state railway administration.[18]

In Austria at this time there were two kinds of public and legally acknowledged *(öffentlich-rechtliche)* corporations representing the interests of the employed: *Personalvertretungen* (shop stewards representing public employees) and *Betriebsräte* (representative organs in private firms). In addition there were also «chambers of labor» *(Arbeiterkammern).* Membership in the chambers of labor was automatic and elections followed corporative lines, i.e. each category voted within its own organizational framework. Because of this strict separation, we have direct access to information on the political alignments of the groups organized by these corporations: the workers in private firms *(Privatarbeiter),* the employed in the private sector *(Privatangestellte),* and the employed in the state communications service, particularly the railways *(Verkehrsbedienstete)*. In 1926/27 in the whole of the country only 2.6 per cent of the blue-collar workers in private enterprises elected representatives belonging to the pan-German unions, whereas as many as 20.4 per cent of those employed in the private sector gave their votes to the *völkisch* unions. Those employed in the public communication sector *(Verkehrsbedienstete)* as a whole gave a 12.5 per cent vote for the pan-German unions. Blue-collar workers in public communications service (post, telephone and telegraph services in addition to the railways and the stateowned bus lines) gave only 4.4 per cent of their vote to the pan-Germans; the white-collar workers in the same sector however, 13.3 per cent.[19] Whereas for the whole country the overwhelming majority in all these electoral blocs voted in favor of the Social Democratic unions, there were strong regional variations. Particularly Vorarlberg, Salzburg and Kärnten proved to be, relatively speaking, areas of diminished Social Democratic dominance.

Table 5. *Results of Elections for the Chambers of Labor in Austria in 1926/27*

Section of the Chambers of Labor	Election Results						
	in Absolute Figures		in Per Cent of Valid Votes				
	Registered Votes	Valid Votes	Social Democrats	Christian Socials	German Nationals	Communists	Others
Workers	516,973	331,000	83.5	9.9	2.6	4.0	–
Employees	168,052	93,996	64.6	13.5	20.4	0.4	1.1
Workers in Transportation	12,687	10,844	90.2	3.5	4.4	1.9	–
Employees in Transportation	127,921	110,929	75.8	9.9	13.3	1.0	–
Together	825,633	546,769	78.8	10.4	7.8	2.8	0.2

Calculated from: *Wirtschaftsstatistisches Jahrbuch 1926* (Vienna 1927), p.69.

As the same elections to the chambers of labor (1926/27) showed, the *völkisch* element among employees and laborers in transportation (mostly in public enterprises) was strongest in Styria and Vorarlberg (over 15 per cent) and in Carinthia (20.6 per cent). These unions showed their weakest spots in Vienna, Lower Austria and Burgenland (altogether 7.6 per cent).

Another, and perhaps more important, pan-German trade union was the German Commercial and Industrial Employees' Union *(Deutscher Handels- und Industrieangestelltenverband)*. It was composed of between 8,000 and 10,000 private employees and gained over 20 per cent of the votes of the section of employees in the 1926/27 chamber of labor elections in Austria as a whole (see table 5). In Carinthia and Salzburg this union obtained as high a figure as 49.8 per cent and 56.3 per cent, respectively. Another very strong occupational group within the *völkisch* trade unions was that of the post and telegraph workers, (5,000 to 6,000 members) and the civil servants. Furthermore, some smaller organizations of the non-self-employed pharmacists, the domestic servants and workers in private enterprises also belonged to the pan-German trade unions.[20]

The distribution of National Socialist votes across local constituencies in the parliamentary elections between 1919 and 1927 corresponded almost perfectly to the vote of the salaried employees and those employed in transportation in the chamber of labor elections. Only later did the votes for the Nazi party spread out more evenly. This lends credibility to the view that until 1927 the main voting blocs in support of the Nazis at parliamentary elections were to a large extent made up by private employees and employees of the railways, especially in Salzburg, Carinthia and Styria. These provinces were the strongholds of German nationalism. In the southern alpine provinces, German nationalist sentiment was intensified by the struggle with the Yugoslavs after World War I. Pan-Germanism and border problems went together, and during the twenties and thirties the areas directly involved in these disputes became a fertile soil for Nazism.

Rise to a Mass Party (1926–1933)

In the second half of the twenties and in the period of the final ascent of National Socialism to a mass party, the occupational structure of the Nazi «militants», but also of the Nazi party members, shifted further towards the petty bourgeoisie. The internal break-up of the German version of fascism, which in Austria started before Hitler's *Putsch,* and the gradual improvement of the economic situation seemed to have resulted in a marked desertion of workers and employees. In 1924 Riehl, the former National Socialist chairman, founded his own tiny group called the «German Social Union» *(Deutsch-Sozialer Verein),* which made little further impact. In May, 1926, came the final break-up of Austrian National Socialism. It was split into two separate groups, one under the new party chairman *Karl Schulz* and another under the leadership of Hitler. The former retained the old party name and a certain democratic slant. Hitler on the other hand tied his supporters strictly to the Munich party leadership and their political principles. He named his party «Austria's NSDAP (Hitler movement)».[21] Not even equal in numbers at the beginning, the Hitler movement gained an ever increasing preponderance. Concomitantly with Hitler's seizure of party power the claim to be primarily a worker's party was gradually abandoned.

Schulz was of the opinion that the National Socialist party, the members of which were mostly organized in the *völkisch* trade unions, had to co-operate with these unions. He criticized Hitler's attitude and argued against the German party leader at their meeting at Passau in August 1926, maintaining that «the ideal of a German Workers' Party was not to gather a 'hundred or thousand desperados' and to cause trouble in a 'mercenary-like manner'. Rather he saw the task as one of penetrating the masses of German workmen with national and socialist ideas . . .»[22] In sum his political line represented primarily the working class wing of Austrian National Socialism, whereas the Hitler movement mainly attracted the urban middle classes.

Heimwehr fascism developed rapidly after 1927. It benefited probably somewhat less from immediate economic dislocation than did National Socialism in Austria or Germany. It gained support more because of the fear of the bourgeoisie precipitated by the riots in Vienna on July 15, 1927, in which socialist workers set fire to the Ministry of Justice building. It also drew increasing support from domestic big business and aristocracy and from abroad, in particular from Hungary and Italy. This support assumed the form of money and weapons. In 1928, when the Austrian economic situation was at its best in the entire period of the First Republic, the *Heimwehr* rapidly rose to a mass movement which in the parliamentary elections of November 1930 gained 228,000 votes.[23] Until 1930 the rise of *Heimwehr* fascism presented a kind of competition which at the same time prevented a massive rise of the NSDAP. The *Heimwehr* not only attracted a proportion of former National Socialist supporters, particularly in Upper Styria, but as long as the *Heimwehr* was a strong and unified movement, it also blocked the expansion of the National Socialists into rural areas.

The Hitler movement had already established itself organizationally in 1926. When, however, in the parliamentary elections in 1927, it competed in a union with another German national splinter group, presenting itself as the *Völkisch-sozialer Block,* it did not even match the success of the DNSAP in 1920.[24] Only when the world economic crisis swept over Austria and one tenth of all able-bodied men were unemployed, did the National Socialists obtain 111,627 votes or 3 per cent in the 1930 parliamentary elections. In Lower Austria alone they got 34,307 votes or 4.2 per cent. In small agricultural-industrial towns such as Langenlois and Marchegg the National Socialists even became the second strongest party, mostly at the expense of the Greater German Peoples' Party and the *Landbund,* the German national farmers' party.[25]

A further, though small, increase in support for the NSDAP could be recorded in the provincial elections in Upper Austria in April 1931. Within five months their proportion of votes increased from 2.2 per cent to 3.4 per cent. Research in this province has shown that the National Socialists scored highest in areas with a predominantly industrial-commercial structure (5.7 per cent). In workers' residential districts, they got 2 to 3 per cent, but in farming districts only 0.6 per cent. As was also the case when the party was founded, at all parliamentary elections thereafter the NSDAP drew more support from men than from women. In 1930 the ratio was 1,000 to 737.[26]

When a *Putsch* of the Styrian *Heimwehr* failed miserably on September 13, 1931, every fifth Austrian was out of work. Gradually the NSDAP started to gain momentum. From July 1931 it was reorganized by Theo Habicht, an emissary sent by Hitler, in accordance with the German party statutes. This further increased its striking power. The Nazis succeeded in making the decisive breakthrough to a mass party in the provincial and council elections on April 24, 1932, when altogether two thirds of the registered voters in Austria cast their votes. At the provincial elections, the NSDAP gained 17 per cent in Vienna, 14 per cent in Lower Austria, 29 per cent in Salzburg. Only in Vorarlberg, on November 6, 1932, did they gain as low a figure as 11 per cent (table 6). In April 1932, at one stroke 29 Nazi representatives moved into the provincial parliaments of three federal provinces, and seven months later two followed suit in Vorarlberg. Altogether, they gained 344,000 votes or 16 per cent in the federal provinces which in 1932 held provincial elections. Local council elections which were also held on April 24, 1932 in Styria and Carinthia (except in the two provincial capitals) revealed the same trend. Extensive reports and analyses of this election result have already been presented by Robert Danneberg and Walter B. Simon.[27] The following statements are based on their results.

Everywhere in Austria, nearly the whole of the Greater German Peoples' Party, the party of urban German nationalism, and a considerable part of its rural equivalent, the *Landbund,* was absorbed by the NSDAP. In Vienna and in other urban centres and in Styria the NSDAP also attracted a great proportion of the voters who had voted for the *Heimwehr* in the last parliamentary election.

Table 6. *Election Results in Vienna, Lower Austria, Salzburg, Vorarlberg and Innsbruck from 1930 to 1933 in Thousands*

Elections	Registered voters	Votes cast	Communists	Social Democrats	Christian Social Party	Grossdeutsche Volkspartei (German Nat.)	Landbund (Peasant League)	Heimatblock (Fascists)	National Socialists	Others
						Schober-Block				
Vienna										
1930a ...	1 280	1 193	10.6	703	283	124.4		26.4	27.5	18.0
1932b ...	1 303	1 158	21.8	683	234	8.8	–	–	201.4	10.0
Difference	+23	−35	+11.2	−20	−49	−115.6		−26.4	+173.9	−8.0
Lower Austria										
1930a ...	912	818	4.1	292	361	70.1		54	34	4
1932b ...	931	783	8.5	272	363	18.4	10.0	–	111	–
Difference	+19	−35	+4.4	−20	+2	−41.7		−54	+77	−4
Ld. Salzburg (Region)										
1930a ...	145	123	0.8	36.9	51	15.6	6.7	7.1	4.5	–
1932b ...	?	117	3.1	29.8	44	2.0	7.4	5.5	24.1	0
Difference	?	−6	+2.3	−7.1	−7	−13.6	+0.7	−1.6	+19.6	–
Vorarlberg										
1930a ...	85.5	77.5	0.17	16.2	44.0	16.2		–	0.88	–
1932c ...	?	76.4	2.61	11.9	43.3	5.2	5.3	–	8.03	–
Difference	?	−1.1	+2.44	−4.3	−0.7	−5.7	–	–	+7.15	–
Innsbruck										
1930a ...	39.0	35.7	0.13	13.4	8.1	9.7		3.5	0.79	–
1931d ...	40.2	30.1	0.40	12.0	9.9	5.1	–	–	1.20	0.7
1933e ...	40.4	36.4	0.47	9.9	9.4	0.8	–	0.8	15.00	–
Difference f	+0.2	+6.3	+0.07	−2.1	−0.5	−4.3	–	–	+13.80	–

a Parliamentary Elections Nov. 9, 1930.
b Provincial Diet Elections April 24, 1932.
c Provincial Diet Election Nov. 6, 1932.
d Council Election 1931.
e Council Election April 23, 1933.
f Difference 1933–1931.
? No data.
Sources: *Statistische Nachrichten*, special issue: *Die Nationalratswahlen vom 9. November 1930*, (Vienna 1931); Walter B. Simon, *The Political Parties of Austria*, (diss., Univ. of Columbia, 1957); *Neue Freie Presse* and *Neues Wiener Tagblatt*, Vienna, April and November 1932 and April 1933.

The NSDAP also made gains at the expense of both the large parties which together traditionally received approximately 80 per cent of the votes. Where the Christian Social party was strong, the National Socialists did not really succeed in breaking into its clerical bourgeois voter bloc. Social Christian losses were compensated for by gains in *Heimwehr* votes. It was where the Social Christians had always done considerably worse than the national average, that their losses were greatest. The same tendency can be noted in the case of the Social Democrats.

The mass success of the NSDAP in Austria, in contrast to Germany, was not primarily the result of the participation of the previous non-voters in the parliamentary elections. Nevertheless absenteeism played a noticeable role, with the exception of Vienna, as a first step in the process of transfer of loyalties to Hitler's party. It remains an open question whether insignificant local fluctuations in the support for National Socialism at the polls are sufficient for arguing the claim that the National Socialist success was a «non-ideological protest vote».[28]

Attempts at tracing the political origins of National Socialist voters have only been made for Vienna. As the turnout in Vienna was 4 per cent lower in 1932 than in 1930, the presumed addition of previous non-voters to the Nazi bloc cannot have played an important role. The 201,000 Nazi voters in 1932 (100 per cent) therefore consisted of 54,000 (27 per cent) voters who had also voted fascist in 1930, (27,500 for the NSDAP and 26,500 for the *Heimwehr*). For the most part, in 1932 the Nazi electorate consisted of 81,000 previous German National voters (40 per cent), of 49,000 previous Christian Social (24 per cent) and of 17,000 previous Social Democratic voters (9 per cent). The 34,000 registered voters who did not take part in the election, beyond the number of non-voters in 1930, were mainly of Jewish origin and had in 1930 probably voted for the German national *Schober-Block*.

Sociologically speaking, the election results in the 1932 provincial council elections and the results of later local elections in Innsbruck and in some small communes in Lower Austria and Tyrol, meant that by and large National Socialism at that time had succeeded in winning over only the middle classes in the large and medium sized towns (tradesmen, professionals, private employees and public servants). In Vienna, Robert Danneberg has shown that the public servants did not behave uniformly. Whereas the bulk of the workers employed by the «red» council and the railway employees voted for the Social Democrats, the civil servants and council employees voted mainly for the NSDAP.[29] It cannot be determined whether the voting behavior of public servants in other federal states of Austria deviated from the findings in Vienna.

In 1932 and also in 1933, the inroads made by National Socialism into rural areas remained limited.[30] The farmers were traditionally more inclined towards Catholic Conservatism and the industrial workers remained for the most part safely within the confines of the socialist bloc. Both proved fairly resistant to the Nazi appeal. Protestants, on the other hand, who in 1934 accounted for only 4.4 per cent of Austria's population, tended to support National Socialism much more than Catholics, as shown by an analysis of the «militants» and of the votes.[31]

In local council elections later in the spring of 1932 the Nazis gained in some small towns in Lower Austria – Schwechat, Strasshof and Krems – 12 per cent, 24 per cent and 32 per cent respectively. On September 25, 1932, in the Innsbruck labor suburb of Hötting the NSDAP received 24 per cent. On April 23, 1933, it gained 41 per cent of the valid votes in Innsbruck (table 6). These election results showed that the progress of the National Socialists in April 1932 had not yet come to an end. Nevertheless, there was a slowdown of the upward trend suggesting that the party was approaching the limits of its electoral potential.

Estimates of the social background of enrolled party members in the same period would require extensive research on the card index material deposited in the Berlin Document Center. This work has not yet been done, but using another source, the Austrian historian Karl R. Stadler has estimated that the number of NSDAP members increased from 4,400 to 43,000 between June 1928 and January 1933. Until June 19, 1933, when the NSDAP was banned, probably another 25,000 new members joined the NSDAP. According to statements by the Vienna Gauleiter, Walther Rentmeister, 50 per cent of the party members in his district were unemployed in 1928, a fact undoubtedly conducive to the party's rapid growth.[32]

Table 3 allows some conclusions as to the social structure of the Nazi «militants» in the beginning of the thirties. This table shows that roughly speaking the petty bourgeoisie (21 per cent) and dependent employees and workers (altogether 73 per cent) were represented among the armed and non-armed activists approximately in the same proportion as in the Austrian working population *(Berufstätige)* as a whole.[33] From the middle of the twenties to the beginning of the thirties, the proportion of self-employed and professionals had increased over the number of students. Compared with the years 1923/25, within the groups of the working class only insignificant changes appear.

Furthermore, the distribution of the Nazi «militants» by occupation in table 4 shows that in comparison with private employees, the proportion of self-employed (16 per cent) and professionals (5 per cent) was many times greater among the ordinary non-armed NSDAP than in the armed formations, SA and SS, whose total numerical strength was estimated to be 30,000 to 40,000 at the end of 1933.[34] The proportion of public servants (9 per cent) was approximately the same across the different party branches, considerably greater only in the SS (18 per cent). In light of the proportion of public servants at the élite level, their lack of public visibility in demonstrations and gatherings is all the more noticeable and was probably due to the fact that their positions were in jeopardy if they showed themselves in armed marches.

On the other hand, private employees and (less clearly) workers were more or less overrepresented in the SS (each 39 per cent) and in the SA (29 per cent and 46 per cent respectively). Thus the supposition is strengthened that the armed formations of the NSDAP were more «proletarian» than the movement as a whole. The SS appears to have been more strongly centred on civil servants and employees, the SA more strongly on manual workers. This does not imply, however, that the SA already had the same proportion of workers as the Social Democratic Republican *Schutzbund* or the defense unions of the Catholic Conservative *Lager*, in particular the *Heimwehr*. In the Social Democratic defense militia the percentage of workers amounted to 88 per cent and in the group of «militants» in the Catholic Conservative *Lager* to over 50 per cent (in the monarchistic *Ostara*, it was even 82 per cent).[35]

The social composition of the Nazi élite can be estimated from the list of people elected in the provincial elections[36] (see the middle column in table 1). Out of 31 representatives to the different *Landtage* and to *Bundesrat* elected in 1932, 10 per cent owned small enterprises in trade and commerce and 6 per cent were farmers, whereas professionals amounted to 13 per cent. By far the strongest group numerically were the public servants (45 per cent), while employees in the state railways alone made up 13 per cent. Teachers and officers made up 6 per cent each, while 16 per cent were private employees, two thirds of them in higher positions. Only 10 per cent were workers in private enterprises.

The fact that this sociographic profile corresponds in detail with that of the DNSAP candidates in the year 1919 deserves special consideration. The reason for this remarkable convergence in the social origins of the members must be sought in the high degree of stability at the élite level: the National Socialist élite remained the same for more than 12 years. This fits in with a complaint from Nazis in Alpine areas who reported to the party administration based since 1928 in Linz, «that practically only Sudeten Germans sit in 'top' positions».[37]

The illegal NSDAP (1933–1938)

Increased terrorist activity led to the prohibition of the NSDAP and their subsidiaries *(Gliederungen)* in Austria on June 19th, 1933. A majority of the leaders of the party immediately escaped to Bavaria and carried on their activity from there. Although in the course of the next few months over 10,000 active members fled to Germany and an «Austrian Legion» was formed there, the NSDAP was soon able to overcome the blow to the organization dealt by the prohibition. Only the unsuccessful *Putsch* on July 25, 1934, carried out primarily by SS and SA groups, led to strong signs of disintegration.[38]

Nevertheless, it seems that membership continued to increase for another period. According to calculations already quoted, the number of party members increased from 67,000 to 87,000 between June 1933 and July 1934 and up to the *Berchtesgaden* agreement between Hitler and Schuschnigg on February 12, 1938 by another 60,000. Admittedly, these numbers are too high, as after the *Anschluss* many new National Socialists obtained a fictitious earlier entry date as a favor from leading Nazis.[39] The fact remains though that the influx into the NSDAP continued in 1933/34 and later.

There are few numerical facts available on the accompanying social restructuring. It can be assumed with some plausibility, however, that the proportion of young people was still increasing. The number of small owners in the non-agrarian sectors did not increase; they held their position as before. Now the NSDAP succeeded in making some inroads into the rural population. Significantly, a report from Carinthia in the autumn of 1934 states that after the July *Putsch* the ripe harvest rotted away on the fields in some regions, because the farmers who had taken part in the attempted *coup d'état* had fled to Yugoslavia.[40] In May 1933, Hitler proclaimed the «1000-Mark-blockade» which forced every German who wanted to travel to Austria to pay a tax of 1000 Reichsmark. In the Alpine areas of Austria this blockade had a strong effect on tourism and the livestock and timber trades. This was probably decisive for the continuing growth of Nazism in the western and southern provinces.

On the other hand the proportion of civil servants most probably decreased because they put their occupational position in jeopardy simply by being members of the NSDAP. It was only because of the increased influx of members in the months just before March, 1938, that civil servants once more came to occupy a strong position along with the professionals.

The industrial working class remained as a whole impenetrable despite attempts by the Nazis to win over former Social Democrats after the unsuccessful uprising of the *Schutzbund* against the Dollfuss dictatorship. Inside certain Nazi sub-organizations the proportion of workers was fairly high, however. In a few cases before, but to a greater extent immediately after February 1934, the National Socialists seem to have

215

succeeded in gaining support from the disoriented and suppressed members of the outlawed Social Democratic party and among the young unemployed.[41] This hypothesis is in no way discredited either by the social composition of the Nazi «militants» in 1933 (see table 3) or by data on the NSDAP prisoners of the concentration camp at Wöllersdorf in May 1934:[42] more than 40 per cent of them were workers (20 per cent skilled, 27 per cent unskilled).

The short-lived readiness of the Linz *Schutzbund* leader Richard Bernaschek, who had started the fighting on February 12, 1934, to enter into a tactical alliance with the Nazis does not seem to have been exceptional either in western Austria or in Carinthia or Styria. One may estimate that one third of the approximately 44,000 members of the *Schutzbund* in these provinces and a considerably smaller proportion of the Vienna *Schutzbund* members (17,500) changed over to the NSDAP in single or in small groups. The latter form of changeover was encouraged by the Nazis. Political persecutions of Social Democrats and Nazis in the prisons and concentration camps of the Dollfuss and Schuschnigg dictatorship diminished political and personal differences between the members of the two antagonistic movements. Also the fact that the Nazis could help some of the unemployed to obtain posts because they were well represented among tradesmen, might have led former *Schutzbund* men to join the National Socialists for a short time.[43] In 1937 the problem of Nazi infiltration into working class strata arose again when National Socialism threatened to break into the Social Democratic youth movement. Thus, the Austrian Social Democrat Edmund Schlesinger reported to Otto Bauer in Brno that «the industrial workers, as far as the older age groups are concerned, have gone through social democratic training and are faithful to the party. The upcoming generation, however, is exposed to Nazi influences».[44]

The National Socialist leadership in illegality broke down into a number of rival groups. As a result, considerable internal tensions and intrigues ensued, which also lasted from 1938 to 1945. A report from the German Embassy stated the causes of these tensions: «the difficulties . . . are mainly based on the contrast between the old National Socialist leaders, who have been freed by the amnesty (of 1936) and who claim the unlimited leadership of the party for themselves, and the young forces in the movement who have run the party in the past two years of fighting and who now do not wish to be excluded from participation.»[45]

In addition, the conflict between the SA on the one side and the SS and the political organization of the NSDAP on the other side, aggravated by the Röhm crisis, played an important part in polarizing the leadership. This conflict, which caused the SA to take no part in the *Putsch* attempt on July 25, 1934, and which quite often took the form of the SA giving information on the SS to the «Christian Corporate state» authorities and *vice versa,* was another expression of the social contrast between the «plebeian» and the bourgeois wing of National Socialism.[46] Altogether, between 1933 and 1938, four leading groups gained influence inside the National Socialist movement. They were 1. the group of the terrorist and exiled «Habicht men», 2. the SA-orientated illegal «revolutionaries» around Captain Josef Leopold, 3. the SS-orientated semi-legal «Carinthians» around Hubert Klausner, and 4. the purely bourgeois and intellectual «Catholic Nationals» around Seyss-Inquart.[47]

National Socialism in Power (1938–1945)

The most important factor in deciding appointments to leading positions in the NSDAP and the state after the *Anschluss* on March 13, 1938 was probably the internal balance of power between these groups. While the *Gauleiters* were in key positions in the long run, the «Catholic Nationals» found themselves at a dead end in the public sector because of the restructuring of the administration. With Seyss-Inquart's retirement in April, 1939, they disappeared completely from the leading positions. Hence it is not surprising that the «Carinthians» and their associates took five seats of a total of thirteen *Gauleiter-* and deputy *Gauleiter*-positions. Himmler's SS had also secured a critical influence. Apparently, it was only due to an explicit order from Hitler that the «Habicht men» and the Leopold group were given two positions by Reichskommissar Bürckel. The other «old fighters» *(alte Kämpfer)* like Habicht and Leopold themselves were left out.[48]

The same distribution of internal party power, i.e. between the SA, the SS and the political organization, is also apparent in the *Reichstagsliste*, the list of candidates to the national assembly which had been put together from considerations of prestige and propaganda value. Out of 55 «elected» *Reichstag* members for the Austrian region in 1938 who had had another public or party function, 12 belonged to the SS, 18 to the SA and just as many to the political organization (among them were all the *Gauleiters* and their representatives). Only four were Austrian *Landesministers* (regional ministers), three others being representatives of corporative organizations.[49]

All 73 *Reichstag* members from the «Ostmark» can be classified as follows according to their original (but no longer practised) occupation (right column of table 1): 23 per cent self-employed and professionals, 25 per cent (mainly higher) employees in private enterprises, 14 per cent workers and – again the largest group – public servants (38 per cent), among them including 10 per cent teachers, 7 per cent police and 8 per cent army officers. Compared with the candidates or representatives in former elections, this list shows, apart from the decline in railwaymen, a surprisingly similar sociological structure as to occupation. In terms of education, 34 per cent had finished their university studies (16 per cent *Dr. jur.* and 8 per cent *Dipl. Ing.* degrees), 29 per cent had the *Matura* (leaving certificate of secondary schools) and 37 per cent had only compulsory or special school education.

The results of the plebiscite on the completed *Anschluss*, in which the German *Reichstag* was also «elected», provide from a sociological point of view little information, although direct forgery of the election results is evident only in special cases.[50] Terrorism, timidity control and indirect influence alone were sufficient to cause the result. In a poll of 99.7 per cent of all registered voters 99.3 per cent voted «Yes». Nevertheless, there are minor regional differences in the distribution of the abstentions and «No» votes. Whereas in Burgenland there was one «No» vote to 2,722 «Yes» votes, in Vienna the ratio was 1 to 249 and in Vorarlberg one «No» vote to 72 «Yes» votes. This indicates a slightly stronger oppositional trend in the western Alpine regions than in the rest of the country. In Vienna there was in working class districts mostly a lower proportion of «No» votes than in other districts. But the ratio of abstentions in the same districts indicates a stronger will to demonstrate political dissent. In bourgeois districts public dissent seems to have been negligible, though camouflaged anti-Nazism seems to have been relatively frequent.[51]

The new men in power were not deluded about the real extent of support for National Socialism. A *Gestapo* report from Tyrol even gave the political attitude of civil servants in June 1938, in figures: only 15 per cent were definitely reliable National Socialists, it said, 30 per cent had become Nazis for personal or economic reasons, 10 to 20 per cent were only sympathisers and 35 to 40 per cent were «either Marxist or clerically inclined and open or hidden opponents».[52]

As long as the economic and foreign political successes of the German *Reich* in the following months drew attention away from the sinister intentions of the Nazis, the signs of opposition and resistance were restricted to single cases. Yet as early as autumn 1938 and spring 1939 there were signs of unrest among the workers and in Catholic bourgeois circles. Even many «old fighters» inside the NSDAP had been disappointed either because they actually had been left out in the distribution of profitable public positions and of «aryanized» Jewish businesses or because they thought they deserved a better deal. These people caused a feeling of dissatisfaction with the German occupation in some circles of the NSDAP.

In May 1945 the Austrian authorities started to record the former NSDAP members on public lists. Each Nazi had to give information on his social position and previous memberships in party organizations. These interrogations were repeated in 1947. The resulting lists of Nazis, which would be of considerable evidential value in delineating the sociological profile of the NSDAP and a valuable addition to the party card-index in the Berlin Document Center, have not yet been subjected to research. Only a preliminary result can therefore be presented here.

In all of Austria 541,727 Nazis were registered. This figure is of minor importance for estimating the social composition of the NSDAP, as after the *Anschluss* the numerical development of party membership was directed from above and guided by considerations among the leading Nazis on what the social composition of the party ideally should be. Between 1939 and 1945 war losses and emigration seem to have changed the social composition and especially the age structure of the Nazi party. The full evidential value of the following figures (see table 7) therefore applies only to the NSDAP membership at the end of World War II. No direct conclusions drawn from this material are applicable to National Socialism before 1938.[53]

Nearly 40 per cent of the registered Nazis were self-employed or members of families where the breadwinner was self-employed. (Usually the family members took part in running the small business.) Compared with all Nazis employed or out of work (except pensioners, students, housewives, etc.) as much as 49 per cent belonged to this social class, though among all persons employed and out of work *(«Berufsträger»)* in Austrian society in 1934 the self-employed and their family members represented only 33.6 per cent. Accordingly, they were overrepresented one-and-a-half-fold (at a ratio of 147 : 100). Within this occupational group, though, the self-employed in agriculture (and forestry) were clearly underrepresented (76 : 100), whereas the self-employed in industry and handicrafts, commerce and transport and particularly in the professions were highly overrepresented. Shopkeepers and owners of small enterprises in transport were not very strongly overrepresented (149 : 100). Artisans were nearly doubly overrepresented as compared with the small owners in commerce and transport (288 : 100), whereas the free professions were again doubly overrepresented as compared with the artisans. «Other trades» in the breakdown, mostly domestic personnel and barbers, were strongly overrepresented as well (466 : 100).

The public servants, 15.6 per cent working as white-collar workers and only 2.4 per cent as blue-collar workers, represented nearly one fifth (18 per cent) of all Nazi members. Compared with society as a whole, they are overrepresented twofold. Nevertheless, the workers in public enterprises were clearly underrepresented

Table 7. *Social Origins of the «Registered» Austrian NSDAP Members in 1945 (up to 24th April 1946) and of all Persons Employed and out of Work in Austria in 1934*

	NSDAP members 1945			persons employed or out of work in whole society 1934 in per cent**	proportion NSDAP-members*: whole society** (=100)
	in absolute figures	in per cent	in* per cent		
Self-employed (and assisting members of family).........	212,764	39.28	*49.32*	*33.55*	*147*
of these in					
agriculture and forestry	69,100	12.76	*16.02*	*21.01*	*76*
industry and handicrafts	70,369	12.99	*16.31*	*5.67*	*288*
commerce and transport	32,534	6.01	*7.54*	*5.05*	*149*
free professions	22,699	4.19	*5.26*	*0.92*	*572*
other trades	18,062	3.33	*4.19*	*0.90*	*466*
Public servants	97,562	18,01	*22.61*	*11.42*	*198*
of these					
employees................	84,576	15.61	*19.60*	*5.36*	*366*
workers..................	12,986	2.40	*3.01*	*6.06*	*50*
Employees in private enterprises	58,560	10.81	*13.57*	*9.49*	*143*
Workers in private enterprises	62,551	11.55	*14.50*	*45.54*	*32*
Sum of persons employed and out of work.............	431,437	79.65	*100*	*100*	
Others	110,290	20.35			
of these:					
pensioners	20,223	3.73			
students..................	6,856	1.27			
housewives	68,331	12.61			
Total	541,727	100			

* Only NSDAP members employed and out of work.

** As exact figures were not available, pensioners, students, pupils, housewives etc. were excluded.

Calculated from: Radomir Luža, *Austro-German Relations in the Anschluss Era*, (Princeton, NJ 1975), p. 381: *Ergebnisse der österreichischen Volkszählung vom 22. März 1934*, (Statistik des Bundesstaates Österreich, no. 2), (Österr. Staatsdruckerei, Vienna 1935), tables 10a and 11a.

(50 : 100). Accordingly, the overrepresentation of employees in the public administration is to be counted very high (366 : 100). Even if a sharply increased pressure for conformity in the Third *Reich* must have played an important rôle in the public service, this result somehow seems to indicate a continuation of the trend of the period before the Nazi acquisition of power.

The private employees, on the other hand, were not very strongly overrepresented at 10.8 per cent (143 : 100). The corresponding data from Vienna show that private employees (19 per cent) were only slightly overrepresented in this city, whereas the public servants (25 per cent) again constituted one of the main Nazi strongholds (threefold overrepresentation). The economic and socio-psychological situation of the private employees and the public servants, both occupational groups characterized by a strong desire to be upwardly mobile, seems to have determined the attitude of these two groups towards National Socialism after 1938 just as during the early thirties.

By contrast, in 1945 the proportion of blue-collar workers in private enterprise who were members of the Nazi party and who made up 11.6 per cent of the entire NSDAP membership that year, was only one third as high as the proportion of blue-collar workers in private enterprise (in work or temporarily out) in Austrian society as a whole in 1934. This result stands in contrast to the available data on the social origins of «militant» Nazis before the seizure of power (see table 4). One explanation could be that the members of armed formations and very active party members more frequently originated from the working class than recruits to the rest of the party. Another explanation could be derived from the fact that the social composition of the NSDAP in Austria underwent a significant shift from the lower to the middle classes between 1938 and 1945. As long as no additional sources of information are available, it cannot here be decided which explanation should be given preference.

The heterogeneous group of non-professionals and 'others' was underrepresented as well, which can mainly be attributed to the relatively low percentage of housewives (12.6 per cent) among the party members. Altogether, only a fourth of the total number of registered Nazis were women.

Much less reliable is the age structure of registered Nazis in 1945. As expected, war and captivity caused a big dropout among the younger age groups. Moreover, only figures from Vienna were available.[54] Whereas the percentages of the twenty- and thirty year olds are at 4.8 per cent and 17.8 per cent, respectively, the percentages of forty- and fifty year olds are 31.6 per cent and 28.3 per cent, respectively. Even the sixty-year olds still reached 14.1 per cent.

This material does not allow any conclusions regarding the extent to which there was an influx of older Nazi party members in the course of its ascendancy to executive power. It can by no means be concluded that the older ones (then 10 years younger) also dominated the Nazi movement in the early thirties, as their preponderance in the material from 1945 seems to suggest.

Only 21,081 or 19.4 per cent of the registered Viennese National Socialists in 1945 revealed themselves to have been *illegale*, i.e. Nazi members before the *Anschluss*. If the registration lists are reliable, this number indicates a remarkably restricted National Socialist mass basis in Vienna before 1938. 20.7 per cent of all registered male Nazi members were *illegale*, the equivalent figure for women being 16.3 per cent. Thus at the time of illegality there were 1000 men to 319 women among the Nazis. Among those who became party members after the seizure of power the ratio was 1000 to 428.

On the Sociological Profile of Austrian National Socialism

The social origins of the four categories of supporters, the Nazi leadership, the «militants», the ordinary members and the voters, changed significantly from 1919 to 1945. Nevertheless, running the risk of slightly oversimplifying matters, it is possible to describe the social foundations of Austrian National Socialism in the following way:

Austria was a developed industrial nation. It is therefore not surprising that the NSDAP consisted mainly of wage earners. This applies both to its élite and to its membership stock. In the population as a whole 66.4 per cent were classified as wage earners, of whom in 1934 51.6 per cent were workers and 14.8 per cent private and public employees. The self-employed constituted 33.6 per cent. In relation to the entire working population, the petty bourgeoisie was overrepresented in the party, especially in the late thirties and forties.

Only until the middle of the twenties did National Socialism have a significant element of wage and salary earners both in its leadership and in its electoral following. The NSDAP was not a party of manual workers like the Social Democrats, but a party of employees and public servants. The appeal of National Socialism to employees in transport and trade enterprises was striking. Railway officials outside Vienna and employees in commerce *(Handelsangestellte)* and to a lesser degree teachers and postal service employees remained pillars of National Socialism, even when it had passed its early phase. Apart from the «militants», National Socialism was never able to sway the industrial workers in any significant measure.

The proportion of self-employed in trade and professionals in the Nazi party was considerably higher from the beginning than in the Social Democratic party. These occupational groups were by no means dominant, however, as in the later NSDAP and in the liberal-democratic and German national parties and in the urban section of the Christian Social party. The proportion of self-employed and professionals increased in 1922/23 and peaked in the middle of the thirties. But Austrian National Socialism never became a party of the petty bourgeoisie to the extent suggested by Austro-Marxist theories on fascism.[55] Likewise, farmers in Austria never played an important rôle within the DNSAP or NSDAP. When, influenced from Germany, the NSDAP became a party of the masses in 1932, an apparent shift in its social composition occurred. Whereas the social origins of the party élite remained surprisingly constant in the following periods, the proportion of voters from the urban petty bourgeoisie increased considerably. The same probably also applied to its members. These recruits were mostly drawn from the German national urban bourgeoisie but did not swell the ranks of the «militants». The petty bourgeoisie was not yet the predominating stratum. Nevertheless, it was highly overrepresented (compared with its share of the entire population). Later, in about 1933/34, National Socialism succeeded in making remarkable inroads into the rural population, which for the most part had persevered in its Catholic Conservative orientation. The workers in big enterprises continued to be anti-fascist, but the NSDAP was successful in reaching the unemployed and the young workers: the percentage of workers particularly in the paramilitary formations showed an increase over time.

In 1938 there was another change in the social composition of party's membership, to a lesser degree also in its leading cadres. Although the NSDAP in its program at this time claimed to represent all social classes and groups, its social profile did not become more similar to that of Austrian society as a whole. On the contrary, the

221

proportion of the urban self-employed and the civil servants increased again at the expense of workers and private employees.

The rôle of former World War I officers and petty officers at any period remained limited within the civil (non-military) Nazi organizations, contrary to what was the case in the *Heimwehr* and among the monarchists.

In all periods, National Socialism in Austria was mainly a movement of the small and medium-sized towns and cities, though in the thirties it also became a movement of the larger provincial capitals. In purely industrial and agricultural areas, in the traditional areas of the Social Democrats and of the Social Christians, it was always weaker than in other parts of the country. The Nazi party was always a party of males, and between 1920 and 1932 this tendency even increased.

Youth from all occupational groups, particularly students and grammar school pupils, played an increasingly important rôle from 1922 to the takeover in 1938, most notably in the paramilitary formations. In these, the proportion of self-employed and academics was relatively low. Apart from the SS, the proportion of the public servants was noticeably even lower among the militants than in the National Socialist movement as a whole. The proportion of private employees and workers was, in contrast, considerably higher. The SA and its predecessors were rather more centered on the workers, the SS more on private employees and civil servants.

Austrian National Socialism was always further to the «left» than German National Socialism and very much further to the «left» than the *Heimwehr*, both in terms of the sociological characteristics of its members and in its programmatic statements. It is true that this leftward trend became continually weaker during the twenties and the second half of the thirties, although there was never a «Röhm crisis» like the one in Germany.

From 1936 onwards, however, concomitantly with the influx of purely bourgeois strata from Catholicism and of state employees, the SS managed to strengthen its position and to solidify its influence after the occupation of Austria. The *Anschluss* led to the decisive weakening of the «left», «anti-capitalist» wing of Austrian National Socialism (especially the SA and the *Betriebszellenorganisation* – the Nazi trade union substitute) which from then on became preoccupied primarily with stirring up anti-Semitic, anti-clerical and even Austrian «separatist» emotions.

In sum, the concepts of *neuer Mittelstand* (new middle class) and *alter Mittelstand* (old middle class) seem more suitable for the understanding of the social character of the Nazis than the concepts «petty bourgeoisie» and «income earners». In this sense, Austrian National Socialism was *first of all a movement of the new middle class and secondly one of the non-agrarian older middle sector.*[56] As long as it was limited to a small splinter party (DNSAP), the Austrian Nazi movement thus seems to have been a party of specific occupational groups, mainly consisting of private employees, especially in commerce, and of higher and intermediate employees in the public service, especially in the railways and the postal service. With the weakening of pseudo-socialist demands and the increase in the Nazi membership, the social spectrum of the party widened from 1921/22 onwards. Therefore, from the beginning of the thirties, the NSDAP can be regarded as a kind of *people's party*, integrating many and very diverse social groups, but succeeding only partially in penetrating the industrial working class and the rural producers, the largest single social groups in Austria.

NOTES

[1] Andrew G. Whiteside, *Austrian National Socialism before 1918* (The Hague 1962), p. 118; Alois Ciller, *Deutscher Sozialismus in den Sudetenländern und der Ostmark* (Hamburg 1939), pp. 77 *seqq.*

[2] Johannes Hawlik, «Die politischen Parteien Deutschösterreichs bei der Wahl zur konstituierenden Nationalversammlung 1919» (unpublished thesis, Vienna 1971), pp. 458 *seqq.*, 485 *seqq.*, appendix, p. 23 *seq.*

[3] The share of votes for the DNSAP (DAP) amounted to 0.6 per cent in constituencies with less than 2000 inhabitans, 1.4 per cent in places with 2001 to 5000 inhabitants, 1.5 per cent in medium-sized and large towns and cities with 5001 to 200,000 inhabitants, and 0.7 per cent in Vienna *(Beiträge zur Statistik der Republik Österreich,* ed. by Statistische Zentralkommission, no. 2 (Vienna 1920), pp. 12 *seqq.* and calculations from pp. 65–75).

[4] By comparison: 571 votes cast by women to 1000 votes cast by men for the Communists, 888 for the Social Democrats, but 1,315 for the Christian Social Party *(ibid.,* no. 10, p. 30).

[5] *Ibid.,* no. 3 (Vienna 1920) and *ibid.,* no. 11 (Vienna 1921).

[6] Cf. Walter Goldinger, *Geschichte der Republik Österreich* (Vienna 1962), pp. 95 *seqq.;* Otto Bauer, *Die österreichische Revolution* (Vienna 1923), pp. 262 *seqq.*

[7] Cf. also Reinhard Kühnl, *Formen bürgerlicher Herrshaft. Liberalismus – Faschismus* (Reinbek bei Hamburg 1971), pp. 80 *seqq.*

[8] *Salzburger Volksblatt,* 16. August 1923, quoted from Adolf Meixner, «Die Anfänge der NSDAP in Österreich bis 1929», 1961, (Seminararbeit, *Institut für Zeitgeschichte,* University of Vienna) pp. 21 *seqq.,* Hans Volz, *Daten der Geschichte der NSDAP,* 11th ed. (Berlin 1943), p. 7.

[9] Rudolf Brandstötter, «Dr. Walter Riehl und die Geschichte der nationalsozialistischen Bewegung in Österreich» (unpublished thesis, Vienna 1969), pp. 183 *seqq.,* 194.

[10] Otto Bauer, *Zwischen Zwei Weltkriegen? Die Krise der Weltwirtschaft, der Demokratie und des Sozialismus* (Bratislava 1936), pp. 113 *seqq.*

[11] For the following paragraph see: Francis L. Carsten, *Der Aufstieg des Faschismus in Europa* (Frankfurt a.M. 1968); Ludwig Jedlicka, «Die österreichische Heimwehr», in: *Internationaler Faschismus 1920–1945* (Munich 1966), pp. 177–299.

[12] As a rule, the different kinds of fascism in Austria found their main core of support within one specific *Lager;* rarely did they recruit across any of the two bourgeois social segments, the German National and the Catholic Conservative *Lager.* Because the *Heimwehr,* with the exclusion of its Styrian wing, was both organizationally and ideologically close to the Conservative *Lager,* we include both the militant monarchists and the Social Christians when we speak about *Heimwehr* militants. With the armed monarchist Squad *Ostara,* the *Frontkämpfervereinigung,* Schuschnigg's *Ostmärkische Sturmscharen* (The Ostmark Storm Bands) and a few smaller paramilitary splinter-organizations, the pro-Austrian *Heimwehr* can be regarded as the armed extension of the Catholic Conservative segment (see also my introduction to this section of the book).

[13] For details of the collection of data and the results of their interpretation see my study: *Gewalt in der Politik. Attentate, Zusammenstöße, Unruhen, Putschversuche in Österreich 1918–1934* (Munich 1976), pp. 251–249.

[14] Cf. Robert Danneberg, *Die Entwicklungsmöglichkeiten der Sozialdemokratie in Österreich. Betrachtungen über das Ergebnis der Nationalratswahlen am 21. Oktober 1923* (Vienna 1924), p. 34 (15 per cent self employed, 3 per cent professionals, 16 per cent employees in private enterprises, 36 per cent workers, 15 per cent public servants, 11 per cent without profession, 3 per cent others).

[15] Cf. Fritz Klenner, *Die österreichischen Gewerkschaften. Vergangenheit und Gegenwartsprobleme,* vol. 2 (Vienna 1953), pp. 973, 1097 *seqq.*

[16] Leo Haubenberger, *Der Werdegang der nationalen Gewerkschaften. –* Gewerkschaftliche Bildungsschriften 7 (Vienna 1932), pp. 28 *seq.;* Leo Haubenberger, «Völkisches Gewerkschaftsleben», in: Karl Wache (ed.), *Deutscher Geist in Österreich. Ein Handbuch des völkischen Lebens in der Ostmark* (Dornbirn 1933), pp. 323 *seq.*

223

[17] *Nationalsozialistisches Jahrbuch,* vol. 1925 and vol. 1926 (Vienna), pp. 99 and 118 *seqq.* (respectively); *80 Jahre Gewerkschaft der Eisenbahner* (Vienna 1972), pp. 375 *seqq.* and *passim.*

[18] *«Der deutsche Eisenbahner»* (Vienna), vol. 3, Aug. 1st, 1923, p. 3; vol. 6, Oct. 7th, 1926, p. 2; vol. 11, Sept. 9th, 1931, p. 4.

[19] *Wirtschaftsstatistisches Jahrbuch 1926* (Vienna 1927), p. 69.

[20] Walter B. Simon, *The Political Parties of Austria,* Ph. D. thesis, University of Columbia 1957 (Microfilm: Doctoral Dissertation Series, no. 121828, Ann Arbor, Michigan), pp. 153 *seqq.,* 160 *seq.,* 171 *seq.*

[21] Alexander Schilling, *Dr. Walter Riehl und die Geschichte des Nationalsozialismus* (Leipzig 1933), pp. 79 *seqq.,* 92 *seqq.*

[22] *Deutsche Arbeiterpresse* (Vienna), August 21st, 1926; Brandstötter, *Dr. Walter Riehl,* pp. 235 *seqq.*

[23] See the article of Bruce F. Pauley in this book. For the riots of July 15th, 1927 cf. also Charles A. Gulick, *Österreich von Habsburg zu Hitler,* vol. 2 (Vienna 1950).

[24] In constituency XI 705 votes for the NSDAP, as *Völkischsozialer Block* in 20 constituencies 27,142 votes: *Statistische Nachrichten, Sonderheft «Wahlstatistik»: Nationalratswahlen vom 24. April 1927,* (Vienna 1927), p. 6.

[25] *Statistische Nachrichten, Sonderheft: Die Nationalratswahlen vom 9. November 1930,* (Vienna 1931).

[26] Josef Sageder, «Soziale Grundlagen des Nationalsozialismus in Oberösterreich» (unpublished *Hausarbeit,* Linz 1971, *Institut für Neuere Geschichte und Zeitgeschichte,* University of Linz), pp. 11, 24.

[27] Cf. Simon, *Political Parties,* chapter VIII; *Jahrbuch der österreichischen Arbeiterbewegung 1932* (Vienna 1933), pp. 113 *seq.;* see also: Walter B. Simon: «Motivation of a Totalitarian Mass Vote», in: *British Journal of Sociology,* vol. 10 (London 1959), pp. 338–345; Danneberg, *Wiener Wahlen;* C. A. Gulick, *Österreich von Habsburg zu Hitler,* vol. 3, *op.cit.* pp. 259 *seq.*

[28] Simon, *Political Parties,* pp. 329 *seq.,* 313, 331; Simon, «Motivation», p. 342.

[29] Robert Danneberg, *Die Wiener Wahlen 1930 und 1932. Statistische Betrachtungen* (Vienna 1932), pp. 68, 60 *seqq.;* see also: *Der Kampf,* vol. 25 (Vienna 1932); Simon, *Political Parties,* pp. 155 *seq.*

[30] The statement that the NSDAP had managed already in summer 1931 to make ground with the rural population (R. Haintz: «Die N.S.D.A.P.», in: *Wache, Deutscher Geist, op.cit.* p. 272) is only partly true.

[31] Simon, *Political Parties,* p. 315 *seq.;* see also pp. 329 *seq.;* Adam Wandruszka, «Österreichs politische Struktur», in: Heinrich Benedikt (ed.), *Geschichte der Republik Österreich* (Vienna 1954), pp. 373 *seq.*

[32] Karl Stadler, *Österreich 1938–1945 im Spiegel der NS-Akten* (Vienna 1966), pp. 34 *seq.;* the same table has recently been published with more details by Radomir Luža, *Austro-German Relations in the Anschluss Era* (Princeton 1975), p. 376.

[33] The comparison is made with: Emanuel Januschka, *Die soziale Schichtung der Bevölkerung Österreichs* (Vienna 1938), p. 13. If one includes assisting members of the family in the group of self-employed (see table 7), the self-employed were strongly underrepresented.

[34] Bundesministerium für Landesverteidigung, sect. 1. Evidenz: «Innenlage – Bewaffnete Verbände», *Kriegsarchiv,* Vienna (I am indebted to Dr. Kurt Peball, who has located these materials and provided me with copies).

[35] For details see chapter IV of my study: *Gewalt in der Politik, op.cit.* p. 243. It should be mentioned that the members in the *Ostara* received payment for participating in demonstrations.

[36] *Ergebnisse der Wahl in den oberösterreichischen Landtag am 19. April 1931* (Linz 1931), pp. 4–12; *Ergebnis der Landtagswahl in Niederösterreich vom 24. April 1932* (Vienna 1932); *Land und Gemeinde,* vol. 1, no. 1, (Linz 1932).

[37] Materials Alfred Proksch, *Berlin Document Center.*

[38] Materials Thomas Kozich, ibid.; see also *Beiträge zur Vorgeschichte und Geschichte der Julirevolution* (Vienna 1934), p. 4.

[39] Hugo Meinhard, *Parteimitgliedschaft und Parteianwärter* (Vienna 1947), p. 18 *seq.;* Stad-

ler, Österreich, pp. 35 seq.; Rot-weiß-rot-Buch. Darstellungen, Dokumente und Nachweise zur Vorgeschichte und Geschichte der Okkupation Österreichs (Vienna 1946), pp. 29 seqq.

[40] Gerhard Jagschitz, «Faschismus und Nationalsozialismus in Österreich bis 1945», in: Fascism and Europe. An International Symposium, vol. 2 (Prague 1970), pp. 76 seqq.; my attention was drawn to these reports from Carinthia by Dr. Gerhard Jagschitz.

[41] See: Evidenz: «Innenlage – Bewaffnete Verbände», Kriegsarchiv, Vienna; Bruce F. Pauley, Hahnenschwanz und Hakenkreuz (Vienna 1972), p. 103.

[42] In a recent publication Gerhard Jagschitz listed the professions of 301 prisoners at Wöllersdorf («Die Anhaltelager in Österreich», in: Vom Justizpalast zum Heldenplatz (Vienna 1975), pp. 150 seq.). To make his figures more meaningful, they have been adapted to conform to the principles of this investigation.

[43] See Helmut Konrad, «Richard Bernaschek», in: Bildungskurier, vol. 25, no. 1 (Linz 1974), p. 4; Inez Kykal and Karl R. Stadler, Richard Bernaschek. Odyssee eines Rebellen (Vienna 1976), pp. 101–170; and Kurt Peball, Die Kämpfe in Wien im Februar 1934. – Militärhistorische Schriftenreihe, no. 25 (Vienna 1974), p. 40; cf. also Karl R. Stadler, Opfer verlorener Zeiten. Geschichte der Schutzbund-Emigration 1934 (Vienna 1974), pp. 93 seqq.; especially p. 97.

[44] Quoted from: Jacques Hannak, Karl Renner und seine Zeit. Versuch einer Biographie (Vienna 1965), pp. 630 seq.; see also pp. 626, 612 seq.; Akten zur deutschen Auswärtigen Politik, series D, vol. 1 (Baden-Baden 1950), p. 451.

[45] Quoted in: Ludwig Jedlicka, «Gauleiter Josef Leopold (1889–1941)», in: Geschichte und Gesellschaft. Festschrift für Karl R. Stadler zum 60. Geburtstag, (Vienna 1974), p. 149.

[46] Cf. materials on Gustav Wächter und Thomas Kozich, Berlin Document Center; see also Die Erhebung der österreichischen Nationalsozialisten im Juli 1934 (Vienna 1965), p. 8 (introduction by Ludwig Jedlicka); Franz Langoth, Kampf um Österreich. Erinnerungen eines Politikers (Wels 1951), p. 314.

[47] Gerhard Botz, Die Eingliederung Österreichs in das Deutsche Reich. Planung und Verwirklichung des politisch-administrativen Anschlusses (1938–1940) (Vienna 1972), p. 93 seq.; Wolfgang Rosar, Deutsche Gemeinschaft. Seyss-Inquart und der Anschluss (Vienna 1971), pp. 259 seq.; for the «Catholic Nationals» see the contribution of John Haag in this book.

[48] Sammlung Schumacher/304 and R 43 II/1359, Bundesarchiv, Koblenz.

[49] Composed from: Der Großdeutsche Reichstag, IV. Wahlperiode. Berlin 1938. Unfruitful on the topic is Nikolaus von Preradovich, Die Führungsschichten in Österreich und Preußen (1804–1918) (Wiesbaden 1955).

[50] See Herbert Steiner, Gestorben für Österreich. Widerstand gegen Hitler. (Vienna 1968), pp. 17 seq., 76.

[51] Statistische Nachrichten, vol. 16 (Vienna 1938), pp. 77 seqq.; see also my introduction to Robert Schwarz, «Sozialismus» der Propaganda. Das Werben des «Völkischen Beobachters» um die österreichische Arbeiterschaft 1938/39. – Materialien zur Arbeiterbewegung 2 (Vienna 1975), pp. 39 seq.

[52] Rot-weiß-rot-Buch, p. 81.

[53] The following results are calculated from: Luža, Austro-German Relations p. 381 and Ergebnisse der österreichischen Volkszählung vom 22. März 1934 (Statistik des Bundesstaates Österreich, no. 2) (Vienna 1935), tables 10a and 11a.

[54] Statistisches Jahrbuch der Stadt Wien, 1943–1945, new series, vol. 7, (Vienna 1948), pp. 17, 268.

[55] Cf. my article «Austro-Marxist Interpretation of Fascism» in: Journal of Contemporary History, vol. 11 (1976), part 4.

[56] See Theodor Geiger, Die soziale Schichtung des deutschen Volkes (Stuttgart 1967 [1st ed. 1932]), pp. 109–122; Martin Broszat, Der Staat Hitlers (Munich 1969), p. 50; Heinrich August Winkler, «Mittelstandsbewegung oder Volkspartei?» and Hans Mommsen, «Zur Verschränkung traditioneller und faschistischer Führungsgruppen in Deutschland . . .», papers submitted to the 30th Deutscher Historikertag at Braunschweig, October 1974.

225

Nazis and Heimwehr Fascists:
The Struggle for Supremacy in Austria, 1918–1938

BRUCE F. PAULEY

Austria between 1918 and 1938 is a fertile field for the study of comparative fascism. Trapped between Hitler, Mussolini, and Gömbös it was exposed to fascist influences from nearly every side, a fact which was reflected in the great variety of forms manifested by Austrian fascism. Most historians who have studied the phenomenon have concentrated on the clerical variant supported by Chancellors Dollfuss and Schuschnigg: the *Heimwehr* (HW) or Home Guard. Austrian National Socialism, when considered at all, has been seen as a mere aspect of the *Anschluss* movement, while the pan-Germans within the *Heimwehr* as well as numerous other fascist groups have been virtually ignored. Equally neglected has been the fascinating struggle for supremacy which raged between the Austrian fascists.

Aside from the disappointment caused by Austria's exclusion from the German *Reich* in 1849 and 1866 the roots of Austrian pan-Germanism, and indirectly fascism, can be traced to the nationalities-struggle along the linguistic borders of the Austro-Hungarian Monarchy, particularly in northern Bohemia, late in the nineteenth century.[1] The rising political, economic, and cultural standards of the Slavs, especially the Czechs, were interpreted by many lower- and lower-middle class German-Austrians as threats to their national existence.[2] Efforts by the *Reichsrat* deputy Georg von Schönerer to «save» the German-Austrians by attaching them to the German Empire had already largely failed by the end of the nineteenth century, although Schönerer left behind a pro-*Anschluss*, anti-Catholic, and anti-Semitic legacy. By no means all Austrian pan-Germans followed von Schönerer's lead uncritically, however. His neglect of working class interests[3] led to a split in the movement, and in 1903 the «German Workers' party» or *Deutsche Arbeiterpartei* (DAP) – not to be confused with Anton Drexler's party of the same name in Munich – was founded. Making little progress before the war, the party depended heavily on trade union support, differing from the Social Democrats chiefly in its opposition to the idea of the international equality of all workers.[4] In place of the Marxist dogma of class struggle, the party called for a *Volksgemeinschaft* or people's community of all «honest» (i.e. non-Jewish) German-speaking workers whether industrial, clerical, or professional (thus broadening the concept of «worker» far beyond the Marxist definition). Here too the party differed from Schönerer's pan-Germanism which appealed only to the middle class.[5] In May 1918, the DAP enlarged its name to «German National Socialist Workers' party,» but a few months later the party was badly hurt when the collapse of the monarchy split it into a Czechoslovak and a much smaller Austrian branch.

In the years between the war and 1923 the Austrian Nazi party was led by Dr. Walter Riehl, a lawyer from Reichenberg (northern Bohemia) and a former Social Democrat. Although Riehl's politics of legality clashed with Hitler's revolutionary tactics (before his Beer Hall *Putsch*) the two men held many similar views. Both favored strong central governments and regarded democratic parliaments as obstacles to vigorous decision-making. Riehl also shared Hitler's anti-Semitism and like Hitler blamed the Jews for all domestic and foreign policy problems. Riehl hoped to limit the influence of Jews in political, cultural, and economic affairs to their proportion of Austria's total population.

In the winter of 1918–1919 the Austrian Nazis established a link with their German counterparts (as well as with their old comrades in Czechoslovakia). But by 1923 this tie already produced a split in Austrian ranks between those who favored Hitler's revolutionary policy and those, like Riehl, who opted for continued campaigning in national elections.[6] Similar tactical disagreements divided the Austrian *Heimwehr* seven years later.

In contrast to National Socialism the *Heimwehr* movement was almost exclusively a post-war phenomenon. Initially composed of people from all social classes, it arose in the southern states of Styria and Carinthia largely as a para-military response to Yugoslav imperialism in 1918 and 1919 and as a protection for German-Austrians from the looting of non-German-speaking veterans of the Austro-Hungarian army returning to their homelands.[7] In those federal states sharing a common border with Bavaria, namely Salzburg, Tyrol, and Vorarlberg, the brief existence of a Bolshevik regime in Munich in the spring of 1919 galvanized an anti-Marxist reaction south of the border and in 1920 and 1921 led to the establishment of loose ties between the several Austrian *Heimwehr* units and the para-military Bavarian groups known as the *Organisation Escherish* (Orgesch) and its affiliate, *Organisation Kanzler* (Orka). Rudolf Kanzler, a Bavarian surveyor, was the supreme commander of this coalition. Although a great many pan-Germans belonged to the early *Heimwehr*, co-operation with the Bavarians was limited purely to anti-Marxist goals since the Bavarian leaders feared that a pro-*Anschluss* course would antagonise the Allies. The «reunification of all German brothers in one Reich» was therefore only a distant goal.[8]

In the more easterly states of Upper and Lower Austria, Vienna, and the Burgenland, the *Heimwehr* developed significantly only after July 1927 when domestic Marxism appeared to reach alarming proportions.[9] Divided by pan-German and clerical wings, by provincialism, and by the jealousy of its various leaders, the Austrian *Heimwehr* movement remained divided in the years after 1921 with the exception of a brief period in the second half of 1922.

After slumbering between 1923 and 1926 the *Heimwehr* suddenly revived and was partially reunited in the latter year when the Austrian Socialists at Linz announced their intention of defending a future electoral victory and a socialized state, if necessary by force. Then the burning of the Palace of Justice in Vienna on July 15, 1927, by workers outraged over the verdict of a political trial frightened the Austrian bourgeoisie and peasantry into joining the *Heimwehr*. In the following two years the *Heimwehr* reached the peak of its popularity.

During this «golden age» the *Heimwehr* depended heavily on war veterans, peasants (especially refugees from those parts of Styria and Carinthia annexed by Yugoslavia) and students from universities and technical schools.[10] In the early days of the *Heimwehr* these students were mostly veterans of the World War. Until 1931, when they began to cross over to the Nazis, they were among the most reliable as well as the most radical members of the *Heimwehr* in Styria.[11] Beginning in May 1928, a substantial number of industrial workers (perhaps fifteen or twenty thousand)[12] from the Alpine-*Montan* steelworks of northern Styria joined the *Heimwehr*, albeit under pressure from their employers.[13] If the social composition of the Austrian *Heimwehr* differed at all from that of fascist movements elsewhere, or from the Austrian Nazis, it was in its relatively high proportion of peasants, estimated in 1928 at seventy per cent. By contrast the middle class may have made up another twenty per cent with industrial workers accounting for no more than ten per cent.[14] On the other hand the leadership was drawn from the small town intelligentsia (Richard Steidle of Tyrol and Walter Pfrimer of Styria, the co-leaders from 1928 to 1930 were both lawyers), aristocrats such as Prince Ernst von Starhemberg, or retired army officers like Emil Fey in Vienna.

In the meantime, the growth of the Austrian Nazis and other pan-German groups was painfully slow during the prosperous middle and late twenties. The Salzburg convention of the tri-state Nazi party in August 1923 resulted in the resignation of Riehl who favored entering an electoral coalition with the Greater German People's party (GVP). His opponent and successor as chairman, Karl Schultz, sided with Hitler in rejecting such a course, although he did so because the party was too small and too poor to afford an election campaign and not as a matter of principle.[15] Ironically Schulz was no more capable of resisting Hitler's growing influence over the Austrian Nazis than Riehl had been before him. In May 1926 a second and even more serious split occurred in the party when the Hitler partisans, at first confined mostly to young radicals in Vienna and to the SA, directly subordinated themselves to Hitler's dictatorial leadership in Munich (thereafter called the NSDAP Hitler *Bewegung*) while the rest of the Austrian Nazis remained loyal to Schulz.[16] At a meeting with Schulz in Passau (Bavaria) in late 1926 Hitler made it clear that he regarded Austria as no more than a *Gau* of the German Reich. Nothing would be tolerated from Schulz short of unconditional obedience.[17] By 1928 the Hitler Nazis had become as numerous as the Schulz group and by the end of 1930, after a period of fierce competition, they far outnumbered them.[18]

Until Hitler's landslide electoral victory in September 1930, however, the Hitler *Bewegung* in Austria was forced to stagger through a political wilderness. Every *Landesleiter* (federal leader) evoked the envy and hatred of the seven *Gauleiters* and for three years (1928–1931) there was no *Landesleiter* at all; each *Gauleiter* was directly subordinated to the party leadership in Munich and acted like a petty princeling in the medieval Reich.[19] Although the party was unified when Theo Habicht was appointed *Landesinspekteur* of the entire Austrian party by Hitler in 1931, it later returned to its divided condition following the disastrous July *Putsch* in 1934 when Habicht was personally dismissed by Hitler. The more moderate Nazis denounced the radicals to government officials and jealousy between local leaders on more than one occasion actually led to murder.

Leadership problems were by no means confined to the Austrian Nazis. Since July 1928 the *Heimwehr*, which had been fully united for the second time only the previous October, was under the dual leadership of Steidle and Pfrimer. This awkward arrangement was replaced by the controversial election of Starhemberg in September 1930. The Prince came from a proud family of soldier-aristocrats and true to his family's tradition, young Starhemberg always remained more of a soldier than a politician. This fact helps explain Starhemberg's vacillation between pan-Germanism and clericalism.[20] As federal leader of the *Heimwehr* for most of the last six years of its existence, he tried to please all factions. Only when he had lost the pan-German wing of the *Heimwehr* to the Nazis did he throw in his lot completely with the clerical supporters of Dollfuss and Schuschnigg.

Immediately after his election the new *Bundesführer* entered the Vaugoin government as Minister of the Interior and shortly thereafter favored the *Heimwehr's* entering the national elections in November 1930 as a separate political party. Both moves were bitterly though unsuccessfully opposed by Pfrimer and his pan-German followers in the *Heimwehr* while the clerical HW leaders in Vienna, Lower Austria and part of the Burgenland campaigned for the Christian Socialist party as they had done in the past. Pfrimer, preferring a *putsch,* saw no value in elections since the Austrian Social Democrats commanded a solid forty per cent of the electorate and a change in the federal constitution in the authoritarian direction demanded by Pfrimer required a two-thirds vote in the National Assembly. Pfrimer's pessimism proved well founded since the *Heimwehr* gained only slightly over six per cent of the votes. But the Styrian leader made matters worse by attacking the Christian Socialist party during the campaign, thus alienating those of its supporters who also belonged to the *Heimwehr*. [21] The 228,000 votes that the HW collected, therefore, probably did not accurately represent the true strength of the organization.

Although the *Heimwehr* managed to outpoll the Nazis (who drew only 111,000 votes) by a ratio of more than two to one, a rivalry between the two groups had begun in earnest during the campaign. Prior to 1930 multiple membership in various fascist groups was not only possible, but commonplace; thereafter the lines were rigidly drawn and rivalries intensified. A favorite HW charge was that the Nazis were a foreign import. The Nazis retaliated by calling the *Heimwehr* the «foreign legion of France» and Starhemberg a traitor for supporting the Lausanne loan of 1932 which carried an *Anschluss* prohibition. A HW dictatorship allegedly would lead inevitably to a Habsburg restoration. The *Heimwehr* was also attacked for entering the Christian Socialist governments of Vaugoin and Dollfuss, not to mention the later Schuschnigg ministry.

A perennial Nazi accusation against the *Heimwehr* (and not without validity) was also that the latter lacked a well-defined ideology. On the *Anschluss* issue, for example, the *Heimwehr* was split between its clerical-monarchists who were clearly unenthusiastic about the proposed union and the pan-Germans who naturally supported it. Consequently, Starhemberg spoke vaguely about an «eventual» association with Germany, but insisted that Allied opposition made the merger impossible for the time being. In the meanwhile, Austria, with the help of the League of Nations (the Lausanne loan), would have to pull itself up by its own bootstraps and not depend on Germany. Although firmly maintaining that he did not favor a Habsburg restoration, Starhemberg did tolerate legitimists in the *Heimwehr's* ranks and favored improved economic relations with the Danubian states. [22] The heterogeneous composition of the *Heimwehr* also forced it to be ambiguous about racial anti-Semitism. Walter Pfrimer once said that Austrian Jews ought to be treated as foreigners and placed under special laws and Starhemberg blamed Austria-Hungary's defeat in the World War on «a foreign race sitting in coffee houses.» But except for the last years of the Styrian *Heimwehr,* when it was competing with the Nazis, the *Heimwehr* as a whole had no clear-cut policy of racial anti-Semitism. [23] The famous (or infamous) Korneuburg Oath of May 1930 did not even mention Jews. On the matter of democracy, which the *Heimwehr* rejected as «Western» at Korneuburg, the Nazis could truthfully point out that the *Heimwehr* elected its leaders, [24] a practice which the Hitlerian Nazis abandoned after their break with Schulz.

The most devastating criticism the Nazis levelled against the *Heimwehr* was that it simply lacked a positive program. The Korneuburg Oath, which was an attempt to correct this deficiency by demanding a *Heimwehr* dictatorship and a fascist-style corporate state, continued to emphasize such negative goals as opposition to liberal-capitalism and Marxism. Far from unifying the *Heimwehr*, however, the Oath's attack on democracy and the «party state» offended the pro-Christian Socialist wing of the organization and deepened the already serious divisions.

The same ideological weaknesses of the *Heimwehr* were also found in other pan-German groups during the twenties and early thirties. The Greater German People's party, the Peasant League (Landbund), and the para-military Front Veterans' Association (FKV) all lacked precise, positive programs. The GVP, founded in September 1920, never overcame its origins as a loose coalition of national and anti-Semitic groups as could be seen in the party's vague and eclectic ideology. Unable to take a positive stand on almost anything for fear of offending one of its components, the party condemned socialism, liberalism, internationalism, and even the Christian philosophy. In their place it could only offer the hazy idea of a *Volksgemeinschaft* (already found in the pre-war German Workers' party) which would presumably overcome the divisions wrought by socialism and liberalism. But this program, along with the *Anschluss* idea, was stolen first by the *Heimwehr* and then in a much more radical way by the Nazis.[25]

The Front Veterans' Association resembled the *Heimwehr* even more than did the GVP since it was not only anti-Marxist and anti-Semitic, but also anti-democratic (despite the fact that its leadership, like the *Heimwehr's* was democratically elected until 1927). Moreover, it was a para-military formation composed at first primarily of World War veterans (although from the beginning in 1920 it permitted non-veterans in its ranks, as did the *Heimwehr)*. Both groups stressed love of the Austrian homeland and the virtues of military discipline. They also regarded themselves as élites who stood above the political parties and as such were entitled to «renew» the *Volk* and State. Consequently, the FKV and the *Heimwehr* favored a change in Austria's constitution to provide for a strong head of state and the abolition of voting for party lists rather than for individuals. Indeed they differed only in so far as the Front Veterans were more uniformly in favor of the *Anschluss* and more vehemently opposed to Jews. (For these reasons many Nazis temporarily joined the FKV after the NSDAP was outlawed in 1933.)[26]

The Peasant League was a purely political and democratic party made up of pan-German peasants mostly from Styria and Carinthia. Although originally anti-Semitic, this aspect of its program was later jettisoned, at least officially. Its anti-Marxism and anti-capitalism were reminiscent of the *Heimwehr* as was its advocacy of corporations and its provincialism. In the two and a half years following the Vienna uprising of July 1927 the *Landbund* was closely associated with the *Heimwehr*, but the increasingly political nature of the HW caused its *Landbund* members to start breaking away beginning in December 1929.[27]

The similar ideologies of the NSDAP and other pan-German groups in Austria made the latter susceptible to Nazi propaganda after the Nazi party began its rapid growth in 1930. Although, as we have seen, the Nazis won only a disappointing 111,000 votes and not a single parliamentary deputy in the national elections of November 1930, this vote nevertheless represented a four-fold increase of the 27,000 votes the Hitlerian Nazis had gained in the national elections in 1927. Further gains came in local elections in Upper Austria and Klagenfurt in 1931. But the big breakthrough occurred in the local elections of April 1932, two weeks after Hitler's impressive showing in the German presidential election. In Vienna alone the Nazis increased their 1930 vote of 27,000 to over 201,000. The Greater German People's party, which had amassed 124,000 votes in the capital in 1930, could garner only a paltry 9,000 votes two years later. On April 30, 1933, in the last democratic elections held in Austria before the war, the Nazis won 41.2 per cent of the vote in municipal elections in Innsbruck. In the intervening twelve months the number of Nazi cells or *Ortsgruppen* throughout Austria grew from a thousand to more than twice that number.[28]

In terms of social origins new members of the Austrian NSDAP were unemployed workers, minor employees *(Angestellten)*, farm hands, peasants, and a few members of «high society.» Beginning in April 1932 and then especially after Hitler's *Machter-greifung* in January 1933 these groups were joined by a veritable invasion from the bourgeoisie: businessmen, professional people (like architects and engineers), and particularly academicians.[29] The latter, however, lost some of their enthusiasm when the party was outlawed in June, only to rejoin in the fall of 1937 when the *Anschluss* seemed imminent. In that year they were joined by major business executives, *Gymnasium* professors, civil servants, and judges,[30] all no doubt hoping to assure their positions in the event of a Nazi takeover.[31]

Although it is impossible to document with any accuracy, there appears to have been a disproportionately large number of Nazis among Austria's tiny (282,000) Protestant minority,[32] a phenomenon which was also true in predominantly Catholic Bavaria.[33] As recently as the 1880s Georg von Schönerer had induced 60,000 Austrians to convert to Protestantism in his *Los von Rom* movement.[34]

The Nazis resembled the Austrian *Heimwehr* in their ability to attract students. Already in February 1931 Nazi students at the Vienna School of Agriculture captured ten of fifteen seats in the student senate.[35] It was certainly no accident that Chancellor Kurt von Schuschnigg raised the voting age from twenty-one to twenty-four in the ill-fated plebiscite of March 1938.[36]

It is once again impossible to prove statistically, but there is considerable evidence that many leaders of both the *Heimwehr* and the Nazis were ethnic Germans from «lost provinces.» Walter Pfrimer came from Lower Styria, annexed by Yugoslavia in 1918; Richard Steidle was born in the South Tyrol as was Walter Oberhaidacher, the *Gauleiter* of Styria. Walter Riehl was a native of northern Bohemia and Alfred Persche leader of the Austrian SA from 1936 to 1938, was born in Spalato on the Adriatic. Alfred Proksch, the onetime Nazi *Landesleiter,* was of Sudeten German extraction. There were also important Reich Germans in both the *Heimwehr* and the Austrian NSDAP such as Waldemar Pabst, the *Heimwehr* chief of staff, and Theo Habicht, the Nazi *Landesinspekteur.* A large share of the Nazi speakers in Austria were Reich Germans as were the most active Nazis in the Austrian universities.[37]

The Austrian Nazis, like all other Austrian fascists, always regarded rival fascists as their prime recruiting material. Consequently, not long after the unsuccessful Pfrimer-*Putsch* in September 1931 the Nazis made obvious overtures to disgruntled pan-Germans in the *Heimwehr.* These moves at first met with little success, but shortly after Adolf Hitler became Chancellor the reorientation of the pan-German wing of the *Heimwehr* was completed. It soon became clear to all Austrian pan-Germans, regardless of their party affiliation, that their *Anschluss* dreams could now be realized only by the Nazi party. So on April 18, 1933, the Styrian and parts of the Carinthian *Heimwehr,* together with the para-military *Bund Oberland* of Tyrol, joined the Nazis in the so-called «Pan-German Front.» This alliance was augmented by the GVP, or what was left of it, followed by the *Landbund* in February 1934. After Schuschnigg dissolved the Front Veterans in 1935[38] many of its members also joined the illegal Nazi party.

231

For Dollfuss, Hitler's appointment as Chancellor together with his electoral victory in March 1933 raised the spectre of the Austrian Nazis also trying to use democratic elections and Parliament as stepping stones to power. To forestall this possibility Dollfuss allowed Parliament to «dissolve itself» on a mere procedural question. Simultaneously the Chancellor forbade all public meetings and marches and began a censorship of the press.[39] A new phase of Austrian fascism had begun. In effect «Millimetternich» (as his enemies called him) was trying to save Austrian independence by destroying Austrian democracy. If in the long run he failed, his record in holding back the «brown flood» at least compares favorably with that of his German counterparts.

The Dollfuss dictatorship was by no means directed against the Nazis alone: the dissolution of the Socialists' para-military Republican *Schutzbund* (defense league) on March 31, 1933, is clear proof of that. But while giving the Nazis some useful propaganda ammunition, the dissolution of Parliament also frustrated them and led directly to the abortive Nazi *Putsch* of July 1934.[40]

The Nazis, of course, were incensed by the Dollfuss dictatorship and inaugurated a series of terroristic acts against governmental installations and supporters. On May 19 Dollfuss responded by unconditionally forbidding the wearing of Nazi uniforms and insignia and Alfred Frauenfeld, the Vienna *Gauleiter,* was prohibited from making future speeches. Shortly thereafter the first house searches and mass arrests of Nazis were made.[41] The climax came on June 19, 1933, when fifty-six unarmed «Christian German Gymnasts,» a police auxiliary, were attacked, allegedly by Nazis. In an emergency meeting the same day Dollfuss disbanded the Austrian NSDAP along with its armed ally, the Styrian *Heimwehr.* Alfred Proksch, the Nazi *Landesleiter,* Theo Habicht, and most of the Nazi *Gauleiters* of Austria fled to Germany and rebuilt the party's directorate in Munich.[42] Thousands of lesser Nazis also fled to Germany following the dissolution of their party. Their property was confiscated and they were made liable to a loss of citizenship.[43]

Taking Starhemberg's advice the Chancellor began to switch from the defensive over to the offensive during the summer of 1933. The fascist prince insisted that the Austrian public had to feel physically secure from Nazi violence and the Nazis had to realize that it would be dangerous to continue their party loyalty.[44] Now the Austrian government turned some of the Nazis' own tactics upside down by arresting and imprisoning them, sometimes without trial. When actual Nazi terrorists could not be apprehended other known Nazis were arrested in their place.[45] Civil servants and soldiers suspected of Nazism were dismissed and replaced by patriots.[46] Enemies of Dollfuss and his successor, Kurt von Schuschnigg, were imprisoned in the relatively comfortable Wöllersdorf concentration camp where Nazis, socialists and communists all nevertheless claimed to be more brutally mistreated than the others.[47]

In following his dictatorial course Dollfuss was by no means an entirely free agent. From the moment he took office in 1932 he was subjected to pressures from every side. His dependence on the *Heimwehr,* which was itself financially dependent on fascist Italy,[48] forced him to follow an ever more authoritarian policy. Similar, though weaker pressure came from the Hungarian strongman, General Gyula Gömbös. Dollfuss was thus faced with the unpleasant choice of favoring the Social Democrats at home with the *hope* of gaining the support of their British and French friends abroad or utilizing the *Heimwehr* and its Italian patron. Given the chronic British disinterest in Central European affairs during the whole inter-war period and France's growing military timidity in the thirties, it is not surprising that Dollfuss opted for Mussolini. The *Duce's* nearby legions looked far more reassuring than the faraway platonic sympathy of Britian and France.[49]

The Austrian Chancellor therefore set to work to build a fascist-style dictatorship which, if it was not an exact copy of either the Italian or German models, was a least a kissing cousin. In a major address on September 11, 1933, Dollfuss denounced the social and economic weaknesses of liberalism, capitalism, and Marxism.[50] Then, having dispatched the socialists during the civil war of February 1934, the Chancellor announced a new constitution for Austria on May 1. Beginning with the words «In the name of God, the Almighty, from whom all Justice derives ...» the new constitution established, in theory at least, a new state system with seven economic corporations replacing the old democratic national Parliament. Much weaker powers were allotted to the provincial governments which, in any case, had already been purged of Nazis, socialists, and communists. Only the government could initiate legislation and all political parties including the Chancellor's Christian Socialist party were forbidden and replaced by the so-called «Fatherland Front.» Even the *Heimwehr,* after a three-year period of rivalry and only limited co-operation with the Front was absorbed into the latter in October 1936. Thus the demands of Dollfuss' former teacher, Professor Othmar Spann, as well as those contained in the Korneuburg Oath (which was also inspired by Spann) were at last realized.[51] This was true only on paper, however, since the new constitution could only become valid by means of a national plebiscite which was never held.

Apologists for Dollfuss and Schuschnigg, including Schuschnigg himself, have frequently argued that Austria between 1933 and 1938 was neither a full-fledged dictatorship nor a fascist state, but rather displayed the characteristics of a form of an old-fashioned bureaucratic absolutism. This contention cannot be dismissed out of hand. As noted above, the Dollfuss-Schuschnigg regime was certainly no exact copy of either Nazi Germany or fascist Italy. Far from being oppressed, for example, the Roman Catholic Church greatly increased its influence.[52] The use of force, although as we have seen by no means non-existent, was generally limited to overt rather than merely to potential enemies of the regime. Any talk of imperialism in a country of 6,500,000 souls would have been ludicrous, although both Dollfuss and Schuschnigg did talk about an Austrian «mission» of creating a true Christian Germandom as a bastion against the secular, pagan-national character of Nazism.[53] Unfortunately for both Austrian dictators the absence of prosperity and a charismatic leader (especially in the case of Schuschnigg) also deprived the regime of the kind of fanatical support enjoyed by the fascist systems in Germany and Italy. And the lack of popular support made it impossible for both Dollfuss and Schuschnigg to establish either a truly successful fascist state or to restore democratic institutions.

However mild the Austrian dictatorship may have been it nevertheless did have some very decided fascist characteristics. The government's Fatherland Front, while never enjoying genuine popularity with the Austrian masses,[54] certainly had many of the trappings of European fascism. The Front made an explicit claim to totality which excluded the possibility of opposition views[55] and in a typically fascist way was built on the leadership principle *(Führerprinzip).* In contrast to the *Heimwehr,* the *Führer* (his actual title) was not elected, – he was simply «there.» As had been true of the NSDAP since 1927 the leader named his deputy and the deputy appointed his subordinates and so on down to the lowest echelons of the hierarchy. The *Führer* had unlimited power over the organization and its members owed him unconditional obedience.[56]

Although the Fatherland Front was launched just before the Dollfuss assassination in July 1934 it was not until the Schuschnigg era that it reached its maturity. Superficially the organization looked impressive; membership was widespread, reaching a peak of 3,000,000 in November 1937.[57] But membership was far from voluntary. Starhemberg, who was the nominal leader of the Front from 1934 to 1936, announced in a speech on December 11, 1935, that everyone who was not a member of the Front was a *Staatsfeind* and a second class citizen.[58] So much pressure was placed on civil servants (such as postal, telegraph and railroad employees, and teachers) to join the Front that even secret Nazis signed up.[59] State contracts went only to companies whose owners were members of the organization.

Typical of Austrian fascism in general, the Front suffered from inadequate leadership particularly before Guido Zernatto took over in 1936. Prince Starhemberg was always far more interested in the *Heimwehr* than in the Front and scarcely even mentions the latter in his memoirs. There was little contact between the sub-leaders of the Front and the ordinary membership and Front propaganda was ineffective. The crux of the matter was, however, that the Fatherland Front failed to win over the sincere enthusiasm of anyone but members of the disbanded conservative parties, mainly the Christian Socialist party.[60]

The philosophy and policies of the Front were clearly designed to take the wind out of the Nazis' sails. While a maximum of freedom compatible with the security of the regime was permitted the more popular aspects of German and Italian fascism were implemented in modified forms. Thus while racial anti-Semitism was rejected, religious and cultural anti-Judaism were fostered and Jews were identified with the rejected philosophies of liberalism, individualism, and socialism.[61] Female employment was discriminated against just as in Nazi Germany; no wife might be employed whose husband was also employed. The Fatherland Front's «Mother Protection Association» *(Mutterschutzwerk)*, likewise inspired by Germany and Italy, was intended to reverse the declining birth-rate in Austria. The Front even had its own fascist-style youth organization, built on the remains of the *Heimwehr's* youth group. There was also an organization for Austrians living abroad (reminiscent of the Nazis' *Auslandsorganisation)*, a *Winterhilfe* for the poor, and a cultural organization called «New Life», an obvious copy of Germany's *Kraft durch Freude* and Italy's *Dopolavoro*.[62] The Front's rallies were decorated with huge symbols *à la* Albert Speer and the Front's ensignia was the medieval *Krukenkreuz*, a slightly modified swastika.[63]

Finally, after the dissolution of the *Heimwehr* in October 1936, a substitute was founded within the Fatherland Front called the *Sturmkorps* inspired by the SS. Organized only in the second half of 1937, it was outfitted with SS-style uniforms. Although designed to have 30,000 to 50,000 members between the ages of nineteen and thirty the usual fascist leadership problems together with the *Anschluss* brought its development to a premature end.[64]

Even this brief survey of Austrian fascists and semifascists reveals many similarities between them, their bitter internecine warfare notwithstanding. Ideologically every organization from the Nazis on the extreme Right to the relatively middle-of-the-road *Landbund* and Greater German People's party was anti-Marxist. The true fascists (Nazis, *Heimwehr*, Front Veterans, and Fatherland Front) were also authoritarian, anti-democratic (except occasionally in their own internal structure), and in varying degrees anti-Semitic. These same groups also claimed to be «movements of renewal» which would revive the fortunes of *all* the Austrian people (except to some degree the Jews). None the less, these same four groups never succeeded in winning the heartfelt support of anything like a majority of the Austrian population, or even its own membership in the case of the Fatherland Front. Industrial workers were almost never won over, except in the Styrian *Heimwehr,* and even there the sincerity of their conversion is open to doubt. All but the Nazis admired the corporativism of Othmar Spann. Only on the role of the Roman Catholic Church and on the question of Austrian independence was the Austrian Right split. While the Nazis, GVP, *Landbund* and at least a third of the *Heimwehr* supported the *Anschluss* idea even after 1933, the clerical fascists in the *Heimwehr* rejected it after Hitler's rise to power, fearing that an *Anschluss* with Nazi Germany would destroy not only Austrian traditions, but also the independence of the Catholic Church. The ideology of the Austrian NSDAP, therefore, was distinctive only in its extremism and its all-encompassing nature. For example, although all Austrian fascists adhered to some form of anti-Semitism, only the Nazis regarded it as an essential part of their *Weltanschauung.*

Austrian fascists also subscribed unanimously to the *Führerprinzip* (with the Nazis carrying the idea to its ultimate extreme), but every group including the Austrian Nazis found it impossible to find a suitable *Führer.* Pfrimer, Steidle, Starhemberg, Riehl, Proksch, Habicht, and after 1934 Josef Leopold (an SA man from Lower Austria who led the illegal Austrian NSDAP) all managed to offend one group or another of their potential followers. All of them also attacked each other with great relish. The Nazis, however, did enjoy the immense advantage of having the charismatic leadership of Adolf Hitler. In contrast to the Austrian fascist leaders Hitler had the power to prevent major ideological debates and could intervene to settle any quarrels between Nazi leaders.[65] Even Hitler, however, was forced, out of foreign policy considerations, to leave day-to-day Austrian affairs in the hands of subordinates. Thus divisions arose within the Austrian NSDAP only slightly less serious than those of other fascist groups.

Despite, or perhaps because of their many similarities, a kind of cannibalism existed within the whole Austrian Right. The *Heimwehr* absorbed much of the Front Veterans' Association, the Greater German People's party, and the Peasant League in the late 1920s only to see the independent remnants of these groups plus the *Heimwehr's* own pan-German wing switch over to the Nazi camp after 1933. The clerical wing of the *Heimwehr* was then incorporated into the Fatherland Front in October 1936, which in turn was destroyed by the Nazis after the *Anschluss* in 1938.

In the final analysis the Nazis therefore succeeded in absorbing all other Austrian fascists because of the success of the German Nazis in carrying out the *Anschluss.* Success was the absolute *sine qua non* for fascists not only in Austria, but also elsewhere in Europe. Nothing else could hold their heterogeneous social groups together.

A NOTE ON THE SOURCES

The student of Austrian fascism is considerably handicapped by a scarcity of documentary materials. Police records and personal letters concerning the Heimwehr and the Nazis for example, are largely non-existent, having been destroyed either in 1938 or in 1945 by men fearing persecution by the Nazis or the Russians. A partial exception for Nazi correspondence is the Schumacher Sammlung at the German Federal Archives in Koblenz. Consular reports can be seen at the archives of the German Foreign Ministry in Bonn and many dissertations, rare books, and various documents, both published and unpublished, are available in the Institute for

Contemporary History and at the Documentation Center of the Austrian Resistance Movement, both in Vienna. Rare newspapers from all over Austria are in the Austrian National Library and a thoroughly indexed collection of newspaper clippings in the *Tagblatt* Archive of the *Arbeiterkammer* in Vienna. The author wishes to take this opportunity to thank the various directors of these archives and libraries for permission to use their manuscript collections. Additional bibliographical information on Austrian fascism can be found in the author's book, *Hahnenschwanz und Hakenkreuz: Steirischer Heimatschutz und österreichischer Nationalsozialismus, 1918–1934* (Vienna: Europa Verlag, 1972). The author has just completed a new book on Austrian Nazism entitled *Hitler and the forgotten Nazis: A History of Austrian National Socialism* which will be published in 1981 by the University of North Carolina Press.

Owing to space limitations the sources cited below refer primarily to the social composition of the Austrian fascists.

[1] Among the many works on the nationalities question see, Andrew G. Whiteside, *Austrian National Socialism before 1918* (The Hague, 1962) and Hugo Hantsch, *Die Nationalitätenfrage im alten Österreich* (Vienna, 1953).

[2] *Linzer Volksstimme*, September 9, 1924, p. 3.

[3] Andrew G. Whiteside, «Reply to the Above Comments» (by Robert A. Kann), *Austrian History Newsletter*, No. 4 (1963), p. 16. Whiteside also says that members of the DAP were chiefly industrial workers. (*Ibid.*, p. 17.)

[4] Rudolf Brandstötter, «Dr. Walter Riehl und die nationalsozialistische Bewegung in Österreich» (University of Vienna, Ph.D. diss., 1970) pp. 54–55.

[5] Whiteside, «Reply,» p. 16.

[6] Brandstötter, «Dr. Walter Riehl,» p. 96.

[7] David F. Strong, *Austria (October 1918 – March 1919): Transition from Empire to Republic* (New York, 1939), p. 149; Reinhard Kondert «The Rise and Early History of the Heimwehr Movement» (Rice University, Ph.D. diss., 1971), p. 2.

[8] Ludger Rape, «Die österreichische Heimwehr und ihre Beziehungen zur bayerischen Rechten zwischen 1920 und 1923» (University of Vienna Ph.D. diss., 1969), pp. 44, 47, 50. See also Kondert, «Rise of the Heimwehr,» p. 33.

[9] On the early history of the Heimwehr see Kondert, «Rise of the Heimwehr,» and C. Earl Edmondson, «The Heimwehr in Austrian Politics, 1918–1934» (Duke University, Ph. D. diss., 1966).

[10] Kondert, «Rise of the Heimwehr,» p. 2.

[11] *Deutsches Grenzwacht* (Radkersburg, Styria), February 1, 1929, p. 1.

[12] Interview with Dr. Walter Pfrimer, Judenburg, Styria, July 2, 1964.

[13] *Ibid,;* Sepp Kogelnik (ed.), *Österreichisches Heimatschutz-Jahrbuch 1933* (Graz, 1934), p. 63; interview with Dr. Karl M. Stepan, Graz, June 30, 1964.

[14] New York *Times*, December 2, 1928, p. 4; C. A. Macartney, «The Armed Formations in Austria,» *International Affairs*, Vol. VIII (November, 1929), p. 627.

[15] Brandstötter, «Dr. Walter Riehl,» pp. 224, 228; *Linzer Volksstimme*, September 15, 1923, p. 1.

[16] Brandstötter, «Dr. Walter Riehl,» pp. 224, 228; *Kampfruf* (Vienna), April 29, 1931, p. 1.

[17] Brandstötter, «Dr. Walter Riehl,» pp. 233, 235–236; *Deutsche Arbeiterpresse* (Vienna), August 21, 1926, p. 1.

[18] Brandstötter, «Dr. Walter Riehl,» pp. 238, 267.

[19] *Ibid.*, p. 256; Federal Archives in Koblenz «Sammlung Schumacher,» 305, II Report by Leo Haubenberger, Vienna, March 19, 1930, pp. 2–3.

[20] Barbara Berger, «Ernst Rüdiger Fürst Starhemberg: Versuch einer Biographie» (University of Vienna, Ph.D. diss., 1967), pp. 196–198.

[21] Charles A. Gulick, *Austria from Habsburg to Hitler*, Vol. II (Berkeley, 1948), pp. 936–937.

[22] *Heimatschutz-Zeitung* (Klagenfurt), February 20, 1932, p. 3; *Heimatschützer* (Vienna), March 3, 1934, p. 3.

[23] Herbert Müller, «Heimatschutzbewegung, Heimatwehr, Heimwehr, Heimatbund, Heimatblock-Partei,» in Karl Wache (ed.), *Deutscher Geist in Österreich* (Munich, 1933), p. 246; *Heimatschützer*, March 3, 1934, p. 2.

[24] Berger, «Starhemberg,» p. 145; Administrative Archive in Vienna, Karton 14. *NS Parteistellen.* Statutes of the Heimatschutz verbandes Steiermark.

[25] Isabella Ackerl, «Die Grossdeutsche Partei» (University of Vienna, Ph.D. diss., 1967), pp. 69–70, 312, 314; Karl Jung, «Die Grossdeutsche Volkspartei,» in Wache (ed.), *Deutscher Geist,* pp. 176–177, 179.

[26] Ingeborg Messerer, «Die Frontkämpfervereinigung Deutschösterreichs. Ein Beitrag zur Geschichte der Wehrverbände in der Republik Österreich» (University of Vienna, Ph.D. diss., 1964), pp. 21, 41, 60, 114, 115, 118.

[27] Anton Gasselich «Landbund für Österreich,» in Wache (ed.), *Deutscher Geist,* p. 228; Angela Feldmann, «Landbund für Österreich: Ideologie, Organisation, Politik» (University of Vienna, Ph.D. diss., 1967) pp. 10, 12, 138, 140, 160; *Landbund-Stimmen* (Graz), May 4, 1933, p. 2.

[28] *Vormarsch* (Klagenfurt), June 2, 1933, p. 2.

[29] Federal Archives in Koblenz, «Schumacher Sammlung,» 305, II, Walter Riehl to Alfred Proksch, April 26, 1932, p. 1.

[30] Resistance Archive (Vienna), document 5116/1. Manuscript by Alfred Persche, «Die Aktion Hudel. Das letzte Aufgebot das Abendlandes», p. 234.

[31] Geoffrey Pridham, *Hitler's Rise to Power: The Nazi Movement in Bavaria, 1923–1933* (New York, 1973), p. 194.

[32] Helene Grilliet, *Eine Französin erlebt Grossdeutschland* (Graz, 1938), p. 19; Oswald Dutch (pseud.), *Thus Died Austria* (London, 1938), p. 110.

[33] Pridham, *Hitler's Rise to Power,* pp. 170–171.

[34] Arthur J. May, *The Habsburg Monarchy, 1867–1914* (Cambridge, Mass., 1951), p. 189.

[35] *Kampfruf* (Vienna), February 3, 1931 (Sonderausgabe), p. 1.

[36] Gulick, *Habsburg to Hitler,* II, p. 1826.

[37] Documents of the German Foreign Office, Bonn. *Gesandtschaft Wien. Geheim Akten betreffend Nationalismus, Faschismus, Heimwehr, Stahlhelm, Monarchismus usw. von 1923 bis 1934,* Band. Unsigned report dated July 30, 1931, K468971.

[38] Messerer, «Frontkämpfervereinigung,» p. 52.

[39] Imgard Bärnthaler, *Die Vaterländische Front: Geschichte und Organisation* (Wien, 1971), p. 10.

[40] Wolfgang Rosar, *Deutsche Gemeinschaft: Seyss-Inquart und der Anschluss* (Vienna, 1971), p. 62; Kurt von Schuschnigg, *The Brutal Takeover* (London, 1969), p. 92.

[41] Wladimir Hartlieb, *Parole: Das Reich* (Vienna, 1939), pp. 38–45, 49.

[42] Brandstötter, «Dr. Walter Riehl,» p. 297.

[43] Ulrich Eichstädt, *Von Dollfuss zu Hitler. Geschichte des Anschlusses Österreichs* (Wiesbaden, 1955), pp. 33.

[44] Ernst Rüdiger Starhemberg, *Memoiren* (Vienna, 1971), 138.

[45] Felix Kreissler, *Von der Revolution zur Annexion. Österreich 1918 bis 1938* (Vienna, 1969), p. 210.

[46] Hans Frisch, *Die Gewaltherrschaft in Österreich 1933 bis 1938. Eine staatsrechtliche Untersuchung* (Leipzig, 1938), p. 78; *Volkskampf* (Vienna), June 17, 1933, p. 1; Mary Margaret Ball, *Post-War German-Austrian Relations* (Stanford, 1937), pp. 99–100.

[47] Frisch, *Gewaltherrschaft,* pp. 72–73.

[48] Lajos Kerekes, *Die Abenddämmerung einer Demokratie: Mussolini, Gömbös und die Heimwehr* (Vienna, 1966), pp. 13–14.

[49] Jürgen Gehl, *Austria, Germany, and the Anschluss, 1931–1938* (London, 1963), p. 61. Gordon Brook-Shepherd, *Dollfuss* (London, 1961), p. 191.

[50] Edmondson, «The Heimwehr,» p. 334.

[51] John Haag, «Othmar Spann and the Politics of 'Totality': Corporativism Theory and Practice» (Rice University, Ph.D. diss., 1969), pp. 109–110, 122–123. See also Haag's contribution to this book.

[52] Brook-Shepherd, *Dollfuss,* p. 157–163.

[53] Max Dachauer, *Das Ende Österreichs* (Berlin, 1939), p. 190; Clyde K. Kendrich, «Austria

237

under the Chancellorship of Engelbert Dollfuss» (Georgetown University, Ph.D. diss., 1955), p. 325.

[54] Gerhard Jagschitz, «Faschismus und Nationalsozialismus in Österreich, 1918–1945,» in *Fascism and Europe. An International Symposium* (Prague, 1969), p. 73.

[55] Kurt von Schuschnigg, *My Austria* (New York, 1946), Fragments from a diary, December 1, 1934, p. 256.

[56] Bärnthaler, *Vaterländische Front*, pp. 56, 58.

[57] Guido Zernatto, *Die Wahrheit über Österreich* (New York, 1939), p. 94.

[58] Gulick, *Habsburg to Hitler*, II, pp. 1167–1168; Frisch, *Gewaltherrschaft*, p. 38.

[59] Bärnthaler, *Vaterländische Front*, p. 26.

[60] Brook-Shepherd, *Dollfuss*, p. 105; R. John Rath, «Authoritarian Austria», in Peter F. Sugar (ed.), *Native Fascism in the Successor States, 1918–1945* (Santa Barbara, Cal., 1971), p. 34.

[61] Heinrich Busshoff, *Das Dollfuss-Regime* (Berlin, 1968), 251–252.

[62] Bärnthaler, *Vaterländische Front*, pp. 189–197; *Stimme der Heimat* (Vienna), June 1935, p. 3.

[63] Vaterländische Front, Bundeswerbeleitung, *Richtlinien zur Führerausbildung*, 2 Auflage (Vienna, 1935), p. IX.

[64] Bärnthaler, *Vaterländische Front*, p. 58; Zernatto, *Wahrheit*, p. 97; Hartlieb, *Das Reich*, p. 458.

[65] Dietrich Orlow, *The History of the Nazi Party: 1919–1933* (Pittsburgh, 1969), p. 305.

The above research was made possible by a Fulbright-Hays fellowship in 1963–1964 and in 1972 by the National Endowment for the Humanities and the American Philosophical Society. Additional support in 1974 was provided by a grant from Florida Atlantic University.

238

Marginal Men and the Dream of the Reich: Eight Austrian National-Catholic Intellectuals, 1918–1938

JOHN HAAG

Although not providing us with the full spectrum of history, biography must be seen as a vital part of the documentation that enables us to understand the dynamics – and ambiguities – of choice operating in individuals and groups. For an understanding of the origins and nature of fascism and Nazism, research into individual lives and motives must continue to be one strongly pursued avenue of enquiry; the empirical and theoretical studies of Peter H. Merkl, Juan J. Linz and others have already provided us with a great fund of material for continued work in the field of Right-radical behavior patterns. But much of this research deals either with the rank-and-file followers or high-level leaders of the various Nazi and fascist movements. An area in which there remains a great need for more intensive biographical research is in the intermediate area of the «fellow-travellers» – those individuals who, while never completely accepting the discipline of a mass movement, nevertheless allied themselves with it, giving it their prestige and support at critical junctures. Almost by definition, such individuals would have to come from those social classes that customarily functioned as opinion-makers and trend-setters for the educated bourgeoisie. In German-speaking Europe, intellectuals and particularly *Akademiker* up to the year 1945 enjoyed immense social prestige; consequently, any political views they might enunciate as individuals or as a group, any loyalties they might take up, would automatically have a profound effect on that stratum of society they were most in contact with, namely the students and the literate and politically active upper middle class. We need hardly add that the latter were groups of crucial importance during the process of social, political and ideological decay preceding the several fascist and Nazi takeovers in Central Europe.

Case studies of individual intellectuals who lent support to Nazi and fascist movements tell us little unless they can somehow be incorporated into the framework of a larger theoretical and historical context. For our study the theoretical framework, to be discussed below, will be the *concept of marginality;* the historical background will be the attempt of intellectuals to restore a lost world, first in the realm of ideas and then in the real world of politics and power. Even with our conceptual demarcations we are prepared to grant that in all of these investigations we are dealing with that most troublesome (and fascinating) element of history, human passions and feelings. Loss of social status is a shattering emotional experience, one that (no matter how much the social scientist would like it to be that way) simply will not allow itself to be completely tabulated or quantified. How does one *weigh* or *count* bitterness, anger, frustration, hopes born of sheer desperation? After the necessary quantification comes the equally necessary appeal to historical intuition. All that we can do as we carry on such studies is to try to re-create, as best we can – given the emotional distance caused by the passage of time, the unique feelings, aspirations and, as it turned out, illusions that an important group of Austrian intellectuals shared during the era of fascism.

In the most general sense, the Austrian National-Catholic intellectuals played a major role in allowing Nazism to become respectable and acceptable in «reasonable» bourgeois circles. They were also instrumental in blurring what had at one time been fairly clearly drawn distinctions between the kind of racism that was at the heart of National Socialist «ideology» so far as it existed at all, and the spiritual, universalistic ideas proclaimed by the Catholic Church to be its sole guiding principles. By being quiet, personally decent men, these scholars and teachers were able to carry on their propaganda activities unmolested throughout the middle years of the 1930s. They were, in effect, parlor brownshirts. Never did they call for an abandonment of Catholic-National conservatism to the forces of Nazi radicalism. Their belief in the ultimate primacy of ideas and *Geist* led them to believe that patience and persistence would in the long run allow Nazism to be «tamed» and endowed with spiritual elements it had initially been deficient in. The Spanns, Srbiks and Eibls of the 1930s saw their function to be that of responsible mediators, *Brückenbauer* able to initiate lasting contacts that would one day culminate in a smooth act of fusion between Hitler's Reich and the Austrian state. As intellectuals, it seemed quite natural to these men that they would play significant roles in this new stage of the national revolution. As Austrians, they hoped that the harsher, more «Prussian» aspects of the Third Reich could be ameliorated as the *Regierungskunst* of the Austrian intellectual and administrative élite was incorporated into the Greater German state apparatus. As Catholics who also felt themselves to be German to their very marrow, they saw their role in terms of effecting a lasting union between the universalistic imperial traditions of the Habsburg realm and the dynamic nationalism and social cohesion achieved by the new German dictatorship.

To throw some light on the significant role played by intellectuals in the process of softening-up liberal, democratic institutions and values in the years before 1933, eight Austrian conservative intellectuals have been chosen for closer scrutiny. The purpose of this inquiry is to present an in-depth investigation into the lives, careers and ideological development of these eight men active during the 1920s and 1930s.

Six of the men chosen taught at the University of Vienna during inter-war period: Hans Eibl (1882–1958), a philosopher; Wenzel Gleispach (1876–1944), a legal scholar; Karl Gottfried Hugelmann (1879–1959), a legal historian; Oswald Menghin (1888–1973), a prehistorian; Othmar Spann (1878–1950), a social philosopher and *Gemeinschaft* theorist; and finally, Heinrich Ritter von Srbik (1878–1951), a historian. Although they did not teach at the University of Vienna, two other figures intellectually active in Austria during these years have been included in the scope of this analysis: Bishop Alois Hudal (1885–1963), an influential prelate; and Father Wilhelm Schmidt, S.V.D. (1868–1954), an anthropologist and ethnologist.

What common values, assumptions and beliefs did these men share? What made their lives and writings more or less a collective experience culminating in the Nazi years? We can begin to answer these questions by pointing out that they were born into the chaos and moral flux that was the dying Habsburg realm. The oldest of this group was born in 1868, the youngest in 1888, so that all of them came of age before the catastrophe of 1914. While Stefan Zweig was to recall this era in a mist of nostalgia as a «golden age of security,»[1] it was in point of fact an extraordinarily turbulent epoch in which to grow to maturity. Our eight intellectuals-to-be had their formative experiences during the closing decades of the nineteenth century. Thus they grew up in a society in which the last traces of a semi-feudal patriarchal order were being destroyed by capitalism. To further complicate the picture, by the last years of the century the seemingly impregnable capitalist regime was itself being challenged by an increasingly confident proletarian socialist movement. In such an environment conflict and turmoil appeared to be the guiding principles of social development.

Young intellectuals of the late Francisco-Josephine era could choose from a bewildering profusion of ideas and *Weltanschauungen*. Unless they were Marxists or grimly determined adherents of the dying ideology of Liberalism, many of them were strongly attracted to the various shadings of neo-Romanticism and a reviving Catholic conservatism. The 1870s and 1880s in Vienna saw the vigorous anti-capitalist (and reactionary as well as anti-Semitic) journalism of Baron Vogelsang and other champions of a corporative way of life.[2] During these troubled decades the corporative *Ständestaat*, an ideal of hierarchical organization that had never died out in Austria, was revived as a viable alternative to both anarchic capitalism and revolutionary socialism. In the realm of more abstract ideas, a new mystical tendency began to assert itself against the positivism of the preceding generations. The axioms of empirical scientific investigation, of Lockean epistomology, and of an unquestioned secular faith in material progress all seemed to contain more problems than answers. In a generation of materialism, idealism began to gain ground among a generation seeking a way out of a desperate situation.

The young men who would decades later become spokesmen for a peculiar variety of radical conservatism – Austrian National-Catholicism – were without exception profoundly influenced by the neo-Romantic currents of thought prevalent in the German-speaking world in the last years of the century. While neo-Romanticism was not confined to the German-speaking areas of Europe, in Germany and more particularly in Austria it often exhibited traits rarely if ever found elsewhere. First there was the intense yearning for a «true» society, an organic state based not so much on social justice as on the stability that only an acceptance of hierarchy and strong differentiation of status and roles could ensure. This desire for a *ständisch* way of life permeated all levels of non-proletarian society in Austria, from the small shopkeepers who voted for the demagogic Mayor Lueger, through the middle classes and bureaucratic strata that feared «Jewish domination of life» and the unleashing of class struggle by the Marxists, to an aristocracy that naturally enough desired a world in which their position would be genuinely secure.

Among intellectuals, particularly those coming from a marginal class or personal environment, a passionate interest in restoring hierarchical structures – whether intellectual, moral or social – became an important, indeed often dominating concern. In the general crisis of culture aptly described by Carl Schorske as a «bourgeois world spinning out of orbit»,[3] many individuals, no matter what external symbols of status they might have been able to achieve, felt themselves to be marginal. In sociology, a marginal man is defined as one whom «fate has condemned to live in two societies and in two, not merely different, but antagonistic cultures.» Such individuals forever exist «poised in psychological uncertainty between two (or more) social worlds.»[4] While heightened rationality results in some cases from this permanent state of tension, in other instances marginality and its closely associated feelings of ambivalence and heightened self-consciousness result in yearnings that appear to outside observers to be clearly impossible of attainment.

In the case of the eight bourgeois intellectuals coming to maturity around the crisis-ridden *Jahrhundertwende*, marginality was a very real issue. The academic professions were entering into a period of intense introspection and loss of confidence. It was, in the telling phrase of Fritz Ringer, the era of the «decline of the German Mandarins.»[5] Professors and scholars were deeply troubled by the increasingly apparent fact that the status and social power of the *Akademiker* in the German-speaking world was plummeting. Where once a Fichte could pull the entire nation into his spiritual orbit, now the rise of the working class and the class struggle that came in its wake virtually confined professorial appeals for idealism and social harmony to lecture halls and seminar rooms.

As did virtually all of the major German intellectuals of the age, these neophyte Austrians in the years before 1914 spent untold hours grappling with the problems of *Macht* and *Geist*. As Germans, these men were part of the dominant and privileged nationality in a disintegrating empire. Since with only two exceptions these eight men were of bourgeois rather than aristocratic background, personal social marginality was combined with professional marginality. To be both bourgeois and academic at a time when Marxism, universal manhood suffrage and various egalitarian ideals were on the march, and when to make matters worse the Czechs and other emerging nationalities were demanding an end to the German-dominated state, was truly to be living in a permanent state of crisis. All of these intellectuals dealt with these problems in a radical fashion: in their several chosen fields, they called for a fundamental restructuring of thought, particularly in terms of putting in place of Western scientific positivism and philosophical materialism some form of specifically German idealism.

«Idealism» for Hans Eibl, Othmar Spann and the others was in large measure the conscious expression of an almost desperate search for absolute and eternal values. Most of these men had early on been attracted to neo-Romanticism because it provided a refuge for sensitive souls suspended between two worlds, one dead and gone but perhaps for that reason even more desirable than when it was still alive, and the horrifying reality of a conflict-ridden modern age built on quicksand. While the others of the group were occasionally to dabble in social theory, it was the indefatigable Othmar Spann who formulated the overall political philosophy of the group.[6] Drawn to philosophy even though ostensibly a social scientist, Spann found inspiration in a great variety of organic conceptions of the world. On the eve of 1914, Spann had in the manuscript of his *Gesellschaftslehre* already drawn the broad outlines of what he chose to call «Universalism».[7] Claiming to be a method of social science, Universalism was in fact a social and political ideology.

Othmar Spann's ideas – and the illusions that increasingly sustained him as he set sail into the rough seas of day-to-day politics – became after 1918 the compass that would guide the small circle of Viennese intellectuals we have chosen to scrutinize. Totally convinced that his system embraced all of the great idealistic systems of time and space from Plato, Aristotle, Confucius and medieval thought up to and including German Idealism and Romanticism, Spann saw Universalism as nothing less than a blueprint for the reintroduction of idealism (that is, clearly drawn hierarchies of thought and social roles) into the German lands. Leaving the real world of strife behind, his turgid writings reveal a straining after a perfect metaphysical realm of *Ganzheit* – wholeness. Spann's «hunger for wholeness»[8] in the political sphere culminated in his demand for the scuttling of popular sovereignty and parliamentary institutions. The Universalistic state would be an uncompromisingly anti-democratic order ruled by a highly trained and motivated élite of «natural» leaders whose high level of spirituality would ensure that the German *Geist* would never again be endangered by the corrosive forces of individualism and materialism. In his revived *Ständestaat*, Spann planned to rigidly exclude the great bulk of the masses, whom he saw as being constitutionally unable to govern themselves, from any participation in political, moral and intellectual concerns. As marginal men dreaming of a world in which they could genuinely be close to the centers of power rather than outsiders, Spann and his seven colleagues found themselves in the early 1920s in the dangerous and poorly defined borderland between pure ideas and political strife.

Vienna in the years after 1918 was, despite the appalling poverty of an Imperical city stripped not only of glory but even of the ability to feed itself, a fascinating kaleidoscope of shifting moods, passions and ideas. At the University, physical impoverishment did not prevent a rich profusion of hopeful, indeed fantastically optimistic schemes for a better Germanic future from being openly proclaimed. Foremost among these ideas was the idea of the *Reich*.[9] While many Viennese intellectuals were skeptical of one aspect or another of the Roman Catholic religious tradition, in the area of politics and society they often drew openly on the vast body of ideas and experiences represented by the Catholic Habsburg experience. In sum, a mood of restoration was in the air.

The key document of the defiantly reactionary atmosphere of Vienna University in the immediate post-war years was Othmar Spann's book *Der wahre Staat (The True State)*.[10] Based on a series of highly successful lectures given at the University in 1920, *Der wahre Staat* boldly attacked not only an Austro-Marxism still flushed with victory, but went on to identify all the disorders of Western civilization since the Renaissance as resulting from the root-cause of materialistic «Individualism». Individualism for Spann sooner or later led to atomism, liberalism, socialism and finally Bolshevism. Obviously only by eliminating the curse of individualism could a «true» social order flourish. And since Spann and those sympathetic to his message took it for granted that the Germans as a nation, and within this nation the intellectuals and «spiritually higher» individuals, had a natural right and even duty to lead Europe out of chaos, in the final analysis *Der wahre Staat* was a thinly veiled manifesto of German imperial domination of Central and South-Slavic Europe.[11]

Der wahre Staat was the first document in a series of increasingly confident assertions of what can best be called the National-Catholic point of view. The National-Catholic intellectuals were convinced that no insuperable gulf existed between the conservative, indeed reactionary, mystical Catholic Romanticist tradition best defined in Austria a century earlier by Adam Heinrich Müller (1779–1829), and the more recent *Machtstaat* of Bismarck. In other words, the National-Catholics aspired to fuse a mystical *Reich* ideology with the dynamism of recent German history. Clearly these intellectuals hoped that the rapid consolidation of German power in *Mitteleuropa*, using both Austro-German manpower (themselves no doubt included) and Greater German economic, political and military might, would radically reverse the process of disintegration and Slavic rebellion that dated back at least to 1848. In their own sphere, they assumed that the creation of a new *Reich* in the heart of Europe would usher in the era they had been longing for – an age in which once again *Geist* would reign supreme. For them, this of course would mean the end of their painfully endured status as near-outsiders.

Throughout the 1920s the Viennese National-Catholic intellectuals concentrated on disseminating their ideas in print and from the class lectern. Hans Eibl, apart from his studies in the history of philosophy, concentrated on agitating for a reborn *Reich* among students and ethnic Germans (particularly Sudeten-Germans, as is understandable since Eibl had himself been born in Austrian Silesia).[12] In the area of history, Heinrich von Srbik analyzed the nineteenth-century struggles between *kleindeutsch* and *grossdeutsch* factions in the Germanies, coming to the rather metaphysical conclusion that transcending these clashes was a higher reality of German unity that had at all times been present and creatively active on behalf of the entire nation. Calling this idea his *gesamtdeutsch* view of the German past, Srbik acted as if he possessed a magic wand that was somehow able to make troublesome facts in the past vanish whenever there was an emotional need in the present for this to occur.[13] Spann with his *wahrer Staat*, Eibl with his *Reich* appealing so strongly to border Germans, and Srbik and his remarkable synthetic treatment of once-violent fraternal struggles all believed in the validity of an «Austrian Mission» in Central Europe. They were convinced that when the Third Reich appeared, as appear it must, Austria (and particularly that special Austrian élite, the National-Catholic intellectuals) would of necessity have an important role to play in the revival of a «true» state of affairs in *Mitteleuropa*, one unequivocally anti-democratic internally and imperialistic externally.

In the sciences, strongly anti-rationalist currents were also running in Vienna during these years. Although Wilhelm Schmidt and Oswald Menghin had received specialized training in their respective disciplines of anthropology/ethnology and prehistory, both men retained an emotional loyalty to the entire complex of ideas and associations derived from the notion of *Ganzheit*. With his so-called *Kulturkreis* theory of cultural diffusionism, Schmidt not only presented to his colleagues a new scientific hypothesis but carried on an unrelenting struggle against what he believed to be the stupidly materialistic natural science, particularly in its Darwinian guise, of the preceding century.[14] Menghin too was at heart a Romantic *Schwärmer* as well as an anti-Semite and occasional supporter of *völkisch* causes.[15]

The University of Vienna presented an almost ideal environment for irrationalist politics; it was, in the words of a contemporary critical observer, a veritable «breeding ground» of fascist and Nazi ideas.[15] The student body had for decades been enamored of violent methods of dealing with ideological opponents – it was no accident that strong-arm tactics were as much in vogue in the days of the fledgling Austrian Republic as in the era of the pan-German rowdies of Georg von Schönerer. It was at the University that two men trained in the law began the fateful involvement of the National-Catholic group with Nazism. Possessed by the desire for participating in the creation of a new, glorious *Reich* based on «race» and emotions rather than dryasdust legal codes, Karl Gottfried Hugelmann and Wenzeslaus Graf Gleispach both allied themselves with the most radical student demands, including those for the *Numerus clausus* for Jews.[17] The racist *Deutsche Studentenschaft* received the open support of professors whose religious and philosophical background at least provided the possibility of opposing on ethical grounds any form of racial or ethnic hatred. A clear sign of the utter moral confusion of these men was the high praise Spann gave Hitler in front of his students when he received the news of the abortive Munich *Putsch* of November 1923.[18]

By 1930, the National-Catholic intellectuals of Vienna could no longer avoid coming to grips with the fundamental problem of their political involvement: how could these men, all of them self-proclaimed conservatives and «idealists», justify any contacts (let alone alliances) between their pure little circle and the National Socialist movement of Adolf Hitler? How could they accept, as an expression of the national spirit of a reviving Germandom, a mass movement that catered to the very basest instincts of fear, hate, and naked greed? Somehow, in a mysterious fashion known only to themselves, men like Hans Eibl were by 1932 able to resolve such issues and hold up the martial spirit of the Nazis as an example for fellow-Catholics. For the philosophy professor Eibl it was a sign of healthy national spirits asserting themselves when brownshirts gleefully smashed opposition newspaper kiosks and newspaper offices,[19] just as for Spann in May 1933 it represented a great triumph for the German *Geist* when «un-German» books were thrown into bonfires.[20]

To the end, the National-Catholics held to their illusions about Nazism. As late as 1937 Bishop Alois Hudal was content to spin an elaborate fantasy, publishing it in book form as *Die Grundlagen des Nationalsozialismus*. Ignoring history and the evidence before him in the real world, Hudal «proved» to his own satisfaction that Nazism and Roman Catholicism were thoroughly compatible historical movements based in both instances on the deepest needs and aspirations of *Deutschtum*. More than once Hudal ventured into the realm of the absurd, claiming for instance that nineteenth-century social Catholicism and the Nazi «social program» had much in common.[21] What had happened to these men? From the very start of their involvement in politics, they had held tenaciously to the idea that as «idealists» they somehow would play a major role in the creation of a Central European «true state» free of the twin scourges of assertive Marxism and a rebellious Slavdom. Nazism, for which these *Akademiker* had no respect, represented a means to an end – the restoration of their moral status. There were many Spanns, Eibls and Srbiks not only in Austria but in Germany as well in the years before and after 1933; all of them shared the naive belief that National Socialism, and indeed Adolf Hitler himself, were the vehicles for the creation of a «reasonable,» i.e. solid fascist regime that would give them the status they had sought for so long.[22] But the Nazis discarded these little men once they had been fully, cynically exploited. Nazism had a dynamism all its own, and refused to be either «spiritualized» or «tamed.»

As late as 1930, most if not all Austrian Catholic conservatives looked upon Nazis as little better than beerhall ruffians and the National Socialist «idea» as street-corner demagogy. By 1933, in part because of the tireless oratorical and publicistic activities of the National-Catholic intellectuals, a significant number of Austrian Catholic students, civil servants and free professionals – the nation's administrative élite – looked with favor upon the Nazi phenomenon. It goes without saying that the German *Machtergreifung* of 1933 was of crucial significance in this dramatic metamorphosis of opinion. From this point on, a bandwagon mentality developed in Austrian circles previously indifferent or hostile to the more primitive aspects of the *Hitlerbewegung*. After 1933, Nazi sympathizers could be found in virtually every important branch of government service. In press, theater and the arts as well as in higher education, most individuals previously loyal, if only halfheartedly, to the Austrian state now ardently hoped for an *Anschluss* (or perhaps better put, a *Zusammenschluss*) that would allow Austrians of the administrative stratum once more to play a dominant role in a German-dominated Central Europe. That these were not idle dreams can be thoroughly documented by the increasing pro-German drift of events after the July 1936 Austro-German accords, a slow but steady erosion of support for the Schuschnigg administration by scores of important individuals in and out of government, many of them fancying themselves to be intellectuals of a *Brückenbauer* persuasion.[23] In this connection, the names of active National-Catholic figures appear again and again in the closing months and weeks of the Austro-fascist state. Seyss-Inquart, Menghin and other National-Catholic personalities played out their roles of smoothing the path for Reich-German domination to the very last scene of the last act of Austria's dissolution-from-within, the sham post-Schuschnigg «government» of March 1938.[24] That these men were almost immediately shelved and discarded by Hitler and his inner circle does not in any way lessen the historical example given by them as fellow travellers of Nazism. Underlying all these rather grotesque events was the sincerely held belief that intellectuals could, and indeed must help infuse a venerable and spiritually rich tradition into what must at times have seemed to them to be a totally ruthless Nazi state, creating in the process a new German order in the heart of Europe that would make ample use of their academic expertise and proven qualities of national idealism. But these eight scholars in search of a perfectly restored world guaranteeing them the prestige and influence they felt was their birthright, thoroughly misread all the signs of the times, never once recognizing the inherent nihilism of the Nazi behemoth. Because of this singular inability to look reality in the face, these men not only shattered their own careers and lives, but by virtue of having actively helped Nazism grow in power, they permanently discredited whatever positive elements the ideology of National Catholicism may have originally offered.

As the last inheritors of an exhausted and by now grotesquely distorted tradition of German Romanticism and Idealism, the Viennese National-Catholic intellectuals needed a myth to live by. That myth was above all else provided by the idea of the *Reich*.

As well as being a cultural ideal, the *Reich* was a reactionary Utopia, a *Gemeinschaft* order so perfectly balanced, ordered and strife-free that it represented that dream of dreams in an epoch of almost unbearable tensions and contradictions, a polity based on synthesis and social cohesion rather than on conflict. That the Nazis cared not at all for these reveries scarcely seemed to bother our eight dreamers-in-politics. For them it was enough that *Geist* seemed to be returning to the German lands, for they never were able to separate their own fates and ambitions from the general movement of what they defined as «idealism.» Had they looked hard at the world around them, they would have had to come to the conclusion that they had been exploited by men who, though German, were capable of the most extraordinary acts of cynicism and brutality. And these eight intellectuals could never admit that the foundation upon which their thinking was built was flawed, for to do so would have meant accepting that as *Edelnazis* they had helped make Nazism respectable; ever the cynic, Hitler had accepted their proffered fig leaf. Remaining rank outsiders to the end, these *Grenzland* intellectuals became superfluous men in the Third *Reich*. The Germany of their dreams, the «true» realm which if truth be told was little more than a fairy-tale version of the medieval First *Reich*, had had no influence on the grim but successful reality that was Hitler's own, Third, *Reich*. Thus it was that rather than diminishing, these men's marginal status increased greatly after the «national revolution» of 1933. In the end they became, like so many others, «cast-off pioneers» of Hitler's state.

NOTES

[1] Stefan Zweig, *The World of Yesterday. An Autobiography* (New York 1943), p. 1.

[2] A sympathetic study of Vogelsang and his circle is Johann Christoph Allmayer-Beck, *Vogelsang. Vom Feudalismus zur Volksbewegung* (Vienna 1952).

[3] Carl E. Schorske, «Politics and the Psyche in *fin de siècle* Vienna: Schnitzler and Hofmannsthal,» *American Historical Review*, Vol. LXVI (July 1961), p. 940.

4 Everett V. Stonequist, *The Marginal Man* (New York 1937), pp. xv-xvii, 74–76 and *passim*. See also Zvi Y. Gitelman, *Jewish Nationality and Soviet Politics: The Jewish Sections of the CPSU, 1917–1930* (Princeton 1972), pp. 108–110.

5 Fritz K. Ringer, *The Decline of the German Mandarins: The German Academic Community 1890–1933* (Cambridge, Mass. 1969).

6 Spann was born in Vienna in 1878, his father a member of the threatened *Handwerkerstand*. Cf. Klaus-Jörg Siegfried, *Universalismus und Faschismus. Das Gesellschaftsbild Othmar Spanns* (Vienna 1974), p. 19.

7 Othmar Spann, *Kurzgefasstes System der Gesellschaftslehre* (Berlin 1914).

8 This useful phrase is from Peter Gay, *Weimar Culture: The Outsider as Insider* (New York 1968), p. 96. Ralf Dahrendorf sees a «nostalgia for synthesis» and a deep aversion toward the real world of conflict as fundamental themes of modern German social and intellectual development. Cf. Dahrendorf, *Society and Democracy in Germany* (paperback ed., Garden City, N.Y. 1969), pp. 188–203.

9 Fundamental for a history of the *Reich* ideology is Klaus Breuning, *Die Vision des Reiches. Deutscher Katholizismus zwischen Demokratie und Diktatur (1929–1934)* (Munich 1969).

10 The full title is *Der wahre Staat. Vorlesungen über Abbruch und Neubau der Gesellschaft gehalten im Sommersemester 1920 an der Universität Wien* (Leipzig 1921). The book appeared in new editions in the crisis years 1923 and 1931 and, inexplicably, in 1938. Interestingly, the only translation of Spann's magnum opus was into Japanese.

11 Breuning, *Die Vision des Reiches*, p. 37.

12 Eibl is a significant figure badly in need of a biographical study. Cf. [Josef Nadler,] «Hans Eibl: Umrisse von Josef Nadler» (undated typescript), Woodson Research Center, Fondren Library, Rice University, Josef Nadler Papers, box 3; Felix Zawodsky, «Hans Eibl: Mehr als ein blosses Einzelschicksal,» *Die Furche*, December 6, 1958, p. 4.

13 Gyula Tokody, «Der Weg der grossdeutschen Geschichtsschreibung zum Faschismus,» in *Etudes Historiques 1970 publiées a l'occasion du XIIIe Congres International des Sciences Historiques par la Commission Nationale des Historiens Hongrois* (two vols., Budapest 1970), vol. I. pp. 427–453; Ronald J. Ross, «Heinrich Ritter von Srbik and 'Gesamtdeutsch' History,» *Review of Politics*, Vol. XXXI, No. 1 (January 1969), pp. 88–107.

14 Paul Honigsheim, *On Max Weber* (New York 1968), p. 56.

15 A representative collection of Menghin's articles appeared in his book *Geist und Blut: Grundsätzliches um Rasse, Sprache, Kultur und Volkstum* (Vienna 1934).

16 Nikolaus Hovorka, *Der Kampf um die geistige Wiedergeburt Österreichs* (Vienna 1946), p. 22.

17 Hugelmann championed Spann's ideas at the University; cf. his article «Der wahre Staat,» *Hochland*, Vol. XX (April 1923), pp. 88–93. Gleispach was the «father» of the anti-Semitic student constitution of 1930; cf. Hans Eckstein, «Das Ende der Gleispachschen Studentenordnung,» *Sozialistisch-Akademische Rundschau*, Vol. IV, No. 7 (July 1931), pp. 88–90.

18 Letter to the author from Viktor Matejka, Vienna, August 18, 1972.

19 Eibl in *Schönere Zukunft*, Nr. 34 (1932), cited in Klaus-Peter Hoepke, *Die deutsche Rechte und der italienische Faschismus* (Düsseldorf 1968), p. 84.

20 Othmar Spann, *Kämpfende Wissenschaft: Gesammelte Abhandlungen zur Volkswirtschaftslehre, Gesellschaftslehre und Philosophie* (Jena 1934), p. 126.

21 Alois Hudal, *Die Grundlagen des Nationalsozialismus: Eine ideengeschichtliche Untersuchung* (Leipzig 1937), p. 17. An earlier attempt by Hudal to show the compatibility of Nazism, *Deutschtum*, conservative authoritarianism and Roman Catholicism was his *Rom, Christentum und deutsches Volk* (Innsbruck 1935). See also «Bishop Alois Hudal: A Controversial Figure,» *Wiener Library Bulletin*, Vol. XVIII, No. 2 (April 1964), p. 17.

22 Hans Eibl summed up these incredibly naive notions in his discussion of the program of Franz von Papen's pro-Nazi alliance of German Catholic intellectuals and politicians, the «Kreuz-und Adler-Bund», which appeared in the Vienna newspaper *Neuigkeits-Welt-Blatt* on April 23, 1933. The classic summation of the attitude prevalent in 1933, namely that the Nazis were barbarians who could somehow be easily domesticated by reasonable people certain of their goals is found

247

in the following fragment in Roger Morgan (ed.), *Germany 1870–1970: A Hundred Years of Turmoil* (London 1970), p. 53:

«Interviewer: 'Who thought that they could use him?' Dr. Ernst Hanfstaengl: 'Oh, millions! Every man and woman I know thought, give me a half-hour coffee chat with him and I will make him *my* Hitler. That was the illusion.'»

[23] Adams Wandruszka, «Österreichs politische Struktur. Die Entwicklung der Parteien und politischen Bewegungen,» in Heinrich Benedikt (ed.), *Geshichte der Republik Österreich* (Vienna 1954), pp. 412–416; Breuning, *Die Vision des Reiches*, pp. 253–265. See also Irmgard Bärnthaler, *Die Vaterländische Front. Geschichte und Organisation* (Vienna 1971), and Ulrich Eichstädt, *Von Dollfuss zu Hitler* (Wiesbaden 1955).

[24] The best study to date of the subversion of Austria by «respectable» men willing to offer their services to Nazism is Wolfgang Rosar, *Deutsche Gemeinschaft. Seyss-Inquart und der Anschluss* (Vienna 1971).

248

The Dollfuss-Schuschnigg Regime: Fascist or Authoritarian?

JOHN RATH AND CAROLYN W. SCHUM

Thus far relatively few scholars have made systematic efforts to apply the ever-increasing body of general theories about right-wing political movements to the Dollfuss-Schuschnigg regime in Austria. With the exception of Grete Klingenstein[1] and, to a lesser extent, Fritz Fellner,[2] historians of the First Austrian Republic have largely ignored the hypotheses of American, German, British, and other social scientists about the intrinsic nature of totalitarianism, fascism, and authoritarianism in their discussions of the form of government prevailing in Austria in the 1930s. At the same time, the theoreticians analyzing the basic attributes of fascism have largely ignored Austria. The historians' lack of interest in the theoretical aspects of fascism and the theorists' lack of interest in «Austrian fascism» is in many ways unfortunate, for both the historians and the social scientists could perhaps learn something of value from each other.

Quite a few of the preconditions for fascism spelled out by the social scientists did indeed exist in the First Austrian Republic. The rapid change in form of government in 1918 amounted to a veritable social revolution in which the upper classes and bourgeoisie lost much of their former affluence as well as their social and political leadership. Moreover, the ensuing disruption of the economy and resulting inflation «led to an emotional extremism in all shades of political opinion.»[3] The situation as a whole aroused in many middle-class youths that feeling of isolation, uprootedness, hostility, and moral resentment which has been emphasized by psychological theorists as an underlying cause of fascism.[4] In addition, there arose among the bourgeoisie those non-intellectual or anti-intellectual reactions against rationalism and liberalism which H. R. Trevor-Roper[5] and George Mosse[6] have spotlighted as forerunners of fascism. And there then existed that tendency to rebel against everything vitally concerned with freedom which Hans Buchheim has argued is the essence of fascism.[7]

The increasing disenchantment with parliamentary democracy exhibited by growing numbers of the bourgeoisie in a capitalist country with a powerful labor movement suggests the existence of an undercurrent of the extremist middle-class variant of fascism described by Seymour Martin Lipset.[8] Francis L. Carsten's description of a class which having lost social position and fearing for the future, was the target of specific appeals by the fascists,[9] accurately describes the Austrian bourgeoisie of the 1920s and early'30s. Influential segments of the bourgeoisie, many of them Catholics perturbed over the anticlerical and pro-socialist tendencies of democracy,[10] were under the spell of that reactionary ideology which Hugh Seton-Watson suggests was basic to fascism;[11] while two fascist parties, the Heimwehr and the National Socialists, each supported by powerful neighboring countries, were ready to provide «a mass organization.»[12] Furthermore, towards the end of the 1920s, as T. W. Mason and

J. Solé-Tura suggest, many big industrialists were taking «a flight into politics» and seeking to destroy the labor movement[13] by financing the Heimwehr.

The strong anti-Marxist prejudices of many upper and middle-class Austrians and the language of the Heimwehr Korneuburg Oath are consistent with the precondition implicit in Ernst Nolte's definition: «Fascism is anti-Marxism which seeks to destroy the enemy by the evolvement of a radically opposed and yet related ideology and by the use of almost identical and yet typically modified methods, always, however, within the unyielding framework of national self-assertion and autonomy.»[14] Moreover, of Nolte's six conditions essential for any fascist movement[15] three existed in Austria: the liberal movement was undergoing a severe crisis; many inhabitants of the country were under the spell of recent wartime experiences;[16] and most of them were dominated by anti-Marxist and anti-liberal ideologies. Two of the other three preconditions – the penchant for defending bourgeois values with non-bourgeois methods and for using methods strangely similar to those of the enemy – were characteristic of both the Heimwehr and the National Socialists. And the sixth, a strong emphasis on nationalism, also characterized the Austrian Nazis.

Reinhard Kühnl's explication of the preconditions for fascism also existed in one form or another in pre-Dollfuss Austria. The capitalist system was definitely undergoing a crisis, and conservatives in increasing numbers were rejecting democratic governing methods and turning to anti-communist, corporative, and «folk-community» ideologies to preserve the existing economic system.[17] Several of Clemenz's «generative dimensions» of fascism also existed: a relative balance of power between workers, industrialists, and property holders and an increase in the popularity of corporative «organic» capitalism.[18]

Clearly, many conditions conducive to the rise of fascism were present in Austria in May, 1932, when Engelbert Dollfuss, the leader of the strongly pro-democratic Peasants' League (Bauernbund) became chancellor. He was a devout Catholic who believed in the ideas of the corporate state as outlined by Othmar Spann[19] and in the papal encyclical *Quadragesimo anno,* and he was a pragmatic, impulsive man who believed in order and authority and acted quickly and decisively.[20] Although Dollfuss was originally pro-democratic, the open campaign of terror launched in Austria by the Nazis immediately after Hitler came to power in Germany,[21] the growing antidemocratic proclivities of an increasing number of Austrian conservatives, and pressures from the Heimwehr, on whom his government was dependent for a one-vote majority in the National Assembly, soon persuaded him that parliament was a frail reed on which to lean in waging what he believed was a life-and-death struggle for his country. Taking advantage of a constitutional crisis on March 4, 1933, to declare that parliament had abolished itself through its own actions, he announced that henceforth he would rule by emergency decrees.[22]

However, the chancellor rid himself of the troublesome opposition in parliament of the Social Democrats only to find himself more dependent than before on the Heimwehr and on Benito Mussolini, who regarded the Heimwehr as an instrument to coerce Dollfuss to set «Austrian internal policies on a fascist course.»[23] In February, 1934, Mussolini and the Heimwehr goaded the Republican *Schutzbund* into taking defensive measures which proved to be the opening shots of a catastrophic civil war whose end was permanent alienation of the workers from the regime.[24] Meanwhile, Mussolini and the Heimwehr had induced Dollfuss, as early as May, 1933, to create a Fatherland Front for the purpose of uniting all political parties and all other organizations wishing to serve their fatherland and to fight for its independence.[25] The defeat of the Social Democrats in February, 1934, speeded the completion of an «authoritarian» constitution to replace the democratic one of 1920. Mussolini and the Heimwehr for a long time had been pressing the chancellor to adopt such a course. Finally, he submitted, aware that he was no longer a free agent but was virtually a prisoner of the Heimwehr and Mussolini, both of whom were increasingly impatient with his delaying tactics.[26]

The preamble of the constitution, which was officially proclaimed on May 1, 1934, declared that Austria was a «Christian, German, federal state, on a corporative basis.»[27] For Dollfuss and his supporters a Christian state was not only a state in which the ethical and moral principles of Christianity were to be stressed but also a corporate state based on the fundamental reforms advocated in the papal encyclical *Quadragesimo anno*. By having all economic and cultural activities directed by corporations which possessed considerable autonomy, the authors of the constitution hoped both to create the social and political order spelled out in the papal encyclical and to avoid the evils of socialist, liberal, and capitalist states. On the federal level, two of four advisory bodies, the cultural and economic councils, were to be corporative in nature. The other two were the council of state and the provincial council. After consulting the proper advisory organs, the government was to submit bills to the federal diet, a body composed of fifty-nine members chosen by the four advisory councils and exclusively entrusted with the making of laws.[28] Only lip service was paid to the principle that Austria was a federal state. The chief provincial official, the *Landeshauptmann*, who selected all the chief officials, was appointed by the federal president, with the approval of the chancellor, from a list of three persons submitted to him by the provincial diet. Moreover, most legislation of real importance was reserved for the federal government. In addition, the chancellor could veto all provincial and local laws and remove all officials at these levels.[29] The federal president was little more than a figurehead. He named and dismissed the members of the federal government, but only upon recommendation of the chancellor. All his other actions required the countersignature of the chancellor.[30] Nearly all real power lay in the hands of the chancellor.

Unquestionably, democracy had no place in «the new Austria» that was officially proclaimed on May 1, 1934. True, the constitution contained a bill of rights guaranteeing many of the personal freedoms already secured in advanced democratic states; however, freedom of speech was carefully circumscribed, freedom of assembly was permitted only «within legal limits,» and no mention whatever was made of suffrage rights or the right to bear arms.[31] Moreover, until corporative reorganization was completed, all representatives were to be selected either by the federal president, on the advice of the chancellor, or by the *Landeshauptmann*, who was appointed by the president.[32] In fact, the restructuring of Austria on a corporative basis was still far from completed when the Schuschnigg regime collapsed in March, 1938.

If the new regime instituted by Dollfuss was not democratic, was it fascist? A superficial examination reveals many characteristics of fascism. Dollfuss undoubtedly fits Carsten's description of the charismatic leader who believed in direct action.[33] Moreover, he contributed significantly to the realization of some of Clemenz's «functional ideological dimensions» of fascism: the political and economic suppression of the proletariat; the popularization of the leadership principle; and the creation of a governing system that left the political influence of the old oligarchy largely unimpaired.[34] Then too, under Dollfuss a truly fascist paramilitary party gained a great deal of influence. More important, the chancellor proved unable to resist Mussolini's and the Heimwehr's pressures to inaugurate that corporative state, patterned on the Italian model, which is usually regarded as necessary to fascism. The Dollfuss government also appears to have condoned actions frequently taken in fascist states: censorship of the press, restrictions on the right of public assembly, proscription of opposition parties, appointment of all key officials by the president upon the advice of the chancellor, establishment of a hierarchical chain of command from the top down to the local commune, and the retention of effective control over legislation and of wide emergency powers by the chancellor. And he even established concentration camps. The Fatherland Front, which was intended eventually to develop into a state party similar to the Italian fascist party, also had many of the attributes of fascism.

Various external trappings of fascism were thus in evidence during the Dollfuss regime. However, a look beneath the surface trappings of the government and the rhetoric of both the enthusiastic supporters and strong opponents of a regime may reveal a discrepancy between the actions of the government and its stated policies. Moreover, various practices frequently dubbed «fascist» may also exist in non-fascist states. The key to the matter is the spirit in which and degree to which a government's policies are carried out and the extent to which individual liberties are effectively curbed. Hierarchical administrative structures and the practice of appointing key governing officials on the nomination of a prime minister are not necessarily limited to fascist countries. The press and certain personal freedoms are also limited in democracies. In Austria they were, of course, curbed more than in democratic states. After the February, 1934, civil war, there were widespread arrests and imprisonments of Social Democrats. But the terms of imprisonment were usually brief. Moreover, various party units and the trade unions continued to exist, although illegally, without suffering more than petty persecution. According to Austrian and to foreign observers living in Austria in 1937–1938 there was nothing even vaguely resembling the mass persecution of socialists that occurred in fascist Italy or Nazi Germany. As for the existence of concentration camps, even G.E.R. Gedye, who was anything but a friend of the Dollfuss regime, admits that life was relatively easy at Wöllersdorf.[35] In regard to efforts to restructure the state on a corporative basis, Dollfuss made no secret of his desire to base the corporative structure on the *Quadragesimo anno* rather than on the Italian fascist model.

The difference between specific practices in Austria and those in genuine fascist countries such as Italy became even more pronounced during the chancellorship of Dollfuss' successor Kurt von Schuschnigg. A reserved and shy «intellectual» who never succeeded in establishing close relations with the masses,[36] Schuschnigg lacked the charismatic personality and popular appeal of a Mussolini or Hitler, or even of a Starhemberg or Dollfuss, which has been a distinguishing mark of successful fascist leaders. Unlike strong fascist leaders, he never succeeded in keeping his key officials from publicly criticizing his government. For instance, it was an open secret that Federal President Wilhelm Miklas frequently criticized the «authoritarian» regime among various circles of personal friends.[37] Of much greater significance to Schuschnigg's image as a fascist was his removal in May, 1936, of Vice-Chancellor Starhemberg from the government and from leadership of the Fatherland Front, the one and only fascist party supporting the regime. When the Heimwehr was dissolved and incorporated into the Fatherland Front the following October, the man frequently denounced as a fascist chancellor no longer even had a fascist party at his disposal. The Fatherland Front, into which the Heimwehr and all other paramilitary formations and political organizations supporting the government were incorporated, never amounted to more than an amorphous body which only vaguely represented a fascist party. At best, it was a facade for the various groups supporting the government; at worst, «a cover under which the old party dissension continued.»[38]

Even though many of the preconditions for fascism existed in Austria prior to 1933, and although various fascist trappings were clearly visible from then until 1938, the supporters of the Dollfuss-Schuschnigg regime were probably right in insisting that between 1933 and 1938 Austria was in essence not a fascist but an authoritarian state[39] – one which, unlike fascist states, does not seek to create a new type of man but allows the individual to act according to the dictates of his own conscience: one which merely limits but does not abolish freedom; and one which changes political institutions for the purpose of preserving or restoring old cultural and economic values rather than implementing cultural and social revolutions.[40] The few social scientists who have formulated general hypotheses about the attributes of fascism and applied them to Austria support this contention. Carsten maintains that Mussolini's efforts to impose a fascist regime in Austria ended in failure.[41] Seton-Watson writes of the government: «It was without doubt reactionary, but it is hard to say whether it was fascist.»[42] Nolte points out that «Austrian Heimwehr fascism» and »Austro-fascism» are not one and the same thing. Although «Starhemberg might be said to have been more of a Fascist than an aristocrat,» he argues, «this would not be true of either Dollfuss or Schuschnigg.»[43] Lipset refers to the Dollfuss-Schuschnigg government as a «dictatorship of Austrian clerical conservatives,»[44] while Clemenz calls it «a bourgeois-conservative dictatorship.»[45]

On the whole, they are right. Dollfuss and Schuschnigg did succeed in resisting the Heimwehr's and Mussolini's urgings to turn Austria into an out-and-out fascist state patterned on the Italian model. Even though fascist leanings are clearly visible in the May 1, 1934, constitution and though some of the policies pursued by the government were quite similar to, or in a few instances the same as, those of fascist states, the actual practices of the Dollfuss-Schuschnigg government generally followed the authoritarian pattern much more closely than the fascist one. At the minimum, the Dollfuss-Schuschnigg regime was basically a bourgeois-conservative dictatorship or a dictatorship of clerical conservatives. At the most, it was what Otto Bauer referred to as a «half-fascist dictatorship.»[46] Ernst Karl Winter probably came closest to the truth when he wrote that the «authoritarian» regime was «a compromise between political Catholicism and Heimwehr fascism».[47]

Certainly, the preconditions for fascism, as spelled out by social scientists, existed in Austria in the 1920s and 1930s. But that did not mean that the rise of fascism was inevitable, for these are also the preconditions for authoritarianism.

NOTES

[1] Grete Klingenstein, «Bemerkungen zum Problem des Faschismus in Österreich,» *Österreich in Geschichte und Literatur,* Vol. XIV (1970), No. 1, pp. 1–13.

[2] Fritz Fellner, «The Background of Austrian Fascism,» in Peter F. Sugar (ed.), *Native Fascism in the Successor States, 1918–1945* (Santa Barbara, Calif.: ABC-Clio Press, 1971), pp. 15–23.

[3] Kurt von Schuschnigg, *The Brutal Takeover: The Austrian ex-Chancellor's Account of the Anschluss with Austria by Hitler* (New York: Atheneum, 1971), p. 35.

[4] See especially G. Germani, «Fascism and Class,» in S. J. Woolf (ed.), *The Nature of Fascism* (New York: Random House, 1968), pp. 73–77.

[5] H. R. Trevor-Roper, «The Phenomenon of Fascism,» in S. J. Woolf (ed.) , *European Fascism* (London: Weidenfeld and Nicolson, 1968), pp. 20–24.

[6] George L. Mosse, «Introduction: The Genesis of Fascism,» *Journal of Contemporary History*, Vol. I (1966), No. 1, pp. 14–15; George L. Mosse, «Fascism and the Intellectuals,» in Woolf, *The Nature of Fascism,* p. 214.

[7] Hans Buchheim, *Totalitarian Rule, Its Nature and Characteristics* (Middletown, Conn.: Wesleyan University Press, 1968), pp. 23–24.

[8] For the whole argument, see especially Seymour Martin Lipset, *Political Man: The Social Bases of Politics* (Garden City, N. Y.: Anchor Books, 1963), pp. 127–148 and 176–178.

[9] Francis I. Carsten, *Der Aufstieg des Faschismus in Europa* (Frankfurt am Main: Europäische Verlagsanstalt, 1968), pp. 273–281.

[10] See especially Erika Weinzierl-Fischer, «Österreichs Katholiken und der Nationalsozialismus,» *Wort und Wahrheit*, Vol. XVIII (1963), No. 5, pp. 418–419.

[11] Hugh Seton-Watson, «Fascism, Right and Left,» *Journal of Contemporary History*, Vol. I (1966), No. 1, pp. 183–184.

[12] *Ibid.*

[13] T. W. Mason, «The Primacy of Politics – Politics and Economics in National Socialist Germany,» in Woolf, *The Nature of Fascism,* pp. 165–195; J. Solé-Tura, «The Political 'Instrumentality' of Fascism,» *ibid.,* pp. 42–44.

[14] Ernst Nolte, *Three Faces of Fascism: Action Française, Italian Fascism, National Socialism.* Translated from German by Leila Vennewitz (New York: Holt, Rinehart and Winston, 1966), pp. 20–21. The author's italics have been omitted.

[15] For good summaries of these criteria, see Ernst Hanisch, «Neuere Faschismustheorien,» *Zeitgeschichte*, Vol. I (1973), No. 1, p. 19; and Manfred Clemenz, *Gesellschaftliche Ursprünge des Faschismus* (Frankfurt am Main: Suhrkampf Verlag, 1972), p. 206.

[16] For a brief but thoughtful analysis of the effects of wartime experiences on the development of right-wing attitudes, see especially Adam Wandruszka, «Die Erbschaft von Krieg und Nachkrieg,» in *Österreich 1927 bis 1938. Protokoll des Symposiums in Wien 23. bis 28. Oktober 1972* (Vienna: Verlag für Geschichte und Politik, 1973), p. 23.

[17] For good summaries of Kühnl's basic ideas, see Hanisch, «Neuere Faschismustheorien,» p. 21; and Clemenz, *Gesellschaftliche Ursprünge des Faschismus*, p. 206.

[18] See especially Clemenz, *Gesellschaftliche Ursprünge des Faschismus*, pp. 213–232. See also Hanisch, «Neuere Faschismustheorien,» p. 22.

[19] For Spann's ideas and influence, see John J. Haag, «Othmar Spann and the Politics of 'Totality': Corporatism in Theory and Practice» (unpublished doctoral dissertation, Rice University, 1969).

[20] See especially Hugo Hantsch, «Engelbert Dollfuss (1892–1934)», in Hugo Hantsch (ed.), *Gestalter der Geschicke Österreichs* (Innsbruck: Tyrolia Verlag, 1962), pp. 619–620; Lajos Kerekes, *Abenddämmerung einer Demokratie. Mussolini, Gömbös und die Heimwehr* (Vienna: Europa Verlag, 1966), p. 105; Ludwig Jedlicka, «Das autoritäre System in Österreich. Ein Beitrag zur Geschichte der europäischen Rechtsbewegungen,» in *Aus Politik und Zeitgeschichte. Beilage zur Wochenzeitung das Parlament*, B 30/70 (July 25, 1970), p. 8; Irmgard Bärnthaler, *Die Vaterländische Front. Geschichte und Organisation* (Vienna: Europa Verlag, 1971), pp. 71-72; and Friedrich Funder, *Als Österreich im Sturm bestand. Aus der Erste in der Zweite Republik* (3rd ed., Vienna: Herold Verlag, 1957), pp. 67–68 and 181.

[21] Julius Deutsch believes that Hitler's coming to power in Germany convinced Dolfuss «that the democratic era was at an end» and that «the hour for totalitarianism had also come to Austria.» See his *Ein weiter Weg. Lebenserinnerungen* (Vienna: Amalthea Verlag, 1960), p. 189.

[22] For an excellent analysis of the evaluations of Dollfuss' abolition of parliament by conservatives and socialists and in recent works of Austrian historians, see Gerhard Botz, «Die Ausschaltung des Nationalrates und die Anfänge der Diktatur Dollfuss im Urteil der Geschichtsschreibung von 1933 bis 1973,» in *Vierzig Jahre danach. Der 4. März 1933 im Urteil von Zeitgenossen und Historikern* (Vienna: Dr. Karl Renner Institut, 1973), pp. 33–59.

[23] Ludwig Jedlicka, «The Austrian Heimwehr,» *Journal of Contemporary History*, Vol. I (1966), No. 1, p. 143.

[24] Among the extensive writings on the civil war, see especially *Das Jahr 1934: 12. Februar. Protokoll des Symposiums in Wien am 5. Februar 1974* (Vienna: Verlag für Geschichte und Politik, 1975); Kerekes, *Abenddämmerung einer Demokratie*, pp. 176–187; Ludwig Jedlicka, «Neue Forschungsergebnisse zum 12. Februar 1934,» *Österreich in Geschichte und Literatur*, Vol. VIII (1964), No. 2, pp. 69–87; Ludwig Jedlicka, «Das Jahr 1934,» in *Österreich 1918–1938* (Vienna: Verlag Ferdinand Hirt, 1970), pp. 73–82; Otto Bauer, *Der Aufstand der österreichischen Arbeiter. Seine Ursachen und seine Wirkungen* (2nd ed., Prague: Verlag der deutschen sozialdemokratischen Arbeiter-Partei in der Tschechoslowakischen Republik, 1934), pp. 14–18; and Rudolf Neck, «Der Februar 1934. Die politische Entwicklung,» in *Österreich 1927 bis 1938*, pp. 107–108.

[25] *Between Hitler and Mussolini. The Memoirs of Ernst Rüdiger Prince Starhemberg* (New York: Harper, 1942) (hereafter cited as «Starhemberg, *Memoirs*»), pp. 101–108. For the organization of the Fatherland Front, see especially Bärnthaler, *Die Vaterländische Front*, pp. 11–12 and 22–27; and Guido Zernatto, *Die Wahrheit über Österreich* (New York: Longman, Green, and Co., 1938), pp. 79–85.

[26] See especially Funder, *Als Österreich den Sturm bestand*, p. 78; Suvich to Dollfuss, Rome, January 26, 1934, Jedlicka, «Neue Forschungsergebnisse zum 12. Februar 1934,» p. 71; Sir J. Simon to Sir E. Drummond, Foreign Office, 10.30 P. M., February 12, 1934, *ibid.*, p. 78; and Sir W. Selby to Sir. J. Simon, Vienna, February 17, 1934, *ibid.*, pp. 79–80.

[27] See *Die neue Bundesverfassung für Österreich samt Übergangsverfassung. Mit Erläuterungen von Dr. Kurt Schuschnigg* (Vienna: Styrermühl Verlag, 1936), p. 95. See also Schuschnigg's explanations of the meaning of the preamble in *ibid.*, pp. 92–93; and my own article on «Authoritarian Austria,» in Sugar, *Native Fascism in the Successor States, 1918–1945*, pp. 24–25.

[28] See articles 46–72 of the May 1, 1934, constitution, *Die neue Bundesverfassung für Österreich samt Übergangsverfassung*, pp. 109–118; Schuschnigg's explanation of these articles in *ibid.*, pp. 48–58 and 90–91; and Eric Voegelin, *Der autoritäre Staat. Ein Versuch über das österreichische Staatsproblem* (Vienna: Julius Springer, 1936), pp. 233–235 and 237–251.

[29] See articles 34–43 and 114 of the May 1, 1934, constitution, *Die neue Bundesverfassung für Österreich samt Übergangsverfassung*, pp. 102–109 and 126–127.

[30] See articles 10 and 73–94 of the May 1, 1934, constitution, *ibid.*, pp. 30–32, 58–62, 76–78, and 120; and Voegelin, *Der autoritäre Staat*, pp. 189–199.

[31] See articles 15–33 of the May 1, 1934, constitution, *Die neue Bundesverfassung für Österreich samt Übergangsverfassung*, pp. 97–101.

[32] See paragraph 21, section 2, and paragraph 29, section 1, of the *Übergangsgesetz* of June 19, 1934, in *Übergangsbestimmungen zur neuen österreichischen Verfassung*, with an Introduction and Explanations by Federal Minister Dr. Otto Ender (Vienna: Österreichischer Bundesverlag für Unterricht, Wissenchaft und Kunst, 1934), pp. 25–28.

[33] See Carsten, *Der Aufstieg des Faschismus in Europa*, especially pp. 274–275.

[34] See Clemenz, *Gesellschaftliche Ursprünge des Faschismus*, pp. 213–232.

[35] G. E. R. Gedye, *Betrayal in Central Europe. Austria and Czechoslovakia: The Fallen Bastions* (New York: Harper, 1939), p. 156.

[36] Ernst Hoor, *Österreich 1918–1938. Staat ohne Republikaner* (Vienna: Österreichischer Bundesverlag für Unterricht, Wissenschaft und Kunst, 1966), p. 116; Oswald Dutch [pseudonym], *Thus Died Austria* (London: Edward Arnold & Co., 1938), p. 131; Elisabeth Barker, *Austria 1918–1972* (Coral Gables, Fla.: University of Miami Press, 1973), p. 98.

[37] See Emmerich Czermak diary, October 15, 1937, and January 10, 1938, in Ludwig Jedlicka, «Aus dem politishen Tagebuch des Unterrichtsministers a. D. Dr. Emmerich Czermak,» *Österreich in Geschichte und Literatur*, Vol. VIII (1964), No. 7, p. 333; and No. 8, pp. 362–363; and the diary of Anton Orel, entry numbers 17 and 44, in Ernst Joseph Görlich «Ein Katholik gegen Dollfuss-Österreich. Das Tagebuch des Sozialreformers Anton Orel», *Mitteilungen des Österreichischen Staatsarchivs*, Vol. XXVI (1973), pp. 393 and 411–412.

[38]Starhemberg, *Memoirs*, p. 195. See also Ernst Karl Winter, «Grossdeutsch-Kleindeutsch,» *Wiener Politische Blätter*, Vol. IV, No. 7–8 (July 5, 1936), p. 255; Bärnthaler, *Die Vaterländische Front*, pp. 201–202; and Emmerich Czermak diary, February 13 and November 22, 1937, in Jedlicka, «Aus dem politischen Tagebuch des Unterrichtsministers a.D. Dr. Emmerich Czermak,» No. 6, p. 271; and No. 8, p. 359.

[39] For examples of their arguments, see Zernatto, *Die Wahrheit über Österreich*, pp. 37–38; Kurt von Schuschnigg, *Dreimal Österreich* (Vienna: Thomas-Verlag Jacob Hegner, 1937), pp. 291–292; Franz Rehrl, «Praktisches und Theoretisches zum staatlichen Neuaufbau», *Der Christliche Ständestaat*, Vol. I, No. 9 (February 4, 1934), pp. 3–6; Wilhelm Böhm, «Staatsform und Regierungsform,» *ibid.*, Vol. IV, No. 17 (May 2, 1937), p. 397; and Rudolf Hausleithner, *Der Geist der neuen Ordnung. Einblicke in das päpstliche Gesellschaftsrundschreiben «Quadragesimo Anno»* (Vienna: Typographische Anstalt, 1937), pp. 97–98.

[40] For good analyses of the basic attributes of authoritarianism, see Buchheim, *Totalitarian Rule*, pp. 22–23; Lipset, *Political Man*, p. 130; and Leonard Schapiro, *Totalitarianism* (New York: Praeger, 1972), p. 39.

[41] Carsten, *Der Aufstieg des Faschismus in Europa*, p. 271.

[42] Seton-Watson, «Fascism, Right and Left,» p. 191.

[43] Nolte, *Three Faces of Fascism*, p. 15.

[44] Lipset, *Political Man,* p. 177.

[45] Clemenz, *Gesellschaftliche Ursprünge des Faschismus*, p. 208.

[46] As quoted in Botz, «Die Ausschaltung des Nationalrates und die Anfänge der Diktatur Dollfuss» p. 57.

[47] Ernst Karl Winter, «Das Ende der Aktion,» *Wiener Politische Blätter*, Vol. III, No. 3 (July 21, 1935), p. 147.

PART 3

THE FASCIST CORE COUNTRIES: GERMANY AND ITALY

Peter H. Merkl   Introduction

Peter H. Merkl   The Nazis of the Abel Collection: Why They Joined the NSDAP

Nico Passchier   The Electoral Geography of the Nazi Landslide ....

Friedrich Zipfel   Gestapo and the SD: A Sociographic Profile of The Organizers of Terror

Renzo de Felice   Italian Fascism and the Middle Classes

Joseph Baglieri   Italian Fascism and the Crisis of Liberal Hegemony: 1901–1922

David D. Roberts   Petty Bourgeois Fascism in Italy: Form and Content

Introduction

PETER H. MERKL

Unlike the smaller fascist movements in recent history, the German NSDAP and the Italian fascist party hardly require an introduction. The NSDAP and the PNF far surpassed other fascist movements in their impact on the domestic political system and the world; they proved more disastrous and brutal than most other similar movements and their growth and ultimate fall have as a result produced a large and still growing literature, much of which is cited in the notes of various chapters of this volume. It includes quite a few speculations about the motives of the average party member, such as the literature on the «authoritarian personality.» There are also biographies of some of the more prominent party leaders of the period, such as Benito Mussolini, Hitler, Goebbels, or Hermann Goering, whose motivation, of course, is likely to differ somewhat from that of their followers.[1] There are even studies of the childhood and adolescence of Adolf Hitler and Heinrich Himmler.[2] There are also, in addition to the wide-ranging literature on the fatal weakness of the republic before the Nazi onslaught, some excellent recent histories of the NSDAP during the «fighting years».[3] These histories tend to be on the macro-political level and rarely concern themselves with local situations and with the motivations of small local leaders and their followers.[4] Despite their informative value, therefore, they still leave us with the impression that perhaps we do not really understand the rank-and file Nazis as people.

To be sure, there are also some accounts of local struggles that were published under the Nazi regime. The Institut für Zeitgeschichte in Munich has a collection of such materials.[5] Although generally unsystematic, highly subjective and biased, they can serve as valuable sources because they reflect the self-image and the sense of purpose the principals possessed, which is needed for confirmation of any sound interpretation of their motives. Some of the local materials date from before 1933,[6] and there are now also a few current attempts to fathom the Nazi phenomenon at the local and personal level on the basis of police reports and local government records.[7]

The rise of Italian fascism has generated no less of a literature in several languages and with varying emphasis on the movement as such. Partly due to the longer duration of Mussolini's dictatorship, there are also more contributions by secret sympathizers and propagandists.[8] Major recent works such as the writings of Renzo de Felice[9] or, in English, Adrian Lyttelton,[10] treat and include bibliographical references on many aspects including the nature of the rank and file of the PNF. By way of an introduction to the contributions in this section, it may be best to concentrate on the three themes that have occasioned particular controversy and occupied contributors to this volume.

The Class Issue

First, there is the so-called *class character* of fascist movements which might be demonstrated either by their «predominantly» bourgeois or petty-bourgeois character or by the support given them or control exercised over them by distinctive elements of «the old ruling classes» such as the land-owning nobility, the industrial entrepreneurs, or the military establishment. Reinhard Kühnl, Alan Milward, Bernt Hagtvet and other contributors to the theoretical section of this volume have explored these questions in considerable depth as well as the existing literature on them, especially with regard to Germany.[11] My study of the Abel Collection also touches on this theme, as does the comparative study of Juan J. Linz.

The three essays on the Italian fascist movement expressly deal with this question, Joseph Baglieri's by linking the movement to the disintegration of the earlier political leadership and those of Renzo de Felice and David Roberts by examining its alleged «middle-class» character. This thesis of the fascist party as a «middle-class» movement goes back to the writings of Luigi Salvatorelli, Mario Missiroli and others who in various formulations preferred to see the black-shirted mass movement as a fighting force of the *ceto medio* or, at least, of the lower middle class of small business and handicraft, against the challenge of the rising socialist labor movement. But even at the very beginning of the fascist party, in 1921, Agostino Lancillo and Giovanni Zibordi already distinguished various strong non-bourgeois elements, such as agriculture and the military, and stressed the mixed social composition of the movement, especially among the «Fascists of the first hour.»[12] Mussolini and his local chiefs emphasized the classless character of their fighting movement of «producers» (both capitalists and workers) and «combatants» (both officers and men), and prided themselves on a fascist identity made up of images of «men of action», especially violent action, in contrast to the «men of words», the politicians. At the bottom of the controversy over the significance of the social composition of the fascist party (PNF), as of the NSDAP, lie fundamental questions of interpretation extending also to other wellsprings of motivation. The student of fascist movements has to decide what might have shed the greatest light on their motivation at the time among such factors as their generally mixed «class character,» their youthfulness, their rural-urban mix, their war- or veteran-related origins, or the more or less violent postures they struck.

Table 1 compares the occupational composition of the PNF of 1921 and the NSDAP of 1930 (1933) at a point when the two parties had grown to comparable size and had not yet succeeded in placing their respective leaders in office. The statistics have obvious limitations owing to their sources, but we have tried to make them comparable and to juxtapose them with the population statistics of those years. The comparison shows not only the expected relative underrepresentation of blue-collar workers and the overrepresentation of white-collar groups and civil service in both movements, as mentioned also by Seymour M. Lipset and many others;[13] it also brings out in spite of its limitations such glaring differences as the larger role of agricultural laborers and urban students in the PNF while the NSDAP appears to have a more disproportionate share of small business and handicraft. Farmers are underrepresented in both parties, probably owing to their low organizability. The working class element, especially if we add agricultural laborers, is far less underrepresented in the PNF than it is in the National Socialist Workers Party (NSDAP) in highly industrialized Weimar Germany.

The same source on the PNF of 1921 also states that about 25 per cent of it were under 21, mostly students, which can be compared with the age breakdowns of table 2 for the NSDAP. About 80 per cent of all males in the PNF of military age were said to be veterans which is about the same as in the NSDAP of 1930, except that by 1930 a whole new generation of younger people had grown up who had not been of military

Table 1. *Occupations of NSDAP and PNF before Takeover*

(a) Abel-Merkl breakdown: NSDAP 1933			(b) PNF 1921		(c) Italian Population 1921 (%)	(d) NSDAP 1930		German Population 1933 (%)
Occupation	n	%	Occupation	%		Occupation	%	
Agricultural laborers	8	1.4	Agricultural laborers	24.3	22.8			
Workers	169	28.6	Workers	15.4	24.0	Workers	26.8	46.3
			Seamen	1.0	2.3			
White collar	106	17.9	White collar	9.8	.9	White collar	24.0	12.4
Public employees	49	8.2	Public employees	4.8	2.0	Civil service	7.7	4.8
Teachers	16	2.7	Teachers	1.1				
Civil servants	64	10.7						
Professions (and students)	25	4.2	Students	13.0	1.4	Business and professions (and students)	19.9	9.6
Small business and handicraft	63	10.6	Entrepreneurs	2.8	1.1			
			Small business and artisans	9.2	12.3			
Farmers	36	6.0	Farm owners	12.0	32.3	Farmers	13.2	20.7
Others (officers)	22	3.7				Pensioners and others	5.3	6.2
Women	36	6.0	Women	6.6	–	Housewives	3.6	–
		100%		100%	100%		100%	100%
n = 594			n = 151,644			n = 129,563		

a Source: Peter H. Merkl, *Political Violence Under the Swastika: 581 Early Nazis*, Princeton University Press, 1975, pp. 13–15, 63–65, also p. 561.

b *Il popolo d'Italia*, Nov. 8, 1921.

c From P. Sylos-Labini in P. Farneti, ed., *Il sistema politico italiano*, Bologna, 1973, pp. 100ff., with some adjustments.

d *NSDAP Parteistatistik*, Reichsorganisationsleiter, 1935.

age in 1918. For the PNF, this high proportion of veterans confirms the impression that Italian fascism in 1921 was composed largely of rather young, able-bodied males. The NSDAP of 1930, by comparison, was not quite that youthful, at least outside of the stormtrooper (SA) ranks. In comparison to the older German parties, the bourgeois parties and the SPD, it may have been a «party of youth.» In the years from the 1930 elections to Hitler's appointment, however, it became distinctly older and more like its moderate rivals.[14]

Table 2. *Age of Members of the NSDAP 1930*[a]

NSDAP 1930 Party Statistics		Abel-Merkl Breakdown		German Population 1939	
14 – 25	36.8%	14 – 20	8.7%	– 20	32.7%
		21 – 23	10.9%		
26 – 35	31.4%	24 – 27	21.3%	20 – 45	39.3%
		28 – 34	28.5%		
36 – 45	17.6%	35 – 44	16.4%	45 – 65 (and over 65)	28.0%
46 – 55	9.7%	45 – 51	6.8%		
Over 56	4.5%	52 – 70	7.4%		
	100.0%		100.0%		100.0%
n = 129,563		n = 321			

a) There is a breakdown of sorts on age among the casualties of the PNF in the years 1919 to 1924 in the obituaries of *Pagina Eroiche della Rivoluzione Fascista,* Rome: PNF, 1925. Of the 471 listed, 163 indicate their age at the time of death: 27.6% were 18 or younger, 53.5% 19–25, 11% 26–30, and 7.9% over 30, according to Joseph Baglieri. However, this flawed sample indicates only the age at which young men are likely to engage in street violence rather than age averages of the PNF.

Changes in Composition

To further complicate any discussion of the origins (whether rooted in class issues, youthful rebelliousness or war) of any particular fascist movement, there is also the record of constant changes in composition. In the few years before the March on Rome, the Italian fascists underwent the most extraordinary metamorphosis from their interventionistic, revolutionary syndicalist antecedents to the «anti-Bolshevik» assault on the socialist establishment, and from short-lived alliances with right-wing socialists and Republicans to dependence on certain industrialists in Milan. Since Mussolini and his revolutionary syndicalist henchmen had failed to attract more than a small élite following both among the urban working class and among veteran *arditi* (shock troops) and officers, it was quite logical that they would rely heavily on the petty bourgeois youth of students, shopkeepers, artisans, and white-collar employees who flocked to them in search of the excitement of combat. The development of the armed squads of the movement, beginning in mid-1919 and culminating in the mass-mobilization phase of 1920/1922, again shifts the character of the movement toward military influence and organization and the recruitment of former army officers to train and lead the *squadristi* in paramilitary action. The nationalist agitation at the ethnic border, in Trieste and Venezia Giulia permitted the fascists to combine convincingly their ethnic patriotism with anti-socialist reaction and the glamor of quasimilitary action against Slavs and «Bolsheviks». In response to the agricultural strikes and socialist seizure of factories in 1920, finally, the rapid expansion of the movement in 1920/1921 created a vast army of students, military men, agrarians and some of their laborers in the provinces and small towns of the North and center which came in time to rival the influence of the metropolitan movement. The agrarian element appears in due proportion (36.3 per cent) in our table above, along with the students (13 per cent) and the more typical urban middle class element (38.3 per cent) which we would identify with a «fascism of the center.»

After the March on Rome, several distinctive groups struggled for influence within the movement: the personal following of Mussolini, the hardfisted élitists of the local and regional «extremist» fascist leaders who came to occupy many leading positions in the party, and the fascist syndicalists whose organizations had expanded greatly under the protection of the anti-socialist violence of the *squadrismo*. Since the local chiefs had taken over the party and, in alliance with the syndicalists, kept Mussolini from dominating his own party, the central leadership embarked on another big membership drive in 1923. These «Fascists of the second hour» mirrored especially the governmental coalitions with the right wing, mergers with various regional parties (e.g. *Partito Sardo d'Azione)*, and the systematic expansion of the PNF in the traditional Nationalist South. The partial absorption of certain veterans and syndicalist groups, and the converts from the Republican and other parties at an earlier stage were new elements that again changed the character of Italian fascism. If Mussolini had had his way in making an alliance with the socialists in 1921, or in bringing in the Socialist Trade Union Federation (CGL) after 1922, the change would have been in a left-wing direction. Instead, the PNF became more bourgeois and more Nationalist, and more southern agrarian, but its change also strengthened Mussolini's faction in the end. With the PNF's emergence as the state party, (and in the wake of another big recruitment drive in 1926) it underwent one more crucial change that tended to make its social composition increasingly irrelevant: the internal election of leaders was replaced with appointment from above. Its members henceforth became merely cogs in the wheels of the totalitarian state, elements whose «class character,» age, military, or regional origins were no longer a motive force behind the regime.

The Changing Nazi Party

Similar if smaller changes complicate any assessment of the NSDAP. The Nazi party was born as a predominantly lower middle-class party with ambitions of attracting urban working class support. Most of its members were independent craftsmen, white-collar employees, and such difficult-to-classify people as Hitler himself or the journalist, Karl Harver. Very soon, in any case, the influx of veterans and army officers, along with the financial support of the *Reichswehr*, gave the party a very different character. The Storm Troopers (SA), under professional military leadership, took in entire Free Corps units and played a major role in determining the course of the party. On the other hand, mergers with more clearly petty-bourgeois groups, such as the *Deutschsoziale Partei* in 1923, and much of the following of the *völkisch Schutz-und-Trutzbund*,[15] not to mention Hitler's personal preferences and connections, again pulled the party in a bourgeois direction. The right-wing turbulence of the year 1923, in any case, involved the NSDAP so deeply in alliances with militant far-right organizations ranging from the veteran *Kampfbund* to Bavarian conservatives, as to obscure any «class character» it might have possessed. When the party was reestablished in 1925, its «northern faction» for a while tended to pull it strongly into a «socialistic» direction.[16] It also became notably more urban, only to shift its weight once more to the countryside in 1929/1930 as the agricultural crisis drove many farmers, lower middle class citizens, and lower officials into its arms. In the late twenties, also, the NSDAP succeeded in attracting (through its student and professional associations) the kind of upper middle-class following that had eluded the movement so far. The role of the educated middle class became very pronounced after 1933 when well-qualified careerists replaced the rough and ready stormtroopers of the «fighting days» in many responsible positions. The Nazi appeal to working-class elements was at first successful only with certain small groups such as a) a labor élite of foremen and skilled workers or dependent craftsmen, b) some traditional groups such as the German Brewers Association, and c) workers hostile to the socialist labor movement (including the trade unions) because of their nationalistic or anti-Semitic views. Even the foundation of the Factory Cell Organization (NSBO) in 1929 did not contribute much to Nazi inroads into the solid ranks of organized blue-collar until the years of massive unemployment, when very young workers, in particular, joined the stormtroopers and sought open confrontation with socialists and communists. The resistance of the organized working-classes to the brown virus throughout most of the «fighting years» made their sudden surrender in mid-1933 all the more puzzling.

Where does the waxing and waning of various class elements really leave the question of «class character» of these two fascist movements? Is it meaningful to reduce this undeniable heterogeneity of social origins and habitats to a single «class character» for the sole purpose of thus fitting it into the clash of capital and labor? Would it not make more sense, perhaps, to look for other wellsprings of political motivation such as the dynamics of social mobility, rural-urban differences, or the generational conflict stressed by both, the PNF and the NSDAP?

Contributors and Supporters

Considerably easier to interpret, though not necessarily without ambiguity, is the record of who supported these fascist movements with money and in other ways. Mussolini's early years of building up the movement were distinguished by so many mindboggling about-faces in appealing alternately to the right and the left that one might be tempted to assume he must have alienated any support he enjoyed from the established forces. However, he and his newspaper, *Il Popolo d'Italia*, could always count on financial contributions from certain Milan industrialists who probably perceived even his more extreme appeals to the left as a skilful attempt to outbid the socialists and to win working-class and veteran support for nationalistic causes such as claiming Fiume for Italy. The fascists also enjoyed a great deal of support and sympathy in their armed assault on socialist and trade union centers from the local police and administrators. At the time of their March on Rome, furthermore, when the king refused to sign the emergency decree prepared by the Facta government, it was probably on the advice of his generals. The sympathy for the PNF of large parts of the officer corps and of whole military garrisons at the time the fascists seized strongpoints and communications centers are well-known.

To put the role of industry in a more appropriate light than is suggested by the simplistic dichotomies of capital and labor, one has to see it as only one among several well-established forces of Italian society at the time, especially the Church, the monarchy, the military, and the bureaucracy, which have never formed anything like a unified «ruling class» except in isolated situations as with the bourgeois-agrarian supporters of fascism in the Po Valley. Within these limitations, however, the evidence of industrial support for the PNF is conclusive throughout from the testimony of various officers of *Confindustria*, the association of Italian industry. There is a consensus among former *Confindustria* leaders and historians alike that Italian industrialists decided to back Mussolini long before the March on Rome and to stick with him throughout the ups and downs of the years until the consolidation of his dictatorship.[17] This is not to say that Mussolini and the PNF were their political instrument or that they were very happy with fascist radicalism and crude behavior generally.

The allies and supporters of Hitler and the NSDAP during the years before 1933 present a picture with far weaker accents on the support of army and industry and, of course, no monarchy. During the first years of the NSDAP in Bavaria, the party maintained good relations with the army there and with well-connected militant organizations of the right, but during the years of expansion throughout Germany the party was viewed with a mixture of disdain and apprehension by the military leadership whose partiality to conservative, authoritarian solutions did not favor the Nazi party. The neutrality of an army which was neither willing to defend the republic nor to destroy it in league with the usurper was the best Hitler could hope for.

As for the support of German big business, Henry A. Turner, Jr. has described tellingly its lack of commitment to the Weimar Republic, but also its general political indecision and ineffectiveness. Industry money found its way into Nazi coffers only in isolated cases such as that of steel magnates Fritz Thyssen or Friedrich Flick and when the Nazis cooperated with better-connected parties, such as with Hugenberg's DNVP during the Young Plan campaign of 1929. Hitler did his best to woo heavy industry throughout the years of the Nazi build-up, only to see its support go again and again to rivals such as von Papen who by any standard of support from the «leading circles» of Weimar society should have won out in the end. German industry came around to Hitler only late in 1932 in reaction against the cabinet of General von Schleicher, whose plans for an alliance of the army with labor they feared. Even then, their backing played a negligible role in the intrigues leading to Hitler's appointment as Chancellor and their funds began to flow only in time for the Nazi election campaign of March, 1933, and after Hitler was already in power.[18] It is hardly factual, then, to speak of Hitler and the NSDAP as an instrument of German big business or of the army, or to describe these two and other elements as «the ruling class» of Germany.

A third question still pursued by scholars is an analysis of who voted for the NSDAP in the numerous national, state, and local elections in which they presented candidates. Bernt Hagtvet in his contribution to this volume has reviewed some of the evidence and cited the relevant literature. Nico Passchier in this section adds to this a sophisticated analysis of the regional context of the Nazi candidates in order to show the sources of Nazi support and how voters were abandoning certain other parties in favor on the NSDAP.

By 1933, when Hitler came to power, the Nazi party had attracted more than a million members and 14 million voters. The key to Hitler's power in 1933 lies in the character of these men and women who joined his movement or voted for it, making it the strongest popular party of the day, though not a majority. Without them and without their motivations, whatever they may have been, he would have remained a powerless figure, a shrieking orator of no consequence. In the case of Mussolini, the number of members was well over 300,000 at the time of the March on Rome and nearly 800,000 by the end of 1923. The following year the PNF and its allies received 65 per cent of the vote in national elections, after a campaign of terror. Who were these people who would not rest until they had plunged their countries into the long night of totalitarian dictatorship and war? What did they want and what were they hoping to achieve?

Who Were They?

To ask who were the German Nazis or the Italian fascists is to ask a question admitting many different kinds of answers. It does not limit us to any particular research method or discipline of social science although we have chosen to strive for an empirical answer rather than to search for a quasi-Platonic «essence of National Socialism.» It has long been popular with writers to manufacture such an essence out of a combination of non-empirical sociological analysis of the movement and a sweeping interpretation of Nazi ideology, especially in the form of a «German tradition from Luther to Hitler,» as one American school of thought used to put it, or of «Italian national character.» One kind of answer to the question *who were they?* is indeed ideological in nature requiring a commitment to another political faith or movement. Another kind of answer deals with individuals and would have to take into account a curious mixture of feelings and ideas which our first essay, among other things, attempts to explore: the latent insecurity of the «national bourgeoisie,» the impact of the war experience on attitudes toward the use of violence, raw anti-Semitic prejudice and other fears, but also the vague *völkisch* ideology and cultural pessimism of countless groups and pre-war publications.

Partial answers to the question *who were they?* can be attempted by an analysis of the social background of the pre-1933 Nazi rank and file, of the leadership, or of a particular group such as the Gestapo (secret police) and SD (security service) after the seizure of power. The NSDAP itself compiled statistics on its membership in 1935 which are very revealing although they may not be beyond challenge. The information on the PNF is much sketchier. Even within such an examination of social origins, there are many different paths of analysis. A social historian might look for changing social milieus or the phenomena of migration and urbanization. An economist might trace the motivating forces of the individual member, leader or voter to the compulsions of unemployment or bankruptcy. A neo-Marxist might seek to link the Nazi behavior with the way a person's occupation and social status relate to the processes of production. A social psychologist again might look for personality types and personal motivations to join or vote for the rising Nazi or fascist movements. And there is also the generational angle which pits the fascist battle cry of youth against the bourgeois gerontocracy of the Weimar Republic or the Italian monarchy.

NOTES

[1] Joachim C. Fest, *The Face of the Third Reich*, New York: Pantheon, 1970 is particularly noteworthy in its portraits of typical Nazi figures. F. L. Carsten, *The Rise of Fascism*, Univ. of California Press, 1967, also brings out the personal features of Nazi and Italian fascist leaders.

[2] Bradley F. Smith, *Adolf Hitler: His Family, Childhood and Youth*, and *Heinrich Himmler, A Nazi in the Making 1900–1926*, both Stanford: Hoover Institution, 1969 and 1971. See also Robert G. L. Waite, «Adolf Hitler's Guilt Feelings: A Problem in History and Psychology,» *Journal of Interdisciplinary History*. II: 2 (Winter 1971), 229–249 and «Adolf Hitler's Anti-Semitism: A Study in History and Psychoanalysis,» in Benjamin B. Wolman, ed., *The Psychoanalytic Interpretation of History*, New York: Basic Books, 1971, pp. 192–230.

[3] Most recently Dieter Orlow, *The History of the Nazi Party, 1919–1933*, Pittsburgh: University of Pittsburgh Press, 1969. See also Georg Franz Willing, *Die Hitlerbewegung: Der Ursprung 1919–1922*, Hamburg: Schenck, 1962; Ulrich Lohalm, *Völkischer Radikalismus*, Hamburg: Leibniz, 1970, on the early period and on the *völkisch* antecedents of the NSDAP, and the first chapters of Karl D. Bracher's *The German Dictatorship*, New York, Praeger, 1969. See also the account in Heinrich August Winkler, *Mittelstand, Demokratie und Nationalsozialismus, Die politische Entwicklung von Handwerk und Kleinhandel in der Weimarer Republik*, Cologne: Kiepenheuer & Witsch, 1972, on the motives of Nazi converts among small businesses and handicrafts.

[4] There are, of course, excellent regional studies such as Rudolf Heberle, *Landbevölkerung und Nationalsozialismus*, Stuttgart, 1963. See also Jeremy Noakes, *The Nazi Party in Lower Saxony, 1921–1933*, Oxford University Press, 1971; Max H. Kele, *Nazis and Workers: National Socialist Appeals to German Labor 1919–1933*, Chapel Hill: North Carolina University Press, 1973, and of course, William S. Allen's *The Nazi Seizure of Power, The Experience of a Single German Town*, University of Chicago Press, 1965.

[5] For example, A. Gimbel, *So Kämpften wir! Schilderungen aus der Kampfzeit im Gau Hessen-Nassau*, Frankfurt: NS Verlagsgesellschaft, 1941; R. Hochmuth, ed., *Koburg, Nationalsozialismus in der Praxis*, Berlin, 1932; Will Hermanns, *Stadt in Ketten, Geschichte der Besatzungs- und Separatistenzeit 1918–1929*, Aachen: J. A. Mayer, 1933; Friedrich Heiss, *Das Schlesienbuch*, Berlin: Volk und Reich, 1938; Wilfrid Bade, *SA erobert Berlin*, Munich, Knorr & Hirth, 1941, and many others.

[6] For example, many of the materials published as documents by the Forschungsstelle für die Geschichte des Nationalsozialismus in Hamburg or discussed in appropriate publications of the *Kommission für die Geschichte des Parlamentarismus und der politischen Parteien in Bonn.*

[7] One illuminating account and document collection deals with the efforts of local and regional agencies in the Mainz-Koblenz-Trier area to control the spreading brown poison. Franz J. Heyen, *Nationalsozialismus in Alltag*, Boppard: Boldt Verlag, 1967, pp. 5–7. There are also detailed accounts of Nazi agitation and propaganda in the villages and of violent clashes with the communists (KPD).

[8] One cannot help reading with sympathy the efforts of the respected historian Gaetano Salvemini, for example in his *The Origins of Fascism in Italy*, New York: Harper & Row, 1973, to repudiate or correct the many misleading interpretations spread by apologists of the regime.

[9] See especially his *Mussolini il fascista; la conquista del potere 1921–1925*, Turin; 1966 and *Il fascismo: le interpretazioni dei contemporanei e degli storici*, Bari: 1970.

[10] *The Seizure of Power: Fascism in Italy 1919–1929*, New York: Scribner's 1973.

[11] See esp. note 54ff. in Hagtvet's essay, *supra*, p. 108ff. and the work of Winkler cited above in note 3.

[12] Adrian Lyttelton, *The Seizure of Power: Fascism in Italy 1919–1929*, New York: Scribner's, 1973, chapter 3 and Renzo de Felice, *Mussolini Il Fascista and Il Fascismo*, Bari: 1972 and 1970 provide an excellent summary of the older interpretations of the fascist movement.

[13] Hagtvet, *supra*, p. 82–83.

[14] See Merkl, *Political Violence Under the Swastika*, p. 599.

[15] This little-known proto-fascist organization which was outlawed in 1922, following the assassination of Walter Rathenau, had a reported membership of nearly 500,000, a size which the NSDAP only reached at the height of the struggle in 1932.

[16] On these factional shifts, see especially Joseph Nyomarkay, *Charisma and Factionalism in the Nazi Party*, University of Minnesota Press, 1967, and his essay in Henry A. Turner, Jr., ed. *Nazism and the Third Reich*, New York: Quadrangle Books, 1972, pp. 21–44.

[17] See especially Piero Melograni, *Gli Industriali e Mussolini. Rapporti tra Confindustria e fascismo dal 1919 al 1929*, Milan: Longanesi, 1972 and the diary of Confindustria President (1920/1922) Ettore Conti, *Dal taccuino di un borghese*, Milan: Garzanti 1946; and Felice Guarneri, *Battaglie economiche tra le due grandi guerre*, 2 vols. Milan: Garzanti, 1953. Also Roland Sarti, *Fascism and the Industrial Leadership in Italy, 1919–1940*, Berkeley: University of California Press, 1971, especially his bibliographical note.

[18] See Henry A. Turner, Jr., «Big Business and the Rise of Hitler» in Turner, ed., *Nazism and the Third Reich*, pp. 89–108, especially the bibliographical footnotes. The author does not deny, however, that the NSDAP received substantial support from small and medium-sized business which was more vulnerable to the economic downturn after 1929.

The Nazis of the Abel Collection: Why They Joined the NSDAP

PETER H. MERKL

Barely three decades have passed since the final breaking of the Nazi stranglehold on Germany and on half of Europe, three decades during which vast numbers of books and articles have appeared about the Nazi and fascist movements in Germany and elsewhere. Not all of this literature could be called research. Much of it has been strongly colored by an understandable ideological revulsion against Nazi deeds and Nazi ideology. Only in the last few years, except for some isolated early attempts, have there been empirical, sociological, and comparative studies of individual cases (other than Nazi leaders), motives, and local situations that probe beneath the broad sweep of national histories and the idle speculations about social conditions for the emergence of Nazi or fascist movements.

This is a report on a major study of the background, political socialization, activities, and attitudes of 581 pre-1933 members of the NSDAP whose *vitae* were collected by means of an essay contest in 1934 by a Columbia University sociologist, Theodore Abel.[1] Our analysis of this material consisted in the computer-aided processing and crosstabulation of 79 items of information from the Abel *vitae*. The codes and many of the tables of this study are now available in book form,[2] augmented with quotations from the *vitae*. This presentation will limit itself to some of the highlights of the larger study.

A sample drawn from an essay contest is unlikely to please a social statistician, and there are also questions as to the reliability of the content of the responses, especially regarding attitudes and activities. We shall set forth below how the basic dimensions of the sample differ from comparable indicators of the *Parteistatistik* of 1935. On the positive side we should emphasize that it is probably impossible to get any comparable source today, not to mention a better sample. The date of the original collection was particularly fortunate, for the Abel respondents report with great pride what they would obviously have been most reluctant to recall after the war and the denazification trials. Also, they were evidently still close enough to the fighting years to be able to remember details and feelings they would have forgotten 30 or 40 years later.

The Abel Sample: How Representative, How Reliable?

The Abel sample deviates from the parameters of the *Parteistatistik* of 1935 in the following ways. It has more respondents of the war generation, a flaw most probably related to the fact that a young activist might be less likely to respond to an essay contest. It is also rather heavy on civil servants and pensioners, probably for the same reason. Since Abel's essay contest was evidently promoted[3] more in some regions than in others, we have an unusual number of respondents from Berlin and from the occupied areas of the Rhineland. Finally, there is a heavy preponderance of members who joined before the 1930 elections to the *Reichstag*, in other words before the first electoral landslide and before the influx of hundreds of thousands of *Septemberlinge* (opportunists) into the NSDAP. The Abel sample is thus a rather pure representation of the activist, fighting strain of the pre-1933 Nazi party and has more than its share of storm-troopers and holders of party offices. If we check the dates of joining, the sample turns out to have one out of every 400 pre-1930 Nazis in it – not a bad percentage for any sample.[4]

What then may have been the motives of the Abel Nazis to become involved in the NSDAP and its activities? Were there socio-economic causes that pushed them into a posture of revolt against the established authorities? Were they militarized by their war experiences or politically mobilized by the «still-born revolution» or the counter-revolutionary drives against domestic insurgents and Polish irregulars? Was it just the rising sap of youth which politicized and socialized the entire youth culture of Weimar? Or did these men feel a secret yen for violence and struggle which drove them into a party that would give them an excuse for doing what they really wanted to do? Or was it their anti-Semitic prejudice, or other psychological obsessions, or even discernible ideological goals that they felt they could realize only through a Nazi victory?

The meaning of motive or causation in the social sciences is in itself a matter of controversy. Even if we elicit clear statements of purpose from a principal, is this really his «motive» or is he not really being «moved» by the socio-economic forces as elaborated in a Marxist analysis, by his Freudian subconscious, or by Hegel's «use of reason»? We will have to return to these questions when we relate the different sets of motives to one another at the end of this essay. For the moment, inductive method demands that we look at the different kinds of evidence before we attempt to close the gap between ideology and empirical method.

Socio-Economic Motives

Our first set of questions addresses itself to the social dynamics among the pre-1933 NSDAP as a reason for joining. Was there a discernible socio-economic cause such as the «lower middle-class revolt», or the fascism of social decline that drove people into the Nazi movement? Was it the Depression, or perhaps the resentment of the «losers of the industrial revolution»? As we might have expected, there is no such simple causation at work among the Abel respondents, but rather a complex set of differentiated reasons for the various age and status groups.

Age sharply separates such groups as the older rural-urban migrants who left the farm or estate in the 1880s and 1890s from the war and post-war generations of pre-1933 Nazis. It also distinguishes what may be a mild sense of frustrated upward mobility among these rural-urban migrants from the much more acute frustration of the second generation of new urbanites who grew up in the city with all the educational advantages their farmer or proletarian parents could give them, but who could not maintain their new status because of the economic crises and stagnation of the Weimar Republic. In fact, at least half of the lower middle class respondents of the Abel Collection are in transit from a lower (proletarian) status or declining from a higher (upper middle or upper class) status rather than representing a traditional petty bourgeoisie in revolt.

The most pronounced socio-economic reason for becoming a Nazi among the generation that grew up under the empire, though not affecting large numbers, was a kind of in-between status between the two major camps of bourgeoisie and proletariat. The class resentments of the Imperial sergeant who could never become an officer, the

269

primary school teacher who felt despised by the academically trained professions, or the half-proletarian by birth are typical examples of this misfit or in-between status. Particularly revealing is the analysis of the substantial number of military-civil servants[5] (one fourth) of the Abel Collection whose «unpolitical devotion» to their duty to the Imperial state and army evidently became politicized with the fall of the old regime. Their chief contribution to right-wing violence seems to have taken place before they joined the Nazi party, in the Free Corps and vigilante organizations of the early years of the republic. The conservative military and civil service personnel notably differed in their views from the anti-capitalistic farmers of the Collection, though both shared an intense and aggressive nationalism. On the other hand, the farmers show far less interest in the myth of «blood and soil» than the military and civil service elements show in a prospective renaissance of German power and military glory. To be sure, some of the young farm-owning respondents were motivated by the agricultural crisis and by the farm revolt of 1929/1930. Others again, however, stress their economically dependent status and derive from it a kind of agrarian socialism. The highly stratified nature of agricultural society suggests careful distinction between the respective exposures of early Nazis to the conservative (DNVP of *Stahlhelm*) right or the socialist-communist left. The evident resistance of Catholic rural society to the brown virus side by side with the fatal weakness of rural Protestantism also underscores the importance of faith and tradition in the rural settings. It is evident that neither the military and civil service group nor the farmers fit neatly into the bourgeois or proletarian camps of those days.

To return to the social mobility patterns, it is significant, for example, that 47.2 per cent of the Abel sample were spatially immobile: they never moved from where they were born, apart from temporary absences such as for education or military service. 22.1 per cent were rural-urban migrants and the remaining 30.5 per cent moved around the country or, in a few cases, could even be called drifters.

Table 1. *Spatial and Social Mobility*

	Spatially Immobile	Rural-Urban Migrant	Mobile	
No attempt to rise	60 (45.4%)	27 (35.1%)	44 (45.4%)	
Upwardly mobile	44 (33.3%)	40 (51.9%)	30 (30.9%)	
Decline	20 (15.1%)	7 (9.1%)	20 (20.6%)	
Other	8 (6.2%)	3 (3.9%)	3 (3.1%)	
Total	132 (43.9) (100%)	77 (24.4%) (100%)	97 (31.7%) (100%)	Total 306 (100%)

Those who never moved from where they were born also tended not to be as upwardly mobile as the rural-urban migrants, nor did so many of them suffer social decline as the spatially mobile.[6] This spatially immobile segment furnished the most virulent and violent Nazis of the sample. Far from being the work of «outside agitators», the Nazi revolt was evidently the work of a political opposition arising in its local communities, especially in small towns and in the contryside.

The collection also allows an examination of the impact of social mobility and economic adversity on particular occupational status groups: the upwardly mobile military and civil service element often coming from the countryside, the rising and the static older middle class, the static farmers, and the socially declining women. The white-collar cases in the sample were either upwardly or downwardly mobile, the blue-collar Nazis stagnant or declining. Each group had indeed a recognizable set of socio-economic motives, but the motives were not the same. It was for this reason, also, that the vaunted *Volksgemeinschaft* slogan meant very different things to different groups. The upwardly mobile solidarists of the middle, in particular, meant by it a social prescription quite different from those who looked at the class antagonism from below or from above. They also showed the most anti-Semitic and ethnocentric prejudice.

The impact of the economic troubles of the Weimar Republic on possible motives for joining, finally, is clearly determined by generational groupings. The pre-war generation of the sample suffered hardly any economic adversity, and the war generation only in the years before 1929. It was the post-war generation (born 1902 or later) and among them especially those moving from city to city who encountered unemployment and bankruptcy with a frequency (up to one third) so high as to suggest an important motive. Many young stormtroopers of the Abel Collection indeed report how unemployment and being thrown out by their parents (for being in the SA) left them little choice but to live in a stormtrooper home *(SA-Heim)* and fight round the clock for the movement. Others tell how bankruptcy radicalized them in the direction of Nazi activism. Yet even there, the economic factor appears to have been only a contributory or aggravating reason to join for people already tending in this direction. After all, millions of other unemployed or ruined persons at the same time joined the communists or other paramilitary organizations, or withdrew into non-political concerns.

War and Revolution

A second set of likely motives for joining was related to World War I and its turbulent aftermath. Not that there weren't plenty of other parties and militant veterans' organizations that appealed to the revanchist or to the person disoriented and disturbed by the war experience: but World War I was a veritable watershed of German popular opinion after which even many of the pre-war class resentments of the older Abel respondents seem to have lost their poignancy. The war also greatly intensified the effect of various foreign contact experiences that frequently seem to have driven people into the arms of the superpatriotic Nazi movement. Among these were the experience of having been born abroad or having resided abroad, or in the German colonies, or having settled among Poles in Prussian-held Poznan or among Frenchmen in Metz and evidently having experienced (if only subjectively) intense nationalistic hostility (31 cases).[7] More than one tenth of the sample grew up or lived in the ethnic border areas of the East and were led by their experiences there to join the movement of a fellow ethnic border German, Adolf Hitler. Nearly one fourth of the Abel respondents, furthermore, report a similarly intense nationalistic animus from hostile encounters with the French occupation in the West, especially from the Ruhr invasion of 1923: All these experiences appear to have induced superpatriotism and recruited activists for the Nazi party.

As for the war itself, it left a potent legacy of bitter political hatreds against civilians and, in particular, against the left-wing mutineers and revolutionaries of 1918 and against the Weimar parties (SPD, DDP, and Center), which for many Nazis were indissolubly linked with them. The wartime attitudes of soldiers wanting to fight to the bitter end, soldiers with decorations and war injuries or years in an allied prison camp, correlate closely with their later involvement in Free Corps and *Einwohnerwehr* activities against domestic insurgents or the Poles. These enthusiastic soldiers of World War I were not only deeply involved in Free Corps violence, but continued their violent activities with the stormtroopers until about 1928. Only then were they superseded as the most violent Nazi troops by the politicized post-war generation of Weimar, especially by the «victory-watchers», young people vicariously socialized by the war experiences of their brothers and fathers. The victory-watchers shared the feelings of the soldiers, but they were not heavily involved in «counter-revolutionary» violence of any sort until after 1923.

The reaction of the Abel respondents to the German defeat is more strongly linked to social dynamics than is generally understood. Rural residents and the sons of farmers, for example, tended to accept the defeat without much ado even though they were generally rather nationalistic and ethnocentric. The sons of military-civil servants instead mirror in their displays of diffuse emotion the great rage or sadness which their fathers must have felt. The children of businessmen and of workers, on the other hand, reacted in a violent, extropunitive way that evidently grew out of their embattled position in either camp of the class struggle. They emphatically blame the Marxists and Spartakists for the defeat, thus giving the legend of the «stab-in-the-back» a specifically anti-socialist note. These anti-Marxists also tended to be far more involved in counter-revolutionary violence than the other early Nazis.

Many respondents report a sense of cultural shock at the incisive changes which war and defeat had allegedly brought upon German society by 1918. Since this sense of cultural shock amounts to a measurement of alienation from Weimar society, we scaled it and arrived at several distinctive attitudinal postures which can easily be related to theories of socialization. One such posture was manifested in complaints about «social disintegration», immorality, loose women, strange clothes and the like, and was mostly adopted by respondents who were older, in social decline or stagnant, poorly educated, and frequently from authoritarian or poverty backgrounds. These respondents were strongly *völkisch* or anti-Semitic, but not particularly engaged in political violence. Toward their political enemies, nevertheless, they exhibit the most *outré* attitudes, calling them subhuman, rodents, etc. Respondents who are shocked at the new Weimar leaders are often similar in age and anti-Semitic prejudice to the social disintegration respondents. Those concerned about «a lack of order and discipline» (authoritarians) by comparison, tend to be of the war generation and younger. Frequently the sons of military men or civil servants, they already liked marching, violence, uniforms, and military training in their youth groups. In the years 1919/1923, they were heavily involved in Free Corps, vigilantes, and militant veterans' organizations. From 1923 on, they flocked into the NSDAP and continued to fight there. They were the revanchist and authoritarian «military desperadoes» of the movement, especially during the middle years of the republic. From about 1925 on, the young respondents who report no cultural shock and those preoccupied with the disparagement of traditional symbols move into the forefront of Nazi action and make their main contribution to the SA and SS. The authoritarians, on the other hand, being men of military experience, supply still more SA and SS officers.

The social-disintegration complaints can be related to the insufficient primary socialization of the respondents who later become paranoid anti-Semites and so patently irrational that only the extremist struggle can hold their personalities together. And then there is the similarly incomplete socialization in the home of the order-and-discipline-conscious who were so warped by the war experience that they could only go on hating and fighting for the decade following 1918, fit for no human company other than the comradeship of fighting men.

Our concern with the impact of the war and its consequences finally turned to the «counter-revolutionaries» of various sorts among the Abel respondents. They naturally fall into the three generations: the Kapp putschists are the oldest, the true reactionaries of the Imperial establishment; the Free Corps and vigilante members were generally of the war generation; those who received para-military training but saw no action and many Free Corps sympathizers were part of the post-war generation. Three-fourths of them were indeed in the war, mostly as enthusiastic soldiers, and the rest were youths vicariously socialized by the war (victory-watchers).

The second counter-revolutionary wave in 1923 was a far more political undertaking for the Abel respondents than that of the immediate post-war years of 1919/1922. The fateful year of 1923 found as many as half of the Kapp putschists and paramilitaries without civil war experience in the NSDAP or other *völkisch* groups who together make up the largest share of the second wave. The Free Corps and vigilante fighters, being less political, are far less often (only one in four) in these groups and also rather unlikely to have been among the local founders of the NSDAP. With the sole exception of *Stahlhelm* members, the counter-revolutionaries of 1923 are also quite attached to the slogan of the *Volksgemeinschaft* which goes well with their urban background and frequent economic troubles. Their involvement in political violence, finally, shows in both duration and character (partisan streetfighting rather than Free Corps-type organized action) a much higher degree of continuity with the Nazi violence to follow than that of the first wave of counter-revolutionaries. If any groups can be said to be the «vanguard» of the brown movement of 1925/1933, it was these right-wing revolutionaries of 1923.

In this differentiated fashion, then, the impact of war and revolution imprinted itself upon the emerging Nazi movement. There were several links to the social dynamics of pre-war society, especially to the military and civil service strain, but also to the class struggle in the form of the reactions of the Abel respondents to the German defeat. There were more direct links between the war experience and the counter-revolutionary activities of 1919/1922. And there was the striking politicization of the counter-revolution and war experience in the second wave of 1923 and the impact of the Franco-Belgian occupation on the Abel respondents.

The Weimar Youth Revolt

A third major factor in swelling the Nazi ranks, in addition to socio-economic causes and war and revolution, was the politicization of Weimar youth. We attempted to relate the youthful strain in the Abel sample to the broader phenomenon of Weimar youth culture. At the outset, we noted the encompassing breadth of organized youth which enrolled no less than seventy per cent of the Abel respondents. Only the oldest respondents (born 1860–1895) had never been in a youth group, a fact that helps to pinpoint the rise of the German youth culture in history and to link it with other social phenomena of the immediate pre-war period and with the war. The war generation and the victory watchers tended to be in quasi-military, conservative, and Youth Movement-related organizations. The latter also enrolled a goodly number of the post-war generation. The youngest cohorts of the Abel collection, a second wave of political youth (after the victory-watchers), directly entered the stormtroopers or Hitler Youth (HJ) without first going through another youth group. The defectors who joined the Nazi youth from socialist or communist youth antecedents were generally motivated by anti-Semitism.

Those joining the SA and HJ directly and the converts from the left sustained the movement with their violence where the quasi-military youth left off, for the second half of the Weimar Republic. The likes and dislikes of the different groups mirror their changes in orientation. The war generation, and especially the members of quasi-military groups, liked comradeship, marching, and violence best; a simile of the *Fronterlebnis*. They disliked the advocacy of class struggle and «unnational views». The post-war generation preferred hiking, folk culture, marching and ideology and disliked a lack of leadership and political direction. There are also striking differences in location experiences: The great urge to march, on which even Hitler comments derisively in *Mein Kampf* («*die ewigen Marschierer*»), came more naturally to young respondents from the occupied areas, the borderland, rural-urban migrants, the urban upwardly mobile, and families in social decline. The spatially immobile, who play such a central role, loved group comradeship instead and gloried in the cultural traditions.

The use of violence among the young Abel respondents exhibits several striking features worth closer examination. The most violent, both in partisan street fighting and in the organized violence of Free Corps and vigilantes, are those who already express a liking for violent action at a tender age. They are also the least-educated and frequently from a poverty or orphaned background, all of which tends to underscore their inadequate socialization. There is also a fairly clear division between those active in organized violence who tend to be hostile militants with little political understanding, and those in partisan street-fighting and «marching with a purpose» who are more often «politically-militarized» or «fully-politicized» youths. Marching with a purpose is evidently a stage preliminary to engaging in political violence, just as the immersion of the «pre-political, parochial youths» in group life is preliminary to marching and violence. All the youthful political postures we have sketched strain toward marching with a purpose and violence even though the life cycles of some permit them to get there earlier and with greater vehemence than the rest.

We took our data on political friction encountered at work to warrant a theory of extremist behavior modelled on the example of social deviancy, that is, a process of external labelling and increasing self-identification with the extremist label. The young extremists of the Abel sample, especially those who directly joined the SA or HJ, tended rather deliberately to stir up political friction by exhibitionistic acts such as wearing a stormtrooper uniform to work. Friction usually intensified their extremist sense of identity and if they got fired for their behavior, they would complain about political persecution. Seeking to separate the external causes from the actions of the respondents, we noted in particular that most of the «economic suicides» got themselves fired long before the Great Depression and that the war and pre-war generations, including many respondents in quasi-military youth groups, rarely complained about a politically «unfriendly» work environment. We are evidently dealing with manifestations of the youth revolt of Weimar, including an explosive generation gap. Friction in the neighborhood, in the family, or at school appears to have a somewhat different character from friction at work which seems to be a favorite locale for extremist self-representation. In neighborhood, family, or school, the external causes are often more pressing.

Coming back to the various types of youthful posture among the Abel respondents, we constructed social profiles for each. The *politically militarized* turned out to be the youngest, spatially immobile («inside agitators») and socially stagnant, or urban climbers much like the portrait of the American ghetto rioter of the 1960s. One out of four lost his father early in life though most of them have no particular reaction to the war and never served in the military. They are rather low in their level of education, but extremely high in their involvement in political violence. They tend to be struggle-oriented and show little ideological concern apart from superpatriotism and Hitlercult. The hostile militants resemble them except that they are older and obviously formed by the inner fears and outer violence of war and revolution. They are also highly mobile and frequently in social decline. Their ideological motives tend to be a mixture of revanchism and anti-Semitism. The fully-politicized, by comparison, are younger, upwardly mobile, better educated, and frequently from a *völkisch* home and school background. Often victims of the *Judenkoller*,[8] they were attracted to the movement by comradeship and by the figure of Hitler and tend to be Nordic-German romantics or solidarists. These are the three main groups among the young activists. The pre-political parochials are less distinctive as a type, but resemble the fully-politicized except for belonging to the war or pre-war generations.

Finally, we took a close look at the childhoods and schools of the young Abel respondents. There appear to be two rather distinctive groupings. Those from a poverty background, orphans, and respondents with a disciplinarian childhood were less eager to get involved and yet a good deal more violent than the rest. The orphaned and disciplinarian cases are particularly anti-Semitic, the orphans Hitler cultists, and the poor solidarists emphasizing the *Volksgemeinschaft*. The economically secure were more eager to get involved and show a curious division into those from a «freewheeling» and those from a sheltered childhood background. The freewheeling, interestingly, are far more inclined toward anti-Semitism while the sheltered are often revanchists and inclined toward violence.

As for the political preferences of the parents of the Abel respondents, there appears to be a significant progression from the militaristic homes of the oldest via nationalistic, conventionally political, or unpolitical homes to the *völkisch* homes of the younger respondents whose indoctrination took place from about the turn of the century onward. It is this *völkisch* generation that best liked ideological direction, marching, and cultural appreciation in their youth groups, (groups that also brought forth most of the hostile militants, politically-militarized, and fully-politicized youths). Its *völkisch* background, furthermore, induced it to embrace anti-Semitism, Nordic-German romanticism, and the Hitler cult after joining the NSDAP. Numerically, and in degree of active service, it was undoubtedly the dominant element within the party during the «fighting years».

With this consideration of the youth factor, we have obviously shifted ground from antecedent to situational factors such as the life cycle and outlook of the respondents.

The Nazi Weltanschauung and Attitudes

There is a rather naive notion abroad of the role of ideology in motivating a person to join an extremist movement such as the Nazi party. According to this notion, the individual starts out already with certain ideas and looks for a party to match them. Such a notion only rarely describes with any accuracy the process by which a movement such as the NSDAP persuaded potential members of its positions, assuming for the moment perfect knowledge and agreement. Judging from the accounts given by the Abel respondents, Nazi propaganda faced a particularly difficult challenge in explaining to potential recruits in plausible language the political incongruities of their times. Most attendants at rallies on their first contact, seem to have brought with them only a burning curiosity along with an aversion to all the unacceptable explanations they had heard from other parties and other politicians.

There are many dimensions to the subject of Nazi ideology that are worth exploring. Of these, the least promising are the ones that have received the most attention in the literature, namely National Socialism as a logically consistent system of ideas, or as the outgrowth of German intellectual traditions. We propose instead to examine the random beliefs and attitudes, in other words, the political culture of the Abel respondents, beginning with the levels of their political understanding of the complex Weimar political system. We found the post-war generation characterized by ideological preconceptions of a low order and containing an abundance of political and often romantic dimwits, especially in rural and small-town areas and under the French occupation. Military-civil servants and white-collar personnel were still among the more intelligent. Social mobility and an urban environment evidently contribute to political intelligence. The most intense ideological obsessions could be found among respondents in social decline, Catholics, and those upwardly mobile from the urban proletariat.

The main ideological themes among the Abel respondents divide the sample along generational lines: The pre-war generation tended to be made up of anti-Semites and of revanchists and superpatriots, especially military and civil service elements and respondents with experience of foreign sojourn or a colonial background living in Berlin. The war generation shared this revanchism, but was more attached to the *Volksgemeinschaft* and especially to the theme dearest to the post-war generation, Nordic-German romanticism, a *völkisch* tenet of faith popular in towns and cities. Hitler worshippers and respondents with no ideological theme round out the picture among the post-war generation, especially in small-town and rural areas. Respondents from the border areas, women, and persons in social decline combine the Nordic-German line with the Hitler cult. Those from the occupied areas are superpatriots and Hitler cultists. The Hitler cult seems to be the ideal stop-gap for empty extremist minds.

The relation between two elements, the monomaniac anti-Semites and the other ideological groupings, shall preoccupy us for a moment. First, to what extent were the other ideological groups free of prejudice? The anti-Semites, of course, exhibit the deepest bias: Half of them have the *Judenkoller,* one fourth are aggressive paranoids, and another fifth tell prejudicial anecdotes. The Nordic-German romantics follow at some distance. The least prejudiced are those without an ideology and the swash-buckling revanchists, followed at some distance by the Hitler worshippers, the superpatriots, and the solidarists who have about half in the «no evidence» and «mild» categories. The bias against aliens, xenophobia, is distributed analogously to anti-

Semitism, except that the superpatriots have more of it and that all the other groups focus their ethnocentricity more on the foreign nations outside (chauvinism) and their «inferiority». The attitudes toward authority, despite the well-known theories fail to follow this pattern of distribution.

Those without ideology and the revanchists, conversely, do most of the fighting in the SA and SS, followed by the Hitler cultists and the superpatriots. The anti-Semites and Nordic-Germans with few exceptions tend to stick to demonstrations, electioneering, and proselytizing. Only half of them are in the stormtroopers and joined them with obvious reluctance. Yet they frequently hold party offices and special organizing functions in the party, while those most involved in fighting do not. This division of labor amounts to a system of stratification between those who do the dirty work and the party organizers and ideologues. It also implies a functional equivalence between the violent acting-out of street fighting and strong prejudice for the inner tensions of the early Nazis. If they discharged their tensions by fighting or by other bizarre behavior they were less in need of the mental contortions of prejudice and *vice versa*.

What were the expectations of the respondents in 1934, after Hitler had come to power? A significant bloc composed of anti-Semites, Nordic-Germans, but also revanchists, coming especially from the war generation, from friction with the occupation, and numbering many military-civil servants, white-collar employees, and farmers, hoped for the establishment of a German racial empire. The post-war generation, and especially the superpatriots and solidarists, borderland Germans, and some military-civil servants with chauvinistic memories of their *Fronterlebnis* wanted to see a national renaissance within. Social and economic restitution was desired by the solidarists, by rural and small-town respondents of the war generation, by many who had been upwardly mobile, and by business and professional people. More crassly, the pre-war generation of Abel respondents and many anti-Semites and persons from metropolitan areas simply hoped for an individual pay-off for themselves. By comparison, the totalitarian utopia of the 1000-year Reich had its clientele mostly among Nordic-Germans, Hitler worshippers, those without any ideology, the victory-watchers, those involved with the occupation or in social decline, white- and blue-collar elements, xenophobes and Catholics. These totalitarians included many strong anti-Marxists and liked to refer to their enemies in gutter language, a chilling forecast of the terror regime descending upon the country. The dreams of racial empire, by comparison, seem more like a revanchism deflected against internal enemies and against the weaker East.

The Role of Anti-Semitism

We have touched upon the role of anti-Semitic prejudice among the Abel respondents so often that it appears to be high time to focus on it more specifically and to explore its internal dynamics. Of all the hazy ideological elements in these Nazi minds, this prejudice seems the most tangible precisely because its object is in the minds of the prejudiced persons themselves, at least at this stage. We distinguished four categories aside from *vitae* with no evidence of bias: mild verbal projections, the *Judenkoller*, anecdote-telling, and aggressive paranoia (speaking of threats and counter-threats). The underlying theory pictures the mild verbal projections as a form of social conformism in the movement; the choler as an outbreak of scapegoating in which the prejudiced mind is still relatively at balance with its own displacement; the anecdo-

277

te–telling phase as a transition to aggressive paranoia; and the latter as a dynamic disequilibrium which drives the disturbed minds on to hectic political action.

How do these prejudice groups of the Abel sample differ from one another? The no-evidence and mild groups were the youngest and tended to be farmers, workers, salaried employees, and women. The more prejudiced groups were much older, often metropolitan, rural-urban migrants, or upwardly mobile within the city. The cholerics were generally over 30 at the time of the outbreak of their choler and, along with the paranoids, frequently in social decline. The anecdote-tellers tended to be upwardly mobile military and civil service personnel, the paranoids business and professional people, upwardly mobile white-collar elements and the children of military and civil service personnel.

Their childhood experiences shed some light on the origins of their prejudice. Poverty origins and a sheltered childhood appear to produce the least bias, disciplinarian and orphan childhoods the most intense prejudice, particularly of the paranoid kind. Theodor W. Adorno's theory of the disturbed relationship to the father thus held up well. A freewheeling childhood, as compared to a sheltered one, turned out to be very high in prejudice of the choleric type, in contradiction to what many American psychologists have suggested about the genesis of a democratic personality. It would be more accurate to say, however, that this finding only drew a distinction among different kinds of Nazi minds. It is entirely possible that a normal mind would benefit rather than break under the strain of a freewheeling childhood, even though our respondents tended to become choleric.

While examining the youth organization membership of the Abel respondents, we discovered that in their younger years they either held youth group offices or engaged in violence, but rarely both. We can now refine also our earlier statement on violence or offices and blend in our findings on prejudice. The prejudiced are low in violence, but this is true mainly of the cholerics and the anecdote-tellers. The paranoids and the mild and no-bias groups are highly involved in stormtrooper violence. The paranoids and the mild group also hold most of the party offices. The cholerics and anecdote-tellers probably were being ruled out as office-holders because they were «running off at the mouth». And those of no bias were used only for the dirty work of street violence precisely because they showed no bias. The important party offices were in the hands of the aggressive paranoids, the embodiment of our theory of dynamic disequilibrium. The mildly verbal were allowed to hold local offices precisely *because* they were conforming to the Nazi rhetoric.

The paranoids and the no-bias group also were struggle-oriented and did the most fighting and «day-and-night» campaigning. The mild group got more satisfaction from the comradeship of the stormtroopers but was not far behind in fighting. The anecdote-tellers fought less and were looking forward to the coming of the racist utopia. The cholerics, instead of fighting, concentrated on electioneering and proselytizing and received their satisfaction from the Hitler cult. Quite typically, many of the cholerics experienced a severe cultural shock (social disintegration and the new leadership) in 1918/1919 which may well have been identical with the genesis of their *Judenkoller*. As much as one seventh of the Abel sample seems to have experienced such a crisis at that time, suggesting something like a mass outbreak of political anti-Semitism under the impact of defeat and «revolution» in Germany.

The interrelations among ideology, prejudice, office-holding, and violence, among other things, also make for an inverse relation between intense anti-Semitic prejudice and involvement in street violence (table 2). We can line up all the ideological groups according to their prejudice and engagement in street-fighting while in the Nazi party and obtain clearly opposite trends. The most likely reason for this inverse relationship again is an equivalence in function between violent acting-out and the more introverted, symbolic acting-out that is violent prejudice. If we assume approximately the same inner tensions in all the early Nazis, some evidently discharged them with their fists or other bizarre behavior while the prejudiced persons discharged them by mental contortions. In either case, the acting-out behavior was likely, and perhaps even intended, to shock society and to bring about retribution of sorts as long as society conformed to common-sense social prerequisites. Once a society is taken over by people given to this kind of autistic behavior, however, there is a wholesale change in the psychological situation. Not only is the society henceforth «mad», but the acting-out behavior loses its point of reference and, thereby, one of its special gratifications, namely a reaction of shock and authoritative punishment. This was one of the reasons for the disorientation of many a Nazi immediately following the take-over of 1933.

Table 2. *Prejudice and Violence in Ideological Groupings*

Anti-Semitic Prejudice		Street-Fighting	
(in per cent paranoid, anecdotic, and choleric)		(in per cent fighting in the NSDAP)	
Anti-Semites	(93.3%)	Anti-Semites	(30.5%)
Nordic-Germans	(54.3)	Nordic-Germans	(34.7)
Solidarists	(50.3)	Solidarists	(36.4)
Superpatriots	(50.0)	Superpatriots	(36.5)
Hitler cult	(46.7)	Hitler cult	(36.4)
Revanchists	(39.3)	Revanchists	(42.9)
No ideology	(7.1)	No ideology	(52.6)

How were the other forms of ethnocentricity distributed over the sample? Generally speaking, the pre-war generation was the most ethnocentric and the post-war generation the least. The «oldest» ethnocentric motif was that all the other nations were «inferior». This was held especially by women, military and civil service personnel, businessmen, and professionals. Chauvinism toward foreign nations and xenophobia were more typical of the war generation. The chauvinists, in particular, tended to be military and civil service personnel, white-collar workers, people who had been in contact with foreigners (for example in border areas), and the socially static, Protestants, Nordic-German romantics and revanchists, bitter-enders and victory-watchers (youths vicariously socialized by the war). The xenophobes, by way of contrast, were highly mobile, white-collar, children of military and civil service personnel and farmers, and upwardly mobile in the city. They tended to be anti-Semites or superpatriots, from border or occupied areas, and to stand out with their all-inclusive hate lists, their *outré* language, their hostility toward authority, and their irrational and insecure personalities.

Next to their hatred of Jews and of aliens, the early Nazis also were anti-Marxists, although their anti-Marxism appears to have been neither particularly ideological nor very intense. To be sure, the anti-Marxists were a very large group and they are also among the youngest Abel respondents. But the feeling seems to have been mostly a reaction to the would-be revolutionaries of the left, as well as to the «outdated legacy» and the monopoly of many unionized jobs by Weimar's well-entrenched SPD and KPD. Anti-Marxists were particularly from Berlin or from rural or border areas, workers of little education and probably resentful of the socialist labor movement, women, military-civil servants, and the sons of workers and military men. They tended to be socially static or in decline, which may explain their envy of some of the SPD careerists of Weimar. They included many victory-watchers and men suffering strong cultural shock at the fall of the old symbols. They blamed the defeat on Marxists and Spartakists and were often brought into counter-revolutionary organizations by the shock of defeat and revolution.

Their parental influences were generally *völkisch* or militaristic, although one out of ten came from a left-wing youth group. They tended to have no ideology at all, or to be Hitler cultists, or Nordic-German romantics. The NSDAP gave them few party offices of any importance and few stormtrooper promotions, even though they were heavily (and masochistically) involved in stormtrooper violence. Evidently, with the stop-gap ideology of anti-Marxism rather than anti-Semitism, they were only the foot-soldiers of the movement, in spite of their gutter language about their political enemies. Here too, a Marxist interpretation of fascism appears to be unsupported by our data.[9]

Conclusion

We have come to the end of our survey of what particular motives may have been most influential in causing the Abel Nazis to join the movement. Now is the time to relate the different categories to one another and to ponder which of them appear to be the most important. One way of doing this is by tabulating the major formative experiences or themes chosen by the authors of the *vitae* in presenting the stories of their lives:

Table 3: *Formative or Influential Experience*

	Number	Per cent
Fronterlebnis, war	101	13.8
Defeat, revolution	175	23.8
Social snub, humiliation	29	4.0
Alleged episode with Jews	37	5.0
Alleged encounter with aliens (including occupation soldiers)	55	7.5
Comradeship in youth organization	75	10.2
Educational, literary influence	131	17.8
Unemployment, economic crisis	43	5.9
Other experiences	88	12.0
Total entries	734	100.0

This procedure, of course, incorporates both the flaws of the sample and the subjectivity of the content of the *vitae*. To the extent that we can rely on this approach, in any case, the most important influences on the lives of the respondents are 1. the impact of war, defeat and «revolution», and 2. ideological influences of an educational or literary character, and the alleged encounter with aliens or Jews. The effect of social snubs or unemployment and the appeal of youthful comradeship appear to play minor roles as compared to the former two factors.

A balanced assessment of the interrelationships indeed can hardly dispute the prominent role of the two first-mentioned factors, but there are additional angles to consider. As for the war and its aftermath, we are obviously dealing with a historical phenomenon limited to particular age groups.[10] Many of the pre-war and war generation respondents indeed explain their lives as if they were simply the products of personal misfortunes or of the great historic drama of war and revolution. On the other hand the vast majority (three fourths) concentrate instead on describing their own political development, step-by-step, until they were Nazi activists. Thus there seems to be plenty of conscious, political will and intent present as we would indeed expect of such a forceful, power-hungry, self-accelerating movement.

As for the purported influence of literary, school, or personal experiences, they deserve to be taken with a grain of salt. The respondents were probably not simply «awakened» to hear the sound of a different drummer, although they appear to be saying something about themselves and their ideological bent of mind through the simile of the literary or personal encounter. Many of the most prejudiced among them, indeed, show every sign of paranoid fears and irrationality to the point of incoherence in their accounts. For the younger respondents, moreover, the Hitler cult and a great urge to merge their «identities» with the fighting movement seem to have taken the place of the irrationality, cultural shock, and prejudice of their elders.

There can be little doubt that the broader socio-economic motives, whatever contemporary literature may say about them, were important to only a few of the older Abel respondents, although the Depression seems to have contributed considerably to bringing existing discontents to a head. There is very little evidence in the Abel Collection to support a Marxist interpretation unless it were to argue in terms of the reactions of dislocated youth against a repressive establishment.

Youth indeed seems to be at the center of possible explanations of the Nazi phenomenon, at least after the «military desperados» of war and Free Corps origin began to yield the stage of violence to the young. The post-war generation was not only beyond the impact of the war experience (except for the victory-watchers); its formative experiences were precisely the literary and personal encounters along with the thrill of youthful comradeship. The young Nazis of the Abel Collection consisted primarily of workers and white-collar employees, the upwardly mobile of the city, and the super-patriots from the border areas and from the occupied Rhineland.

Generational differences also appear to be the major matrix of the seemingly disjointed elements of Nazi ideology we have found. The compulsive engagement in street violence, finally, was also the monopoly of the young whose thirst for fighting and struggle evidently was not to be quenched except by encounters with the equally thirsty young members of the Communist Red Front. After the NSDAP came into power, in fact, many of these young toughs went on to sinister careers in the higher SS, in SD, RSHA, concentration camp guards, Gestapo and in other enforcer functions of the Third Reich.[11] It was the misfortune of the Weimar Republic that this explosive political youth revolt happened to develop in a right-wing direction and that it occurred at a time of nationalistic humiliation and painful economic dislocations. It could hardly have happened under worse circumstances and with more fateful consequences.

281

NOTES

[1] See his book *Why Hitler Came to Power* (1938) which was reissued in 1966 under the title *The Nazi Movement,* New York: Atherton. The original documents were deposited at the Hoover Library on War and Revolution at Stanford, California.

[2] Peter H. Merkl, *Political Violence Under the Swastika : 581 Pre-1933 Nazis,* Princeton University Press, 1975.

[3] The Ministry of Propaganda and the Nazi Party itself helped Prof. Abel to solicit *vitae* and collected them for him. This procedure is an obvious source of possible bias. For a discussion of the sample and of the weak points of their material, see pp. 6–21 of the book, and the tables in the introduction above, p. 260–261.

[4] Statistically speaking, the frequency distributions are not very reliable in this sample, but this need not detract from the reliability of secondary analyses such as cross-tabulations.

[5] Under the Empire it was common practice to transfer «other ranks» among the professional military to a civil service career such as the railroad or postal service, or local government.

[6] With regard to the urban upwardly mobile segment among the spatially immobile, there are some telling parallels to the «portrait of a rioter» in the Kerner Commission report on American race rioters in the 1960s where the typical rioter is also described as a second generation urbanite, upwardly mobile, and frustrated with unemployment and barriers to his advancement.

[7] A number of prominent Nazis such as Rudolf Hess, Walter Darré, Alfred Rosenberg and Joachim Ribbentrop had similar backgrounds.

[8] Many respondents report a violent outbreak of anti-Semitic prejudice at or shortly after the end of the war, frequently associated with a personal crisis of some sort.

[9] See, for example, the discussions in Wilhelm Alff, *Der Begriff Faschismus und andere Aufsätze zur Zeitgeschichte,* Frankfurt: Suhrkamp, 1971, pp. 29 ff.

[10] The war generation, as the reader may recall, also is overrepresented in the sample at the expense of younger members.

[11] We looked up the Third Reich careers of the Abel respondents in the NSDAP membership files and found 42 cases of this description. See *Political Violence Under the Swastika,* pp. 634–667.

The Electoral Geography of the Nazi Landslide

The Need for Community Studies

NICO PASSCHIER

To a considerable extent the end of the Weimar Republic was brought about by the explosive growth of the Nazi party in the elections. At that time fascist movements in many countries spread their propaganda industriously but nowhere was a fascist party able to gain as much support in free elections as in Germany. In about three years (1929–32) the NSDAP developed from the small, marginal party it had been throughout the twenties into a mass movement representing over one third of the electorate and organizing hundreds of thousands of partisans (table 1).

Without this popular support for Hitler one cannot imagine the later *Machtergreifung*, irrespective of the extent to which the last stage of the Republic was affected by the ignorance and insincerity of the professional politicians. Hitler became a political factor only after unprecedented landslides in the elections. His party undermined the Weimar Republic not only by ideology and violence but also by its sheer weight. It disturbed the traditional patterns of representation and, in the end, crippled parliamentary government.

Ever since the first Nazi success in the 1930 *Reichstag* elections, the social roots of this sudden electoral landslide have been discussed. It seems, however, that up to the present only fragmentary explanations of the extraordinarily rapid and successful penetration of the electorate have been established. Most studies, including the present one, concentrate on the identification of social groups which supported Nazism «more (or less) than average». Support or resistance to the Nazi appeal is then explained by reference to the (supposed) interests, social or economic positions, ideologies or emotional dispositions of the groups under consideration. Although the arguments are often based on accurate observations of German conditions, they have remained very broad and general. Only seldom has detailed empirical research been conducted to explain why and how individual voters became members of the party or supporters at the polls.

This is due, of course, to the general scarcity of data on mass behaviour before World War II when opinion polls and survey research were still in their infancy. Thus, a considerable amount of work has been necessary only to establish which kind of Germans were attracted by the NSDAP (see e.g. Heberle 1963; Gerth 1952; Schäfer 1957; Milatz 1965). And the discussion on this matter is still continuing (cf. O'Lessker 1968). Because of this scarcity of data, interpretations of the attraction of Nazism to voters in agriculture (Heberle 1963; Loomis & Beegle 1946), and to those with middle class backgrounds (Geiger 1930, 1932; Riemer 1932; Lipset 1960), or about the resistance of Catholics and workers (Loomis & Beegle 1946; Lepsius 1966) remain largely hypothetical.

As the link between broad social categories more or less favouring Nazism and individuals abandoning or holding fast to political convictions has yet to be established

283

theoretically and empirically, thorough studies of voting and party membership at the «grass roots» level are needed. Such local studies could reconstruct the *process* of Nazi recruitment and change in party adherence by concentrating on individuals and what influenced them. Research of this kind has to include the traditional identification of the social bases of Nazism in terms of class and properties of the persons involved, but we need to go further and try to analyse the micro-level mechanics which impelled people to become Nazis and the changing of their opinions and commitments[1].

A small number of local studies have been written about Nazi mobilization, the best-known example being Allen's research on a small town in Northern Germany (Allen 1965). However, in order to generalize about the whole of Germany detailed studies have to include all discernible regional contexts, exploring a diversity of social categories, environmental arrangements and influence systems, and encompass regions where the Nazis were successful and where they failed. In large countries regions will often represent different political climates and traditions. In addition, the regional balance of power will have an influence on the strategies of parties and on the options of voters. As to dominant religion, economic base, level of modernization, class relations, etc., local communities within such regions can differ, but nevertheless the region as such adds a contextual property which must also be considered[2].

In Germany, regions were independent units of state before the unification in 1870, and even under the Weimar system many *Länder* had some autonomy. Local and regional governments and parliaments; *Reichstag* constituencies following old administrative boundaries; the constraints of communication and individual mobility; all these factors made political parties much more dependent on regional organizations than in the present era of mass mobility, mass communications and centralizing government. Furthermore, regional differences in speech and culture, in religious traditions and dominant economic structures were considerable at that time (cf. Dickinson 1945, p. 32–36). Therefore, the parties in Germany experienced large geographical differentiation, both in their appeal and in the efficacy of their party organizations. Many of the German parties depended on regional strongholds since Imperial times. Several parties even aimed only at regional support and the promotion of regional interests. After 1919 this pattern continued as can also be observed in the penetration of Nazism which showed striking regional differences.

The purpose of this paper is to assess the relative importance of these regional differences in the Nazi vote and to show their stability throughout the period 1930–33. The variation of the Nazi vote through time and space will be broken down into the national trend during these years and into specific regional electoral trends, which can be related to the social composition of the electorate and earlier voting behaviour. Finally, a classification of German regions as socio-political contexts is presented that will be relevant for the selection of localities for «grass roots» studies of the Nazi recruitment process.

The Degree of Regional Variation in Nazi Voting

At the end of World War I Imperial Germany collapsed and gave way to a republican régime. As the change of power did not grow into a social revolution, the most important result of the events in 1918–19 was a constitutional reform: the establishment of parliamentary democracy.

The political parties functioning in this new constitutional system originated for the most part in the Imperial era. Many names were new, but there had not been a major realignment in positions and electoral support, apart from the revolutionary year 1919. Only the communists and the growing number of marginal parties can to a certain extent be considered new elements. The major change had been a reversal of the basic constitutional positions among the parties. The Empire had leant on Conservatives, Nationalists and National-Liberals, leaving the Social Democrats, Liberals and Catholics a more peripheral role. In the Republic, however, the latter parties became the *staatstragende Parteien* (the state supporting parties), a fact which influenced their actions even after the breakdown of the «Weimar Coalition». On the other hand, the nationalist parties developed very strong anti-republican attitudes, although they sat in parliament and took part in governments.

In addition to issues like nationalism, war, and the constitution, the party system was polarized on socio-economic matters. Most observers (e.g. Neumann 1932) indicate that the parties, apart from the Catholics, were strongly geared to specific strata and their organizations. This not only applies to the minor parties articulating special professional and regional interests, but also to the larger ones like the Social-Democrats, Communists, Liberals, and Nationalists. Table 1 gives an outline of Weimar parties and their performance in the *Reichstag* elections.

Table 1. *Distribution of votes in national elections during the Weimar Republic (Nationalversammlung 1919; Reichstage 1920–33)*

Parties	Elections								
	1919	1920	1924a	1924b	1928	1930	1932a	1932b	1933
	%	%	%	%	%	%	%	%	%
NSDAP	–	–	6.5	3.0	2.6	18.3	37.3	33.1	43.9
DNVP	10.3	15.1	19.5	20.5	14.2	7.0	5.9	8.3	8.0
Wirtschaftspartei	–	–	1.8	2.1	4.5	3.9	0.4	0.3	–
Other special interest parties	1.0	2.5	4.4	4.1	6.4	8.8	2.1	2.4	1.6
DVP	4.4	13.9	9.3	10.1	8.7	4.5	1.2	1.9	1.1
DDP (DSP)	18.5	8.3	5.7	6.3	4.9	3.8	1.0	0.9	0.8
Zentrum/BVP	19.7	18.0	16.6	17.4	15.2	14.8	15.7	15.0	14.0
SPD	37.9	21.6	20.5	26.0	29.8	24.5	21.6	20.4	18.3
USPD	7.6	17.9	0.8	0.3	–	–	–	–	–
KPD	–	2.1	12.6	8.9	10.6	13.1	14.3	16.9	12.3
Others	0.6	0.6	2.3	1.3	3.1	1.3	0.5	0.7	0.0

Source: Milatz (1965, pp. 38, 151). For more information on the parties, see Neumann (1932) and Matthias and Morsey (1966). Just to give an impression of what the parties stood for, a short characterization is given here:

NSDAP: Fascists, against democracy and republic, nationalist, striving for a vague social revolution by propaganda vehemently anti-capitalistic as well as anti-socialist.

DNVP: Nationalists and conservatives, anti-democratic and anti-republican, aiming at restoration of the pre-1914 system.

Wirtschaftspartei: Platform for the interests of the older independent middle classes, tradesmen, artisans, etc., often small town inhabitants.

Other special interest parties: A host of small parties that managed to represent farming interests (e.g. *Landbund, Landvolk, Deutsche Bauernpartei*) or regional and minority interests (e.g. *Deutsch-Hannoversche Partei, Polen-partei*) or both (e.g. *Bayerischer Bauernbund, Sächsisches Landvolk, Württemberger Bauern- und Weingärtnerbund);* to this category also belong some smaller right-wing parties like the *Christlich-Sozialer Volksdienst* and the *Konservative Volkspartei* that depended on the same rural and small town middle classes.

DVP: National Liberals, sceptical about the republic but co-operative in practice, support from industrial circles but also from the modern white-collar middle classes.

DDP: Liberal Democrats, with more parliamentary and republican attitudes than the right-wing liberals, but depending on about the same social basis.

Zentrum/BVP: Catholics, with large regional strongholds, Bavarian *BVP* showing autonomous tendencies now and then, no official class commitment, represented in all republican governments up to Papen.

SPD: Social Democrats, parliamentary and republican labour party striving for social reform, strong urban orientation.

USPD: Independent Social Democrats, short-lived separation from SPD developing out of its pacifist left wing during the World War.

KPD: Communists, grown out of revolutionary *Spartakus*-movement since 1918, anti-parliamentary, revolutionary ideas increasingly restrained by dogmatism and Komintern-problems.

Since the Weimar coalition had already lost its majority in 1920 the Republic was governed by an unstable system of changing coalitions or minority cabinets. During the twenties, the Liberal parties could attract only a decreasing proportion of the vote. Initially it was the Nationalists who profited from their losses, later the special interest parties, and finally Hitler. Throughout the period the Catholics and the Social Democrats held over a third of the electorate. At the end of the decade, however, the Weimar system could no longer overcome the problems of political fragmentation and economic crisis, which from 1930 onwards led to government by presidential emergency decrees and to a reduction of parliamentary influence (the Brüning period). It was in this situation that Nazism, which in 1929 had begun to rise in local government elections, reached an extraordinary peak, crushing the Liberal and special interest parties and also absorbing a good deal of Conservative support.

If this Nazi landslide is analysed by regions, a striking difference can be observed (Fig. 1). The following analysis relates to 68 regions occupying the whole of Germany in its 1933 boundaries. Most of the units are large administrative areas which in German statistical sources appear as *Länder, Landesteile,* or *Regierungsbezirke.* Some small units have been aggregated with neighbouring areas, some larger units have been split (e.g. Berlin, Ruhr) in order to attain more comparable units of analysis. They contain between 100,000 and 1,000,000 voters, on the average about half a million[3]. For each of the units the results of the *Reichstag* elections have been gathered for May 1928 (before the rise of Nazism) and for September 1930, July 1932, November 1932 and March 1933 (the mobilization period). The average regional NSDAP vote in the last four elections is shown in Fig. 1, the national over-all average being 33.13 per cent and the areas ranging from a minimum 16.05 per cent in the Münster area up to a maximum 49.26 per cent in the region of Upper Hesse.

The large gap between maximum and minimum averages suggests that during the four elections of Nazi mobilization the nature of the regional differences remained fairly constant, so that national and regional electoral trends can be separated clearly. By using a version of a model developed by Ştokes (1966) for the analysis of regional

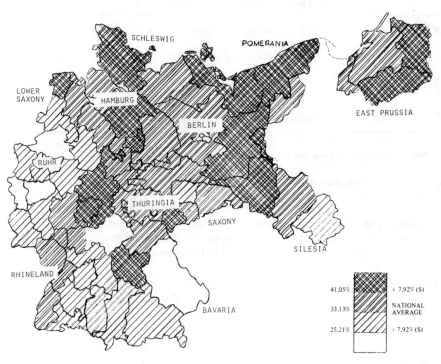

Fig. 1. *The average regional NSDAP vote, 1930–33*

SCHLESWIG

POMERANIA

LOWER
SAXONY

HAMBURG

EAST PRUSSIA

BERLIN

RUHR

THURINGIA

SAXONY

SILESIA

RHINELAND

BAVARIA

41.05%   + 7.92% (S)

33.13%   NATIONAL
              AVERAGE

25.21%   ÷ 7.92% (S)

political effects, the differing regional trends ban be made visible and weighted against the national trend.

The crux of the method is a tautological expression, also used by Alker (1969a) and MacRae & Meldrum (1960), in which the Nazi vote in a single area *i* in one election *t* is shown as:

$$(X_{it}-X_{..}) = (X_{.t}-X_{..}) + (X_{i.}-X_{..}) + [(X_{it}-X_{.t}) - (X_{i.}-X_{..})]$$

Total	National	Regional	Residual deviation for
deviation	trend effect	effect	this unit in this
(A)	for this	for this	election
	election	unit	(D)
	(B)	(C)	

The basic parameters of this formula have been defined in table 2. The idea behind it is that all NSDAP scores (X_{it}), for all 68 areas in all four elections considered, can be expressed as deviations from the overall national average NSDAP percentage in the four elections $(X_{..})$. This total deviation for each area and election (A) is conceived to be the resultant of tendencies specific to the election and of tendencies specific to the region. First, all regional scores will be influenced by the national trend of the moment (B) which is the deviation between the national averages for that election *t* $(X_{.t})$ and for all four elections $(X_{..})$. The remaining total regional deviation $(X_{it}-X_{.t})$ will reflect the regional peculiarity, but it is useful to break it down into a long-term and a short-term

287

Table 2. *Definition of parameters*

X_{it}	The percentage of NSDAP-voters in area i in election t
$X_{.t} = \underset{i}{\Sigma}\ X_{it}$	The national average percentage of NSDAP voters in election t*
$X_{i.} = \underset{t}{\Sigma}\ X_{it}$	The regional average percentage of NSDAP voters during the four elections 1930–33.
$X_{..} = \underset{i}{\Sigma}\ \underset{t}{\Sigma}\ X_{it}$	The national NSDAP- average 1930–33*

* Averages calculated over the regions have to be weighted for the sizes of the electorates.

effect. A long-term regional effect, stable through the four elections, can be measured by the difference between the regional $(X_{i.})$ and national $(X_{..})$ averages during the elections. Fig. 1, in fact, portrays this regional effect (C), which can be related theoretically to other protracted institutional and cultural characteristics of the region. The residual effect (D), only working in this region and in this election, could possibly be related to-social change, local political issues, etc.

Fig. 2. *Decomposition of the regional variation of the NSDAP vote: the example of Regierungsbezirk Trier*

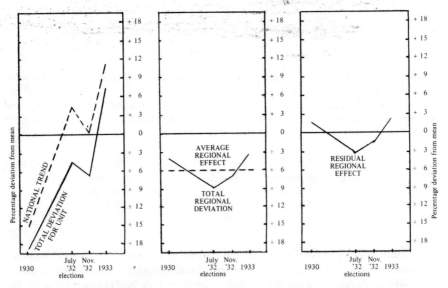

Now that national and regional effects have been made visible for each area and election, the relative importance of the total of regional effects can be weighted against the national mobilization trend of the NSDAP. Such a generalization has to take into account all observations on all units and moments of analysis. Using the elements of the breakdown formula, a variance-components model can be presented, defining the variance of the Nazi vote in an area i through the four elections as:

$$Var\ (A) = Var\ (B) + Var\ (C) + Var\ (D) + 2\ [Cov\ (BC) + Cov\ (BD) + Cov\ (CD)]$$

If the variances for all areas are added, the result will be a breakdown of the total variance of the NSDAP vote through four elections over 68 areas into components of national trend, regional effect, residual regional effect and the covariances between several effects and trends. Stokes (1966) believes that such covariances in totality will always be very slight in magnitude, which is almost confirmed in the calculations reported here. By standardization of the resulting components the latter can be compared for the proportion they contribute to the total variance. The result is summarized in table 3.

Table 3. *Variance components of the Nazi vote in Germany 1930–33, 68 areas, four elections*

Component	Variance	Proportion
National trend	354.8	0.53
Regional effect	251.2	0.38
Residual regional effect	34.6	0.05
Covariance terms	26.2	0.04
Total variance	666.8	1.00

It can be concluded that strong regional factors have influenced the Nazi mobilization of voters in the four *Reichstag* elections. About 43 per cent of the variance through time and space is due to regional deviations from the national trend. Most of this came from the regional effect, i.e. the average regional deviations through time (about 38 per cent). This means that rather stable, enduring regional characteristics are important in the detailed study of Nazi mobilization. Thus, for a reliable picture of German politics at the end of the Weimar Republic, studies at the grass-root level must be conducted in a diversity of «mobilization regions».

Related Factors

Now that it is established that regional differentiation in the Nazi vote was considerable – even at the level of the large areas studied here – the obvious problem is how to classify the areas as significant contexts for selecting localities for further research. Clearly, the areas should be ranked according to level of Nazi success but, as such levels can have different backgrounds of social composition, institutions or political tradition, some further analysis seems necessary. The problem comes down to the choice of variables which can permit a simple classification of the research units into socio-political regions of diverging levels of Nazism.

Earlier studies of the social basis of Nazism suggest such variables, and it will be useful to summarize some of these and to test them using the data of this study.

Middle-class and Farmers' Support

The electoral mobilization of the NSDAP matched the decline of the traditional centre and right-wing parties (DDP, DVP, DNVP) and later of the special interest parties as

289

well (cf. table 1). As the rural and urban middle classes in the Protestant areas had been the most important clients of these parties for years, contemporary observers identified these categories as the most important supporters of Nazism. Later research has strengthened this opinion.

Especially among Nazi party members, the more urban middle classes dominated the scene. As Gerth (1952, p. 106) and Schäfer (1957, pp. 17–19) have shown, both the traditional urban middle classes, such as small but independent businessmen, artisans or professionals, and the numerically increasing modern strata of white-collar employees and civil servants were highly overrepresented among NSDAP-members. For the Nazi voters the same relationship has been indicated by correlational analyses in some cities (Pratt, cited by Lipset 1960, p. 144, 252) as well as in smaller towns (cf. Heberle 1963, p. 108). As early as in 1932, Riemer labelled the NSDAP the «*Front der revolutionären Mitte*».

Interpretations of this middle class support all point at some special emotional state among these classes in Germany during the twenties. It has been contended that feelings of «displacement» between big business and labour with their huge organizations may have made them desperate and resentful (Lipset 1960, pp. 132–137). Other authors argue that an inadequate assessment of the realities of class society may have caused their panic (Geiger 1930, p. 637 ff.), or that the escape into radical nationalism is a general tendency among middle classes in crisis, the result of their self-image as the guardians of national virtues and normalcy (Lepsius 1966, pp. 13–18).

Rural, and especially agrarian, support for Nazism was extensive. The growth of the Nazi vote in a Protestant rural area has been described in detail by Heberle (1963). He reports the special success of the NSDAP in areas with small farms, a rather homogeneous social structure, strong feelings of local solidarity and social control. There the Nazis destroyed the original representation by liberal and/or special interest parties, as they did in Protestant small farm regions in Southern Germany. But even in the areas of large-scale agriculture in the East Nazism was successful, draining the traditional support for the conservative DNVP.

Interpretations of this Nazi take-over start from the opinion that farmers are a separate category, part of rural subculture, and much less directly integrated in the national social and political system than the urban tradesmen and craftsmen. Although some authors consider farmers part of the older middle classes (Geiger 1930), most interpretations treat them as a separate phenomenon and deal with the representation of farmers' interests and the ways they are integrated into the German political system. The process to be explained can be outlined as the breakdown of traditional agricultural representation during the agricultural crisis about 1928/29, the emergence of spontaneous movements and organizations for mutual aid during that crisis, the capture of these farmers' leagues by the Nazis, and the re-integration of the farmers into national politics, this time in a negative sense: against the Republic.

On the basis of a comparison of regions where Nazism did or did not succeed some theories have been proposed. Nilson (1954, p. 302) contends that, unlike their counterparts in Protestant Germany, the Norwegian fascists could not attract and hold the support of new agrarian movements in the long run since the Norwegian Social Democrats developed an effective and credible agricultural policy, which the German left-wing parties did not. He believes that the rural origin of the Norwegian socialist leadership can explain such a difference; German SPD leaders had almost entirely an urban-industrial background which they could not overcome. Loomis and

Beegle (1946) compare Catholic and Protestant small farmers' communities which were very different in their degree of nazification. The farmers' movements can be considered as the response to the crisis of rural populations without experience with *Gesellschaft*-type organizations. In Protestant areas, the Nazis could penetrate these movements with their appealing pretence of bringing back the good old times; in Catholic areas, however, these farmers' movements could join the familiar *Gesellschaft*-type organizations of the *Zentrum*, as could urban workers with trade unions and socialist parties (Loomis & Beegle, p. 734).

Catholic and Workers' Immunity

Why these groups were less receptive to the Nazi appeal has not been the subject of many studies. Only Loomis & Beegle (1946, pp. 731–733) and Lepsius (1966, pp. 26–37) attempt an explanation, although most other authors register the fact. However, for understanding the process of Nazi penetration, its speed and its mechanics, the study of such groups having functional alternatives in their response to the economic and political crisis seems very important.

That urban workers were less receptive to Nazi ideology has been observed from Nazi membership figures (Gerth 1952, p. 106; Schäfer 1957, p. 17) as well as from ecological analysis of voting statistics (cf. Heberle 1963, p. 111). Since the Nazis were more successful in rural areas and small towns than in large cities (Pratt cited in Lipset, p. 144; Bracher 1955, p. 646–655) nobody doubts the resistance to Nazism of the left-wing parties, which had dominated the large cities for years. Although the working class supporters of these parties were severely hurt by the crisis, their organizations were not drained by the Nazi effort like the organizations of farmers and craftsmen. As a party the Social Democrats had lost voters since 1928, but a good many of the defectors went over to the Communists who aimed at the same social strata. In a sense they stayed in the same working class environment. In its traditional form, this working class subculture remained unimpaired up to the dissolution of the Republic in 1933. (For a discussion of socialist parties and strongly tied ancillary organizations, see Hunt 1964).

The same can be observed for the Catholics. Their parties held on to their electoral support until 1933 as well as did the left-wing parties. Although the basis was not social class but religion, their organizations, covering the same broad field as did the Social Democratic groups, remained functional until the Concordat and the Nazi regimentation *(Gleichschaltung)*.

A theory to explain the resistance of both groups to Nazism can start from this remarkable similarity. Both categories were more than just population segments; they were separate subcultures organizing the majority of the members of their class/religion in a host of organizations and associations with strong relationships among the leaders. They were self-contained; the ideology of unity, characteristic of emancipation movements, produced strong ties from years of socialization, and loyalty was enforced by frequent interaction. The direct and effective representation of the Catholics and the working class up to the highest level of state, combined with their cultural isolation, prevented according to Lepsius (1966, pp. 26–37), a loss of legitimacy and breakdown of their organizations[4].

In their interpretation of the Nazi vote of the rural Protestants Loomis & Beegle (1946, pp. 732–734) considered a more general application of this theory of mediation and representation. They argue that the effect of the economic and political crisis

291

could have caused a state of *anomie*, especially among the rural population living in *Gemeinschaft*-type groups threatened with disruption. Under these circumstances the Catholics and the workers could call on the effective and legitimate organizations of their immediate social environment, whereas the traditional representation of the middle classes and farmers appeared to be too fragmented and too small-scale to be effective. This offered the great opportunity for Nazism[5].

Regional Social Diversity and the Nazi Vote

For the purpose of tracing significant contexts for community studies of recruitment for the NSDAP, it will be necessary to consider differences in the social composition of the areas under study. Apart from special regional conditions, the Nazi vote in a particular area will be the outcome of diverging tendencies among various social categories. Since everywhere the mixture of social groups with high or low Nazi propensity will be different, areas can be classified according to their level of nazification and the related composition of their population. In a study conducted some years ago on the same 68 areas analyzed earlier, multiple regression and correlation techniques have been applied to variables describing Nazi performance and socio-economic composition of the population of the areas (Passchier 1972). The dependent variables (the percentage increase in the NSDAP vote between the *Reichstag* elections of 1928/30 resp. 1930/July 1932, cf. table 1) were somewhat different from the variables used here, but of course they are both closely related to the average regional effect (C) in the first formula, $(X_{i.}-X_{..})$. Since the product-moment coefficient of correlation is +.83 resp. +.86, some results of that study can be used to trace relevant factors correlated with the regional propensity to vote for Nazism.

Table 4. *Multiple regression analysis of the increase in Nazi voting 1928–30 and 1930–32 on the percentages of Catholics and Farm Population in the total population*

Increase in % NSDAP voters	Partial correlations		Regression coefficients		Regression constant	Coefficient of determina-tion (R^2)
	Cath.	Farm Pop.	Cath.	Farm Pop.		
1928–30	÷.64	+.35	÷.104	+.100	16.6	.43
1930–32	÷.78	+.65	÷.160	+.240	19.1	.66

As independent variables the percentages of Catholics, farm population, industrial labour force, unemployed, voting turnout, farm size, etc. were available. Since many of these variables appeared to be intercorrelated at this level of data-aggregation, it was not necessary or useful to take too many variables into account. As is shown in table 4, half or more of the variance could be related to the variables Catholics and farm population. Addition of more variables of this kind improved the coefficient of determination only slightly, producing very bad regression coefficients because of multicollinearity. (For the method and problems of ecological regression, see Alker 1969a,b and Boudon 1963.)

The result of this statistical analysis allows two conclusions. First, an interesting estimate can be made of the proportions of Catholics and farmers that may have been attracted by the NSDAP in September 1930 and July 1932. According to the method proposed by Goodman (1953, 1959) and Duncan *et al.* (1961, p. 73 ff.) these proportions can be derived from the regression parameters. Table 5 gives these estimated proportions. Some typical areas have been added in which one of these social groups is overrepresented; for these areas, the expected outcome of Nazi voters (according to the regression equations) can be compared with the observed percentage.

Table 5. *Estimated increase in the percentage of NSDAP voters 1928–32 among Catholics and farmers.*[a]

Social category	Estimated % increase 1928–30	Estimated % increase 1930–32	Total 1928–32	Increase in % Nazi voters in some typical areas		
				Exp.	Obs.	Area
Catholic/Non Farm ..	6.2	3.1	9.3	16.7	14.3	Aachen[b]
Catholic/Farm	16.2	27.1	43.3	28.9	27.1	Trier[c]
Non-Catholic/Non-Farm	16.6	19.1	35.7	37.6	34.1	Leipzig[d]
Non-Catholic/Farm ..	26.6	43.1	67.7	51.7	49.0	Köslin[e]

[a] The percentages have been estimated on the basis of the regression coefficients and constants given in table 4.
[b] Reg.Bez. Aachen, Catholics 91.6%, Farm Population 15.4%.
[c] Reg.Bez. Trier + Oldenburgisches Birkenfeld, Catholics 82.0%, Farm Pop. 43.7%.
[d] Kreishptm. Leipzig, Catholics 3.1%, Farm Population 8.1%.
[e] Reg.Bez. Köslin, Catholics 3.0%, Farm Population 49.3%.

For the purpose of this paper the second conclusion is most important: as the larger part of the variance is related to the variables Catholics and farm population, these can be used to classify the areas in large-scale Nazi mobilization contexts from which smaller units might be picked for detailed studies.

In principle there are two ways to arrive at such a classification: one can use a computerized linkage procedure in which the 68 units are grouped step-by-step according to their similarity, or one can use a divisive approach in which the units become divided step-by-step according to their dissimilarity. Since we have an insight into the relevant variables associated with Nazi voting in our areas, the second procedure is chosen for reasons of economy.

Every classification procedure has its subjective aspects, the first being the selection of the variables to be taken into consideration. Since our purpose is the generation of contexts of diverging levels of Nazi voting the variables must be positively or negatively correlated with Nazi support. As we have seen, two sets are available: first, variables depicting gross social backgrounds of Nazism at this level of aggregation, i.e. the proportions of Catholics and farm population; secondly, variables describing the political situation on the eve of the Nazi landslide, i.e., the proportions of voters in the 1928 elections of both parties which melted away in later years and of parties which remained stable. Both classifications will be produced and compared.

Religion and Agriculture
In respect of the percentage of Catholics and of farm population the areas under study show considerable variation that can be related to Nazi voting (tables 4 and 5). Besides, the theories about the social basis of Nazism offer interpretations to be researched in further studies. Therefore these variables are relevant for classification.

Table 6. *Classification of areas into Nazi mobilization regions according to percentages Catholics and Farm Population (1933)*

Start	Step 1	Step 2
	Criterion: Areas have more/less than 32.5% Catholics	*Criterion:* Areas have more/less than 21.0% Farm Population
		Urbanized Catholic Germany N=10, Nazi vote 27.2%
	Catholic Germany N=29, Nazi vote 28.6%	
		Rural Catholic Germany N=19, Nazi vote 29.8%
Germany N=68, Nazi vote 33.1%		
		Urbanized Protestant Germany N=18, Nazi vote 32.5%
	Protestant Germany N=39, Nazi vote 36.3%	
		Rural Protestant Germany N=21, Nazi vote 40.6%

N= number of areas involved. Nazi vote= Average NSDAP percentage 1930–33.

In our procedure, contrasting groups of units have been formed by successively dividing the population (table 6). Units with more than the average percentage of Catholics (32.5 per cent) have been separated from units without this proportion. Then these categories have been divided again into groups in which the farm population did or did not exceed the national average (21 per cent). The location of the areas of the resulting four types is given in Figure 3.

For each of the types, the average Nazi vote in 1930–33 has been calculated, showing – as was to be expected – clear contrasts in the tendency toward Nazism: from 27 per cent in the Catholic-urban areas of Western Germany up to 40 per cent in the Protestant-rural areas in the North and East.

Politics on the Eve of the Landslide

Concomitant with the Nazi landslide was the rapid «demobilization» of the other right-wing and centre parties in the Weimar Republic. Their downfall was a necessary condition for the rise of fascism, giving Hitler the «opportunity space» to penetrate the electorate. These parties as well as the resistant Catholic and left-wing blocks had established their regional strongholds before 1930, hence the opportunity for Nazism differed regionally. The second classification tries to map this divergence in fascist opportunity space by considering the vote cast in the 1928 elections for the parties which gave way to Nazism as well as for the parties which were obstacles for Nazism by their stability. Thus useful mobilization contexts can also be distinguished. It may

Fig. 3. *Four Nazi mobilisation regions according to % Catholics and Farm Population*

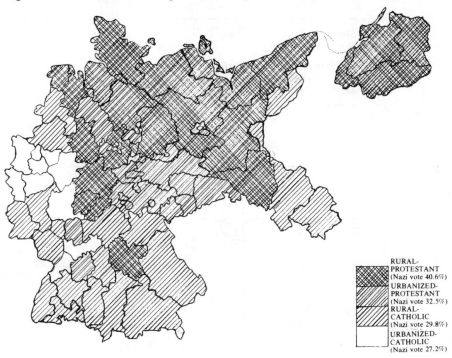

RURAL-
PROTESTANT
(Nazi vote 40.6%)
URBANIZED-
PROTESTANT
(Nazi vote 32.5%)
RURAL-
CATHOLIC
(Nazi vote 29.8%)
URBANIZED-
CATHOLIC
(Nazi vote 27.2%)

be expected that the regions found in this classification will overlap considerably with the contexts distinguished earlier.

In our procedure, the parties to the right of the *Zentrumspartei* (the Catholic Center Party) have been considered as the demobilizing parties, i.e. in 1928 the block of the Nationalist party (DNVP, 14.1 per cent) on the one hand, and the block of the small centrist parties (Liberals, special interest parties, etc., 27.6 per cent) on the other hand. It is assumed that domination by one of these blocks indicates a difference in socio-political structure, small party areas being more fragmented and also economically more heterogeneous than Nationalist areas. Therefore, after separating areas with a high propensity for Nazism (NSDAP + demobilizing parties in 1928 stronger than the average 44.5 per cent), these areas have been split into areas dominated by either the Nationalist party or the smaller parties.

As the opportunity space for Nazism was also determined by the strength of the resistant parties, their performance in 1928 is entered into the classification to distinguish demobilization areas with smaller and larger opportunities for Nazism (smaller opportunities where the total vote for Catholic and left-wing parties in 1928 was over 50 per cent). It appeared that in this way the small party areas were concentrated in two clearly observable regions (Fig. 4).

Furthermore, the areas where Nazism had the smallest opportunity space in 1928 have been divided into one group dominated by left-wing parties and one group where the *Zentrumspartei* had more voters than the socialists together.

295

Table 7. *Classification of areas into Nazi mobilization regions according to voting behaviour in 1928*

Start	Step 1	Step 2	Step 3
	Criterion: Areas have more/less than 44.5% centrist and right-wing voters	*Criteria:* Resistant vote dominated by *Zentrum*/left-wing parties or opportunity vote dominated by DNVP/ small parties	*Criterion:* Opportunity areas had a resistant vote more/less than 50%

Germany
N=68,
Nazi vote
33.1%

Resistant areas
N=29, Nazi vote 28.0%

Catholic Germany
N=14, Nazi vote 24.4%

Socialist Germany
N=15, Nazi vote 30.2%

Opportunity areas
N=39, Nazi vote 37.3%

Small Party Germany
N=29, Nazi vote 36.1%

Average Germany
N=14, Nazi vote 34.7%

Small Party Germany
N=15, Nazi vote 37.8%

Nationalist Germany
N=10, Nazi vote 41.2%

Fig. 4. *Five Nazi mobilisation regions according to opportunity space 1928*

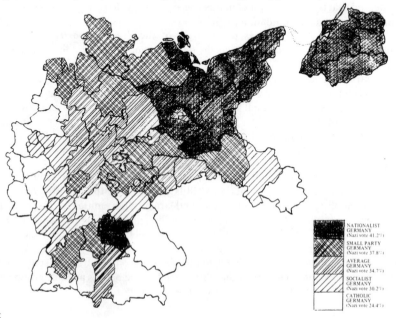

NATIONALIST GERMANY (Nazi vote 41.2%)

SMALL PARTY GERMANY (Nazi vote 37.8%)

AVERAGE GERMANY (Nazi vote 34.7%)

SOCIALIST GERMANY (Nazi vote 30.2%)

CATHOLIC GERMANY (Nazi vote 24.4%)

The resulting regionalization of Germany (Fig. 4) shows five types of areas, again each with a different average Nazi-percentage (from 24 per cent in the *Zentrum*-areas up to 41 per cent in the former DNVP-areas).

As expected there is considerable coincidence between both classifications, as can be seen from the maps. Cross-tabulation produces a clear correlation of .44 (Guttman's λ). Therefore, it seems appropriate only to give the types of the last classification a label and a short description.

A. *Nationalist Germany* – The provinces of East-Prussia, Pomerania, the *Grenzmark* Posen–West-Prussia clearly stand out as the classical lands of East-Elbian Prussia. Only the capital Berlin is not contained in it, whereas one distant area in Central-Franconia has to be added. The DNVP had been dominant in these areas for years, especially in the heavily rural areas where often half of the labour force was still on the land in 1933. Agriculture was dominated by large holdings, the average level of prosperity being very low. Raupach (1967, p. 14–17) considered these poor, agricultural regions outside the influence of the big cities the «German periphery». Apart from the more urbanized surroundings of Berlin, and despite the poverty in these emigration areas, the left-wing parties could not profit politically there.

B. *Small Party Germany* – A more diverse group of areas in which already during the twenties the special interest and regionalist parties had been supported. It consists of the rural Protestant areas along the Northern seaboard and the Weser-Elbe region, areas treated in a very detailed fashion by Heberle (1963) and Noakes (1971), both in terms of their nazification histories and the role of the minor parties. Other farming regions with strong small-party traditions are Upper Hesse and most of Württemberg. Small family farms and specialized production characterize these regions. Even in the more urbanized areas in this class, Thuringia, parts of Saxony, and Lower Silesia, small-scale enterprise has been important; hence, perhaps, the tendency to support the special interest parties. South-west Berlin with its upper-class and white-collar population traditionally supporting liberal parties was a special case here.

C. *Average Germany* – This classification contains, apart from Catholic and agricultural Swabia, mostly Protestant areas in Central Germany, somewhat more urbanized than the other small party regions, and with a greater left-wing element in the electorate. Cities like Bremen and Hamburg had large white-collar populations, not always supporting the Labour party; Saxony was industrial with an emphasis on small enterprise. Mixed populations without dominant party blocks in 1928 and an average Nazi vote later on are typical for this category.

D. *Socialist Germany* – Urban areas along the Rhine and its tributaries form the core of this type, e.g. the Ruhr and Rhine-Main region, together with most of the city of Berlin. Several areas with considerable farm populations are also found in this group, like parts of Lower Silesia, Upper Franconia, and the Palatinate region. Most of these areas have Protestant populations, although some have large Catholic minorities as do most West German regions.

E. *Catholic Germany* – Finally the majority Catholic areas of Western and Southern Germany, urban as well as rural districts in Westphalia, Rhineland, Bavaria, Baden and Württemberg. In these parts of the country, the *Zentrumspartei* could secure its vote in industrial as well as agricultural districts, often competing with left-wing and other class parties. The tendency towards nazification was lowest in these areas in later years. In the East, only Upper Silesia was a Catholic stronghold, being also of a mixed urban-rural nature.

Conclusion

This paper started by expressing the view that more community studies are necessary to explain the decline of several of the Weimar parties and the subsequent Nazi landslide. We have argued that in order to select communities for such studies, contextual differences at the regional level have to be considered. Comparison of details from such different contexts could yield fresh insights into conditions governing the process of Nazi mobilization.

We have aimed to show the relative importance of regional differences in Nazi voting and to trace the relevant contexts. By breaking down the variance of the Nazi vote through time and space into national and regional trend factors, we have shown that a considerable proportion of that variance has been contributed by regional deviations from the national trend. These deviations were stable over time, so that they can be related to structural or cultural characteristics of those regions.

Following theories about the social bases of Nazism we have put forward two sets of characteristics in order to trace relevant mobilization contexts by classification. Both theoretically and empirically, the variation in the Nazi vote can be related to the composition of the areas' populations with regard to religion, living on farms, and earlier voting behaviour. By using these variables, two contextual classifications have been produced which partly coincide. The contexts which are thus singled out, although few, represent different levels of Nazi voting *and* different factors behind that pattern.

NOTES

[1] It has to be emphasized that the study of the Nazi landslide should be as much a study of the rise of the NSDAP as of the complete downfall of a number of Weimar parties.

[2] The influence of differences between regions within one country has been extensively treated by Linz & Miguel (1966). They also make an interesting attempt at distinguishing such regions.

[3] Apart from my own modifications these units as *grössere Verwaltungseinheiten* (larger administrative units) often appear in the statistical sources as levels of aggregation. They have been chosen for that reason and for their limited number. Their large size is a disadvantage as much variation is concealed within the units. The alternative of sampling smaller units of analysis at the levels of *Kreis* or *Gemeinde* did not seem appropriate in relation to the classificatory purpose of this paper.

[4] At this stage it is possible to draw a parallel with the Dutch situation of 1934–36 in which a growing fascist movement – taking 8 per cent of the vote in its first election – was blocked by the existing political system. In this system of vertical pluralism, brought about by a process of *verzuiling* or «pillarization» (cf. Goudsblom 1967, pp. 120–127; Lijphart 1968), each «pillar» is a self-contained, close-knit organization, representing its religious or class segment up to the highest political level. When the Dutch Nazis grew into a mass movement, they did not succeed in making major and prolonged inroads in the electorates of the «pillars». They simply did not have the «opportunity space», not because of the pillars' successful representation, or because of the plain deference of the people to their leaders, but precisely because of the power of the pillars to enforce a policy of isolation of the Nazis. Dutch Nazis became socially and politically

isolated by effective counterpropaganda within the pillars, by stigmatization, by prohibition of membership for civil servants, etc. For further information on Dutch Nazism, see the paper by Smit & Van der Wusten in this book.

[5] This theory is related to the theory of politics in mass society (Kornhauser 1959) concerning the atomization of individuals in industrial society, making them ready for totalitarian movements. Application of this theory to the Weimar situation has been disputed recently by Oberschall (1973, pp. 108–113), also by Hagtvet in his paper in this book, on the grounds of the high degree of organization and integration of the middle classes and farmers in Germany at that time. This criticism may also apply to the *Gemeinschaft*-thesis of Loomis & Beegle.

LITERATURE

ALKER, H. R. Jr. (1969a), A Typology of Ecological Fallacies. *In:* M. DOGAN & S. ROKKAN (eds.), *Quantitative Ecological Analysis in the Social Sciences*. Cambridge, Mass., pp. 69–86.

ALKER, H. R. Jr. (1969b), Statistics and Politics: The Need for Causal Data Analysis. *In:* S. M. LIPSET (ed.), *Politics and the Social Sciences*. New York, pp. 244–313.

ALLEN, W. S. (1965), *The Nazi Seizure of Power: The Experience of a Single German Town*. Chicago.

BOUDON, R. (1963), Propriétés individuelles et propriétés collectives: un problème d'analyse écologique. *Revue Française de Sociologie 4*, pp. 275–299.

BRACHER, K. D. (1965), *Die Auflösung der Weimarer Republik*. Villingen.

DAHRENDORF, R. (1968), *Gesellschaft und Demokratie in Deutschland*. München.

DICKINSON, R. E. (1945), *The Regions of Germany*, London.

DUNCAN, O. D., B. DUNCAN & R. P. CUZZORT (1961), *Statistical Geography: Problems in Analyzing Areal Data*. Glencoe.

GEIGER, Th. (1930), Panik im Mittelstand. *Die Arbeit 7* (10), pp. 637–654.

GEIGER, Th. (1932), *Die soziale Schichtung des deutschen Volkes*, Stuttgart.

GERTH, H. H. (1952), The Nazy Party: Its Leadership and Composition. *In:* R. BENDIX *et al.* (eds.), *Reader in Bureaucracy*. New York.

GOODMAN, L. A. (1953), Ecological Regression and Behavior of Individuals. *American Sociological Review* 18, pp. 663–664.

GOODMAN, L. A. (1959), Some Alternatives to Ecological Correlation. *American Journal of Sociology* 64, pp. 610–625.

GOUDSBLOM, J. (1967), *Dutch Society*. New York.

HEBERLE, R. (1963), *Landbevölkerung und Nationalsozialismus: Eine soziologische Untersuchung der politischen Willensbildung in Schleswig-Holstein, 1918–1932*. Stuttgart. (1st. English ed. 1945).

HUNT, R. N. (1964), *German Social Democracy, 1918–1933*. New Haven.

KORNHAUSER, W. (1959), *The Politics of Mass Society*. Glencoe.

LEPSIUS, R. M. (1966), *Extremer Nationalismus: Strukturbedingungen vor der nationalsozialistischen Machtergreifung*. Stuttgart.

LIJPHART, A. (1968), *The Politics of Accommodation: Pluralism and Democracy in the Netherlands*. Berkeley/Los Angeles.

LINZ, J. J. & A. DE MIGUEL (1966), Within-Nation Differences and Comparisons: The Eight Spains. *In:* R. L. MERRITT & S. ROKKAN (eds.), *Comparing Nations*. New Haven, pp. 267–319.

LIPSET, S. M. (1960), *Political Man*. New York.

LOOMIS, C. P. & J. A. BEEGLE (1946), The Spread of German Nazism in Rural Areas. *American Sociological Review* 11, pp. 724–734.

MACRAE, D. & J. A. MELDRUM (1969), Critical Elections in Illinois, 1888–1958. *American Political Science Review* 54, pp. 669–683.

MILATZ, A. (1965), *Wähler und Wahlen in der Weimarer Republik*. Bonn.

NEUMANN, S. (1932), *Die politischen Parteien der Weimarer Republik*. Stuttgart.

NILSON, S. S. (1954), Wahlsoziologische Probleme des Nationalsozialismus. *Zeitschrift für die gesamte Staatswissenschaften* 110, pp. 279–311.

NOAKES, J. (1971), *The Nazi Party in Lower Saxony, 1921–1933*. London.

OBERSCHALL, A. (1973), *Social Conflict and Social Movements*. Englewood Cliffs.

O'LESSKER, K. (1968), Who Voted for Hitler? A New Look at the Class Basis of Nazism. *American Journal of Sociology* 74, pp. 63–69.

PASSCHIER, N. (1972), *De benadering van samenhangende individuele kenmerken uit geaggregeerd materiaal via ecologische regressie*. Unpubl. ms.

RAUPACH, H. (1967), Der interregionale Wohlfahrtsausgleich als Problem des Deutschen Reiches. *In*: W. CONZE & H. RAUPACH (eds.), *Die Staats- und Wirtschaftskrise des Deutschen Reiches 1929–33*. Stuttgart, pp. 13–34.

RIEMER, S. (1932), Zur Soziologie des Nazionalsozialismus. *Die Arbeit* 9 (2), pp. 101–118.

SCHÄFER, W. (1957), *NSDAP: Entwicklung und Struktur der Staatspartei des Dritten Reiches*. Hannover/Frankfurt.

STOKES, D. E. (1966), A Variance Components Model of Political Effects. *In*: J. CLAUNCH (ed.), *Mathematical Applications in Political Science*. Dallas, pp. 61–85.

Gestapo and the SD: A Sociographic Profile of The Organizers of Terror

FRIEDRICH ZIPFEL †

When Hitler moved into the Reich Chancellory on January 30th 1933, he assumed control of a state apparatus which was largely paralyzed. Trust in democracy, if it had ever existed, had been destroyed in large sections of the population. Hopes turned to the strong leader; people were ready to exchange freedom for order. There was a widespread feeling that only through dictatorial measures could the crisis be overcome. Despite intimidation and terror, the results of the election held on March 5th seemed to indicate that more than half of the German population favored the «government of national concentration» which was formed by Hitler's National Socialists and other nationalists.

During the election campaign, in the evening of February 27th, the German *Reichstag* went up in flames. This event proved to be of momentous importance in the period to follow. For some time the current interpretation of the fire has been to blame the Dutch anarchist van der Lubbe and him alone. The hypothesis cannot yet be said to be fully confirmed, as recent research into the incident has shown. Most certainly, the Nazis themselves were the instigators of this arson, though certain details are still far from clear. For our purposes, deciding the actual responsibility for the fire is less important than analyzing how the Nazis made use of the incident. The day after the fire the President of the republic issued an ordinance for «the protection of People and the State», repealing the basic civil rights laid down in the constitution. Thereafter there was no effective legal protection against arbitrary rule by the state.

The Reichstag fire was not the only basis for unleashing full-fledged terror in Germany. In fact, the fire only accelerated a process which was to establish the SA and the SS, as well as the German Nationalist *Stahlhelm* organization, as auxiliary police forces acting not only with the consent of the state but also on explicit instructions from it. A case in point is the well-prepared action against the communists even before the decree had been issued, leading to the arrest of about 4,000 Communist party functionaries during the night of the fire. The decree did nothing more than legalize acts of violence that were already a familiar part of the German political scene. It also formed the legal basis for future terror.

In this paper we shall address ourselves to the question of the social origins of the men carrying out the persecution, first in Germany and later in other parts of Europe. Anyone investigating this matter is faced with a series of problems. For a thorough examination, thousands of isolated cases in Germany would have to be analyzed. Written documents exist, however, only in a few cases, so that a complete answer cannot be expected. On the whole, it is easier to examine the leadership strata because files on them are more complete and more systematically organized. The following material is based on the organizational plans and the personal files of the SD *(Sicherheitsdienst)*, the Gestapo *(Geheime Staats-polizei)* and the *Reichssicherheits-*

hauptamt (RSHA), the Security Service of the Reich, the secret political police, and the Central Bureau for Security of the Reich, respectively.[1] The regional and local police and the SS authorities are not included here, nor are the commanders, officers and guards in the concentration camps and members of the mobile execution squads, the *Einsatzgruppen*.

The Political Police in Pre-Nazi Germany

A few comments on the institutions of police surveillance in pre-Weimar Germany will provide a background for a better understanding of the traditions on which the Nazi organizers of terror could draw.

After the Karlsbad revolutions of 1819, the police authorities in the German Confederation developed joint anti-subversive activities. Having then gradually diminished in importance, these early co-ordination efforts again proved crucial when, in 1878, Bismarck had his anti-socialist laws passed in the German parliament. In Berlin, the Prussian government established an office headed by the city head of police, and empowered it to collect information on members of illegal political parties. This office made agreements with other state police forces whereby local police were obliged to pass on information on subversive elements to the head office in the Prussian capital. Thus in spite of the federal structure of Germany, a central office for the fight against Social Democrats was established. Its jurisdiction was limited to the compilation of information; actual prosecution had to be carried out by local authorities. The Berlin office continued to perform these functions until the Anti-Socialist laws were repealed.

The unrest after World War I again made surveillance of political activists desirable. Rather ironically, the men in charge of the new police authorities were for the most part Social Democratic politicians. Early in the year 1919 a department IA was set up at the Berlin headquarters camouflaged as an appendage to another office. Its task, besides compiling information on potential state enemies, was to keep a watchful eye on the allied Armistice Commission. Although its authority only extended to Prussia, and despite the lack of any formal agreements with other state governments, cooperation between police forces in different German states was common. Under the Social Democratic chief of police and Ministers of the Interior, the department IA remained a small branch of the entire police force working within the bounds of legality. In 1931 it still consisted of 7 higher and 7 subordinate officials. Only as late as the summer of 1932 was it expanded.

Except in Bavaria, the development of political surveillance in the rest of Germany took more or less the same form as in Prussia. In the Bavarian constitution of 1919, the Munich chief of police was entrusted with special authority by the *Land* government as head of political intelligence, not only in the city of Munich itself but in the whole administrative region of Munich. As a rule, however, authority over the political police was exercised directly by the Bavarian Ministry of the Interior. It was not until the end of 1932 that the chief of police in Munich was assigned powers of this kind for the whole of Bavaria. The department of political intelligence in the Munich police headquarters seems to have been very active and staffed with qualified officials. Reports on Hitler's meetings in the year 1920, for example, were compiled here.

The Prussian Secret State Police

Immediately after the seizure of power, Herrmann Göring was provisionally charged with the administration of the Prussian Ministry of the Interior. One of the first acts he performed in this new capacity was to appoint Rudolf Diels as director of the department for the persecution of communists. Also among Diels' duties was conduct of the campaign to purge the Prussian state administration of politically «unreliable» elements. Diels' popular image has to a large extent been formed by his memoirs *Lucifer ante portas*. Even in the long tradition of self-adulatory memoirs, there are probably very few books of this genre in which truth has been so thoroughly turned upside-down as in the Diels memoirs. Presenting himself and his colleagues as loyal Prussian officials, trained in the spirit of Severing, the SPD Minister of the Interior, and accidentally making Göring's acquaintance, he asserts his own innocence in the period of persecution. Together with his friends, he maintains, he tried to save as much as possible of the rule of law.

The records of the ministry and his own personal files reveal quite another picture, however: from March 1932, Diels had been a supporting member of the SA (being a Prussian civil servant he was barred from becoming a regular SA member); and on July 20th, 1932, he participated directly in von Papen's plot against the Prussian government, accusing his immediate superior, Dr. Abegg, the Secretary of State in the ministry, of plotting with the communists. In view of these actions it is hardly surprising that the man was on good terms with von Papen and was promoted to the rank of senior government councillor before his turn had come. In his SS curriculum vitae Diels boasts about these achievements, in particular his pre-1933 coordination of the political police and the NSDAP for the purpose of fighting the Communist party. Göring no doubt knew that he took a reliable man into his confidence when he entrusted Diels with the powers of heading the political police in Prussia.

Diels' right-hand-man in those days was Heinrich Schnitzler («Lucifer» as he was called). He had also taken part in the plot against the Prussian government and had since August 1932 been in contact with high officials in the NSDAP. In the party, Schnitzler was supported by Helmut Heisig, who played an important part in the investigation of the fire in the *Reichstag*. He too was a member of an illegal «Nationalsozialistische Beamten-Arbeitsgemeinschaft» (National Socialist Work Group) which had been founded by Arthur Nebe. Nebe was at first Diels' colleague in the Gestapo and later the chief of the German criminal investigations department. Diels, moreover, brought two other high officials from Breslau into his Gestapo who had also been members of the «Arbeitsgemeinschaft». Nevertheless in his memoirs he writes: «In the whole Land of Prussia you could count the higher officials who showed an inclination towards National Socialism on the fingers of your hands.»

When, at the beginning of 1933, Göring conferred the administration of the department IA upon his confidant, its powers were expanded to include executive tasks. This involved an essential expansion of personnel. The «Karl-Liebknecht-Haus», the former Communist party centre, temporarily served as accommodation. Diels' department found its final home in a confiscated school in the Prinz-Albert-Strasse. On April 26th, 1933, Göring separated the department from the police headquarters. He put it directly under his own control and named it *Preussische Geheime Staatspolizei* (the Prussian Secret State Police). The 32 year old Diels also forgot to mention in his memoirs that from 1932 he happened to be married to a sister-in-law of Göring.

Diels now actively set out to consolidate his position. In addition to the experts from the Ministry of the Interior and the department IA, officials from other departments of the Prussian police and administration were transferred to the Gestapo. Added to them were also a number of men who had not hitherto been employed in the civil service. In the name file of the persons employed by the Gestapo in July 1935, we find that even during Diels' term of office (until April 1934) a great number of men who were strangers to officialdom were taken into this organization. Among the 340 men employed in the department at that time, there were 85 «employees», i.e. persons who did not have the qualifications necessary for public service. Regarding a number of these officials, we find the additional comment «on probation». Thus they must have been newly admitted to the police services. The majority of these «employees» were members of the SS.

In his memoirs, Diels reports that he had serious conflicts with the leaders of the party and the SA because he allegedly turned against terror in the interests of preserving the rule of law. In most cases this proved to be futile, he writes, as he did not get the necessary backing from his superior, Göring. Events may have taken place in approximately this manner, but Diels' motive was likely to have been a different one. It was more a question of the personal prestige involved in controlling the administration of the political police force. For this reason he could not tolerate any arbitrary acts by SA-leaders or any «illegal» concentration camps.

Diels was a successful administrator. The act establishing a secret police office on April 26th had made the Gestapo a Prussian central office, entitled to «request» police cooperation from all police authorities on November 30th, 1933; another one provided that from now on the Gestapo was to be directly under the control of the Minister President, Göring, and that the subordinate officials had to comply with his directions. Diels had asserted himself in the administration; the basis for further consolidation had been established.

The Bavarian Political Police

While Diels in Prussia was scuffling with individual SA-leaders and building up his office, Himmler and Heydrich were deliberately consolidating their powerful positions in Munich. Their basis was the SS which had developed out of the bodyguards of Hitler and other high party leaders. When the agricultural manager Heinrich Himmler, son of a grammar-school teacher, became the leader of the SS in the end of 1929, he took over a small group of 280 people who were under the command of the SA-leadership. At once Himmler began his expansion. He did not want to form yet another mass organization beside the SA, but an élite unit. Only those with certain biological and character qualities as Himmler understood them could be members of the SS. Above all this organization was meant to attract the young intelligentsia. By January 30th, 1933, the ranks of the SS had swelled to 52,000 members.

Beside its traditional task, the protection of the party leaders, the SS was commissioned to build up the central party organization and to safeguard party meetings. But Himmler was not content with this. He also wanted his own efficient intelligence service, to protect himself against other intelligence services (especially that of the police), gather his own information and control competing party leaders. He won over Reinhard Heydrich for the task of establishing the IC-service – to give it its original name. Heydrich (a music-teacher's son) was a dishonourably discharged naval officer. Talented and ruthless, this man developed just the instrument Himmler needed, the *Sicherheitsdienst* (SD) (Security Service), at first mostly with unpaid help. No fighting qualities were demanded for membership in the SD, but intelligence, attentiveness and influence. Membership in the NSDAP and in the SS was not necessarily required. Heydrich succeeded in recruiting confidants in the various political parties and also from business. Thus the chief of the SD became one of the best-informed men in Germany.

On March 9th, 1933, the Bavarian government was removed by a coup d'état. The new commissar of the Reich, Ritter von Epp, appointed the NSDAP-Gauleiter Wagner as Minister of the Interior on the same day, and Himmler was made chief of the police in Munich. Himmler in turn made his SD-chief Heydrich chief of the political department in the Ministry of the Interior, by which move he acquired the power to give instructions to the police commissioners installed by the SA. He was now in possession of total police authority in Bavaria, and when he was officially appointed political police commissioner of Bavaria on April 1st, it was but a formal act confirming a power position then unrivalled anywhere in the Reich, unless perhaps by Diels in Berlin. He again promoted Heydrich, this time to the top of the Bavarian police (BPP), and as Commissioner he was in charge of all police work in the field of political surveillance, as well as of the auxiliary police and the concentration camps in Bavaria.

The Establishment of the First Concentration Camps

In Prussia the first wave of arrests and the introduction of «preventive detention» had been organized regionally or locally. In the early phase, Diels failed to get things under control. In Bavaria, on the other hand, Himmler very rapidly brought the execution of terror under his command. «Illegal» concentration camps were already in existence, but Himmler wasted no time in putting the official seal on the establishment of these institutions. On March 20th, Himmler issued a decree announcing the establishment of the concentration camp in Dachau with a capacity of 5,000 prisoners, the central detention centre to which all prisoners in Bavaria were to be sent. Its first commander, Hilmar Wäckerle, developed the regulations of the camp and its penal system, later put into practice by his successor, Theodor Eicke. Subsequently, Dachau became the model for all German concentration camps. As an institution of the state, it was equipped and paid for by the Ministry of the Interior. Similarly, the SS members employed in the administration and as guards were on the state payroll. While the SA chief, Röhm, more and more involved himself in opposition against the state officialdom and was finally ruined by this conflict, Himmler chose to integrate his SS into the state. He fashioned a militarily-organized and trained unit out of the guards at Dachau which became an integral part of the SS and had the support of the Bavarian government: Eicke's first SS *Totenkopf-Standarte*.

Himmler's career did not always go smoothly. He had to transfer the Munich police headquarters to his personal enemy, the SA-leader Schneidhuber, though without the political police functions. A permanent conflict arose with the Minister of Justice, Hans Frank, the future Governor-General in Poland, because of the conditions in Dachau, the maltreatment and the murders. But Himmler had established himself in the essential positions before the others had realized the importance of the respective offices. Heydrich's SD spies kept him reliably informed about the intentions of his rivals. More vitally, he controlled the SS, an instrument making him superior to all his rivals, a kind of personal power unit. It was sufficiently independent of the state but could also if necessary be used as a semi-governmental organization against other party branches (as for example on June 30th, 1934). He was considered, after all, the most loyal supporter of Hitler, from whom all the men in the brown shirts and in the various offices derived their power.

Himmler's and Heydrich's Career

As early as the summer of 1933 some authorities outside of Bavaria had sent their political prisoners to the «model camp» Dachau. Himmler's reputation as an efficient chief of police was spreading. Whether it was due to his cleverness in negotiating with the governments of the states or to the activities of the SD, in November 1933 Himmler was appointed commander of the political police by the authorities of the smaller German states as well.

Still the most important state was not yet under his authority: Prussia. Here Göring did not intend to relinquish the Gestapo. But their common rivalry towards the SA chief, Röhm, brought him together with Himmler, who cleverly played on Göring's vanity. He let the Minister President have the title Chief and contented himself with being the Deputy Chief. Thus on April 20th, 1934, the Prussian Gestapo was also conferred upon Himmler. Heydrich was made the leader of this force. His former superior, Diels, was promoted to district president and sent off to Cologne.

In the Prinz-Albrecht-Strasse Heydrich at once established a new office, The Constituent States' Political Police Headquarters (Der Politische Polizeikommandeur der Länder), which was in charge of political surveillance in all states other than Prussia. This expansion made it possible for the head of this office to call non-Prussian officials to Berlin. Now the fight against political opponents could be coordinated throughout the whole of the *Reich*.

The efficiency of this coordination was proven on June 30th, 1934, when the SS and the political police took an essential part in the execution of the hated SA leaders and other troublesome persons. After these actions, which finally secured Himmler the independence of his SS from the SA leadership and gave him command over all German concentration camps, Heydrich energetically started reorganizing the Gestapo. The plan of organization of October 1934 shows that a general upgrading in rank was intended. The departments were made main departments, the minor departments were made sub-departments etc. By October 1935, The Constituent States' Police Headquarters had been expanded to 607 officials. Diels had started with about 40. By the end of 1934, most of his leading officials had been replaced by Bavarian officials or by young Prussian SS officials. Qualified officials still were in the majority, but only in non-political, administrative offices could they be found in leading positions. Some were men who could hardly be discharged because of their accredited services to the SS. The essential positions were held by a group which Heydrich had brought with him from the BBP, persons such as Heinrich Müller and Franz Josef Huber. Both of these had been of lower rank in the Munich police headquarters. In Bavaria they had even been considered opponents of the NSDAP, but both had made themselves indispensable to Heydrich by their faithful services. In Berlin their lack of qualifications as higher officials was made up for by conferment of a corresponding rank in the SS. Thus subordinate officials could be placed at the top of a department in which university-trained lawyers had to carry out the expert work. Müller rose to be the chief of the whole German Gestapo with the rank of Lieutenant-general. Huber was made chief of the Gestapo in Vienna in 1938, rising to the rank of major general.

The need for specialists continued. From 1935 on, however, qualified officials could be found who had gone through the school of the *Hitler Youth* and the *NS-Student Federation*, or who had gained the necessary qualifications by their university studies, or received their training in Heydrich's offices. More and more they pushed out the old specialists from the Weimar police and also many of Heydrich's favourites from Munich. Of course there were many offices in Germany to which they could be relegated with full honours. By the end of 1938 Heydrich's secure position was based almost without exception on men who owed their promotions to him. The few older survivors had adapted themselves sufficiently to be agreeable to their superior.

In the meantime, development of the police continued. In 1936 Himmler was able to free himself from the inconvenient authority of Göring. A decree by Hitler of June 17 made him the chief of a new, comprehensive office with the title Reichsführer SS and Chief of the German Police in the Ministry of the Interior. From now on the Prussian and Bavarian police forces no longer existed as such. His new title did not mean that Himmler was subordinate to the Minister of the Interior. In police matters his decision was considered that of the Minister. His title meant that here the party organization (SS) and the state organization (police) were united in one institution and in one man, a combination which was also applied to Heydrich's office. In 1936, Heydrich became the chief of the security police in Himmler's new office, into which the criminal investigation office and the Gestapo were incorporated. The Chief of the General Police, the Prussian police general and SS leader Kurt Daluege obtained command over all the other police functions.

As the chief of the security police, Heydrich had a state function. At the same time he was the chief of the SD. The cooperation of the two institutions which had begun earlier, now reached its culmination in the establishment of the *Reich* Security Main office (RSHA). Here the SD (department III, VI, VII), the Gestapo (department IV), and the criminal investigations department (department V) were united under Heydrich's leadership, though under joint administration and each keeping its personal files. During the war the persecution of opponents was organized on a large scale in Heinrich Müller's department IV, while the departments III and VII provided auxiliary services.

The Organizers of the Persecution

This development makes it clear that men of very dissimilar origins were employed in the RSHA, men whose relationship to the NSDAP varied greatly.

Diels had built up the Gestapo through a preponderance of experienced officials of the Prussian police and administration, some of whom had already made contact with the NSDAP or had given money to it. Others, however, had been taken into the office simply as specialists without any political commitments. Because of the personnel requirements, Diels had also been forced to accept individuals who did not belong to the police, mostly members of the SS. Yet he did not allow them to occupy leading positions. Only in the Berlin local chapter which was developing at the same time were these SS-men important.

Heydrich accepted the old officials to the extent that they were willing to adapt themselves in the manner required. To the key positions, he appointed his colleagues from the Bavarian political police, members of the subordinate official ranks who had so far had nothing to do with the NSDAP. One of them, Huber, had even fought against the NSDAP. The old officials were now pushed aside; Bavarians or proven SS men with some office experience were made their superiors. Without any sentimentality Heydrich got rid of officials and also of unqualified SS-leaders whom he found inconvenient. They were replaced by technocrats who had been trained in the meantime and of whose loyalty he was assured.

In 1939, the several offices of the RSHA were thus assigned:

1. Organization, administration and personnel were in the hands of Dr. Werner Best, 36 years old, a lawyer, who in 1931 had caused a stir by publishing the «Boxheimer Dokumente»; in 1933 he had built up the Hessian state police, was taken into the RSHA by Heydrich and had finally become chief of the administration of the Gestapo;
2. Ideological investigation and analysis, i.e. literature, the humanities and the sciences was led by Dr. Franz Six, 30 years old, granted a professorship in 1937 on Himmler's urging, a party member since 1930, a member of the SS since 1935;
3. *Deutsche Lebensgebiete*, a spy organization in the Reich, was headed by Otto Ohléndorf, 32 years old, a specialist in economics, a member of the party since 1925, a member of the SD since 1936;
4. The Gestapo was under the command of Heinrich Müller, 30 years old, a petty official admitted to the SS as late as 1934. He had in the meantime attained the rank of colonel. The Bavarian party authorities had energetically objected to his admittance into the NSDAP, though in vain;
5. Chief of the criminal investigation department was Arthur Nebe, 45 years old. He was the oldest departmental chief, and experienced Prussian crime investigator promoted from a subordinate position. He had already discovered his inclination for the NSDAP, but had joined the party and the SS as late as 1933;
6. At the top of the *SD-Ausland*, i.e. the foreign intelligence service, was the lawyer Hans Jost, 35 years old, party henchman since 1923, who in 1933 had played an important part in the Hessian police and had in 1934 entered the SS with the rank of major.
7. Heydrich, finally, the chief of the RSHA, had established the SD when he was 27 years old. He entered the Gestapo at 30 and was now 35.

The extraordinary youthfulness of these leading officials is noteworthy. Their subordinates were mostly of the same age group. Of the leaders of groups and minor departments exercising authority in the field of political persecution and identified in the organizational plans of 1941 and 1943, 9 were born before 1900, 32 between 1900 and 1910 and 5 even later.

Already in 1933, Diels had appointed certain of his contemporaries to his new Gestapo and conferred leading positions upon some of them, but the older career officials still dominated until mid-1934.

On the whole we can say that the organizers of the repression had almost without exception been born after 1900, and did not belong to the generation that had served at the front in World War I. Even if some of them had temporarily served in volunteer corps or student troops after the war, they lacked real «front» experience. This handicap was made up for by a special flair, by harshness, and by total contempt for fairness. By their youth, and lack of combat experience, the Gestapo élite differed profoundly from the leaders of the SA and the top officials of the party.

Since, according to German law, university graduation was usually required for the higher administration positions, it is not surprising that in the Gestapo many leading positions were occupied by lawyers. Of 135 officials examined, 46 were lawyers. There were other graduates as well: 8 philologists, 5 graduated economists, 3 Catholic and 1 Protestant clergymen, 2 physicians (they had become policemen) and 1 graduate in agriculture. Among these 66 graduates, only 10 had been born before 1900. 28 of the younger ones had entered Heydrich's services even before they had finished their studies. 5 others gave as their profession «student» when first entering the office. Among the non-graduates in leading positions, 23 came from subordinate positions in the police or the administration. 12 officials indicated other professions. In their case, as well as in the case of the subordinate officials, we repeatedly find in their curriculum vitae the remark that financial reasons had forced them to abandon their studies.

This survey of their professions conveys the impression of a somewhat unusual bureau. One third at the most had the qualifications required for these positions. It must be pointed out, however, that as a group they were intelligent and proficient, and knew their business well. This also applies to the promoted subordinate officials such as Heinrich Müller: he was uneducated and had no ambition to cut a fine figure in society. But in his office he was perfect, a good organizer, a clever negotiator, smooth and brutal at the same time, a loyal henchman for his superiors, a tough chief for his subordinates.

We cannot find out much about the social origins of these men. Their statements about their parents are often vague. The subordinate officals mostly originated from the lower middle-class, the higher officials from the higher middle-class. The professions of their fathers range from university-professors to physicians, from officers to merchants. But there are also master craftsmen and teachers. Both of these latter occupations have often been starting points or intermediate stages of social climbing. Most of the men with such fathers had gone through school and university with remarkable success.

What could have induced these men from families in orderly if plain circumstances, and generally with good educations, to assume offices in which they became the organizers or henchmen of mass murder?

Regarding their attitude towards the NSDAP the evidence is unreliable. In some of the personal files there are enthusiastic declarations for Hitler and the party. They may have been inspired by the wish to please a future superior. We also cannot rely on statements to the contrary, made after the war and for reasons of self-protection. Although we do not know their beliefs, some data may be helpful. Among those who had been members of the NSDAP before January 30th, 1933, the members of the «Alte Kämpfer» (old fighters) are estimated at one fourth and this is probably too high rather than too low. In the Weimar Republic they were not allowed to become members of the NSDAP. Yet there were quite a few NS adherents among them. In 1933 they and many others who had previously been neutral at once joined the party. Many of them quickly realized that the future was with the SS. Among the 32 SS leaders, named in the file of names of 1935, 10 joined this organization only after 1933; 6 of them had not even been members of the NSDAP. In 1937 Himmler initiated «equity promotions» i.e. the automatic conferment on officials who were members of the SS (or later joined it) of the SS rank corresponding to their position as civil servants. Conversely, the SS leaders obtained the titles and prestige of the corresponding official class. By 1941 almost all persons in the RSHA were thus «adjusted». There was one exception: Adolf Eichmann and the members of his Jewish department remained merely SS leaders. No official rank was ever conferred upon them.

To understand the meaning of joining the SS, we should point out the discordant character of this organization. It was considered a union of the élite and it did what it could to give the public this impression: strict selection, hard discipline, cultivation of certain sports which enjoyed a special prestige (horse-riding, fencing) etc. Thus Himmler especially appealed to the young intelligentsia and to men with influence. If he could not put them under his command he at least granted them an equivalent honorary rank which carried with it the right to wear the elegant black uniform. It was considered an honour to be allowed to be a member of the SS.

On the other hand «the order of the death's head» (Orden unter den Totenkopf) did the dirty work of the dictatorship: spying on fellow citizens, fighting political, racial, and religious opponents and finally getting involved in mass murder. Anyone who devoted himself to the SS and displayed some personal capability, had a splendid career open to him, and that irrespective of personal conviction in Nazi ideology.

But opportunism and vanity are hardly sufficient to explain the attitudes of the men belonging to the Gestapo élite. There must have been other motives as well. The educated members of this generation had at least been in intellectual contact with the «Youth Movement», with its attitude of protest against bourgeois society at the beginning of the century. National ideals and romanticism, including worship of nature, belonged to the intellectual legacy of these groups, and they became the pioneers, if not the propagandists, of anti-Semitism. Hitler's «ideology» now seemed to show a way out, a way to overcome the old, despised bourgeois world, and to attain a new, ideal future.

The Post-War Fate of the Organizers of Terror

What has become of these men who were responsible for a decade of barbarism? Here we can offer only a general answer; unfortunately, the complete documentation is not available to historians.

The fire-eaters of the early years (pre-1930) rarely got promoted to leading positions. Some of them were removed from office because of misconduct, others because of drunkenness.

A number of persecutors lost their lives during the war. The concentration camp inspector Eicke, for example, was killed at the Eastern front; others, e.g. Heydrich, were killed by partisans. One man from this group, Arthur Nebe, was executed because of his links with the German anti-Nazi opposition. Heinrich Himmler and a number of high Gestapo leaders and SD functionaries committed suicide at the end of the war. The last chief of the RSHA, Ernst Kaltenbrunner, appeared in the court at Nuremberg. There, and in other cities, other members of the secret police were brought before the courts, not so much because of their activities in Berlin but because of their activities as police commanders of mobile execution units (Ohlendorf is a case in point.) Up to the present, no trials of the organizers of terror have taken place before German courts. At first these cases were considered settled by the allied jurisdiction. Then the prosecution of the men planning crimes against humanity behind their desks was found to be legally difficult. Against one of them, Werner Best, investigations have been going on for years.

Some of the men in the sample have been presumed dead since the end of the war. Once again rumours have surfaced regarding the whereabouts or the discovery of the body of Heinrich Müller. The public does not seem to concern itself with his less important subordinates.

None of the leading organizers of the terror has played a part in the public and political life of the Federal Republic of Germany. Some of them have been employed in industrial firms or business enterprises after their dismissal from allied arrest, e.g.

Werner Best. One of them has made a career in education: the SS lawyer Reinhard Höhn was a teacher at a school of economics. Yet even in the cases where the courts have not succeeded, nature will soon ensure that the murderers will no longer be with us.

NOTES

[1] The files on which this paper is based are deposited in the Berlin Document Centre. The dissertation of Shlomo Aronson «Reinhard Heydrich und die Frühgeschichte von Gestapo und SD» has been of great help in the preparation of this manuscript. I am also indebted to Mr. Cristoph Graf of the University of Bern who allowed me to read his paper on the role of the political police in connection with the Reichstag fire.

Italian Fascism and the Middle Classes*

RENZO DE FELICE

As my research on Italian fascism and my critical study of the interpretations of fascism have shown,[1] no single interpretation of fascism so far can claim absolute validity. Although common factors among the various fascist experiences undeniably exist, we have reason, with certain reservations, to take all these interpretations into account. Instead of generalizing about some features of fascism, we must concentrate on those aspects of fascism which are essentially national, and which are linked to the historical, economic, social, cultural, and political experiences of each country, of each regime, and of each fascist movement.

This contribution is not meant to be a new interpretation of fascism reduced to a simple expression of the middle classes – though the crisis of the middle classes is indeed essential to an understanding of fascism both at its beginning and after it became a «regime», particularly in Italy and in Germany.

There is a large body of literature on the social bases of fascism, and especially on the relationship between the middle classes and fascism. There is no need here to review the main arguments about Italian fascism and the other fascist movements before World War II.

The essential points of the relationship between the middle classes and fascism are the following:

1. After World War I, the middle classes in several European countries, both victors and vanquished, entered a crisis. This crisis was especially important in Italy and in Germany, and had several causes. Some of these causes were already present before the war and were linked to the processes of change and «massification» in industrial society. Others were directly linked to the war and centered around the acceleration of social change in general and of social mobility. Of particular importance were the consequences of the economic and social crisis in the immediate post-war period and the great crisis in 1929.

2. As far as the economic and social aspects are concerned, the crisis of the middle classes assumed different forms depending upon the occupations of the individuals who made up these middle classes. On the one hand, there were the traditional middle classes – the farmers, the tradesmen, the professions and the small entrepreneurs, who enjoyed a certain personal autonomy and constituted a social entity which was both homogeneous and integrated. On the other hand, there were those who had of late been upwardly more mobile – white-collar employees, retail clerks, salaried intellectuals. These were relatively lacking in personal autonomy and less integrated. Without going into much detail, one may say that all the middle classes were confronted with rapid changes and with the emergence of a proletariat and an upper bourgeoisie. They had to face adverse economic conditions – inflation, a rising cost of living, a reduction of their fixed incomes, rent freezes and so on – and in most cases they did not have the means of defense provided by the unions. Hence they gradually lost their economic and social status.

312

3. At the psychological and political levels, the crisis of the middle classes manifested itself as social frustration. This frustration in turn became a deep anxiety, a confused desire for revenge, and a protest which often took destructive and revolutionary forms against the society in which the middle classes felt themselves to be the main victims, if not the only ones. They had often believed that the war would allow them to dominate this society with *their* democracy and *their* values. At the very beginning this frustration could have been used by the socialist movement in order to create an alliance with a part of the middle classes, but the mistakes of the workers' parties and the fear of Bolshevism led the middle classes toward fascism which they considered *their* own revolutionary movement, able to defend them at a political and social level against the proletariat and the upper bourgeoisie.

4. In that sense, according to some authors, fascism was an attempt to give political life to a *third force* opposed both to parliamentary democracy of the capitalist countries, and to communism. The prime mover of fascism was thus the middle classes because of their emergence as an autonomous social reality. These interpretations are not undermined by the fact that fascism directed its main attack against the proletariat. In the beginning, the offensive against the proletariat is explained by the fact that the middle classes felt socially and politically more threatened by the proletariat than by the upper bourgeoisie, and therefore reached a temporary «modus vivendi» with the latter against the former. Later, this basic tendency would reappear in the economic policies of the Italian and German fascist regimes. Without harming the principle of private property, this policy aimed at imposing its own control on the economy, at increasing the activities of the public sector, and at transferring the management of the economy from the capitalists and entrepreneurs into the hands of the higher civil servants of the state.

As an interpretation of the fascist phenomenon, even in the case of Italy and Germany, this analysis of the relationship between the middle classes and fascism is, in our opinion, too one-sided to be acceptable. Like any other historical interpretation of fascism, it does not take into account other important aspects of the fascist reality. It neglects especially the way the mechanisms of the fascist dictatorship grew increasingly independent of the social forces which had contributed to its creation. This independence of the regime was achieved especially at the expense of the petty and middle bourgeoisie which had made up the striking force of the *squadre d'unione* in the period of the armed struggle. After the fascist takeover, they would have liked to manage the internal life of the fascist party democratically and to make the party a means of imposing their own economic and social claims from top to bottom.

Conservative authoritarian regimes have always had a tendency to demobilize the masses and to prevent them from taking any active part in political life. These regimes offer the masses values and a social model derived from the past which might avoid the horrors of some recent revolutionary upheavals. On the other hand, fascism had always had a tendency – and this had been its strength – to create among the masses the feeling of always being mobilized, of having a direct relationship to the leader, viewing him as someone capable of interpreting their own aspirations and translating them into action. Fascism creates the feeling of participating and contributing not to the restoration of a social order of historical limitations and inadequacies but to a revolution from which a new social order, better and fairer than the previous one, can originate. This is the reason why fascism managed to retain mass support for such a long period of time. This mass-based support can be appreciated only if we point out the moral and cultural values which nourished it and the hypothetical social order propelling its clientele to join. Both the values and the promised ideal society were embodiments of middle class aspirations.

The support for fascism was great, but not total. It declined during the prolonged period of social stagnation and then had to be supported by irrational palliatives and projected outside the national society, either as in Germany, through the myth of Aryan superiority or, as in Italy, through a doctrine about the rights of the «proletarian» and «young» nation vis à vis the «plutocratic» and «old» nations. No wonder both myths originated in the petty bourgeoisie, and expressed their particular point of view.

Obviously, an analysis of the relationship between the middle classes and fascism may explain other riddles such as the problems of the fascist ideology and its origins, or the existence in fascism of *old* and conservative elements, inherited from the past, and of *new* and innovative elements, all of them being features of the modern mass society. Both are typical of a mentality, of a culture, and of interests which are derived solely from the middle classes. A fair consideration of the role of the middle classes in the political and social crises of some countries between the two wars can contribute to a less doctrinaire assessment of the mistakes of the workers' parties in the emergence and ultimate take-over of the fascists. To what extent were those mistakes due to an underestimation of the strength of the middle classes, and to a narrow refusal to see any valid claims in the grievances expressed by the fascists and instead regard them as mere adventurers, as mercenaries in the service of agrarian and industrial capitalism? Today, this problem is merely a historical one, but would it not have been better at the time of that dramatic political struggle, to have avoided such errors (more especially their repetition in other countries after the initial experience in Italy) by means of a careful analysis of the problem of the middle classes?

In the case of Italy, the basically petty bourgeois features of fascism are clear. They can be confirmed at all levels, in the writings of the shrewdest contemporary observers, in the documents of the police and of the fascist party, and in the mounting number of research studies in recent years.

Unfortunately there are no comprehensive statistics of the social make-up of the fascist party, but the partial data we have leave no real doubt. Most of the party members who enrolled first in the *«Fasci di Combattimento»* and then in the *«Partito Nazionale Fascista»*, the fighters as well as their leaders, came from the petty or middle bourgeoisie.

At the end of 1921, a survey made by the secretariat of the *Fasci* provided the following percentages:

Cultivators (farm labor)	24.3
Workers	15.4
Seamen	1.0
Students	13.0
Employees from the private sector	9.8
Public employees	4.8
Teachers	1.1
Liberal professions	6.6
Tradesmen and artisans	9.2
Industrialists	2.8
Farmers (large, small and medium landowners, tenants)	12.0

The data on the *Fasci* and on the individual executive committees are even more interesting. Here the middle class forms about ninety per cent of the party members enrolled, even in essentially rural areas where the landowners and many simple peasants and day-laborers belonged to the party. These partial data have been confirmed by a large sociological and statistical survey on the fascist ruling class.[2] It is therefore safe to conclude that until after the regime was consolidated as a dictatorship, when membership in the PNF became a practical necessity for everybody, the fascist party was composed of the middle classes and the petty bourgeoisie.

These quantitative data become even more significant in view of the character of press and party propaganda in the period between the wars. The press and the propaganda oscillated between conservatism (it was anti-proletarian) and general subversion (in attitudes toward the upper bourgeoisie), between free trade and protectionism, between dictatorship and social democracy, between realism and romanticism. In many ways it reflected the mentality, the aspirations, the interests, the culture, the self-contradictions, and even the phraseology of the Italian middle classes of those years. It also promised the hegemony of the middle sector over other sectors of the nation such as the upper bourgeoisie and the proletariat.

Although Mussolini and the new fascist rulers (moderate fascists, nationalists, sympathizers and general civil servants as well) tried to eliminate this promised hegemony after the takeover, and after the two compromises of October 1922 and October 1925, this hegemony was decisive for fascism in the period of the March on Rome. At that time Italy allowed fascism to become a mass party and to keep its own political autonomy (but contrary to the wishes of Giolitti and most of the old liberal ruling class). It allowed fascism to penetrate in depth into the bureaucratic and military apparatus of the state while destroying its connective tissues such as cutting off the links of authority between the center and the periphery.

On another level it enabled fascism to attract a large part of the members and voters of more typically «petty bourgeois» parties, the traditional parties, as well as the «Partito Populare» towards which a substantial section of the more traditional and internally cohesive middle classes belonged to right after World War I.

This is our explanation of the fact that just after the takeover by Mussolini, such a careful observer of the Italian social and political scene as Luigi Salvatorelli[3] not only asserted that the petty bourgeoisie was the characteristic and decisive element for an understanding of fascism, but (in contrast to other observers who had seen the importance of the same class) went on to maintain that the petty bourgeois element was not merely «numerically preponderant» in fascism, but «characteristic and directive». One must understand the economic, moral and historical reasons for the adherence of the middle classes to fascism to have a real idea of the features of fascism and of the successive phases of middle class support.

For the later historians of fascist Italy, fascism from 1922 to 1923 represents «the class struggle of the small bourgeoisie framed between capitalism and the proletariat, like the third man between two litigants». There was no doubt that the fascist petty bourgeoisie had the psychology of a revolutionary class and wished an «autonomous and radical» revolution; but this psychology had no real underpinning since the petty bourgeoisie «was not a real social class, with its own functions and its own forces, but a conglomeration lying outside the productive process essential to the capitalist civilization». According to Salvatorelli, this had entailed the notion of «revolt» and not of «revolution» underlying fascist action and its vain demagoguery. From this also he derives these two basic appraisals of fascism:

1. The petty bourgeois revolt had been made possible by the complicity of the upper bourgeoisie which wanted to use fascism for its own class interests;

2. Because of its heterogeneity the only ideological element common to the petty

bourgeoisie was nationalism. Finally, from this Salvatorelli deduced the accusation of anti-historicity he made about fascism:

«Nationalism which constitutes its ideology, is neither the physical product of capitalism, nor the political projection of the capitalist economy, but a laggard ideological stage compared with that economy. We find such a lack of synchronization between economic reality and the ideology of the so-called cultured classes (like the petty bourgeoisie) during and after the war in Europe – we cannot imagine a definitive victory of national fascism without the fall of the capitalist economy, which, in our opinion, is not going to take place.

Today, after the changes which have taken place since then in the advanced capitalist societies, it is hard to deny, as Salvatorelli does, that the middle classes constitute a precisely defined social reality with its own functions.[4] But where he refers to Italian society in the period just after the war, I think that Salvatorelli's analysis and judgment are more acceptable, especially if they are integrated with the theories of Guido Dorso about both the impact of fascist power during the March on Rome and the establishment of the real fascist «régime».

As I showed in my biography of Mussolini, as soon as fascism has become a «régime», the policy of the fascist ruling group and of Mussolini is characterized by the repetition of and improvement in the compromise made in October 1922 with the old political and economic pre-fascist ruling class and the social forces behind it (that is, the upper bourgeoisie and the remaining aristocracy). A direct and important consequence of this new compromise was that Mussolini and the régime made a change in the PNF by removing many of the most uncompromising fascists (in general former *squadristi*) – those most linked to a destructive socio-political perspective like that of the petty bourgoisie. Thanks to this removal (which took place especially between 1926 and 1928), the PNF changed its social character and was reduced to a mere instrument having no autonomy.

The change in the PNF shows two important things: 1. the original basis of fascism which more typically reflected the crisis and the desire for change in the middle classes was too radical for the «régime» and almost incompatible with it; 2. on the other hand, this element was unable to face its own political liquidation. While the first of these two findings may be obvious, the second one is explained by Salvatorelli: The middle classes, especially the petty bourgeoisie, were not able alone to produce a tangible alternative, and their revolutionary aspirations were only pipe-dreams. One may add to this explanation another more detailed one: Like a large part of European society during the birth and the emergence of fascism, Italian society was about to go through a period of intense social and psychological mobilization, and therefore through a period of protest (both revolutionary and authoritarian) against the structures which had been legitimized so far. At this point, even the middle classes wished for their own «revolution», and in Italy they had expected to be able to achieve it through fascism. But the mobilization was followed by a process of traditionalist reintegration and of demobilization. Besides, in Italy, the first years of the fascist government had caused some of the hopes pinned on fascism to disappear and raised in their place a fear of new disorders and an uncertain future. A new climate was formed, where few people dared challenge the unpopularity and the repressive apparatus of the fascist state.

The demobilization of the middle classes was at once voluntary and compulsory, and the formation of the fascist regime in the second half of the 1920s was like a sociopolitical compromise between the old ruling class and a successful and moderate élite. Although it was already substantially integrated, we must not believe that the

316

Italian fascist regime of the 1930s had completely lost its original features. Despite the political and social compromises of the Mussolinian ruling class, and the ever-increasing autonomy of the social forces that had contributed to its creation, there is no doubt that the real social basis of the Italian fascist regime was still the middle class. Nor could it have developed otherwise, considering its origins (and those of its main representatives) and the attitudes of the two other Italian contemporary social forces toward it.

In spite of the undeniable benefits that the middle class drew from fascism, the upper bourgeoisie never completely accepted it. For this there were psychological as well as cultural reasons – reasons of style and even of taste – but there were also the fears derived from a) the tendency of the fascist state to control economic activities; b) the tendency of the fascist élite to change into an autonomous ruling class and to alter the balance of the compromise in its own favor; and c) Mussolini's foreign policy, which was becoming more and more aggressive and corresponded less and less to the real interests of Italy and of the upper bourgeoisie itself. As for the proletariat, its adherence to fascism was very limited (quantitatively speaking), precarious, and characterized by large areas of discontent and of latent opposition even during the greatest successes of the regime. In such a situation, the most massive support of fascism was always given by the middle classes which even today have the largest number of «neo-fascists» and of «nostalgics». This is not only because they were psychologically and culturally the most receptive to the nationalist and social demagogy of fascism, but also because they received, or believed they did, the greatest «moral» and economic advantages from the fascist régime. They always believed in their own social promotion and in their participation in civil society.

These aspects are basic to an understanding of the fascist phenomenon in general, and of Italian fascism in particular, and one must not be misled either by the «proletarian» rhetoric of fascism, or by the episodic attacks against «the bourgeois spirit», especially aimed at the upper bourgeoisie and its cultural hegemony over the middle classes.

NOTES

*Original title: *Le Fascisme italien et les classes moyennes*. Presented first at An International Symposium, Prague 28–29 August 1969.

[1] For a listing of the author's work on Italian fascism, see the 'Notes on contributors'.
[2] This research has been conducted here under the auspices of the National Research Council.
[3] *Nazionalfascismo*, (Turin 1923).
[4] It is enough to think of the studies by Frits Croner and Michel Collinet.

Italian Fascism and the Crisis of Liberal Hegemony: 1901–1922

JOSEPH BAGLIERI

The rise of Italian fascism has to be seen among other things, against the background of the Liberal hegemony that preceded it. This study will focus on the quest of the Italian Liberal élites for hegemonic rule,[1] the breakdown of the Liberal model of economic development under the impact of the Great War, and the post-war mass mobilization. In the process the nature of the opposition to the Giolittian system will be assessed, in particular the quest of the Italian industrial élite for an alternative model of economic development and political organization.

Liberal Italy experienced greater collective violence than any other period in the history of the country. Strikes, both political and economic in nature, riots, outright revolutionary attempts on the State, a long and bloody war, and political and social strife throughout the period 1901–1922 steadily undermined the Liberal projects of the Giolittian political class and eventually brought about the collapse of the Liberal system. To what extent all of these factors contributed to the demise of the Liberal state is a question which has long been debated among scholars. However, broad consensus has been reached regarding the determinant role which fascism played in fatally compounding the crisis of the Liberal system and bringing about its downfall. Fascism will here be considered as the *decisive* factor in the breakdown of the Liberal state, a new political and social force which was capable not only of destroying the institutional differentiation which had developed under Giovanni Giolitti, but also of subordinating all social groups to a self-proclaimed «totalitarian» state.

Giolitti's System

Giovanni Giolitti came to power in 1901, following the turn-of-the-century crisis which had caused the demise of the *Destra*. Under his leadership, the government adopted a more tolerant attitude towards the Socialist party and especially the trade unions, which grew very rapidly.[2] This strategy was part of the price which the Liberal élite was willing to pay in its attempt to build a new coalition whose major components were to be the Northern industrialists and the Northern industrial workers, with the outside support of the Socialist party. These policies resulted «. . . in the rapid growth of an industrial- entrepreneurial class which gave its support to a model of economic development based on the strengthening of the industrial sector, a policy of higher wages and concrete benefits to the working class and on the acceptance of the Giolittian policy of freedom for all and neutrality of the State in labour disputes . . .».[3]

Giolitti's ability to carry on this mediating role, to keep in check both allies and adversaries and to pursue with a fair degree of success his socio-economic program hinged primarily upon his ability to control parliament. He had a rather narrow view of politics, dominated by a nineteenth century, pre-mass party conception which largely restricted the political process to the parliamentary arena. «He followed time-honoured parliamentary practices. Bribing the deputies with legislative favours, he continued the nineteenth century system of politics as the activity of notables, politics based on personalities, rather than on political parties.»[4] The task of controlling parliament was defined by the size of the electorate, whose political choices Giolitti often succeeded in restricting, especially in the South, and by continued access to resources with which to smooth the political process.

The seamy side of Giolittian Italy was characterized by a continuation of repressive and authoritarian practices by the state, aimed largely at marginal revolutionary groups (i.e., the anarchists and the revolutionary syndicalists) and at the bulk of the rural population, particularly those peasants living in highly politicized areas like the Po Valley, Tuscany and Apulia.[5] The South itself became the object of a vast operation aimed at maintaining the status quo. Since the control by Giolitti of an amenable parliamentary majority hinged upon the decisive contribution made by Southern notables to the Liberal slate, the Liberal Prime Minister was willing to use the state apparatus and an open-ended migration policy in order to preserve the status quo in that region. As Giancarlo Provasi has noted,

the [Liberal] reformist historical bloc was founded essentially on a class alliance between the industrial-financial bourgeoisie and the Southern landed aristocracy. This front was capable of hegemonizing the urban working class, of dominating the marginal social strata (especially the peasants) while using as a supportive element for the state an ascending petty bourgeois class. The working class, mobilized by the industrial development, was being subjectively integrated through its participation in the industrial sector and the ideological use of socialist reformism . . . The alliance with the Southern landowning class . . . would guarantee [the Liberal system] the necessary social and political base for its ideological and repressive control of the peasant masses . . . The political mediation of the aristocracy and of the absentee landed bourgeoisie would make possible the social domination of the work of the peasant masses and the continued extraction of agricultural surplus . . This process was a fundamental element of the socio-political equilibrium of the Giolittian bloc.[6]

In order to carry out his policy of ensuring high wages and concrete benefits for the Northern industrial workers, Giolitti had to rely on the more advanced sectors of Italian capitalism. In return, the latter received state support in the form of subsidies and tariffs. The recession of 1907 threw this model of economic development into a severe crisis. Italian capitalism, despite its protected status and its privileged access to state resources, was still subject to serious fluctuations whose gravity was compounded by a dual squeeze: the reformist model of high wages and the objective demands for capital accumulation and expansion.[7]

The period 1907–1912 was characterized by the economic crisis of 1907, the political crisis of the reformist wing of Italian socialism, the collapse of the original Giolittian system of alliances and the Libyan war. This period also saw the progressive alienation from Giolitti's position of some of the social forces which had supported him from the very beginning. Significantly, the break-up of the Giolittian equilibrium on which the Liberal model of economic development rested, was initiated by the entrepreneurial sector of the Italian bourgeoisie. This sector, in fact, had gained the least from the liberal-reformist model. Their integration into the world market and the demands of competition narrowed down the space available to them in the realm of wages and normative benefits to the working class. The strategy of this group was embodied in the Turin Industrial League and in particular in the consortium of the auto sector,[8] and was essentially an alternative to the Giolittian model. Central to the aims of the group was a reassessment of two key issues: first, the function of the capitalist factory, which they saw as the source of hegemonic and political power over society; and second, the role of working class organizations in the country's social and political development. The Giolittian model had in fact subordinated the factory organization and the requirements of the capitalist mode of production to a hegemonic project to be carried out at the political level. The more advanced sectors of Italian industry, however,

> sought to secure, by means of an operation aimed at «capturing» the industrial working class in reformist syndical organizations, the latter's acquiescence in the adoption of the newest techniques of «concentrated accumulation» and the rationa-lisation of the process of production, i.e. Taylorism and the most advanced methods of production and of industrial organization offered by American industry.[9]

This maneuver aimed a) at transforming the industrial firm into the real base of power of the capitalist class; b) at creating the preconditions for the subordination and the long-term integration of the working class into the fabric of the rapidly growing capitalist order. A precondition for this particular project was the abandonment of the politically-mediated Giolittian model of economic and political development and a shift by the state to more conservative, openly repressive positions. In the move away from the Giolittian project, Adolfo Pepe sees

> the dissonance between two phases and two historical stages in the development of the Italian bourgeoisie. On the one side, [we find] the democratic principles of the political class, aiming at containing and regulating the country's economic devel-opment in order to prevent profound cleavages and violent social reactions capable of upsetting the social equilibrium and causing the convergence of all social classes onto the political-parliamentary plane; on the other, [the emergence of] the authori-tarian principles articulated by the industrial entrepreneurial groups . . . [the latter] held as a major goal the expansion and the acceleration of the productive capacity of society . . . They became very sensitive about their right to regulate the factors of production according to rules dictated by the technical requirements of the industri-al process . . . in effect, the first model aimed at maintaining the predominance of the political class over the State and the rest of society. The second wanted to destroy this equilibrium and to assign to the entrepreneurial groups the task of hegemonizing and guiding the entire national bourgeoisie.[10]

Politically, the Giolittian coalition continued to deteriorate following the break-down of the original system of alliances in 1910. The extension of universal suffrage in 1912 compounded the problem of electoral control by the Liberal political class, leading to the progressive deterioration of the political base of the Constitutional parties. The crisis of the reformist wing of the Italian Socialist Party (P.S.I.) prompted the assimilation of the Catholics, long alienated from the Italian state, into the new system of political alliances which Giolitti was attempting to build. With the Gentiloni Pact, which allowed Liberal candidates who accepted the program of the Catholic Union to receive Catholic support, Giolitti aimed at substituting for the now defunct northern bloc an alliance composed of the northern industrialists, the Catholics and the southern landowners. As Gramsci pointed out, «Giolitti changed his rifle to his other shoulder; for the alliance between the bourgeoisie and the worker, he now substituted an alliance between the bourgeoisie and the Catholics, who represented the peasant masses in northern and central Italy».[11]

This new alliance, which excluded the participation of the Left, was also a concession to those industrial groups which had slowly abandoned the reformist model and had adopted a policy of technical rationalization and market-regulated behaviour toward the industrial work force. As a result, large sectors of the Left came to regard the assault on the state by revolutionary means as the only alternative open to them. The Great War and the Russian Revolution reinforced this effort.

Interventionists and Nationalists

The Great War sealed the fate of the Liberal-reformist historical bloc, as the issue of intervention created havoc among the system of alliances and opposition at every point of the political spectrum. During the nine months which preceded Italy's entry into the war, political and social forces realigned along an Interventionist-Neutralist axis, largely irrespective of ideology and class.

As an independent variable, nationalism can provide a wide range of explanations for the mass mobilization and the enthusiasm characteristic of the early phase of the war. If it can help explain the behaviour of large sectors of the petty bourgeoisie and the working class, it can hardly provide a «scientific» explanation for the behaviour of the political leaders who staged a virtual coup d'état against parliament and Giolitti, or for the pro-war stand taken by the most powerful social and institutional élites in the country: industrialists, landlords, the aristocracy, the monarchy. Fundamentally, the latter's attitude had been defined by the advanced stage of decomposition which the Liberal-reformist model had reached.[12] Universal suffrage threatened to take the state away from the political class which had often used it to define the limits of its own liberal policies. Serious economic contradictions had arisen due to the highly uneven

Table 1. *Political Alignments in the Italian Parliament: 1913–1919 and 1919–1921*

A
1913 – 1919

	LEFT	Number of seats	RIGHT		Number of seats
Interventionists	Radicals	73	Constitutional-Democrats		29
	Republicans	17	Democrats		11
			Non-Giolittian Liberals		70
	Independent-Socialists	8	Catholics		20
	Social-Reformists	19	Conservative Catholics		9
Interventionist Left	total	117	*Interventionist Right*	total	139
Neutralists	Socialists	52	Giolittian Liberals		200
Neutralist Left	total	52	*Neutralist Right*	total	200

Total = 508

321

Interventionists {	Republicans	9	Salandra Liberals	23
	Radicals	57	Partito Economico, Partito Agrario,	
	Independent Socialists and Social- Reformists	22	Gruppo Misto	15
	Rinnovamento	33		
Interventionist Left	total	121	*Interventionist Right* total	38
Neutralists	Socialists	137	Giolittian Liberals	91
	Communists	17		
Neutralist Left	total	154	*Neutralist Right* total	91

Popolari (Left and Right) : 99
Total = 503

Source: Paolo Farneti «La Crisi della Democrazia Italiana e l'Avvento del Fascismo: 1919–1922.» *Rivista Italiana di Scienze Politiche,* Anno V, 1, April 1975 p. 57.

pattern of industrial development: key industries were too large for the internal market and unable to compete abroad, which in turn resulted in the stagnation of numerous other sectors.

The war brought to the political forefront the petty bourgeoisie, whose potential as a countervailing force to the pressures of the Left came to be appreciated by the Interventionist bloc. Because of its anti-nationalist and anti-clerical positions Italian socialism was particularly vulnerable to the conservative charges of being a foreign implantation in the body of the nation. Its influence in society could easily be circumscribed by these charges. In fact, socialist support was largely limited to the working class and to some sectors of the agricultural workers, also regionally defined. Socialist exclusion from influence on other social strata, especially the rapidly growing middle strata,[13] did not mean that the Liberal state had firmly «captured» these important sectors of Italian society. Here Giolittian Liberalism encountered formidable competition from the Nationalists.[14] Nationalists called for the pursuit of an *Idea,* by which they meant the creation of a new empire, capable of rallying the Italian people, regardless of socio-economic status, different interests, or conflicting aspirations. They saw war as a purifying force which could revitalize a decrepit society immersed in liberal-bourgeois mediocrity. Liberalism, with its underlying assumptions about man and society, was regarded by the Nationalists as a destructive force, capable of arousing the basest passions in man: the pursuit of material gain, individualism in the field of material production, the promotion of class conflict which weakened the nation and prevented its pursuit of imperial grandeur, and the degradation of the authority of the state (seen by the Nationalists in Hegelian terms) and of social hierarchies.

Organized in the Nationalist Association, the Nationalists attempted to make an impact on the major cleavages in Italian society by asserting the «proletarian character of Italian imperialism». As Salvadore Saladino points out, the concept of the proletarian nation made possible the rapprochement between the Nationalist movement and the revolutionary wing of the Italian Left, on the grounds that Italy's imperial expansion would in fact be a form of proletarian imperialism.[15] As an intellectual and emotional movement, it had a tremendous impact and deprived the Giolittian system of the support of numerous social groups. «The Nationalists – writes Adrian Lyttelton – . . . . operated like a reactionary version of the Fabian society. Permeation [was] their most effective method; their ideas had taken hold in the universities, in the law courts, the Army and the Civil Service.»[16] But the problem of state power was never resolved in the Nationalists' mind. Intellectuals usually make bad revolutionaries and the Nationalists were no exception. It was the convergence of the revolutionary wing of socialism-turned-nationalists under the impact of the war with revolutionary syndicalism and Republicanism, plus the mass of demobilized soldiers and officers *who knew how to fight* which created the condition that fatally compounded the crisis of the Liberal State.

The War and Lower Class Mobilization

The Great War exacerbated the sharp cleavages which had arisen in the previous decades. The country was brought into war by ministerial decree and royal effort, which bypassed parliament and was supported by both a vociferous nationalist minority and a powerful agrarian and industrial bloc. Vast socio-economic and institutional changes took place under the impact of the conflict. Hundreds of thousands of new workers were suddenly needed by the war industry, millions of peasants were mobilized in the army and new burdens fell on the lower classes. All of this added to the already vast problems of the Liberal state and delineated the scenario for the post-war social and institutional crisis. At the same time, «the sheer momentum of the military and economic effort strained the administrative social structure of Italy . . . A vast new military bureaucracy was improvised with the almost inevitable concomitants of waste, corruption and Parkinsonian multiplication; the civilian bureaucracy also grew in quantity but not in quality, and the war industries . . . profited fully from the weakness of parliamentary and administrative controls. The result was the birth of a new military-bureaucratic-industrial complex accustomed to bypassing Parliament.»[17]

The expansion of the industrial base, natural under the requirements of the war effort, was led by the metallurgical, auto-mechanic, electrical and chemical industries – that is exactly by those industrial-entrepreneurial groups who had been the first to abandon the Liberal-reformist model and to reject the political mediation of Giolitti. This sector acquired a close relationship with the state apparatus, pushing the interpenetration of the state and the economy to such an extent that «by 1918 the entire process of production was taking place under the State . . . the State . . . had become the center, the engine of the national economy, the sole customer of a multitude of industries. The process of industrial expansion was accompanied by just as rapid a concentration of industrial strength».[19] In brief, the war provided the industrial-entrepreneurial groups with the financial, industrial and technical *potential* for the realization of those goals which had induced them to abandon the Giolittian model: first, the transfer of the real base of capitalist power from a politically-mediated process to the industrial firm; and second the objective integration and hegemonization of the lower classes into the structures of a rapidly advancing capitalist society. This project was to take place within the conservative parameters of the interventionist bloc and its newly acquired relationship with the bureaucratic-military structures

323

of the state. The timing, however, was at least a decade too late. The advantages which the Italian industrial groups had enjoyed in the first decade of the century (a relatively small and geographically defined working class, organized in reformist trade unions, a largely dormant agrarian sector under the hegemony of the Catholic Church and a relatively strong state to act as «ultima ratio» in all eventualities) had all but disappeared by the end of the Great War.

With the end of the war and the cancellation of the military contracts, the industrial sector, geographically concentrated in the industrial triangle of Milan, Turin and Genoa, began to decline. The state had to intervene to save numerous industrial concerns from sudden collapse, without, however, being able to turn the economy around. The steady, war-related expansion of the money supply sparked off an inflationary spiral which was violently destabilising to numerous social groups.[20] The latter had few if any defences against inflation, and while a small number of individuals profited from it, the many turned from hapless victims to willing participants in food riots, as in July 1919, and in the long wave of strikes and social unrest which have come to be known as the «Red Biennium». Of dire consequence for the future of the Liberal regime was the rapidly deteriorating status of the petty bourgeoisie, that very class that had thrown its full support behind the war and which was now becoming the unwilling target for a whole host of economic, political and emotional letdowns. Economic ruin was only one of the many problems which beset large sectors of this class and finally mobilized them against the Liberal state. The «mutilated» victory of Versailles, Gabriele D'Annunzio's Fiume adventure, the post-war mobilization of the Catholic and socialist masses and the polarized political atmosphere provided the context for the mobilization of the petty bourgeoisie and the triumph of fascism.

Concomitant with the above process was a massive mobilization of the lower classes as they organized to press their claims for change and fulfillment of the promises made by the government during the war. Socialist party membership and parliamentary representation underwent a huge increase. From 58,000 members before the war, P.S.I. membership climbed to 200,000. In the 1919 general elections, the socialists succeeded in winning almost a third (156 to be exact) of the seats in Parliament, as compared to 52 in 1913.

Of more serious consequence, however, was the founding in January 1919 of the Partito Popolare Italiano (P.P.I.), a Christian Democratic party. An heir to the Catholic Union, the new party's major strength lay exactly among those popular forces which had been voted by Conservative Catholics in that vast geo-political maneuver known as the Gentiloni Pact, a maneuver which had saved the Giolittian system from political collapse in 1913. The Popolari supported a Wilsonian, anti-imperialist international policy and a populist domestic program which called for a drastic change in the land tenure system in favour of the smallholder. The P.P.I.'s social base was largely interclassist, as the party attempted to integrate numerous disparate interests whose only commonality was Catholicism. This situation became a constant source of policy disagreements and ideological and political infightings. In 1919 the Popolari elected 100 deputies.

The post-war mobilization was visible most dramatically in the explosion of union membership. The Confederazione Generale del Lavoro (C.G.d.L.), of socialist orientation, expanded from 347,000 members in 1914 to 2,2 million members at the end of 1920. This included almost half a million farm workers, organized in Federterra.[21] A final feature of the post-war scenario and an indication of the strong centrifugal forces operating the political parameters of the faltering Liberal system, was the proliferation

324

of political associations, veterans' groups and outright secessionist movements, as in the case of Sardinia.[22] Politically, the Constitutional parties had been greatly weakened by the post-war mobilization of the lower classes and the implementation of universal suffrage coupled with proportional representation. The transition to mass politics had fully exposed the Liberals as structurally weaker than the Socialists and the Popolari, whose strength lay in their local organizations and the appeal of their ideologies and programs.

The electoral results of 1919, as reproduced in table 1, part B, produced a highly fragmented parliamentary arena, which became progressively unable to function for reasons ranging from sharp ideological differences to personal idiosyncracies.[23] More important, the results irremediably weakened the position of the Liberal political class in the eyes of those powerful industrial and agrarian groups which felt the need for state action in order to avoid economic collapse and to promote social discipline. In their eyes, civil society had clearly failed to hegemonize and integrate the lower classes. The Liberal state had not only allowed within itself the growth of the seeds of its own destruction, in the form of the P.S.I. and the P.P.I., and the trade unions. More critically, its political class appeared inclined to form coalitions which would have led inevitably to the implementation of an array of reforms contrary to the interests of the powerful agrarian and industrial groups. As Carlo Vallauri has pointed out,

> [in the post war period] the character and composition of the State [had] experienced profoundly radical changes: the old state, impervious to popular influence and politically unassailable thanks to a restricted suffrage . . . [was] rapidly being supplanted by a state in which the pressures of large popular movements . . . the strength of well-organized and disciplined parties could lead to radical political and economic reforms, to programs aiming at achieving further social transformations . . . The 'imponibile di mano d' opera' new taxation criteria, the political price of consumer goods are alterations of a system which the dominant groups no longer intend to accept.[24]

It is in this context of a *systemic* crisis, taking place at the political, structural and hegemonic level, and its impact on the system of power relations among social classes, that fascism will be discussed.

The Emergence of Fascism

The men who gathered in Milan in March 1919 to found the Fasci Italiani di Combattimento shared a number of common experiences. Most of them had been on the fringes of Italian political life as revolutionary syndicalists, futurists, revolutionary socialists, and anarchists as early as at the time of the first Giolittian government. Interventionism had led them to align themselves with the «hated» bourgeois parties in the hope that the war would have accelerated the process toward the socialist revolution.[25] The only tangible result, however, had been, aside from the general disarray of society, the tremendous growth of those very parties and organizations which had opposed the war. More seriously, their own «revolutionary practice» had alienated them from those very parties to which the masses were turning in 1919. At the same time, their particular ideological predilections made most of them reluctant to form alliances with those parties with which they had shared the interventionist experience. This was the «late-comer's dilemma», a situation so named by Juan J. Linz in which the political space has been pre-empted by existing political parties and the political spectrum has largely crystallized.[26] In such a situation of lack of «opportunity space» as Nico Passchier puts it in his article in this volume, a new political group might either subsist on the fringes of political life, with the prospect of turning into a sect or becoming an appendage to some major political party with which it shares broad ideological goals. Or it might travel whatever road leads to political growth and power, regardless of any previous programmatic or ideological commitments. In the process it is bound to lose a few of its original members, the so-called «idealists», but it will pick up numerous new «realists» and it will arrive at its goal of political power substantially transformed both in terms of its internal composition and of its ideological and programmatic parameters.

In the case of Italian fascism, the late-comer's dilemma was solved by the existence of a political dualism in which the Center and the Left of the political spectrum were rapidly crystallizing while the traditional Right was progressively crumbling under the impact of the post-war mobilization and its own organizational and ideological deficiencies. The war veterans who formed the Associazione Nazionale Combattenti,[27] the Catholic masses who rallied to the P.P.I., and those who swelled the ranks of the Socialist party and its labour organizations shared with the early fascists a desire that change be achieved outside the structure of traditional politics. Several traits differentiated the fascists from the latter organizations. The fascists had a common revolutionary and interventionist experience, which largely served to reinforce an *ésprit de corps* and a sense of camaraderie capable of withstanding temporary setbacks; a vague and confused ideology whose multiple strains were less a source of tension and more a system of beliefs which strongly contributed to the reinforcement of the movement and its political myths;[28] and finally an organizational structure based on military principles and a political style whose rhetorical apparatus, keen sense of activism, and direct involvement with the «enemy» were vestiges of previous movements, most prominent among them Futurism and Revolutionary Syndicalism.[29]

The Milan meeting produced a program which vigorously opposed any imperialism of other nations harmful to Italy, called for the integration of all Italian «national territories» into the nation, and pledged to sabotage all neutralist politicians, of whatever party.[30] Nationalism formed the underlying bond within this heterogeneous political group, whose unity seemed more the product of the «anti» themes in their ideology than the result of a coherent political program. Nevertheless, they produced a popularly-oriented domestic program which proposed, in the words of Paolo Vita-Finzi,

> vast and almost subversive reforms: workers' participation in the management of industry, partial expropriation of wealth by means of special taxes, confiscation of goods belonging to religious congregations and almost total seizure of the profits of war. It was an emphatically radical programme aimed largely at the 'parasitic bourgeoisie', and it is characteristic of Fascism that it followed in the footsteps of Sorel in its loathing for the prevailing electoral system and parliamentary rule; in its place we find a yearning for dictatorship by a bold, resolute minority, to be expressed in workers' associations, and with a well-defined hierarchical structure. Beyond such generic pronouncements they did not go. The rest would follow 'by the miraculous generating power of action' in the words of the fascist historian Gioacchino Volpe.[31]

In fact, right from the beginning, the fascists participated in demonstrations and fights against what they considered an unpatriotic, internationalist socialism. In April

326

1919, the fascists took part in an anti-socialist demonstration which culminated in the burning of the headquarters of the Socialist newspaper *Avanti!*. In mid-1919, during the food riots and the general strike of July, the fascists and other veterans' groups offered their services to the Nitti government to counter what they perceived as socialist and anarchist threats to order. The government ambiguously warned that while autonomous action from groups was unacceptable, it would welcome their cooperation in maintaining order. «On that occasion [writes Roberto Vivarelli] a harmonious relationship arose between the authorities and the Fasci di Combattimento. The latter put themselves at the disposal of the government . . . and were extremely active and efficient; by this process . . . the Fasci took their place among those groups recognised as «forces of order».»[32]

Although there was a rapid proliferation in the number of Fasci, the movement did not grow as quickly as their leader, Benito Mussolini, had hoped. Fascism was largely an urban phenomenon and it did not aim at expanding into the rural areas. Mussolini himself had recognized the limits of the movement as early as July 1919, when he wrote, «Fascism will always remain a minority movement. It cannot expand beyond the cities».[33] In fact by the end of 1920, the Fasci amounted to 88 largely urban sections with 20,615 members.[34]

Subjectively, early fascist activism was the expression of a myriad of personal hatreds against socialist internationalism, Left-inspired strikes and political protest, the Socialists' devaluation of the Great War, and the spinelessness of the Liberal government in dealing with the «mutilated» victory of Versailles. Their own functional activity as *objective* allies of the crumbling Liberal state against the popular masses led numerous contemporaries to regard fascism as strictly a counter-revolutionary force.[35] This ideological and motivational heterogeneity gave fascism an objective duality which renders the orthodox communist equation capitalism = fascism quite untenable. John M. Cammett has correctly stated that this definition «reinforced some negative tendencies in communist historiography and bolstered the earlier propensity to reduce fascism to a capitalist conspiracy *from the very beginning.*»[36] (emphasis in original).

Agrarian Fascism

The growth of agrarian fascism followed the end of the last great agricultural strike in Emilia and the simultaneous mobilization of the industrial working class in Piedmont and Lombardy. Both events took place under a Giolitti government, which true to its Liberal philosophy and still hoping to attract the moderate wing of the P.S.I. within its orbit, refused to intervene repressively, despite the urgings from industrialists and landowners. The government's inaction when confronted with outright instances of land seizure and factory occupation fatally delegitimated it in the eyes of the industrial and agrarian élites.

> The occupation of the factories [writes Angelo Tasca] gave the bourgeoisie a psychological shock . . . The sense of property and the authority of the industrialists was hit; evicted from their factories, they saw work go on, for better or worse, in their absence . . . After a few days of bitterness and uncertainty, during which their chief feeling was a deep grudge against Giolitti who 'had failed to back them up' . . . their reaction took the form of a fight to the death against the working class and the 'Liberal' state.»[37]

The shift of large sectors of the industrial bourgeoisie toward positions of extreme conservatism and reaction already adopted by major industrialists (such as the owners of ILVA and Ansaldo and numerous other state-dependent industries) led to a linking-up with rightist dissenting groups in parliament, such as the Salandra Liberal faction, the Nationalists and the Agrarians. Ideologically, this group came to appreciate the Nationalist reactionary vision of a new state capable of «encapsulating» the lower classes into structures that would eliminate social conflict and promote class cooperation, a position also supported by the Agrarians.[38] In this situation, fascism, with its productivist ideology, its nationalism and its promotion of class co-operation, became an important factor in the political arena. At the same time, its military tactics subverted the rules of political competition and put the question of power onto a new plane.

Agrarian fascism was from its very inception a reaction against the mass mobilization in the countryside, the land occupations, the socialist leagues and their labour practices (especially the so-called «imponibile di mano d' opera», a practice which forced landowners to hire landless peasants according to the acreage which they owned rather than their real need for them), the boycotts and fines against those who broke class solidarity, and the general upsurge of socialist and Popolari power in the countryside.[39] The component parts of agrarian fascism are more difficult to discern, as its more visible parts vary from region to region and even from city to city. The phenomenon, however, was largely the result of the confluence of the following elements:

I. Completion of the demobilisation of the army in the second half of 1920. Thousands of war veterans, many of them non-commissioned officers and interventionists from the very beginning of the war, returned to a society in the throes of a profound social crisis. During the two years following the Great War, they had watched impotently the social turmoil, the degradation of their war experience by numerous political forces, the phenomenal upsurge of «anti-national» socialism and the «mutilation» of the victory by an «inept» Liberal class.

II. The end of Gabriele D' Annunzio's occupation of Fiume in December of 1920. His followers, mostly members of the élite army group Arditi, disbanded and made their way to their towns and cities. «Part of them [writes Gaetano Salvemini] found in the fascist ranks fresh and well-paid jobs . . . They imported into the fascist movement the black shirt, the dagger, the club, the song 'Giovinezza', the Roman salute, the castor oil, the cruelty – all the implements, slogans and practices.»[40]

III. The post-war economic crisis, which led to the dismissal of workers who had been temporarily recruited from the countryside for the war effort. Thousands of peasants returned to their villages, only to find the labour market monopolized by the socialist leagues. Here they discharged the double function of numerically pressing against the labour monopoly and providing the muscle for the incipient agrarian reaction.

IV. The tremendous increase in the number of smallholders in those very areas of socialist and Popolari strength. The further parcelling of land was vehemently opposed by the socialists, who aimed at its collectivization. Their ideological premises led them to assume a hostile attitude toward small landowners and anyone aspiring to acquire some land, subjecting them to the same vexations and contract clauses as the larger landowners. This policy inevitably led numerous

smallholders into an alliance with the large landowners and the fascists who seemed the only ones willing and able to withstand the socialist onslaught in the countryside.[41]
V. The political consequences of the local elections of October 1920. Popolari and socialists succeeded in capturing 3,635 communes and cities out of a total 8,327. More important, their strength was concentrated in the most important regions: Piedmont, Lombardy, Veneto, Emilia Romagna, Tuscany. In the latter two regions the socialists captured respectively 65.2 per cent and 52.1 per cent of the vote in the cities and communes.[42]

The 1920 Local Elections

The results of the local elections came as a shock to many who still felt that the Constitutional parties were the most effective defence against the Popolari and especially the socialists. In one stroke the outcome of the 1919 national elections was confirmed. These elections had not been a temporary aberration, but they represented the beginning of a continuing leftward trend. Moreover, the elections resulted in the transfer to the local level of a political force largely hostile to the principles of private property and armed with a great number of laws with which to enforce radical resolutions. To numerous members of the petty bourgeoisie (who feared greater «co-operativization» of essential services) and the Radical political parties, both of which had opted for intervention in 1915, the entry into office of the socialist local administrations represented a most essential betrayal of the ideals of the Great War and another proof of the spinelessness of the Liberal political class which did nothing to prevent the taking of seats by elected socialists.

The conquest of local power opened up great possibilities for many basic reforms. The socialists, in fact, did not waste any time in passing laws aimed at expropriating uncultivated lands, raising taxes on property holders, and setting up co-operative stores in order to break up local monopolies in essential goods, such as bread and medicines. This form of participation in running sectors of «bourgeois» society was not alien to the ideology of the reformist wing of the P.S.I. In fact,

> the commune had always been considered by the reformist wing [of the P.S.I.] as the highest point of conquest by the proletariat within the structures of bourgeois society . . . [They saw in it] the platform from which to carry out a program of social transformations which would eventually have led to the collectivization of private property. The management and municipalization of vital sectors of the urban economy, especially in the field of distribution, combined with the activity of the socialist co-operatives and the support of syndicalist organizations, were to constitute the basis for an attack on bourgeois profit in the realm of production and distribution.[43]

Social and political polarization first became an ugly reality in the countryside. Here, greater social homogeneity, the breakdown of mediating mechanisms, the overwhelming presence of radical parties striving to fill up all political space, and the long tradition of violent conflict combined to give fascism its political place in the sun. While closely linked to urban bases, such as Milan, Cremona, Ferrara and Bologna, the fascists directed their efforts at the conquest of the countryside, especially the Po valley, which was a major area of Popolari and socialist strength. The use of trucks, liberally furnished by the large landowners and, in some instances, by the army gave the fascists mobility, long-range striking power, and the element of surprise. Albert Szymansky has irrefutably pointed out the extent to which the socialists were the primary target on the fascist reaction.[44] What is striking, however, is that fascist reaction took its most violent forms exactly in those areas where social reformist traditions were strongest.

> Logically [writes Claudio Giovannini] the fascists should have attacked the maximalist and communist wing of the P.S.I. In reality, what caused great concern to the landlords and the shopkeepers were the syndicalist organizations and the agricultural and service co-operatives. The former because they protected the interests of the workers, the latter because they were threatening to destroy the private monopoly in the distribution sector and bringing downward pressures on prices, thus contributing to lower profit margins.[45]

As regards the future course of the Liberal regime, the political consequences of agrarian fascism can hardly be overestimated, even though its relationship to the urban wing and Mussolini are still the object of profound disagreement.[46] Between March 1921 and May 1922, fascism, now constituted as a party, increased its membership from 80,476 to 322,310; northern Italy, including Emilia and Tuscany, accounted for 251,783 members.[47] In the process of expanding, fascism underwent substantial ideological and programmatic changes of a conservative nature. Regional power bases emerged and many able leaders arose, such as Italo Balbo in Ferrara and Dino Grandi in Bologna, any of whom could have presented an alternative to the leadership of Mussolini. This situation further restricted Mussolini's freedom of action who, once in power, used the state to redimension the party and impress his authority on the movement.

The rapid swelling of the fascist ranks led to the marginalization of the original fascists. Numerous fascists of «the first hour», baffled and confused by the purely reactionary role that the movement was assuming in many regions, quit. Others attempted to control what seemed at times «a chaotic ensemble of local phenomena of reaction».[48] Renzo de Felice, in his monumental biography of Mussolini, has observed that

> if we compare the list of names of those who attended the founding session of the Fasci in Milan in March 1919, and the first national congress of the Fasci di Combattimento the following October in Florence, with a list of those who participated at the Rome Congress [November 1921] and that of Naples just before the march on Rome [October 1922], we cannot fail to notice the extent to which the fascist leadership had drastically changed in the course of two or three years. This was not due so much to the admission of new elements – which would be considered normal – but to the disappearance of over ninety per cent of the original leadership . . . It is interesting to note the social and political origin of the new one: [we no longer find] old socialists, anarchists, revolutionary syndicalists, republicans, all of these having either retired or gone over to the ranks of anti-fascism, but Liberals, Constitutionalists, Nationalists, all of whom gone over lock, stock and barrel to those very Fasci which two years earlier they had denounced as subversive . . . [we no longer find] workers, craftsmen, petty bourgeois, but members of the middle and upper classes, of the aristocracy, industrialists, landowners . . .[49]

During this period, the potential functions of the movement, as an ideological pole for the industrial and agrarian élites in crisis and as a structural constraint upon the rebellious masses, were shaped by two determinant factors: «the demonstrated incapacity of the working class and the P.S.I. to fight fascist violence with violence, to overcome its own maximalist visions, and to cooperate in the strengthening of the government in order that it might be capable of withstanding the reactionary-fascist wave . . . [secondly] the aid and the encouragement given to fascism by the Liberal class and by Giolitti himself».[50]

The Trojan Horse

In fact, Giolitti, still tied to his pre-mass politics vision of parliamentary equilibrium, sought to revive his old Liberal model of class alliances. This time the pillars of the political alliance were to be the more progressive sector of the industrial class, the Popolari and the reformist wing of the P.S.I., Giolitti's handling of the factory occupation had created an irreparable rift with the industrialists. At the same time the old cleavage of Clericalism – Anticlericalism, along with personal divergencies between the old Liberal statesman and Don Luigi Sturzo, leader of the P.P.I., precluded Giolitti from receiving Popolari support. Finally, the persistence of maximalism among the ranks of the P.S.I., which, following the Leghorn Congress in January 1921, had broken away *to the left*, deprived him of the last strategic pillar for his prospective alliance. In the spring of 1921, Giolitti decided to gamble. He welcomed the fascists into the Constitutional ranks and called a general election. By inviting the fascists into the Blocchi Nazionali, Giolitti sought to realign the socialists, still clinging onto old anti-bourgeois myths, and the Popolari, who wanted to fight against socialism but without allying themselves to the conservatives. «Giolitti thought of using fascism to give the Liberal state a breather . . . [for him] the constitution of the Blocchi Nazionali was meant to achieve what he had in vain hoped for at the Socialist Congress of Leghorn, a realignment within the Socialist party to the advantage of the reformist wing . . . On the whole, the maneuver was far from successful.»[51]

Even though the elections showed the impact of fascist extraparliamentary activity, especially in Emilia Romagna and Tuscany where most fascist violence had occurred, the socialists managed to retain 123 seats which, when added to the 14 seats won by the newly-formed Communist party, confirmed the limits of electoral maneuvering in stopping the Left. The Popolari actually increased their representatives to 106, while the fascists themselves gained a foothold in Parliament with 35 deputies. The Giolittian attempt at altering alignments within the Left by using the fascist movement had utterly failed. In the process, Giolitti had allowed an essentially subversive, anti-liberal and fundamentally anti-democratic movement to insinuate itself into the political arena. In the course of this operation, fascism acquired legal political status in the eyes of numerous elements of the Italian ruling élites and demonstrated its availability for further political projects. At the same time, even after its constitution as a political party in December 1921, fascism maintained a uniquely independent political base in the form of armed squads and thereby introduced an entirely new dimension into the competition for political power. Its continuous expansion among institutional élites, in particular the Army and the bureaucracy, and marginal radical parties, such as the Republicans[52], widened its social base, isolating at the same time the socialists, the communists, and the Popolari.

The nationalist obsession, the rabid anti-socialism, the call for order, hierarchy and class cooperation, the flexibility of its program, the political style and the military tactics contributed to make fascism the new axis along which an old ruling class in crisis realigned itself. Politically, this realignment emerged from the crisis which followed Giolitti's gamble at the general elections. In the course of 1921–1922, the political arena became further fractionalized by splits within the Liberal groups, some of which moved to the Right. Table 2 illustrates the degree of fractionalization of the political spectrum and the compatibility – incompatibility factor among the various political factions.

The making of a political crisis: the fragmentation of parliamentary groups 1921 – 1922

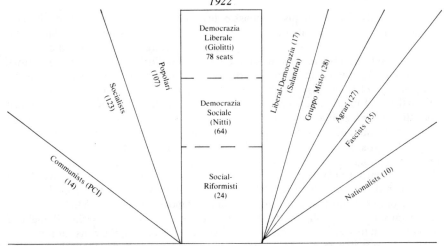

The fragmentation of the political arena following Giolitti's failure to realign the only two mass parties in the country created new political «compartments» which made it impossible for the Liberal parties to create new coalitions.[53] The socialists continually refused to enter the government and the Popolari, while anti-socialists were unwilling to lend their support to the Liberal parties. At the same time, they could prevent the formation of any government based on the center parties thanks to their control of over one hundred seats in Parliament. The impasse which arose from this situation led the political axis to move to the Right, where numerous small and contradictory factions were available. They were not only united by the «anti» themes of their ideology and the political mentalities of their leaders, but also shared common experiences (i.e. interventionism) and a confused political philosophy based on common values of order, hierarchy, nationalism and a strong faith in Italy's future greatness.

These right-wing groups hoped like Giolitti to use fascism for immediate reactionary purposes and continued to think in terms of a parliamentary equilibrium, with the possibility of using Mussolini's movement as an instrument to reestablish social discipline and the authority of the state. Fascism, however, had projects of its own, which contained multiple ideological strains and conflicting programs, and thus sharply differentiated it from traditional conservative reaction.[54] In fact, part of the success of the fascists in attracting numerous social groups to their cause was due to the multifarious aspects of their ever-changing program and their ability to monopolize at the *mass* level as volatile and emotional an issue as nationalism and the myths of

Table 2. *Political Crisis of 1922*

Left	Center	Right
Partito Popolare (106)	*Democrazia (Giolitti) 42*	*Democrazia Liberale (23) (De Nava)*
Partito Socialista Unificato (83) (Filippo Turati)	*Democrazia Italiana (Nitti) 36*	*Democrazia Sociale (41) (De Cesaro')*
Gruppo Socialista (GM Serrati) 40	*Social-Riformisti (Bonomi) 26*	*Liberal-Democrazia (21) (Salandra)*
P.C.I. 14		*Gruppo Misto (32)*
		Agrari (23)
		Fascists (32)
		Nationalists (11)

– – – – – potential aggregation lines
——————compartmentalization lines
Source: Derived from Paolo Farneti, «The Crisis of Parliamentary Democracy and the Take-over of the Fascist Dictatorship: 1919–1922.» Table VII in Juan J. Linz, Alfred C. Stepan, Eds., *Breakdown and Crisis of Democracies,* Baltimore, Johns Hopkins Press, 1979.

the Great War, using them both in their delegitimating attacks on the Liberal State and in rallying support against the socialists and the communists.

Fascism, with its slogans, political style and confused programmatic statements attracted thousands of war veterans, students, white-collar workers, small property-owners – in brief, that stratum of society which formed what Luigi Salvatorelli has so aptly referred to as «the humanistic petty bourgeoisie, which made the Myth of the Nation the banner of its revolution . . . Its class struggle against capitalism and the proletariat consisted in the negation of the concept of class and the substitution for it of the concept of Nation.»[55] The movement's functional role against the socialists and the Popolari attracted the sympathies and the support of all those interests which felt threatened by the post-war mobilization of the lower classes, the incipient process of economic and political democratization and the breakdown of traditional authority. In the process of crushing the Left, the fascists succeeded in offering these interests an alternative sovereignty which successfully stood in for the crumbling Liberal state. It was around this sovereignty that social classes aligned themselves, eventually to be realigned by it. The mediating functions of the old Liberal political élite were slowly taken over by a personalistic dictatorship,[56] which, having succeeded in stamping out whatever vague progressive notions existed in the fascist movement, became the hallmark of the inter-war period.

333

NOTES

[1] The concept of hegemony is here put forth in Gramscian terms. In his analysis of Liberal-democratic states, Antonio Gramsci distinguished between two superstructures of society on the basis of their different functions: *civil society*, which he defined as consisting of all the organizations commonly called «private» (i.e. parties, churches, intellectual organizations etc.) and which competed to attain the intellectual and moral leadership of society; the *State*, which had the function of direct rule expressed in the legal government. The function of the organizations of civil society is to create support for the present organization of society by cultural and ideological means, thus allowing a particular ruling class to exercise hegemony over the rest of the population. The function of the state is to secure the maintenance of the current political, economic and social arrangements by coercion or threat of coercion. The two superstructures compliment each other, as all liberal-democratic societies attempt to establish some sort of balance between consent and coercion. This was largely the essence of the project of the Giolittian political class: the transition to a form of hegemonic control over the lower classes by enlarging the realm of *civil society* and restricting the role of the state to one of «ultima ratio». See Antonio Gramsci, *Prison Notebooks*. Edited by Quintin Hoare and Geoffrey Nowell Smith. (New York: International Publishers 1971.) pp. 206–276.

[2] For the earlier period of Giolittian Italy, see Giampiero Carocci, *Giolitti e l'Età' Giolittiana*. (Torino: Einaudi 1971) *passim;* Christopher Seton-Watson, *Italy from Liberalism to Fascism*. (London: Methuen 1967); Adolfo Pepe, *Storia della CGdL* 2 vols. (Bari: Laterza 1971–1972).

[3] Adolfo Pepe, *Storia della CGdL. Dalla Fondazione alla Guerra di Libia*. (Bari: Laterza 1972) p. 2.

[4] Sandor Agocs, «Giolitti's Reform program. An Exercise in Equilibrium Politics». *Political Science Quarterly,* 86, 1971, # 4 p. 646.

[5] G. Neppi Modona, *Sciopero, Potere Politico e Magistratura (1870–1922)*. (Bari: Laterza 1969) pp. 215–230. Also Luigi Preti, *Le Lotte Agrarie nella Valle Padana*. (Torino: Einaudi 1955), *passim*.

[6] Giancarlo Provasi, «Considerazioni sullo Sviluppo del Capitalismo nell' Italia Post-Unitaria». *Rassegna Italiana di Sociologia* Vol. VIII, (1) 1973 pp. 303–304.

[7] Salvatore LaFrancesca, *La Politica Economica Italiana dal 1900 al 1913*. Roma: Edizioni dell' Ateneo. 1971. chs. I–III. Also Alberto Caracciolo (ed.) *La Formazione dell' Italia Industriale*. (Bari: Laterza 1969.)

[8] Valerio Castronovo, «Potere Economico e Fascismo». *Rivista di Storia Contemporanea* Vol. II, (3) 1972 pp. 273–274.

[9] *Ibid* p. 275.

[10] Adolfo Pepe, Storia della CGdL . . . *op. cit.* p. 15.

[11] Antonio Gramsci, «The Southern Question.» in *The Modern Prince and Other Writings*. (New York: International Publishers, 1957), p. 39.

[12] See Arno J. Mayer, *Dynamics of Counterrevolution in Europe, 1870–1956*. (New York: Harper & Row 1971), *passim*.

[13] Paolo Sylos-Labini, «Sviluppo Economico e Classi Sociali in Italia.» Quaderni di Sociologia, vol. 21, (4), 1972 Appendix, Table I.

[14] For the Nationalists, see Christopher Seton-Watson, *op.cit.* pp. 349–365; John A. Thayer, *Italy and the Great War* (Madison: U. of Wisconsin Press 1964), pp. 192–232 and 271 ff. Francesco Gaeta, *Nazionalismo Italiano*. Napoli 1965.

[15] Salvatore Saladino, «Italy» in Hans Rogger and Eugen Weber, (eds.) *The European Right*. (Berkeley: U. of California Press 1966), pp. 233–234.

[16] Adrian Lyttelton, *The Seizure of Power*. (New York: Charles Scribner's Sons 1973), p. 120.

[17] *Ibid* pp. 25–26.

[18] Renato Bachi, *L' Italia Economica nell' Anno 1918*. Roma 1919. pp. V–VI.

[19] Renzo Paci, «Le Trasformazioni ed Innovazioni nella Struttura Economica Italiana.» in Alberto Caracciolo et al., *Il Trauma dell' Intervento 1914–1918*. (Firenze: Vallecchi 1968), pp. 35–36.

[20] See Luigi Einaudi, *La Condotta Economica e gli Effetti Sociali della Guerra Italiana*. (Bari: Laterza 1933), pp. 337–358.

[21] For a history of the agricultural unions, see Idomeneo Barbadoro, *Storia del Sindacalismo Italiano. Vol. II. La Federterra*. (Firenze: La Nuova Italia 1973.)

[22] Salvatore Sechi, *Il Movimento Autonomistico e le Origini del Fascismo in Sardegna*. (1920–1926.) Torino: Annali della Fondazione Luigi Einaudi 1967.

[23] See the same article by Paolo Farneti, «La Crisi della Democrazia Italiana e l'Avvento del Fascismo: 1919–1922.» *Rivista Italiana di Scienze Politiche* Anno V, 1, April 1975.

[24] Carlo Vallauri, *Le Radici del Corporativismo* (Roma: Bulzoni 1971), p. 134.

[25] See Renzo de Felice, «I Sindacalisti Revoluzionari» in Alberto Caracciolo et al., Il Trauma dell' Intervento . . . *op. cit.*

[26] Juan J. Linz, «Some Notes Toward a Comparative Study of Fascism in Sociological-Historical Perspective» in Walter Laqueur (ed.) *Fascism. A Reader's Guide.* Berkeley, University of California Press, 1976.

[27] For this important veteran group, mistakenly accused by some of having been a source of fascist support, see Giovanni Sabbatucci, *I Combattenti nel Primo Dopoguerra.* (Bari: Laterza 1974.)

[28] For the function of political myth and ideology in social movements, see Barry McLaughlin, ed, *Studies in Social Movements.* (New York: The Free Press 1969).

[29] Emil Oesterreicher, «Fascism and the Intellectuals: the case of Italian Futurists». *Social Research* vol. 41, 3, 1974.

[30] For the full program, see Renzo de Felice, *Mussolini il Rivoluzionario.* (Torino: Einaudi 1965), pp. 742–743.

[31] Paolo Vita-Finzi, «Italian Fascism and the Intellectuals» in S. J. Woolf, ed. *The Nature of Fascism.* (New York: Vintage Books 1968), p. 229.

[32] Roberto Vivarelli, *Il Dopoguerra in Italia e l' Avvento del Fascismo.* Vol. I (Napoli: Istituto Italiano per gli Studi Storici, 1967), p. 453.

[33] Quoted in Angelo Taşca, *Nascita e Avvento del Fascismo.* (Firenze: La Nuova Italia 1950), pp. 54–55.

[34] Renzo de Felice, Mussolini il Rivoluzionario . . . *op. cit.* p. 607.

[35] See the various assessments of fascism made by its contemporaries in Renzo de Felice, ed. *Il Fascismo e i Partiti Politici Italiani.* (Rocca San Casciano 1966).

[36] John M. Cammett, «Communist Theories of Fascism: 1920–1935.» *Science and Society* Vol. XXXI, 1967, p. 167.

[37] Angelo Tasca, *Op. cit.* p. 123.

[38] See Valerio Castronovo, «Potere Economico . . .» *op. cit.* passim.

[39] The literature on Agrarian fascism is vast. For a good synthesis of the character of the northern Italian countryside on the eve of the fascist reaction, see Frank M. Snowden, «The Origins of Agrarian Fascism in Italy». *Archives Européennes de Sociologie,* vol. XIII, 2, 1972, pp. 268–295.

[40] Gaetano Salvemini, *The Origins of Fascism in Italy.* (New York: Harper & Row 1973), p. 292.

[41] See Arrigo Serpieri, *La Guerra e le Classi Sociali in Italia.* (Barri: Laterza 1933), pp. 484 for data on property shifts in the post-war period.

[42] See Ugo Giusti, *Le Correnti Politiche Italiane Attraverso due Riforme Elettorali dal 1909 al 1922.* (Firenze: Alfani e Venturi 1922), p. 32.

[43] Rolando Cavandoli, *Le Origini del Fascismo a Reggio Emilia. 1919–1923.* (Roma: Editori Riuniti 1973), p. 161.

[44] Albert Szymanski, «Fascism, Industrialism and Socialism: the case of Italy». *Comparative Studies in Society and History* vol. XV, 4, 1973 pp. 396–404.

[45] Claudio Giovannini, *L' Italia da Vittorio Veneto all' Aventino.* (Bologna: Patron 1972), p. 242.

[46] The controversy between Renzo de Felice and Alessandro Roveri, briefly synthesized by

Mario Bernabei, «La Base di Massa del Fascismo Agrario». *Storia Contemporanea* Vol. VI, I, 1975 p. 123–153.

[47] Data calculated from Renzo de Felice, *Mussolini il Fascista. La Conquista del Potere.* (Torino: Einaudi 1966), pp. 8–11.

[48] Quoted from a letter by Dino Grandi to Mario Missiroli in Renzo de Felice, Mussolini il Rivoluzionario . . . *op. cit.* p. 607.

[49] *Ibid,* pp. 505–506.

[50] Renzo de Felice, Mussolini il Fascista. La Conquista . . . *op. cit.* pp. 11–12.

[51] Gabriele De Rosa, *L' Utopia Politica di Don Luigi Sturzo* (Brescia: Morcelliana 1972), pp. 126–127.

[52] The Republican Party, anti-Liberal and Interventionist, provided numerous cadres to the fascist movement (i.e. Italo Balbo, who as late as February 1921 was a card carrying member of the party). See also Luciano Casali, «Fascisti, Repubblicani e Socialisti in Romagna nel 1922.» *Il Movimento di Liberazione in Italia,* vol. 20, 93, 1968.

[53] For a micro-political discussion of the 1922 crisis, see Paolo Farneti *op. cit.*

[54] See Edward Tannenbaum, «The Goals of Italian Fascism» *American Historical Review* vol. 74, 1, 1960 pp. 1183–1204.

[55] Luigi Salvatorelli, *Nazionalfascismo.* (Torino: Gobetti 1923) pp. 18–19.

[56] Alberto Aquarone, *L' Organizzazione dello Stato Totalitario.* (Torino: Einaudi 1965) *passim.* esp. chapter 5, pp. 290–311.

Petty Bourgeois Fascism in Italy:
Form and Content

DAVID D. ROBERTS

In confronting the problem of Italian fascism, we tend to ask first about social composition, because we assume that if we can find social categories enabling us to distinguish fascists from non-fascists, we have the key to explaining the phenomenon. Although we have surprisingly little solid evidence about social composition during the rise to power, and although the composition of fascism varied over time, there has been general agreement since 1922 that its mass base came from the lower-middle class, that some sort of petty bourgeois revolt made fascism possible. What evidence we have does indicate the overrepresentation of lower-middle class groups, especially among the creators of fascism in 1920–1922, and the most sensitive students of Italian fascism, from Luigi Salvatorelli in 1923 to Renzo de Felice today, have made the petty bourgeoisie category the keynote of the reigning interpretation. Even though class analysis raises thorny theoretical and definitional questions, we can usefully approach the problem of who the fascists were from within this familiar and well-established tradition, accepting the overrepresentation of the lower-middle class as a fact. The serious deficiencies that we will find in the standard interpretation stem not from the insistence on the petty bourgeois role in fascism, but from the inferences about motivation that are made from this fact of social composition. Conversely, if we are to improve our understanding of Italian fascism, it is not enough to continue asking the same questions about social composition – through local studies, for example. It is more important that we establish a more flexible framework for explaining what the petty bourgeois elements in fascism were trying to accomplish.

Ever since fascism rose to power, discussion of the lower-middle class role in the movement has focused on the thesis of Luigi Salvatorelli, who collected his articles on the subject in his classic *Nazionalfascismo* in 1923. Salvatorelli emphasized the autonomy and internal consistency of petty bourgeois fascism; since it opposed industrial capitalism as well as the working class, fascism could not be explained in simple, dualistic terms as bourgeois capitalist counterrevolution. On the contrary,Salvatorelli argued, fascism «represents the class struggle of the petty bourgeoisie, squeezed between capitalism and proletariat, as the third party between the two conflicting sides.»[1] He sought to give his categories greater precision by distinguishing between the «technical» petty bourgeoisie – those with a place in modern industrial society – and the «humanistic» petty bourgeoisie – pre-industrial groups like school teachers, lower government officials, and marginal lawyers, often university-educated, but lacking the solid economic roles of their «technical» counterparts. It was this humanistic petty bourgeoisie, threatened economically, socially, and psychologically, which created fascism. Since they lacked modern productive roles, Salvatorelli went on, these groups were too weak to struggle openly with the industrial classes and to develop a genuine «ideology,» or political program, of their own.[2] They relied instead on hollow rhetorical ideals, especially the myth of

337

the nation, as a way of denying the modern world of class and class struggle altogether; but such ideals, derived from their superficial humanistic education, were simply ever more irrelevant as modern industrial civilization developed. It was only because Italy was relatively weak economically, Salvatorelli concluded, that these marginal, pre-industrial sectors of the lower-middle class could attempt through fascism «to play the primary role on the political scene.»[3]

It is surely testimony to the force of Salvatorelli's argument that it has a central part in the major interpretations of Italian fascism even today, although there is some difference in the way his thesis is used. Enzo Santarelli, Franco Gaeta, Roberto Vivarelli, and Alessandro Roveri employ Salvatorelli's categories to show how the petty bourgeoisie could be manipulated by irrational and rhetorical nationalism and made the mass base for a reaction in defense of restricted economic interests.[4] On the other hand, Renzo de Felice strongly endorses Salvatorelli in order to emphasize the autonomy of the petty bourgeois role in fascism, which was more, he argues, than a mere counterrevolution.[5] Despite this difference in emphasis, however, these inter-pretations, as well as others which do not explicitly use Salvatorelli, all explain the petty bourgeois role in fascism in terms of socio-economic crisis and the traumas and frustrations which industrial modernization causes the lower-middle class.

Although social composition, in itself, does not reveal motivation, it seems plausi-ble to assume that socio-economic concerns underlie the common response in a movement whose membership can be characterized in terms of socio-economic grouping. Moreover, in our customary conception of the movement of history, indica-ted by the short-hand term «modernization,» the petty bourgeoisie includes those losing out as modernization proceeds: and by implication these elements, since they are losers, can play no progressive role in history. It is easy to assume that fascism attracted elements from the lower-middle class who were discontented because the universal process of modernization was either leaving them behind or threatening to drag them along, undermining their traditions, their status, and their self-esteem. Edward Tannenbaum's view is typical: «What makes a revolution specifically fascist is its slogans and its appeal to certain kinds of people who see themselves as losers in modern technological civilization.»[6]

Although it would be possible to raise theoretical objections to this schema and to the rather indiscriminate uses that have been made of it, it hardly seems necessary, for the nature of the crisis from which fascism emerged, and the nature of the fascist response, seem striking confirmation of the socio-economic interpretation. Italy's post-war crisis did include severe socio-economic problems which caused the classic strains on the petty bourgeoisie. High rates of inflation, stemming from government financial policies during the war, meant a redistribution of wealth in favor of the industrial classes. And this included Italian industrial workers, who managed to hold their own or even improve their position during the war and during the difficult readjustment to peacetime.[7] The dislocations of this post-war readjustment, including unemployment or the threat of unemployment, reached their peak early in 1921, just as discontented petty bourgeois elements were making fascism a mass movement. During 1919 and 1920, moreover, Italy experienced the most extensive and militant strike wave in her history, culminating in the factory occupations of September 1920. Italian socialists, infatuated with the Bolshevik example, fanned expectations and fears by proclaiming that the dictatorship of the proletariat was imminent in Italy, and the fascism of 1920–21 emerged, on the immediate level, in violent reaction against the socialist labor movement.

338

The fascist response to this post-war situation also seems to support a socio-economic interpretation of petty bourgeois fascism. In their vicious assault on the labor movement, it would seem, resentful fascist squadristi were seeking to undermine the source of the workers'relative economic advantage. But the fascists did not merely destroy the existing labor movement; they also tried to force the workers into new fascist organizations, which included non-manual «intellectual labor» from the middle class as well. Adrian Lyttelton sees this pattern as the attempt of threatened middle class groups to defend themselves against the two-sided squeeze from capitalists and workers.[8] In calling for some sort of syndicalist or corporativist state, Lyttelton argues, these sectors were attempting to reverse this disadvantageous position and to become, in fact, the arbiters of conflicts between labor and capital.

A Cultural or an Economic Revolt?

Fascist slogans and myths seem to indicate a backward-looking orientation, an attempt to cling to and defend the traditional values of the culture in the face of modernization. In glorifying the romantic pre-industrial nationalist Giuseppe Mazzini, and in proclaiming the superiority of Mazzini to Marx, petty bourgeois fascists were apparently seeking to deny the modern world of class and class conflict represented by Marxism and repudiated by Mazzini.[9] It is certainly true that these fascists called for class solidarity – and had misgivings about Italian capitalism. At the same time, fascism stressed the values of the war and the nation, thereby offering, it would seem, a kind of irrational psychological reassurance or compensation to those whose place in society was eroding.[10] Since their position was declining, their pretensions were apparently futile; thus their ideals tended to become irrational and rhetorical. Consequently, many historians argue, petty bourgeois fascists proved easily manipulated for the reactionary purposes of others.[11]

Fascist polemics focused not only on socialism, but also on the Italian political system. According to Enzo Santarelli, the fascism of 1921 opposed political parties and the parliamentary system because its declining petty bourgeois nucleus was unable to get its interests represented through the existing parties and factions in parliament.[12] Fascism thus became an anti-party movement, denying the legitimacy of political parties and the whole parliamentary system. Although the political stance of this early petty bourgeois fascism was not wholly negative, historians have found no difficulty explaining fascist proposals for a political alternative in terms of the usual schema. For example, Renzo de Felice portrays Dino Grandi's call for a national syndicalist «democracy», to bind together the «producers» in Italian society and to bring the masses into political life, simply as confirmation of the Salvatorelli thesis.[13]

So a strong case can apparently be made for interpreting petty bourgeois fascism in terms of the classic socio-economic problems of the pre-industrial middle classes. But while there was certainly a socio-economic dimension to Italy's post-war crisis, the central issues were political and cultural; they stemmed from long-term problems of national integration and cultural self-confidence that reached a climax because of the way Italy experienced World War I. Especially with the defeat at Caporetto in October 1917 and the remarkable recovery that followed, the war experience raised the national-political consciousness – and self-confidence – of people left out of Italy's restrictive transformist political system.[14] The political side of the post-war crisis did not stem primarily from the socio-economic strains we have discussed but had deeper roots – in the way Italy was put together as a nation, in the limits to parliamentary government in Italian practice, and in the perceptions and priorities of the restricted liberal political class which had governed Italy since 1861. Seeking to keep the badly fragmented young nation together, and pessimistic about the political capacity of the Italian people, the liberal élite devised a political system which reinforced the corruption and fragmentation in the society while keeping the state aloof and restricted. Even though the new country held together and the parliamentary system continued to function, after a fashion, political alienation and cynicism, and the oft-noted divorce between the citizens and the state, continued to plague liberal Italy.

Italy's performance in the war seemed to indicate that the Italian people were better than the pessimistic political class had thought and were now worthy of a fuller political role. The old political expedients no longer seemed appropriate or necessary, and some sort of radical political change in a populist direction was widely expected after the war. Although proportional representation was instituted in 1919 in an attempt to encourage a more healthy and popular kind of party system, the old ruling class ultimately proved incapable of renewing itself and of bringing about the essential changes from within the liberal parliamentary framework. Sensitive liberals like Guido de Ruggiero and Adolfo Omodeo have left us much eloquent testimony that the old system and political class were bankrupt and could not bring to fruition the hopes for political renewal bound up with the war experience.[15] Moreover, the Socialist party blithely anticipating the dictatorship of the proletariat, saw no value in the war experience and had no interest in leading a nationalist-populist challenge to the system itself.

Under the circumstances, those seeking solutions to Italy's long-term national and political problems might plausibly doubt the value of both liberalism and socialism. Indeed, parliamentary liberalism and Marxist socialism each failed to come to terms with the Italian crisis not only because of accidents of personality or the anomalies of the Italian situation, but also because both were subject to genuine deficiencies which had already come to light in Europe but which were especially evident in Italy's situation of political crisis. There were questions about whether a liberal parliamentary systems could bring about meaningful popular participation and about the relationship between interest groups and the collective interest. At the same time, there were questions about the utility of Marxism for analyzing national and political problems and about whether the proletariat could make itself worthy of a universal role. Given the genuine problems in the two traditions, it was not irrational to repudiate both and to cast about for alternatives.

Outsiders Against the Establishment

Since the Italian crisis was not only socio-economic, fascist themes and actions which at first seemed to confirm the prevailing interpretation could have had more than one meaning, so we have to approach the assault on socialism, for example, and the revival of Mazzini, and the glorification of the war and the nation, more flexibly and imaginatively. Under the circumstances, individuals from pre-industrial middle class backgrounds could have been more concerned about Italy's political and cultural problems than about their personal socio-economic position. In fact, a variety of concerns contributed to the petty bourgeois revolt as a whole – and could even be combined in the same individual; some of those subject to the standard socio-economic traumas were seeking a more legitimate political system at the same time. Concerns no doubt varied greatly from one individual to the next. If we are to

340

characterize petty bourgeois fascism accurately, we need an interpretive framework pluralistic enough to account for this variety of motives and purposes.

The petty bourgeoisie was overrepresented in fascism, but obviously many with this social background were not involved in the fascist revolt. Those who did help to create fascism constituted a kind of vanguard best characterized in terms of two substantially overlapping categories. First, they were political outsiders. Some had been politically indifferent or alienated before; others had been active in pre-industrial populist and Republican groupings hostile to the political establishment; many were young people just coming of age politically. Second, they were war veterans, often from the ranks of the junior officers. In the current as a whole, socio-economic traumas were surely at work, but petty bourgeois fascism was above all the creation of young, politically alienated war veterans who claimed to embody the moral legacy and promise of renewal bound up with Italy's war experience. Their enemy was not industrial capitalism but the Italian political system; they were alienated not because of declining economic prospects and social status, but because they felt excluded politically. Their resentments were directed less at the industrial classes than at the old political class, with its lack of confidence in the Italian people. Since political power and confidence in the political process are to some extent a function of socio-economic position, it is not surprising that the petty bourgeoisie was overrepresented in this «populist» reaction against the old Italian political system. And this overrepresentation was especially pronounced because most of the political discontent among the other «populist» sectors, the workers and the peasants, found an outlet in socialism or political Catholicism.

The young veterans in fascism are generally described as «military desperadoes» unable to readjust to civilian life, especially in a situation of socio-economic dislocation, or «dropouts» from the established order, which they rejected because they could find no acceptable place in it.[16] But when we consider what the war experience had meant, and determine what these young veterans did not like about the established order, it becomes obvious that these customary categories are too facile. These fascists revolted against the old Italy not because it had no acceptable socio-economic place for them, but because they were outsiders politically. To say they could not readjust after the war is trivial and tautological: they chose not to adjust – first, because they believed, quite plausibly, that the situation called for significant political and cultural change instead; and second, because they believed, much less plausibly, that they themselves could spearhead that change, because of their role in the war. Whatever their prospects of success, it was not merely petty bourgeois prejudice to insist on the value and the political implications of the war experience; and to return to normal, to the traditional patterns of Italian life, was neither desirable nor possible for the society as a whole. When the old liberals, the new politics of mass parties, and the «normal» socialist alternative to the system all failed to fill the developing political vacuum, lower-middle class outsiders and veterans set out on the perilous course of trying to develop their own political challenge – and political alternative – through the fascism of 1921. Insofar as the Italian political system was genuinely in crisis, and insofar as the liberal parliamentary system in general has genuine defects, these young fascists could at least attempt to make their own political discontents the basis for a new political program – transcending narrow class interests and having validity for the whole society. And indeed there was a struggle for coherence, universality, and autonomy in petty bourgeois fascism, but the current remained weak and fragile, its program clumsy and in some ways superficial, in large part because of the social

341

insecurities, the deficiencies of education, and the lack of experience with the modern industrial world that resulted from the social background of those involved.

Motives of Fascist Leaders

In fact, of course, individuals with similar social backgrounds differed in the quality of their vision of the political alternative, so our interpretive framework must enable us to differentiate even among those whose concerns were primarily political rather than socio-economic. Some were primarily place-seekers who envisioned a mere change in personnel or circulation of élites. Young fascists like Roberto Farinacci lacked the idealism, the intelligence, the education, or the breadth of vision necessary to grasp the basis of present problems and to propose institutional alternatives. They championed the new Fascist party *vis-à-vis* the old state apparatus because they were seeking to establish an institutional power base for themselves, not because they believed new institutions essential for implementing a more genuinely populist political system. From their perspéctive, the coming to power of new, energetic men of the people like themselves was in itself the essence of the fascist revolution.

But this was not the only petty bourgeois perspective on fascism; for other alienated young war veterans – like Dino Grandi, Augusto, Turati, Curzio Suckert, Giuseppe Bottai, and those whose goals they articulated – the fascist revolution would be populist in a different sense. In fascists like these, we find a more coherent critique of the liberal parliamentary system and more sensitive consideration of what fascism was for, what it was to do with the power it sought. The petty bourgeois revolt did produce a political program, envisioning not merely change in personnel but change in institutions – a kind of Mazzinian and populist national syndicalism derived primarily, directly or indirectly, from syndicalist publicists like Sergio Panunzio, A. O. Olivetti, and Agostino Lanzillo.[17] By 1921 these syndicalists had become nationalist populists claiming to offer an alternative to liberalism, not to capitalism, and now they mixed with the populist current in fascism, seeking to give it direction.

Despite its heterogeneity, the petty bourgeois current did manage to develop a program with modernizing, post-liberal elements. But if we are to understand this current as a whole, we must avoid assuming that those whose political ideas had a measure of coherence were not petty bourgeois, an assumption which simply forecloses the possibility that petty bourgeois fascism could have given rise to something other than the expected myths and prejudices. Relatively articulate and intelligent fascists like Grandi and Bottai were young populist veterans speaking for and to a populist middle class constituency, but one whose members obviously varied greatly in intelligence and commitment.

An Alternative Path to Modernity

A second look at what the petty bourgeois fascists said and did – including the assault on socialism, the plebeian nationalism, the ambivalence about Italian capitalism, and the opposition to parliamentary liberalism – reveals a plausible but ultimately inadequate attempt to lead, and not merely a reaction against socio-economic strains and modernization. Although the fascist struggle with socialism stemmed in part from socio-economic resentments, it was above all a dispute over the value and meaning of the nation and the war – and over the kind of change appropriate for Italy at that moment. In evaluating this bitter conflict, we must remember that the socialists were not yet offering the sensitive, flexible alternative which Antonio Gramsci later elaborated, partly in response to the inadequacies of the socialists' post-war strategy. Rather, they proposed an alternative which historians have portrayed, with a rare measure of unanimity, as inflexible, insensitive, and inappropriate.[18] Since socialists and workers during the post-war crisis ridiculed the veterans and the war and eschewed any national-political leadership role, the discontented young veterans did not have the option of following the socialists. Indeed, their alternative movement inevitably took shape first in opposition to socialists and workers. In the short term, of course, this movement could be exploited for the purposes of others, especially reactionary landowners, but these fascists did not deny labor's right to full citizenship, nor were they seeking to erect a permanent apparatus of repression. It was not the workers' rising socio-economic position that appalled them, but their denial of the war and the nation, their pretensions to superiority and leadership, their indifference to Italy's longstanding national and political problems at a time when solutions seemed possible.

At the same time, however, these fascists sensed that they needed labor's involvement if they were successfully to challenge the old Italy and to create a viable alternative. They sought to transcend a restricted class perspective and to find a basis of accommodation with the workers, a common denominator of basic goals and socio-economic roles, to make possible a common political challenge. By using the umbrella «producer» category, they insisted – somewhat defensively, to be sure – that they too were valuable, productive members of society, just like the workers. They destroyed the existing unions not simply to undermine the relatively advantageous economic position of some sectors of labor, but to force the workers into new unions, organized for a different set of purposes – to force the workers into this alliance of populist «producers.» And by the same token, they included petty bourgeois «intellectual labor» in their new organizations not simply as a means of static socio-economic defense, but to forge this alliance with the more obviously modern, productive workers as the basis for a new order.[19] Of course the initial conflict between petty bourgeois fascists and socialist workers deformed the post-war popular political challenge from the outset, but only subsequent development could make clear whether this would be fatal.

The evidence does not indicate that these petty bourgeois fascists were trying to preserve traditional values and repudiate the modern industrial world; the more coherent of them saw quite clearly that the new Italy they envisioned required continued industrial progress and a greater commitment to productive values throughout the society. A contemporary observer of fascism, Giovanni Ansaldo, raised some telling objections to Salvatorelli's thesis in 1922 and 1923, pointing out that the petty bourgeois elements which formed the core of fascism were very much taken with modernity and industrial development, but in a superficial and rhetorical way.[20] Ansaldo pointed to a dilettantish fascination with the modern industrial world in the movement: fascists emphasized change, dynamism, and the future, and dreamed of the great modern and productive Italy which fascism would create. In response to Ansaldo's critique, Salvatorelli began to back off, explaining that he had intended to link fascism to the superficial and rhetorical mentality characteristic of the Italian petty bourgeoisie, and not to a specific social grouping.[21] Salvatorelli dismissed Ansaldo's examples – including the fascist cult of speed, dynamism, and modernity – as new manifestations of the traditional rhetorical mentality of the pre-industrial Italian middle class. Indeed, Salvatorelli went on, it was evidence of the relative

backwardness of her middle classes that in Italy even interest in industrial modernization tended to assume an artificial and rhetorical character. But Salvatorelli was giving
up most of his original argument: he was offering a useful explanation of the rhetorical
forms of fascism, but if petty bourgeois fascists were not opposed to modern industrial
society, if they were not clinging to traditional, pre-industrial values, then his original
explanation of their motives in creating fascism was no longer valid.

In fact, we can make better sense of this component in fascism by portraying it not
as the losers' revolt against modernity, but as an awkward, often superficial attempt to
make Italy more modern and productive on the part of people whose background and
experience gave them little concrete sense of the modern industrial world.[22] These
fascists were troubled by their own nationality and suffered traumas about national
character and worth – no doubt to an irrational degree. But these concerns, typically
petty bourgeois in some ways, led them to favor modernization, not to cling to
tradition. They longed to be part of a more modern, efficient, and productive nation
and saw fascism as the vehicle for the desired change.

Producers Versus Parasites

Petty bourgeois fascism did include rhetorical attacks on the financial plutocracy, and
Salvatorelli cites them as confirmation of his thesis; but given the questionable, highly
speculative role which large financial groups played in Italy's industrial development,
especially during the war, it was perfectly possible for Italians to deplore the machina-
tions of big finance capital out of a desire to promote productivity and healthy
industrial development.[23] In the same vein, Adrian Lyttelton portrays early fascist
support of free trade as a manifestation of the concerns of static middle class consumers; but the relationship between protection and Italian industrialization had been
problematic at best, and consequently it was possible to support free trade in Italy out
of a desire for a healthier kind of economic development.

If we pre-judge these fascists by making *a priori* assumptions about the concerns of
the petty bourgeoisie, then anything they say about the economy can be used to
dismiss them in terms of the standard socio-economic interpretation. Insofar as they
objected to any of the features of Italian industrial capitalism, these fascists can be
taken as losers unable to adjust to modernity. On the other hand, insofar as they
favored large-scale industrial development in Italy and insisted on the progressive role
which capitalists could play, we assume they must have swallowed the Nationalist
line, which can be explained only because of their susceptibility to irrational factors.[24]
And ambivalence and hesitation, of course, merely indicate the incoherence we
expect to find in sectors being left out as modernization proceeds. But ambivalence
about Italian capitalism, especially given its contradictory performance during the
war, when solid productive development and speculative financial manipulation took
place side by side, was no doubt the only rational stance. To promote healthier
industrial development in Italy, it really was necessary to attack some sectors of
Italian capitalism and to favor others. And this is basically what petty bourgeois
fascists hoped to do. Their understanding of the situation was superficial, and they
were not sure how to make the necessary distinctions in practice, but they wanted to
distinguish between «producers» and «parasites» and to overcome the old unproduc-
tive patterns of Italian life. The most coherent of them sought to promote productive
values by creating a new relationship between economics and politics through the
corporativist system.

Of course the relationship between populism and productivism in a country like Italy, with its uneven industrial development, was problematic, to say the least. The country did not yet have enough modern productive roles to go around, so more political power «for the people» could end up an obstacle to real streamlining. Petty bourgeois fascists certainly did not succeed in solving this problem, which is by no means confined to Italy, but some of them tried. Their approach was to organize the «people», not just the workers, according to economic function and to make the resulting economic organizations the basis of political life. Renzo de Felice explains Dino Grandi's national syndicalism, and the more general «anti-political anarchism» of early fascism, in terms of Salvatorelli's initial framework, but only the rhetorical and exaggerated forms of Grandi's proposals, not their content, can be understood in Salvatorelli's terms.[25] Grandi was responding to the political crisis, trying to suggest how fascism, through national syndicalism, could mobilize and politicize the masses more effectively and thereby create a more productive society and a more legitimate and popular state.[26] Other young outsiders, like Suckert, Turati, and Bottai, had essentially the same objectives, although their commitments were sometimes fragile and they often disagreed sharply over strategy.[27] The post-liberal direction they proposed pointed to a kind of totalitarianism, with private behavior and experience becoming more public and with the newly popular state strong enough to impose the collective interest on a traditionally undisciplined society.

National Integration

The Mazzinian nationalism in petty bourgeois fascism was undeniably exaggerated and rhetorical, but it responded to genuine, long-standing, and widely recognized problems of inadequate national integration and political awareness in Italy. Despite the rhetorical forms of this nationalism, it cannot be simply dismissed as a «myth», serving to deny the modern world of class struggle and providing irrational psychological compensation to petty bourgeois losers. In Italy, after all, nationalism was hardly traditional for the society as a whole, and it could still have progressive consequences in such a context. Since these fascists were seeking alternatives to the political patterns that had developed because of the way Italy was unified, it was plausible for them to turn to Mazzini, who represented all the unfulfilled promise of the Risorgimento; his vision of a more popular kind of Italian unity had not been achieved, so it was not merely reactionary nostalgia that led fascists to look to him for ideas and inspiration as they sought solutions to contemporary problems.

Historians have generally recognized that the young veterans in fascism had vague ideals, but they have underestimated the measure of coherence these fascists achieved and the potential their ideals had for practical implementation. According to Renzo de Felice, for example, the «confused and contradictory amalgam» of aspirations in early petty bourgeois fascism, including the anti-political impulse, stemmed from a psycho-social crisis comprehensible in terms of Salvatorelli's categories, and not from genuine political awareness.[28] Inevitably, such aspirations were too absurd to have had any potential for practical development. But while the deep resentment of the Italian political system which De Felice describes was indeed its essential impulse, this fascism did not remain merely negative: it gave rise to an alternative which, confused and superficial though it was, did to some extent transcend the social concerns of the petty bourgeoisie and respond to the genuine political crisis. And this thrust toward political change had an important effect on the regime itself. Most obviously, fascism

345

began to dismantle the liberal parliamentary system and to move toward mass mobilization and corporativist organization. The populist thrust was not the only source of fascist corporativism, nor did the corporate system ever amount to much in practice, but the intention was real and did have some practical effect. Neither the motivating goals nor the impact on the shape of the regime can be understood in terms of the standard petty bourgeois traumas. And further progressive development would have been possible from within the proposed program; above all, the fascist organizations gradually had to be given serious things to do, real decisions to make, without constant interference from above.

The Unfulfilled Promise

Nevertheless, the current as a whole failed to develop sufficient coherence to establish its hegemony within fascism and to implement a successful program. And so it ended up providing a mass base and a populist veneer for a regime which turned out to be only a hollow personal dictatorship. Of course, we cannot know how effective a more coherent populist fascism would have been – especially since the fascist regime included powerful enemies of populism. In fact, however, problems on three levels undermined this current's political effectiveness and made it relatively easy to tame and twist to other purposes. First, there was too much superficiality, there were too many tensions and unanswered questions even in the most coherent expressions of the program. Partly because these fascists were confronting genuine dilemmas, partly because of their limited experience, partly because of the paradoxes in their own socio-economic position, the best they could produce was a confused and awkward fusion. Second, many of those involved in this political rebellion remained stuck on the level of resentment and place-seeking and failed to grasp even this program, such as it was. At the same time, some of those at first motivated by a long-term vision ended up settling for places in the regime or for Mussolini's superficial dynamism and the mere trappings of change, especially militarized trappings. And third, this current lacked sufficient support in the society as a whole because the split with the workers never healed. Ultimately, petty bourgeois fascism was strong enough to destroy the weakened liberal parliamentary system, but not strong enough to replace it with a viable populist alternative. The personal dictatorship which finally filled the post-war political vacuum managed to fragment the populist current in fascism, turning its once-meaningful ideals into myths giving the illusion of purpose to a haphazard regime.

NOTES

[1] Luigi Salvatorelli, *Nazionalfascismo* (Turin, 1923), p. 16.

[2] *Ibid.*, pp. 18–19.

[3] *Ibid.*, p. 26.

[4] Enzo Santarelli, *Storia del movimento e del regime fascista*, Vol. I (Rome, 1967), pp. 218–24; Franco Gaeta, *Nazionalismo italiano* (Naples, 1965), pp. 23–26; Roberto Vivarelli, *Il dopoguerra in Italia a l'avvento del fascismo (1918–1922): I, Dalla fine della guerra all'impresa di Fiume* (Naples, 1967), pp. 253–59, 266, 278–80, 329n., 498–500; Alessandro Roveri, *Le origini del fascismo a Ferrara 1918–1921* (Milan, 1974), pp. 56–58, 110n., 134–36.

[5] Renzo de Felice, *Le interpretazioni del fascismo* (Bari, 1969), pp. 157–60; Renzo de Felice, *Mussolini il fascista: I, La conquista del potere 1921–1925* (Turin, 1966), pp. 117–24.

[6] Edward Tannenbaum, *The Fascist Experience: Italian Society and Culture 1922–1945* (New York, 1972), p. 4; see also De Felice, *Mussolini il fascista: I*, p. 118.

[7] Piero Melograni, *Storia politica della grande guerra 1915–1918* (Bari, 1969), pp. 359–69; Vivarelli, *Il dopoguerra in Italia*, pp. 397–98, 410–11.

[8] Adrian Lyttelton, *The Seizure of Power: Fascism in Italy 1919–1929* (New York, 1973), p. 50.

[9] Adrian Lyttelton, for example, portrays the cult of Mazzini as a romantic petty bourgeois leftover from the past. *Ibid.*, p. 56.

[10] *Ibid.*, p. 50; Salvatorelli, *Nazionalfascismo*, pp. 16–23.

[11] For example see Vivarelli, *Il dopoguerra in Italia*, pp. 259, 266, 274, 278–80, 329n., 498–500.

[12] Santarelli, *Storia del movimento e del regime fascista*, I, pp. 220–22.

[13] De Felice, *Le interpretazioni del fascismo*, pp. 160–61.

[14] Vivarelli, *Il dopoguerra in Italia*, pp. 24–33; Costanzo Casucci, «Fascismo e storia,» in Costanzo Casucci (ed.), *Il fascismo: Antologia di scritti critici* (Bologna, 1961), pp. 444–49.

[15] Guido de Ruggiero, «Il problema dell' autorità,» in *Scritti politici 1912–1926* (Bologna, 1963), pp. 421–24; Alessandro Galante Garrone, «Introduzione» to Adolfo Omodeo, *Momenti della vita di guerra: Dai diari a dalle lettere dei caduti 1915–1918* (Turin, 1968), pp. xxi–xxv.

[16] Wolfgang Sauer, «National Socialism: Totalitarianism or Fascism?» *American Historical Review*, LXXIII:2, Dec. 1967, pp. 419–22; Tannenbaum, *The Fascist Experience*, p. 50.

[17] See for example Curzio Suckert, «La conquista dello Stato nella concezione organica di Sergio Panunzio,» *Corriere Padano*, I:217, 16 Dec. 1925, p. 1.

[18] Casucci, «Fascismo e storia,» pp. 444–47; Vivarelli, *Il dopoguerra in Italia*, p. 323; Santarelli, *Storia del movimento e del regime fascista*, I, pp. 221, 223n.; Gaetano Salvemini, *The Origins of Fascism in Italy* (New York, 1973), pp. 164–68, 181; Pietro Nenni, *Il diciannovismo (1919–1922)* (Milan, 1962), pp. 59, 66; Antonio Gramsci, *Passato e presente* (Turin, 1951), pp. 53–54.

[19] See for example Dino Grandi, «Il mito sindacalista,» in *Giovani* (Bologna, 1941), p. 220; «I compiti del sindacalismo e le finalità immediate delle organizzazioni politiche e sindacali (Nostro intervista col Prof. Sergio Panunzio)», *Il Giornale del Popolo* (Rome), IV:234, 2 Oct. 1921, p. 1.

[20] See the two articles by Giovanni Ansaldo, «Ceti medi e operai» and «La piccola borghesia,» in Nino Valeri (ed.), *Antologia della «Rivoluzione Liberale»* (Turin, 1948), pp. 345–62, 417–22.

[21] Luigi Salvatorelli, «Risposta ai critici di nazionalfascismo,» in Valeri (ed.), *Antologia della «Rivoluzione Liberale»*, pp. 425–27.

[22] See for example Augusto Turati, *Il partito e i suoi compiti* (Rome, 1928), pp. 117, 160; Curzio Suckert, «Il sindacalismo è forza espansionistica,» *L'Impero*, I:27, 11 April 1923, p. 1.

[23] Bruno Caizzi, *Storia dell'industria italiana dal XVIII secolo ai nostri giorni* (Turin, 1965), pp. 314–453; Alberto Caracciolo, «La grande industria nella prima guerra mondiale,» in Alberto Caracciolo (ed.), *La formazione dell'Italia industriale* (Bari, 1969), pp. 198–219.

[24] This is the implication of Roberto Vivarelli's interpretation in *Il dopoguerra in Italia*, pp. 235–39, 253–59, 266, 272–74, 329n., 498–500.

[25] De Felice, *Mussolini il fascista, I*, pp. 46, 116–19, 158–59; De Felice, *Le interpretazioni del fascismo*, pp. 160–61.

[26] Dino Grandi, «Le origini e la missione del fascismo,» in Adolfo Zerboglio and Dino Grandi, *Il fascismo* (Bologna, 1922), pp. 53–69: Dino Grandi, «Verso il Congresso,» *L'Assalto*, II:52, 22 Oct. 1921, p. 1.

[27] See for example Curzio Suckert, «Il problema fondamentale,» *La Conquista dello Stato*, I:1, 10 July 1924, p. 1; Giuseppe Bottai, *Scritti* (Bologna, 1965), pp. 168–77; Augusto Turati, *Ragioni ideali di vita fascista* (Rome, n.d.), pp. 77, 108, 144.

[28] De Felice, *Mussolini il fascista, I*, pp. 46, 116–19, 158–59.

347

PART 4

FASCISM IN EASTERN EUROPE

Stephen Fischer-Galati   Introduction
Jerzy W. Borejsza   East European Perceptions of Italian Fascism
Yeshayahu Jelínek   Clergy and Fascism: The Hlinka Party in Slovakia and
     the Croatian Ustasha Movement
Zeev Barbu   Psycho-Historical and Sociological Perspectives on
     the Iron Guard, the Fascist Movement of Romania
Miklós Lackó   The Social Roots of Hungarian Fascism: The Arrow
     Cross
György Ránki   The Fascist Vote in Budapest in 1939

Introduction

STEPHEN FISCHER-GALATI

In their attempts to justify the legitimacy of their existence within the framework of the national state, the leaders of the contemporary communist regimes of Eastern Europe have evolved the doctrine of «separate roads to communism.» The clear intent is acceptance of the master form as developed and practiced in the Soviet Union, albeit with such variations as may be rooted in the specific historic conditions which have shaped communism in the various states of Eastern Europe. The doctrine, in the case of communism applies both to communism as such and to communism triumphant in the national communist state itself.

Without stressing the parallelism between communism and fascism, it seems fair to say that one may also speak of «separate roads to fascism» in Eastern Europe in the historical period antedating the advent of totalitarian communism in that region. In fact, fascism in Eastern Europe, while sharing in and frequently borrowing from the experience and lessons of the master Western European phenomena – the Italian and the German – was rooted in the historic experience and specific historic conditions of the various countries which emerged at the end of World War I from the legally-defunct body politic of the Habsburg, Ottoman, Russian, and German empires. If anything, most of the elements which were to be found in the Italian and German fascist doctrines and manifestations of the inter-war years were to be found – often at an earlier date – also in those of the East European fascist movements. This is not surprising since the roads to Italian and German fascism had a common starting point with many of their East European counterparts, in the Holy Roman Empire of the Habsburgs. This is not to say that the Habsburg Empire was the root source of twentieth century fascism. After all, several of the structural characteristics of that underdeveloped empire were shared, often in exacerbated form, by the even less developed empires of the Turks and of the Romanovs, as well as by the more developed one of the Hohenzollerns. And the same was true of the underdeveloped or semi-developed nation states which emerged from these empires in the nineteenth and early twentieth centuries such as Italy, Romania, or Bulgaria. Rather, it is our belief that the East European manifestations were the prototype of the fascist phenomena which became identified with Italy and Germany in the nineteen-twenties and thirties and also that the relative lack of success and consequent lack of recognition of the significance of the East European movements in the history of European fascism in general, are a function of the political, economic, and military strengths of Italy and Germany relative to those of the underdeveloped states of Eastern Europe. In short, twentieth century fascism is essentially a political phenomenon rooted in the historic experience of Eastern Europe and, in most respects, is the culmination of that experience in the specific historical conditions which prevailed in certain parts of Europe in the inter-war period.

What then were the basic elements common to all fascist movements and what were the specific East European elements as such? In general we tend to accept the conclusions reached by Francis L. Carsten who distinguishes several common elements in all fascist movements (contrasted with traditional authoritarian or reactionary movements of the right wing.) Carsten contends that all fascist movements shared the goal of creating single-party monopolies of political influence and activity. All fascist movements emphasized paramilitary organization and aggressive action against opponents, combining mass appeal with élitist postulates that placed political participation in a strictly hierarchical framework under dictatorial leadership. All contained elements of love and hate (e.g. anti-Semitism), and all celebrated a glorious past and a correspondingly glorified future for the particular nation. All relied on dynamism and violence of action. Finally, Carsten believes that the rise of fascist movements was directly related to the existence in various social groups, but notably among the lower middle class, of a profound dissatisfaction with prevailing socio-economic and political circumstances.[1]

All these elements were, of course, to be found in the fascist movements which flourished in Eastern Europe. They are, in most respects, characteristic of the historic experience of underdeveloped authoritarian societies in transition. Nowhere in Europe, however, were these factors more prevalent than in historically underdeveloped Eastern Europe. The historic retardation of Eastern Europe was at the end of World War I manifest in all pertinent areas – social, economic, political. The countries, mostly creations of the war and of subsequent peace settlements, retained the essential characteristics of the empires from which they were born. The area was overwhelmingly agrarian with a largely illiterate peasant population. Industrial development was limited and the industrial working class was also largely illiterate. And this general illiteracy was political as well. Capital was in the hands of landlords, wherever they were able to retain control of the land, and of commercial and industrial entrepreneurs, more often than not foreign and frequently also Jewish. It was also in the hands of various religious organizations, primarily Catholic, and of various ruling establishments, whether monarchic or not, whose individual or collective authority over the masses was infinitely greater than that of private capitalists and, as such, exploited for political advantage at all times. The confrontation between the normally politically-allied church and ruling establishment on the one hand and the native and «foreign» capitalists, misallied into a specious middle class on the other, was translated into continuing political turmoil directed against *de facto* implementation of democratic principles and practices imposed on Eastern Europe by the peace treaties. The struggle for power involved also the anti-democratic armed forces and state bureaucracies which had supported and continued to support authoritarian forces. Ostensibly, the retention of power by traditional élites even in countries such as Romania, where at least a partial restructuring of the ruling class was dictated by agrarian reform, or Czechoslovakia, where the same phenomenon resulted from the advent of an industrially-oriented establishment, was based on their ability to protect the national interest against external revisionism and anti-national and anti-Christian Communism. Thus, the governing principles of «Autocracy, Orthodoxy, and Nationality,» which accurately characterized the historic experience of Eastern Europe, were readopted, usually with artificial or superficial changes, by nearly all ruling establishments which emerged at the end of World War I.

The myth of democracy, as it is generally known, was dispelled in all of Eastern Europe, with the partial exception of Czechoslovakia, by the early thirties. The true

351

political confrontations were not among «democratic» and «anti-democratic» forces vying for power but rather among anti-democratic, authoritarian, and totalitarian groups seeking control of every country in Eastern Europe save, again, Czechoslovakia. The fascists, who emerged in the twenties, were only one of the many anti-democratic forces which sought authoritarian alternatives to prevailing authoritarian solutions, which wanted to recast the existing pseudo- or non-democratic regimes in a totalitarian manner more compatible, in their view, with the realities of the times and the aspirations of the people. The fascists' revolt was specifically directed against (to them) unrepresentative authoritarian forces and was designed to bring into power the true representatives of the dissatisfied elements of the nation: the intellectuals, the unemployed students, the lower middle class, the exploited workers, the impoverished peasants, and all others who could not identify their interests with those of the existing establishments. Their success, therefore, was a function of specific conditions prevailing in the various countries of Eastern Europe after World War I and of the measure of success which competing authoritarian groups met with in their attempts to solve the problems of their respective nations.

As the contributions to this section reveal, the roads to fascism were not identical yet all fascist movements shared similar goals and used comparable tactics. In all countries the fascist movements relied on their nation's youth to provide the clout, both spiritual and physical, for the proposed rejuvenation and remolding of the political order. In all countries anti-Semitism was the principal instrumentality for rallying the masses in support of the fascists and of their programs and promises. In all countries the fascists sought to exploit the grievances of the restless and the underprivileged. In all countries the fascists posed as the saviors of the nation from communism. In all countries the creation of a «corporative-Christian state» was one of the final goals. And yet there were differences among the fascist movements, the significance of which, however, should not be exaggerated.

Among the most comparable fascist organizations and movements are the Hungarian Arrow Cross and the Romanian Iron Guard. This is clearly explained in the contributions of Miklós Lackó and Zeev Barbu. The programs and aims of the two were almost identical. The principal differences were qualitative: for instance, the Romanian fascists were more mystical and peasant-oriented than the Hungarian and more violent in their outward manifestations. Yet these differences were primarily reflections of the relative degree of development of Hungarian and Romanian societies and the specific consequent political and socio-economic conditions prevailing in the two countries in the inter-war years. Comparably, as Yeshayahu Jelinek states in his study, the similarities between Hlinka and his followers in Slovakia and Pavelic and his in Croatia were striking; the differences again reflected the relative degrees of development and the specific issues prevailing in Czechoslovakia and Yugoslavia. Lesser fascist movements, such as those centering around Roman Dmowski in Poland, Hristo Lukov in Bulgaria, Dimitrije Ljotic in Serbia, and a few of the others discussed in Jerzy Borejsza's study, were rooted in societies coping with specific problems of their own, yet offering similar solutions and relying on similar methods and sources of support for the attainment of their totalitarian goals.

In the last analysis, success or failure of the various fascist movements and organizations in Eastern Europe was predicated on two factors: 1. the ability of the native authoritarian regimes to pre-empt the platform of the fascists as compatible with their own interests while attempting to split or destroy the fascist organizations as such and 2. the degree of support given the East European fascists by fascist Italy and particu-

352

larly by Nazi Germany. As a rule, the native authoritarian regimes, especially in the Balkans where royal dictatorships were prevalent in the thirties, were able through the use of a variety of methods to control the fascists. As a rule, also, neither Italy nor Germany supported fascist organizations whenever the governing authoritarian regimes were willing to come to terms with Hitler and Mussolini. And even when, as in the case of Romania the Iron Guard was allowed to seize power in 1940, Hitler was ready and able to destroy the Guard when its extremist actions were incompatible with his own political and military interests.

This is not to say that fascist organizations and movements in Eastern Europe were not supported by, or that their historic evolution was unrelated to, fascist Italy or Nazi Germany. The interactions, as Borejsza points out, were numerous and often profoundly significant. Nevertheless, the fascist movements in Eastern Europe were native movements, frequently antedating the Italian and the German and in most instances more representative of the historic realities of Eastern Europe than those of Italy and Germany. The question of whether Mussolini and Hitler enjoyed genuine support in their own countries and in those countries of Eastern Europe where authoritarian and totalitarian movements of the right flourished, may very well be asked again. No matter what the answers to this question may be, they are relevant to our analysis only to the extent they help us assess the popularity of fascism in Eastern Europe and the relative impact which fascist movements had outside of Italy and Germany. In our view the experience of the East European movements and the support they were given by their Italian and German counterparts are peripheral to our understanding of the significance and realities of East European fascism.

The fascists, as shown in the contributions comprising this section, scored major successes everywhere in Eastern Europe, with the notable exception of parts of Czechoslovakia, in direct confrontations with democratic forces in the thirties. Their failure to secure power by electoral means was not necessarily indicative of their actual or potential strength. Rather, it was the result of the ability of authoritarian regimes – themselves rooted in the non-democratic traditions of Eastern Europe – to retain the support of conservative forces which could not identify their own interests with those of the fascists as fully as with those of established regimes.

NOTES

[1] Francis L. Carsten, *The Rise of Fascism* (Berkeley and Los Angeles: University of California Press, 1967). The last chapter spells out the conclusions summarized here.

353

East European Perceptions of Italian Fascism

JERZY W. BOREJSZA

Poland in the Face of Authoritarianism and Fascism

In the Polish language the notions of 'fascist' and 'fascism' have since World War II taken on an unambiguously pejorative connotation. Fascism, in the Poles' current understanding of the word, is identified with Nazism.

In Poland, the figure of Adolf Hitler, his crimes and his conquests, completely overshadowed the figure of Benito Mussolini, reducing the latter to but 'a black shadow of the Brown *Führer'*. The image of fascism in its original Italian version has further been obscured by political polemics in which, from the 1930's up to the present day, epithets like 'fascist' and 'fascism' have been used all too freely.[1] People tend to forget that there have indeed been many kinds of fascism and that there have been many political movements outside Germany and Italy which, while officially deprecating Hitler and Mussolini and even formally opposing them, have nonetheless drawn considerable inspiration from their teachings.

In Poland between the two world wars the glory of Italian fascism was sung in dozens of pamphlets and books. Adolf Hitler was the head of a hostile, predatory power next door, but Mussolini's distant realm never posed a threat to Poland. Hitler lashed out against Roman Catholics, whereas Mussolini patched up differences with the Vatican. Mussolini's Italy presented a much more inviting model for emulation by the Polish right wing, including fascist-type groupings, than Hitler's Germany.

Between 1918 and 1939 the political system of independent Poland clearly first evolved from parliamentary democracy, fragile and unfulfilled from the outset, then towards more authoritarian forms of government. However, ruled by Pilsudski's marshal's baton and by his adepts, Poland never became a fascist state. The overwhelming majority of the Polish people had traditionally been opposed to all forms of totalitarian rule, a tradition deeply ingrained during the nearly 150 years of foreign subjugation. Further, there were the freedom-seeking traditions of a nation which had on many occasions in the 19th and 20th centuries risen up in arms to fight foreign oppression. Therefore, even though democratic freedoms in Poland were curtailed following Jósef Pilsudski's March on Warsaw in May 1926, neither the multiparty system nor the influential opposition press was crushed by the new regime. The vocal opposition press in fact survived up to the outbreak of World War II, despite the introduction on April 23, 1935, of an authoritarian Constitution. After all, even a segment of the new government grouping, the so-called 'sanacja' opposed the idea of having Poland remoulded into a fully authoritarian state.

True, authoritarian and fascist tendencies within 'sanacja' between 1926 and 1939 were self-evident, much as they were within the powerful opposition grouping of National Democrats. Moreover, while emphasis was perhaps placed differently in the two cases, the political programmes of both the Pilsudski followers and of the National Democrats were in many aspects convergent. They were at one in their slogans of anti-communism, anti-Bolshevism, and social solidarity, in their acclaim

354

for corporate undertakings, their anti-parliamentarism, their cult of arbitrary exercise of executive powers, and their reliance on Catholic tradition. 'Sanacja' trumpeted the slogan of great-power Poland, frequently resorting to nationalistic forms of argument, but in the National Democrats' version Polish nationalism was even more intense and unrelenting.

The National Democrats were notorious for their fervent anti-Semitism and their constant struggle against a mythical freemason enemy. The government grouping on its part was second to none in propagandizing the ideals of a militarized society. The Pilsudski cult and the leadership principles were seen by it as axiomatic. This sort of personality cult never surrounded Roman Dmowski, the leader of the National Democrats. His reputation as a master in cabinet negotiations rather than leader on the barricades and trenches was clearly incompatible with such a cult.

'Sanacja' and the National Democrats were divided more by dint of past tradition, different social origins and tactical differences than by different political programmes. That became especially evident when a process of rapprochement between the two began following Pilsudski's death in 1935.

J. Pilsudski and his associates had their roots in the left wing, largely in the Polish Socialist Party (PPS). They were steeped in the legendary tradition of armed combat, the 1905 revolution and, above all, the rise of the 'Polish legions' which fought, side by side with the armed forces of the Central Powers, for Poland's independence. Some of Pilsudski's followers did not abandon the tradition of their youth until 1939: they were not readily given to using nationalistic and anti-Semitic slogans. Rather, they were more sensitive to the social and economic demands advanced by the masses than were the leaders of the National Democrats, a traditional right-wing party which prior to 1918 had been staunchly oriented towards the Russian Empire and the Entente.

Even shortly after World War I, the National Democrats were taking an interest in the new European phenomenon: Italian fascism. National Democratic newspapers eulogized Mussolini and his execution of the coup. On the contrary, papers representing the left wing or related to Pilsudski condemned the March on Rome. And yet, the Italian envoy to Warsaw had his good reasons when, received by Mussolini on November 3, 1922, and asked, «what do people in Poland think of fascism?», he replied: «They are very much interested in this movement because certain elements of the extreme right wing, intent on toppling Pilsudski are trying to imitate fascism, thereby causing bad blood between the followers of the head of state and other left-wing groupings.»

He also added that «. . . there is no analogy between Italian fascism and its Polish imitation . . . and if anyone sought such an analogy in Poland he would have to look for it among the followers of Pilsudski, a born leader, an extraordinarily courageous man, prepared to accept violent changes in politics».[2]

Between 1922 and 1926 the National Democrats tried to establish the closest possible ties with Italian fascists.[3] Stanislaw Kozicki, one of Roman Dmowski's closest associates, was named as Poland's envoy to Rome. Another National Democratic leader, Wladyslaw Jablonowski, remained within the sphere of influence of the *Partito Nazionale Fascista,* conducting all-out propaganda for the new regime. After the P.N.F. Congress in 1925 he wrote enthusiastically about that 'reassembly of soldiers': «Fascism revived and stimulated in the nation its better instincts and sentiments: love of the motherland, respect of religion, a sense of family bonds, the capacity for self-sacrifice, love of work and social order, realization of the need of discipline and a sense of hierarchy in the state, and finally – national pride.»[4]

Roman Dmowski himself, while visiting Rome in the early spring of 1926, did not conceal his admiration for Mussolini. He decided to set up his own party after the pattern of the P.N.F.: the O.W.P. (*Obóz Wielkiej Polski* – Greater Poland Grouping). But Pilsudski pre-empted the possible 'March on Warsaw' by Dmowski and his right-wing affiliates.

What were the similarities and differences between Pilsudski and Mussolini? Both had had a long tradition of work in the socialist movement, both realized the enormous role of patriotic and nationalistic slogans in the attitudes of the masses, both were adept in leading the masses, and both frequently and contemptuously alluded to those volatile, blind masses which allowed themselves to be led by the collar. But Pilsudski's vision of a future Poland was coherent and consistent from the start, and he never conceived of Poland as the mother country of one social class alone. Mussolini, on the other hand, performed essentially an about-face, from his early repudiation of Italy – «the bourgeois motherland» – and from his pre-1914 description of the national flag as «a rag sticking out of a cess pool», down to his latter-day slogans of an imperial Italy and to his implementation of racist legislation, the like of which Pilsudski never contemplated in his political programme.

If we are to go by the opinion of the brilliant Italian diplomat Carlo Sforza, Pilsudski was an 'outdated type of dictator'. On the other hand, Mussolini was no doubt a modern politician who, in a way, pioneered 20th-century techniques of practical government. The former was a true continuator of the basic traditions of the Polish nobles, whereas the latter throughout his lifetime retained the complete set of habits and sentiments of a Romagna peasant or an Italian petty bourgeois.

Mussolini, who had from his early years lived in an independent country and had first-hand knowledge of the tribulations and hardships experienced by the Italian peasants, bricklayers and unemployed, never forgot the importance of economic and social requisites in his political activities. Pilsudski, born only three years after the debacle of the 1863–1864 rising, was obsessed by one great idea, the regaining of independence.

Pilsudski's March on Warsaw had some common features with the March on Rome. Not that it was in any way an imitation of the latter. Many similarities were quite simply due to similar circumstances in which the two events took place.

Similar were also their relations to the parliament, their methods of instigating aversion among the masses against the incumbent government, and their tactics aimed at lending the anti-government strife a national character. Both the March on Rome and the March on Warsaw had been prepared well in advance. On the eve of their respective coups, both Mussolini and Pilsudski declined participation in their legitimate parliamentary governments. Neither gave a thought to sharing power with others. They both preferred to take power by sheer force.

Pilsudski believed that he would take over power without too much bloodshed, exactly like Mussolini, and that the authority and pressure brought to bear by the masses would force the government to resign. That was a misjudgment. Eventually he had to secure dictatorial powers by sword and bayonet, running up a toll of 379 dead and 920 wounded in the streets of Warsaw. Lloyd George once described Pilsudski as a 'socialist Bonaparte'. Pilsudski took over power with the help of mutinous troops and industrial workers, in fratricidal combat with loyalist troops; he was aided by a railwaymen's strike and applauded by the entire left wing, initially including the communists.

The cutting edge of Mussolini's takeover was directed against the left wing: he feared to the very last minute that a general strike might be called. He secured power for himself by means of his own party and armed forces while neutralizing the regular army. He achieved success by terror and blackmail but avoided actual street fighting.

Pilsudski, much like Mussolini in 1922, urged Parliament to give legal sanction to his coup. But changes in Poland's political system after 1926 bore only fragmentary resemblance to those in fascist Italy. Even five years after the May 1926 coup, Curzio Malaparte stressed that it had yet to succeed as a genuine coup against a parliamentary state.

Il Duce and his entourage saw Pilsudski's negative attitude towards parliament, his hailing of the veterans' traditions from the Great War, and his aversion to the multiparty system and to freemasonry, as evidence of the Polish leader's gravitation towards the objectives of Italian fascism. After 1926 Rome quite clearly gave preferential treatment to relations with the ruling grouping rather than with the National Democrats and their offspring organizations. However, genuine rapprochement never really came about in bilateral state and party relations.[5] Certain attempts in that direction were undertaken by Giuseppe Bastianini, Italy's ambassador to Warsaw in 1932–1936, and by Józef Beck and Adam Koc. Characteristically, they only gained some momentum after Pilsudski's death.

Personal dislikes are, as is known, one of the driving forces of history. Pilsudski used to shrug off with disgust all attempts at comparing him with Mussolini. In reply to the question by a correspondent of the Paris Le Matin, «Are you an adherent of fascism?», Pilsudski said on May 25, 1926: «I think nothing of the sort could ever take root in Poland. The people are patient, but they sincerely need confidence in their leaders and would not bear such an abuse of force by small local organizations. No, that's not our cup of tea».[6]

Pilsudski's anti-fascist declarations, expressed to representatives of French public opinion, so hated by Mussolini, did not dispose the Duce favourably. When in the summer of 1926 the new councillor of the Polish legation, Wladyslaw Günther, having been sent out specifically to tighten relations with fascist Italy, turned up in Rome, the Duce talked with him mainly about Turkey and Kemal Atatürk, with whom the Polish guest was familiar. «Those were», Günther later commented, «questions asked by one confrère about another, by one dictator about another».[7] Apparently, Mussolini did not regard Pilsudski as exactly his own kind. For him Pilsudski was an outdated type of dictator with a still lingering itch for democracy. One gets that impression by reading Polish-Italian diplomatic correspondence between 1926 and 1935 and by recalling the Duce's reticence on learning of Pilsudski's death. In a briefing for the Italian press on May 13, 1935, a recommendation had to be issued to «treat Marshal Pilsudski's figure with sympathy».[8]

Pilsudski was merely a Mussolini-watcher. Augustinas Voldemaras, Antanas Smetona and Antonio Carmona were Pilsudski-watchers.[9] Technical similarities in taking over power did not mean an immediate similarity in political systems.

It was only after Pilsudski introduced police methods for fighting the opposition on a wider scale (1930) and after the setting up of the B.B.W.R. (Bezpartyjny Blok Współpracy z Rzadem – Nonparty Block of Cooperation with the Government), active between 1928 and 1935, that the Polish state could indeed be called authoritarian. At the peak of its power in 1930, the B.B.W.R., helped by appropriate pressures applied through the state apparatus, was able to secure more than 55 per cent of the popular vote in a parliamentary election. The B.B.W.R., which disintegrated shortly after Pilsudski's death, and its successor, the O.Z.N. (Obóz Zjednoczenia Narodowego,

National Unification Grouping), which functioned between 1937 and 1939, could count from time to time on passive acceptance by the broader social groupings, but they never became truly mass-compelling organizations. Nor did they ever assume the form of a party.

Pilsudski's system never relied on a mass party. When the National Democrats succeeded in forming a political party of several dozen thousand members – the O.W.P. – which was on the way to becoming a mass party, the government ordered it dissolved. Shortly after the demise of the O.W.P. the youth wing of the National Democrats founded what was to become the most notoriously fascist organization of pre-war Poland: *Obóz Narodowo-Radykalny – Falanga* (National-Radical Grouping – Falange). Active from 1934 to 1939, it was an élite cadre organization, emulating Nazi and Italian patterns, strictly observing the principles of authority, hierarchy and leadership. Its social bedrock consisted of university students and it was mainly active in the universities, propounding the slogans of a totalitarian state based on a world outlook of combined Roman Catholicism, nationalism and anti-Semitism. The O.N.R.-Falanga terrorized Jewish students and destroyed Jewish shops and quarters.

In an economically underdeveloped country such as pre-war Poland, in which national minorities accounted for 31 per cent of the total population (Jews, Ukrainians, Belorussians, Germans), the breeding ground for Polish nationalist and fascist organizations was to be found mainly, though not exclusively, among the petty and upper bourgeoisie and, to a notably lesser degree, among the peasants and some strata of the working class.

If we compare Poland's situation in that respect with that of Mussolini's Italy and Hitler's Germany, we shall be struck by the relatively small number of war veterans among the rank and file of Polish extreme right-wing organizations. The Polish war veteran was different from his German and Italian colleagues in that during the Great War he fought not in the name of an existing state but for the rebirth of a state of his choosing. Consequently, he had no accounts to settle with pre-1918 Polish governments as there had been no such governments. For most Polish troops in the Great War the call for independence was inseparable from more general ideals of liberty.

Even such a superficial characterization of the situation in Poland between 1926 and 1939 shows how complex that situation was and how precipitate and incorrect it would be to call it a fascist state. Full justice must be done to the typology devised by the Polish scholar and expert on fascism, Franciszek Ryszka, who holds that Spain in 1923–1930, Poland in 1930–1939 and Austria in 1934–1938 shared the following features, characteristic of authoritarian states: «First, the assumption that nothing but the state, as a self-contained force, was capable of surmounting 'anarchy and chaos' which, in the opinion of authoritarianists [i.e. proponents of dictatorship], were identified with 'Bolshevism', that is, with a broadly conceived political movement of the working class . . . Second, the conviction that parliamentary representation essentially works against the interests of the state if based on the pluralist [multiparty] system. The very notion of a party being a part of a whole was incompatible with the requirements of 'totalitarianism' [a term meaning the same as 'authoritarianism'] if totalitarianism was conceived as the projection of authority onto citizens' attitudes. . . . Third, and the most important perhaps, the striving to achieve political and state unity in the face of centrifugal tendencies stemming from regional or national differences . . .», and also «the authority of the state, regulating the interests of all [citizens], prevailed over nationalistic mystique. Hence the inevitable conflicts between authoritarian regime and extreme nationalists, later amplified by the social-class factor».[10]

The constraint and elimination of extreme nationalistic groups by an authoritarian-ruling right wing was the common feature of Poland, of the Baltic states, and of Bulgaria under King Boris III.[11]

To offer a schematic picture, we might say that under Polish conditions the National Democrats and the extremist organizations stemming from them were to the right of the Pilsudski grouping. The numerical strength and power-range of notoriously fascist organizations was relatively small in Poland, but the influence of fascist ideology reached far beyond their organizational framework. Therefore, when speaking about fascism, we must introduce a strict distinction between the movement and its ideology on the one hand, and the state systems where fascists actually ascended to power on the other.

The Italian Model of Fascism and East-Central Europe

Italian fascism and German Nazism were mass phenomena, whereas the authoritarian currents either did not want to or were not able to command mass support. Unlike most of their dictator contemporaries of South and East Europe, Mussolini in 1926–1936 and Hitler after 1933 enjoyed the active support of millions of their fellow countrymen.

Italian fascism and German Nazism were distinct from most authoritarian movements in Europe in that they relied on mass parties and on strong para-military organizations linked to those parties. A distinctive trait of fascism was the subordination of the state apparatus to the party apparatus. This subordination was total in Hitler's Reich, while in Italy it was more subtle as shown when Mussolini, in his circular of January 5, 1927, formally declared the state to be above the party and the province prefect to be above the province party secretary.[12]

Unlike Hitler or Mussolini, Miklós Horthy, Ion Antonescu, King Boris III and Antanas Smetona consolidated their power principally by means of the armed forces and the police apparatus, the masses remaining largely passive. Identifying themselves with the traditional nationalistic right wing, they consolidated their power in a struggle against the anti-traditionalist extreme right wing, i.e. fascist organizations, which they gradually restrained or completely broke up. Later on, during World War II, German Nazis in Lithuania and Latvia reactivated those 'retired' fascists, and the *Führer* himself used to play off the surviving Iron Guards, the Romanian fascist emigrants whom he had given asylum in Germany, against his ally Ion Antonescu.

The Mussolini system of 'one leader – one party – uniform corporations – one nation' was never transplanted detail for detail to any of the East-Central European countries. Nonetheless, in view of similar social structures and many similar national traditions, it was clearly the most popular model for emulation by the right wing up to the late 1930s. The Italian model of fascism proved to be attractive for right-wing groups in that European territory which Tomas Masaryk, the first president of Czechoslovakia, used to call «the small nations' zone»: the area tucked in between Germany, Italy and the Soviet Union.

Italy offered East and Central Europe the example of a state which, pitted against communism, promulgated and partly implemented a definite programme of economic reform and social reconstruction. This was being done in an essentially backward country, more closely identifiable with Hungary, Romania, Yugoslavia, Bulgaria or Poland, than Germany could ever be.

The Italian answer to the 'Red danger' was more attractive to the more distant nations, to whom it was a purely ideological and political proposition, not brought home by force of arms as it was in Yugoslavia, Albania and Greece. Distant Lithuania and Latvia looked to Italy as a model of relations which promised to eschew the constant pressures being brought to bear by their more powerful neighbours. An expert on the history of the Baltic states writes:

«The relationship between Smetona's Lithuania and Mussolini's Italy is to be defined as close friendship, based on a similarity of ideological premises and on the community of state interests. Lithuania was wide open to doctrines pouring in from fascist Italy. They were disseminated by means of books, pamphlets and very frequent press enunciations . . . On the government level, the relations between Lithuania and Italy were also good and lively.» [13]

The fanatical Italian fascist, Alessandro Pavolini, winding up his propaganda visit to Latvia on the heels of the coup by Karlis Ulmanis, the Peasant Union leader, on May 15, 1934, stated that Latvia showed a distinct 'fascist-type orientation' in that «1. Premier Ulmanis was elevated to the status of a dictatorial and providential leader, in a word, he was made a 'duce' (this was attempted in especially characteristic ways at the 'mass spectacle' for 42,000 viewers, whereby the new government resumed contacts with the people of Riga); 2. The entire official press publicized the need for and intention of setting up a strong, viable government; 3. Demands were made on many occasions for a totalitarian type of concord of all citizens above and outside the political parties; 4. Anti-parliamentarism was encouraged; 5. Nationalistic sentiments were stimulated; 6. Propaganda was stepped up for creating a militarized nation, and incentives were provided for setting up voluntary, sports and youth organizations». [14]

The coup in Latvia, much as those in Poland and Lithuania (December 1926), was, according to official explanations, directed against the abuse of parliamentarianism and a looming menace of civil war. In Poland only half-seriously, in Lithuania quite openly, the Bolshevik bogey was used. In Latvia the Social Democrats and communists were the *bête noire*, though actual terror affected much broader segments of society.

The anti-Bolshevik function of the Italian fascist model was essential in winning for Mussolini the interest and sympathy of politicians otherwise not even remotely connected with fascism. This can be read from the diplomatic reports of the Polish ambassador to Rome, Alfred Wysocki, by no means a fascist himself. At the beginning of 1937 he reported from Rome: «Although Communist action in Italy was not recently a menace to the fascist system, rather reflecting isolated instances of sympathy for the Caballero government and dissatisfaction over heavy taxes and charges, Mussolini's foresight made him react even to these relatively innocuous manifestations. The social policy of the fascist leader has accordingly been oriented in the following directions: a. paying the greatest respect to the village people as that social class which can be regarded as the mainstay of imperial Italy; b. winning over the working-class rank and file both by material and cultural means; c. tightening the corporate screw which is to free the worker from the yoke of what is here called 'capital Communism'; d. Mussolini's striving, *coûte que coûte*, to improve the national economy, and thereby to enable the state to provide better care of the people. Mussolini has, moreover, turned special attention to the plight of women who had hitherto been assigned the Cinderella role in his social welfare plans». [15]

Ten months later Wysocki reported: «Recently Tribunale Speciale in Rome tried a number of workers, intellectuals, communists and liberals, and sentences ranged between 3 years and 18 years in prison . . . In comparison with other dictatorial regimes, notably Moscow, the Rome court showed relative leniency, thereby indicating the strength and confidence of the fascist regime . . .».[16] That view was characteristic of large circles of intellectuals – university professors, men of letters and the arts – in the 'small nations' zone'. In their fight against the Soviet Union and communism they acquiesced in the Italian alternative.

The dictators of Central European states realized that popularization of an Italian-style programme was in itself not enough but that mass parties should be set up to implement that programme. That was not an easy task in countries with populations dominated by politically-passive peasantries. In fact, it was an impossible task. A. Smetona, who was a true follower of Mussolini, managed to bring together not more than 8,000 members in his incoherent party, L.T.S. Not many, considering that Lithuania had a population of 2,500,000.

Receiving the Italian chargé d'affaires at the beginning of 1938, King Boris III of Bulgaria told him that, all his admiration for the fascist regime notwithstanding, «Bulgarian conditions were too different from those of Italy». Outside of established traditional groupings, Bulgaria had no political party which could count on a guaranteed support among the masses. At that point in the conversation, the Italian diplomat notes, «His Royal Highness alluded with only lightly veiled contempt to Professor Tsankov's national socialists».[17]

The absence of mass fascist-style parties in East-Central European countries is a recurrent theme in reports sent out by Italian diplomats from Belgrade, Warsaw, Athens and Bucharest.

For example, on July 16, 1942, Italy's ambassador to Bucharest, Renato Bova Scoppa, wrote to Ciano: «the problem of eventual succession to the Marshal [Antonescu] presents extraordinary difficulties . . . the Romanian system has no solid basis, no party, no mass organization on which it could count».[18] Italian journalists, reporting in 1941 on Ante Pavelić and his new-founded authoritarian little state, found «near-absolute indifference, coolness and abulia among the general public» to be striking.[19] Even more striking perhaps was how swiftly Ante Pavelić set about loosening Italian controls, trying to play Rome against Berlin.

Ideological and political divergences between Rome and Berlin helped to increase the interest in fascist Italy. This could be seen clearly in the case of Lithuania, forever threatened by German aggression, where official orientation towards fascist Italy was not merely an anti-Bolshevik but also anti-Nazi political instrument. In the case of Finland, during the 1939–1940 Soviet-Finnish war Italian party leaders decided that faithfulness to the tenets of fascist ideology made Italy duty-bound to aid Mannerheim's Finland in the name of an anti-communist crusade, much as they had aided Horthy and Franco on previous occasions. On the other hand, Hitler and Ribbentrop showed a far more pragmatic approach by, among other things, blocking Italian supplies to Finland.[20]

In April 1939, a month after the creation of the Slovak state, Vojtech Tuka, vice-premier of the puppet government, told an Italian envoy plainly: «of the two types of authoritarian state, fascist and Nazi, the Italian type fits Slovakia better in that it reconciles the totalitarian concept with the Nation's Catholic tradition».[21] Tuka requested Italian assistance in drafting the Constitution of the new state. Proclaimed on 21 July, 1939, the document indeed borrowed heavily from Italian legislation. But a year later, the ruling triumvirate of Tiso-Tuka-Mach reoriented Slovakia towards the Nazi model.

For politicians of the cast of Tuka, Dollfuss, Horthy, Ulmanis, Päts, Laidoner, Smetona, and Mihail Antonescu, it was easier to accept or emulate Mussolini than that notorious destroyer of established tradition, Hitler. Bulgaria, Romania, Yugoslavia and Greece were ruled by monarchs, Hungary by a regent. Mussolini tolerated monarchy, whereas Hitler never concealed his utter contempt for that institution. The Italians and their Balkan allies saw the monarchy as an institution linked to the tradition of national revival. Therefore Mussolini tolerated the monarchy albeit reluctantly, knowing that the king and his entourage were no real assets towards making the state fully totalitarian. (We note in this connection that the coup of 25 July, 1943, which toppled Mussolini, and the overthrow of Ion Antonescu on 23 August, 1944, were both hatched in court circles and that the many features they had in common cannot have been accidental.)

Mussolini presented the model of a dictator, respecting monarchy, religion, the officers' corps and many elements of established national tradition, combining the elements of the old and new systems; a dictator who, up to the Ethiopian war, did not employ methods of repression and terror to the extent that Hitler did. He appeared to serve better as a model for emulation by his East European colleagues, many of whom had graduated from former imperial universities and military academies.

In the years 1922–1929 Italian fascism exerted some influence by the mere fact that it existed. It was a case of foreigners seeking contacts with the P.N.F. rather than of the Italian party seeking contacts abroad. Only after 1929, the year of the Concordat with the Vatican, did the dictator, now feeling deeply entrenched, decide the time had come to start exporting fascism. Five years later, on March 18, 1934, he was able to state: «. . . between 1929 and the present day fascism has developed from a purely Italian phenomenon to become a universal phenomenon». The lessons of the initial 18 months of Hitler's rule in Germany in 1933–1934 caused Mussolini to fight what he regarded as deviations from the ideals of fascism by the 'German imitator'. The resounding failure of Mussolini's first meeting with Hitler in Venice on June 14–15, 1934, the 'night of the long knives' in the same month, and the Dollfuss assassination on July 25, 1934, created strong tensions between the two dictators, tensions that did not subside until two years later.

In this historical context it is true that, for some time beginning in 1933, fascism was presented by Mussolini «more than at any other time as the best remedy, a panacea for European afflictions . . . attempts were made, not without success, to give a pleasant, orderly appearance to a system which had overcome all contrast, a true mediator . . . In such 'openings' of fascism one could read between the lines: in the face of Nazism, which cut loose to sow terror as soon as it grabbed power and which immediately started persecutions, especially anti-Semitic ones, Mussolini intended to tell Europe, as it were: yes, authority is necessary, and so is a strong government, but a level attitude must be kept and Latin, Italian, fascist humaneness preserved. This is the true recipe, my very own! I avoid the weaknesses of democracy as well as the excesses of Nazism».[22] The dictator managed to impress this image on many naive observers like Emil Ludwig.

Fighting for priority treatment for Italian fascism and opposing Goebbels with his propaganda machine, Italy centralized its propaganda apparatus. A *Sottosegretariato per la Stampa e Propaganda*, headed by Galeazzo Ciano, was set up, later to be transformed into *Ministero della Cultura Popolare*.[23] In the same burst of initiative the C.A.U.R. (*Comitati d'Azione per l'Universalità di Roma*) was formed under the baton of Eugenio Coselschi, former personal secretary of Gabriel d'Annunzio and an

362

enterprising expert in propaganda bluffs. In their programmatic declaration the C.A.U.R. founders stated openly: «There are movements which don the name of fascism but which are merely the result of some personal ambitions, or exacerbated nationalisms, or accidental economic circumstances».[24] In December 1934, a congress of representatives of fascist organizations was held under the aegis of C.A.U.R. at Montreux, Switzerland. Italian fascists there strove to set up a Fascist International which would counter the Communist International.[25]

Coselschi's emissaries employed a wide range of means and methods to disseminate fascist ideology. They negotiated secretly with Croatian and Macedonian terrorists, with the Finnish Lapua movement, with Ioannis Metaxas and his opponents, and with Vidkun Quisling. The latter received outright financial aid through the Italian legation in Oslo.[26] Coselschi was directly involved in the assassination of King Alexander I in Marseilles.[27] Hiring assassins with one hand, with the other he raised toasts at dinners given for European intellectuals.

Through the channels of the C.A.U.R., the *Ministero della Cultura* and numerous cultural organizations (the I.R.C.E., *Società Luce, Dante Alighieri* among them), Italians disseminated fascist ideology by means of books, press articles, free films and film newsreels, exhibitions, lectures, etc. It is enough to glance at the list of works translated from Italian into Croatian between 1931 and 1941 to understand that the Italians were not wasting time.[28] Their propaganda effort did not subside during the war, even after the defeat at Stalingrad: at the beginning of 1943 about a thousand copies of anti-Bolshevik publications were sent to Athens «in connection with intensified communist propaganda in Greece».[29] Close attention was paid by the Italians to scholarships offered to Romanian and Bulgarian students whom the Germans invited by the hundreds to their universities.[30]

Following two years of considerable propaganda successes up to 1935, there came the war in Ethiopia, economic sanctions and the Spanish Civil War. The Italians redoubled their propaganda effort to substantiate their African claim and to impress on the world their military prowess. But from 1935 onwards the Italian model lost most of its peaceful attractions. Later, when Austria was abandoned to German claims, Mussolini's essential weakness became evident, and when racist legislation was introduced and the society militarized, differences became blurred between the state run by the N.S.D.A.P. and the state run by the P.N.F. Then came the invasion of Albania and the remaining illusions about Italy's protecting small European nations were gone.

The dossiers of the Italian representations in Budapest, Sofia and Bucharest in 1941–1943 prove the continuous nature of the effort to export ideology. In a special report, an I.R.C.E. emissary complains in 1942 that in Croatia «only 37,500 copies of [Italian] dailies and 35,000 copies of periodicals (exclusive of the Croatian edition of Tempo) are sold every month, and in Hungary the corresponding figures are barely 12,900 dailies and 4,300 periodicals (excluding the Hungarian Tempo»).[31] But another set of statistics tells us that within a dozen or so months at the turn of 1940 and 1941 some ninety titles of propaganda books and pamphlets by Mussolini, Virginio Gayda, Giorgio Pini, Gioacchino Volpe and others were distributed in Hungary.[32] In 1942 the Romanian Vice-premier M. Antonescu wrote the preface to a Romanian book on the Italian corporate movement while in 1943 the Bulgarian university professor Vladykin, who had already published the works of Hitler, rushed through the printing press a single-volume anthology of Mussolini's works. These are significant facts. The ruling élite of the Balkan countries was not at all willing to give the Germans a monopoly in ideology.

However, the Italians themselves were in the long run incapable of meeting the formidable propaganda challenge of the Reich. Their film propaganda, dynamic up to 1930 or so, was later beaten back by the German film output. In Bulgaria in 1939, for instance, 120 German films were shown, 70 French, 50 Soviet, 30 British, but only 12 Italian.[33]

Italy could ill afford propaganda expenditures that would match Germany's. Moreover the Germans had always been at the top of the league in the economic competition in Eastern Europe. The following table shows the share (in percentage points of total) held by Germany and Italy in the imports of six countries from this part of Europe:[34]

	1928		1937	
	Germany	Italy	Germany	Italy
Bulgaria	21	15	55	5
Czechoslovakia	24	3	17*	1*
Hungary	20	4	26	7
Poland	23	3	15	2
Romania	24	8	29	4
Yugoslavia	14	12	32	8

*1936

It is to be assumed that the extent of overt economic penetration reflected more or less accurately the degree of covert penetration by the two powers' intelligence services, and their political and military influences on the countries in question. The subsequent war years swung that disproportion even further to the advantage of the German Reich. Apart from obvious objective factors, this process was helped considerably by Mussolini himself when he discarded all pretense of defending small nations and oppressed minorities and instead started kindling interstate animosities in the Balkans. True, Hungary, Romania and Slovakia did accede to the Axis in quick succession on November 20, 23 and 25, 1940, to be followed by Bulgaria on March 1, 1941, but they were only made allies by the threat of German bayonets. All parties concerned knew about that: Ciano in his «Diario» called those states «vassals or near-vassals of Germany».

Mussolini overlooked the chance which was presented to him by Romanian, Bulgarian and Hungarian strivings in 1942–1943 to break away from Hitler's sphere of influence. He was loath to accept hegemony of neutral states. From 1935 onward, ever new conquests were on his mind. His wars declared on Ethiopia, Albania, Greece and Yugoslavia made the Italian model of fascism as unattractive in the eyes of many as the German. The crucible of World War II proved the truth contained in the words of Romanian Foreign Minister Grigorie Gafencu: «The Axis is a political euphemism which meant Germany, both in East and West».[35]

The years 1943–1945 brought utter defeat to the fascist and old authoritarian systems in Italy and in East and Central Europe. But vestiges of those systems linger on in the attitudes of millions of people. They can yet be seen in people's vulnerability to nationalist and racist propaganda, in their submission to totalitarian authority. This poses for a modern scholar a query of enormous weight: can one possibly speak of a 'genetic predisposition' of certain countries to accept dictatorial rule? Why, within more or less the same part of Europe, did some nations, notably the Czechs and the Finns, prove more resistant than others to pressures from authoritarian power? Why in France over the past century did no dictatorship succeed in establishing itself for an appreciable period of time even though several attempts were made, starting with General Boulanger? And why, on the other hand, have there been, in Romania since 1861 and in Bulgaria since 1878, several pretty durable dictatorial regimes?

In attempting to answer these questions we must turn our attention to many internal factors which seem to condition a nation's predisposition to accept authoritarian and totalitarian regimes. These are: democratic and constitutional state tradition or its absence, the mode of operation of the parliamentary and multi-party systems, social structures (with special reference to the potency or underdevelopment of the middle class and the extent to which it has developed attachment to civil liberties), the importance and degree of emancipation of the working class and the peasantry, something that can be vaguely termed «national mentality», moral-religious traditions, and the presence or absence of national minorities. The importance of all these internal factors should be duly appreciated even in such totalitarian systems as have been imposed from outside.

NOTES

[1] Cf. Renzo de Felice, *be interpretazioni del fascismo* (Bari 1972), p. 16–18.

[2] F. Tommasini, *Odrodzenie Polski* (Rebirth of Poland), (Warsaw 1928), 338–339.

[3] Cf. Jerzy W. Borejsza, *Mussolini byl pierwszy* (Warsaw 1979).

[4] Wl, Jablonowski, *Amica Italia,* (Poznań, 1926), p. 25,99.

[5] Cf. Philip V. Cannistraro, «Poland and Fascist Italy, 1922–1939». Paper presented at the IIth Conference of Slavic Studies. October 14, 1972, Miami, Florida.

[6] J. Pilsudski, *Dziela* (Works), vol. IX, (Warsaw 1937), p. 21.

[7] W. Günther, *Pióropusz i szpada* (Memoirs), (Paris 1963), p. 86.

[8] ACS – Archivio Centrale dello Stato, Roma, Agenzia Stefani.

[9] R. Fajans, *Hiszpania 1936 – z wrażeń korespondenta wojennego,* (Spain. From a War Correspondent's Notebook), (Warsaw, 1937), p. 217; P. Lossowski, *Kraje baltyckie od demokracji do dyktatury* (The Baltic Countries between Parliamentary Democracy and Dictatorship), (Warsaw, 1972), p. 254–255.

[10] F. Ryszka, «Państwo autorytarne» (Authoritarian State) in: *Dyktarury w Europie środkowo-wschodniej 1918–1939* (Dictatorships in East-Central Europe 1918–1939), (Wroclaw 1973), p. 119–120, Cf. by the same author, *Państwo stanu wyjatkowego* (Emergency State System), II ed. (Wroclaw), 1974.

[11] J. Bardach, in: *Dyktatury w Europie, op. cit.* p. 208–214.

[12] Cf. Alberto Aquarone, *L' organizzazione dello Stato Totalitario,* (Torino 1965).

[13] P. Lossowski, *op. cit.,* p. 254–255; See J. W. Borejsza, «Wlochy wobec tendencji faszystowskich w krajach baltyckich» (Italy and Fascist Tendencies in Baltic Countries), *Kwartalnik Historyczny,* LXXXI, vol. 1, (Warsaw 1974), p. 44–75.

[14] ACS, Ministero della Cultura Popolare, MCP, parte VI, b. 301.

[15] A. Wysocki to J. Beck, 3 I 1937, Archiwum Akt Nowych (New Documents Archives), Warsaw.

[16] A. Wysocki to J. Beck, 30 X 1937, *ibid.*

[17] Telegram No 736/219, II II 1938, Archivio del Ministero degli Affari Esteri/AMAE/, Roma, Bulgaria, vol. 16.

[18] Telegram No 3002/947, Romania, vol. 17, AMAE.

[19] Viaggio a Zagabria 16–20 V XIX, ACS, Agenzia Stefani, vol. 2, fasc. 5.

[20] J. W. Borejsza, «Wlochy a tendencje faszystowskie», *op. cit.*, p. 70–72.

[21] Report Lo Faro from Bratislava, 13 IV 1939, ACS, MCP, parte VI, Cecoslovacchia, vol. 286.

[22] L. Salvatorelli, G. Mira, *Storia d'Italia nel periodo fascista,* (Verona 1972), vol. 2, p. 202–203.

[23] Cf. Philip V. Cannistraro, *Burocrazia e politica nello stato fascista:* Il Ministero della Cultura Popolare, Storia Contemporanea, VI 1970.

[24] Comités d'action pour l'universalité de Rome. Réunion de Montreux. 16–17 décembre 1934 – XIII, Roma, p. 10.

[25] CAUR, Ministero dell' Interno, Pubblica Sicurezza 1920–1945, G I 148/34, ACS.

[26] Reports from Oslo, October 12 and 17, ACS, MCP, Norvegia, vol. 387–388.

[27] E. Coselschi from Paris, 10 X 1934, *ibid.* parte III, vol. 170, fasc. 16.

[28] ACS, MCP, parte VI Jugoslavia, vol. 371.

[29] *Ibid.*, Grecia, vol. 349.

[30] Report from Bucharest, 20 VII 1942, *ibid.,* Romania, vol. 412.

[31] *Ibid.*, Ungheria, vol. 474.

[32] *Ibid.*, parte III, vol. 161, f. 15.

[33] *Ibid.*, parte VI, Bulgaria, vol. 283.

[34] Cf. J. Tomaszewski, «Gospodarka krajów Eurepy srodkowej i poludniowo-wschodniej w latach miedzywojennych» (The Economy of Central and South-East European Countries between the Two World Wars), in *Dyktatury w Europie, op. cit.,* p. 78.

[35] E. Collotti, T. Sala, Giorgio Vaccarino, *L'Italia nell'Europa danubiana durante la seconda guerra mondiale,* (Monza 1966). Cf. N. Smirnowa, *Balkanskaja polityka faszistskoj Italii* (Balkan Policy of Fascist Italy) (Moscow 1969).

Clergy and Fascism: The Hlinka Party in Slovakia and the Croatian Ustasha Movement*

YESHAYAHU JELINEK

In some of the countries of East Central Europe, the extreme right-wing movements exhibited a curious combination of secular and ecclesiastic elements in their élite and following. This essay, however, is concerned only with the role of the clergy in these movements. An attempt has been made to elaborate on this subject by presenting two cases: that of Hlinka's Slovak People's Party and that of the Croatian Ustasha Revolutionary Organization.

The Clergy in Hlinka's Slovak People's Party (HSPP)

With the creation of Czechoslovakia, the Slovak People's Party came into existence. From the very first, the clergy played a leading role in it. In the period between the two world wars, Father Andrew Hlinka dominated and guided the party, the most important item in its program being the demand for territorial autonomy for Slovakia. The program also included defense of the Catholic Church's interests, use of Christian-Social slogans, and the urging of conservative views on various aspects of life. The party did not display tolerance towards Protestants and Jews. Its lack of internal democracy was due to the parochial outlook of its leaders, and above all, of Andrew Hlinka, not to an ideology. Certain party personalities already supported authoritarian and anti-democratic ideas in the early twenties.[1] The People's Party showed strength in many Czechoslovak national and local elections, polling about 30 per cent of the votes cast in Slovakia (perhaps 50 per cent, or slightly more, of all Slovak votes).[2]

Parish clergy constituted the backbone of the party. The senior lay leaders were influenced by the Church and emphasized its interests; they were, so to speak, clerically-minded. But the young activists who were slowly advancing in the party hierarchy were different. Nationalistic aims pushed their faith into the background and they would not have minded seeing a smaller proportion of clerics among the party notables. These young people were wide-open to the totalitarian ideologies spreading over Europe. To them, the autonomy of Slovakia began to appear as a step on the way rather than as the final goal in the life of the nation.[3]

The party drew a great deal of support from small-town bourgeoisie all over the country. Workers, with some notable exceptions such as the railway employees, turned a deaf ear to it. The richer peasantry preferred the powerful Czechoslovak Republican («Agrarian») Party. Evident was the strong regional support in Western and Northern districts, whereas Eastern Slovakia displayed a rather nonchalant attitude.

On March 14, 1939, the extremist elements in the party, in close cooperation with the Nazis, proclaimed the Slovak state.[4] By applying to the Third Reich for protection, Slovakia became the first German satellite *(Schutzstaat)* and Nazi intervention in Slovak internal affairs was not infrequent.[5] From then on Slovakia had a one-party system, though the HSPP was far from being a closely knit party. With the passing of time polarization occurred in Slovakia. The clerical bloc led by Father Dr. Jozef Tiso ruled the state. A radical, SS-supported, Hlinka Guard of stormtroopers served to offset the clericals. Being small in number and poor in talent, the Guardists could hardly have challenged their clerical adversaries unaided, but with German support they could and did rock the state. Nonetheless, Berlin realistically preferred the clericals to the radicals, so that an ostensibly unified government ruled the country, while the real power lay in the hands of the President, Dr. Tiso.[6]

In this way a close satellite of the Reich came under predominantly clerical rule. Tiso's bloc included, besides the numerous clergy, «*Ludak*» laymen of various ages – «Ludak» was the partymembers' nickname – several personalities from the abolished parties, industrial entrepreneurs, and commanders in the Army. The opposing group included the SA-like Hlinka Guard, a phalanx of radical intellectuals, a few young priests, and declassé elements from Slovak society.

In the clerical bloc, and consequently in the state, the clergy held many positions of power. The president of the Republic was a parish priest, and the Party Presidium included clerics. In 1940, out of 61 Members of Parliament, twelve were priests. Eighteen State Counsellors included three churchmen, among them the Chairman, the Bishop of Spiš, Msgr. Ján Vojtaššák.[7] The same year, priests led twenty-seven county branches of the party out of fifty-eight, and two district organizations out of six.[8] The clergy provided the mayor of the capital, Bratislava, as well as mayors of other localities. Priests supervised countless local branches of the party, parent-teacher associations, and schools. They sat on managerial boards of business and industrial firms. They had an important voice in many voluntary and not-so-voluntary organizations. Several of the party ideologists were ordained priests. Some of the most important – if not necessarily the best – writers and poets were priests and friars. In fact, there was hardly a single aspect of life in the state where the clergy was not conspicuous. In 1943, the ecclesiastic hierarchy put pressure on politically engaged priests to relinquish their posts to laymen, and although the official explanation pointed to negligence in parish work by certain pastor-politicians, it was obvious that changing fortunes in the war induced the hierarchy to take a hand.[9] While the regime permitted Roman Catholic clergy to take public office, protestant ministers were hardly to be seen in public service. Greek Orthodox (Uniate) priests were suspect of «anti-Slovak» inclinations, and therefore told not to meddle in politics.[10]

The Vatican was never enthusiastic about the deep involvement of the clergy in Slovak state politics.[11] The fate of the Church in changing circumstances was of great concern to the Holy See. Slovakia compromised the Church and its teachings, and the Jewish policy constituted only one, though the most obvious, example[12] of this. Extensive powers, formal and informal, were concentrated in Father Tiso's hands[13] and many of his trusted advisors were priests.[14] As the Dean of the Banovce parish, he was under Church discipline, which could be exercised in ways both positive and negative. But to the best of our knowledge, Tiso's superior, Archbishop Msgr. Dr. Karol Kmet'ko, did not exercise the prerogatives given him by Canon Law. The clergy had no actual representation in the cabinet, but we may be sure it was influential behind the scenes.

The clerical impact was likewise remarkable in education, legislation and exercise of matrimonial rights, in supervision of morality, and in cultural policies; it was felt, too, in innumerable acts and orders concerning every phase of life. The Church as an

368

institution, its monastic orders and secular clergy, drew material advantages from the prevailing conditions.[15] The army and other branches of the state added to the prestige of the Church and its hierarchy in a variety of ways. The state outlawed dissident sects, such as the Baptists, Adventists, and the so-called Czechoslovak Church.[16] It was natural, therefore, that regardless of the benefits accruing to the Church in Slovakia, papal concern over the future developments increased.

Slovakia was functioning on quite a solid basis: it had a constitution, a more or less efficient administration, and the public generally respected the law. The clerical leadership could claim much credit for this situation and the Nazis preferred orderly clericals to chaotic radicals.[17] The Church might well suspect that a different government would curb its freedom. The radicals and their SS advisors branded the existing regime as influenced by «political Catholicism»,[18] since the Church opposed numerous radical ambitions, which it regarded as conflicting with its teaching. It so happened that both the Vatican and Berlin supported the Slovak regime, but with important reservations, and each for different reasons.

Of the fascists and radically-minded clerics, some eventually left the Church, and others lived under the threat of being unfrocked.[19] Curious allies of the radicals were the democratically minded anti-clerical intellectuals, many of them Lutherans. The secular intelligentsia suffered from the circumscription of Slovak cultural life in the spirit of Catholic doctrine, and attempts to intervene in the freedom to produce and consume cultural commodities aroused resentment. Radical intellectuals felt uneasy in the face of the Church's endeavors to prevent them from spreading pro-Nazi thought, though such intellectuals retained functions in the state and public institutions, regardless of their *Weltanschauung*, since Slovakia and the Church were short of educated specialists. The resulting tension took the form of State-Church rivalry, with a variety of anti-clerical intellectuals representing the state, and the clergy the Church.

It so happened that leading state institutions such as the University of Bratislava and *Matica Slovenská* (the «Slovak Mother-Bee», an establishment for the support of Slovak language and literature) turned into centers of opposition to clerical domination.[20] The Church had to contain itself within its own institutions, among them the Catholic Academy of Art and the St. Adalbert Foundation, managed mostly by the clergy. Consequently these institutions stood in a sense in opposition to the state. Tiso's efforts to purge and to replace the rebellious intellectuals with men of his choice, failed.[21] The cultural scene well illustrated the problems of the clergy: although decision-making was in its hands, the clergy could not enforce its wishes completely because of the shortage of qualified manpower on the executive level.

The need to reconcile state and Church could also be seen in the efforts to conclude a concordat with the Holy See, which would confer added prestige on the regime. The Vatican was reluctant to sign a concordat during the war, however, and the informal character of Church-State relations persisted, based as it was on the clerical permeation of the state and the intimacy between the hierarchy and the ruling élite headed by the priest-President. One may assume that existing conditions persuaded the hierarchy to abstain (with some exceptions) from publicity criticizing the State and its leaders.[22]

The Clergy and the Ustasha Revolutionary Organization in Croatia

The Zagreb lawyer Dr. Ante Pavelić founded the Ustasha («Rising») Revolutionary Organization on January 7, 1929, after royal dictatorship had been introduced in Yugoslavia. With a small coterie of friends, he set up a closely knit organization, led from outside of Croatia, with branches spread all over the country. Centers of activity abroad were located in Italy and Hungary. The Ustashi specialized in acts of terror against Yugoslav personalities and properties, culminating in the assassination of King Alexander in Marseilles in 1934.

Pavelić's political flirtation with Mussolini was a love – hate story. Italy's relations with the Ustasha moved from ardent support to imprisonment and internment, and back again to support. With the signing of the Italian-Yugoslav treaty in 1937, several leading Ustashi returned to Croatia from exile. With their arrival, the home chapter of the Ustasha expanded. Nevertheless, before 1941 it never surpassed a following of 40,000[23] out of a population of 6,663,157.[24] This was a far cry from the dominant Croatian Peasant Party, which had captured the hearts and minds of most Croatians.[25] During its short career, the Ustasha enjoyed the support of a host of Yugoslavia's enemies, including the Bulgarians, the Hungarians, the Italians, and eventually the Germans. The Germans handed over power in Croatia to Pavelić's men on April 10, 1941, after the defeat of Yugoslavia. In Zagreb, a retired K.u.K. colonel, Slavko Kvaternik, who headed the Home Ustasha, proclaimed the «Independent State of Croatia» *(Nezavisna Država Hrvatska,* NDH). A few days later, Pavelić with the «Ustasha from abroad» unit arrived, and took over the government.[26]

The Ustasha ideology followed ideas of the 19th Century Party of Pure Right and of some later thinkers, advocating a revival of Croatian statehood. The movement claimed all Yugoslav territories populated by Catholics and Moslems, as well as certain locations inhabited by the Orthodox. The Ustasha explained that the Orthodox were Catholic apostates or immigrants from Serbia. The movement was devoutly Catholic, anti-Serbian, racist, and intolerant of other people and political groups. It denounced social injustice, and favored a strong authoritarian regime.

The new state faced many problems, finding itself pinched in between the competing Italian and German influences. Shortly after the creation of the NDH, the Serbs took to the sword, joining the Chetnik resistance *en masse.*[27] The communist-led partisans raised their flag after the Nazi invasion of the Soviet Union.[28] In spite of the wave of enthusiasm which followed the establishment of the State, the Ustasha remained a poor minority in it. Massacres of the Serbs, forced conversions of the Orthodox, extermination of Jews, gypsies and anti-fascists, arbitrary transfers of population – all these were deeds which revolted many and stamped a black mark on the consciousness of the Croat people, who turned hostile to the Ustasha. Orgies of murder occurred among all groups operating in Croatia.[29]

The Ustashi were quarrelsome. A latent hostility pulsed between the Home Ustashi under Slavko Kvaternik and those who came with Pavelić from abroad; and between pro-German and pro-Italian segments. Some veterans of the Peasant party who joined the regime, remained unassimilated. The Moslems – celebrated as the purest of the Croats – clashed with the rest of the Croats.[30]

The cabinet and a short-lived Parliament *(Sabor)* were both powerless and uncoordinated.[31] Actual authority rested in the hands of the Ustasha Supreme Command. This was challenged by the Poglavnik's (to give Pavelić his official title as leader) own Chancellery. Then there were fairly independent *Grand Župans* (district Lieutnant Generals), the *Domobrana* (Home Guard, armed units), and the Military Ustasha (comparable to the *Waffen* SS). Municipal authorities and party regional organizations vied with each other for influence. Over this hornets' nest, Pavelić sometimes ruled with an iron hand and terror, sometimes by intrigue, and sometimes by just relying on the Germans and on Hitler in person. After paying off his political debts to

Mussolini with huge pieces of Dalmatia, the Poglavnik moved more and more into the Nazi orbit.[32]

The Ustasha recruited its members predominantly from the lower income stratum of the urban population. The peasantry was poorly represented in it.[33] A disproportionate number of members came from certain regions such as Lika and Herzegovina.[34] In opposition to the Ustashi from abroad the home Ustasha attracted numerous young intellectuals, students, and clergy.[35]

Seminaries for priests and Church-owned high schools were among the Ustasha strongholds. Newly consecrated priests could easily be got at. The Faculty of Theology at Zagreb University and the monasteries housed numerous friends of the Ustasha. In the ethnically and denominationally mixed Bosnia and Herzegovina, the Franciscans acted as *Ecclesia Militans*. In this region where an Orthodox was regarded as a Serb and a Catholic as a Croat, the Franciscans turned into flagbearers of Croatian nationalism. They were easily accessible to the Ustasha ideology.[36]

The armed forces of the NDH called a large number of priests to the colors to serve as military chaplains. This happened contrary to the wishes of the bishops, and consequently many parishes were deprived of their pastors.[37] It was not unusual for friars and young priests to enroll directly in the Military Ustasha, and to win dubious fame as the most dreadful concentration camp guards.[38] Heavy accusations linger about the participation of some clerics in the forced conversion of the Orthodox, and in mass murder.[39] Clerics were to be found among high ranking civil servants and Party ideologists[40] as well. Out of the 20 deputies[41] he appointed to the *Sabor* in 1942, Pavelić nominated eleven priests (among them the Archbishop of Zagreb, Msgr. Aloysius Stepinac, and the Bishop of Djakovo, Msgr. Dr. Antun Aksamović).[42]

The clergy's contribution to the enforcement of Ustasha policies is recorded in depositions at Stepinac's trial. The Archbishop claimed to have disciplined his subordinates and to have encouraged them to abstain from political involvement,[43] though often to no avail. Even if we accept this claim, there were still many priests left free in other dioceses, including those of the outspoken pro-Ustasha Archbishop of Sarajevo, Msgr. Dr. Ivan E. Sarić. Provincials of monastic orders, such as the Franciscans, were responsible for their friars. This writer feels that one should accept in good faith at least some of the indictments concerning the clergy's share in atrocities committed by the Ustasha, and its cooperation with the organization. Many ecclesiastics, however, remained passive or even opposed the regime. No one is able to determine the number of Ustasha collaborators among the sacerdotes. Priests also joined Tito and were among the victims of the Ustasha.[44] One may go as far as to say that certain Croat priests became «schizophrenic» when national and religious demands called for split loyalties; and in nationalistic zeal often breached the Ten Commandments.

The Church hierarchy took a very cautious stand vis-á-vis the NDH, and although several documents testify to its sympathy for independent Croatia,[45] it remained highly circumspect about the regime.[46] Not all bishops were alike in their attitude. There were indeed agressively pro-Ustashi prelates like the aforementioned Sarić or the Greek Orthodox (Uniate) Bishop of Križevci, Msgr. Dr. Janko Simrak, but others, such as the old Franciscan Bishop of Mostar, Msgr. Aloysius Mišič, and Aksamović, were said to have taken a reserved line. The Croat Catholic hierarchy, which resented the Serb-Orthodox supremacy in pre-war Yugoslavia, was nationalistically inclined and sympathetic to a Croat national state, so that the paraded Catholicism of the Ustasha leaders made a strong appeal.[47] Being the outpost of Roman Christianity, the Croat clergy and hierarchy were inspired with missionary zeal to return the «Byzantine schismatics» to the bosom of the Mother Church. The German Minister to Croatia, SA *Obergruppenführer* Siegfried Kasche reported that the Croat Catholic Church « . . . *hatte wahrscheinlich die Absicht, Kroatien zu einen Bollwerk des Katholizismus dem Orient gegenüber zu machen.»* (. . . was probably aiming to make Croatia a bastion of Catholicism facing the Orient).[48] The anti-orthodox acts of the NDH, if not always admirable, were regarded as moving in the right direction.[49] The spectre of communism was always looming, and the Ustasha propagandists charged to Serb Orthodoxy with being Bolshevik.[50] It was, therefore, quite natural that the Church appreciated the new state, although its sympathies for the regime declined as time passed.

State policies caused some of the bishops (and probably the Vatican as well) no little concern. A study of the documents leaves the impression that the hierarchy had a relatively limited say in the decision-making process.[51] One even discovers a certain amount of mutual hostility, at least between individual Ustashi and members of the Catholic élite. There were also several irritating issues. The intervention of the state in matters of conversion caused frictions, and racism was incompatible with Church doctrine. The horrors of the concentration camps and the extermination of the Serbs could not and did not escape the attention of Church leaders. Likewise, there were problems with education, censorship of the Catholic press (including Papal pronouncements), freedom of action for Catholic lay organizations, discrimination against converted Jews, and other matters. The ecclesiastical dignitaries knew well that the secular leadership of the state was glad to exploit any prestige the Church was willing to bestow. But in taking decisions, the lay Ustashi followed above all their own aims and needs. Consequently, the Church also took care of its own interests. Ustasha notables, when visiting Hitler, were quick to denounce «political Catholicism» and to emphasize the unity of the nation regardless of faith. This was done not only to satisfy the suspecting and knowledgeable Hitler.[52] German agencies kept close track on Church activities and were not short of material to report.[53]

The Vatican was also familiar with the issues at stake. Although anxious to please the NDH indirectly, it was extremely careful in every official move. The nomination of two new bishops in 1942, which was a gesture of good will, was illuminating.[54] The Vatican snubbed Zagreb in a twofold way: it omitted to seek the agreement of the local government and installed a Jesuit in one of the sees previously held by the pro-Ustasha Franciscan order.[55] Zagreb's protests were of no avail. The Vatican's course of action was not lost on either the clergy or the Ustashi. Both the Church as a whole and individual clerics benefited from the situation in the country. In several cases, the Church received confiscated properties of outlawed bodies, e.g. the Old-Catholics or Orthodox. Priests were permitted to receive fees for conversion.[56] Nor was there any lack of other means of benefiting form the conditions in the country.

The Clergy in Slovakia and in Croatia: a Comparison

Historiography on the World War II period in Eastern Europe tends to compare Slovakia and Croatia, concentrating on the similarities between the two countries.[57]

Although the Catholic Church was important in both countries, in Croatia it took second place. In Zagreb, the secular Ustasha was dominant. It was independent in decision-making (except when orders of the Axis intervened) and at least in theory able to dictate to the clergy as well. The Ustasha was free to shape the Croat people and mold their destiny, yet had the misfortune to constitute only a pitiful minority at home. The banned Peasant party continued to wield power. Nazi support cemented

Ustaha rule in the NDH, and Pavelić knew this well. He badly needed all the prestige the Church could grant, without allowing it to share his supremacy. Pavelić favored those of the clerics who were willing to accept his leadership and execute his policies. The Poglavnik argued that he was serving the interests of the Church and the nation by Catholicizing Croatia. The hierarchy and the priests could not dismiss this argument; many of them felt uneasy, however, with his brutal methods. Sacerdotal capacity to influence the Ustashi was limited mostly to carrying out policies decided upon elsewhere. Possible later repercussions worried the Church and the Vatican.

How fluctuating and insecure the Croatian Church was can be seen by a comparison to Slovakia. Here the clergy was firmly in the saddle. It was able to influence decision-making in directions favorable to the Church and its doctrines, and later to see to it that the decisions were carried out. The value attached to human life offers another example. Bratislava's government also deported Jews to *Niemehrwiedersehn in den Osten* (a one-way trip East).[58] Even after the horrible truth filtered into the country, deportations still continued. Jews could be manhandled and killed in the streets, communists would jump to their death from prison windows in order to escape further torture. But not a single person was ever legally executed in Slovakia. The priest-President did not sign any death sentences since such an act would not be in line with his calling. In Croatia thousands of victims succumbed without a written sentence.[59] Important historical and ethnic differences existed between Slovakia and Croatia, and the problems they faced were not similar. Nevertheless these differences do not wholly explain the contrast in regard to matters of life and death. In my opinion, the degree of sacerdotal impact on decision-making and administration account for this contrast.

The clerical entanglement in the implementation of government policies weakened the cohesion of the Croat Church. In a country with at least five conflicting forces (German, Italian, Partisan, Chetnik, and Ustasha), and with chaotic political, social, economic, and communication conditions, it was difficult for a bishop effectively to supervise his flock. This impaired discipline paved the way for clerics to attach themselves to the administrative machine of the state and the Ustasha. By the same token, they could more easily escape the supervising eye of their superiors and act as they pleased. The foregoing by no means diminished the responsibility of the *Ordinarius* to guide his clergy in the spirit and letter of Canon law.

In conducting public and Church affairs, the Croatian Episcopal Collegium could not close its eyes to the nationalistic feelings among sections of the general public, among the clergy, and in its own ranks. In supporting the NDH, the Collegium could not disregard the clear and often ostentatiously pro-Catholic bent of the regime. The Croatian clergy was only glad to shake off what it regarded as a pro-Byzantine Yugoslav government. It hoped for a greater share of power in the nation and for extension of privileges and prerogatives; and some of these expectations did materialize. In Croatia the bishops could not influence the government from within; since the Collegium could not know what was going to happen, it was forced to shield the Church from unseen and unidentified dangers. As a result the bishops were on the defensive, and in their attitude to the government, support mingled with suspicion. They had to approach the ruling administration from without. Their line of action was negative; the Episcopacy was anxious, not so much to achieve positive results as to prevent harm to the Church and to Croatian Catholicism. The hierarchy sought to change decisions, to alter agreed-upon measures, and to modify results of steps already taken. Naturally, the Episcopacy aroused misgivings and anger in the ruling circles. Ustasha leaders considered some Church pronouncements offensive to the regime. To make things worse, the Croatian hierarchy gave an impression of only limited uniformity of mind and unobtrusively determined individuality of action. Particularly the radical bishops such as Šimrak and Sarić broke the common front. The controversial personality of Stepinac constituted a particular problem: in the NDH he seemed to personify the cautious policy of the Church. He supported the regime from without, liked some acts and criticized others, and would probably have preferred a less extremist and more clerically-minded administration.

In contrast to that of Croatia, the Church of Slovakia suffered much less from the political situation in the country. Quieter internal conditions prevailed there. Also unity of purpose prevented disintegration of the sacerdotal corps, as the ideology of the People's party bore a heavy Catholic imprint. Hence the HSPP avoided certain utterances and deeds incompatible with the Church teaching. In addition, the regime granted the anti-fascist clergy some living space, provided it remained politically passive. The conflict between national and religious goals in Slovakia was less evident.

The Slovak Republic had almost unconditional Episcopal backing. As in Croatia, the bishops were aware of nationalism among considerable segments of the population, including the clergy. They were also happily rid of the Czechoslovakia they considered anti-Roman and appreciated the advantages of the new state. The Slovak Republic was generous in bestowing upon the Church rights and benefits and in promoting its interests. The bishops had a say in state matters from the inside. They acted in a clear-cut, constructive, and even uniform and carefully directed fashion. State-Church cooperation was close and mostly satisfactory to both sides, so that even the more radical bishop Vojtaššák hardly stepped out of line.

The Vatican's stand must have been taken into account by the clergy. In Bratislava, only the radicals offered open resistance to the Papacy.[60] The Zagreb authorities sought its support or good-will; at the same time they did not hesitate to quarrel with and offend the Vatican.[61] Repercussions were not slow in coming. It is safe to say that the extremists approached the Holy See with a certain toughness. Naturally, Father Tiso's administration was more open to Vatican communications than the Poglavnik's. Tiso (whose official title was *Vodca*, the Leader) was not well liked, being often criticized in Rome and by the Holy Father himself.[62] But Tiso's was a pro-Catholic regime, and the Holy See bestowed upon the *Vodca* official gestures of favor.[63] Gestures toward the NDH were less formal and less official.

Several ideologists in Slovakia and Croatia took Holy Orders. Nonetheless, the impact of Nazi ideology on the Ustasha was evident. The HSPP was not free from Nazi influence either, but the Hlinka Guard expressed its Nazi sympathies more strongly. The NDH welcomed ideas from the Third Reich, and ecclesiastic opposition to these was also more determined and open.[64]

A comparison of the Slovak and Croat cases shows clearly the importance of clerical elements in these extreme right-wing movements.

Summary and Conclusions

In the HSPP the clergy played a crucial role, imprinting upon it both a world outlook and a course of action in a very determined way. The fact that priests shared the decision-making and executive levels of the administration, promoted understanding between Church and State.

374

The clergy was of little influence in decision-making in the NDH. The Ustasha was basically a secular movement, which through its nationalistic appeal was able to recruit a number of churchmen and use them in executing decisions made by its own organs. The Church hierarchy, although in support of the regime, was not happy with conditions in the State, and with its own limited ability to influence decision-making. The totalitarian NDH endangered the Church in several ways, and conflicts between the two were clearly apparent.

Of major importance for the development of right-wing thought and action in a Catholic nation is the position of the radical fascists. In Slovakia, the hierarchy and its allies kept the Hlinka Guard out of business. In the case of Croatia, however, the needs of the occupying powers and the complaisance of the Episcopacy allowed the radical Ustasha to rule. Therefore Croatia differed from Slovakia, and the results were self-defeating for the Ustasha supporters.

NOTES

* I would like to express my appreciation to Professor Dan Segré-Avni of the University of Haifa for reading this paper and commenting on it. Needless to say, I bear the sole responsibility for the views and details included.

[1] Ladislav Šuško, «Hlinková garda od svojho vzniku až po salzburské rekovania (1938–1940),» *Zbornik Muzea Slovenského Narodného Povstania,* II (1969), pp. 173, 174; Yeshayahu Jelinek, «Storm-troopers in Slovakia: the Rodobrana and the Hlinka Guard,» *Journal of Contemporary History,* VI, 3 (1971), pp. 99–102.

[2] For returns of general elections, see in František Vnuk, «Slovakia in Pre-Munich Czecho-Slovakia (1918–38)» in Joseph M. Kirschbaum, ed., *Slovakia in the 19th & 20th Centuries,* Toronto, 1973, pp. 103, 123.

[3] For the People's Party before the war, see Jörg K. Hoensch, *Die Slowakei und Hitlers Ostpolitik,* Cologne-Graz, 1965, pp. 1–77.

[4] For the period from Munich until March 14, 1939, see Hoensch, *Die Slowakei,* pp. 78–314; Josef Anderle, «The Establishment of Slovak Autonomy in 1938,» in Miloslav Rechcigl, Jr., *Czechoslovakia, Past and Present,* The Hague, 1969, pp. 76–97; Milan S. Ďurica, «The Slovak Secession of March 14, 1939, Some Aspects of the Czecho-Slovak Crisis,» *Il Politico,* XXIV (1959), pp. 131–144; František Vnuk, «Slovakia's Six Eventful Months (Oct. 1938 – March 1939),» *Slovak Studies,* IV, 1964, offprint.

[5] On the Slovak state, see Hans Dress, *Slowakei und die faschistische Neuordnung Europas,* Berlin, 1972; Jozef Lettrich, *History of Modern Slovakia,* London, 1956, pp. 110–227; Joseph A. Mikus, *Slovakia, A Political History: 1918–1950,* Milwaukee, Wisc., 1963, pp. 67–154; Gilbert L. Oddo, *Slovakia and its People,* New York, 1960, pp. 236–302; Milan S. Ďurica, «The Republic of Slovakia, Its Origin and Existence,» *Slovak Studies,* 1 (1961), pp. 105–121. See also my dissertation, *Hlinka's Slovak People's Party, 1939–45,* Indiana University, Bloomington, Ind., 1966.

[6] Joseph M. Kirschbaum, «The Politics of Hlinka's Slovak People's Party in the Slovak Republic,» *Slovakia,* I, 1 (1951), pp. 43–49; Yeshayahu Jelínek, «Slovakia's Internal Policy and the Third Reich, August 1940 – February 1941,» *Central European History,* IV, 3 (Sep. 1971), pp. 242–270; the same, «The 'Final Solution' – The Slovak Version,» *East European Quarterly,* IV, 4 (Jan. 1971), pp. 431–441.

[7] U.S. National Archives, Washington, WWII Records Division, T-120, R 1450, 588242, List of the Members of Parliament; T-81, R 527, 5294541, *Frankfurter Zeitung,* Aug. 8, 1940.

[8] T-175, R 531, 9402998-99, A list of leaders of regional organizations. Oct. 15, 1940.

[9] T-175, R 514, 8380837, Note, March 31, 1943; 8380841, Note, Apr. 4, 1943; *Pred súdom národa,* 3 vols. Bratislava, 1947, Vol. II, p. 18.

[10] T-175, R 515, 9382651, *Zeitungschau der DPS,* Nov. 7, 1940.

[11] About Chairman of the State Council, Msgr. Vojtaššák, see Secretaire d'Etat de sa Saintete, *Actes et Documentes au Saint Siege relatifs à la Seconde Guerre Mondiale*, Citta del Vaticano, Vol. IV, Chargé d'Affaires in Bratislava to Cardinal Maglione, Note of Msgr. Tardini, Aug. 17, 1940, p. 102, doc. No. 40; About the President, see *Actes et Documentes*, Vol. I, Nunzio in Berlin Orsenigo to Cardinal Maglione, March 18, 1939, pp. 99-101; Karol Sidor, *Šest'rokov pri Vatikáne*, Scranton, Pa., 1947, pp. 60–62.

[12] See John S. Conway, «The Churches, the Slovak State and the Jews 1939–1945,» *The Slavonic and East European Review*, LII, 126 (Jan. 1974), pp. 85–112; Yeshayahu Jelinek, «The Vatican, the Catholic Church, the Catholics, and the Persecution of Jews During World War II: the Case of Slovakia,» in G.L. Mosse and B. Vago, ed. *Jews and Non-Jews in Eastern Europe, 1918–1945*, Jerusalem, 1974, pp. 167–208.

[13] See my dissertation, pp. 92–94; for another view, see Milan S. Ďurica, «Dr. Joseph Tiso and the Jewish Problem in Slovakia,» *Slovakia*, VII (Sept. – Dec. 1954), p. 4.

[14] Jozef Paučo, *Tak sme sa poznali*, Middletown, Pa., 1967 pp. 56; Sidor, *Sest'*, p. 60; T-175, R 119, 2643771–74, Report, Nageler to Himmler, Feb. 11, 1943; Vilém Prečan, *Slovenské Národné Povstanie, Nemci a Slovensko 1944, Dokumenty*, Bratislava, 1971, p. 42, doc. No. 8, Report of Dr. Böhrsch, Oct. 1943.

[15] *Pät' rokov slovenského školstva 1939–1943*, Bratislava, 1944, pp. 435, 436. T-175, R 514, 9380942, Report, Nageler to RSHA, Dec. 29, 1943. For «aryanization» of Jewish property see *Proces proti vlastizradným biskupom*, Bratislava, 1951, p. 53.

[16] *Slovák* (Bratislava), Apr. 22, 1939; Decree of the Minister of Interior of Sep. 12, 1940, on measures taken against religious sects, No. 3690/1940. Political Archives of the German Foreign Office, Bonn (hereafter PA), *Inland 1-D, Slowakei, Kirche*, Letter, Reichsprotektor in Bohemia-Moravia to the German Foreign Office (hereafter GFO), Prague, Aug. 5, 1942, No. DXII 400/42.

[17] Yeshayahu Jelinek, «Bohemia-Moravia, Slovakia, and the Third Reich During the Second World War,» *East European Quarterly*, III, 3 (June 1969), pp. 237, 238.

[18] T-120, R2198, 338254, *Politischerlagerbericht*, von Killinger to GFO, Oct. 27, 1940; T-175, R 119, 2643751-61, Report on Slovakia, Berger to Himmler, Feb. 19, 1943. Cf. US Library of Congress, Himmler Files, Container No. 390, Foulder No 6, Ludin: *Beurteilung des politischen Lage in der Slowakei*, Jan., 1945.

[19] T-175, R 514, 9380517, Report, SD agent, June 25, 1939; 9381509, The case of Viliam Ries; R 533, 9404923, The case of Fraňo Boháč.

[20] Vlado Clementis, *Usmerňované Slovensko*, London, 1942, pp. 28, 44–48, 89; Štefan Pasiar and Pavel Páska, *Osveta na Slovensku*, Bratislava, 1964, p. 293; *Katolické Noviny*, January 4, 1942; T-175, R 514, 9381506-09, Report, SD agent, Feb. 1942.

[21] *Čas* (Bratislava), Nov. 5, 1947, Trial of members of the Slovak government.

[22] Diary of the Chief Rabbi Armin Frieder (held privately), entry of March 8, 1943; Yad Vashem Archives, Jerusalem, Microfilm No. JM 2218, K213048, Text of the pastoral letter, criticizing the treatment of Jews.

[23] *Naša domovina*, 2 vols., Zagreb, 1943, Vol. I, p. 117.

[24] Gert Fricke, *Kroatien 1941–1944*, Frieburg, 1972, p. 10.

[25] On the Peasant Party, see short, but penetrating assessment in Jozo Tomasevich, *Peasants, Politics, and Economic Change in Yugoslavia*, Stanford, Cal., 1955, pp. 254–260.

[26] Kruno Meneghello-Dincic, «L'etat 'Oustacha' de Croatie (1941–1945)», *Revue d'Histoire de la Deuxième Guerre mondiale*, 74 (Apr. 1969), pp. 46–49. Other works on NDH: Ladislav Hory and Martin Broszat, *Der kroatische Ustascha-staat, 1941–1945*, Stuttgart, 1964; Edmund Paris, *Genocide in Satellite Croatia, 1941–1945*, Chicago, 1960; Carlo Falconi, *The Silence of Pius XII*, London, 1965, pp. 259–391; Franjo Tudjman, «The Independent State of Croatia as an Instrument of the Occupation Powers in Yugoslavia, and the People's Liberation Movement in Croatia from 1941 to 1945,» in *Les Systèmes d'Occupation en Yougoslavie 1941–1945*, Belgrade, 1963, pp. 135–262; Rudolf Kiszling, *Die Kroaten*, Cologne-Graz, 1956, pp. 128–223; Dinko Tomasić, «Croatia in European Politics,» *Journal of Central European Affairs*, I, 2 (Apr. 1942), pp. 64–82.

[27] Toko A. Marić, *General Dragoljub-Draža Michajlović*, Milwaukee, Wis., 1971, p. 17.

376

²⁸ *Komunistički pokret i socijalistička revolucija u Hrvatskoj,* Zagreb, 1969, pp. 210, 211.

²⁹ On the chaos and beginning of the massacres, see the conflicting versions: *Serbian* Marić, *General,* p. 15; David Martin, *Ally Betrayed,* New York, 1946, pp. 47, 48; *Croat-Ustasha,* Matija Kovačić, *Od Radića do Pavelića,* Munich-Barcelona, 1970, p. 129, *Kroatien baut auf,* Zagreb, 1943, pp. 12, 25; *Croat non-Ustasha,* Vladko Maček, *In the Struggle for Freedom,* University Park and London, 1957, pp. 231, 232, 234; *Communist,* Milan Basta, *Agonija i slom Nezavisne Države Hrvatske,* Belgrade, 1971, pp. 91, 92; *German,* Fricke, *Kroatien,* pp. 32, 33.

³⁰ Tudjman, «The Independent,» pp. 176, 177, 190, 191; Kovačić, *Od Radića,* pp. 150–152; Basta, *Agonija,* pp. 90, 91.

³¹ *Ibid.,* Hory & Broszat, pp. 75–80, Fricke, *Kroatien,* pp. 68–71.

³² Jere Jareb, *Pola stoljeća Hrvatske politike,* Buenos Aires 1960, pp. 94, 95; Kovačić, *Od Radića,* pp. 163–165, 168, 189, 179, 180; Ivan Mestrović, *Uspomene na političke ljude i dogadjaje,* Buenos Aires, 1961, pp. 293, 321–325; Vlado Strugar, *Jogoslavija 1941–1945,* Belgrade, 1970, p. 303; Fricke, *Kroatien,* pp. 77, 78.

³³ Tudjman, «The Independent,» p. 218; Hory & Broszat, pp. 82–84; Paris, *Genocide,* pp. 52, 95; Basta, *Agonija,* pp. 26, 27; Fricke, *Kroatien,* p. 36.

³⁴ Meštrović, *Uspomene,* pp. 301, 302, 308.

³⁵ Viktor Novak, *Velika optužba,* Sarajevo, 1960, pp. 40–42; Basta, *Agonija,* p.388; Paris, *Genocide,* pp. 25, 51; PA, *Inland ID,* 8/8-20, Letter, the German Legation (hereafter GL) in Zagreb to GFO, *Katolische «Kreutzbrueder» Organization in Kroatien,* Pol. 4, Nr. 6–2816/42, Dec. 18, 1942.

³⁶ Paris, *Genocide,* pp. 194, 219; Falconi, *The Silence,* p. 298; Viktor Novak, *Magnum Crimen,* Zagreb, 1948, p. 601; *Tajni dokumenti o odnosima Vatikana i Ustaške «NDH»,* Zagreb, 1952, Report, Rusinović to Lorković, March 6, 1942, photocopy, PA, *Inland ID,* 8/8–20, Letter, GL to GFO, *Kirchenpolitische Lage in Kroatien,* Kult. 4–677/44, July 28, 1944; *Inland IIg,* 290, Letter, Command of the 2nd Italian Army to the Foreign Ministry, *Violenze degli Ustasci,* No. 824/AC/Segreto, July 1, 1941.

³⁷ Richard Pattee, *The Case of Cardinal Aloysius Stepinac,* Milwaukee, 1953, pp. 184, 190; Paris, *Genocide,* p. 165.

³⁸ Nikola Nikolić, *Taborišče smrti Jasenovac,* Ljubljana, 1969, pp. 316–320; Maček, *In the Struggle,* p. 235; Basta, *Agonija,* p. 382; Novak, *Velika,* p. 165; PA, *Inland ID,* 8/8–20, Letter GL to GFO, *Kirchenpolitische Lage in Kroatien,* Kult 4–677/44, July 28, 1944; Paris, *Genocide,* p. 137, «Of twenty-two concentration camps in Croatia, nearly half of them had ecclesiastics as commanders.»

³⁹ Zdenko Loewenthal, ed., *The Crimes of the Fascist Occupants and their Collaborators Against Jews in Yugoslavia,* Belgrade, 1957, pp. 95, 96, 125; Falconi, *Silence,* p. 382; Nikolić, *Taborišče,* p. 51; Pattee, *The Case,* pp. 115, 131, 173.

⁴⁰ For example, Fr. Božidar Bralo, *Grand Župan* of Sarajevo; Msgr. Dr. Vilim Cecilja, Supreme Army Chaplain; Fr. Radoslav Glavaš, Chief of the Dept. for Religious Affairs in the Ustasha Ministry for Justice and Religions; Msgr. Kerubin Segvić undertook a mission to the Holy See for the Ustasha government on Sep. 7–Sep. 24, 1941. Ideologists were Father Dr. Ivan Guberina, Msgr. Kerubin Segvić, Father Dr. Krunoslav Draganović.

⁴¹ Fricke, *Kroatien,* p. 68.

⁴² Paris, *Genocide,* p. 169. Stepinac prevented four priests from his diocese from taking their seats, Pattee, *The Case,* p. 209.

⁴³ Pattee, *The Case,* pp. 79–82, 107, 131–133, etc.; Cf. Maček, *In the Struggle,* p. 235.

⁴⁴ Pattee, *The Case,* pp. 49, 131; Basta, *Agonija,* p. 115; Nikolić, *Taborišče,* p 216.

⁴⁵ PA *Inland ID,* 8/8–20, Letters, GL to GFO, *Katolischer Erzbischof Dr. Sarić,* Pol 4, Nr. 6–2836/42, Dec. 23, 1942; *Aktion des kroatischen Bischopats,* Kult 4–148/44, March 7, 1944; *Kirchenpolitische Lage in Kroatien,* Kult 4–677/44, July 7, 1944; *Tajni dokumenti,* Letter, Rusinović to Lorković, May 9, 1942, Photocopy, and report Lobkowicz to the Croat Ministry for Foreign Affairs, No. 8/43, June 10, 1943, photocopy. See also Pattee, *The Case,* doc. No. D., pp. 239, 240.

⁴⁶ *Actes et Documentes,* Vol. IV, doc No. 347, p. 491, Notes du cardinal Maglione, May 15,

1941; PA, *Inland,* ID, 8/8–20, Carbon copy, GFO to GL, *Aktion des kroatischen Episkopats,* *Inland* ID 1501/43, Aug. 18, 1943; Letter, The Police Attache of the GL to RSHA, Meeting of Dr. Cecilja with Archbishop Stepinac, No 2218/42, Nov. 21, 1942.

[47] See the banning of the Old-Catholic Church: PA, *Inland* ID, 8/8–20, Verbal note, Croatian Ministry for Foreign Affairs, to the GL, No. K-24. 984/42, Sep. 21, 1942.

[48] PA, *Inland* ID, 8/8–20, the letter quoted in ft. 39. Cf. *Inland* ID 22/1, Letter, *Der Chef der Sicherheitpolizei und SD to GFO,* No. VII–VII B2, B. Nr. 6000/42, July 15, 1942.

[49] PA, *Inland* ID, 22/2, *Kirche Allgemein, Kirchenpolitische von Tagepresse, Sept./Okt. 1942,* Sep. 24, 1942; *Inland* ID, 8/8–20, Letters, GL to GFO, *Prawoslaven in Kroatien und römisch-katolische Kirche,* Pol. 2 Nr. 3 Serb-A645/42, Oct. 22, 1942; *Aktion des kroatischen Bischopats,* Kult 4–148/44, March 7, 1944.

[50] PA, *Inland* IIg, 404, Telegram, Neubacher, Belgrade, to GFO No. 371, Feb. 20, 1944; Tudjman, «Les Systems,» p. 189; Sima Šimić, *Prekrstavanje Srba za vreme drugog svetskog rata,* Titograd, 1958, pp. 51, 52.

[51] PA, *Inland* ID, Letter of the Police Attache, see note 46; *Inland* ID, 8/8–20, the letter quoted in note 39; Letter, the Police Attache of the GL to RSHA, *Katolische Aktion,* No. 1963/42, July 12, 1942; *Documents of German Foreign Policy* (DGFP), London, 1964, Vol. XIII, doc. No. 603, pp. 881–977; Meeting Hitler- Pavelić, June 9, 1941; *Meštrović, Uspomene,* pp. 281, 325–326; Patee, *The Case,* pp. 61, 128.

[52] *DGFP,* Vol. XIII, doc. No. 603, pp. 891, Meeting Hitler – Pavelić, June 9, 1941; doc. No. 511, pp. 865–867, Meeting Hitler – Lorković, Nov. 28, 1941.

[53] PA, *Inland* IIg. 86, Letter, Kasche to GFO, *Dienstelle Polizei-Attache,* Pol. 2, Nr. 2–17430/42, July 20, 1942; Memorandum of Joachim Heinrich, *Kirchensachbearbeiter für Kroatien,* July 29, 1942.

[54] Falconi, *The Silence,* p. 331.

[55] PA, *Inland* ID, 8/8–20, Telegram No. 1376, Kasche to GFO, June 13, 1942; Letter, German Embassy by the Holy See to the GFO, *Katolische Bischofe in Kroatien,* No. A505, June 23, 1942; Letter, German Embassy by the Holy See to GFO, *Kirchliche Verhältnisse in Agram,* No. A 613, June 19, 1943.

[56] PA, *Inland* ID, 22/2, *Kirche Allgemein,* see note 49; Paris *Genocide,* p. 176.

[57] See book review by Lubomir Lipták *(Historický Časopsis,* 1, XII/1964/, pp. 15–127) of *Le System d'Occupation en Yugoslavie 1941–1945.*

[58] An expression used by Slovak officials, Jelinek, «The 'Final'» p. 433. One should remark, however, that non-Catholic Christians in Slovakia were not forced to embrace the Roman faith. The fate of local minorities is too extensive a topic to be discussed here.

[59] Meštrović, *Uspomene,* p. 323.

[60] Sidor, *Šest'* pp. 13, 108.

[61] See note 56.

[62] *Actes et Documentes,* Vol. V, doc. No. 123, pp. 273, 274, Notes de Msgr. Tardini, Oct. 21, 23, 1941. Cf. Kirschbaum, *Slovakia,* p. 54.

[63] Sidor, *Šest',* pp. 31–41, 63–66, 100–105, etc.; Jozef Kapala, *Spod Roháčov po Vatikán,* Galt, Ont., 1972, pp. 97–106, 137–142.

[64] Pattee, *The Case,* pp. 267–286, documents XIII–XVI; PA, *Inland* ID, 8/8–20, Letters, GL to GFO, *Schreibweise des kat. Blattes «Katolicki tjednik» Agram* (Sic!); DP inf-1364/42, May 22, 1942; *Schreibweise des «Katolicki tjednik» Sarajevo,* P3, Nr. 2a-2793/42, Dec. 3, 1942.

Psycho-Historical and Sociological Perspectives on the Iron Guard, the Fascist Movement of Romania*

ZEEV BARBU

Introduction

In the present paper I propose to discuss the fascist movement in Romania, generally known as the Iron Guard, with special reference to the first two questions with which this volume is concerned, i.e., «who joined the movement, and for what reason?». Two points have to be made clear from the very outset. First, because of its predominantly analytical orientation this paper may fail to provide the reader with a sufficiently clear descriptive account of the subject; for this purpose he is advised to consult E. Weber's admirable monographic study «The Men of the Archangel».[1] Second, methodologically speaking, not only have I not been able to consult the membership archives of the Iron Guard, but as far as I know such archives no longer exist. In the absence of more detailed sources I have endeavoured to form a general idea about the social composition of the Iron Guard by extrapolating from small samples extracted either from the 1937 electoral lists which contain brief references to 350 Iron Guard candidates, or from a few records left by the Romanian police or army. In this respect the subject is obviously under-documented.

Regarding the second question, the position is slightly more encouraging. For one thing, «confession of motives» was a routine admission-recruitment procedure and the Iron Guard publications are practically littered with essays bearing the title «How and why I have become a legionnaire» (The Legion was one of the esoteric names of the movement). Similarly, like most people serving long terms of imprisonment, many legionnaires became compulsive writers of memoirs and diaries, most of which contain important material on motivations. In addition, I had the opportunity of interviewing, informally of course, a small sample (19) of former members.

Since the procedure just outlined resembles a non finished manner of painting, highly suggestive but representationally ambiguous, a brief explanatory comment is necessary. In the present research I started, as most researchers do, from a series of basic observations, or primary intuitions, one of them being that the Iron Guard was socially more homogeneous than were most other European fascist movements; consequently, generalizations from relatively small samples were methodologically speaking more tolerable. But, empirical generalization apart, there are other ways of arriving at valid conclusions concerning the motives and the dominant social characteristics of those who became members of the Iron Guard. As we hope to show later, a detailed study of ideologies, specific forms of organization, style of life, and even dominant vocabulary could and should yield significant results in this respect.

The Historical Background

The origins of Romanian fascism, like those of European fascism in general, can be traced back to the period of social turmoil following World War I. The Romanian

379

fascist movement stands out in three main respects. First, it was born in universities as a student protest movement, and it preserved throughout its existence the character of a youth movement. Second, despite its remarkable electoral successes (between 1927–1937) it never assumed the form of a true political party: it remained a «movement» exhibiting a combination of elements of a fascist, liberationist, and religiously nativistic character. Thirdly, if it is true that fascist movements or regimes have strong autochthonous roots, then Romanian fascism should be considered as a paradigmatic case. Although not entirely immune to external influences, the Iron Guard was an essentially «home made» branch of fascism, almost obsessively concerned with its original, unique if not outright odd character. As late as 1929, on the eve of his departure for Germany to meet Hitler, C. Z. Codreanu, the leader of the Iron Guard, boasted that he could teach Hitler a few things on how to be a fascist. To understand this exaggreated self-awareness we need a brief account of the historical and social context in which the Iron Guard developed.

Since present-day Romania is normally considered a developing country, early twentieth century Romania cannot be described as anything else than a backward nation making its first steps towards modernization. Despite some feeble and spasmodic impulses towards industrialization, the economy of the country was overwhelmingly agricultural, with over 80 per cent of the population exlusively employed, or rather under-employed, in this sector. To the extent that production exceeded the subsistence level (on large private estates) it was due to what Barrington Moore calls a «labour exploitative system» rather than modernized techniques.[2] Throughout this period, Romanian society was a typical agrarian traditionalist society with a small, heterogeneous, and largely absentee landed upper class at the top, with the peasants constituting over 80 per cent of the total population at the bottom. As late as 1939 only one tenth of the population worked in industry. As for the so-called middle-classes, they consisted of small professional and commercial groups mainly of recent foreign origin i.e. Greek, Turkish and Jewish, in the South and East, and Hungarian and German in the North and West of the country. Briefly, one is here dealing with a tense and unstable social structure characteristic of most agrarian traditional societies facing the need, but lacking appropriate means for modernization. Thus, economically speaking, Romania entered and remained throughout the modern era a semi-colonial country, its condition being similar to that of present-day Latin American countries, and one which sheds direct light on Romania's perennial social problem; an over-exploited and increasingly disoriented peasantry. And yet the main source of tension and conflict lay somewhere else.

Few other European countries, with the possible exception of Poland, had a more frustrating political history. An ethnically homogeneous population constituting a fair majority throughout the territory of present day Romania, had, until the late nineteenth century, lived divided under four foreign occupations, that is, Turkish, in the South, Russian, in the East, Hungarian and Austrian, in the West and North. The first politically independent state, the so-called Old Kingdom of Romania came into being in 1877, while more than half of the population continued to live under foreign rule until 1918, when Romania reached the take-off point for political modernization by becoming a nation state. Although the significance of this for the rise of Romanian nationalism is on the whole obvious, the following points deserve to be emphasised.

Despite prolonged political fragmentation the Romanians have shown, at least from the beginning of the eighteenth century, an ever-growing awareness of their being a distinct and remarkably homogeneous ethnic community. By far the most important factor in this connection was their common language which, being a Latin language, fulfilled simultaneously three main psycho-historical functions: a. it was a unifying force in that it was spoken with very few and insignificant local variations by all Romanians; b. it performed a differentiating function in that the Romanians were the only Latin-speaking community in that part of Europe, and c. it fulfilled a prestige function for obvious although not necessarily legitimate reasons. It is relevant to note that there was and maybe still is a strong feeling among the Romanians that given the adverse circumstances of their history, their Latin language fulfilled more than a natural function; it performed a «miracle» to which they owe their survival as a nation.

What has just been said throws light on a series of aspects in the rise and development of the so-called Romanian nationhood which are particularly important here. First, like most colonial or semi-colonial nations, the Romanians have forged their identity, their sense of solidarity, under conditions of stress, a fact which needless to say has left the scar of inferiority, of what I would call a defensive type of group identity which normally asserts itself by a strong negative reference to other groups, and the oppressor in particular. Only a few years ago the Romanians were at pains to demonstrate to the world that they were *not* Russians. This has implicitly led to a no less strongly positive self-reference, as for instance, a strong emphasis put on their Latinity, Christianity, or their traditional way of life. All this, and especially a prolonged political fragmentation, has in the long run overstimulated what may for short be called the national consciousness of the Romanians. From the middle of the 19th century onwards a series of notions such as «liberty», «independence», «unity», «nationhood», «romanity» and many others have become more and more «dreamlike» or magic words, a sort of collective obsession dominating the cultural life of the country.

This leads to another, and perhaps the most important, point regarding the formative context of Romanian fascism. It refers specifically to the process of modernization, which, in Romania, as in most «late developers» was initiated and largely carried out under the impact of Western Europe. The westernization of Romania began in the upper classes towards the beginning of the last century and has been growing ever since. As this is a kind of socio-cultural process which is better known in its Russian version, it is helpful to bear in mind that, in Romania, it followed approximately the same course and had similar results. The modern intelligentsia of Romania was a product of westernization and, in likeness to the Russian intelligentsia, disclosed in its development all the main symptoms of a marginal group. Until the last decades of the nineteenth century the Romanian intelligentsia saw itself as a progressive group whose mission was to transform a backward traditional community into a modern society on the model of France. This resulted, of course, in its gradual alienation from the native culture. Thus, already towards the end of the nineteenth century, one could see the first signs of marginality among Romanian intellectuals who became aware that they belonged neither to the West because of their origin, nor to their native culture and society because of their education. The crisis was solved in a manner which has by now become a well-known phenomenon. Many Romanian intellectuals began to identify with the people, with their traditional way of life and culture. This triggered an intense process of revival, reappraisal and indeed exaggeration of native, hence specifically Romanian traditions, values, and, generally speaking, Romanian ways of life. The village and the peasant became symbols of honesty, sanity and primeval purity, the strongholds of national life. Christianity itself became a Romanian virtue. From the beginning of the century, up to World War II, the Romanian cultural scene was dominated by «populist» movements, literary, political and religious, so many hot-beds of nationalism and anti-Semitism.

But, needless to say, neither nationalism nor anti-Semitism must necessarily lead to fascism, a much more complex phenomenon, which can perhaps be defined as follows: Fascism is first of all a type of social-political movement developing within a nationalistic, and often populist, climate of opinion. If a social movement is defined as a collective reaction to a «problem», then the specific problem of fascism consists of a crisis of social solidarity and identity normally attributed to the decline of the traditional and ethnic characteristics of the community. Secondly, as a political movement fascism displays strong tendencies towards an authoritarian and para-military type of organization. Thirdly, it contains visible totalitarian elements in that the movement, or party, constitutes a concrete model, indeed, an archetype of society as a whole. Fourthly, as a model of society, fascism includes emotional, revivalist and, on the whole, regressive forms of social organization. It is backward-looking, using traditional and often primeval symbols of social solidarity. The image of a primary group constitutes a central motivational force among the members of such a movement.

If the above definition is borne in mind, there was only one movement and one party in Romania to which the term «fascist» can unambiguously be applied. This had various names corresponding to various stages in its development, but it was generally known as the Iron Guard. What follows is a brief interpretative account of the main characteristic traits of this movement which for more than one decade played an important, often dominant role on the political scene of inter-war Romania.

Xenophobia, «Estrangement» and Anti-Semitism: A Psycho-historical Perspective on Romanian Modernization

As mentioned, Romanian fascism was born in the period of social turmoil following World War I. Considering its formative context the first thing to be borne in mind is that Romania was not a defeated country. Nor was she a disappointed victor, as was Italy. On the contrary, by a stroke of luck, Romania came out of the war somehow dizzy with her success: as the result of the peace treaty of Versailles all the provinces in which the Romanians constituted a majority – Transylvania, Bucovina and Bessarabia – were united in a new Romanian national state with a population of over seventeen millions. Thus, Romanian fascism was not the outcome of national defeat. This does not mean, however, that Romanian fascism was in no way the child of collective confusion and anxiety. As recent studies of mental disorders and of suicide in particular have shown, sudden riches and sudden poverty produce similar results. If the analogy can be stretched so far, Romania found herself in the position of the *nouveau riche,* with a territory more than twice the size of that of the Old Kingdom, and with a population not only considerably larger, but also highly heterogeneous in traditions and ways of life. The problem, therefore, was one of organization and unity. What were the unifying factors, and what was the basis for consensus and solidarity in the new community? Questions such as these aroused considerable anxiety. This was reflected in the political situation of the country which was marked by vague democratic populist ideologies and even vaguer democratic reforms – with one exception, the extension of electoral rights to all males over the age of 21. The spectrum of political parties was rich, colourful and highly changeable. One structural feature, however, seemed to be constant: an almost empty «centre», with the large traditional political parties to the Right, and a very small Social Democratic and even smaller Communist party to the Left. Electorally, there was no sign of political radicalization.

The political instability, or better, fluidity of the country had a series of causes all of them contributing indirectly to the rise of fascism. To start with, the level of political education was alarmingly low and the socialization of the majority of the population contrasted sharply with the basic requirements of parliamentary democracy. A few years of febrile activity and rough competition among a dozen or more of political parties resulted in political confusion and apathy rather than enlightenment. In addition, as in all newly born nations and young democracies, the party system was very much of an artifical creation. With possibly two exceptions (the Liberal and National Peasant parties) the political parties of post-war Romania had no firm social base and no stable electorate. Moreover, most of them were hastily built and amounted often to no more than spasmodic organizations around some outstanding personality, such as a celebrated poet, a great general, a famous lawyer, with a woolly programme of government and an even woollier ideology drawing heavily on dominant cultural stereotypes, such as «Romanity», «Christianity», «peasant-ism», «All for the fatherland» and many others. Thus, an electoral campaign in post-war Romania looked like a war of ghosts, each party being concerned with itself or with other parties rather than with the needs and aspirations of the community at large. Briefly, democracy meant schismocracy and politics politicianism.

Two other aspects of political life added to the confusion in the newly born democracy: communism and the so-called Jewish problem. Regarding the former it seems important to emphasise that although Romania, unlike Germany or Italy, never had a strong Marxist party, communism as an idea and a threat from outside played a considerable part in the rise of the Iron Guard. The fact that the movement's birthplace was Moldavia and its first successes were achieved in Bucovina and Bessarabia, three provinces bordering Soviet Russia, can be adduced as an evidence of this. This has additional relevance. Bessarabia, Bucovina and Moldavia were not only more exposed to the communist threat, they also had a relatively large, and (because it was less assimilated) certainly a more evident Jewish population. Consequently, in these regions there was a long tradition of anti-Semitic movements, political and cultural. In this way, in Romania, as in Austria and Germany, anti-communism and anti-Semitism constituted a powerful cluster in the ideology of fascism. Moreover, the leaders of the Iron Guard took considerable pains to produce, admittedly shaky, statistical evidence to prove that Jewishness and communism were one and the same thing.

At this stage one point of qualification is necessary. While being an important ideological feature of Romanian fascism, anti-Semitism was in fact only one symptom in a larger syndrome which for lack of a better word can be called xenophobia. This ought to be stressed because from the first to the last day of its existence, the Iron Guard has been involved in a bitter struggle, ideological and political, against all minority groups of Romania, be they Hungarians, Turks, Greeks, Bulgarians or even Germans (Saxons). This explains why Transylvania, with her large Hungarian and German minorities, became relatively soon one of, if not the main electoral stronghold of the Movement.[3]

As to the question whether the Iron Guard was a racist movement the answer is neither an easy, nor a simple one. To be sure, it was not racist in the manner in which Hitlerism was, for Romanian fascists had neither a naturalistic, pseudo-scientific concept of race, nor an imperialistic ideology or policy. Central to their ideology and policy was the concept of «nation», more accurately, the conceptual cluster *nation* →

Romanian people → Romanian soil, signifying or rather symbolising a historic spiritual entity (all Romanians who had lived, are living, and will live on the Romanian soil in a manner epitomised by the traditional community of the village).

In this respect Romanian fascism shared some features with Italian fascism in that both extolled the historical past of the nation, its «noble origin», with the important difference that the Iron Guard concept of the nation had a strong mystic-Christian component and a distinct rural-bucolic flavour. To go back to the main point, the Iron Guard nationalism, its xenophobia was visibly rooted in a vision of the world characteristic of a closed community in which a highly differentiated category of people – a minority group, for instance – is normally perceived as an out-group. Anti-Semitism should, therefore, be seen as an aspect of this. As has been frequently noticed, the Romanians did not hate the Jews because they were Jews, but mainly because they were «different», less assimilated, and hence, more foreign than in most other European countries. One should nonetheless bear in mind that owing to the cumulative effect of a colonial past this xenophobic vision could, and at times did reach nightmarish proportions, as the Iron Guard clearly shows. This constitutes an important psycho-historical aspect of the Romanian community which has to be included in any systematic study of the rise of the Iron Guard. For the moment, I can do no more than briefly outline its nature and significance.

No one seriously concerned with the cultural history of the Romanian community can fail to notice the prevalence, and indeed the centrality, of a series of symbols, verbal or otherwise, connoting with various degrees of intensity and complexity a human condition of «estrangement». This may be a relatively simple feeling of regret or nostalgia aroused by a concrete experience of separation from a familiar environment, and the environment of childhood in particular, or a more complex mental state of disquietude and free-floating anxiety which in its cultural expression includes a series of compensatory states, and above all, a compound of hope, desire and longing for a lost world, or unattainable happiness, as well as a profuse manifestation of death fantasies thinly disguised under an ethic of resignation, of acceptance if not identification with the great rhythm or cycle of nature. Most Romanian studies of the phenomenon insist on its literary, mainly poetic expression, and above all on the key position of the word «dor», a singularly polysemic phoneme, conveying a strong feeling of homelessness and estrangement associated with vague hopes and desires, briefly, a mode of existence with no eschatological vision or at best a very obscure one.[4] None of the studies known to me pays the slightest attention to the social and political expression of this phenomenon, more precisely, to the functional correlation between the notion of «dor» and a series of more specific words, such as «strange», «stranger», «estrangement». This is all the more surprising as even from a cursory examination of the main contexts in which the latter words are used, one can infer a series of mainly negative emotional states (mistrust, suspicion, avoidance, withdrawal, hostility) which underline the typical Romanian attitude to society. For not only did the Romanians (as perhaps they still do) perceive their political society as something external, oppressive and alienating, but they entertained throughout the nineteenth century the belief that an expression, such as «a stranger in his own country» was a more or less accurate definition of their existence as individuals or as a community.

Now, the main point is that the above attitude has a definite historical dimension which can briefly be described as follows: Up to the last decade of the nineteenth century, the dominant note was one of passivity and total resignation. The feeling of an implacable fate was generally considered as a basic component of the Romanian vision of the world. This could be inferred from a great variety of cultural expressions, poetry and music in particular – as well as from the behavioural placidity of the peasant which was often regarded as a Romanian variety of the Stoic attitude. But as the century drew to a close, the symptoms of a great transformation became clearer and clearer. «Transformation» is not quite the right word because the beginning of the twentieth century brought about a «rupture», an inversion of signs in the Romanian culture and character. Lacking better terms and bearing in mind the limitations of psycho-analytical vocabulary, this can be described as a transition from a dominantly schizoid to a dominantly paranoid vision of the world, more specifically, from a mental structure dominated by mechanisms of withdrawal and avoidance, to a mental structure dominated by mechanisms of attack, and a moral system based on aggressive assertion and power. The social historian will undoubtedly have little difficulty in collecting and connecting a great variety of significant events taking place in this period, such as, for instance, the rise of the small nativistic intelligentsia discussed above, together with an infinite variety of populist and nationalist ideologies and movements, the dawn of a Romanian socialist movement, and last but not least, the peasant rebellion of 1907, the only true peasant revolt recorded in the modern history of the country.[5] For the sake of clarity it is necessary to refer to the symbolic, hence hyperbolic expression of the phenomenon, namely, one of the best known poems by Mihai Eminescu, a romantic, nationalistic poet of the period, written in popular verse-form and bearing the title *Doina*. To grasp the point one should bear in mind that Doina – the nearest Romanian equivalent to the «blues» – is an archetypal cultural expression (lyrics and song) of that kind of sensibility and world view which were characterized above by the word «dor», that is, a dominantly schizoid world view. By comparison to its traditional model, Eminescu's Doina sounds like a beat version of Bach's Passacaglia; it is shockingly aggressive, and certainly one of the most xeno-phobic poems ever written. It starts with a provocation «From the banks of Dnister to those of Tisza every Romanian cries out that he can hardly breathe because of so many foreigners . . .», and ends with a curse «If any shall cherish the stranger may the dogs eat his heart; may the weeds destroy his house; may his kin perish in shame».[6]

It is undoubtedly true that this poem and Eminescu in general constituted a main source of inspiration for the Iron Guard. On the other hand, the real nature of the Movement and above all its ethno-centric orientation cannot be properly understood without taking into account the pre-Eminescu schizoid stage of the process outlined above. As will be shown later, the mythology of the Iron Guard is basically a gloomy and apocalyptic one. Not even in their most sober moods were the Iron Guardists able to offer a simple solution, a scape-goat solution of an anti-Semitic type, for instance. Since the enemies were so many and powerful they were more often than not inclined to resort to a religious-eschatological vision in which «transcendence», «death and resurrection» were basic notions.

Leaders, Ideology and Organization

Historical circumstances apart, the Iron Guard owes its existence to two men, C. Z. Codreanu, student at the University of Iasi (1919–1925) and Ion Mota, student at the University of Cluj (1920–1924). Space allows but a short biographical and political portrait of the former, but before I do this I should like to record here a general idea arrived at a relatively advanced stage in my research. To use a Weberian notion of causality, I am now firmly convinced that the existence of the Iron Guard is intrinsically bound up with that of Ion Mota, fervent Iron Guard activist. Lest this should appear as a naive if not unwarranted application of the rule *sublata causa tollitur effectus* (remove the cause, and the effect disappears). I should like to make a further suggestion which I hope will be worked out in detail somewhere else – that it is possible to argue that the Iron Guard was a bicephalous authoritarian movement. To understand this, it is necessary to distinguish between the formal organizational structure and the symbolic structure of the movement. With regard to the former, the Iron Guard was undoubtedly a monolithic authoritarian organization, C. Z. Codreanu being its undisputed leader for almost twenty years. With regard to the symbolic structure the Iron Guard revealed a basic polarity, more precisely a life/death polarity. While no less active and creative in practical political terms, Mota stood for everything that had to die, to be sacrificed in order to enhance life. In his thirties and at a time when the Movement was visibly within reach of political success, Mota decided to join the Spanish Civil War as a simple soldier where he died. His body was brought back and canonized by his followers.[7]

Though retrospective interpretations should always be regarded with caution, there is hardly anything in Codreanu's biographical background which can throw serious doubts on the assumption that he had strong authoritarian traits in his personality. His father, a school teacher in a provincial town of Moldavia who became a well-known political figure, displayed throughout his life unmistakable signs of strong disciplinarian impulses and heroic fantasies wrapped up in bombastic nationalistic language. The relationship between father and son is best illustrated by an incident which is often mentioned by the latter in his autobiographical writings. At the beginning of World War I the father, despite his advanced age, volunteered for the army. This was a signal for the son, then a schoolboy, to leave home and wander for a few weeks from one military unit to another offering his services. He was refused and so returned home. Thus his first heroic «flight» ended in disappointment. In this context, it is worth mentioning that before going to university he studied at the military school of Manasti-rea Dealul.

One other relevant biographical detail concerns Codreanu's mother, who was of German origin, a fact which certainly had something to do with his demonstrative nationalism. As has often been suggested, his need for achievement coupled with a mystic faith in human will may also have come from her. I hasten to specify, however, that Codreanu was not a voluntarist in the manner in which Hitler was, nor was he a master of words and a fluent conceptualizer as was Mussolini.

This being said, it must be admitted that biographical details can tell relatively little about a man who was not only a mystic but also a mystery, a kind of man who defies, consciously or unconsciously, any attempt to draw a clear distinction between his public and private face. To start with, Codreanu was a highly dedicated man revealing a particulary high rate of interference between an ideal-ego (the saviour of the nation) and a real ego. In addition, one has to bear in mind that one is here dealing with a tradition-controlled type of mental structure and motivational system totally dominated by national stereotypes: «My enemies, the country's enemies» was a banal, but effective shield-formula for Codreanu's violent, often murderous political convictions and activities. But there is something else, namely, the close, almost symbiotic, tie between Codreanu and Mota which, strange as it may be, was of such significance that it would be difficult to present a meaningful psychological portrait of Codreanu, the leader of the Iron Guard, without including in it some features dominant in Mota's personality. Briefly, Mota, the «saint» and «Martyr», re-enforced the religious spiritual side of Codreanu's rationalization-sublimation system to that extent that in the end one can reasonably speak about a *folie à deux*, a mental merger between a primitive-impulsive (Codreanu), and a highly repressed aggressive (Mota) who rationalized their murderous actions by the formula «my enemies are my country's and God's enemies». If one wanted to size up this mental structure in a formula (for the sake of brevity I shall from now on refer to it as Codreanu's personality) one would say that Codreanu was a sentimental and mystic authoritarian. The paranoid streak in his personality reached theomanic proportions and the basic motif in his life was *Imitatio Christi*. But this also revealed a duality, or rather a precarious balance between two diametrically opposed views of man and political conceptions, one based on action and deeds, the other on faith and contemplation. The Christ of *Theologia Gloriae* and the Christ of the *Theologia Crucis*, the mystique of life (Codreanu), and the mystique of death (Mota) were brought together in the symbolic world of the Iron Guard.

The Iron Guard: Its Development and Organizational Features

Between 1920 and 1923 the Iron Guard consisted of student groups organized outside the official unions, first in Iasi and then in the other three universities of the country, Czernovitz, Bucharest and Cluj. There was only a small minority in each university but all three were well-organized and ready to use threats and other terrorist methods, hence they became an awkward and often dominant group at many student meetings. Their programme can be summed up in two points, violent anti-Semitism demanding the application of a *numerus clausus* for the admission of Jews, and a vague Christian reformism. Much more important than their programme, however, was their way of life as individuals and as a group – their dedication, discipline and readiness for action.

The period from 1923 to 1927 can in many ways be considered as the period of political consolidation. In 1923, Codreanu and A. C. Cuza together formed a political party, the League of National Defence, which, in 1926, won six seats in the Romanian Parliament.[8] Two events of 1923 are crucial for the understanding of Romanian fascism. As a result of increased anti-Semitic agitation and above all of a plot to punish (by shooting) a number of liberal MPs, Codreanu and a few of his friends were arrested, tried, and as often happened in those early days, acquitted. But on leaving prison Mota shot dead the man suspected of having betrayed the plot. This brought to light the essential organizational and ethical features of the movement. For it appeared that the victim was previously tried and sentenced by the «secret tribunal» of the organization, which also designated the executioner. Expressions such as «traitors» and «heroes» as well as the «blood baptism of the Guard» were used in this context.

The second event relates to Codreanu's life. During the short term of imprisonment, in 1923, he had his first vision: the Archangel Michael came to him and urged him to dedicate his life to God as revealed by the Romanian Christian tradition. Soon after, on the day Mota was released (1923) Codreanu appointed him the head of the «Brotherhood of the Cross», an élitist body, which he placed at the centre of the movement. To indicate the nature of this organization it is necessary to mention that, apart from the Archangel's revelation, Codreanu was inspired by an old Romanian tradition. Such forms of privileged and mystic associations, or rather communions, between two or more people existed and maybe still exist among Romanian peasants. The association is highly ritualized and often those entering upon it have to taste each other's blood in order to become brothers, «unto life and death». The Brotherhood of

387

the Cross was the mystic body of the Iron Guard, open only to the few and the elect. Those worthy of membership had to undergo a primitive ceremony, a *rite de passage*. They were summoned to a secret place, and after an incantational ritual which took place at a late hour of the night they made a formal vow pledging their life to the cause and the «Captain».

In 1928, the League of National Christian Defence was dissolved, and, in 1927, there came into being the first independent political organization of Codreanu's movement, the Legion of the Archangel Michael. This was a prototype of the fascist organization. To start with, it had no political programme. «The country is dying for lack of men and not for lack of programmes» were the words used by Codreanu at the foundation meeting of the Legion. The basic trait of the organization was a state of mind, succinctly expressed by the following four points: «Faith in God», «Faith in the Mission», «Love for each other» and «Love for songs». All these were «cultist» in character, and required specific tests and trials and particularly specific states of mind.

The Legion had a conspiratorial type of organization. The basic unit was the «nest», a small group consisting of seven, rising to a maximum of twelve members, who called each other *camarazi,* a term which was used, not by the Romanian communists (who called themselves *tovaresi*), but by the Romanian army. Above the level of the «nests», the Legion consisted of a semi-military and semi-mystical organization with a rigid hierarchy. At the top was the «Captain» and a small number of «great commanders of the Legion».

The «nest» as the structural unit of the party was a model for totalitarian groups. Even the name was chosen to appeal to the needs of dependence and security of the young. In it, the legionari received their basic training, which consisted of some knowledge of the history and martyrology of the Guard, instructions about rules of conduct expected of them, and above all unconditional obedience to the Leader. The «nest» had a monolithic internal organization, with all decisions made unanimously. Though in principle and overtly Codreanu was not against democracy in the same sense as Hitler, on the question of leadership he had always held extreme, authoritarian views. 'I was a leader from the beginning', he often said, meaning that a leader should have obvious and compelling qualities which make election and, on the whole, formal delegation of authority unnecessary. Consequently the leaders of the 'nests' emerged eruptively, as Max Weber would put it; they were the obvious choice on account of their loyalty to the cause. The leaders were also religious people with a Manichean vision of the world in which – following the example of their patron, Saint Michael – they were the angels of light. Since the mission of the legionari was nothing less than the moral regeneration of the nation, the distinctive mark of their leaders was a high sense of mission and martyrdom.

This throws light on one of the most characteristic organizational and psychological features of the Iron Guard. I know of no other fascist movement which incalculated in its members a deeper sense of personal dedication and sacrifice. To start with, one of the main élite groups within the Iron Guard was the so-called 'death team', consisting of young fanatics ready to kill and be killed. Their status and mission were highly institutionalized, or rather ritualized. It was said that they used to wear around their necks a tiny bag of Romanian soil and that there was nothing in the world which they would not do at the sight of it. There were also other less magic expressions of their sense of sacrifice. Most outstanding in this respect were their songs with the mystique of death as the basic motif. Here is an example:

Legionari do not fear
That you will die young

For you die to be reborn
And are born to die

For we are the death team
That must win or die

Death, only the legionari-death
Is a gladsome wedding for us.

Two powerful motifs of the mystique of death inflamed the mind of the legionari. One, explicitly stated in the last quotation, is traditional-native, constituting the central theme in one of the best known Romanian ballads, Mioritsa, where the hero, threatened with imminent death, overcomes his fear by comparing death to a wedding, the bridegroom being himself and nature his bride. It was often said that this was the «typical» Romanian attitude to death. Even more powerful is the other motif, the Christian mythology of resurrection and victory through death.

While the main slogan of the legionari was «victory or death», this religious formula seems to reveal more adequately the deep motivation of their behaviour. The more and the heavier they had to pay for their murderous violence, the more they practised it. These are a few figures illustrating this tight chain of action which can be formulated either as «kill and be killed», or «kill to be killed». Between 1924 and 1937 they committed eleven murders – mainly important political personalities.[9] During this period, however, over 500 legionari were killed, mainly by the police. Between April and December 1939, the year of martyrdom, some 1,200 legionari were arrested, imprisoned and killed. To this, one should add another incident, the significance of which can hardly be overestimated. In the summer of 1936, in one of Bucharest's hospitals, there took place an event which cannot be described as anything else than ritual killing. While Stelesco, a prominent legionari leader who had just left the Iron Guard and joined another nationalist organization, was lying in bed, a group of four legionari broke in and fired 120 shots at him. Afterwards, they chopped his body in small pieces, danced around it and kissed each other.

The Membership

From the very beginning the membership of the Iron Guard was dominated by two categories of people, youth and intellectuals. In 1922, Codreanu was twenty-two, Mota, twenty, and the average age of their followers must have been somewhere in between. According to a rough estimate, the average age in a group of 350 Iron Guard candidates (in the 1937 elections) was definitely under thirty even if one took into account some 20 venerable figures, such as, for instance, Codreanu's father who was in his late sixties at the time. Even as late as 1942–44, the average age in a group of legionaries interned in Buchenwald was 27.[10]

The samples are obviously not representative. On the other hand, considering the dominant organizational traits and above all the recruitment procedure of the Movement one can reasonably infer that the average age of the rank and file was lower than that just mentioned. As an organization, the Brotherhood of the Cross was set up to

389

enlist «students, school boys and village youth», and train them stage by stage until they became fully fledged legionaries. Thus, from the age of ten (minimum requirement) the enlisted members were pressed through the following stages and organizational unities: from 10 to 14, the preliminary stage, a relatively loose organization normally referred to as «The Little Brothers», from 15 to 18 (?), the Brotherhood, rigorously organized in small groups «fascia» (seven members, minimum). The Legion was the next and final stage and as such it consisted of the end-product, the most dedicated and active members of the movement. Thus, the movement as a whole was a militant organization with strong proselytizing tendencies, rapidly indoctrinating its members and organizing them into «nests», the basic organizational units of the Legion. In this way the Movement spread out from universities and schools, which remained its most powerful formative centres, into other areas of urban and rural life. And as the leaders and activists were young, so were the rank and file. At no time in the existence of the Iron Guard was the average age of its members higher than twenty. As for the size of the Legion's membership, the only evidence I can mention is that according to official figures the number of nests was 4,200 in 1935, 12,000 in 1937, and 34,000 later in the same year. By the end of 1937 total membership could not be lower than 200,000, perhaps considerably higher.

The question of the social origins of the Iron Guard leadership and membership in general presents some difficulties. The two samples analysed by E. Weber (251 interned in Buchenwald, and 31 executed in Vaslui, in 1939) show an overwhelmingly dominant middle-class element (state employees, professionals, and even tradesmen (6 per cent) and shopkeepers (5 per cent)). However, Weber is quick to qualify such a conclusion by pointing out that two samples together included 75 students, and above all, the average age of Iron Guard membership as a whole was considerably lower than that of the NSDAP membership. This leads him to stress the relevance of the age factor in understanding the social composition of the Iron Guard. This important point deserves further elaboration.

Before arriving at any definite conclusion with regard to the class composition of the Iron Guard, we should go back to a point made earlier which may be re-stated birefly as follows. First, Romania of the inter-war period was a developing country emerging from a long colonial past, and hence facing all the main problems characteristic of a post-liberation period. Second, in terms of social structure, Romanian society was a typical traditional agrarian society; throughout this period, the middle class was numerically small, ideologically and politically ill-defined, and above all divided between foreign and indigenous elements. To this we should add the disrupting impact of modernization, all the more obvious as the process was initiated from above and from outside. The inroads made by urbanization, industrialization and democratization were regarded by the majority of the population and peasants in particular with suspicion and mixed feelings.

Seen in this broad context, the class character of the Iron Guard becomes considerably more problematic than it would appear at first sight. Admittedly, their economic and educational status indicates a middle-class position in a large majority of its members. But the significance of this cannot be fully assessed unless one takes into account their direct, almost uninterrupted connection with the traditional community and way of life. As mentioned, Codreanu was the son of a schoolteacher and the grandson of a peasant; Mota, the son of a country priest and the grandson of a peasant. This applies to the leadership at all levels and on the whole to the so-called middle-class element in the Legion.

All this throws considerable doubt on the class specificity of the membership, let alone the class identity of the legionaries. It is very likely that we are dealing here with a psychological rather than a social group. Most of its members were climbing up the ladder of social hierarchy in the direction of the middle class. But the point is that they had not yet arrived, they had not yet broken away from their rural traditional background. On the whole they were a marginal group, and it was their condition of marginality rather than their class position which determined their political behaviour.

The prominent part played by the intelligentsia in the rise of the Iron Guard can in itself be taken as a symptom of marginality, of classlessness. Moreover, this should be taken in a far more concrete and straightforward sense than that implied in the famous Mannheimian thesis, for the obvious reason that the kind of intelligentsia we are dealing with belonged to an emerging, newly born society without a clear sense of solidarity and identity. Furthermore, the intelligentsia belonged to a society in which the middle strata were perceived as fulfilling an ambivalent role (positive, to the extent they were Romanian by origin or reference, and negative, to the extent they were foreign). This says a great deal about the social position, objective and subjective, of the Romanian intelligentsia and the legionary intelligentsia in particular. In reality they could not and did not belong anywhere, and escaped reality by inventing their society and reference group. For example, Codreanu identified himself with the «people», an idealized community which he never defined except in vague and abstract terms, such as, «unity», «purity», «Christianity». Even more characteristically, Mota, after rejecting the corrupt social reality of his time, identified himself with the «old world», the legendary past of his nation. Thus, the reference group of the legionaries was an imaginary one. It was an ideal society in which the legend of an old traditional Romanian community loomed large. The predominant utopian element in this image of society was of a moral/religious character, with brotherly unity and love as the basis of communal life.

The Question of Motivation

The training procedures and organizational framework of the Iron Guard were so designed as to appeal to the young. Moreover, the Movement offered an instant substitute, a concrete alternative to anyone who for one reason or another had cut himself off from the primary sources and implicit framework of his social existence. I say «concrete» because the ultimate goal of the Movement, the so-called legionary society and man, was not in the least a conceptual construct. It was a mode of being, a «new life» accessible to feelings and faith rather than reflexion and will-power.

Any complete study of the motivational structure of the legionaries has to pay attention to legionary language and mythology, and above all, to a series of key signs, verbal and otherwise, such as, «cross», «soil» (two legionary amulets), «cradle», «home-coming», «estrangement», «revenge», not to mention, the «love/death» polarity so dramatically expressed by the double image – the sword and the cross – of the Archangel Michael, and in more concrete terms, by the Codreanu/Mota leadership. This is a complex idea which requires further elaboration.

According to a well-known thesis, drama as a literary phenomenon as well as the theatre as an institution rose and developed in those historical periods and societies in which intense conflicts or disruptive structural changes stimulated in the members of the community the need to restore and re-enforce their sense of solidarity by imagining or representing an alternative society.[11] The process could be, needless to say, either past-oriented, i.e., a reactualization and idealization of a legendary and mythic social past, or future-oriented. Now, most fascist movements are dramatizations of social life, more precisely, rituals of solidarity and myth – re-enactments focused on the theme of salvation and resurrection. None of them, however, have gone so far and so overtly in this direction as the Iron Guard. Nobody who lived in Romania in the inter-war period can forget the anachronistic and at the same time vivid character of a legionary demonstration. It was something between a political protest, a religious procession, and a historical cortége. The middle and indeed the core of the demonstration consisted of a well-organized body of young people in uniforms – «the green shirts». It was normally headed by a group of priests carrying icons and religious flags. Finally, all this was followed and surrounded by men and women in national dress. Briefly, it was the Romanian community recreating its past, or in more technical terms, a mystery play in which the drama of the Romanian people was acted out in the street.

Since some of the words just used many appear too strong, I should like, finally, to refer to one of those «confessions of motives» mentioned at the beginning of this essay. This confession should have more credibility because, unlike most others, it was written neither on the spur of the moment, nor for the purpose of admission, but at a time when the Movement was dead. Its author is Horia Sima, the last leader of the Movement who, unlike Codreanu and Mota did not need to have prophetic charisma. He was a skilled and unscrupulous manipulator, an almost second generation routinizer. Sima joined the Movement in 1926 as an undergraduate at the University of Bucharest. As already mentioned, 1926–1927 constituted the take-off point of the Movement. Sima points to a critical precondition for the rise of the Movement when he writes that «. . . in 1926–1927, our Universities were flooded by a big wave of young people of peasant origin . . . who brought with them a robust national consciousness and were thus destroying the last strongholds of foreign spirit in our universities». This flood of country boys had also introduced a radical change in the conventional role for the student, for they were anxious «not only to learn from books», but also to analyse the spirit of the New Romania so as to establish «the purpose of their own existence *as Romanians*». [12] Since their highest aspiration was to know «what is to be done», their main heroes were the nationalist gurus of the time. But by far the most revealing part of the confession is the part in which Sima describes the impact made on him by the ritual of admission as the following string of quotations shows: «A feeling of self-transcendence and transfiguration of daily life»: «a mystic union between nation and God»; a «sensation of power coming from afar and the feeling that the whole country moves at the same time, and in the same direction with us»; «an expansionist and creative impulse with the inner certitude that a few years from now Codreanu will be acclaimed by the whole country»; «a volcanic passion for action . . .». [13]

That such a Movement should appeal to the young, the uprooted and the marginal elements of society makes good psychological sense. It also makes fairly good sociological sense if one takes into account some of the main conclusions arrived at by a series of recent comparative studies of revivalist messianic movements in underdeveloped and developing countries. But the Iron Guard was something more and something else than a simple revivalist movement. It was a political movement, one of the few wholly fascist movements to come to power and form a government. Moreover, it had a widespread electoral support – nearly 500,000 votes, in 1937 – which included peasants and a Workers' Brigade over 13,000 strong (in 1939). Given this can one still maintain that the concept of marginality constitutes a suitable analytical tool?

The short answer is yes, and regretfully it has to be only a short answer. A survey of the 1937 elections shows sufficiently clearly that the success of the Guard was greatest in those districts which fulfilled two or more of the following conditions: 1. Remote, isolated and neglected; 2. containing large minority groups; 3. affected by industrialization or commercialization; 4. dominantly «middle-range» peasant communities, downwards moving (Razesi, in Moldavia), or upwards moving (Transylvania).

I am, needless to say, fully aware of the limitations of such an interpretative model. The concept of marginality, like a whole series of kindred concepts (relative deprivation, for instance) could be and normally is embarrassingly elastic, both in an objective and subjective sense. Motivationally speaking, a mental condition of marginality could lead to organized violence, or moral re-armament, to a religious, or a political movement, to radicalism of the right, or of the left. That is why the kind of motivational analysis which is offered here can never be exhaustive. This may readily be illustrated with the case in point, for owing to the circumstance discussed on the foregoing pages, the situation in which Romania found herself during the inter-war period cannot be described as anything but an example of marginality, more precisely, of stress verging on despair. Now the point is that the Iron Guard was not the only expression of this complex situation. Romania, whose history and culture were particularly poor in holy figures, had now produced a prophet. In the summer of 1935 the Romanian public was quite overwhelmed by the news, eagerly spread by most newspapers, that a miracle had taken place in the village of Maglavit. While grazing his sheep the shepherd Petrache Lupu saw «the Old Man with his white beard» appearing from nowhere and commanding: «Go and preach love and peace to your sinful countrymen». Millions of people from all walks of life went to see and listen to him.

Of course, there is a great deal of difference between the crowd attracted by Petrache Lupu and a fascist movement. The Iron Guard had a stable organization, and a well articulated reactionary framework in which anti-Semitism, anti-democracy and anti-politicianism played a major part. All this, and much more else has to be taken into account in a proper study of motivation. But the point I am trying to make here is more specific, and hopefully, more useful: motivationally the Iron Guard may be seen as a combination of Petrache Lupu's crowd and a fascist movement. Its specific if not unique character may briefly be described as follows: The Iron Guard represents in a highly compressed yet well differentiated form what is normally known as a two-phase phenomenon, that is, the transition from a religious to a political movement in developing countries. Apart from being an exemplary case of agrarian fascism, the Iron Guard has another not less important theoretical significance: it illustrates and to a certain extent foreshadows a kind of anomaly occurring in most societies with a high rate of change. This phenomenon may for lack of a better expression be called relative-marginality. The anomaly consists of a boundless appetite for power, a never-to-be-satisfied desire to be included in the decision-making processes and structures aroused by a free and rapidly changing society in greater and greater numbers of its members.

NOTES

* The present study is based on the research carried out a few years ago under the auspices and with the financial assistance of the Columbu. Centre at the University of Sussex. Apart from the sources referred to in the text I have made use of documentary material found in: *Österreichische Nationalbibliothek*, Vienna; *Rumänisches Kulturhaus*, Freiburg: *Academia de Stinte Sociale*, Bucharest.

[1] In *Journal of Contemporary History* vol. 1, no. 1, 1966. An even more detailed treatment of the subject can be found in H. Rogger & E. Weber (eds.), *The European Right* (London 1965). Other relevant sources are E. C. Carsten, *The Rise of Fascism* (London 1967) and S. J. Woolf (ed.) *European Fascism* (London 1967).

[2] Cf. *The Social Origins of Dictatorship and Democracy* (London 1967).

[3] Concerning the Iron Guard attitude towards the Saxons, see I. Mota, *Cranii de Lemn* (Bucuresti 1936) pp. 181–186.

[4] The best known and by far the most perceptive work in the field is L. Blaga, *Spatiul Mioritic* (Sibiu 1936).

[5] The two famous rebellions (1784 and 1848) of the rural population living in the mountainous areas of western Transylvania cannot be described as peasant rebellions for the simple reason that the population in these areas, the so-called *Motsi,* lived on the fringe of agrarian economy and can be best described as a marginal social group gaining its subsistence partly from agriculture, partly from trade.

[6] A penetrating account of the socio-cultural climate of the period can be found in Z. Ornea: *Samanatorismul,* Bucarest 1971. It is interesting to note that the author manages to interpret the violent fervour of the period in terms of class struggle.

[7] Mota was the son of an orthodox priest from Transylvania, famous for his nationalistic activities. Soon after the war he went to Paris to study law where he was closely associated with the activities of the *Action Française.* On his return to the University of Cluj he founded the Romanian Action group. At the time when he met Codreanu (1923) he had just finished translating the *Protocols of the Elders of Zion.* Unlike Codreanu, who was a practising Christian, but took a political view of the Church and religion, Mota was a religious fanatic. His anti-Semitism was basically Christian («Jews are murderers of God»). In his writings *(Cranii de Lemn* i.e. Wooden Skulls) he reveals alarmingly strong symptoms of self-alienation vaguely disguised in religious fantasies and myths. The contrast between a pure (Christian) traditional past and a corrupted anti-Christian present creates an irremediable rift inside his own existence: he imagines himself as having lived two lives, one under the name of Nutu Doncii, a happy village boy, and the other, under his proper name. The Movement helped him to bring the two existences together, or rather, to impose the past upon the present.

[8] A. C. Cuza, a sort of Romanian Julius Streicher, was Codreanu's political mentor during his student years at the University of Iasi (1919–25).

[9] In 1926 Codreanu murdered the prefect of Galatsi, Manciu.

[10] E. Weber, *op. cit.* p. 108.

[11] J. Duvignaud, *Sociologie du théatre* (Paris 1961).

[12] Italics mine.

[13] From *Marturii Despre Legiune* (Rio de Janeiro 1967).

The Social Roots of Hungarian Fascism: The Arrow Cross

MIKLÓS LACKÓ

The emergence of the first extreme rightist movements in Hungary, openly calling themselves National Socialists, dates back to the time of the great economic crisis from 1929 to 1933. But the National Socialist movements in Hungary represented no considerable force before 1935–36. Leaders, groups and parties emerging in the first half of the thirties, sometimes separating, sometimes fusing, were not able to gain substantial influence. Most of them were «modernized» variants of the old racist gatherings and were active within the middle-class or backward peasant strata in various rural districts. It was only Böszörmény's *Scythe-Cross* movement – also initiated by sections of the gentry – that was able for a while to attract larger numbers of the most destitute, most backward have-nots of the agrarian proletariat on the Hungarian Plain. As a result of the 1935 elections, only two national socialist deputies were seated in Parliament.

By the second half of 1937, the strength of the National Socialist movements showed a considerable increase. This, however, was not the result of any substantial broadening of their mass influence; it was rather correlated with two characteristic developments: on the one hand, further elements of the extreme right wing of the genteel middle-class approached the Arrow Cross movement; and on the other there were endeavors to form a coalition of the various fascist parties and groups.

The Arrow Cross movement in Hungary showed a marked upswing and became a mass movement during the period from early 1938 to the middle of 1939. The decisive factor behind this upturn was the further increase of large-scale political, ideological and, last but no least, material support by Nazi Germany.

Of all the Arrow Cross parties, it was only the one led by Szálasi and Hubay that grew into a broadly based mass movement. This was made possible by an unprecedented influx into the Arrow Cross, starting from the lower strata of the middle class after the *Anschluss*. In 1938–1939, a considerable part of the leading echelon of the movement was recruited from the stratum of army officers. The other leading political group of the movement emerged from the civil servant-intellectual stratum of the middle class. Their numbers mounted appreciably in 1938–1939, partly through the influx of leaders of extreme rightist groups that merged with the Hungarian movement, partly through political climbers who had been in the government party, or had been royalists and now tried to exploit the fascist boom. Besides these people, some déclassé members of the aristocracy were among the leading cadres of the Arrow Cross movement. In addition to all these, a few petty bourgeois and «laborers» were also found among the Arrow Cross leaders.

Within the party a particular place and function was assigned to a group of so-called activists. They held no leading posts, most of them were active as «worker» organizers. They constituted the «radical»-anarchist core of the movement and were the leaders of semi-legal activities: leaflet distribution, demonstrations, etc; and of terrorist acts. They were also the participants in the anti-Jewish hate campaigns: the more «daring» slogans of social demagogy were their inventions. It was this group that regarded itself as the «revolutionary conscience» of the movement, as the mobilizer of the masses. Regarded from the social angle, this praetorian guard was recruited from the scum of society in the strictest sense – from among criminals, psychopaths and the «lumpen» elements of the various classes. Pimps figuring in the police registers, sadistic noncommissioned officers, jobless, depraved clerks of private firms were to be found in this group.

To specify clearly the social pattern of the broader masses – attached members and «fellow-travellers» – that were dragged into the movement is much more difficult than to picture its uppermost layer. No data are available for analysing the social basis of the party: we may only try to reconstruct its social composition from police reports, from the information of local organizations of the Social Democratic party, and from the fragmentary documents of the Arrow Cross movement.

What must be emphasized first of all is that the Arrow Cross party gained ground not by some steady, gradual developmental course, but by a sudden breakthrough in mass influence reaching its peak in as short a time as one, or one-and-a-half years. As for the registered party members, their number in July 1938 was not much above the ten-thousand footing; but membership was well above 200,000 a year and a half later. At the culminating point of the success of the Arrow Cross movement, Szálasi estimated the number of members to be 250,000. In this evidence given at the People's Tribunal, Emil Kovarcz gave an estimate of 300,000.

This mass movement was made up of elements of extremely mixed social background. This is why it is so difficult to make generalizations as regards the social basis. To the overwhelming majority who joined it, the Arrow Cross movement could offer no more than a distorted form of political attitude pushed towards the extreme reactionary line. This attitude was not dominated by even a small measure of real and sensible social considerations. It was rather the reactionary innovation, the prospect of easy pillage, the longing for illusory ways of breaking loose from hopeless subordination, and the expectation of the miracle of a rapid rise which so decisively spurred its growth. The basis of the movement was altogether heterogeneous, labile and accidental, subject to a multitude of momentary effects and counter-effects, to the local balance of power, and accidental events. Still, there are four principal layers which can be more or less differentiated in this muddled, reactionary convolution.

One was the numerically important layer of army officers of the gentry, civil servants and intellectuals to be found in the lower strata of the genteel class. The majority of the local leaders of the movement came from these elements, and they maintained their relations with the higher classes.

The other layer forming the social basis of the movement came from the lumpen element of the various strata of society. Such a layer is the inevitable product of any modern social system; their role in society and in political struggles is an important sociological problem that has so far hardly been analysed. This layer played a most active role in the fascist movement in Hungary: most of the Arrow Cross activists emerged from it. This is confirmed clearly by police statistics illustrating the role in the fascist movement of the extreme aberrations of this lumpen layer, and of the various criminal elements of society. An investigation of the past records of 4,292 office-holders or activists proved that 1,228 of them had previously been convicted; the number of sentences in these cases was 1,779, mostly for common-law crimes. The distribution of the crimes committed was this:

Theft	284	16.0%
Fraud	137	7.7%
Embezzlement	128	7.2%
Receiving stolen goods	52	2.9%
Indecent assault	17	1.0%
Slander and defamation	120	6.7%
Insulting the head of state	26	1.5%
Assault on private persons and on officers of the law	167	9.4%
Military crimes	81	4.6%
Assault and battery	163	9.2%
Conspiracy for the violent overthrow of state and social order	304	17.0%
Others	300	16.7%

«Other» crimes include manslaughter. Sentences imposed for penal idleness and begging were frequent.

If we deduct from these statistics the sentences of a more or less political character, about 1,300 criminal cases are left; so the estimate is that about one-fourth of the investigated activists can be classified as criminals, or at any rate people of a criminal disposition.

The third basis of the movement was drawn from the petty bourgeois elements of towns and – to a smaller extent – of villages. This layer was made up of large numbers of artisans and shopkeepers (including publicans) many of whom were hovering on the fringes between independent and proletarian status; and groups of intellectuals and clerks (underpaid private employees, intellectuals holding inferior positions, small pensioners, etc.) who were dragged into the Arrow Cross party in considerable numbers and are best placed in this group.

Finally, the fourth basis was made up of the large backward stratum of urban and village semi-proletarians and proletarians. Two layers deserve attention within this stratum. One was that of the railwaymen, postmen and «assistant personnel» working in public utilities. In Hungary these people can be regarded as a particular type of semi-proletarians; as people with a proletarian class background whose circumstances of life were mixed with a number of typically bourgeois features (fixed salary, pension, complete dependence on the high-class members of the state machinery, etc.). The other layer consisted of the most backward elements of the proletariat: of ever more sporadically employed daily workers at the lowest grade of class consciousness and education, living on the verge of abject poverty and starvation; of the considerable number of proletarians with a rural background for whom the way back to their village was practically blocked, of the perpetually changing groups of laborers coming from the villages, etc. It must be admitted that, especially in 1938–1939, Arrow Cross influence was not restricted to these layers; it involved also other, more stable groups of workers, the new generation of skilled workers brought up in the atmosphere of counter-revolution; a segment of the workers in smaller industries (mainly in rural districts) and especially the inflated numbers of miners who were of radical leanings but who remained practically unorganized.

The general elections were held on May 28, and 29, 1939. The most important result was the great success of the various extreme rightist groups, the Arrow Cross first of all.

The distribution of seats was as follows:

Government party candidates	183 seats	(70%)
Christian party candidates	4 seats	
National Socialist parties and candidates	49 seats*	(18%)
Smallholders' party	11 seats	
Social Democratic party	5 seats	

* Of which the Arrow Cross party had 31 seats.

There were thus substantial changes in the distribution of seats compared to 1935. The government party showed essentially the same proportion of seats as in 1935. But the government party of 1939, the Party of Hungarian Life as it was called then, was much more rightist than the Party of National Unity of 1935, both in its policy and in the attitudes of its deputies.

The distribution of parliamentary seats showed further that the number of deputies of the Christian party, standing close to the government party and entering into an electoral alliance with the latter, decreased from 14 to 4. The collapse of the Christian parties at the 1939 election – their former followers for the most part were casting their votes for the government party or the Arrow Cross parties – was one reflection of the extreme rightist, fascist activation of the middle class and the petty bourgeoisie.

But the most spectacular change took place within the composition of the opposition.

With regard to political attitude and parliamentary importance, the oppositionist Smallholders' party and the Social Democratic party were rather weak already in 1935; in the 1939 elections they lost more than half of their seats. As contrasted with 26 seats in 1935, the Smallholders' party obtained 11 seats, the Social Democratic party only 5 instead of the former 14. Hence the opposition parties virtually collapsed, while the extreme rightist Arrow Cross movement advanced dangerously: the overtly fascist parties and groups increased the number of their deputies from 2 to 49, with 31 seats for the Arrow Cross party proper.

The extent of the shift to the right is shown even more clearly by the distribution of the votes, and this permits the drawing of further conclusions regarding the social basis of the Arrow Cross movement. The number of votes was well over three million, but this meant actually much less – about 2,600,000 voters – since a number of voters were voting twice: for the county and municipal lists and for individual candidates. The political parties shared the votes cast as follows:

MEP (Party of Hungarian Life)	50%
Christian party	3%
National Socialists (including Arrow Cross)	25%
Liberals	2%
Smallholders' party	15%
Social Democratic party	4%

Of all votes cast the Arrow Cross and similar groups obtained more than 900,000.

The success of the Arrow Cross was most conspicuous in the suburbs of Budapest, in Budapest and in Pest County. In the suburbs of Budapest the parties shared the votes percentagewise at the two elections thus:

	1935	1939
Government party	35.7	27.5
Christian party	13.5	6.9
National Socialists	–	41.7
Social Democratic party	33.3	17.1

The situation in the great proletarian suburbs of Budapest however, is as follows:

	Government party	Arrow Cross	Social Democratic party
Kispest	6 364	6 722	4 152
Pesterzsébet	3 839	4 187	3 539
Pestlórinc	3 646	5 034	2 339
Rákospalota	4 331	5 453	2 728
Ujpest	3 238	6 524	2 712
Csepel	1 614	1 515	1 213
Pestujhely	792	1 072	482

The result in Budapest in percentages:

	1935	1939
Government party	26.0	33.1
Christian party	25.8	5.5
National Socialists	–	29.9
Liberals	19.0	16.4
Social Democratic party	22.3	12.7

The results of the elections in the country were much less characteristic of the actual balance of power. The Smallholders' party, the opposition group that had set up candidates in the largest number of constituencies, held their ground in their traditional districts, counties such as Bihar, Hajdu, Szatmár, in part of the «Stormy Corner» (in Southern Hungary), in the southern part of Pest County, etc., but suffered severe losses elsewhere. It is a remarkable phenomenon in this connection that in the constituencies where the Arrow Cross had not set up candidates, the Smallholders remained as a rule the strongest oppositionist party with a considerable number of votes; but where the Arrow Cross were competing with the Smallholders' party, the former scored second behind the government party in most cases and the Smallholders' had to put up with a smaller proportion of the votes. Also it was the Arrow Cross movement that profited from the oppositionist sentiment of the voters.

We may sum up the result of the elections in the provinces in the following manner:

1. The influence of the Arrow Cross party was considerable in territories near Budapest, mainly in the counties Pest, Fejér and Szolnok.

2. The party had an influence better than average in the most underdeveloped parts of the country, in the county of Szabolcs-Szatmár and the politically retrograde parts of Transdanubia.

3. At least the most surprising lesson was the great success of the Arrow Cross in the industrial and mining parts of the country, in countries like Veszprém, Nógrád and Komárom-Esztergom.

Summing up, we may point to three special features of the social basis of the Hungarian fascist mass movement.

1. The great number of plebeian and proletarian elements among the members, followers and supporters of this mass movement;

2. The characteristic fluctuations in party membership and support – the instability of the «popular» basis of fascism. As by the sudden and rapid rise of the movement, this instability is also illustrated by its rapid decline: in 1943 the number of Arrow Cross party-members sank to 1/3 and finally 1/4 of the 1939 figure.

3. The relatively minor proportion of convinced fascists in the movement. The social basis of the fascist movement – mainly between 1938–1940 – was large in Hungary. But the number of fanatical National Socialists who embraced the fascist ideology and firmly adhered to it, was in the Arrow Cross by no means as vast as suggested by the data cited above. The «fascism» of the large, pauperised masses who followed the Arrow Cross movement expressed an effort to solve urgent social problems, albeit in a confused way. In Hungary the main reason for the fascist mass movement lay not in the disillusionment of politically active masses with democracy. It was rather the result of the activation of the masses by an autocratic, anti-democratic regime; these people had to an overwhelming extent a low political consciousness and had until then been passive. This occurred under circumstances whereby the regime tolerated only rightist movements, and allowed the possibility of political activity to larger masses only in the direction of the right. All this does not imply underestimating the extent of retrograde, chauvinist and anti-Semitic infection of the masses which adhered – if only in a transient manner – to the Arrow Cross movement. It only means that after the defeat of fascism in Europe, the majority of these masses were ready to support other political tendencies which seemed able to solve the social conflicts which originally impelled them to turn to the extreme right. In this sense there were no real difficulties in the way of their integration into a democracy or a new social system. Their integration into the developing system was complicated, but not blocked, by fascist influences.

SOURCES AND LITERATURE

Home Office Archives. Trials of Ferenc Szálasi, Kálmán Hubay, László Endre, László Baky, Béla Imrédy eds.

Home Office Archives and National Archives. József Sombor-Schweinitzer: History of the Hungarian National Socialist Movement. (Manuscript.)

National Archives. The Diary of Szálasi.

Archives of the Institute for the History of the Communist Party. Summary Reports of the Gendarmerie 1937–1943.

National Archives. Parliamentary Archives 1935–1939. Records of elections.

György Ránki. «Reflections on the Social Base of the Counterrevolutionary Regime in the 1920's», in *Revue Historique* (Budapest), 1963. N° 3–4.

Miklós Lackó, *Arrow Cross Men, National Socialists. 1935–1944.* Budapest, 1966. 347 pages (Abridged version of this monograph is available in English in *Studia Historica.* Budapest, 1969. 112 pages.)

The Fascist Vote in Budapest in 1939

GYÖRGY RÁNKI

Despite various attempts at finding new sources of data on the Hungarian Arrow Cross movement other than the frequently used membership list of 1940, no new documentation has become available for research. The failure to obtain new direct evidence has prompted the search for indirect evidence. Such evidence has become available through the discovery of two very important sources in the Budapest municipal archives. The first is the results of the 1939 election, not only in the three main areas for which published data exist (Buda, Pest North, and Pest South), but in all the small voting districts, almost 320 in number. This election marked the pinnacle of Arrow Cross success. One of the reasons for this success was the fascists' ability to make a breakthrough even in the capital, where the parties of the left, either liberals or social democrats, had previously achieved significant successes.

The break-down of the electoral results of 1939 provides better insight into the behaviour and attitudes of the different social strata comprising the 14 administrative districts of the Hungarian Capital. Our task was made easier by the discovery in the same archives of election lists for all of the 320 districts of Budapest. The importance of these lists lies in the fact that they contain the names of the voters as well as voters' dates of birth and occupations. By comparing the structure and age groups of the electors with the results of the elections we may draw certain conclusions concerning those who voted for the fascist party.

First, we tried to ascertain in how many of the 14 administrative districts in Budapest the government attained a majority, and in how many the fascist or the left-wing parties came out strongest. Second, in each administrative district we chose one characteristic local area, mostly one which gave a majority to the Arrow Cross party, and tried to relate the results to the social structure. In this we encountered many difficulties. In the first place we are not certain whether we chose the voting districts correctly; furthermore, it may not be possible to draw truly meaningful conclusions by using only 10,000 names from a total of 280,000 which appear on the lists; and lastly, the determination of social composition is limited by the available data. Frequently it was not easy to assign the given occupation to any social class or stratum and for this reason our results are probably subject to correction.

In our scheme we tried to classify the electors into nine different classes:

The largest unit everywhere was the family. (We did not try to divide this unit despite the fact that in many cases the husband's occupation was given and there was thus a possibility to determine the social class of the women also).

The ruling class comprised the entrepreneurs, executive managers of companies, some landowners, generals of the army and some of the merchants. (The majority of the merchants were regarded as belonging to the middle class.)

The middle class was divided into four different sub-groups:

a. Small property owners, shopkeepers, artisans, petty bourgeoisie;
b. civil servants belonging to the state apparatus or to the city administration;

401

c. clerks, employees in business (white-collar workers);

d. professional people, intellectuals.

We do not think it is any argument against classifying small property owners as a special group that they are stratified internally and divided professionally, including as it does both rich merchants from the inner city and poor, marginal craftsmen from the outskirts.

Public and private employees were treated separately in accordance with Hungarian historical traditions, even though by doing so we subsumed under the same class scribes and ministerial secretaries, lower and higher ranking public functionaries, policemen and officers unable to advance beyond the rank of colonel. Public employees, when the modern Hungarian state apparatus was built, came to be dominated by the so-called gentry. These people, mostly from the ranks of the ancient nobility and impoverished landowners, after losing their wealth and income, sought to preserve their status and influence by occupying positions in the state apparatus, the rural administration and a good part of the city administration. On the one hand, they were not willing to enter into any other middle class grouping such as business or industry. On the other hand, the abundantly-created posts in the civil service became a thick network of gentry kinship. The rising members readily adopted the right-wing political ideas of the dominant gentry. While the public sector was dominated by the gentry from the turn of the century onward, the growing demand for clerks and officials in business was met by the Jewish middle class. In the inter-war period the share of Jews declined in proportion with the increase in the number of non-Jewish employees. Yet on the eve of World War II, over 50 per cent of business employees were still Jews.

Finally, even among professional people there were sharp differences between, for instance, the rich bourgeois solicitors in the city and the poor teachers in the outskirts.

With regard to the lower classes, we found it necessary to divide even the urban proletariat into three different groups.

In the first we placed workers in industry, regardless of whether they worked in small industries or in factories, and of whether their work was skilled or unskilled.

In the second group we put those who worked either in commerce or in transport. (The latter, belonging mostly to the public sector, was one of the hotbeds of the Arrow Cross movement in Budapest).

In the third sector we placed those labourers who composed a servant class like concierges, office messengers and domestic staff recruited chiefly among peasants looking for work in the city. In our view, this stratum belonged to the class of servants rather than to the proletariat. In the fourteen voting districts in which we tried to compare the distribution of the votes between the parties and the social composition of the voters, we found that workers were underrepresented: $6.6 + 2.3$ per cent vs. $6.9 + 2.6$ per cent.

Finally, in the three districts where the Arrow Cross party received over 35 per cent of the votes, industrial workers accounted for between 28 and 35 per cent of the total population. (Including other workers, the total was between 33 per cent and 50 per cent).

We may conclude that in most cases a positive correlation is found between the percentage of workers and the percentage of Arrow Cross votes. To account, however, for Arrow Cross influence, a positive correlation must have existed between Arrow Cross votes and other strata of the population as well.

If we consider the four districts where no proportional relationship between Arrow Cross influence and workers is to be found, i.e. where Arrow Cross votes are higher than the proportion of workers represented in the social composition of the district, we may draw the following conclusions: disregarding housewives (between 25 and 35 per cent) there are three districts in which the civil servants have a relative majority, (15 or 18 and 21 per cent), while in one district the petty bourgeoisie (minor artisans) have one (17 per cent). May we conclude that those were the other strata in which the social effects of the fascist movement made themselves felt?

Arrow Cross votes	Civil servants	Small businessmen
Under 15 per cent	4–16 per cent	3–16 per cent
15–25 per cent	7–15 per cent	4–17 per cent
25–35 per cent	2–21 per cent	6–13 per cent
Over 35 per cent	6– 8 per cent	6–11 per cent

These numbers indicate that no general correlation exists between four different groups according to the results achieved by the Arrow Cross party:

under 15 per cent: 3 districts
     15–25 per cent: 3 districts
     25–35 per cent: 5 districts
over 35 per cent: 3 districts

What are the characteristics of the three districts in which the Arrow Cross received less than 15 per cent of the votes (two of which were in Pest, one in Buda)? These are middle class or petty bourgeois districts with relatively large Jewish populations, together with the district of Buda, inhabited by high ranking civil servants. In all of these districts the Arrow Cross obtained under 3 per cent, in the other two between 10 and 15 per cent. Even taking workers in transport and commerce into consideration, the Arrow Cross share did not exceed 20 per cent. The same conclusion is valid also for the three districts with a proportion of Arrow Cross voters ranging from 15 to 25 per cent. In two districts, industrial workers amounted to about 5 per cent, with other workers even less than that. Only in one district did industrial workers reach 20 per cent of the total population.

Of the five districts where the size of the Arrow Cross vote was between 25 and 35 per cent, one was an overwhelmingly working class district with 51 per cent of the total population industrial workers plus 5 per cent of workers in other sectors; in the two other districts, workers were relatively important (20 or 25 per cent industrial workers in addition to 10 to 20 per cent of workers in trade and transport in each district). However, in two districts with 26.6 and 25.2 per cent Arrow Cross votes was a positive correlation between these two strata and Arrow Cross votes.

In some districts a rather large percentage of state employees and petty bourgeois voted for the fascists, but in many districts these strata supported other parties as well. The data have been split up.

A negative correlation could be traced between Arrow Cross votes and the number of white-collar business employees, intellectuals, and members of the ruling class (entrepreneurs, industrialists).

403

	Entre-preneurs	White collar workers	Profes-sionals
	per cent		
Districts with highest Arrow Cross votes	0.5–2	8–10	2–6
Districts with large (25–35 per cent) Arrow Cross votes	1–7	3–12	1–15
Moderate Arrow Cross votes	2–10	10	5–13
Arrow Cross votes less than 15 per cent	5–15	6–13	5–22

Let us consider another aspect of the election – the relationship between high Arrow Cross votes and votes for the most important parties:

Arrow Cross votes:	Social-democrats	Liberals	Government party
	per cent		
over 35 per cent	10–20	3–7	20–30
25–35 per cent	3–30	5–20	16–50
15–25 per cent	4–22	20–40	20–38
under 15 per cent	6–15	10–62	19–48

The correlation is not quite clear. However, one may conclude that as a rule, in the districts in which the Arrow Cross party was strongest, the liberals were at their weakest. More diverse is the correlation between the influence of the government party and the Arrow Cross men. Broadly speaking, those districts in which Arrow Cross influence was strongest did not always support the government as well. However, no negative correlation existed. In other words, the Arrow Cross and the government were both well supported. If there was any negative correlation it occurred in strong liberal districts. There the government party secured majorities whether or not the Arrow Cross obtained small or large support from the voters.

The showing of the Social Democrats essentially parallels that of the Arrow Cross. Where the Arrow Cross is weak so are the Social Democrats; where the Arrow Cross is on top, the Social Democrats are also stronger than in other districts. The Labour party is stronger in those districts where the Arrow Cross is also strong but not the strongest party.

This correlation is related to the social structure in the districts. Two districts with 25 to 35 per cent Arrow Cross votes had 17 to 30 per cent votes for Labour and in their social composition workers were very important. But there were two other districts in which 25 or 35 per cent of the votes went to fascists whereas only 3 per cent went to Social Democrats. However, in these districts (which were in Buda) workers were extremely underrepresented, since the majority of the inhabitants were either civil servants or white-collar workers or small businessmen.

This table shows that in those areas where workers represented only a small proportion of the residents, even the number of Labour (i.e. Social Democrat) votes was insignificant; however, in most of these very same districts the fascist party was

Voting districts with industrial workers	Arrow Cross	Social democrats	Liberals
	per cent		
less than 10 per cent	25.5	3.1	8.6
	6.5	11.0	62.0
	16.8	8.5	20.3
	19.8	4.1	21.5
	26.6	3.9	10.3
more than 10 per cent	11.2	5.9	10.4
	13.4	15.8	45.8
	29.4	22.2	19.6
	32.2	17.6	7.7
more than 25 per cent	35.0	17.4	7.0
	33.4	30.3	5.0
	36.1	19.2	2.6
	46.2	10.5	7.0
	28.6	21.4	21.4

supported by a rather large proportion of the inhabitants. On the whole, we may conclude that the workers' votes were almost evenly divided between the Labour and the Arrow Cross parties. But while the Social Democrats were not able to gain important support from other strata (except a few districts with mostly Jewish population) the Arrow Cross party was successful in appealing to different groups, especially civil servants, the lower middle class, artisans and the *lumpen* elements (domestic servants).

Some have maintained that fascism is basically a middle class movement. To be sure, its ideology was very attractive to the lower middle class suffering heavily from insecurity of income. There is no doubt that the party élite was composed of middle and lower middle class elements as well; but in its backing, working class elements must have had almost an equal role with the middle class if they were not actually in the majority.

Very likely a more detailed examination of the stratification of the working class would give more information concerning its distribution between the Arrow Cross and the Social Democrats. However, at this moment we are not able to conclude more than that in the traditional working-class areas the proportion between the two parties was more favourable to the Labour party than in the new industrial districts.

In the election campaign there was practically no difference between the party of the government and the Arrow Cross candidates concerning the condemnation of liberalism and social democracy. Politically, the government party was a right-wing party as well; however, its slogans concerning social problems were less radical, less anti-Semitic, more traditional.

In the fourteen districts in which we tried to examine the social composition of voters, we can compare the results of the Arrow Cross and the government party with the support gained by the Liberals and by the Social Democrats:

	Left wing	Right wing
	per cent	
Districts with large left-wing majority	73.0	20.5
	61.6	27.5
Districts with almost equal proportion	41.8	49.5
	48.8	39.4
	35.4	49.8
	42.8	49.2
Districts with right-wing majority	28.5	62.1
	17.2	69.8
	25.8	58.5
	16.9	59.6
	17.5	73.9
	29.9	54.1
	11.7	75.3
	21.8	61.4

In the two districts with a left-wing majority, the proportion of workers was relatively small (20 per cent, of which 12 per cent in industry, trade and transport) but in both districts the winner of the election was the Liberal party (with 46 and 62 per cent of the poll) partly owing to its petty bourgeois/upper middle class backing. The situation was the same in the third (Jewish) district where left-wing parties had a relative majority (workers less than 10 per cent compared with 8 per cent well-to-do businessmen, 17 per cent small businessmen, 13 per cent professionals, 10 per cent business employees). The heavy losses of the left-wing parties to the right-wing, disregarding other important factors, could be explained by the fact that Liberals were totally unsuccessful in winning working class support; in the middle class or petty bourgeois areas, the Social Democrats were not able to compete either with the government or with the Arrow Cross party. It is certainly true that the government party did not enjoy much support from the working class.

Per cent workers in district	Votes for government party
3 districts with 30–40 per cent workers	20 per cent (2) 27 per cent (1)
1 district with 40–50 per cent workers	25 per cent (1)
1 district with more than 50 per cent workers	16 per cent (1)

Or, presenting the same data in another way:

Votes for government	Percentage of the workers
More than 30 per cent /1 district/	6
more than 40 per cent /2 districts/	9 or 17
more than 50 per cent /1 district/	9

These data confirm that the right-wing parties were able to win the election in Budapest for two obvious reasons: 1. Because they were able to gather considerable support, even if not a majority, among the working class; 2. with the exception of the Jewish sector, the Arrow Cross party was able to reach almost every stratum of the population. If we compare the results of this election with the election of 1935, it is quite apparent that the Arrow Cross party must have won votes partly among former non-voters (number of voters in 1935, 250,000, in 1939, 360,000).

But a more important source of increase may be examined: a proportion of those formerly voting for the Social Democratic party. The loss of votes was very heavy in the case of this party. The Social Democrats obtained roughly 55,000 votes (22.5 per cent of total number of votes cast) in 1935; in 1939 it only secured 35,000 votes, roughly 10 per cent of the total poll. If we had examined only the number of votes, the defeat of the Labour party would not have been so serious, taking into account that the so-called Catholic party lost almost 50,000 votes (64,000 or 25.8 per cent in 1935 as against 13,000 or 4 per cent in 1939). But the Catholic party belonged to the traditional right wing which had always been heavily supported by civil servants, artisans and lower middle-class elements. It is very likely that some of its former supporters switched to the Government party whose net again amounted to 31,000 new votes. Another sector definitely stronger in Pest than in Buda now supported the Arrow Cross party. This party, almost unrepresented in 1935 (0.6 per cent of the votes), gained 72,000 votes, or 20 per cent of the total votes cast in this election. The Liberals were able to preserve their numerical strength at 47,000 votes; this represented 19 per cent in 1935 and only 13 per cent in 1939.

Among the lower middle-class voting behaviour was influenced by feelings of deprivation, insecurity of income and discrepancies between status, prestige and income. In this stratum, voting behaviour was also influenced by religion and traditional political attachment. A prestige hierarchy was based on religious or ethnic differences as well; especially in Hungary where anti-Semitism had been part of the official government policy since 1919. It especially affected Budapest where 20 per cent of the inhabitants were Jews. Among them, even the relatively well-to-do were politically less conservative than their non-Jewish fellows of the same social group. The inferior status and position of the Jews induced them to back, in the case of the working class elements, the Labour party and in that of the middle-class – whether higher or lower – the Liberal party. It is almost certain that no Jews supported the Arrow Cross party or, with the possible exception of «top people», the Government party either. Thus, the Arrow Cross and the government (the former more than the latter) were able to gain support among the workers and the middle-class because of their anti-Semitic statements aimed at discrediting «Jewish parties», these denunci-ations having a basis of truth in them inasmuch as upper middle-class Jewish votes did go to the Liberals, while non-Jewish ones went to the Government party. Such propaganda was also effective with the lower middle class which in fact backed the Arrow Cross primarily because of the party's slogans directed against Jews and Jewish capitalism.

It is entirely justifiable to ask the question whether this drastic change in the electoral pattern may be accounted for by changes in the political atmosphere in Europe in general or in Hungary in particular. Probably it is attributable not only to stratification but to the change in composition of age groups among the voters as well. It was a rather well known fact in Hungary that among the younger generation educated in the traditional conservative educational institutions, left-wing ideas did not spread very easily. Taking the same 14 voting districts, we tried to draw conclusions based on the correlation between electoral results and the age structure of the voters. This attempt failed, however, to provide conclusive data. A reading of the press and the literature tends to reveal the young voters' preferences for the fascist party. The results arrived at through our own analysis are not reliable enough either to support or to disprove this impression.

For example let us compare two districts. In the first one, the Arrow Cross party received 46 per cent of the votes; in the second just 6.5 per cent.

	I	II
	per cent	
Voters over 50 years	36.4	40.8
Voters between 40–50	25.5	30.8
Voters between 30–40	28.1	22.8
Voters under 30 years	10.0	5.6

One might argue that in the second group the average age of the voters was certainly higher. But the differences – 38 per cent under 40 years in one case and 28 per cent under 40 years in the other case – are not large enough to account for the striking differences of 6 vs. 46 per cent. Even if we were to disregard the two extreme poles and take into account districts with moderate discrepancies instead, our results remain just as disputable. Let us take case No. III and No. IV: in district No. IV Arrow Cross gained 13 per cent, in No. III 36 per cent of the votes.

	III	IV
over 50 years	29.6	30.0
between 40–50	26.8	26.8
between 30–40	32.5	31.7
under 30	11.1	11.5

The two age group compositions are almost the same. Further analysis of other districts is also not helpful. Although the old hypothesis that younger people voted for the fascist party more often than the older ones did might still be valid, our research did not bring up any new arguments or data to support this thesis.

Our examination enabled us to draw some conclusions from the correlation between social composition and results but even these conclusions were premature because of various other factors influencing the voters' behaviour were left out. It is well known that in the same social group, family tradition, political tradition, security of livelihood, effects of religion are important factors determining the voters' behaviour. In the working class more highly skilled workers with greater job satisfaction, creativity, and class consciousness were in favour of the Labour party; unskilled workers expressed their discontent by voting for fascists.

Working on the material – recently found in the Municipial Archives of Budapest – we were not able to correlate the social composition of the 14 boroughs or districts of Budapest with the election results. Our method – partly due to lack of time was also defective because the analysis of 300,000 names and occupations would have required the use of a computer, which was not available for this study. However, for the purpose of getting some rough idea of the voting behaviour of the 14 large districts comprising 320 voting areas, we were able to use general statistical information concerning the occupation of flat-tenants in 1940 in every administrative district of the capital. It is almost certain that discrepancies do exist between this grouping and ours because we did not know what classification criteria were used in the former. But in spite of this difficulty we have ventured upon rough comparison between social composition and proportion of voters in the 14 administrative districts of the capital with a view to spotting any correlation that might exist.

Social structure of the administrative districts

	I	II	III	XI	XII	IV	V	VI	VII	VIII	IX	X	XIII	XIV
Ruling classes	5.0	4.2	2.2	3.4	3.5	6.8	4.2	3.2	1.8	1.7	1.2	1.0	0.7	2.4
Artisan shopkeepers	8.7	9.1	7.5	7.7	7.6	24.7	17.9	15.9	19.7	17.0	11.7	5.6	7.4	9.3
Professional people	3.8	4.6	1.2	2.6	3.1	7.8	8.3	4.3	2.3	2.2	1.2	0.6	0.4	1.2
Employees	14.2	15.1	7.6	13.9	12.9	12.3	21.0	13.2	9.1	8.5	8.8	5.9	5.1	8.9
Civil servants	33.0	30.6	12.6	31.6	36.5	19.5	14.7	12.5	9.7	16.8	15.7	12.3	4.6	16.3
Industrial workers	12.8	15.2	45.3	20.6	16.6	10.9	12.2	23.7	29.4	39.6	33.4	50.4	58.4	36.1
Tradesmen	1.6	1.6	2.2	2.1	1.4	3.2	5.1	6.7	7.3	6.0	3.1	1.9	2.6	2.9
Other workers & servants/	8.9	7.8	12.4	11.9	11.4	3.6	4.6	6.3	6.6	7.3	9.5	14.0	12.2	16.2

Result of 1939 election

District	Government party	Social-Democrats	Liberals	Arrow Cross
		per cent		
I.	48.6	3.3	12.1	23.5
II.	39.6	5.0	16.8	24.1
III.	31.2	13.1	0.9	33.2
XI.	44.6	5.1	9.0	27.5
XII.	43.7	4.1	10.6	26.7
IV.	37.0	5.4	24.8	19.9
V.	24.5	7.4	42.2	15.6
VI.	21.7	13.8	33.0	19.8
VII.	23.4	18.1	26.6	21.3
VIII.	31.8	14.3	14.8	25.7
IX.	32.5	11.2	8.09	28.3
X.	37.4	14.2	3.5	29.4
XIII.	26.8	20.8	20.2	21.8
XIV.	35.2	13.6	8.2	29.6

District I [Buda] (8 voting areas)

Characteristics of social composition: residential area of upper middle class, aristocracy, civil servants, rather high share of servant classes; Jewish population: 6.4 per cent.

	Government party	Arrow Cross	Liberals
Winner	8	–	–
2nd place	–	7	1
3rd place	–	1	7

District II [Buda] (21 voting areas)

Characteristics of social composition: very wealthy area, upper and upper middle classes, bourgeoisie, civil servants; 10.5 per cent Jewish population.

	Government party	Arrow Cross	Liberals	Social-Democrats	National Front /Fascist party/
Winner	20	1	–	–	–
2nd place	1	15	4	1	–
3rd place	–	4	12	3	2

District III [Buda] (11 voting areas)

Characteristics of social composition: poor area; 50 per cent working class, intellectuals with low income, civil servants with low income, high share of German elements (Swabian), low income artisans; Jerwish population 9.2 per cent.

	Government party	Arrow Cross	Social-Democrats	Liberals
Winner....................	5	6	–	–
2nd place....................	6	5	–	–
3rd place	–	–	8	3

District V [Pest] (27 voting areas)

Characteristics of social composition: upper middle class, well-to-do businessmen, intellectuals (lawyers), better-off white-collar (business employees); Jewish residential areas (37 per cent Jews).

	Liberals	Government party	Arrow Cross	Social-Democrats
Winner:	24	3	–	–
2nd place....................	–	23	3	1
3rd place	2	–	16	9

District XIII [Pest] (20 voting areas)

Traditional working-class areas, skilled workers, artisans, low paid white-collar, slums; Jewish population: 8 per cent.

	Government party	Arrow Cross	Social-Democrats
Winner	12	5	3
2nd place	5	10	5
3rd place.............................	3	5	12

District VI [Pest] (31 voting areas)

Characteristics of social composition: Jewish petty bourgeois residential areas, Jewish small businessmen (merchants and artisans), high share of workers in trade and in handicraft; Jewish population 39.3 per cent.

	Liberals	Government party	Arrow Cross	Social-Democrats
Winner	24	4	3	–
2nd place	2	16	10	3
3rd place	4	8	14	5

District VII [Pest] (39 voting areas)

Characteristics of social composition: Jewish working-class and petty bourgeois area; workers in trade and in handicraft, artisans, white-collars; Jewish population 43 per cent.

	Liberals	Government party	Arrow Cross	Social-Democrats
Winner	20	13	5	1
2nd place	3	10	16	10
3rd place	9	7	11	12

District XI [Buda] (24 voting areas)

Characteristics of social composition: more middle-class core than upper middle class, high share of civil servants, white-collars, some new working class areas; Jewish population 7.2 per cent.

	Government party	Arrow Cross	Liberals	Social-Democrats	Christian opposition
Winner	23	1	–	–	–
2nd place	1	23	–	–	–
3rd place	–	–	19	4	1

412

District XII [Buda] (19 voting areas)

Characteristics of social composition: very rich residential areas, upper classes (industrialists, entrepreneurs), high ranking civil servants, large share of servants (gardeners); Jewish population 7.6 per cent.

	Government party	Arrow Cross	Christian opposition	Liberals	National Front
Winner	17	2	–	–	–
2nd place	2	16	1	–	–
3rd place	–	1	–	17	1

District IV [Pest] (10 voting areas)

Characteristics of social composition: the City, business area, merchants and artisans with high income, aristocracy, industrialists, well-to-do intellectuals and white-collar workers; Jewish population 18.3 per cent.

	Government party	Liberals	Arrow Cross
Winner	6	4	–
2nd place	4	2	4
3rd place	–	4	6

District XIV [Pest] (23 voting areas)

Characteristics of social composition: new residential area; artisans, workers, civil servants, small businessmen; Jewish population 12.3 per cent.

	Government party	Arrow Cross	Liberals	Social-Democrats	National Front	Christian National independent
Winner	17	6	–	–	–	–
2nd place	6	14	3	–	–	–
3rd place	–	3	8	10	1	1

District VIII [Pest] (42 voting areas)

Characteristics of social composition: special mixture of working class and petty bourgeois residential area. Inner part civil servants, outer part Jewish small businessmen, employees and non-Jewish workers and artisans. Jewish inhabitants 21.5 per cent.

	Arrow Cross	Government party	Liberals	Social-Democrats
Winner:	9	28	4	1
2nd place.....................	26	10	4	2
3rd place	7	1	18	16

District IX [Pest] (29 voting areas)

Characteristics of social composition: large part of working class new-comers, without Labour movement tradition, small property owners, artisans with low income, politically right wing; Jewish population 12 per cent.

	Government party	Arrow Cross	Social-Democrats	Liberal	Christian Independent
Winner	17	11	1	–	–
2nd place	10	16	–	1	2
3rd place	1	1	13	10	4

District X [Pest] (24 voting areas)

Characteristics of social composition: Working class areas, food and textile industry, artisans, civil servants: Jewish population low, 5.5 per cent.

	Government party	Arrow Cross	National Front	Social-Democrats
Winner.......................	16	8	–	–
2nd place.....................	7	14	2	1
3rd place	1	2	3	18

On the whole the Government party won in 190 districts. Of these, 74 were located in Buda, 116 in Pest. The Arrow Cross party dominated 59 areas: 10 in Buda, 49 in Pest. The Liberals were successful in 76 areas, all in Pest. The Social Democrats gained the plurality in 6 sectors, all in Pest.

Winner in percentage of voting districts

	Buda	Pest	Altogether
Government party..........................	88	47	57
Arrow Cross	12	20	18
Liberals.....................................	–	31	23
Social Democrats	–	2	2
	100	100	100

Taking into account that the Arrow Cross party received 50 per cent more votes than the Liberals, it might seem surprising that the Liberals received majorities in more districts. However, this is the same phenomenon to which we have already made reference; namely that the Liberals had strong support in some areas and were absolutely unsuccessful in others, while the fascist party was strong everywhere. This important difference shows up clearly if we consider the distribution of second places as well.

Second place in percentage of voting districts

	Buda	Pest	Altogether
Government party..........................	12.1	38.2	32.2
Arrow Cross	79.5	45.4	52.8
Liberals.....................................	6.0	6.0	6.5
Social Democrats	1.2	8.8	6.8
Other	1.2	1.6	1.7
	100.0	100.0	100.0

Who, then, voted for the fascists in Budapest in 1939 and who did not? If we view the question according to districts, we may reinforce our earlier conclusion. Generally, we might say that the Arrow Cross party was more successful in the poor districts. In Buda, the upper and upper middle-class residential, district III, (Altofen), an industrial area, brought success to the Arrow Cross party. In Pest, the Arrow Cross had little influence in the two rich districts (IV and VI). In working-class areas (district XIII and district X) they were more successful, but while in the Labour movement's stronghold, district XIII, they were able to break more or less even with the Labour party, in district X their influence was overwhelming against Social Democrat opposition. In the petty bourgeois areas with lower income groups, Arrow Cross ranked second behind the Government party (districts XIV and IX). In previous elections these districts supported the Christian party. In districts where a Jewish population was significant and where the Liberals had deeper roots (districts VI and VII), the Arrow Cross was unsuccessful. To conclude: deeper analysis of the 1939 election results seems both to reinforce and offer more convincing support for some previous hypotheses regarding the social roots of Hungarian fascism. It rejects the validity of two extreme views, one regarding fascism as a typical middle-class movement and the other interpreting it as particularly apt to appeal to working-class elements. The comparison of election results and social components, as far as the data allow conclusions, tends to show that the Hungarian Arrow Cross party had a very specific support.

By adapting many of its popular slogans from traditional counter-revolutionary right-extreme nationalism, anti-Semitism, anti-urbanism and anti-capitalism, the Arrow Cross was successful in gaining the support of discontented middle-class elements – gentry, army officers, bureaucrats on the one hand, and artisans and small businessmen with uncertain economic roots on the other. Had the Arrow Cross party restricted its disseminating activities to those strata alone, it would have been hardly more successful politically than the former Christian Social or Catholic parties had been. The success of the Arrow Cross was based on the adaptation of all the ideas of its predecessors and on pursuit of a very active and very aggressive anti-capitalistic campaign aimed at winning the support of at least parts of the working class. Its hard, revolutionary-like methods and its new élite successfully fused the two varieties of anti-capitalism, that from above and that from below.

In Budapest, with its social structure and its authoritarian political system, the success of the Arrow Cross would have been impossible had its activity or influence been limited to winning over either the middle-class or the unorganized workers alone.

PART 5

THE DIFFUSION OF FASCISM IN SOUTHERN AND WESTERN EUROPE

Stanley G. Payne	Introduction
Stanley G. Payne	Social Composition and Regional Strength of the Spanish Falange
Philippe C. Schmitter	The Social Origins, Economic Bases and Political Imperatives of Authoritarian Rule in Portugal
Beat Glaus	The National Front in Switzerland
Zeev Sternhell	Strands of French Fascism
Luc Schepens	Fascists and Nationalists in Belgium, 1919–1940
Daniéle Wallef	The Composition of Christus Rex
Herman van der Wusten and Ronald E. Smit	Dynamics of the Dutch National Socialist Movement (the NSB): 1931–1935
John D. Brewer	The British Union of Fascists: Some Tentative Conclusions on its Membership
Maurice Manning	The Irish Experience: The Blueshirts
Yannis Andricopoulos	The Power Base of Greek Authoritarianism

Introduction

STANLEY G. PAYNE

With the major exception of Spain, the politics and society of inter-war Western Europe offer much less substance for the study of fascistic parties and their following than do Central and East Central Europe. The reasons for this are not mysterious. In general, fascist movements enjoyed success only in countries experiencing status deprivation or humiliation and/or grave problems of national identity and cohesion. The largely industrialized states of the West, either victorious or neutral in the war, were satisfied powers during the two decades following Versailles. Their dominant international position coincided with either an advanced degree of industrialization or mature commercial and financial status (except for the economically marginal regions of Spain, Portugal and Ireland). They were, with the same exceptions, already among the handful of happy states to have achieved functional and relatively balanced liberal democracy, almost equally immune from revolutionary left or reactionary right. Hence it is not difficult to understand why the diverse fascistic parties of Western Europe failed to mobilize any significant portion of their respective societies.

The initial problem involved in talking about diverse «fascist» parties, i.e., whether or not there really existed a common identity and if so, how it may be defined, has still not been resolved. This is a problem not merely for scholars, but was also a dilemma for Italian fascists themselves when they began to promote the notion of international fascism in the early 1930s and then had to identify precisely which kindred movements in other countries were truly or generically «fascist».[1] One of the few scholars to have given us a serious working definition is Ernst Nolte, whose «fascist minimum» posited the following characteristics:[2]

> Anti-Communism
> Anti-Liberalism
> Anti-Conservatism
> Leadership Principle
> Party Army
> Aim of Totalitarianism

The problem here is that this constitutes primarily a typology of German National Socialism and its imitators, and cannot identify or include most of the political groups commonly considered «fascist». Indeed, it cannot even include the Italian National Fascist party during its formative period of 1919–24, when significant sectors of the party were neither altogether anti-liberal, anti-conservative, proponents of the *Führerprinzip* nor aiming at «totalitarianism».

This has led scholars such as Karl D. Bracher and Renzo de Felice to suggest that in fact we have no topic to study, that generic European fascism cannot be categorically identified on a comparative basis. As against this extremely nominalistic position, we are still left with the evident reality that a new kind or kinds of radical nationalism emerged in Europe during the inter-war period, manifested itself in almost every country and exhibited characteristics that did not fully exist either before or after the 1919–1945 period.

The common distinguishing characteristics of these groups may perhaps be most clearly identified in terms of three major aspects: their common negations, their common ideological principles and goals, and their common features of style and organization.[3] Groups that may be identified as generically fascist were all anti-communist, and also largely (though not in every case exclusively) anti-liberal, as well as being relatively anti-conservative (though usually more willing to compromise at least to some extent initially with rightist organizations and principles).

They aimed at the creation of a new nationalist authoritarian state not merely based on traditional rightist principles or models, and proposed to achieve some sort of new multi-class integrated economic structure, whether more or less strongly controlled by the state and whether called corporatist, national socialist or national syndicalist. They aspired to empire or at least a radical change in the nation's relationship to other powers, and specifically espoused a philosophy and epistemology that was idealistic (in the metaphysical sense), vitalist, non-rationalist or non-positivistic, voluntarist and not primarily grounded in traditional religious culture.

They struggled to achieve mass mobilization, attended by the militarization of political relationships and style, with the goal of a mass party militia. They emphasized the aesthetic structure of meetings, symbols and political choreography, stressing romantic and/or mystical aspects. The principle of youth was given inordinate importance, and there was a specific tendency toward an authoritarian, charismatic style of command, together with a positive philosophical evaluation of violence (not merely a practical willingness to use it). Such a description of salient characteristics may provide the working outline of a criterial definition of fascist movements that makes it possible to identify clearly the groups in Western Europe that properly belong to such a genus, while avoiding confusion either with the revolutionary left or the radical bourgeois or traditionalist right.

If none of the West European fascist groups ever achieved major importance, Zeev Sternhell in his essay in this volume reminds us that the ideological constituents of generic fascism were more directly present in France than in Italy at the time that World War I began. Elsewhere he has pointed out that, just as the ideas of revolutionary socialism, communism and anarchism were first voiced in France, the major constituents of a kind of pre-fascism appeared in France in the wake of the defeat of 1871, when status deprivation, an atmosphere of domestic political malaise and the growing economic problems of the lower middle classes gave momentary bouyancy to the Boulanger movement in the 1880s.[4] The latter was a political novelty, altogether precocious for its time. In post-World War I France, however, the major social, economic and political incentives for fascism were either weak or missing. The numerous attempts to form a French fascism are more a tribute to the variety and imagination of French politics than to the political support or effectiveness enjoyed by their protagonists.

Some students of comparative fascist movements have suggested that the genus may be divided into two general subtypes, the Central European or German, and the Southwest European or Italian.[5] According to this interpretation, a distinction may be drawn *grosso modo* between the radical, fanatical, hyperviolent and anti-Semitic fascism of the Nazis and some of their imitators in Eastern and Northern Europe who were little interested in social and economic development, when compared with the more moderate, practical and «modernizing» fascism of Italy and some of the fascist movements of Southwestern Europe, particularly in Spain and France. The latter were not racist, somewhat more objective and instrumental in their outlook, and seriously concerned with issues of modern development and transformation.

There is something to be said for this «two faces of fascism» approach, so long as the interpretation remains cautious and flexible and is not made into an exclusive mold. Some of the major West European fascist movements were indeed concerned with economic modernization and the transformation of a new society in practical terms, as in the cases of the Spanish Falange, and several of the major French groups (those of Déat and Doriot) and also Mosley's British fascists. However, some of the latter were also racist and anti-Semitic, so that only certain general tendencies rather than a clear-cut differential typology can be distinguished.

If West European fascist groups in various ways exhibited dissimilar features, one common limitation, with only a few exceptions, was the difficulty they had in mobilizing support outside the middle classes. This is repeatedly borne out by the several case studies that follow. No significant West European fascist movement was able to sustain for any period of time the approximately 30 per cent worker support of Nazism in 1933 or the overall 40 per cent worker-peasant membership of both the Italian and German parties in the last phase of the struggle for power. The other general social characteristic that they all had in common (and with all other fascist movements) was generational: they all made a vigorous and primary appeal to the young and drew a disproportionate amount of their support from men under 30.

The limitations on the capacity of fascist movements to mobilize social support in France also obtained in most other parts of Western Europe. The nature of and limitations on fascist social mobilization in advanced democracies such as Holland and Switzerland are analyzed in the studies by Herman van der Wusten and Beat Glaus. In Ireland, a new polity was just being established during the 1920s and 30s, yet the social pressures of radical politics on the European continent were largely absent. In his study of the Irish Blueshirts, Maurice Manning demonstrates that the true form and content of fascism was basically lacking.

The case of Belgium might seem an exception, for there the two principal putative fascist parties, the Walloon Rexists and the Flemish VNV, together polled more than 17 per cent of the popular vote in the 1936 elections. If the Rexists seem to have relied primarily on the French-speaking middle classes, there is some indication that the VNV drew more grass roots support from some of the ordinary agrarian population and from workers. Yet here some questions should be asked, the chief of which is whether or not either the Rexists or the VNV had really developed into full-scale fascist movements by 1936, or whether they did not still function as more conservative Catholic nationalist movements in Walloon and Flemish society. The more radical and identifiably fascist Verdinaso movement of van Severen proved much less successful in electoral mobilization. Moreover, the Rexist-VNV vogue began to pass as quickly as it had come, and support had waned considerably by late 1937. Only after this point did the two groups develop the full radical doctrines and characteristics of what has been defined above as generic fascism. The studies by Luc Schepens and Daniéle Wallef effectively demonstrate the ambiguities and limitations of both the fascist identity and the social support of the putatively fascist movements in Belgium. Moreover, Mlle Wallef indicates that to the extent that the Rexist movement progressively moved toward a specific fascist identity it proportionately lost its initial support and even its parliamentary representation.

Western Europe may be considered a unit in terms of geography and religion, and also in terms of formal culture, but not in terms of social and economic structure, at least until recently. If there has been a cultural and religious dividing line between Western and Eastern Europe (somewhere east of Germany), there is another dividing line of social structure and economic development that has cut north and south, and has separated Spain and Portugal from the rest of Western Europe for the past 300 years. If most of Western Europe was politically too stable and experienced and economically too advanced to be seriously tempted by fascism, somewhat the opposite might supposedly be said for Spain and Portugal. The fact of the matter was, however, that fascist movements in Spain and Portugal drew even less ordinary political support than did their counterparts in France and Belgium. This may at least in part be explained by examining certain apparent pre-conditions for fascism. These seem to include a sizable lower middle class that is at least partially secularized, an open competitive political system that permits mobilization, and strong currents of nationalism. In one way or another, these factors did not obtain in Spain and Portugal.

Moreover, the historical importance of fascism has tended to obscure what were two important new authoritarian anti-leftist forces in inter-war Europe: radical fascism proper and what, for lack of a better definition, may be called the «new right» (or modern twentieth-century authoritarian right). The new right paralleled fascism in a stress on authoritarianism and opposition to liberalism and the left. Unlike fascism it was not anti-conservative save in its opposition to moderate constitutional or legalistic conservatism. Its orientation in political economy was toward corporatism, but it used corporatism primarily to reinforce the existing social forces and rejected the radical proposals for social change made by fascist national syndicalists and national socialists. The new right in its philosophy tended toward official piety and established religion, rejecting the vitalism, anti-clericalism and Nietzscheanism of the fascists. The new right had little hope of radical mass mobilization – always the fascists' goal – and relied much more on established élites and the support of the military. Forces of the new right emerged in the 1920s and 30s in most European countries, but were strongest in the socially and economically backward lands of Southern and Eastern Europe, where the older social sectors and élites retained greater influence and the new radical social forces were least developed. The new authoritarian regimes created in Spain, Portugal and Greece were basically the work of military and civilian sectors of the new right. Only that in Spain had a significant organizational component of fascism.

Philippe Schmitter's study presents a great deal of new information about the formation of the new élite structure of the corporatist *Estado Novo* in Portugal. It also makes clear that the new Portuguese regime was basically a right-wing conservative system that repressed mobilization and maintained the status quo. The only specifically fascist movement in Portugal. Rolão Preto's «National Syndicalists» of 1932–35, was ultimately eliminated by the Salazar regime itself, which drew a categorical distinction between right-wing pro-Catholic corporatism and radical, secular fascism.

Greece in some ways resembled Portugal because of the rural, highly familial, emigration- and clientage-oriented qualities of its society. Neither country had experienced full-scale mass political mobilization by the 1930s and in both the predominant role was frequently played by the military. The Greek and Portuguese revolts of 1909–10 may be said to represent the climax of nineteenth-century liberal South European praetorianism, ushering in major new liberal reforms. After World War I, a growing reaction in the direction of right authoritarianism occurred among sectors of

421

the military in both countries, and the new dictatorships in both countries were established in the first instance by generals, not caesaristic fascist leaders. The movement toward a new military-led right authoritarianism in Greece is narrated in the paper by Yannis Andricopoulos.

Spain was not so backward and ultra-conservative as much of Portuguese society, but it was singularly wanting in nationalist fervor (compared with such disparate countries as France, Italy or Greece). Its middle classes largely preferred conservative Catholicism to radical, secular fascism. Faced in 1936 with the first major breakthrough of the revolutionary left in twentieth-century Europe, they rallied round a conservative counter-revolutionary general. Significant structural similarities did exist between the Mussolini and Franco regimes in the years 1937–43, but one of the main differences was the absence of a major fascist movement in Spain, since the Falange had never won strong independent support on its own.

Thus in Southwestern Europe, as in other parts of Southern and Eastern Europe, the new authoritarian systems that had developed by 1940 were essentially syncretic, semi-pluralist, rigtht-wing corporate systems rather than radical new fascist systems. The new right corporatist regimes of Salazar, Franco and Pétain either directly repressed domestic fascists, as in Portugal, encouraged their emigration, as under Vichy, or thoroughly subordinated them to an authoritarian state that was at best only semi-fascist, as in the case of Spain. Unlike Pétain's Vichy system, neither the Franco nor the Salazar regimes were a product of World War II. Both survived for many years after the war because the passing of the so-called «fascist era» at first held only limited implications for them; one had never been specifically fascist while the other moved progressively to divest itself of most – though not all – of its fascistic accoutrements.

NOTES

[1] Cf. Michael Ledeen, *Universal Fascism* (New York, 1972), and Renzo de Felice, *Mussolini il Duce* (Turin, 1974), 872–919.

[2] Ernst Nolte, *Die Krise des liberalen Systems und die faschistischen Bewegungen* (Munich, 1968).

[3] It should be pointed out that the utility of the triadic structure in the definition of fascism was emphasized by Juan J. Linz at the Bergen conference in June, 1974.

[4] Zeev Sternhell, «Paul Déroulède and the Origins of Modern French Nationalism», *Journal of Contemporary History*, 6:4 (Oct., 1971), 46–71.

[5] Eugen Weber, *Varieties of Fascism* (New York, 1962); Wolfgang Sauer, «National Socialism: Totalitarianism or Fascism?», *American Historical Review*, 73:2 (Dec., 1967), 404–24; and Alan Cassels, *Fascism* (New York, 1974).

Social Composition and Regional Strength of The Spanish Falange

STANLEY G. PAYNE

Generic fascism in Spain was originally the product of the radical intelligentsia. The common denominators of the ten young men who formed the first fascistic association in Madrid early in 1931 were youth (all were in their twenties) and a background as students at the University of Madrid. All those whose social background was identifiable came from various strata of the middle classes.[1] The title of their weekly organ, *La Conquista del Estado*, was derived from an Italian fascist journal, but their doctrine was dubbed «national syndicalism» (also of course, originally formulated by Italian fascists), and they completely eschewed the use of the term «fascist». The subsequent JONS (Juntas de Ofensiva Nacional-Sindicalista), organized in October 1931, was composed of two tiny nuclei: the Madrid circle of radical nationalist middle-class university or post-university youth, led by the young intellectual and white-collar postal employee Ramiro Ledesma Ramos,[2] and an almost equally exiguous provincial group led by the lawyer and nationalist ideologue Onésimo Redondo Ortega in Valladolid. Though the Valladolid sector relied primarily on a small following among provincial middle-class youth at the University of Valladolid, Redondo also represented small farming interests as organizer and promotor of a smallholder syndicate of *remolacheros* (sugar beet growers) in León and Old Castile, a smallfarmer pressure group somewhat analogous to the *betteravier* interests in France.

The most direct parallel between the two sectors of *jonsismo* was their common reliance on a radical nationalist (mostly middle class) student intelligentsia for support. Ledesma's Madrid group harped on the theme of revolutionary national syndicalism and made one of its strongest appeals to the CNT, the anarcho-syndicalist worker confederation, espousing vague goals of economic revolution and seeking to nationalize Spanish anarchism just as some sectors of Italian anarchism had gone nationalist between 1911 and 1922. This effort was a total failure despite the sometimes strident economic-revolutionary tones of Ledesma's propaganda. Spanish anarchism could not be nationalized since genuine Spanish nationalism even among the middle classes ranged from feeble to non-existent. *Jonsismo* remained primarily a radical movement of a few hundred university and secondary school students.

The tonality of Valladolid *jonsismo* was considerably different, for it remained rooted in lower-middle class provincial Catholicism, largely eschewing socioeconomic radicalism. Redondo's appeal to healthy rural and peasant interests as opposed to the decadence of the cities and the seduced and debauched urban workers paralleled the fascist appeal to the peasantry in other countries, but differed in its extreme religiosity, which gave it a strong traditionalist tinge. However, the Valladolid group drew only the most marginal support from provincial society and continued to rely mainly on its small university nucleus.

Falange Española

The origins of the main fascist group, Falange Española, in October 1933, can be traced to a somewhat different background. By 1933 the honeymoon period of left-liberal Spanish Republicanism had ended, several para-revolutionary offensives had been launched against state and society by the anarchosyndicalists, and the mass Socialist party was beginning to withdraw from semi-reformist parliamentary collaboration toward a posture of increasing «bolshevization», as they themselves termed it *(bolchevización)*. To this had been added the passage of a statute of partial regional autonomy for Catalonia, the effect of which was not to pacify but to radicalize Catalan regional nationalism, while a similar movement developed on a more narrow base in the Basque country. By mid-1933 a reaction had begun to take place among middle- and upper-class society against the influence of anti-clericalism, social revolutionary agitation and the threat to national unity. Its chief protagonist was a new movement of middle-class political Catholicism, the CEDA (Confederación Española de Derechas Autónomas), which in many ways paralleled the program, base of support and political ambiguities of the Austrian Christian Social party. In the elections of November 1933, the CEDA emerged as the largest single party in Spain, adopting an ambivalent semi-collaborationist, semi-oppositionist policy toward the Republican political system. The CEDA functioned as a normal political movement, eschewing street violence. Nonetheless, like the more radical movements it had its own green-shirted youth which symbolized the party's inherent ambiguity by adopting a half-fascist salute that only extended the right arm at a right angle from the shoulder. CEDA spokesmen espoused a vague sort of corporative reorganization of Spain's government and economy and were universally denounced by the left as the chief movement of «Spanish fascism». However, given the party's devotion to parliamentary tactics and legality, together with their general timidity of doctrine and style, perhaps the best interpretation has been given by Ricardo de la Cierva: «Gil Robles and his movement were not fascist, but on occasion they were affected – sometimes intensely – by the vertigo of fascism».[3]

For a very few proponents of the upper-class extreme right and nationalist élitism, this was not enough. Such elements coalesced around José Antonio Primo de Rivera, eldest son of the former dictator, who had determined to extend and complete his father's attempt at the regeneration of Spain by an organized form of integrative radical nationalist authoritarianism that would replace the parliamentary system and coordinate social and economic interests. Money for such a movement – conspicuously lacking in the case of the radical and obscure *jonsistas* – was at least momentarily available from certain sectors of high finance. Several key figures interested in the promotion of a «Spanish fascism» met in San Sebastian in August 1933, apparently in the company of agents or associates of one or two big Bilbao banks. Ramiro Ledesma, who attended, refused association with a «right fascist» movement that might be financially dependent on big business.[4]

In his keynote address at the founding of the Falange in Madrid on October 29, 1933, José Antonio explicitly acknowledged the bourgeois or upper-class background of the organizers of the new nationalist movement («Yes, we wear neckties and you may say of us that we are *señoritos*»)[5]. In the same breath, however, he pledged the new party to a dramatic social and economic transformation that would revolutionize the condition of the lower classes.

The Falange particularly drew support from radicalized monarchists or ex-monarchists, former members of the Unión Patriótica (front organization for the Primo de Rivera dictatorship) and comparatively young army officers who had voluntarily retired from the military under pressure of the new Republican army policy. This amounted to a following of several thousand people centered in Madrid, the Primo de Rivera home district of Western Andalusia and a few scattered provincial capitals, accompanied by temporarily adequate financial support. Compared with this, the JONS counted a bare thousand followers at most and suffered from a perpetual scarcity of funds. It then found the new Falangist organization competing, and not unsuccessfully, for its own radical nationalist university following in Madrid. For these reasons, Ledesma and Redondo agreed to a fusion with the Falange in February 1934.

Between 1933 and 1935 the Falange faced the problem of defining itself as an effective and genuinely Spanish form of radical integral nationalism while mobilizing a significant base of support. It achieved at best limited success in the first enterprise and failed altogether in the second. Right-wing middle-class anti-leftism was thoroughly monopolized by the CEDA and to a much lesser extent by the Carlist and Alfonsine monarchist groups, leaving no outlet for Falangism on the right. Thus it tried increasingly to appeal to the left, adopting and at times accentuating the *jonsista* line of nationalistic revolutionary syndicalism. In the process the upper-class rightists who had patronized the birth of Falangism and even organized its first direct-action squads began to fall away,[6] and the economic doctrines of José Antonio Primo de Rivera became more «leftist». A Confederation of National-Syndicalist Workers was launched, but languished utterly for lack of support. Further financial subsidies were briefly obtained from the upper-class right through a secret agreement with the Alfonsine monarchists (Renovación Española) in August 1934, but the latter soon found their own resources strained and discontinued the subsidy.[7] By 1935 the Falange had failed to mobilize on either the left or the right.

Nearly all original Falangist records were destroyed in 1936, and the only surviving membership lists of the pre-Civil War party that I have found contain the background of the approximately 1,100 members of the Madrid Falange at the beginning of 1936:

Table 1. *Professional Background of the Primera Línea of the FE de las JONS of Madrid, January 1936*

Laborers and service employees	431
White-collar employees	315
Skilled Workers	114
Professional men	106
Women	63
Students	38
Small Businessmen	19
Officers and aviators	17

Source: Madrid province membership records, FE de las JONS.

The proportion of 50 per cent workers might at first glance seem striking, for it is higher than in the NSDAP of 1933 and much higher than in the Italian PNF. More important are the microscopic dimensions of the general Falangist membership, which at that point scarcely numbered 10,000 in a country of 25 million. Since the total Madrid work force numbered several hundred thousand, the fact that 545 workers were Falangist was insignificant. The vast majority of Madrid workers were vehemently opposed, and the great majority of the middle classes indifferent. The only other areas in which the party had any following at all to compare with Madrid were Valladolid, Santander, the Seville-Cádiz area of Western Andalusia and a few Estremaduran towns.

The bulk of the Falangist following never appeared on the official membership lists, however, for the main support continued to be drawn from students, and a law of the Republic prohibited students below minimal voting age from officially joining political parties. The true Falangist base in Madrid at the beginning of 1936 numbered between 2,000 and 3,000, more than half of it associated with the SEU, the Falangist student syndicate. This was the principal corps of Falangist militancy.[8] The Falange thus resembles the Romanian Legion of the Archangel Michael in being a radical authoritarian nationalist movement based primarily upon student support and also in being ideologically grounded in the traditional national religion rather than in a primarily secular ideology. The difference was that by 1937, if not before, the Legionary movement had begun to achieve a degree of mass mobilization, particularly in some sectors of peasant society.

For the Falange this was altogether impossible. With middle-class Catholic support denied to it by the vigorous organization of a semi-traditionalist middle-class right, Falangism completely failed to find alternative sources of support. The more radical anti-clerical middle-class sectors of opinion were completely non-nationalist and totally committed to secular Republicanism. Anti-clericalism propelled them leftward and into a Popular Front, inducing a *pas d'ennemis à gauche* political psychology that overrode fears of social revolution and prevented any mobilization of latent anti-leftist feeling. The electoral performance of the Falange was thus less than insignificant. The party could not win a seat on its own either in the elections of 1933 or in those of 1936. In the latter campaign, after two and a half years of propaganda, it garnered only 1.74 per cent of the national vote, in comparative terms the poorest electoral performance by fascism in any of the larger continental European countries save Poland. Under anything approaching normal political conditions, the possibilities of a Spanish fascism were completely pre-empted by the middle-class Catholic right.

The situation began to change with the incipient breakdown of the Spanish constitutional system in the spring of 1936, which brought rapid polarization between the heterogeneous para-revolutionary left and the variegated elements of a counter-revolutionary right. For much of the latter, Falangism gained enormously in prestige and came to appear the youthful shock force of nationalist counter-revolution. For the Falange, this opportunity came too late and in the wrong circumstances, for the party was outlawed by the Republican government in March 1936 and driven underground, ending all possibility that the Falange could mobilize mass support on a normal political basis. Again, the situation of the Iron Guard in 1938 provides some parallel.

Breakdown of ordinary political life was a crucial variable, for the European fascist parties, so often middle-class in nature, seem to have required conditions of political freedom to develop. Though Falangism attracted the active or passive support of thousands of middle-class, mostly Catholic, youth in the spring and early summer of 1936, this support was channeled into random terrorism and poorly organized clandestine meetings. It did not contribute to a potent, organized mass political movement.

The Civil War that began in July 1936 quickly developed into a clear-cut revolutionary/counter-revolutionary struggle. I have elsewhere made the point that counter-revolutionary coalitions in situations of total civil war are led by the military,

426

by professional military commanders like a Kolchak, a Mannerheim, a Horthy or a Franco, not by political corporals such as Hitler or Mussolini. The Spanish Nationalist effort was controlled from beginning to end by the army, soon united under the complete leadership of Franco. The Falange was in no way a partner or an equal ally in this effort, but a subordinate civilian auxiliary. Once more the parallel with Romania is striking. The Iron Guard leadership was mostly murdered by the Caroline dictatorship in 1938; many of the Falangist élite, including its top four leaders (Primo de Rivera, Ledesma, Redondo and Ruiz de Alda) were shot by the left during the first four months of the Civil War. A reorganized state-bureaucratic Falange was then made a political organ of the military regime in 1937, just as the Iron Guard was made a secondary associate of the Antonescu military dictatorship in 1940. Franco's takeover of the Falange was accompanied by a brief, bloodless rebellion, while the Iron Guard revolt of January 1941 was much more gory, but the outcome was much the same, ending in both cases in total control by a rather syncretic military regime.[9]

Falangist and Nationalist Recruiting in the Civil War

One of the Falange's main functions during the crucial phase of the Civil War was to mobilize both front-line volunteers and rearguard militia for the Nationalist war effort. This was particularly important during the first nine months or so before the Nationalist army had fully organized its mass mobilization structure. Falangist volunteering, accompanied by the lesser recruitment of Carlists, constituted a crude plebiscite of political enthusiasm in certain districts, though in some instances it may actually have sprung from the opposite motivation, for in a few provinces leftists trapped behind the Nationalist front volunteered for the Falange as a shield from potential persecution.

Thus no very precise conclusions about the support for Falangism may be drawn from the social basis of the Spanish Nationalist cause during the Civil War. Many pro-Nationalists were not pro-Falangists, and apparently many of those who did join Falangist organizations during the war did so not for specific ideological reasons, but because it was the most active para-military force. After April 1937 it had the official sanction of the Franco government, but the same action converted it into an increasingly heterogeneous patriotic assembly that steadily lost its original character.

The anti-Republican revolt first achieved success in the conservative Catholic smallholder provinces of North-Central Spain, and from his jail cell in Alicante the imprisoned José Antonio Primo de Rivera quickly inferred that

> this rebellion is above all of the middle classes. Even geographically the regions in which it has most firmly taken root (Castile, León, Aragon) are regions petty-bourgeois in character.[10]

However, the pattern of volunteering for the Falangist and Carlist militia during the Civil War does not altogether bear out the interpretation that Falangist units mobilized among the more «lower-middle class» provinces, if the statistics in table 2 are analyzed in terms of the socio-economic structure of the regions included.

The region of Old Castile and León, Spain's lower-middle class rural district par excellence and the target of much of the propaganda of the original JONS, as well as home of one of the few notable Falangist nuclei, failed to contribute its proportionate share. Neither did Galicia, but the latter is more a mixed rural proletarian/lower middle class district. Genuinely «proletarian» regions such as Estremadura and Andalusia contributed their approximate share, while the greatest proportionate contributions were made first by Navarre and then by Aragon.

Table 2. *Contributions of Different Regions of the Spanish Nationalist Zone to the Volunteer Falangist-Carlist Militia 1936–38*

Province or Region	Percentage of Total Volunteers	Percentage of Total Population in Nationalist Zone
Navarre	19.9	3.5
Western Andalusia	19.6	24.0
Castile-León	14.3	30.0
Aragon	9.7	5.0
Estremadura	4.6	5.0
Galicia	3.0	24.0

Sources: Unofficial Statistics of Excombatientes Organization; 1930 Spanish Census.[11]

The factors that seem to have been dominant were not those of «class background» so much as the local military and political situation and in the case of Navarre, the traditional provincial culture. There was at times very heavy regular army recruiting in Old Castile and Galicia, which could provide some of the most reliable troops for the Nationalist forces, and this cut into Falangist militia recruiting there.[12] The reverse was the case in Aragon, where the regular army was extremely weak and para-military militia forces were formed on a larger scale to shoulder more of the normal military burden. While it is true that Navarre may be classed as a lower-middle class rather than proletarian-peasant rural province, its torrent of volunteers was not due primarily to its social structure – not much different from half the others in the Nationalist zone – but to its local institutions and history and its strongly conservative Catholic/Carlist culture. Of the Navarrese volunteers, approximately two-thirds were Carlists and one-third Falangists, the latter coming proportionately much more from urban communities than from the countryside.

Membership and Composition of the Franquist Movimiento-Organización

When Franco seized control of the Falange in April 1937 and made it the official state party of his regime, he also merged it with all other political forces (mainly monarchist) supporting the Nationalist struggle. The new state party's name then became «Falange Española Tradicionalista de las JONS». Beyond that, however, Franco made it clear in his founding speech that the new organization would become a synthesis of all forces supporting the regime, and that its ideology and structure would not be limited to the ideas and configuration of early 1937. Accepting the term «totalitarian», his use of it nonetheless seemed to mean merely authoritarian, for he said that a Spanish totalitarianism system would be based on the political norms of the monarchy of Fernando and Isabel. If that were taken seriously, it would mean a form of semi-pluralist, semi-constitutionalist state authoritarianism. Although it is very doubtful that Franco's political and historical ideas were anywhere near that exact in 1937, he made evident the complete independence and syncretism of his ideology and policy.

Thus, the FET was transformed into an increasingly bureaucratic state party at the service of a syncretic military regime over which it had no direct control whatsoever. No Falangist entered Franco's cabinet until 1938, and the party became to some extent a patriotic front organization for supporters of the regime, its ideology increasingly blurred and indistinct. There did remain an ideologically fascistic hard core to the Falangist organization through the early 1940s, and if Germany had won the war these forces would undoubtedly have gained much greater significance.

However, the formal downgrading of the very term and concept of totalitarianism began in 1942 (coinciding with the turn of the tide in the World War), and by 1945, the regime had entered a period of full-scale «defascistization», made easier by the fact that it had never been more than partly fascist. The fascist salute was abolished, Spain was declared a «social and Catholic state» in May 1945, and the formal succession of the monarchy was arranged in 1947. The very name Falange began to disappear, and soon the state party was being universally referred to as simply «Movimiento» or «Movimiento Nacional». In 1958 a new set of «Principles of the Movement» officially replaced the original fascistic Twenty-Six Points of the Falange without even mentioning them, proclaiming an anodyne set of principles that merely endorsed unity, patriotism, morality and national welfare.

The official FET Movimiento-Organización was steadily downgraded, limited in its activities and bureaucratized into low-level routine activities, but it was never abolished either in the regime's attempt to escape the wrath of the antifascist powers in the late 1940s or during the more genuine liberalization of the late 1950s and 1960s. Universally ignored by most Spaniards and scorned by critics as an impotent, irrelevant relic, the Movimiento was nevertheless both retained and sustained by the regime for nearly forty years because it was the only formal political organization that had always been completely and officially committed to the Franquist state. Without the Movimiento, the regime would have been deprived of any organized political support whatever and would have been reduced to the bureaucratic structure of a South American or inter-war East European dictatorship.[13]

The only statistics concerning the membership of the official Falange-Movimiento are those provided by an organizational report in 1963.

Table 3. *Official «Active Membership» (Militantes activos) of the Falange-Movimiento, 1936–63*

1936[14]	35,630	1950	938,000
1937	240,000	1951	944,000
1938	362,000	1952	946,000
1939	650,000	1953	952,000
1940	725,000	1954	951,000
1941	890,000	1955	950,000
1942	932,000	1956	928,251
1943	925,000	1957	923,305
1944	922,000	1958	926,514
1945	908,000	1959	914,057
1946	934,000	1960	918,950
1947	933,000	1961	925,729
1948	941,000	1962	931,802[15]
1949	940,000		

Source: Joaquin Bardavio, *La estructura del poder en España* (Madrid, 1969), 117–18.

Several aspects of these membership figures should be noted. One of the most obvious is the stagnation of FET membership after 1942, which may be considered the turning point in the history of European fascism. A second is that part of the membership is attributable to bureaucratic functions pure and simple. The process of bureaucratization in Spain has never been carried as far as in the Italian PNF of 1933–40, but a tendency in that direction developed in the latter part of the Civil War. Army officers automatically became members of the organization and a considerable following was recruited among the expanding government bureaucracy of the following decade.

A strong suspicion exists that many of those defined as *militantes activos* are not at all active members. During the past twenty years there have been comparatively few signs of mobilized organizational activity in Spain. From my interviews in 1958–59 I talked with scores of early enthusiasts from the years 1934–37 who declared that they largely or entirely dropped out of FET activity at the end of the war. In some instances this was clearly the case, though its extent may have been exaggerated. At any rate, there seems to be a high rate of paper membership in the FET, and the official decline of 1955–56 was attributed to a readjustment of records, removing the names of members who had either died or completely dropped out of activities.

The major figures of local administration in the Franquist state are *ipso facto* local leaders of the Movimiento, beginning with the civil governors of provinces, who are also *jefes provinciales* of the Movimiento. However, they have often become nominal FET leaders by being named to official positions, rather than vice versa. Only 20 of the 50 members of the first National Council of the FET in 1937 were members of the original Falange. As the Franquist bureaucracy expanded in the post-Civil War period, the percentage of Falangists was steadily diluted. The most striking example was given by the secretary of the Falange-Movimiento in 1956, José Luis de Arrese, reporting the results of a survey conducted at that time:

Table 4. *Proportion of Falangists among Office Holders in 1956*

Offices	Total Number of Office Holders	Falangists	
		Number	Per cent
Cabinet Members	16	2	12
Under-Secretaries	17	1	6
Directors-general	102	8	8
Provincial Governors (jefes politicos of FET)	50	18	36
Mayors of Provincial Capitals	50	8	16
Presidents of Provincial Deputations	50	6	12
National Councillors of FET	151	65	43
Procuradores (Deputies) in Cortes	575	137	24
Provincial Deputies	738	133	18
Mayors	9,155	776	8
Municipal Councilmen	55,960	2,226	4
Total Office Holders Surveyed	66,864	3,380	5.5

Source: José Luis de Arrese, *Hacia una meta institucional* (Madrid, n.d.), arranged by Juan J. Linz, «From Falange to Movimiento Organización» in S. P. Huntington and C. H. Moore, eds., *Authoritarian Politics in Modern Society* (New York, 1970), 120–203.

There is little indication that the situation has changed much in recent years. Of the forty members of the FET National Council in 1968 studied by Juan J. Linz, only twenty were found to have any Falangist background, even in the broadest sense. Linz's study also demonstrates that the Movimiento leaders seated in the Spanish Cortes (assembly) represent both an older-age group and a more urban background than do most other sectors of the Cortes, accentuating their status as a relatively static bureaucratic sector and also one little representative of Spanish society as a whole. On the other hand, in terms of ordinary membership, the Movimiento seems to be relatively strongest in small towns (up to 20,000 population) and particularly in Old Castile-León, one of its earliest recruiting grounds, and weakest in the large cities, where the traditional patriotic lower-middle class ethos is probably weakest.

Only in the regular membership category, reinforced by the loyalties of middle-aged faithful and a certain degree of bureaucratic backing, has the Movimiento retained anything approaching the support of the mobilized FET at the end of the Civil War. Even there, a decline of nearly one-third has occurred in proportion to the growth of Spanish population, for in 1939 four per cent of the population were adult male Falangists while in the 1960s and '70s the figure seems to have fallen well below 3 per cent. Auxiliary groups among students, women, and the youth have all declined greatly.

This is most striking in the case of university students, the only solid core of pre-1936 support. The SEU enjoyed a monopoly of student organization in the 1940s but soon ossified, dwindling rapidly to a small minority in the 1960s and to microscopic proportions in the 1970s. In 1962–63, the last year for which official statistics are available, only 4 per cent of university students (3,310 out of 80,000) could even be listed on paper as SEU members. The nominal figure may not have declined greatly since then, but the great expansion of the number of university students in the past decade has reduced the proportion of neo-national syndicalist youth almost to the vanishing point. During recent years the general swing of student intelligentsia opinion to the left has in some cases imposed an almost catacomb-like existence on Falangistic students.[16]

The Feminine Section claimed 580,000 members at war's end in 1939 but dropped to 207,000 in 1959 before rising again to 294,000 in 1962. The decline in youth organizations was more precipitous. In 1941 the FET youth organizations enrolled a total of 564,399 boys and 371,538 girls, which were respectively 18.9 and 12.3 per cent of the boys and girls of minority in Spain.[17] This total of less than a million in a country of 25 million population during the aftermath of the Civil War could not compare with the degree of youth mobilization in Germany and Italy, but nonetheless represented not inconsiderable organization. Yet by 1962 it stood at only 172,000, a decline from about 16 per cent of the youth population to scarcely more than 2 per cent. Since then, it has apparently dropped even further.

Remaining in or joining the post-1945 Movimiento-Organización has meant a largely ceremonial and bureaucratic activity in most cases, with few opportunities for genuine political initiative. There are numerous examples of prominent «dropouts» since the period 1939 to 1945. The most notorious is that of Dionisio Ridruejo, the «Spanish Djilas», sometime propaganda chief of the FET under the Ministry of the Interior, who has been a social democratic opposition leader for the past twenty years.[18] José Ma. de Areilza, once an aggressive neo-Falangist, has become a principal spokesman for liberal democratic monarchist reformism. Other notables, such as Ridruejo's close associate, Antonio Tovar, a noted philologist, simply returned to their professional activities. General Agustín Muñoz Grandes, the most important army officer among Falangist leaders during the semi-fascist era, later devoted himself exclusively to military and bureaucratic duties.

More typical, however, are the cases of leading Falangist politicians who withdrew completely from official political life to lucrative positions in law, industry, commerce or finance. Leading this list would be Franco's brother-in-law, Ramón Serrano Súñer, the first political coordinator of the FET as official party, who has since 1942 devoted himself exclusively to an influential law practice. Pedro Gamero del Castillo, a leading young neo-Falangist of the post-1937 period and briefly acting secretary of the party at the close of the World War, soon withdrew altogether to become a major figure in Spanish shipping and finance, and also in reformist monarchist politics. Gerardo Salvador Merino, the chief of syndicalist «left» Falangism in 1939–40, was forced out of politics due to his somewhat radical ambitions but allowed and even encouraged to become a very prosperous businessman. This paralleled the situation of Manuel Hedilla, last independent leader of the party,[19] who was imprisoned for seven years (1937–44) for resisting Franco's political requests but later permitted and even assisted in developing an affluent portfolio of business interests in the 1950s. Many lesser Falangists with whom I have talked followed much the same pattern. Some remained on the membership lists of the Movimiento-Organización; others did not. Most extraordinary of all, perhaps, was the case of a maverick idealist, the physician and early Seville activist Narciso Perales, who resigned all his official posts in the 1940s but tried to remain true to his early Falangist ideals by operating a charity clinic for workers partly out of his own income.

Finally, it is necessary to ask what was the purpose of a post-fascist state political organization for a rightist authoritarian regime in contemporary Europe. The functions of the Movimiento-Organización were in fact several: a) as mentioned earlier, it was the regime's own political party, and even an apathetic, relatively weak and inactive organization seemed to be better than no organization at all; b) the new Organic Laws of 1966–67 gave the Movimiento's National Council a more specific function within the state by making it a sort of appointive senate with consultative and even partial veto powers, as well as the constitutional watchdog of the regime with the capacity to suspend dangerous or deviant new laws or rulings as instances of *contra-fuero;* c) in the latest phase of nominal liberalization, as announced by prime minister Carlos Arias Navarro in February 1974, the Movimiento was designed to provide the representation of several diverse political tendencies – some more conservative or liberal, some statist or individualist – in lieu of an elective party system.[20]

Whether or not so moribund an organization could really be mobilized for the genuine representation of even restricted differences of opinion was always doubtful, but in the Franco era it remained the only vehicle for any form of legitimate political activity.

NOTES

[1] Juan Aparicio, ed., *La Conquista del Estado* (Barcelona, 1939).

[2] There is no adequate study of Ledesma. His own political memoir for the years 1931–35; ¿ *Fascismo en España?* (Madrid, 1935; Barcelona, 1968), is fundamental. Some clues to his personality and emotions are given by his friend Emiliano Aguado, *Ramiro Ledesma en la crisis de España* (Madrid, 1943). I have presented a synopsis in «Ledesma Ramos and the Origins of Spanish Fascism», *Mid-America,* 43:4 (Oct., 1961), 226–41. The major biography is Tomás Borrás, *Ramiro Ledesma Ramos* (Madrid, 1971).

³ Ricardo de le Cierva, *Historia de la Guerra Civil española* (Madrid, 1969), I, 509. For a good account of the CEDA and the entire Spanish right, see R. A. H. Robinson, *The Origins of Franco's Spain* (London, 1970). Gil Robles' own memoirs, *No fue posible la paz* (Barcelona, 1968), are illuminating if apologetic.

⁴ Ledesma, *¿ Fascismo en España?* (1935), 104.

⁵ José Antonio Primo de Rivera, *Obras completas* (Madrid, 1951), 68.

⁶ For the memoirs of a right-wing, upper-class monarchist activist who was briefly a member of the first wave of Falangism, see Juan Antonio Ansaldo, *¿ Para qué?* (Buenos Aires, 1953).

⁷ From a copy of the agreement in the author's possession, supplemented by an interview with Pedro Sáinz Rodríguez (Lisbon), May 1, 1959.

⁸ There is a lively narrative of the SEU's activities by David Jato, *La rebelión de los estudiantes* (Madrid, 1967).

⁹ The only attempt at a comparison of the Falange and Iron Guard is Horia Sima's *Dos movimientos nacionales* (Madrid, 1963), but it is mainly a comparison of the personalities and ideologies of Jose Antonio Primo de Rivera and Corneliu Zelea Codreanu. The book makes no attempt at a systematic structural and historical comparative analysis of the two movements. It might be noted that Codreanu's *Pentru legionari* was translated and published in Spain in 1939, to my knowledge that volume's only appearance in a West European language.

¹⁰ Partial photocopy of letter of José Antonio Primo de Rivera, August, 1936, in the author's possession.

¹¹ It must be emphasized that any attempt to divide up the proportionate populations of the main districts on which the Nationalist zone was based at the time of the original recruiting in 1936–37 is guesswork. The lines were constantly shifting and in the Southern regions, particularly, part of the population fled into the Republican zone. Excluding peripheral regions that contributed only a minimal number of Falangist units, the estimates in my table are based on the calculation that these regions altogether constituted about 90 per cent of the base population of the Nationalist zone. (The percentages of volunteers were calculated by Prof. Juan J. Linz.) Slightly different statistics on militia volunteers have since been published by J. M. Resa, *Memorias de un Requeté* (Barcelona, 1968), Appendix.

¹² For example, the records of José Andino, Falangist *jefe provincial* of Burgos, show that during the first nine months of the Civil War the Falange recruited 9,120 militiamen in that Old Castilian province, but of these 4,252 were drafted directly into the Nationalist army.

¹³ An excellent study of the evolution and function of the Falange-Movimiento in the post-fascist period has been made by Juan J. Linz, «From Falange to Movimiento-Organización», in S. P. Huntington and C. H. Moore, eds., *Authoritarian Politics in Modern Society* (New York, 1970), 128–203.

¹⁴ The exact date in 1936 is not specified. Membership in the Falange was from five to ten times greater in December than in January of that year.

¹⁵ In a report of March 9, 1963, the total following of the Moviemiento was given as 1,986,084 (in a country with approximately 30 million inhabitants), composed of the following groups:

Active membership	931,802
Feminine Section	294,931
Ex combatientes	372,069
Excaptives (of the Republic)	43,419
Servicio Español de Magisterio (Schoolteachers)	47,043
Servicio Español de Profesorado	2,351
Vieja Guardia (pre-1937 members)	37,534
Guardias de Franco (youth militia)	80,037
Youth Groups	173,588
SEU (University students)	3,310

There is considerable overlap between some of these categories. The weakness of the youth groups is particularly striking, as is the great decline in student following.

[16] In 1971, I was invited to talk with a group of (mostly left-wing) students at the Autonomous University of Barcelona about the historical problem of fascism. On my way to this discussion in the Economics building, I was stopped in the hall by a student with overcoat lapels pulled up over his face who surreptitiously asked me to talk with the neo-Falangist student group. The latter were but a handful and felt it necessary to meet off-campus in quarters provided by a Movimiento agency.

[17] *Anuario Español del Gran Mundo* 1942, in Linz, «From Falange to Movimiento-Organización».

[18] Ridruejo's chief memoir is *Escrito en España* (Buenos Aires, 1962).

[19] For Hedilla's version of the 1937 crisis in the party, see Maximiano García Venero, *Falange en la guerra de España: La Unificación y Hedilla* (Paris, 1967).

[20] For the political attitudes of a handful of more active young neo-Falangists, see the opinions expressed in M. Veyrat and J. L. Navas-Migueloa, eds., *Falange, hoy* (Madrid, 1973).

The Social Origins, Economic Bases and Political Imperatives of Authoritarian Rule in Portugal*

PHILIPPE C. SCHMITTER

The coup of April 25, 1974, which liberated Portugal from over forty years of authoritarian rule has yet to liberate scholars from the very limited information which is available to them to explain and evaluate the bases of that protracted political experience. In fact, the sort of data which might belatedly tell us why Portugal suffered so long under such a mode of domination – e.g. membership rolls for the governmental party, para-military *Legião* and youth organizations; lists of the employees and informers of various police forces; information on regime opponents from the files compiled by these agents; *organigramas* of overlapping directorates and interlocking public-private collaboration in industry, commerce, and finance; lists of officeholders in the various functional and territorial agencies of the state; documentation on government loans, subsidies and other economic policies – all this has become a political weapon eagerly sought by contending forces within the Revolution. As a result, we may never have access to these data, or only to those parts of them which best incriminate opponents or ingratiate supporters. It seems to take defeat in war and foreign occupation to open up the coffers of the state to impertinent scholarly postmortems on the bases of authoritarian rule.

One reason why this material is so sensitive is quite simply that such a substantial proportion of the population, especially of the relatively privileged, educated and politicized élite, is in some way or another «incriminated» by its contents. Ironically, a regime which was manifestly exclusionist, repressive and unpopular seems to have managed to include, if not incorporate, at great many citizen-subjects at some time in its manifold activities, whether by material self-interest, ideological conviction, youthful self-delusion or just plain personal prudence and fear. Narrowly based as the rule of Salazar and Caetano surely was, it did draw upon and subsist on a wide range of class, regional, sectoral, institutional, ideational, and personal interests.

What then were the social, economic and political bases of authoritarian rule in Portugal? As indicated above, a compelling empirical answer cannot presently be given to this question. The best we can offer is a statement of the *problématique* involved and a few tentative conclusions. Given the nature of the other contributions to this volume, we will concentrate upon the social dimension, although for reasons discussed below, a brief treatment of economic *structure* and political *conjoncture* will be included.

Much of the literature on authoritarian rule (or more specifically on fascism and/or National Socialism) places heavy emphasis on the *social origins* of individual recruits to parties and movements, individual voters for relevant parties or plebiscites, individual appointees to the state or para-state roles, and/or individual leaders in the formulation of ideologies and policies. Presumably, the root hypotheses are 1. that the social relations of production as well as those linked to ethnicity, religiosity, center-periphery, status re-definition, spatial and occupational mobility determine a given country's propensity for authoritarian rule and 2. that identification of individuals within this manifold matrix permits one to infer that they «represent» in some sense underlying collective interests and forces. Hence, if a given authoritarian movement is found to have recruited more individuals of a given social category to its ranks than were proportionately present in the society as a whole, it is said to have been, at least in part, a product of that category's needs, aspirations or illusions.

A second trend in the literature stresses the *economic context* within which authoritarian rule emerged and/or the functional impact which policies followed·by a given regime had upon that country's economic development. From this objectivist, «who needed it» and «who benefited from it», perspective, heavy emphasis is placed on such conjunctural factors as depression, inflation and unemployment, and such structural ones as capital accumulation, concentration of ownership, sectoral competition, shifts in technology and scale of production and international competition. These macro-systemic imperatives of the mode of production in a particular stage of its capitalist development and in relation to that of other economies are seen as inducing crises and, thereby, producing an objective need for a change in the form and role of state power – whether or not this is subjectively and accurately perceived by relevant «needy» individuals. Hence, it is argued that authoritarian *régimes d'exception* are governed by certain constraints and opportunities intrinsic to the capitalist mode of production, even if many of their recruits, supporters and ideologues do not come from «the capitalist-bourgeois class», and even when many of them may be genuinely convinced that they are acting to overthrow or at least overcome the contradictions and irrationalities of that system of economic exploitation.

Yet a third major interpretative trend suggests that the roots of authoritarian rule are more specifically *political*. In an era of generalized expectations of legal, political and social equality and of mass aspirations for economic «progress», fueled by invidious intersocietal comparisons and fed by the global diffusion of revolutionary ideologies and insurrectional techniques, liberal-parliamentary bourgeois democracies find it difficult to contain their influence and decisional processes within the structured confines of «normal» politics. Caught in a bind between increased demands and stable or even declining political resources, electorates get fickle, party systems fragmented, leaders indecisive, negotiations protracted, policies incoherent, implementation ineffective, and legitimacy doubted. A pervasive sense of estrangement between the *pays réel* and the *pays légal* emerges, making political life appear epiphenomenal or artificial to much of the population. Into this breach rides the providential man-on-horseback or steps the more prosaic parliamentary dictator, and these forms of transitional, «caretaker», rule frequently pave the way for more protracted and institutionalized authoritarian regimes. This perspective suggests that, radically mobilizational or conservatively demobilizational in form or intent, these regimes are uniquely rooted in both their origins and subsequent policies in «the primacy of the political.» Hence, they emerge in different countries backed by quite different social alliances and motivated by substantially different economic conditions. Inversely, they do not manage to seize power in countries at a similar level of capitalist development and societal complexity where political structures and class hegemony are sufficiently strong to enable ruling groups to survive comparable economic and social crises.

Even with the best of data, no single historical case study would permit us to choose definitively which of these three «regions» of determination best explains the emergence of authoritarian rule.[1] In the specific case of Portugal, the data are manifestly insufficient. So, the best we can hope for is an empirically tentative and conceptually heuristic discussion of the social origins, economic functions and political imperatives which seem to have led up to and subsequently sustained the regimes of Antonio de Oliveira Salazar (1933–1968) and Marcelo Caetano (1968–1974). On the purely «politico-logical» level, none of these sets of factors seems (to me) exclusively compelling and all three contain highly plausible elements of explanation. For reasons of space and the general theme of this collection, they will, however, receive unequal treatment.

Social Origins

The pattern of *emergence* of authoritarian rule in Portugal in the latter half of the 1920s had certain very distinctive features which make it virtually impossible to analyze its *social origins* in the manner routinely used in such cases as Italy, Germany, Romania, Austria, Spain, or even Norway, Switzerland, Belgium and the Netherlands. Ironically, the *consolidation and perpetuation* of Portuguese authoritarian rule possessed other unique features which make it fairly easy to establish its subsequent *social bases*. Why, then, such a paradox?

Unlike all other regimes of this type or sub-type which successfully or unsuccessfully attempted to seize power in Europe in the inter-war period, the Portuguese *Estado Novo* was *not* the product of prior activity by a militant, self-conscious movement or party. While there were minor groups of «integral nationalists», militant «Christians», aggressive monarchists, and even a «Young Turk» youth movement active in Portuguese politics during the republican period (1910–1926), these were directly responsible neither for the 1926 coup nor for the eventual accession to power of Antonio Salazar in 1932/3.

Elsewhere, authoritarian-fascist movements organized to distribute propaganda, to compete in elections, to control the streets and plants through para-military violence and/or to attempt armed seizures of power. In so doing they left a «social trace» in the form of voting patterns, arrest records, membership lists of *alte Kämpfer*, even casualty reports and obituary notices in the event of violent confrontation up to and including civil war. The general pattern observed in several detailed empirical studies seems to be one of authoritarian movements, especially those of the radical-mobilizational (fascist) sub-type, «vacuuming up» discontent from a great variety of sources: class conflict, urban-rural cleavages, generational discontinuities, confessional differences, ethnic competition, national animosities, status shifts, etc. in a broad historical context of instability and uncertainty. Often beginning in what was socially a fairly homogeneous and geographically concentrated *milieu*, such movements, where they were more or less lineally successful in the inter-war period, tended to become increasingly heterogeneous in composition as they approached the seizure of power. Once they acquired control of the state, their social bases shifted even more dramatically under the impact of bandwagonners. Where these movements never broke through the established barriers to entry in the political process (e.g. Great Britain, Norway, Sweden, Switzerland, the Netherlands) or where they peaked early and/or fell short of posing a credible threat to those in power (e.g. Finland and Belgium), an inverse dialectic can be observed of a very dramatic progressive narrowing of their recruitment basis until individual psychological, if not psychotic, disorder becomes the major factor.

Nothing of this sort of continuous socio-political dynamic can be said to have existed with respect to Portuguese authoritarian rule. Take, for example, the closest thing to a forerunner which the *Estado Novo* possessed,[2] *Integralismo Lusitano*. Although one distinguished scholar of the Republic could claim in 1969 that «Integralism was the oldest of existing fascisms» (it was founded in 1914) and that it «provided the bulk of fascist ideology after 1930»,[3] there is little evidence of its participation in the coup of 1926, although *integralistas* had apparently infiltrated the military officer corps and helped to write the proclamation of the armed forces after their successful uprising.[4] In fact, their movement as a political force had crested already in 1919, was internally divided over support for different monarchist factions, and had lost its principal intellectual leader, António Sardinha, in 1925. Summarizing its position «on the eve of the 28th of May (1926)», Carlos Ferrão described them as «dispersed and disillusioned . . . dominated by a sense of patent frustration in their publications and conferences, a reading of which leaves no doubt as to the decadence of the movement already ripe to accept compromises with the winners.»[5]

From all accounts, the coup which put an end to parliamentary rule in Portugal was primarily organized as a military affair, but initially enjoyed widespread «popular» support. The ambiguity and breadth of its social and political base is rather well illustrated, on the one hand, by the fact that actors ranging from the extreme left to the extreme right and representatives of very varied social groups seem to have welcomed its success[6] and, on the other, by the subsequent persistence of sharp factional conflicts within the military establishment over personnel, ideology and policy. The ensuing two years of military dictatorship were marked by repeated coups, continuous plotting, contradictory public policy and even greater instability than had plagued the parliamentary republic. Despite the patent bias of his monumental study on *The Portuguese Revolution*, Jesús Pabón was undoubtedly correct in observing that one «would fall into an understandable and curious anachronism by attributing, in general, to the [Movement of the] 28th of May the purposes which later were to lead to the creation of the Estado Novo».[7] It would be similarly anachronistic to assume that knowledge of the social origins of those who actually led or indirectly inspired this anti-democratic and anti-liberal military uprising in some way explains the emergence and consolidation of civilian authoritarian rule in that country after 1932. In fact, some of the latter's most vigorous (if unsuccessful) opponents played a role in the former.[8]

In 1928, Salazar was again «invited» to become Finance Minister[9] and imposed such stringent conditions upon his acceptance that he in effect became *de facto* head of government. Not until four years later (1932) did he get around to establishing the formal constitutional outlines of his «New State» and not until 1935 were its publicly «representative» bodies: the Legislative Assembly and the Corporative Chamber, first installed. While it would certainly be an exaggeration to claim that Salazar created authoritarian rule in Portugal *tout seul et de toutes pièces,* the evidence suggests that he played a very personal and imperious role in both the direction of policy after 1928 and the selection of personnel after 1932. Of course, he must have accommodated his choices to the demands and «advice» of various privileged classes, conservative and reactionary political forces, as well as those entrenched institutional actors, most notably the military and the Church, which had not been jailed, exiled or cowed into submission by the repressive policies of the military dictatorship; but to an extraordinary degree Salazar could create from above the «élite» to which he felt the (New) state could or should be held accountable. After a ritualistic plebiscite in 1933[10], the first legislative elections were held in December, 1934 and the electorate of

478,121 (only 6.7 per cent of the total population)[11] was invited to vote for a single list of candidates set forth by the *União Nacional,* a governmental party which had been established only shortly before and long after Salazar had firmly gathered the reins of state in his hands. All «representatives» to the Corporative Chamber were hand-picked by the executive (presumably Salazar himself). Elsewhere, I have argued that this *Câmara Corporativa* closely resembled «a sort of National Honor Society or functional-administrative-intellectual College of Cardinals whose members had been anointed for their service to the State,» and that «given this peculiar (genesis and) composition, one could argue that an examination (of it) affords a virtually unique opportunity to peer into and analyze the dynamics of élite formation (since) the Chamber represented precisely those interests, collective and individual, which Sala-zar wished to reward for their fidelity to the system, or to co-opt in an attempt to ensure their future fidelity.»[12] While it is possible that the composition of the Legisla-tive Assembly more closely reflected Salazar's need to accommodate and co-opt the motley assortment of monarchists, national syndicalists, Catholics, renegade republi-cans, «Sidonistas» and military officers left over from the fall of the First Republic, it shared many of the appointive-anointed features of the Corporative Chamber. The social backgrounds of the founding individual members of these two «representative» bodies provides the primary empirical raw material from which we will attempt to infer the social base of authoritarian rule in Portugal[13] – along with some fragmentary data on ministerial appointments.

In view of its manifestly traditionalist if not reactionary ideology, its extolment of the virtues of pre-industrial society and its pretense to promote a *via tertia* between capitalism and socialism, the regime in Portugal has been «identified» as a «dictator-ship of notables» and its supposed class origins «at least at the beginning» have further caused it to be labelled as a «dictatorship of large landowners».[14] Elsewhere, it has been suggested that these large landowners were closely allied with a «comprador bourgeoisie», i.e. urban financial and commercial interests acting as local agents for foreign capitalists and traders, in a dominant «historical bloc» which provided the social base for the Estado Novo.[15]

Such affirmations, common and reasonable as they may seem, are based on vague impressions or aprioristic assumptions. Table 1 provides an admittedly very incomple-te basis for testing them empirically. Its breakdown of the reported occupations of members «invited» to the first sittings of the Legislative Assembly and Corporative Chamber (1934–1938) casts some doubt on the identity of this founding historical bloc. Agrarian landowners were not particularly prominent – no more so than in the Constituent Assembly that began the republican experiment twenty-three years earli-er. Granted that the veterinarians (2), a few of the engineers and physicians, and many of the lawyers may have been agents of agricultural interests, nevertheless, the proportion of *terratenientes* hardly seems excessive since over 50 per cent of Portu-gal's population was employed in agriculture at the time. Combing the biographies for any mention of an agrarian connection, only 18.7 per cent (17 members) of the Assembly could be so identified. Incidentally, most of these appear to have come from the North where relatively small landholdings are the rule rather than the *latifundista* South. Although no member reported his occupation as «industrialist» or «mer-chant», seven of the ninety-one had some positions in industry, civil construction, and transport. Banking and insurance, however, had thirteen «representatives» in the Assembly, almost as many as agriculture. Contrary to the «comprador» label, these propertied interests were connected to notably «domestic» enterprises – at least at

Table 1. *Occupations of Members of the First Session of the Legislative Assembly and Corporative Chamber: 1934–38*

Member's Reported Occupation	Legislative Assembly	Corporative Chamber	Constituent Assembly (1911)
Workers	0.0	8.4	1.8
Landowners*	8.9	10.3	8.4
Military Officers**	16.7	9.3	20.8
Professors & Educators	8.9	15.9	10.2
Lawyers & Judges	41.1	6.5	14.2
Civilian Engineers	10.0	8.4	0.1
Physicians & Veterinarians	6.7	3.7	21.7
Industrialists***	0.0	15.0	0.0
Merchants	0.0	6.5	3.5
Other liberal professions	7.8	14.0	****19.0
Unknown	0.0	1.9	0.0
	100.1	99.9	99.7
N	(90)	(107)	(226)

* includes agronomists.
** includes military physicians & engineers.
*** includes construction.
**** includes 25 «government employees».
Source: Portugal, *Anais da Assembléia e Câmara Corporativa*, Lisbon, 1935.

this early stage in the regime's consolidation. Particularly striking in both the Assembly and Chamber is the high proportion of engineers and lawyers, and the low proportion of physicians, especially when compared to the 1911 Constituent Assembly. Reinforcing this impression of the prominent role of middle-class professionals (in a later period these specialists might have been called technocrats or *técnicos)* is the fact that an extraordinarily large number of the new deputies were or had been employees of the state – sixty-eight or 74.6 per cent of the total! Granted that many of these had been civil governors of provinces or administrators of municipal governments (and, here, possibly closely linked to rural local notables), about one-half were working for specialized agencies of the central government.

In a sense, membership in the Corporative Chamber is less revealing. Its formal composition more or less «guaranteed» a broader sectoral spread. Hence, it contained a lot less lawyers and judges, a few more professors and educators (from a wider variety of disciplines and establishments – five of the eight in the Legislative Assembly were from the two law faculties), many more industrialists and merchants, and a token ten per cent of «workers» (most of whom were middle level employees). However, when it came to public employment, the Chamber rivalled the Assembly. Fifty-two per cent of its members worked for the state in some capacity and at some level.

Before considering other aspects of the social background of this founding élite, let us make a further distinction. Given that it was the first attempt to put together a representative component for a regime which itself was barely getting started, one can infer that mistakes were made and that not all the selections «worked out». What particularly interests us are those who left after serving only a single term and those of proven reliability who went on to serve numerous terms.[16] As table 2 testifies, the *procuradores* of the Corporative Chamber proved less reliable (or more occupied with other affairs). Almost one-half left in 1938 and only nine per cent served as many as five terms; whereas nearly one-quarter of the *deputados* settled in for more than twenty years of representative duty. Comparing the occupations of the short-termers and those of the long-termers, one discovers that among the latter were no workers or merchants and very few landowners, military officers, engineers or industrialists. The physicians, lawyers, judges, and professors were most likely to go on to have lengthy careers as representatives. We will return to this notion of hard core supporters with their great longevity and multiple careers within the public and private sectors later.

Table 2. *Tenure of Members of the First Session of the Legislative Assembly and Corporative Chamber: 1934–1938*

Length of Term in Office	Deputados in the Legislative Assembly	Procuradores in the Corporative Chamber
1. Remained only one term	28.9	46.7
2. Served two terms	28.9	27.1
3. Served three to four terms	18.9	16.8
4. Served five or more terms	23.3	9.3
	100.0	99.9
N=	(90)	(107)

Source: *Anais*, 1935.

Table 3. *The Survival Rate of First Session Representatives by Occupation: Legislative Assembly and Corporative Chamber, 1934–1938*

Occupation	Percentage of Both Legislative Assembly and Corporative Chamber Members who served	
	One term	More than five terms
Workers	66.7	0.0
Landowners	47.4	10.5
Military Officers	32.0	12.0
Professors & Educators	16.0	24.0
Lawyers & Judges	33.3	26.2
Civilian Engineers	33.3	11.1
Physicians & Veterinarians	20.0	30.0
Industrialists	90.9	9.1
Merchants	42.9	0.0
Other liberal professionals	54.6	13.6

Source: *Anais*, 1935.

The tumultuous political life of the First Portuguese Republic was marked by repeated clashes between the interests and style of Lisbon and those of the rest of the country, especially the more traditional, Catholic, small-peasant landowners of the North of the country. The coup of 1928 was a sort of imitation of the March on Rome and it began in the Northern cities of Braga and Porto. Although not a country having very distinctive regional, ethnic or linguistic subcultures, it could be argued that formation of the *Estado Novo* in the early thirties involved the mobilization of Portugal's periphery – its provincial towns and rural masses – against its center or more particularly against Lisbon. The above observations concerning the role of provincial and municipal officials in both Houses and the relative absence of direct spokesmen for metropolitan industry and commerce (with the notable exception of finance and insurance, which were well-represented), and the broad similarity in occupational background with the 1911 Constituent Assembly, all suggest that geographic location (and with it, differences in cultural values, degree of modernization and scale of production) may have played an independent role.

Table 4. *Place of Birth of Members of the First Session of the Legislative Assembly and Corporative Chamber, 1934–38*

Place of Birth	Legislative Assembly	Corporative Chamber	Total Population (1930)
1. Lisbon	13.3	29.0	8.8
2. Porto	3.3	8.4	3.4
3. Rest of the country, including colonies, Atlantic islands and foreign countries	83.3	60.7	87.8
	99.9 N=(90)	*98.1 (107)	100.0

* two places of birth unknown.
Source: *Anais*, 1935.

Table 4 demonstrates that despite treating the country as a single electoral district, the places of birth of *deputados* very closely matched the general population distribution. Although the data are not available for the 1911–1926 sessions of the Chamber of Deputies for comparison, one suspects that this represents quite a change. In any case, the functionally recruited Corporative Chamber was a good deal more metrocentric. Unfortunately, the hand-written cards from which these compilations were made are not sufficiently legible to identify the names of some of the less well-known cities and villages so that a full and detailed geographic breakdown is impossible. From those which can be read, the impression is one of heavier than proportionate representation from the North (but not from the city of Porto itself). This does not support the contention that Portuguese authoritarian rule was primarily a reflection of latifundist-domination, most of which is concentrated in the South.[17] We are reminded, however, that place of birth is not the same as place of residence and work (although the modest rate of urbanization in Portugal from 1911 to 1930 – an increase from 17 to 19 per cent of the total population – implies that internal migration was not very great) and that lawyers, engineers, and physicians from other parts of the country could act as agents for *latifundistas*.

442

Youths, university students, junior military officers, recently demobilized soldiers, even juvenile delinquents play a rather prominent role in most descriptive accounts of the emergence of authoritarian or fascist movements in inter-war Europe. There is more than just a suspicion that the collapse of liberal parliamentary rule was somehow related to a breakdown in the intergenerational transmission of political values and partisan allegiances. Old parties and old politicians failed to attract youthful followers and these relatively *déclassé* new participants were recruited in droves by promises of a new order and the thrill of a more virile style of political activity.

Portugal was no exception. Most of the proto-authoritarian movements which preceded Salazar's consolidation of power had their origins in university student politics. What is less well known is that Salazar and the men he gathered about him in the early thirties also represented the emergence of a new political generation. Because Portugal later developed into an extreme gerontocracy, observers tended to forget that old men were young once – and that their youth was once an important factor in their strategy of domination. At the ministerial level, Oliveira Marques has already demonstrated the significance of differences in the average age of appointments as Portugal changed from monarchy to republic to «New State.» During the monarchy, the mean age of ministers was over fifty and increased with time. With the advent of the republic, it dropped to 46.5 years and then rose gradually to 49.5. The dictatorship of Sidónio Pais (1918–1919) saw a dramatic but short-lived rejuvenation (to 42.8 years) after which republican ministers tended to get older. The military dictatorship (1926–1932) only increased that trend, but when Salazar put together his «own» cabinet in 1932 its average age was only 43.7 years. More important, it brought to power the «Generation of 1910» which had come of political age precisely at the moment the Republic was founded.[18]

Table 5. *Age and Generational Difference among Members of the First Session of the Legislative Assembly and Corporative Chamber, 1934–38*

Date of Birth	Age in 1934	Legislative Assembly	Corporative Chamber
1. Generation of 1880 (born 1851–1860)	83–74	0.0	2.9
2. Generation of 1890 (born 1861–1870)	73–64	2.2	11.4
3. Generation of 1898–1900 (born 1871–1880)	63–54	17.8	21.0
4. Generation of 1910 (born 1881–1890)	53–44	25.6	31.4
5. Generation of 1920 (born 1891–1900)	43–34	48.9	22.9
6. Generation of 1930 (born 1901–1910)	33–24	5.6	10.5
		100.1	100.1
N=		(90)	*(105)

* two unknowns.
Source: *Anais*, 1935.

An age and generational breakdown of the 1934–38 «representative» élite shows an interesting difference between the Assembly and the Chamber. The former was much younger – very young in fact– bringing a whole new generation into politics. Almost one-half of its members came from the same generation and its average age was only 45.4 years. The Corporative Chamber was older and had a more normal distribution across generations. As we shall see later, this meant that more of its *procuradores* had had previous political experience during the Republic. The *deputados,* however, were more likely to have been neophytes or to have held previous government positions only during the military dictatorship (1928–1932).

So far, in our quest for the social origins of Portuguese authoritarian rule, we have paid attention exclusively to the 197 members of the first sessions of the regime's representative bodies. Elsewhere, I have presented data on members of subsequent sessions of those two chambers. These data show a substantial continuity in social composition over the next thirty-five years[19], despite the fact that both the Legislative Assembly and the Corporative Chamber increased monotonically in total size and experienced a rather high rate of turnover in personnel.[20] Average age increased, of course, as did the proportion of «workers». Landowners and lawyers increased in the Chamber and decreased in the Assembly – the inverse occurring with physicians. Military officers, industrialists and merchants became less well-represented in both, as did the proportion of «metropolitans», i.e., those born in Lisbon and Porto. A substantial amount (10 per cent by 1965–69) of shuffling back-and-forth between the two Houses also took place.

Let us take a closer look at the second session of these representative bodies (1939–1942). In 1935/36, the *Estado Novo* took a markedly «fascist» turn. A para-military Portuguese Legion and a compulsory youth organization were established; the infamous PVDE (later PIDE) secret police was created; large numbers of «volunteers» *(viriatos)* were sent to fight in the Spanish Civil War; the rhetoric and symbols of the regime became more aggressively nationalistic and anti-democratic. Perhaps in the social composition of the 95 newcomers to the Assembly (33) and the Corporative Chamber (62) in 1938 we can find a clue to the nature of the «ultras» that accompanied, if not encouraged, this process of fascistization.

Table 6, however, offers very little evidence of any dramatic shift in response to these emergency conditions, existing or impending. They did manage to find some more «workers» to fill seats in the Corporative Chamber. Physicians (mostly from small towns) seem to have regained something of the representative role they had played under the First Republic. Somewhat surprisingly, the proportion of military officers declined, despite the increased emphasis on military preparedness. The second session newcomers to the Assembly were much more likely to have come from Lisbon (36 per cent vs. 13 per cent), but this merely compensated for the fact that previously «elected» metropolitans were less likely to have survived the first-term cut. Their total representation, therefore, remained fairly constant. Nor was there any distinctive juvenation. In fact, the median age hardly changed. Only a trickle of the new «Generation of 1930», i.e., those born 1901–1910, managed to enter the Assembly (9) or the Chamber (12) in 1938. So, as Portugal appeared to move toward a more mobilizational and militant form of authoritarian rule (a stance from which it prudently retreated after 1945), and thousands voluntarily joined or were compulsorily enrolled in the new fascistoid organizations, the core of social support at the individual élite level seems to have remained the same.

444

Table 6. *Occupations of New Members of the Second Session of the Legislative Assembly and Corporative Chamber, 1939–42*

	Legislative Assembly		Corporative Chamber	
	New	Previous	New	Previous
Workers	0.0	(0.0)	19.4	(8.4)
Landowners*	9.1	(8.9)	9.7	(10.3)
Military Officers**	9.1	(16.7)	9.7	(9.3)
Professors & Educators.......................	12.1	(8.9)	6.4	(15.9)
Lawyers & Judges	39.4	(41.1)	6.4	(6.5)
Engineers	6.0	(10.0)	8.1	(8.4)
Physicians & Veterinarians.....................	18.2	(6.7)	8.1	(3.7)
Industrialists***	0.0	(0.0)	12.9	(15.0)
Merchants...................................	3.0	(0.0)	8.1	(6.5)
Other liberal professions	3.0	(7.8)	11.3	(14.0)
N=	(33)	(90)	(62)	(107)

* includes agronomists
** includes military engineers & physicians
*** includes construction
Source: *Anais*, 1939–1942.

Table 7. *Scoring the Founding Political Élite in Authoritarian Portugal: 1934–42*

	«Hardcore points»
1. Each Term in Legislative Assembly or Corporative Chamber ..	1
2. President of Municipal Council, Subsecretary of State, Chefe de Gabinete do Ministro, Pres. de Junta, Directorio Geral	2
3. Civil Governor of Province, Head of PSP, Ambassador to major country, National-level leader in União Nacional, Legião Portuguesa, Mocidade Portuguesa	3
4. Member of Conselho Político Nacionál, Conselho do Estado. ..	4
5. Minister of State	5
Types of Regime Activists-Supporters	N
Total of ten points or more=hardcore	(48)
Five to nine points=semi-hardcore.........................	(63)
Four or less points=softcore...............................	(181)
total	(292)

Of course, not all the representatives in the first two sessions of the two chambers belonged to the «hard core» of regime supporters and activists. We have already identified some important differences between the single and multiple-termers. Now, let us push this search a bit further and extend it over ministerial, upper administrative and higher party positions. In table 7, I have devised a system of weighted scores for various political and administrative positions held by this founding élite and then divided the aggregated totals into three categories of supporters-activists: «hardcore», «semi-hardcore» and «softcore». Arbitrary though these quantitative manipulations may be, they do provide us with a replicable and verifiable way of distinguishing different degrees of «service to the authoritarian regime.»

The 48 hardcore, 63 semi-hardcore and 181 softcore activists do not, however, constitute a total enumeration of all those who served to put together the *Estado Novo*. A very few top leaders, including Salazar himself, never held a seat in either the Assembly or the Chamber. Some who did, left early for protracted tenure in a single politico-administrative position, e.g. Adm. Henrique Tenreiro, the «czar» of the Portuguese fishing industry, and are therefore penalized by the scoring system of table 7 which gives a sort of quantitative premium to job switchers and multiple officeholders. Finally, not all those who played a prominent founding role in the New State remained loyal to it. For example, Henrique Galvão merited classification as a «semi-hardcore» supporter for his recorded activity before, during and after his tenure as a *deputado*. In 1961, he led a revolt involving the seizure of the liner *Santa Maria* in midocean in one of the most colorful and well publicized efforts to overthrow Salazar.[21]

These caveats notwithstanding, table 8 provides an illuminating picture of the socio-economic bases of the regime in its formative phase. The softcore consisted of temporarily co-opted workers, physicians, industrialists, merchants and a varied assortment of liberal professionals: clerics, architects, journalists, even a sculptor and a librarian. These relative outsiders were more likely to come from Lisbon or Porto and to have had positions in the relatively modern private industrial, transport, communications or commercial sector, although there was a sizeable proportion of landowners and others linked to the agricultural sector among them. The high proportion (15.9 per cent) whose sectoral activity was unascertainable consisted mainly of lawyers who listed no private economic connections or public sector positions.

The semi-hardcore supporters-*cum*-activists overlap in some ways with the softcore e.g., a few co-opted workers and liberal professionals, but are distinguished especially by two characteristics: 1. their dependence upon the state for a livelihood; 2. their status as agents, intermediaries or brokers for or between other interests. This was the role occupied primarily by lawyers and secondarily by small town physicians or veterinarians. One suspects that the semi-hardcore of the *Estado Novo* was not composed of the direct owners of the means of production (as was much of the softcore and the hardcore in their different ways), but of relatively self-made men who saw an opportunity to mediate between the state and private propertied groups. These were the most likely to «militate» in the *União Nacional*, the *Mocidade Portuguesa* or the *Legião Portuguesa* and to have been rewarded with a few terms as a *deputado* or *procurador*, an administrative position as president of a municipal council and/or a national agency directorship, maybe even as a subsecretary of state.

The hardcore of regime personnel seems to have been a sort of amalgam of the first two subgroups of supporters with additional definite characteristics of its own. It too had a large percentage of career public officials (48 per cent) but these tended to be

Table 8. *The Formative Political Élite in Authoritarian Portugal: 1934–42*

	«Hardcore»	«Semi-hardcore»	«Softcore»
I. Occupation:			
Workers	0.0	4.8	8.8
Landowners	6.2	11.1	8.8
Military Officers	22.9	11.1	8.3
Professors & Educators	27.1	11.1	7.7
Lawyers & Judges	25.0	30.2	17.1
Engineers	10.4	9.5	9.4
Physicians and Veterinarians	4.2	7.9	8.8
Industrialists	2.1	3.2	11.0
Merchants	0.0	1.6	7.2
Other liberal professions	2.1	9.5	12.7
N=48	100.0	100.0	99.8
II. Sector of Activity:			
Agriculture	13.5	11.1	18.1
Industry & Transport	13.5	9.5	22.9
Commerce & Publishing	3.8	1.6	10.6
Finance & Insurance	19.2	6.3	4.3
Public Service	48.1	63.5	28.2
Other or unknown	0.0	7.9	15.9
N=52	100.1	99.9	100.0
III. Place of Birth:			
Lisbon	16.7	22.2	27.6
Porto	4.2	3.2	8.8
Rest	79.2	74.6	63.5
N=48	100.1	100.0	99.9
IV. Age:			
born 1851–1880	14.6	28.6	23.2
born 1881–1890	33.3	23.8	28.2
born 1891–1900	39.6	33.3	36.5
born 1901–1910	12.5	14.3	12.1
N=48	100.0	100.0	100.0

Source: *Anais,* 1939–42.

higher level civil servants, e.g. ministers «inherited» from the military dictatorship or even from ex-republican governments. Officers, upper echelon and older, from the armed services – both Army and Navy – were prominent, as were tenured university professors.[21a] In fact, this *catedrocracia,* especially from the University of Coimbra, constituted the major source of recruitment to the hardcore. Even by 1942 many of these had already acquired important directive positions in major private firms. Which brings us to this élite's most distinctive «sectoral» characteristic: the marked importance of finance and insurance, followed in a more «balanced» way by industry and agriculture. Rounding out the distinctive attributes of the hardcore in this sample were its greater provinciality and its relative youth (in 1934–1942).

Our examination of the social relations which might have promoted, if not made ineluctable, the advent of protracted authoritarian rule in Portugal, has led to some tentative conclusions. Some are supportive of «established wisdom»; others less so.

The absence of workers' and even lower middle class representatives, except in the most minimal and perfunctory manner, confirms the suspicion that the emerging *Estado Novo* had little or no support from «popular» classes or even the *mesoi*. The high proportion of provincials, especially among the regime's hardcore, suggests that its rise to power involved a mobilization of relatively privileged groups on the geographic, cultural and developmental periphery of that society against the more sophisticated, cosmopolitan, «progressive» elements of its metropolitan center. Rural landowners were present in substantial numbers in the founding élite but appeared to have played a rather affaced role amid the soft and semi-hardcore of supporters. At least in terms of personnel, the *Estado Novo* was certainly not a «regime of *terratenientes*».

Nor does the foreign-dependent «comprador» element loom very large. Unless one extends the term quite incongruously to cover those with interests in the Portuguese colonial empire, very few of the propertied elements within its ranks seem to have had extensive foreign interests or even connections. Quite the contrary. They were a narrowly provincial and rather introverted *national* élite and, as we shall see *infra*, they followed correspondingly nationalist and exclusivist economic policies, at least until quite recently.

The other most distinctive social characteristics of this founding élite (especially its hardcore) were: 1. its youth and narrow generational base; 2. its dependence on public employment; 3. its close relationship with the financial and fiscal sector of Portugal's weak and dependent capitalist economy.

The conclusion that the *Estado Novo* was founded and staffed in large measure by a new generation composed mainly of civil servants, technicians and professors of fairly provincial origins who, with the important exception of the financial sector, do not appear to have *initially* been controlled by or held accountable to either a liberal, internationally-linked, modern industrial-commercial bourgeoisie or to a conservative, provincially-bounded, feudal-landed aristocracy does not by any means resolve the issue of the social bases of *subsequent* authoritarian rule in Portugal, or its relationship to the development of capitalism in that country. To infer from the indisputable fact that by the time of its overthrow in 1974 this regime was intimately connected with Portugal's industrial, commercial, financial, and agrarian bourgeoisie that such a relationship must always have existed is to commit an elementary fallacy, that of *nunc pro tunc* or «presentism».[22] It is to ignore the historical process and sequence by which this came about. In the Portuguese case, there is evidence that the interpenetration of public and private power came from above rather than from below – by the deliberate and systematic placement of ministers, colonial and civil governors, higher military officers, subsecretaries of state, even *chefes de gabinete*, in private or mixed enterprises *after* their period of service to the state. Often of rather modest social origins and personal fortune, these men (there were virtually no women) received specialized training in law, economics, and engineering in one of the country's few university faculties and often held teaching positions there. If loyalty, ideological orthodoxy and professional performance were found satisfactory, they were «rewarded» with a series of ill-paying governmental positions. At the end of this *cursus honorum* lay much more financially rewarding positions as directors of major banks, memberships on the board of metropolitan and colonial enterprises and presidencies of mixed corporations.

In one of the very few studies which provide some data on the economic roles of ex-political officials, Raul Rego manages to capture some of the dynamics of this process of growing interpenetration: «the men of the *Estado Novo*, with rare exceptions, interpenetrated the large economic organizations and installed themselves within them . . . One can find whole companies transformed into veritable beehives of ex-ministers, subsecretaries of state, directors-general and colonial governors . . . [With dismissal from high government position] the nominations were, as a rule, not long in coming. Weeks, even days, after ministerial remodellings, commenced the dance and counter-dance of placing the outgoing ministers and subsecretaries. A few go back to the places they occupied before, others go into companies for the first time, leaving their law firms, their clinics, or previous public agencies . . . It is evident that, in most cases, these men do not enter the boards of directors because of their technical competence. It is enough to see how they pass from one company to another with completely different functions to know that the capacity that promotes them is always the same – that of being an ex-minister . . . It appears that Portuguese public life, for many, is only a passage to the private sector, from official administrative functions they go to lucrative positions in private companies.»[23] Rego followed this description with a list of 46 ex-ministers and 23 subsecretaries and the private jobs they then held.

The social basis of authoritarian rule in Portugal seems to have been based on a very complex pattern of recruitment and élite circulation. Its hardcore, far from being a mere executive committee named by a comprador bourgeoisie and/or rural landlords, was composed of a distinctive generation of largely self-made men, liberal professionals and technicians, who used their control over the public apparatus of coercion to penetrate (but not subordinate) the private sector. Portugal may have had the least developed, formally public productive sector in Europe, but no other country had as extensive and systematic a system of *pantouflage* from leading public to private sector positions. The end result was the sort of élite symbiosis between the state and the dominant economic class described in the most vulgar of Marxist treatments of the Capitalist State, but it was the product of a very different historical process and masked rather different relations of influence.

Complementing this hardcore symbiotic process were other «circulatory arrangements» connecting Portuguese civil society to the state. In the semi-hardcore, this seems to have involved local notables from the provinces, relatively minor industrialists and merchants, medical and legal professionals as well as an assortment of priests, architects, journalists, etc. who were offered multiple-term representative roles, positions in provincial and municipal governments, and middle-level national administrative posts in return for their support or acquiescence. This group also seems to have provided most of the active participants in the fascistoid *Legião* and *Mocidade* organizations. The soft outer core was filled with a constantly renewed set of opportunity-seekers recruited from a wide variety of social groups, but less territorially dispersed than the other two. Positions in the syndicates and guilds of the corporative system along with minor administrative jobs seem to have been sufficient to attract and retain them. When these three core «representative» elements are combined with other regime recruits (employees in ministerial and para-state regulatory agencies, members of the National Republican Guard and the several police forces, not to mention a very sizeable contingent of paid informants), one begins to understand how this regime could have been unrepresentative and unpopular, isolated from virtually all social formations and undefended when the crunch came, even by its most privileged beneficiaries; and yet could have managed to implicate in its folds such a substantial portion of the population. While this analysis of social relations indicates *how* authoritarian rule may have worked in Portugal, it does not inform us very satisfactorily about *why* it occurred. For that, we must turn to other explanatory factors such as economic functions and political imperatives.

Economic Bases

Limitations on space, time and data make it impossible to explore thoroughly here the economic needs which may have made authoritarian rule imperative in the Portuguese case. We can only touch briefly on the issues involved.

Much of the speculation on the nature of the relationship between the mode of economic production and the form of political domination in societies such as the Portuguese has focused on two issues: their *delay* in developmental timing and their *dependence* on imperial, earlier developing, capitalist countries. These themes are interrelated, in fact often treated indistinguishably. Both emphasize the three central problems of capitalist development: 1. How to accumulate capital in ever expanding amounts from a population whose precarious command over resources inclines them to immediate consumption; 2. How to realize profitably and privately the fruits of production given great inequality in distribution of property and its benefits and hence structural restrictions on the size of the market; and 3. How to accomplish the above within national economies in the context of growing economic competitiveness and diffusion of expectations across international boundaries. Delay, however, draws our attention more specifically to changes in the scale of production and hence of capital requirements due to ensuing technological change; discontinuities in the process of import substitution; shifts in the historical-political role of economic sectors and social classes given differences in the timing of industrialization and commercialization; and «distortions» in both production and consumption patterns inspired by emulation and mimicry of earlier developers. Dependence tends to focus more on changes in the quantity and nature of foreign capital investment; secular trends and irregularities in the volume and price of export and imports; crises in the balance of payments and value of national currency; discontinuities and opportunities created by inter-imperial competition and war; penetration and subordination of «national» classes by external interests; financial vulnerability of the state due to the need for foreign loans; and manipulation of preferences through external control of media and cultural symbols.

Both of these structural perspectives suggest that at particular conjunctures of delayed-dependent capitalist development, major contradictions emerge which necessitate a change in the nature of political domination, and more specifically in the nature of the regime and policy role of the state. In a nutshell, the embryonic national bourgeoisie is rendered so weak and internally fragmented that it can no longer control the processes of accumulation and profit realization through privatistic action under an established set of legal guarantees, through a stable monetary system, and within the confines of a liberal-pluralistic political process. The direct coercive power of the state must be increasingly brought to bear to replace the loss of hegemony by these

450

propertied élites and to repress the threat to «order» contained in the demands of non-propertied, exploited classes.

Is it plausible to argue that the emergence and consolidation of authoritarian rule in Portugal correspond to the structural imperatives of such a crisis in its delayed-dependent development? The answer seems to be a qualified «yes», but not for the reasons most frequently advanced. No one can deny that Portuguese development was «delayed» relative to that of the rest of Europe, but much of the contemporary literature focuses specifically on the way changes in the scale and type of production during a process of industrialization through import substitution produce contradictions which can only be resolved through «imperative coordination» by the state.[24] Portugal in 1926 or 1932, however, was a long way from having exhausted the easy, initial stages of import substitution. Twelve per cent of its imports were still textiles, not to mention 8.9 per cent in assorted manufactures (mostly finished consumer products). Capital goods (including armaments) constituted only 11.9 per cent of the country's foreign purchases. Not until 1936 did these figures begin to change under the impact of the regime's protectionist policies. Textiles fell to 3.4 per cent; capital goods remained more or less constant at 11.1 per cent while imports of consumer goods increased to 13.0 per cent.[25] Nor can one find any evidence of an impeded or impending shift in the scale of production and, hence, need for greater capital accumulation. Industrial production was and remained mostly artisan-based (two-thirds of all establishments employed less than 10 workers); total industrial employment (only about 130,000) had showed no marked tendency to increase prior to 1926.[26]

Nor can external dependence straightforwardly provide an alternative answer.[27] When, in 1932, the British Embassy's commercial secretary felt it necessary to explain why Portugal had escaped relatively unscathed from the Great Depression, he argued:

> In many fundamental aspects commerce, industry and finance in Portugal are isolated from the conditions which have developed or have been created in many other countries since the war. There has been until quite recently relatively little restriction in the operation of the normal tendencies of supply and demand for her principal exports such as wine, cork and sardines. She has not suffered the creation of abnormal conditions arising out of industrialization on such a scale that a fall in commodity prices, the contraction of demand and monetary disturbances, have imperilled the safety of the structure . . . The opportunities for foreign capital are relatively limited. . . Portugal has never issued a foreign loan with the minor exception in 1896 of the unissued balance of the 1891 loan. The whole of the state's and the country's foreign commitments have been met out of her own resources . . . The fact that the state has not had recourse to foreign loans and that foreign capital has not sought investment here can now be seen to have eased her burdens during the depression.[28]

To the extent that there was a structural crisis in the development of Portuguese capitalism which made a change in the mode of political domination «necessary» by the end of the 1920s, it must, therefore, have been different from the one which seems to lie behind the rash of authoritarian «revolutions from above» which have afflicted Latin America in the 1960s and 70s, and is perhaps closer to those which produced «populist dictatorships» in the same area during the 1930s and 40s. One of its elements was a severe banking crisis. In 1924–25 twelve banks failed and almost as many new ones were founded. This chaotic reorganization of the private banking sector was, in turn, linked to a growing extension of public authority. A very strict governmental supervision of banks was decreed in early 1925. Equally important had been the rapid and steady expansion of two quasi-public banking institutions, the *Banco de Portugal* and the *Caixa Geral dos Depositos*. The former was beginning to compete in regular banking services and had acquired a near monopoly of foreign currency transactions; the latter had become by far the largest savings bank in the country and was, in effect, fixing interest rates and the volume of loans. «The result was that the Government and the state-guaranteed *Caixa* absorbed between them practically all the capital which had not fled the country. For the normal working of Portugal's economic system, much less for its development, little or nothing was left».[29] To this must be added the imposition of new, higher taxes on property after 1922.

This threatening absorption of available surplus by the state was compounded by the spectre of an eventual extension of public activity and authority over industry. The «hottest» political issue at the time of the 1926 coup was what to do when the monopoly granted to a private (Franco-Portuguese) firm for the production of tobacco products came to an end that year. The parliamentary republican regime was ready to implement a *régie*, state-owned, system in the teeth of fierce opposition. The issue of public vs. private ownership of railways was also in contention at the time.[30] Moreover, in 1916 a labor ministry had been established for the first time and compulsory social insurance instituted three years later. More social and redistributive measures seemed sure to follow.

The mid-1920s also witnessed a major crisis in the regime's economic and political relationship with its Empire. Administrative and fiscal decentralization and economic liberalism in the Republic's colonial policy had led to some developmental changes in Angola and Mozambique, stimulated in part by the introduction of foreign capital, but by 1924/25 there came a monetary collapse in the value of Angolan currency, a sizeable decline in exports and the near bankruptcy of the two private *Companhias* that were exploiting Mozambique. The metropolitan state was faced with the need for large budgetary subsidies and, of course, loss of previous surplus extracted from these possessions.[31]

Finally, while Portugal did not have a large-scale foreign debt, it did have the immediate problem of paying off its accumulated war debt to Great Britain. Some £ 22,000,000 were owed and the British were pressing for payment.

The salience of these issues is well demonstrated by the attention paid to them between 1926 and 1930. Banking regulations were drastically changed. The *Caixa* was limited in its role of lender to the state and some of its functions transferred to the Banco de Portugal or to a newly created *Caixa Nacional de Crédito* aimed at lending to the private agricultural and industrial sectors. The Bank of Portugal itself was given a new constitution making it less of a threat to private banks. The tobacco *régie* was extinguished after a few months of existence, the concession put up for auction and repurchased by the former concessionaries. Part of the state-owned railway system was turned over to an existing private line. In 1928, the military dictatorship even went so far in its privatizing zeal as to decree private ownership for the post office, along with all telegraph and telephone services, but this was never implemented. Once Salazar had come to power, this drive to divest the Portuguese state of its economic role disappeared and was replaced by the more modern, «neo-physiocratic» one, of using public regulatory and extractive power to subsidize the expansion of private property.[32]

The creation of a separate *Banco de Angola* in 1926, a new status for the *Banco*

Nacional Ultramarino, the bank of issue for the other colonies, coupled with tighter budgetary control over colonial government expenditures and the dissolution of one of the private Mozambique companies began to clear up the imperial mess. The attempt to do so was capped in 1931 by a completely redrafted Statute for Colonies which reasserted centralized, metropolitan control and raised the level of intra-imperial economic preferences. In 1928 an important convention was signed in Preto-ria «regulating» South African recruitment of labor in Mozambique and assuring the *métropole* of a sizeable annual payment in gold for the transaction. From a drain on public finances and private capital accumulation, the African possessions again began to make a positive contribution to both, although Angola remained in a depressed state throughout the 1930s. Finally, the British accepted a favorable Portuguese offer resolving the war debt issue in 1926.

Fragmentary as these data are, they do support the hypothesis that the advent of authoritarian rule coincided with a structural crisis in the development of Portuguese capitalism and that policies followed by the military dictatorship and the succeeding «financial» dictatorship permitted the stabilization and eventually the growth of this «delayed-dependent» mode of economic production.[33] To two generic conflicts within the capitalist growth process: 1. Between concentrated accumulation of savings in private hands and the fiscal and monetary imperatives of a modern state; and 2. Between «natural» private monopolies which emerge strongly in the earlier stages of development and the need for public regulation, even ownership, of this basic infra-structure of transportation, communication and production in order that its exploita-tive operation will not distort or endanger further capitalist development, was added another conflict, specific if not unique to the Portuguese case: the conflict implied by Portugal's simultaneous dependent development on the periphery of Europe *and* its attempt to reap the benefits of imperialist exploitation in an even more remote periphery of the expanding world capitalist order. Portugal's participation in World War I (and the dislocation this provoked in its economic, monetary and fiscal situation – not to mention the direct impact this had on civil-military relations) was in no small measure a product of the desire on the part of its ruling élite to demonstrate that they were entitled to membership in the «European Concert» and, hence, entitled to maintain their colonial possessions and imperial practices.[34]

Political Imperatives

This tentative finding, that both the advent and subsequent policies of authoritarian rule in Portugal were closely related to an «overdetermined» structural crisis in that country's capitalist development, by no means precludes the possibility that the emergence of this form of political domination also had its roots in more «superstruc-tural» imperatives. In fact, the conflicts mentioned above were peculiarly «political» in the multiple sense that they tended: 1. to reflect differences of interest between and *Koalitionsfähigkeit* among fractions of the same class, e.g. financial vs. industrial bourgeoisie, «old» vs. «new» middle-class, privately-employed vs. public service workers; 2. to focus on alternative uses (or non-uses) of state power rather than on differences in class hegemony; and 3. to involve (at least indirectly) the asymmetric impact upon Portugal of the unequal distribution of power among nation-states. They did not involve the sort of confrontation between polarized, self-conscious *Klassen für sich* which may characterize both much earlier and later stages of capitalist development, e.g. feudal aristocracy vs. urban bourgeoisie, industrial bourgeoisie vs. industrial proletariat.

These «fractional» conflicts and efforts at alliance formation normally find political expression within the confines of a single regime-type, but, as Karl Marx had already argued convincingly in his *Eighteenth Brumaire* under certain circumstances, they can lead to regime change (without change in the mode of production) *via* the breakdown of previous influence and authority relations. Sterile ideological disputes, atavistic historical attachments, resurgence of regional loyalties, provincial resentment against metropolitan predominance, «inorganic» intellectuals and interest representatives cut off from their class connections, «parliamentary cretinism», praetorianism, violence and illegal political activity by *lumpen* and *déclassé* elements are but some of the «epiphenomenal» manifestations Marx observed in mid-nineteenth century France before Napoleon III's seizure of power. Early twentieth century Portugal exhibited many of these signs of political collapse and several others.

Another reason for stressing the relatively autonomous role of political factors is that, in terms of specific economic *conjoncture* (as distinguished from *structure* discussed above), Portugal was not in such desperate shape. The balance of payments was not further in the red than it had been for several decades: the exchange rate for the *escudo* had levelled off and had even appreciated a bit; 1925 was a relatively good agricultural year and wheat imports were no higher than usual; inflation had slowed down and even stopped by 1924; many industries were in crisis (e.g. textiles, cork, flour, milling and canning) but some were expanding (e.g. cement, mining, ceramics); unemployment does not appear to have been more serious than usual; emigration remained heavy but declined; wages and prices had returned to their relative levels in 1914. Most of these indicators of current economic performance became worse rather than better in the two years following the 1926 coup! These facts by no means annul the importance of the more deep-seated impasses and conflicts but they do suggest that authoritarian rule did not come to Portugal in the imminence of economic collapse.

The most generic political cause of the collapse of democratic parliamentary rule in Portugal was, as the current jargon would have it, the loss of hegemony over the society by its dominant classes. Conversely, this implies that one reason for the relative longevity of subsequent authoritarian rule lay in its ability to put together a viable «political formula» which convinced significant social groups of the naturalness or appropriateness of its domination. Of course, given the ambiguity of the concept of «hegemony», and the fact that its loss can only be ascertained retrospectively, this is not a very enlightening argument. Its analytical weight is comparable to that of the claim that «the regime fell because it was insufficiently: a. powerful; b. popular; c. self-confident; d. internally coherent to sustain itself; e. some combination of the above; or f. all of the above.»

«Conquering bourgeoisies» capable of providing the material and ideational bases for their preferred, liberal-parliamentary, mode of political domination have been notoriously rare in delayed-dependent developing economies.[34a] Compromised by their continued and intimate association with traditional agrarian and commercial élites, unable to compete in price and quality with products exported by earlier developers, penetrated by highly visible foreign interests, badly divided internally over further import substitution, derivative in their ideas and technology, forced by a more militant and conscious working class to cope with «premature» and inflated demands for immediate personal benefits and expanded public goods, these capitalists have trouble protecting their «right to make money», much less asserting their «right to rule.» In particular, hegemony within a «bourgeois-democratic» polity depends on managing at least three general problems: 1. creating and sustaining a minimal winning supportive coalition; 2. extracting sufficient resources from civil society to cover state activities; 3. creating and sustaining the illusion that other modes of economic production and forms of political domination are impossible or inappropriate. In all three of these «management dimensions», the Republic experienced great difficulty, and the military dictatorship which replaced it in 1926 performed even more poorly. It was Salazar's ability to combine and co-opt disparate elements into his National Union, to reorder public finances and to take advantage of the fascist ideological trend in inter-war Europe and the anti-communist wave of the Cold War that accounts for his relative success.

Table 9. *Electoral «Support» for Governing Party: Per cent of Legislative Seats won by «Democrático» Party (PRP), 1910–26*

	1911 (Constituent Assembly)	1912–15 (approx)	1915	1918	1919	1921	1922	1925
Democrático Seats as per cent of Total in Chamber of Deputies	97.9	44.4	67.9	–	52.8	33.1	46.5	51.3
N = ...	(234)	(153)	(156)	(155)	(163)	(163)	(159)	(156)

Source: A. H. de Oliveira Marques, *A Primeira República Portuguesa* (Lisbon: Livros Horizonte, n.d.), pp. 179–181.

Table 10. *Electoral Support for the President: Per cent of Electoral College Vote for Winner on First Turn: 1911–1925*

	1911	1915 (May)	1915 (Aug.)	1918 (April)	1918 (Dec.)	1919	1923	1925
	55.8	96.1	37.6	*–	96.8	48.1	54.8	72.5
N = ...	(217)	(102)	(189)		(125)	(181)	(197)	(171)

* Plebiscitary Election of Sidônio Pais. 513,958 votes in favor.
Source: *Ibid.*, pp. 182–184.

The Portuguese Republic was notorious for its political instability. There were 8 presidents, 45 major cabinet shuffles, 20 «revolutions», 325 «terrorist» incidents and 518 strikes[35] during the regime's 15 year existence. The Republic, however, had a rather successful experience in political machinebuilding. The Republican party (PRP), or «Democráticos» as they were more commonly called, managed to combine an urban petty bourgeois and working class following with the support of rural *caciques* and their dependent clients. This heterogeneous coalition won every election it contested, as can be seen from tables 9 and 10, though it rarely enjoyed a clear majority and suffered endemically from factionalism which made cabinet formation and legislative support difficult. The high point of this perpetual game of «musical chairs» (many politicians were reappointed to ministerial positions they had recently vacated) came in 1920–21 when there were 15 major cabinet reformations and 146 ministers! By 1925–26, however, instability in top-level personnel had declined markedly, as had the strike rate and acts of terrorism.[36] More significant in terms of maintaining broad coalitional support was the defection shortly before the coup of the left-wing of the Democráticos. Previously, all «hiving-off» had involved defections from the right.[37] For the first time, the machine seems to have lost the support of the urban masses who appear to have initially welcomed the military seizure of power.

The chaotic state of Portuguese public finance rivaled the country's ministerial instability for international notoriety in the post-World War I period. Much of the public debt was inherited from the profligate monarchy and war expenses did throw the budget balance badly out of kilter, but republican politicians found it virtually impossible to contain expenditures within the extractive capacity of the state. Nevertheless, the standard, contemporary arguments about the fiscal crisis of the capitalist state hardly apply. Public welfare spending was virtually non-existent so that one cannot attribute it to concerted pressure from an aroused proletariat. Rather it was demands for government employment and pork-barrel public works from petty bourgeois and provincial notables that inflated that side of the ledger.[38] Public subsidies and credit for industry were not a major source of disequilibrium, although there were enough «political capitalists» around to have made charges of illicit enrichment through government favors and funds a credible moral weapon for tight-wing «integralists».[39] Nor was the regime so tightly bound by accountability to propertied groups that it could not extract more revenue from them. The fiscal reforms of 1924 were «progressive» and successful enough so that by the time of the Republic's overthrow the budgetary balance had markedly improved. The specific conflict-*cum*-contradiction which contributed most to the regime's demise was the decline in purchasing power of civilian and military employees to less than one-half of previous levels. The fiscal crisis of the Portuguese State in the mid-1920s was to a large extent internal to it, rather than externally imposed by «popular masses».

Finally, hegemony was weakened by the proliferation of ideological alternatives (mostly on the Right) amplified by a free and greatly expanded press,[40] and encouraged by the «success» of fascist or fascistoid experiences elsewhere (especially those of Mussolini and Primo de Rivera). As long as these alternatives were divided into multiple and competing currents of monarchism, nationalism, clericalism, conservatism, integralism, corporatism, personalism on the one side, and socialism, anarcho-syndicalism and communism on the other, the core republican dogma of popular suffrage, parliamentary rule, secular education and culture, defense of private property and social justice through gradual reform and redistribution remained that which divided the Portuguese the least. The «victors» of 1926 seem to have embraced almost all these ideological divergences and to have had no clear intention to replace parliamentary republican rule with a new hegemonic order. Only after their abject failure did Salazar and his allies manage to synthesize and syncretize a new political formula from several of these disparate components.

The first political imperative tackled by Salazar was the fiscal crisis. So many accounts of his financial wizardry have been published, it hardly seems necessary to describe how he accomplished the «miracle» of putting Portuguese public finances in order.[41] Ruthless centralization of control, improved accounting and collection measures, a few new direct and regressive taxes, cuts in expenditures for the Navy (but not the Army), the National Republican Guard and education plus some internal borrowing made the books balance.[42]

From at least 1933 until the 1960s, the Portuguese State accumulated fiscal surpluses and paid for investments and extraordinary expenses from these «earnings». The impact of these austerity measures on capitalists was softened by a reprivatization of the banking system, new credits for agriculture and industry, higher protective tariffs and imperial preferences, subsidized prices (e.g. for wheat) and, of course, efficient repression of working class demands.

Putting together a dominant political coalition was a more difficult imperative to satisfy. If in retrospect the transition from «exceptional dictatorship» to consolidated authoritarian rule appears to have occurred smoothly at the time, the outcome was anything but foreordained. Resistance to Salazar's gradually unfolding scheme to abolish all political parties and incorporate all «right-thinking patriots» into a single National Union, to disband all class associations in favor of singular, subsidized and state-controlled syndicates and guilds, to convert parliament into an assembly of hand-picked notables and experts, to render executive power unaccountable, not only to the whims of competitive choice, but also to a concerted élite action, to institute permanent censorship and regime control over «the ideological apparatus» came from the left, the center and the right. Armed insurrections, *pronunciamientos,* personal resignations and general strikes came from a wide variety of groups: some who had supported the 1926 coup; some who had opposed it; some who felt the measures were going too far in destroying the nation's political life; others who felt that Salazar was not going far enough in establishing an integral, syndicalist-fascist state.

Table 11. *Ex-deputies Serving in the First Session of the Legislative Assembly and Corporative Chamber: 1934–38*

	Sessions in which first served		Republic (1918–1919)	Republic (After 1920)
	Monarchy (before 1910)	Republic (1910–1914)		
Legislative Assembly	5	0	6	5 (16)
Corporative Chamber	5	6	5	0 (17)*
total	10	6	11	5 (33)

* one unknown.
Source: *Anais,* 1934–1936.

The political compositon and complexion of those first sessions of the Legislative Assembly and Corporative Chamber are indicative of the sort of hodge-podge of tendencies from which Salazar compiled «his» winning coalition, which he then retained for the next thirty years or so. Of the ninety *deputados* in the founding Assembly, sixteen (17.8 per cent) had previously been deputies, only three had been ministers in the Republic and some eighteen (20 per cent) had been ministers during the 1926–32 dictatorship. Among the corporatist *procuradores*, seventeen (15.9 per cent) had already been deputies or senators, ten (9.3 per cent) republican ministers and only seven (6.5 per cent) «dictatorial» ministers. What is even more indicative than this co-optation of past politicians is the date at which the hold-overs first acquired their representative position. About one-third entered politics before 1910, i.e. under the monarchy. The next cohort from which Salazar recruited his representatives was first elected under the peculiar circumstances of the Sidónio Pais «popular dictatorship» (1918–19). In fact, five of the previous monarchists re-entered politics during this period. Over one-half of the ex-republican ministers seated in the Corporative Chamber also held their positions under this proto-typical dictatorship. The final cohort of any importance consisted of those elected after 1920. Of these five, two served in the short-lived parliament of 1921 when the *Democrático* proportion of seats fell exceptionally to 33.1 per cent. In short, the representative élite of the New State, while composed predominantly of new men without previous governmental or elective experience or of those who had held high appointive office during the frequent shifts after the 1926 coup, did manage to recruit important figures from monarchist, nationalist and various conservative parties previously active in Portuguese politics. The link with *Sidonismo* was especially strong. By the second session of the Assembly and the Chamber, recruitment from these pools of previous talent and experience virtually stopped (only 2 in the former, 4 in the latter), and the proportion of alumni from the monarchy and republic dropped thereafter monotonically – despite the fact that new entrants were as a rule no younger than these *anciens*.

Another interesting facet of this co-optation process concerns the regional origins of the hold-overs. All those for whom data are available (13 of the 16 in the Assembly) came from the peripheral regions of Portugal: seven from the North, two from the South (Beja and Evora), none had previously represented Lisbon or Porto! This is not evidence that the *Estado Novo* «inherited» the *caciques* who had been so important to

Table 12. *Electoral Support for Authoritarian Rule: Elections for the Legislative Assembly, 1934–73*

	1. Actual Votes	2. Inscribed Electorate	3. Total Population	4. Turnout (1/2)	5. Participation (1/3)
1934	377,792	478,121	7,148,046	79.0	5.3
1938	649,028	777,033	7,505,554	83.5	8.6
1942	668,785	772,578	7,830,026	86.6	8.5
1945	569,257	992,723	8,045,774	57.3	7.1
1949	948,695	?	8,333,400	?	11.4
1953	991,261	1,351,192	8,621,102	73.4	11.5
1957	1,030,891	1,427,427	8,908,766	72.2	11.6
1961	1,112,577	1,440,148	8,932,000	77.3	12.0
1965	1,211,577	1,609,485	9,234,400	75.3	13.1
1969	1,115,248	1,784,314	9,582,600	62.5	11.6
1973	1,320,952	1,965,717	*8,564,200	67.2	15.4

Source: Antonio Rangel Bandeira, *As Eleições em Portugal* (Toronto: Brazilian Studies, July 1975), p. 3; *Anuario Estadístico*, 1957, p. LVI; *O Século* (11 November, 1973); *Keesing's Weekly*, various numbers.
* The 1965 and 1969 values were interpolations. The 1970 Census revealed an unanticipated net decline in population since the previous decennial census.

republican politics, since so many of these provincials were monarchists or *Sidonistas*, but does show its lack of interest in or accountability to urban masses and their historic political leaders.

Elections, of course, continued to be held after 1934 – more regularly and predictably in fact than under the parliamentary republic. They were not, however, plebiscitary devices for arousing and certifying majority support. One cynic even claimed that their principal function was to enable the police to update their records on regime opponents. Table 12 shows that the *Estado Novo* began with a constitutional plebiscite in which only 5.3 per cent of the population voted. By World War II the registered electorate and actual voters had stagnated at 11 to 13 per cent. Little or no effort was made to expand the electoral rolls until Caetano came to power (many more were eligible than actually enrolled) and the extraordinary constancy of the turnout may have had something to do with the fact that a high proportion of those enrolled were civil servants, employees of para-state agencies and other public dependents.

Nevertheless, regional or better provincial breakdowns of voting could be interesting proximate indicators of régime support, especially when analyzed in terms of patterns of abstention and even overt opposition on the rare occasions when candidates were run against the official state. Unfortunately, however, such breakdowns are only available for the last two legislative elections (1969 and 1973) and only in the former did opposing candidates present themselves.

The data in table 13, despite temporal shallowness, demonstrate a point we advanced earlier about the social origins of the authoritarian élite. The center of gravity of regime support as measured by both relatively high turnout and low opposition vote (the rank-order correlation between the two is almost unity) lay in the lesser-developed, Catholic North and interior – the region of small landholding peasants *par excellence*. The more developed, but still more Catholic, «coastal» region occupied an intermediate position. The latifundist South showed higher abstention rates (in 1969 not 1973), but slightly less opposition electoral support. The Azores and Madeira had a more inconsistent pattern with the exception of Ponta Delgada, the most populous of the Azorean Islands.

The seedbed of opposition was clearly situated in Lisbon and, more particularly, the relatively industrialized district to its south, Setúbal. In both forms of rejection, namely abstention and opposition voting, they were far in the forefront. Whatever impact this might have had upon the regime was, however, systematically distorted. In addition to the usual districting arrangements rigged to overrepresent rural areas, the electoral rolls were manipulated to the benefit of those regions most likely to support the regime. Hence, in Lisbon and Setúbal, the 1969 registered electorate constituted only 74 and 36 per cent of the number of families and 22 and 16 per cent of the total population, respectively. For Bragança and Guarda, the two most supportive districts, the corresponding proportions were 102 and 95 per cent of families and 28 and 29 per cent of the population.

To fiscal order and electoral manipulation, the New State added a third element for its hegemonic formula: ideological control. No aspects of Portuguese political life were perhaps as well-known and documented as its oppressive censorship, sycophantic press, docile academe and pretentious claims to exemplifying a natural organic corporatist order, historically and culturally appropriate to that country's society and traditions.[43] The Spanish Civil War and Axis victories in the early stages of World War II intervened exogenously to bolster these claims and practices. After a very «uncomfortable» period marked by the Allied victory and attempted quarantine of

Table 13. *Regional Support for Authoritarian Rule: Elections to the Legislative Assembly. 1969–1973*

	Turnout		Opposition Vote	
	1969	1973	1969	1973*
1. North & Interior:				
Bragança	79.3	81.0	0.1	
Guarda	76.9	78.9	4.2	
Viana do Castelo	76.6	86.8	13.2	
Vila Real	71.8	77.3	3.4	
Castelo Branco	69.7	74.3	5.6	
Viseu	68.3	70.6	4.5	
Braga	67.9	72.2	10.9	
Portalegre	67.7	79.7	0.0	
2. Coastal:				
Porto	63.0	65.9	13.1	
Aveiro	65.1	67.2	12.9	
Coimbra	62.8	72.0	12.4	
Leiria	61.7	69.1	11.0	
3. Central:				
Lisbon	48.1	54.6	24.5	
Setúbal	47.0	56.3	36.3	
Santarem	57.6	67.7	12.6	
4. South:				
Evora	55.2	64.9	9.7	
Beja	59.8	68.5	10.2	
Faró	59.9	71.9	9.8	
5. Islands:				
Horta	79.3	65.3	0.0	
Angra do H.	59.4	61.3	0.0	
Funchal	58.2	53.5	6.6	
P. Delgada	49.0	50.0	22.2	
Global Average for Continent and Adjacent Islands	61.6	67.2	12.0	

* Opposition slate withdrew from election.
Source: se Table 12.

Spain, the regime's plausibility was again given an exogenous transfusion by the Cold War. The initial emphasis on anti-liberalism and extreme nationalism switched to international collaboration with the Western-Christian world against Soviet and communist aggression. Not until several decades did the isolation produced by protracted colonial war and the loss of *raison d'être* occasioned by American-Soviet *détente* begin to unmask and undermine this façade, as well as promote the emergence of a strong, left-radical alternative vision of Portuguese society.

460

Ironically, the only previous serious challenge to its ideological and political formula came from the extreme Right. As different groups jockeyed to determine what kind of regime would succeed the obviously transitory military dictatorship, an authentically fascist and radical movement emerged from the ranks of *Integralismo*. Calling itself «National Syndicalism», it advocated an anti-liberal, anti-bourgeois, anti-capitalist, anti-internationalist, anti-Bolshevik mobilizational solution – a corporatist *revolução*, not just a corporatist *enquadramento*. Its social base would have been the rural-provincial middle class, the peasantry, the working classes and *técnicos,* and their mobilized efforts would have aimed at breaking the power of «citified bourgeois», «pseudo-intellectuals», «local caciques», «parasitic intermediaries», etc.[44] With its cross-like symbol expressing its «Christian» vocation, its adoption of the red flag pre-empting communist imagery, its blue-shirted militia attracting youth, its verbal violence and xenophobia reflecting its *Integralista* origins, its assurance of a harmonious corporatist order within the existing property system drawing the support of some privileged groups, its promise of social welfare and a more equal distribution of income appealing to some segments of the working class, and its emphasis on technical expertise appealing to professionals[45], the National-Syndicalists seemed in 1932 to represent the wave of Portugal's future. Despite rigid censorship, its propaganda circulated freely, even in a daily newspaper, clearly indicating official sympathy and even complicity. Its leader, Rolão Preto, was a personal friend of Salazar.

Despite or because of its meteoric success in attracting followers and penetrating governing and military circles, it very quickly came into conflict with Salazar's own plans for consolidating a more moderate form of authoritarian rule around a loosely structured «honorific» single party and an impotent, state-controlled set of corporatist institutions. Preto's demagogic leadership qualities may have seemed a threat to the more self-effacing, technocratically-efficient, paternalist image of Salazar. In any case, National Syndicalism's «welfarism» and verbal anti-capitalism would have severely compromised the plan of financial and fiscal reconstruction which was the policy core of the *Estado Novo.* In 1934, in a series of confused events, Preto was arrested and exiled. Shortly thereafter «the purged executive committee of national syndicalists decided to terminate its existence and called upon its members to join the *União Nacional».*[46] A quixotic attempt at a coup by some of its die-hards (in collaboration with anarchosyndicalists[47]) the following year was easily suppressed. Ironically, the Salazar regime appropriated many of the symbols and organizational forms of the Blue-Shirts when, in conjunction with the Spanish Civil War, it entered its own fascistoid period.

Conclusion

The social origins, economic bases and political imperatives associated with the emergence and consolidation of authoritarian rule in Portugal were hardly unique in inter-war Europe. Their combination, however, was rather distinctive as was the eventual outcome. Not only did authoritarian rule survive longer than elsewhere, but it lacked or deliberately avoided many of the features which elsewhere constituted the «fascist minimum».[48] Radical, anti-bourgeois and anti-capitalist motivations, while present, were relatively mitigated and easily transformed by co-optation. The political authority of the bureaucratic apparatus of the state was never undermined or even challenged by a «party-army». Demobilization rather than mobilization was the intended goal of most of its «representative» institutions; obedient compliance rather

461

than enthusiastic support was the preferred role for its citizenry. Leadership was personal and concentrated, but hardly dynamic or charismatic. The regime's nationalistic policies were aimed at cautiously conserving rather than agressively extending its imperial domain.

In common with analogous Eastern European experiences, this form of conservative-bureaucratic authoritarian rule emerged in conjunction with a crisis of financial accumulation at a very early stage of capitalist development and a double crisis in the fiscal management and ideological hegemony of the liberal state. Many, if not most, of its *cadres* were recruited from within the state bureaucracy and the ideological apparatus of its universities. To the limited extent that mass support was involved, peasants, provincial *mesoi* and local notables on the geographic and social periphery of Portuguese society were «mobilized» against its more cosmopolitan, secular and developed center. The absence of linguistic or ethnic minorities, the weakness of a credible communist or proletatian threat, and the *éloignement* of Portugal from great power competition all contributed to moderating if not obliterating some of the scapegoating, xenophobia, violence and other extremist *bizarreries* which characterized authoritarian movements and regimes with similar social origins, economic functions and political imperatives elsewhere in Europe.

However, the Portuguese New State did share in common with virtually all fascist and authoritarian responses to capitalist development and bourgeois modernization a number of profoundly paradoxical characteristics.[49] True, the social origins of its individual leaders and supporters were not dramatically different from those who founded and ran the «bourgeois parliamentary» regime they displaced – a bit younger and more provincial, yes; but basically similar in class and occupation. Nevertheless, once in power, they created new patterns of élite recruitment, circulation and interpenetration which, in the long run, did radically restructure the relation between Portuguese civil society and the state. In terms of economic functions the *Estado Novo* ostensibly aimed at creating a harmonious and organic *tertium genus* avoiding the excesses of both liberal capitalist and bureaucratic socialist development. Instead, it presided over the establishment of an economic system with the worst features of both: extreme inequality in the distribution of wealth and income, and deep-seated class enmity and exploitation on the one hand; stultifying administrative control and reduced capacity for innovation and initiative on the other. Politically, authoritarian rule in Portugal responded to imperatives for fiscal balance, stable coalitional dominance and ideological hegemony. It ended in financial and intellectual bankruptcy supported in the crunch by only a handful of its own secret police.

NOTES

* A grant from the Social Science Research Council in 1971 gave me an initial opportunity to conduct research on Portugal. Since then, support from the Social Science Divisional Research Fund and the Committee on Latin American Studies of the University of Chicago has enabled me to continue that research.

[1] A related difficulty concerns the «exemplary» nature of the case being analyzed. While one could hardly question the *bona fides* of Portugal as a generically authoritarian regime from 1973 to 1974 (see Juan Linz «Spain: An Authoritarian Regime» in E. Allardt & S. Rokkan (eds.), *Mass Politics* (New York; Free Press, 1970), pp. 251–283 for the general model), one could ask whether this type of political domination is not so broadly defined that it encompasses numerous

subtypes, each with its own origins and genealogy. Hence, whatever generalizations are suggested by the Portuguese experience may, at best, only be valid for a subset of similar authoritarian regimes – «demobilizing, bureaucratized and exclusionist», as I have labelled it elsewhere. «Liberation by Golpe: Retrospective Thoughts on the Demise of Authoritarian Rule in Portugal», *Armed Forces and Society* II, (Fall, 1975), pp. 5–33.

² Leaving aside the small intellectual *coterie* of «Social Catholics» which grouped around Salazar and Pe·Cerejeira (future Archbishop of Lisbon) first in the Academic Center for Christian Democracy at the University of Coimbra and later (1917) in a political party, the Portuguese Catholic Center. Salazar ran and won a seat in 1921 on this party label but made only a brief appearance in the Chamber and then resigned. H. Kay, *Salazar and Modern Portugal* (London: Eyre and Spottiswoode, 1970), p. 32.

³ A. H. de Oliveira Marques, «Revolution and Counterrevolution in Portugal – Problems of Portuguese History, 1900–1930» in M. Kossok (ed.) *Studien über die Revolution* (Berlin: Akademie Verlag, 1969), p. 416, fn. 27.

⁴ Hermínio Martins, «The Breakdown of the Portuguese Democratic Republic», paper presented at the Seventh World Congress of Sociology, Varna, Bulgaria, 1970.

⁵ *O Integralismo e a República,* Vol. I (Lisbon: Inquérito, 1964), p. 12.

⁶ For a lengthy list of those who welcomed the downfall of the regime (or more accurately, of the Democrático machine, see A. H. de Oliveira Marques, *History of Portugal,* Vol. II (New York: Columbia University Press, 1972), p. 174. Also his *Historia de Portugal,* Vol. II (Lisbon: Palas Editores, 1973), pp. 286–7 for a slightly different version. Also Stanley Payne, *A History of Spain and Portugal,* Vol. II (Madison: University of Wisconsin Press, 1973), pp. 559–577.

⁷ *A Revolução Portuguese* (Lisbon: Editorial Aster, 1961), p. 574.

⁸ Of the thirty-three opponents active in opposing the installation of authoritarian rule from 1928 to 1931, whose brief biographies were given, nineteen were military officers. A. H. de Oliveira Marques, *A Unidade de Oposição à Ditadura* (Lisbon: Europa-America, 1973), *passim.* Marcelo Caetano has admitted very candidly that «within the Dictatorship (of 1926) in both civilian and military circles, there were plenty of non-believers as well as believers (in Salazar)». *Paginas Inoportunas* (Lisbon: Livraria Bertrand, n.d.), p. 170.

⁹ Previously (in 1926) Salazar had held the post for a very short time but resigned when it became clear that the government would refuse to accept his policies. According to an eyewitness account, General Gomes da Costa, head of the victorious military junta, appointed Salazar without knowing who he was. H. Kay, *op.cit,* p. 38–9.

¹⁰ According to the official results as reported in *ibid.,* 719, 364 voted «yes», only 5,955 voted «no» and some 488,840 abstained (p. 49). Other published versions have given rather different figures. In any case, abstention was high but the regime had the nerve to claim that those not sufficiently motivated to vote «no» supported its position and, therefore, counted the 40% abstaining as voting in favor of the proposed constitution. See Antonio de Figuereido, *Portugal and its Empire: The Truth* (London: Victor Gollancz, 1961), p. 40 for a description of the conditions under which this «popular» consultation took place.

¹¹ In these first legislative elections, some 377,372 reportedly voted (79% of those eligible and 5.3% of the total population). Unfortunately, for neither of these elections are district breakdowns available. For these and several succeeding contests, the country comprised a single electoral district.

¹² «Corporatism and Public Policy in Authoritarian Portugal», *Contemporary Political Sociology Series,* Sage Professional Series, Vol. I, No. 06–011, 1975, p. 31.

¹³ The primary source for this analysis is the short biographies contained in the *Anais da Assembléia Legislativa e Câmara Corporativa* (1934–1975). Dr. Manuel Cabeçada Ataíde has kindly made available to me his collection of handwritten 3"×5" cards which record this and other information. The tabulation presented herein should be considered tentative, given problems of legibility and manual sorting.

¹⁴ André et Francine Demichel, *Les dictatures européennes* (Paris: PUF, 1973), pp. 17, 32.

¹⁵ Nicos Poulantzas, *La crise des dictatures* (Paris: Maspero, 1975), pp. 55 et seq.

¹⁶ Therefore, we are assuming that the probability of decease was equal for all categories at the

beginning of the session. Obviously, some of the one-termers did not get re-anointed for the simple reason that they had died or become ill. Since the *procuradores* of the Corporate Chamber were significantly older than the *deputados* of the Assembly, this assumption could be a source of systematic distortion.

[17] Although the compilation must be considered very tentative due to legibility problems with the names of small towns, it seems that only nine members of the Assembly and six from the Chamber were born in the southernmost provinces. With 10.5% of Portugal's population residing in Evora, Beja and Faró, as of 1930, the south was slightly underrepresented in these founding sessions. Stanley Payne, *op.cit.*, p. 574, has calculated that under the parliamentary republic «the number of leaders from the (more conservative north) was 25 to 30 per cent less than its population warranted».

[18] A. H. de Oliveira Marques, «Estudos sobre Portugal no Século XX«, *O Tempo e O Modo* (March-April, 1967), pp. 270–295.

[19] «Corporatism and Public Policy in Authoritarian Portugal», pp. 32–3.

[20] The Assembly which initially had a lower rate of turnover gradually became more of a revolving-door institution. By the eighth session (1961–65) almost one-half its members were newcomers and of these 80% left at the end of the term. The Corporative Chamber «lost» only 56% of its 101 newcomers.

[21] Henrique Galvão, *Santa Maria: My Crusade for Portugal* (Cleveland & New York: World, 1961). Also Warren Rodgers, Jr., *The Floating Revolution* (New York: McGraw-Hill, 1962).

[21a] This *catedocracia* – prominence of tenured university professors in the élite structure of the *Estado Novo* – raises the issue of *agencement,* the role of these professionals in relation to other interests. Apparently, a high percentage of them were directors of financial, commercial and industrial companies (or became so subsequently). For a listing, see Armando Castro, *A economia portuguesa do século XX: 1900–25* (Lisbon: Edições 70, 1973), pp. 197, 276–7.

[22] David Hackett Fischer, *Historians' Fallacies* (New York: Harper Torchbooks, 1970), pp. 135–140.

[23] *Os Políticos e o poder económico* (Lisbon: Edição do Autor, 1969), pp. 15, 16, 18, 22, 25. In his *Depoimento* (Rio: Record, 1974), p. 112, Marcelo Caetano acknowledges (and defends) these practices. He even suggests that they constituted a sort of functional substitute for pensions!

[24] Cf. Guillermo O'Donnell, *Modernización y Autoritarismo* (Buenos Aires: Paidos, 1972) and his «Desenvolvimento Político: Novas Perspectivas de Pesquisa» paper presented at the Conference on History and Social Sciences, Campinas (SP) 26–30 May, 1975 for Latin American cases; Ludovic Garrucio, *L'industrializzazion tra nazionalismo e rivoluzione* (Bologna: Il Mulino, 1969) for a more Eurocentric discussion.

[25] Portugal, Instituto Nacional de Estatistica, *Comercio Exterior 1947,* Vol. I, pp. xxi-xxv. Also A. H. de Oliveira Marques, «Revolution and Counterrevolution», p. 406.

[26] A. H. de Oliveira Marques, *op.cit.* Vol. II., pp. 119–29 for a general résumé of the *conjoncture.* Also Stanley Payne, *op.cit.,* Vol. II, pp. 573–5. Actually, industrial employment decreased in proportional terms from 1920 to 1930, as did agriculture. The residual «services» category increased from 22 to 37% of the economically active population. For a more complete analysis of Portugal's relatively slow structural transformation during this period, see Armando Castro, *op.cit.*

[27] Portugal, like most dependent economies, did tend to have a dominant trading «partner». The United Kingdom accounted for 24 to 30% of imports and 21–29% of exports in the 1926–29 period. With «invisibles», this concentration may have reached 40–50% of Portugal's foreign exchanges. British interests also controlled important public utilities, much of the wine trade and some industries. The UK also held Portugal's war debts.

[28] A. H. W. King, «Economic Conditions in Portugal. Dated July, 1932», Department of Overseas Trade (London: HMSO, 1932), pp. 9–10. Other United Kingdom Consular reports by S. G. Irving (1926), Leonard H. Leach (1928) and A. H. W. King (1930) were important sources for the brief description of the economic situation which follows. Also Ch. H. Cunningham & Ph. M. Cap, «Portugal: Resources, Economic Conditions, Trade and Finance». *Trade Information Bulletin,* No 455, U. S. Department of Commerce, Washington, D. C., 1927.

[29] A. H. King (1932), p. 19.

[30] The most detailed description of political events and issues during this period is Damião Peres, *Historia de Portugal*, Suplemento (Porto: Portucalense, 1954).

[31] The best general account of colonial developments is A. H. de Oliveira Marques, *Historia de Portugal*, Vol. II, pp. 355 *et seq.* Also A. H. W. King (1930), pp. 57ff.

[32] Although one of Salazar's «fiscal decrees» upon his taking up the Finance Ministry in 1928 ordered the devolution to private enterprise of all state activities having «a purely commercial or industrial character», there is little evidence after that date of this having occurred.

[33] For a similar emphasis on the «instrumentality» of fascism for capitalist development, see J. Solé-Tura's article in S. J. Woolf (ed.) *The Nature of Fascism* (New York: Vintage, 1969), pp. 42–50.

[34] Cf. A. H. de Oliveira Marques, *A Primeira República Portuguesa* (Lisbon: Livros Horizonte, 1970), p. 78.

[34a] In his *Depoimento*, Marcelo Caetano aims some of his most bitter remarks at the «lack of culture», absence of risk-taking, monopolistic instincts and political timidity of Portugal's bourgeoisie.

[35] See A. H. de Oliveira Marques, *A Primeira República Portuguesa* for documentation on cabinet shuffles and strikes. The other data on instability are contained in R. V. Gersdorff, *Portugals Finanzen* (Bielefeld: Verlag Gieseking, 1961), pp. 6–9.

[36] A. H. de Oliveira Marques, *A Primeira República*, p. 161. Also David Ferreira, «Greves», *Dicionário de Historia de Portugal*, Vol.II (Lisbon: Iniciativas Editoriais, 1965), pp. 379–86.

[37] Cf. James O'Connor, *The Fiscal Crisis of the State* (New York: St. Martin's Press, 1973).

[38] Especially crucial was the substantial increase in state employment under the Republic and the decline in purchasing power of civil servants, A. H. de Oliveira Marques, *A Primeira República Portuguesa*, pp. 58–9. The Portuguese case before and after the *Estado Novo* appears to confirm «Director's Law» which states that «Public Expenditures are made for the primary benefit of the middle classes, and financed with taxes which are borne in considerable part by the poor and the rich», George Stigler, «Director's Law of Public Income Redistribution,» *The Journal of Law and Economics*, XIII (April, 1970), pp. 1–10.

[39] Raul Rego *(op.cit.)* takes indignant exception to these charges apparently repeated as late as the 1960s in campaign speeches by Marcelo Caetano. Also A. H. de Oliveira Marques *op.cit.* Vol.II, refers to moralistic reaction to corruption, scandal and «political capitalism» as a factor in the generalized rejection of the parliamentary republic (pp. 172–4).

[40] Hermínio Martins in his «Breakdown» essay *(op.cit.* fn. 4) attaches considerable significance to this communications explosion. In a country which was 80% illiterate and had a population of only 5 million there were almost 600 periodicals in 1900 – more per capita than the U. S. or the U. K. In 1926 there were 35 dailies and 283 weeklies being published.

[41] For his own account, see A. de Oliveira Salazar, *A reorganização financeira* (Coimbra: Coimbra Editôra, 1930). A very comprehensive treatment is Araújo Correia, *Portugal Econômico e Financeiro*, 2 vols. (Lisbon: Imprensa Nacional, 1938). Also useful is *Doze Anos na Pasta das Finanças: 1928–1940*, 2 vols. (Lisbon: Corporação do Crédito e Seguros, 1968).

[42] The League of Nations, however, refused until the mid-1930s to certify that Portuguese public finances were in fact balanced since the nominal equivalence of receipts and expenditures was accomplished by domestic borrowing and juggling of categories. To make his fiscal miracle more impressive, Salazar always used the first year of military dictatorship (1926/7) as the base-year, rather than the last fiscal year under the Republic (1924/5).

[43] For example, Peter Fryer & P. McGowan Pinheiro, *Le Portugal de Salazar* (Paris: Ruedo Ibérico, 1963); Fernando Queiroga, *Portugal Oprimido* (Rio: 1958): Rudi Maslowski, *Der Skandal Portugal* (Munich: Hanser Verlag, 1971): Mario Soares, *Le Portugal Baillonné* (Paris: Calmann-Levy, 1972).

[44] A. Neves da Costa, *Para alem da ditadura I:Soluções Corporativas* (Lisbon: Nacional Sindicalismo, January, 1933).

[45] Cf. «Portugal's Blue-Shirt Fascism,» *The Literary Digest* (June 3, 1933), p. 14. For an

excellent but brief analysis of National Syndicalism see Herminio Martins, «Portugal» in S. J. Woolf (ed.) *European Fascism* (London: Weidenfeld and Nicolson, 1968), pp. 319–22.

[46] *Ibid.*, p. 320.

[47] Stanley Payne refers to a similar attempt in Spain at virtually the same time in which a «fascistic group» of «national syndicalists» (later JONS) made an unsuccessful appeal to the anarchosyndicalist worker confederation. «Social Composition and Regional Strength of the Spanish Falange» this volume, p. 423. Presumably, both the Spaniards and the Portuguese were inspired by the success of Italian nationalists in recruiting syndicalists to their cause a decade earlier.

[48] For a listing of «the fascist minimum», see Ernst Nolte, *Die Krise des liberalen Systems und die faschistischen Bewegungen* (Munich: Deutscher Taschenbuch Verlag, 1966). A more limited but more reactive and negative definition of generic fascism can be found in his *Three Faces of Fascism* (New York: Holt, Rinehart, and Winston, 1965). Even more *ad hoc* are the listings in Paul Hayes, *Fascism* (London: George Allen & Unwin, 1973), F. L. Carsten, *The Rise of Fascism* (Berkeley: University of California Press, 1969) and N. Kogan «Fascism as a political system» in S. J. Woolf (ed.) *The Nature of Fascism* (New York: Vintage, 1969), pp. 11–18.

[49] The paradoxical nature of fascism has been noted by others. For example, in Nathaniel Greene's «Preface» to his *Fascism: an Anthology* (New York: Thomas Y. Crowell, 1968).

The National Front in Switzerland*

BEAT GLAUS

The Social Structure and Origins of a Swiss Fascist Movement 1930–1940

The fascist movements in Switzerland play no great part in the international discussion of fascism. Various surveys do not even mention them.[1] Ernst Nolte deals with them only briefly.[2] The anti-fascist backlash in Switzerland produced the first comprehensive study of the largest of these movements, the National Front.[3] In the immediate post-war years, various officially documented reports supplied answers to open questions of civil and military justice.[4] In 1966, Peter Gilg and Erich Gruner dealt with the national preconditions of these currents.[5] Subsequently, Walter Wolf assessed the importance of the National Front and other fascist groups from the standpoint of modern Swiss democracy.[6] I myself published a sociological examination of the National Front in 1969.[7] Klaus-Dieter Zöberlein supplemented the early history of the Front with his valuable work of biographical research.[8]

The External Course of Events

The beginnings of the National Front are to be found in the intellectual and political unrest which took hold of the student population of the university and of the Federal Institute of Technology in Zurich around 1930. The foremost subject of contention was the task and the future of higher education; the chief spokesmen were the student-councellor Dr. Julius Schmidhauser[9] and the medical student, Walter Robert Corti[10]. But the discussion broadened, and the values of a democratic society and a liberal economy were themselves called into question. The impetus for these debates had been given by two conferences of academics staged by the Swiss Radical-Democratic Party.[11] After the meeting of June 1930, the younger generation of politicized academics in Zurich – with the exception of a few Marxists – joined forces in the New Front («Neue Front») political group to carry out these discussions. It was here that the political outlook of the more active students was molded over the next two years. Some of their number were also involved in the activities of the Young Liberals («Jungfreisinnige»). The New Front group had little connection with fascism, even though Robert Tobler[12], later a party-member, chaired its meeting from the start. In the autumn of 1930, Hans Vonwy[13], dissatisfied with the New Front, set up the National Front which aimed at winning support among the populace at large. In the years from 1931 to 1933, its appeal was strengthened by «Der Eiserne Besen» (the Iron Broom), an anti-Semitic newspaper, and by agitation along the lines of Austrian National Socialism. Thanks to the economic crisis, political uncertainty at home, and Hitler's so-called seizure of power, other «fronts» sprang up like mushrooms in 1933. In this «springtime of fronts» the National Front numbered serveral hundred members, chiefly in Reformed Church German-speaking Switzerland. By now, the New Front had also become more one-sided in its membership and its ideology. With

Robert Tobler's corporativism, Paul Lang's[14] organic view of the state, and Hans Oehler's[15] foreign policy which rejected the League of Nations and leaned towards Germany, it had come very near to a fascist ideological system on all essential points. It had access to an important publishing organ in the «Schweizer Monatshefte» (Swiss Monthly) edited by Oehler and having close links with the Popular League for the Independence of Switzerland (Volksbund für die Unabhängigkeit der Schweitz). In April 1933, the New Front and the National Front came together in a combative alliance and organized themselves as a party. The Schaffhausen New Front group obtained the services of the Stein Frontier Messenger newspaper («Steiner Grenzbote»).[16] The first mass-meetings were held, and retired Coloned Divisionnaire Emil Sonderegger who had made his name in the general strike of 1918, campaigned for the party.[17] On 13 May, the New Front was absorbed into the National Front. The New Front academics laid claim to the leadership. Fascist institutions and devices were adopted. The aim was to be not one party among many, but the organized nucleus of a restored state.

Intensive publicity and initial popular support guaranteed a rapid expansion. On 1 August 1933 in Schaffhausen, with the authorization of that town's Federal Commemoration Committee (Bundesfeierkomitee), the provincial leader Dr. Rolf Henne[18] called officially for the re-establishment of the folk-community («Volksgemeinschaft»). One month later, in special election to the Council of states, the second chamber of the federal parliament, the same man won the support of a considerable number of previously bourgeois and socialist voters. In the elections for the Zurich municipal council in September 1933, the National Front was one of the factions linked together in the «Patriotic Action» citizens' bloc (Vaterländische Aktion) that campaigned against «red Zurich». The Front won 10 of the 125 seats on the municipal council.

Table 1. *Composition of the Most Important Elections*

Year	Election	Votes gained by NF	Per cent	Mandates
1933	Schaffhausen special election for Council of States on 3.9.	2 949	27.1	
	Zurich Municipal Council elections on 24.9	6 085	7.7	10 out of 125
1934	Berne Cantonal Council elections on 6.4. Electoral district Bern-Stadt	373	1.6	
1935	Zurich Cantonal Council elections on 7.4	9 211	6.2	6 out of 180
	Elections for National Council, 27.10:			
	Berne[19]	2 428	1.6	
	Schaffhausen	1 544	12.2	
	Thurgau	812	2.7	
	Zurich	5 678	3.7	1 out of 28
1936	Schaffhausen Cantonal Council elections on 1.11 in Schaffhausen, Neuhausen, Stein and Schleitheim	1 411	21.9	
1937	Aargau Cantonal Council elections on 14.3. Electoral districts Aarau, Baden, Brugg	826	3.3	1
1938	Zurich Municipal Council elections on 20.3	1 913	2.4	
1939	Zurich Cantonal Council elections on 19.3	3 559	2.4	

(The percentage-figures in this table represent the share of the respective electorate)

Even the secession of the Basel Major Ernst Leonhardt[20] and his North-West Swiss following did little to check the party's growth. «Die Front» and other combative papers were founded.[21] In 1934 the party was able to launch a widely-supported campaign in Schaffhausen for the reduction of mortgage-interest and of rents, as well as a national campaign for the total revision of the federal constitution. «Front» and «Grenzbote» became daily papers, supervised by a party publishing-house. Hans Oehler, pushed out by the «Monatshefte», started up the independent National Monthly («Nationale Hefte») as a platform of his own Publications of the National Front («Schriften der Nationalen Front») aimed at propagating the main ideas of the movement.[22] The first large-scale provincial party conference («Gauparteitag») was held. Whilst various other right-wing movements had already begun to stagnate, the National Front continued on its upward path. The well-known writer Jakob Schaffner (1875–1944) espoused its cause. When the legislative body of the canton of Zurich was elected in April 1935, the Front gained 6 out of around 80 urban seats (out of a total of 180 seats on the cantonal council). In the autumn of the same year, the National Front installed its own printing-press in the party headquarters in Schaffhausen.

But the anti-fascist backlash in the towns was gathering momentum as well. One example was the socialist reaction to the Front's pronouncements on the riots in the working-class districts of Töss bei Winterthur and Zurich-Aussersihl, while the liberal response manifested itself *inter alia* in the defamation-suits filed by the Federal Councillor Schulthess and the National Councillor Schüpbach. And when the National Front demonstrated on the streets of Zurich against Erika Mann's «Pfeffermühle» cabaret and Friedrich Wolf's play «Professor Mannheim», the police took swift action. An ever-increasing proportion of the Swiss public rejected the Front as something «un-Swiss» and «imported». But the real swing away from the Front began to make itself felt only in the summer of 1935. The plebiscite's clear rejection of a total revision of the constitution marked the beginning of the end for indigenous frontism and the assorted movements that aimed at national renewal under the aegis of conservative revolution. At this time, the National Front had a maximum strength of around 10,000 registered party-members, while the Social-Democrats numbered over 50,000. A quarter of the Front's members were to be found in the Zurich township alone, and around 1,000 each in the remaining area of Zurich canton, in Schaffhausen canton, in St. Gallen canton and in Aargau canton. The rest were divided up mainly between Thurgau and Berne cantons, and French-speaking Switzerland.

The movement fought against its decline by reorganizing and by strengthening its fascist traits: reorganization of the militia, ideological national-socialism, etc. In the early spring of 1937, the National Front, the fascist Union Nationale in Geneva and the fascist Lega National Ticinese divided Switzerland up between themselves in accordance with language-boundaries. The Front pulled out of the Romance cantons in favor of the other two groups. Various critical symptoms served to confirm, however, that the tide had turned against the Front. In the Zurich elections for the National Council in 1935, the Front had just managed to scrape in with a single seat in the first chamber of the federal parliament although it had fielded candidates in the cantons of Schaffhausen, Thurgau and Berne as well. In Zurich canton, its fortunes had been particularly adversely affected by the competition of the Independents («Landesring der Unabhängigen»), led by the MIGROS businessman Gottlieb Duttweiler.[23] In June 1936, former party-members who had resigned from the Front founded the Federal Social Workers' party («Eidgenössiche Soziale Arbeiter-Partei»), although this never achieved any importance. In the same summer, the Frontist businessman Friedrich

Eisenegger made his way to the German Ministry of Propaganda to release frozen Swiss funds for his fascist publishing-house in Lausanne, and by this action brought discredit upon the movement. In 1937, before the vote on a fascist ban on free-masonry, it was revealed that individual Front-members had benefited from semi-private German support during the 1935 law-suit in Berne about the so-called «Proto-cols of the Elders of Zion».[24] Some of the Front's most valuable members turned their backs on the party in the wake of these disclosures. Vehement internal wranglings completed the party's troubles, and the national leader Henne was dismissed. The chief criticism voiced was that ideological national-socialism had done the party more harm than good. As a result, the numerically small circle around Oehler, Henne and Schaffner, which was nonetheless politically and financially important, split off. The League of Loyal Swiss of National-Socialist Ideology came into being («Bund treuer Eidgenossen nationalsozialistischer Weltanschauung»), a movement which was to end in collaboration.

Only with difficulty could the National Front maintain the framework of the party. Begging campaigns were necessary to revitalise the party-press. All the seats the Front had gained were lost in the Zurich communal elections of March 1938 and in the Zurich cantonal elections of March 1939. The number of members dropped to a fraction of its former size. Widespread police action and federal criminal proceedings against two extreme right-wing groups showed that, in the face of the international crisis, the authorities intended to keep Frontism as far as possible under control. During the Sudetan crisis, the National Front had to bear the brunt of public anger. The new leader of the party, Dr. Robert Tobler, tried to reach some accommodation with the authorities and the press, but his efforts met with scant success. On the outbreak of World War II, most of the active members entered military service, and henceforth the daily papers were able to appear only once a week. When Leader Tobler was briefly imprisoned on suspicion of espionage at the end of February 1940, the party quickly decided upon its own dissolution, to hold its forces ready «for a new engagement» («für einen neuen Einsatz») as was said at the time. The newspaper-concern and the cooperative undertakings continued in existence.

This new engagement took the form of founding surrogate organizations, like the Federal Union («Eidgenössische Sammlung») and the Schaffhausen National Community («Nationale Gemeinschaft»). In the years of German success in the war, these groups managed to attract between two and three thousand members. Not a few erstwhile National Front members engaged in actual military or political collaboration with Nazi Germany, however, and Tobler himself received a few thousand francs by way of German financial assistance for his paper. The surrogate and surviving organi-zations of the National Front were wound up in the summer and autumn of 1943 by the Federal Council.

Organizational Development

For the National Front, fascism signified a combination «of the socialist and military principles». This was reflected in the fascist party-structure. Like its socialist and communist counterparts, it was based on the organizing of masses who could be directed and influenced through a rigid system of local groups, through party-officials, regular payment of membership contributions, leisure-organizations, etc. A system of vertical dependencies, autocratic methods of leadership, unremitting and vociferous propaganda and agitation, a kind of party-militia, the maintenance of a claim to power

470

in the state, irrational dedication and military discipline among the members: these were the chief characteristics of the movement.

Local groups, regular contributions, a national secretariat and cantonal leaders had been features of the National Front as far back as the years 1930–1932. With the «Eiserne Besen», it had adopted the fascist style of propaganda. Specific campaigns of agitation were carried out, special youth- and sports-groups were envisaged. An open-air party-assembly displayed the beginnings of paramilitary formations and uniform-wearing. In the «springtime of fronts» («Frontenfrühling») in 1933, the unified party enshrined in its statutes its commitment to «the spiritual and political renewal of the Swiss folk-community through national and social policies» («die geistige und politische Erneuerung der schweizerischen Volksgemeinschaft durch nationale und soziale Politik»). It intended to make its stand not on democratic foundations, as the New Front had formerly done, but «on Swiss soil». Significantly enough, it adopted as its flag the elongated cross of old Switzerland, as its membership-badge a little Swiss cross with «inlaid morning-star», and as its clothing a gray shirt with black tie. The Front's fascist greeting added to the foreign salute the Swiss cry: «Haruus».[25] Membership was restricted to «Aryan» Swiss citizens who were prepared to engage themselves unsparingly for the party's aims. The organizational units were: local group, province and country, («Ortsgruppe . . . Gau . . . Land»); their legislative bodies were the assembly of the active members of the local group, the provincial council, and the diet («Aktivenversammlung . . . Gaurat . . Tagsatzung»); their executives the local group-leader and the provincial and national leaders with their staff. The first group-leader of the fascist leader-principle also appeared. A triumvirate with equal powers stood at the head, consisting of two members of the New Front and Dr. Ernst Biedermann[26] of the National Front as the national leader («Landesführer»).

In February 1934, Biedermann was replaced by Rolf Henne. A revision of the statutes ensued. The name people's movement («Volksbewegung») made the nature of the party's challenge clearer. Confirmation and recall henceforth regulated the relationship between the national directorate and the provincial leader, and between the provincial leader and the subordinate local leaders. The «Landesführer» chose the national directorate, although his choice was «subject to confirmation by the diet»; he was also in charge of organization and the conduct of the party's business and its policies. Henne performed his duties on a full-time, unpaid basis.

The indoctrination of party-members was carried out at more or less cyclical assemblies, at training-courses and at mass-meetings. From 1933 onwards, Frontist students were organized in a special university-group, for younger followers there was the National Youth («Nationale Jugend»), and for the ladies the National Women's League. Music-and theatre-clubs and similar societies took care of leisure activities. The party also planned for specific institutions to deal with social and economic life which aimed at systematization according to profession. Industrial cells were created in various firms, and in individual branches the Frontists formed employer- and employee-groups. An insurance-fund for the unemployed was set up, though never a trade-union. The industrial economist Dr. Hans Bachmann[27] formulated the outlines of a party arbitration tribunal which was intended to function «as a settlements authority, or in the language of the bourgeois legal code as an arbitration tribunal, or as an agreements office for employers and employees». After the tribunal was set up in Schaffhausen, however, it did little to justify its existence. The vanguard-formations («Harst») of the National Front were in action from the «springtime of the fronts» onwards. They were used primarily for practical purposes, i.e. for defense and for propagandizing, but their organization was along paramilitary lines and tied in with sporting activity. In spite of the federal ban on wearing of uniforms, «Harst»-members were not averse to appearing in gray-shirts. Like the party, the «Harst» had a national leader and several provincial leaders. In February 1934, the formation was banned in the canton of Zurich.

Definitive regulations were fixed in 1936, together with an «Unalterable 26-Point Program». The «Harst» was replaced by the so-called «Auszug» (selection[28]), to which all the active members now belonged. This step meant that the National Front was in theory a completely militarized movement, and more evidently so than either German or Italian fascism. The leader-principle was given greater validity as well. The national leader was henceforth autonomous in his appointment of the national directorate, as well as being the last court of appeal in exclusion-cases. The local group-leaders were chosen by the provincial leaders, who in turn were picked by the «Auszug». As before, the regulatory committee – that is, essentially the provincial leaders – also decided upon the national chairman. Nonetheless, the customary predominance of the legislative body had been seriously eroded, and the membership's power of influence restricted to the form of the plebiscite.

The financial foundations of the party were laid by regular contributions from members, one Franc per person per month. In these circumstances, the selfless dedication of the active members was of immense value. Party-offices were filled on an unpaid basis. Members of the vanguard and other officials often placed not just their leisure, but also their cars and other possessions at the disposal of the party. Party-projects like the insurance-fund, the publishing-house, the Schaffhausen headquarters and the printing-press could only be realized because the wealthier, middle-class members gave them cooperative support. Donations from industry and from private individuals can have been of only secondary importance.

Class Disposition and Age Structure

Because of the positions regarding sources, I can give only an incomplete documentation of the social stratification and age-structure of the Front's adherents. My statements are essentially based on analyses of a number of party-members, electoral candidates, and signatories of Frontist campaign-petitions.

In respect of membership, the only available figures were those of the Schaffhausen group, that is, a more or less representative selection of 126 out of the approximately 500 Frontists who lived in rural Schaffhausen between 1933 and 1935; 345 of the total of 346 urban members around 1938, and 237 of the 238 members of the surrogate «Nationale Gemeinschaft» organization.

All these groups were dominated by the dependent, wage-earning classes – employees and workers – a pattern roughly in accord with the Swiss social structure. These two strata provided around two-thirds of the membership, and the proportion of workers was greater than that of employees. The patterns of membership for rural Schaffhausen were dominated by the representatives of the old middle-class, the farmers, tradesmen and artisans. Conversely, the 111 élite members of the urban group were drawn from this stratum to an even lesser extent than the urban party-members. The proportion of farmers was very small in all cases. One wonders whether the figure for rural Schaffhausen was really only 7 per cent. Around 5 per cent

Table 2. *Social Composition of the National Front in Schaffhausen*

Area	(Percentage proportions of social classes)			
	Upper Class	Self-employed (Farmers)	Employees	Workers (Unskilled)
Rural Schaffhausen (Land)				
Membership of National Front 1933–35 (n=126)	6.3	36.5 (7.1)	24.6	32.6 (15.9)
Urban Schaffhausen (Stadt)				
Entire membership of National Front 1937/38 (n=345)	4.6	28.4 (0.6)	31.0	36.0 (9.3)
Of these, members who belonged to the «Auszug» (n=111)	7.2	18.9	31.5	42.4 (9.9)
Schaffhausen Canton				
Entire membership of «Nationale Gemeinschaft» 1942 (n=237)	5.1	22.3 (2.1)	26.2	46.4 (8.9)
Of these, women (n=26)			11.5	88.5 (15.4)

of members belonged to the upper class, in which are here included industrialists, directors, doctors and other academics.

The upper class and the old middle-class seem to have been over-represented in urban Schaffhausen. This can be attributed, in part at least, to the powerful socialist presence in the town, which gave the citizens reason to fear for their property. While it is also true that a greater number of the National Front's members in Schaffhausen came from the employee- and worker-strata, the percentage was lower than the proportion of dependent wage-earning men in Schaffhausen or indeed Switzerland at the time. It is fair to see a kind of middle-class character in the Schaffhausen groups, if the employees, the new middle-class, are also included in the concept. There again, workers accounted for almost half the membership of the later «Nationale Gemeinschaft». These observations cannot of course simply be extended to the party's other cantonal groups, but by and large they probably apply to them as well.

Table 3. *Social Composition of the Candidates Fielded for the Zurich Cantonal Assembly Elections of 1935*

	(Percentage proportions of social classes)			
	Upper Class	Self-employed (Farmers)	Employees	Workers (Unskilled)
Average (n=1068)	16.8	24.9 (8.1)	40.4	17.9 (2.5)
Radical Democrats (n=141)	46.8	22.0 (1.4)	27.7	3.5
National Front (n=111)	17.1	21.6 (5.4)	40.5	20.8 (3.6)
Social Democrats (n=155)	11.0	12.9 (1.9)	41.9	34.2 (5.2)

Because a party's electoral candidates embody a certain selection, they present only an imperfect reflection of that party's social stratification. But an analysis can still be instructive since there is such good material for comparison. In 1935, the National Front fielded 111 candidates for the Zurich cantonal legislature. On average, two-fifths of all candidates were employees, a good fifth middle and lower self-employed, slightly less than a fifth workers, and the rest belonged to the upper stratum. While for example the old middle-class was over-represented in the Farmers' party («Bauernpartei»), the employee-class in the Democrats, the proprietorial upper-class in the Radical Democrats («Freisinn»), and the worker-stratum in the Social Democrats and communists, only the candidates of the National Front and the Social-Christians («Christlichsoziale») represented all the social strata fairly equally according to the mean values. Thus at least the selection of candidates matched up to the movement's claim to embody the «folk-community». The same is true of the elections for the Zurich municipal council in 1933. At the beginning of 1934, the Schaffhausen National Front presented a cantonal initiative calling for a reduction in mortgage-interest and in rents (to my knowledge, never submitted to the plebiscite). In doing so, it addressed itself primarily to certain disadvantaged sections of the population, but practically all the members and many of the 1933 Front-voters must have signed the petition as well. Of the signatories, 45 per cent were workers, 36 per cent middle and lower self-employed, 18 per cent employees and 1 per cent members of the upper class. In urban Schaffhausen and in Neuhausen the employees and workers were strongly predominant among the signatories. In the rest of the canton, the middle and lower self-employed predominated. Almost two-thirds of the latter worked in agriculture in the farming villages. Particularly interesting is a comparison with the Front-voters of September 3, 1933 (cf. table 1). The 2286 signatories from

Table 4. *Social Composition of the Signatories of the Initiatives Launched by the National Front in Schaffhausen Canton*

	(Percentage proportions of social classes)			
	Upper Class	Self-employed (Farmers)	Employees	Workers (Unskilled)
1934 initiative:				
Entire canton (n=3091)	0.7	36.6 (15.2)	18.1	44.6 (13.7)
Urban Schaffhausen (n=1176)	1.4	18.2 (0.4)	28.0	52.4 (12.7)
Neuhausen (n=397)	0.8	20.9	21.2	57.1 (12.8)
Stein am Rhein (n=206)	0.5	46.7 (5.3)	11.6	41.2 (17.9)
Farming villages (n=1312)	0.1	56.2 (34.3)	9.4	34.3 (14.1)
Places with comparable number of Front voters (n=2286)	0.9	30.9 (9.2)	20.4	47.8 (13.6)
1935 initiative:				
Entire canton (n=1317)	2.0	46.5 (11.5)	23.6	27.9 (10.5)
Schaffhausen (n=657)	2.9	32.6	34.1	30.4 (9.6)
Neuhausen (n=191)	1.6	36.7 (1.0)	19.9	41.8 (15.7)
Stein am Rhein (n=67)	1.5	52.2 (4.5)	14.9	31.4 (28.4)
Farming villages (n=402)	0.7	73.2 (36.6)	9.7	16.4 (8.2)

places with a similar number of electors (where the number of signatories was no higher than 12.5 per cent of the number of Front-voters) largely accorded with the average finding: the old and new middle-class were well represented in both instances. The remaining villages (where the proportion of signatories to Front-voters was 5:4 and higher) consisted mainly of agricultural workers. We can therefore assume that it was above all farmers who were prepared to sign the petition but that they had not voted for the Front in the same numbers.

In August 1935, the Schaffhausen provincial leadership drew up another initiative – also withheld from plebiscite «concerning the maintenance of the independence of the judiciary's powers». With 1300 valid signatures, it came very near to the cantonal total of members (around 1,000). It is fair to assume that party-adherents supported the campaign more or less en bloc. Only 28 per cent were workers, as against 46 per cent middle and lower self-employed, 24 per cent employees, and 2 per cent members of the upper class. The social stratification of the signatories in urban Schaffhausen corresponded fairly closely with that of the 345 urban members at the beginning of 1938 (cf. table 2). Seen as a whole, the signatories of 1935, like those of 1934, seem to have exhibited a stronger middle-class character than the membership ranks of the National Front.

The «Schweizer Monatshefte» made these comments on the age-structure of the movement in the summer of 1933: «In the main, the ranks of the National Front are today filled by men aged between 20 and 40. But this is by no means a strict limit. There is no shortage of recruits from the older sections of the population, and younger men follow closely on their heels.» In early 1938, the party presented the following picture in urban Schaffhausen: the 345 members of the local group had an average age of 38.8, and of these, the 6 women averaged 25.5 and the 111 members of the «Auszug» élite-formation 37.6. Most of those who were still in the party in 1938 must have been members as far back as the «springtime of fronts». It is thus reasonable to assume that in 1933 the average age of this core-group was around 34. An analysis according to age and party of the Zurich national council candidates of 1935 affords us an insight which, while exaggerated, is nonetheless highly informative. On average, the 269 aspirants were 44 years of age. The representatives of the Radical Democrats and the Protestant People's Party («Evangelische Volkspartei») averaged 50 to 51. Between 45 and 49 was the average age of the candidates for the Social Democrats, the Democrats, the Social Christians and the Farmers' party, and around 41 that of the nine independents and the Young Farmers. The Communists fielded an average age of 38, the Free Economy Union («Freiwirtschafter») 37, and the Frontists 35. The Front's mean-age was undercut only by two candidates of the National Democrats. It seems that the National Front's claim to represent the younger generation was borne out in terms of age.

In summing up, emphasis should be laid on the strong middle-class bias of the National Front. In the towns the new the middle-class was dominant, in the country or the villages, its older predecessor. The proportion of workers was not inconsiderable, both in respect of the membership and in respect of the electorate. In the Schaffhausen party at least, this proportion stood at around one third. It seems that the National Front's following reflected by and large the stratification of Swiss society, whereas most other parties had a more one-sided structure. Frontist ideology consciously addressed itself to all sections of society. Not the least part of the Front's intake came from the ranks of those who had grown dissatisfied with other parties. By comparison with these other parties, the average age both of members and voters appears to have been lower in the case of the National Front, and the proportion of young followers greater. The leadership had a strong academic impress and the party's cadre was essentially drawn from the erstwhile New Front.

Style and Policy

The National Front surely found its truest embodiment in dynamic action: charged with romantic energy which was like the atmosphere in the youth-movement, stiffened by military discipline and military feeling – credere, obbedire, combattere! It expressed itself in noisy proclamations, marching columns, drums and music, in flags and in uniform-attire, but also in robust resistance and attack, in dirty tricks and street-brawls. Mass-meetings like the provincial conference («Gautage»), a march on Berne, a night-time commemoration of the Confederation on the Rütli (the legendary birth-place of Swiss independence) – such events generated images that could not fail to make a mark. In the sphere of ideology, the National Front claimed to be the Swiss expression of a pan-European phenomenon. A society which had disintegrated under the impact of liberalism and socialism was to be led back into the «natural bonds»: folk, home, station in life, and soil («Volk. . .Heimat. . .Stand. . .Scholle»), through fascist rule and discipline.[29] Religious motives played a not inconsiderable part in justifying this mission. Actual opponents like the socialist parties and eventually the bourgeois parties too, as well as purely theoretical enemies like «Jewry», were condemned root and branch. The National Front looked for its models primarily in the Switzerland of a former age, for example in the thing democracies («Landsgemeinde-demokratien»[30]) or among the founding-fathers of Swiss liberalism.

«We have no program, we are the program» was the party's political slogan for years. It was only the reverses of 1935 that led to the elaboration of a 26-point program, which did no more than embody existing tendencies in pregnant formulations. «The people elects the federal government and dismisses it», parliament is assigned a purely advisory role, legal initiatives and constitutional jurisdiction are new correctives. «The economy must serve the people», unions and firms are accountable to the government as «trustees of the country». Social welfare measures include among others the revolutionary «right to work and to bread», compulsory old-age- and bereavement-insurance (introduced only in 1948), and the closing-down of single-price stores. Subsequent paragraphs deal with «effective national defense», the «physical and personal improvement of the people», and the protection of state and people against the «disintegrating» influence of cultural Bolshevism, Jewry, free-masonry, socialist parties, and a free press. Finally, «all international treaty-obligations that are at variance with neutrality» are to be revoked.

It would surely be wrong to see the National Front as no more than an assortment of reactionary aspirations and achievements. The Front certainly expressed a clear desire to create a social and state-structure that was in keeping with the industrial age, even if this structure was to be built up along totalitarian lines, according to the fascist concept.[31] From the first, the party was loud and clear in its advocacy of national defense policies, and in this field its agitation was not without merit. In its foreign policy, the National Front originally administered the inheritance of the Germanophile Swiss bourgeoisie. After the Axis was established, the Front aligned itself ever more closely with the aims of the fascist Internationale, which it saw as the bulwark that would protect Europe against Bolshevism. It supported a fascist new order, even a new division of the continent, although it was never prepared to sacrifice the independent status of Switzerland. Nolens volens, its official contribution necessarily limited itself to declarations of solidarity and was accordingly of scant political or military value.

NOTES

This essay has been translated by Paul N. Bristow.

[1] e.g. Eugen Weber, *Varieties of Fascism* (Van Nostrand ANVIL Book 73: N. Y. 1964) «International Fascism, 1920–45» in *Journal of Contemporary History*, vol. I (1966).

[2] E. Nolte, *Die faschistischen Bewegungen* (DTV No. 4004: 1966). Idem, *Die Krise des liberalen Systems und die faschistischen Bewegungen* (Munich 1968).

[3] Bruno Grimm, *Das Ende der Nationalen Front* (Zurich 1940).

[4] «Bericht des Bundesrates an die Bundesversammlung über die antidemokratische Tätigkeit von Schweizern and Ausländern in Zusammenhang mit dem Kriegsgeschehen 1939–1945», Part I, 28 December 1945, in *Bundesblatt der Schweiz, Eidgenossenschaft*, (Berne 1946). «Bericht des Bundesrates an die Bundesversammlung über die Verfahren gegen nationalsozialistische Schweizer wegen Angriffs auf die Unabhängigkeit der Eidgenossenschaft», 30 November 1948, in *Bundesblatt der Schweiz. Eidgenossenschaft.* (Berne 1948). «Bericht des Regierungsrates des Kantons Aargau über die Abwehr staatsfeindlicher Umtriebe in den Vorkriegs-und Kriegsjahren sowie die Säuberungsaktion nach Kriegsschluss, dem Grossen Rate des Kantons Basel-Stadt vorgelegt am 4. Juli 1946», (Basel 1946). «Bericht des Regierungsrates des Kantons Aargau über die im Jahre 1946 erfolgte Entlassung des Herrn Dr. Hektor Ammann als Staatsarchivar und Kantonsbibliothekar», communication to the «Grosser Rat» on 3 April 1950 (Aarau 1950).

[5] P. Gilg & E. Gruner, «Nationale Erneuerung in der Schweiz 1925–1940», *in Vierteljahreshefte für Zeitgeschichte* (1966) No. 1. p. 1.

[6] W. Wolf, *Faschismus in der Schweiz. Die Geschichte der Frontenbewegungen in der deutschen Schweiz, 1930–1945* (Zurich 1969).

[7] Beat Glaus, *Die Nationale Front. Eine Schweizer faschistische Bewegung 1930–1940* (Benziger: Zurich 1969). With the kind permission of the publishers, the present essay is based essentially on the source-material set out and referred to in this book. The tables and relevant commentary were incorporated in part literally.

[8] K. –D. Zöberlein, *Die Anfänge des deutsch-schweizerischen Frontismus* (Meisenheim a.G. 1970). Cf. my review in the Zurich «Tages-Anzeiger» of 7 December, 1970.

[9] Dr.Jur., 1893–1970. Writer and philosopher. Main early works: *Der Kampf um das geistige Reich* (Zurich 1933); *Die Schweiz im Schicksal der Demokratie* (Zurich 1931); *Das Reich der Söhne* (Berlin 1940). Cf. Dino Larese, *Julius Schmidhauser* (Amriswiler Bücherei: 1965).

[10] Dr.phil. h.c., 1910-. Writer. Founded the Pestalozzi children's village in Trogen, planned an academy. Cf. Corti, «Das Archiv für Genetische Philosophie», in *Librarium, Zeitschrift der Schweiz. Bibliophilen-Gesellschaft*, No. 5 (1962), p. 33.

[11] For the Swiss party-system, see Erich Gruner, *Parteien in der Schweiz* (Berne '69). Gruner's verdict (p. 237) that, ideologically, Frontism turned out to be «quite simply an imitator of National Socialism» is inaccurate.

[12] 1901–1962. 1922 teacher of musical theory. Stay in Italy. From 1927, stud.jur. at Zurich University. 1930 founded the New Front. 1931 Dr.jur., substitute in law-court. 1931–1933, editor of official periodical «Zürcher Student». From 1934 lawyer. 1935–39 National Councillor, 1938–40 Leader of National Front.

[13] 1899– 1928/9 stud.phil., then jur. at the universities of Zurich, Vienna, Basel and Freiburg i.B. 1929–31 editor of the official periodical «Zürcher Student». 1929 founded the «Patria» student-association, 1931 founded the paper «Der Eiserne Besen» (1931–33). 1933–34 on journalistic staff of National-Socialist «Alemanne» (Freiburg i.B.). 1934 Dr. jur. at University of Freiburg i.B. After the war, worked some time on communist magazine «Vorwärts» (Basel). Inter alia, wrote the antifascist pamphlet *Ein Schweizer erlebt Deutschland* (Zurich 1938) and the anti-

communist *Meine Odyssee durch den kommunistischen Sumpf,* 16 instalments in the Independent paper «Die Tat», from 29 May to 16 June 1946.

[14] 1894–? Dr. phil., ideologist of the New Front and the National Front. Teacher at the Zurich cantonal commercial school. Inter alia, wrote «Karl Bürkli, ein Pionier des Schweiz. Sozialismus» (diss. phil.: Zurich university 1920); *«Tote oder lebendige Schweiz?»* (Zurich 1932).

[15] 1888–? Dr. phil. Co-founder and director of the periodical «Schweizerische Monatshefte für Politik und Kultur» (later: «Schweizer Monatshefte»), the mouth-piece of the Germanophile Swiss bourgeoisie who opposed the League of Nations. 1934–45 in charge of the Frontist «Nationale Hefte». After 1945, he is supposed to have handled the «editorial direction in Switzerland» of «Nation Europa».

[16] 1869–1943. Frontist from 1933. Originally a typical rural Swiss paper, middle class and petty-bourgeois, appearing 3 times a week.

[17] 1868–1934. Originally in embroidery business. Commander of the 4th division. Commandant in Zurich during national strike of 1918. 1919–23, head of the General Staff of the Swiss army. Wrote *Ordnung im Staat* (Berne 1933).

[18] 1901–1966. Dr. jur. Until 1934 a lawyer; 1934–38, Leader of the National Front. Finally a lecturer, later owner of the «Argus der Presse» press-cuttings agency.

[19] «Liste Nationale Erneuerung der Heimatwehr und der Nationalen Front».

[20] 1885–1945. Businessman. 1933–38 head of the «Volksbund», National Socialist Swiss Workers' Party. After 1939 involved in conspiratorial action in Germany.

[21] «Die Front», Zürich-Schaffhausen 1933–1943; «La Voix Nationale», Lausanne 1933–34; «Front National», Lausanne 1935–36; «Jung-Thurgau», Kreuzlingen 1934–36.

[22] Zurich 1934–44: Robert Tobler, «Wesen und Ziele der Nationalen Bewegung» (i). Rolf Henne, «Der Standort der jungen Generation und anders politische Schriften» (ii). Max Leo Keller, «Die Organisation von Landesunternehmungen und Grossbetrieben» (iii). Hans A. Wyss, «Die Jüdische Situation. Ein Betrag zur Judenfage» (iv). Alfred Zander & Wilhelm Brenner, «Erziehung, Schule und Volksgemeinschaft» (v). Hans Kläul, «Der Kampf um die Volksgemeinschaft» (vi). Ernst Wolfer, «Streit um die Demokratie» (vii). Ernst Braendlin, «Korporativer Aufbau und landwirtschaftliche Entschuldung, zwei Wege zur Volksgemeinschaft» (viii). Max Leo Keller, «Der Neuaufbau der Wirtschaft» (ix). Paul Lang, «Lebendige Schweiz»(x). Rolf Henne «Eidgenössischer Sozialismus» (xi). Rolf Henne, «Kampfruf» (xii). Alfred Zander, «Was will die Nationale Front?» (xiii).

[23] Cf. Karl Hanns Maier, «Die antiliberalen Erneuerungsbewegungen in der Schweiz und das Enstehen des liberal-sozialen Landesrings der Unabhängigen» (diss. phil.: Tübingen university 1956).

[24] Cf. Norman Cohn, *«Die Protokolle der Weisen von Zion»* (Cologne 1969). In my judgement, Cohn fails to deal as exhaustively as he might have done with the main source, the court-records. . .

[25] Old Swiss night-bird challenge: «Heraus», meaning «come out».

[26] 1902–. Dr.phil. II, Cantonal school-teacher. 1932–34, Leader of the National Front.

[27] 1898–? Dr. rer.cam. Manager in the Swiss aluminium industry. Professor at the commercial university in St. Gallen, director of the Swiss institute of foreign trade and market research («Aussenwirtschaft und Marktforschung»).

[28] In the Swiss army, the Auszug military class basically consisted of soldiers aged from 20 to 32 («Wehrmänner vom 20. bis zum zurückgelegten 32. Altersjahr»).

[29] Thus for example according to the Frontist writing *Amerika und der Faschismus* (Berne 1937), by Walter Adolf Jöhr, 1910–. Dr.jur. & phil. From 1940–53, his father was director of the Swiss Credit Bank. Professor at the commercial university in St. Gallen. Also wrote *Die ständische Ordnung* (Leipzig-Berne 1937).

[30] Cf. Wolfgang Wirz (1910–69. Dr. Jur., party-speaker), «Die Träger der verwaltenden Staatsgewalt im Kanton Unterwalden ob dem Wald im Laufe der staatsrechtlichen Entwicklung» (dissertation at Zurich university, 1938).

[31] As set out by Peter Drucker, *The Future of Industrial Man* (Mentor Books No. 625: N.Y. 1965), with reference to German National Socialism.

Strands of French Fascism*

ZEEV STERNHELL

Precursors of Fascism in France: the Continuity with the Pre World War I Traditions

In February 1936, the fascistic review *Combat* published an article entitled «Fascisme 1913». In it, Pierre Andreu, one of the most faithful and authentic disciples of Georges Sorel, touched on the strange synthesis of syndicalism and nationalism which on the eve of World War I took place around the author of *Reflections on Violence* and the nationalist circles close to the *Action Française*. About the time this article appeared, the same fact was noted by Pierre Drieu La Rochelle, who some months later, in company with the young leftist economist Bertrand de Jouvenel, would be one of the leading intellectuals of France's largest fascist party, the *Parti Populaire Français*, (P. P. F.). He said: «When one thinks back to that time one can see that several elements of the Fascist atmosphere had come together in France by 1913: earlier than elsewhere. You had young men of every social class burning with love of heroism and violence and dreaming of fighting what they called the two-faced evil – capitalism and parliamentary socialism – and of getting the best of both sides. . . . The marriage of nationalism and socialism was already in the offing.»[1]

Here we have the very formula Georges Valois, founder of the first fascist movement outside Italy, was to employ in 1925 to express the essence of the phenomenon: «Nationalism + Socialism = Fascism».[2] Fifteen years after him – in September 1940, on the eve of founding the *Rassemblement National Populaire* – Marcel Déat was to sum up his idea of the essence of fascism in the words «basically I feel all can be reduced to this remark: the engine of revolution has ceased to be class interest and has become the general interest. We have moved from the notion of class to that of the nation». And Déat would add: «I'm not interested in how much of this enterprise is national and how much is social. All I know is that .. . . the mixture is explosive in the good sense of the term: that it can set off all the motors of history».[3] It is in precisely this synthesis which Valois, right after making long quotations from Sorel and Corradini, said he saw not only the common denominator of all fascist movements – the most perfect expression of their European character – but also that which is specifically French in the roots of fascism.[4]

It is no accident that Valois, in the very act of launching *Le Faisceau,* harked back to Barrès, Boulangism and turn-of-the-century nationalism. Barrès, who had been one of the first to see the possibility in modern terms and the necessity of merging socialism and nationalism, can indeed be considered one of the first – if not the first – of the national socialists in Europe. And the Boulangists and nationalists had from the late 1880s been in rebellion against liberal democracy and bourgeois society in the name of a strong and authoritarian state, an organic, hierarchical and disciplined society – in short, in the name of a body of principles which were the negations of the values inherited from the Revolution and the philosophy of the Enlightenment.[5]

For it was in France that fascist ideology first matured, as indeed it had by the eve of World War I, as an articulated body of thought presenting quite clearly practically all the familiar features. Only two things were lacking: the name which was yet to come, and the proper external conditions – the enormous mass of unemployed and of frightened bourgeois – which it needed to become a political force. The solid conceptual basis was already there.

This is a little-known fact, but one of which the fascists of the inter-war period were perfectly well aware; and it is also one of prime importance if we are to understand the nature of French fascism.

To a great exent the answer to the question «Who were the fascists and why were they fascists?» lies in the nature of the period which preceded World War I. The same is true for a whole series of questions on how fascism came to take root in France. Was it, like the Stalinist form of communism, a graft from a foreign body – an importation, even a vague imitation, of Mussolinian fascism and later of Nazism? Or was it rather a phenomenon well rooted in French political, social and cultural reality – the native outgrowth of a particular political culture? How are we to tell which is fascism and which simple reaction? How, without recourse to the heritage of the pre-War years, can we explain that fundamental feature of French fascism – the effortless ease with which so many eminent men of the left found their way to the extreme right? For it is in the very midst of left-wing, and extreme left-wing organizations that we can clearly discern, from the beginning of the 'thirties, individual men and whole groups which show a good number of fascist characteristics – men who are in fact already fascists, even though they still belong to their original organizations. In 1935, Marcel Déat would be a minister in a government paving the way for the Popular Front while at the same time having already worked out a thoroughgoing fascist ideology considerably closer to the fascist ideal than anything the Colonel-Count de La Rocque could have dreamed up.

The phenomenon we see here is far too broad to suffer reduction to a matter of a few special cases – of renegades or mere opportunists – just as it cannot be limited to France alone: the well-known examples of Mussolini, Mosley and de Man bear witness to its European dimension. But in France it reached dimensions unknown elsewhere: and certainly not because of simple opportunism. Indeed, there the shift from left to right took place in peacetime, just as the left which had produced the turncoats was reaching the height of its power, and the break generally marked the end of a political career which had begun with particular brilliance. No one can doubt today that Jacques Doriot could have continued to play a key role in the P.C.F. even after seeing himself passed over in favor of Thorez for the post of Party Secretary-General; nor can we doubt that Marcel Déat could easily have been a Minister under Léon Blum, or that Gaston Bergery could have made a respectable Prime Minister of the Fourth Republic. Such giants of socialism's heroic age as Hubert Lagardelle or Gustave Hervé surely had nothing to gain in cutting themselves off from their origins. Their intellectual evolution, commonly called treason, is one of the great constants of French politics from 1885 to 1939; it is also an essential element in understanding fascism in France.

For French fascism is in fact marked by an extraordinary degree of continuity with the pre-War situation. World War I was not a watershed for France as it was for other countries in Europe: neither ideological systems nor political structures and behavior were shaken up in a comparable manner, and there was no real break on the ideological or personal level. We must therefore look neither to the success of Mussolini nor to the rise of Nazism for the starting-point of the fascist take-off. The War did, to be sure, play an infinitely important role as catalyzer – in producing the psychological, social and economic conditions conducive to the rise of fascism; but it did not, in France, produce fascism.

It was back in the French 'nineties that an alliance formed between a kind of non-Marxist, anti-Marxist or already post-Marxist socialism, on the one hand, and nationalism on the other. This turn-of-the-century nationalism, marked by the debacle of 1870 and the consequent loss of Alsace-Lorraine, had precious little in common with the traditional Jacobin nationalism of Michelet or of the generation of 1848; indeed, the moral climate of the last quarter of the century is strangely reminiscent of what the world was to see among the losers of 1918. France had been struggling vainly throughout the 'seventies and 'eighties to shake off the psychology of a defeated nation. By the time of the Boulangist outbreak, French nationalism, as personified by Déroulède and his *Ligue des Patriotes*, had lost much of its humanitarian, universalist and messianic character.

For the turn-of-the-century nationalists, the Republic's inability to avenge the humiliation, to recover the lost provinces or even simply to prepare for war, arose from the fundamental weakness of liberal democracy. And in consequence, nationalism was above all a revolt against democracy, a negative critique of the system's weakness, incoherence and impersonal character. This populist, authoritarian and anti-parliamentarian nationalism was also one which ranted against the rich and against economic injustice. At the same time that it was attacking liberal democracy as political system and form of society, and demanding an authoritarian reform of the state, it was also attacking economic injustices in the name of national solidarity.

At the end of the 'eighties, nationalism came together with a protest movement born on the far left; the Boulangism which resulted constituted the first wave in that series of assaults which liberal democracy was henceforth to suffer. Here, we see for the first time what is to become the classic fascist mechanism set in motion – the shift from extreme left to extreme right of elements which are socially advanced but hostile to liberal democracy.

The Boulangist experience was of tremendous importance for the future, as it showed that great slices of the population would subscribe, with alacrity, to a program which borrowed its social values from the left and its political ones from the right. Boulangism had enjoyed its greatest success in the working-class Paris suburbs, the industrial North and the textile industry; we can thus see how this audacious mix foreshadowed the mass movements of the twentieth century.

Ten years later, in May 1898 – in the midst of the violent agitation which formed the basis of the Dreyfus Affair – the term «nationalist socialism» was created by Maurice Barrès, nationalist candidate for the Nancy seat in Parliament.[6] This «nationalist socialism» was already violently anti-Semitic, having realized that anti-Semitism was the surefire way not only to bind the proletariat to the national·community but also to rally a lower middle class menaced with proletarianization. Here was the «popular formula» which would make it possible to replace class warfare with a struggle against foreign elements. Social and racist anti-Semitism gave nationalism a popular basis among the masses it sought to mobilize; the resulting anti-Semitic outbreaks marking the last years of the century[7] are, both in intensity and in scope, strangely reminiscent of the later Nazi pogroms.

Another milestone in the prehistory of fascism was the founding, in 1903, of Pierre Biétry's *Parti Socialiste National,* replaced a year later by the *Fédération Nationale*

481

des Jaunes («Yellows») *de France*. A true forerunner of fascism, «Yellow» socialism, unlike the Red variety, preached national solidarity instead of class warfare, accession to property instead of expropriation, profit-sharing by workers, and a syndicalism within which workers' syndicates and employers' syndicates would coexist; the whole edifice was to be capped by a strong state in which national and regional representation would be according to trades and guilds. The «Yellow» movement was, to be sure, violently anti-Marxist; it worshipped a leader who was in fact its quasi-dictator, and it was anti-Semitic; indeed, it is within the ranks of the *Fédération des Jaunes de France*, «welded to this notion of prising the working class out of its socialist rut», that we see for the first time the whole fascist ideological apparatus set in motion.[8] It should, by the way, be kept in mind that this «Yellow» variant was an authentic movement of workers and clerks, and that it was by no means numerically insignificant. Biétry himself was elected to the Chamber of Deputies from Brest in 1906.

At the same time we cannot really understand the French fascism of the 'twenties and 'thirties, or the presence of many important leftists at Vichy, unless we come to grips with the nature of French syndicalism and the influence – often nearly invisible but nevertheless extremely important – of revolutionary syndicalism. In the first few years of the century, syndicalism came out against the official social democracy, as well as against the bourgeois republic and its parliamentary system. This had been one of the results of the Dreyfus Affair, which had ended with the socialist movement becoming in effect the watchdog of the Republic. Indeed, under the influence of Jaurés, French socialism had gradually been transformed into a parliamentary party impossible at all but a few points to distinguish from any of its bourgeois rivals; the first noted socialists to turn their coats, Millerand and Briand, were simply the first to draw all the conclusions from this new state of affairs. One should recall that they made their departure at a time when the Dreyfusard Clemenceau, then Prime Minister, was regularly giving orders to shoot down obstreperous workers.

At that time the bourgeois Dreyfusards, put into the driver's seat of a liberal democracy by the socialists, were arousing uncommon hatred in working-class circles. On May Day, 1908, the republic was hanged in effigy in the Paris Bourse de Travail; it was a symbolic finish to a lost revolution – to what (to use Sorel's term) could have been the Dreyfusard revolution. And in the reaction of the syndicalist far left wing we can at once see the preparation for and the explanation of the subsequent rise of fascism: its revolt against the bourgeois state now merged with the rebellion nationalism had been conducting. After all, both syndicalism and nationalism shared a hostility towards liberal democracy and bourgeois society; their analyses of that society's mechanisms were very much alike. That is, they shared the same vision of a society dominated by a powerful minority which had made the state apparatus the servant of its will. Changing material conditions might dismiss one élite and put another in its place, but there would always be some élite mobilizing the masses to achieve its ends.

In the first years of the new century this theory gained in favor among the avant-garde of socialism – among that part which was in violent revolt against parliamentary socialism and calling for direct action. In opposition to the kind of socialism which preached the takeover of power through universal suffrage and which postponed the revolution to some indeterminate future – the year 3000, its enemies said – the movement's radical wing propounded the theory of the avant-garde of the working class, the thesis that a self-aware and activist minority could lead the proletariat on to revolution. Against a housebroken and morning-coated socialism ensconced in ministerial chambers – one which accepted the passwords and the rules of the liberal-democratic game – syndicalism raised the standard of revolutionary violence led by a proletarian élite.

The fascists-to-be Roberto Michels and Arturo Labriola represented abroad a current of thought that in France was to assume still greater proportions. Sorel was, it is true, better known and appreciated in their Italy than in his own France; but Hubert Lagardelle was a considerable personage. Director of *Le Mouvement Socialiste,* the celebrated theoretical organ of anti-parliamentarian and anti-democratic Marxism, he fought against any compromise over or deviation from the class war. Lagardelle, the personification of doctrinal purity at every socialist congress, was in April 1907 saluting as «the culminating fact of the history of these last few years» the «disaffection of the French worker with the republicanized State.» For him, the struggle against liberal democracy was the first and greatest aim of socialism. Hubert Lagardelle would be Minister of Labor under Pétain.

It was during this same period that the head of the C.G.T., Victor Griffuelhes, communing with himself over the future of universal suffrage, declared: «It seems quite clear to me that it will have to be left in the lumber-room»[10] and replaced by the syndicalist method of direct action. According to another ranking syndicalist leader, Emile Pouget, Direct Action «can express itself in benevolent and peaceful ways, or in very vigorous and very violent ones.» The enormous difference between syndicalism and «democratism» lay in the fact that «the latter, through the mechanism of universal suffrage hands the direction of society over to the unthinking and backward . . . . and stifles the minorities who carry the future within them.»[11] We thus see the socialist far-left planting the seeds both of distrust of parliamentary democracy and of the cult of violent revolt conducted by conscious and activist minorities.

Among the ranks of the collaborators and fascists of the 'forties, syndicalists, socialists and communists were to play an extremely important role, one far more decisive than that of the men of the *Action Française.* The number – and the level – of the militants who went over to fascism can only be understood as a function of that long tradition of opposition to liberalism and social democracy which took root in France at the turn of the century. Indeed, the moment the regime emerged victorious from the long confrontation imposed on it by the Dreyfus Affair, an enormous effort was initiated to cut the working class off once and for all from parliamentary democracy. Socialism's far-left wing decided it was vital to instill in the proletariat a mistrust for everything having the slightest relation to the bourgeoisie; for middle-class virtues and morals, and for respect of the law, legality and the democratic system. The syndicalist theoreticians exalted instead military virtues and violence and the purifying role of social struggle. With Georges Sorel syndicalist thinking was fused with a murky stream of anti-intellectualism and irrationalism.

Sorel's works are well known today; but it is perhaps less well known that when his *Reflections on violence* appeared in France in 1908, the book represented nothing out of the ordinary; merely a more or less systematic restatement of the universally known writings of socialist and syndicalist leaders. It was this systematization that constitutes his real importance, and that explains why he played a rather important role (especially in Italy) in converting syndicalists to the right. In and around Sorel there crystallized ideas and currents of thought whose common denominator was rebellion against bourgeois society and its moral and political values – against the doctrine of natural rights, liberalism and democracy. In his teaching, revolutionary syndicalists, nationalists, anti-democrats and anti-liberals of every stripe found common ground: the shift from revolutionary syndicalism to nationalism or vice versa had never been theoretically impossible; on the eve of World War I it became almost natural.

In 1911–1912 the one-time revolutionary syndicalist, Sorel, was publishing a nationalist and anti-Semitic review called *L'Independance*. And it was just at this time that the most interesting and significant, intellectually speaking, of pre-fascist publicistic efforts was made – *Les Cahiers du Cercle Proudhon*.

The *Cercle Proudhon* itself, a coming together of syndicalism and *Action Française* – style nationalism, was founded – at the inspiration of Sorel – in December, 1911, under the nominal presidency of Charles Maurras. A month later the *Cahiers* appeared, offering both *Action Française* thinker Georges Valois, once a revolutionary syndicalist but by then better known for his *La Monarchie et la Classe Ouvrière*, and the Marxist Edouard Berth, a disciple of Sorel who, in the 'twenties, would move over to the far left. About these two poles both nationalists and syndicalists could unite in proclaiming that «democracy was the last century's biggest mistake,» that it had allowed the most abominable exploitation of the workers, and that it had substituted for the «law of blood the Capitalist law of Gold.» From this followed that «to preserve and increase the moral, intellectual and material capital of civilization, it is absolutely necessary to destroy democratic institutions.»[12] The *Cahiers du Cercle Proudhon* lay somewhere in the middle of the long road from the 'nineties' national socialism to fascism. On the one hand it strongly recalls the part played by *La Cocarde* and its editor Barrès, who had run two election campaigns on a platform of national socialism; on the other hand, it prefigured the tendency in the 'thirties to break out of established opposition frameworks and to merge formerly hostile traditions. In 1894 *La Cocarde* had rallied socialists, syndicalists and nationalists around Barrès; for Valois, writing in the 'twenties, it had been the first fascist paper.[13]

When, in 1925, the first fascist movement in France, indeed, the first outside Italy, was founded – and by a former member of the *Cercle Proudhon* – it was hardly an accident that the date chosen for the event was the highly significant one of November 11, anniversary of the Armistice. For the war and its aftermath had just given an added push to the fascist upsurge. Nevertheless, the *Faisceau* came of a long lineage which insured continuity both of ideology and personnel; what its creation really represented was an attempt to resume the work of the *Cercle Proudhon*, brutally halted by the War, by Sorel's death and the Bolshevik Revolution. It was in part a defensive reflex brought on by the electoral victory of the *Cartel des Gauches*, and as well a rebellion against the political immobilism and fundamentally reactionary nature of the *Action Française* and the various «ligues nationales.»

The *Faisceau* made its appearance in the form of a double split within the *Action Française*: that is, through the departure on the one hand of some of that movement's most militant and ardent elements, and on the other hand of a certain number of figures who were more «to the left» than the leadership. Georges Valois, for example, had before the war been in charge of mobilizing working-class support for the *Action Française*; he had also been the one who had taken the *Cercle Proudhon* effort most seriously. Now, a true fascist could only be repelled by the complete lack of a will to action which characterized Maurras' movement, by the salon atmosphere and royalism which, willy nilly, had made it the party of the squirearchy, the cavalry officers and the Lady Bountifuls. Indeed, from Valois at the time of the *Cartel* until Déat and Doriot in occupied Paris, the real fascists were loud in expressing their profound distrust of *Action Française*'s extremely narrow social base, its class character and its very nature as a movement which only existed as a species of journalism. The fascists, or more simply, the men of action, were no fools. They knew that behind that unconvincing screen of bitter, incendiary, invictive-laden rhetoric Maurras and his fellow *Action Française* journalists were sitting comfortably in their editorial offices, quite at home in the liberal democratic system – the system that provided the perfect framework for their one and only talent. Action was not merely something the *Action Française* never dreamed of taking; it was something of which it was completely incapable. For the only thing it had ever thought about bringing out on the streets was its paper.[14]

Valois' defection touched off a battle to the death between Maurras' movement and the *Faisceau:* the two were now competitors and Maurras did everything he could to break his rival. For the *Action Française,* the main danger presented by the fascists was the possible loss of members, especially of the younger and more activist ones, and of quite a few subscribers. For a movement which lived only through its paper and the journalistic talents of its leaders, this last was no small matter.

But the *Faisceau* was no less of a menace to all the other leagues, starting with the venerable *Ligue des Patriotes* which Déroulède had founded back in 1882. Here again it was the most pugnacious, and least elderly, elements – the vast majority of whom were fresh from the trenches – who were affected, while the leadership, mostly old and established parliamentarians, remained violently hostile to the new movement. The old *ligues* were by now an integral part of the political system and had a cold welcome for the newcomer. Valois' *Faisceau* would therefore only be able to carve out a place in the sun for itself at the cost of unremitting warfare with the organizations already on the scene, since it nibbled away not only at their clientele but at their resources – at the moneybags whose favor they hoped to attract.[15] Indeed, the launching of the *Faisceau* had only been possible due to powerful financial support. And this essentially only came their way after a group of rich industrialists, all former *Action Française* members or sympathizers, became convinced of Maurras' impotence to deal with the danger presented by the left's electoral victory in May 1924 and got together to finance first a fascist-style publication called the *Nouveau Siècle,* and then a fascist movement.[16]

By February 1926, the *Faisceau,* less than three months after its first appearance, had, according to police reports, some 10,000 members and by April there were some 15,127 in Paris alone. (Valois was at that time claiming 20,000 followers for all of France). By September, according to the same sources, the number had reached 48,000.[17] The middle of 1926 represented the numerical peak for the *Faisceau.* Assuming the figures furnished by the *Renseignements Généraux* are accurate, its strength, six months after its founding, exceeded that of *Action Française* in the Paris area. For the latter could muster only 13,500 members in the Department of the Seine, to which we should add 1,000 *Camelots du Roi* – its shock troops, or, more modestly speaking, its mobilizable cadres. These are but feeble figures to set beside the 65,000 members, organized nationwide in 225 sections, of Pierre Taittinger's *Jeunesses Patriotes – La Legion,* the most powerful of the various movements with frankly authoritarian ideology and dictatorial aspirations. On the other hand the *Ligue des Chefs de Section,* out of whose ranks the *Croix-de-Feu* would a few years later emerge, at the time could count only 7,000 members.[18] All together the three great leagues could muster an impressive minimum of 100,000 activists – enough to have made them a force to be reckoned with, had they only been able to agree on some common course of action.[19]

Now, it was nothing new in France to have antiparliamentary leagues advocating the overthrow of the liberal state: the oldest of the leagues, the *Ligue des Patriotes,* had in fact gone into open revolt during the Boulangist episode and even been briefly dissolved by the authorities. In 1926 it could still count 10,000 members, headed by former President of the Republic, Alexandre Millerand. To be sure, by the 'twenties its influence was zero, but we should nevertheless not forget that Déroulède's and Barrès' venerable *Ligue* had been France's first extra-parliamentary movement: the first republican organization to rebel – back in the 'eighties – against liberal democracy.[20] It had been the *Ligue des Patriotes* which, nearly fifty years earlier, had at the time of the Boulanger affair organized street demonstrations which had posed a real threat to the regime. The fertile soil it plowed had soon brought forth Jules Guérin's *Ligue Antisémite,* the *Ligue de la Patrie Française,* and the most famous of them all, the *Ligue d'Action Française.* In 1899, the *Ligue Antisémite* had sustained a veritable siege right in the heart of Paris. To be sure, the Fort Chabrol affair did not rock the republic to its foundations, but it bore out the fact that the *Ligues'* para-military activities had become implicitly legalized, and that the *Ligues* were already an integral part of French political life.

Where the *Faisceau* differed from all this was in the fact that it was a true fascist movement, resolutely national socialist, violently anti-bourgeois and anti-conservative, seeking to win away the left just as much as the right. At the same time, it would only remain believable if it put its proclaimed revolutionary intentions into practice within the shortest possible time. Here there is no room for doubt: the *Faisceau* had gathered in the most pugnacious elements of the old *Ligues;* and they would be the first to leave once its impotence to act became clear.[21]

In Antoine Redier and his *Légion,* the *Jeunesses Patriotes* had lost their most radical elements. Redier, a former member of the *Action Française,* had set up the *Legion* in June 1924 as a sort of radical ginger-group, to prod the national *Ligues* out of their politicking and their fundamentally defensive stance. In contrast, he organized his Legion as combat troops commanded by a chief, all on the purest lines of the *Führerprinzip.* The *Légion* counted about 10,000 of these stormtroopers, and its merger with the *Faisceau* was considered a great coup for Valois.[22]

The *Jeunesses Patriotes* did not as it happens follow their erstwhile colleagues into the *Faisceau,* but this was for essentially petty reasons bound up in personal rivalries: Pierre Taittinger was particularly jealous of his authority. Then too, the leaders of the *Ligue des Patriotes* – Marcel Habert and General Castelnau – who were supposed (at least officially) to exercise a certain authority over the *Jeunesses,* were fiercely opposed to Valois. The latter was never able to impose his authority, and French fascism was never to find its Leader.

As for the *Action Française,* it appears to have been suffering particularly heavy losses at this time, assuming the figures collected by the Interior Ministry's Services to be accurate. Between December 1925 and April 1926 some 1,800 members quit its ranks in the capital to go over to the *Faisceau,* and in the Southwest it lost 30 per cent of its following to the fascists. In December 1925 a shiver of panic ran through the *Action Française* headquarters: it seemed that the Camelots were defecting in particularly large numbers.[23] Perhaps it is these figures, rather than the difference of ideology, that explain Maurras' and Daudet's ferocious hatred of Valois.

Nevertheless, with all its success on the recruiting front, the *Faisceau* suffered from the fundamental contradiction between its financial needs on the one hand and its leftist tendencies on the other. As a true fascist movement it was seeking to get some

486

purchase on part of the working class – on the would-be non-conformist intelligentsia and the youth who were spitting on the world of their parents; and it had therefore developed a violently anti-bourgeois and anti-capitalist ideology. Throughout his campaigns, Valois preached distrust of old bourgeois Europe. The fascist would be the gravedigger of all the bourgeois virtues just as he would of all the evils which bourgeois rule had created; he was the harbinger of a new morality.[24] The main trouble with this fine program lay in the fact that, pending the coming of the New Order, it was still the bourgeois who had the money. Valois' incendiary appeals aimed at communists and socialists soon managed to frighten off both the moneybags on the scene and those who would have to be solicited later: the right took fascism's revolutionary tendencies seriously and feared their socialistic aspects. Some of his first and richest supporters withdrew their aid from Valois, exasperated at his «leftism». Leading the exodus was Eugène Mathon and his group of Roubaix industralists. As soon as it became clear that Valois was toying with giving his movement a relatively popular and even «socialistic» character, the number of defections increased and with them the incessant financial difficulties which finally killed the movement.

Threatened thus on his right, Valois turned to his left to redress the balance. «There's nothing more to expect from a rightist movement», he told his militants during a confidential meeting in June 1927 at which some of them accused him of flirting with the extreme left.[25] The hostility of the upper middle class, or better, its lack of enthusiasm, immediately produced an insurmountable money-problem, and the first to be his was *Le Nouveau Siècle*. Valois had launched his journal in February 1925, but six months later it could show only 4,700 subscribers as against 40,000 for the newspaper *Action Française*.[26] Newsstand sales were always poor and the paper piled up heavy losses: income never managed to cover even 20 per cent of expenses and the returns from the stands ran between 60 and 90 per cent.[27] This was extremely characteristic of the real nature of the two movements: the *Faisceau* had more members but nearly eight times less readers than *Action Française*.

If he never managed to break through the wall of hostility on his right, Valois was no more lucky on the left. His only real success was to lure away Delagrange, the communist mayor of Perigueux, and a small number of former C.G.T. stalwarts. On the whole the *Faisceau* remained a middle class movement: its socialistic ideology made no real impression on the working class, and this meant that all it could do was poach on the preserves of the already existing *Ligues* without being able to add to their traditional public.

Thus it happened that the ranks of the *Faisceau* pretty much reproduced the picture in the older *Ligues*, if with a larger proportion of workers. Here too we have no precise figures, but this is the impression which emerges from the police reports. For example, we learn that in June 1926 a «French Workers Study and Mutual-Aid Group» was formed in Le Havre, with 150 members drawn from various Catholic Socialist and Christian Syndicalist associations. According to the local *Commissaire Spécial*, the group was a new fascist propaganda organization. In the East we read of the accession, in October 1926, of 26 railwaymen signed up by Bardy, himself like Dalagrange, a former C.G.T. man. It seems, moreover, that it was in the provinces – mainly in the North and East – that the *Faisceau* made what progress it did in the second half of 1926: in Paris it had reached a dead end by July. But then the provinces, less aware than the capital of the way the political wind is blowing and less influenced by passing fashion, are generally slower to react, and also to release their grip once it is fastened.[28]

If the number of authentic proletarians in the *Faisceau* was small, there was nevertheless a large number of technicians, engineers, middle-management and other white-collar types. The police reports also reveal a sizeable number of industrialists and plant managers, along with retired officers. On the other hand, we find very few of the old landed aristocracy.[29] It appears very likely that the *Faisceau's* basic attraction was for persons in the more dynamic areas of the economy – for technicians and members of the free professions, drawn by the corporate organization (its most original feature) which made the movement appear vigorous, efficient and modern. In the present state of our documentation, an analysis of the *Faisceau's* corporate structures will unquestionably give us the best picture we can hope to obtain of the movement's social composition.

The *Faisceau* of corporations, set up in April 1926, by Valois' lieutenant Pierre Dumas (a former revolutionary syndicalist and C.G.T. stalwart who like his leader had passed through the *Action Française*), comprised at its founding thirteen constituent corporations, with 2,500 members.[30]

1. Engineers .... 360 members
2. Travelling salesmen...................................... 250 members
3. Mechanical and Electrical (automotive and aviation) .... 220 members
4. Insurance... 150 members
5. Retail and Wholesale employees .... 150 members
6. Banking and Securities .... 150 members

Total: 1,280 members

The remaining half of the total membership was divided among seven other organizations, all of them considered less dynamic and important than their aforementioned brethren. These were the:

7. National Union of Musical Artists
8. Professional Union of Pharmacists
9. Book Guild
10. Professional Union of Accountants
11. Building Guild
12. Legal Professions
13. Corporate Union of Physicians

The Engineers' Corporation was the most active, lively and homogeneous of these organizations. It was also the largest. Furthermore, two other corporations – Building, and Mechanical and Electrical – were included within it *de facto,* making it far and away the dominant element. There can be no doubt that the *Faisceau's* new, modern style, with its appeals to efficiency and know-how, had a certain appeal for professional men ready to respect competence.

Nevertheless, the *Faisceau* never really scored a breakthrough. Valois lacked charisma; it was the same problem that had dogged the French Radical Right since the days of Boulanger and of anti-Dreyfusard nationalism. What he did manage was to impose a new political style: a quasi-military organization and uniformed toughs to keep order at rallies: he also succeeded in arranging monster demonstrations to which thousands of militants were brought by special trains. The techniques were already at hand – but the socio-economic conditions were not: the *Faisceau,* like the fascist

488

movements which would succeed it, lacked the necessary background of inflation and unemployment: or, alternatively, of fear of revolution.

Valois had thought he could succeed where Boulanger and his Radical militants had failed – to get the right to finance an essentially non-proletarian political movement with a revolutionary ideology. But the structures of French society would not permit this; the right was strong enough to look out for itself unaided.

Indeed, the same phenomenon can be seen throughout Europe: fascism scored its greatest successes where the right was too weak to maintain its own position. Where this was true the right would, in times of great crisis, turn to the new revolutionary movement – the only one capable of meeting the challenge of communism – albeit without taking the fascists very far into its confidence. But where it possessed sufficient self-confidence to stand up to the Marxist left on its own – where its positions were comfortable enough and its social base adequately wide – the right did all in its power to see to it that the fascist adventure did not get out of hand. Above all, it made sure that it would manipulate its own following, and dispense its own money. It was not a strong right but on the contrary a relatively weak and fearful one that was essential if fascism were to succeed. And such was not the case in France; both electorally and socially, the right was there a power which fascism never managed to shake.

The upsurge of the *Faisceau,* like that of the *Jeunesses Patriotes,* had been the direct result of the fear inspired by the left's victory in the May 1924 elections; with the installation of the Poincaré cabinet on July 27, 1926, the danger was exorcised and the crisis resorbed into the structure of the existing system. It had been a classic victory for the whole traditional right: this had been so powerful that it needed no recourse to extra-parliamentary solutions. And with the economic status quo and the health of the franc quickly restored, inflation halted, and power solidly lodged in the hands of an intransigent nationalist, the *Faisceau* had lost its *raison d'être:* it thereupon quickly fell to pieces.

The Second Generation of French Fascism in the Twenties and Thirties. The Solidarité Française and the Francistes

The elections of 1928 were favorable to the right; not so those of 1932, which saw a spectacular recovery by the left and the formation of a new Cartel. This leftist majority, however, was divided and fragile, and had to face the grave economic and financial problems caused by the Depression as well.

The deteriorating economic situation, coupled with ministerial instability and financial scandal, had thus prepared the ground for a renewal of fascist or fascistic agitation; and this finally came about in the bloody outburst on February 6, 1934. In principle, then, a set of conditions had come together which favored the rise of fascism; but in France, for a large number of reasons, the situation was to work itself out differently.

To begin with, although there were serious economic difficulties, these never reached the dimensions of the German crisis; the French middle and peasant classes never had to face a similar disaster; nor was there ever a serious threat that the political structure would collapse, as it had in Italy. Second, the political system of the Third Republic, which had weathered first the Boulanger and then the Dreyfus affairs, once again showed its solidity. (It would in fact take the debacle of 1940 to knock it down.) The third element in explaining French fascism's failure to take hold in the thirties lies in the restoration of the «Republican defence reflex». This, eroded by the end of the nineteenth century and shattered by the founding of the Communist party, was revived by the Soviet volte face: the end of the «class against class» strategy made possible the creation of a socialist-communist alliance. Thus the resurgence of fascist agitation, far from helping to bring down democracy, only contributed to the rise of the Popular Front and to the latter's victory at the polls in June 1936.

The second generation of post-World-War I fascism – the first having been the *Faisceau* – consisted of two small movements: the *Solidarité Française* and the *Francistes,* each the creation of men who had been associated in one way or another with Valois' earlier venture. The *Solidarité Française,* launched in 1933 by the millionaire industrialist François Coty, has as its moving spirits Jean Renaud, once a major in the colonial forces and now writing editorials for Coty's paper *L'Ami du Peuple,* and two other members of the Coty team at the same daily: Jacques Fromentin and the prominent attorney Jacques Ditte. The movement was thus the offspring of a mass-circulation daily, one which the famed perfume-maker had set up after earlier acquiring *Le Figaro* and *Le Gaulois* and attempting a political career in Corsica.

Coty had founded *L'Ami du Peuple* in 1928, far underselling his competitors at 10 centimes a copy; with its appeals to the anti-privilege sentiments of the man in the street, and its crusades against Judeo-American High Finance, the trusts and the Freemasons, this populist and fuzzily fascistic sheet soon had a large circulation. What the founder of the *Solidarité Française* had in mind was to gather up all these readers and fashion them into a political force; once again, France was to see a political movement born out of a millionaire's printing presses.

The *Solidarité Française's* lesser leadership, mainly young, was made up of ex-soldiers, young intellectuals – some of them writers of ability such as J.P. Maxence and his brother Robert Francis – a few lawyers and a small number of physicians, but above all of journalists and literary men, of very unequal attainments. Quite a few of these were men who, as the years went by, were to be seen passing from one movement, and one publication, to the other. As to the latter, there was at this time an enormous number of ephemeral publications circulating in France, in and outside of Paris, creating the not entirely illusory impression of strength of numbers on the extreme-right. And indeed, the *Solidarité Française* claimed at various times from 180,000 to 250,000 followers – no inconsiderable number. But these were readers, vague sympathizers. It is certain that the number of active followers hardly exceeded 15,000 to 20,000, and that the number of «mobilizables» – those who could be got out on the streets – came to barely 5,000, 3,000 of them concentrated in greater Paris.[31] Nevertheless, as Léon Blum said at the time of Coty's death. *L'Ami du Peuple* always had more subscribers than *Le Populaire.* This gap between the fascist ideology's power of attraction and fascist movements' severely limited capacity to act – their inability to mobilize their masses of sympathizers – was one of the basic features of French fascism.

At the recruiting level the *Solidarité Française* was a faithful replica of the *Faisceau:* financed by a multi-millionaire and led by journalists, men of letters, lawyers and other members of the free professions. Down in the ranks the movement was essentially made up of reserve officers, clerks, small proprietors and a limited number of workers. It was clearly aimed at the little man, but appeared not to have made any real impact on the working class.[32]

490

In this respect the *Solidarité Française* hardly differed from the *Francistes*, a small movement also founded in 1933, by another former *Faisceau* stalwart, Marcel Bucard. The *Francistes* were to enjoy considerable prestige abroad, but very little in France. Bucard himself, although he had represented France in September 1935 at the International Fascist Congress in Montreux – and even after being received, at the head of 250 comrades, by Mussolini – could never put together a following of more than 10,000. He was chronically short of money, little thought of personally, and had the distinction of being the sole far-rightist leader never to attract a single first-rate intellectual to his movement.

The *Francistes* nucleus was a group of former colleagues of Gustave Hervé, a leading pre-1914 socialist who, right after the war, had founded a *Parti Socialiste National*. Indeed, immediately below the signature of Bucard, that authentic hero of the War, on the movement's founding manifesto, we find those of two one-time members of *La Victoire* group. Among the other signatories – insofar as it is possible to identify them socially – we find a few journalists, some students, shopkeepers, a few manufacturers, some engineers and artisans – and a small number of workers.[33] Like the *Solidarité Française*, Francism, which sought to wage war simultaneously on «reaction, capitalism and Judeo-Marxism», combined an anti-bourgeois and quasi-revolutionary ideology with an essentially petty-bourgeois membership. Like Marcel Déat's *Rassemblement National Populaire* and Doriot's *Parti Populaire Français*, Francism would, after 1940, be one of the main movements advocating ideological collaboration with Germany. Violently anti-Vichy, the legions of Bucard, Doriot and Déat were to battle for a true French national socialism.

The Third Generation: Doriot's P.P.F.

If Francism, with its vulgar and incendiary language, never managed to become a credible mass movement, such was not the case with French fascism's third generation – that of the *Parti Populaire Français* (P.P.F.), which was founded in 1936 by one of the most outstanding figures in French communism. Here indeed was a phenomenon without parallel in Europe. Doriot who had been secretary-general of the *Jeunesses Communistes* in 1923, a Communist Deputy since 1924, and a candidate for the P.C.F. secretary-generalship, was at the time of his exclusion from the party in 1934, Mayor of the industrial town of Saint-Denis, one of the finest jewels in Paris' Red Belt. Thanks to the support of the majority of the town's communist «Rayon» he was able in the 1936 legislative elections to win out over the official party candidate, by 11,587 to 10,887. In fact, Doriot only lost his Saint-Denis seat on August 1, 1937, when he tried to turn a by-election in his precinct into a show of strength.[34] At any rate, at the time of the P.P.F.'s foundation it was the famous Saint-Denis «Rayon Majoritaire» that provided the new fascist party with its most fiery elements – and with a large part of its leadership.

A glance at the composition of the party's higher echelons reinforces this impression: of the eight members of the politburo elected at the 1936 Saint-Denis party congress (held on November 9–11, making this the third fascist party to choose to be born on the fateful day), seven – including Doriot – had come from the far left, and five were industrial workers. Their pasts are not without interest, as they were an uncommonly odd group to find at the head of a fascist movement.[35] The party's

491

Number Two, Henri Barbé, had fought side by side with Doriot within the Communist party: from April 1929 to May 1932, he had served on its Politburo. Paul Marion, who would be a Vichy minister, was a former communist and *Jeunesses Communistes* activist, educated in 1928–1930 at the International Leninist School in Moscow. Victor Arrighi, former head of the *Banque Ouvrière et Paysanne* (a Communist party enterprise) had quit the party in 1929. Alexander Abremski, a working mason, had come to Doriot from that noted leftist body, the Amsterdam-Pleyel Committee. Jules Teulade, a building worker, was a former C.G.T. stalwart and had been secretary of the *Confédération Nationale des Ouvrièr du Batiment*. Marcel Marshall had been Doriot's second-in-command at the Saint-Denis city hall, and was a metal-worker. The eighth member of the politburo, Yves Paringaux, was an engineer, and had come over from the *Croix-de-Feu*. In 1939 the Communist party was to lose a third member of its politburo to the P.P.F. – Marcel Gitton. The party Central Committee – note how the P.P.F.'s organization imitated that of the communists – was made up of 46 members (including the eight on the Politburo), of whom 12 were former communist activists, another four came from various other leftist groupings, three were from the *Croix-de-Feu* and two came from the *Action Française*. The political origins of the remaining 27 Central Committee members cannot be determined, but they appear to have been new men whose first political activity was in the ranks of the P.P.F. This impression is borne out by what we can learn from the organ of the *Union Populaire de la Jeunesse Française,* the P.P.F.'s youth wing.

In its May 30, 1937 issue, *Jeunesse de France* gave the original political affiliation of the 277 delegates to its first National Congress. Almost half – 134 to be precise – had never belonged to any party. More than a third came from various leftist and extreme-left groupings – 61 from the *Jeunesses Communistes,* nine from the *Jeunesses Socialistes* and eight from the *Jeunesses Radicales.* Only a mere 45 delegates had a far-right background – 23 former *Jeunesses Patriotes,* 14 from the *Volontaires Nationaux* and eight graduates of the *Action Française.* Of the remaining ascertainable delegates, seven had come out of the the *Jeunesses Ouvrières Chrétiennes,* and 12 from various other parties. To be sure, we must be careful in using figures supplied by a single source; but they do not appear greatly exaggerated. Bearing this out is the number of known former *Jeunesses Communistes* activists who changed over to Doriot's *Jeunesses:* two former *Jeunesses Communistes* cell-secretaries can be identified, as well as G. Deshaire, the secretary general of the Doriot youth, and R. Grandjean, their treasurer, both of them also former communists. It is also perhaps worth mentioning that Professor Maurice Duverger, today a noted leftist political scientist, sat on the administrative committee of Doriot's *Jeunesses.* As for Bertrand de Jouvenal (originally a Radical Socialist), the future author of *Du Pouvoir* and *De la Souveraineté* was then a member of the Party Central Committee and one of the most assiduous contributors to the Doriotist press. Dr. Ben Tami, the P.P.F.leader in Algeria, would in the 1950s be an F.L.N. activist.

It is, and will probably always be, impossible to obtain accurate information as to the social make-up of the P.P.F. In the absence of this, we can only extrapolate from the data furnished by the Doriotist press; these for example enable us to more or less establish the social composition of the party's Constitutive Congress, in November 1937.

The 736 delegates can be divided into three main categories:[36]

1. Workers (more or less skilled) and various lower-grade clerks:

Occupation	Number
Metal-workers	87
Technicians	82
Clerks (retail, banking, insurance)	63
Industrial laborers	54
Public services, including officials	16
	302

2. Free professions (journalists, lawyers, physicians)	78
Students	19
	97

3. The third category of activists was the object of a certain amount of camouflaging: it consisted of 337 delegates classified solely according to sector of the economy rather than occupation. Given, however, that workers and clerks were classified elsewhere, and exactly, these can only have been various members of the middle classes. Thus the rubric Agriculture cannot mean farm laborers nor can the entry Building and Public Works refer to building workers: they clearly involve, respectively, landowners and contractors. These 337 bashful members of the bourgeoisie were distributed by sector as follows:

Agriculture	62
Transport	43
Chemicals	41
Building and Public Works	32
Textiles	28
Mines and Quarries	22
Books and Stationery	12
Lumber Industry	10
Food	9
Others	78
	337

Up to the founding of Déat's *Rassemblement National Populaire* in 1941, the P.P.F. remained the anti-Marxist grouping to have attracted the largest number of workers and former communists and socialists. Nevertheless, it is quite certain that former communist activists never made up more than ten per cent of its simple rank and file. They were thus enormously fewer than at the level of the Politburo: even on the Central Committee they made up only 25 per cent of the membership as against the 90 per cent of former communists at the party's topmost level. At the same time, the P.P.F. certainly knew how to give itself the framework and style of an authentic «people's» party while getting big business to finance it. But Doriot never managed to attract to his cause the hard core of French industry, which clearly preferred the *Croix-de-Feu*. In the final analysis Doriot, that friend of the people and former communist, gave them the willies.

Doriot did of course manage to secure the support of part of business – that represented by Pierre Pucheu – and up to Munich his financial situation was most comfortable. But from the beginning of 1939 a large number of his leading associates, opposed to their chief's policy of appeasement, walked out, cutting the party off from its sources of supply. The most obvious symptom was the disappearance of a large part of the Doriotist press, including *La Liberté* and *Jeunesse de France*. Had it not been for the war the P.P.F. would unquestionably have succumbed to the same malady that had earlier carried of Valois' *Faisceau* and which killed the *Solidarité Française* and the *Francistes*. Fascist movements never had any staying power in France, because, mere crisis expedients that they were, they could neither make the revolution that was their sole reason for being, nor, failing this, retire behind the high walls of a full-fledged «counter-society» as could the communists.

The Croix-de-Feu

The bourgeoisie, for which fascism was hardly more than an expedient, a lesser of two evils, would always prefer to employ its own shock troops: and this was the function of the *Croix-de-Feu*. Founded in 1928 to bring together those decorated for valor under fire, the *Croix-de-Feu* (Cross of Fire) Association did not at the start have a well-defined political program. It did of course lie to the right, inasmuch as it defended national values, but it had no pretensions beyond that of grouping together the fighting élite. However, the new association very quickly caught the eye of François Coty, who opened to it the pages of his newspapers and, no doubt, the pages of his check book as well. The millionaire perfume-maker encouraged the rise of Lieutenant-Colonel (Reserves) Comte de La Rocque, who in 1931 became president of the movement. The movement – after La Rocque had cut his ties with Coty (who would soon found *Solidarité Française*) – rapidly developed and took on a clear political coloration. It mobilized in addition a whole series of satellite groups which at the end of 1932 could show about 36,000 members.[37]

From the very beginning La Rocque placed the movement at the service of the parliamentary and bourgeois right. At the end of 1931 he threw his support behind Laval and seems – according to the testimony in 1937 of former Prime Minister André Tardieu – to have bitten into a sizable chunk of the *fonds secrets*.[38] This would have been nothing new, as the way had undoubtedly been paved by the *Jeunesses Patriotes* under the Poincaré ministry. And here we touch on the vital element of explanation: the two most important rightist mass-movements of their time – the *Jeunesses Patriotes* in the 'twenties and the *Croix-de-Feu* in the 'thirties – far from being organizations of rebels, were actually in the pay of the traditional right: for both shared the same essential aim – preservation of the existing political and social structures. That is why the French bourgeoisie turned to La Rocque and Taittinger, rather than to Valois, Bucard or Doriot. The latter were real revolutionaries, who hated the bourgeois order; they could thus never be more than a makeshift which one jettisoned as soon as ever possible.

It was therefore not just personal rivalries that made the *Jeunesses Patriotes* reject all forms of alliance or collaboration with the first fascist movement or which made La Rocque turn a similar cold shoulder to Doriot's proposal that all nationalist movements join forces in a «Front de la Liberté». To put it plainly, the P.P.F. refused to let itself be dragged along by a policy which could amount to nothing more than opposition *à outrance* not just to the regime but to the very social structures on which that regime rested.[39]

It is thus not surprising that the *Croix-de-Feu* repeated in the 'thirties the experience the *Jeunesses Patriotes* had already undergone in the 'twenties: the loss, after the summer of 1935, of its most active elements. Bertrand de Maud'huy's exit was

494

followed by those of Laroche, Pucheu – head of the *Volontaires Nationaux* – and of an indeterminated number of members. The leave-takers were not numerous, but they clearly belonged to a significant category: that of true national socialists who, fed up with the movement's inactivity and passivity, had openly criticized La Rocque's «softness» towards the authorities and accused him of letting Laval lead him by the nose.[40] The immediate cause for the split in the leadership was its chief's refusal to permit publication of a manifesto in which Maud'huy and his friends had outlined a vigorous program of social and economic reform for adoption by the *Croix-de-Feu*. Bertrand de Maud'huy, son of the famous general, had in fact been a member of the S.F.I.O., which he had quit right after the sixth of February. Authoritarian nationalist that he was, he could hardly be expected to adapt himself either to proletarian internationalism or to the democratic socialism of a Léon Blum. But he nevertheless possessed some extremely advanced ideas on social policy. Maud'huy's manifesto advocated the abolition of class distinctions and the creation of a state-controlled labor market which would provide work for all, fixed wages and a forty-eight hour week; employers were to be answerable to a higher authority. The manifesto attacked capitalism, and promised reform of the whole economic system as well as establishment of an all-powerful state.[41] This was too much for the *Croix-de-Feu*, and very much too much both for the colonel-count and for the phalanx of big-businessmen on which he depended.[42]

It is nevertheless not without interest to note that, according to the *Renseignements Généraux*, La Rocque was also in touch with the Count of Paris and had, as of 1934, worked out an agreement for possible future cooperation with the Pretender. This agreement did not foresee an immediate restoration; but it would, in the event of a seizure of power by the *Croix-de-Feu*, have provided initially for «relations of trust» between the French Crown and the French State.[43]

Having quit the *Croix-de-Feu*, Maud'huy made contact with Gaston Bergery.[44] This eminent leftist politician and one-time member of the Radical Party's Young Turks had, through his non-conformism and ardor for a regeneration of the left, begun vaguely working out a political doctrine which quite soon took on a clearly fascist tinge. Bergery, however, stopped in midstream, and would end his career as Vichy ambassador to Moscow and later, Ankara. The contacts between his *Front Social* and the *Croix-de-Feu* breakaways came to naught, and we therefore find Maud'huy at Doriot's side at the founding of the P.P.F. He would be a member of its Central Committee, where he would be joined in 1938 by Pucheu.

Thus, by July 1935, everything was quite clear; the way was open for the P.P.F., which had drained off the *Croix-de-Feu's* fascistic elements. Colonel de La Rocque's movement, on the other hand, became each day more and more the praetorian guard of the traditional right; just what authentic fascism – let us hear how Brasillach put it – refused to be:

«. . . We haven't a great deal in common between us, in spite of appearances, Mr. Conservative. We defend certain truths in the way we feel they ought to be defended, that is, with violence, impetuosity, and lack of respect; with life. You've found that useful at times, Mr. Conservative. You may again. The minute you think you don't need these compromising bodyguards you prefer to talk of other things and to look at them from very far off. After all, they run their own risks, don't they? After all, they're on their own, aren't they? It's not your business. You're the one who's said so, Mr. Conservative. They run their own risks. Not yours. We're not mercenaries. We're not the shock-troops of the right-thinkers. We are not the S.A. of conservatism.»[45]

And yet it was the *Croix-de-Feu* which was the real mass movement of the 'thirties: in July 1935, Interior Ministry estimates of its membership varied between 250,000 and 400,000.[46] We have no trustworthy figures for 1936–1939: but it is fair to guess that the number must in that time at least have doubled.

In 1938 the movement claimed three million adherents; even if most of these were just sympathizers, it still remains an impressive figure. This considerable potential enabled it to organize demonstrations involving tens of thousands of followers, able among themselves to mobilize some five thousand private automobiles for a single demonstration, plus several dozen airplanes. A good illustration of the social origins of the *Croix-de-Feu* men: we are certainly not dealing here with the denizens of Paris' industrial suburbs.[47]

Well organized and deploying a considerable following, the movement enjoyed enormous financial backing, having among its patrons some of the largest fortunes in French industry. But despite all this, it never managed to get more than a dozen men into Parliament.

The *Croix-de-Feu* was potentially the strongest political movement in France. The P.P.F., which claimed to have a following of 250,000 can never have had more than 150,000.[48] But even that was considerable: let us note in comparison that the Communist party in 1933 could show less than 29,000 adherents, and the S.F.I.O. about 130,000. In January 1936, the communists still had only 81,000. It was only in December of that year – the year of the Popular Front – that there would be 284,194 French communists, and a slightly smaller number of S.F.I.O. members.[49]

It would be inexact to speak of the failure of the *Croix-de-Feu*. It is much more in line with reality to say that there was never a question of its being put to the test because, even in the first days of the Popular Front, neither the structure nor the political system of French society were ever in danger. Such was the stability of French society as a whole, and the solidity of its right-wing, that the latter had no need to use the new weapon it had joined together to form.

It is important to stress here that, in the critical months which followed the disturbances of the Sixth of February, 1934, the liberal right was ready to hedge its bets; even the *Solidarité Française* enjoyed its secret support. In fact, it was the National Republicans' Propaganda Centre that supplied the posters with which Jean Renaud's movement plastered Mulhouse, and it was Henri Kerillis who took the initiative for a great recruiting campaign in Alsace.[50]

Nevertheless, Colonel de La Rocque's movement got the traditional right's most direct and vigorous support and the *Crox-de-Feu* was never a fascist movement: it never possessed either fascism's power to disrupt and will to revolution or that national socialist ingredient without which there is no true fascism. In France, real, authentic fascism was always born on the left, never on the right. This had been true for proto-fascism, and it remained true in the inter-war period – from Gustave Hervé, founder of the ephemeral *Parti Socialiste National,* through Georges Valois (who in the 'thirties returned to the left and was to die in Buchenwald) and Jacques Doriot, the one-time communist leader who was to serve on the Eastern Front in the uniform of a German officer, right up to Marcel Déat, the former socialist minister who would, in 1941, be reunited with his former socialist syndicalist cohorts in the *Rassemblement National Populaire.* To be sure, we are not trying to say that the bulk of followers came from leftist movements, but at the activist level the proportion of former leftists – of former socialist and communist officials – was considerable.

The Rassemblement National Populaire

The last-born of these movements, Déat's *Rassemblement National Populaire*, bore out the rule. Déat, in 1926 a Socialist Deputy and in 1932 re-elected against Jacques Duclos, in 1931 published his *Perspectives Socialistes*, brought out by Valois' publishing house. This work, which attacked the essence of orthodox socialism and put in its place the idea of a great anti-capitalist coalition, marked the birth of a new kind of socialism – national, authoritarian and violently opposed to the Marxist notion of class struggle. Déat quickly emerged as the theoretician of the party's right wing. Two years later the S.F.I.O. split and, at the famous Mutualité Congress, neo-socialism was born. The formula launched by Déat, Deputy for Charonne, in collaboration with Montagnon, Deputy for Clignancourt and Marquet, Deputy for and Mayor of Bordeaux, constituted nothing less than the birth – in the very bosom of a great Marxist party – of the most authentic sort of fascism. Léon Blum was one of the first to realize this, even as the «neos» were elaborating their program from the Congress dais. By 1936 Déat was Minister of Aviation in the Albert Sarraut Cabinet, formed that January, and when, on May 7, the Nazis marched into the Rhineland he was to oppose all mobilization measures and call for appeasement at any price. Henceforth squarely in the pacifist camp, he was to be one of the main supporters of Munich and, later, with Doriot, the embodiment of ideological collaboration with a Nazism he saw as the great social revolution of the twentieth century. In December 1941, he formed the *Rassemblement National Populaire*, intended to be the great single party which, in imitation of the Hitlerites in Germany, would forge the Second French Revolution. Déat called for an authoritarian and populist national socialism, a vague but virulent anti-capitalism based largely on the ideas expressed in *Perspectives Socialistes*, and for unreserved collaboration with Hitler's Germany. The R.N.P. managed to bring together a significant number of former socialists and syndicalists who thought to find again in fascism a socialism purified of that which had falsified its true nature – namely, democracy.

Including Déat, the movement's guiding body – the Permanent Commission – counted some 14 members, eight of whom had come from the left or the far-left. The R.N.P. leader was surrounded by a number of important figures of the inter-war left; Ludovic Zoretti, creator of the C.G.T.'s worker-education centre; Georges Dumoulin, one-time candidate to succeed Jouhaux as C.G.T. secretary-general; Pierre Vigne, former president of the Fédération International des Mineurs; and the former neo-socialist Deputies Gabriel Lafaye and Barthelémy Montagnon. It is, and will always remain, impossible to get a broad idea of the R.N.P.'s recruitment, as the movement's archives have disappeared and its weekly maintained a total silence as to the social origins of the movement's following. Of course, right from its first appearance in June 1942, *Le National Populaire* set off on a long campaign for an authentic national socialism, for a Charter of Labor centred on the rights of the workers, and for a syndicalism which, while corporative, would be potent and effective. The R.N.P. clearly placed itself on the extreme left among those who collaborated with the Germans: it denied nothing of its leaders' socialist past, kept up the cult of Jaurès and of May Day, and fought the reactionary spirit of Vichy without letup.[51]

In the Europe of those war years, the R.N.P. could only be compared with the fascism of the Salò Republic: a fascism free of compromises with power and thus of the essentially alien admixtures which that would bring to its doctrine, but for the same reason an unreal fascism, one unable either to put flesh on its bones or to approach the corridors of power. The traditional right had remained too strong to have to make way for the national socialism of a Déat or a Doriot; the 1940 defeat had not created a political vacuum in France – it had merely brought about the replacement of one élite by another. And the traditional right, having come to power, had no intention of sharing this with the fascists – nor were the latter strong enough to take it for themselves. It was indeed the weakness, not the strength, of the right that lay at the root of fascist successes; and in France the right, even under the worst conditions, was always far too good at safeguarding the essential interests of its following to ever have to call in the fascists.

NOTES

* I am deeply indebted to the Warden Fellows of St. Antony's College, Oxford, for having elected me to a Wolfson Visiting Fellowship for the 1973–1974 academic year. It was during the year I spent in Oxford that I was able to prepare this study.

Abbreviations

A.N. = Archives Nationales, Paris
P.R.O.= Public Records Office, London
P.P. = Archives of the Paris Prefecture de Police

[1] Quoted in Michel Winock. «Une parabole fasciste: *Gilles* de Drieu La Rochelle», *Le Mouvement Social*, no. 80, July 1972, p. 29.

[2] Georges Valois, *Le Fascisme,* (Paris, Nouvelle Librairie Nationale, 1927) p. 21.
On Valois cf. Jules Levey «Georges Valos and the Faisceau: The making and breaking of a Fascist», *French Historical Studies*, vol 8, no 2, Fall 1973, pp 279 – 304, and Yves Guchet, «Georges Valois ou l'illusion fasciste» *Revue Française de Science Politique*, Vol. XV, no 6 December 1965, pp. 1111–1144.

[3] 25 September 1940.

[4] Georges Valois, *op. cit.,* pp. 5–7.

[5] Cf. Zeev Sternhell, *Maurice Barrès et le Nationalisme français*, (Paris, Armand Colin, 1972) and Robert Soucy, *Fascism in France: The Case of Maurice Barrès,* (Berkeley, Univ. of California Press, 1972).

[6] Maurice Barrès, «Que faut-il faire?» *Le Courrier de l'Est* (2nd series), 12 May 1898. See also *Mes Cahiers* (14 vols. 1929–57) II, p. 197 and «Socialisme et Nationalisme», *La Patrie*, 27 February 1903. It is by no means an accident that French fascists of the 'twenties and 'thirties constantly referred to Barrès.

[7] Cf. Stephen Wilson, «The Antisemitic Riots of 1898 in France», *The Historical Journal,* XVI, 4, 1973, pp. 789–806.

[8] Pierre Biétry. *Le Socialisme et les Jaunes,* Paris, Plon – Nourrit, 1906, pp. 99 and *passim.* See also George L. Mossé: «The French Right and the Working Classes: Les Jaunes», *Journal of Contemporary History*, vol. 7, nos. 3–4, July–October 1972.

[9] Hubert Lagardelle, «Le Syndicalisme et le Socialisme en France» in *Syndicalisme et Socialisme,* (Paris, Marcel Rivière, 1908,) p. 36.

[10] Victor Griffuelhes, *L'Action Syndicaliste,* (Paris, Marcel Rivière, 1908) p. 37.

[11] Emile Pouget, *Le Confédération Générale du Travail,* (Paris, Marcel Riviere, 1909,) pp. 35–36.

[12] «Déclaration», *Cahiers du Cercle Proudhon*, I, January 1912, p.l.

[13] Georges Valois, *Le Fascisme,* p. 6.

[14] On the other hand, Ernst Nolte considers *L'Action Française* as an authentic form of fascism. See his brilliant *Three Faces of Fascism,* (New York, Holt, Rinehart and Winston, 1966.)

15 A.N. F⁷13208, 6 December 1925, January 1926.

16 A.N. F⁷13208, November 1925. *Le Nouveau Siècle* was launched on 26 February 1925 by a group of industrialists led by the millionaires Eugène Mathon and Franz van der Broeck: they had no difficulty in raising ten million francs for the project – a considerable sum at the time. Among the other partners were Serge André, Antoine Cazeneuve, Count de Laperouse, Jacques Arthuys, the Sterne family, de Fontaine, de Verville – all people of considerable wealth. Valois, when his *Nouveau Siècle* was turned into a daily, also enjoyed a subsidy – of more than a million francs, from the noted perfume-maker, François Coty (14 January 1926).

17 A.N. F⁷13208, Reports on the effective membership of the various Leagues: February, 13 April, 24 September, and 13 October 1926.

18 Cf. the Reports for February and April, 1926.

19 It is not without interest to compare these figures with the effective membership of the Communist party and the S.F.L.O. In 1926 the P.C.F. could show only about 55,000 members, half the strength of the S.F.L.O. (Annie Kriegel, «Le parti communiste français sous la Troisième République (1920–1939). Evolution de ses effectifs», *Revue française de Science politique*, vol. XVI, no 1, 1966, p. 35). Of course, there is little value in making mechanical comparisons, and one can hardly compare a socialist or communist militant's degree of commitment with that of a member of the *Faisceau* or the *Jeunesses Patriotes*, to say nothing of the lack of a common measure for comparing the two workers' parties with the nationalist *Ligues* in terms of apparatus and effectiveness.

20 Cf. Zeev Sternhell, «Paul Déroulède and the origins of Modern French Nationalism», *Journal of Contemporary History*, vol. 6, 4, 1971, pp. 46–70.

21 Cf. A.N. F⁷13209, 14 December 1926.

22 A.N.F.⁷ 13208, January 1926, cf. also the text of the lecture-outline prepared for Legion activity in F⁷ 13209 and the special report of the *Jeunesses Patriotes – La Légion* of 9 January 1926, as well as that for 18 December 1925.

23 A. N. F⁷ 13208, 10 April 1926. At Bordeaux *Action Française* lost Bertrand de Lur-Saluces, one of the most notable royalists of the twentieth century. Among the other breakaways recorded were Roger de La Porte, Barral, and the industrialists Mathon and Van den Broeck; cf. 10 December 1925.

24 Georges Valois, *La Révolution Nationale*, (Paris, Nouvelle Librairie National, 1924) pp. 81–97.

25 A.N. F⁷13209, 24 June 1927.

26 A.N. F⁷13208, 25 July 1925.

27 A.N. F⁷13208, 14 December 1925, 16 March 1926, 25 July 1925.

28 A.N. F⁷13210, Reports of the police special intelligence officer for Le Havre, 24 June, 18 July, 30 October 1926.

29 A.N. F⁷ 13209, 12 December 1925, 6 January 1926, 6 February 1926.

30 A.N. F⁷ 13210, April 1926.

31 A.N. F⁷13239 and more particularly 18 October 1934, P.R.O., F.O. 371, 17656, March 15 1934 (Lord Tyrrell to Sir John Simon). *Solidarité Française* also possessed an élite «*Corps franc*» of about 180 men, under a Colonel Sallerin, designed for the dealing out of hard knocks. Like Valois' *Faisceau*, Coty's movement was based essentially on greater Paris, the East, the North and the Bouches-du-Rhône: see the special report on the movement's membership and the geographical distribution of same in F⁷13239.

32 Cf. various police reports in the F⁷13239 file.

33 Cf. the official Party organ, *Le Franciste*. Only by minutely combing the Francist monthly (later weekly) have we been able to establish the origins of the Francist *cadres*. Issue no. 7 for June 1934, in announcing the first fascist congress, provides information which amplifies that in the paper's first number. On the other hand, the file (F⁷13241) deposited in the *Archives Nationales* is astonishingly poor, containing next to no information as to the organization's rank and file. On the *Solidarité Française* and the *Francistes*, see important details in Henry Coston, *Partis, Journaux et hommes politiques d'hier et d'aujourd'hui*, special number of *Lectures françaises*, December 1960, pp. 9–64, 113–118.

[34] Doriot's aim in forcing this by-election was to show that the trend of the 21 June balloting had been reversed. (In the municipal elections held a month after Doriot's removal from office as Mayor of Saint-Denis, the Doriotist list had lost to the Popular Front by 6,966 to 10,524). But the trend was in fact amply confirmed, with the P.P.F. losing a further 2,500 votes – the Communist Grenier winning 9,222 as against 4,563 for the Doriotists and 2,570 for the socialist candidate. The Communist party had thus reconquered Saint-Denis.

[35] The list is given in the order of precedence established by the Party: cf. *L'Émancipation Nationale*, 14 November 1936, which immediately following the closing of the first Party congress furnished the details on which our analysis is based. On the same sources, is also based Dieter Wolf's analysis: see his *Doriot: Du Communisme à la Collaboration*, (Paris, Fayard, 1969) pp. 186–192.

[36] *ibid.*

[37] Cf. René Rémond, *La Droite en France de la Première Restauration à la Cinqième Republique*, (Paris, Auber, 1963,) p. 220.

[38] It is true that La Rocque has always had his defenders; but it seems from the evidence furnished by the authorities that the charge was in order. It is worth noting that so impartial an observer as the British Ambassador thought the charges against La Rocque clearly proven: P.R.O., F.O. 371, C8403, letter of Cripps to Eden of 7 December 1937.

[39] *Le Parti Social Français et le Front de la Liberté – Rapport présenté par Fernand Robbe suivi de l'Ordre du Jour voté au Conseil National extraordinaire du Parti*, 9 June 1937, Paris, Société d'éditions et d'abonnements, no date.

[40] Cf. A.N. F^{7}13241, reports of 12 July 1935, 13 June 1935.

[41] Cf. P.R.O., F.O. 371, C5599: Clerk to Hoare, 24 July and 5 October 1935.

[42] Among the great names of French business who unquestionably gave La Rocque more or less direct financial aid we find the Mallet Frères et Cie. bank, which administered the greatest noble fortunes in the land; Pierre Mirabaud, de Wendel, Schwob, d'Héricourt, Jacques de Neuflize, and Otto. We also know, according to the overall picture established by the Interior Ministry's intelligence service, that he was «in perfect agreement» with Finaly, Béghin and Puyerimhoff. Cf. A. N. F^7 13241, reports of 29 June and 6 July 1935.

[43] A. N. F^{7}13241, reports of 20 June and 12 July 1935.

[44] A. N. F^{7}13241, report of 12 July 1935.

[45] «À un conservateur», *Je Suis Partout*, 23 February 1940.

[46] A. N. F^{7}13241, reports of 1 and 10 July and 12 August 1935.

[47] A. N. F^7 13241, reports of 27 June, P.R.O., F.O. 371, C4986, Clerk to Foreign Office, 27 June 1935.

[48] This is also a former fellow–traveller's estimation: see Henry Coston, *op. cit.*, p. 126.

[49] Cf. Annie Kriegel, *loc, cit.*, pp. 26–35.

[50] A. N. F^{7}13239, report of Prefect of Haut-Rhin to Minister of the Interior, 10 November 1934.

[51] Cf. the R.N.P.'s weekly, *Le National Populaire* and more particularly the first 12 numbers (6 June – 5 September 1942), giving the basic elements of Déat's ideology, and, thanks to the Party's *Conseil National* of 11–12 July 1942, some details on its organization. Cf. also Claude Varennes (pseud. Georges Albertini) *Le Déstin de Marcel Déat*, (Paris, Editions Janmery, 1948.)

Fascists and Nationalists in Belgium 1919–1940

LUC SCHEPENS

Like all the Western European countries, Belgium was shaken by a series of crises between World War I and World War II. The first was a crisis of conscience which affected mainly the army veterans who had personally endured the ravages of World War I. In order to avoid (the) repetition of such a slaughter, some became anti-militarist in the name of human dignity; others turned militarist in order to reinforce the defense of the country to deter any possible aggressor. This crisis extended to another level when fascism was on the rise in Europe and obtained spectacular results by means of force. Should one draw inspiration from it, agree with it, imitate it, or fight it?

Added to this was the crisis of the political system in Belgium, caused by the «aging» of the traditional political parties and their ineptitude in the new situation created by the introduction of universal male suffrage from 1919 (although the Constitution was amended to that effect only in 1921). For the first time in its history Belgium was ruled by coalition governments. This implied negotiations between the leaders of the parties and gave increasing influence to the parties headed by aged leaders who were still influenced by 19th century notions of politics and who were not in a hurry to resign. Youth became impatient and, unable to gain acceptance for its views among the parties, gathered at the fringe of the parties in study groups or pressure groups with names like the *Ligue de la Jeunesse nouvelle* (League of the New Youth) or the *Ligue pour la restauration de l'ordre et de l'autorité dans l'État* (League for the Restoration of Order and Authority in the State), and its opposite, the *Action socialiste et révolutionnaire* (Socialist and Revolutionary Action). This conflict between the generations within the parties was not solved in favor of the youths till after 1935.

Finally, there was the economic crisis and the accompanying social crisis involving in particular the middle classes and the workers, and also the financial crisis involving banks and other financial institutions which cast a vivid light on the coalition bonds between the higher political and financial circles.[1] Numerous politico-financial scandals emerged. Discontent, indignation, and popular disgust was pervasive.

The Catholic Church also played an important role. Under the influence of Italian fascism it established the festival and cult of «Christ the King» in 1925. At the same time in Belgium a lot of Catholic youth movements were created. They aimed at consolidating the hold of the ecclesiastical hierarchy over the popular masses and reinforcing the struggle against communism and socialism by enrolling youths in strongly hierarchical organizations with paramilitary appearance and terminology.

All this created in Belgium a pro-fascist atmosphere, although the country had always been ruled by democratic governments. From 1919 to 1940 the country was dominated by the traditional parties rather than by militant and noisy minorities. In this respect it is instructive to examine the results of the legislative elections to parliament.

Table 1. *Election Results for the Chamber of Representatives 1919–1939**

	Catholics		Socialists		Liberals		Flemish Nation-alists		Com-munists		Rex		Others	
	%	seats	%	seats	%	seats	%	seats	%	seats	%	seats	%	seats
1919.....	38.8	73	36.6	70	17.6	34	2.6	5	–	–	–	–	–	4
1921.....	41.3	80	34.8	68	17.8	33	3.0	4	–	–	–	–	–	1
1925.....	38.6	78	39.4	78	14.6	23	3.9	6	1.6	2	–	–	–	–
1929.....	38.5	76	36.0	70	16.6	28	6.3	11	1.9	1	–	–	–	1
1932.....	38.6	79	37.1	73	14.3	24	5.9	8	2.8	3	–	–	–	–
1936.....	28.8	63	32.1	70	12.4	23	7.1	16	6.1	9	11.5	21	–	–
1939.....	32.7	73	30.2	64	17.2	33	8.3	17	5.4	9	4.4	4	–	2

* The number of seats in proportion to the population was from 1919 to 1921: 186; from 1925 to 1932: 187; from 1936 to 1939: 202.
Source: Theo Luykx, *Politieke Geschiedenis van België van 1789 tot heden* (Brussel, Amsterdam, Elsevier 1964) pp. 540–542.

In the last elections before the war (in 1912), the Catholic party which had been ruling the country since 1884, obtained 51.5 per cent of the votes and 101 seats. However, in 1919 it lost considerable ground to the Socialist party. The Catholic party's share of votes fell to 38.8 per cent giving it 73 seats, while the Socialist party almost doubled its representation: it got 70 seats instead of 37 in 1912. The elections of 1921 did not greatly change anything: The dissidents of 1919 entered the Catholic party which increased its representation by 7 seats at the expense of the Socialist party. The elections of 1925 brought more noticable changes. The Socialists won ten seats at the expense of the Liberals. This was a popular response to the militarist policy of the Liberals, and the opposition of the Socialists to the occupation of the Ruhr by Belgium and France. For the first time, the Communist party obtained two seats. The elections of 1929 were marked by increased representation for the Flemish Nationalists, who increased their seats from 7 to 11 at the expense of both the Catholic and the Socialist parties. The Liberals regained some lost ground taking 5 seats from the Socialists. The sudden improvement in the fortunes of the Flemish Nationalists was due to discontent in Flanders over the government's refusal to grant linguistic concessions promised by the King in 1918, and the refusal to grant amnesty for former activists. The elections in 1932 took place at the beginning of the great depression but did not revolve around this issue. The Catholic party cleverly focused its electoral campaign on the defense of Free Catholic Schools (always a sensitive issue in Belgium). Its opponents felt obliged to defend the official state schools. The Catholic party won three seats at the expense of the Flemish Nationalists (thanks to the linguistic laws which had been passed in the meantime). Among the other parties there was a further shift to the left as the youth became more and more radical. The Liberal party lost 4 seats to the Socialists who themselves lost two seats to the Communist party. The election of 1936 was characterized by the Rexist tidal wave which all at once carried 21 seats. This success was mainly at the expense of the Catholic party which had been shaken by the economic crisis and politico-financial scandals. The Socialist party leaned more and more towards its left wing. The Flemish Nationalists doubled the number of their seats. This was due mainly to the gains in the rural areas which were suffering from the financial difficulties of the powerful Catholic agricultural association in Flanders, the *Boeren-bond*.

By 1939, everything was back to normal. In the traditional parties the old leaders had given way to young ones; a strong government had succeeded in rectifying the economic situation by applying a program that took into account some of the aims of the *Rex;* and finally the external threat and the attitude of the fascist movements inside Belgium provoked a reaction among most Belgians. They wanted a return to the traditional parties and to rally around King Leopold III who by temperament and position took on the appearance of a leader.

The Liberal and Catholic parties still had almost the same number of seats as in 1919. The Socialist party lost some seats to the Communist party.

Nationalist and Fascist Movements after the War

Two peak periods for the birth of fascist parties or similar movements can be distinguished. There are the movements born just after World War I, and those born during the great crisis of the 1930's. The former were all nationalist movements, but of two kinds: on the one hand there were the Flemish Nationalists, who were confined to the Dutch-speaking part of the country; they demanded cultural and political autonomy for Flanders either by changing Belgium into a federal state or by attaching Flanders to the Netherlands. On the other hand, there were the Belgian Nationalist movements which appeared in the French-speaking part of the country (that is the Walloon county and Brussels) and in some towns of Flanders, among the bourgeoisie who generally are French-speaking. These movements sought to reinforce the Belgian unitary state under the King's leadership, and to maintain the linguistic *status quo* (in fact also a social *status quo)* of Flanders, contrary to the Flemish autonomist movements.[2]

The main Flemish nationalist movement, the *Vlaamsche Front* or *Frontpartij* (Party of the Front) came directly from the clandestine movement which took shape in 1917 among the Flemish soldiers of the Belgian army as the *Frontbeweging* (Movement of the Front). This movement was essentially a reaction to the Frenchification of the Belgian military and political establishment. In its program the *Frontpartij* took over the claims of the *Frontbeweging*: complete autonomy of Flanders in the fields of administration, education, administration of justice and conscription (constitution of separate Walloon and Flemish regiments). It was a democratic party made up mainly of veterans and former activists, that is the Flemish who had collaborated with the enemy in order to achieve the aims of the pre-war Flemish movement. But it also had ties with the majority of the former Christian-Democrats who had seceded from the Catholic party before the war. A small part of the Christian-Democrats were later to enroll in the Socialist party.

In the towns of Gent and Antwerp, the *Frontpartij* had a majority of Flemish leftist intellectuals among its members. Its recruits came from the middle classes:Small tradesmen and industrialists, liberal professions, employees, small farmers, lower clergy, and the workers who had once followed the Christian-Democrats. In other words, except for the last category, this was the milieu where the Flemish movement developed in the second half of the 19th century. Oddly enough, while the success of Flemish Nationalism increased with each election, disagreements arose among the members of the *Frontpartij* in such a way that by about 1930 the party was composed of as many more or less autonomous small groups as there were Flemish Nationalist leaders. In 1931 one of these leaders, Joris van Severen, broke away from the *Frontpartij,* founding his own movement the *Verdinaso (Verbond van Dietsche Nationaal-Solidaristen* (Federation of Dutch National-Solidarists)). This split provoked a crisis among the other small groups which resulted in a *rapprochement* between them, and the establishment on October 1, 1933, of a federation (rather than a new party) under the name of *Vlaamsch Nationaal Verbond* (Flemish National Federation) or *V.N.V.* It had as leader Staf Declercq, whose main task was to establish again a minimum of agreement for the purpose of coordinated political action. At the beginning, the direction of the *V.N.V.* was unquestionably democratic and parliamentary. But under the pressure of some extremists coming from outside (the *Verdinaso)* or from within the federation, and under the influence of Nazi Germany which, since 1937, provided money, the direction of the federation evolved more and more toward fascism while the parliamentary group of the *V.N.V.* remained democratic. It should be noted that, except for some individuals, the *V.N.V.* as a whole was neither anti-Semitic nor anti-parliamentary but strongly anti-militarist (which ultimately was to Germany's advantage).

Next to Flemish Nationalism, there was also a Belgian Nationalism rooted in the war experience. It developed in the Belgian governmental milieu in exile at Le Havre and among some Belgian refugees in France, identifying the struggle against Germany and the fear of Flemish Nationalism which was considered pro-German. Under the influence of French extremists, some Belgians even proposed to increase the national territory at the expense of Germany, the Netherlands (which remained neutral in the conflict), and the Grand Duchy of Luxembourg, which they wanted to annex. One of the champions of this Belgian expansionism was Pierre Nothomb who in 1919, after the failure of these expansionist claims at the conference of Versailles created a *Comité de politique nationale* (National Policy Committee) concerned with the domestic situation of the country. The Committee strove for the maintenance of national unity and the linguistic *status quo* in Flanders, the reinforcement of the executive, the limitation of legislative power and the corporate organization of the workers and employers' unions. Recruitment to this *Committee* took place essentially among the Catholic and Liberal bourgeoisie and by organizing monthly dinners during which speakers presented their proposals. In 1921, it changed into the *Parti National Populaire* (Popular National Party) for the elections. This proved a complete failure, and the party was soon dissolved. The *Comité de politique nationale* continued in another form, however, as the *Ligue pour l'Unité belge* (League for Belgian Unity) which in 1923 changed into *Ligue nationale pour la défense de l'Université de Gand et de la liberté des langues* (National League for the Defense of the University of Gent and for the Freedom of Languages), and in 1924 became the *Action nationale.* This *Action nationale* presented itself as anti-democratic, anti-Bolshevist, anti-socialist and anti-Flemish, in favor of a strong government responsible to the King (and not to parliament) and in favor of a corporate organization, modelled on Italian fascism.

The *Action nationale* manifested itself especially through its *Jeunesses nationales* (National Youth), an organization which included from 2,000 to 3,000 high school students who put into practice the «anti» part of the program of the movement. It never really succeeded in commanding much attention, and was partly absorbed by the Catholic party, which since 1925 reserved a place to Pierre Nothomb on its list of candidates for the Chamber. He had to wait until 1936, however, to get elected as a Catholic provincial senator by the Provincial council of Luxembourg. The other part of the *Action nationale* was absorbed by the *Légion nationale*, a movement created by Belgian nationalist veterans in 1922 in Liège. When Paul Hoornaert became the leader, in 1927, it was transformed into a movement which claimed kinship with fascism. Paul Hoornaert seems to be the first one to talk about *The New Order*. Its *Groupes mobiles* (later *Jeunes Gardes*, Young Guards) wore uniforms, helmets and sticks. Faithful to the King's person, the *Légion nationale*, which never accounted for more than 4,000 members, was opposed to any parliamentary party, including *Rex*, and prepared the «National Revolution» by assaulting the *Young Socialist Guards* and the Flemish Nationalist militia. It founded about 15 «National Houses» over the country, even in Flanders, and published a newspaper in French and in Flemish. It should be noted, however, that the fascist *Légion nationale* was totally on the side of the armed resistance in 1941, and its leader Hoornaert died in a Nazi concentration camp in 1944.

All these Belgian nationalist movements took inspiration from Charles Maurras and the *Action Française*, whose influence in Belgium was strengthened by the fact that the Belgian monarchy emerged stronger from the war. They were all bourgeois movements. The hitherto dominant bourgeoisie felt threatened in Flanders by the Flemish Nationalists, and in all of Belgium by the Socialist and Communist parties which flourished under universal suffrage. As a result, a part of the bourgeoisie turned toward anti-democratic movements, and wanted to reinforce the executive power that it still commanded at the expense of the legislative power that it no longer controlled.

The Verdinaso and the Rex

The economic crisis of the 1930's and the victory in Germany by the Nazis led to the creation of two Belgian movements which were akin to fascism: The *Verdinaso* and the *Rex*. The *Verdinaso* was officially founded on October 5, 1931, by Joris van Severen, as a dissident movement of the *Frontpartij*. It took Italian fascism as a model. The foundation of the movement was preceded, in fact, by the establishment of a militia in September 1930, the *Vlaamsche Nationale Militie*, later *Dietsche Militanten Orde* (Dutch Militant Order) which never included more than 800 members, and by a Flemish nationalist union, a successor of the Christian-Democratic unions, which was based on corporatism (Van Severen called it solidarism). In 1934, however, the Belgian government decided to stop its subsidies to this nationalist union, which consequently was unable to pay the unemployed (in the midst of the crisis!). This decision of the government dealt a deadly blow to that union.

Born in Wakken on July 19, 1894, in a bourgeois French-speaking family, Van Severen studied in a Jesuit school, then began attending the university, but did not finish because of the war. He was drafted and sent to the front in March 1915 where he remained for two years as a sergeant, then as a warrant-officer because of his evident capacity to provide leadership. In June 1918, however, he was demoted because of a (minor) infraction of discipline. At the front he discovered the élitist doctrine of the *Action Française* and became enthusiastic about it. He also became aware of the intellectual and spiritual situation of the Flemish soldiers. He enrolled in the Flemish movement and became one of the leaders of the clandestine *Frontbeweging*. After the war, he made his way toward a career as a publicist by publishing the magazine *Ter Waarheid* (To the Truth) with other former activists, aiming to bring to the Flemish people echoes of artistic and philosophical developments all over Europe. (Articles on Charles Baudelaire, Maurras, Romain Rolland, but also Zoltan Kodaly and Le Corbusier). Committed thoroughly to the struggle for the rights of he Flemish people, he was a candidate for the *Frontpartij* in the elections of 1921. Elected to the Chamber of representatives, he attracted attention both by his lack of parliamentary zeal and his verbal violence in the two or three speeches he made to condemn the Belgian unitary state and to glorify the activists' attitude in the war. Defeated in the elections of 1929 thanks to the calculations and intrigues of the Catholic party, he then became a resolute enemy of the parliamentary system. He ordered the members of the *Verdinaso* not to vote in the elections and after 1928 openly advocated revolution and the destruction of the Belgian state and its replacement by a new state including the Netherlands and Flanders. An unexpected turn occurred in July 1934 when he proclaimed the «nieuwe marschrichting» or the «new marching direction» for the *Verdinaso*. Now he no longer wanted to destroy the Belgian state, but non-violently to take over power in Belgium as well as in the Netherlands (where the *Verdinaso* had a few hundred members) for the purpose of reconstituting an enlargened national territory like the Burgundian state, including the Netherlands, Flanders, Wallonia, French Flanders and the former Burgundy.

An enemy of Germany, Van Severen did not conceal his sympathy for Italy and Portugal. However, in contrast to the *V.N.V.* and *Rex*, he never asked for, nor accepted any financial aid from the outside. The *Verdinaso* did not want to be a party, but a movement, an order (in the religious sense of the word), and a «mystique». It never had more than 5,000 members and recruited mainly from the middle classes: small tradesmen, private employees (public servants being not allowed to become members by the Belgian government), liberal professions and very oddly Christian-Democrat workers who followed one of their leaders, Jules Declercq, when he left the *Frontpartij* to follow Van Severen into the *Verdinaso*.[3]

After the «new marching direction» had been launched Van Severen lost a significant number of Flemish Nationalists. On the other hand he won the sympathy of some people in the high society of Brussels, who were susceptible not only to his personal charm, but also to his attempts at a *rapprochement* with the Netherlands, a policy which corresponded with their own opinions on the possibilities for such an alliance to strengthen the defence of the national territory.

Van Severen and his *Verdinaso* exhibited typical fascist features in their public manifestations: their annual gatherings were imitations of the Nazi party days, and they organized a paramilitary militia. The movement also resembled fascism in its doctrine: cult of the Leader, suppression of the parliamentary system, corporatism, racism, anti-Semitism, anti-Bolshevism, anti-masonism. In addition to this, the *Verdinaso* freely accepted a degree of discipline which included individual financial sacrifices of each member. Van Severen also agreed to negotiate with the *V.N.V.* and the *Rex* but his conditions were always uncompromising. The others had to accept his requirements, which made any dialogue impossible. Toward the end of his life threats of dissension appeared in the movement; but it was only after the Belgian government had turned Van Severen over, along with other prisoners, to French soldiers who murdered him on May 20, 1940, that the *Verdinaso* fell apart, some joining the collaboration, others the resistance.

Like the *Verdinaso,* the *Rex* movement was primarily a one-man show: Léon Degrelle's. Born on June 15, 1906 in Bouillon into a bourgeois family, Degrelle (like Van Severen) was educated by the Jesuits in the college of Namur, one of the bastions of the *Action Française* in Belgium. He also started his studies at the University of Louvain, but (like Van Severen) did not finish, being too busy with his activities as a student publicist. A gifted writer and journalist, Degrelle attracted the attention of the General Chaplain of the *Action catholique de la Jeunesse belge* (Catholic Action of the Belgian Youth) and was asked to be the manager first of a student magazine, then of a publishing company named *Christus Rex*. He created a literary review, *Rex*, then bought a family review, then a religious magazine; finally he added a collection of literary works, and a series of monographs about national history, the «Collection nationale». In order to manage this huge enterprise, he set up an advertising organization which covered five areas in Belgium and had 500 propagandists who had to report their activities to their respective chiefs.

In 1932, the Catholic party, suddenly faced with imminent elections, asked Degrelle to organize its propaganda. Having tasted politics in an auxiliary capacity, he did not long resist the temptation to enter the political arena on his own account. He added a political review, *Vlan*, to his other publications and began giving advice to those who were elected thanks to his efforts. From giving advice, he went on to take a critical position, joining some Catholic maverick deputies like Paul Crockaert and Gustave Sap, who were launching a campaign to expose scandals in their own party. Degrelle always dreamed of taking over power in the Catholic party. But things did not work out: mainly for financial (but also for political) reasons the *Action catholique de la Jeunesse belge* withdrew from the Rex publishing company in 1934. In 1935, Degrelle began building the structure of a political movement. The advertizing organization for the Rex company was changed into *C.A.P. (Cadres Actifs de Propagande* or Active Propaganda Staff) and *F.P. (Front Populaire* or Popular Front) which consisted of political and professional discussion groups. Then «sections» were added, that is, internal organizations for the maintenance of order. Having everything prepared, Degrelle crossed the Rubicon on November 2, 1935 by mobilizing his «sections» in order to disturb a meeting held by the *Fédération des Cercles catholiques* in Courtrai, where he went himself to attack publicly the respectability of the president of the federation. The Catholic party then broke off its relations with Degrelle, who, with all the means at his disposal, embarked upon a continuous electoral campaign, based on the exposure of all the politico-financial scandals which the economic crisis had revealed during the last years.

Like Van Severen, Degrelle balked at the label of «party» and preferred that of a rally or a movement or even a «mystique». His program was pro-fascist and demagogic: A strong government; reduction (but not suppression) of the role of parliament; corporate organization; replacement of universal suffrage by an integral familial and feminal suffrage (with more than one vote for the head of the family); popular referendum; de-proletarization of the masses; making capitalism «march in step»; establishment of a magistrature on labor and of a «charta of labor»; a proclamation about the corporate organization of labor; a campaign against unemployment; the regulation of foreign workers; finally «a physical and moral reform of the whole nation, a return to the profound virtues of the family, of labor, of the Earth, of the economy, of honesty, solidarity and human fraternity». The program was elaborated not by Degrelle but by the theoreticians of the movement José Streel and Jean Denis. It was vast, vague, and indeed nobody, or almost nobody, cared much about it. Degrelle did not personify a program. He was first of all a bigmouth, a gifted propagandist, an orator who knew how to convince the people and who possessed a good dose of so-called «rex-appeal». He could count on powerful sympathies in the Belgian business world, among people who believed that «the time had come» and who hurried to pay for 20,000 two-month subscriptions to *Le Pays réel*, the newspaper launched just before the elections in May 1936. Even some members of the magistrature also gave him their support by condemning one of his Catholic opponents just before the elections. He was viewed with sympathy by the military, some of whose members offered him their services for a coup in October 1936, but he refused. Finally, he received the moral and financial support of Mussolini.

In Wallonia *Rex* obtained more than 25 per cent of the votes in the province of Luxembourg (where Degrelle was born), from 15 to 25 per cent in the provinces of Liège and Namur, between 5 and 15 per cent in the province of Hainaut, and from 10 to 15 per cent in the Walloon *arrondissement* Nivelles in the province of Brabant. The mixed Brussels *arrondissement* in the same province gave 15 to 20 per cent of the votes.

In Flanders, *Rex* obtained between 5 and 15 per cent in the province of West-Flanders, and less than 10 per cent in the three other Flemish provinces of East-Flanders (except the *arrondissement* of Audenarde situated between West-Flanders and Hainaut, were *Rex* obtained from 10 to 15 per cent), Antwerp and Limburg. In the Flemish *arrondissement* Louvain of the province of Brabant, *Rex* obtained between 5 and 10 per cent.

In the Walloon provinces (with the *arrondissement* of Nivelles) Rex obtained 13 seats, in the *arrondissement* of Brussels, 5 seats, and in Flanders, 3 seats.

It is remarkable that *Rex* obtained the best scores in the non-industrialized *arrondissements* of Wallonia, and in the industrialized *arrondissements* of Flanders, where the *Verdinaso* was implanted, (which, however, had instructions not to vote), and where the most of the French-speaking bourgeoisie lived. Elsewhere it seems that the middle classes and the civil servants practically guaranteed the success of *Rex*. In fact, the success of *Rex* was essentially a defeat for the Catholic party, an expression of disillusionment with the crisis management of the party faced with the depression.

Dazzled by his success of 1936, Degrelle hoped to stir up the political life of the country and to create a situation of permanent crisis by forcing a series of by-elections through the successive resignation of Rexist deputies and their assistants. This tactic was used some years earlier by the socialist Paul-Henri Spaak. Thus Degrelle hoped to be able to take over power peacefully, as if he were elected through a plebiscite by the people. He started in Brussels and brought about the by-election of April 11, 1937, with himself as a candidate. His opponents, including the communists, presented an outstanding candidate, the later Prime Minister Paul Van Zeeland, who was not yet member of the parliament. He was a Catholic. The Flemish Nationalists decided to support Degrelle's candidacy. Completely lacking in realistic perception, Degrelle addressed a meeting at which he dealt with a pastoral letter of the Belgian Episcopate in which communism and every form of totalitarian or dictatorial government was condemned. His comment was that *Rex* was not concerned with this letter, and that if the Church had disagreed with *Rex*, it would have said so already. This was a real provocation. Two days before the election, the Archbishop of Malines published a statement condemning *Rex* «which constitutes a danger for the country and for the Church». It was a hard blow but essentially a result of Degrelle's imprudence. However, this statement does not seem to have had a great impact on the election of April 11, since out of a total of 363,000 votes, *Rex* finally achieved only 6,000 votes, less than in 1936. Degrelle obtained 69,000 votes, that is 19 per cent. Paul Van Zeeland won easily with 276,000 votes, that is 75.8 per cent and there were 5 per cent blank ballot-sheets.

508

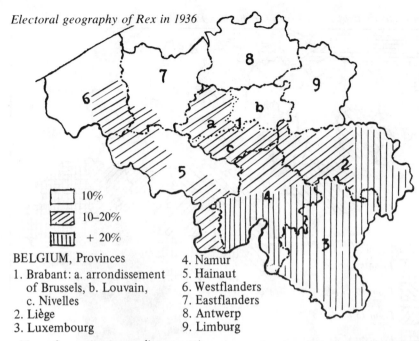

Electoral geography of Rex in 1936

10%

10–20%

+ 20%

BELGIUM, Provinces

1. Brabant: a. arrondissement
   of Brussels, b. Louvain,
   c. Nivelles
2. Liège
3. Luxembourg
4. Namur
5. Hainaut
6. Westflanders
7. Eastflanders
8. Antwerp
9. Limburg

Map of counties (arrondissements)

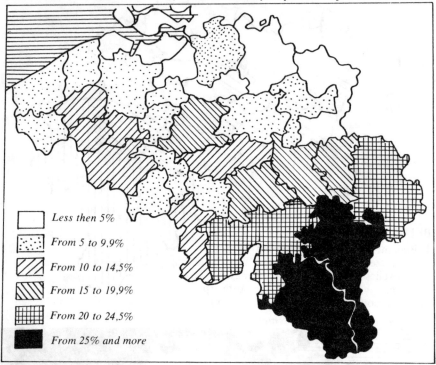

General elections of 1936. Votes for the Rex Party in per cent of total vote

Less then 5%

From 5 to 9,9%

From 10 to 14,5%

From 15 to 19,9%

From 20 to 24,5%

From 25% and more

In absolute figures, *Rex's* votes increased by comparison with 1936:at that time there were only 53,000 votes in the Canton of Brussels. There had certainly been some falling-off in support for the Nationalist Flemish, who had obtained 22,000 votes in 1936. The main problem in 1937 was that Degrelle did not obtain the majority on which he counted. The elections in Brussels of April 1937 were regarded by everybody, including *Rex* and Degrelle, as an immense defeat, because it was not the percentages so much as the moral implications of the elections which counted. Degrelle had not succeeded and in addition he came in for that fatal condemnation by the Ecclesiastical authorities. It was not long before he had to face the consequences. From June 1937, there was a rout among the deputies and leaders of *Rex*. In 1939, none of the «historical leaders» who had played a rôle in 1936 were still in office. At the same time a reorganization of the movement took place: A great Nazi-style congress was organized, the political council of *Rex* was changed from the ten members of March 1936 to the Executive Bureau of *Rex* with only 5 members. A political Control Committee was set up with disciplinary powers. All this gave the movement a more clearly fascist character. To continue to attract the public's attention, the movement was obliged to become more and more radical. The «sections», now «guards», became more aggressive, the theme of anti-Semitism, practically unknown until then, appeared in Rexist propaganda. Since 1937 some Rexist writers had refused to distinguish between the «Rexists» and the «Degrellians». However, it seems that the distinction was clearly made within the movement, the Rexists being the sympathizers in the period before April 1937, the Degrellians being the sympathizers in the period after April 1937. In other words, one could call «Rexists» all those who voted in favor of *Rex* in reaction to the other parties, and «Degrellians» the real fascists of the later movement.

The communal elections of October 1938 confirmed the defeat of *Rex*. In Brussels the movement again got almost 11 per cent of the votes. However, the legislative elections of 1939 decreased the representation of *Rex* from 21 to 4 seats, and the number of votes for the whole country from 11.5 per cent to 4.4 per cent. Thus Rexism was reduced to its true proportions, that of an active minority along with other minorities. Together with the communists, Rexists made up almost 20 per cent of the Belgian electorate, just before World War II.

Conclusions

We have stressed several salient facts: **a.** Nationalism functioned as a catalyst in World War I. The invasion of Belgium by Germany provoked a double awareness, in the occupied country as well as among the soldiers on the front and among Belgian refugees abroad. Most Flemish intellectuals enlisted in the war were convinced that the Flemish bloodshed for Belgium would constitute an obligation to give rapid satisfaction to Flemish claims for autonomy. They very quickly realized that the Belgian government would not make any serious concessions, whereas the German occupants (for the sake of German influence after the war) granted the Flemish all the rights they had been claiming for years.

This double discovery, together with the severe repression unleashed against the collaborators after the war, exasperated the Flemish Nationalists, who now kept their distance from the traditional political parties (forcing the Catholic party, for example, to be reorganized into a Flemish wing and a Walloon wing), Flemish Nationalism became a political movement rather than a new political party. This nationalist movement eventually gave birth to fascist tendencies.

As for the French-speaking Belgians, the threat of the Flemish movement, even before the war, was reinforced by the events taking place during the occupation (the establishment of a Flemish university at Gent by the Germans, the administrative and judicial separation of the country etc.), and on the Belgian front (the subversive action of the Flemish *Frontbeweging*). These events gave birth to an intense Belgian nationalism, influenced by the *Action Française*. Here too nationalism appeared in movements outside the framework of the ordinary political parties and gave rise to fascist tendencies.
b. Fascism in Belgium was essentially inspired by Italian fascism. The influence of Nazism was limited to the formal manifestations, to style rather than to doctrines. Only the *V.N.V.* was more distinctly influenced by Nazism. This is partly explained by the Germanic character of the Flemish people (so often invoked by the *V.N.V.*). The *V.N.V.* seems to be the only movement to have received money from Germany before the war.

The predominance of the Italian model in Belgium is explained both by the cultural kinship of the French-speaking Belgians to Italy (including Van Severen), their «Latinity», and by the attitude of the Roman Catholic Church which without any doubt was looking with sympathy to the education in moral rectitude taking place in fascist Italy, and which applauded the struggle of fascism against the common enemy: Bolshevism and the Free Masonic lodges.
c. One can hardly talk about Belgian fascism, but rather about fascism in Belgium and

511

about small fascist groups. In the elections of 1939, the Flemish Nationalists and the Rexists together received 297,349 votes out of 2,667 341 registered voters, that is 11 per cent (or 12.7 per cent of the valid votes). The number of active members of the different fascist or pro-fascist movements can be estimated to be less than 40,000 out of an overall Belgian population of 8,409,000 people (that is 0.47 per cent). The numbers can be broken down as follows: 12,500 members of *Rex;* from 12,000 to 13,000 members belonged to the *V.N.V.;* less than 5,000 to the *Verdinaso;* less than 5,000 members to the *Légion nationale;* and some hundreds of members or small groups which belonged more to folklore than to politics, like the *Nationaal-Socialistische Vlaamsche Arebeiderpartij* (The Flemish National-Socialist Workers Party) of a certain leader, Segers, in Antwerp.

d. Who, then, were the real fascists in Belgium? In an excellent article H.W. Von der Dunck has shown how the notion of fascism has been gradually extended over the years. Defining the fascist phenomenon, he writes that fascism is «a political current which, in place of parliamentary democracy and its proliferation of political parties, and instead of its communist alternative, wants to establish a kind of homogeneous national communitarian state under the leadership of a powerful leader or of a dominating élite.»[4]

In applying this definition to the Belgian situation, we can proceed by elimination. The parties or the movements which only want to reinforce the executive power and to decrease the legislative power are not fascist. In other words, the cult of a leader and a program aiming at decreasing the role of parliament are not enough to make a movement fascist. In that respect, the major Belgian political parties which experienced the leadership cult– one only has to think of the publicity given to Hendrik De Man and his «Plan», or of the attitude of the parties vis à vis Leopold III– are not fascist. Neither are the many study groups for the reform of the state, or the various Catholic youth movements where the cult of a leader (the Christ-King, Pope or bishop) was very strong. All of them were influenced by the «fascist style», however. They were children of their times.

It is much more difficult to form an opinion on the *V.N.V.* and the *Rex.* Neither movement rejected the parliamentary system, but they tended toward a drastic decrease in the role of parliament, whose prerogatives they wanted to reduce to budgetary control. On the other hand, both of them were nationalist, but adhered to mutually contradictory nationalism, and both clamored for a reform of the state according to the corporatist principle.

The hierarchical structure of the *V.N.V.*, with the leader at the top of the pyramid, was much more an efficient device for action, a strategic necessity, than a political doctrine aiming at the transformation of the state. The notion of an élite was certainly absent from the *V.N.V.* which essentially was a nationalist and democratic movement. In a certain sense, the same can be said of the *Rex,* originally a movement concerned with the middle classes and soliciting their electoral support. The character of Degrelle, his pride, his lack of insight into the real causes of his success made *Rex* a movement with a leader, but did not provide a political direction or a real political program. For Degrelle there was not to be a revolution and a new state; his aim was a legal seizure of power by himself in the office of prime minister appointed by the King.

It is certain that after 1936 – 1937 the *V.N.V.* as well as the *Rex* evolved in a more fascist direction: anti-Semitism, racism in general, fascist liturgies became commonplace. The financial support from Nazi Germany was a part of this evolution. In our opinion, before 1940, the *V.N.V.* and the *Rex* must be classified as proto-fascist rather

512

than as fascist movements. It is not surprising that they settled down to fascism after 1940. Everything was ready for this evolution, and the presence of a fascist occupant could only accelerate it. Still the motives that made the *V.N.V.* a collaborationist movement were not at all the same as those impelling the *Rex* to collaborate. The former made use of the German presence to realize the aims of the Flemish Nationalists (just as during World War I); the other cherished being a part of the new Europe that was to be established after the defeat of Bolshevism.

Finally, there remain the two real fascist movements which have always been compared to Italian fascism: the *Légion nationale* and the *Verdinaso*. There is no doubt here: All the elements of Von der Dunck's definition are present in these cases, including the convergence of styles. Very strangely, however, during the Nazi invasion of Belgium, both movements organized armed resistance against the enemy. After the occupation of the country, the whole *Légion nationale* and many individuals coming fom the *Verdinaso*, whose leader was no longer alive to command, went into the resistance.

e. Let us also point out that none of these movements had a foreign policy program of real substance. The field of foreign policy was reserved to the traditional parties, if not exclusively to the Crown. The military pact between Belgium and France (1920) gave rise to strong opposition among the Flemish Nationalists. But when in 1936 the Belgian government renounced the pact and Paul-Henri Spaak proposed the policy of the «free hands» (active neutrality), all the parties supported him unanimously, hoping that the threat of a new invasion which hung heavily over the whole country, would disappear.

This pacifism, inspired by the horror of the bloodshed during World War I also characterized the behavior of the fascist movements in Belgium. In principle, everybody advocated non-violence, even though they did not always succeed in maintaining this standard. Every fascist movement in Belgium advocated a legal and peaceful seizure of power without abolishing the monarchy. With his open disdain for some of the parliamentary practices of the political parties, King Leopold was seen as no stumbling block for attempts to replace it with a more authoritarian form of government.

f. Why did fascism never become a mass phenomenon in Belgium? All of Lipset's preconditions for the rise of the «extremism of the center» were present: the collapse of the old political structures and the existing economic and financial system; economic crisis hitting the middle classes especially hard; a widespread feeling among these strata that they had no spokesmen or support within the traditional party system. The middle classes formed a floating mass between the Liberals and the Catholic party, sceptical towards the upper bourgeoisie, increasingly out of reach for the Catholics which in their party had fused groups of very diverse origin, often irreconcilable in their interests: blue-collar workers, farmers, the middle self-employed sector, commercial and entrepreneurial bourgeoisie, members of the professions. Religion had always been the unifying bond between these groups rather than a clear-cut economic and social program. On the left, the middle classes were threatened by the socialists and the communists. This horizontal cleavage which could have been conducive to the rise and success of fascism was cross-cut by a vertical cleavage: nationalism, or better: several nationalisms, the contradictory national sentiments of the Flemish and the Walloons. Flemish nationalism was fundamentally of a romantic kind, advocating the establishment of an autonomous or federal Flemish state. On the other hand, nationalism in the French-speaking parts of Belgium was on the whole an anti-

513

nationalism, triggered by a fear of becoming a minority through the demographic dominance of the Flemish. It was at the same time a rational, calculating nationalism aiming at the preservation of economic and political stability and securing the prospects for the future in a nation threatened by division and by the dominating, propertied classes in Flanders. The administrative structures in the unitary Belgian state had been favorable to the French-speaking section of the population, as were the electoral laws, which aimed at giving the traditional and unitary parties a competitive edge over secessionist political formations.

In these nationalisms the discontent of the two ethnically based middle classes found different expressions. In Flanders dissatisfaction was primarily of a political nature, whereas in the Francophone parts of the country nationalism took on a more economic and social flavor. These two nationalisms neutralized each other. The attempts by the fascists to suppress or downplay the antagonism between the two groups (as witnessed for example by the agreement on October 6, 1936, between Rex and the V.N.V. and the negotiations between Rex and the *Verdinaso*) all eventually failed and produced among a great many of the sympathizers of both movements considerable uneasiness and suspicion towards the nationalist orthodoxy displayed by the leading circles in the two movements. The nationalist contradictions proved too entrenched for the fascist common bonds to have any chance of uniting the two groups.

Similarly, at the same time efforts to form a Flemish «common front» between the V.N.V., the *Verdinaso* and the Flemish wing of the *Catholic party* and the agreement between the V.N.V. and the Flemish Catholic party on December 8, 1936, also proved unsuccessful. This showed the internal divergencies of the Flemish nationalist movement. The moves were felt, rightly or wrongly, by the population to be maneuvers instigated by Catholic politicians to lead vacillating and potentially democratic voters away from the V.N.V.

The agreements between the V.N.V. and *Rex* and between the V.N.V. and the *Flemish Catholic party* diminished the prestige and the credibility of the Flemish nationalist leaders. They were never put into practice.

Unquestionably, nationalism which should have formed the driving force behind fascism in Belgium instead became its weakness and one of the causes for its failure. The division between the two forms of nationalism gave, moreover, the traditional parties a comparative advantage in allowing them time intermittently to concede to the demands of the Flemish nationalists and to implement some of the economic and social reforms espoused by the *Rex*, while at the same time upholding the repressive measures against the fascist movements (among which were a decree banning civil servants to become members in one of the fascist organizations and a prohibition of armed militia, etc.). The ethnic cleavage splitting nationalism in Belgium gave the government the opportunity to proceed slowly by progressively disarming its enemies. At no point in the inter-war period did the government find itself confronted with a bloc which could seriously endanger the existence of the parliamentary system and the unitary state.

NOTES

[1] J. M. Étienne, *Le Mouvement Rexiste jusqu'en 1940*, Paris 1968, p. 46. 59 Catholic deputies held 245 positions as directors of banking, industrial or commercial firms; 19 Liberal deputies held 113 of such offices and 17 of the Socialist deputies, 53.

[2] It should be pointed out that in the 19th century all the levels of control in Belgium were held by the bourgeoisie, and that in Flanders this bourgeoisie had assimilated the French culture entirely. During the second half of the 19th century, thanks to the liberalization of the electoral laws and to economic development, the lower middle classes tried to get a share of the power.

In Flanders, these lower middle classes were divided into two sections: One tried to imitate the bourgeoisie by assimilating French culture and by speaking French; the other tried to distinguish itself from the bourgeoisie and even to oppose it by making common cause with the working class which at that time was under-developed and largely illiterate. This last tendency was typical of the Flemish movement which, under the influence of romanticism and nationalism, struggled for equality between the languages (French being the official language in Belgium) and the recognition of the identity of the Flemish people. Because of the social stratification in Flanders, this linguistic and nationalistic struggle was a social challenge to the hegemony of the bourgeoisie.

[3] J. M. Étienne, op.cit., p. 64 establishes the sociological structure of the Rex on the basis of the lists of candidates in the parliamentary elections of 1936 and in the communal elections of 1938. See also Wallef's article in this volume. In a study about «Joris Van Severen – Een Raadsel», in Ons Erfdeel, 18 (1975) pp. 221 – 239, we presented a table on the composition of the Verdinaso in Bruges in 1940.

We are comparing the two tables by taking for the Rex the figures of 1936.

	Rex	Per cent	Verdinaso	Per cent
Small business	57	24.5	20	18.0
Industrialists	33	14.2	5	4.5
Employees	28	12.0	24	21.6
Liberal Professions	27	11.6	20	18.0
Executives	25	10.7	9	8.1
Farmers...........................	27	11.6	*–	–
Craftsmen	17	7.3	21	18.9
Workers	13	5.6	11	9.9
Others	6	2.6	1	0.9
Total	233	100.1	111	99.9

* Since Bruges is a town where agriculture does not exist.

[4] H. W. Von der Dunck, «Het fascisme. Een tussenbalans», in Internationale Spectator (January 1975) pp. 32–50.

LITERATURE

Rachel Baes, Joris van Severen. Une âme (Zulte, Oranjeuitgaven, 1965).

Arthur De Bruyne, Joris van Severen. Droom en Daad (Zulte, Oranjeuitgaven, 1961).

Pierre Daye, Léon Degrelle et le rexisme (Paris, Fayard, 1937).

Eric Defoort, Charles Maurras en de Action Française in België (Brugge, Grion, 1978).

Luc Delafortrie, Joris van Severen en de Nederlanden (Zulte, Oranjeuitgaven, 1963).

Jean Denis, Principes rexistes (Bruxelles, Rex, 1936).

Jean-Michel Étienne, Le Mouvement Rexiste jusqu'en 1940 (Paris, A. Collin, 1968).

Ursmar Legros, Un homme, un chef, Léon Degrelle (Bruxelles, Rex, 1938).

Jean Stengers, «Belgium» in The European Right. A Historical Profile. H. Rogger and E. Weber, editors (Berkeley and Los Angeles, University of California Press, 1965) pp. 128– 167.

José Streel, Ce qu'il faut penser de Rex (Bruxelles, Rex, 1936).

M. Van Blankenstein, *Woelig België*, (Amsterdam, Nederlandsche Keurboekerij, 1937).

Herman Von der Dunck, «Het fascisme. Een tussenbalans», in *Internationale Spectator*, January 1975, pp. 32 – 50.

Eugen Weber, *L'Action française* (Paris, Stock, 1962).

A. W. Willemsen, *Het Vlaams-Nationalisme. De geschiedenis van de jaren 1914–1940* (Utrecht, Ambo, 1969 2nd ed.).

Jacques Willequet, «Les fascismes belges et la Seconde Guerre Mondiale», in *Revue d'Histoire de la Deuxième Guerre Mondiale*, (Paris, Presses Universitaires de France, 17 (1967) n°66) pp. 85–109.

Jacques Willequet, La Politique intérieure de 1926 à 1965, in *Histoire de la Belgique contemporaine 1914 – 1970*, (Bruxelles, La Renaissance du Livre, 1975) pp. 101– 174.

J. Wullus-Rudiger, *En marge de la politique belge 1914 – 1956* (Paris, Berger-Levrault, 1957).

The Composition of Christus Rex*

DANIÉLE WALLEF

In 1935 Leon Degrelle created a new party from a group of youths at the Catholic University of Louvain under the name of Christus Rex. Its goals were authoritarian and aimed at renewing Belgian public life under the banner of «Christ the King». In the 1936 general elections, this new party got 11.5 per cent of the vote, and 21 deputies (out of 202) in parliament, at the expense of all the traditional parties, but especially at the expense of those parties which recruited their following from among the middle classes (the bourgeoisie).

Instead of discussing all aspects of Rexism thoroughly, we have chosen to focus on two subjects. The first will be the socio-economic composition of the Rexist movement, a brief study too sketchy in our opinion because we have only very partial evidence at our disposal. Our second topic is the tensions between internal sections from 1938 to 1940 which resulted in the decline of the movement, and the causes and consequences of its march toward fascism.

If in 1936 Rexism won 21 seats in the Chamber of Deputies with a fascist program, does this really mean that one Belgian out of ten – that is 270,000 voters – was fascist? Historians' opinions diverge on this point. For some, since the beginning of the movement, Rex was a classical fascist movement; for others, it was only at a later stage that it became more like a fascist movement. According to the historian J. Stengers[1], «Those who in 1936 did not see that Rex was sailing on fascist waters, showed little political sense». To the young Italian historan G. Carpinelli[2], Rex also appears as a fascist movement from the beginning according to the following criteria:

1. It arose in the context of bourgeois democracy.
2. It was supported by a mass basis essentially recruited from the middle classes.
3. Its nationalistic ideological conception aimed at solving the conflicts between classes on the internal level leaving intact the basic social structures.
4. It used as a method of action the recourse to elections and to demonstrations of force and violence.

According to Carpinelli, Rex was taken for a classical fascist movement from the beginning. Therefore, he maintains, there was no passage from one political position to another, as for example, Étienne[3] claims, but rather at the most consolidation of a position already assumed at the outset.

For other historians, such as Étienne, Rex was a Catholic, nationalistic, authoritarian, conservative movement, and it tended to identify itself with fascism only in its period of decline. Especially after Munich, European fascist and para-fascist movements which had not succeeded in taking over power, were condemned to be the servile imitators of the Mussolinian and Hitlerian models.

The analysis made by Étienne of the Rexist newspaper, *Pays Réel* and the internal situation of Rex incline us toward this second hypothesis.

Indeed, after the success of 1936, the inability of Rex to elaborate a real political program, the inexperience of the Rexists elected, the absence of social organizations supporting the party, and finally the failure of the party to generate popular enthusiasm very soon became apparent.

Degrelle then tried to resort to a plebiscite which would have led him to power. He brought about a by-election by asking the Rex deputy of Brussels, Olivier, to resign with all his assistants. But the other parties rose to the challenge and presented a single candidate, Prime Minister Van Zeeland. On April 11, Degrelle's every hope fell apart: only 20 per cent of the votes were in his favor. Van Zeeland received 80 per cent of the votes.

The failure of April 11 marks the end of the ascendancy of the movement, but this is also the failure of the first kind of Rexism, Catholic, nationalist and authoritarian but not really fascist. For the movement, this date accelerated its march toward fascism.

At about the end of 1937, new themes – racism and pacifism – appear in the newspapers and in the propaganda of Rex. *Pays Réel* no longer withheld its praise for the authoritarian regimes and missed no opportunity to criticize the democracies, such as France and Great Britain. These new tendencies made plausible the slogan «Rex-Hitler» which in 1938 was more and more widely accepted. The Nazi danger was now visible to everybody. Degrelle became the «Fourex» and these slogans were very effective.

In 1938, also, the non-violence of the origins of the movement was abandoned, and if they had not been prevented from doing so by the laws, the Rexists would have constituted fighting squads at this point. In November 1939, the General Council of Rex studied a project proposed by the leader of Rex-Flanders, de Bruyne, which envisaged the creation of «Strijd Formaties» and rejected it on November 30. Although, according to Carpinelli, those violent tendencies had existed from the beginning, the order and protection squads, replaced by the Rexist guards in January 1937 were unarmed. For Étienne, it was only in 1938 that Rexism could be taken for a classical fascist movement, or at least was strongly resented as such, and this is what is important. To support this hypothesis, the following developments can be presented:

1. The 270,000 voters who voted for Rex in 1936 cannot be considered fascists. They were ordinary citizens, most of them coming from the middle classes. They were depressed by the crisis of 1930 and not yet able to receive the benefits of the economic recovery of the 1935–36 period. When in 1938 they perceived more clearly the fascist tendencies of the movement, they moved away from it. A wave of resignations started in 1938 and coincided with the more fascist orientation of *Pays Réel*, a phenomenon that we are going to study. There were many individual breakaways and almost constant conflict between the parliamentary group and the chief of Rex and *Pays Réel*.

2. The communal elections of 1938 showed the increasing gap between *Pays Réel*, the expression of the movement, and its electorate. The results obtained for the Canton of Brussels showed this trend: 10.9 per cent in favor of Rex as opposed to 18.7 per cent in 1936. An additional factor explaining this decline was Rexism's disinterest in communal needs and local problems. The voters finally concluded from the unfolding of the flags and the display of the escort at all the meetings of Rex, as well as from the demonstration in Germany and Italy, that Rex wanted to introduce Hitler's methods in Belgium. From that moment, Rexism was reduced to bare survival. On the eve of the elections of March 1939, 8 of 21 deputies resigned as well as 3 of 12 senators. Among the regional leaders in 1939 those who were already established in 1936 did not remain in the movement. The first two editors of *Vlan*, Ydewalle and Vroylande, left. The movement was dying. In fact, it was reduced to a group of sympathizers and of

militants gathered in the publication of a newspaper, *Pays Réel*. At the elections of 1939, the Rexist representation was reduced to 4 deputies and 4 senators. But soon, Degrelle's increasingly authoritarian personality and the increasingly fascist inclinations shown by *Pays Réel* provoked further resignations: Two of the four senators resigned in April 1940, when Degrelle supported Hitler during the German invasion of Denmark and Norway. This sparked a wave of resignations among Rexist leaders and communal and provincial counselors. Just before the war, only a few original militants still remained with Degrelle: Denis, the ideologue of the movement; the *Pays Réel* editor Matthys, active from the beginning of the «Rex will Vanquish» campaign; Meulenijzer, editor-in-chief of *Pays Réel;* and Bailly, the one editor from 1936 who would not stop writing during the war. Degrelle's collaboration during the war caused the resignations of the last sympathizers: For instance, de Schittere de Lophem of the Executive Bureau of Rex (June 1937-November 1939), who was Rex chief of Western Flanders, resigned from the movement when Degrelle started signing his articles «Heil Hitler», according to testimony at the trial of *Pays Réel* after the war.

The Socio-Economic Composition of Rexism

The sociological analysis of Rexism is particularly difficult because of an almost complete lack of documentation. Nothing has been published on the social origins of the members of Rex. We approach this problem armed only with the electoral lists and lists of the Rexist members from St. Josse-Ten-Noode, a mainly lower class and commercial commune in Brussels with a 1938 population of 28,756.

In 1937, St. Josse registered 433 Rexists, that is 1.5 per cent. However, some of these were registered as mere sympathizers and not as adherents. The fees a new adherent had to pay to the party were low (five francs) while a subscription to *Pays Réel* cost 35 cents per issue. For the same commune, we also have the number of subscriptions to *Pays Réel*: 15.

Not all the enrolled members were necessarily active members. While we do not know the number of active members in St. Josse, J. M. Étienne counts only 40 active members out of the 300 enrolled in the section of Liège, a number which can be extrapolated to all of Belgium.

The St. Josse list shows the following distribution along class and occupational lines:

Small business	101
White-collar workers	55
Skilled workers	29
Craftsmen	28
Liberal professions	22
Executives	19
Industrialists	12
Industrial workers	8
Students	4
Pensioners and those having no regular occupation	56
Others	26

(including 6 barbers,
8 sales representatives,
3 musicians, 2 nurses,
7 ladies-in-waiting.)

In the category 'small business', we put 10 café-owners, 3 restaurant owners and 7 hotel owners who were among the Rexist militants in St. Josse.

This list confirms the exceptional importance of the business class which represented 28.4 per cent of the voters of this party. Second on the list are the white-collar employees. The small percentage of workers is also striking. In rural areas (as opposed to St. Josse), support from farmers was quite substantial, but obviously the petty bourgeoisie (trade professions and white-collar employees) and the craftsmen are more representative of the Rexist electorate. At least in the beginning, Rexism often appeared as a poujadist movement, registering the discontent of a bourgeoisie hit first by the 1914–1918 war, and then by the crisis of the 1930s.

Having considered its socio-economic composition, it is also interesting to look at the political origins of the Rexist electorate. Nothing can be deduced from the list of members in St. Josse since their former political opinions are not mentioned. On the list of the Rexist candidates in the municipal elections of St. Josse in 1938, there are, however, indications of previous political opinions:

Of 21 candidates, 9 were Catholics, 7 Liberals, 3 Christian-Democrats, and 2 Socialists.

If we add to this that in the legislative elections in 1936, the majority of the Rexist votes came from Catholic backgrounds, our earlier finding that the peasantry and the small bourgeoisie formed the bulk of the Rexist voters, supplemented from the liberal professions and the top levels of management, is corroborated.

At first sight, it could be dangerous to extrapolate to the socio-economic composition of the Rexist electorate from the lists of St. Josse, which, as mentioned, is an essentially commercial commune. Data from another commune of a very different composition, for instance a residential commune, would strengthen our position.

However, our approach seems valid because other statistics, presented by J. M. Étienne from an analysis of the electoral lists, serve to corroborate our first hypothesis. They are electoral lists for the 1936 legislative and provincial elections of the Cantons of the District of Brussels, Ostende, Furnes, Courtray, Charleroi, Huy-Waremme, Ciney, Rochefort (List A) and the lists of the candidates running for the communal elections in October 1938, in the District of Brussels: St. Josse, Jette, Brussels, Ixelles, Anderlecht, St. Gilles, and Koekelberg (List B).

	List A	List B
Small business	57	58
Industrials	33	17
White-collar	28	31
Liberal professions	27	33
Executives	25	8
Farmers	27	2
Craftsmen	17	8
Industrial Workers	13	24
Others	6	6
Total	233	187

As in the first case, figures taken from the lists of candidates published in *Pays Réel* must be used with caution. First because in some cases there is no indication of a profession, and second because occupations indicated cannot be confirmed. Anyhow, if we compare the material from these two regions, the similarity between the Rexist electorate and the list of the candidates for the elections is borne out clearly.

As a third resort, we may try to analyze the composition of the Rexist group in parliament. Here the liberal professions (lawyers, journalists, etc.) are more important than small business. This can be explained by the fact that in Belgium, Rexism was represented especially by a group of very young people who were almost always ineligible to stand for office – more than 400 candidates and their deputies had to be found in a period of a few weeks. All the sympathizers, all of them local notables who seemed to be in agreement, were candidates. Nevertheless, the composition seems representative enough of the socio-economic make-up of the Rexist electorate: out of 21 deputies, there were seven lawyers, five businessmen, four journalists, one metal-worker, one industrialist, and Robert Motteux, the mayor of Lombeek-Notre-Dame, one of the leading Rexists. In the Senate, the representation was different: The Rexist senators had only one thing in common: they were all war veterans. They came form very different areas, however. Xavier de Grünne, an outstanding mountain climber, one of the great names of the Belgian nobility; Charles de Fraipont, professor of paleontology at the University of Liège (unlike most of the Rexists, he was not a Catholic), Louis Rhodius, a lawyer at the Court of Appeal in Namur; Joseph Mignolet, a Walloon regionalist writer; Misson, a medical doctor; Joseph Carette, a lawyer at the Court of Appeal in Brussels: R. Boon and Jean Lekeux, both Captain-Commanders in the Reserve; Mr. De Schrijnmaekers, the mayor of Dormael.

Two main feelings seem to have motivated the Rexist voters: fear and indignation. The middle classes, who had come through a rather difficult period, feared that the regime wanted them to disappear. By voting for a new party that promised to protect them against both communism and capitalism, they hoped to escape the crisis. These feelings were typical of the petty bourgeoisie and in particular of the tradesmen.But indignation was the essential reason for the success of Rex. The financial scandals and the impotence of parliament disgusted some people, ready to vote without any hesitation for a new, young, apparently honest party which claimed independence of the financial powers. Disgust was the common denominator of very different social groups. At the beginning, Rex received much support from lawyers and the magistracy, which explains some amazing judgments (the Segers trial, for example). A part of the military establishment also seems to have been responsive to Rexist views, both nationalist and anti-parliamentary. The war veterans were also firm supporters of Rex. Initially, their support was moderate because they regarded Rex as a movement with very young leaders, who were for a long time taken to be only 'kids'. Then there were some teachers and professors who were attracted to Rexism. A detailed examination of Rexist leaders from the working class seems to show that they rarely came from the Socialist or Communist parties, but almost solely from the Christian-Democrats. Besides, this finding is corroborated by the zeal with which the union and political representatives of the Christian-Democrats used to fight Rexism. Their tenacity was much greater than that of the other parties, and most certainly came form the feeling of being much more threatened than the others.

Finally, it is interesting to note that the Rexist parliamentary group knew its electorate well, and that its main concerns in parliament were determined by this. There were many interventions and special bills aimed at protecting small tradesmen.

521

Out of 43 bills proposed in the Chamber during the period 1936–1938 (15 of which were only discussed within committees, whereas 23 were not even taken into consideration). Eight concerned the middle classes, the tradesmen and the farmers, while the remainder corresponded to other Rexist preoccupations: Defense and protection of the family, and protection of the Belgians against foreigners.

The Rexist Movement During the War

As we have seen, at the outbreak of the war, Rexism seemed to be more than ever a one-man show, with Degrelle's «supporting cast» consisting of personal friends. And during the weeks following the Belgian surrender, Rex did not conduct itself as a party. The elimination of Rex-Flanders, the failure of 1939, and Degrelle's statements about the invasion first of Poland, then of Norway and Denmark had left the group in limbo, while mobilization deprived the party of polemicists and spokesmen it could ill afford. The Rexist movement was in decline and Degrelle was arrested and taken to France.

Soon, however, he brought Rexism around to collaboration. Having come back to Belgium at the end of July, Degrelle declared that the time had come for Rex, and that therefore Rex was going to take its place in the new order. It would be interesting to see who among the Rexist militants followed him into this collaboration with the enemy until the end. To find out, we would have to consult the files in the legal archives opened after the war in connection with charges of collaboration. But since those files were not made accessible to the public, we can only give some glimpses of what is known. When Degrelle began his collaboration by moving from his Italian fascist model to National Socialism, thereby recognizing the primacy of Hitler's role, and when this course led him to sign his New Year's editorial of 1941 with the greeting «Heil Hitler», some veteran Rexist leaders were again alienated, among them Schiettere de Lophem (chief of the Province of the Western Flanders in 1939) and one of the oldest sympathizers, Englebienne. But Degrelle did not care: «Rex is getting rid of its 'ugly fat'«, he said, and kept on actively reorganizing his movement. At the end of August the Rexist fighting squads were reconstituted. *Pays Réel* re-started publication on the 25th of August 1940. Matthys, Streel, Doring and Denis played an important role with their articles on political and ideological matters. Odiel Daem (who later – in January 1942 – became an alderman of Grand-Anvers) came back to head Rex-Flanders. Antoine Le Clercq accepted the position of Chief of Rex-Wallma. Degrelle himself was Chief of Rex-Brussels. The Rexist youth organization was reorganized, it had been rather weak before the war because the youthfulness of the Rexists then limited its utility.

Many young people who were not active before 1930, now took an active part in the movement because of the war. This was the case with Pety de Thozée, born in February 1920, who entered the fighting squads of Rex in September 1940, was with the N.S.K.K. in August 1941, and by the end of the occupation had the position of Secretary of the Chief's Staff, just below Matthys.

The evaluation of the Rexist forces during the war is difficult, but if the youths and the women are included, the number of members in the organization would probably be between fifteen and twenty thousand persons. However, there was a wave of former Rexists returning, attracted by the possibility of taking vacant positions in the communes or organizations of the new order. Their number was not that important.

An example is Teughels who was arrested and maltreated in 1940 and came back to Belgium, putting himself again at Degrelle's disposal. He became the mayor of Charleroi.

Conclusion

Apart from the small group of loyal friends around Degrelle and *Pays Réel*, Rexism in the period 1938–1940 appears essentially different from that of 1936 as far as its militants and its officials are concerned. Unfortunately, we cannot evaluate exactly the attitudes that the people in power in 1939 adopted during the war. Did they remain loyal to Rexism when the movement began to collaborate? We saw that some resigned, but to what extent did others follow their example? What is striking is the fact that because of the war, a certain number of «new» Rexists emerged and occupied important positions. They were probably either «youths» or early militants who until that moment had not played any role, but they could also have been completely new recruits.

The Rexism of the war therefore has little to do with the Rexism of 1936, but how does it relate to the one of 1939?

This question deserves further study.

NOTES

* This study is not intended to be original research, but rather a synthesis of the works cited below, except for the analysis of documents at the Center for Research and Historical Study of the Second World War in Brussels.

[1] J. Stengers, «La Droite en Belgique avant 40», *C.H. Crisp*, Jan. 30, 1970.

[2] G. Carpinelli, «Les interpretations du réxisme», *Cahiers Marxistes*, July/Sept., 1973.

[3] J.M. Étienne, *Le Mouvement Réxiste, jusqu'en 40*, (Paris 1968).

Dynamics of the Dutch National Socialist Movement (the NSB): 1931–35*

HERMAN VAN DER WUSTEN AND RONALD E. SMIT

Introduction

The *Nationaal Socialistische Beweging* (National Socialist Movement – NSB for short) was one of a series of efforts to introduce fascist or national socialist movements into the Netherlands in the inter-war period. All of these movements, except the NSB, failed to win significant support. Whereas the NSB obtained nearly 8 per cent of the votes in 1935, other parties with a similar ideology never won the support of more than 0.8 per cent of the electorate. In terms of membership, the NSB was one of the largest political organizations in the Netherlands a few years after its inception, but only for a short while.

The first phase of the NSB lasted from December 1931 until the summer of 1935. The movement was successful during most of this period. However, from mid-1935 it declined in membership and in electoral support up to the beginning of World War II. At that time it was not much larger than most of the fringe groups on the Dutch political scene. During the first year of the German occupation the NSB got a new wave of members that made it even larger than at its pre-war height. But many of these new entrants quickly turned their backs upon the NSB when the tide turned against the Germans on the battlefields.[1]

In this paper we are only concerned with the first phase of the NSB (1931–1935). Our aims are, first to describe the build-up of the movement during this phase; secondly, to link electoral support in 1935 with the strength of the organization in various parts of the country; and thirdly, to give some explanations for its success during this phase and its decline during the following years. Before turning to these topics, we shall describe some characteristics of the socio-economic structure and political situation in the Netherlands relevant to the understanding of the rise and growth of the NSB.

Dutch Society and the Segmentation of Alignments

In socio-economic terms the twenties were a period of quiet expansion. The economic world crisis made itself felt rather slowly and comparatively late for many groups. The Netherlands were definitely an industrialized and urbanized society by this time. In 1930 only 26 per cent of the employed male population worked in agriculture and 49 per cent of the population lived in urban centres with more than 20,000 inhabitants. During the twenties large new housing areas were built in urban fringe areas. Environmentally attractive, these countryside villages not too far from the cities doubled or even trebled in population because of the influx of well-to-do urbanites. The total number of dwellings increased by 38 per cent during the twenties. Spatial sorting out of social categories according to income, age and allegiance towards one of the large cultural segments in Dutch society, had started earlier and continued at an accelerated rate. Cultural segmentation, also called *Verzuiling* ('pillarization') resulted from the bulding of communities organized around each of the three larger segments in the country (mainly Protestant, Catholic and Social Democrat). These will be discussed shortly.

The impact of the economic crisis made itself felt rather late. This is shown by the trends of trade and industrial production. If we take the situation in 1929 in the world and in the Netherlands as a base, we can discern a smaller fall in the volume of industrial production and trade in the Netherlands than in the world as a whole until 1932 or 1933. But because unemployment increased at about world rates right from the beginning this does not apply to all groups in society. The continuation of the crisis, however, was more serious in the Netherlands than in most other countries. The fall in trade, industrial production and employment was deeper and lasted longer. Partial recovery was only visible at the end of the thirties.[2]

All that has been said applies to industry and to most of the service sector. Agriculture, however, did not prosper during the twenties. The economic world crisis only aggravated a situation that had been unenviable for most farmers for a long time.[3] Consequently, various types of farmers had been involved in protest movements even before the economic crisis struck.

Politically, the twenties and the thirties were primarily a period of consolidation.[4] The power of the religion-based parties (two Protestant, one Catholic) became consolidated and with it their preferred division of labor between private initiative and public administration, a division which resulted in the entrenchment of the already existing socio-cultural segmentation. The way in which the 'school struggle' was solved at the end of World War I provided the model for this governmental involvement. Legislation was introduced, based on the freedom of mainly Protestant and Catholic associations to start and operate their own primary schools within a set of general rules and financed by public expenditure. Apart from this 'private sector' as it was called, there was also to be a 'public sector' directly under the supervision of public authorities. This way of recognizing and formalizing socio-cultural differences by allowing separate institutions to be financed by the government could be used again and again. Similar rules were applied to broadcasting and building-societies, and were also used in the field of health care and social welfare. Gradually, not only religion-based associations but other organizations as well, and in particular social democratic ones, gained access to the public purse. In this way the élites of a few religiously based segments imposed the system of *verzuiling* on Dutch society, although it can not be said that they encountered an all-out opposition from all the others in their endeavor.

The concept of *verzuiling* refers to the process whereby society is being divided into segments. The word itself is derived from the noun *zuil* which means pillar. The social ideal of *verzuiling* has found expression in the image of a series of pillars supporting a common roof. Each pillar should ideally isolate itself as much as possible from the others and communication with others should only take place through its leadership in order to maintain the central institutions which formed the common roof. Under this system all spheres of life were locked, so to speak, within one specific segment. Catholics, for example, had their own church, party, trade union, building-society, leisure associations, radio broadcasts, certain medical services, schools and so on. One could stay within one's own milieu from the cradle to the grave. Multiple leadership positions in different organizations within one segment guaranteed a large amount of control and coordination of action on occasions in which other segments or outsiders in general were involved.

525

The system of *verzuiling* was originally elaborated for two segments: orthodox Protestants and Catholics. These two segments also had their political parties. Along with the second big Protestant party whose supporters were found in the less severely orthodox general Protestant Church, these parties controlled slightly over half of the seats in Parliament in the twenties and thirties. All prime ministers were drawn from the ranks of these parties as were the majority of cabinet ministers.

The principal opponents of *verzuiling* had been the Liberals but they had been defeated and had split up in several parties of which two were still significant. Together these had 20 per cent of the seats in 1918 and they declined continuously until they had reached 10 per cent at the eve of World War II. The Liberals did not have a pillar of their own, but in several instances there were so-called 'neutral' associations that attracted a disproportionately large number of Liberals. The Liberals participated in several of the cabinets between the wars, but their role was necessarily limited.

The Social Democrats were the last of the leading six parties on the Dutch political scene. They had been involved in the negotiations which led to the introduction of universal suffrage with proportional representation, the safe-guarding of trade unions rights and the solution of the «school struggle» at the end of World War I. The Social Democrats controlled between 20 and 25 per cent of the seats in parliament during the inter-war period, but they entered the cabinet as late as 1939. Their alliance with the most important trade union and their control of the municipal councils in some of the largest cities gave them a certain amount of influence before that date, however. The Social Democrats built up the third pillar during this period. In their internal organization and external relations they resembled at several points the Protestant and Catholic segments.

The big six – the three religion-based parties, the two liberal parties and the Social Democrats – controlled around 90 per cent of the seats in all parliaments of the period. Many other parties participated in elections, a few (always some communists) obtained seats, but they could not play a central role in parliamentary politics.

Under these conditions, with three religion-based parties in stable coalition, together in command of a slight majority and with other parties willing to join the government if necessary, cabinets were rather long-lived. During the twenties there was only one cabinet formation beside those taking place as a consequence of regular general elections. These were held three times during the later part of the thirties. At no time was parliament prematurely dissolved.

In our view the Dutch support of fascism and national socialism was to a large extent embodied in the NSB. From what has been said it should be clear that the NSB in the first years of its existence could not tap the same sources of discontent as were available in Germany and Italy. On the one hand, social life had been comparatively orderly and the economic crisis, although eventually very serious, came slowly and unevenly. On the other hand, the massive blocs of voters organized by the *zuilen*-parties could not be won over very easily to a new organization. This clearly restricted the political space available for NSB activity.

The NSB: Organization and Electoral Support

Early History

The NSB was publicly launched in the city of Utrecht (fourth-largest city in the Western part of the country) on December 14, 1931, by two civil servants, A. Mussert and C. van Geelkerken. Mussert, 37 at the time, was a civil engineer who had made very rapid headway in the Ministry for Roads and Waterworks. Politically, he had a record of public involvement in some controversies in the field of civil engineering. He came from a liberal background and had only maintained superficial connections with the existing fascist, ultra-conservative and ultra-nationalist groups when he started the NSB. Van Geelkerken was a low-ranking civil servant in another ministry. Though younger than Mussert, he had more experience with earlier fascist organizations. But he was to remain Mussert's second in command.

At the initial meeting, which was attended by twelve people of whom four eventually joined, Mussert presented a document which was published shortly afterwards and remained the immovable foundation of the movement until the bitter end in 1945. Many of its principles were directly translated from Gottfrid Feder's NSDAP-program. The name of the movement and the source of its inspiration could give rise to the belief that Mussert made clear distinctions between national socialism and fascism and tried to organize a specifically national socialist movement. This was not so. Mussert probably preferred national socialist to fascist terminology mainly because it was felt to be less alien.

The NSB showed its kinship with German and Italian movements in its name, preference for corporatism in economic life, nationalism, radical rejection of parliamentary democracy and hierarchical organization. In the Dutch political context, the NSB opposed the series of compromises on which the political order of the inter-war period rested. It opposed the multiplicity of parties and the leading part the Social Democrats could play as a result of proportional representation and universal suffrage. It also opposed the way in which the working men's associations were incorporated in the political system and it was against *verzuiling*. It favored the unity of the *volk*, and emphasized national symbols like the Queen, the flag and the national anthem. It did not present a clear-cut program to alleviate the economic crisis but neither did other public bodies, parties or associations at that time. There was no anti-Semitism in Mussert's document.[5]

From the very beginning everybody who joined the movement was given what was called a 'number in the genealogical register'. The number itself (indicating the date of entry) was a recognizable source of prestige within the movement and reference to it was made in all sorts of connections. Later joiners of importance sometimes got a low number from someone who had left in order to provide them with the necessary status tokens. Mussert received the title 'general leader' and became no. 1 in the genealogical register of the NSB. Van Geelkerken became secretary and got no. 2. The NSB had the legal form of a foundation in which Mussert was the only officer. Headquarters were established in Utrecht and from here Mussert and Van Geelkerken made an effort to spread the NSB throughout the country.

After the first meeting there was a period early in 1932 when Mussert tried to gain a foothold in other large cities.[6] To this end he organized a number of small meetings similar to the inaugural convention and efforts were made to form 'groups' on the basis of some common features. Among the labels given to these 'groups', occupational descriptions were prominent. The category 'professions' probably indicating self-employed professionals as well as highly qualified people in large bureaucracies, was especially notable. There were also, however, some student and youth groups, a few workers' groups and groups named after an individual. We should not take the claims of intra-group homogeneity too seriously. But these labels nonetheless indicate that the NSB drew its first members mainly from the better educated and wealthier parts of society. The first press reports on the NSB also appeared in the two most distinguished dailies in July 1932.[7]

On January 1, 1933, the NSB started the publication of a weekly paper called *Volk en Vaderland,* generally abbreviated VOVA. In the issue of April 4, 1933, a nation-wide organizational basis for the movement was presented. According to these plans, 'groups' organized on a functional basis were to be brought together on a territorial basis in 'rings'. The first rings had at the time of writing been in operation in Amsterdam and Rotterdam for more than a month and others followed in due course. What in fact also happened was that the functional groups gradually changed into territorially-based units but on a lower level than the rings. At the end of 1933 new directives dictated the division of groups into 'blocks'. The increasing spatial differentiation of the movement (blocks, groups, rings) created an enormous number of official positions. Their number was further enlarged by the functional division of labor within each unit. This proliferation of officials probably did not improve administrative efficiency at all, but it certainly tied a lot of people more strongly to the movement. Not all the posts were filled and a lot of people had more than one position. Many units apparently existed only on paper.

The Development of an Organizational Base

The information on the overall growth of the NSB during the period 1931–35 has been summarized in table 1.[8] Data on membership and subscriptions to the VOVA show on the whole the same trend. After a modest start in 1932 the NSB grew rapidly during most of the rest of the period until it reached its pre-war peak of nearly 50,000 members in the summer of 1935. The question why growth accelerated around the beginning of 1933 is largely a matter of speculation at the moment. But the following factors should be taken into consideration:

Table 1. *The growth of the NSB 1931–1935 (approximate figures)*

Date	Member-ship	Subscrip-tions VOVA	Circu-lation VOVA
Jan. 1932	start	–	–
Jan. 1933	1,000	start	5,000
Aug. 1933	7,000	6,000	–
Jan. 1934	21,000	14,000	50,000
March 1934	20,000	—	—
Jan. 1935	33,000	23,000	58,000
April 1935	36,000	34,000	80,000
Jan. 1936	47,000	—	—

First, during 1932 the NSB had won a certain renown and an enthusiastic following that now started recruiting new people on its own. These two developments spurred larger growth-rates. Secondly, the campaign for the general elections in 1933 provided a clear target for the anti-political party propaganda of the NSB. The Liberals seem on this occasion to have lost votes to the A.R.P. (Anti Revolutionary Party) one of the Protestant parties whose leader Colijn's campaign contained clearly authoritarian overtones. If this type of appeal attracted voters, it may be argued that the NSB plea for a more authoritarian type of political order was not lost on many of these people either. Thirdly, Hitler's rise to power may have prompted the thought that something similar might now be possible in Holland as well.

The decrease in growth during the early part of 1934 may be due to the first instance of resistance by the Dutch government to the development of the NSB. From the beginning of 1934 civil servants were no longer allowed to be members of a number of organizations, among which was the NSB. This prohibition induced considerable numbers of members, probably civil servants in particular, to leave the organization. Very few chose to give up their employment. Mussert and Van Geelkerken, however, did make such a choice, and in a much publicized move left their jobs and became full-time professional organizers of the NSB.

From comparisons between membership, subscriptions to VOVA and its circulation, an element of levelling-off in the growth is discernible. The number of subscribers moves closer to the membership figures over time and the difference between the number of subscribers and the circulation figures in relative terms decreases. This probably means that an ever smaller part of the circulation came into the hands of potential recruits to the movement. Assuming that the growth in subscriptions primarily takes place among members, we guess that the number of VOVA's sold outside the organization between January 1934 and April 1935 increased in absolute terms (from 29,000 to 36,000 copies), but decreased when related to membership figures from 1,5 copies per member to somewhat less than 1 copy.

The spectacular growth of the NSB was not only caused by the influx of new members. The important net growth was the result of a larger in-flow than out-flow of members. As time went on the NSB became less capable of permanently attaching new recruits to its organization. Half the number of people entering the movement in 1932 stayed for at least 4 years. Out of all those who entered during 1933, 50 per cent had disappeared after nearly 3 years. The cohort of 1934 had been halved in less than 2 years, and out of the entrants in 1935 at the end of the year only 40 per cent were still on the membership books.[9]

The headquarters had much difficulty in coping with the large number of people moving in and out of the NSB. We know from the slow execution of new directives that it was not easy to keep abreast. At the end of 1933 this must have been so urgent a problem that a provisional membership of three months was introduced in order to get better control of the new entrants. The strains resulting from the incorporation of so many people in the movement can also be gauged from the irritated tone in a lot of correspondence between local organizers and headquarters regarding delays in the procurement of membership cards, in the allocation of numbers in the genealogical register of the NSB and in the official recognition of local proposals to limit the number of rings and groups. Nonetheless headquarters managed in a remarkably short time to build up one of the largest political movements in the country. Its effectiveness was later demonstrated in election campaigns.

We now change our focus to the spatial diffusion of the NSB. The distribution of members within the Netherlands was remarkably stable after the first year. In its early days the NSB was very much a big city movement. In October 1932 the support it received came solely from the four largest cities, apart from a few people in a small university town. Less than a year later, in the summer of 1933, 50 per cent of the greatly enlarged movement still lived in this area. About 20 per cent lived in the rest of the three most urbanized Western provinces (N. Holland, S. Holland and Utrecht), and 30 per cent lived in the rest of the country.

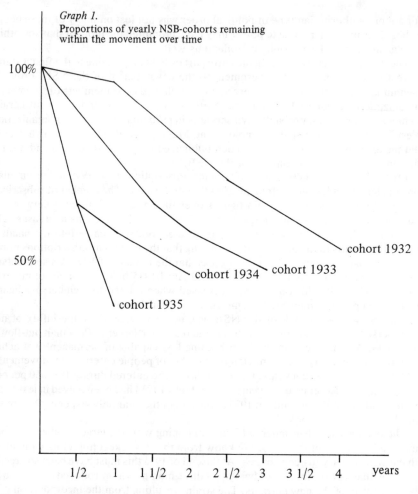

Graph 1.
Proportions of yearly NSB-cohorts remaining
within the movement over time

100%

50%

cohort 1932

cohort 1933

cohort 1934

cohort 1935

1/2   1   1 1/2   2   2 1/2   3   3 1/2   4   years

These approximate figures can be compared with the distribution of the total population (table 2, see also map 1) and they show the overrepresentation of the big cities in relative terms as well. These figures become even more significant when one considers the fact that most of the support in the urbanized provinces in the West came from wealthy commuter areas, especially around Amsterdam. Large groups and rings existed in Kennemerland (along the North Sea coast) and in het Gooi (to the South East of the city).

Here again the lack of adequate information makes any attempt at a clear-cut explanation premature, but some factors come to mind. The first is that Mussert directed his first canvassing efforts there. The second is that a new message like that of the NSB, primarily attacking the political order, stating a general ideology and not obviously representing direct material group interests, will in most cases get its first audience, if any, in the relatively varied, secular, open atmosphere of parts of the urban population. And thirdly, one should think of the limits of political space as outlined above. NSB support, in our view, was not likely to be forthcoming from the

Table 2. *Regional distribution of NSB-members and population (in per cent)*

	Approx. distribution of members Aug. 1933-June 1935	Population distribution according to census of population 1930
Four big cities	50	24
Rest Western provines........................	20	25
Rest country	30	51

well-organized segments, the Protestant, the Catholic and the Social Democrat *zuil*. It would have to come from Liberal and fringe party-supporters. Given the background of its leadership, the nature of its appeal and the direction of its first recruiting activity, our tentative conclusion is that many of the members of the NSB during the period 1931–35 came from Liberal backgrounds, held relatively prominent positions in society and were worried about the democratization of politics which seemed to threaten their political influence. Their worries had possibly been augmented by the exclusion of the Liberal parties from the cabinet in 1929. A more radical alternative may then have seemed the most attractive to them. People of this type were to a large extent concentrated on the fringes of big cities and in commuter areas.

One of the issues NSB propaganda capitalized on was the disgust with the existing party system. The NSB emphasized its desire to stay outside the existing party framework and the parliamentary arena. From this point of view it was difficult to have a clear policy with regard to electoral participation. The movement did not take part in the 1933 general election. It was decided some time during 1934 to enter the Provincial Estates-election of April 1935 (people elected to the provincial councils determine the composition of the Senate; therefore this election also had a certain significance at the national level) but to stay out of the municipal elections two months later.[10]

The NSB extended its activities considerably during the period preceding the elections. The number of meetings increased and NSB speakers turned up in all parts of the country. The movement clearly made efforts to win electoral support outside of the existing kernels of strength in the West, and to gain a foothold in the peripheral parts of the country.[11]

Electoral Support: Regional Variations and Social Origins

This brings us to the NSB election results and their relation to the organizational build-up. The NSB received 7.94 per cent of the votes which is the highest percentage that any party under universal suffrage ever secured in its first electoral contest. These votes were very unevenly distributed over the country and apparently came from several political quarters. To get an impression of the origin of the NSB votes the results of the 1935-election can be compared with those of the general election of 1933.[12] The electorate did not change very much between those two dates, and as voting was compulsory by law turn-out was very high. Differences are therefore nearly exclusively to be ascribed to changing preferences of voters. The figures do not show the flows of voters but only the net-changes resulting from in- and out-flows, and in the case of the NSB only the in-flows. Summarizing the election results by taking the

percentages of different parties together into the blocs presented earlier, we get a Protestant, a Catholic, a working-class and a Liberal bloc and finally the support of fringe parties in a separate category.[13] All blocs lost votes between 1933 and 1935. There is no way to know if all these losses went straight to the NSB, but we think that the differences between these losses give a fair indication of the origin of the NSB vote.

Table 3. *Electoral loss of party-blocs 1933–1935*

	Difference 1933–35 as a percentage of support in 1933	Difference 1933–35 as a percentage of total electorate
Protestant	5.4	1.5
Catholic	2.5	0.8
Working-class parties	2.9	0.8
Liberals	14.2	1.7
Rest	77.7	3.3

These losses can be expressed in two ways. First, they can be seen as a proportion of the support of the different blocs in the election of 1933, thus offering an opportunity to compare the attraction of the NSB in the different blocks. Secondly, from the differences between the two elections expressed as a proportion of the whole electorate one gets an impression of the composition of the NSB support. Table 3 shows that the NSB was mainly attractive to fringe party voters. It also attracted a fair proportion of Liberals. The NSB vote was to a large extent but less overwhelmingly composed of former fringe party voters. Expressed as shares of the total NSB vote the last column in table 3 gives about 40 per cent originating from fringe parties and 20 per cent each from Liberal and Protestant parties. Voters who had supported the Protestant parties in 1933 may have originated from two quarters. On the one hand they may have come from the Protestant party whose supporters were less closely tied to the Protestant *zuil*, on the other hand there may have been some ex-Liberals who voted for the Protestant leader (Colijn) who posed as the strong man in 1933 and were now moving on to the NSB because their hopes and expectations in 1933 had not materialized. The regional voting pattern of the NSB followed the distribution of members up to a certain point. Electoral support was high in the four big cities and in two of the three Western provinces in which they are located and relatively low in most of the other provinces. In two of the big cities (Rotterdam and the Hague) and also in a smaller provincial city in the West (Alkmaar) for which we have data, voters were mainly from outside working class areas.[14] In a number of municipalities with commuters the NSB polled very highly (over 15 per cent). It is clear therefore that the NSB drew a large part of its voters from the same districts as its members. More detailed information would be necessary to prove that the distribution of the organizational network affected the results of the election, but these data suggest that it did matter.

There were two exceptions to the relatively low level of support in the provinces outside the West. These were the provinces of Limburg and Drente, both located in the Eastern part of the country adjoining Germany. In some other areas along the German border the NSB received many votes as well. The proximity to Germany may have helped to persuade people that the NSB was an attractive alternative even at this early stage of the movement's existence, when it was relatively unknown.

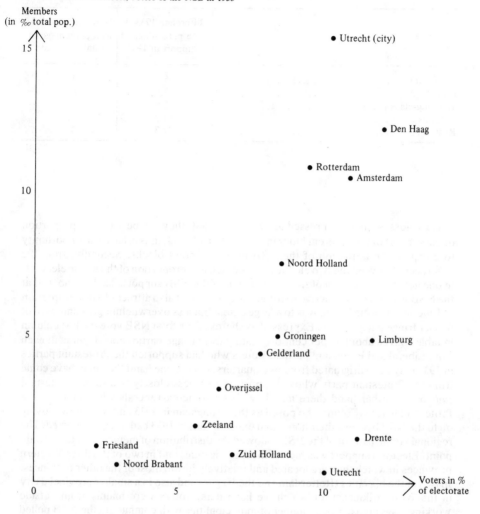

Graph 2.
The Relation Members/Voters of the NSB in 1935

Members
(in ‰ total pop.)

15   ● Utrecht (city)

                                      ● Den Haag

                        ● Rotterdam
                          ● Amsterdam

10

                        ● Noord Holland

5   ● Groningen   ● Limburg
                      ● Gelderland

                ● Overijssel

               ● Zeeland
                            ● Drente
  ● Friesland   ● Zuid Holland
    ● Noord Brabant   ● Utrecht

                                         Voters in %

0   5   10   of electotate

There is also some evidence to suggest that the NSB reached a lot of people, partly the same people along the border, in other indirect ways as well. In both provinces many of the votes for the NSB must have come from small farmers. This may seem strange. There was not a word about agriculture in Mussert's program. But as mentioned, agriculture had been depressed even during the twenties when the other economic sectors had expanded, making the farmers volatile, unleashing a wave of mistrust with regard to the Dutch political order. A lot of them had been sensitive to the appeals of special interest farmers' parties. By 1933 the NSB leadership was aware of the possibilities of attracting support from these quarters. Special articles on the plight of the farmers soon appeared in the VOVA along with a party pamphlet directed to farmers. The NSB received its electoral support in Drente mainly from the influence exerted by NSB members in a very active new pressure group started in 1932 among small farmers.[15]

For homogeneously Catholic Limburg other explanations must be discussed. The main cause for NSB voting in a recent study[16] is low incorporation in the Catholic segment. In municipalities where ties with the segment were weak (e.g. because farming pressure groups or Catholic fringe parties had earlier been supported instead of the big Catholic party or because the clergy was not as active as elsewhere), susceptibility to the NSB appeal was higher. But it is not clear how the NSB was presented as an alternative in this province where few members resided. The only obvious factor inducing people to support the NSB was awareness of and sympathy for what happened in Germany.

In conclusion, the following factors seem to be relevant in understanding the social foundations of the NSB electoral following. 1. A position in life outside the mental seclusion of the socio-cultural segments *(zuilen)* seems to have been important. These positions were to be found among those who had been part of or had paid allegiance to the older élite – the previous followers of the Liberal parties. They were the secular, wealthier and better educated groups in society. 2. But there were also groups who had been alienated or had never been properly incorporated in their respective segments. They had supported various types of fringe parties before. These two categories formed the main part of the political space from which the NSB drew its voters.

We have, then, indicated three factors that may have induced voters to switch their allegiance to the NSB. The first is the proximity of voters to the NSB organizational network, the second is membership of an organization in which the NSB had influence, and the third is geographical position in relation to the German border. Of course these factors may in a lot of cases have prevented people from voting NSB, but the figures seem to show that in most cases they were contributory to mobilizing people to vote for the NSB.

The NSB on the Local Level: Reports on a Western City and an Eastern Border Region

Now that we have followed the growth of the NSB during its take-off phase in a national perspective, it may be useful to add some information taken from two of the few monographs devoted to the local strength of the movement.[17] Both studies focus on areas where the NSB was very successful in the election of 1935. One concerns the Hague, the third-largest city in the country with somewhat less than 500,000 inhabitants and a few adjoining villages with commuters. The other deals with Winterswijk, a municipality including both the centre of an agricultural region with some recently developed industries and part of its rural hinterland – the whole area having slightly less than 20,000 inhabitants.

Both places are fairly representative of the main types of contexts where the NSB proved to be a success, as shown in our analysis. The Hague represents the big city milieu but it should be said at the outset that it had the reputation of being more «distinguished» than the other big cities. Traditionally the Dutch government is located in the Hague, which is also the residence of the Royal Court. Hence a large number of civil servants live there. In the thirties the city also had a large number of people who had returned from the Indies with a fortune or a pension. The impression from the sources is that the NSB in the Hague suffered less from internal strife than, for example, the party chapter in Amsterdam. This intra-city difference underlines the dangers of generalizing too easily to all big Western cities.

Winterswijk is located along the German border, but not in one of the two provinces discussed earlier. The NSB received a large percentage of the votes here, especially from the farming population. Winterswijk may, however, be a bit atypical for the Eastern regions we discussed in that it had a fairly large and active local section of the NSB. The movement also held one of its largest rallies in the Eastern part of the country during the election campaign in Winterswijk.

The Hague

The general pattern of growth in the Hague was very much in line with the national trend. The NSB had about 100 members in 6 groups at the end of 1932 and 5,738 members in 48 groups in June, 1935. Many early members were in groups labelled «professional». In August, 1933, about half the membership belonged to groups of this sort. It seems that the upper level of the organization in the Hague, the ring, was mainly run by people from one of the «professional» groups. The ring had been formed at about the time the national organization statutes were published in April, 1933. The switch from functional to territorial groups occurred during the first months of 1934 and the first blockleaders were also nominated at that time. The one ring was then divided into two rings.

During the following year there was a continuous process of group formation, accelerating in the autumn of 1934. In June 1935 after the elections, there was a new reshuffle at the ring level. The number of groups increased between March 1934 and June 1935 from 16 to 48. New directives then brought the number of rings up from two to seven. All these splits kept the mean group size at somewhat over 100 and the mean ring size at about 900. Some central decision-making body apparently had a fairly firm grasp of the situation and made general decisions on the desired optimal group- and ring-size.

The NSB was by no means equally strong in all parts of the Hague. It is difficult to get an accurate picture of the diffusion of the movement. As we stated earlier, the first groups were not narrowly based territorially. Therefore, it is difficult to pinpoint the location of groups during the first stages. And apart from that, our data on the addresses of individual members have serious gaps.

Nevertheless, when we put the existing groups at different points in time on a series of maps a fairly clear picture emerges. The NSB definitely won its first support overwhelmingly from the wealthier neighborhoods of the city. And although it tended to get somewhat larger backing from less wealthy areas as time went on, the spatial distribution of support for the movement in 1935 was still heavily skewed in favor of neighborhoods with a higher standard of living.

Groups were supposed to meet every month, but even during the election campaign more than a third of the groups did not meet at all and only just over 10 per cent met according to the rules. Older groups were usually more active than newer ones, which seems to be in line with our earlier observation that the NSB had much difficulty in keeping later entrants attached to the movement. The frequency of group meetings was not associated with the socio-economic characteristics of the group's membership. The proportion of groups having meetings was about equal in all types of neighborhoods.

536

The election figures for the Hague as a whole were impressive. The NSB captured 12 per cent of the valid poll. However, we have only a rough idea where the voters came from. No electoral result broken down by polling district seems to have been preserved. There is only an impressionistic newspaper account. From this we know that high percentages only occurred in the wealthier parts of the city. At this level the relation between members and voters also holds.

In Voorburg, a village adjoining the Hague with a lot of commuters but also some middle-class and working-class blocks, it is possible to study the variation in the NSB vote for polling districts (with an electorate somewhat under 1000 as a rule). Whereas 12 per cent of the voters in the Hague supported the NSB, 17 per cent did so in Voorburg. Within Voorburg there is again an association between wealth and voting for the NSB, now at the level of the polling district. But the relation between NSB-members and voters is very weak. The polling district being about the size of one or a few blocks in the NSB organization, the significance of this lowest level of the organization as a vote-winner is therefore very doubtful.

Winterswijk

In Winterswijk an NSB group started in July 1933, a year-and-a-half after the movement was launched. Membership was 85 in mid-August 1933 and about 300 in April '35. This is reasonably in line with the national trend which was also reflected in a stagnating growth-figure during the first half of 1934.

The first leaders of the group were two local businessmen, but from the end of 1933 two new entrants seem to have been most influential. These were a Protestant clergyman whose church had deprived him of his ministry shortly before because of a scandal in his parish, and a veterinary surgeon, who had recently become a municipal councillor for the Liberals by way of preference votes and who was also a key person in the new agrarian pressure group in Drente and in which NSB-influence was pervasive. The minister brought some of his own supporters into the movement, the veterinary surgeon had a personal following among the farming population which he switched to the NSB.

Personal information on a lot of members is available from a membership list captured after the liberation in 1945. For our purpose it has serious disadvantages because probably more than half of the members joining the NSB during the period 1933–1935 left the movement before the list was composed. Therefore, tables with an entry as to date of joining contain only a large minority of the members that actually were in the NSB during its first phase in the period 1933–1935. Besides, not all published tables have such an entry. When the data apply to the list as a whole, it concerns NSB-membership during the war only. Our analysis can therefore only be tentative.

With regard to religion, members came from all denominations, but non-Christians and the less regular church-goers were overrepresented. Few members had been firmly tied to the Protestant or Catholic segment. In terms of occupations, middle-class people, shopkeepers and self-employed professionals in particular were heavily overrepresented among the joiners during the period under consideration. Only at a later stage did farmers accede to the point where they were finally represented according to their proportion of the employed population. Wage- and salary-earners were underrepresented at all times. From this one may conclude that only a small proportion of those who switched their allegiance to the NSB came from the Social Democratic segment.

In Winterswijk the elections in April 1935 took a favorable course for the NSB. The movement got 20 per cent of the vote. Although the party membership was concentrated in the urban core, the party polled only 16 per cent in this area, whereas the mean vote for the rural polling districts was more than 10 per cent higher. Many of these rural votes were apparently due to the personal influence of the veterinary surgeon. There is a nearly perfect correlation between the number of preference votes for him in the municipal elections of 1931 and the figures for the NSB in 1935. But it should be added that the figures for the NSB in the various rural polling districts are much higher. It is not clear if this is the consequence of the heightened popularity of the veterinary surgeon or of other factors.

However this may be, it is clear that in Winterswijk again a bridge was being built between the former Liberals concerned about the political order and their social position within it and the farmers who had felt economically neglected by the government over a long period. Both types of anxieties were aggravated at the time of the world economic crisis. In Winterswijk the bridge between the two groups seems to have been built by the compassion of the veterinary surgeon for his small farmer clients. Unfortunately, it is not quite clear in what way the proximity to Germany influenced the bonds between the vet and his farmers.

During these first years the NSB seems to have been one association out of many as far as the people of Winterswijk were concerned. The movement at this time neither attracted undifferentiated wholesale support nor complete suspicion or distrust. This is evidenced by the coalition important local NSB-people made with definitely non-NSB farmers just after the Provincial Estates elections in April, 1935, for the municipal council elections coming up in June. They announced it as an a-political list of 'Municipal interests'. This list presumably received the support of a lot of NSB voters and a lot of others. The NSB leaders acted similarly against headquarters directives and well-known non-NSB people were prepared to cooperate with NSB-people and the members in these respective groups did not seem to object.

The First Phase and Beyond

The NSB in its first phase was a movement of the non-religious middle class who had been part of or had identified with the Liberal élite that had lost a considerable part of its influence at the end of World War I. It was directed against the new political order of *verzuiling* and working-class power and pinned its hopes on a new more authoritarian political system, vague in outline but certainly decorated with the most obvious signs of Dutch nationality: Queen, flag and national anthem. Mussert did not start the NSB to solve the economic crisis. It was started at that time because the representatives of the new political forces then in charge were apparently unable to provide solutions to the crisis and must have looked weak and vulnerable to the NSB leadership. One factor that may have reinforced this radicalization was the composition of the cabinet, which at that stage consisted of ministers from the religious parties only.

The NSB refrained from proposing clear-cut solutions to concrete problems. People signalled their support because of its rejection of the existing political order wrapped up in radical jargon. At the same time the development of the organization seems to have been a most important aim in itself for many of the members. Sometimes one gets the impression that the NSB was a means to provide the shelter of a *zuil* for those who had not yet got one well organized. During its first phase, the NSB was definitely dominated by trim professionals and businessmen, ex-officers and rentiers who formed the core of its membership. Significantly, in the early correspondence there is a disproportionate number of double family-names, in most cases indicating gentry or noble background. Despite the radical tone of its propaganda Mussert always asserted that he felt himself obliged to stay within the bounds of the law. The WA (an abbreviation for *Weerafdeling,* defense section), a uniformed corps organized along military lines to patrol marches, canvassing activities and guard meetings, was disbanded after an uneventful existence. Neither in the Hague nor in Winterswijk was the NSB a movement composed especially of young people. No generational cleavage was involved in its formation as far as we are aware. The movement was a very respectable-looking body from the start.

Its vague but authoritarian program, its radical jargon, its respectable outlook and its organizing ability probably ensured the initial success of the NSB. In particular it grew in and around the big cities in the Western part of the country outside working-class areas. In the secular atmosphere of these places the Protestant and Catholic segments did not 'immunize' people from the attractions of the new movement, nor had the Social Democrat *zuil* been an alternative for the social groups attracted to the NSB. The voting support for the NSB in 1935 came from the same sources. The territorial organization of the movement was probably useful here although we saw in Voorburg that the relation between members and voters nearly broke down at the level of the polling district. But in other places other factors influenced the size of the NSB vote: the economic depression affecting the small farmers who had supported other fringe parties before, and the proximity to Germany.

During the summer of 1935, the NSB was at its pre-war height. We have seen certain signs of a decline in growth before. The part of the circulation of the VOVA sold outside the movement receded, and ever more people left the NSB after very brief contacts. During the latter part of 1935 the NSB actually decreased in size. This is rather curious as long as we rely on the explanatory factors invoked so far. We reckoned at the beginning of this paper that the NSB would have to operate in about a quarter of the total political space outside the grip of the tightly organized socio-cultural segments. In the elections of 1935 the NSB won 8 per cent of the vote, mainly from this part of the population. Why should its powers of attraction have been exhausted when it had won about a third of its initially available clientele? To find an answer to this last question, other factors will have to be introduced. We would like to focus on three of them:

The first and probably most important factor was the growing resistance of many institutions to the NSB. Left-wing organizations as well as some churches had protested very early. The state had also reacted (prohibition of membership for civil servants, disbanding of the WA). As time went on, more and more institutions pronounced themselves against the NSB and special associations were formed to combat the influence of fascism. Of special importance were probably the activities of the Liberals for they competed most directly with the NSB.

There were three reasons for the growing resistance to the NSB. First, success at the polls had brought the NSB support into the open and the movement was recognized as a major contender for political power. Secondly, events in Germany, Spain and Italy sharpened the resistance. And thirdly, with its pronouncements of solidarity with fascist and Nazi-activities on matters of public concern, and with its growing racism with regard to Jews, the NSB was moving to a quite separate position from the rest of Dutch society.

It is uncertain how the increasing radicalization of the NSB and its growing identification with fascists in other countries in itself affected the composition of its membership. But one can imagine that this reduced possibilities of recruiting more support among the social groups forming the core of its first supporters. It is very doubtful if this change of policy enhanced its attraction among other groups.

The last factor to have diminished the growth potential of the NSB was the gradual disappearance of the economic crisis, in itself the most important factor facilitating (though not causing) its rise. This factor was not important in 1935 but may have been influential in the later thirties when the economy gradually recovered.

One of the ironies in the situation was that the Germans probably harmed the growth potential of their Dutch supporters in two ways. To the extent that their war economy boosted Dutch economic activity, they undermined the size of the NSB's potential audience. To the extent that Nazi policy inspired Dutch resistance, the Germans helped to raise the barriers against joining for those who still had any inclination to do so. The question whether proximity to the German border played a role different in the later thirties to the one it apparently had during the first years of the NSB, is still to be answered by future research.

NOTES

* This report is based on an ongoing research program at the Social Geographical Institute, University of Amsterdam. It is intended to study the overall diffusion of the NSB-movement as well as the development of the organization and membership in a number of places.

Data have been mainly collected from the archives of the NSB headquarters. These are fairly complete. No membership cards etc. have been preserved, however. The study was made possible by the permission and kind operation of the *Rijksinstituut voor Oorlogsdocumentatie*, Amsterdam, the present keepers of the archives.

[1] J. F. Vos, *Het ledenverloop van de nationaal-socialistische beweging in Nederland* (Rotterdam: thesis Erasmus University, History Dept. 1971).

[2] J. Beishuizen and E. Werkman, *De magere jaren. Nederland in de crisistijd 1929–1939* (Leiden: Sijthoff 1968), pp. 66/7.

[3] G. Minderhout, De crisis in de Nederlandse landbouw, in: n.a. *Prae-adviezen over de landbouwcrisis als element der algemene economische depressie* ('s-Gravenhage 1931), p. 123.

[4] I. Schöffer, De Nederlandse confessionele partijen, 1918–1938, in: L. W. G. Scholten a.o., *De confessionelen. Ontstaan en ontwikkeling van de christelijke partijen* (Utrecht: Amboboek 1968), pp. 41–60; A. Lijphart, *The politics of accommodation. Pluralism and democracy in the Netherlands* (Berkeley and Los Angeles: University of California Press 1968), chapters 2, 3, 4, 6; J. Goudsblom, *Dutch society* (New York: Random House 1968), pp. 120–127.

[5] The whole document was printed in: n.a., *Voor volk en vaderland. Tien jaren strijd van de nationaal socialistische beweging der Nederlanden 1931 – 14 december – 1941* (Amsterdam 1943²), pp. 455–501. An analysis of the document is in: L. de Jong, *Het Koninkrijk der Nederlanden in de tweede wereldoorlog. Deel I. Voorspel* ('s-Gravenhage: Staatsuitgeverij 1969), pp. 258/9. The history of ideas of the period is in: A. A. de Jonge, *Crisis en critiek der democratie. Anti-democratische stromingen en de daarin levende denkbeelden over de staat in Nederland* (Assen: Van Gorcum 1968).

[6] Accounts of the first activities are found in: A. A. de Jonge, *Het nationaal-socialisme in Nederland. Voorgeschiedenis, ontstaan, ontwikkeling* (Den Haag: Kruseman 1968), p. 69 a.f.; J. F. Vos, *op.cit.*, pp. 5, 60; n.a., *Voor volk en Vaderland, op.cit.*, pp. 131–177.

[7] A. A. de Jonge, *Het nationaal-socialisme, op.cit.*, p. 73.

[8] This table has been compiled from several sources: L. de Jong, *op.cit.*; A. A. de Jonge, *Het nationaal-socialisme . . . op.cit.*, and files on the number of VOVA copies sold.

[9] This is one of the main subjects in J. F. Vos, *op.cit.*, in particular p. 16; also: L. de Jong, *op.cit.*, p. 284.

[10] During a policy meeting of the NSB-leadership in 1933 one of those present stated that 200,000 members would be enough to win an absolute majority in parliament (L. de Jong, *op.cit.*, p. 277). This clearly implies a willingness to enter the electoral arena, even at that stage. But in public a certain aloofness was maintained. Mussert in his preview for 1935 in VOVA 1935, 1, barely mentioned the elections at all and then wrote: «I hardly think of the election for the Provincial Estates as the most important field of work and defense of interest the way political parties see them. But to us national socialists elections have only the significance of being an incident on the road to a stronger and better organized NSB that will enable all our fellow-countrymen to return to the nation's womb.»

[11] File 207, NSB archives.

[12] For the rest of the paragraph we rely mainly on: G.a. Kooy, *Het échec van een 'volkse' beweging. Nazificatie en dénazificatie in Nederland 1931–1945* (Assen: Van Gorcum 1964), chapter 5.

[13] In this case Social Democrats and Communists have been taken together as a working-class bloc and the two big Protestant parties from the Protestant bloc. The basic table has been printed in G. A. Kooy, *op.cit.*, p. 293.

[14] R. E. Smit, *Kring 5 en kring 32, de nationaal-socialistische beweging in Den Haag en omgeving (van december 1931 tot april 1935)* (Amsterdam: thesis University of Amsterdam, Dept. of Social Geography 1975), pp. 77, 101/2; M. O. van Ossenbruggen, *De ontwikkeling van de Nationaal Socialistische Beweging in Rotterdam van december 1931 tot april 1935* (Amsterdam: thesis University of Amsterdam, Dept. of Social Geography 1975), p. 85; D. J. Hagtingius, *Groei en afval van de NSB in Alkmaar en het Geestmerambacht* (Amsterdam: thesis University of Amsterdam, Dept. of Political Science 1976), p. 80.

[15] P. Loogman, *De NSB in Drente* (Amsterdam: thesis University of Amsterdam, Dept. of Social Geography 1976), pp. 50–59.

[16] S. Y. A. Vellenga, *Katholiek Zuid Limburg en het fascisme. Een onderzoek naar het kiesgedrag van de Limburger in de jaren dertig* (Assen: Van Gorcum 1975), pp. 145/6.

[17] These are the studies by R. E. Smit, *op.cit.*, see note 14 and by G. A. Kooy, *op.cit.*, see note 12. Kooy's study on Winterswijk is the most penetrating social science study on the NSB so far.

The British Union of Fascists: Some Tentative Conclusions on its Membership

JOHN D. BREWER

The study of fascism is at the crossroad of many disciplines and can be approached through various perspectives which complement one another. One of the aims of a sociological perspective is to delineate the «social base» of fascism. In terms of the British Union of Fascists[1], one approach would be to document the societal context within which the BUF's ideology operated: to interpret its ideology in the context of depression, unemployment, World War I and Jewish immigration.[2] Another approach is to analyse the BUF's relationship to major British social institutions and values in the nineteen–thirties: to the established forms and centres of authority; to the conventional political parties; the Monarchy; Church; trade unions; in short, to British political culture.[3] In a more restricted sense, the «social base» of the BUF can also be analysed by studying the social origins of the leadership of the movement[4], and by an analysis of its membership in relation to certain social parameters – class, occupation, locality, age and education.

The aim of this paper is to attempt a brief analysis of this latter facet of the BUF, for which there is a manifest need. In view of the great wealth of information to be had about the membership of continental fascist movements, the dearth of knowledge on BUF membership is striking. The student of British fascism meets certain difficulties which help explain this. BUF records were seized in 1940 and along with other Home Office material are closed by order of the Lord Chancellor under Section 5(b) of the Public Records Act for one hundred years. No samples of membership have been obtained and in consequence few works have attempted any analysis of the social and general characteristics of the membership.[5] Very little is known about the movement's mass support. In the light of the lack of research material this can be rectified only by a sample of members. The sample on which this paper is based[6] is small – fifteen in total – which restricts the conclusions to this sample alone. The sample has a high scarcity value, however, being the only one of its kind. It is therefore interesting in its own right, but the information can also be instructive if treated as a prolegomenon to further research using larger samples. While the smallness of the sample prevents any broader generalization, in being the first of its kind, it is important in that it can help to formulate what generalizations need to be tested in larger samples.

In analysing the movement's membership this paper is organized in two parts. The first is a discussion of the sample's social and general characteristics seen in light of what has been the consensus of agreement concerning the social composition of the movement as a whole. The second is a discussion of the motivations of the respondents to join the movement and how these are related to individual and social conditions.

Social and General Characteristics of the Membership

The most striking characteristic of the Blackshirts on which students of the movement agree,[7] is the youthfulness of its cadres. This was in part the result of its leader's deliberate tactic of appealing to the young. For Sir Oswald Mosley World War I created a radically new situation. Out of death must come purpose, and Mosley always thought of himself as the spokesman of the war generation. The war had produced «modern» problems which must be met by the «modern mind». The war produced the «modern age» and this was dynamic not static; the problems of this age could not be handled by perpetuating the divisions of the past. The two mentalities, outlooks and approaches to problems were simply «the mind of 1914 and the mind of today». The redivision of the political system was between the type that merely demanded a return to the pre-war life and the type that longed to march forth. With this belief Mosley arrived enthusiastically at fascism. Fascism was the new political alignment free from the trammels of the past: «it brings to post-war politics a new creed and a new philosophy. It has produced not only a new system of government but also a new type of man who differs from the politicians of the old world as men from another planet».[8] Youth had paid the price in 1914 and now youth must build. As Mosley warned, «the enemy is the old gang of our present political system. No matter what their political label, the old parliamentarians have proved themselves to be all the same. The real political division of the present decade is not a division of parties but a division of generations».[9] This launched the BUF as the pioneer of the modern youth racket, the champion of all those whose sole moral and intellectual asset was youth.

As a leading authority on fascism recognised, in Britain, «the years between the wars were dominated by old men and by mediocrities. Like families, like business, like the literary and artistic world, political parties were led by men of the nineteenth century whose age made them timid and reluctant to change».[10] Youth felt it was not trusted. As a young novelist described it «in England youth is mistrusted. The idea of young Bill giving orders to old Bill is regarded with indignation.»[11] The movement aimed deliberately to exploit this feeling. It correctly perceived the wave of revolt in Britain during the thirties as one essentially of youth versus age brought about by the aftermath of war and economic depression. The one factor the leaders of all political parties had in common was their age.[12] It was a factor the youth of England could appreciate and understand; age was blamed for the evils of society. As George Orwell provides testimony, «throughout almost the whole nation there was a wave of revolutionary feeling. Essentially it was a revolt of youth versus age. . .everyone under forty was in a bad temper with his elders. At that time there was among the young, a curious cult of hatred of old men. The dominance of old men was held to be responsible for every evil known to humanity».[13]

Fascist ideology attempted to express this. «Beware», Mosley intoned, «lest old age steals back and robs you of your reward. . .lest the old dead men with their dead minds embalmed in the tombs of the past creep back to dominate your new age, cleansed of their mistakes in the blood of your generation».[14] This message to the youth of England evoked a response. A Gallup Poll in 1937 asked respondents to choose between fascism and communism and 56 per cent chose fascism compared with 44 per cent who preferred communism. But more important, 70 per cent of those under thirty chose fascism.[15] It is not surprising that the sample should be predominantly young.

Table 1. *Age at Time of Membership*

Age cohort	15–20	21–30	31–40	41–50
Total numbers	5	7	1	2
Per cent of whole	33	47	7	13

As one respondent thought, the typical Blackshirt, «had to be young»; Mosley's appeal, «was to the young». Indeed, as a percentage of the total sample, 80 per cent were under thirty. This figure might not be as large in the movement as a whole because only the relatively younger members would still be available for study today. Nevertheless, the movement was significantly one of youth.

The typical Blackshirt was also thought to be middle class, as recent studies of the BUF confirm.[16] This is merely an adumbration of the common opinion in the thirties. Communist intellectuals saw it as the rearguard of capitalism populated by the middle class: «it was almost the rule in the past for the sons of the middle class to join the army if they failed to win any intellectual distinction for university. Now the BUF was able to offer them the attraction of full-time employment in a movement which offered them the same excitement and just as much scope for the practise of leadership and discipline».[17] In fact the sample was predominantly middle class.[18]

Table 2. *Class Distribution*

Class	Total	Percentage of whole
Lower	5	34
Middle	10	66

However, it is not enough to describe them as merely middle class young. In analysis of those members under thirty one finds that 42 per cent were of lower class and 58 per cent of middle class status, a proportion much less than the one in every two for the sample as a whole. This would suggest that the younger members were more evenly distributed in their class status. This proved not to be the case, however. In the youngest age cohort, rather than equilibrium, the proportion was reversed. The members here were mainly of lower class status.

Table 3. *Age and Class*

Age Cohort	15–20	21–30
Lower class	60%	29%
Middle class	40%	71%

Only as the age cohorts advance does the middle class bias emerge. This can be illustrated when comparing the age and class characteristics of the sample as a whole.

Table 3a. *Age and Class*

Age cohort	15–20	21–30	31–40	41–50
Lower class	60%	29%	0%	0%
Middle class	40%	71%	100%	100%

The generality of this must await larger samples, but the implication is that describing the movement as predominantly middle class is too simple, for the class characteristics of the membership are too complex for this. The age of the member needs to be considered.

So does the locality of his membership, for the movement made a concerted effort for support in certain working class areas, and this was forthcoming with different degrees of success. In some areas the movement showed a working class bias, while in others, notably the agricultural areas and the South-East, it was significantly middle class. In the autumn of 1934, the BUF launched a big campaign in industrial Lancashire revolving around the declining textile industry centred in the area. This attracted a great deal of support among the workers there. The movement also campaigned strenuously in South Wales in the depressed coalmining industry and in impoverished Welsh mining valleys. But it was among the working class of East London that the BUF received its greatest support. The campaign here featured the movement's violent anti-Semitism, resulting in a 19 per cent average poll in the local elections of 1937. In communication with the author, Sir Oswald recalled his support in this working class area. He remembered, «the vigour, vitality and warm responsiveness to any appeal for personal action or high idealism» among the workers. With whom, «my personal relations were close and warm».

This deliberate effort to appeal to the working class came from his view of fascism. Mosley was locked in a contradiction: he wanted to preserve and destroy. One the one hand there was a desire to introduce necessary reforms to preserve the existing society, while on the other there was a profound dissatisfaction with that society. In fascism alone Mosley found the perfect union of patriotism and nationalism coupled with revolutionary political dynamism. A radical intent was strong in the BUF. Fascism in Britain at least, was not mere economic reaction. It was an attempt to hook the capitalist leviathan, to be master of the complex of finance and industry, not its hireling. It amounted to a reconstruction of society, an alternative to socialism rather than its plain negative. The aim was not merely to oppose the Left's theories of change, but to offer an alternative that appealed to both Right and Left. As a result the appeal was restricted to neither class alone. Sir Oswald warned those who sought to abuse the BUF ideology as reactionary: «we have no place for those who have sought to make fascism the lackey of reaction. In fact fascism is the greatest constructive and revolutionary creed in the world. In objective it is revolutionary or it is nothing».[19]

It was however a subtle and tenuous combination of progress and stability. To replace what was seen as the traumatic utopia of progress in communism, it offered a new orderly, ordered reconstruction by combining the dynamic urge for change and progress with the authority, discipline and order of the Corporate State. The progress it offered was not that of the social democrat, nor the Marxist socialist, but rather of a cooperative conception of the state with a revolutionary foundation along with conservative stability. The notion of ordered, organized revolution was recognised by a

545

respondent who seemed to be searching for the expression of this idea. Fascism was «utopian socialism», «conditions such as back to back slum houses which existed in parts of Birmingham brought the realisation of urgency and reality. To me it seemed that Mosley was putting forward socialism at national level as opposed to pie in the sky socialism of the International Socialists. Britain needed things doing now and the time seemed right for a new dynamic creed like fascism.»

These attitudes and views of fascism enabled Mosley to aim his appeal at one and the same time to the Right and Left, the working and middle classes; and the patriot and radical. A measure of support from each was received in return. However, this says little of the nature of his working class support. The sample suggests that, as far as the respondents are concerned, the working class supporters were marginal[20] in the sense of being separated from traditional supports of working class life. One individual was later socially mobile and the attitudes and outlook contributing to his being so must have influenced his life while he was a fascist. Another was a «working class Tory»[21] whose attitudes and outlook were similarly different from those typical of the working class. However, the one factor which indicates a marginality above all is their employment in the unorganized labour market. Of those with lower class status, 80 per cent were free from the working class support of trade unionism.

This marginality has been hypothesized to be a characteristic of the movement as a whole. Given the small numbers involved and the rapid turnover in membership, a recent author concluded, «it seems in order to assume, short of more substantial data, a high degree of social and economic marginality».[22] Some brief data were provided by a Home Office committee surveying the membership which suggested that the stable membership was comprised of marginal members of all social and economic classes, occupational groups and ages.[23] One can see why this should be the case. Fascism in Britain concentrated on certain occupational groups, specifically on those intermediate groups which fell outside the labour-capital confrontation. It was the «small men», the *petite bourgeoisie,* offering individual services independently yet precariously in an increasingly mass-production, mass-service economy, who were the focus of the ideology. They were the people of all classes who were outside big business and trade union supports: the working class domestic servant, the lower middle class shopkeeper, the middle class cinema owner in conflict with larger competitors. The BUF analysed their problems and made an appeal for their support. In the fascist press, Alexander Raven-Thomson wrote of the small man being caught between big business and trade unions; between, «the millstone of trustification and the millstone of unionization».[24] So it aimed its appeal at the tailors, cabinet makers, small bakers, taxi-men, barbers and small restaurant proprietors.

Apart from its support in Lancashire and South Wales, the BUF's main contact with the working class was through the service sector of the economy. Shop assistants, cinema usherettes, barmaids, waiters and domestic servants were the type to whom the appeal was aimed. It was claimed that nearly every hotel and restaurant in the West End had BUF members.[25] Efforts were made to win the support of those generally in the non-industrial working class, with weak unionization and in close «paternalist» contact with their employers.

The sample reflects this, 60 per cent being in the unorganized sector of the labour market (including a commercial traveller, a shop manager, a private detective, a houseman in domestic service, a trainee chef and a van driver). In addition, 34 per cent worked for themselves in small independent firms (including a cinema owner, a fruit grower and two farmers). Only one individual worked in a large plant, as a steel worker, and he was unemployed at the time. Moreover, those members who were in the organized labour market belonged to predominantly non-industrial unions – the teacher's and journalist's unions. These were highly middle class and non-radical in the nineteen-thirties. Analysis of the membership characteristics of the Birmingham branch echoes this. Among its members were shop assistants, a railway clerk, a teacher, farmers, a retired soldier, a solicitor's clerk, a son of a small independent brewing family and the son of a shirt manufacturer. Exposed to a combination of forgotten-man propaganda and a deepening economic crisis, they supported the BUF.

The characteristics thought to be those of the membership as a whole are reflected in the sociological profile of the sample. This suggests that the membership was predominantly young, with a tendency to be of middle class status and employed in the non-industrial, non-organized sector of the economy. What is interesting in the sample is how the possession of these characteristics correlates with the possession of official position within the local branches in which the members served. Six members (40 per cent) held official position, varying from Prospective Parliamentary Candidate, District Leader, Propaganda Officer and Women's Organizer. The majority of these (67 per cent) were under thirty. Analysing this further one finds the following distribution.

Table 4. *Position in Branch and Age*

Age cohort	15–20	21–30
Those with position as per cent of age cohort	20%	43%

Those in the 21–30 age cohort are those more likely to hold official position: they are young enough to be in line with the movement's youth orientation, yet of an age to be experienced enough in life to warrant official position. Those under twenty would seem to lack this experience. In the sample as a whole, a proportion approaching one in every three members came from this youngest age cohort, whereas in terms of holding official position, the proportion is only one in six.

The middle class bias of these is also striking, 84 per cent being from this class. Only one individual from the lower class held any official position. This is significantly different from the ratio of the classes in the sample as a whole. With a proportion of two middle class members to every one lower class member in the sample, in a total of six members with official position, one would expect only 67 per cent to be middle class, whereas the observed rate was 84 per cent. One can perhaps understand why this should be the case. Those who decide who is going to hold official position are the national leadership in the case of the Prospective Parliamentary Candidate, but in all other cases the decision is made by the local leadership. As studies of the leadership indicate, they were middle class themselves and there does seem to have been a prejudice against the working class. Members of the middle class local leadership chose others of their class for any official positions they could endow. The significance of these correlations however, is reduced by the small numbers involved. They remain valid in terms of the sample but any broader significance must await larger samples.

The Membership's Motivations

It is not enough to show the appeal of the cosh and castor oil, the uniform and excitement and think thereby one sums up the reason impelling people to join the BUF. Normally, there were higher motives in most of the rank and file. In the sample these motives reveal how individual and social conditions combine to result in support for the BUF. The motivations indicate in fact, how a societal context affects the individual and influences his behaviour. This does not imply, however, that individual behaviour is a simple response to social stimuli; to the influence of this societal context must be added certain unique features of the individual himself. The motivations of BUF members were dominated by the perception of a social crisis and the search for a solution. This perception induced in the individual a response in which the search for a solution led to support of the BUF and its ideology. Support among the sample is related to three variables: the perception of a crisis, the nature of the ideology which presents itself as a solution and the individual's view of fascism.

This societal context of crisis was used deliberately as a strategy for power. The BUF was outside the parliamentary arena and normal political rules did not apply. Power could be achieved only by extra-parliamentary means. The crisis triggered a feeling of urgency and prepared the ground for this abnormal tactic. It was a genuine belief of Mosley's that to achieve power he needed only the ideology and the men to fit the crisis. This belief had three causes. The first was his view that historical example showed Hitler and Mussolini coming to power in the wake of crisis.[26] Sir Oswald Mosley, by extrapolation from history, was to do the same. The second rationale stemmed from his first experiences as a «revolutionary leader» in the economic depression which saw his greatest measure of success. The third cause and by far the most crucial was Mosley's genuine crisis view of politics, a conception of political change and electoral behaviour which saw crisis as the animus behind politics.[27]

The consequence of this belief was that fascism in Britain became dominated by the need to manufacture, exaggerate or predict a crisis. Success would come from getting people to actually believe this and perceive that society was in disarray and in need of salvation.[28] The sample is indicative of this. As one respondent thought, «we lived in an age of crisis and selfless efforts were needed to save our country». The relationship between crisis and the movement was recognised by all: «the BUF came into being because of a social and economic crisis». There was a strong element of «salvation» in their remarks. This is described well by one respondent. «Britain was in acute danger. To me it seemed that the BUF was determined to act as a modern St. George.»

A crusading spirit inspired them, but what Britain was to be saved from varied. Some respondents (20 per cent) interpreted the crisis to be rooted in economic and social conditions. Seeing the poverty-stricken, the unemployed, the utterly bereft in the cities of England, the utter degradation and struggle of the masses, respondents had been both alarmed and embittered. As one said, «it was then that I saw the utter sham of party politics». He supported the movement thinking here was a leader who «thought much as I thought and was applying in a constructive way a cure for some or most of the evils of the thirties». A young female teacher echoed this concern. «Conditions such as back to back slum houses. . . brought a realisation of urgency and reality. Britain needed things doing now. . .» Yet in the many individual crises related to the economic and social position of Britain in the thirties, the crisis of unemployment looms by far the largest. Of the sample, 47 per cent mentioned this crisis when discussing their motivations. This is hardly surprising. Unemployment was widespread. The fears it could arouse, the hopes it could shatter made it tragically suited to generate an atmosphere of crisis.[29]

Many respondents bear witness to the effects and fear of unemployment, and the fascist ideology's preoccupation with cutting down unemployment seemed to offer a welcome salvation. A respondent, himself unemployed, described it precisely in these terms. «Unemployment is the most degrading thing that can happen to you», «a loss of self-respect». «The collection of the dole is the most degrading thing.» The BUF recognised this and concerned itself with aiding the unemployed. It organized the Fascist Union of British Workers in 1933. This ran a register of unemployed workers and encouraged employers to consult them for labour. The movement was ready to act as referees to the unemployed before the adjudicators in means test cases, and frequently members could be seen outside Employment Exchanges handing out free cigarettes to the unemployed. But more than this, Mosley's economic policy saw unemployment as unnecessary and proposed a massive injection of funds for public works, increased benefits and greater protection against world economic trends. In both a practical and policy sense, unemployment featured prominently in the movement. This was recognised by the respondent who continued, «fascism was my salvation. It provided hope for the future. We unemployed knew of this crisis. Mosley knew of this crisis and gave us hope.»

However, both fascism and communism provided this hope. In understanding why this respondent supported fascism and not communism, the importance of the individuals' view of fascism becomes evident. This respondent was deeply patriotic and joined Mosley in thinking communism unpatriotic, with fascism not conservativism as the true mantle of patriotism. Being unemployed yet devoted to the country that placed him in that situation caused a dilemma. How to fight for his right to work while still being patriotic? The «revolutionary patriotism» of the BUF was the solution. The traditional patriotism of the Conservative party was superseded by the militant patriotism of fascism, where love of King and Country was cemented with a determination to build a country free from unemployment, poverty and despair and worthy of their patriotism. Protest and patriotism coexisted in the BUF which allowed the respondent to say in spite of his fight for the right to work, «I love Britain. I would do anything for her. It was natural for me to be attracted to Mosley's policy of keeping Britain great».[30]

It is with the crisis of a loss of Empire that patriotism comes to the fore. The Empire was the symbol of patriotism and the devoted interest of Mosley and his movement. The spectacle of «Little England» on a huge world stage, ever humiliated, increasingly belittled and bewildered, her former glory and power diminishing angered the BUF members. This crisis was to be resolved in economic autarky, making Britain an Empire-oriented, self-sufficient economic unit. Britain was to be made «great» again. The District Leader for Eye expressed this in the following way: «My support was connected with a crisis which I summed up as all-is-finished. I was aware of the many lickspitting pawns ready to follow the history of the annihilated empires of the Greeks, Romans, Egyptians, Spaniards and others. The proof of this came in 1942 by which time the British Empire has been sold to America for a pottage.» The respondents perceiving this crisis of Empire (20 per cent) thought the movement was the only one interested in maintaining and even enhancing faith in the colonies. This feeling was described: «I joined the BUF because it was the only movement that put the interests of Britain and the Commonwealth first.» This appealed to one respondent so much that he was prepared to take to the parliamentary hustings. Thus he could say, «I did feel that I was stressing something I honestly believed in myself.» He was a man who fervently believed in Britain, in the superiority of her armed forces, in the divine right for her to colonise and spread her Civilization to grateful minions who can be nothing but enriched by this imperialism. Fascist ideology recognised these same virtues. Indeed Mosley was later to claim that patriotism was the one unifying factor in his movement.[31]

In fact, Mosley believed that with fascism he had found the creed to achieve the rebirth of British glory. It would be the vehicle to drive Britain along the road her forefathers once trod, a road that led to Empire, to Britain leading the world. «We have lit a flame in England which nothing can extinguish», he claimed, a flame which, «will burn until England returns to her place of greatness.»[32]

Patriotism within the BUF was subtly different from patriotism in other fascist movements because British patriotism had recently been a force representative of the largest empire and the greatest traditions. It was of a type that had experienced greatness and the growing depths of despair and now demanded greatness again. Always it was associated with the return of former glory albeit by positive action; not to capture something new but to recapture something lost. The tenacity of the belief is thereby explained for it was fed by the history of former glory. Theirs was «the epic generation» once more, «to hold high the head of England, lift strong the voice of Empire. Our flag shall challenge the winds of destiny. The flame still burns. This glory shall not die. The soul of empire is alive and England again dares to be great».[33]

The individuals' view of fascism is relevant here. The PPC for Evesham joined the BUF because he saw fascism as Britishness and patriotism writ large, whereas another respondent did not join precisely because it was viewed as the negation of patriotism. This individual confessed himself «Royalist and Church of England», «patriotic, Royalist and steeped in Britishness», yet he did not join because supporting fascism «would be like supporting Germany».

The impact of domestic crisis and impending Imperial decline coupled with the view of fascism as upholding the great traditions of Britain made itself felt again among those who saw the root of Britain's malaise in the conflict of generations, symbolized in the procrastination of the «old gang» and in particular its inability to tackle the depression quickly and decisively. This age-versus-youth theme is an impatience common to all times and to all generations and is transitory in nature. It finds its expression in different ways and is moulded partly by the fashion of the times. For some individuals this impatience acquired a particular sense of urgency because of the intensifying effects of the war and depression. A respondent recognised this. «I think all young folk tend to be impatient with their traditional political figures and this impatience is channelled in different ways according to the times.» This member's impatience was magnified into a crisis of generations in which the established political figures, «significantly failed to catch the allegiance of the young».

What made the respondents different from the many more who have perceived a crisis as they did yet remained loyal to traditional parties? As already established, important to the answer is the individuals' view of fascism. A further explanation could be provided by the political consciousness of the respondents. The notion of political consciousness used in this context is not defined in terms of an interest in politics or political issues or the possession of political attitudes, but the possession of a partisan framework which accepts loyalty to established parties. The index to establish this is whether the individual has had any previous political affiliation prior to supporting the BUF.

The contention is that it is much easier for individuals without a developed political consciousness in the sense defined to support the BUF because they lack a partisan framework which accepts loyalty to established parties. In the face of a crisis that many perceive, only some will support an unconventional movement like the BUF, and those that find this support easier are those with a poorly developed political consciousness. If this is the case, the nature of the respondents' previous political support becomes of interest.

The essence of this emphasis on crisis is that the perception of a crisis «politicized» those with a poorly developed political consciousness into support of a movement whose ideology offered a solution. The over-representation of the politically inexperienced is evident in the whole sample. Of the total, only 13 per cent professed any previous political support. In other words, only 13 per cent had a partisan framework which accepted loyalty to an established party. This means that thirteen of the fifteen members had not supported any other party prior to joining the BUF. As one sardonically put it, «my only previous activity in politics was to vote for the National Government. This turned out to be a lie (i.e. that it was «National»).» Another described it rather more eloquently than most, but his sentiments hold true for them all:

«I was interested in politics only as an observer of its trickery, sham and hypocrisy, a sophistry of the devil trading as Party Politics. In my early examination of extreme poverty and wealth, avarice, greed and usury, it was compulsive to see that party politics and religion were the main dividers of the allegiances of man. I did not support another political party as there was nothing in them that I could intelligently support. The Conservative Party had sold itself to the vultures. The magnificent ideals of the early Labour Party had succumbed to the same financial masters. The Liberal Party, then as now, was the coward of both sides, and the socialists were so wrapped up in International mysticism that they remained unconscious of all National interests and quickly became the pawn of outside enemies.»

In the sample there is a significant relationship between membership of the movement and the lack of previous political support. It is possible to test the sample for its statistical validity on this point based on the observed rates complying with the relationship in the sample and the expected rates in the population as a whole. A number of limitations are obvious. There is no evidence of the proportions or numbers in the electorate who lack a partisan framework. Short of a blanket poll of the whole electorate the nearest gauge to this figure could be the percentage of those who do not vote in a general election. On an average poll of 70 per cent at least 20 per cent of the remainder deliberately decided not to vote. This figure is itself inadequate, for the same twenty per cent need not fail to vote on every occasion. Moreover, consistent failure to vote may not indicate a lack of a partisan framework. Equally, the consistent voter may only vote because he perceives it as his duty and not because he possesses any partisan framework. Irrespective of these difficulties this figure is the only one available, but because of them the following analysis should be taken as a guide only.

On the assumption that 20 per cent of the general population can be expected to lack a partisan framework, the sample's corresponding observed figure of 87 per cent is significant. What this means is that one in every five voters can be expected to lack any party loyalty compared with the observed rate of four in every five for the sample. Another factor is relevant however. If BUF support and the lack of a partisan framework are related, one must compare the expected number of those in the general population who lack a partisan framework with those who can also be expected to be fascist. Those that can be expected to be fascist total only 0.001 per cent of the population (worked on the assumption of fifty thousand fascists in a population of fifty million). Those who can be expected to lack a partisan framework total 20 per cent of the population. On these figures, if no relationship existed between the two factors one could expect only one individual in every five thousand to be fascist and lack a partisan framework. Unfortunately the sample is too small to provide an observed rate of such magnitude. But on the hypothesis that the relationship is important and repeated for the movement as a whole, generalizing the observed rate for the sample to a population of five thousand, one would expect five hundred and thirty three to be fascist and lack a partisan framework.

However, if one brings the analysis back to the sample, statistical evidence indicates that if there is no relationship between BUF membership and the lack of a partisan framework, one could expect in a random sample of fifteen BUF members not even one individual (0.003 of a member!) to lack a partisan framework. The observed rate was thirteen. In other words, if there is no relationship one would need a random sample of one thousand fascists to obtain only three members without a partisan framework. The relationship therefore does seem significant for the sample. The reason why it should be important has been previously mentioned. Those without a partisan framework find support for unconventional movements easier because they lack any previous allegiance or loyalty to established parties. Because they find it easier, there will be an over-representation of them in the ranks of such movements. It is not that support is inevitable, only that support is easier. One would not expect all those with a poorly developed political consciousness to be fascist but that the BUF should have an over-representation of them within its ranks. This over-representation is evident in the sample.

Why do they find it easier? What are the mechanisms involved? For the answer to these questions one can turn to political sociology where it has become an established premise that what determines the strength and unchangeability of partisan ties is not so much the voter's age as the duration of his attachment to one party.[34] This is expressed in the theory of «political immunization»[35] which maintains that those immunized to disturbances, crises and events are those with the political experience of support and loyalty to a specific party. Those with this experience, are immunized to the political effects of disturbances, while those without this are more susceptible to current political stimuli and change therefrom.[36] Such a pattern was found in all American elections.[37]

Another factor in immunization, other than political experience, is identification with one's partisanship. In a study of the American voter it was found that his party identification is a function of the time a person has been associated with the party. The stronger the identification, the stronger his sense of loyalty becomes and as time passes, stress of increasing severity is required to induce him to shift his allegiance.[38] Psychological attachments become stronger the longer they are held, so that the longer the identification with a party, the harder it is to overthrow. Conversely, the shorter the identification, the easier it is to overthrow.

What the theory of «political immunization» implies is that those more amenable to change their support in favour of the BUF were those without any allegiance to or identification with a party, or without one of duration. A pool of marginally indifferent and politically unconscious voters, who have not cultivated any attachment to parties and who are not immunized to political stimuli, vote for «heroes in an heroic period»[39] and being uncommitted they remain a pool of potential voters for the next new and unconventional movement. What reflects the lack of attachment, experience and identification is a poorly developed political consciousness of the kind possessed by many of the respondents.

On this basis one can account for the youthful bias of the sample. The obvious youth orientation of the ideology explains in part this over-representation. One can also refer to the notion of political consciousness since the young, because of their political virginity, have less opportunity to form an established partisan framework, less time in which it could have functioned and less opportunity for it to operate. Hence they find the acceptance of new and unconventional movements easier. Older people have had more time to cultivate tenure in their partisanship, and as they settle in their choice their tenure grows and they become increasingly less susceptible to change. Nevertheless, older voters who have supported a party for as brief a time as the young, and have as yet not formed a partisan framework, are just as weak and changeable in their partisanship. In changeability what counts is not so much age as the development and duration of a partisan tie.

It is now possible to present diagramatically the process of becoming a member in the BUF for the sample.

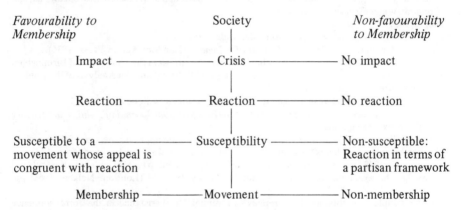

An individual will not join by leaving at any of the four exits – crisis, reaction to the crisis, susceptibility and movement. The two sides are obviously not mutually exclusive. Thus an individual may have favourable responses until the final stage: he may perceive a crisis, react to it and be susceptible to a movement because of the lack of a partisan framework, yet still not join for any number of reasons. These come freely to the imagination: the movement's image may be unacceptable; it may be un-British to the patriot; too conservative for the radical; it may meet on a day when the individual cannot attend; or he may simply not like the local leader. Any number of serious or trivial reasons may prevent membership. This reaffirms the point constantly stressed. It is not that the perception of crisis results in support for the BUF, or that having a poorly developed political consciousness implies that one must support the movement. It is only that these factors make *favourability* to membership greater. They are predispositions to membership rather than prerequisites: they indicate those who are predisposed to support rather than those who will inevitably do so.

Such conclusions from a sample of this size are naturally only a prolegomenon to our knowledge of the membership of the BUF. But they are useful in that they are the first conclusions to be drawn from first-hand, objective data with actual members.

They may be useful in another sense too, for they could provide the beginnings of further work with larger samples. If these tentative conclusions provoke this work, which up to now has been sadly lacking, they have served their purpose, irrespective of whether later they may be found valid or not.

NOTES

[1] Formed by Sir Oswald Mosley in October 1932 in an amalgam of his New Party and the British Fascisti. Changed its name in 1936 to British Union of Fascists and National Socialists. For a general history see the following:
Colin Cross *The Fascists in Britain* (London: Barrie & Rockcliffe: 1961), R. Benewick *The Fascist Movement in Britain* (London: Allen Lane: 1972), F. Mulally *Fascism Inside England* (London: Claud Morris: 1946), W. Rudlin *The Growth of Fascism Inside England* (London: George Allen & Unwin: 1935), 'James Drennan' (W.E.D. Allen) *BUF: Sir Oswald Mosley and British Fascism* (London: John Murray: 1934).
General works on fascism containing historical data on the BUF include: Eugene Weber *Varieties of Fascism* (Princeton: D. Van Nostrand: 1964) and S.J. Woolf (ed.) *European Fascism* (London: Weidenfeld & Nicolson: 1968).
Biographies of Mosley are:
R. Skidelsky *Oswald Mosley* (London: MacMillan: 1975)
A.K. Chesterton *Oswald Mosley: Portrait of a Leader* (London: Action Press: 1936).

[2] This is the approach taken in the author's M. Soc. Sc. thesis at the University of Birmingham «The British Union of Fascists, Sir Oswald Mosley and Birmingham: An Analysis of the Content and the Contexts of an Ideology», 1975.

[3] This is greatly under-researched. It is briefly mentioned in Benewick, *ibid.* 7–9, 12–13.

[4] See W.F. Mandle «The Leadership of the BUF» *Australian Journal of Politics and History* vol. 11/12 1965/66 pp. 360–383.

[5] As an illustration of the difficulties involved, not even the approximate size of the membership can be gauged with any agreement. Estimates of the total size in 1934 vary from 17,000 to 40,000 and in 1938 from 15,000 to 40,000. The difficulty is added to by Mosley's steadfast rule not to divulge the exact numbers. See his autobiography *My Life* (London: Nelson: 1968) pp. 310–311.

[6] The sample was obtained from replies to a request for assistance in the correspondence columns of Birmingham newspapers and Union Movement's *Action*.

[7] Skidelsky *ibid.* p. 317/18.

[8] Sir Oswald Mosley quoted by Cross *ibid.* p. 57.

[9] Sir Oswald Mosley *The Greater Britain* (London: BUF Publications: 1932) p. 15.

[10] Weber *op.cit.* p. 107.

[11] Beverley Nichols *News of England* (London: Jonathan Cape: 1938) p. 48.

[12] See A.J.P. Taylor *English History 1914–1945* (London: Penguin: 1965) pp. 771–778 for evidence as to how the individuals in the different Cabinets of 1914–1932 changed little.

[13] George Orwell *The Road to Wigan Pier* (London: Victor Gollanez: 1937) p. 121.

[14] Sir Oswald Mosley *My life op.cit.* p. 128.

[15] *Cavalcade* 13:11:1937.

[16] Skidelsky *ibid.* p. 317 and Cross *ibid.* p. 70.

[17] Mulally *ibid.* p. 237.

[18] Their class status was determined by self-designation and thus is a subjective rather than objective classification. This is just as valid because it is the class status they feel they possess and in which terms they view themselves. The relative value of objective and subjective class measures is an on-going debate in Sociology. See for example Mayer and Buckley *Class and Society* (New York: Random House: 1970) pp. 42–60.

[19] Sir Oswald Mosley *The Greater Britain op. cit.* p. 15.

[20] For a discussion of marginality see H. Dickie Clarke *The Marginal Situation* (London: Routledge and Kegan Paul: 1966).
Classic studies are:
S. C. Lenski «Social Participation and Status Crystallization» *American Sociological Review* 1956 pp. 458–464.
A. C. Kerokoff «Group Relations and the Marginal Personality» *Human Relations* 1958 pp. 77–92.
E. C. Hughes «Social Change and Social Protest: An Essay on the Marginal Man» *Phylon* 1949 pp. 58–65.

[21] For a discussion of the working class Conservative and his differing attitudes and social outlook see:
Frank Parkin «Working Class Conservatives: Theory of Political Deviance» *British Journal of Sociology* vol. 18 1967.
McKenzie and Silver «Conservatism, Industrialism and the Working Class Tory in England» *Transactions of Fifth World Congress of Sociology* vol. 3 1962.

[22] Benewick *ibid.* p. 129.

[23] Advisory Committee On Persons Detained Under Defence Regulation 18b report to Home Secretary (1940). For further illustration, John Wynn, himself interned in 1940, wrote a pamphlet on his experiences, from which the following passage is taken. «Very few people realise that 18b has drawn a representative cross section of the British public . . . the Admirals, Colonels, Majors and other officers and many rankers and ex-servicemen, doctors, dentists, solicitors, school and college tutors, manufacturers, journalists, geologists, steel workers, soldiers, sailors, airmen, civil defence workers, laboratory technicians, farmers, labourers, pathologists. . .» *It Might Have Happened To You* (Glasgow: Strickland Press: 1943) p. 13. This indicates their non-industrial employment.

[24] A. Raven Thomson *Action* 21:5:1936.

[25] *The Blackshirt* 3:1:1936.
A further illustration of this is *The Blackshirt's* attempt to appeal to the working class by having articles written by members of this class, but they were predominantly of the non-industrial kind. Articles read «Furniture Trade and British Union», «Smithfield Market and National Socialism» and were signed by such as «Blackshirt Butcher», «Furniture Worker», «Cinema Engineer» and «Porter».

[26] For an example of this simple view of fascist success abroad: «Both Italy and Germany suffered economic collapse. The Italian disintegration was extreme and brought Mussolini to power as rapidly as the conditions of war brought Lenin to power in Russia. Can anyone think that any of these events would have occurred without collapse? Political fortune in terms of economic crisis is measured more exactly in the German struggle where there is not the slightest doubt that the rise in unemployment brought them to power.» Sir Oswald Mosley *My Life op. cit.* p. 278/9.

[27] For example: «Fascism comes to all great countries in turn as their hour of crisis approaches.» Sir Oswald Mosley *The Greater Britain op.cit.* p. 13 «You do not need fascism until the crisis which is inevitable in the modern world comes. When the crisis comes, fascism is the only salvation». Sir Oswald's broadcast on radio March 15th 1933. See *The Listener* vol. 9 March 22 1933 pp. 433–435. See also the author's MS *ibid.* where this conception has been formulated into the concept of crisis determinism and used to interpret fascist ideology in Britain.

[28] This is why membership fell after the economic crisis of the thirties improved. There was simply no evident, obvious, recognisable crisis. In which event Mosley sought to manufacture his own in the form of violent anti-Semitism.

[29] There is a wealth of psychological evidence showing the stress of unemployment. See for example: R. Cochrane and A. Robertson «The Life Inventory: A Measure of the Relative Severity of Psycho-Social Stresses» *The Journal of Psychosomatic Research* vol. 17 1973 p. 135–141. P. Eisenberg and P. Lazarsfeld «The Psychological Effects of Unemployment» *Psychological Bulletin* vol. 35 1938 p. 358–390. Zawadski and Lazarsfeld «The Psychological Consequences of Unemployment» *Journal of Social Psychology* vol. 6 1935 p. 224–251. E. Rundquist

and R. Sletto *Personality in the Depression* (Minneapolis: University of Minnesota Press: 1936). Tiffany, Cowen and Tiffany *The Unemployed: A Social-Psychological Portrait* (Englewood Cliffs: Prentice Hall: 1970).

[30] Correlating the perception of this crisis with the sample's social charactristics, one finds that 80% of the lower class respondents perceived it, compared with only 30% of the middle class. This is not surprising for it is upon the lower class that the first ravages of depression fall. But certainly this figure for the middle class is low, for one can imagine the situation in the 1930's where for the first time, the middle class were having the yoke of economic depression and insecurity press upon them. What is interesting is that of those mentioning this crisis, all were under thirty and 72% were under twenty and in the youngest age cohort. This could well be caused by the standard practise in depressed times of laying off the youngest and most inexperienced first. In addition, since many firms are reluctant to employ new staff, school leavers find great difficulty in obtaining employment. It is notable that the only schoolboy of the sample mentioned this crisis. In such circumstances the fears of unemployment are intensified among the young.

[31] Radio interview BBC Radio 4 25:8:1974.

[32] Speech at Birmingham Rotary Club reported in the *Birmingham Gazette* 10:11:1936.

[33] Speech at the Albert Hall March 1935 reported in *The Times* 11:3:1935.

[34] See for example D. Butler and D. Stokes *Political Change in Britain* (London: MacMillan: 1969) pp. 56–58.

[35] For an elaboration of this see: Campbell *et al.* *The American Voter* (New York: John Wiley: 1960) pp. 161–164. W. McPhee and J. Ferguson «Political Immunization» in McPhee and Glaser *Public Opinion and Congressional Elections* (Glencoe: Free Press: 1962) pp. 155–179.

[36] McPhee and Ferguson *ibid.* p. 156.

[37] Campbell *ibid.* p. 162 «the immunizing effects of previous experiences are clearly visible».

[38] *Ibid.* p. 163. Furthermore, it is easy to sense how the recurrence of political issues, campaigns and elections progressively deepens the partisanship of the committed voter. Each confronts the individual with the necessity of acting on abstract and complex matters about which he is imperfectly informed, and an established partisanship provides the individual with a simple means of sorting the diverse information he is fed. This process was described well by Campbell *ibid.* p.,165 «Once a person has acquired some embryonic party attachment it is easy for him to discover that most events rebound to the credit of his chosen party. As his perception of his party's virtue gains momentum, so his loyalty to it strengthens and this in turn increases the possibility that future events will be interpreted in a fashion that supports his party inclination.» Every time a partisan framework functions in this manner it becomes stronger. The point to be made is that those with a poorly developed political consciousness lack this experience and are therefore less likely to interpret new political stimuli in terms of established parties.

[39] McPhee and Ferguson *ibid.* p. 172.

The Irish Experience: The Blueshirts

MAURICE MANNING

Background

In 1932 the Irish Free State was ten years in existence. During that decade its politics had been dominated by the issues, memories and continuing acrimony of the civil war which had attended its birth. The major political parties were based on the civil war division and each election during this time was fought on the civil war question in an atmosphere that was always bitter and unforgiving and in which political violence was always close to the surface.

The years 1922–32 had seen the Free State firmly established. In spite of the civil war, the usual post-revolutionary problems of setting up an administration, organizing a police force and bringing the army under civil control had been successfully tackled. In addition by 1932 the Protestant minority, traditionally hostile to Irish independence, had accepted the changed order, friendly relations had been established with Britain and a limited but real prosperity, largely based on agricultural exports, had been achieved.[1]

Two big and critical problems, however, remained to threaten the stability of the state. The first was the outright refusal until 1927 of the main opposition group – de Valera's *Fianna Fail* party – to accept the legitimacy of the state and their very limited recognition of this legitimacy after that date.[2] De Valera's partial acceptance in 1927 had been totally rejected by the IRA which aimed at overthrowing the state by armed force, attacking Northern Ireland and establishing a 32 county Republic – and for some sections of the IRA this would be a socialist republic. During all this time the IRA, which represented a strong tradition and which, with its propensity to violence and sympathetic links with *Fianna Fail*, had an influence out of all proportion to its size.[3] The second problem facing the state was its unresolved border dispute – an issue which simmered dangerously during all of this period.

The dominant political party during these years was *Cumann na nGaedhael* – originally that part of *Sinn Fein* which had accepted the Treaty in 1922 and which had then gone on to establish the new State. Under the leadership of W.T. Cosgrave it had developed into a conservative political party, drawing its support from, and reflecting the values of the propertied and business classes, the bigger farmers, the Catholic hierarchy and senior clergy and, later in the decade, the reluctant support of the former Protestant 'ascendancy' – or that section which stayed after Independence. The other major party, *Fianna Fail*, was based on the defeated civil war group and by the end of the 1920's had developed into a highly organized, professional mass political party. Its political philosophy was a mixture of 'Republicanism', intense nationalism and populist social policies and it drew its support from the less well-off sections. Its attitude to the legitimacy of the State was ambiguous and it maintained a relationship of cordiality and shared aims with the outlawed IRA.

These were the main parties but partly because of the presence of proportional representation and partly because of the generally confused and unsettled political climate, the type of two and a half party system which has characterised the Irish political system since the 1930's had not yet fully taken shape. Thus there was also a small Labour party, isolated by the dominance of nationalistic issues and unable to compete with de Valera's combination of republicanism and social reform. There was a loosely organised Farmers' party, a collection of ex-Unionist 'Independents', a handful of ephemeral smaller parties and dozen or so unattached deputies. As a result no one party had a majority between 1922–32, but *Cumann na nGaedhael* managed to provide stable one-party governments, helped between 1922–27 by the abstention from Parliament of *Fianna Fail* and from 1927–32 by support of Farmers and ex-Unionists who deeply feared the 'revolutionary' tendencies of *Fianna Fail* and the 'threat' of the IRA.[4]

The dominant characteristic of Irish politics in this first decade of the Free State was one of distrust. Each of the major groups totally distrusted the democratic intentions and good faith of the other. The memories of the civil war had been exacerbated by years of unforgiving bitterness. *Cumann na nGaedhael* blamed *Fianna Fail* for the civil war and saw it as having no loyalty to the State or to the democratic process. *Fianna Fail* blamed *Cumann na nGaedhael* for having 'betrayed' the revolution and for being 'pro-British' and 'anti-national'. This chasm of distrust was not to be bridged for thirty years and in it can be found the key to the emergence of the Blueshirts.

De Valera in Power

After the general election of 1932, *Fianna Fail* emerged as the biggest single party and with the support of Labour de Valera formed his first government. De Valera in power meant radical changes – as much in style and attitude as in policy. He released all IRA prisoners, set about removing the remaining elements of British constitutional dominance and withheld the land-annuities due to Britain under the Treaty.[5]

The change of government and implementation of these policies, especially the release of IRA prisoners, was viewed with alarm and apprehension by the supporters of *Cumann na nGaedhael* – and this alarm increased as the IRA's rhetoric grew more bellicose and as opponents to the IRA were singled out for abuse and attack under the general slogan of 'No Free Speech for Traitors'. In addition the material interests of many *Cumann na nGaedhael* people were seriously affected when the first effects of de Valera's 'Economic War' with Britain began to be felt – a war which effectively closed the British market to Irish agriculture at a time when over 95 per cent of total exports were to Britain. The IRA joined enthusiastically in this Economic War hoping to destroy at once the cattle industry and the big 'ranchers', then to take over the farms, divide them up among small farmers and labourers and establish an economy based on tillage.

A New Organisation

It was against this background of fear and impending disaster that an organisation called the Army Comrades Association (ACA) was founded in early 1932. This new organisation claimed to be 'non-political' and 'non-sectarian' and to be concerned with the welfare of widows and dependants of ex-members of the army. Two points, however, are significant. The nucleus of the new organisation was those who had fought against de Valera in the Civil War and, secondly, the association came into existence at a time when there was good reason to think that the new government might embark upon a vindictive policy against its old enemies.

558

At first the ACA made little public impact but within a matter of months it had set up branches in all parts of the country. And as soon as this was done the ACA changed both its objectives and methods and took on a 'political role'. This change took place in August 1932 and according to its leaders was a direct response to the intimidation of its supporters, the breaking up of public meetings addressed by Cosgrave and others, and the general aggression of the IRA.[6]

The ACA elected a new leader, Col. T.F. O'Higgins, a leading member of the *Cumann na nGaedhael* party and enlarged the scope of its activities to 'uphold the lawfully constituted government of the state' and to «wholeheartedly oppose communism». The ACA would protect the 'right to free speech' and in order to achieve these objectives they announced they were about to establish a 'volunteer division' made up of «all who feel the need for the existence of a powerful, steadying, moderate body of opinion in the country».

This new development was seen as sinister by *Fianna Fail* and the IRA who quickly dubbed the new organisation the 'White Army'. From this point on, too, the level of violence escalated sharply and the presence of ACA men as bodyguards at political meetings was seen as provocative by the IRA/*Fianna Fail* group who needed little excuse to step up their activities.

In January 1933 Mr. de Valera, whose parliamentary majority was slender, called a sudden general election. The campaign was an extremely bitter one with civil war issues and memories raised to a new level of intensity. There were frequent and serious clashes between ACA members and their IRA/*Fianna Fail* opponents and the situation degenerated to such an extent that the Government threatened to call in the army to maintain order.

The election resulted in a resounding victory for *Fianna Fail:*

	Fianna Fail		Cumann na nGaedhael		Labour		Others	
	Seats	Per cent Votes	Seats	Per cent Votes	Seats	Per cent Votes	Seats	Per cent Votes
1927	57	35.2	62	38.7	13	10.4	21	15.7
1932	72	44.5	57	35.3	7	9.3	17	11.0
1933	77	50.3	48	31.4	8	5.3	20	13.1

De Valera now had an overall majority and a clear mandate to press ahead with his controversial policies. In addition, shortly after this election he dismissed the Chief of Police, General Eoin O'Duffy, and established an auxiliary police force drawn largely from his own supporters. And at this point too the farmers began to become increasingly perturbed at their worsening situation. Exports in August 1932 were £1.8m. down on the same month in 1931 and these losses were concentrated in the cattle, sheep and general agricultural sectors. As there were no alternative domestic outlets, farmers now found themselves without markets for much of their produce and able to get only loss-making prices for what they could sell.

The Blueshirt Appears

It was against this background that the ACA which was now seen as having close ties with *Cumann na nGaedhael* and which included many prominent *Cumann na nGaed-hael* politicians in its leadership but which as yet had no formal ties with that party, decided on a new structure and course of action. The most important development was the decision to adopt a 'distinctive uniform' for the movement – the blue shirt. This decision was taken by the ACA's executive and, it appears, for two main reasons. One was a desire to help 'discipline' and aid identification at public meetings and this was the reason made public at the time. The other reason was that a number of members on the executive were looking to the Continent and were anxious to emulate the fascist idea – though this was emphatically denied, at least in public.

From this point on events moved rapidly. The new movement – quickly called the Blueshirts – began to attract members throughout the country and within a matter of weeks Blueshirt parades and meetings were being held in all parts. The 'crusade against communism' was loudly proclaimed with the IRA seen as the vanguard of the Irish communist movement while farmers, suffering the consequences of the economic war, began to join the new movement in large numbers.

A New Leader

In July 1933, the energetic and rumbustious ex-chief of police, O'Duffy, was offered, and accepted the leadership of the movement and immediately changed the name of Army Comrades Association to that of the *National Guard*. The National Guard proclaimed itself to be independent of all political parties, to be 'outside politics' – even though most of its leaders and members were also members of *Cumann na nGaedhael*. At this point too the first traces of Corporate thinking begin to appear in Blueshirt policy as a number of Catholic intellectuals influenced by continental fascism and especially by *Quadragesimo Anno* joined the movement and sought to give it a distinctive ideology.

O'Duffy set out to organise a 'non-political mass movement' throughout the country and his early success quickly alarmed the Government. His strictures on the uselessness of parliament aroused apparent enthusiasm and when O'Duffy announced a commemorative parade to the Parliament House, the Government alleged he was seeking to emulate Mussolini's March on Rome (for which there was no evidence), and threatened to outlaw the movement if O'Duffy persisted. O'Duffy did, and just one month after he had taken over, the Blueshirts, or National Guard, were banned by the Government.

The banning of the Blueshirts was to mark an important turning point in the history of Irish fascism. O'Duffy, in order to survive, now had to abandon his earlier stand on political parties and seek out new allies. The conservative and discontented *Cumann na nGaedhael* party and the new Centre party each of whom totally distrusted de Valera and feared the IRA would seem to have been O'Duffy's natural allies.

Certainly de Valera's victory in 1933 had alarmed these groups and special concern was expressed about the effects of the economic war, the growing lawlessness of the IRA and the Government's dictatorial tendencies. To the *Cumann na nGaedhael* newspaper de Valera was

«leading the country straight into Bolshevik servitude. We do not say that he has set out with the object of creating a communist state . . . but whatever his intention may have been, or may now be, he is proceeding along the Bolshevik path almost as precisely as if he was getting daily orders from Moscow. His Government is unmistakably out to demoralise the police force, and render them incapable of dealing with armed terrorists. His financial policy is leading inevitably to despoliatory taxation, which, rounded off with a dose of inflation, may be trusted to dispose of our Irish Kulaks».[7]

Given these fears and given the pervading sense of distrust among the opposition groups there were compelling reasons for a common front and the banning of the Blueshirts made this common front all the more urgent. Negotiations began, and in September 1933 agreement was reached to form a new political party *(Fine Gael)*, and to incorporate the Blueshirts, now renamed the *League of Youth* into this party as an ancillary section. O'Duffy, who did not have a seat in parliament, was to lead both *Fine Gael* and the Blueshirts (a move opposed by Cosgrave). In return O'Duffy promised to abandon his *fascist* ideas. The new party did, however, incorporate some aspects of Corporate thinking («The Pope's social programme» as it was called by O'Duffy) into its policy document.

A New Party

The new party began vigorously, and the Government's action, instead of destroying the Blueshirts, seemed to give it a new vitality and strength. The next ten months were to see the escalation of Blueshirt activity on a number of fronts. Its organisation was extended to all counties, it began to champion the case of the farmers whose economic plight was worsening, it continued to hold marches and parades and its members continued to act as bodyguards at political meetings.

Not surprisingly, this increased activity was accompanied by growing hostility between the IRA (which was itself breaking with de Valera) and the Blueshirts, and between the Blueshirts and the State. As far as the Blueshirts were concerned, the IRA was not just an extreme nationalist movement, it was something much more sinister, as in this editorial in the *Fine Gael* paper:

> «the object of the IRA is to impress on us here a Soviet Regime, with all power and complete control of all activity in the hands of the few whom the upheaval would throw on top».

The IRA saw the Blueshirts in equally clear-cut terms – «defenders of British imperialism, lackeys and fascists» and with the added incentive of civil war memories the hostility between the two groups was total.

The Government, professing to see in the Blueshirts a fascist and anti-democratic threat, was also fierce in its hostility. Its attempts to outlaw the movement, however, were less than successful. These attempts included the arresting and jailing of some leaders, the banning of the organisation and finally a bill to make illegal the wearing of uniforms. This last attempt in early 1934 was defeated by the conservative Senate, which in turn was shortly afterwards abolished by de Valera.

Before discussing the nature of Blueshirt activity it is necessary at this stage to return to a point which was made earlier and that is, that the merger of these three groups changed the whole nature of the Blueshirt movement. The Blueshirt movement, as it developed between April and September 1933 had a number of classical fascist characteristics. It originated from a nucleus of discontented ex-soldiers, was unhappy with the developing political scene, had an obsession with the 'growing communist threat', was impatient with parliamentary democracy («all parliaments gabble too much»), was infatuated with Corporate ideas, had a contempt for political parties, placed an emphasis on youth and renewal and exalted the role and place of the leader. There were no elections within the movement – all appointments were made by O'Duffy. In addition the movement was seen by the threatened farming and business class as their best bulwark against communism, economic ruin and incompetent government, and of course, the movement had adopted the liturgy of continental fascism.

The merger with *Cumann na nGaedhael* and the Centre party meant a radical change. The Blueshirts were now part of a political party, were obliged to work within the existing legal and constitutional structures and the governing body of the movement now included men like Cosgrave, McGilligan, FitzGerald of *Cumann na nGaedhael* and Dillon and McDermott of the Centre party, all unequivocal in their adherence to democratic and constitutional methods. This meant that if O'Duffy were tempted to return to his fascist ideas or if his lieutenants were tempted into illegal or unconstitutional activities the presence of Cosgrave, Dillon and company would act as a brake. And in fact it was the contradictions inherent in this situation which led to the disintegration of the movement.

In the early stages after this new development, these contradictions were not apparent. O'Duffy seemed to totally dominate the new *Fine Gael*-Blueshirt movement. The initiative on almost all fronts was now being taken by the Blueshirts rather than by *Fine Gael*. O'Duffy began a personal organisational drive, a whirlwind tour with mass meetings, making vigorous and often inflammatory speeches, appointing new organisers, explaining the Corporate idea, warning against the dangers of communism and expressing frequent words of admiration for Europe's «leading bulwarks against communism» Mussolini and Hitler. Before long it became clear that O'Duffy saw himself primarily as a Blueshirt and only secondly as a constitutional politician. The wearing of the blue shirt now spread to parliament, much to the embarrassment of the Cosgrave section, and at local level it was O'Duffy's men rather than traditional *Cumann na nGaedhael* men who took over the organisation.

The Corporate Ideology – Irish Style

The Blueshirt dominance soon became apparent in policy also. A number of Catholic intellectuals had sought to transform the National Guard into a vehicle for *Quadragesimo Anno*. Two of them, Drs. Tierney and Hogan now became members of the executive of the new party and their influence was soon obvious, with an evergrowing emphasis on Corporate ideas. The sophisticated political analyses of Tierney and Hogan, both of whom were opposed to Hitler and had strong reservations about Mussolini,were lost on O'Duffy whose admiration for European fascism grew with the passing months and who was unable to stick to the texts prepared for him by Hogan and Tierney. As far as policy was concerned there were differences of emphasis within the party. At one level were the traditionalists like Cosgrave who wanted to get back to the pre-1932 status quo. At a second level were the intellectual theorists, seeking to reconcile *Quadragesimo Anno* with the existing democratic institutions. And at the third and most vociferous level was O'Duffy – muddle-headed, demagogic and infatuated with the movements of Mussolini and Hitler. And without much doubt it was O'Duffy and his followers who overshadowed the others.[8]

On the one big socio-economic issue available to those opposed to de Valera – the economic war – the initiative was very decidedly taken by the Blueshirts. The economic war meant an almost total collapse in the cattle trade and in face of this the Government neither could nor would find any solution, other than paying a small bounty for every animal slaughtered. And as the Government insisted on collecting the rates (local taxes) and annuities from the farmers even though the farmers claimed their inability to pay, *Fine Gael* and the Blueshirts at local level – urged on by O'Duffy – began to organise resistance to the police who were seizing the property of rates defaulters. This resistance was at times violent and the year 1934 saw a huge rise in the number of Blueshirts convicted and jailed by the Military Tribunal – and in almost all cases the charges related to economic war activities.

The Local Elections

O'Duffy's first big test as leader came in the local elections of 1934. His campaign was vigorous and flamboyant and the elections took place against the background of escalating economic war violence. Shortly before the election a number of Blueshirts were killed – the movement now had its first «martyrs». The elections showed, however, that de Valera's party was still the strongest and that *Fine Gael*, under O'Duffy, had done little better than *Cumann na nGaedhael* under Cosgrave.

The election results, instead of sobering O'Duffy made him more extreme. Gone now were any inhibitions about expressing admiration for Hitler and Mussolini; gone too was any attempt to control the violent actions of some of his subordinates.

In early September the dissatisfaction with O'Duffy's style of leadership came to a head. O'Duffy was accused by his national executive of being autocratic, financially reckless, inconsistent in policy and unconstitutional in his methods. He was also a loser – as the local elections had shown. The executive sought to impose conditions on O'Duffy's leadership. He refused to accept the conditions and resigned.

The initial post-resignation period was characterised by confusion and bitterness but very quickly two distinct patterns were obvious:

In the first, the *Cumann na nGaedhael* – Centre party section of the movement seized upon the opportunity to defuse much of the Blueshirt activity. This section had been disturbed by O'Duffy's intemperate behaviour and speeches and disapproved of the activities of many local Blueshirts. In addition they now (1934) saw that de Valera was taking a strong stand against the IRA, that he was no radical revolutionary, that he was just as conservative as Cosgrave and that there was no fear of a revolution. And shortly afterwards when de Valera negotiated a Coal-Cattle pact with Britain – something which eased the economic war to some extent – they felt that much of the earlier justification for the Blueshirts had disappeared. Hence from 1935 on there was a deliberate attempt to play down the Blueshirts, to phase them out, something which eventually occurred in 1936. But as an effective and relevant political force, this, the majority section of the Blueshirts, ceased to be of importance by mid-1935.

O'Duffy, himself, sought to create a new movement – this time unequivocally fascist. He met with no success. His political party – the National Corporate Party – flopped, his newspaper floundered, his followers dwindled away and he, himself, became involved in the affairs of international fascism. It was only when the Spanish Civil War broke out that he came to life again, but his hastily organised brigade made little more than a nuisance of itself in Spain during its six months tour of duty. It was after the return of the brigade in June 1937 that O'Duffy finally wound up this section and left politics completely.

Thus it was that a movement which burst dramatically upon Irish politics in 1933, which looked as if it might radically alter the whole structure of Irish politics, slid quietly and ignominiously from the stage in two surreptitious movements in 1935 and 1936. From that point on the term 'blueshirt' was no more than a term of political abuse to be stored in the folk memory for use in later times.

The Blueshirts – Who Were They?

Any attempt to reconstruct an accurate picture of Blueshirt membership is made difficult by a number of factors, most of which spring from the fact that the movement had an effective life of little more than two years. No attempt was made to preserve organisational or membership records either at national or local level, police records are not accessible and the passage of time has blurred memories. There are, however, a number of ways which taken together give us a reasonably accurate profile of Blueshirtism and these are elaborated briefly below.

The fact that the Blueshirt movement had its *origins* in the ACA is significant. The core of members who founded the ACA and the bulk of its early supporters were ex-members of the Irish army, most of whom had been demobilised in the years following the civil war. Even when the ACA opened its membership and extended its aims in August 1932 its leadership at national and local level remained firmly in the hands of ex-soldiers – and mainly ex-officers. It should be noted, however, that in contrast with many continental situations most of these were steadily employed and many were citizens of substance.

Then, secondly, there was the *Cumann na nGaedhael* connection. Not all supporters or leaders of this party supported the Blueshirts – Cosgrave for example was never enthusiastic – but in general almost all Blueshirts were *Cumann na nGaedhael* supporters. And as has been noted earlier *Cumann na nGaedhael* was by 1932 the party of the farming and business classes, professional and established groups. It was also of course the party of the Treaty and as such numbered among its supporters many labourers and lower middle class groups whose allegiance owed nothing to economic interest – but was none the less total or partisan for that.

Then there was the question of *Blueshirt violence and activism*. The only significant socio-economic issue championed by the Blueshirts was the cause of the farmers hit by the economic war. This 'war' had meant a drastic drop in agricultural exports and as a result farmers found themselves unable to sell their goods except at ruinous prices. As a result many felt not just threatened with economic extinction but believed – with some reason – that the Government was determined on their extinction as a matter of principle. It is significant but hardly surprising that the bulk of Blueshirt activism which usually consisted of non-payment of rates, violent resistance to rate-collectors and attacks on bailiffs and on their police protectors was most frequent in the big-farm, cattle-intensive counties. It is even more significant that the level of violence was highest in those counties which had both this type of structure and a strong tradition of agrarian and republican radicalism and where IRA radicalism was particularly marked. This was especially true of counties like Cork, Waterford, Limerick and Kilkenny, and in all of these areas Blueshirt activity was spearheaded by farmers and farmers' sons who were reacting against both central government and local IRA/*Fianna Fail* opponents.

564

As far as *contemporary observers* were concerned there was almost universal agreement on the nature and composition of Blueshirt support. *The Round Table* which was probably the most reliable contemporary observer was emphatic that the bulk of Blueshirt membership was drawn from *Cumann na nGaedhael* supporters, from ex-servicemen, from farmers and shopkeepers and from the sons of farmers and shopkeepers – and that in many cases these categories overlapped. And even *An Phoblacht,* the IRA newspaper which was bitterly opposed to the Blueshirts, was in general agreement with this assessment.

A *reconstruction of Blueshirt branches' membership* in different parts of the country (based on the recollections of survivors)[9] confirmed that Blueshirts were drawn for the most part from the families of bigger farmers, shopkeepers and professionals and that it was essentially the sons of these groups who took the lead in local activism. Incidentally this reconstruction also showed that the 'Blueblouses' – the female Blueshirts – invariably came from strong Blueshirt families and it showed too that leadership at local level was usually provided by ex-army men. What is interesting about this reconstruction of branch membership is that it showed that local branches also included substantial numbers of labourers, shop-assistants and unemployed – as much as twenty five per cent of membership. The presence of shop assistants is explained by their background – mainly farming – and by the 'influence' of their employers. Some labourers were undoubtedly 'influenced' by their employers but the majority owed their membership to the intensity and persistence of civil war partisanship and this also explains the presence of some unemployed.

The Blueshirts – Social Reintegration

For most Blueshirts the question of social reintegration after serving in the movement did not prove to be a problem. Indeed the question hardly arose. There had never been a Blueshirt regime and the effective life of the movement had been less than three years. There had been very few full-time Blueshirts and most activity had been carried out at week-ends or after-hours. Most of those who were jailed were farmers' sons who simply returned to their farms after being released. The same was true of the small number of shop-assistants jailed – sympathetic employers took them back without question. There is no evidence to suggest that former members of the movement were ever discriminated against or socially ostracised because of their Blueshirtism.

Nor as far as leaders were concerned were there any real problems of social re-integration. With the exceptions of O'Duffy and Cronin, both of whom had difficulty in re-establishing careers, all other members of the Central Council of the movement simply continued in their careers and – for the most part – prospered. Four of them later became Cabinet Ministers when *Fine Gael* got back to power in 1948 and 1954, one became a judge (and part-time book censor), another a university president, yet another was managing director of the Abbey Theatre, while seven served in Parliament. And even in the case of O'Duffy and Cronin it can be said that their problems were due more to temperamental difficulties than to any hostility on the part of Irish society.

The Blueshirts and Fascism

That, very briefly, was the Irish Blueshirt movement, and hardly surprisingly the first and most difficult problem facing any study of this movement is the question of

565

definition: Were the Blueshirts a *genuine* fascist movement? If so, what *kind* of fascist movement was it?

Most fascist movements were pleased to describe themselves as such, and whether the word 'fascist' was incorporated in the name of the movement or not, there was little doubt or ambiguity in the minds of either leaders or rank-and-file on the nature of the movement. This however, was not the case with the Blueshirts, whose leaders always denied that the movement was fascist, who never used the word and resented it being applied to their movement. And yet, what do we call a movement which burst into the highly charged, if isolated and insulated, arena of Irish politics in 1932, developed around a nucleus of discontented and apprehensive ex-army officers, found itself a demagogic and (to himself at least) messianic leader, adopted a shirted uniform, organised itself into para-military formations, gave itself a Corporate ideology, pledged itself to fight to the end against 'atheistic' communism, put its faith in youth and action and fought the fight of a prosperous economic class threatened with extinction?

On the face of it, such a movement, while not meeting Ernst Nolte's requirements for the 'fascist minimum' does appear to have most of the characteristics of a classic fascist movement.

And yet the doubts remain. Can a movement which lacked such «hard» fascist characteristics as opposition to democracy (the majority of its leaders and supporters being in fact totally committed to parliamentary democracy), which was strongly anti-totalitarian, which was not particularly nationalistic, which rejected the leadership principle, which was never anti-Semitic and which most of all did not see itself as fascist, qualify as a genuine fascist movement? This problem is compounded by the short life of the movement. It lasted for little more than three years, disappearing almost as suddenly as it appeared and it is this more than anything else which makes it so difficult to assess the degree and extent to which the movement was, or was not, a genuinely fascist one.

All that can be said with certainty is that had the movement continued along the lines it was going before the merger with *Cumann na nGaedhael* and the Centre party in September 1933 it might well have developed into a full fascist movement, and had O'Duffy had his way in October 1934 it certainly would have. And finally the total failure of O'Duffy to bring any significant group with him along his fascist path in 1934–5 is possibly the best indicator of the extent and commitment to fascism either in practice or ideology of the great majority of those who donned the blue shirt in 1933.

NOTES

[1] The best account of the constitutional development of the new Irish state is to be found in D.W. Harkness, *The Restless Dominion* (London 1969). The problem of policing is covered by Conor Brady's *Guardians of the Peace* (Dublin 1974) while the setting up of a parliamentary regime is dealt with by Brian Farrell in *The Founding of Dail Eireann* (Dublin, 1972). The best overall account of this period is F.S.L. Lyons, *Ireland Since the Famine* (London 1971).

[2] For an account of Fianna Fail's early attitude to the legitimacy of the state, see M. Manning *Irish Political Parties* (Dublin 1972) pp. 34–43.

[3] The best account of the IRA is in J. Bowyer Bell, *The Secret Army* (London 1970 and 1980).

[4] For the development of the Irish party system see Manning *op.cit*.

[5] The land annuities were payments made by the Irish government to the British government twice yearly to finance the purchase of land from landlords under various Land Acts from 1870 to

1920. The money was collected by the Irish government which then paid it to the British government.

⁶ For a more detailed account of this episode see M. Manning *The Blueshirts* (Dublin & Toronto 1971), pp. 20–27.

⁷ Cited in Manning *The Blueshirts op.cit.* p. 44.

⁸ For a full discussion of these ideas see Manning *The Blueshirts* Chapter 13.

⁹ The areas were: Bagenalstown, Co Carlow, Cashel, Co Tipperary, Graignamanagh, Co Kilkenny and Macroom, Co Cork.

The Power Base of Greek Authoritarianism*

YANNIS ANDRICOPOULOS

The power base of authoritarianism in Greece has consistently been the military, acting as an agent for the monarchy and/or the bourgeoisie, or in its own interests as a power *élite*. A fascist mass movement did not appear in Greece until World War II, when Greece, occupied by the Axis, possessed no army apart from a few units stationed in the Middle East. The quisling government of John Rhallys then set up the «Security Battalions», a professional anti-communist body armed and equipped by the Germans to fight the *antartes*, the guerillas of the National Liberation Front (EAM). Terrorist activity of anti-communist para-military gangs increased in the years after the liberation, when the nationalist army, challenged by the communist-led «Democratic Army», could not fully exert its authority over the territories it controlled. But by 1950, although nationalist para-military bodies such as the National Security Battalions (TEA) were institutionalised, the authoritarian movement became once again a «family affair» of the military and has remained so until today. Anti-communism in Greece obtained mass support only in the forties, i.e. at a time when fascism in Europe had been defeated and anathematised. Yet, contemporary Greek authoritarianism did not emerge from post-war developments; it sprang from the thirties, when actual power was fully transferred into the hands of a small group of the extreme right and the contemporary model of «fascist» control established.

The Asia Minor Débâcle

Greek political life during and after World War I was dominated by the traditional conflict between republicanism and monarchism. In 1915, Prime Minister Veniselos, favouring Greece's entry into the War on the side of the Allies, clashed with Constantine, the pro-German King of Greece, who stood for neutrality. Constantine, claiming that he was the embodiment of the nation and the elected government only the «accidental» leadership of the country,[1] forced Veniselos to resign. In 1916, Veniselos established a rival government in Salonica, and, in 1917, with Allied support, forced Constantine to abdicate. The outcome of World War I, into which Greece had intervened on the side of the Allies, vindicated Veniselos' policy of territorial expansion: by the treaty of Sèvres, Greece was assigned Western and Eastern Thrace and the town of Smyrna with its Ionian hinterland in Asia Minor. But soon after, Veniselos was defeated in the elections and Constantine returned to the throne to face the refusal of nationalist Turkey to accept the proposed peace settlement. Graeco-Turkish hostilities re-opened, and the royalists committed themselves to a policy of conquest. Eventually, in 1922, after impressive initial successes, the Greek army retreated from Asia Minor defeated and in disarray. This was a turning point for both Greece and the monarchy.

The defeat had a number of effects whose political significance was only partially clear at the time. The Greeks of Asia Minor were totally uprooted, and Greece was faced with the huge task of absorbing 1,200,000 refugees. The peasant element among these refugees was chiefly settled in Macedonia, strengthening its Greek character, and the town dwellers settled in Athens, the Piraeus, Salonica, Cavalla and Volos, creating an urban proletariat. Furthermore, the exchange of population between Greece and Turkey – and also Bulgaria – left Greece with no large national or religious minority groups. The shock of the defeat also killed forever the romantic nationalism which the Greeks had nourished for centuries: Greece renounced the *Megali Idea* of recovering Constantinople and replacing the defunct Ottoman Empire by a renascent Byzantine Empire. An immediate political result of the defeat was that an army revolutionary committee, led by the Veniselist Colonels Plastiras and Gonatas, assumed office and executed the leaders of the royalist government which had conducted the Asia Minor campaign. In 1923 the committee formed an anti-monarchist Military League under the leadership of Kondylis, Pangalos, Hadjikyriakos and Othonaios. In the same year, following an abortive royalist *coup d'Etat* led by Metaxas, Leonardopoulos and Gargalides, they deposed King George, who had succeeded his father to the throne. In 1924, Greece was declared a Republic.

Republicanism, opposing the absolutism of the Crown, expressed both the new aspirations of the bourgeoisie and the old liberal traditions of the country. It was upon these two pillars that the strength of the Republic rested. Furthermore, it drew support from the refugees, who were overwhelmingly republican because of the responsibility of the monarchists for instigating the war which had led to the enforced abandonment of their homes. The whole constitutional, political and social structure was supported by the republican army. Conversely, the Republic drew strength from the ideological bankruptcy of its opponents and the disarray they were thrown into following the Asia Minor disaster. «Cast-offs of Veniselos' party and old discredited politicians of Old Greece», as the British Minister described them, they were «half-hooligan and half-aristocratic, devoid of principles, extremely vocal and unscrupulous in using street rowdyism as a means to their ends».[2] But the balance achieved was affected as soon as new factors made their impact felt. These were chiefly the steps towards industrialisation, the growth of fascism in Europe, and, above all, the economic crisis.

Until 1922, Greek capitalism invested exclusively in traditional and more profitable sectors such as international banking, commerce and shipping. The Greek «industrial revolution» began only in the years after 1922, owing to the inflow of foreign and refugee capital and the availability of cheap refugee labour. New industrial units opened and the value of industrial output (exclusive of olive oil, wine and flour) increased from $59 million in 1921 to $93 million in 1929.[3] The growing industrialisation, halted because of the economic crisis only in 1932, spurred the growth of an industrial proletariat.* It also signalled the emergence of a new national bourgeoisie alongside the Greek international bourgeoisie. The political outlook of this new bourgeoisie reflected its dependence on the exploitation of labour rather than financial opportunities: it had both a greater attachment to the country and a greater interest in political stability. It tried to safeguard this stability by rallying to the cause of

---

* In 1928, in a total population of 6,205,000, there were 2,745,500 gainfully employed. Industry absorbed 430,000, communications and transport, including the sailors, 107,000, commerce 185,500, liberal professions 86,000, public services 44,500, banking 23,000, mines 6,000 and others 388,000. Agriculture employed 1,476,000, who were primarily smallholders.

republicanism, but it also greatly undermined it by the ruthless exploitation of its labour force.*

The rise of fascism in Europe encouraged authoritarian elements in both the old royalist party and the senior leadership of the republican army to seek extra-parliamentary solutions. These tendencies signified the beginning of a new era for the army. The army, which had always been used as an instrument to retain or obtain political power, had been involved in all major political changes in Greece since independence and had become a power-conscious force. Until 1922, however, it saw itself primarily as a force destined to liberate still unredeemed territories; it attracted many idealists and intellectuals from the middle class and was a relatively progressive political force. The situation changed after the partial fulfilment of the nationalist dreams and the ensuing Asia Minor disaster which killed the old patriotic idealism. While retaining its power-consciousness, the army then limited its interests to internal developments and began to attract both peasant and petit-bourgeois elements, who saw in it only a career prospect, and to look for a new ideology in the place of the now defunct nationalism. Fascism began to sweep Europe and the old republican military leaders fell under its spell. Pangalos, Kondylis and Hadjikyriakos came close to National Socialist ideas and worked with the monarchists to overthrow both democracy and the Republic; Plastiras and Othonaios retained their republicanism, but the former became an admirer and would-be disciple of Mussolini and the latter flirted with the idea of a military dictatorship; and Gonatas, during the Axis occupation of Greece, led the fascist Security Battalions.

Economic Crisis and Fascism

Neither the industrial growth and its social effects, nor the rise of authoritarianism in Europe would, however, have produced, at least in the short term, any serious repercussions had it not been for the economic crisis. The impact of the crisis was felt in Greece in 1932. Her exports suffered a disastrous diminution; for instance, the sale of tobacco, her chief export item, brought in only 3 million gold pounds in 1932 as compared with 12 million in 1929. Remittances from emigrants, which had reached 22 million gold pounds in 1920, fell in 1932 to 3 million, and income from Greek capital abroad was likewise diminished by 67 per cent. The foreign exchange of the Bank of Greece dried up, and on April 26, 1932, the Greek drachma went off the gold standard and suffered a fall in value equal to 55 per cent.[5] To restore the financial position, the

---

* In a 1932 report of the *Bereau International du Travail* it was stated that generally the duration of a working day was 10 hours, and in many cases, particularly in Macedonia, 12 hours. A sample survey in a number of factories, carried out in Athens, the Piraeus, the Peloponnese, etc. in 1927–28, revealed that the working force comprised 14,238 women, of whom 2,309 were girls aged 9 to 14, and 1,748 men, of whom 214 were boys aged 13 to 14. In several instances children aged 7 to 8 were working by the side of their mothers. In Athens and the Piraeus children aged 10 to 15 were paid 12 drachmas a day, women 28 drs, unskilled male workers 40 drs, and skilled male workers 70 drs. Outside Athens and the Piraeus wages were lower by 20 to 30 per cent. To meet the cost of living, the minimum wage of a worker with a wife and two children should be 100 drs a day. These insufficient wages, attributed by the industrialists to a crisis of demand due to the diminishing purchasing power of the peasants, as well as «disastrous» conditions of work and hygiene resulted, *inter alia,* in a high rate of mortality, particularly from tuberculosis. No statistics were available.[4]

Liberal government under Veniselos suspended payments to foreign bondholders, restricted imports, reduced public expenditure, and reimposed a tax on agricultural production. But the population was on the verge of collapse. The peasants could sell only part of their produce and at reduced prices; commerce and industry suffered a serious setback; the number of unemployed rose to 237,000;[6] and inflation in the first few months of 1932 alone was 30 per cent.[7] Starving workers, particularly in northern Greece, took to the streets demanding bread, and on several occasions – in Salonica, Cavalla, Xanthe or Naousa – the army was called out either to prevent or to quell riots.[8]

However, in spite of the unprecedented economic and social crisis, the people did not step out of their traditional bourgeois party framework. In the September 1932 elections, the Liberal party and the conservative Popular party together won 198 of 250 seats in Parliament. Nine Communist party deputies were elected. The fascists, with the exception of General Metaxas whose party of Free Believers increased its representation from 1 to 2, made no impact at all.

The fascist movement at the time was virtually non-existent. There were nevertheless a few organisations inspired by the National Socialist rather than the fascist example. The best known among them was the *Nationalist Union of Greece* (EEE), a semi-military organisation. Based in Salonica and led by a certain Cosmides, a merchant, it consisted chiefly of NCOs and remnants of the anti-Slav nationalist bands active in Macedonia during the Ottoman occupation. The EEE, violently anti-communist and anti-Semitic, invited public attention in 1931, when it provoked anti-Semitic riots in Salonica.[9] In 1932, it carried out further attacks on the Jewish community in Salonica, but when it attempted, in 1933, to transform itself into a political party, it split into many sections and lost its impetus. The *Greek National Socialist party,* established in Athens in 1932 under the leadership of George Merkouris, a royalist politician, drew its support from ex-officers and exerted no influence whatsoever, while the *Iron Peace,* an organisation under the leadership of retired Colonel Niklambos, and the anti-Semitic *National Socialist party of Macedonia-Thrace* existed only on paper. The anti-communist *All-Student Union,* active at Athens University, claimed an exceedingly small membership.[10] Metaxas, the only pro-British fascist, remained a lone wolf.

The Republic had no desire to assist the fascist/National Socialist movement, but did not actually oppose it. The activities of Leagues «tending to organise society against subversive communist activity» were «irreproachable», Prime Minister Veniselos told Parliament on December 10, 1931.[11] But it did not back it either: «the big businessmen were not prepared to support it financially».[12] Communism was not a «menace», for the working class movement remained disorganised, and any potential threat to bourgeois privileges could be dealt with within the existing political and legal framework. Veniselos enacted in 1929 a series of «measures for the security of the prevailing social order» – the Idionym Law – on the basis of which in 1932 alone 544 persons were convicted to sentences of up to five years imprisonment.[13] Where this law proved insufficient, the army could always be called in, as it had been on several occasions. To activate workers against «plutocracy» and «capitalism» in order to rally them under the fascist banner was, for the bourgeoisie, both uncalled for and politically non-expedient. And fascism could not grow independently. It could find no breeding-ground in national frustration over lost territories or unfulfilled expansionist expectations; it could not campaign against national minorities since they were insignificant; it could stir no hatred against the Jews – the 80,000 strong Jewish community of Salonica was too small and too uninfluential to sustain the development of a national anti-Semitic movement; it made no appeal to the Greek character, essentially undisciplined, individualistic, and unmartial.

Militarism on the Ascendant

While the economic crisis did not transform the traditional political framework, it did shift the existing equilibrium of power between the two opposing bourgeois factions, the Liberals and the Populists. Although the Liberal party had emerged once again as the largest single party, its seats in Parliament were reduced from 189 to 102, while the Popular party's seats increased from 19 to 96. Veniselos let Tsaldaris, the Popular party leader, form a government with his acquiescence. Tsaldaris was himself a mild conservative, but the key positions in his first minority government were given to right-wing extremists like Kondylis, Metaxas, John Rhallys and Hadjikyriakos. They immediately began to interfere with the composition of the republican armed forces with a view to establishing a dictatorship.[14] Tsaldaris did not favour a dictatorship and before assuming office, he had explicitly recognised the Republic, but the removal of the Veniselist officers from the army command was in his own party's interests; political power was, as ever, identified with control of the army. Veniselos withdrew his acquiescence, but the new elections, held on March 5, 1933, were won by the Populists. Upon hearing the results, Plastiras proclaimed a republican military dicta-torship; the parliamentary system, he declared, had brought about a situation in which government was impossible. His dictatorship lasted for only fourteen hours: it was not supported by the majority of the republican army officers, and was denounced by all the political parties.[15] His clumsy and abortive move dealt, however, a heavy blow to the Republic, the parliamentary institutions and the Liberal party; it gave the extre-mists the long-awaited chance to begin wholesale purges in the army. Two new elements were immediately introduced in the political conflict: the threat of a royal restoration, pursued by one section of the anti-Veniselists as the only means to preclude the return of the Veniselists to power, and the threat of a military dictatorship considered to be the prerequisite of such a restoration.

Due to its pronounced anti-Veniselist character, the pro-dictatorship movement found no support in the Veniselist social, economic, political and military establish-ment. The social and economic establishment particularly disliked it because it was likely to add to the troubles of the country before taking over, should it ever do so. Moreover, Tsaldaris, the politically vulnerable and temperamentally weak Prime Minister, endorsed neither its aims nor its tactics, although he succumbed to its political blackmail. In spite of this, the existence of this movement was not a negation of the political role previously assigned to the army by the ruling class, but its reaffirmation, and it did not contradict the principles upon which the army had functioned in the past; it perpetuated them. But, although consonant with past and present practices, this movement was not now controlled by the ruling class. Its leaders, socially despised by the bourgeoisie, politically rejected by the people, ambitious yet uncertain about their political future, conscious of army power and unscrupulous enough to want to employ it for their own personal ends, impressed by the rising power of fascism in Europe and quick to take advantage of the political implications of the economic upheaval, had emancipated themselves from the tutelage of the political parties. They sought the support of the army against the political parties, pitted army power against political power, and proposed a militarist solution to the political problems. In effect, they made it their aim to «steal» the bourgeoisie's army from it. They had no ideology besides hostility to parliamentary institutions, and no acknowledged leader, although several aspired and conspired after the job. However, soon they found a leader in the person of ex-King George, who, in April 1933, declared that only a «supreme mind» and a «firm hand» could protect Greece from the manifold evils of the time.[16]

From March 1933 to March 1935, the militarists considerably increased their power by obtaining control of key positions in the army and the security forces. The ex-King's known and publicised connexions with its leaders fostered the alliance between the militarist element, led by Kondylis, and the monarchist element led by Theotokis, an aristocrat from Corfu, and this constellation was joined at a street level by the National Socialists. A new National Socialist organisation, the *Panhellenic National Front*, emerged and according to its own claims comprised 70 nationalist organisations.[17] Acts of terrorism increased, including a Nazi attack on the Athens offices of the Communist party in November 1934 and an attempt on Veniselos' life made by the Chief of the security police at the instigation of John Rhallys and Metaxas[18] in June 1933. Eventually, on March 1, 1935, Veniselos began his fateful Liberal-Republican revolt, which, ill-planned and badly executed, was crushed by the government forces within a few days. Its failure marked the beginning of a new era, namely, that of extreme right-wing authoritarianism, from which Greece has not yet escaped. Upon its defeat, the militarists and the monarchists began a new ruthless purge in the army, the administration and the judiciary and in all walks of intellectual and economic life.[19] They then forced new elections which the Opposition parties, except for the communists, boycotted. These elections, notable for their corruption, returned 287 government deputies, of whom, however, only 37 and 7 were followers of Kondylis and Metaxas, respectively.

At about the same time, the economic crisis made its second major contribution to developments by re-introducing into active politics both the workers and the peasants. The new class awareness, tracing its roots not only to the 1931–32 crisis, but even further back to 1923, when the Plastiras government brutally suppressed the first General Strike and banned the trade unions,[20] manifested itself forcefully. Numerous workers' and students' strikes in Athens in the first months of 1935 were followed in August by workers demonstrations at Herakleion in Crete. The troops which interfered in the latter were disarmed and the workers dispersed only after reinforcements opened fire with machine-guns causing numerous casualties.[21] In the same month, thousands of peasants, many of them armed, clashed with gendarmerie and troops in Southern Peloponnese.[22] The new movement, partially under the influence of the communists, encountered the hostility of both the Populists and the Liberals. This, in turn, accelerated the process of alienation of the working class from the traditional political parties which had already begun in 1932, when the disastrous social consequences of the economic crisis had failed to attract the interest of the two bourgeois parties. Although still very weak, the socialist movement in 1935 became for the first time a force to be reckoned with.

From Dictatorship to Dictatorship

Following the June 1935 electoral *coup*, the pro-dictatorship forces, under the leadership of Kondylis, arranged for a plebiscite on the question of the King. Open and officially encouraged acts of terrorism – in addition to the official discrimination against republican propaganda – assumed for the first time alarming dimensions. A republican meeting was banned in Athens four times, and when one, organised by the Liberals, was allowed in Salonica it was attacked by both terrorists and the cavalry. The same happened in Patras and elsewhere. Terrorists in Athens destroyed the offices of the Veniselist newspaper *Patris*. The terrorist mob acted in the name of the «King». Nevertheless, the people refused to rally to the royalist cause. Epirus, Macedonia, Thrace, Crete and the islands – the new Greece – remained predominantly and stubbornly republican and democratic,[23] while the Peloponnese, the traditionally royalist district of the Old Greece, demonstrated such an apathy to the royalist cause that even die-hard royalists were disheartened.[24] The militarists and the monarchists then took a final step: on October 10, 1935, with the ex-King's connivance,[25] they staged a *coup d'Etat*. They overthrew the conservative government of Tsaldaris, imposed a military dictatorship, and decreed the abolition of the Republic. Leaders of the *coup* appeared to be General Papagos, a «respectable nonentity», General Reppas, an «obscure adventurer of unsavoury reputation», and Admiral Oeconomou, an officer «whose incompetence was a danger to the Greek navy».[26] The real leader of the coup, and now dictator and Vice-Roy of Greece, was, however, General Kondylis. General Metaxas was not a party to it, having been outmanoeuvred in the battle for its leadership. The dictator was supported only by the army, and used it indiscriminately against all his opponents, including the bourgeoisie itself. For, as the British put it, «the best elements in the country, both royalists and republicans», i.e. the bourgeoisie, «refused to support» the dictatorship.[27] More than that, the Populists and the Liberals, and also Metaxas for his own reasons, tried, though unsuccessfully, to organise a joint front against it.[28]

While isolated inside the country, the dictatorship found a powerful ally outside its frontiers – the British. Britain had made her choice in favour of the anti-Veniselist State long before the Greek bourgeoisie did. Days after the Veniselist revolt of March 1935, Waterlow, the British Minister at Athens, publicly congratulated Tsaldaris for the steps he had taken to preserve «public order»,[29] convinced that failure to restore the monarchy might lead to anarchy. «Since anarchy», he stated to the British Foreign Secretary on May 30, «which means communism here, would be a danger to the British interests, I feel that we ought to consider . . . whether we cannot help Greece to become a monarchy».[30] However, Britain refused to become officially involved in Greek affairs until the Abyssinian crisis broke out. The line then adopted was that nothing should be done to alienate the Greek government, and on October 15, Foreign Secretary Hoare instructed his Minister at Athens: «You should enter at once into personal relations with General Kondylis and other Ministers».[31] The British were well aware that Kondylis was, as Sargent of the Foreign Office put it, a «gangster»,[32] and that the monarchist movement in Greece was, as Hoare blatantly told ex-King George, «in the hands of extremist fanatics in the army».[33] Still, they supported it because the restoration was «inevitable»; because Greece was behaving «really rather well at present and [was] indeed trying to order aeroplanes in this country»; and because Britain might have «real need of Greece in the present emergency». Besides, ex-King George, in return for the British support, should be expected to give Britain «the maximum cooperation from his country».[34] Hambros Bank in London, with interests in the National Bank of Greece, was believed to have already begun to support the monarchists financially.[35]

The confirmatory plebiscite on the question of the King's return was held on November 3, 1935, and produced a 95 per cent majority in favour of the restoration. No more fraudulent voting has been held in Greece[36] either before or since. On

November 25, King George returned to the throne. Soon after, he dismissed Kondylis and his government, re-established «parliamentary institutions», and appointed a new Cabinet of «non-party» personalities under Demerdjis to conduct new elections proclaimed for January 26, 1936.

The King's paramount concern was, in fact, to put the armed forces under his undisputed personal control. For him, too, as for his predecessors and successors to the throne, the army, as opposed to the people, the political parties or the «democratic» institutions, was the only reliable instrument of control. He, therefore, refused to reinstate the officers of the armed forces, as well as the police and the gendarmerie and the civil servants,[37] dismissed since March 1933. Further, while he dismissed the government, he did not dismiss the militarist element from the army. The militarist element, as opposed to the monarchist, immediately formed secret societies,[38] and began from then on to challenge the monarchist predominance; it actually succeeded only in 1967 under Col. Papadopoulos. The anti-democratic army, security forces and administration, established by the militarist element and perfected by King George and his successors, has comprised the social basis of Greek «fascism» until today. From this so-called «apolitical» power structure, not only the Liberals but also the conservative Populists were excluded. Whoever challenged it would be branded a traitor to his country, an enemy of the state, a communist.

With the army under his own personal control and on the condition that this influence would not be challenged,[39] the King tried to effect a reconciliation with the political establishment and secure its appeasement and cooperation. It was with this end in mind that he dismissed the Kondylis government. Kondylis' removal proved an easy task. He enjoyed the confidence neither of the bourgeoisie nor of the political parties; he did not, in spite of the never-ending purges, command the full support of the army; he was not trusted by the King himself, whom Kondylis had destined for the role of Victor Emmanuel with himself in the role of the «Duce»; and he was not as reliable to the British as the King. Moreover, as soon as the King returned, the cohesion of Kondylis' camp was shattered, for a large section, under Papagos, deserted him and granted the King support, though not unqualified. The monarchy's position vis-à-vis the militarist element was further strengthened among the military because the throne, seen as the institutionalised and lasting element in Greek politics as opposed to the yet uninstitutionalised, personalised and unstable power of Kondylis, exerted a powerful unifying appeal. The King's decisions were, however, violently attacked by both the militarist element under Kondylis and the royalists under Theotokis. Both denounced the «bastard dictatorship» of Demerdjis, the Premier of the new «non-party» government, and were responsible for several attacks with dynamite against property of pro-George royalists and Liberals.[40]

The King proclaimed elections under the system of proportional representation. Demerdjis explained to Waterlow that this system was chosen because «under the ordinary majority system, it was quite certain that the former republicans would be returned with a very large majority indeed, and should this happen now, the country would at once be split again over the question of the control of the army».[41] The Liberals and their republican allies won 143 seats, the Populists and their «allies», i.e. the militarists, the monarchists, and Metaxas, won 142 seats (Metaxas' party of Free Believers won 7 seats) and the communists 15 seats. As a result no government could be formed. The Populists and their allies, even if they agreed to combine their forces in spite of the bitter hatred which now separated them, could produce no majority. The Liberals could produce a majority only if they combined with the Populists or the communists. Negotiations between all parties concerned led, however, to no result. Once again the main dispute concerned the control of the army. The Veniselists would make no deal whatsoever with the Populists unless the reinstatement of all the cashiered army officers was agreed upon.[42] The Populists, desiring to balance the influence of the militarist-monarchist element in the army and to reinstate Populist officers also dismissed, were prepared to meet their demand, but only partially.[43] Following the deadlock, the «non-party» government of Demerdjis, with Papagos as Minister of War, continued to hold office. Meanwhile, the King's authority was strengthened owing to the sudden eclipse of the major contestants of his power. Kondylis died on January 31, Veniselos on March 18, and Tsaldaris on May 17. But the deadlock continued, and this gave the enemies of the parliamentary system a chance to attack it again as if the deadlock were due to parliamentarism. On March 5, the militarist element, this time under Papagos, acting, he claimed, on behalf of the armed forces, delivered to the King an ultimatum demanding the instalment of a dictatorship. The King called his bluff; Papagos resigned, and the King appointed Metaxas as Minister of War. Metaxas was no longer connected with the militarists, had no influence with the military, so he could not conspire against the King, and could be counted upon as the King's ally against the militarist element.[44] His appointment as Minister of War signified a new defeat for the militarists, whose pressure on the King did not, however, decrease.

Yet, the Liberals and the Populists continued their negotiations, unable to agree on the question of the army. They failed to realise the magnitude of the dangers emanating from both the militarist element and the palace, and they seemed unaware that the new confrontation transcended party disputes, being a confrontation between democracy and totalitarianism. They were utterly out of touch with their time. Instead of defending the remnants of democracy, they tried once again to build up their party machinery: to regain control of the army in order to re-establish traditional patterns of power structure and class exploitation. Their concern with the army question was due not to a principled opposition to dictatorship, but to the fact that they had lost control over the army and thereby the means to exert their authority. Hence, when Metaxas deceitfully promised the Liberals to reinstate Veniselist officers, the Liberals gave him their support. With their vote of confidence, Metaxas became Prime Minister when Demerdjis died on April 13. However, the crisis of the regime did not subside. The King had «a rooted determination, almost amounting to a mental kink, not to re-admit to the army even a selection of the Veniselists ejected»;[45] and the re-admission of the officers was a *sine qua non* for the cooperation of the political parties with the King. Their attitude, implying refusal to accept the politically decorative role the King had assigned for them, destroyed both the basis of his policy and his plans for the future. There was a complete deadlock, and this sealed the fate of democracy.

The pretext for abolishing parliamentary institutions was furnished by new working class manifestations against the rising cost of living and the threat of a new dictatorship. To these the government responded with unprecedented brutality. On May 2, gendarmes opened fire against textile workers in Volos, Central Greece, killing one person and wounding several others. On May 9, gendarmes and troops opened fire in Salonica against a workers' demonstration, killing twelve people and wounding over a hundred. These acts, which constituted a deliberate provocation, caused widespread indignation, and on May 13 the workers throughout Greece staged a General Strike in protest. When the government announced its intention to introduce a system of compulsory arbitration for the settlement of labour disputes, a new General Strike in protest was proclaimed for August 5. The trade union movement was, in effect, coming out in the open against the Metaxas government and the oncoming dictatorship. But on August 4, the King established a military dictatorship, with General Metaxas at its head, to prevent a «communist uprising» and a «repetition of events in Spain».[46]

Parliamentary institutions did, thus, disappear, not under the pressure of a mass fascist movement; such a movement did not even exist. They were destroyed, instead, by the monarchy, supported by the army and the British – the triple alliance which dominated political life also in the post-war era until 1947, when the USA slipped into the shoes of Britain.

The Regime of the 4th of August

Britain rallied to the support of the new regime chiefly because King George, British by sentiment, had fully committed himself to a pro-British foreign policy and to what became a scandalously favourable treatment of British financial and economic interests in Greece. Waterlow, the British Minister at Athens, disagreed only with the time the dictatorship was set up; the King, he reported, ought to have given the parties more rope to hang themselves with.[47] In March 1937, the opinion in the Foreign Office was that, since his return, the King had done «very well»,[48] and in May 1937, Vansittart, the Permanent Under-Secretary of State, wrote to his Foreign Secretary: «We have found the Metaxas regime a good deal more satisfactory to deal with than many of its predecessors». Therefore, «we deprecate criticism of it».[49]

A power behind the dictatorship was also the financial capital, and particularly the National Bank of Greece under Drossopoulos, its Governor, who had «for many years rendered great services to British vested interests».[50] The National Bank financed most of the businesses of the country and controlled about half of them: the textile factories, the mining enterprises, the chemical and fertiliser companies, the Bodosakis munitions plants, the Peloponnese Railways and many other interests were under its sway. Employees or former employees of the Bank such as Apostolides, Arvanitis, Karanikas, Korizis and Kozonis, controlled the principal economic Ministries of the Metaxas government.[51] On the other hand, industrial capital, mostly in the hands of Veniselists, neither trusted nor liked the new regime, but it nevertheless supported it. The republicanism to which it had rallied was already outdated by events, and political stability, as well as stability in industrial relations, heavily disturbed by the growth of the working class movement, could now be offered only by the dictatorship.[52] Having secured the support of the bourgeoisie, the dictatorship in the first months won the acquiescence of the Liberal party, too.[53]

On this powerful combination of interests, Metaxas began to build his «anti-communist, anti-Parliamentarian, totalitarian and anti-plutocratic state».[54] For a dictator, he found himself in a most peculiar position. He assumed such exceptional power despite having no mass following, no party machinery, and no influence with either the army, the British or the bourgeoisie. His authority could be asserted only in the King's name – a weakness which was the very reason why the King made *him* a dictator. Still, Metaxas, viewing himself, as Kondylis did in 1935, in the role of the «Duce» of Greece, with the King powerless in the background, refused to be the King's man. In this he was motivated by an instinct for political survival, but also by his perception of the bourgeois State which differed considerably from that of the King as well as that of the militarist element. Generally speaking, while the militarist

577

element stood on the «right» of the King, demanding a savage military dictatorship controlled by the army as opposed to a «gentle» military dictatorship controlled by the King, Metaxas, being the only fascist in the lot, stood on his «left» striving for a fascist, «anti-capitalist» dictatorship able to command some support from the masses. From the very beginning, Metaxas attempted to obtain a power base of his own. He built up the security forces, transforming them into a most formidable, and exclusively Metaxist, instrument of control; he attempted to create a fascist movement of a paramilitary nature by setting up the National Youth Organisation (EON) and the Labour Battalions, his «guard»;[55] and he tried to win over the workers and the peasants politically by introducing «socialist» reforms.

The police and the gendarmerie, under the jurisdiction of Maniadakis, Minister for Public Security, soon became a state within the state. Its most select, and most notorious, section was the Special Security branch, which developed the closest relations with the German Gestapo.[56]* The strength of this branch consisted of 45 officers, 400 others ranks, some 30 political advisers and a security battalion of 1,200, equipped with machine guns and motor cycles. The Special Security branch was primarily responsible for the atrocities committed against political prisoners, including forced suicides. It was also the most trusted force on which Metaxas was believed to rely in order to obtain control of the capital in case of trouble.[58]

By comparison with the security forces, the fascist youth movement, which Metaxas later established, was only a toy; a balloon which burst as soon as he died – in January 1941. The National Youth Organisation (EON), into which the Labour Battalions were later incorporated, was brought into existence on November 7, 1936, but its first phalanx appeared in public only on December 31, 1937. Its aims were described as being «the useful employment of the free time of the young, tending to the improvement of their physical and intellectual condition, the development of national sentiment and religious faith, and the creation of a spirit of cooperation and social solidarity». The oath bound the members to be obedient to the «leader» and to strive with all their might for the national ideals of the 4th of August.[59] Wearing navy blue uniforms and carrying rubber truncheons, the members bore the insignia of the organisation – the double Cretan axe, resembling the Italian fasces, encircled with laurel and surmounted by a royal crown. They greeted the «leader» with the «Roman Salute». The organisation provided for the active membership of all Christian Greek citizens – the Jews were excluded – between ages of 14 to 25. The «educational» programme of EON included military drill, air raid defence, political education, etc. Special activities for boys comprised operation of motor vehicles, aerial gliding, rifle shooting, horse-back riding, and fire-fighting.[60] All state services were called upon to lend their support to the organisation, and the State itself was its primary financial contributor. Additional funds were supplied by «voluntary» contributions. In 1939, its membership rose, according to Metaxas, to 600,000. However, the youths joined its ranks only because refusal to do so meant expulsion from schools, having their parents under police surveillance, loss of social benefits to the needy etc. Threatened by the state, the young people were also bribed to join in by special benefits awarded

---

* Michalopoulos, its General Director, and Bombolas, his deputy, along with Angelides and Zanglis, its directors in Athens and the Piraeus respectively, were «full of sympathy» for the German Nazis and worked hand in glove with them. The same was true of Vavouris and Vassilopoulos, the city police directors of Athens and the Piraeus respectively, and Drossopoulos, the General Director of the gendarmerie.[57]

to the members, such as free admission to all cinemas in Greece (Emergency Law no. 1510 of December 8, 1938). EON was, in fact, hated by the people and caused such distress that, as Waterlow reported, there could hardly be a home in which tears were not flowing.[61] This potentially powerful fascist organisation, which in the absence of any means to resist it was made subject to ridicule by the people, [62] totally collapsed when Metaxas died.

The «Third Hellenic Civilisation»

The dictatorship aimed at consolidating the existing social order, or, as Metaxas himself repeatedly said, at strengthening the bourgeois regime. To achieve this, he brutally suppressed the trade union movement and all manifestations of social and political discontent, he made extensive use of the most up-to-date brainwashing techniques, and transformed Greece into a veritable *Polizeistaat*. In return for the iron stability he imposed, he asked the bourgeoisie to make, in its own long-term interests, some «sacrifices», in effect to modernise industrial relations policy by lifting some of the most notorious features of class exploitation.[63] Class cooperation, which was his aim, would not otherwise be possible, he argued. The «socialist» reforms he introduced, were looked upon by the bourgeoisie with abhorrence. He enforced a minimum wage to protect the notoriously underpaid workers and imposed some price controls; however, the rate of inflation – 30 to 40 per cent in the first year of his dictatorship – outweighed the benefit from these measures.[64] He introduced the system of collective labour contracts which was, however, inoperative in conditions of dictatorship, and of compulsory arbitration which gave the state power to intervene in labour disputes. He further extended both the eight-hour day and the six-day week to more industries and allowed a fortnight's holiday a year on full pay. In most cases, none of these measures were or could be enforced.[65] The greatest «achievement» of Metaxas was the enforcement of compulsory social insurance. This nevertheless turned out to be a most profitable business since the funds of the Social Security organisations were used to finance the police and propaganda activities of the regime or its rearmament schemes.[66] These measures did not leave the workers better off than before; some even argued they left them worse off, taking also into account both the inflation and the numerous deductions in the form of contributions, «voluntary» or otherwise, from the wages enforced.

Class cooperation, as viewed by Metaxas, was to be ultimately effected within a Corporative State. This would be based on organisations of employers and workers in each sector of economic activity[67] which were entrusted with still undefined tasks. These organisations would be represented in a national council which would operate in a purely advisory capacity; decisions would be made by the dictator. In this system, industry would be controlled by the state in a form and to a degree never precisely indicated: Zavitsianos, his principal early theoretician, declared himself in favour of control of the economic life by the syndicates,[68] Metaxas himself believed in state intervention, and an Athens newspaper wrote once that «State Socialism» was in the process of realisation. In December 1937,[69] Metaxas seemed ready to develop the state into a «States General» in which the power to legislate in each field would rest with the appropriate congresses of syndicates. The system he had in mind, he then told a British visitor, would be close to that of Portugal under Salazar.[70] Soon after, he abandoned this idea, too, in favour of a «democratic dictatorship», or, alternatively, an «authoritarian democracy» based on voting by acclamation in public meetings held for the express purpose of acclaiming him as a leader greater than Pericles. In December 1940, following the Italian attack on Greece and his disillusionment over the policies of Hitler and Mussolini,[71] Metaxas, rejecting all his previous utterances, finally endorsed the principle of universal suffrage for the election of national councils entrusted with an advisory mission.[72]

The nationalism of Metaxas did not find expression in expansionist aspirations – his foreign policy was pro-British – or in the cultivation and display of a militarist spirit. It had nothing to do with racism and it did not encourage persecution of the Jews. His nationalism, mild by comparison, aimed instead at creating a «Third Hellenic Civilisation» – the first being the classical and the second the Byzantine – in continuity with the millenary traditions of the race. Significantly, the era of the «Third Hellenic Civilisation» began with nationalist students burning books in front of Athens University. His «cultural» nationalism was coupled with an economic nationalism. Performing what the German termed «Hellenic industrial chauvinism»[73] and the British, «nationalist megalomania»,[74] he repeatedly attempted to nationalise important economic activities of foreign interests in Greece and to build up a national industry against the wishes of both the Germans and the British. Mention should be made here of his attempts, all in 1937, to nationalise the British-controlled Eastern Telegraph Company and the Blackburn Aeroplanes factory in Phaleron; to set up a Greek Oil monopoly and a State reinsurance monopoly with which all foreign insurance companies should reinsure 45 per cent of their business; to build a naval yard at Scaramanga and to construct an iron nickel industry; or to penetrate, through Bodosakis' munitions factory, the Near Eastern market. All these attempts encountered the fierce opposition of the foreign interests involved, backed, on the one hand, by the British government and the King of Greece,[75] and, on the other, by the German government, and were eventually frustrated.

By 1938, Metaxas, intended as «an instrument in the King's hand»,[76] had already pushed the King into the background. He became the leader of an overtly Metaxist regime. The King conveniently accepted the state of the 4th of August, without relaxing his own authority over the army and after persuading Metaxas to abandon both his Corporative State plans and his economic nationalism. Meanwhile, Metaxas' own zeal for «socialist» reforms had run out of steam, particularly as his «anti-capitalist» drive had caused an outcry from the bourgeoisie.[77] Metaxas was accepted by Britain, too, since his regime, as a Foreign Office official minuted, «suits us very well».[78] But the regime of August 4 never took root. It remained an artificial creation never intended to express the will of the people but only to «instruct» them, imposed from above when the King and the army had silenced all opposition, and founded on and developed in violence and corruption. When Metaxas died, everything he had built, save for the Police State, collapsed. The Police State was the legacy the «Third Hellenic Civilisation» left. Such a collapse had, in fact, been anticipated even by Metaxas himself.[79]

An Inevitable Split

Meanwhile, as soon as the dictatorship was declared in 1936, other important developments occurred in the army. The militarist element, refusing to accept a dictatorship under Metaxas, never ceased to try to bring about his downfall. A first step in this direction was taken in 1936, when Skylakakis, the Minister of the Interior and a representative of the militarist element in the government, attempted to rally the army commanders in Macedonia against Metaxas. He was discovered and, in December 1936, forced to resign.[80] The militarist element, including now many officers of the lower ranks, did not rest, however. Under the leadership of General Reppas, General Apostolopoulos and John Rhallys, and in alliance with both the old royalist party under Theotokis and Michalacopoulos, the right-wing Veniselist leader, it planned once again to overthrow Metaxas in 1937.[81] Its plans, involving some 500 officers, were frustrated and, in December 1937, the leaders of the movement were deported to islands.[82] The split within the army subsequently widened: the monarchist element rallied around the General Staff, under Papagos, once again a monarchist, and Yalistras, and the militarist element around various commanders of Armies, under Drakos and Pitsikas.[83] In July 1938, a new army plot was discovered: Generals Drakos, Diamesis, Manettas, Demestichas, Tsangarides and Matalas, as well as about sixteen colonels were arrested.[84]

The second consequence of this split appeared soon after, when the militarist element began to plot together with the German Intelligence to overthrow Metaxas. The King was now faced with a thorny choice. In order to support his pro-British policy and protect the independence of his country against Germany, he needed to reinstate the cashiered republican and democratic officers, for it was they who were pro-British. But in doing so he ran the risk of undermining his dictatorship and endangering his throne. He chose to protect his dictatorship. The measures he and Metaxas took to check the growth of the pro-German tendencies in the army were thus only of a restrictive nature, i.e. totally insufficient: In June 1940 the government banned Skylakakis to an island, and in July banned also General Platis, second deputy chief of the General Staff, and other officers.[85] But the militarist element, in its pro-German course, found, meanwhile, powerful allies within both the monarchist and the Metaxist camps and grew considerably in strength. In December 1940, the leadership of the pro-German militarist group consisted of Generals Reppas, Drakos, Pitsikas, Pakopoulos, and Politis, actively intriguing with the German Nazis through Nikolopoulos, the director of the Lufthansa in Athens. Their aim was not only to replace Metaxas, but also to bring about «an occupation of Greece by the German Wehrmacht without a struggle».[86] Other groups under John Rhallys and General Pangalos in Athens, General Tsolacoglou, the monarchist army commander, on the Macedonian front, and General Plastiras,[87] exiled in Paris, were also actively engaged in plotting with the Germans. Fifth-column activity, corruption and defeatism spread, in fact, so much that in the three months from Metaxas' death to the collapse of the military front, both the King and the British lost control of developments. Amid chaos and treachery in the highest government echelons, Korizis, the King's new Prime Minister, committed suicide in despair.[88]

Authoritarianism in Sunday Clothes

The powerful national liberation movement under the auspices of EAM, which rapidly grew in the armed struggle against the Nazi occupation, did not thus seek merely to expel the invaders, but also to liberate Greece from her tyrants and establish the rule of democracy. The EAM met, however, fierce opposition both from the monarchists and the British, on the one hand, and the militarists and the Germans, on the other: the militarists, together with the Metaxist security forces and functionaries of the Metaxas regime, fought alongside with German troops against it, and the monarchists helped the British to quell by force of arms the republican and democratic revolt of the

Greek armed forces in the Middle East in April 1944. In October 1944, the Germans withdrew from Greece. But, although the militarists closed ranks with the monarchists again, their former power had vanished, and it was the British who, in the Anglo-Greek war of December 1944, militarily crushed the EAM and then installed King George on the throne of Greece. The pre-war regime was now fully re-established, but with a parliamentary façade. The bourgeois parties, passive spectators all along to the struggle between the left and the King, did not now challenge the King's «right» to exclusive control of Greece's new, but once again anti-democratic, army. George Papandreou, the Liberal Prime Minister, the only one who did challenge it in the post-war era, was in 1965 summarily dismissed by the King. This autocratic army in 1967 once again abolished parliamentary institutions, and soon after that its militarist wing abolished the monarchy and cashiered the monarchist army officers.

The Metaxas dictatorship was only one phase in the history of twentieth century Greek authoritarianism, and not the most important. The battle against democracy, a battle whose key objective was control of the army, had to all intents and purposes been won by Kondylis and the King before Metaxas assumed office. Metaxas had no connexions with the mainstream of the pro-dictatorship forces, i.e. the army, and came to power almost accidentally. It was, in fact, his marginality which led the King to select him, and the King could in theory have equally well chosen another marginal figure, or even a non-marginal monarchist had he found one he could trust. Hence Metaxas' fascism represented only Metaxas himself and not the Greek authoritarian establishment. Hence also he was propelled out into the open to attempt the creation of a fascist mass movement; not having control of the army, he needed a power base of his own. And hence his non-conformist actions were rejected by the anti-democratic establishment, while the rest was preserved long after his death. Still, Metaxas made his contribution to the development of Greek authoritarianism by consolidating the political, legal and administrative structure within which the most reactionary forces have, since 1935, dominated Greece.

These forces are indeed still today so powerful that even a government with the unprecedented electoral power of liberal-conservative Prime Minister Karamanlis is unable to master them. The army, which remains anti-democratic and above government control, allows for no substantial changes in the pre-war power structure; the threat that it will intervene again openly should Karamanlis attempt to alter anything of importance is well known and ever present. Political life is thus a matter of blackmail at gunpoint, authoritarianism is still present though in Sunday clothes, and the people, while free to argue and demonstrate, are debarred from making real choices. But the day will come, that the people or the government will become too impatient with the tutelage the military exerts over the political life, and this will certainly be the day of another showdown between democracy and authoritarianism in Greece.

NOTES

* I am indebted to Dina Glouberman and George Catephores for their help and advice.

Unpublished documents of the British Foreign Office will be identified by the preface *BR*, those of the United States Department of State by *US*, and those of the German Ministry for Foreign Affairs by *GR*.

[1] John Campbell and Philip Sherrard, *Modern Greece*, (London: Ernest Benn, 1968), p. 120.
[2] BR: Waterlow, Athens, 1 April 1936, R 2033/220/19.

[3] Institute of Finance, Bulletin no 56, New York, 12 September 1932.

[4] Report by Tixier, Bureau International du Travail, 1932 (included in BR C 2886/324/19/1932).

[5] Report by Maximos, League of Nations, Journal of the Monetary and Economic Conference, London, 1933, p. 39.

[6] Dimitratos, A., Elatosis tis anergias en Elladi, *To Neon Kratos*, (Athens 1938).

[7] BR: Ramsay, Athens, 19 May 1932, C 3999/324/19.

[8] BR: Chick, Salonica, February 1932, C 2092/462/19.

[9] GR: Salonica Consulate, Salonica, 24 June 1933, L 1024/L 301048–49.

[10] GR: Eisenlohr, Athens, 9 May 1934, L 1024/L 301051–52.

[11] US: American Legation, Athens, 12 December 1931, 868.00/660.

[12] GR: Salonica Consulate, Salonica, 24 June 1933, L 1024/L 301048–49.

[13] Koundouros, Roussos, unpublished thesis, Brunel University, Britain, 1974.

[14] BR: Ramsay, Athens, 13 January 1933, C 140/6/19.

[15] *The Times*, London, 8 March 1933.

[16] *Eleftheron Vema*, Athens, 23 April 1933.

[17] GR: Eisenlohr, Athens, 23 November 1934, 6625/E 502648.

[18] BR: Foreign Office minutes, London, 7 June 1933, C 5327/399/19.

[19] BR: Waterlow, Athens, 22 March 1935, R 2008/34/19.

[20] KKE, *Episema Keimena*, 1964, Vol. I, p. 562.

[21] BR: British Consulate, Herakleion, 6 August 1935, R 4962/34/19.

[22] BR: Walker, Athens, 27 August 1935, R 532/34/19.

[23] BR: Waterlow, Athens, 27 May 1935, R 3421/34/19.

[24] US: MacVeagh, Athens, 9 October 1935, 868.00/915.

[25] BR: Waterlow, Athens, 11 October 1935, R 6160/34/19.

[26] BR: Waterlow, Athens, 15 October 1935, R 6289/34/19.

[27] BR: FO minutes, London, 11 October 1935, R 6108/34/19.

[28] BR: Waterlow, Athens, 17 October 1935, R 6250/34/19.

[29] BR: Waterlow, Athens, 7 March 1935, R 1499/34/19.

[30] BR: Waterlow to Vansittart, Athens, 30 May 1935, R 3597/34/19.

[31] BR: Hoare, London, 15 October 1935, R 6173/34/19.

[32] BR: Sargent, London, 5 November 1935, R 6675/34/19.

[33] BR: Hoare, London, 16 October 1935, R 6249/34/19.

[34] BR: Hoare to Vansittart, London, 14 October 1935, R 6249/34/19.

[35] US: MacVeagh, Athens, 9 October 1935, 868.00/915.

[36] BR: FO minutes, London, 4 November 1935, R 6580/34/19.

[37] BR: Waterlow, Athens, 12 December 1935, R 7593/34/19.

[38] BR: Waterlow, Athens, 6 March 1936, R 1345/220/19.

[39] GR: Eisenlohr, Athens, 6 January 1936, 5873/E 429640–44.

[40] BR: Waterlow, Athens, 12 December 1935, R 7593/34/19.

[41] BR: Waterlow, Athens, 20 December 1935, R 7730/34/19.

[42] BR: Waterlow, Athens, 1 February 1936, R 599/220/19.

[43] BR: Waterlow, Athens, 27 April 1936, R 2558/220/19.

[44] BR: *Ibid.*

[45] BR: Waterlow, Athens, 12 August 1936, R 4920/220/19.

[46] BR: Waterlow, Athens, 6 August 1936, R 4815/220/19.

[47] BR: Waterlow, Athens, 7 August 1936, R 4819/220/19.

[48] BR: FO Minutes, London, 29 March 1937, R 2296/349/19.

[49] BR: Vansittart, London, 25 May 1937, R 4073/2970/19.

[50] BR: Palairet, Athens, 7 July 1939, R 5532/46/19.

[51] US: MacVeagh, Athens, 18 February 1937, 868.00/1033.

[52] BR: Waterlow, Athens, 13 November 1936, R 7014/220/19.

[53] BR: Waterlow, Athens, 3 May 1937, R 3177/349/19.

[54] Metaxas, Ioannis, *To prosopiko tou imeroloyio*, (Athens: Govostis, not dated), p.553.

[55] *Ibid.* p. 299.

[56] Maniadakis-Himmler correspondence, May–November 1937, R 8049/2312/19.

[57] GR: Erbacht, Athens, 18 June 1937, 921/245327–28.

[58] BR: Waterlow, Athens, 10 January 1939, R 330/64/19.

[59] BR: Waterlow, Athens, 21 March 1938, R 3532/170/19.

[60] US: MacVeagh, Athens, 9 January 1939, 868.00/1068.

[61] BR: Waterlow, Athens, 18 December 1938, R 10301/726/19.

[62] BR: Waterlow, Athens, 1 December 1938, R 9819/726/19.

[63] Metaxas, *op.cit.*, p. 804.

[64] BR: Roberts, Athens, 31 July 1937, R 5224/349/19.

[65] Metaxas, *op.cit.*, p. 791.

[66] BR: Hopkinson, Athens, 2 November 1938, R 8839/169/19.

[67] *Völkischer Beobachter,* 25 September 1936.

[68] *Ethnos,* Athens, 14 October 1936.

[69] BR: Waterlow, Athens, 18 June 1937, R 4454/349/19.

[70] BR: Waterlow, Athens, 23 December 1937, R 8687/349/19.

[71] Metaxas, *op.cit.*, p. 553.

[72] *Ibid.,* pp. 862–66.

[73] GR: Kordt, Athens, 7 July 1937, 7869/570217–23.

[74] BR: Waterlow, Athens, 3 May 1937, R 3178/349/19.

[75] *Ibid.*

[76] BR: Waterlow, Athens, 8 December 1936, R 7731/220/19.

[77] BR: Waterlow, Athens, 23 February 1938, R 2102/726/19.

[78] BR: Sargent, London, 25 February 1938, R 1210/64/19.

[79] Metaxas, *op.cit.*, p. 321.

[80] US: MacVeagh, Athens, 22 January 1937, 868.00/1004.

[81] BR: Waterlow, Athens, 28 October 1936, R 6606/220/19.

[82] US: MacVeagh, Athens, 10 December 1937, 868.00/1024.

[83] BR: Levy, T., M. P., London, 5 March 1938, R 2096/726/19.

[84] US: MacVeagh, Athens, 25 July 1938, 868.00/1046.

[85] BR: Palairet, Athens, 19 July 1940, R 6807/118/19.

[86] GR: German S. D., Berlin, 20 December 1940, 863/285980–84.

[87] GR: Picot, Berlin, 14 January 1941, 863/285975–76.

[88] US: MacVeagh, At sea, July 19, 1941, 868.00/1124.

PART 6

FASCISM AND NATIONAL SOCIALISM IN THE NORDIC COUNTRIES

Stein Ugelvik Larsen   Introduction

Stein Ugelvik Larsen   The Social Foundations of Norwegian Fascism
                            1933–1945: An Analysis of Membership Data

Jan Petter Myklebust
and Bernt Hagtvet   Regional Contrasts in the Membership Base of the
                            Nasjonal Samling

Hans Hendriksen   Agrarian Fascism in Eastern and Western Norway:
                            A Comparison

Sten Sparre Nilson   Who Voted for Quisling?

Hans-Dietrich Loock   Support for *Nasjonal Samling* in the Thirties

Risto Alapuro   Mass Support for Fascism in Finland

Reijo E. Heinonen   From People's Movement to Minor Party: The
                            People's Patriotic Movement (IKL) in Finland
                            1932–1944

Henning Poulsen and
Malene Djursaa   Social Bases of Nazism in Denmark: The DNSAP

Bernt Hagtvet   On the Fringe: Swedish Fascism 1920–45

Asgeir Gudmundsson   Nazism in Iceland

Introduction

STEIN UGELVIK LARSEN

The Nordic countries constitute a distinct historical, cultural and geographical region within Europe. They also have a common ethnic background except for the Finnish people and the Lapp minorities in the far North. In many respects the study of fascism in the Nordic countries possesses a unique interest because of the stress upon the Nordic race, Nordic mythology and medieval (especially the Viking) culture in Nazi ideology. Since the Nordic emphasis was so central to fascist propaganda, it is of interest to see how native fascism developed in these countries. Studies of fascism in the Nordic countries acquire added interest because the domestic forces intent on furthering its growth can be seen more in their purity: all the countries were small nations that were not, except as strategic stepping stones, linked to the great powers on the continent and not really involved in the struggle for hegemony in the world arena. Outside of Finland, irredentism and imperialism were marginal both in their emergence and their varying success in obtaining wider support.

I shall here give a brief overview of five main factors in the Nordic countries relevant to the development of fascism. In this way I hope to provide a framework for explaining the formation and development of the various movements in the pre-war period. Such an overview is intended to give a general introduction to the Nordic scene, so providing the reader with the background necessary to appreciate the arguments of the following articles. A brief review of the case of Iceland is presented separately.

Constitutional Development

The steps in the constitutional development of the Nordic countries were very much dependent on how far the latter experienced large and lasting political unions with one another. The historical trend in nation-building can be divided into four stages: 1. From scattered petty kingdoms they developed into three nation-states in the eleventh and twelfth centuries (Finland as a unified part of Sweden and Iceland recognizing Norwegian supremacy); 2. In 1398 all three were united in a single political union with the Danish queen as the formally accepted head. 3. The break-up of this union occurred in phases, with Sweden seceding in 1521, and Norway finally in 1814 (though forming a new union with Sweden until 1905). Finland was handed over to Russia in 1809 after the Swedish defeat in the war, and political independence for Finland was established in 1917 after the Russian revolution. 4. By the end of World War I all four nation states had achieved national independence to become politically, economically and culturally sovereign states.

The overall trend in democratization and the introduction of parliamentary government developed very differently. Norway and Finland are the two extremes. The former developed as the earliest democratized nation in Scandinavia: an extended suffrage and a parliament *(Storting)* with wide powers were established in 1814, with full male suffrage coming in 1899, and female suffrage in 1913. The principle of parliamentary government was accepted as early as 1884. Finland, which enjoyed relative autonomy as a Russian province until 1898, did win a short-lived parliamentary and democratic constitution in 1906 after the first abortive revolution in Russia in 1905. Shortly afterwards Finland was again suppressed by the Russians and a fully democratized and parliamentary republic was finally introduced after the end of the civil war in May 1918. By the time both countries faced the threat of fascist movements in the twenties and early thirties, the Norwegian polity had experienced a long lived and stable governmental system, while Finland had just violently overcome forces which in the civil war had tried to destroy the system in order to establish a Finnish radical regime. These two different positions in constitutional and state development certainly gave fascism radically different opportunities for support.

In Denmark and Sweden the struggle for constitutional reforms in the early 19th century was very hard. In both countries it took more than 40 years after the first constitutional breakthrough – in Denmark in 1849 – and in Sweden in 1866 – before parliamentary and more democratic constitutions were established. In both countries the two-chamber assemblies were soon divided with a lower chamber striving for reform against an upper chamber resisting it. In Denmark liberal suffrage regulations had been enacted in 1849, but in 1866 the suffrage to the upper chamber was limited and representation was basically controlled by the King and a small section of the population. It was not until 1918 that full adult male suffrage was introduced. Parliamentary government was established in 1901, but even as late as 1920 the King tried to obstruct the system by extra-parliamentary mobilization against the cabinet.

The struggle for the democratic right to vote for parliamentary government in Sweden succeeded with the introduction of male suffrage in 1909 and for women in 1921. In 1906 the King appointed the first government based upon a parliamentary majority, but eight years later he acted against his government by openly criticizing the cabinet in a broadly based public meeting called to oppose the cabinet on principles of policy.

In this respect Denmark and Sweden followed a similar course in constitutional development. By the time fascist ideas entered the scene, far right-wing forces and conservative politics had become so stigmatized that they could not easily mobilize or enjoy a wider public appeal. There were no strong anti-democratic forces that could be mobilized behind a fascist revolution. The conservatives, having accepted reform, now focused on securing a liberal capitalist economy instead of trying to reverse the system of government.

If we compare the four nation-states and their long road to democratic and parliamentary government systems, it can be argued that Norway was the earliest to introduce political citizenship and the most gradualist and stable. Denmark and Sweden came in the middle as systems which developed slowly and with a stronger opposition to reform, while Finland was the least stable system with the shortest experience of democratic and parliamentary government in the Nordic countries, containing a high potential of defeated and frustrated people after the civil war of 1918.

The Importance of Nationalism

The nation-building processes within the Nordic countries took shape gradually inside or outside the various unions, and the sense of national identity and nationalism as a

587

political force was formed in line with the situation experienced by each country in the union. Finland and Norway developed the strongest nationalist ideas and nationalist movements, since each had been the weaker partner in various unions. As older, more imperialistically inclined countries, Denmark and Sweden could not mobilize people to fight for a special national identity in the same way. They forced or persuaded the other nations into the unions and strove to keep the latter effective.

When fascism came to Scandinavia, the flavor of nationalism was only one basic part of their ideology. However, in both Norway and Finland nationalism had been so integral to the political movements demanding democratic government and political independence that it could not so easily be turned into a new ideology that was not only anti-democratic, but also in some way part of a new scheme of comprehensive, foreign dominance from Germany. Nationalism in fascist ideology and propaganda had to go far beyond the ideas of the most nationalistic period in Finland and Norway (from the 1830's onwards) to seek inspiration from the old tribal and Viking periods. It was too difficult to attempt to build on the strong and well established nationalist ideology or to penetrate the organized movements which had brought so much success on questions of nationhood in Finland and Norway. The position in Finland on this issue was not the same as in Norway, since the civil war and the turmoil immediately afterwards did in some way provide extreme nationalistic forces with an opportunity to advance propaganda in favor of a «Greater Finland» extended eastwards. Extremist nationalism flourished much more freely in Finland than it ever did in Norway, and thus made for greater susceptibility to fascist appeals.

In Denmark nationalism developed in relation to the Schleswig-Holstein issue in 1864, 1918 and 1946. Many Danes wanted most of the two duchies to be integrated into the Danish state, and there was much agitation, especially in the neighboring districts in Jutland and in the two duchies themselves, for bringing the areas «home» to Denmark. However, the disputes were settled by international agreements and a referendum in 1920 which took most of the emotional strength away from any lasting nationalist claims. The puzzling problem for the fascists in Denmark was that they had their highest relative strength in Schleswig and the neighboring districts, – but the supporters of fascism were Danish nationalists and oriented towards Germany.

Sweden was the least nationalistic state. Since its great imperialist era before 1809, Sweden had taken a neutralistic attitude in international politics and withdrawn to her mainland. Swedish nationalism in the nineteenth century was directed against Norway, its fellow partner in the union. When the union was dissolved in 1905, there did not exist any sizeable nationalist claims to be pushed forward. The diplomatic quarrel over the Åland islands during 1917–22 and also during World War II, inspired some commitment to a nationalist cause, but it could not become a lasting issue after the international agreement over the neutral status of the islands had been arrived at in 1922, and confirmed in 1949.

Social Structure and the Economy

At the time of the great fascist successes in Continental Europe the Nordic societies were structurally rather different from each other. Today we find that they present a much more homogeneous picture, but during the inter-war years several structural changes took place.

Denmark was the most urbanized society followed by Sweden and Norway. In contrast, Finland was clearly the least developed nation with a high percentage of the population living outside the main towns. During the years when fascism was emergent, all four underwent structural changes with a relatively high rate of influx from countryside to town. This mobilization had started in the first years of the century, but its social effects were felt strongly when the economic crisis struck both the new immigrants in the towns, and the remaining population in the countryside.

During this period Sweden overtook Denmark to become the most highly industrialized of the Nordic countries; Norway experienced a very rapid industrial growth, not only in the first two decades in the century, but also in the 1930's. Finland also had a very rapid industrial growth from the early twenties and during the whole inter-war period. But Finland was the least industrialized and least modernized Nordic society.

As a cross-national impulse at a fixed point in time fascism therefore developed in a different setting in Finland compared to the other countries. We may also observe that it became a movement of a very different nature in its first effective years and it was most serious and also most savage in that least modernized country.

The Great Economic Crisis

Many writers exploring the background of the early development of fascism take the great crisis in the world economy as the most important single event in explaining the growth and success of such movements. The timing of the crisis and its effects on the support for fascism give an interesting, comparative perspective of the Nordic scene.

In all four countries the groups that were most severely hit by the crisis seem to have been the farmers and the industrial workers. There are no easily comparable data on the overall situation of the farmers, but the unemployment figures, which are limited to industrial and other workers, provide some clues as to the timing of the crisis and its culmination. We can see from the table below how unemployment figures in Norway and Sweden reached their peak two years after the peak in Finland, and Denmark one year after Finland.

Table 1. *Yearly Average of Unemployment**

	Denmark (per cent)	Finland (in thousands)	Norway (per cent)	Sweden (per cent)
1928	18		19	11
1929	16	23	15	10
1930	14	56	17	12
1931	18	88	22	17
1932	32	84	31	22
1933	29	42	33	23
1934	22	20	31	18
1935	20	18	25	15
1936	19	3	19	13

* Source: «Kriser og krispolitik i Norden under mellankrigstiden». Nordiska historikermøtet i Uppsala 1974. Møtesrapport. Uppsala 1974. s. 313. (Crises and Crisis Politics in the Nordic Countries in the Inter-War Period).

Thus the Finns first experienced the shock of the crisis and also immediately faced its fascist reaction in form of the Lapua movement. When the other countries entered their darkest years, the crisis may have been seen as part of a general international problem, and not one that could so easily be solved by an internal political turnover. Thus the extremist movements would have had less chance to win internal support for their cause.

In all countries the fascist movements gained some support among the farmers, who were most severely affected by the crisis. Very soon, however, there developed a close cooperation between the main Agrarian parties and the Social Democrats which averted a possible split between industrial workers and farmers on economic issues. The fascists could not therefore utilize the whole farming sector and the farming organizations as potential partners. Sweden, which had one of the strongest agrarian parties (Bondeförbundet) saw the least agrarian support for fascism. Nevertheless, the strongest initial support from any single occupational group seems to have come from the farmers in all four countries. This is reflected in the voting figures from farm areas and from party membership figures. Middle class groups of various kinds also joined the fascists in varying proportions all through the fascist era, but they were apparently not motivated by economic issues in the same way as the farmers and workers.

The Development of Communism and Social Democratic Politics

One main impulse to the stimulus of fascism in the twenties and the thirties was the development of international communism after 1917. Communism took a very different form in the various Nordic countries. Denmark and especially Sweden were marked by possessing, in the critical years of 1917–18, very stable and well organized Social Democratic party organizations, which even served in coalition governments with liberal or centrist parties. Shortly after the end of the war they also formed their own governments after successful electoral contests. This situation seems to have weakened the opportunity for a radicalization of these parties and the development of communism.

By contrast, Finland fought a civil war that was directly influenced by the Russian Revolution in 1917 and the close ties between Soviet communists and radical Social Democrats in Finland. Thus both the Finnish Communist party, which organized itself within Russia shortly after the war, and the Social Democrats were extremely discredited for a long time afterwards.

In Norway the Labor party was strongly radicalized both by previous internal (Fagopposisjonen av 1911 [Union opposition in 1911]) criticism as well as by the events in Russia, and a majority vote in the party led to the party's becoming a full member of the newly organized Communist International. This decision split the party: a small right wing fraction seceded in 1921 taking the name Norwegian Social Democratic party, leaving the majority to continue as the Labor party. The majority group stayed in the Third International until 1923 when it completely severed its ties with Moscow. A third group then seceded to form the Communist party. In 1927 the two first groups merged and gradually the united Norwegian Labor party began to follow the same tactics and program as its Social Democratic neighbors. In 1928 it formed its first, short-lived government, and after 1933 a stable Social Democratic policy was adopted as its platform.

590

Like Norway, the other Nordic countries experienced the split within the Social Democratic camp after 1917, but only in Finland did this split produce a very serious communist contender in the political system. The Danish and Swedish splinters never had any probability of success. In Norway the split within the Labor party was rapidly healed and the reversal in the attitude to the Third International was too strong to enable the communist commitment in the party to endure for any length of time. The small Norwegian Communist party did not therefore succeed in attracting any strong support among the working population in the twenties and thirties when it started out in 1923 as the only «pure» communist alternative.

Finland was different altogether. After 1918 communism became a lasting force in Finnish politics either as a non-resident Soviet organized fraction or as a party organization on Finnish territory. Both in terms of numerical size and also in terms of Moscow-tied revolutionarily oriented politics, it was always feared as a real revolutionary force in Finland. Thus fascist movements and fascist appeals could always count on anti-communism as a strong and living threat among the ordinary citizens. The Lapua movement from 1929 onwards was mainly an anti-communist movement with a policy directed towards prohibiting any communist activity, and in this they succeeded. In the other Nordic countries anti-communism could never attract such interest and fear, given the small and often fragmented nature of the communist parties. Some success was gained by the fascist parties in their anti-communist propaganda, but nothing that could compare with the easy mobilized antagonism in Finland.

Another important factor was the way the other parties took up the ideological and tactical fight with the communists on much the same scale as the fascists themselves. The communists, especially after the Strasbourg theses in 1928, regarded the Social Democrats as their main antagonists, and therefore did not leave the field open for the fascists to profit from being the only opponents to international communism and revolution.

This short description of five main factors in the development of the political and social systems of the Nordic countries can serve as a brief introduction to some of the main questions concerning variations in fascist success in this region. An outline of the factors is presented in the comparative table below.

The Situation in Iceland

Iceland is a small country which had only 70,000 inhabitants in 1930. This corresponds to 1.14 per cent of the population of Sweden (6,140,000 in 1930). In the same year the populations of the other Nordic countries were in Denmark 3,550,000, in Finland 3,460,000 and in Norway 2,815,000. The land area of Iceland is rather large. Except for the town of Reykjavik, the population is very scattered with many small, rural settlements.

In the 1930s the Icelandic economy was characterized by a low degree of industrialization, with production concentrated on the primary products of fishing and farming. The most important single export-product was fish, and lacking a domestic industrial base, Iceland inevitably became dependent on imports for a whole range of items. With one single export product, and with heavy imports, Iceland thus became strongly tied to developments in the international business cycles. As a consequence, when the crisis came in 1930, it hit the economy of Iceland severely, despite the country's low rate of industrialization and modernization.

	A Constitutional Development	B Special features of Nationalism	C Structure of Population and economy	D Timing and impact of the Economic Crisis	E Development of Communism and Social Democratic Politics
Denmark	Continuity in state- and nation building since 11th century. Estate assembly and first constitution in 1849. Revised constitution in 1864. Strong First Chamber. Adult male suffrage in 1849, restricted in 1864. General male and female suffrage in 1915. Parliamentarism in 1901. King's effort to disrupt parliamentarism in 1920. New effective constitution from 1953.	Strong nationalist period from 1834 to 1864. Effort to integrate Schleswig and Holstein ending in defeat. Strong nationalist movement in 1918–1920 when North Schleswig became a part of the Danish state, after a referendum. Renewed nationalism in 1948 on issue of integrating South Schleswig. Danish minority in German South Schleswig and in Holstein in 1930: 8.000. German minority in Danish North Schleswig in 1930: 20–25.000.	1930– 35 % in primary sector 1930– 57 % in rural areas 1930–27 % in industry.	Peak of unemployment in 1932. Three years of highest unemployment 1932–1933–1934. Protest party Agrarian protest party (Landbrukernes sammenslutning) formed in 1935. Dansk samling (Danish Unity) formed 1939. Economic agreement on crisis management 1933. (Kanslergadeforliget) among Social Democrats. Venstre (liberals) and Radicals.	First Communist party formed in 1919. Various splits in 1925/1926. Communist voting strength in 1929: 0.2, 1932:1.4, 1935:1,4. Social Democrats first organized 1876. First social Democratic minister (in coalition) 1916. First Social Democratic Government 1924 Social Democratic strength in 1929: 41.8, 1939: 41.9. 1935: 45.9.
Finland	Political union and part of Swedish kingdom until 1809. Province under Russia until 1917. Independent nation state from 1917. Estate assembly and constitution in 1809. Effective estate and political representation from 1866. Parliament and constitution in 1906. Suffrage for men and women 1906. Parliamentarism from 1906, not effective before 1918. New effective constitution from 1918. Changed in 1944.	Strong particularist Finnish national movement beginning in 1839. Partly anti-Russian (especially from 1899) and basically anti-Swedish. Strong Swedish nationalism (as minority) to counteract Finnification. Merging of the two from 1899 until 1917. Greater Finland movement in 1918–20. Strong anti-Swedish nationalism 1935–39. Russian minority in Finland: 8.216 (0.24 per cent) Finnish minority in Russia in 1930: 2.984.800 (1926: Finnish relatives): Swedish minority in Finland in 1930: 342.916(10.1 per cent).	1930 69% in primary section 1930– No information on rural areas. 1930– 15% in industry.	Peak of unemployment 1931. Three years of highest unemployment 1930–1931–1932. Protest parties Lapua Movement from 1929. Continued as the IKL movement after 1933. 3–4 smaller protest parties in the thirties. No specific political agreement on solution of economic crisis.	First Finnish Communist party formed in Russia 1918. No later splits or fractions in the party. Voting strength of Communists before the anti-communist act in 1927:12.1, 1929:13.5, 1930:1.0. Social Democrats first organized in 1903. First Social Democratic government 1927. Stable Social Democratic coalitions partners in Government 1937. Social Democratic strength 1927: 28.3, 1929: 27.4, 1930: 34.2, 1933: 37.3.
Norway	Political union with Denmark until 1814. Political union with Sweden until 1905. Independent nation-state from 1905. Parliament and constitution in 1814 – still in force. Liberal male suffrage in 1814. Male suffrage in 1899. Female suffrage in 1913. Parliamentarism in 1884.	Strong particularist nationalist movement from 1830s. In the beginning partly anti-Danish influence, and prolonged efforts to establish own national identity culturally. Later anti-Swedish and with other nationalists merging as a general independence movement from 1890–1905. Greater Norwegian sentiments in 1920/30 to extend jurisdiction in arctic fields (Greenland). Nationalism revived as mutual dominance/ equalization-movement after 1905 between nynorsk and bokmål contenders. 1930: nynorsk minority ca. 20 per cent.	1930– 37% in primary section. 1930– 72% in rural areas 1930– 25% in industry.	Peak of unemployment 1933. Three years of highest unemployment 1932–1933–1934. Protest parties Bygdefolkets Krisehjelp (Farmers Relief Association) formed in 1933. Close cooperation with the Nazi party in 1933. Samfunnspartiet (Social Consciousness) 1933. Economic agreement on crisis policy in 1935 between Social Democrats and Agrarian party (kriseforliket).	First Communist party formed in 1923. Norwegian Labor Party (later Social Democrats) attached to Communist International from 1919 to 1923. Communist voting strenght 1930: 1.7, 1933: 1.8, 1936: 0.3. Social Democrat labor party formed 1887. First Social Democratic government from 1928 (28 days only). Stable Social Democratic government from 1935. Social democratic strength 1930: 31.4, 1933: 40.1, 1936: 42.5.
Sweden	Political union with Denmark/Norway until 1521. Independent nation-state from 1523. Estate assembly and constitution in 1809. Restricted manhood suffrage 1866. Male and female suffrage in 1918. Parliamentarism from 1906. King's effort to disrupt parliamentarism in 1914. New constitution from 1974.	General support for Swedish minorities in Finland in eighteenth century. Strong mobilization in Sweden for Swedish speaking population on Åland islands in 1917–1920, and also during Second World War.	1930– 37% in primary section 1930– 68% in rural areas 1930–31% in industry.	Peak of unemployment in 1933. Three years of highest unemployment 1932–1933–1934. Protest parties: Several minor fascist groups. Economic agreement on crisis politics in 1935 between Social Democrats and Agrarian party.	First Communist party formed 1917. Various splits etc. in 1921, 1924, 1929, 1934. Communist voting strength 1928: 6.4. 1932: 8.3, 1936: 3.3. Social Democratic party formed in 1889. First Social Democratic minister (in coalition) 1918. First Social Democratic government in 1920. Social Democratic strenght 1928: 37.0, 1932: 41.7, 1936: 45.9.

Politically Iceland was tied to the Danish system of government, but had gradually achieved semi-independent status. First in regard to economic policy in 1883, and then culturally by establishing its own university in 1911. Finally, during World War I Iceland became isolated from Denmark and enjoyed actual independence for four years. This resulted in the status of 1918 which gave Iceland almost complete sovereignty except in foreign policy matters. Iceland had been first united with Norway until 1398, then with Norway-Denmark until 1814. It won complete freedom as late as 1944, – in another phase of de facto separation from Denmark as a consequence of World War II.

Iceland claims to have the oldest enduring parliament in the world dating from 930 A.D.. The *Allting* has functioned more or less continuously and with varying degrees of power since then. But it was only in the mid-nineteenth century that national politics came to revolve around specific contents: political parties date from that period. In 1903 parliamentarism was introduced in Icelandic politics, and «normal» political democracy developed within the limits set by the Union with Denmark.

In 1916 the Social Democratic party was formed. The communist split followed in 1930. Surprisingly, the communist alternative experienced a rapid growth, and very soon it was able to compete in strength with the Social Democratic party. The other parties, *Selvstendighetspartiet* and *Framstegspartiet*, (The Independence Party and The Progress Party) are the two larger parties, respectively, resembling a liberal/conservative nationalist party, and an agrarian nationalist party elsewhere in the Nordic area. In relative strength the combined Communist and Social Democratic parties never gained a position approximating the strength of their counterparts in the other Nordic countries. The basis for Social Democratic trade-union and communist class-struggle politics was smaller in Iceland than in the other Nordic countries because industry was already to a high degree state-owned, or cooperatively-owned, and there was a relatively low proportion of people employed in industry.

Given this background, one would not expect to find an atmosphere conducive to fascist success. However, as Gudmundson's article shows, we find the familiar ideological components present in the Icelandic fascist party, and an actual fascist movement having its ups and downs. Anti-communism, racism, nationalism, anti-parliamentarism, state power etc. were used as slogans by Icelandic fascists. The failure to become a real threat or challenge to the Icelandic system of politics has, however, to be explained by much the same factors as have been relevant for the other Nordic and European countries that saw the emergence of small and fragmented fascist movements.

In the first article on Nazism in Norway Stein Ugelvik Larsen examines the total recruitment process to the *Nasjonal Samling* and analyzes the timing and growth of the party. The next article by Jan Petter Myklebust and Bernt Hagtvet examines the regional distribution of the NS and the historical determinants of this development. This article is followed by contributions by Hans-Dietrich Loock, Sten Sparre Nilson and Hans Hendriksen who try to explore how local factors determined the success of the NS before and during the war. In their article on Denmark, Henning Poulsen and Malene Djursaa discuss the growth of Danish Nazism in the countryside and the towns and show how it never won any appreciable support outside the capital and the border areas with Germany. Its failure to gain political power in the war years is also clearly documented. Risto Alapuro shows how the Lapua movement first won support in a specific region in Finland before spreading into other areas. He also describes how this most important of the fascist movements in the Nordic countries acquired its mass support. The continuer of fascism in Finland after the Lapua movement was the IKL-party (The Fatherland Movement) along with the Academic Karelia Society. The IKL is analyzed and described by Reijo Heinonen who points out some of the determinants of its recruitment strength and its political achievements.

Sweden did not experience any important fascist movement at all. Numerous small and short-lived groups did emerge, but they never won any serious backing from the people. Bernt Hagtvet gives a description of the various parties and movements in Sweden and offers some explanations why fascism failed completely. In the final article Asgeir Gudmundson illustrates the kind of fascism which emerged in Iceland, – the small inhabited island far out in the North Atlantic. This article demonstrates how fascism as an international impulse spread even to the most peripheral country of Europe.

The Social Foundations of Norwegian Fascism 1933–1945

An Analysis of Membership Data

STEIN UGELVIK LARSEN

Introduction

In this study I will survey the recruitment of members to the Norwegian Nazi Party, the Nasjonal Samling* (NS) over the entire period of its existence (1933–45). I will describe the socio-economic *background* of its membership, trace the *growth* of the membership and demonstrate how at different stages in the life of the party, before and after the German occupation of Norway, *various social groups were recruited disproportionately to their relative size in the Norwegian population*. In the second section I will give a summary of the two waves of mobilization into the party. The third section analyzes the age and sex composition of the NS over time. The fourth part of the paper describes how, after an Oslo-based upper-middle class nucleus had founded the party, the lower classes gradually swelled the ranks. The final section reports some findings from a post-war survey on individual motivations for becoming a member of the NS.[1]

In this book we have used the terms «fascism» and «fascist» to describe a wide variety of ideas, tendencies, parties and movements which themselves neither used this term in their party name, nor described themselves as such. Thus we use the term «fascist party» of the Nasjonal Samling, even if Quisling himself, the NS leader, once positively declared that he was *not* a fascist, but a Norwegian nationalist.[2] The concept of fascism would also have been a strange concept for many of the rank and file members of the Nasjonal Samling. But, in order to be able to generalize across all the diversified parties and movements in Europe which apparently were aiming at roughly the same political goal during the fascist epoch – and which to a large extent utilized the same set of ideas and methods, we will use the concept of fascist party when analyzing the NS in Norway from 1933 to 1945. This does not mean that we accept that the NS was completely similar to all the European parties of the fascist kind; but at a minimum it was similar to such parties on some crucial points of comparison, having e.g. adopted some of its party program and organizational structure from the NSDAP. For a more extensive discussion of the common concept of fascism we refer the reader to the theoretical section.

The study of fascist movements and parties has for a long time been dominated by what may be described as the «voter-approach». In most studies of this kind the analysis has concentrated upon the kind of people who *voted* for the various fascist parties in *normal elections* either before a fascist takeover of government or before the outbreak of war. Such studies formulate theories of the fascist potential in terms of the conditions under which certain parts of the electorate will prefer a fascist government. But it may not be correct to designate an average voter for a fascist party at one election as a typical fascist. By the term fascist I rather mean a person who is a member of a fascist party and as a member carries out propaganda or other kinds of political activity on its behalf.

* In English normally rendered as 'National Unity' or 'National Unification'. – i.e. the opposite of the devisive effect of the presence of competing political parties or deepened class cleavage.

595

Thus, in the study of fascism, it is important to differentiate between studies which try to formulate theories or generalizations concerning the potential for fascist support, and studies which try to formulate generalizations about potential fascists proper. In the Norwegian project we found that there were many fascist voters who later became party members, but the material also revealed that a considerable number of people who later became NS members had previously given their vote to other parties.[3] However, many of the fascist members were recruited from the same contextual environments from which the party gained its strongest support before the war: thus there is an indirect connection between the potential for fascist support and the potential for fascist membership.

In our study of such phenomena we therefore found it illuminating also to confront our findings on the national level with the microstudies carried out in different local constituencies and on different material as a part of the Bergen Project on the Nasjonal Samling.[4] Some of these findings are reported in Hendriksen's chapter and the other Norwegian contributions to this volume.

In general, for most of the countries in Europe which during the war experienced fascist regimes or fascist collaboration of some kind, and for countries which early suppressed their fascist alternative, there exist vast archives and documentary material on individual membership which either are available or will become so in the near future. The main problem will be to secure complete access to the documents (and possibly also to be able to inverview some of the former fascist members who are still alive), and when faced with the vast numbers involved, to have sufficient resources to work efficiently with the files. Fascist movements were treated as parties of a revolutionary or treasonable character. As such, information on them was gathered and stored for use in court proceedings or in various administrative tribunals that might deny ex-members certain citizens' rights. No other kind of political party has ever been investigated or has experienced systematic registration on such a large comparative scale as the fascist parties. Not even the communist groups or parties, when treated as potential revolutionaries, have been so well documented. The potential for comparable membership studies in the future has thus by no means been exhausted.

In Norway we were able to plan a complete membership study of the NS after obtaining access to material from the trials of NS members after the liberation. Due to far-reaching legal provisions of the Norwegian government in exile in London, all actual and many previous NS-members were closely scrutinized by the police and the courts. Under these provisions membership in the NS was subject to a sentence ranging from a fine to lengthy imprisonment for the most active.[5]

From information in the vast archives, we have built a comprehensive file of the entire membership stock based on standardized information concerning the social background of information and we were able to conduct various kinds of statistical analyses on the NS party members, as well as analyzing the membership stock in relation to their social environment. By using standardized files of data from the Official Bureau of Statistics we can trace these social groups in the various regions of the country, and over the periods in which the NS enjoyed its greatest success.[6]

Since none of the authors who have contributed to this book were able to build their studies on such complete membership material, it is our hope that, on the basis of this comprehensive material, we might in the future be able to join with similar large projects in other European countries. With such comparative projects we should be able to generalize on a more firm basis how such movements attracted their support. It is of particular importance to analyze developments in the parties over time, since what made someone a fascist varied considerably from the early days, through the periods of opportunism, to the last-ditch enrolments when there were no signs of victory but only plain signs of dissolution and defeat.

In this chapter we try to give neither a broad description of the history of the NS, nor any kind of extensive theoretical treatment of the analyses. For more details on the history of the NS we also refer to the broad outlines of Norwegian historical research on this period, and to the articles in this book on recruitment to the NS in local areas in Norway.[7]

Recruitment Trends: The Two Waves of Mobilization

Nasjonal Samling (NS) was founded on May 17, 1933 (Norway's National Day, the anniversary of the Constitution of 1814), a decade after its Italian counterpart and a few months after Hitler's accession to power in Germany. The depression, as measured in numbers of bankruptcies, foreclosures, and unemployed had reached its peak late in 1932/early 1933, but the consequences of the economic crisis were still being felt, especially in the countryside.

At first the establishment of the party was greeted with great enthusiasm, and the General Secretary later said that the first organized recruitment was simply a result of presenting the first ideas about the party in public.[8] In the first years the organization was fairly loose. Quisling himself stayed rather aloof from day-to-day affairs. The organizational talent in the party belonged to Quisling's close companion, the Oslo lawyer Johan B. Hjort. His main strategy was to present the NS as a new party alternative, and he energetically wrote articles on reasons why he thought certain occupational groups should support the NS.[9] Special attention was focused on the middle classes, i.e. farmers, fishermen with their own boat, artisans and smaller businessmen. Hjort explicitly stated that a people who wanted to survive had to take care of its middle class:

> «It not only provides the healthy economic foundation for the people, but it is also the class that fosters the leader each nation must have.»[10]

The number of registered members in the NS was always reported by the party in a way that created doubts about the accuracy of the numbers. In 1935, just before the annual rally in Hafrsfjord, the party newspaper reported that there were 15,000 registered members in the party.[11] Later, however, the headquarter stated that the party had only 8,542 members in 1935/36.[12] Even with the easing of the depression there remained much frustration and discontent that could be and was utilized by the NS for propaganda recruitment appeals. In the months after its founding, the NS was able to run an election campaign that brought it 27,850 votes in the general election to the Storting in October 1933. These votes comprised only 2.23 per cent of the total poll, but were regarded as an exceptional gain after so little preparation.

In some rural areas, as well as in some towns, the party gained quite strong support. For this early stage of the party's development we can map out regional contrasts in its support, contrasts which later became even more accentuated (see map 1 on the percentage of votes for the party in 1933). In 27 of the 330 voting districts contested (approximately one-half of the constituencies) the party won more than 10 per cent of the votes cast, several of these in joint lists with *Bygdefolkets krisehjelp* (Farmers' Relief Association).[13] Some of these districts also remained strongholds of the party during the war.

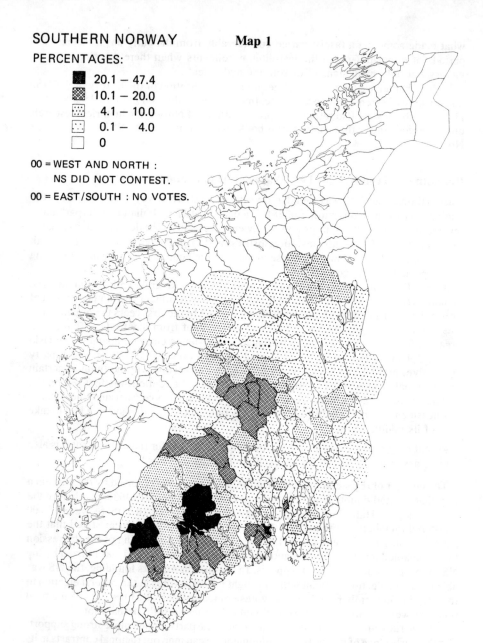

SOUTHERN NORWAY   **Map 1**

PERCENTAGES:

- ■ 20.1 – 47.4
- ▨ 10.1 – 20.0
- ▦ 4.1 – 10.0
- ⬚ 0.1 – 4.0
- ☐ 0

00 = WEST AND NORTH :
    NS DID NOT CONTEST.

00 = EAST/SOUTH : NO VOTES.

GENERAL ELECTION 1933:
PERCENTAGE OF VOTES FOR NASJONAL SAMLING

NOTE: IN SOME PROVINCES COOPERATION WITH
THE EMERGENCY AID FOR THE RURAL PEOPLES' MOVEMENT.

Norwegian Social Science Data Services.

The next test, the local elections in October 1934, did not, however, sustain the hopes for rapid growth: the party won 16,130 votes, equaling only 1.5 per cent of the total number of votes cast. The general election of 1936 was regarded as a challenge for the NS, since by then the party headquarters should have had sufficient time and experience to spread the party's message more effectively. But it won only 26,577 votes or 1.83 per cent of the poll, a heavy disillusionment both for Vidkun Quisling himself, who had hoped to win a seat in the capital, and also for the rest of the members. Soon afterwards internal disputes in the party erupted, leading to a major confrontation between Quisling and his second in command, the lawyer J. B. Hjort. After attempts at reconciliation had failed, the latter, accompanied by many others, left the party. In its last election – the 1937 local election – the party did not put up lists in many communes, and polled only 1,422 votes corresponding to 0.06 per cent of the poll. Only the most ardent supporters around Quisling kept up their spirits and sustained the idea of an organization intact. The next electoral fight should have taken place in 1940: with the coming of war this opportunity never arose.

If the figure of 8,542 is accepted as the membership total in 1935/36 our number of about 2,200 in Fig. 1 is clearly too low. The pre-war membership in our data-file is clearly less than the party's total estimates, but the trend in timing of enrolment, as illustrated in Fig. 1, is reasonably accurate. It shows that the NS secured a high proportion of its pre-war members in its first three years. Thereafter, the curve flattens out and approaches a level of about 2,200 in 1936 with almost no entries afterwards.

If the other 6,000 estimated members did not join in a very different way, we may regard the recruitment process as a sudden wave, rising from nothing in 1933, and culminating after 1934/35.[14]

If it is true that the membership level reached its peak at 8,542, the Norwegian politicians should have had no fears of this anti-democratic alternative. After Quisling's negotiations with Hitler and Rosenberg in Berlin in the autumn and winter of 1939, the situation was definitely altered. From then on, financial support for the party started to flow from foreign sources, and a new wave of mobilization was prepared.[15]

The German occupation of Norway began on the morning of April 9, 1940, and at noon when the Germans had assumed control in Oslo, Quisling supposedly on his own initiative, established a National Socialist (NS) government and appealed over the German controlled radio in Oslo to the Norwegian forces asking them to surrender. He tried to exploit the chaotic situation of the first week, but on April 15, he was replaced by a German appointed Reichskommissar Joseph Terboven, who took over the civil administration. The first attempt to put the NS in power by *putschist* tactics thus failed, but during the following spring and summer-months the party membership slowly began to grow.

After negotiations between the new Reichskommissar and the remaining administrative and political leadership in Norway broke down on September 25, 1940, the NS was declared to be the only legal political party – to be the only road to political power along with the German controlling forces.[16]

Immediately thereafter there began a rapid and accelerating expansion of NS membership. Within three or four months the party had acquired more members than it had votes before the war. After a short set-back in February 1941, during the German state of emergency, recruitment to the NS grew steadily. In 1941 the NS could also claim that it compared in actual membership with the size of the two or three largest Norwegian parties before the war.[17] Using this comparison, it tried to present itself as a power-base for establishing a genuine Norwegian National Socialist Government, supported, or tolerated, by the Germans. The «State Act» of February 1, 1942, gave legal status to such a government official by appointing Quisling 'Minister-president» and head of a NS-government.

However, the Germans never permitted the experiment to go too far: the general steering of the country remained totally in the hands of the military and the civil German authorities. When the Germans' various setbacks in the war became known, and the hopes for some real elements of independent, NS-self-government were broken, the recruitment wave started to recede. After the summer of 1943 the number of new entrants did not match up to the number leaving the party, and the NS started a process of slow decline. There was no mass exodus, partly because there was «nowhere else to go», since the social milieu for long had stigmatized all NS people, and also because their stubbornness and pride, as well as their ideological commitment, seems to have kept them on the sinking ship.

The second wave of recruitment thus ended in 1943. There would never be another chance.

From Fig. 1 we can see the overall recruitment trend of the NS. For the years before the war we have plotted the estimated membership at two points in time and the number of votes at the two general and two local elections. From September 1940 we have plotted four curves. Pi describes the information given by the official party sources on the size of the adult membership, and gives the actual membership when resignations are taken into account. PiT plots the party information on adult party membership plus the members of the youth and child organizations. BP is the curve drawn from the data in the Bergen Project. Finally there is a cumulative curve giving only new entrants without subtracting the people who left the party. NST (NS-total) assigns the maximum total of all those calculated by the Bergen Project as members of NS from 1933 to 1945.

Let us summarize some of the steps in the recruitment process. The NS developed from a party with no members to one of some size in 1935–36. Let us call this phase the «nationalist fascist» period. During this phase the party grew out of a mixed set of problems connected with economic crisis, a lost faith in the traditional party system and parliamentarism, and fears of communism. The period is also characterized by a set of vague ideas of nationalism with regard to recovery of «lost territories» in Greenland which since the dissolution of the union with Denmark in 1814 had been left to Danish control.

The next phase may be described as the «national socialist» period and it shows the NS in decline and (late in 1939) seeking contact with Germany and thus preparing for its role under a possible occupation. This period is the more typical Nazi period. The party's ideas and propaganda took a more anti-Semitic turn and the leaders seem to have been strongly influenced by German models and by the NSDAP.

The third phase from 1940 until the culmination of membership recruitment in 1943 is the real «revolutionary» period. Under the circumstances many Norwegians turned to the party as a plausible alternative during the events of the first war-years. In the turmoil created in Norway by the war and afterwards by the often vague lines of resistance and continued war effort by the Norwegian government in exile, the NS gained a heavy inflow of new members and soon intimated to the Germans that they wanted to take on a revolutionary role on behalf of the Norwegian people.

The last phase from 1943 until the end of the war on May 8, 1945, is a period of slow

Fig. 1.

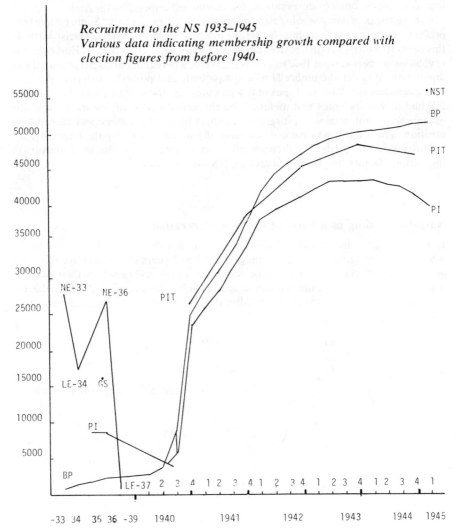

Recruitment to the NS 1933–1945
Various data indicating membership growth compared with
election figures from before 1940.

NE 33/36: National Elections in 1933 and in 1936.
LE 34/37: Local Elections in 1934 and in 1937.
GS   : The NS-Secretary General's estimates by 1935.
PI   : Data from Party information on actual membership (withdrawals excluded).
PIT   : Data from Party information on actual membership with the Youth organization
          included (withdrawals excluded).
BP   : Data from the Bergen Project.
NST   : NS total membership as cumulative figure with withdrawals included. (In 1945
          added all members with no information on data of entry.)

decline and also the phase in which Quisling and his associates produced their most ingenious plans, born of desperation, for staving off impending disaster.

Can we speak of *one genuine fascist* party during all these years? Some people may prefer to designate the first phase as the one in which we have a typical fascist party. In this period it won its maximum strength under «normal» circumstances. However, the revolutionary period from 1940 to 1945 is the phase where the real fascist potential was demonstrated under the umbrella of a sympathetic and powerful external ally.

We can thus speak of two types of fascist potential: the *normal* potential when the NS had to win its votes and members on the general political «market», and the *extraordinary* potential when it recruited people by having a monopoly recruitment position, and when it was backed economically and militarily by the Germans.

Both fascist potentials have their specific points of interest, and we shall now turn to the various factors involved in analyzing NS membership.

Nasjonal Samling as a Party of the New Generation

In Fig. 2 we have drawn a curve showing percentages of the total recruitment to the NS for different age cohorts. The youngest are 5 to 7 years old: at that age boys and girls were enrolled in the *Småhird* (the equivalent to Hitler-Jugend) by their parents. The curve has a sharp rise between those aged 13–15 to those aged 18–22. Then there is a rapid decline to the 28–45 age group. After the age of 45 the curve gradually declines.

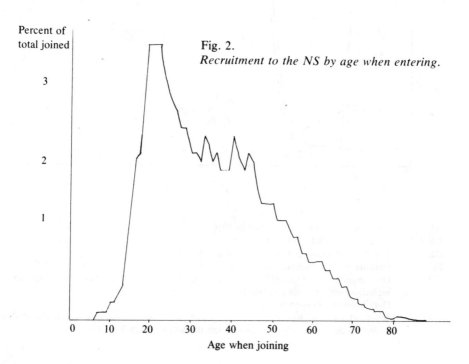

Fig. 2.
Recruitment to the NS by age when entering.

Percent of total joined

Age when joining

Table 1. Recruitment to CNS by age and time

Year joined	1870/79	1880/89	1890/99	1900/09	1910/19	1920/29	1930	Year of birth not known	Total
1933	71	128	199	268	149	5	0	24	844
	2.7	2.4	2.2	2.4	1.1	0	0	2.5	1.5
1934	41	81	116	198	172	31	0	17	656
	1.6	1.5	1.3	1.8	1.2	0.3	0	1.5	1.2
1935	10	24	61	102	112	33	0	10	352
	0.4	0.5	0.7	0.9	0.8	0.3	0	1.1	0.6
1936	20	48	56	129	161	58	0	4	476
	0.8	0.9	0.6	1.1	1.2	0.5	0	0.4	0.9
1937	2	2	8	8	18	10	0	0	48
	0.1	0.0	0.1	0.1	0.1	0.1	0		0.1
1938	1	3	9	9	8	17	0	1	48
	0.0	0.1	0.1	0.1	0.1	0.2	0	0.1	0.1
1939	2	3	10	16	26	63	0	1	121
	0.1	0.1	0.1	0.1	0.2	0.6	0	0.1	0.2
1933–39	147	289	459	730	646	217	0	45	2,537
	5.5(5.8)*	5.5(11.4)	5.0(18.1)	6.5(28.8)	4.6(25.5)	1.9(8.6)	0	5.7(1.8)	4.6
1940	1,153	2,543	4,560	5,369	5,853	2,635	146	291	22,448
	43.8(5.1)	48.5(11.3)	49.9(23.5)	46.7(23.5)	42.5(26.1)	23.4(11.7)	29.4(0.7)	37.0(1.3)	41.1
1941	624	1,166	1,956	2,436	3,182	3,096	181	218	12,859
	23.7	22.2	21.4	21.6	23.1	27.5	36.5	27.1	23.5
1942	433	807	1,385	1,723	2,475	2,847	88	134	9,892
	16.4	15.4	15.2	15.3	18.0	25.3	17.7	16.7	18.1
1943	144	233	384	446	682	1,040	26	55	3,010
	5.5	4.3	4.2	4.0	5.0	9.2	5.2	8.1	5.5
1944	46	71	127	139	269	492	12	23	1,179
	1.7	1.4	1.4	1.2	2.0	4.4	2.4	2.9	2.2
1945	4	6	15	81	76	142	11	0	335
	0.2	0.1	0.2	0.7	0.6	1.3	2.2		0.6
1941–45	1,251	2,283	3,867	4,825	6,684	7,617	318	430	27,275
	47.1(4.6)	43.5(8.4)	42.3(14.2)	42.8(17.7)	48.5(24.5)	67.6(27.9)	64.1(1.2)	54.8(1.6)	49.9
Year joined not known	102	131	255	458	591	805	32	19	2,391
	4.0	2.5	2.8	4.0	4.3	7.1	6.5	2.6	4.2
Total	2,653	5,246	9,141	11,282	13,774	11,274	496	785	54,651
	100%	100%	100%	100%	100%	100%	100%	100%	100%
	4.9	9.6	16.7	20.6	25.2	20.6	0.9	1.4	

If we compare these data with the general trend in turnout at normal elections we know that high mobilization among people between 30 and 50 is a typical feature of all elections. There is usually lower participation among those aged under 30 years or over 45. In view of this general pattern the most striking success in the case of the NS was its high rate of mobilization among the «new generation», i.e. people in their late teens and early twenties.

There is no doubt that the NS was able to attract a lot of young previously non-mobilized people to an extent unknown among other Norwegian political parties. In this respect it resembles most of the fascist movements elsewhere in Europe.

However, the recruitment of youth to the NS was very much dependent upon the actual political situation at the time. The younger age groups came to the party later than older groups. This is illustrated in table 1 which gives the chronological development of the party since 1933 and the age distribution of the party membership in three intervals 1933–39, 1940 and 1941–45. In the 1933–39 period 1.9 per cent of the people born between 1920 and 1930 had joined the party (some had to be very young). In 1940, 11.7 per cent of this group had joined, while as many as 67.6 per cent joined between 1941 and 1945. For the older groups born before 1920, the chronological sequence of entry is not very different from the overall entrance rate.

Consequently we can establish that the NS secured its strongest support among young people, and that they came to the party later than the older members. The adults can be said to have formed the NS in Norway, and then mobilized the younger to support it. If we look at the question of who in the young generation came first, we find a marked contrast between the sexes, as Fig. 3 clearly demonstrates. Here we have drawn one curve for men and one for women, describing the chronological development of the total number of persons entering the party at three-monthly intervals from the pre-war period and throughout the war. The graph shows that a much higher proportion of men than of women acceded to the party in the early period, while the recruitment among women is higher than the recruitment of men for the whole period of the war after the first quarter of 1941. The high peak for recruitment of women in the first part of 1942 is a typical example of time-lag in the process of mobilization.

This effect is even more pronounced when recruitment is aggregated to three periods of time as shown in table 2.

Table 2. *Members in the NS according to time of joining by sex and party leadership*

Time of joining	Men	Women	Total	Party leaders
Joined before April 1940	5.8	3.4	4.9	46.3
Joined later in 1940.............................	49.1	25.3	41.0	42.9
Joined 1941–1945................................	45.0	71.3	54.1	10.8
(and no inf.)				
Sum	100%	100%	100%	100%
N	35,568	19,083	54,651	250

The table clearly confirms the trend described above. Before the end of 1940, 54.9 per cent of all men who were to join had already registered, as compared to 28.7 per cent of women members. The table also shows an interesting trend with regard to the

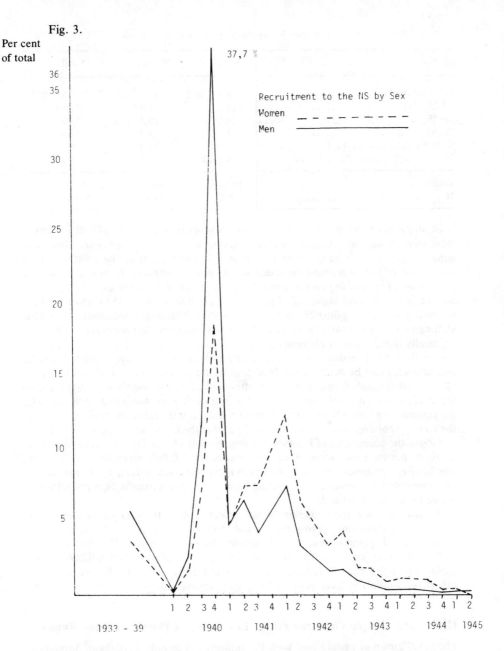

Fig. 3.

Per cent of total

37,7 %

Recruitment to the NS by Sex

Women – – – – – – –

Men ─────────

1933 - 39   1940   1941   1942   1943   1944   1945

party leadership: 46.3 per cent had joined the party before the war and another 42.9 per cent became members in 1940, leaving only 10.8 per cent of the party leadership to be recruited after 1940 as against 50.1 per cent of the total membership.

One very interesting fact about this sex difference in the recruitment process is the difference in the age structure at the time of joining:

Table 3. *Age when joining by sex*

	Men		Women		Total	
18 or younger..........................	8.4	28.2	11.8	37.7	9.6	30.5
19–25	19.8		25.9		21.9	
26–35	21.9		20.5		21.4	
36–50	27.5		24.5		26.5	
Over 50	17.9		13.9		16.2	
N.i	4.5		4.0		4.2	
Totals	100%		100%		100%	
N	35,568		19,083		54,651	

Of all members 9.6 per cent were below 18 years of age at time of entry: most of these were members of the *Småhird*. Almost one third, 17,222 people joined the party before their 25th birthday. Remarkable in this connection is the relatively high proportion of young women recruited to the party compared to young men. The percentage of men of 18 years or less is 8.4 per cent while the corresponding figure for women is 3.4 per cent higher: 37.7 per cent of the women were 25 years or younger when they joined as against 28.2 per cent of the men. This might be connected with the shifting profile of the party from the early thirties onwards. At later stages of the war, politically inexperienced elements joined the party.

Why the NS succeeded in mobilizing many of the previously non-mobilized females and juveniles can be briefly explained first by its novel, radical and revolutionary appeal, and secondly by more «hard» or «trivial» factors. Among these we will mention the effect of growing isolation of whole families during the war when stigmatized by the surrounding non-NS, or growing anti-NS-milieu. If the father or mother, and even the younger children became members– the rest of the family lost their social contacts and found the acceptance of NS-membership the only channel for contact with others. Thus one person's enrolment in the party forced other family members to follow suit. The family-recruitment mechanism, which is normally less effective, is important in explaining why the young, those getting on in years, and a usually high proportion of women became mobilized.

We have also pointed to one immediate effect, namely the way young women and also, for other reasons, young men found their way into the NS by virtue of the immediate and appealing presence of German soldiers in Norway. The German forces in Norway were numerically large and impressed people by their military organization and efficiency. This both frightened and attracted many Norwegians who otherwise would not have bothered engaging themselves in any political activity.

High Status People Form the Party, Lower Status People «Fill the Ranks»

The small group of people who took the initiative of founding *Nasjonal Samling* in 1933 were largely drawn from what are traditionally called the middle and higher strata of Norwegian society. Quisling himself was a retired officer in the Norwegian army, and some of the others were businessmen able to provide a certain, though not very substantial, financial support to the organization. Among the founding fathers we find typical middle class people, and few, if any, workers.[18] Unlike their counterparts in

Italy and Germany, and some of the other fascist movements in Europe, the NS did not try to exploit working class potential or actively seek to attract people from that segment, nor did it grow out of a concern with the plight of the working class.[19] Ideological statements before and after the formal constitution of the party clearly reveal the authoritarian, corporative and nationalistic sentiments which formed its platform. Its appeal was directed to those groups which held the same ideals, particularly farmers and «responsible people» like policemen, military officers, doctors as well as active representatives of Norwegian culture and society: teachers, artisans, managers in industry, and employees in the civil service. Fiercely anti-communist and also clearly anti-labor, the NS would never have become a broad social movement comprising all sections of the Norwegian society, as the party purported to be.

The decision to take part in the general election of 1933, some months after its foundation, compelled the party to work out a more general class appeal. Joint lists with one farmers' group (Bygdefolkets krisehjelp) and one local conservative party branch (Høire) in Bergen, contributed towards making the NS a more broadly based nationalist and probably a more open middle class party.

As shown in table 4, the list of NS candidates in the Storting election of 1933 reveals a predomination of people in higher status brackets (– people with professional or business management backgrounds –) a low proportion of workers and a high proportion of farmers and white-collar employees. But new hopes and expanded organizational activities before the next election in 1936 produced a new situation with a broadened class composition in the candidate group. The NS presented lists in all constituencies as against approximately 40 per cent of the constituencies in 1933. This new strategy produced a shift from a typical farming and middle class party to one with almost twenty per cent of its candidates drawn from a working class background.

This change between the two elections confirms one of our main hypotheses, *that high status people were instrumental in establishing the party, whereas low status people filled the ranks.* Involvement in the national electoral process, where vote maximization is always the primary goal, and the necessity of widening the social and occupational profile does, at least in Norway, force a party to «open» or «soften» its specific social appeal. When the failure of the 1936 campaign was a fact, the more ardent members argued that it was precisely the party's failure to become sufficiently national socialist which had produced the setback and had made the other party alternatives equally attractive to Norwegian voters. The NS was not a new alternative, and had not been able to utilize the fascist potential in the Norwegian class structure.[20]

Within the party organization itself we can see the same general trend: in the membership structure from the pre-war years, throughout 1940, and continuing in the next four war years there was a shift from high status people to a lower class clientele. In table 4 we have tabulated the composition of the party membership in these three periods. The striking change from «early» to «late» entrants in the composition of the party's membership demonstrates even better than the change among the candidates in the two pre-war elections how the widened mass appeal produced a party consisting of men and women from all sections of Norwegian society, though in the period from 1933 to 1939 we find a very low proportion of workers. In the period 1941–45 the porportion of workers increased by more than 30 per cent, combining with a drastic reduction in the proportion of white-collar employees and people with higher status occupations. Farmers were most numerous in the party in 1940, and the proportion of housewives, students and other groups increased in the final period (1941–1945). The

Table 4. *Occupational background for party candidates at two national elections. Party headquarters personnel, and organizational membership at three points in time*

Occupation	Candidates on election lists			Party Head-quarters 1940–45	Membership 1933–45			
	1933	1936	Both		1933–39	1940	1941–45	1933–45
1. Unskilled workers .	11	54	65	4	171	3,135	5,910	9,479
	7.6	19.8	15.6	1.6	6.8	14.0	21.7	17.4
2. Skilled workers				7	215	2,191	2,515	5,033
				2.8	8.4	9.8	9.2	9.2
3. Farmers and fishermen	50	63	113	9	221	3,179	2,416	5,952
	34.5	23.1	27.0	3.6	8.7	14.2	8.9	10.9
4. Lower white collar .	45	88	133	77	539	5,144	4,327	10,288
	31.0	32.2	31.8	30.8	21.2	22.9	15.9	18.9
5. Higher white collar				42	283	1,890	808	3,061
				16.8	11.1	8.4	3.0	5.6
6. Professionals	16	23	39	58	115	646	310	1,106
	11.0	8.4	9.3	23.2	4.5	2.9	1.1	2.0
7. Business directors, owners of private enterprises	15	20	35	5	193	1,357	847	2,467
	10.3	7.3	8.4	2.0	7.6	6.1	3.1	4.5
8. Housewives, students, pupils, pensioners, other occupations	8	25	33	48	472	3,797	7,705	12,254
	5.5	9.2	7.9	19.2	18.6	16.9	28.3	22.5
9. No information on occupation ...	–	–	–	–	346	1,109	2,437	5,021
					13.6	4.9	8.9	9.2
Totals	145	273	418	250	2,545	22,448	27,275	54,651
					100.0	100.0	100,0	
	100.0	100.0	100.0	100.0	(4.7)	(41.1)	(49.9)	

development of the membership structure of the NS is shown in detail in table 5. The number of people registered as joining the party before 1940 is too low to give any safe annual description of enrolment. Recruitment in 1933–36 was even for most of the occupational groups, but by 1937–39 there were very few new members in any category. After 1940 the numbers increased rapidly until they were again reduced to very few in 1944 and 1945.

If we again take as a point of departure the development from high status party to general all-class mass-party, we can see from table 5 how this status change occurred. Let us take the 3 stages of development within each status group. In the lower status occupations (workers: unskilled and skilled) only 1.8 and 4.3 per cent were recruited

Table 5. Recruitment to NS by year of recruitment and by occupation

Year of joining	Unskilled workers	Skilled workers	Lower white-collar employees	Higher white-collar employees	Farmers and fishermen	Professionals	Business directors, owners of private enterprises	Housewives, students, pupils, pensioners, other occupations	No information	Total
Year of joining not known	263	112	278	80	136	35	70	280	1,129	2,383
	2.8	2.2	2.7	2.6	2.3	3.1	2.8	2.3	22.5	4.4
1933–39	171	215	539	283	221	115	193	472	346	2,545
	1.8(6.7)	4.3(8.4)	5.2(21.2)	9.3(11.1)	3.7(8.7)	10.4(4.5)	7.8(7.6)	3.8(18.5)	6.9(13.6)	4.7(100.0)
1940	3,135	2,191	5,144	1,890	3,179	646	1,357	3,797	1,109	22,448
	33.1(14.0)	43.5(9.8)	50.0(23.0)	61.7(8.4)	53.4(14.2)	58.4(2.9)	55.0(6.1)	31.0(16.9)	22.1(4.9)	41.1(100.0)
1941	2,381	1,235	2,256	473	1,118	183	451	3,584	1,178	12,859
	25.1	24.5	21.9	15.5	18.8	16.5	18.3	29.2	23.5	23.5
1942	2,336	874	1,459	272	917	97	296	2,818	823	9,892
	24.6	17.4	14.2	8.9	15.4	8.8	12.0	23.0	16.4	18.1
1943	790	275	388	46	266	21	76	877	271	3,010
	8.3	5.5	3.8	1.5	4.5	1.9	3.1	7.2	5.4	5.5
1944	271	95	187	15	81	5	17	388	120	1,179
	1.4	0.7	0.4	0.1	0.6	0.4	0.3	0.3	0.9	0.6
1945	132	36	37	2	34	4	7	38	45	335
	1.4	0.7	0.4	0.1	0.6	0.4	0.3	0.3	0.9	0.6
1941–45	5,910	2,515	4,327	808	2,416	310	847	7,705	2,437	27,275
	62.4(21.7)	50.0(9.2)	42.1(15.9)	26.4(3.0)	40.6(8.9)	28.0(1.1)	34.3(3.1)	62.9(28.2)	48.5(8.9)	49.9(100.0)
Totals	9,479	5,033	10,288	3,061	5,952	1,106	2,467	12,254	5,021	54,651
	(17.3)	(9.2)	(18.9)	(5.6)	(10.9)	(2.0)	(4.5)	(22.5)	(9.2)	100.0

to the pre-war NS (1933–39). In the single best year of 1940, 33.1 and 43.5 per cent of the unskilled and skilled workers were recruited, and in the last period from 1941 until 1945, 62.4 and 50.0 per cent were recruited. Thus very few of the total numbers of lower status occupations in the NS were recruited before the war: a very high percentage came in 1940, and the highest share in the last four years.

The higher status occupations (higher white-collar grades, professionals, businessmen, directors etc.) show a different pattern. In the pre-war NS (1933–39) they joined the party in percentages of 9.3 and 7.8. In 1940 61.7, 58.4 and 55.0 per cent of them joined. In the last four years recruitment to the NS from higher status occupations were 26.4, 28.0 and 34.3 per cent.

The proportions of entry within the farming groups and lower white collar groups do not fall «in between» these two, but have a more constant profile with less variation over the three periods. The most general and most vague occupational group (but also the single largest) – housewives, students, pupils, etc. – has a development profile which corresponds well with that of the unskilled group. In this group we find many of the young people and most of the women.

The tendencies described in table 5 can be seen more clearly when restructuring the material as in table 6. In our archives, each member's occupational label was also given, producing a total of approximately 800 different labels. These have been grouped into a more detailed classification scheme in table 6, where we have distributed the NS members according to their occupational background and have compared their dates of entry with those of the party élite.

By looking at the various classifications we can easily see that the higher occupations join the party to a much greater extent in the «pre-war NS» than later. The lower status occupations instead increased their relative strength after April 1940.

One particularly interesting phenomenon bearing upon the thesis of upper-status origin and the later spread to lower status as a mass-party is the composition of the NS leadership group. In table 6 we find the occupational composition of the NS national executive (Riksledelse) from 1940–45. This central leadership group was very small and showed a high degree of continuity throughout the war: the war leaders were on the whole the same people who occupied leadership positions in the thirties. The composition of the national executive contrasts clearly with that of the party candidates, and especially with that of the rank and file. The party executive was drawn preponderantly from the groups of white-collar employees and professionals. Workers and farmers were insignificant at this level. People in occupations with low and uncertain status have a relatively low share in the leadership, but account for one third of the members registered during the war. This clearly shows the difference between the leaders and their followers.

It might be asked whether the NS was a middle class party and whether the Norwegian middle class was strongly responsive to the NS' political appeal. To answer this we turn to data on the occupational structure of the Norwegian population derived from two censuses, one taken in 1930 before the NS was founded, and one in 1946, a year after the war and after the NS had been dissolved. Some change in the occupational structure of the gainfully employed population over 15 years of age had occurred during the sixteen-years period. The proportion of workers declined, as did the proportion of farmers and fishermen, while the proportion of white-collar employees, housewives and students increased. The proportion of professionals and business managers remained relatively stable.

Table 6. *Occupations of the members of Nasjonal Samling according to their date of joining. Compared with occupations in the party leadership*

Occupation	Joined before April 1940		Joined April 1940 or later in the War		Party Leadership*	
Farmers	9.0		10.9		3.6	
Lower white-collar employees	15.3		11.2		28.0	
Lower and middle public servants	3.3		2.7		7.6	
Police	1.4	6.9	4.0	8.0	–	7.6
Civil Servants	2.2		1.3		–	
Teachers	1.4		1.7		4.0	
Technicians and engineers	3.3		1.2		5.6	
Free professionals	2.9	7.4	1.1	3.1	15.2	26.0
Artists	1.2		0.8		5.2	
Managing private	8.1		3.6		9.2	
Businessmen	3.5	11.6	2.2	5.8	2.0	11.2
Skilled workers	7.6		8.5		2.8	
Unskilled workers	8.9	16.9	18.2	30.4	1.6	8.0
Servants	0.4		3.7		3.6	
Students	4.6		3.7		13.6	
Pensioners	0.4		0.8		–	
Housewives	13.5		18.6		2.0	
N.i.	12.9		6.8		–	
Totals	100%		100%		100%	
	2 691		49 437		250	

* M. A. thesis Arnt Ove Aune: *NS Riksledelse 1940–1945. Organisasjon og rekruttering.* Institute of History, Bergen 1975. Table 3.8. (p. 70) gives an occupational structure which is compressed in our table. In Aune's further analyses we find that the Riksledelse had a higher education (p. 65), were middle aged (p. 62) and recruited preponderantly from the Oslo area (p. 61).

The question of which of the classes or occupational groups were most susceptible to fascism can be answered in two ways:

1. By comparing the percentage of each occupational group in the population at large with the percentage of the same group in the NS. The discrepancy between the percentage of white-collar people in the NS and in the population at large can then be taken as an indicator of white-collar susceptibility to Nazi propaganda. If we look at table 7 we find that the white-collar groups are heavily over-represented: white-collar groups made up 9.9 per cent of the population in 1946, but formed 24.5 per cent of the NS membership, a difference of 14.6 per cent. We can also see that the group of housewives and students are heavily under-represented. This can be a product of a too broad categorization in the census. In this table the farmers are under-represented by 4 per cent and the workers by approximately 2 per cent. Professionals are represented in the NS in proportion to their share of the population, while factory owners show an over-representation of about 1 per cent.

Table 7. Comparison between the Norwegian adult population 1933–1946 and occupational recruitment to NS

Occupation	Census 1930		Census 1946		NS (1933–45)			NS as per cent of adult population-45	
1. Unskilled workers	604,679	30.0	692,599	28.4	9,479	17.4	26.6	$\frac{14,512}{692,599}$ × 100	2.1
2. Skilled workers		17.8			5,033	9.2			
3. Farmers and fishermen[1]	357,702	17.8	361,287	14.8	5,952	10.9		$\frac{5,952}{361,287}$ × 100	1.7
4. Lower white-collar	158,024	7.9	240,426	9.9	10,288	18.9	24.5	$\frac{13,349}{246,426}$ × 100	5.4
5. Higher white-collar					3,061	5.6			
6. Professionals	43,790	2.2	50,724	2.1	1,106	2.0		$\frac{1,106}{50,724}$ × 100	2.2
7. Business directors owners of priv.ent.	66,222	3.3	79,581	3.3	2,467	4.5		$\frac{2,467}{79,581}$ × 100	3.1
8. Housewives, students, pupils, pensioners, others	780,805	38.8	1,009,187	41.3	12,254	22.5		$\frac{12,254}{1,009,187}$ × 100	1.2
9. Occupation not known	1,423	0.1	8,080	0.3	5,021	9.2		$\frac{5,021}{8,080}$ × 100	(62.1)
Total	2,012,645	100.1	2,441,884	100.1	54,651	100.2		$\frac{54,651}{2,441,884}$ × 100	2.2

NOS xl 155 – 1946   Tab. m. – s. 32–33 og Tab. ad – s. 51
NOS lx 61 – 1930   Tab s. 14 – 15

[1] Family members working on farms are grouped with farmers, but not hired workers on the farms. Fishermen-owners and independents are grouped together.

2. By calculating the percentage of NS members in each occupational group. This implies taking NS members in each group as a percentage of the entire group of the population in that occupation. This is illustrated in column three of table 7, and we can see that the relative percentages reveal the same general tendencies as described above. If we range the percentage of NS members in the various occupational groups we obtain the following result: The highest NS-percentages are found in the white-collar groups (5.4 per cent); businessmen (directors/managers) come second with 3.1 per cent; and professionals and workers rank almost even with 2.2 and 2.1 percentage respectively. Farmers range fifth with 1.7 per cent, and housewives, students etc. lowest with 1.2 per cent.

It has previously been argued that the NS-support and potential in Norway was based on the crisis-stricken farmers and the frustrated «technicians» and professionals who had lost confidence in parliamentary politics. The results in table 7 do not lend credence to such assertions. The truth is actually quite the opposite. The farmers did not join the NS in large numbers relative to their share of the population, and the professionals (probably including many of the «technicians») were recruited to the NS in equal proportion with workers. Even if there was more evidence for the customary statements to be found in the very first NS-groups in the early thirties, for example by using the general election candidate-lists in 1933, this was certainly not the case when fascism really became a political force of some magnitude.[21]

Why did so many white-collar people join the NS? The question of motives will be discussed in the next section, but we shall point out one crucial factor explaining public sector white-collar adherence to the NS when the party was in a power-position during the war: the strategic positions of these white-collar groups in public administration.[22] They were strongly exposed to pressures for joining both from NS governmental employees and from the Germans. A breakdown of the figures according to public employment shows that the police was strongly represented. This was explained as a strategic move early in the war to prevent a take-over of the police by the Quisling Hird.[23]

Motivation for Joining: A Post-War Survey on Previous NS-members

The analyses in the preceding sections have mainly been based on what are termed socio-economic background variables – i.e. collective properties of groups of individuals which characterize their objective social and political situation. We have made various inferences on the basis of these characteristics, e.g. that people became members of the NS because they were of a certain age, engaged in a certain occupation, or living in a certain part of the country, etc. Inferences of this kind do not postulate that the causes thus assigned should be «felt» or «understood» by the individuals concerned. A social «force» does not necessarily have to become a perceived «reason» or motive when «translated» into the psychological reality of individuals. Inclination towards joining the NS would naturally manifest itself as a vague sentiment of dissatisfaction with the existing situation, but would not be perceived as a specific «need» based on youth, occupation, immediate social environment, etc.

It is this individually perceived experience that we shall discuss in this section. The two forms of analysis, one based on objective and collective properties of a socio-economic kind, and the other on individually expressed motives for joining, may often appear as two explanations that have no clear connection with each other. One example that illustrates this point is the reason for becoming a member given by a young farmer from the East of Norway who said that he joined the NS because he felt that it was important to prevent the Germans taking complete command in all Norwegian civil affairs. He said he felt it was necessary to join the NS, not because he perceived the effects of his own (internalized and latent) socio-economic characteristics, – but because he thought the NS was a better political alternative at the time than a fully-fledged German civil administration along with the occupation forces.

In order to illuminate the question of why people became members of the NS we shall illustrate some of the individual motivations as expressed in a series of interviews. These interviews were conducted with previous members of the NS in 1972–1973, thirty to forty years after they had made the decision to join the party. Many of the explanations were obviously in part retrospective and defensive in character.[24]

From the list of 25 motives in the table we can see that only some were dependent

Table 8. *Motives for joining NS as expressed in interviews with previous NS members in 1972–73*

	N	Per cent
1. Because of Quisling's personal appeal	15	3.1
2. Against Bolshevism and the Soviet Union	57	11.8
3. Tired of old parties and parliamentarism	36	7.5
4. Had a nationalistic atttitude, «was NS»	26	5.4
5. NS program and NS propaganda	57	11.8
6. Unemployed, wanted a job	2	0.4
7. So as not to lose job in public service	5	1.0
8. To avoid German influence in Norwegian civil administration	82	17.0
9. Because of Reichskommissar Terboven's speech – 25th of September 1940 – NS only party	14	2.9
10. Disappointed by the Norwegian military defeat	6	1.2
11. Wanted to become member of Norse Legion or Waffen SS	1	0.2
12. Impressed by the Germans and Germany	7	1.4
13. Friends and family were members	17	3.5
14. The British aggression at sea in 1940	1	0.2
15. Frustration of social and economic policy in Norway during the «dark thirties»	25	5.2
16. Had been a member of «Fedrelandslaget» (Patriotic League)	2	0.4
17. Frustrated with the Norwegian Social Democratic Party (Arbeiderpartiet) and its politics	25	5.2
18. Attitude towards the Jews	1	0.2
19. Pressure from others	1	0.2
20. Had intended to join the Homefront	1	0.2
21. To avoid losing radio (Radios were confiscated)	3	0.6
22. Because others said they already were members	1	0.2
23. Individual protest against Homefront activities	1	0.2
24. Disappointed with the action of the King and the Government in leaving the country – and with the neutrality declaration	25	2.5
25. The general impression of what happened in Norway around the 9th of April 1940	12	2.5
26. Various other motives	43	8.9

N=483

upon the actual political situation at the time (nos. 6, 7, 8, 9, 10, 11, 14, 20, 21, 23, 24, 25).

Some of the motives are genuinely of Nazi origin, i. e. the respondent expressed belief in the ideology, the persons and their program (nos. 1, 2, 4, 5, 11, 15, 16, 18). Others relate more to general social mechanisms at work in the environment in which the person lived (nos. 12, 13, 19, 22).

Altogether the list of individual motives is heavily dominated by those arising out of the specific political situation of 1940 when the occupation began, by those connected with the Norwegian efforts and activities in the war-months in 1940, and later by motives connected with the tactical maneuvers of the German Reichskommissar Joseph Terboven. The party's tactical use of the situation, expressed as an appeal to «responsible» Norwegians to join the NS in order to prevent the Germans staging a complete takeover, (no 8) also turned out to have a marked effect.

In the list we find very few people, or none, whose motivation for joining the party relates to «anti-modernism», as exemplified by the «threat of industrialization in the countryside», or to «middle class defence», exemplified by being «afraid of decline of one's own social status». The connection between *cause* of recruitment to NS as described by collective properties of socio-economic structural characteristics, and the conscious *motives* for joining described in table 8, is not direct. Which of the two, the «cause-approach» or the «motive-approach» is «best» or the most «true»?

Without giving any direct reply to this question, we shall illustrate the connection between one of the socio-economic background characteristics and individual motivations.

In table 9 we have analyzed various motives by occupational categories. The lower-white-collar occupations have the highest percentage of motivations that derive from Nazi ideology (1), with none mentioning economic favors (3). They also have a relatively low proportion motivated by a concern for preventing Germans from taking over the whole system (5).

On the other hand, workers did not that often express ideological motives (1). But they were relatively more frequently «frustrated» by social and economic conditions(2) or were intimidated into joining (6). The most «independent» occupational groups, farmers, professionals and businessmen, were motivated to join by ideological considerations (1) and relatively frequently express the need to prevent a German takeover of the Norwegian civil administration (5).

The farmers had the highest proportion of members motivated by the social and economic situation from before the war (2).

However, because of the retrospective/defensive character of the interviews and the small sample (which gives few entries in many of the cells in the table), one should not rely too much on the exact differences in percentage totals between the various occupational groups. The table reveals a rough tendency which points to a possible relationship between socio-economic background and individually expressed motives. In the higher-status occupations, ideological and tactical motives occur more frequently as reasons for joining the NS than in the lower status occupations. Workers more often than others justify their membership in the party by referring to problems more closely related to their daily existence. To sum up the two tables, we can conclude that the individual motivations for joining the NS add up to a rather mixed bunch. It is impossible to speak of a single genuine and easily discernible ideological justification. This may prove that the NS members came from many different backgrounds and joined the same party for very different reasons.

Table 9. *Motives for joining the NS, by occupation before joining. Data from interviews with previous NS members 1972–73 (weighted by sex – Compare N = 483 in table 8)*

Motive / Occupation	Workers	Lower white collar	Higher white collar	Farmers/ fishermen	Professionals, business directors, owners	Housewives, students, others	No information on occupation	Total
1. Agreed with NS program. Favored a strong leader. Believed in Quisling. Were nationalist	32 / 33.3	30 / 53.6	45 / 38.5	94 / 47.2	18 / 45.0	54 / 49.1	16 / 53.3	289 / (44.6)
2. Were tired of old parliamentarism. No trust in old parties. Protest against Norwegian system of politics and government. Frustrated by the economic and social system before the war. Memories from the «dark thirties»	19 / 19.8	7 / 12.7	18 / 15.4	41 / 20.6	1 / 2.5	11 / 10.0	1 / 3.3	98 / 15.1
3. To obtain economic or social favors from NS	3 / 3.1	0	3 / 2.6	3 / 1.5	3 / 7.5	0	1 / 3.3	13 / (2.0)
4. Impressed by Germans Positive attitude to Germany	2 / 2.1	0	3 / 2.6	0	4 / 10.0	1 / 0.9	1 / 3.3	11 / (1.7)
5. To prevent German influence in Norwegian affairs. To prevent Germans taking over Norwegian civil administration, Terboven' speech	17 / 17.7	13 / 23.2	37 / 31.6	49 / 24.6	13 / 32.5	14 / 12.7	8 / 26.7	151 / (23.3)
6. Were threatened – persuaded to join	14 / 14.6	1 / 1.8	8 / 6.8	3 / 1.5	0	14 / 12.7	2 / 6.7	42 / (6.5)
7. Various other motives	7 / 7.3	5 / 8.9	0	2 / 1.0	0	11 / 10.0	0	27 / (4.3)
8. Motive not given. Not identified	2 / 2.1	0	3 / 2.6	5 / 2.5	1 / 2.5	5 / 4.5	1 / 3.3	17 / (2.6)
Total	96 / 100 / (14.9)	56 / 100 / (8.6)	117 / 100 / (27.3)	199 / 100 / (30.7)	40 / 100 / (6.2)	110 / 100 / (17.0)	30 / 100 / (4.6)	N=648 / 100

If we compare the findings of our survey with the Abel-Merkl study, we find some striking similarities as well as some obvious differences. First, it is important to remember that Abel conducted his study as an essay contest when Hitler already had seized power, while our survey was carried out 27 years after the demise of the NS. Secondly, the different historical and political contexts of the two countries clearly influenced the individual experience. The crisis went deeper in Germany; there was a higher rate of unemployment. On the whole Norway was a more stable nation. The occupation by the Germans, the depression and the disillusionment with parliamentary government in the thirties account for almost 40 per cent of the answers given by the Norwegians. In Germany, the memory of defeat looms large, and also the revolutionary upheavals afterwards. Along with the instability of the Weimar republic, these two are the reasons most commonly given for joining the NSDAP.

In Norway we find that the largest group of motives (no 1) centers around the ideological, nationalistic, pro-Quisling appeal. This group comes second in the Merkl/Abel table, but in both countries this set of motives is more important than anti-Semitism and social pressures.

Interestingly, economic hardship or unemployment rank very low in the motivational universe of the members of the two parties. This brings us to a puzzle concerning the impact of the economic crisis on decisions to become involved in anti-democratic activism. The lack of complaints about economic misery in the two samples may of course be a reflection of the need to idealize the commitment: in retrospect it is of course more honorable to have joined out of idealistic or ideological motives than for reasons of poverty, or anticipated loss of status. If the members of the two samples really said what they meant, it was not the unemployed themselves who flocked to the parties, but instead the people who experienced the crisis more indirectly – people who *saw* the long queues of unemployed and feared the repercussions but were not among the hardest hit.[25]

In arguing thus we are quite aware of the problems of using the motive approach, and of the possible weakness of research-projects utilizing retrospective interviews and pre-arranged essay contests. However, we do think that this research illustrates how the indirect impact of the environmental context, and of the contemporary political situation, has to be understood when explaining fascist support. Both the people who were individually caught in a difficult situation arising out of current events, and those who felt some kind of collective responsibility for the fate of their own country – though without themselves being directly threatened – would support the NSDAP or the NS. But the findings from both countries suggest that the latter joined the parties in greater relative proportions than the former.

The 'cause-approach' and the 'motive-approach' have therefore to be taken together when trying, in a very broad sense, to explain why people became fascists. The blend of the two approaches also brings us into the well known (and unresolved) debate between the so-called «positivists» (objectivists) and the «subjectivists» (those emphasizing «understanding»/«Verstehen») and their followers. But that is a topic for another article.

NOTES

¹ This is a preliminary report from the Bergen Project on *Nasjonal Samling* organized jointly in 1969 by the Institutes of history and sociology at the University of Bergen, Norway. Directors of the project are Rolf Danielsen and Stein Ugelvik Larsen. The author wishes to thank Bernt Hagtvet, Jan Petter Myklebust and Derek Urwin for their many comments and suggestions for revision of earlier draft of this chapter. Thanks are also due to F. G. Castles and M. Djursaa for their critical comments on earlier drafts. None of them are responsible for the final version, of course.

² In an article in *Fritt Folk*, no. 7, 1939. In the inaugural issue of the paper *Nasjonal Samling* (No. 1, 1933) Quisling emphatically rejected any comparison with foreign models, saying that the movement used the Norwegian greeting «Heil og sæl» as the Norsemen in the Middle Ages had done. The party's symbol, the Sun Cross, or the Olav Cross was Norse in origin and had nothing to do with the swastika. In the thirties Quisling was at pains to underscore this independence from Italy and Germany. The NS was rooted in Norwegian history and traditions and did not see its task to defend the NSDAP in Germany or its racial policies (*Framsyn*, no. 17, 1935).

³ As a part of the Bergen Project we undertook a survey analysis of previous members of the NS. This was done partly in the form of oral interviews and postal questionnaires. In this chapter we have used a sample of 483 respondents from the postal survey who represents a cross-section of the membership from all over the country.

Among the questions we asked was which party the former NS-member voted for in the 1936 Storting election. In this election the NS nominated candidates in every constituency. For the total sample the electoral preferences in 1936 were as follows: Labor (DNA) 3.9 per cent; Liberals (Venstre) 2.3 per cent; Farmers Party (Bondepartiet) 27.8 per cent; Conservatives (Høire) 13.9 per cent; Moderate Conservatives (Frisinnede Venstre) 1.9 per cent, NS 19.4 per cent; «did not have the right to vote» 21.9 per cent; «did not vote» 2.6 per cent. This information clearly shows that there was a rather weak correspondence between the previous party choice and later party membership. See also S. U. Larsen, *Recruitment to Nasjonal Samling (NS) in Norway*, Paper to the Bergen Conference on Comparative European Fascism, 1974, pp. 53–59.

⁴ These studies of local areas are in the form of M. A. dissertations (mimeographed) and cover a series of topics: Finn Hestvik: *Nasjonal Samling i Salten under Okkupasjonen* (The NS in Salten during the Occupation), 1972. Hans Hendriksen: *Mennesker uten Makt* (People without Power), 1972. Svein Rognaldsen: *NS medlemmene i Bergen 1940–1945* (The NS Members in Bergen 1940–1945), 1971. Bodil Wold-Johnsen: *Nasjonal Samling i Stavanger 1933–1937*. (The NS in Stavanger 1933–1937), 1972. Arnt Ove Aune: *NS Riksledelse 1940–1945 Organisasjon og rekruttering* (The NS National Executive 1940–1945. Organization and Recruitment), 1975. Nina Nordberg: *Kvinner i Nasjonal Samling. En undersøkelse i Bergen* (Women in the NS. A Local Study of Bergen), 1977. Torgeir Tunshelle: *NS i Sogn og Fjordane 1933–1945* (The NS in Sogn og Fjordane 1933–45), 1972.

Excerpts from some of these studies are published in Rolf Danielsen and Stein Ugelvik Larsen (eds.): *Fra idé til dom* (From Idea to Sentence), Bergen 1976.

⁵ The first principal enactment was issued on January 22, 1942 *(Den opprinnelige landssvikanordningen)*. It stated that enrolment in the NS or continuation of membership after April 9, 1940 qualified as treason and those found guilty would be indicted. See: Department of Justice, *Om landssvikoppgjøret* (On the Trials for War-time Collaboration), (Oslo 1962), pp. 39–57. For a general description of the proceedings; see Johs Andenæs: «The Post-War Proceedings Against Enemy Collaborators», in Olav Riste (ed.): *Norway and the Second World War* (Oslo 1966).

⁶ Our data source is *Erstatningsdirektoratets kortarkiv*, (Card catalogue from the Bureau of Retribution) in The National Archives, Oslo. The card for each person contains the following information: Name, address (1945), occupation, birthplace, date of birth, date when registered as member, date of withdrawal (if such), and assorted information on sentences. The card catalogue

contains about 92,000 cards, of which we found 54,561 related to people registered as members of NS. The information on NS members has been transformed into a general data-file for statistical analysis.

[7] The literature on the NS in Norway has grown quite appreciably since 1945. In his paper «Fascismen i Norge etter 10 års forskning» (Fascism in Norway after 10 Years of Research) Hans Fredrik Dahl gives an overview covering the main works. He also discusses the historical context of the NS in the inter-war period.

The two most comprehensive books analyzing the development of the NS are Hans Olaf Brevig: *NS – fra parti til sekt* (The NS: From Party to Sect), (Oslo 1970) and Hans Dietrich Loock: *Quisling, Terboven und Rosenberg* (Stuttgart 1970). The journal *Kontrast* published a whole issue devoted to Norwegian fascism in 1966 (no. 3). One study of the electoral support of the NS is Sten Sparre Nilson: «Wahlsoziologische Probleme des Nationalsozialismus», *Zeitschrift für die gesamte Staatswissenschaft* CX, 1954, pp. 279–311. Magne Skodvin *Striden om okkupasjonsstyret i Norge* (The Struggle for the Occupation Administration in Norway), (Oslo 1956) and Thomas Chr. Wyller: *Nyordning og motstand* (Reorganization and Resistance), (Oslo 1957), are two larger doctoral theses which provide considerable information on the party's war-time history.

For a discussion of various psychological and cultural theories that have been developed to explain the conduct of Vidkun Quisling and popular susceptibility to fascism in Norway, see: Bernt Hagtvet: «Norwegian Fascism – the Emergency Defence of the Bourgeoisie, or Utopian Anti-Modernism?» Mimeographed. (New Haven: Department of Political Science, Yale University 1972).

[8] Expressed in letters to Quisling (in the *Quisling Archive*) *Riksarkivet*. Also repeated by former Secretary General of the party Jørgen Fuglesang in a meeting in a seminar in Bergen 1972.

[9] Appeared in several articles in *Nasjonal Samling* (The Party Weekly) in 1934/35; 26.7. 1934; 21.6. 1935; 23.5. 1935.

[10] *Ibid.*, 23.5. 1935.

[11] Nasjonal Samling, no 30, Oslo 3.8. 1935, p. 1.

[12] Information in *Riksarkivet*, NS-statistiske kontor kass. Title heads on tables: «Zum Bereicht von 12.12. 1940. NS Mitgliederbestände in der Zeit von 1.7. 1935 bis 1.4. 1936 (Angaben NS). *Der Einsatsstabes Wegener*. Numbers in totals: 1/7-35: 8556, 1/10-35: 8511, 1/1-36: 8369, 1/4-36: 8542. See also: *Om landssvikoppgjøret, op. cit.* p. 15.

[13] This was a semi-vigilant voluntary association created to prevent forced foreclosures in the countryside not unlike the *Schicksalsgemeinschaften* that appeared in Schleswig-Holstein in the twenties and early thirties. For details see S. S. Nilson's contribution of this volume.

[14] The precise number of members in the NS in the inter-war period will never be established with complete accuracy. The sources are lacking, and the few efforts to trace local organizations indicate that the specification and actual keeping record of members was rather unsystematic. There are good reasons to believe that the membership never reached anything near 1/3 of their votes in Norway. By contrast, in Denmark the voters of the Nazi party were most probably drawn from the membership. See H. Poulsen and M. Djursaa's article in this volume.

[15] Both Magne Skodvin *op.cit.* and Hans-Dietrich Loock *op.cit.* cite much evidence on Quisling's commitment to German occupation plans. More details are given in: *Straffesak mot Vidkun Abraham Lauritz Jonssøn Quisling i Eidsivating Lagmannsrett* (The Trial against V. A. L. J. Q. in Eidsivating Appeal Court), Oslo 1946. In Jerzy Borejsza's article in this volume there is material showing that financial support came from Mussolini to Quisling as early as in 1935. (See note 26 of this paper.)

[16] Magne Skodvin, *op.cit.* pp. 80–93 and Helge Paulsen, «Reichskommissariatet og «motytelsene» under riksrådsforhandlingene» (The Reichskommissariat and the Demands for Norwegian «Reciprocity» during the Negotiations for an Occupation Settlement), In Helge Paulsen (eds.) *Fra nøytral til okkupert* (From Neutral to Occupied), Oslo 1969, pp. 285–356. The Norwegian occupational system by a Reichskommissar was more like the Dutch war-time administration than any of the other types of German administration in occupied European countries.

[17] This comparison was given by the NS to Mr. Wiese and Mr. Wegener in the Reichskommissariat in August 1941. *Om landssvikoppgjøret, op.cit.*, p. 20.

[18] Hans Olaf Brevig, *op.cit.*, pp. 24–39, Bjørn Vidar Gabrielsen: «De gode middagers tid. Noen glimt fra norsk mellomkrigsaktivisme» in *Kontrast*, nr. 3, 1966, pp. 71–81.

[19] The *NS program* from 1933, points 8 to 12, (there were 30 in all) outlines the structure of a completely state-dominated labor market and a state- (i.e.party) dominated corporative system consisting of non-political branch-corporations *(laug)*. The position of the workers in the system was expressed at a local meeting in Ålesund in the following way: «The NS works towards a working state (en arbeidets stat) – not a workers' state» (en arbeiderstat). Danielsen/Larsen (eds.), *Fra idé til dom, op.cit.*, p. 167–168.

[20] Dag Olav Bruknap, «Idéene splitter partiet», (The Ideas Split the Party) in *Fra idé til dom, op.cit.*, pp. 9–46.

[21] See Hans Olaf Brevig, *op. cit.*, p. 108–111. Brevig makes no distinction between the categories of 'lower technical personnel' (repairmen, laboratory assistants, etc.), and artisans including the latter in the general category. This excludes examination of the very segment which in Germany has been labelled the primary crisis stratum in the support for fascist parties. In his category 'higher technical personnel' Brevig includes engineers, architects, pharmacists, chemists and military officers. For an extensive discussion of Brevig's methodology, see Jan Petter Myklebust, «Hvem var de norske nazistene? Sammenheng mellom sosial, økonomisk og politisk bakgrunn og medlemskap i Nasjonal Samling» (Who Were the Norwegian Nazis? The Relationship Between Social, Economic and Political Background and Membership in the NS), M. A. dissertation in Comparative Politics, Mimeographed, Institute of Sociology, University of Bergen 1974, pp. 63–66.

[22] Magne Skodvin, in *Om landssvikoppgjøret, op.cit.*, Historisk Innleiing (Historical Introduction), pp. 8–35. See also *NOS Statistiske meldinger*, nr. 12, 1953: «NS medlemmer og andre som viste unasjonale forhold under okkupasjonen» (NS Members and Others in the Governmental Services that Displayed un-Norwegian Behavior During the Occupation), p. 357.

[23] Signy Arctander: «Opprenskning i offentlig tjeneste» (Dismissals of Civil Servants in Public Service), *Nordisk Administrativt Tidsskrift*, 1952, gives a thorough report on the extent of nazification in the civil service. But it is difficult to establish from her figures how many of the new entrants in the service during 1940–45 were appointed because they already were members and as such were awarded the job by way of booty.

[24] Details of the questionnaire are described in: *Paper 1. NS Prosjektet. Intervjuhistorie* (Description of the Survey Procedure). Institute of Sociology, University of Bergen 1973. Mimeo.
See also: Stein Ugelvik Larsen: Paper to the Bergen Conference, *op.cit.*, p. 77.

[25] This *indirect* impact of the crisis is also found by W. S. Allen, *The Nazi Seizure of Power* (Chicago 1965), p. 214.

Regional Contrasts in the Membership Base of the Nasjonal Samling*

A Study of the Political Ecology of Norwegian Fascism 1933–1945

JAN PETTER MYKLEBUST AND BERNT HAGTVET

Previous research on the socio-cultural and socio-economic cleavages in the Norwegian political system has revealed a great deal about the development and timing of party choice and political mobilization in Norwegian elections.[1] These studies have illustrated the marked contrasts in partisan alignments over time between the various regions in the country, between the areas of the East, the South West, Trøndelag (mid Norway) and the North. Since the advent of party politics in the 1880's, the South-Western parts of the country have remained distinct in terms of electoral choice, identifying far more with the non-socialist center parties and with region-specific cultural values such as revivalist religion, language and temperance than the rest of the country. As we shall see, this persistent rejection of polarized urban class politics affected the opportunities for *Nasjonal Samling* appreciably.

This essay is an attempt to trace the regional variations in the membership base of Norwegian fascism. We will proceed by first discussing the urban-rural differences in the recruitment of members to the party. Then we shall analyze the various strongholds of the party, suggesting several local determinants which may have affected the susceptibility of certain regions towards the N.S. In particular we shall argue that any explanation of N.S. strength must take into account the interplay between cultural and economic factors. Finally, we shall attempt to summarize the reasons why fascism in Norway never managed to transcend its narrow political base.

Urban-Rural Differences in the Party Membership

Table 1a and 1b present the growth in party membership across regions and indicate the differences in recruitment between urban and rural districts.

They bring out clearly that the N.S. was *overwhelmingly an urban-based party*. Its best recruiting grounds were found in the capital Oslo and the counties around the Oslo Fjord. If we include the neighboring areas in the East Inland these regions account for almost two thirds of the total number of members. The breakdown on regions in table 1a demonstrates that the South and West recruited only about 15 per cent of the party's members, Trøndelag approximately 10 per cent and Northern Norway only 7 per cent. As is seen in table 1b, the differences between urban and rural areas remained almost 14 per cent for the entire period. The substantial inroads made by the N.S. in some rural districts in the East Inland are particularly noteworthy. We will return to the question why these areas provided the party with a relatively hospitable environment.

Table 1a. *Percentage Breakdowns of the New Entrants in the NS. Broken down by Region and Time*

Regions	Year joined					Proportion of Population in 1930
	1933–39	1940	1941–45	No inf.	Average for the whole period	
Oslo Fjord	49.2	43.7	35.3	38.2	39.5	28.1
Rest of Eastern Norway	20.8	27.6	23.1	25.1	24.9	20.1
South and West	13.4	14.8	17.0	15.9	15.9	30.2
Trøndelag	6.9	7.3	12.7	9.2	10.1	9.6
North	3.0	4.4	9.4	7.9	7.0	12.0
No information	6.7	2.1	2.6	3.6	2.7	—
N	2,691	22,302	27,275	2,383	54,651	2,814,194
Total	100%	99.9%	100.1%	99.9%	100.1%	100.1%

Table 1b. *Percentage Breakdowns of New Entrants in the NS. Broken down by Urban vs. Rural*

	1933–39	1940	1941–45	No inf.	Average
Urban	53.5	41.7	40.7	43.2	41.8
Rural	39.8	56.2	56.7	53.5	55.5
No inf.	6.7	2.1	2.6	3.6	2.7
N	2,691	22,302	27,275	2,383	54,651
Total	100%	100%	100%	100%	100%

In table 1a we have divided the people who joined the N.S. according to their date of joining. The year 1940 provides the dividing line. The table gives the *percentage of the net numbers of new members for each period (1933–39, 1940, and 1941–45), broken down by region*. Thus of all the people who became attached to the N.S. in the period 1933–39, 49.2 per cent came from Oslo. The capital accounted for 39.5 per cent of all the members in the N.S. over the entire period of the party's existence, but this share declined from 49.2 per cent in the years 1933–39 to 43.7 of those recruited in 1940 to only 35.3 per cent of the net inflow from 1941 to 1945. In other words, there was a marked shift in the pattern of recruitment to the party: *the regions outside Oslo increased their share of incoming members after 1941*. This is the *geographical* counterpart to the *social* lag in the sociological profile of the party described by Stein Ugelvik Larsen. Just as the party was initiated in upper-middle-class circles in Oslo and then attracted middle and lower class people, so it also reached out geographically from the same center. Most remarkable in this respect are Trøndelag and Northern Norway (Trøndelag increased its share of new members from 6.9 in the pre-war period to 12.7 during the occupation). The most stable region over time seems to have been the Eastern Inland which, except for the extreme case of 1945, kept its proportion of incoming members to around 20 per cent of the annual total. The diffusion process from Oslo is also indirectly indicated by the over-all urban-rural difference (table 1b). In the pre-war period urban areas provided 53.5 per cent of all the new members entering the party, a proportion that declined to less than 30 per cent in 1945 alone. The last few who enrolled in the N.S. in 1945 came predominantly from rural areas: the ratio of rural to urban new recruits in that year was 3:1.

In table 2 we have analyzed the regional distribution of the party members from a different perspective. The table shows the *timing of attachment to the N.S. within each region*. Of *all* who joined in Oslo, 6.1 per cent enrolled in the period 1933–39, 45.1 in 1940 and 44.6 during the occupation. Again, the lag in the provinces of the South and West, Trøndelag and Northern Norway is borne out with the upward trend exceptionally sharp in the case of Trøndelag and Northern Norway.

Setesdal, Northern Gudbrandsdal, Mid-Oppland and Østerdal: Four Core Areas of N.S. Strength

By giving information on each individual suspected of collaboration during the war, our original data base allowed us to analyze the internal composition of the party's following over time.[2] In order to be able to use this data base for ecological study, we had to leave the individual units out and aggregate our data to the commune level (the *kommune* is the smallest administrative unit in Norway). In this way we arrived at *type of locality* as our independent variable and political response, i.e. the total number of people registered in the N.S. as members, as the dependent variable. To avoid a series of empty cells in our matrix we decided to exclude information on age and sex, and limited the study to the total number of N.S. members in each locality, and the proportion of members to the population.

A word of caution: We are naturally under no illusion that the relationship between socio-economic background variables and support for the N.S. is a *direct* or straightforward one. It is possible to imagine two exactly similar communities with the same background variables in operation producing different political alignments. This word of methodological caution is especially appropriate in our case since we are dealing with small numbers and fringe phenomena. To understand why the N.S. gained support in one locality but not in another requires particular sensitivity to *mediating* and *precipitating* factors locally: specific traditions, isolation from external influences, the presence – and idiosyncracies – of respected leaders in the community,[3] who, by enrolling, lent legitimacy to the Quisling movement, a particularly active newspaper, etc. Many of these intervening variables made a difference, although they might have had only a tangential relationship to the socio-economic structure *sensu stricto*. There is a level of analysis problem here.[4] What a statistical treatment can do is to provide important clues towards explaining susceptibility of different kinds of communities to the N.S. Once tendencies in this quantitative material are brought out, other aspects can be introduced. Our aim is here to use socio-economic structure as a vantage point while remaining sensitive to less tangible influences in each community, trying to weigh the two against each other. It should also be pointed out that our

Table 2. Percentages of Total Number of Entrants in the NS Broken Down by Time and Region

Date of joining	Oslo	Rest Eastern Norway	South and West	Trøndelag (Mid.-North)	Northern Norway	Urban areas	Rural areas	No infor- mation	Total
1933–39	1,325 6.1	559 4.1	360 4.2	186 3.4	82 2.2	1,441 6.3	1,071 3.5	179 12.3	2,691 4.9
1940	9,745 45.1	6,164 45.3	3,296 38.0	1,633 29.6	985 25.9	9,304 40.7	12,519 41.3	479 33.0	22,302 40.8
1941–45	9,626 44.6	6,288 46.2	4,629 53.4	3,473 63.0	2,551 67.0	11,104 48.6	15.463 51.0	708 48.8	27,275 49.9
No info.	911 4.2	599 4.4	379 4.4	219 4.0	189 5.0	1,019 4.5	1.278 4.2	86 5.9	2,383 4.4
Total number recruited from each area	100% 21,607 39.5	100% 13,610 24.9	100% 8,664 15.9	100% 5,511 10.1	100% 3,807 7.0	100% 22,868 41.8	100% 30,331 55.5	100% 1,452 2.7	100% 54,651 100%

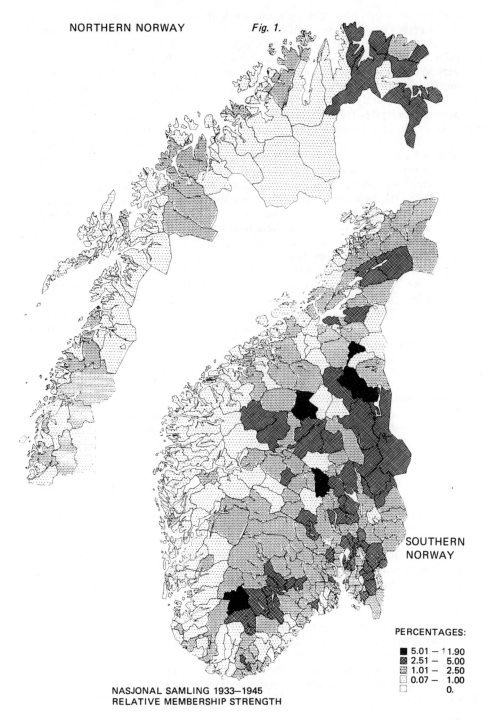

NORTHERN NORWAY   *Fig. 1.*

SOUTHERN
NORWAY

PERCENTAGES:

- ■ 5.01 – 11.90
- ▨ 2.51 – 5.00
- ▦ 1.01 – 2.50
- ⬚ 0.07 – 1.00
- ☐ 0.

NASJONAL SAMLING 1933–1945
RELATIVE MEMBERSHIP STRENGTH

625

regionalization may blur significant contrasts within the regions. Our main contention is that people became associated with the N.S. for a variety of reasons: it became a vehicle for structuring the world into which all kinds of needs and aspirations were projected. It was a response to *multi-dimensional* strain assuming different forms depending on each member's life conditions and place of residence. Hence its sources must be sought on separate levels: economic, socio-structural, ideological and personal.[5] And, evidently, the timing is crucial: April 9, 1940, marks the transition of the party from a legal political alternative to an object of nearly universal condemnation.

This multi-causal approach will be our basic theme in the subsequent presentations.

Fig. 1 reproduces graphically the regional variations in the membership of the Nasjonal Samling 1933–45. In 1930 Norway was divided into 746 communes. Of these 681 were classified as predominantly rural. The total number of people living in each commune was deduced from the census taken in 1930, the last available before the war. Using the 1930 census will exaggerate the relative share of N.S. members in relation to the total population, but we are more interested in the *tendencies* found in the material than the accuracy of these relative measures.

By relating the number of people who joined the N.S. in each commune to the total population, we found a proportion of N.S. members ranging from a maximum of 11.9 per cent (Valle in the Setesdal region in Aust Agder county) to none in 19 of 746 communes. The list of localities with a high ratio of N.S. membership is given in table 3.

Together Fig. 1 and table 3 provide the groundwork for an analysis of the contrasts in N.S. strength in Norway. The material yields a few striking results: first it shows the *relative proneness of the Eastern Inland* and the *immunity of the South and the West to the N.S.* Second, it demonstrates the *preponderance of primary economy-type localities.*

Besides the region of *Setesdal* (in addition to Valle, the neighboring commune of Hyllestad further south occupies no. 18 in table 3), Tolga in the *northern part of the Østerdal valley* scores highly. The party also enjoyed substantial support in the *Northern Gudbrandsdal* valley and the commune of Dovre in the *county of Oppland*. This is a mountainous agricultural area. The *southern and middle part of the same county* (the communes of Torpa and Nordre Land) also rank as relatively strong N.S. areas. In addition there was a rather strong belt of communes with a high N.S. percentage in the Oslofjord area. *(Aurskog, Hølen, Drøbak, Blaker) through Hedmark to Southern Trøndelag* along the Swedish border with *scattered pockets of N.S. strength in Nord-Trøndelag* (Levanger, Beitstad, Skatval). In the county of *Østfold* a few localities had a sizeable N.S. following as well (Mysen, Rakkestad). In *Finmark*, in the northern tip of the country, the party made a fairly strong showing in the communes closest to the Soviet Union.

To show the preponderance of agriculture and forestry in the communes which gravitated towards the N.S., it should be pointed out that among the 30 communes showing the highest N.S. presence, 22 had farming, forestry and cattle breeding as their primary means of livelihood, while the remaining 8 were small trading centers. All of the first groups of communes (the 22) are located in the Southern and Eastern Inland regions. In the rank ordering of N.S. communes, the first entry of a Western locality is no. 53, the next is no. 82 and the one then following no. 162 (out of 746). Conversely, of those 19 communes where no member in the N.S. is recorded, 14 are found along the Western coast. Of the 384 communes with less than 1 per cent of the population enrolled in the party, 196 were clustered in the Western region. In all there were 218 communes in this region. This implies that only 22, or one tenth, were in the

Table 3. *Municipalities with a High NS Ratio: Geographic Location, Percentages of NS Members to Population and Socio-Economic Structure of the Localities*

Commune (kommune)	County (fylke)	Percentages of NS Members to Population	Type of Primary Economy
1. Valle	Aust-Agder	11.9	Cattle breeding (c.b.), forestry (f.)
2. Finsland	Vest-Agder	8.5	Agriculture (agr.), c.b.
3. Tolga	Hedmark	8.2	C.b., f.
4. Levanger	Nord-Trøndelag	7.1	Commerce, industry
5. Aurskog	Akershus	7.0	F., agr.
6. Åsgårdstrand	Vestfold	6.8	Commerce
7. Haltdalen	Sør-Trøndelag	6.7	Agr., f., copper mining
8. Torpa	Oppland	6.6	F., c.b.
9. Hølen	Akershus	6.6	Commerce
10. Dovre	Oppland	6.5	C.b., home crafts
11. Beitstad	Nord-Trøndelag	6.5	Agr., f.
12. Øvre Rendal	Hedmark	6.2	C.b., f.
13. Hovin	Telemark	5.7	Agr., f.
14. Kongsvinger	Hedmark	5.6	Commerce, industry
15. Mysen	Østfold	5.5	Commerce, industry, agr.
16. Skatval	Nord-Trøndelag	5.4	Agr., f.
17. Drøbak	Akershus	5.0	Small commercial center
18. Hyllestad	Aust-Agder	5.0	C.b., f., home crafts
19. Brønnøysund	Nordland	5.0	Commerce, fisheries
20. Rakkestad	Østfold	4.9	Agr., f., industry
21. Mo i Rana	Nordland	4.9	Small commercial center
22. Nordre Land	Oppland	4.8	Agr., f.
23. Krødsherad	Buskerud	4.8	Agr., f.
24. Åmot	Hedmark	4.6	Agr., f., industry
25. Blaker	Akershus	4.6	Agr., f.
26. Trysil	Hedmark	4.6	F., agr., c.b.

group of communes with more than 1 per cent of the population as card-carrying N.S. members. Among the statistical correlations established between various variables in our material, these differences between the N.S. base in the Eastern and Western parts of Norway are the most significant. In absolute numbers, over 35,000 members, or 64.4 per cent of those who joined the ranks of the N.S. lived in Eastern Norway. To account for these intra-national differences has long been one of the main tasks of Norwegian political sociologists.[6] In a later section we shall make a systematic attempt to locate the N.S. within these traditional regional contrasts in Norwegian politics. Next, however, we shall review the explanations that have been given for the concentration of N.S. members in the Eastern Inland and Setesdal. To understand why these areas deviated from the national average of very low N.S. adherence, we shall proceed along two dimensions. First, we intend to analyze the impact of *Nazi anti-modernist utopianism* which in our view must gain priority in explaining the N.S. strength in Setesdal and Northern Gudbrandsdal, and to a limited extent also in Tolga.

Second, we shall focus on the repercussions of the *economic crisis* and the social tensions produced by the depression. This approach better explains the N.S. following in mid and South Oppland, the forestry districts in South-Eastern Hedmark and the scattered cases in Akershus and Østfold. These two dimensions are clearly not distinct. Social tensions sharpened by economic depression may produce upper-class defense in different forms, from the more clear-cut interest-based reactions to more specific 'anti-modernist' responses in which attempts to safeguard acquired positions are moulded by culture-bound reflexes invoking tradition, hierarchy and stability. These two forms of defense intermingle, but for analytical purposes we propose to keep them apart.

Hans Hendriksen's analysis of Elverum, Åmot and Trysil in this book is in itself an indication of the need to be sensitive to localistic traditions. Compared to the forestry communes along the Swedish border, Valle and Northern Gudbrandsdal were only mildly affected by the depression.[7] As a result, cultural explanations must take precedence over economic in these areas. Valle and to a certain extent Hyllestad in Setesdal and the localities in Northern Gudbrandsdal shared one decisive characteristic: their primordial *Bauernkultur* in the setting of a vertically divided social structure. In both Setesdal and Gudbrandsdal there are isolated, partly mountainous agricultural communities with strong ancestral pride. Edv. Bull, the noted Norwegian historian, noted in 1921 that as late as 1840 Setesdal was in many respects «entirely medieval».[8] The farm and the family were the central social units, and some of the farmers had an almost sacred feeling of belonging, by uninterrupted inheritance, to the soil. Habits and customs had remained stable for a long time; industrialization had only had a marginal effect, although the stirrings of lower-class unrest had been felt occasionally. In fact, social divisions between the large landowners and the crofters had run deep, but in suppressed forms, and the legacy of this antagonism surfaced again in the form of N.S. support. The N.S. was able to exploit these sentiments through its conscious appeal to traditionalism and hierarchy. Like so many of its Central European brethren, the party capitalized on the resentments against the modern world among the wealthier strata in the countryside by propagating a distinctive backward-looking ideology which in Norway assumed the additional connotations of a «Viking» cult. The Norwegian Nazis did not, to be sure, seek any historically correct understanding of the past. Rather, the image of the past was consciously romantic, mythic and eclectic. What the Norwegian Nazis proposed had very much in common with the Germanic paganism of the N.S.D.A.P.: it was, in Henry A. Turner, Jr.'s words, «an escape from the modern world by means of a desperate backward leap toward a romanticized vision of harmony, community, simplicity, and order of a world long lost».[9] The propaganda of the N.S. exhibited a form of mental posture which best can be described as 'utopian anti-modern' – utopian because it implied a kind of retrospective wishful thinking, and also because the heroic past thus projected could not be re-created in the modern age. It is important to grasp this imagery in order to understand why these rural communities were drawn towards the N.S. The party made a conscious link to this golden age: it used the old Norse symbol of the sun and the cross as its emblem; it introduced the old Viking greeting of *Heil og Sæl* as a nationalistic substitute for the Hitlerite *Sieg Heil;* Quisling renamed his residence *Gimle,* the home of the old Norse gods, and called his equivalent to SA forces *hird* after the guards of the Viking kings.[10] The party held its annual convention at historical sites such as Borre, Stiklestad and Hafrsfjord – the latter connected with Norway's unification as a state under King Harald Fairhead in the 9th century. Quisling took on the whole old Norse symbolism of *ting,* legislative and adjudicative assemblies in the Middle Ages; *heim og ætt* (home and family) became the Norwegian equivalents to *Blut und Boden.* In addition, the N.S. singled out the farmer as the country's main resource: «He was the bearer of the good seed».[11] Occasionally, this propaganda would assume absurd proportions: «It is the people from the Nordic countries that have dominated in the world until this date. The conqueror of the world is the white man, for instance a Norseman from Setesdal.»[12]

Eggen[13] has suggested that in Northern Gudbrandsdal, fear of the modern world – of industrialization, commercialization, concentration, and socialism – led the wealthier families to join the N.S. They reacted with political extremism to what they perceived to be a *long-term* threat to their status and power. Threatened from two sides, from encroaching industrialization and an increasingly impatient rural proletariat, they saw in the N.S. a hope for a reactivation of the past. Eggen's interpretation is supported by a contemporary observer, Tor Jonsson, a poet and writer who grew up in Northern Gudbrandsdal. He saw the underside of these communities, belonging as he did, to a crofter's family in revolt against the local agrarian establishment. After the war he wrote:

«It is worth pointing out that in the mountain communities with a deep reverence for traditions, the N.S. gained wide support. One should note that excessively nationalistic groups *(heilnorske grupper)* usually stand in opposition to the labor movement. Many aspects of local patriotism and nationalism are irrational, but the mixture of national mysticism and old Norse mythology seems to have attracted many. This characteristic is often found in strong measure among the farmers in the mountain valleys, and it is reasonable to believe that it is inherited from the old clan community. The struggle for social emancipation is to these people something alien and non-national... What has happened during the last 15 years ought to be a warning against too much dancing around the golden calf of nationalism. In Nazism we discover the same national ethnocentrism, and among the farmers there are still strongly reactionary elements at work. In general, farmers have a tendency to be hypnotized by everything from the past.»[14]

Conditions in Setesdal resembled those found in Gudbrandsdal and our data lend much support to the interpretation that fascism in these valleys was an expression of anti-modernist sentiments made more acute by the economic crisis, or, more accurately, by the *feeling* of impending crisis.[15] This hypothesis complements other variables such as relative deprivation as explanations for the comparatively strong N.S. showing in these primary communes. In our view, what caused the fears about status loss to assume such an extreme form was the ideological filter through which the processes of cultural standardization and lower class ascendancy were interpreted. Pseudo-pagan nationalism was very alien to the farmers in the West, but there the social structure did not require this kind of defense. The existing local power hegemony in these valleys may not have been in jeopardy in the short run. In this respect there are interesting parallels to the German *Mittelstand* panic: it was not fear of *revolution* that drove the *Mittelständler* and the traditionalist Norwegian mountain farmer into fascist atavism; it was a reaction against the whole *Zeitgeist,* the *evolutionary* trends towards mechanization, equalization, urbanization and industrialization.[16] Thus a case can be made that this rural center of gravity of Norwegian fascism was, in Wolfgang Sauer's phrase, «a revolt by those who lost – directly or indirectly – by industrialization»,[17] the *déclassés* or the potential *déclassés.* This perspective on Norwegian rural fascism as an anti-labor and anti-industrial defense reaction is shared by other writers on the subject.[18]

Whereas cultural predispositions may take us far in understanding Setesdal and Gudbrandsdal, Tolga in the Østerdal region represents a rather intricate case. Tracing the high proportion of N.S. members in this locality (8.2 per cent of the population) to class antagonism seems far-fetched since the size of holdings was very even throughout the area. Further, the economic depression was in fact lighter in Tolga than in the neighboring Os which had very few people inscribed as members in the N.S. Tolga is an agricultural and mountainous region, hence the labor market conflicts following in the wake of falling timber prices and unionization as in Trysil were non-existent. Before any systematic study of this interesting case is carried out, we tend to support the observations of local historians. They view the high N.S. membership in the Tolga community as the result of the specific conditions of mistrust in representative bodies which arose out of a political conflict inside the Tolga township over economic pledges made to the commune of Os in connection with the partition of the two localities in 1926.[19]

On the other hand, depression and peripheral status provide the best explanation for the high N.S. score in the commune of *Torpa* in the county of *Oppland*. Conditions were miserable in Torpa. As early as 1928 the local administration had been suspended for lack of money and the Ministry of Justice in Oslo had taken over the day-to-day affairs of the local administration (this was a common procedure in communes hardest hit by the depression). In the first half of 1931, the 300 unemployed in this tiny community had received N.kr. 1125 (approx. $ 215 by the current exchange rate) in unemployment benefits, which meant 10 *øre* (about 2 cents!) per family a week.[20] These figures convey the air of desperation prevailing in this area. This poverty, intensified by the anti-centralist reaction against bureaucracy and the impersonal control from the capital, produced a vehement political reaction which gave the N.S. the mayoralty after the 1934 municipal elections. Torpa was the only commune in Norway where that happened.

Our map also reveals an interesting trend in Finmark: in this region close to the Soviet Union the N.S. had, again in relative terms, a sizeable following.[21] Finmark was well below the national average in terms of debts on holdings (on farms over 50 decares the percentage was 21.32: on farms below 50 decares the figure was 33.60 as against the national average for both categories of 45.20). But, importantly, the county was *second only to Hedmark* in the number of foreclosures per 1000 holdings in 1931/32 (Hedmark had 103.54 foreclosures per 1000 holdings, Finmark 50.66. The national average was 23.47.[22] For a more extensive discussion, see next section). It is reasonable, then, to assume that reaction to the agricultural depression was mingled with fear of communism, made more present and clear by the proximity to the Soviet Union. For a variety of reasons, this phenomenon of fascism as a border movement has interesting parallels in other countries: in Austria, the struggle of the *Heimwehren* derived an additional impetus from the border disputes with Yugoslavia in Carinthia; in Germany, the N.S.D.A.P. had its decisive breakthrough in the crisis-stricken periphery of Schleswig-Holstein. Obviously, the question of the relative importance of geographic location as against internal conditions arises in each of these cases, but the phenomenon deserves further study.

So far we have tried to elucidate the sources of N.S. strength by pointing to the interaction between anti-modernist defense reactions and economic depression. We have placed our emphasis differently in our discussion of Setesdal, Gudbrandsdal,

630

mid Oppland and Østerdal. Another dimension, or rather a refinement of the economic dimension is found in Hendriksen's study of Trysil: embittered anti-socialism
arising out of the protest against class struggle imported from outside, a culturally
founded 'lumberjack individualism' which saw socialist unionization as the last confirmation of social degradation. Coupled with the fall in prices of timber, this made for
virulent animosity between competitors for jobs in the forests and provided the N.S.
with a fertile ground for recruitment. This conflict was revived during the war when
the losers in the struggle against unionization joined the N.S.[23] In the next section we
shall delve more deeply into the mechanisms of N.S. support in the fertile agricultural
areas of Hedmark and see this county as a whole.

Debts on Holdings and Class Polarization: Two Clues to N.S. Affiliation

The depression assumed different forms: unemployment, falling prices and inability of
debtors to pay back their loans. When some or all of these appeared in conjunction,
the resulting crisis drove people to despair and changed their political loyalties. The
crisis gave extremism a chance. But what people and where?

In this section we shall try to uncover the connections between the debts crisis in the
countryside and support for the N.S. Our line of explanation concentrates on the
following characteristics of the communities:

1. *The impact of the depression.* The depression struck unevenly, both in class
terms and geographically. Some areas were more exposed than others; some
farmers less fortunate than others. A probable inference is that the deeper the
vulnerability *(as measured by the percentage of debts on holdings)* the stronger the
N.S. We shall also make an attempt to break down our information according to
class, trying to trace propensity to join the N.S. to size of holdings (our distinction
here will go between *gårdsbruk* which include farms over 50 decares, and *småbruk,*
holdings with less than 50 decares).

2. *The rural class struggle.* We would expect a stronger N.S. presence in areas of
intense polarization between large owners of land *(storbønder)* and landless farm
laborers and smallholders dependent on seasonal employment in the forest industry
(landarbeidere, småbønder). One way to identify areas where the social structure is
likely to be politically polarizing is to examine the *proportion of large farms in the
area.* The rural structures most likely to prove polarizing between socialists and
non-socialists are those where majorities of smallholders, forestry workers and
farmhands confront a few dominant forest owners and large-scale farmers. Our
main task will be to see whether, in deeply split localities of this kind, the N.S. gain
from the divisions. The next task will be to see *who* were swayed by the Nazi
ideology, *storbønder* or *småbønder.*

3. *Type of economy.* Sensitivity to market fluctuations is related to both the degree
of monetization and the extent to which the economy is subsistence vs. export
oriented. The more explicitly subsistence oriented the local economy, the lesser its
likely vulnerability to price fluctuations.

We have constructed a set of social indicators which are cross-checked over all
Norwegian communes in an ecological test. Our first task is to explore if there is any
relationship at all between our measure for economic vulnerability in the depression,
percentage of debts on holdings, and N.S. affiliation. Concentrating on the commune
as the unit of analysis, a comparison between Fig. 1 and Fig. 2 confirms this.

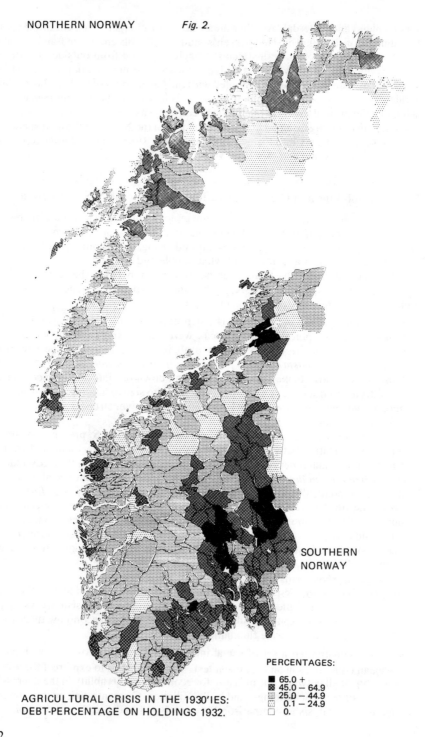

SOUTHERN
NORWAY

PERCENTAGES:

- ■ 65.0 +
- ▨ 45.0 — 64.9
- ▧ 25.0 — 44.9
- ▦ 0.1 — 24.9
- □ 0.

AGRICULTURAL CRISIS IN THE 1930'IES:
DEBT-PERCENTAGE ON HOLDINGS 1932.

This illustration of loan commitments makes clear that *the most heavily indebted areas are also among those areas where the N.S. found its strongest sources of support*. Regrettably, we have no material on individual wealth among the members of the N.S. Our archive did not record this information. Hence we are in no position to establish any relationship between personal wealth and political loyalties. This might, of course, have been very illuminating. But in itself, this tendency towards a correspondence between areas of heavily indebted people and N.S. strength may be taken to have some significance.

Why was the East Inland so encumbered by debts?

After World War I many new farms were built in this area. They were cleared on previously non-productive land and financed by taking out loans from local banks. When the economic slump brought unemployment to the forest industry, it also affected many of the farm workers in the area. The larger farms reduced their intake of labor. Many smallholders were dependent on the additional income they could gain from working as lumberjacks. Thus indebted farmers on the newly established farms could not obtain sufficient revenue to pay interests and instalments. The pre-Keynesian economic policy of the government was a reflection of the prevailing economic wisdom of the day, namely, that the Norwegian currency should follow sterling, which meant a de facto revaluation of the *krone*.[24] In consequence, the farmers had to repay their loans in production equivalents two to three times higher than the rate in operation when they first obtained their loans. This, in short, is the background for the debts crisis afflicting the East Inland.

How severe the crisis was in the county of Hedmark can be gauged from the following information: The number of foreclosures in this region was five times higher than the average in the country. An average of 103.5 holdings were sold at mortgage sales per 1000 holdings in 1932 as against 23.5 for the whole country. In absolute numbers 2072 farms were auctioned in 1931/32 compared to 628 in 1926/28. The corresponding figures in neighboring Oppland were in 1931/32 35.7 per 1000 holdings, 627 in absolute numbers, as against 260 in 1926/28. The county north of Oppland, Sør-Trøndelag, and Hedmark's southern neighbor, Akershus, showed these numbers respectively: 13.2/192 and 14.9/423. The drastic differences between the East Inland counties and the West and South in 1931/32 are brought out clearly by these numbers: Møre og Romsdal: 7.6/131; Sogn og Fjordane 5.3/63; Hordaland 2.7/57, Rogaland 7.5/114; Vest Agder 4.1/48 and Aust Agder 8.4/76. (See note 22.) We shall return to the significance of the East/West discrepancy. Here it will suffice to add that the debts had been accumulated at different rates by different people in the rural communities. On the whole, *the farmers on the smaller holdings were more deeply committed to the banks than were the owners of larger farms*. For instance, available information on percentages of debts in relation to assets indicate that in Hedmark among the large-size farms (over 50 da) the percentage of debts was 55.7 as contrasted to 66.7 in the small-holding category. The average for the whole country was 45.2. The corresponding figures for Oppland are 49.6 vs. 65.5, an even greater disparity.[25] The smaller farms were hit harder and this pattern is repeated throughout the country with varying degrees save in three counties. The effect of this is easy to imagine: the disparities in debt commitments, made even more visible by the crisis and compounded by the smallholder's lack of resources in comparison to the larger farms, fuelled traditional class resentments and deepened the polarization in these communities. The N.S. was one of the beneficiaries of these divisions.

Yet the question remains: who exactly in these debt-ridden localities were drawn to

633

the N.S.? Conventional guesswork would of course have it that despite the heavy burden of debts among the smallholders, their loyalties would remain on the left. One would expect that the prime recruiting field of the N.S. would be in the higher strata. That, in other words, under the impact of increasing strain, the smallholders would be reinforced in their radicalism, whereas higher up in the social structure the N.S. would be seen as the last bulwark against lower class unrest.

One way to approach this question is to develop measures on agricultural diversification and run these measures against selected indicators of N.S. support. In table 4 we have presented this material. The table contains information on members in the N.S. as a percentage of total population and the proportion of farmers in the N.S. as percentages of all farmers, correlated to farm size and average wealth broken down according to type of farm and ratios of debts on each type of farm.

Table 4. *Correlations Between Support for the N.S. and Selected Indicators on Farmer's Wealth and Debts Broken down by Size of Holding*

	Members in N.S. as Percentage of Total Population	Farmers in N.S. as Percentages of all Farmers
1. Per cent of total holdings in the *småbruk* category (under 50 decares)	÷ 0.30	÷ 0.24
2. Per cent of total holdings in the *gårdsbruk* category (over 50 decares)	0.30	0.24
3. Average wealth on the *gårdsbruk* (in Norw. *Kroner*) ..	÷ 0.06	÷ 0.02
4. Average debt on the *gårdsbruk* (in Norw. *Kroner*)	÷ 0.01	0.04
5. Average wealth on the *småbruk* (in Norw. *Kroner*)	0.24	0.21
6. Average debt on the *småbruk* (in Norw. *Kroner*)	0.30	0.22

Pearson correlation coefficients, rural communes only: N = 681.

These figures of course mirror a complex social reality and it is necessary to express reservations with respect to the degree of association established. But the existence of a *tendency* might be argued: Support for the N.S. correlated positively with a high proportion of large holdings in the area *(gårdsbruk)* and negatively with the proportion of smaller holdings *(småbruk)*. The commune is here the unit of analysis. In other words: the *more pronounced the concentration of large holdings in a commune, the stronger the N.S.* The degree of association between farm size in the community and N.S. support is a statistical measure and does not convey any information on *who* joined, either large scale farmers or smallholders. One probable inference is supported: class antagonism was stronger in communities with a high proportion of large farms. Here the disparities in wealth could more easily be perceived.

When examining the co-variance between average wealth and debt relations on both *småbruk* and *gårdsbruk* on the one hand and N.S. support on the other, we find no association at all for the *gårdsbruk*. There is, however, a positive relation between both average wealth and average debt (in *kroner*) for the *småbruk* on the one hand and degree of support for the N.S. This seems to give credibility to the view that the relationship between economic crisis and political mobilization is very unpredictable and capable of upsetting 'normal' alignments. The crisis-ridden smallholders in des-

634

pair seem to a surprising degree to have been swayed by the N.S. The tentative conclusion to be drawn from these data is that in communes with a *larger concentration* of larger holdings, there was an upsurge of support for the N.S., but that the root of this support was not clear-cut. We shall have to develop new indicators to be able to say exactly who joined in these strata, but our data lend credence to the interpretation that the N.S. had a rather wide appeal which might have swayed people deep down in the social structure. It should be remembered that we are here talking only about *those who went over to the N.S.* It is in the *membership* we find this trend of smallholder representation. In relation to the entire *småbruk* segment in Norway this membership group was small. We say nothing about the behavior of the smallholders as a group. As such they continued to give the socialist parties heavy surpluses, but those among the farmers who joined the N.S. seem to have been recruited to a large extent from the less wealthy echelons of the rural community. We would argue this is an interesting finding, understandable in view of the heavy burden of debts accumulated by those who could least withstand an economic downturn. Indeed, in this context of crisis it becomes all the more surprising that the traditional alignments persisted to the extent they actually did. It is a promising new task to study the political alignments of the Communist Party (C.P.) members in this area, who also were recruited from debt-ridden smallholders. Here we can only raise the question: what made one segment of this group join the C.P., another the N.S.?

Another way of looking at the relationship between class antagonism sharpened by economic setbacks and adherence to the N.S. is to compare the results from the general elections in 1933 and 1936 with the support for the N.S. both measured in votes and in members. In table 5 we have correlated the vote for various parties with several indices for N.S. strength. As expected there is some correlation between our indices of class polarization and support for the N.S. Both elections were mobilizing elections which brought the Labor party close to the majority point in the national assembly. The assumption behind this design is that class polarization was higher in areas where the crisis was most pervasive. As measures of class conflict we used three indicators: 1. the proportion of valid votes for the Labor party; 2. the turnout level, and 3. the polarization index proposed by Stein Rokkan.[26] Contrasting the proportion of valid votes for Labor in the two elections with the proportion of valid votes for the N.S. we end up with a correlation coefficient of .27 and .30. With regard to turnout level the coefficient is .36 and .30. Using Rokkan's polarization index against N.S. electoral support in these two elections gives a correlation coefficient of .33 and .31. This indicates a correlation, although not a particularly strong one. Again it is the *relative* degree of association which is of primary interest.

We have in this section used two approaches to scrutinize political divisions in the rural Norwegian communes. We have established support for two assertions: 1. That a high concentration of large farms in a commune tends to increase the strength of the N.S. We showed this by using membership data drawn from our archive. 2. That there is a discernible, although not very strong, relationship between a high number of votes to the Labor party and electoral support for the N.S. As to the question of who the people drawn to the N.S. were, we used our membership files to argue that, contrary to our expectations, the data show a significant smallholder element in this grass root base.

635

Table 5. *Correlations Between N.S. Strength and Turnout and Voting for other Parties in the General Elections in 1933 and 1936*

	NS relative membership strength 1933–1945	NS proportion of valid votes 1933	NS proportion of valid votes 1936
1. NS-indicator of relative membership strength ..	1.00	0.40	0.47
2. Proportion of valid votes for the *Liberals* 1933 .	÷ 0.39	÷ 0.25	÷ 0.34
3. Proportion of valid votes for the *Liberals* 1936	÷ 0.40	÷ 0.22	÷ 0.28
4. Proportion of valid votes for the *Labor* party 1933	0.27	0.08	0.27
5. Proportion of valid votes for the *Labor* party 1936	0.30	0.12	0.30
6. Proportion of valid votes for the *Agrarian* party 1933	÷ 0.03	÷ 0.04	÷ 0.03
7. Proportion of valid votes for the *Agrarian* party 1936	0.06	0.06	0.06
8. Proportion of valid votes to the *Conservatives* 1933	0.03	÷ 0.06	0.03
9. Turnout 1933	0.36	0.11	0.36
10. Turnout 1936	0.30	0.11	0.28
11. Polarization index 1933*	0.33	0.22	0.26
12. Polarization index 1936	0.31	0.15	0.31

*) Polarization index = Socialist + Conservatives + National Socialist vote as ratio of the total votes cast for all major party groups. See Rokkan and Lipset, *Party Systems and Voter Alignments*, note 46, p. 441.

Social Structure, Economy and Anti-Centralism: Three Clues to the Immunity of the West and the South

In the preceding parts we demonstrated how the N.S. failed almost completely to win adherents in the Western and Southern coastal areas both before and during the war. We have already had occasion to present the three indicators which we see as crucial for any comparative analysis of this phenomenon. They were: percentage of debts on holdings *(the economic crisis variable);* the preponderance of large farms *(the political polarization variable);* and the type of economy *(monetization vs. subsistence orientation).* Here we shall make an attempt to account for this striking immunity to extremist politics by using these three indicators.

1. The most important factor in making the population in these regions immune to any Nazi inroads is probably the *relative equality of social conditions* in the Western rural communities. Holdings were roughly equal. We have shown how internal size differentials gave impetus to political polarization. In 1959 the agricultural census reported these regional variations in size of farms:[27]

	Mean size in decares	Proportion of units over 100 decares
East and Trøndelag	61.01	18.4%
South and West	35.99	3.4%
North	30.11	1.7%
National Average	46.95	8.9%

The important point is that since poverty – or prosperity – were shared, the social structure did not give room for any extremist appeals. It is essential to distinguish between *absolute* and *relative* size. While smallholders are likely to be polarized in areas of substantial size differentials, in areas where their fellow citizens are basically equal there will be no basis for class hatred. In addition, because of the size of the farms there was relatively little need for hired labor, hence no resentment between farm laborers with no land and the local *storbønder*. The familiar pattern of large majorities of forestry workers, smallholders and other seasonal workers facing a small group of powerful forest-owners and large-scale farmers was absent from the West.

2. The Southwestern rural communities were often *isolated* and *tightly integrated* with a high degree of social control. Large proportions of the people lived in mountainous parts along the fjords or scattered on the many islands along the coast. In the thirties, with the exception of a few industrial towns, the area was rural or based its income on fisheries. The Southwest, in Rokkan's view, has not only been more *egalitarian* in social structure. These regions have also exhibited a marked *cultural distinctiveness* in relation to the rest of the nation. This socio-cultural distinctiveness can explain the deviance of these areas from the national political alignments, in particular the trend towards support for the middle parties and the rejection of class ideologies. Rokkan singles out three sets of policies more strongly advocated in the regions of the South and West than elsewhere:[28]

– the defence of Lutheran revivalist orthodoxy and pietistic fundamentalism against radicalizing and secularizing influences from the urban centres;
– the strong support for temperance and prohibition movements; and
– the protection of the rural language *nynorsk* against the standard *riksmål* identified with the capital and foreign influence via the Danish civil servants.

This Southwestern «counter culture» is in our view crucial in understanding the immunity to the N.S. The N.S. was at best seen as lukewarm towards religion. One of the most persistent advocates of resistance to National Socialism at home or abroad was the Bergen religious newspaper *Dagen*. Fiercely revivalist, it detested the N.S. not only as an import from a city center, Oslo, which had long been the target of the Southwestern religious communities, but also as a *pagan* movement. Its Viking symbolism and its blend of millenarism and explicit espousal of pre-Christian names and values was bound to alienate the Southwestern fundamentalists. Attempts to tie the Nazi form of nationalism to traditional religious values in these regions failed miserably: the people remained immune.[29] With its belief that men are unequal before God, that their fate is determined by their racial inheritance and not by divine grace and their own merits and by their invocation of an inherently pre-Christian social philosophy, the N.S. offered little the religiously committed could identify with. People in the Southwestern communities were already integrated in a web of supportive social networks often concentrated around the local religious meeting house *(bedehus)* and the low church congregations. To them, the N.S. was heathen, associated with city folks and anti-democratic. Hence the stiff resistance.

It may be enlightening to discuss whether this rejection of Nazism in the South and West is a phenomenon similar in structure to that observed in Schleswig Holstein by Heberle[30] and Loomis and Beegle,[31] and in German elections by Lipset[32] and Dean Burnham:[33] in those areas and among the layers of the population where the Catholic *Zentrum* was strong, the N.S.D.A.P. gained considerably less electoral support. The *Zentrum* was the only non-socialist party which kept its relative share of the votes in the elections in the Weimar Republic. Burnham's explanation is that the *Zentrum* – and the SPD – were 'political churches'. Within the Catholic camp there were strong religious commitments. The presence of the Church in everyday life added to the cohesiveness of the Catholic communities and «immunized» people against extremist appeals. Such an «immunization» mechanism was probably at work in the Southern and Western part of Norway as well, most clearly in the primary economy communes. In the cities, in particular Stavanger and Bergen, this phenomenon is less prominent.

We have tested this hypothesis by correlating our indicators of Nazi support with indicators on «counter-cultural» attitudes. The result is presented in table 6.

Table 6. *Correlations between «Counter-cultural» Attitudes and N.S. Affiliation*

	N.S. membership as percentage of the total population	
1. Percentage of voting for prohibition on alcoholic beverages in the national referendum over this issue in 1926	÷ 0.39	
2. Percentage voting for the Liberal *(Venstre)* party of total number of votes cast in the general elections in 1933 and 1936	÷ 0.39	÷ 0.40

Pearson correlation coefficients (N=746)

As expected, there is an *inverse association between these measurés of counter-cultural loyalties and indicators of N.S strength.*

3. Closely related to the size of holdings which made large-scale production difficult and removed the need for extensive hiring of farm hands, there was the added factor of an economic ideology of *thrift, independence* and *economizing.* People were on the whole less apt to accumulate debts on their holdings. Indeed, topography put restrictions on any large-scale program of land-clearing which would have required further mechanization and capital outlays. More vital yet, the *type of economy was different in the West and the South.* As Hendriksen and Thunshelle have pointed out, the farmers in these regions were less incorporated into the market economy than their counterparts in the East. The degree of capitalization was relatively low; very few were in debt (see note 25 for the figures). Based on small, flexible units and local industries which converted raw materials from the primary sector into products for local consumption, the economy remained relatively shielded from international business cycles.[34] The number of people receiving unemployment benefits was both

638

in absolute and relative terms very low; in 1930 Sogn og Fjordane ranked lowest in this respect. In sum, the misery of unemployment, foreclosures, debt burdens and municipal poverty, so familiar in the East, were to a large extent absent from the West and South.

4. Finally, there was a crucial *political dimension* to the resistance to Nazi influence in the West and South. By incessantly attacking parliamentary institutions, downgrading popular rule in favor of rule by «professionals» or «competent men» *(fagstyre)*, Quisling struck a raw nerve.[35] The N.S., while never making up its mind whether to advocate free enterprise or a *dirigiste* economic system, always espoused corporatism. Decision-making should be transferred to a *næringsting,* a corporate assembly of representatives from industry and the professions. This was bound to evoke resistance in the peripheries. In the rural areas in the West and the South, and also in the North, people had worked to increase grass-root control over the central administration. The capital and the central core of Nowegian 'nation builders' had historically been the adversaries of the peripheries. Through parliament, the population in the Western, Southern and Northern periphery had won influence in the center. The principle of electoral equality and geographical representation gave the districts a number of seats out of proportion to the size of population. This bias was built into the system to counteract the effects of an unfavorable position in relation to the central decision-making agencies. The peripheries had used *voice,* to use Hirschman's standard expression,[36] and they intended to protect this important channel of influence. It did not help that N.S. extolled the simplicity, decency and order of rural life: no *Mittelstand* propaganda could undermine the defense of the political access already won. In the alliance with the urban intelligentsia, the peripheries had formed the backbone of the drive towards parliamentarization from the middle of the 19th century. Any attack on the Storting was, indirectly, an attack on the political aspirations of the majority of the people in the regions.

Fascism in Norway: Why it was Deprived of Political Space

The NS reached its electoral peak in 1933, polling 2.23 per cent of the vote. After its second try in a general election, in 1936, the failure was irrevocable. It slid downwards, internally split, hopelessly discredited and increasingly prone to anti-Semitic sloganeering. It became a political dead-end only to be resurrected under German auspices.

Why was the N.S. so inept in carving out a niche for itself in a country so beset by crisis as Norway was in the early thirties?

The three Scandinavian countries all showed a basic immunity to fascism as a mass phenomenon. They all shared a series of fundamental characteristics which go a long way towards explaining why fascism had no chance. Or put differently: Scandinavia lacked many of the requisites commonly held to be crucial in preparing the ground for mass support for fascism. Here we shall discuss some of these characteristics. Our prime focus will be Norway, but what holds for Norway is, with minor variations, equally true for the other two countries. What remains of differences shed interesting light on each political system, but they did not affect the chances of fascism to expand beyond its original nucleus of activists. (For a comparison between Norway and Sweden, see Bernt Hagtvet's paper on Swedish fascism in this volume.»)

The failure of fascism to gain a foothold in Scandinavia requires explanations on several levels. First, it will be necessary to discuss the mobilizing potential of *the issues* presenting themselves to the political system of the day. The second task will be to account for the limited *political space* afforded to fascism in these countries. The availability of alliance partners for fascism proved very restricted. This requires elucidation. And third, there was no illiberal political culture in these countries which could nourish fascist sentiments. We will end by suggesting a few general features of the prevailing *political culture* in the inter-war period.

As to the question of issues, it is easy to see that the problems which proved so effective as mobilizing agents in the Central European countries were conspicuously absent in Scandinavia. Norway, like Denmark and Sweden, was neutral in World War I and had not suffered any national humiliation. Hence the *potential for appealing to frustrated nationalism was simply not there*. The state corresponded closely to what the majority perceived the boundaries of the nation to be. As a result, there were *no irredentist sentiments*. When, in 1931, a case emerged which could have offered opportunities for a flare-up of nationalism, *the population as well as the majority of the parties refused to become involved*. That year Norway challenged Danish jurisdiction over parts of Greenland. Towards the end of the 19th century Norwegian fishermen and seal hunters had built settlements on East Greenland, but in 1919 the Norwegian government had committed itself not to claim sovereignty over the island. Quisling tried to foment «grossnorwegische» sentiments over the issue, but on the whole he only reached marginal groups. Neither the Labor party nor the majorities in either of the non-socialist parties were willing to turn the issue into a national cause. When the Hague Tribunal ruled in favor of continued Danish control over the territory, the result was readily accepted.[37] Attempts by Quisling to revive the issue proved futile.

Save for the Lapp minority in the North, Norway was *culturally and ethnically homogenous*. Although the state was young (independence gained from Sweden in 1905, domestic sovereignty in 1814), the nation was old. Therefore, *national identity was no problem*. Another feature of the fascist core countries, the *accumulation of crises* syndrome, was likewise absent: mass politics had been established before the onset of industrialization; the state was consolidated and the administration centralized at low levels of mobilization. In Norway, there was *no absolutist heritage and no remnants of feudal power*, as in Germany, which could create barriers for the gradual enfranchisement of the lower classes. The 1814 Constitution was one of the most liberal of the time. The country had not, like Italy and Germany and to a lesser extent Austria, experienced a *failed revolutionary attempt* after the war. Despite its verbal intransigence well into the thirties and its membership in the Comintern (1920–23), the Norwegian Labor party had no plans for an armed overthrow of government. The use of the socialist bogey did strike a responsive chord in the Norwegian bourgeoisie, however, but the menace of revolution was a too one-dimensional issue over time, especially after the DNA had proved its *Salonfähigkeit* in 1935. When it entered the scene, the N.S. had, in effect, to campaign against a Labor party which had ceased to be revolutionary and a C.P. with less than 1 per cent of the vote. In order to make its appeal credible, the N.S. had to conjure up an image of an imminent revolutionary take-over at a time when the radical wave of the post World War I years had long subsided.

The most burning issue confronting the parties in the inter-war period was, of course, the depression. By 1932 the crisis had peaked, however, making the N.S. a late-comer also in this respect. When, after 1935, the party attempted to use anti-Semitism to bolster its political fortunes, it seized on the wrong issue in the wrong country. Norway had its share of anti-Semitic journals, and anti-Semitism found a certain resonance in conservative and agrarian newspapers and among a small group of literati.[38] The vigilante strike-breaker organization *Norges Samfundshjelp* (Norway's Community Relief) also included anti-Semitism in its anti-democratic propaganda.[39] But projecting the Jews as a threat to the national community could easily be rejected by checking the actual number of Jews in the country. The census taken in 1920 estimated that 1457 Jews had taken up residence in Norway. Ten years later the number had declined to 1359. On the whole *anti-Semitism had little to thrive on* in Norway and remained insignificant as a politico-cultural force. There was considerable resistance among medical students against allowing Jewish doctors to settle and practice freely in the country,[40] but the openly anti-Semitic demonstrations found in Sweden at the time had no equivalent west of the border. Similarly, no student body passed any anti-Jewish or racist resolutions like those passed in the Swedish student unions in Lund, Uppsala and Stockholm. Approximately 500 Jews were given entry visas to Norway between 1920 and 1940. At the outbreak of World War II about 300 of them still lived in the country.[41] Quite a few of these refugees from Germany used Norway only as a stop on their way to other nations, most notably the U.S. When the N.S. resorted to vociferous anti-Semitic campaigns after 1935, this was alien to Norwegian political and cultural traditions and only deepened the isolation of the party.

In sum there was relatively little for the N.S. to gain from the prevailing resentments of the age. Issues which had galvanized and given direction to anti-democratic sentiments in Central Europe were either nonexistent or soon lost their relevance in Scandinavia. This holds true with minor variations for the whole inter-war period. The polarization and the segmented divisions found for instance in Germany and Austria were prevented in Scandinavia by a series of complex *compromises between the primary sector in the economy and the urban industrial working class.*[42] Through these re-alignments the fascist movements were deprived of political 'space' in which to gain credibility for their alternative. Since its inception, fascism had come to power either on the shoulders of the farmers or through compromises with the existing economic and political élites. The success of fascism depends in large measure on the penetrability of the barriers between the fascist party and immediate political environment: the conservatives and the agrarians. In the Scandinavian case, despite substantial ideological affinity, no *lasting* organizational co-operation between a fascist party and a major non-socialist party came into being (an exception must be made for the SNU, *Sveriges Nationella Ungdomsförbund*, which started as the youth organization of the Swedish conservatives).[43] The underlying reasons why alliance-building on the Right proved such an unrewarding task at the same time give important clues for understanding the entire Scandinavian political scene. We shall here give a brief overview of the relations between the N.S. and its neighbors in the party spectrum, drawing parallels with Sweden and discussing further why the N.S. never succeeded in breaking out of its fringe existence.

The compromises worked out between the agrarians and the urban industrial proletariat are important in Norway and Sweden because they *pre-empted* political space for fascism. On the parliamentary level these crises deals laid the foundation for more stable majorities and paved the way for Labor governments more willing to use economic planning and deficit spending on the Keynesian model to combat the slump. In Norway, the compromise was essentially a pledge by Labor to protect the agricultural sector in return for Agrarian support in parliament. In the course of the depression, the gap between the Labor and Agrarian proposals to deal with the slump in the countryside had narrowed considerably. The improvement in the economy had started before Labor took office in 1935 with Agrarian support, but the new alliance had deep symbolic significance.[44] It showed that «the system» was capable of acting; a mere reacting to events had been succeeded by conscious expansionary policies. Although the first budget from the Labor government proposed additional funds for agriculture and fisheries to be financed by a new sales tax, it did not break radically with established economic wisdom. This had been traditional Agrarian policy. But the compromise showed that there was considerable room to manoeuvre in the Norwegian political system. In Germany, a rural-urban alliance of this kind never came about, with disastrous consequences for the stability of Weimar democracy.

The compromise was made possible by the existence of a rural wing inside the Labor party consisting of fishermen and smallholders. Wanting immediate alleviation of their conditions, they made the Labor party more amenable to working out a deal. These rural Labor leaders represented a lower socio-economic stratum than the Agrarians, but this internal split in the rural population proved less important than their common interest in arresting the full fledged exercise of market forces in the primary economy.[45] The crisis compromise in 1935 was an example of Norwegian 'radical conservatism': 'radical' because it increased the role of the state in the economy and brought a party pledged to socialism to power; 'conservative' because it in a sense was designed to preserve a great deal of the *status quo*, to soften the impact of industrialization and market relations in the countryside.

In an attempt to fuse various groups on the extreme Right, the N.S. had initiated talks in 1934 to form a 'national bloc'. The partners in this endeavor were the Agrarians, the National Liberals *(Frisinnede)*, the Fatherland League *(Fedrelandslaget)* and the N.S. The Agrarians had the key to success, but pressure from the other non-socialist parties proved too strong. When the party was promised economic support from a common non-socialist electoral fund only on the condition that N.S. was excluded, the party withdrew. The next year its alliance with the Labor party confirmed the isolation of the N.S.[46]

The other potential alliance partner for the N.S., the Conservative party *(Høire)*, were primarly motivated by a desire to keep a unified front against the Labor party. The leadership in the Conservative party regarded the N.S. as a splinter party, a «grampus» or a «killer whale» as one of the leaders put it, making a living by eating the flesh off other parties.[47] When a local party branch in Bergen formed an electoral alliance with the N.S. in 1933, it drew criticism from the party headquarters although no one was excluded for this breach of party discipline. The leading conservative daily *Aftenposten* showed a baffling insensitivity to reports about cruelty in Germany but remained firm in its resistance to Quisling at home.[48] As an editorial put it in 1922: «. . . while fighting the socialist dictatorship of the Norwegian Labor party on the main scene, we have no intention of letting another socialist dictatorship in backstage».[49] *Aftenposten* equated socialism with Quisling's brand of fascism; their common point of reference, as the editors saw it, was the strong state. This economic liberalism which found its clearest expression in the fear of an omnipotent state and intervention in the economy, provided the best defense against flirtations with the ultra Right. Here is an interesting difference between Norway and Sweden which deserves further comment. These differences over the concept of the state can best be studied in the conservative youth organization which for a time shared the authoritarian views of the Swedish counterpart SNU.

Both the Danish (KU, *Konservativ Ungdom)*, the Swedish (SNU) and the Norwegian conservative youth organizations *(Unge Høire)* went through periods of corporatist and authoritarian activism. The strategy of the Norwegian young conservatives in 1933 and 1934 was to convince the elders in the party that co-operation with the N.S. could strengthen the anti-marxist front. By 1936, however, the attempts at *rapprochement* had cooled and the young conservatives joined the official party line. In their ideological affinities with the N.S., the young conservatives concurred that National Socialism had recognized the most basic principle in the conservative ideology – «a strong authoritative state by and for the people». In March 1934 the conservative student magazine *Minerva* put it bluntly:

> «An authoritarian state to which everybody must yield, commanding obedience through a powerful government independent of other organs of the state and local self-government, that is what we need. But such a government, which also has to govern the economy of the country, cannot be rooted in our existing parliamentary system. It must be based on and paralleled by an assembly of representatives, as an advisory council, from the interest organizations and certain other associations and institutions. What we need, in other words, is the fascist system.»[50]

These departures from the laissez-faire liberalism espoused by the official party line were regarded with increasing anxiety from the elders. In 1934 the two groups within the conservative camp were close to a break. What made a fusion with the N.S. difficult, however, were disagreements over the *Führer*-principle and a feeling on the part of the young conservatives that there was hope of winning over the elders. The pseudo-fascism of Unge Høire remained an episode, an intermezzo in the twilight of democracy. The critical factor in keeping the Norwegian conservatives away from Quisling was *the lack of an indigenous 'organic' conservative* tradition of the kind epitomized by the geo-political thinker Rudolf Kjellén in Sweden. In Sweden, under influence from Kjellén and his 'Young Conservatives', the conservative resistance to democracy lasted far longer than in Norway. As late as 1929 prominent conservatives in Sweden expressed reservations about the legitimacy of democracy which was seen as «fundamentally alien to conservatism». In Sweden, the concept of the state as the strong, authoritative focus for the defense of the nation had lingered on and taken precedence over the liberal notion of the state. This blurred the distinctions between the fascist notion of the state and the 'organic', and made Swedish conservative ideology less of a stumbling block for anti-democratic activism.

The different character of conservatism in Norway and Sweden is indicative of a more general feature of the Norwegian political system: the weakness of the upper classes and their willingness to backtrack once new rules of the game have been established. Ulf Torgersen makes this capacity for «painless institutional change» a prominent characteristic of Norwegian political development.[51] The «crises of legitimacy» in Norwegian political history (1814, 1884, 1920's and 1940–45) were all quite rapidly overcome without anyone resorting to extreme solutions (except on the verbal level). The liberal predispositions of the upper classes, the predominance of egalitarian values, the gradualness of the extensions of the franchise, a pattern which diverge from the path followed by Sweden, and the consensus, despite doctrinal commitments to the contrary, on democratic rules of the game – these features made the Norwegian political system very resistant to the extreme, dictatorial alternative presented by the N.S. Not even the depression threatened the basic legitimacy of the system. The N.S. was doomed to failure.

The N.S. offered the path which was not followed. It bears a striking resemblance to the fate of Mosley's B.U.F.: its proposed way out of the crisis was too alien for the country's political traditions and institutions. How, then, can Norwegian fascism most appropriately be defined?

In this study we have argued that the social locus of the N.S. varied considerably. Any coherent *Mittelstand* hypothesis fails to come to grips with the extremely varied, often contradictory, influences which impelled people to join the N.S. This remains our main contention: the N.S. was used as a vehicle for structuring a confusing world; it became a repository of ideals of reconciliation and escape for people who had experienced disruptions and disappointments in their aspirations and in their daily lives. What the fringe groups found in the party was essentially a projection of their own frustrations, and they were not uniform. There are *tendencies* in the material presented in our and Stein Ugelvik Larsen's study, but they do not warrant any conclusion that the N.S. was the response of *one distinct class* to political strains. Neither does the question of *cui bono* allow any simple answer. Dahl argues that the activists in the N.S. gravitated towards shipping and the export industry, sectors vulnerable to the international business cycles. But there were also other influential industrialists less dependent on exports who provided support.[52] How much is unclear. Generous financial support from industry was at no time available. The N.S. cannot be seen as the political arm of aggressive and crisis-stricken industrialists. By contrast to Germany, the Norwegian business segment, though clearly conservative, was not anti-democratic as a whole. The diversification of support makes it difficult to determine the party structurally to the level of class. Instead it can be located primarily at the *political* level, as «the hot-headed reaction against . . . acknowledgment of the Labor party as a legitimate partner in the political realm».[53] This definition of the N.S. as fundamentally a political *rear-guard action* aginst Labor party ascendancy with its geographical center of gravity in the capital, is a view common to several writers on the subject.[54] This perspective makes the N.S. part of a longer tradition of Norwegian anti-parliamentarism,[55] the most extreme version of an ideology of preventive *coup d'état* which had lingered on in rightist circles in Oslo ever since Labor threatened the political balance of forces, even before.[56] The common focal point of this anti-laborite formation was to weaken the plebiscitary channel and replace it with some form of corporatism bypassing the *Storting*. With the collapse of the negotiations about the 'national bloc' in 1934 this anti-labor alliance between the Fatherland League, the Agrarians, the National Liberals and the N.S. had run its course. It had proved impossible to establish a bourgeois government alternative outside the Liberal and Conservative parties. From this date the fate of the N.S. was sealed. Only after the invasion could Quisling manage what he had hoped to do a decade before: declare the establishment of a national government «above parties» and dissolve the representative organs which, in his view, had so long lent legitimacy to the enemies of the constitution and sown the seeds of discord in the country.

NOTES

* We would like to thank Stein Ugelvik Larsen especially for his advice at different stages of this work, and Trygve Bull, Michael J. Clark, Malene Djursaa, William M. Lafferty and Sten S. Nilson for comments on earlier drafts. They are of course absolved of responsibility for any remaining shortcomings.

[1] The best guide to the literature on Norwegian political development and electoral mobilization is found in Stein Rokkan's work. See in particular his *Citizens, Elections, Parties* (Oslo/New York 1970) especially ch. 6. The best introduction to Norwegian politics for the English-speaking reader is still his «Geography, Religion and Social Class: Cross-cutting Cleavages in Norwegian Politics» in Seymour Martin Lipset and Stein Rokkan (eds.) *Party Systems and Voter Alignments* (New York 1967). This work and Rokkan's discussion of «Norway: Numerical Democracy and Corporate Pluralism» in R. A. Dahl (ed.) *Political Oppositions in Western Democracies* (New Haven & London 1966) provide the underpinnings for our discussion of the regional contrasts in the social bases of Norwegian fascism.

[2] On the data archive used as the basis for this study, see note 6 in Stein Ugelvik Larsen's contribution to this volume.

[3] In Tolga in the Østerdal region, for example, one of the strongholds of N.S., the party benefited from one extraordinarily active recruiter, Ivar Sæter, a colorful local «opinion leader» of considerable influence, well known for his admiration for Bjørnstjerne Bjørnson, the prominent Norwegian nationalist, poet, novelist, playwright and publicist (1832–1910). On this point, see Eystein Eggen, «Norsk nazisme» (Norwegian Nazism), in *Samtiden* vol. 79, no. 7, p. 450 and footnote 19.

[4] The most perceptive discussion of the level of analysis problem as a challenge in Norwegian ecological studies, is found in W. M. Lafferty's work on the reponse of the Scandinavian labor movements to processes of industrialization. See his *Economic Development and the Response of Labor in Scandinavia: A Multi-Level Analysis* (Oslo 1971), especially ch. 1, and *Industrialization, Community Structure and Socialism: An Ecological Analysis of Norway 1874–1925* (Oslo 1974) ch. 1.

[5] For an analysis of individual perceptions conducive to support for the party, see Stein Ugelvik Larsen's article, in this volume.

[6] Cf. Stein Rokkan and Henry Valen, «Conflict Structure and Mass Politics in a European Periphery: Norway», in R. Rose (ed.) *Electoral Behavior* (N.Y. 1974), and S. Rokkan, «Regional Contrasts in Norwegian Politics», in E. Allardt and S. Rokkan (eds.) *Mass Politics* (N.Y. 1969).

[7] Setesdal is the neighboring district to Fyresdal, the birth-place of Vidkun Quisling. Significantly, the N.S. was strong in the elections in Setesdal before the war: a joint list of N.S. and the militant debtor's organization *Bygdefolkets Krisehjelp* (Farmers' Relief Association) gained 29.7 per cent of the total number of valid votes in 1933. The electoral alliance with the *Krisehjelp* puts the specifically *fascist* character of this support into doubt. Elsewhere, for example in Telemark, the farmer's alliance with the N.S. through this vigilante protest organization was short-lived and opportunist in nature, and did not produce any high percentages of N.S. members after the expiry of the electoral arrangements. In Valle, on the contrary, the persistence of N.S. support suggests a certain continuity of alignments. Besides S. S. Nilson's article in this book, material on this Norwegian version of the North German peasant *Schicksalsgemeinschaften* can be found in Nilson's earlier work, «Wahlsoziologische Probleme des Nationalsozialismus» in *Zeitschrift für die gesamte Staatswissenschaft*, vol. 110 (1954) pp. 295 ff., «Aspects de la vie politique en Norvège» in *Revue française de science politique* vol. III, 1953 pp. 556 ff., and his «The Political Parties» in Joseph A. Lauwery's (ed.) *Scandinavian Democracy* (Copenhagen 1958), pp. 107–126.

[8] Edv. Bull, «konomisk og administrativ historie», in Hans Aall *et al.* (eds.) *Norske Bygder*, Vol. I, Setesdalen, p. 46 (Oslo 1921).

[9] Henry Ashby Turner, jr., «Fascism and Modernization», p. 120, in *ibid.* (ed.), *Reappraisals of Fascism* (N.Y. 1975).

[10] The extent to which Quisling himself was influenced by this tradition-conscious nostalgia is reflected in the testimony he gave at his trial in 1945:

«I was brought up among Viking graves, amidst scriptural history and the sagas. I belonged to an ancient house and was steeped in family pride, family history and a sense of responsibility to our people. Bjørnson and Ibsen were of the same stock, so dishwater did not run in my veins. The name Quisling is no foreign name, but an ancient Nordic name, meaning a cadet branch of a royal house. Q is not an outlandish Latin letter but an ancient protective rune.»

From *Straffesak mot Vidkun Abraham Lauritz Jonssøn Quisling* (Oslo 1946) pp. 327–28, in English translation by Paul M. Hayes, *Quisling: The Career and Political Ideas of Vidkun Quisling, 1887–1945*, p. 12 (London 1971).

[11] *Vår kamp* (Our Struggle) no. 15, 1936.

[12] *Nasjonal Samling,* no. 44, 1935.

As an example of the warnings against the intrusion of «new times» in the countryside found in party propaganda, the following quotation from a brochure conveys some of the flavor of the argument:

«. . . look to our countryside to-day and see how it is ravaged by the Swiss style (of architecture); enter the homes of farmers and see how the chairs with spindled backs *(pinnestoler)* and plush sofas have forced their way in; go into the kitchen and notice how artificial cooking has ousted for the healthy farmer's diet; attend the meetings of the local associations and listen to the decadent cabaret songs performed there; look at the clothing of the people and see how it is marred by mass produced garments.»

J. B. Hjort and T. Hustad, *Nasjonal bondepolitikk* (National Agrarian Policy) in the series *Nasjonal Samling opplysningsskrifter,* no. 1, 1934.

[13] Eggen, *op. cit.,* pp. 446–453.

[14] Tor Jonsson, *Nesler* (Nettles), published in Oslo 1952, pp. 26–27.

[15] The N.S. publication *Norsk jord* (Norwegian Soil) describes Valle in this way: «In the small district of Valle . . . times have passed unnoticed for centuries, and here live and blossom the old Norse customs to-day», no. 17, 1942.

This notion of the *setesdøl* as a conservative «aristocrat» and a staunch guardian of old Norse culture was expressed as early as 1922 by a comtemporary observer with no Nazi leanings:

«. . . the character of the *setesdøl* (inhabitant of Setesdal) is conservative and he is a distinguished aristocrat. There are, in spite of equal material conditions, strong class differences. The upper class is made up of the farmers, those who own their land; the lower classes are the cottiers and the workers. The ancient Germanic conceptions prevail here and leave their imprint on the customs marking the great events of life, such as marriage. Being of a good family is much valued and the feeling of family belonging and family ancestry is strong. The *setesdøl* has been acquainted with a culture that is like a vital breath from those days when we were brave men and the name of Norway was mentioned with respect among the nations. The *setesdøl* is the last guardian of the remaining parts of our *medieval culture*. It is with great pain that we acknowledge that time is conquering this survivor. The day will come and it is unfortunately not far away when the marvellous lofts with their beautiful bold ornaments will have been removed from the valley to rot in the damp ocean gusts beside the sea, in the folk museums or in rich people's gardens; when the last silver smith will have to see girls buy fake gem stones from the local grocery; when folk dances and the sounds of the fiddle will have been replaced by vulgar cabaret songs and the noise of grammophones.» *(Our italics.)*

Setesdal og setesdølene. Et Rids af Olav Benneche. (Oslo: Den Norske Turistforenings Årbok 1922.)

This folkloristic description, however unsupported by hard data, in our view reveals quite a lot: how people outside perceived these isolated valley areas and how the people in these communities regarded themselves. This kind of propaganda, cleverly directed by the N.S. towards these communities in times of profound change, must have had an impact.

[16] On this fear of evolution exhibited by the *Mittelstand,* see Heinrich A. Winkler, «Extremismus der Mitte? Sozialgeschichtlicher Aspekte der nationalsozialistischen Machtergreifung», in *Vierteljahreshefte für Zeitgeschichte* (20), 1972 pp. 175–191, and his survey of the field, «From Social Protectionism to National Socialism: The German Small-Business Movement in Comparative Perspective» in *Journal of Modern History,* 48 (March 1976) pp. 1–18.

[17] Wolfgang Sauer, «National Socialism: Totalitarianism or Fascism?» in *American Historical Review* LXXII (1967), p. 417.

[18] Cf. G. Ousland, *Fagorganisasjonen i Norge* (The Trade Union Movement in Norway), vol. II, p. 514, and S. Tveite, «Krisa i nord-europeisk jordbruk i mellomkrigsåra», *Syn og Segn,* 6, 1974, p. 365.

[19] Specifically, the conflict revolved around a pledge of N.kr. 90,000 made by the Tolga municipal council to Os on the partition of the two communes. The commune had co-signed for large sums for the construction of hydro-electric power plants in the twenties in the belief that there would never be any question of actually having to pay these sums. With the onset of the depression, however, the commune, then consisting of Tolga and Os, was forced to fulfill its obligations. Some local people, among them the activist mentioned in note 3, later to become the most prominent N.S. recruiter in the community, thought that the Tolga representatives in the municipal council had been far too generous with the demands from Os when the common debts had to be divided. A feeling of mistrust towards the politicians responsible for the decision was growing and a climate created in which typical N.S. propaganda about the 'incompetence of parliamentary bodies' found ample nourishment. The activist was also a leading spokesman for the *Bygdefolkets Krisehjelp* in the community, and on his farm there were Olsok (July 29) gatherings with displays of N.S. symbols in the style of the N.S. conventions at the historical sites of Borre and Hafrsfjord. In the municipal elections in the early thirties this mistrust led to the replacement of most of the members of the municipal council. It is reasonable to assume that the N.S. could capitalize on these local problems. Some local observers have also noted the strength of the *Hird* in the community and takes this to be the result of the conversion of some influential athletes and youthful 'opinion leaders' in the community. These observations are all very tentative, but in the absence of clear-cut structural determinants they seem to offer interesting possibilities for further research. For a discussion of the socio-economic conditions in these two communities, see Kåre Bakosgjelten, *Krise i fjellbygder. Tolga og Os i mellomkrigstida*, M. A. dissertation, University of Trondheim, Institute of History, Spring 1976. (Crisis in the Mountain Communities. Tolga and Os in the Inter-War Period.) We are also indebted to Steinar Simensen for discussing these points with us.

[20] Hans Fredrik Dahl, *Norge mellom krigene* (Norway Between the Wars), p. 72–73 (Oslo 1973).

[21] The influence of individuals should again be noted. One of the founding fathers of N.S. in Vadsø in the county of Finmark was the local minister. He worked energetically for the party in the whole Northern region, and, as Dag O. Bruknapp puts it, «(t)he party's good result in the municipal elections in Vadsø in 1934 is mostly due to him». Another minister played an important role in the N.S. stronghold of Åmot in the Østerdal region. He was chairman of the local party branch from 1933 to 1940. Cf. D. O. Bruknapp, «Ideene splitter partiet. Rasespørsmålets betydning i N.S.'s utvikling». (Ideas Split the Party. The Significance of the Racial Question in the Development of the N.S.) in S. U. Larsen & Rolf Danielsen (eds.) *Fra idé til dom* (From Idea to Sentence), p. 20, 21 (Oslo/Bergen/Tromsø 1976).

[22] The table (p. 648) is reproduced by H. Hendriksen and T. J. Thunshelle in their article «Den mislukka samlinga. N.S. i Sogn og Fjordane fylke 1940–1945» (The Unsuccessful Unification. The N.S. in the County of S. & F. 1940–45), p. 112, in Ugelvik Larsen and Danielsen, *op.cit.* Their source is NOS (Norwegian Official Statistics) IX 18, «Gårdbrukernes og småbrukernes gjeld» (The Debt Burdens of the Farmers and the Smallholders), Oslo 1933. These data have now been transferred to the *Norwegian ecological data archive*, cf. J. P. Myklebust *et al. Kommunearkivet 1905–1940 (The Ecological Archive 1905–1940)* NSD Publication no. 8 from the Norwegian Social Science Data Services, Bergen, 1976 pp. 93–96.

[23] For an amplification of the argument presented in this book, see his «Mennesker uten makt» (People without Power) in Ugelvik Larsen & Danielsen (eds.) *op.cit.*, 68.104.

[24] On Norwegian financial policy in the 30's, see F. Sejersted, *Ideal, teori og virkelighet. Nikolai Rygg og pengepolitikken i 1920-årene* (Oslo 1973). (Ideal, Theory and Reality: N.R. and Montetary Policy in the 1920's.)

[25] The whole table provides the folliving debt profile broken down to counties. (p. 648.)

[26] For details, see S. Rokkan, «Geography, Religion and Social Class . . .» in Lipset/Rokkan, *op.cit.*, p. 408 ff.

[27] N.O.S. (Norway's Official Statistics) XII, 79, *Jordbruksteljinga i Norge, 20. juni 1959* (The Agricultural Census) I, 1961, Table 1, quoted from Rokkan, *op.cit.*, p. 410.

[28] *Ibid.*, p. 415.

Number of Foreclosures

County	Number of Foreclosures Annually per 1,000 holdings in 1931/32
Østfold	14.27
Akershus	14.97
Hedmark	103.54
Oppland	35.74,
Buskerud	21.30
Vestfold	9.00
Telemark	32.06
Aust Agder	8.46
Vest Agder	4.17
Rogaland	7.50
Hordaland	2.73
Sogn og Fjordane	5.38
Møre og Romsdal	7.63
Sør-Trøndelag	13.25
Nord-Trøndelag	25.27
Nordland	23.04
Troms	42.54
Finmark	50.66
National Average	23.47

Percentage of Debts in Agriculture at January 1, 1932

County	Gårdsbruk (Over 50 decares)	Småbruk (Under 50 decares)	Both categories
Østfold	46.77	54.91	47.50
Akershus	47.47	58.23	48.13
Hedmark	55.77	66.73	57.16
Oppland	49.55	65.50	51.11
Buskerud	52.82	50.69	52.66
Vestfold	51.30	51.42	51.31
Telemark	49.48	63.30	50.58
Aust Agder	38.43	46.10	38.04
Vest Agder	28.32	24.54	27.76
Rogaland	37.13	47.95	37.87
Hordaland	34.65	39.48	35.77
Sogn og Fjordane	39.09	42.06	39.36
Møre og Romsdal	31.12	40.26	32.62
Sør-Trøndelag	34.64	46.21	36.26
Nord-Trøndelag	43.47	59.44	45.99
Nordland	33.84	39.66	36.00
Troms	39.95	50.15	44.84
Finmark	21.32	33.60	30.49
National Average	44.48	49.99	45.20

[29] In the county of Sogn og Fjordane, the propaganda leader in charge of Western Norway made explicit attempts to attach the party to the prevailing religious fervor. The party intended, he stated, to make people understand that «N.S. precisely wants to encourage personal conduct in harmony with the beliefs and the norms upon which they built their lives». Quotation from a letter dated November 12, 1941, in the judicial archives, Akershus, Oslo, from Thunshelle & Hendriksen, *op.cit.*, in Ugelvik Larsen & Danielsen *Fra idé til dom*, p. 117. Sogn og Fjordane had the lowest proportion of N.S. members (0.4% of the entire population) as against Oppland which had the highest (2.6% of the population). Corresponding figures for the whole of Western Norway are: Rogaland: 1.1%; Bergen and Hordaland: 0.7%; Møre og Romsdal: 0.9%.

[30] R. Heberle, *From Democracy to Nazism* (Baton Rouge 1945).

[31] C. P. Loomis and J. A. Beegle, «The Spread of Nazism in Rural Areas», in *American Political Science Review*, 11, 1946, esp. p. 733.

[32] S. M. Lipset, «Fascism – Left, Right and Center», in *Political Man* (N.Y. 1960).

[33] W. D. Burnham, «Political Immunization and Political Confessionalism: The United States and Weimar Germany», in *Journal of Interdisciplinary History*, vol. III, 1972, pp. 1–30.

[34] Thunshelle & Hendriksen, *op.cit.*, p. 110.

[35] We are indebted to Professor Ulf Torgersen for calling our attention to this dimension.

[36] Albert O. Hirschmann, *Exit, Voice and Loyalty* (Cambridge, Mass. 1972).

[37] The best account of the Greenland issue is found in Ida Blom, *Kampen om Eirik Raudes land. Pressgruppepolitikk i Grønlandsspørsmålet 1921–31* (Oslo 1973). (The Struggle for Eirik Raude's Land: Pressure Group Politics over the Greenland Question 1921–31). A short summary of the events surrounding this controversy is found in Paul M. Hayes, *op.cit.*, pp. 69–70 and 80–81.

[38] The best known among the anti-Semitic periodicals was *Nationalt Tidsskrift* edited by Mikael Sylten, launched in 1916 and published until World War II. Other magazines of the same kind were *Fronten* and *Ragnarok*. A good discussion of the scattered anti-Semitic articles appearing in agrarian and conservative papers in the inter-war period is found in Oskar Mendelsohn, *Jødenes historie i Norge gjennom 300 år* (The History of the Jews in Norway During the last 300 Years), volume I (Oslo 1969), chapters XVII, pp. 482–509, XIX, pp. 531–584, and XX, pp. 584–665, especially pp. 557 ff. He emphasizes that anti-Semitism was very limited, but quotes in detail from recurring articles, in particular from *Aftenposten*, the largest national newspaper, published in Oslo, indicating that the issue concerned fringe groups.

[39] Sverre B. Johansen, «Borgersamfundets nødverge: En studie i Norges Samfundshjelp» (The Emergency Defense of Bourgeois Society: A Study of *Norges Samfundshjelp*) in *Kontrast*, no. 3, 1966, p. 23.

[40] The issue was raised in January 1939. At that time aprox. 60–70 foreign doctors had applied for license. The Norwegian Medical Association (*Lægeforeningen*) approved of the proposal to give them license and then make their stay dependent on willingness to go to scarcely populated areas to practice. The majority in favor was one vote. At a meeting of medical students in Oslo the proposal from the Medical Association which recommended authorization to 20, preferably 10 foreign doctors, was rejected by a vote of 182 against 82. The most commonly used argument was fear of indigenous unemployment. Mendelsohn, *op.cit.*, p. 645.

[41] *Ibid.*, p. 641.

[42] For a comparative discussion, see *Kriser och krispolitik i Norden under mellankrigstiden. Møtesrapport. Nordiska historikermøtet i Uppsala 1974*, (Crises and Crisis-politics in the Nordic Countries in the Inter-War Period. Reports to the Nordic Historical Convention, Uppsala 1974) which brings together a series of papers on the crisis compromises, see especially chapters III and VII (Uppsala 1974).

[43] Cf. Bernt Hagtvet's paper on Sweden for a discussion of the S.N.U.

[44] A good description of the Norwegian crisis compromise (*kriseforliket*) is given by Berge Furre, *Norsk historie 1906–1940* (Oslo 1971) which also contains further bibliographical references.

[45] For a discussion of the dilemmas of Labor party strategy, see Stein Rokkan, «Norway: Numerical Democracy and Corporate Pluralism», in Robert A. Dahl, *op.cit.*, p. 81 ff.

[46] The standard work on these negotiations is H. O. Brevig, *NS – fra parti til sekt* (N.S. – From Party to Sect) (Oslo 1970). See also H. F. Dahl, «Behind the Fronts: Norway», in *Journal of Contemporary History*, vol. 5, no. 3, 1970, pp. 37–49.

[47] Expressed by *Høire's* leading spokesman C. J. Hambro. See Hans Fr. Dahl, *Norge mellom krigene*, op.cit., p. 107.

[48] For an analysis of *Aftenposten's* position towards National Socialism, see A. Kokkvoll, 'Det prektige tyske folk. Aftenposten og nazismen». (The Noble German People. Aftenposten and Nazism) in *Kontrast*, no. 3, 1966, pp. 43–54.

[49] Ida Blom, «Unge Høire – mellom konservatisme og fascisme. Forholdet mellom Nasjonal Samling og Unge Høire 1933–1936» *(Unge Høire* – Between Conservatism and Fascism. The Relationship Between N.S. and *Unge Høire* 1933–1936) in Ugelvik Larsen & Danielsen, *op.cit.*, p. 48.

[50] Minerva 17.3. 1934, quoted from *ibid.*, p. 52.

[51] Ulf Torgersen, «Political Institutions», in Rogoff Ramsøy (ed.), *Norwegian Society*, pp. 194–225, translated by S. Høivik in co-operation with N. R. Ramsøy (Oslo 1974).

[52] In his stimulating paper *Fascismen i Norge etter 10 års forskning* (Oslo, mimeo, n.d.) (Fascism in Norway after Ten Years of Research), p. 9.

[53] Ulf Torgersen, «Våre helter og høvdinger» (Our Heroes and Leaders) in *Kontrast*, no. 3, 1966, p. 29.

[54] It is for example the main thrust of H. F. Dahl's essay, *op.cit.*

[55] On this tradition, J. Nerbøvik, *Anti-parlamentariske straumdrag i Noreg 1905–14* (Anti-Parliamentarian Currents in Norway 1905–1914) and Ulf Torgersen, *The Anti Party Ideology. Elitist Liberalism in Norwegian Social and Political Structure (Mimeo:* Institute of Social Research, Oslo 1966).

[56] Cf. Dahl, *op.cit.*, and his «Quisling's statskupp 9. april i forfatningshistorisk perspektiv» (Quisling's *coup d'état* on 9 April: A Historical and Constitutional Perspective), in *Historisk Tidsskrift*, 1976, pp. 267–87.

Agrarian Fascism in Eastern and Western Norway: A Comparison

HANS HENDRIKSEN

Introduction

In a speech broadcast on September 25, 1940, the German *Reichskommissar,* Joseph Terboven, proclaimed *Nasjonal Samling* the only legal political party in Norway and declared that it was to form the cornerstone of the state.[1] For the rest of the war this party was to act as spokesman for co-operation between Norway and the German occupation forces. For this reason, the members of the party were morally condemned after the war and tried under Norwegian laws as traitors.[2]

In the course of the war *Nasjonal Samling* had approximately 54,000 members[3], i.e. about 1.8 per cent of the 1930 population of Norway. The geographical distribution of the membership was very skewed, however. The party had most of its members in the Oslo area and in the hinterlands of Eastern Norway, but failed to attract members in Southern and Western Norway.

This article deals with the problem of explaining the regional divergencies in *NS* membership. We shall here analyze two extreme cases: the province of Sogn og Fjordane in Western Norway, and South Østerdalen, a part of Hedmark province which is situated along the Swedish border. During the war *Nasjonal Samling* had only 396 members in Sogn og Fjordane,[4] or 0.4 per cent of a population of 95,000. This was by both absolute and relative standards the poorest result to be achieved by the party in any part of the country. In South Østerdalen the *NS* had 1,028 members during the war out of a total population of 23,000: that is 4.5 per cent, which makes this district among those in which *Nasjonal Samling* had the greatest success. What is the reason for these great differences?

Earlier studies on this problem have concentrated on the social and economic conditions in the local communities under discussion. We shall therefore begin by taking a look at the aforementioned two local milieus as they appeared about 1920.

The Sogn og Fjordane province was at that time one of the least urbanized areas in Norway. The province had a sparse and scattered population and poor communications. Most of the population lived in small villages of less than 3,000 inhabitants. Agriculture and fishing were the main occupations of the province. More than 70 per cent of the population was involved in these primary sectors of the economy as opposed to 40 per cent in Norway as a whole. There was little industry in the province, and the existing small plants converted raw materials from the primary sectors in the area into products for local consumption. The economic system of the province was based on small flexible units largely independent of international fluctuations. The communities appeared to be closely knit with an economy of few capital intensive enterprises. Very few of the fishermen and the farmers in the area were in debt. The environment was socially and politically egalitarian; conflicts within the local community were more often than not geographic (e.g. conflicts between the northern and the southern parts of a community over the location of a road). Only on rare occasions did they assume the form of a class conflict. The province exhibited a political tradition dominated by liberal and nationalistic sentiments. The cultural and political core of society consisted of the Protestant low-church movement, and support for both the New Norwegian language *(landsmål)* and the teetotaler movement. In Stein Rokkan's words this was the area of the rural «counter-culture». Each village had two fundamental pillars: the local religious meeting house *(bedehus)* and the school. The teacher was often a member of the Liberal party *(Venstre)*. On the whole, the labour movement, both the trade unions and their political wing, the Norwegian Labour party, *(DNA)* found far less support here than in the rest of the country.

South Østerdal in the province of Hedmark is quite different. The area consists of three municipalities *(kommuner)*, Trysil, Elverum and Åmot which were the largest forestry communes in Norway in the inter-war period, both in terms of number employed and productive forest acreage. Almost half of all adult males in the area were employed in forestry, and a great many of the farmers in the district were also dependent on income from seasonal work in the forest. Industrial activity was negligible in the district; only about 5 per cent of the population were industrial workers, and most of this local industry consisted of pulp and paper plants. A large percentage of the forest area was owned by non-local companies that were not under the control of the local community. Many of the harvested trees from the forest had to be floated down rivers which ran towards Sweden and sold there. Hence the local community had no part in the sale of a large portion of the timber.

Until 1920, the forestry industry in the area had experienced a great boom which had lasted almost without interruptions since 1860. The economy in South Østerdal was nevertheless extremely sensitive to business cycles and dependent on export markets. If these failed, it would mean a catastrophe for the local community. Politically, South Østerdal of about 1920 was marked by great advances for the labour movement, and the gradual eclipse of the Liberal party.

We have sketched two agrarian rural communities in Norway. How did they react to the international economic crisis in the inter-war period?

The Crisis

Naturally, people in Sogn og Fjordane felt the impact of the hard times, but if we can rely on our sources, the economic and the social conditions in the province remained stable. The producers continued to sell mainly food – potatoes, butter and cheese. It was easy for such an economy to re-organize itself in a crisis, especially since these products were given high priority by consumers and were easy to sell. As a result the rate of unemployment was the lowest in the country. Since industry in the province was not very capital intensive with small creditor claims, there were few public auctions caused by changes in the value of the *krone*.

Labour conflicts were few, and the crisis had little effect on political alignments. The province did not undergo the political polarization which so often is a by-product of a tense social situation. In other words, in the inter-war years the *Venstre* party lost little ground in the province. In contrast, the economy of South Østerdal was hit very hard by the international crisis. The slump in international demand brought about an almost continuous fall in the price of lumber from 1920 to 1932. In 1920 the price of lumber was 47,59 *kroner* per cubic meter; it had dropped to 11,62 *kroner* per cubic meter in 1932. The work in the forests was either cut back sharply or stopped completely. The communities in South Østerdal were especially hard hit by these measures. Dependent on floating their timber into Sweden, they were forced to accept prices 25 per cent lower than in Norway. Hence mass unemployment ensued in the district. The unemployment rate continued to rise from 1921 until the winter of 1932/33 when 75 per cent of those who had been employed in the forestry industry in this area were out of work. In addition, those who had work had to accept shortened hours. Many of the smallholders and farmers who relied on work in the forests for supplementary income lost this additional support. It should also be mentioned that the wages of forestry workers – they were to a large extent unorganized – were much lower than wages for industrial workers. In 1932, a forestry worker earned about 4 *kroner* a day while a worker in the mechanical industry earned 1,57 *kroner* per hour.

The crisis became acute when the smallholders, worker-farmers, and farmers were unable to pay their debts. Throughout the district the small villages experienced one public auction after the other. These foreclosures or mortgage sales hurt the small farms first and hardest: dependent on cash income in order to pay the mortgages on their farms, the small farmers immediately felt the impact of the economic crisis. Furthermore, the economy of the communes was ruined, which in turn reduced greatly the efficiency of local self-government. From 1931 to 1933 there was a definite feeling of crisis in South Østerdal. It was this district the Norwegian Prime Minister, Jens Hunseid, was talking about when, in the winter of 1931, he said in Parliament *(the Storting)* «The rural villages are now being proletarized . . . people are beginning to lose faith in «bourgeois society»»[5]. But if one loses faith in «bourgeois society» what alternatives remain?

One result of the crisis was a great increase in support for the labour movement, both politically and via trade unions in the district. The Labour party increased its vote: In 1924 it had received 36.5 per cent of the vote, but at the 1936 elections, it received 59.6 per cent of the total vote in the area. The Communist party had fairly strong support in some parts of the region: its share of the vote in this period ranged between 5 and 10 per cent. At the same time there was an expansion in the process of organizing the forestry workers into unions; the Norwegian Farm and Forestry Workers Union was founded and joined the National Federation of Labour (LO) in 1927. Organizing the forestry workers was difficult, however. As late as 1933 more than half of the forestry workers in the area were not union members. There are many explanations for this, but one of the main reasons was the lack of a proletarian tradition. Most of those employed in the forestry industry had roots in the rural farm society and its tradition, either because they were sons of farmers who hoped one day to have a farm of their own, or because they owned a farm which they operated intermittently alongside their work in the forests.

For many of the forestry workers in the area, membership in a socialist labour organization would mean the ultimate recognition of social defeat, which was hard to admit.[6] In addition, the Norwegian Farm and Forestry Workers Union was dominated by communists and thus represented ideals and views of society foreign to many of the forestry workers in South Østerdalen. Indeed the ultra-nationalistic youth organization enjoyed a very strong position in that region. Therefore, when the forestry workers tried to force wage negotiations around 1930, it was difficult for the labour union to gain wholehearted support for their call for strikes. Many of the forestry workers did not understand the demands for action which they viewed as an unfitting interference from Oslo in a free labour market. As a result the working class in the area was divided into two camps: the members of the union, and the «eager to work» group. During the tense labour conflicts between 1928–1935 large police and military forces were used to protect the strike-breakers. For this reason the labour conflicts symbolized in such names as Julussa, Austmarka and Trysil became famous in history as some of the most bitter and hardest fought labour disputes in Norwegian history.

These conflicts were characterized by violent rhetoric and in certain cases the open use of violence, a political style not typical in labour conflicts in Norway.[7] These disputes were so bitter because a large part of the working class in the area did not accept the attempt by the socialists to monopolize the organization of workers. The strikebreakers were forced to organize their own unions: between 1928 and 1935 so-called «yellow trade unions» were established under such names as «Liberty of Work», «Free Worker» etc.

The Norwegian Federation of Labour saw in these attempts to organize workers a serious threat to their monopoly, and directed all their strength towards fighting the yellow trade unions. The yellow trade union in Trysil was especially strong. In one period, it had more members than the Trysil Federation of Labour (local branch of the LO). The socialists labelled the yellow trade unions as «fascists», but the renegade unions did not conceive of themselves as such. Significantly, however, they called themselves the *Lapua Movement,* with a clear allusion to their anti-socialist counterpart in Finland. The yellow trade union movement collapsed when the depression was over in 1933. But prior to 1933, a bitter enmity was established between the leaders and active members of these unions on the one hand, and organized labour on the other. The conflict was reinforced by the strict demands of the LO labour unions that the strikebreakers apologize and make amends for their «misdeeds».

The labour movement finally assumed power after 1935. The severe economic crisis, however, had prepared the ground for radicalism in South Østerdal. The electoral program of the labour movement was a response to the crisis and was accepted by a majority, though the yellow part of the labour force in the area remained actively and bitterly opposed to the labour movement. This group satisfied its need for radicalism in the newly established party, *Nasjonal Samling,* which in the summer of 1933 demanded new solutions to the problems of society, although it did not give specific solutions in its own program. The most active members of the yellow trade unions joined *Nasjonal Samling* and found there a new alternative.

Nasjonal Samling 1933–1945

In contrast to other areas in Norway, the *Nasjonal Samling* managed to construct a relatively effective party organization in South Østerdal, and established a small local newspaper *Frihetskampen* (The Struggle for Freedom). In the elections the party mustered 8 per cent of the votes of the area which was a great deal more than it managed to obtain elsewhere during the 'thirties. In this region the party had a core of active and loyal members and in the local elections of 1934 gained representation in the municipal councils in all three communes. With the use of propaganda they made the ideas of the NS known throughout the district. The party also arranged parades with music and speeches in the villages and established sections of the *Hird,* the Norwegian parallel to the SA. The backbone of the local organization of the party seems to have been members of the yellow trade unions. Of the appr. 250 members of the pre-war NS which we have managed to uncover in our materials from the treason proceedings after the war, about 40 per cent had been members of the competing unions. Our sources may be a bit skewed but they tend to confirm information available from other sources.

Nasjonal Samling had a much higher percentage of proletarian members in South Østerdal than in the rest of Norway in the inter-war period. Other analyses of the Norwegian Nazi party seem to show that it was by and large a middle class movement.[8] Why did so many workers join the party in South Østerdal? This was to a great extent the result of the party's program which was so loosely formulated that it could be interpreted in several ways. Not unexpectedly, the local section of the NS in South Østerdal interpreted the party program in its own way. The section viewed itself as national socialist, emphasizing the *socialist* aspects of the movement. Reminiscent of the NSDAP left wing, the local newspaper *Frihetskampen* contained many attacks on «big business» and placed responsibility for the crisis on the forestry industry and on the large forestry owning companies. «The reason for all this misery lies in the pulp and paper industry. Borregaard (a leading combine) has large profits and exploits the forestry owners.»[9]

The agitation carried out by the South Østerdal section of the NS had a strong emphasis on the common interests of rural society vis-à-vis their two chief enemies, which were both a part of the centralized urban society: big business and the centralized socialist labour movement. This special interpretation of *Nasjonal Samling's* program caused tension inside the central leadership to refute the agitation in *Frihetskampen*. When the *Nasjonal Samling* declined after the electoral defeat in 1936 and 1937, the section in South Østerdal managed to keep the party organization intact until the outbreak of the war in 1940. South Østerdal was one of the few places in Norway where there was an organized NS chapter in 1940. In other words, there was in South Østerdal a continuity from the fringe party in the 1930's to the «state» party of 1940.

In Sogn og Fjordane, on the other hand, the situation was completely different. *Nasjonal Samling* never managed to break into the local society with its party organization. It was not until 1936, three years after the party was founded, that it managed to mobilize enough members to set up a party list in the local elections. The result was as miserable as possible: the NS received 0.2 per cent of the vote in the province. This was not more than the votes of those whose name appeared on the list. The Western Norwegian society of the inter-war period does not seem to have «needed» the type of radicalism represented by the Norwegian Nazis.

Conclusion

We must now make an attempt to answer our introductory question: What was the reason for the great regional differences in NS membership?

When the war came to Norway and the NS-leader Vidkun Quisling initiated his collaboration with the occupation forces, the party was totally unknown in Sogn og Fjordane. It did not even have the small core of active members necessary for building up a party organization. Everything had to be done from the party headquarters in Bergen. When the party collided with the pillars of society, the Church and the local educational establishment, the teachers and their defense of the culture of the rural periphery, the party had absolutely no chance of success. The nationalist feelings and trends in the society were instead turned against the NS.

On the other hand, in South Østerdal the party was relatively well known at the outbreak of the war. Its members were represented in the local municipal councils, and the party had a small but stable organization. The party was thus able to exploit the chaotic period from April 9, 1940, until Terboven held his speech on September 25, 1940 – after which the first icy front was raised against it. It should, however, be noted that the conditions in these two regions were a-typical. Most of Norway looked upon «the fascist threat» as something written about in the newspapers and experienced distantly. The economic crisis did not lead to political polarization in Norway but rather to a very moderate social democracy. When the economic crisis had reached its peak in the 1930's the Labour party departed from its revolutionary rhetoric. The parliamentary election in 1933 broke *Nasjonal Samling* as well as the Communist party. The economic crisis ended in Norway in 1935 when the Labour party and the Agrarian party agreed on a great political compromise *(Kriseforliket),* in reality a rallying to the centre, confining *Nasjonal Samling* to the twilight of the far right.

NOTES

[1] For developments prior to September 25, 1940, see Magne Skodvin: *Striden om okkupasjonsstyret i Norge* (The Struggle for the Occupation Administration in Norway) (Universitetsforlaget, Oslo 1956).

[2] More on this in Johs. Andenæs: *Rättsuppgjörelsen i Norge efter andra världskriget.* (Verdandis småskrifter nr. 512).

[3] Data from Stein Ugelvik Larsen in this volume.

[4] One consequence of this was that local elections were politicized through party lists much later here than in the rest of the country.

[5] *Stortingstidende* (The Norwegian Storting Hansard), Dec. 12, 1931.

[6] In the novel *Styrkeprøven* (The Test of Strength) by the Trysil author Sven Moren (1929) there is a vivid description of these attitudes.

[7] Norway is one of the few countries in Europe which did not have a single death connected with a labour conflict in the inter-war period.

[8] Hans Olaf Brevig: *NS – fra parti til sekt 1933–1937* (NS – from Party to Sect) (Pax, Oslo 1969).

Bodil Wold Johnsen: *Nasjonal Samling in Stavanger 1933–1937,* Unpubl. M.A. thesis in History, Bergen 1972.

[9] *Frihetskampen* March 26, 1936.

Who Voted for Quisling ?

STEN SPARRE NILSON

Two Theses: Nazism an Extremism of the Centre or a Reaction to Multidimensional Stress?

According to Seymor M. Lipset bitter struggles along the functional-economic line of conflict will tend to bring forth one or the other of three different kinds of extremism, depending on their social origin. The extremist movements of the left, right, and centre, Lipset says, are based on the working, upper, and middle classes respectively.[1] The term «fascism» has been applied at one time or another to all of these varieties, but an examination of the social base and ideology of each reveals their different characters. The classic fascist movements have represented the extremism of the centre, and Hitler was a typical «centrist extremist».

The question can be raised whether this is not a rather one-sided view. It is true that Lipset makes a reservation. He admits that fascist politicians, and Hitler not least, have been highly opportunistic in their efforts to secure support: consequently such movements have often encompassed groups with the most widely divergent interests and values.[2] However, according to Lipset this is a phenomenon of secondary importance only.

A different view has been presented by Walter Dean Burnham, who points to the fact that opportunism characterized not only the Nazi *leaders* but also many of the people who *voted* for this rapidly increasing «flash party». They were ready to desert their former parties in favour of the new movement almost as soon as it began to assume some slight importance on the national scene. The composition of this volatile section of the electorate was markedly heterogeneous. Nazi voters were activated by *multidimensional stress*.[3] Hitler's movement may not have won quite as much backing from former conservative voters as from people who had previously supported the centrist parties. But the difference was slight indeed. Nor can it be said, according to Burnham, that working-class elements are necessarily immune to such «centrist extremism.»

We shall analyze the record of Nazi voting in Norway, seen against the background of these two theses. Although the party in question, Vidkun Quisling's *Nasjonal Samling, NS* was anything but successful at the four elections in which it took part, some aspects of its electoral record are not without interest. There were a few localities in which it did receive a number of votes sufficient for a statistical analysis to be undertaken.

On a nationwide basis the party obtained only 2.2 and 1.8 per cent of the total vote at the 1933 and 1936 parliamentary elections, respectively, and even less at the municipal elections which took place in 1934 and 1937. There were, however, some places in which it did considerably better, at least for a short time. Three in particular may be mentioned. One was the coastal town of Stavanger, where the decline in prosperity made itself felt rather strongly during the first half of the 'thirties. Quisling also experienced a certain success in some rural communes in two other provinces, rather far from Stavanger. It seems natural to consider these three cases separately. They represent three different phenomena.

The Appeal to Urban Conservatives

Controversy over questions of economic policy dominated Norwegian politics in the 'thirties. It is true that the antagonism of religious people to «godless Marxism» played a role, particularly along the Western coast. Nationalist traditions were also alive, *inter alia* in some places near the Eastern border, but relations with other countries presented no problems on which a nationalist movement could capitalize to any noticeable extent. Racial questions had even less importance, the number of Jews in Norway being extremely small and the only minority of any size, the Lapps, presenting no problem at all.

Table 1. *Elections in Stavanger 1930–1937. Township level*

Year and type of election	Valid votes	Votes cast for				
		Socia- lists	Libe- rals	Conser- vatives	Nazis	Others*
1930, parliamentary	20,201 (100%)	6,223 (31%)	6,271 (31%)	7,583 (38%)	–	124 (0.5%)
1931, local	17,672 (100%)	6,305 (36%)	5,206 (29%)	5,817 (33%)	–	344 (2%)
1933, parliamentary	22,290 (100%)	9,236 (41%)	6,136 (28%)	5,333 (24%)	788 (3.5%)	797 (3.5%)
1934, local	21,067 (100%)	8,734 (41%)	5,266 (25%)	4,202 (20%)	2,559 (12%)	306 (1.5%)
1936, parliamentary	25,962 (100%)	10,233 (39%)	6,455 (25%)	6,470 (25%)	906 (3.5%)	1,898 (7.5%)
1937, local	22,642 (100%)	9,174 (41%)	5,879 (26%)	6,552 (29%)	–	1,037 (4.5%)

* These include: the non-socialist «Samfundspartiet» («Party of Social Unity») which obtained some 3 per cent in 1933, did not participate in local elections but succeeded in gaining more than 7 per cent of the total in 1936; the People's party, which obtained 3 per cent in 1937; and the Communist party of Norway, which received less than 2 per cent but took part in every election except the one held in 1936.

In table 1 are given the results of the elections held in the town of Stavanger from 1930 to 1937. Here Quisling obtained 3.5 per cent of the vote in the 1933 parliamentary elections, more than in most other constituencies. The party had then been launched just a few months before, and its electoral campaign was improvised. In the following year local elections were held. The party leadership decided that «the main battle» would have to be fought in the parliamentary election of 1936. Local organizations were advised to take part in local contests only if they felt it would not be a waste of resources. The Stavanger organization was among the few which decided to make a try, and it succeeded much better than any other, obtaining between 12 and 12.5 per

Table 2. Elections in Stavanger 1930–1937. Precinct level.
Percentage of total vote cast on election day for:

Year**	Socialists				Liberals				Conservatives				Nazis				Others*			
	N	Bl	Ba	T	N	Bl	Ba	T	N	Bl	Ba	T	N	Bl	Ba	T	N	Bl	Ba	T
1930	50.-	38.-	22.-	15.-	30.-	26.-	38.-	32.5	19.-	34.5	39.5	51.5	-	-	-	-	1.-	1.5	0.5	1.-
1931	58.5	42.5	27.-	18.-	23.5	23.-	37.-	32.5	15.-	33.-	34.-	48.5	-	-	-	-	3.-	1.5	2.-	1.-
1933	64.5	48.5	33.5	22.-	22.-	22.-	34.-	32.-	8.5	21.-	24.5	37.5	1.-	3.5	4.-	5.-	4.-	5.-	4.-	3.5
1934	64.5	50.5	32.5	22.-	20.5	19.5	31.5	28.5	7.-	17.5	21.5	31.-	5.5	11.-	13.-	18.5	2.5	1.5	1.5	0.5
1936	61.5	46.5	33.-	21.-	20.5	19.5	30.-	29.-	9.5	22.5	26.5	37.-	1.5	2.5	4.-	5.5	7.-	9.-	6.5	7.5
1937	62.-	47.5	34.-	22.-	21.-	21.-	30.5	30.5	13.-	26.-	29.5	42.5	-	-	-	-	4.-	5.5	6.-	5.-

* See table 1.
** N = Nylund precinct, Bl = Bethel precinct, Ba = Bethania precinct, T = Turnhallen precinct.

cent of the total vote cast in the town. It appears that the Nazi gain was mainly at the expense of the Stavanger Conservatives *(Høire)*. Further, it has been contended that Quisling's party did best «in those precincts where the Labour party was strong, *i.e.* among the segments of the population in which antagonism between socialists and non-socialists was felt most acutely».[4] Clearly the statement accords with the view that Nazi voting is essentially a by-product of struggles between capitalists and proletarians; but the figures do not support this contention.

The town of Stavanger was divided into four precincts of roughly equal size. Electoral statistics were given officially only for the town as a whole, but data from each precinct were published in the local newspapers.[5] Table 2 shows the percentage of the total vote obtained by the different parties within each precinct in each election held during the nineteen-thirties.

While it is not possible to draw conclusions with complete certainty on the basis of this kind of data, it does seem that the Nazis took the bulk of their votes from the conservatives, and more particularly in precincts where the socialist Labour party was weak (Turnhallen, Bethania), not where it was strong (Nylund). Quisling may also have received a certain support from previous non-voters. The development of electoral participation is shown in tables 3 and 4. The former is based on the official records, the latter on information in the newspapers. In all four precincts a certain increase in turnout occurred, from which the Nazis may to some extent have profited. The figures in tables 1 and 2 seem to indicate that there may also have been some people among Quisling's supporters who had previously voted with the Liberals *(Venstre)*. But it appears as if the Conservatives lost considerably more in this way. Moreover, it was their situation which was most strikingly improved after Quisling's party had left the scene.

Table 3. *Electoral participation in Stavanger 1930–1937. Township level*

Year	Rate of voting		
	Both sexes	Men	Women
1930	78.–	79.–	78.–
1931	71.–	74.–	69.–
1933	80.5	82.–	79.5
1934	78.5	79.–	77.5
1936	89.–	89.5	88.5
1937	79.–	79.5	78.–

This does not in itself allow us to make any conclusive statements. Only the *net* changes in the party balance have been recorded. It is conceivable that other and perhaps equally significant shifts could have taken place without leaving any trace in the final result. However, there is information of a different kind available which supports the tentative conclusion reached above.

A study of newspapers and an analysis of campaign material from the period indicate that the new party did not at first present itself as either tough or aggressive; its propaganda was generally conservative in tone, vaguely idealistic, but with no very specific features.[6] The party seems to have derived its main appeal from the fact that it represented a fresh element, a new team of would-be leaders whose style and symbo-

Table 4. *Electoral participation in Stavanger 1931–1937.* Precinct level, votes cast on election day only*

Year	Rate of voting (both sexes) in			
	Nylund precinct	Bethel precinct	Bethania precinct	Turnhallen precinct
1931	67.–	72.5	70.–	73.–
1933	80.–	79.5	78.5	78.–
1934	73.5	77.5	77.–	77.–
1936	88.–	87.–	86.5	86.5
1937	77.5	79.–	76.5	77.5

* Data from 1930 not available.

lism seemed refreshingly unorthodox. Also they enjoyed the advantage of having an energetic local organizer (who later became Quisling's Minister of Propaganda). He was a young engineer educated in Germany and possessed considerable powers of persuasion, which he used in full. But the European scene was rapidly changing. Mussolini attacked Ethiopia in 1935 and anti-Semitic measures were taken in Germany. Quisling's NS approved of these events, but certainly not the Norwegian public in general. It is difficult to know, however, to what extent voters were repelled by such references to somewhat disturbing but distant political developments. It may have meant more to them that economic conditions improved at home. No longer could hard times be blamed on the established parties. The new movement seemed rather superfluous, while its lack of success anywhere else also made it appear ineffectual. Stavanger was the only town in which it had any success worth speaking of; and in the rural districts it mostly abstained from presenting itself at local elections. The Stavanger story was not duplicated in any other town in 1934, and the result of the 1936 parliamentary election proved to be just as discouraging in Stavanger as in the rest of the country. When elections were held locally in 1937, the last before the war, there was an almost total NS failure to put up lists in the communes, and Stavanger was no exception.

Agrarian Indebtedness

In another place Quisling scored a momentary electoral success under conditions which were quite different from those in Stavanger. In 1933 he succeeded in allying himself with a movement of indebted farmers, *Bygdefolkets Krisehjelp*, which had been launched two years earlier. As its name indicated, this «Farmers' Relief Association» had originally an *ad hoc* character. Its aim was to alleviate the rural debt burden during the period of depression. The necessity of a reduction in the rate of interest and a temporary suspension of payments was stressed, and members gave a pledge not to bid at mortgage foreclosure sales.

Bygdefolkets Krisehjelp (often abbreviated *Bygdefolket)* was launched at two mass meetings held in March and April, 1931, and formally instituted in October of the same year. A member of the Agrarian party was elected president of the organization, while a Labour party farmer presided over its Council. The intention of the founders was no

661

doubt to galvanize these two parties into more energetic action to relieve the burden of indebtedness. Not unnaturally, however, both parties from the very beginning looked askance at the new organization, which could easily become a political competitor. They feared it might degenerate into an instrument of the desperate elements among the debtors, the people clamouring for direct action, and they soon found their apprehension confirmed.

In the course of the year 1932 and the first months of 1933, *Bygdefolket* succeeded in strengthening its position in a couple of provinces, especially that of Telemark, where its weekly paper was started in July, 1932. Here was carried through a rather successful boycott of forced sales, culminating in some dramatic riots in the beginning of May, 1933.

With the approach of the general election to be held in the autumn of that year, the leaders of *Bygdefolket* redoubled their efforts to put pressure on the political parties. Meeting in Oslo, they went to Parliament on May 23rd to present their claim for the ending of forced sales and a moratorium on debts. The Speaker, the Labour party farmer Chr. Hornsrud, answered that Parliament certainly was animated by a wish to give assistance – but, he added, «The extent of the wish is often greater than the capacity to fulfill it». None of the existing parties would give any assurance of support. Certain measures of debt relief, introduced by the Agrarians, had recently been adopted by Parliament with the backing of the Labour party, but did not satisfy *Bygdefolket*. Its leaders looked around for support from other quarters and found it in the new NS party which had just been launched in the middle of May by Major Quisling, a disappointed Agrarian politician who had quarrelled with his former colleagues and now embarked on an adventure of his own. This was the year of Hitler's coming to power in Germany. Quisling had not had time to organize his new party properly before the election, but he hoped for votes from not a few of those who were dissatisfied with the hard times. He was eager to ally himself with *Bygdefolket*.

According to the Norwegian electoral law of the time, parties could make an electoral alliance or present a joint list of candidates for the Storting. A joint list of Quisling's *Nasjonal Samling* and *Bygdefolket* was presented in five provinces, natur-ally the ones where they believed their chances of success to be the greatest. Quisling's party also presented its lists in a number of other provinces and cities. The result was a complete failure. Nowhere did any candidate come near to being elected. Only in a few communes of Telemark province, which had become the centre of the *Bygdefolket* movement, was an appreciable share of the votes obtained by the joint list. The figures for the four neighbouring communes of Bø, Hjartdal, Seljord and Kviteseid are given in table 5a.

Although Quisling obtained a larger share of the vote in Telemark than in any other province, his percentage in rural Telemark as a whole was less than 10 per cent in 1933. But in the four communes mentioned above, nearly 30 per cent of the vote was polled by his party, or rather by the candidates on the common list of *Nasjonal Samling* and *Bygdefolket* (designated as «Nazis» in the table). Just as in Stavanger, however, nearly all that had been gained was lost in the 1936 election.[7]

The same reservation must be made here as was made with regard to the Stavanger figures: a greater or smaller number of individual shifts between the various parties are certainly not revealed in the aggregates, which exhibit only the net changes. Still, with the aid of information from other sources it is possible to draw conclusions with reasonable certainty in this case as in that of Stavanger. Clearly, voters gave support to Quisling in the interior of Telemark province for other reasons than in the coastal

Table 5a. *Parliamentary elections in Central Telemark 1930–1936**

Year	Votes cast for					
	Valid votes	Socialists	Liberals	Agrarians	Nazis	Others
1930	4,891 (100%)	1,578 (32%)	1,693 (35%)	1,433 (29%)	–	187 (4%)
1933	4,720 (100%)	1,589 (34%)	896 (19%)	761 (16%)	1,393 (30%)	81 (1%)
1936	5,526 (100%)	2,289 (41%)	1,623 (29%)	1,095 (20%)	226 (4%)	293 (6%)

Table 5b. *Electoral participation in Central Telemark 1930–1936**

Year	Rate of voting		
	Both sexes %	Men %	Women %
1930	75.5	81.–	70.5
1933	70.5	78.5	62.5
1936	81.5	86.5	76.5

* Communes of Bø, Hjartdal, Seljord, and Kviteseid.

town. Also, it should be noted that whereas a certain mobilization of new voters took place in Stavanger, the rate of participation declined somewhat in Central Telemark between 1930 and 1933 (see table 5b). The votes obtained by *NS/Bygdefolket* in 1933 seem to have come from people who had formerly voted in favour of other parties – presumably the Agrarians and the Liberals.

Anti-Union Attitudes

A third element of Nazi support, still smaller than in Stavanger and Central Telemark but of a more durable character, is to be found in the forest region of South Østerdal in Hedmark province. Here, in the four adjacent communes of Vaaler, Elverum, Trysil, and Åmot, near the Swedish border, Quisling's party obtained its highest share of the vote in the 1936 and 1937 elections. It is true that the figures were very small: 380 votes in 1933, 988 votes in 1936 and 542 votes in 1937, amounting to 3 per cent, 7.5 per cent and 4.5 per cent, respectively, of the total vote cast in these four communes.[8]

The whole thing scarcely seems worth mentioning at all. But the fact is that Quisling's percentages were still more pitiful elsewhere, especially in 1937. So few were the isolated places in which the party thought it worth while to put up any lists at all, and so ludicrously small was the number of votes they received, that the 542 ballots mentioned above accounted for more than a third of the total Quisling vote in 1937. After the 1936 defeat the party found itself in a state of virtual dissolution. Actually, these little Hedmark communes were among the few in which it still maintained something like the remnants of an organization.

The background of its relative success in this area was the sharp antagonism existing between the labour unions and certain elements within the rural population. The Norwegian Farm and Forestry Workers' Union was on the offensive but had not yet succeeded in recruiting more than about half of the forestry workers in the area around the middle of the nineteen-thirties. For years times had been hard. Because of the continual decline in timber prices on the world market there was little activity in the forests. Wages were low. Many workers saw unionization and strikes as the right way to achieve an improvement, but there were others to whom the call for strikes appeared as an unwelcome interference from outside, instigated by union leaders in the cities, making it even more difficult to obtain employment than before. Not only did those local farmers who were owners of forests resent union activity. There was also great bitterness between loggers who declared themselves «willing to work» and those who went in for strikes. Some ugly incidents occurred in connection with labour disputes.

It should be added that nationalist traditions were strong in the region, which was certainly one of the reasons why some would reject with such vehemence the unions and their international socialist ideology. Also, acceptance of Marxism and of membership in a labour union seemed like a degradation, the final recognition of a social defeat which some would stubbornly refuse to admit. Quisling's appeal met with response from wealthy farmers whose property would include wooded areas, but also from forestry workers. The social background of party adherents apparently differed from one locality to another. In Åmot persons of rather high social status in the rural community were attracted, whereas in Trysil the local party group hardly included any owners of substantial farms, being composed mainly of smallholder-workers. These were people who found themselves if not in a truly proletarian, then at least in a «proletaroid» position. For their living they depended on the wages they could earn as loggers, working part of the year in the forest, no less than they looked to the proceeds from the small homesteads which they might have inherited, or which they hoped one day to inherit or to acquire. However, whether smallholders themselves or propertyless sons of farmers or smallholders, they still wanted to be farmers rather than labourers. They felt no solidarity with urban workers and refused to support what they regarded as city-influenced unions. In their own way they were as antagonistic to the union movement as were the forest owners.[9]

At any time Quisling's adherents in Hedmark were so few in number as to constitute no more than a small sect. But they were convinced adherents. The indebted farmers in Telemark had tried to use Quisling's party as an instrument, and as soon as it proved useless they threw it away.

Adherents in Hedmark were different, they held on to the party, voting for it and also maintaining their membership. In this connection reference can be made to certain figures which were compiled in the central party organization during the war period, when Quisling collaborated with the occupying power, all other parties being declared illegal. The data should be used with caution, but it may be worth mentioning that members seem to have been, relatively speaking, much more numerous in the Hedmark strongholds of the party than elsewhere. The maximum was reached by one small commune with a membership equal to some five per cent of the population, according to the party register. Elsewhere the figures were much lower. In the four Telemark communes where Quisling, in collaboration with *Bygdefolket,* had once obtained his largest share of the vote, only one and a half per cent of the population were registered as members.

Support for Nazism Seen Partly, but not Solely, as an Aspect of the Left/Right Struggle

Vidkun Quisling failed miserably in his attempt to create a viable movement, and the percentage of votes cast in his favour was always small, not to say infinitesimal, except in a strictly limited number of localities. However, in spite of its failure the NS does seem to present an equivalent to similar phenomena in other countries. The conclusions that can be drawn from an analysis of the party's electoral history point in a direction which is not the one intimated by S.M. Lipset in his *Political Man*.

There is no indication that the majority of those who voted for Quisling belonged to the lower middle rather than the upper or upper middle class. The Agrarians in the countryside, the party of the more substantial farmers, and the urban Conservatives seem to have lost no less – and the latter rather more – of their vote to Quisling than did the centrist Liberal party. We quoted the figures from Stavanger and Central Telemark; these were the only urban and rural localities in which the Nazi share of the vote was large enough to permit some tentative conclusions regarding the transition of voters from other parties to the NS on the basis of electoral statistics. There are some additional facts which could be mentioned, such as the social background of the candidates presented on Quisling's electoral lists. They were rather similar to the candidates of the Conservative party. It should be pointed out, however, that the composition of the joint *NS/Bygdefolket* lists was a different one. Here the candidates were predominantly farmers. The relative success of the latter lists merits attention, because it illustrates the ability of the Nazis to derive profit from controlling or infiltrating special-interest organizations, in Norway as elsewhere.[10]

With regard to voters, what is particularly striking about the majority of those who cast their ballots at one time or another in favour of the NS is their volatility, their willingness to try now one party alternative, now another. Here it seems natural to speak, as does Rudolf Heberle with respect to Germany, about the development of a pronounced political opportunism on the part of the middle classes.[11] Only in the South Østerdal district of Hedmark province is it possible with the aid of electoral statistics to trace a hard core of steadfast Quisling adherents.[12] This region, in contrast to places such as Telemark or Stavanger, was characterized by a bitter antagonism between capital and labour which certainly explains why certain elements within its population turned to the NS.

Some would say, perhaps, that the Nazi members in Hedmark embodied the very essence of Nazism in Norway. However, the phenomenon in question is of such a strictly limited local character that it provides but a fragile basis for any attempt to reach general conclusions. It may be of interest to note that Quisling's following in the area included both an upper middle and a lower middle or rather working-class element, but it is an open question whether this fact can be said to have any wider implications.

We started by referring to the opinion of Walter Dean Burnham. He thinks that where working-class people are not absorbed in political socialism they will tend to behave like the lower middle classes, providing support under conditions of stress for movements representing what others have called the «radical center» or the «extremist center». Burnham refers in this connection to recent events in the United States.[13] Perhaps the case of South Østerdal in Norway could be cited in support of his view. But then it must be added once more that the Norwegian experience with Nazism between the wars was of a strictly limited kind.[14]

NOTES

[1] Lipset, *Political Man*, London 1963, p. 131. For a critique, see H. A. Winkler «Extremismus der Mitte», *Vierteljahresheft für Zeitgeschichte* 20, 1972, pp. 175–191.

[2] *Ibid.*, p. 139.

[3] Burnham, «Political Immunization and Political Confessionalism», in *Journal of Interdisciplinary History*, Vol. 3 (1972), p. 30.

[4] Hans Olaf Brevig, *NS – fra parti til sekt*, (NS:From Party to Sect), Oslo 1970 p. 55.

[5] These include only votes cast on election day, not votes deposited by mail. However, the latter accounted for no more than about one per cent of the total.

[6] The Quisling party's propaganda in Stavanger has been analyzed by Bodil Wold Johnsen (unpublished Master's thesis, University of Bergen, 1972).

[7] Quisling's party presented no list in Telemark at the local elections (1934, 1937).

[8] The result of the local elections of 1934 was recorded only at the level of the rural province, the number of Quisling votes in Hedmark amounting to 965 or 1.6 per cent of the provincial total. In 1937 it amounted to 608, less than 1 per cent.

[9] See H. Hendriksen's contribution to this volume, pp. 651.

[10] For a similar phenomenon in Germany, see Rudolf Heberle, *From Democracy to Nazism*, N.Y. 1970, p. 77: Hitler's electoral success was due largely to his «method of obtaining control of economic interest organizations». Cf. Bernt Hagtvet's discussion of the Nazi take-over of the *Landbund* in this volume pp. 89 ff.

[11] *Ibid.*, p. 119.

[12] «Hard core» being defined in this connection as people who still did not abandon Quisling after his electoral defeat in 1936. Best known among his steadfast supporters was the novelist Knut Hamsun, who wrote a public appeal canvassing support for Quisling at the 1936 election. Its lack of effect could be seen very clearly in Hamsun's home commune of Eide, where NS obtained only one single vote – obviously his own. (See the author's *Knut Hamsun und die Politik*, [Villingen 1964] p. 202).

[13] Burnham, «The United States: the Politics of Heterogeneity» in Richard Rose, ed., *Electoral Behavior*, N.Y. 1974, p. 703.

[14] For further details on the elections in Norway and their background see Hans-Dietrich Loock, *Quisling, Rosenberg und Terboven*, Stuttgart 1970, pp. 112 ff., as well as the author's article «Wahlsoziologische Probleme des Nationalsozialismus» in *Zeitschrift für die gesamte Staatswissenschaft* Vol. 110 (1954), pp. 295 ff., and in *Scandinavian Democracy*, ed. Joseph A. Lauwerys (Copenhagen 1958) pp. 111 ff.

Support for Nasjonal Samling in the Thirties*

HANS-DIETRICH LOOCK

The Road to Defeat: Nasjonal Samling from 1933 to 1936

When *Nasjonal Samling* (NS) was formed during May and June 1933, its central figure was Vidkun Quisling.[1] He had spent many years of his life in the Soviet Union, first as Norwegian military attaché, then as an expert for the Nansen Aid program during the famine in the Ukraine, and finally as a businessman in Moscow. In early 1931 he and a few friends founded a union named the Nordic People's Movement in Norway *(Nordiske Folkereisning i Norge)* in Oslo. In this circle he developed his political philosophy which was meant to be a synthesis of communism, National Socialism and democracy. Striving for an economic organization after a transformed Soviet model, his aim was to reconcile capital and labour directed by instructions from a centrally led popular movement. Quisling called this organization of society «Soviets without communism»[2] and declared that it was in accord with the nature of the Nordic race.

From May 1931 to March 1933, when Quisling was Minister of Defence in the minority cabinet of the Agrarian party *(Bondepartiet),* he attracted public attention mainly because of his vehement attacks on the Norwegian Labour party. After the fall of the Agrarian government he hoped to use the Agrarian party or part of it as a basis for his new party *Nasjonal Samling.* Among the groups he hoped to attract were the National Liberals *(Frisinnede Folkepartiet)* which had originated in 1909 as the conservative wing of the Liberal party *(Venstre).* The National Liberals had been able to survive during the twenties only with the help of the *Høire* (Conservative party) by forming electoral alliances on the local level. In addition, Quisling hoped to win over the *Fedrelandslaget* (Patriotic League) which had been founded in 1925 with the purpose of protecting bourgeois democracy. The Patriotic League wanted to support the non-socialist parties by propaganda and wanted to create for them a common ideological basis. Since the beginning of the thirties, sympathy for Mussolini's fascism as well as for National Socialism became noticeable in its propaganda. Quisling also sought alliance with the *Bygdefolkets Krisehjelp* (Farmers' Relief Association) which had been founded in 1931 as a pressure group of small farmers to enforce legal measures to prevent the forced sale of indebted farms.[3] Under the impact of the economic crisis this group had become activist and militant rather quickly.

Three small associations in Oslo, *Norges Nasjonalsosialistiske Arbeiderparti* (NNSAP) (National Socialist party of Norway), the National Legion and the National Club, consisting almost exclusively of students, showed an independent interest in having Quisling as the head of the party. These three groups were in touch with the Patriotic League but demanded a clear Nationalist Socialist program. Since Quisling's efforts to win the Agrarian party, the National Liberals and the Patriotic League over to his *Nasjonal Samling* failed, he was left with little more than the three student groups. Only with the Relief Association was an agreement reached but a large part of this group refused all cooperation. Quisling succeeded only in introducing into the new party the Nordic People's Movement which consisted of hardly more than thirty members.[4]

By the fall of 1933, regional organizations of the *Nasjonal Samling* were founded in most counties.[5] In the elections of September, 1933, the party appeared with its own lists in 17 out of the 29 electoral districts. It received only 2.2 per cent of the votes (27,850), however, and thus was not able to gain a single seat in parliament. The Norwegian Labour party (DNA) received 40 per cent of the votes and won the election. All other parties suffered considerable losses.

The unsatisfactory results of the election caused serious discussions within the leadership of the *Nasjonal Samling*. The younger members in particular wanted to increase their influence on party leadership and to force Quisling to accept a National Socialist program. Quisling succeeded in defending himself against this inner opposition.

The victory of the Labour party caused those parties which Quisling had tried to win over to the NS during the spring to reflect on how to prevent further successes by the Labour party. The leaders of the Patriotic League in particular tried to bring about a collaboration with anti-Marxist groups. A coalition with Quisling's NS now seemed possible. Quisling's opponents within the party no longer were adverse to an alliance with other groups. The question whether the Agrarian party should be included in this alliance or not, however, triggered new dissension. The Patriotic League and the National Liberals insisted upon its inclusion. The Agrarian party, in which the alliance was vehemently discussed, withdrew shortly afterwards from the National Bloc. The opponents of the alliance within the Agrarian party welcomed a declaration by the Conservatives and the Liberals according to which parties which joined a coalition with the *Nasjonal Samling* would not receive subsidies from an election fund administered by the non-socialist parties. The project of a national bloc failed. The Patriotic League also withdrew from the *Nasjonal Samling*.

In 1935 the Liberal government was overthrown by the Labour and Agrarian parties. The Agrarians tolerated the minority government which was subsequently formed by the Labour party although one of the Agrarian's wings had only shortly before tried to collaborate with the *Nasjonal Samling* in the National Bloc.[6]

It is usually assumed that the NS attracted disproportionately many new members during the years 1935/36.[7] Its public agitation seems indeed to a certain extent to have attracted attention at that time.[8] But the adverse publicity created by the Labour newspapers also contributed to the impression that the party was relatively influential. At the elections of 1936, however, the *Nasjonal Samling* obtained only 1.8 per cent of the votes. The number of votes in all had decreased to 20,577. The Labour party again increased its percentage of votes. The elections of 1936 confirmed the mandate of the Labour and Agrarian parties. The leadership of the *Nasjonal Samling* fell apart. Afterwards Quisling led the party in name only.

The Organizational Development and Statutory Formalization of the Nasjonal Samling

In May, 1933, Quisling had offered to his collaborators a plan for the organization of the party. Its headquarters had yet to be established. Some believed, however, that elements of the plan resembled statutes of the Soviet Communist party. The plan was as a result soon rejected.[9] During the first few months the party thus worked without any statutory organization, though in each province *(fylke)* a *Fylkesfører* (province leader) was to be in charge of the regional organization.[10]

After the 1933 elections, however, Quisling published party statutes.[11] According to these the party was to be led by a select and an enlarged executive committee: the National directorate *(Riksstyret)* and the Council *(Råd)*. The National directorate consisted of the «leader, the general secretary and up to four other members, appointed by the leader in agreement with the Council». The Council comprised the National directorate and the province-leaders. The leader, Quisling, was authorized to appoint and dismiss the province-leaders, while he himself could not be removed from office.

Two levels of organization below the level of the party headquarters were envisaged: the main organization and factory cells. The main organization followed the official administrative division in the country: the province *(fylkes)* organization covered the province-level: the district organizations, the municipalities *(kommuner* in Norwegian), the *lag,* the local communities within the *kommune,* and the *rode,* the neighbourhood areas. At the head of each regional unit stood a leader who was appointed by the next highest leader in rank and confirmed by the party's headquarters.

Attached to the main organization were the Women's Organization, the Youth Organization and a semi-military organization called the *Hird.*

A factory cell of the *Nasjonal Samling* was to be established in each plant.[12] The factory cells were to appoint regional economic advisory councils and in turn a central economic advisory council, the *Næringsting.* In each unit of the main organization there was to be a deputy for the factory cells, in the headquarters there was to be a national leader of the factory cells. This organizational structure was to be the beginning of the future economic structure of a state controlled by the *Nasjonal Samling,* in accordance with Quisling's idea of «Soviet without communism».

These statutes were never put into practice. Although Quisling appointed a national leader, he did not take up his office.[13] There is reason to believe that there was no plant at all in which a factory cell of *Nasjonal Samling* was established. Although the strength of the main organization differed regionally, it was nowhere set up completely.

Marginalia on the Question of the Nasjonal Samling Membership in the Period from 1933 to 1940

Quisling's archives at the University Library in Oslo contain only incomplete and inaccurate data about the social origins of party members. The statements about the number of members differ widely. In 1935 the publicity department of the party declared that the Nasjonal Samling had 15,000 members.[14] Shortly before the occupation, the German embassy in Oslo informed the Foreign Office in Berlin that there were 1,500 members registered, 500–600 in Oslo and Akershus alone.[15] The real number, however, was much smaller. In Oslo the last general meeting had been attended by only eight people.[16] During the occupation, agents of the NSDAP tried to determine the number of members as of April 1940. They reported that membership lists had not been kept in order since 1937. The books relating to membership dues were badly kept. Nevertheless, NSDAP agents estimated the registered members at 3,000. They were not able to make statements about the number of active members.[17]

Contemporary reports from the provinces only seldom mention numbers and there-fore give few clues. According to these reports, one third of the members were in Oslo and Akershus.[18] Here there was a unit of the semi-military *Hird* with about 100 members.[19] In Stavanger, where the party had a rather large following, 946 members were registered in 1935.[20] From the province of Hedmark, however, which was also a stronghold, it is reported that four district organizations had been established. Furth-ermore, 14 communal *lag* organizations are mentioned – the district had 30 commu-nes. Only for one *lag*, the largest of the district, is an absolute number reported: 132 members. This *lag* was the only one subdivided into *roder* in accordance with the statutes. The Women's Organization in Hedmark had 32 members, the Youth Organi-zation «about 25». There was no unit of the *Hird* in Hedmark.[21] From the province of Aust-Agder there is a 1935 report for the Grimstad district from which it may be concluded that there were other district organizations of the party in Aust-Agder. In Grimstad, according to the report, there were «10 to 12 members».[22] In the province of Møre a *Fylkes*-group had been founded in 1934. Apparently nothing happened afterwards, however. A collaborator of Quisling who had been sent to Møre in 1936 was able to find the minutes of the founding session but no membership list or other notes.[23]

From the few data available, it can be concluded that the party had few members and that the official number for the year 1935 – 15,000 – was highly exaggerated. In addition, it is highly improbable that three quarters of the voters for the party should have been recruited as members.

It is questionable whether with such low membership this party represented a specific social group of Norwegian society at all. Regional as well as chance factors probably had interacted to form the social composition of party members. The fact that in Trondheim the majority of the founding committee of the province organization were students seems to have discouraged older persons. These circumstances are pointed out in two letters written in 1933.[24] Other reports confirm that the *Nasjonal Samling* in Trondheim was a student party which assembled around Professor Ragnar Skancke.[25] From Bergen, Hans Hansson, the son of a ship-owner, wrote several letters during the year 1935, in which he described enthusiastically how he mobilized «wives and daughters of the most outstanding men of the town» – probably mostly the daughters – for Quisling's cause.[26] In 1934 a leading official of the shipping company Westfal & Larsen, Georg Vedeler, took charge of the matter. He aimed at a good relationship with the conservatives.[27] In Bergen, a common list of Conservatives and *Nasjonal Samling* was drawn up at the municipal elections. This was probably due to the good reputation of Vedeler. For the Conservative party headquarters in Oslo the NS was, as has been said, not acceptable. In Østfold and in Buskerud, officers and teachers led the party. This is apparently due to the fact that in these districts Quisling's older friends from the Nordic Peoples' Movement took the lead at the founding of the *Fylkes* Organization.[28] Conversely, in the urban areas of Telemark province the younger members from the NNSAP or the National Club seem to have had a decisive influence.[29] Here the youth group of the Liberal Conservatives joined the *Nasjonal Samling* and formed the main body of the party.[30] In the rural areas of Telemark there was a joint list of *Nasjonal Samling* and the Crisis Relief.[31]

The relative success of the party in Hedmark seems to have been less influenced by such purely random factors. In this province lived a third of Norway's forestry workers; in addition, it had the biggest percentage of large farms and a good number of unprofitable rural perquisites. In this province with its strong social tensions, the

Labour party had had great success in the elections of 1933.[32] The leading group of the *Nasjonal Samling* undoubtedly consisted here of bourgeois and rural dignitaries; the province leader of the party was a well-known attorney who demanded the consideration of the big farmers' interests in the program debate of the party.[33] At the same time the party in Hedmark turned to the «small people» *(småfolk)*, in order to alienate them from the Labour party. The province leader triumphantly reported to Oslo that in the biggest *lag* in the province, 30 per cent of the members were former supporters of the Labour party.[34] A regional study here could well contribute to an understanding of the social origins of members in the *Nasjonal Samling* and the needs it came to satisfy in this district.

A regional study of the situation in Stavanger could also be rewarding. The relative strength of the party there is thought to have been due to the free church groups located there and to the clever propaganda of the local leader Gulbrand Lunde. Reports and expositions about atheism in the Soviet Union stimulated anti-Marxist attitudes among the population of this area.[35] As to the social structure of party members in Oslo, one is told only that in the *Hird* students and workers stood side by side.[36]

Turning to the founding group of the NS, a distinction emerges between the «old» and the «young». Best known are those old members who had already joined Quisling in the Nordic People's Movement in Norway 1931. The documents mention 22 people. Among them were three majors (one of them Quisling) and nine captains, none of them however in active duty. Moreover, there were three scholars (one biologist, one researcher on genetics and one constitutional lawyer). Three were directors or business executives apparently active in management. Two were consul-generals, two were lawyers. Two were contractors.[37] One of them, Captain Frederik Prytz, had greatly profited from his activities in the timber trade during the NEP-period in the Soviet-Union. He was now involved in a whaling enterprise.[38] The business of the other consul-general, Dietrich Hildisch, was threatened during the years of his political activity by severe competition from the Unilever combine and was on the brink of being taken over.[39] A detailed biographical analysis of the «old» members would probably reveal that they were outsiders in their own social group. They are not representative of their group but indicators of emerging disintegrational factors that became noticeable in other social groups as well.[40]

Similar facts seem to hold true for the members in the provinces, although partially on a different social level. In any case, the party had difficulties in naming sufficiently well-reputed candidates at elections. In a report from Aust-Agder this fact is expressly deplored by the owner of a gardening business. One of the nominated candidates had neglected his business «because of private affairs» and was near bankruptcy, another had come in conflict with the law because of an illegal distillery.[41]

Among the «young» who had the leading position in the headquarters – the youngest among them was 24, the oldest 32 years old – the percentage of persons with a university education was high. Engineers, economists and chemists were, for instance, prevalent. Whether the young members were affected in their professional development by the economic crisis cannot be stated on the basis of the material at hand. The percentage of those who were educated for business professions was strikingly high.

Aside from the generation problem which is, more generally speaking, also a question of social integration, the members of the NS seem to have come from all social levels – from the contractor to the labourer – with the common characteristic that they represented outsider groups from each social level which were already disintegrating or threatened by disintegration. This would not be surprising in view of the object of investigation, a splinter party with a program of total opposition. Of course, this finding is very general. If the existence of a very small opposition party gives evidence of the social and political situation in Norway, it could be asked whether among the members of the *Nasjonal Samling* there were one or more identifiable social groups which were distinctively overrepresented in relation to the whole of society or to the region in question. The material at hand is insufficient to answer this question.

Hypotheses about the Social Dimension in Recruitment to the Nasjonal Samling

It is probably safe to assume that at all times and in all social segments there are signs of social disintegration. Among the motives impelling a person to join a party or another kind of organization is often the desire to overcome subjectively experienced disintegration. When, however, a party emerges – perhaps a small one – presenting a program of integration designed to encompass the whole of society, this may indicate 1. that the existing parties and organizations in themselves no longer are able to satisfy the needs of all social groups to become integrated, and also 2. that the political system represented by these parties has lost its ability to perform integrative functions. With regard to the *Nasjonal Samling* it is important to note that it in fact did have contact with a variety of smaller and larger groups, among which the largest was the Agrarian party (15.9 per cent of the vote in 1930) and the Patriotic League. The latter had a more or less extremist, that is disintegrative, program in relation to the established political consensus. Moreover, Norwegian historiography tends to describe the period between the two wars as a time of «economic, social and political crisis». Frequently one speaks of a «crisis of confidence». Under these circumstances it does not seem irrelevant to turn our attention to the question of social disintegration in the inter-war period. Two sets of hypotheses may be formulated to facilitate understanding of the integration crisis.

a. In the first set of hypotheses one could start from the fact that in democratic societies social and political integration of society is accomplished through several parties. The appearance of new parties would signify that the former parties have lost at least some of their integrational power. The appearance of working-class parties in early bourgeois society is a classic example of the inability of the old parties to integrate new social groups.

Moreover, it could be supposed that new parties not only turn against older parties, but at the same time against the social and political order maintained in consensus by the older parties. The increase of such new parties would put to test the integrational power of the former political order as a whole. The problems of integrating working-class parties into the social and political order of representative democracy, illustrates this clearly.

Finally, it may be supposed that the ability of the old parties to integrate their traditional voters and therefore to maintain the order represented by the parties, threatens to slacken at the moment when a democratic victory of the labour parties draws closer. Then new parties will emerge whose integrative power in part will depend on their promise to implement a form of integration comprising all of society.

This integration implies the abolition both of the socialist and the non-socialist parties and therefore means the end of the democratic order as such. The feared upheaval through majority rule is to be contained by just another and «better» upheaval. In this context, the new anti-democratic and anti-Marxist parties usually labelled «fascist» can be interpreted to be a sign of disintegration. Politically speaking, they are a disintegrative secondary effect of the integration problem which gave rise to the labour parties.

b. A second set of hypotheses could start out from the fact that new parties require such a new social basis. It is already included in the first set of hypotheses with regard to the labour parties. Since, according to our first set of hypotheses, the new fascist parties are politically a secondary effect, the question of their social basis is more difficult to answer. In hypotheses of this type one must therefore start with the assumption that the propensity for disintegration is linked to changes in the economic and social situation of at least part of those social groups which had up till then been integrated by the old parties. It may further be assumed that those changes of the economic and social situation perceived as being disintegrational were in a larger sense connected with those economic conditions which had also brought forth the working class. The political turn of those groups against the labour parties may be interpreted as a socio-psychological projection of fear under threat of social disintegration. But this would mean that the attempt to overcome their social and political disintegration did not necessarily have to imply fascist methods or to assume a fascist character. If the political integration of the labour parties is successful, at least sections of the disintegrated groups from the bourgeois parties may well be absorbed by the labour parties. Furthermore, in this way the old bourgeois parties would be relieved of their struggle to preserve the political system. In this case an inner, systemically immanent transformation would have taken place allowing all parties again the opportunity to compete freely. This corresponds to the hypothesis of fascism as a secondary effect formulated in the first set of hypotheses. With due allowance for the problems inherent in such general hypotheses, the Norwegian development may be interpreted in the light of both sets of hypotheses (due to the fact that the hypotheses are only an attempt to generalize the anticipated interpretation).

Two political events of the thirties are important in connection with the above-mentioned hypotheses.[42] The Norwegian Labour party obtained more than 40 per cent of the votes in the election of 1933. That means that it was no longer elected by labourers but began to act integratively within Norwegian society, beyond the limits of its own initial social base. According to our hypotheses, it should therefore have reached those groups who had been disintegrated from the traditional parties. This can hardly be doubted where party management was concerned. The leaders of the Labour party had young economists and advertising experts develop the election campaign. Keynes' ideas were also introduced by «new men» and influenced the practical planning of the Labour party. These were people who probably belonged to the same social group as the young members of the *Nasjonal Samling*. During the election campaign the Labour party in addition addressed itself to fishermen, small farmers and employees.

The second important event was the agreement between the Labour party and the Agrarian party of 1935 which caused the fall of the Liberal minority cabinet. The Labour party took charge of the government by setting up a minority cabinet which was consented to by the Agrarian party. The agreement between the two parties concerned a national economic policy of deficit spending in order to overcome the

673

economic crisis and certain measures to secure the income of the rural population. The alliance of the parties is important for several reasons: the two parties had previously presented themselves as irreconcilable adversaries: the Agrarian party had shortly before acted as standard-bearer of a vehement anti-Marxism and had also employed Quisling as its Minister of Defence, and the Labour party had dwelt on the theme of Agrarians with «fascist» leanings in the electoral campaigns. Now they formed an alliance with the purpose of solving the economic crisis in the interest of their voters and therefore in the interest of the entire Norwegian society.

This political alliance was apparently the beginning of the solution of the social and politically integration crisis. The Norwegian voters confirmed this solution in the elections of 1936. It is significant that the Agrarian party could win support from its supporters for its policy of toleration towards the Labour government. It lost only 2.3 per cent of the votes in the election. Splinter parties like the *Nasjonal Samling* declined further. The Conservative party, on the other hand, increased its electoral support by 1 per cent, the first such increase for many years.

A statistical confirmation of this interpretation of events would lead to the question whether there were one or more social groups which turned from the traditional parties, i.e. the Conservatives and the Liberals, to the *Nasjonal Samling* or its related groups. Did they join the Labour party, or did they return under certain circumstances to the old parties?

The material at my disposal is insufficient to answer this question. It should be pointed out that, by examining candidate lists from the years 1933 and 1936, Hans Olaf Brevig found out that the social origins of candidates of the Conservatives and the *Nasjonal Samling* were almost the same.[43] This result would not be surprising in view of our hypotheses since the Conservative party had been steadily losing votes (1921 = 33 per cent; 1933 = 20 per cent) during the twenties. For many of its supporters, the party lost its integrating power. The loss of votes was particularly high in 1933 when it lost 7 percentage points. (The Liberal party which in 1933 also lost 7 percentage points of its votes was, on the whole, more stable than the Conservative party during the twenties.) The steady loss of votes for the Conservatives and the similarity in social origins of the candidates from the Conservative party and the *Nasjonal Samling* could be a confirmation of the assumption that there were socially identical groups which disintegrated from the non-socialist parties and sought a new integration with the other parties – including the Labour party. This assumption is not yet validated, though. A clue to this process may be found in a stronger differentiation of social classification than Brevig could devise.

As a marginal note it should be mentioned that the managing director of the Patriotic League, Joakim Lehmkuhl, declared after the elections of 1933, that the Labour party had used a «typically fascist battle cry» and therefore won «on a false basis».[44] (The slogan was «Work for all people»). Similarly Quisling declared in 1933 that the victory of the Labour party proved «that the people sought new ways, a radical redress of the crisis», therefore the victory of the Labour party was the signal for the future victory of the *Nasjonal Samling* which showed the «right» radical way.[45] Quisling also thought that the Labour party «had won on a false basis». The remarks of Lehmkuhl and Quisling show that the parties and groups like the *Nasjonal Samling* and the Patriotic League gained from social disintegration. The Labour party did not win on a false basis; its victory and the agreement with the Agrarian party signified that the old «basis» was lost, that the notion of the class society in this sense had become ideological.

674

Our concluding hypothesis about social recruitment to the *Nasjonal Samling* could be expressed in the following way: The members and voters of the *Nasjonal Samling* before the war belonged to those social groups which also furnished members and voters for all other parties. To correlate the social origins of the members of *Nasjonal Samling* with right-wing parties or the whole population of Norway cannot yield satisfactory results. For a sociological inquiry to be successful it must single out a relatively equivalent group of shifting voters and bring these into relation with the voters and members of the *Nasjonal Samling*. But for the time being there are not enough socio-statistical data to fulfil this requirement. Scholarship must take detours to arrive at valid results, or it must rest content with partial insights.

To the question «who were the Nazis?» we can only answer, as Sigurd Hoel does: We meet them at the milestones.[46]

An old word about historiography says: *historia scribitur ad narrandum, non ad probandum.* I agree with this ancient opinion. History must be narrated. Sometimes the telling does prove something, but seldom by making us aware of some comprehensive general conclusion. The people encountered are not neat embodiments of our theories, and do not fit their actions to our preconceptions. They remain their complicated selves.

NOTES

*The following presentation is based on the material which I have collected for my book *Quisling, Rosenberg und Terboven – Zur Vorgeschichte und Geschichte der nationalsozialistischen Revolution in Norwegen* (Stuttgart 1970) (Norwegian edition Oslo 1972). It is restricted to the time before the occupation of Norway by German troops on April 9, 1940. It was Hans Olaf Brevig's book *NS – fra parti til sekt* (From Party to Sect), (Oslo, 1970) that inspired me to reflect on the history of *Nasjonal Samling* during this period.

Since the results of the joint projects at the Institute of History and the Institute of Sociology at the University of Bergen are probably based on other material and precise socio-economic methods, I quite acknowledge that my hypotheses can be rejected. There would, however, be no harm in this. I would like to express my gratitude to Mrs. Hildegard Möller for translating the German manuscript and to Mr. Bernt Hagtvet for comments on earlier drafts.

[1] For the history of *Nasjonal Samling* and the life of Vidkun Quisling cf. *inter alia* Hans Olaf Brevig, *op.cit.*, Sverre Hartmann, *Fører uten folk. Quisling som politisk og psykologisk problem* (Führer without people. Quisling as a Political and Psychological Problem) (Oslo, 1959); Benjamin Vogt, «Quisling: the Man and the Criminal»; The American-Scandinavian Review XXXV, 1947; Benjamin Vogt, *Mennesket Vidkun og forræderen Quisling* («The Man Vidkun and the Traitor Quisling), (Oslo, 1965); Loock, *op.cit.*

[2] Vidkun Quisling, *Russland og vi* (Oslo, 1930), p. 211; (English edition: *Russia and Ourselves* (London, 1930)); The German edition *Russland und wir* (Berlin, 1942) does not contain the cited sentence).

[3] Kaare Frøland, *Krise og kamp. Bygdefolkets krisehjelp* (Crisis and Combat. The Farmers' Relief Association) (Oslo, 1962).

[4] Cf. the papers of *Nordisk Folkereisning* (The Nordic People's Movement) in Quisling's archives in the Oslo University Library. In it 22 persons are mentioned by name. No information of the club's activities after Quisling's nomination as Minister of Defence is found in his archives. A number of the names appears again in the papers of the *Nasjonal Samling* as well as in the papers of the *Folkereisning* movement.

[5] Cf. «Stenografisk referat av major Quisling's foredrag den 26. oktober 1933» (Stenographic report of major Quisling's lecture on October 26, 1933). Quisling's archives, Oslo.

⁶ Edvard Bull, «Kriseforliket mellom Bondepartiet og Det norske Arbeiderparti» (The Crisis Agreement between the Farmers' Party and the Social Democratic Party) in *Historisk Tidsskrift*, Oslo, Vol. 39, 1959. See below.

⁷ Brevig, *op.cit.*, p. 56.

⁸ *Ibid.*, p. 51.

⁹ Hartmann, *op.cit.*, p. 277.

¹⁰ Cf. Letters from the provinces to Quisling; cf. also *NS-Partimeddelelser* (NS-Party information), 1933. Quisling's archives.

¹¹ Cf. the papers on the quarrel about the project statuses have been printed in Orvar Sæther, *Vår Organisasjon. Nasjonal Samling, NS ungdomsfylking* (Our Organization. Nasjonal Samling, NS Youth Organization), (Oslo, 1936).

¹² Cf. «Bestemmelser for NS-Støttepunktvirksomhet» (Rules for NS support activity) by Orvar Sæther, *op.cit.*

¹³ Cf. correspondence between Albert Wiesener and Vidkun Quisling, February 1937. Quisling's archives.

¹⁴·*Nasjonal Samlings historiske kamp 1933–1940* (Nasjonal Samling's historical struggle 1933–1940). Halldis Neegård Østbye (ed.), Vol. 1 (Oslo, 1943), p. 222; Hereafter cited *NS' kamp*. Cf. Brevig, *op.cit.*, p. 56.

¹⁵ Report Attaché Lehmann, 8.4.40. Auswärtiges Amt, Bonn: Politisches Archiv. Gesandtschaft Oslo: Besetzung Norwegens, Okkupationspolitik.

¹⁶ *Ibid.*

¹⁷ «Entwurf zu einer Geschichte der Nasjonal Samling» (Maschinenschrift 1.ca. 1943). Ausw. Amt. Pol. Archiv: Parteidienststellen, APA.

¹⁸ Circular, *NS' Hovedkontor* (NS's central office) 9.1.37. Quisling's archives.

¹⁹ *NS' kamp*, p. 153.

²⁰ Jan Petter Myklebust, «Hvem var de norske nazistene? Sammenheng mellom sosial, økonomisk og politisk bakgrunn og medlemskap i Nasjonal Samling» (Who were the Norwegian Nazis? Social, Economic and Political Background related to Membership in the NS). Master's thesis in comparative politics, University of Bergen, 1974, p. 67. Cf. also Bodil Wold Johnson, «Nasjonal Samling i Stavanger 1933–37» (Nasjonal Samling in Stavanger 1933–37). Master's thesis in history, University of Bergen, 1972.

²¹ «Rapport 1935 fra Hedmark fylke» (Report 1935 from Hedmark county), 24.7.35. Quisling's archives.

²² Letter from Sjur Fuhr to Quisling 19.11.36. *Ibid.*

²³ Letter from Andreas Brokstad to Quisling 14.9.36. *Ibid.*

²⁴ Letters from Thor Tharum to Quisling 17.7.33 and 19.9.33. *Ibid.*

²⁵ Letter from NS-studentergruppe Trøndelag to Quisling 7.2.34. *Ibid.*

²⁶ Letters from Hans Hansson to Quisling, autumn 1933. *Ibid.*

²⁷ Letters from Georg Vedeler to Quisling 1933/34. *Ibid.*

²⁸ Letters from Jacob Ihlen, Trygve Tellefsen *et al.* 1933–36. *Ibid.*

²⁹ Letters from Eggen, Ihlen, Lunde *et al.* 1934. *Ibid.*

³⁰ Telemark Arbeiderblad 18.8.33, printed in *NS' kamp*, p. 71.

³¹ Kaare Frøland, *op.cit.*, p. 180.

³² Arne Bergsgård, *Frå 17. mai til 9. april. Norsk historie 1814–1940* (From May 17. to April 9. Norwegian History 1814–1940) (Oslo, 1958), p. 388.

³³ Letter from W. F. K. Christie to Quisling 12.2.34. Quisling's archives, Oslo.

³⁴ «Rapport 1935 fra Hedmark fylke», 24.7.35. *Ibid.*

³⁵ Brevig, *op.cit.*, p. 55.

³⁶ *NS' kamp*, p. 137.

³⁷ Cf. note 22.

³⁸ Article on Frederik Prytz in *Norsk Biografisk Leksikon* (Norwegian Biographical Dictionary), Volume XI, Letter from Prytz to the King 21.11.32. Quisling's archives. Cf. also Benjamin Vogt, *op.cit.* p. 41.

³⁹ Hartmann, *op.cit.*, p. 129. – Sammlung Grossadmiral Raeder 28, Handmaterial Generalin-

spekteur, Rechtsstreit Generalkonsul Hildisch. Militärgeschichtliches Forschungsamt, Freiburg, Dokumenten-Zentrale. Throne Holst was a promoter of the *Nasjonal Samling*. The founder of the food combine «Freia», Holst was also Chairman of the Norwegian Industrial Association. He was affiliated with the National Liberals and financed their newspaper «Tidens Tegn» (Signs of the Time) which was frequently put at Quisling's disposal. The assumption that this connection was at the same time a connection between the *Nasjonal Samling* and the industrial association can be denied with certainty. In this context it should be noted that the *Nasjonal Samling* always had financial difficulties. Only 26,000 N.kr. were at the party's disposal for the election campaign from May till September, 1933. The Patriotic League had spent 16,000 N.kr. per month during the same period of time.

[40] For an elaboration, see pp. 70–71 in the German edition of my book *Quisling, Terboven und Rosenberg* (Stuttgart 1970).

[41] Cf. note 22.

[42] For the following cf. *inter alias* Edvard Bull, *Arbeiderklassen i norsk historie* (The History of the Working Class) (Oslo, 1947); Einhart Lorenz, *Arbeiderbevegelsens historie II 1930–1973* (The History of the Working Class II 1930–1973) (Oslo, 1974); Arne Bergsgård, *op.cit.;* Hans Fredrik Dahl, *Norge mellom krigene. Det norske samfunn i krise og konflikt 1918–1940* (Norway Between the Wars. The Norwegian Society in Crisis and Conflict 1918–1940) (Oslo, 1971); Berge Furre, *Norsk historie 1905–1940* (Norwegian History 1905–1940) (Oslo, 1971); Jorunn Bjørgum, *Venstre og kriseforliket* (The Liberal Party and the Crisis Agreement) (Oslo, 1970); Edvard Bull, cf. note 6.

[43] Brevig, *op.cit.,* p. 108.

[44] Joakim Lehmkuhl, *Norges vei. Et angrep på norsk borgerlig politikk og et forslag til nasjonal arbeidsplan* (Norway's Way. An Attack on Norwegian Non-Socialist Politics and a Proposal for a National Work Plan) (Oslo, 1933), p. 96.

[45] Cf. note 5.

[46] The reference is to one of the most well-known Norwegian novels about the occupation: Sigurd Hoel, *Møte ved milepælen* (Encounter at the Milestone) (1947).

Mass Support for Fascism in Finland

RISTO ALAPURO

Several mainly Marxist-inspired interpretations of fascism imply that fascism between the two World Wars was a phenomenon inherent in the prevailing stage of development of capitalism in certain countries: a reaction to threats against the foundations of the capitalist system in these countries.[1] But these interpretations usually include another element as well. Fascism was not only a reaction of dominant classes but also a mass movement. It was not only a reaction but, more specifically, «an attempt to make reaction and conservatism popular and plebeian», as Barrington Moore puts it.[2]

The emphasis both on the necessity of fascism for the dominant classes and on its character of being a mass movement highlights the importance of the *relation* between these two elements in studying fascism. It also implies, among other things, that in the comparative study of fascism, the focus should be directed to this relation and not only on the comparison of different fascist-type phenomena as such. «In order for the *coup d'état* to have a chance to materialize, a supply, i.e. a fascist mass movement created by socio-economic crisis, must be met by a corresponding demand, i.e. the hope of the ruling class for a fascist power system».[3] In characterizations of this kind the relative autonomy of the fascist mass movement clearly appears. Its specific character can be seen for example in its ideological traits, which to some extent differed from the ideology of the dominant classes owing to differences in traditions, and in threats caused by the economic crisis of the 1930s.[4] It is also known that the fascist movements drew their support mainly from the middle classes and in the countryside from the small farmers, i.e. not only from outside the working class parties but also from outside the traditional conservative parties.[5]

Of course the degree of autonomy of the mass movement is an empirical question, and a central one in considering the relation between the two elements. The review of support for the fascist movement in Finland, which is the main aim of this paper, throws light on that problem. The extent to which the support came from outside the working class parties and especially from outside the traditional conservative parties gives an indicator of the degree of autonomy of the movement vis-à-vis the dominant classes.

Another important factor for the relation between the mass movement and the dominant classes is naturally enough the sheer strength of the movement. Many commentators have pointed out that fascism in Germany came to be looked upon by the dominant classes as a potentially valuable ally against the workers only after it had proved its strength, its right to be taken seriously.[6] In Finland, too, the movement was relatively strong. The Finnish variant of fascism, the so-called Lapua movement, powerfully affected Finnish politics and almost seemed to dominate the country in 1929–32, eleven years after an attempted socialist revolution and the Civil War in 1918. The movement succeeded in having all public activities of communists banned and effected the disintegration of the trade union movement. In 1932, the Lapua movement attempted a *coup d'état*. Its failure led to the founding of a political party, the People's Patriotic Movement (IKL), which held 8–14 of the 200 parliamentary seats from 1933 up to World War II.[7]

The evidence on mass support for fascism in Finland seems to indicate that this exceptionally strong movement was not nearly so autonomous as the fascist movement in Germany. Is was largely a general bourgeois reaction. In inter-war Finland, where the bourgeois front was relatively unified, fascist-type phenomena were largely lacking an independent profile. The strength of the movement and the relation between the two elements paradoxically contributed to a situation where, under pressure from the mass movement, the interests of the dominant classes came to be well catered for in the framework of the existing political system.

The Farmers

The Lapua movement was from its very beginning in the fall of 1929 considered to be basically a peasant movement – a rise of peasants against a conception of a communist doctrine which damned everything the peasant folk *(talonpoikainen kansa)* held sacred. The term «peasant folk» is derived from the common ideological arsenal of the nineteenth century nationalist movement and from its ideological heir, the Conservative party and, on the other hand, from the strong agrarian party, the Agrarian Union which became so prominent in Finland and the Scandinavian countries after the mass political mobilization at the turn of the century. But the term also refers to the fact that the population of Finland was still heavily agrarian. In 1930, 60 per cent of the population worked in the agrarian sector, and 68 per cent of the agrarian population were farmers and members of farming families.[8]

These facts make it clear that the role of the countryside and especially of the farmers is crucial in analyzing the fascist mass movement in Finland. The main rural backing of the movement came from the big farmers and the middle-sized farmers with family farms, not from small farmers.[9] As well as the self-proclaimed «peasant character» of the movement, three features are illustrative of this situation.

First of all, although the Lapua movement received rural support all over the country, it also had a clear-cut regional stronghold, the province of Ostrobothnia. The commune of Lapua which gave the name to the movement, is situated in this province. Ostrobothnia had a long tradition of peasant revolts and other activities directed against the national center, often manifested in religious terms. It has been compared to the French province of Vendée with the stubborn individualism and independence of its peasants. The Lapua movement in Ostrobothnia was a reaction of well-to-do farmers. The land was evenly distributed and middle-sized farms dominated in the province.[10]

The immediate origins of the movement go back to anti-communist riots in the end of the year 1929 where farmers were the most conspicuous participants. But the two major bourgeois parties, the Coalition party (called below also the Conservative party) and the Agrarian Union, immediately expressed their strong support for the movement, and were to back it in the following period. This stand was of course due to several factors, but among other things, it indicates the significance of the support of the big farmers who were an important backing-group for the Conservative party.[11]

The ideological characteristics of the movement also point in the same direction. Its ideology was more conservative than has usually been the case in fascist movements. It is rather exceptional, for example, that there were no explicitly anti-capitalist demands in the proclamations of the movement. It was based in the peasant world outlook, which is alien to capitalism. However, it did not focus on the working of the capitalist system and on threats resulting from it, but focused almost solely on its manifestations in the form of class struggle. It strongly attacked communist and socialist working class movements.

In explaining the structure of the rural backing of the movement as a national phenomenon not confined to Ostrobothnia, it is important to note, first, the impact of the depression in the 1930s on the medium and large-scale peasant farmers. «The development of the depression showed the wealthy strata of the peasantry to be natural allies of the bourgeoisie. By the first blow of the depression they lost a third of their forest incomes, and were threatened with total loss of them.»[12] Although the loss of forest incomes indicated in this quote is not precise, it underscores an important point. Finland had been linked to the international capitalist system from the 1870s especially through timber. No less than 86 per cent of the exports in the period 1920–29 were pulp or timber products. The biggest losses of forest income outside of the export industry were suffered by the wealthy forest-owning farmers; the decline started already in 1928, before the international depression broke out.[13] In the same year there was a crop failure. Indicative of the damage suffered by the middle and large-scale farmers is the fact that compulsory auctions of farms more frequently imposed losses on these groups than on the small farmers.[14]

The economic losses of farmers as such do not give an appropriate explanation for their *fascist*-type reaction. To be sure, the specific Finnish linkage of the (large and medium-scale) farmers to the main export industries of the country could be used as an explanation for the fact that the farmers were so prone to a rightist reaction. But the legacy of the Civil War in 1918 must be emphasized, too. In the Civil War all the bourgeois groups had been united against the revolutionaries led by the Social Democratic party. The farmers and their sons (excluding the small farmers and crofters) had been the main mass basis for the government army – the «white peasant army».[15] In 1929–32 the Lapua movement understood the situation in the same terms, i.e., as a continuation of the Civil War («War of Freedom») against the communists and to a lesser extent the Social Democrats, and even against the Russians. The depression called forth the same reaction among the farmers as the situation eleven years before. The conservative ideological flavor of the Finnish fascist movement is indicative of the Civil War legacy: the two main symbolic figures of the movement were also the two most prominent white leaders in 1918, General C.G.E. Mannerheim, and P.E. Svinhufvud who was to be elected the president of the republic in 1931 under pressure from the Lapua movement.

The role of the small farmers in the Lapua movement has not been studied properly, and undoubtedly there are regional differences. It should also be taken into account that there is no clear-cut distinction between small farmers and other farmers. But still it seems that the main reaction of small farmers to the depression was channelled through the so-called Depression movements, which remained separate from the Lapua movement.

Small farmers were also dependent on the international market through timber. They too owned forests, but the significance of selling timber was smaller than among wealthier farmers. More importantly, the small farmers worked part of the year as lumberjacks, and owing to the depression their income from forestry declined from 1929–30 onwards.[16] Naturally, the declining prices of agricultural products affected them along with all other farmers.

The small farmers in Finland were the last group to be linked to the capitalist market. The process was still going on throughout the 1920s and 1930s. Only in the earlier independence period after the Civil War did a major part of them become affected by capitalist exchange relations. The crofters (a residue from the pre-capitalist period) became «independent farmers» through redemption, and many previously landless families redeemed land for farming.[17] They became directly dependent on the market as owners of farms, but they were dependent on it also as wage-workers in the forest industry. In other words, they were or became linked to the capitalist market in two different ways. Characteristically, the small farmers usually voted not only for the Agrarian Union but also for the Social Democrats.[18]

The Depression movements demanding relief to the indebted farmers which erupted in the winter of 1931 recruited mostly small farmers, who had recently cleared land for cultivation, became indebted through crop failure and were consequently forced to give up their farms at executioner's sales.[19] As has been pointed out by a commentator, the supporters of a Depression movement had only recently been living in a rather self-sufficient natural economy, and were still trying to return to this earlier situation without understanding their dependence both on the capitalists, and on the workers – the group with the biggest share in the consumption of their products.[20] In contrast to the Lapua movement some of these amorphous and dispersed eruptions displayed anti-capitalist features, and the supporters of the Depression movements stayed outside of the Lapua movement. Their political significance lies in the fact that they alerted the Agrarian Union to the discontent of the farmers and for their part helped the Agrarian Union to dissociate itself from the Lapua movement, which consequently came more than before under the control of the Coalition party.[21]

In sum then, mass support for the Lapua movement came mainly from the large and medium-scale farmers. An immediate explanation for this is their economic position during the depression years. Ideologically the movement drew heavily upon the ideological arsenal of the Whites in the Civil War of 1918. The small farmers, on the other hand, did not belong to the core supporters of the fascist movement. More illustrative of their attitudes were the Depression movements with their frequently anti-capitalist tone, and their impact on the Agrarian Union.

The Middle Classes

The heterogeneity of the so-called middle classes makes it difficult, in the absence of detailed analyses, to assess the extent and strength of their support for fascism. It has often been argued that these groups gave considerable support to the fascist movement in Finland like comparable groups elsewhere.[22] It is true, for example, that a middle class party, the liberal National Progress party, to a large extent went along with the Lapua movement in its initial phase. But only the attitudes of the academically trained middle class groups, i.e. the young academics and the students, have been at all thoroughly studied.

That there was support for the Lapua movement among the university-educated can be seen for instance in the composition of the leading organs of the movement – a third of the members of the central council and of the district boards came from the professional and governmental groups with higher education. Together with the people from managerial and proprietary groups they constituted a strong majority.[23] More indicative still is the students' support for the movement. Academic Karelia

681

Society (AKS), the student organization which was overwhelmingly dominant among the Finnish-speaking students and the young educated class, supported the Lapua movement.[24]

However, the support for fascism among the educated middle classes differed from the peasant support in one important respect. It is very obvious that the farmer support was linked to the depression: the rural movement slowed down around 1932 if not earlier, with the easing of the depression and with political setbacks for the movement. But after the breakdown of the strong mass movement – and simultaneously after Hitler's rise to power – fascism continued to attract the educated middle classes in particular. The new party, the IKL, which considered itself the heir of the Lapua movement, remained a small party, indicating the waning of the rural support, and it had a strong academic color. Only two of the 21 MPs the party ever had were without higher education or training as military officers. The close connections between the AKS and the IKL, and other evidence of extensive support for the party by younger members of the educated class, make it plausible to argue that in few European countries did the educated class so widely accept fascism as in Finland. Also, the IKL ideology was less conservative and more overtly fascist than the ideology of the Lapua movement. In the IKL program there were minor direct borrowings from German and Italian fascism.[25]

We have referred to the significance of the Civil War for ideological articulation among the peasants in the Lapua movement. The Civil War experience was pivotal for the educated middle class, too, in the sense that the latter presumably experienced the breakdown of the pre-Civil War *Gemeinschaft* solidarity, finding it a most agonizing problem to cope with. The status of the Finnish-speaking educated class had been particularly based on nationalist ideology which portrayed the national educated class as one valued and accepted by the people, but in 1918 this conception had proved illusory.[26] With the rise of the fascist mass movement the attempt at restoring integration was transformed into a fascist movement and was to remain one or become even more so after the coming to power of fascism in Germany.

On the other hand, the educated class was increasingly viewed as a middle class only after World War I. Therefore, the extreme nationalist and fascist reaction among the educated class can be seen not only as an attempt to integrate the rebellious working class, or to mask class conflict; it was also a sign of opposition against the educated part of the upper classes, which largely spoke Swedish. Both of these tendencies were most distinct among the students.[27]

Briefly, the consequences of the depression were not essential in mobilizing the middle classes for fascism. On this point there is a difference from the farmers. What was decisive for the bourgeois turn towards the extreme right was rather the breakdown of nationalist integration in the Civil War in 1918, and the weakening of the class position of the well-educated vis-à-vis the predominantly Swedish-speaking upper class.

The Relation Between the Mass Movement and the Dominant Classes

At the beginning of this paper a generalization was presented maintaining that mass support for fascism usually came from outside the working class parties and traditional conservative parties. The latter part of this assertion does not apply to Finland. In addition to support from the farmers backing the Agrarian Union and apparently to some extent from the middle classes, the Lapua movement was from the very beginning also supported by conservatives, including big farmers. As the movement went on, this conservative or reactionary character became increasingly clear. On the other hand, the small farmers, the backbone of rural fascism in several other countries, remained outside the movement, expressing their dissatisfactions through dispersed riots.

Finnish fascism assumed a more middle class character only after the mass movement had slowed down. The IKL decidedly bore the stamp of the educated middle class. But it seems to have been supported mainly by former conservative voters,[28] and it also cooperated closely with the Conservative party up to the latter half of the 1930s.

The question of the structure of support for fascism bears on the degree of autonomy of the movement. As was mentioned above, several students have presented fascism as an agent which was called to restore order once it had proved its right to be taken seriously. In Finland the movement was *from the very beginning* strongly supported by the established parties, especially by the Conservative party which, through several of its representatives, was involved in the leadership and control of the movement. Although it remained organizationally unaffiliated with the parties, the Lapua movement was fundamentally a general bourgeois reaction.

Both of the above statements point to the fact that in Finland the relation between the fascist mass movement and the dominant classes was already very close in the initial stage. The export industry and the biggest banks gave considerable financial support to the movement.[29] It has been a subject of controversy whether the mass movement arose spontaneously or was created and pushed forward by the dominant classes.[30] If our delineation of the Lapua movement as a rather general bourgeois reaction is valid, it is not very helpful to put the question this way. In any case, the rise of the mass movement and dominant classes' need for it were closely interconnected.

What accounts for the specific character of Finnish fascism? Here only general comments will be offered.

We have already mentioned an important factor, the significance of the Civil War of 1918. Its outbreak was largely due to the Russian Revolution, which in Finland (then a part of the Russian empire) meant a sudden disappearance of the armed control force which had till then upheld the authority of the dominant classes. In Finland no serious cleavages divided the élite, as has generally been the case in other revolutionary situations. It can be argued that due to the Civil War and the conditions leading to its outbreak, the upper classes in Finland were more united after the war than is usually the case in post-revolutionary situations. One salient feature of the situation after the Civil War was the Civil Guard organization, which, in contradistinction to many armed unofficial groups elsewhere, was a force supported by all bourgeois groups. In contrast with the situation in Germany and Austria, *all* non-socialist parties in Finland backed *one* armed organization, which was also to become loosely tied with the state machinery. In the early 1920s there were 100,000 armed men in the Civil Guards while the corresponding number in the army was 20,000–25,000.[31] Another feature was the overwhelming domination among the students and the young educated class of one nationalist and semi-fascist organization, the AKS.

This background presumably accounts for the fact that in Finland between the two World Wars, a strong but also very *united* nationalistic political culture existed – a more unified bourgeois hegemony than is found in most countries with a history of insurrections. The cultural unity probably had consequences important for the structure of the fascist mass movement. There were large bourgeois strata who were prone to

683

react similarly and sensitively to all threats against some symbolic national values. This unified reaction – as a reaction against the communists – was brought about by the depression. Basically, of course, the bourgeois unity and its Civil War background reflect the significance of the geo-political position of Finland – first as a part of the Russian empire and then as a neighbor of the first socialist country in history, the Soviet Union.

But there seem to be more fundamental factors underlying the character of mass support for fascism in Finland. The fact that the Finnish farmers and especially the wealthier among them were closely linked to the main export industry of the country through timber was mentioned earlier. They were directly affected by the international depression, concomitantly with the pulp and timber industry. It is reasonable to hypothesize that the rapid and general bourgeois reaction both in the countryside and among the capitalists is connected with this fact.

Also, from a more general point of view, the nature of the connection between the wealthy farmers and landowners, and, on the other hand, the capitalist class, appears relevant. Finland did not have a strong landed aristocracy in the initial stages of the development of capitalism in the nineteenth century. Therefore, and presumably also because of the close linkage of the peasants to the industrial and commercial classes through timber, commercialization of agriculture essentially came about through reliance on the labor market, and not by preserving the traditional peasant society and simultaneously squeezing more surplus out of it as was the case in many Eastern European countries. This development was, if we follow Barrington Moore, conducive to the strong adherence of peasants to the parliamentary political system.[32] In this context, the strength of the farmers' party, the Agrarian Union, is especially important. True, the party went along with the fascist mass movement in its initial phase, but it also withdrew from it not later than 1931.

This fact, which differentiates the agrarian party in Finland from its counterparts in Eastern European countries,[33] also throws light on the character of Finnish rural fascism. The involvement of the Agrarian Union in the fascist movement in 1929–31 is illustrative of the nature of the movement as a general bourgeois reaction in Finland. On the other hand, it implies that the small farmers stood aloof from it: they were inactive in the bourgeois nationalist reaction during the depression exactly as they had been eleven years earlier in the Civil War, in which they took part only passively.[34] The fascist potential of the small peasants and farmers was not channelled through fascism in Finland. Rather, the dispersed and inarticulate Depression movements of the small farmers in 1931 contributed to the dissociation of the Agrarian Union from the movement.

NOTES

I wish to thank Matti Alestalo and Erik Allardt for their helpful comments in preparing this paper.

[1] Different interpretations in this vein are e.g. Reinhard Kühnl, *Formen bürgerlicher Herrschaft. Liberalismus – Faschismus* (Reinbek bei Hamburg: Rowohlt, 1971); Barrington Moore, *Social Origins of Dictatorship and Democracy* (Boston: Beacon, 1966); Karl Polanyi, *The Great Transformation* (Boston: Beacon, 1957 [1944]); and Nicos Poulantzas, *Fascisme et dictature* (Paris: Maspero, 1970).

[2] Moore, *Social Origins*, p. 447.

[3] Kühnl, *Formen*, p.103.

[4] Hans Fredrik Dahl, *Hva er fascisme?* (What is Fascism?) (Oslo: Pax, 1972), pp. 137–146; Kühnl, *Formen*, pp. 84–99; Moore, *Social Origins*, pp. 448–452.

[5] Dahl, *Hva er fascisme?*, pp. 58–91; Moore, *Social Origins*, pp. 448–449.

[6] E.g. Dahl, *Hva er fascisme?*, pp. 129–136; Paul M. Sweezy, *The Theory of Capitalist Development* (New York: Monthly Review Press, 1968), pp. 329–330, 334.

[7] A detailed account on the Lapua movement and the IKL is given in Marvin Rintala, *Three Generations: The Extreme Right Wing in Finnish Politics* (Bloomington: Indiana University Press, 1962).

[8] See Kosti Huuhka, *Talonpoikaisnuorison koulutie* (School Attendance of Peasant Youth) (Helsinki: Suomen Historiallinen Seura, 1955), p. 201.

[9] See Jorma Kalela, «Torparna och småbrukarna i finländsk politik från storstrejken till 1930-talskrisen» (Crofters and Small Farmers in Finnish Politics from the General Strike to the Crisis in the 1930s), *Historisk Tidskrift för Finland* 59 (1974), p. 206; Einari Laaksovirta (under the pseudonym N. Tähti), *Fasismi ja Suomen maaseutu* (Fascism and the Finnish Countryside) (Leningrad: Kirja, 1935), especially pp. 70–89; Paula Oittinen, *Pulaliikkeiden alueellinen levinneisyys* (Regional Support for the Depression Movements) (unpublished Master's thesis, Institute of Political History, University of Helsinki, 1975). Cf. Risto Alapuro, *Akateeminen Karjala-Seura* (The Academic Karelia Society) (Helsinki: WSOY, 1973), pp. 42–44.

[10] On the structure of the agrarian population in Ostrobothnia see Eino Jutikkala, *Bonden i Finland genom tiderna* (The Peasant in Finland from the Past to the Present) (Helsingfors: LTs förlag, 1963), pp. 387–389.

[11] Göran von Bonsdorff, *Samlingspartiet* (The Coalition Party) (Helsingfors: Nyliberala Studentförbundet, 1947), pp. 120–122, 134.

[12] Laaksovirta, *Fasismi*, p. 36.

[13] See Klaus Waris, *Kuluttajain tulot, kulutus ja säästäminen suhdannekehityksen valossa Suomessa vuosina 1926–1938* (Incomes, Consumption, and Saving of Consumers in the Light of Economic Trends in Finland in the Years 1926–1938) (Helsinki: Kansantaloudellinen Yhdistys, 1945), p. 91 and table I in the Appendix.

[14] Hannes Gebhard, «Det finska jordbrukets skuldbörda och åtgärder för dess lättande» (Burden of Debt in the Finnish Agriculture and Measures for Relieving It), *Ekonomiska Samfundets Tidskrift* 26 (1932), pp. 38–39.

[15] E.g. Viljo Rasila, «The Finnish Civil War and Land Lease Problems», *The Scandinavian Economic History Review* 17 (1969), especially p. 121.

[16] Lauri Haataja et al. *Suomen työväenliikkeen historia* (A History of the Working Class Movement in Finland) (Joensuu: TSL, 1976) Laaksovirta, *Fasismi*, pp. 17, 29–32; Waris, *Kuluttajain*, pp. 83, 87–88, 137 and table I in the Appendix.

[17] Cf. Huuhka, *Talonpoikaisnuorison*, pp. 202–203; Kalela, «Torparna», p. 205.

[18] Arvo Santonen, *Pienviljelijäin järjestäytymiskysymys ja pienviljelijäjärjestöjen vakiintuminen Suomessa* (The Problem of Organizing the Small Farmers and the Consolidation of Small Farmer Organizations in Finland) (Helsinki: Suomen Historiallinen Seura, 1971), especially pp. 288, 313.

[19] Oittinen, *Pulaliikkeiden*.

[20] The commentator was an Agrarian politician and later the president of Finland, Kyösti Kallio. His comment is cited in Lempi Linna, *Konikapina* (Hack Revolt) (Helsinki: Tammi, 1965), p. 133.

[21] Kalela, «Torparna», pp. 206–207.

[22] See e.g. Krister Wahlbäck, *Från Mannerheim till Kekkonen* (From Mannerheim to Kekkonen) (Stockholm: Aldus, 1967), p. 108.

[23] E.g. Alapuro, *Akateeminen*, p. 223.

[24] Risto Alapuro, «Students and National Politics: A Comparative Study of the Finnish Student Movement in the Interwar Period», *Scandinavian Political Studies* 8 (1973), pp. 128–129.

[25] Marvin Rintala, «An Image of European Politics: The People's Patriotic Movement», *Journal of Central European Affairs* 21 (1963), pp. 308–310; Alapuro, *Akateeminen*, pp. 53–54, 144–146.

[26] Alapuro, *Akateeminen*, pp. 45–46.

[27] Alapuro, *Akateeminen*, pp. 164–165.

[28] See e.g. von Bonsdorff, *Samlingspartiet*, pp. 81–82.

[29] See Haataja et al., *Suomen*.

[30] On the different interpretations and emphases in explanations see Krister Wahlbäck's review in Wahlbäck, *Från Mannerheim*, pp. 107–110.

[31] Wahlbäck, *Från Mannerheim*, p. 103.

[32] Moore, *Social Origins*, especially pp. 422, 433–438.

[33] See e.g. Henry L. Roberts' very illuminating account relating to Romania: Henry L. Roberts, *Rumania: Political Problems of an Agrarian State* (New Haven: Yale University Press, 1951), pp. 89–91, 337–338.

[34] On the role of the small farmers in the Civil War see Rasila, «The Finnish Civil War», pp. 118–121, 134–135.

From People's Movement to Minor Party: The People's Patriotic Movement (IKL) in Finland 1932–1944

REIJO E. HEINONEN

Introduction

The study of European fascism is hampered by one crucial difficulty: the limited value of the term «fascism» owing to its ambiguity. In the words of Wolfgang Wippermann, «(f)ascism is dictatorship, and all current attempts at definition are derived from this understanding, but beyond this point of common agreement there is no consensus at all».[1] In the East as well as in the West, because definitions of fascism in themselves became inextricably linked to the day-to-day political struggle, the history of the term is replete with examples of definitions according to political expediency. The result is loose usage and confusion as to its usefulness for historical analysis.

The linkage is nowhere clearer than in the case of the communist movement. Marxist theory of fascism, particularly in its Comintern version, influenced political developments in every country with a communist party facing the fascist threat. Finland is no exception to this rule. The identification of social democracy as fascism's «left wing», its «twin brother», not its opponent, as Stalin phrased it[2], critically affected Finnish domestic politics in the thirties. Using the theory of «social fascism» in 1929, Stalin did not anticipate the rise of fascism as an Italian-style mass movement from below, but rather expected it to assume the form of a dictatorial regime from above.[3] The Stalinist conception of the gradual fascistization of liberal democracy from above was later attacked by proponents of the Comintern theory. Thus Dimitrov, speaking at the 5th international Comintern meeting in 1935, criticized the Finnish Communist party for allowing itself to be led astray by this theory of fascism from above. This strategic shortcoming had resulted, he argued, in the party's failure to notice the preparations for a fascist coup taking place inside certain nuclei in the bourgeoisie.[4] His remarks referred probably to the Mäntsälä rebellion in February 1932, which, however, was quelled by the government, without bloodshed, in less than a week.

In Germany, the Comintern theory of social fascism led the KPD chairman Ernst Thälmann to believe that fascism in the form of Herman Müller's government was taking command as early as 1930. By thus branding a large coalition government «fascist», Thälmann prevented possible left-wing co-operation, or as Wippermann puts it, cried 'fire!' before anything was burning.[5]

The term «social fascism» had similar repercussions in Finland. It affected the relationship between the Social Democrats and the Communists, two parties which could possibly have co-operated after their common struggle in the Civil War. But the stigma of «social fascism» as it was generally being circulated internationally also drove a wedge into the Finnish leftist camp.

It is also possible that imprudent accusations of fascism and concomitant communist strike activity gradually blinded the centre and the right to the ideological parallels between indigenous extremism on the one hand and Italian fascism and German National Socialism on the other. At party conferences in 1926 and 1927 the Finnish Communist party labelled all bourgeois parties active in the country as fascist supporters, particularly the Coalition party and the Agrarians. Deep suspicions were also aired about the Civil Guard.[6]

From the Marxist viewpoint, Finnish extreme right-wing movements were also seen as consequences of economic development. According to the Soviet ambassador in Finland at the time, I. M. Maiski, the Lapua Movement was made dangerous precisely because of the economic base from which it sprang. Purposes declared in patriotic-religious terms were viewed only as window dressing.[7] In our view this is one-sided. While the significance of the economic crisis and its impact on the agrarian population in the late twenties must not be overlooked, domestic and foreign politics as well as ideological factors should be taken into account in explaining the birth and development of extreme right-wing movements in Finland.

On the advent of European fascism, Finland had been independent only a few years. When Mussolini marched on Rome the independent nation was only four years old. Its system of government found its form at a time when fascist movements were emerging in Europe and the Bolsheviks had seized power in neighbouring Russia. The country's democratic traditions were not well entrenched. Its parliamentarism, based on several parties competing in full suffrage elections, was in the thirties attacked both from the left and from the right.[8]

The peasantry proved to be a volatile segment in Finnish society. For centuries they had lived in village communities in a state of relative seclusion from the rest of society and under the ideological dominance of the local clergy.[9] In pietism they found an ideological articulation of their aspirations. These pietist movements had remained within the sphere of the church and had, unlike the pietistic influences in the 18th century, risen from below as popular movements. Their combination of religious-patriotic and social ideas laid the foundations for a popular national identity.[10] Southern Ostrobothnia, which was particularly dominated by the pietist *herännäisyys* revivalist movement, became the heartland not only of the national activist liberation group *Jääkärit* around the time of World War I, but also later of the Lapua movement. Despite rapid social and economic development, religious values remained unchanged and represented a stable hierarchy of values. For more than a century the basic doctrines did not change perceptibly.[11]

Rigorism, which in a religious sense found expression in a radical aloofness from the «worldly» and «the unrepenting», was also evident in uncompromising doctrines concerning state and society. With the emergence of national identity and in an atmosphere of state oppression this attitude also involved constructive activism towards an independent Finland. But this rigoristic attitude was fraught with danger in a situation where it was important to find solutions through compromise between various political and social identities in support of Finnish democracy.

Although Lenin's government was the first to recognize Finnish independence in 1917, the secession and subsequent Civil War of 1918 indicated for many that the danger of a closer union with the eastern neighbour was still not removed. The bloody fratricidal conflict left the seeds of fear and bitterness and weakened the country internally.[12] For this reason many saw in national integration a pre-condition for preserving independence. During the 1920's it became a key slogan of university students.[13] The Soviet Union was seen as a threat to independence both territorially and ideologically. The borders established in the Peace of Tartu in 1920 were the results of a compromise committing both countries to apply their influence towards neutralizing the Baltic. The Soviet Union for its part guaranteed wide autonomy for the people of East Karelia and later consented to self-government for the Finnish population of Inkeri. It was believed in Finland, however, that the negotiations were carried out in a period of Soviet internal and external weakness and that with the recovery of political strength the desire to expand westwards would grow. Swedish and Norwegian fears of Soviet expansion towards the Atlantic were transferred to Finnish politics as well, and centered particularly on Soviet intentions with regard to the Northern Petsamo area gained at Tartu.

Pressure on the Karelian Isthmus and the islands in the Gulf of Finland was once more brought to bear through the question of Leningrad's security.[14]

Thus considerations of inviolability of the state and national identity formed the broad background against which single political events and ideological directions were shaped.

The Heritage of the Lapua Movement and the Founding of the Isänmaallinen kansanliike, the IKL

The People's Patriotic Movement (IKL) was founded at Hämeenlinna on June 5, 1932, as a continuation of the Lapua Movement which was dissolved after an abortive attempt at rebellion in Mäntsälä. Its purpose was to continue by legal means the political line of the Lapua Movement in support of the tradition of the bourgeois White front in the Civil War. From the very beginning, patriotism was articulated strongly in the IKL programme. The movement saw as its task «the protection of the independence and freedom of the country» which it thought was being threatened, not only by communism but also by «international socialism».[15] Particular attention was given to two social groups; the working class and the agrarian population. The socialist strike activity of the 20's provided the basis for the attempt «to protect the right of the white worker to work freely», whereas calls for «the improvement of means to secure a livelihood for the agrarian population» was aimed at meeting the interests of the majority of Lapua Movement supporters.[16] The return on investment in agriculture was at its lowest (2.9 per cent) in 1929/30 when the numerical strength of the Lapua Movement was at its peak. With economic recovery it clearly lost support. When the IKL was founded the rate of return was already 3.5 per cent and rose to 8.1 per cent in 1937–38.[17] It becomes important, therefore, to know what impact economic recovery had on the social composition and ideological priorities of the supporters.

The educated classes did not have a significant position in the Lapua Movement which was for the most part controlled by farmers, although many of the highly educated expressed their sympathy for it. As the economic situation of the agrarian population began to ease, more educated strata came to the forefront of rightist radicalism and began to shape it. The co-operation of the educated younger generation and the older conservative right, however, did not last.[18]

The initiative to establish the IKL was taken by the Swedish-speaking chairman of the League for Independence, Erkki Räikkönen, and the former Finnish ambassador to Rome, the historian Herman Gummerus. These two, however, as well as several other prominent Swedish-speaking conservatives, including General Mannerheim, left the movement soon after its adoption of the Academic Karelia Society's pure

Finnish principles which replaced the Lapua Movement's bilingualism.[19] The Finnification programme advocated by the Academic Karelia Society (AKS), especially in the universities, thus became the first distinctive departure from the Lapua Movement. The organizational structure of the movement was to become the second. The clergy in the leadership of the IKL considered its organization as a party in 1933 a fateful mistake.[20] In contrast to the rather amorphous form of a people's movement, the party structure enabled the leadership to supervise the activities of members better. Although the farmer Vihtori Kosola, the leader of the Lapua Movement, also held leading office in the IKL, he never exerted significant influence on the movement.[21] The most important leader was the IKL caucus chairman Vilho Annala who borrowed the doctrine of corporatism from the Italian fascists and advocated the establishment of a new representative system along fascist corporate lines.[22] From 1934, the director of the movements' organizational activities was a professor of criminal law, Bruno Sundström (Salmiala).[23]

Helsinki, the capital, became the focal point of the IKL after its organization into a party. This geographical point of gravity became even more pronounced when more highly educated elements assumed the leadership. The parliamentary caucus also met in Helsinki. As a result, demagogues and public speakers were no longer able to direct the movement as before.

With the urbanization of the environment there was a change in ideological emphasis. Whereas patriotic anti-communism formulated in religious terms dominated the Lapua, the tenets of the IKL in relation to communism were more specific, and religious thought more strongly related to the total world view of the movement. While the anti-Marxist slogans of the Lapua movement had included exhortations like «On these plains God shall not be mocked», pitting religion against the communist value system,[24] the IKL's political goals were considerably wider: «The creation of a nationally strong Finland internally and externally».[25]

Common to both movements was their examination of Finnish democracy from the point of view of national morality. The question of political system was not seen as a politico-juridical matter. In politics the IKL saw an expression of «party thinking and party factionalism that weakens society», of a form of partisan pursuit of interest it sought to destroy.[26] From this moral decision many demands derived their comprehensive and uncompromising nature.

Anti-Communism and National Integration

As well as by its Finnification programme, the IKL differed from the Lapua movement on the question of national integration. The concept of national integration was derived from the Academic Karelia Society's social theory of the state and distinguished the position of the IKL from both the right-wing radicalism of the Lapua movement and the traditional conservative right. As early as the 1920's, the ideal of national integration was the central political and social concept of the Academic Karelia Society. In his work «A New Direction», 1920, Yrjö Ruutu, a doctor of Political Science, conceived the main objective in social policy to be the consolidation of independence.[27] The main threat to the independent state, as he saw it, was the social rifts aggravated by the Civil War in 1918. The solution could not be found in the supremacy of either party, neither victor nor vanquished, neither capital nor labour; an integrating whole could be formed only by the middle classes. It had the tools for spiritual reconciliation and its representatives possessed «the greatest competence

690

FINLAND

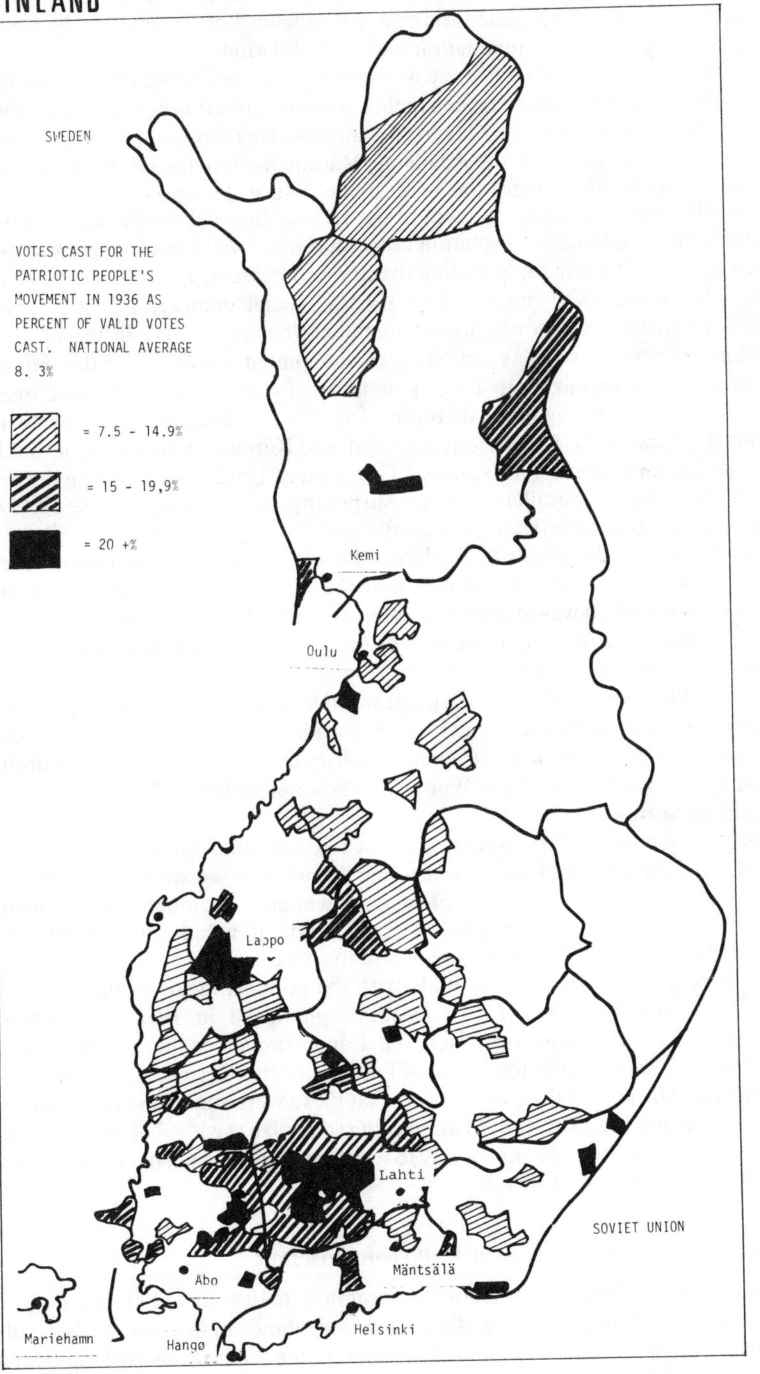

SWEDEN

VOTES CAST FOR THE
PATRIOTIC PEOPLE'S
MOVEMENT IN 1936 AS
PERCENT OF VALID VOTES
CAST. NATIONAL AVERAGE
8. 3%

= 7.5 - 14.9%

= 15 - 19,9%

= 20 +%

Kemi

Oulu

Lappo

Lahti

Mäntsälä

Åbo

Mariehamn   Hangø   Helsinki

SOVIET UNION

691

and knowledgeability in political, economic and social questions».[28] The Academic Karelia Society felt itself called to form the vanguard of the middle classes in their task of forging national rejuvenation and consolidation.

Central to achieving this objective was winning the confidence of the working class. The academic youth did not succeed in this, however, overburdened as they were with utopian thoughts of a Greater Finland and immersed in theoretical university modes of thinking. Some members of the Academic Karelia Society hoped that a strengthened IKL could realize the integration programme on a wider basis.

A month before the establishment of the IKL an internal shuffle took place within the AKS which led to the resignation of a group which later became politically active within the Agrarian Union, including the future president, Urho Kekkonen. Some of those who broke away may be reckoned as social democrats.[29] A considerable number of Academic Karelia Society members became active in the IKL and the founding member Rev. Elias Simojoki was appointed the leader of the movement's unofficial youth organization. Later a member of parliament, he became one of the most noteworthy demagogues of the period. The spokesman for a purely Finnish solidarity policy, R. G. Kallia from the Academic Karelia Society became chief editor of the IKL's party organ *Ajan Suunta* ('Direction of Time'). Considering the personalities and ideological parallels, it is not surprising that many saw in the IKL «a new birth» for the Academic Karelia Society.[30]

In the opinion of the Swedish-speaking right which supported the Lapua Movement and which was represented in the IKL by Erkki Räikkönen and Herman Gummerus, the idea of integration was interpreted as an attempt to fight communism with socialist notions. They contended that one was of necessity either white or non-white as the colour white does not permit shades.[31]

R. G. Kallia gave a different viewpoint when he wrote: «We view the development of closer relations with our great Finnish working population as many times more important than relations with the small Swedish upper class».[32] Thus the heritage of the bourgeois side from the Civil War was interpreted differently in conservative than in National Socialistic groups

Ruutu's programme of socialization advocated a gradual programme of nationalization of all means of production and was otherwise based on the idea of a strong national state and a programme of general welfare. Although this form of state socialism amounted to a nationalistic theory, it did not include a romanticizing of the peasantry and country life as was the case in Sweden.

In this respect the IKL was at odds with the populist ideals of the Lapua Movement.[33]– In his book *The Times Demand* published in 1932, the year of the Mäntsälä rebellion, Ruutu criticised the Lapua movement as a class movement which had not understood the socialist features of the German and Italian national movements. His personal viewpoint was that these were socialistic parties in evolution.[34] The further the IKL went in attempting to realize the ideal of political integration, the more it was forced to find a way to redefine its position in the political spectrum and clarify its relation to labour.

The Parties and the Ideal of a Volksgemeinschaft

The publication of the IKL's labour programme in 1934 meant stepping out of the bourgeois political realm and signified a new acceptance of the state socialist ideas of Ruutu.[35] The programme was aimed at winning the support of working people.

Integration and the elimination of the animosities from the Civil War could only be accomplished by improving the living conditions of the workers. The relationship to the state and the Fatherland was viewed to a great extent as dependent upon the living conditions of each individual.

«It is stupid to argue that workers are by nature less nationalistic than the bourgeoisie. If the working class lived in the same conditions as the so-called bourgeois majority, it would be just as patriotic as the bourgeoisie and conversely, if the bourgeoisie lived in the same conditions as the working class, it would be equally red . . . the truth, which cannot be denied, is that hunger breeds communism»[36] («nälkä on punikki»). The elimination of private property was not advocated because according to the programme private property was «irrevocably rooted in the human sense of justice».[37] It was found desirable, however, to grant the states right to limited supervision of private enterprise. In the name of «national community» it was demanded that «economic activity, be subjected in whatever degree is deemed necessary, to state inspection and, in case of need, submitted to state guidance».[38] In place of a capitalist market economy the IKL wanted to create «mandatory planning in the service of the whole».[39] From the upturn which began in 1932 economic improvement continued until 1934 when it peaked. In the economic programme of the IKL which appeared in the same year, the declining demand for labour as result of mechanization and unemployment was anticipated. The alternative solutions advocated by the IKL included shortening the hours for industrial workers or transferring the unemployed to the land by intensifying settlement efforts in the countryside. The latter solution was preferred. In this way agricultural policy became the key to reducing unemployment.[40]

The rural farming population which had only joined the new movement in small numbers after the Mäntsälä revolt, could not be easily swayed, however. Economic dissatisfaction in the countryside began receding with the rise in the profitability of agriculture to 6.6 per cent in 1934–35 as contrasted with 2.9 per cent in the heyday of the Lapua Movement in 1929–30.[41] These improvements raised expectations. In Finland the right wing was too small to make the IKL widely influential. Therefore the attitude of the Centre and particularly the Agrarian Union was to determine its political momentum. With continuous attacks the Agrarian Union sought to maintain a clear separation between itself and the IKL both in terms of ideology and with regard to practical political objectives.

The emphasis laid on the concept of integration by the IKL, using a term in Finnish close to the German word «Volksgemeinschaft» (kansakokonaisuus), set the stage for closer political co-operation between the Academic Karelia Society and the IKL.[42] In the 1936 election speakers of the society assisted the IKL, making separation of the two increasingly difficult for the general public. The 14 seats gained in the 200 member assembly did not ultimately satisfy expectations. There was increased pressure to re-evaluate policy. Internal power struggles in the IKL raged between the movement's Helsinki leadership and the extremist faction demanding «direct action».[43] This faction was led by a person who had been in charge of the contacts abroad. That the leadership included a professor of criminal law may to some extent have limited the number of unpremeditated extra-parliamentary acts.

In the early thirties the Agrarian Union tried relentlessly to retain its own group of supporters from the Lapua Movement. A similar struggle within the Coalition party occurred over its relationship to the IKL after 1933. This strategy included re-evaluations of its own policy. In revisions of its party programme in 1933, 1936 and

1939, the Coalition party re-evaluated its ideology more frequently than any other party during the thirties.[44]

When the Coalition party lost votes in the elections of 1933 to the IKL on a combined ticket, the chairman and later President of the Republic, J. K. Passikivi issued a warning on the danger of co-operating with the IKL.[45]

In the following national elections the party accused the IKL of drifting towards new policies, making co-operation in a bourgeois front no longer possible. From the right-wing viewpoint the IKL had in 1934–36 transformed itself into a «labour party» whose radical proposals were seen to represent «leftism».[46] The Coalition party was therefore prepared to condemn the movement as a disrupting force in the right-wing bloc. This opinion seemed to be confirmed by several former social democrats and communists who declared themselves IKL election candidates.[47]

Ideological parallels with the left were seen in the theme of national solidarity as well as in Ruutu's theories of state socialism.

It seems that even with the ascent of Hitler to power Ruutu was still not clear whether his socialism was brown or red. The National Socialist Society of Helsinki, which he founded in 1932 gravitated towards the former. Two years later, however, he felt the similarity to be too apparent and disadvantageous and changed the society's name to Helsinki Finnish Socialists which then participated in national elections with little success.[48]

Another ideologically unifying term which in addition to the concept of the *Volksgemeinschaft* indicated the kinship with continental fascism, was the leader principle.[49] Italy was the favourite among foreign models. This was partly due to Mussolini's early success in seizing power and his radical condemnation of communism, partly to the respect paid to religion in Italian fascism.[50]

According to the leader principle, the organization, which had nearly 100,000 members in 1935, was a hierarchical organization.[51] Lower echelon party officers were directly appointed by those above them. The organization's constitution was not completed until 1936.[52] Its most prominent feature was centralization of the leadership into fewer hands. The leadership which was responsible only to the party caucus was reduced from an original six to three. Under the direction of Lt. Col. Paavo Susitaipale and Professor Sundström the IKL developed into a militaristic tightly disciplined citizen's organization on the model of the Academic Karelia Society.[53] The oath which initiated new members into the organization did not, however, assume the same high significance in the IKL as it did in the Academic Karelia Society.[54]

Religion and the IKL

As the Lapua Movement was felt to be a movement in support of the church and clergy because of its pro-religious slogans, a great part of the clergy reacted favourably to it. Archbishop Lauri Ingman attributed the rise of the movement to the moral indignation which the rejection of religion by the communists had caused in pietistic areas.[55] Incipient illegalities and particularly the Mäntsälä rebellion led him as well as many other church representatives to change their attitude and condemn the Lapua Movement. Although clergy members held the organization of the IKL into a party to be an error, they were active within it in large numbers from the very beginning. Activism in a people's movement was not viewed as political activity in the same way as participation in other parties.

694

In the 1933 elections four clergymen were elected as IKL representatives. After transfers from the Agrarian Union and the Coalition party the IKL had 6 clerical representatives in 1935. This was nearly half of the 14 members in the IKL parliamentary group.[56] More of them had official functions in the parliamentary group than in other parties. With the exception of the unofficial youth organization in the organizational activities of the IKL, the role of the clergy was therefore very significant.

One reason for the clergy's strong participation was the stress on religion within the movement. Thus clergymen were apt to consider themselves capable of pursuing spiritual goals with the aid of the movement. Activism inside the IKL was tantamount to «battle against sin and iniquity».[57] In Action Principles 12 and 15 the importance of «religious-patriotic education» was emphasized, the objective being to create «a clear comprehension of the purpose of life» and «a sensitive national conscience».[58] Religious education, therefore, had its value in the service of national goals. However, compared to the Coalition party's church policy in the 1933 and 1936 elections the difference was not great.[59] The difference was more pronounced in the manner in which religion was related to party propaganda. In the IKL, politics was formulated in religious terms and political speeches easily became sermons, whereas in the Coalition party these subject-areas were kept more clearly separate. In the IKL, religion became part of the movement's ideological expression.[60] Although the IKL declaration was worded in such a way as to make politics religion and religion politics, Marvin Rintala's contention that religion was used *intentionally* as a party propaganda technique must be viewed critically.[61] Many IKL speakers did not know and were unable to use anything but a religious speaking style. As far as they are concerned, they cannot be accused of conscious calculation.[62] The misuse of religion and its fusion with ideology in the movement was more an unconscious process due to the influence of the social ideals of the revivalist movements.

Soviet church policy which was assessed against the background of Finnish Civil War hostilities, apparently played a significant part in the formation of the clergy's political opinions. In 1924 the Constitution of the Soviet Union had guaranteed the same rights to religious and anti-religious citizens. It stated that «Freedom to religious and anti-religious propaganda is recognised for all citizens».[63] In 1928, as the focus of Stalin's planning turned to industrialization and collectivization of agriculture, the church fell under increased pressure.[64] Although the Metropolitan Sergei and the interim Holy Synod had issued a proclamation of loyalty to the Soviet government, the section on religion in the Soviet constitution was changed in 1929 to read: «The freedom to religious confession and freedom to anti-religious propaganda belongs to every citizen»,[65] making propagation of religion no longer possible. Refugees crossing the eastern frontier added to the clergy's concern with their accounts. A preacher named Aatami Kuortti, a native of Inkeri who had fled the concentration camp at Solovetsky, gave a distressing picture of this Finnish-speaking home church at the Scandinavian church conference at Visby in 1936. The number of natives of Inkeri deported was then estimated to have risen to 30,000 or 40,000.[66] Acts of violence against the clergy and, more significantly, the Stalinist purges of 1936-37 increased uncertainty and fear in Finland.[67] This naturally gave new impetus to the anti-communist propaganda of the IKL.

In the national elections of 1936 more clergy than previously were candidates. Five were elected. From the standpoint of the church the coming together of the various social classes, emhpasized in the IKL programme, was an important objective because the Civil War and the years preceding it had created a chasm between the church and the working class.[68] The IKL clergy deemed the unity of spirit and ideals between various citizens to be more important than the economic system. The Rev. S. Tapaninen described capitalism and Marxism as equally «immoral» and «godless», because they were both founded on a materialist mode of thought.[69] Christianity thus provided a critique of social and economic conditions. The 14 seats gained with the campaign support of the Academic Karelia Society fell short of the expected success. The new integration programme had not struck a responsive chord; the results rather anticipated the shattering defeat at the next election. While continental fascism was celebrating its triumphs the support for the IKL caved in and the number of seats fell to 8 in 1939. The shift in electoral support was felt most strongly by the clergyman. Only one clergyman was elected as representative. The church-attending voters seem to have played a role in the declining support of the movement and the decisive reduction in the party's parliamentary strength.

Reasons for Failure

The continued rise in prosperity which peaked in 1937–38 also improved the situation of the middle class and brought relief from its feelings of social vulnerability. Domestic political factors also limited the opportunities of the IKL. The emphasis of the Social Democrats on a national policy and the government coalition with the Agrarian Union and the Progress party in 1937 removed or at least weakened prejudices towards the left. During the National Front government Ruutu's Finnish Socialists joined the Social Democratic party. It had changed to such an extent over the years that «even former Whites of the year 1918 might join it», as Ruutu said.[70] Social Democratic criticism of the Soviet Union also reduced suspicions of the party's internationalism. Despite disagreements over the size of the defense budget, the threat from the east was felt across party lines.

To preach an anti-communism of the kind the IKL did, predicting the day when «airplanes from our eastern neighbour will darken the sun»[71], was not only unnecessary but also dangerous, from the point of view of Finland's external neutrality (1938). It was pivotal that all political groups showed restraint.[72]

As Finnish social democracy swung strongly towards a national line, the borrowings of the IKL from abroad must have begun to taste sour. Among the church members in the electorate the church policies of National Socialism had aroused scepticism. The experience of struggle in the church had shown that in a fascist society Christianity would be replaced by political pseudo-religion.[73] National Socialism could not give the desired protection of religion.

The criticism of German Christians (Deutsche Christen) from a pietistic viewpoint in the IKL press is noteworthy although its own clergy produced a similar mixture of religion and ideology in their speeches. The IKL clergy sought to assure a firm and continuing religious base for the movement. This was indicated in youth leader Elias Simojoki's critical words: «Without God the nation, despite its burning national spirit and shining organizations, shall sooner or later be stricken from the pages of history».[74] He saw the relationship to religion as the most significant difference between the Hitler Jugend (HJ) and the unofficial youth-organization of the IKL, the Blue Blacks («Sinimustat»). Whereas the HJ professed a disguised form of secularism, the Blue Blacks were committed «unconditionally to honour the sacred faith inherited from our forbears».[75] But the involvement of Elias Simojoki in a right-wing rebellion in Estonia in 1935 made it clear that the respect for the law displayed by several IKL members deviated ominously from what was regarded normal in a constitutional democracy. It became, in short, increasingly difficult to believe that the lofty principles of the Blue Blacks would also be followed in practice. Both communism and fascism posed a threat to religion. The decisions of the church leadership as well as the church policies of the parties seem to have played an important role in determining the reaction of the church-attending electorate.

Erkki Kaila who became archbishop in 1935 stressed the priority of congregational work over social activism and condemned in his pastoral letter the party activity of the clergy which fell outside the sphere of parliamentary work.[76] The Coalition party's church policy resolution of 1935 stressed the difference between political and congregational work.[77] The protection of the spiritual identity of the church was held to be important and confidence was expressed that if the church remained faithful to its principles its work would also wield a social influence. There was an attempt to show that the religious-patriotic ideology of the IKL and its labour and economic programme which contained socialist and fascist aspects, was unnecessary.

The election results of 1939 increased the Coalition party's representation from 20 to 25 seats. Its clerical representatives rose in number to five, while seats held by farmers numbered four. The IKL elected one clergyman and one farmer. It seems that Coalition party supporters were moving from the IKL back to their former party and IKL support was becoming more restricted to a narrow academic stratum.[78]

The Social Democratic party had demanded prohibition of the IKL since 1935. The decision to disband the IKL, made by the Council of State on November 22, 1938, with Urho Kekkonen as Minister of the Interior, was to a large extent motivated by foreign policy considerations, although it was formally enforced by reference to the statute prohibiting certain political symbols. Adequate supporting evidence had not been accumulated, however, and the courts overruled the decision the same autumn.[79]

Finland's entanglement in World War II took the edge off domestic political conflict. The integration which had been sought since the Civil War seems to have been attained during the Winter War days of 1939–40. Finland's vulnerable situation also forced a return to the values of a national community. Battle for Religion, Home and Fatherland which the IKL also had proclaimed, was approved in wide national circles but without any importation of foreign ideology.

The IKL shared the responsibility of government with Dr. Vilho Annala acting as Minister of Transport and Public Works during the period of co-operation with Germany, 1941–43. The war years could not reverse the process of decline which had been started in the thirties. The game was finally over. On the signing of the cease-fire with the Soviet Union in 1944, the party was dissolved.

NOTES

[1] Wolfgang Wippermann, *Faschismustheorien. Zum Stand der gegenwärtigen Diskussion.* (Theories of Fascism. The Position of the Present Discussion.) (Darmstadt, 1975), p. VII.

[2] *Ibid.*

[3] *Ibid.*, p. 15.

[4] Georgi Dimitrov, *Arbeiterklasse gegen Faschismus.* (Working Class against Fascism. The Offensive of Fascism and the Task of the Communist International in the Fight for Unity in the Working Class against Fascism) (Moscow, Leningrad, 1935), p. 28. Quoted in Wippermann, *op. cit.*, p. 18.

[5] Wippermann, *op. cit.*, 15, 16.

[6] Lauri Hyvämäki, *Sinistä ja mustaa. Tutkielma Suomen oikeistoradikalismista.* (Blue and Black. A Contribution to Finnish Right-Wing Radicalism), (Helsinki, 1971), p. 203.

[7] Keijo Korhonen, *Naapurit vastoin tahtoaan* (Neighbours against their Will) (Lahti, 1966), p. 203.

[8] Risto Alapuro, *Akateeminen Karjala-Seura. Ylioppilasliike ja kansa 1920- ja 1930-luvulla.* (The Academic Karelia Society: Student Movement and People in the Twenties and Thirties), (Helsinki 1973), p. 41.

[9] Matti Klinge, *Vihan veljistä valtiososialismiin. Yhteiskunnallisia ja kansallisia näkemyksiä 1910 – ja 1920 – luvuilta.* (From «Brother of Hate» to State-Socialism. Reflections on Nation and Society in the 1910's and 1920's.) (Porvoo, 1972), p. 163.

[10] Kirsti Suolinna, *Uskonnollisten liikkeitten asema sosiaalisessa muutoksessa.* (The Role of the Religious Movements in Social Change.) Research Reports, Institute of Sociology, University of Helsinki No. 0203, 1975 p. 10.

[11] Mikko Juva, *Suomen kansan historia IV. «Kansallinen herääminen».* (History of the Finnish People. National Revival.) (Keuruu 1966), pp. 242–254.

[12] Eino Jutikkala-Kauko Pirinen, *History of Finland.*(Stuttgart, 1963), pp. 351–357.

[13] Klinge *op. cit.*, p. 113.

[14] *Ibid.*, p. 159.

[15] Olavi Borg, *Suomen puolueet ja puolueohjelmat 1880–1964.* (The Parties and their Programmes in Finland 1880–1964.) (Porvoo, 1965), pp. 208–210.

[16] *Ibid.*, p. 210.

[17] Risto Alapuro, *op. cit.*, p. 53 quotes Kosti Huuhka, *Talonpoikaisnuorison koulutie. Tutkimus talonpoikaisnuorison koulunkäynnistä ja siihen vaikuttaneista sosiaalisista tekijöistä Suomessa 1910–1950.* (The education of farmers' children. A Research Report on the teaching of farmers' children in relation to their social background in Finland 1910–1950.) Historiallisia tutkimuksia 43, (Forssa, 1955), p. 191.

Return of capital in Finnish agriculture in fiscal years (July 1 to June 30)

1921/22	9.3%	1930/31	3.0%
1922/23	4.7%	1931/32	3.5%
1923/24	1.8%	1932/33	4.6%
1924/25	4.9%	1933/34	5.3%
1925/26	5.8%	1934/35	6.6%
1926/27	4.9%	1935/36	5.8%
1927/28	4.4%	1936/37	7.0%
1928/29	3.5%	1937/38	8.1%
1929/30	2.9%	1938/39	6.8%

[18] Alapuro, *op. cit.*, p. 53, Matti Klinge, «Integration of our people. A slogan of [Finland's] academic youth in the 1920'ies». *Journal of History*, vol. I, (1963), pp. 3–4.

[19] Marvin Rintala, *Three Generations: The Extreme Right Wing in Finnish Politics.* (Bloomington, Ind., 1962), p. 223.

[20] Reijo Heinonen, «The Role of the Priests at the Beginning of the Patriotic People's Movement 1932–36». (unpublished Master's thesis, Faculty of Theology at the University of Helsinki. 1965), p. 14.

[21] Ajan Suunta no 2, December 7, 1932. Ajan Suunta was the main organ of the IKL.

[22] Rintala, *op. cit.*, p. 239. The idea of a corporatist form of representation adopted by the IKL in 1935, was not initiated by Annala personally, as Rintala asserts, but advocated primarily by Lt. Col. Aarne Somersalo, who was responsible for the party's foreign affairs and had been in favour of this idea since 1933. Heinonen, *op. cit.*, p.43.

[23] *Ajan Suunta* no 96, April 27, 1934; cf. Sakari Virkkunen, *Elias Simojoki Legenda jo eläessään.* Elias Simojoki. (Living Legends.) (Porvoo 1974), p. 143.

[24] K. R. Kares, «The Religious Base of the IKL». *Ajan Suunta* no 178, August 5, 1935; Heinonen, *op. cit.*, 34.

[25] Borg, *op. cit.*, p. 210.

[26] *Ibid.* cf. The guiding Principles of the IKL, § 5 in Appendix.

[27] Klinge, *op. cit.*, (1972) p. 116.

[28] *Ibid.*

[29] *Ibid.*, p. 131.

[30] *Ajan Suunta* no 44, Febr. 24, 1933. A speech by Elias Simojoki in the AKS 22.2. 1935; cf. Klinge, *op. cit.*, p. 129 who quotes a speech by Arvo Sipilä February 2, 1933.

[31] Herman Gummerus, «Finland and National Socialism», *Itsenäinen Suomi* no 5, May 18, 1932, pp. 86–88; Heinonen *op. cit.*, p. 14.

[32] Klinge, *op. cit.*, p. 124.

[33] *Ibid.*, p. 148.

[34] *Ibid.*, p. 150.

[35] Borg, *op. cit.*, p. 214.

[36] *Ajan Suunta* no 60, March 13, 1934. A speech by Dr. Martti Hertz in Heimola March 12, 1934.

[37] Borg, *op. cit.*, p. 215.

[38] *Ibid.*, p. 216.

[39] *Ibid.*

[40] *Ibid.*, pp. 217–221.

[41] Alapuro *op. cit.*, p. 190; cf. Reino Lento, *Maastamuutto ja siihen vaikuttaneet tekijät Suomessa vuosina 1878–1939.* (Emigration and Connected Factors in Finland 1878–1939.) (Helsinki 1951), pp. 120–121.

[42] Heinonen, *op. cit.*, p. 27. The convergence on the labour issue between the AKS and the IKL is explained by the fact that the author of the labour programme, Heikki Peltola, was a member of the AKS.

[43] *Ibid.*, p. 46.

[44] Borg, *op. cit.*, p. 224; cf. p. 20.

[45] J. K. Paasikivi, «Demokratia vai diktatuuri? Mitä kansallisen Kokoomuspuolueen periaatteet sisältävät?» (Democracy or Dictatorship? The Founding Principles of the National Coalition Party.) A speech by J. K. Paasikivi in Tampere October 25, 1934. In *Paasikiven linja II J. K. Paasikiven puheita ja esitelmiä vuosilta 1923–42.* (The political programme of J. K. Paasikivi. Speeches and lectures.) (Porvoo, 1965), p. 55.

[46] Heinonen, *op. cit.*, p. 26; cf. K. J. Kalliala, *Kokoomuspuolue ja IKL.* (The National Coalition Party and the IKL.) (Helsinki 1936), pp. 1–18.

[47] Heinonen, *op. cit.*, p. 26; *Ilkka* no 172, June 30, 1936.

[48] Klinge, *op. cit.*, p. 149.

[49] Rintala, *op. cit.*, p. 237.

[50] Rintala. «An Image of European Politics. The People's Patriotic Movement». In *Journal of Central European Affairs*, vol. XXI, (1963), pp. 308–316.

[51] A statement by B. Sundström (Salmiala) in Parliament, in the Parliamentary Records for the year 1935. Vol. III, p. 258.

[52] *Ajan Suunta* no 248, October 26, 1936.

[53] *Ajan Suunta* no 43, February 21, 1933: *Ajan Suunta* no 96, April 27, 1934.

[54] *Ajan Suunta*, no 30, February 6, 1933. The oath of the IKL: «In the name of all that is dear and precious to me, I swear ceaselessly to work for the goals of the IKL. I promise to work diligently to spread the IKL's ideas in my home districts. I promise to counteract to the best of my ability forces working to split the people's movement. May God and my belief in a great future for Finland help me in these endeavors.» cf. Alapuro, *op. cit.*, pp. 93–95. The swearing-in ceremony in the AKS had stylistic and rhythmic similarities with the Christian declaration of faith.

[55] *Kotimaa* no 18, March 4, 1932; Lauri Ingman, «Tämän kaiken minä annan sinulle». (I give you all this.) *Kotimaa*, no 10, February 7, 1933.

[56] Among the 21 elected officers in the IKL in the years 1933–39 there were 6 teachers and professors, 3 civil servants, 3 farmers, 2 party officials, 2 military officers. cf. *Suomen eduskunta*

1933–41, incl. Biographical notes of the MP's in the Finnish parliament 1933–41. (Helsinki 1933, 1936, 1939.)

[57] Y. E. Kivenoja, «IKL and the clergy». *Ajan Suunta* no 217, November 19, 1934; cf. Heinonen, *op. cit.*, p. 51.

[58] Borg, *op. cit.*, p. 211.

[59] *Ibid.*, pp. 242, 249.

[60] Heinonen, *op. cit.*, pp. 94–101.

[61] Rintala, *Three Generations: The Extreme Right Wing in Finnish Politics.* (Bloomington, Ind. 1962), p. 240. «The powerful role of the clergy within the party was evidenced by the fact that appeals to religion were regarded as an indispensable part of the party's technique.»

[62] A statement by K. R. Kares in Parliament, in the Parliamentary Records for the year of 1934. Vol. I, p. 415; Heinonen, *op. cit.*, p. 100.

[63] Erkki Kaila. *Kristilliset kirkot nykyisessä henkien taistelussa. Kertomus arkkihiippakunnan synodaalikokousta varten 19.–21.10. 1937.* (The Christian Church in the Contemporary Religious Conflict. A report to the Synode of Episcopal council 19.–21.10. 1937). (Helsinki 1937), pp. 85, 88; cf. Konstitutsija Soyuza SSR i Sojuznyh Respublik (Constitutions of the USSR and the Union Republics) (Moscow 1932), p. 22 quoted by R. Conquest, *Religion in the USSR.* (London 1958), pp. 19, 22.

[64] Dimitry Konstantinow. The Church in the Soviet Union after the war. Successes and failures. (München 1973), p. 18.

[65] Kaila, *op. cit.*, p. 85.

[66] *Ibid.*, p. 87.

[67] Religion in history and today. (RGG)/5, 1244.

[68] Heinonen, *op. cit.*, p. 54.

[69] *Ibid.*, p. 24.

[70] Klinge, *Vihan veljistä valtiososialismiin*, op. cit., p. 150.

[71] Address to the Finnish Army by Elias Simojoki at the Annual meeting of the AKS, February 2, 1938, in Elias Simojoki, *Palava pensas. Elias Simojoen puheita.* (The burning bush. Speeches by Elias Simojoki). (Porvoo 1943), p. 214.

[72] Einar W. Juva, *Suomen kansan historia.* (The History of the Finnish People). Vol. V (Keuruu 1967), pp. 314, 315, 320.

[73] Osmo Tiililä, «Mitä tapahtuu Saksan kirkollisessa elämässä.» (What happens in the life within the Church in Germany). *Ajan Suunta* no 70, March 23, 1935.

[74] E. Simojoki, «Gott mit uns». (God be with us) *Sinimusta* no 10, May 17, 1935.

[75] *Ibid.*

[76] Heinonen, *Työ ja yhteys. Suomen kirkon pappisliitto 1918–1968.* (Work and Solidarity. The Priests Society in the Finnish Church 1918–1968). (Pieksämäki 1969), pp. 54–56.

[77] Borg, *op. cit.*, p. 257.

[78] *Suomen Eduskunta, 1939–41.* Biographies of the MP's in the Finnish Parliament 1939–41. (Helsinki 1941.)

[79] Klinge, *op. cit.*, p. 186.

APPENDIX

The Guiding Principles of the People's Patriotic Movement (Programme adopted at the founding convention, in Hämeenlinna, June 5, 1932).

Programme

The People's Patriotic Movement, which traces its origins to the great popular awakening of 1930, takes as its ultimate objective the creation of an internally and externally strong Finland. To this end, the avowed purpose of the people's movement is:

1. to create a firm White Front to carry on the War of Independence, and to protect the independence and freedom of the nation;
2. to combat not only communism, but the equally dangerous threat posed by international socialism which incites class hatred, tears down patriotic ideals and denigrates the religious and national spirit;
3. to support unreservedly the development of the national defence forces, both the Army and the Civil Guard;
4. to protect the citizen's right to work without hindrance and especially safeguard the White worker's right to work freely and remain secure in his employment;
5. to destroy the party ideology and the party conspiracy which threatens the best interests of our country and weakens society, to strengthen the power of government and to devise a better division of responsibility between government and parliament;
6. to improve the means of livelihood of those sections of the citizenry presently confronted with difficult conditions, and especially the farm population.

Social Basis of Nazism in Denmark: The DNSAP

HENNING POULSEN AND MALENE DJURSAA

In Denmark fascism was represented by many tiny groups, but by only one single party of any numerical significance, the DNSAP – *Danmarks Nationalsocialistiske Arbejder Parti* (Denmark's National Socialist Workers' Party). It was founded in 1930 and survived until the German collapse in 1945. Small fascist groups based on the Italian model were formed in the twenties, but they counted their followers in scores rather than hundreds, their lifetimes in months rather than years. So also did a dozen Nazi splinter parties which appeared in the thirties. As these parties were commonly formed by members who left the DNSAP, it may be assumed that their membership to a high degree is included in the number of people who at some time joined this party. DNSAP's total was about 42,000[1] – roughly the same as the highest number of votes it obtained in any election. This means that Danish democracy was never seriously threatened from within by fascist movements.[2]

The Nazis took part in three nation-wide parliamentary elections, but each time received only a very small proportion of the votes cast. (See maps, pp. 703–705). In 1935 the DNSAP received 16,300 votes, i.e. 1.0 per cent of all votes cast; in 1939 it attracted 31,000 votes, or 1.8 per cent. In the elections in the spring of 1943, when the German occupation restricted the election campaigns of all other parties and excluded the Communist party altogether, the DNSAP reached its peak with 43,300 votes, or a mere 2.1 per cent. Moreover, the party did not to any significant extent compensate for these low levels of electoral support by cooperation with other parties, or by Nazi influence in stronger organizations.[3]

The general history of the DNSAP is short and inglorious. The party was founded in the autumn of 1930 under the impact of Hitler's success in the Reichstag elections in Germany. The initiative was taken by a few men, some of whom had earlier made fruitless attempts to build up fascist groups on the Italian model, and the new party was openly declared to be a Danish counterpart of the Hitler movement.

Knowledge of Nazi ideology within the DNSAP was slight, however, and the Danish party was from the start a primitive imitation of the NSDAP. In addition to the similarity of names and abbreviations, the Danish party's stormtroopers were called SA, the swastika was used as its party symbol, the upright arm served as its form of greeting, and the poets of the DNSAP translated the Horst Wessel *Lied* and other German party songs into Danish. Even the first program was mostly a translation. Since some of the points – revision of the treaty of Versailles, for instance – could not apply to Denmark, others were inserted to match the 25 points of the NSDAP. Imitation was the basic strategy of the party. «What the German youth has managed to do might also be possible in Denmark», the party stated at its foundation. A single reservation – concerning anti-Semitism – was swiftly overcome. The plan was to obtain the same results by the same means, and because the founders of the DNSAP did not distinguish in importance between single features of their model, they took pains not to omit any.

The Nazi approach did not work at all. In the depth of the economic depression the

DNSAP Votes in Parliamentary Elections – per cent of valid votes.

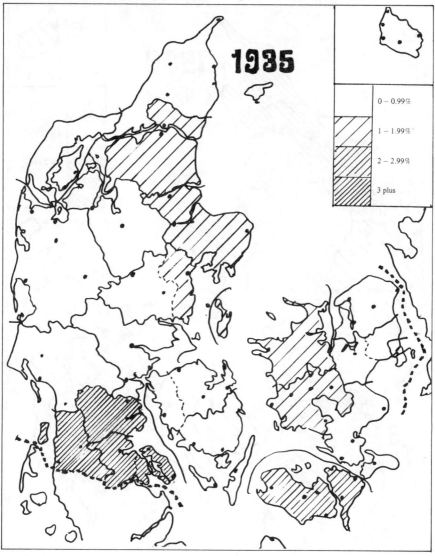

1935

0 – 0.99%

1 – 1.99%

2 – 2.99%

3 plus

Danish Nazis attracted only a few hundred members, and in the parliamentary elections of 1932 the party was unable to collect the 10,000 signatures necessary for national participation. Special rules for North Schleswig allowed the DNSAP to present a party list there, but it received only 700 votes (1 per cent). Individual candidates in Copenhagen and other parts of Sealand received approximately 200 votes altogether.[4]

The fiasco was obvious and caused bitter strife within the party. In 1933 the first leader Cay Lembcke, an ex-officer and former head of the Danish Boy Scouts, was forced to resign. He was succeeded by Fritz Clausen, a formerly Conservative

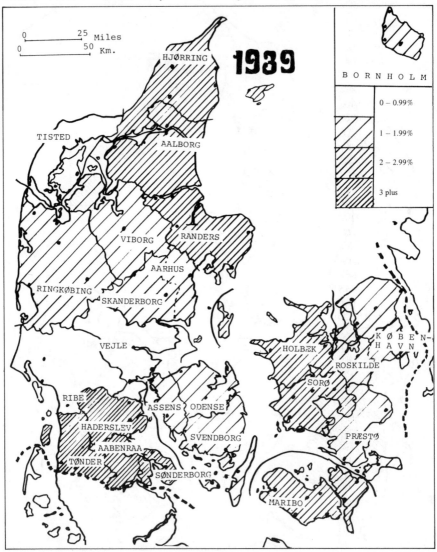

medical doctor in a country district in North Schleswig, who had become the leader of the DNSAP in this part of the country.

Support for the DNSAP fluctuated in the different regions (see maps), but North Schleswig was to remain the stronghold of the party. In 1935, 22 per cent of its votes came from this district, which contained only 5 per cent of the nation's population. In North Schleswig 4.4 per cent voted for the DNSAP, against 1 per cent nationally. In 1939 it received 4.7 per cent of the votes in North Schleswig against 1.8 per cent, and in 1943 5.7 per cent against 2.1 per cent in Denmark as a whole. In some areas of North Schleswig the party attracted 10 or even 20 per cent of the votes cast.

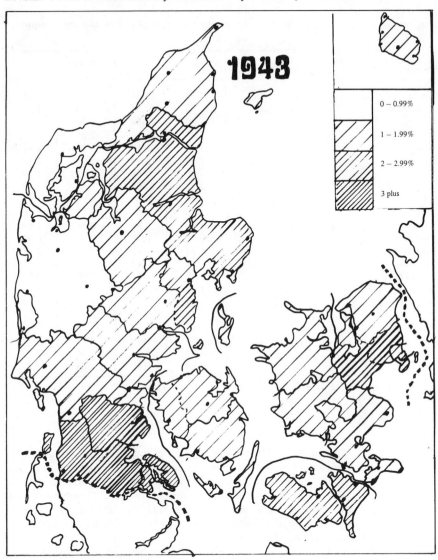

This overrepresentation might be regarded as the result of the special conditions in this border region, in particular the presence of a strong German minority, and the marked Danish national consciousness of the region. But it is not obvious that this was really so. First of all, the strength of the DNSAP in North Schleswig was mostly a rural phenomenon. In the elections of 1935 it got 1.5 per cent of the town votes compared with an average 0.8 per cent in similar towns elsewhere (under 20,000 inhabitants), but outside the towns it obtained 5.3 per cent compared with 1.3 per cent elsewhere.[5] Having been under Prussian rule since 1864, North Schleswig was reunited with

705

DNSAP votes in Parliamentary elections – per cent of valid votes.

Percentage votes given to the DNSAP in individual counties in the three national elections:

	Average	1935	1939	1943
Capital	1.82	0.61	1.70	2.91
København	1.93	0.82	1.80	2.79
Fr.borg	1.36	0.58	1.58	1.80
Holbæk	1.45	1.15	2.05	1.19
Sorø	1.75	1.17	2.19	1.87
Præstø	1.45	0.88	1.93	1.55
Bornholm	1.10	0.96	1.25	1.08
Maribo	2.17	2.08	2.00	2.39
Odense	1.29	0.69	1.52	1.57
Svendborg	1.10	0.61	1.37	1.29
Hjørring	1.76	0.90	2.69	1.69
Thisted	0.77	0.78	0.58	0.93
Aalborg	1.74	1.05	2.02	2.07
Viborg	1.03	0.63	1.32	1.11
Randers	1.92	1.54	2.20	2.00
Aarhus	1.67	1.04	1.81	2.04
Skanderborg	1.24	0.37	1.74	1.53
Vejle	0.98	0.65	0.91	1.31
Ringkøbing	0.75	0.31	1.02	0.87
Ribe	0.85	0.59	0.57	1.27
Haderslev	4.94	4.39	4.74	5.70
Average	1.69	0.99	1.83	2.15

Sources: Danmarks Statistik, Statistiske Meddelelser, 4. række.
1935: 99. bd., 2. hf.
1939: 109. bd., 1. hf.
1943: 120. bd., 1 hf.

Denmark after a referendum in 1920. It still had a considerable German minority who demanded a revision of the border. This minority organized its own party – nazified like other German minority organizations after 1933 – which was just as strong in the towns as in the countryside. Neither is there a significant correlation between the electoral performance of the German minority party and of the DNSAP. The German minority party did not take part in the elections of 1943, but this had no significant influence on the results of the DNSAP.

It is also improbable that the DNSAP benefited from the marked Danish national consciousness in North Schleswig. Firstly, the sentiment was no weaker in the towns than in the countryside. Secondly, with Fritz Clausen as a rare exception, no leading person in the Danish nationalist movement joined the DNSAP, which was regarded as nationally suspect due to its admiration for Hitler's Germany and its uncertain attitude towards the border issue.[6]

Two other factors may have been of importance. Firstly, North Schleswig was the first part of the country in which the DNSAP waged regular campaigns. From 1931 its weekly newspaper was edited here, and in 1933, when Fritz Clausen became leader of the party, its head office was located in North Schleswig. Thus the local activity was able to benefit from the resources of the whole party. Fritz Clausen's prominence as «The Leader» might also have meant something. The area around Bovrup, where he was living, had a higher percentage of Nazi votes than any other.

Secondly, the DNSAP was in the thirties a predominantly rural party benefiting from the agricultural crisis, and its overrepresentation in North Schleswig corresponds to an underrepresentation of another new party, *Bondepartiet* (Agrarian party) formed around the same issues. This party was established in 1934 by some members of parliament elected by the traditional farmers' party, *Venstre* (The Liberals). But not all the MP's who broke with the Liberals joined the Agrarian party. The exception was the most prominent of them, Count Bent Holstein, who was elected in North Schleswig. He did not join the DNSAP either, but he gave it moral support – a factor which may explain why radical circles in the rural population of this part of the country alone were more apt to vote for the Nazis.

Fritz Clausen's leadership lasted until 1944, i.e. throughout the whole of the period when the party had any political strength. The overall failure of the DNSAP is often ascribed to his lack of political skill. «God save the King and Fritz Clausen» was a saying during the German occupation. An explanation on such lines is always dubious, however. It is not always wise to evaluate a politician in terms of his degree of success, and there is no obvious reason to regard Fritz Clausen as a particularly bad leader, despite the electoral feebleness of his party. At any rate the DNSAP did not have a better man. His position inside the party was already quite strong, and his prestige rose further in 1939 when the party had 3 representatives elected to parliament and began publishing a daily newspaper.[7] The problem he was unable to solve was a basic dilemma in Danish Nazism: How to reconcile Danish nationalism – traditionally and basically anti-German – with admiration for the German rulers.

The German occupation in 1940 made this problem acute. Even if Fritz Clausen managed to give the DNSAP a slightly more independent image and often tried to explain that the swastika was not German but Nordic in origin, it was still obvious that Danish Nazism was imitating the German brand and was connected to it by strong sympathies. There is no doubt that Fritz Clausen represented the rank and file of his party when he clung to the German side in 1940. But he failed to obtain the indispensable support of the occupying power: In spite of some hesitation in the autumn of 1940 when the war seemed likely to be won by the German Nazis, they chose to continue their arrangement with the constitutional government. Unlike the Norwegian and Dutch Nazis, the Danish Nazis received no power at all. Politically they were placed in reserve, waiting for Germany to win the war. In the meantime they were given money to expand their organization and propaganda, while they in turn co-operated by recruiting volunteers for the Waffen-SS. German money enabled the DNSAP to hire a staff of professional functionaries and multiply its activities. Its slight progress in the elections of 1943 was a poor return for this investment and was viewed as a considerable defeat by the Danish population at large, by the party itself, and by the German authorities. As a consequence, close co-operation between the two parties came to an end and German support was reduced. In 1944 Fritz Clausen was succeeded by C.O. Jørgensen, a landowner who tried to extricate the DNSAP from German influence in a desperate attempt to prepare the party to survive the collapse of Nazi Germany.

The socio-geographic distribution of Nazi votes shows a marked trend from 1935 to 1943. This can be seen in the table below, which shows the number and percentages of votes obtained by the DNSAP in the three elections:

	1935		1939		1943	
	No.votes	per cent	No. votes	per cent	No.votes	per cent
Copenhagen with suburbs	3,028	= 0.6%	8,165	= 1.7%	17,264	= 2.9%
Towns over 20,000	1,247	= 0.7%	2,497	= 1.3%	4,807	= 2.0%
Towns under 20,000	2,378	= 0.8%	4,799	= 1.7%	6,206	= 1.9%
Country districts	9,577	= 1.3%	15,571	= 2.1%	15,032	= 1.8%
Total	16,257	= 1.0%	31,032	= 1.8%	43,309	= 2.1%

Initially the party was strongest in the countryside, with 59 per cent of all Nazi votes coming from rural districts in 1935. But this share declined to 50 per cent in 1939, and fell even further, to 35 per cent, in 1943, when the percentage of votes for the DNSAP in country districts was less than the national average. In Copenhagen and the bigger industrial towns the DNSAP had relatively few votes in 1935, but ended up with an overrepresentation in 1943.[8] This pattern calls for more than a single explanation of adherence to the Nazi party.

The general trend of increase is most likely due to Nazi Germany's growing prestige combined with a slow but steady development of party activity. Recruitment to the DNSAP peaked in the autumn of 1940, when between 1,000 and 2,000 new members joined it every month. The 43,000 votes in 1943 might be considered a result of this increased base of potential voters, even if there is no simple relationship between members and voters, as will be discussed below.

The special trend in the rural districts corresponds to the economic conditions of Danish agriculture, which suffered much in the crisis of the early thirties, but whose situation had eased by the end of the decade. During the war it recovered further as a result of the big German demand for food. We find a similar trend in the development of the purely agricultural Agrarian party, which suffered a minor loss of votes in 1939 and was halved in 1943. In the industrial towns, by contrast, economic conditions were bad during the occupation because important supplies of raw materials were cut off. Unemployment was almost as widespread in 1940–41 as in the early thirties.

This difference in the economic development of agriculture and industry helps to explain why Copenhagen, which contributed only 19 per cent of the Nazi votes in 1935 and 26 per cent in 1939, supplied no less than 40 per cent in 1943. Other factors may have worked in the same direction. From 1940 the party's daily newspaper was moved to the capital, and most of the new staff of party functionaries paid by German contributions were transferred to propaganda activity in Copenhagen. It is even possible that a considerable number of Nazis moved from rural districts and minor towns in order to get jobs where their political views were unknown.

We have only a few reliable figures showing the actual number of members in the DNSAP. The first can be found in the party archives in a cash-registration from April 1937 of members in each district.[9] It shows a total of 2,740 members. Since the collection of entry forms shows that by 1937 8,500 members had joined the party, this means that 2 out of every 3 newcomers had already left it by that time.

The geographic distribution of members is roughly similar to the distribution of voters. North Schleswig contributed 18 per cent of the members against 22 per cent of the votes in 1935 and 14 per cent in 1939. But Copenhagen was underrepresented with only 16 per cent of the membership against 19 and 26 per cent of the votes. In a speech before an assembly of party leaders in 1943 Fritz Clausen stated that the number of members by the election of 1939 had been 5,000[10]. This is just possible since 3,500 newcomers had joined since April 1937, but 4,000 may well be more correct. All figures from before the occupation must be regarded with suspicion, as the party archives from that period contain a rich collection of complaints about inaccurate registration.

During the occupation the party bureaucracy was reorganized and extended. As a result we have detailed and reliable information for 1942 and 1943, the years when the party membership reached its highest points. For each month in 1942 an account of members in the various districts was compiled, on the basis of which the head office collected its share of the party dues from the districts. That means that some members are not included, as party members in German military service were exempt from payment. Their number can be estimated at between 1,500 and 2,000. For 1943 we have monthly accounts of net gains and losses. Together this material gives the following figures:[11]

1942	Members	+/÷	1943	Members	+/÷
January	16,400		January	18,700	+ 300
February	16,500	+ 100	February	18,700	–
March	16,600	+ 100	March	19,000	+ 300
April	16,900	+ 300	April	19,100	+ 100
May	17,100	+ 200	May	18,600	÷ 500
June	17,400	+ 300	June	17,900	÷ 700
July	17,600	+ 200	July	17,200	÷ 700
August	17,800	+ 200	August	16,600	÷ 600
September	18,100	+ 300	September	15,800	÷ 800
October	18,300	+ 200	October	15,300	÷ 500
November	18,300	–	November	15,000	÷ 300
December	18,400	+ 100	December	14,300	÷ 700

This shows that membership reached its highest point during the election campaign of 1943 (the increase in April is certainly due to the late arrival at the head office of information on earlier recruits). After that time the gains gave way to rapid losses. The number of paying members peaked at 19,100. Compared with only 43,000 votes in the election this number is very high and reveals the character of the latest increase. A closer investigation of the figures will confirm that this recruitment probably occurred within established circles of followers.

If we compare the figures from Copenhagen between April 1937 and January 1942 there is an increase from 442 members or 16 per cent of the total membership, to 4,703 or 29 per cent. This development corresponds to the increasing share of votes, reaching 40 per cent in 1943. With the year 1942, however, this trend ceases. The membership in Copenhagen rose about 600, no faster than in other parts of the country. Its share remained 29 per cent.

In 1942 more than half of the net gains in total membership were registered in the women's section. Of the 2,000 additional members, 1,165 were women (an increase from 3,662 or 32 per cent), 270 were added to the youth organizations (under 18 years, = an increase of 16 per cent), and 573 to male members and SA, an increase of only 5

709

per cent. Even if we take into account an artificial reduction in the number of men due to recruitment for German military service, which may at most have cut their increase in half, the growth among women was still three times greater. The women's share of adult members grew in the year 1942 from 25 per cent to 30 per cent of the paying members.

Together these features present a picture of an organization which had already reached its political peak. It could still draw more members from family circles, by recruiting wives and children, but it could not do much more. Unfortunately it has so far been impossible to trace this state of affairs farther back for the whole country, but statistics from a single district in Jutland (Ringkøbing Amt) show a similar trend, beginning as early as November 1940. From November 1940 to January 1942 the number of men rose by a third while the number of women trebled.

This impression of a party recruiting new members within established circles of followers accords with the general impression gained from the party archives of the social situation in which the Danish Nazis found themselves during the occupation. The archives contain many complaints of various kinds of ostracism by the surrounding population, often quoted by members as a reason for wanting to leave the party; grocers lost their customers, workers their jobs, children were beaten by comrades, and neighbours would no longer play cards with Nazis. Some of these incidents may in fact have been personal rather than political persecution, but on the whole there is no reason to doubt that the Nazis were isolated and distrusted by a considerable part of the population.[12] Positions became more black and white, they had to either get out or resort to each other for company. Thus joining the party was a natural response for women as well as for men. A membership comprising nearly half of the voters was most probably a reflection of these circumstances.

The social composition of the DNSAP membership has recently been the subject of a detailed investigation.[13] Below some broad outlines of the first results are presented, dealing with the basic descriptors, age, sex, social class, and degree of urbanisation.

It has already been established that the party evolved from being overwhelmingly rural and small-town in the early and middle thirties, to being predominantly urban in the late thirties and during the occupation, and this presents us with an immediate problem when setting out to describe the membership in aggregate terms – for there is not much reason to believe that average figures based on the whole membership were typical of the party for any significant length of time.

And in fact we do find that most of the really noteworthy features in a simple aggregate description emerge only when the material is broken down over different periods. This point is well illustrated with a table of age-group distributions, measured at the beginning and the end of the party's existence:

Age groups	15–20	21–25	26–30	31–40	41–
DNSAP 1935	17%(+)	21%(+)	18%(+)	19%(÷)	26%(÷)
DNSAP 1945	11%(÷)	15%(+)	15%(+)	24%(+)	35%(÷)
Total Population	14%	11%	11%	21%	43%

Two features in this table are noteworthy. The first is what might be expected, a distinct overrepresentation of the younger generation,[14] a feature characteristic of fascist parties, or perhaps of any new party. The second is the increasing average age of the party.[15] This seems to be due to the young staying a shorter time in the party, rather than the age of recruits getting generally higher.

It has already been remarked that the recruitment of women increased over time. How big an increase we are talking about can be seen from the fact that whereas women's overall percentage of the membership was 21 per cent, this conceals an increase from about 10 per cent in the early thirties to about 30 per cent at the end of the period. This increase did not affect the party's age distribution, as sex cross-tabulated against age at entry gives almost identical distributions for men and women.

Whereas the rising recruitment of women must be assumed to have little bearing on the age distribution of the party, it is possible that there is a connection to be found with the increasing urbanisation of the membership – for it appears that women constitute more than twice as high a percentage of the town members as of the country members; from the capital and suburbs 29 per cent were women, from towns and suburbs 24 per cent, but from rural areas only about 13 per cent. Establishing the nature of the connection between increasing urbanisation and female recruitment could be more problematical, however, as it can't automatically be assumed that town women were politically more active. Maybe a line of argument combining 're-cruitment in closed circles', as outlined previously, with the fact that the recruitment drive in the last phases of the party's existence centred on the urban areas, could prove satisfactory.

The first results on the distribution of the DNSAP membership over different social classes show that the dimension of time also here reveals a set of results different from that achieved by statistic averages. The class distribution of all DNSAP members was practically identical to the class distribution of the Danish population in 1953[16]; taken as a whole, no social class was more strongly represented in the party than others. If the period is divided up, however, it becomes evident that the higher classes joined earlier than the lower:

	Per cent which had joined by the end of 1940
Lower upper class	85
Upper middle class	72
Middle middle class	68
Lower middle class	63
Upper working class	57
Middle working class	50

The election results from Copenhagen further confirm this trend. In 1935 the Nazi party had a larger share of the votes in well-to-do districts dominated by the Conservatives, while they were quite insignificant in the working-class districts. In 1939 and especially in 1943 this difference was no longer discernible.

Taken as an average, a very large number of DNSAP's members left again before May 1945, when the party was dissolved – as many as 67 per cent approximately. Some groups were more likely to pull out than others, however; whereas 80 per cent of

711

the functionaries and 75 per cent from the trade category got out 'in time', just under 60 per cent of housewives, schoolchildren/students and the agricultural group left the party.

Another way of looking at who was likely to leave the party again is equally interesting. If we take the rural-urban split once more, the figures are approximately these:

	Per cent from area which left party
Capital + suburbs	76
Towns + suburbs	66
Country districts	55

Some of the apparent faithfulness of country members compared to town members must be attributed to the rural-urban trend in the party, since early entries were more faithful party members than later entries. A final reminder that we are dealing with a very small group of people may be called for.

For all main groups in Danish society, by whatever criteria they are selected, adherence to any of the Nazi parties remained the exception rather than the rule. The vast majority of all major groups in Danish society rejected Nazism, both before and during the occupation by the Germans.

Danish Nazism was a political effort that had no roots and left no traces in Danish political life. It was an experiment which demonstrated the inadequacy of an imported ideology. As we begin to know more about where and how the DNSAP failed, it will hopefully become possible to say more about the reasons for and the implications of its failure.

NOTES

[1] This total includes approximately 3,000 re-entries – i.e. there were approximately 39,000 different people in the party.

[2] The literature on Danish Nazism is very restricted. A brief outline of its history until 1939 is given in Henning Poulsen's book: *Besættelsesmagten og de danske nazister* (Copenhagen 1970), which is primarily an investigation of its political relations with German authorities during the occupation. Niels Alkil: *Besættelsestidens Fakta I-II* (Copenhagen 1945–46) gives a view of the various Nazi organizations especially during the occupation. A selected bibliography of Nazi publications in Denmark is found in the list of literature in Henning Poulsen's book mentioned above.

[3] The detailed results of the elections to parliament are found in *Danmarks Statistik – Statistiske Meddelelser* vol. 99, 109 and 120 (Copenhagen 1935, 1939 and 1943). Briefer accounts are available in *Danmarks Statistik – Statistiske Aarbog* 1935, 1939 and 1943.

[4] *Danmarks Statistik – Statistiske Meddelelser* vol. 92 (Cop. 1933).

[5] See note 2.

[6] Concerning North Schleswig see Troels Fink: *Sønderjylland siden Genforeningen i 1920* (South Jutland since the 1920 Unification) (Copenhagen 1955), Sven Tägil: *Deutschland und die deutsche Minderheit in Nordschleswig* (Stockholm 1970), J.P. Noack: *Det tyske mindretal i Nordslesvig under besættelsen* (The German Minority in North Schleswig during the Occupation) (Copenhagen 1974).

[7] The method of election was very favourable to small parties, which normally secured a proportional representation in parliament, if they achieved more than about 1.5 per cent of the

votes (depending on the geographical distribution). For the Nazi press see Niels Alkil *op.cit.* and Henning Poulsen's article «Fædrelandet – tysk understøttelse af danske Dagblade 1939–1945» –*Historie* ny rk. VII, 2 (1966).

[8] The results from Malene Djursaa's analysis of the membership of the DNSAP confirm the rural-urban trend suggested by the voting figures. This table shows year of entry cross-tabulated against degree of urbanisation.

	Year of entry						
	31–33	34–35	36–37	38–39	40–41	42–43	44–45
Cap. + sub	5%	16%	20%	28%	39%	33%	32%
Towns + sub	27%	32%	31%	29%	32%	31%	46%
Rural areas	60%	51%	50%	42%	20%	13%	10%
Abroad (Germany workers)	8%	1%	0	1%	9%	23%	12%
Approx:	100%	100%	100%	100%	100%	100%	100%

[9] Bovrup-arkivet (Archives of the DNSAP head office) pk. 33. (Rigsarkivet – The National Archives).

[10] *Ibid.* 1c – B.

[11] *Ibid.* 4d. Centralkartoteket (Rigsarkivet) pk. 295.

[12] Four people in the 10% sample being analysed (see note 13) were 'liquidated', i.e. killed by the resistance movement during the occupation.

[13] Malene Djursaa has since this article was written completed her Ph. D. thesis, the main emphasis of which is on the social composition of the DNSAP membership. (See bibliography). The source material is the so-called 'Bovrup-kartotek', primarily the original membership forms, supplemented by various other files giving information on annulments, leadership, etc.

A lot of membership cards are missing for the first three years of the party, 1930–33, but for the later years the material is remarkably complete. From the existing cards a 10 per cent random sample has been selected, and the information coded and fed into a computer. Some of the more interesting variables coded are: Sex, birthdate, occupation, address, dates of entering and leaving the party, former party affiliation, trade union and club membership, and reason for leaving the party. For the party leadership which happens to be part of the sample, we have information on rank achieved, no. of leadership posts held, and dates of taking up and leaving leadership posts.

When this article went to press, the computer analysis of this material was just beginning, hence what results we have been able to present are limited. Readers interested in subsequent results are referred to the thesis. Previous work on the social composition of DNSAP membership (except a study of age distribution, in Carl O. Christiansen, *op.cit.*) has been based on an illegal volume of names, published 1946 on the basis of the 'Bovrup-kartotek', but unfortunately containing only about half the names, and with many other methodological and substantive problems making reliance on it impossible.

[14] Note, however, that the very youngest age-group, 15–20, moves to *under*representation by 1945.

[15] This is clearly illustrated by the bracketed crosses (overrepresentation) and minuses (underrepresentation) in the table; the overrepresented age-groups move one to the right over the ten years.

[16] Kaare Svalastoga, *Prestige, Class and Mobility,* Copenhagen, 1959.

A Short Bibliographic Note

The following are the standard works on Danish Nazism:

Bovrup-bogen (1946).

Knud Brix og Erik Hansen: *Dansk Nazisme under Besættelsen*. (Danish Nazism During the Occupation) (1947).

Karl O. Christiansen: *Landssvigerkriminaliteten i sociologisk belysning* (Crimes of Treason in Sociological Perspective) 1955.

Henning Poulsen: *Besættelsesmagten og de danske nazister* (1970) (The Occupation Forces and the Danish Nazis).

Statistiske Meddelelser 1932, 1935, 1939, and 1943 (Statistical Surveys).

Scheduled for publication in 1981:

Malene Djursaa, *DNSAP. Danske Nazister 1930–1945*. Gyldendal, Copenhagen. With English Summary. Original Ph. D. thesis available (in English) through the British Lending Library's Monograph Division: *Danish Nazism: The Membership of «Danmarks National-Socialistiske Arbejder Parti», 1930–1945*. University of Essex, 1979.

On the Fringe: Swedish Fascism 1920–45*

BERNT HAGTVET

The Electoral Insignificance of Swedish Fascism

Fascism in Sweden was a dispersed phenomenon, eclectic in ideology, imitative in style and marginal to the mainstream of Swedish politics in the 1920's and 30's. Unaided by foreign invaders, it remained a fringe movement, fading out in the 40's, totally discredited and leaving no legacy.[1] At no time was a seat in the *Riksdag* within reach of any of the small groups calling themselves fascist or Nazi, nor did they otherwise pose any serious threat to the stability of Swedish parliamentary government. Its marginal nature is the most basic fact about Swedish fascism. This is clearly borne out in table 1 which covers all the elections in which parties of a fascist persuasion competed.

Table 1. *Electoral Strength of Fascist Parties in Sweden in General Elections 1932–1944**

Name of Party, Name of Leader		Number of Votes		Percentage of Total Number of Votes Cast
Sveriges Nationalsocialistiska Parti (Joint leadership B. Furugård/S.–O. Lindholm)	1932	15,170		0.6
Nationalsocialistiska Arbetarpartiet (Lindholm)		17,383		
	1936		20,408	0.7
Sveriges National-Socialistiska Parti (Furugård)		3,025		
Fascist parties did not compete in the 1940 General Election				
Svensk Socialistisk Samling (Lindholm)	1944	4,204		0.14

Sources: Electoral data compiled from Stein Rokkan and Jean Meyriat, *International Guide to Electoral Statistics,* vol. 1 «National Elections in Western Europe», (The Hague 1969); Eric Wärenstam, *Fascismen och nazismen i Sverige* (Stockholm 1972, the paperback edition) and *Sveriges officiella statistik* (SOU) *Almänna val 1925–1940.* There are some minor discrepancies between these sources.

It should be added that fascists also participated in municipal elections in Stockholm in 1931 and won 279 votes out of a total of 219,638 votes cast. They also competed in the Landsting and municipal elections in 1934 and the *Landsting* elections in 1938. The results were: 1934 (I) 8,170 (0.5); 1934 (II) 15,645 (0.9) and 1938 9,925 (0.5).

* These data do not reflect in full the electoral strength of anti-democratic parties in Sweden in the inter-war period. After the break with the Conservatives in 1934, the SNU (The Swedish National Youth League) grew steadily more pro-Nazi and corporativist. Under the name of *Sveriges Nationella Förbund* (SNF, The Swedish National League) this group competed as a party in the 1936 general elections and got 26,750 votes in the 22 constituencies in which it presented lists. The best results were obtained in Skåne in Southern Sweden, in Stockholm and in Norrland. This support had declined to 3,819 votes in 1944.

A special problem is posed by the Socialist party *(Socialistiska Partiet)* which under the leadership of Nils Flyg was transformed in a fascist direction during the war. Discredited and deserted by its original supporters, this party got 5,279 votes in 1944, of which 2,500 were cast in the capital.

In absolute numbers, the peak of Swedish fascism was reached in the general elections in 1936 when 20,408 Swedes gave their vote to the two fascist parties which participated in that election. In terms of relative share of the poll, the best result came in the municipal elections in 1934 when the fascists polled 0.9 per cent of the vote. These numbers are too small to allow any broader generalizations about the regional distribution and exact social locus of the vote, but a closer analysis of the 1932 result can give some clues. In that election altogether 2,495,106 Swedes went to the polls. The 15,170 votes cast in favor of the fascists were utterly insignificant even in comparison with the two communist parties on the opposite wing. Together they got 8.3 per cent of the vote. The Social Democrats got 41.7 and the Conservatives 23.5 (1,040, 689 and 583, 248 votes respectively). In the 1932 elections the fascists competed in 11 constituencies out of a total of 28. Their voter lists were concentrated in south and south-west Sweden. Throughout the history of Swedish fascism the city of Gothenburg remained its main urban stronghold: in 1932 fascists got 5.7 per cent of the vote in this city (6, 071 votes), in 1936 the Lindholm party got 2.6 per cent. The fascist vote in Stockholm in 1932 was 1, 940. Outside the cities, the highest percentage occurred in the county of Värmland in south-west Sweden close to the Norwegian border. Here the fascists in 1932 got 2.9 per cent of the vote (3, 097 votes). Of these, 717 votes were cast in the urban centers of Arvika, Karlstad, Kristinehamn and Filipstad.

The Relationship to the Traditional Right: Affinities and Rejections

Viewed in isolation, these numbers do not go far in explaining the nature of Swedish fascism. They only show that the different fascist nuclei never gained mass support. Yet in retrospect it can be argued that all the tiny organizations which used the fascist label in the 30's deserve more attention than their sheer numerical strength would suggest. Several reasons can be given for this judgment;

First, many of their political acts were illegal and posed problems of public order. Equally important, their mere existence reminded the authorities and the political parties of the fascist potential within their own population. The turnover of fascist organizations was very high: often the same people regrouped and emerged under a new name. One survey includes the names of about 90 organizations of a fascist type. A similar list of fascist publications which at one point or another were published in Sweden contains 64 names.[2] We know that the *fear* of a further growth of indigenous right-wing extremism influenced political developments in the inter-war years. Most important, it helped change alignments and trigger self-defense measures. When, for example, the Agrarians decided to turn to the alliance with the Social Democrats, bringing Labor to power as a minority government with Agrarian support in the legislature from 1933, the depression was of course the precipitating factor. The compromise was the end-result of a slow process whereby traditional Agrarian resistance to economic planning and state control was relinquished. But the suddenness with which this deal was concluded cannot be explained without reference to the fascist threat. As Olle Nyman has showed, the agreement, or «cow trade» as it came to be called, was also prompted by a desire to show the workability of parliamentary government in the face of growing disillusionment with democratic procedures.[3] Indirectly, then, and contrary to their own stated goals, the fascists helped to galvanize resistance to anti-democratic activism. In this way they pre-empted political space among the farmers which might have given them a chance.

Second, fascism in Sweden must be seen within the context of a broader upsurge of militant nationalism. The fascist parties were not the only ones active on the anti-democratic right in this period. Arguably, as critics of democracy, they were not even the most important. Their initial identification with foreign models and their more vulgar racism limited their clientele and made them less acceptable to circles who otherwise might have concurred in their criticism of democracy. Although the Conservative party officially denounced fascism in a brochure in 1933, there were significant affinities between that party and the fascist fringe. These affinities were crystallized with particular clarity in the case of the Swedish National Youth League *(Sveriges Nationella Ungdomsförbund, SNU)*. Organizationally distinct from the conservatives, the SNU served for all practical purposes as their youth organization. The political program of the SNU in 1934 demonstrates the interpenetration between fascism proper and the traditional right. The program contained attacks on economic liberalism and Marxism (both were seen as impotent in solving the 'economic-cultural crisis of the country'). It also called for a 'national sense of purpose' and urged national unification. The program also contained proposals for a strong government. This meant restricting the legislature to passing the budget and generally confining its task to supervisory functions. The political program of the SNU also demanded prohibition of communist organizations; an end to 'Marxist capital exploitation' and 'speculative capitalism'; a corporate economy and a restrictive immigration policy based on the protection of the Swedish race. In 1929 this organization had 31,500 members. It reached its peak in 1936 when 40,000 were registered. In 1940 this number had dwindled to between 12 and 15 thousand.[4] Anti-democratic sympathies were expressed by prominent conservatives throughout the whole period.[5] The years from 1918 to 1933 were on the whole a time of ambivalence for the conservatives: the critique of democracy was widespread in the party. When the Conservative leader Arvid Lidman drew the distinction between Nazism and his own ideology, he did not defend democracy. In 1933 he even accepted an 'emergency dictatorship' although he rejected dictatorship as a permanent form of government. Against democratic principles, Lidman introduced the principle of 'popular rule' *(folkstyre)*. The exact content of this alternative remains unclear. Democracy was seen as one form of this 'popular rule', but not necessarily the best. «The attacks on democracy were numerous, expressions of hatred and contempt equally prominent . . . . The principle of democracy was not accepted by any of the rightist groups participating in the debate.»[6] In a comparative perspective, this delay in recognizing democratic procedures on part of the Swedish conservatives is significant. In Norway the consensus on constitutional democracy as a 'supra ideology', a common frame within which political disagree-

717

ments could work themselves out, came earlier and was more gradualist. It can be argued that this deep-seated ambivalence reduced the distinctiveness of the fascist groups in Sweden; that, in fact, anti-democratic ideology had several outlets in Swedish public life and that much of the anti-democratic potential was absorbed by the traditional right. Subsequent developments on the right lend a certain credence to this view. After a series of skirmishes with the Conservative party, the SNU ceded from the party in 1934. But it did not leave the political scene. It set off on a new path as an independent youth organization and later emerged as a party under the name *Sveriges Nationella Förbund* (The Swedish National League). As such it participated in the 1936 general elections but never came close to obtaining representation in the national assembly (see table 1). This organization existed in parallel with the fascist groups but was reduced to insignificance during the war.

Nor were the Agrarians free of fascistoid elements in their ideology. In the program from 1933, the Agrarians stated for example that protection of the Swedish race was among its main tasks. The racially «sound» people were often identified with the farmers; racial purity could go well with the image of the ideal peasant. The party declared itself against 'inferior racial elements' and advocated restrictions to the immigration of 'undesirable aliens'. That this program could be used to rather pernicious political purposes was demonstrated by the Agrarian MP, Otto Walén, who used this passage in the party program to legitimize his own anti-Semitism and give an air of respectability to his efforts to fight Jewish immigration to Sweden from Germany.[7].

Advocacy of corporativism or a strong government, a racialist immigration policy and an end to both Marxism and liberalism do not necessarily make a party 'fascist'. Definitions which are excessively inclusionist rarely increase the usefulness of the concept of fascism as an analytical tool. The aim of this exercise is not to brand other parties than the self-proclaimed ones as 'fascist'. Rather, it is simply to show that there were significant affinities. Core elements of fascist political thinking found a climate of acceptance outside the narrow fascist circles. We can speak of a constellation of assumptions and ideas that were grouped and regrouped on the right in this period and congealed into a system clustered around these *leitmotifs:* impatience with parliamentary government; longings for a common purpose, a desire often expressed in fierce nationalist language; demand for an end to the divisiveness of class struggle and interest in questions of racial purity. It is important to note, as Rolf Torstendal has shown, that although racism was common in the AVF (The Swedish Conservative Party), it rejected the use of racial arguments for specific political ends as the NSDAP did. «Racism», he writes, «was more of a common frame of reference on the Swedish Right than a motivation for certain political actions».[8] These reservations were not taken as wholeheartedly by the Agrarians. To them, genetic concerns should be taken into account in official family policies. In sum, then, fascism as it emerged in Sweden can be seen as a more plebeian extension of themes already found on the right and among the Agrarians; it took to *the extreme* ideas that were nurtured quite openly within these organizations themselves.

The resonance fascist predispositions found in wider groups can be illustrated further. Two points deserve comment:

1. The fascists had considerable success in instigating or capitalizing on political movements of a broader nature. The demonstrations in the late thirties against immigration, particularly of academic manpower, mostly Jews from Germany, is a case in point. The extent to which anti-Semitic propaganda struck a responsive

chord in the academic youth at the time is a rather embarassing aspect of Swedish history of the period. Naturally, unemployment and the slim prospects of finding work commensurate with expectations prepared the ground, but it cannot explain away the relative ease with which fascists and nationals imposed their frame of reference on the discussions. The respect for the 'national' attitude was pervasive, as was the belief in the need to preserve the purity of the Swedish race. The alleged need for rigorous control of immigration remained largely unchallenged.[9] In February, 1939, the fascists arranged a demonstration in Stockholm directed against work permits to political refugees. One writer contends that a petition against further immigration was signed by 25–30 thousand people.[10] Even more pronounced was the influence of the extreme right among students, demonstrated in the three meetings which took place in February and March, 1939, in Uppsala, Stockholm and Lund. The Stockholm meeting which was arranged by Lindholm's party *Svensk Socialistisk Samling* (SSS – Swedish Socialist Unity), was attended by representatives of several disciplines, all protesting against allowing Jews to practice their disciplines in Sweden. The Uppsala rally was preceded by an intense public discussion where the representatives of the student union made an effort to present the issue as an expression of unpolitical professional concern. A resolution stating that Sweden should *not* diminish its efforts in the campaign to aid the victims of persecution was rejected by a vote of 549–349. The adopted resolution took the view that compassion with the sufferings of other people ought not lead to measures which might have fateful *(ödesdiger)* and unknown consequences for Sweden in a longer perspective. Stripped of its euphemisms, this was racialism in pure form.

In Lund the meeting was attended by around 1,000 students. The resolution speaking of 'alien elements' supported by the nationals and the SSS's student association was overwhelmingly passsed 724–342.[11]

2. The period produced a variety of semi-vigilante strike-breaker organizations directed against the labor movement. *Centralförbundet för arbetets frihet* (The Central Association for the Freedom of Work) was established in 1923 in Hälsingborg and headed by the paper and pulp industrialist A.O. Fränden.[12] Its aim was to protect 'those willing to work', as it stated, its target the forest industry in Northern Sweden. Another was The Swedish National Protection Squads *(Svenska Nationella Skyddskåren)* in Stockholm[13] and the *Föreningen för teknisk samhällshjälp* (literally 'The Association for Technical Societal Assistance'). The Conservatives established *Byrån for arbets-och näringsfrihet* (The Bureau for Free Enterprise), a propaganda instrument designed to collect information about the «terror and monopolism» of the labor movement.[14] The specifically fascist character of those organizations is of course an open question, but they are indicative of the tension and polarization of Swedish political life in the thirties, a reaction which has its parallels in other Scandinavian countries and in which fascism was an important element.

Intellectual Antecedents: Rudolf Kjellén and the Young Conservatives

Fascism thrives on a climate of cultural and political illiberalism. As a whole, Sweden provided a rather unhospitable environment for an ideology of this kind. But the country had an indigenous right-wing tradition of considerable intellectual sophistication, far more extensive and Teutonic in style than anywhere else in Scandinavia. To trace the pedigree of this anti-democratic right in detail would exceed the limits of this essay, but since it can render the conservative ambivalence towards democracy more comprehensible, an analysis of its main figure, Professor Rudolf Kjellén (1864–1922) is necessary. Kjellén, along with a few minor figures, provides the intellectual background of pro-German and pro-Nazi sentiments against which Swedish fascism must be understood.[15]

Rudolf Kjellén, a political scientist first in Gothenburg, later in Uppsala, probably wielded more influence in Germany than in Sweden. Through the Nazi ideologue Karl Haushofer he provided the theoretical foundations for Germany's *Lebensraum* doctrine. Kjellén's *geo-political* theories, his biological view of inter-state relations and his Social-Darwinian view of the importance of war and struggle gave intellectual ammunition to the Nazi *Weltanschauung*. More specifically, Kjellén's political thinking is characterized by the following components:

1. *Nationalism*. The nation, according to Kjellén, was more than the sum of its parts. The nation was seen as a more biological organism whose right to live could only be won by prowess in the struggle for existence. «The iron laws of history» can only accept «those acts of proof that are written in blood.»[16] Egotism is justified between the nations, history is merciless to those unwilling to defend and fight. Nationalism is to Kjellén a power 'beyond good and evil', an instinct.

2. *High regard for war*, a view traceable to the influence of Social Darwinism. Struggle is normal, war «a tool of development used by history to sort out nations incapable of survival like dried-out branches on a tree.»[17] In this Kjellén echoes Treitschke, though his enthusiasm for war was dampened after WW I.

3. *Geo-political justifications for outward expansion*. Nations are propelled forward by their 'biological' needs. Large nations are justified in their expansionism by virtue of their status and needs as big powers. In their case even geo-political laws are suspended. Related to this geo-political ideology, Kjellén advocated *economic autarchy*.

4. *Anti-individualism*. Kjellén frequently attacked what he termed debilitating individualism and supported the primacy of state interest. This super-individual organism represented interests superior to particular individual interests. In line with this Kjellén argued that the onslaught of the masses in democracy threatened 'independent individualism'.

5. *Critique of democracy*. Kjellén predicted that the historical pendulum would swing back from the democracy he had seen emerging in the preceding centuries to autocracy again. He thought the despotism of the masses would be replaced by personal rule: the *leader* was entitled to interpret the true will of the people, even in the cases where his interpretation of this will ran counter to the expressed desires of the people in elections. Here he clearly anticipated the fascist *Führerprinzip*.

6. *Corporativism* he saw as a sound collectivist form of elevating the individual into a higher sphere. He wanted class affiliation, not profession, to be the criterion according to which people should be represented in the corporate assembly.

7. *A special appeal to the middle classes*, bound as they were to the national area, in contrast to the international forces, socialism and capitalism.

8. *Anti-capitalism*. Kjellén distinguished between capitalism supported by banks and the kind of capitalism which was found locally and was rooted in ordinary people's work. This distinction comes very close to the later Nazi concepts of 'exploitative' *(raffende)* and 'creative' *(schaffende)* capital. In the same vein Kjellén advocated a *national* socialism, not a *class* socialism, an idea he hoped would replace liberalism.

Kjellén's political thinking was explicitly anti-liberal with anti-intellectual over-tones. He saw his own ideas as the synthesis between the political foundations of the *ancien régime* and the excesses of 1789. Against equality, Kjellén posited justice, against fraternity, national unity.

9. In his concept of *race*, Kjellén was aware that no clear and distinct races in a biological sense existed. As a result, he did not see blood as constitutive of a nation's unity. Instead language and the cultural traditions made up the common bonds. Although he regarded the Germanic race as the most valuable, he did not use pan-German arguments to justify the territorial expansion of the *Reich: Lebensraum* ventures could only be justified on the grounds of geo-political necessities or by virtue of being a super-power, not legitimized by race.

His views on race set him apart from the later Nazis. He was also largely free from anti-Semitism. It should be noted, too, that his ideas on corporations never included the use of these organizations as a passive instrument of power by the state. Kjellén never broke with the ideals of humanity and due process of law. There was a constant tension in his thinking between the a-moralism of his *Staatsraison* doctrines and the Judaeo-Christian and humanist ethical heritage. Kjellén prepared the ideological climate which fascism could use as a vantage point, but he did not set himself apart from the fundamental political and cultural traditions of the West. The voluntarism, brutality and sheer nihilism of the fascists he would probably have detested. We know that the Swedish fascists were avid readers of him, and through his influence of the Swedish right he came to provide the intellectual justifications which in turn help explain the affinities between these groups and fascism. The phalanx of the 'Young Conservatives' who derived much of their inspiration from Kjellén became a vocal part of the right in Sweden, critical of the lethargy of the established right. The Conservative leader Arvid Lidman was also influenced by Kjellén in the period before and during World War I.

The Furugård Brothers and Early Swedish Fascism

The first fascist organization in Sweden was formed in Älvdalen, Dalecarlia, in August, 1924. The men behind the Swedish National Socialist League of Freedom (*Svenska Nationalsocialistiska Frihetsförbundet, SNF*) as it was called, were the three Furugård brothers Birger, Gunnar and Sigurd. Birger Furugård, the first Nazi leader in Sweden, was a veterinary surgeon from the county of Värmland. His brother Gunnar, a medical doctor, was employed in the state health services in the region, and the third, Sigurd, a journalist, later became editor of the party newspaper «The National Socialist» (*Nationalsocialisten*), a weekly launched in September that year. The leadership of the party at the time of its establishment was composed of one high school teacher, one principal, one lieutenant, one mason and one farmer, in addition to the Furugård brothers themselves. Sigurd had for some time been in contact with the anti-Semitic magazine *Vidi* in Gothenburg and also in the autumn of 1923 been the guest of General Erich Ludendorff and Adolf Hitler, a visit which gave added impetus to his plans for spreading the Nazi ideology in the Nordic countries. The biography of this man is not without interest. He shared a formative experience with Vidkun Quisling, the Norwegian Nazi *Führer:* they had both been active in Russia. From 1916 to 1918 Sigurd Furugård was a representative of the Red Cross in Siberia. Acting as a deputy to the Norwegian polar explorer and diplomat Fridtjof Nansen, Quisling worked with the League of Nations relief organization to famine-stricken Ukraine in the early twenties. While the Norwegian returned with feelings of ambivalence towards the Bolsheviks, reluctantly admiring their skill as political organizers and later offering to train Red Guards for the Norwegian Labor party[18], Furugård left Russia a fervent anti-communist. Struck, as he later wrote, by the preponderance of Jews in revolutionary organizations and the brutality of the Bolsheviks, he remained a staunch anti-Semite and anti-communist for the rest of his life.

The first meeting of the SNF issued an appeal to «all honest Swedes» to join in a united struggle against intrusion of alien races and deterioration of the Swedish stock, a theme which was to become a common feature of later fascist programs in Sweden. The program also included calls for a strong defense, a government independent of the «narrow self-interest» of political parties and big business, protection of small-scale private property, and struggle against trusts, cartels and syndicates. Immigration of inferior races was to be outlawed, and all Jews who had been granted stay in Sweden after 1914 expelled. For the remaining parts of the Jewish population, special laws were to be enacted. In an appeal to the farmers, the program advocated land redistribution schemes and promised subventions to local industry and handicrafts. Agriculture was to be the backbone of the nation, a source of strength and pride. Reminiscent of the 1920 program of the NSDAP, the appeal also included a passage on the «slavery of rent.» Interest should be limited and imposed only for a specified period. As a whole the program was directed to the urban lower middle classes and the farmers, with German racialism and corporativist ideas woven in. Interestingly, it took care in distinguishing between «National Socialism» and «fascism», accusing the latter of downplaying the threat from international Jewry. As could be expected, the program was sensitive to the tactically appropriate in a country with no violent political traditions and a massive Protestant majority: it avoided open conflict with the official Lutheran church and denounced fascist and communist violence. The many revivalist religious movements came in for a heavy attack, however. Finally, in a familiar exercise of Manichean reductionism derived from Gottfried Feder, the program envisaged a secret Jewish world conspiracy in the form of international Jewish capital: through state loans and high interest rates each nation found itself at the mercy of this brotherhood of moneylenders. As a first measure of defense, the appeal urged the nationalization of the large banks and the separation of smaller banks from high finance.

The party had serious problems getting off the ground. In 1925 its weekly ceased publication and Sigurd Furugård had to leave his post as editor. In an attempt to specify its appeal the name was changed to Swedish National Socialist Farmers' and Workers' Party (*Svenska Nationalsocialistiska Bonde- och Arbetarpartiet*). During a visit to Germany in 1927 Birger Furugård paid a visit to Josef Terboven, then *Ortsgruppenleiter* in Essen, later to become the notorious *Reichskommissar* in occupied Norway, with whom he kept in close contact thereafter. He was also received by Georg Strasser, Himmler, Julius Streicher and Hitler himself. Confidently, Hitler told Furugård that he reckoned twenty years active party work was required to win over the masses in Sweden to the National Socialist cause.

Elof Eriksson and the Anti-Semitic Tradition

The first fascist organization explicitly modelled after the Italian original was intimately associated with the name of Elof Eriksson, originally a political agitator and journalist in the farmer's organizations and a fierce anti-Semite. In 1925 he founded in

Stockholm the newspaper «The Nation» *(Nationen)* which throughout the inter-war years became one of the main propagators of anti-Semitic and anti-democratic thought in Sweden. The year before he had been instrumental in establishing the National Unity Movement *(Nationella samlingsrörelsen)* which adopted as its program elimination of class distinctions, creation of strong state authority, strict economizing in state and municipal budgets and further colonization of Norrland in Northern Sweden. In contrast to the rather far-flung character of Furugård's propaganda, Eriksson concentrated more directly on Swedish problems. He fervently fought the state monopoly on tobacco and spirits and attacked the rule of «cosmopolitans» in government, i.e. Jews who through the national debts exercised ultimate control of the government. Election of members to parliament, he argued, should be conducted on the basis of «qualifications». In the same vein he lashed out against disarmament and warned against the threat from the left. He kept in touch with General Erich Ludendorff, who in his later years spent his time attacking free masonry and the international Jewish plot. After a series of attacks on the wealthy Wallenberg family and the free masons, inspired by Ludendorff, Eriksson's paper was banned by the government in the autumn of 1935. Undaunted, Eriksson continued to cultivate his relations with Julius Streicher and *Der Stürmer.* Through Streicher he was offered material from the *Deutscher Fichte-Bund,* a virulently anti-Semitic organization and the *Institut zum Studium der Judenfrage* in Berlin, along with pamphlets from a series of similar German groups. In April 1932 Eriksson maintained that his paper had a circulation of «close to» 10,000. The printer, on the contrary, stated that between September and December 1933 only between 6,500 and 8,000 copies came off the press.[19]

The Swedish Fascist Combat Organization (SFKO) and the Merger Between the two Strands of Swedish Fascism

These initial developments set the stage for a series of complex inner feuds leading to the formation of mutually hostile groups within Swedish fascism. Only a few of these transcend the level of personal idiosyncracy. In the haze of rivalries and factionalism four points are worth emphasizing:

1. Around 1930 there was a *shift in the direction of the movement* as a whole towards a more conscious exultation of German National Socialism. This is apparent both in the aesthetics of the meetings, in the formation of a protection squad (the SA, *Skyddsavdelningar,* which remained unarmed), in the color of the uniform (from black to brown) and in ideology.

2. The movement went through a phase of internal dissension related to *different conception of fascism's relationship to property and wealth.* In diluted form, this struggle reflects the factional strife between the Northern 'anti-capitalist' Strasser wing of the NSDAP and Hitler which crested in the Röhm killings in 1934.

3. This left-right struggle was early manifestations of a *quest for respectability* in the form of efforts to establish a National Socialist Bloc (1933–34) with no socialist trappings. This struggle revolved around the Nazi leader S.O. Lindholm who never wanted to accommodate with the traditional right.

4. Concomitant with foreign aggression and increased brutality towards the Jews in Germany, the identification with the Southern neighbor became more and more

Table 2. *Major Swedish Fascist Organizations 1924–1945: Leaders, Ideology and Social Support*

Date of Founding, Name of Organization, Place of Origin, Newspaper and Essentials of Party Development	Founder(s) or Prominent Figures & Short Background Details on Party Development	Main Ideological Tenets	Available Data on Circulation of Publications and Social Origins of Members (Complete Electoral Data in table 1)
1924: Svenska Nationalsocialistiska Frihetsförbundet (Swedish National Socialist Freedom League), Älvdalen, Dalecarlia. Name changed in 1925 to Svenska Nationalsocialistiska Bonde- och Arbetarpartiet (Swedish National Socialist Farmers' and Workers' Party). Newspaper: *Nationalsocialisten.* Symbol: Swastika.	Birger, Gunnar and Sigurd Furugård, veterinary surgeon, M.D. & journalist.	Anti-communism, racialism (protection of the Swedish race, anti-Semitism). *Blut und Boden* ideology (land distribution schemes and support for local handicrafts, glorification of «healthy» farmers), *Führer*-principle, anti-monopolism.	Reliable figures missing. Newspaper published only spasmodically. Propaganda directed at farmers and lower middle class. Minimal support, limited to the Värmland region.
1924: Nationella Samlingsrörelsen (National Unity Movement), Stockholm. Newspaper: *Nationen.*	Elof Eriksson. Active publicist organizer within farmer's league, failed to organize a fascist movement.	Strongly anti-Semitic and anti-monopolistic; advocated strengthening of state power, public economizing.	*Nationen,* printed: 6000, sold: no more than 4000 on an average. Banned 1935.
1926: Sveriges Fascistiska Folkparti (Swedish Fascist People's Party). Name later changed to Sveriges Fascistiska Kamporganisation (Swedish Fascist Combat Organization). Stockholm. Newspaper: *Spøknippet* (Fasces) Name changed again 1930 to Nationalsocialistiska Folkpartiet (The National Socialist People's Party). Name changed 1930/31 to Sveriges Nationalsocialistiska Parti (Swedish National Socialist Party). Newspaper: *Vår Kamp* (Our Struggle).	Lieutenant K.O. Hallgren, artillery officer S. Hedengren, sergeant S.-O. Lindholm. Furugård and Lindholm movements merged after visits to Germany. Swing to the German Nazi model.	Corporativism, elimination of rule of «international lending capital», anti-communism, racialism, strong defense, preservation of religion, «Swedish» culture and educational policies, «Swedish» foreign policy.	*Spøknippet* circulation between 3–4000. Claimed 7000 members in 1930, 4000 more probable. Members clerks, small business owners, lower civil servants, military officers of lower rank, some working class youths, pupils. Local chapters in Gothenburg, Uppsala, Umeå, Östersund, Gävle, Västerås, Linköping, Lund, Karlskrona.

1933: *January*. Split between Lindholm and Furugård. L. establishes Nationalsocialistiska Arbetarpartiet (National Socialist Worker's Party). Newspaper: *Den svenske Nationalsocialisten* (The Swedish National Socialist). Youth Organization: Nordisk Ungdom (Nordic Youth). This party remains the leading representative of Swedish fascism. *October:* Furugård ousted by own party branch in Gothenburg. 1936: Furugård dissolves the remnants of his own party. 1938: October. Lindholm attempts to create a more Swedish brand of fascism. Drops German symbolism. Adopts old historical Swedish symbols (Vasakärven). Name changed: Svensk Socialistisk Samling (Swedish Socialist Unity). This party fizzles out at the end of WW II. Finally dissolved shortly after the war.	Causes for the split predominantly personal, but reminiscent in content of the Strasser/Hitler conflict. Revolved around the issue of the «anti-capitalist» character of Swedish fascism. Gothenburg chapter of the Furugård party more conservative than the leader, wanting to join the National Socialist Bloc to create a broad, more traditionalist fascist front with no socialist colorings. This split precipitated the decimation and final dissolution of the Furugård party.	Program of the victorious Lindholm party mostly a repetition of previous statements, but more explicitly, «anti-capitalist»: more stress on lower middle class issues, (control with chain stores, nationalization of the banks, profit-sharing schemes, employee representation on company boards).	Municipal elections in 1934, the Furugård party got 6 seats in the Tärendö municipal council, Nothern Dalecarlia. Gothenburg municipal elections same year: 4343 votes, 2 delegates.
1933: Nationalsocialistiska Blocket (The National Socialist Bloc). Newspaper: *Riksposten* (The National Gazette).	Colonel M. Ekström. Attempt to make Sw. fascism more respectable.	Program with a toned down socialist profile, reduced emphasis on bank nationalization, generally closer to traditional right than Lindholm's party.	Regional strongholds Umeå, Rockelsta, Gothenburg. Pretention to be above classes; prime targets, lower middle class, white collar workers, retailers, farmers.
1930: October. Föreningen Det Nya Sverige (The Association «New Sweden»), Uppsala. Journal: *Vägen Framåt* (The Way Ahead)	Per Engdahl. This leader becomes the focal point of the «New Swedish» movement which under different names has existed until today. 1941: Organized as Svensk Opposition (Swedish Opposition).	Mussolini admiration: corporativism, anti-Semitism very pronounced, ideology of «New Swedishness», attempts to unify the fascist-fringe.	«Herrenklub» character. Local chapters Uppsala, Gothenburg.

disadvantageous for the Swedish fascists. Hence Lindholm tried to *dissociate himself from the German model* and weaken the impression of his party as a political import. In 1940, Lindholm privately denounced the German invasion in Norway.[20] There was a *partial swing back* to the pre-1929 ideological orientation around the SFKO.

In table 2 an attempt has been made to chart the main fascist groups in Sweden in the inter-war period and to summarize what is known about their social support. In the chapters to follow I shall trace these internal feuds in more detail.

In October, 1926, the first issue of the weekly *Spöknippet (Fasces)* appeared in Stockholm. The paper presented itself as the voice of a new organization, The Swedish Fascist Combat Organization *(Sveriges Fascistiska Kamporganisation, SFKO)*. It originated from the circle around Elof Eriksson and was headed by three military men: K.O. Hallgren, a volunteer in the German army in World War I, Sven Hedengren, a lieutenant in the Swedish armed forces and himself the son of a lieutenant-colonel, and Sven-Olov Lindholm, the future leader, a sergeant. The paper departed somewhat from Eriksson's anti-Semitism, branding communism, not the Jews, as the main danger in Sweden. This was primarily a shift in emphasis and did not signify an end to the party's general animosity towards Jews. The SFKO must be seen as a typical reflex-phenomenon, a reaction against Swedish communism at the time. The communists, after a turbulent decade following the familiar pattern of splits and accusations of ideological deviationism, were in the midst of a bitter fraternal struggle between two wings, one which can somewhat inadequately be described as national communist, the other Moscow-oriented. The SFKO, which perceived the national loyalty of the communists to be dubious at best, established a group charged with spying on the left. The fascists wanted to check if their revolutionary rhetoric ever materialized into anything more tangible than words. After three years of organizing, the SFKO had succeeded in founding nuclei of supporters around Sweden. The Stockholm group, never strong in any sense, consisted of some white-collar employees, a few retailers' assistants, lower civil servants, some working class youngsters and military officers of lower rank. If there is any pattern in the recruitment to this organization, it must be that of the *declassé military*. This was probably due to the reform of armed forces completed by the Social Democratic Minister of Defense Per Albin Hansson in 1925. The military regarded this reform with suspicion. Some officers lost their commissions, in itself a rather grave problem in view of the unemployment at the time. Fears, particularly among the lower ranks, that there would be further lay-offs made some susceptible to the nationalist propaganda in the fascist weeklies. We know that this reform was formative in Hedengren's conversion to fascism.[21]

In the general election in 1928 the *Fasces* urged its readers to abstain. In their propaganda, the SFKO patterned itself on Italian fascism, wearing the black shirt, appearing in groups surrounded by banners and Swedish flags, talking in the exhortatory style so familiar to continental fascism.

The journal never reached a wide audience. Its average circulation remained between 3–4000 copies.[22] Despite their obvious needs, the SFKO never succeeded in obtaining any sizeable financial assistance outside their own ranks. One exception was the banker Arvid Högman who was impressed with the SFKO pamphlets and thought the movement could fulfill a national purpose. Like his counterparts in Germany, Högman may well have wrongly interpreted the willingness of these groups to protect the status quo. Denying that they were a private police for existing bourgeois society, the *Fasces* wrote in 1928: «We will not risk our lives to protect the bonds and the stocks of the rich and their money bags in the bank vaults. Over and over again: no! We are a patriotic party (not a class party) aiming at the overthrow of the rotten parliamentary misrule in order to build a new Sweden on a firm basis with a strong government, with just laws and strict controls. This is something completely different from (rendering) a police service. The fact that we will clash with the Bolsheviks and crush them in the process is no more than a consequence of our more general purpose.»[23]

In 1927 the *Fasces* called for an armed insurrection against the existing «insane governmental system», but no one took notice. The police evidently believed that the SFKO was unable to muster anything stronger than exhortations and left the fringe to express itself as it pleased. The SFKO founded a women's group within the organization specializing in nursing, arms instruction, combat practice and outdoor life. In 1930 the organization as a whole claimed to have 7,000 members, but there is no way to validate this estimate.[24]

The merger between the SFKO and the Furugård movement occurred in 1930, most probably after initiatives by Hitler. In 1929 a few representatives of the SFKO paid a visit to the Nazi assemblies in Nuremberg. They met Hitler and left impressed by the style and size of these rallies. Birger Furugård was also visiting Germany at the time. After their return there was a significant shift away from Italian ideals. The SFKO changed its name to The National Socialist People's Party *(Nationalsocialistiska Folkpartiet)*, started wearing brown shirts and deliberately imitated Nazi symbolism. When this reformed Nazi group and Furugård's movement united, they tried to bring into the party a small group in Uppsala headed by Per Engdahl, later one of the leading ideologues of Swedish fascism. In line with this objective, they kept the name «New Swedish» *(nysvensk)* in the name of the new organization for a while, but to no avail. The Uppsala group stayed out and was later to form a dissident core within the movement. A *nysvensk* group in Gothenburg decided to join, however. The exclusion of the Uppsala group was indicative of ideological disagreements which eventually, in 1933, split the party. The issue of 'New Swedishness' impinged on the controversy whether the movement ought to be 'fascist' or 'Nazi' and what the relationship to the traditional right should be. After this failure to broaden the basis of the government the final name of the new party became The Swedish National Socialist Party *(Sveriges Nationalsocialistiska Parti)* (SNP). The headquarters were located in Gothenburg, Furugård was elected *Führer* and Lindholm deputy in charge of organization affairs. Under this name the party competed in the 1932 general elections, the most successful for the party in relative terms. (See table 1.)

In its program the new party advocated the substitution of corporativism for parliamentary government, protection against alien races, support for Christian values, strengthened defense and unflinching opposition to 'international moneylending capital'. Relations with Germany continued to flourish. In the fall of 1931, Furugård joined the political campaigns of the German Nazis, speaking over a period of several months in Essen, Düsseldorf and Cologne and seeing party branches at work in Munich and Berlin. Likewise, Lindholm was invited by Himmler in 1932 to study organization and propaganda. This visit included talks with Hitler.

The continental European pattern of a preponderance of youth in the fascist parties repeated itself in Sweden: in 1931, 88 per cent of the voters of the party were between 23 and 27 years of age. The closest approximation to this age distribution can be found in the two competing Swedish communist parties at that time: compared to the Swedish average of between 6 and 12 per cent of the voters in the age cohorts between

23 and 27, the two communist parties recruited 24 and 20 per cent of their members in these groups respectively.[25]

It should also be noted that the SNP organized a large number of people below the voting age. The leader Furugård was quite active at this time. With Lindholm he toured southern and southwest Sweden. Later, after the split, Lindholm went on his own, speaking on «Capitalists and other Non-Working People».[26] In January 1932, he appeared in central Stockholm addressing an audience variably estimated by the newspapers to have been between 2,000 and 10,000 people (the latter being the fascist newspaper's estimate).[27]

The Furugård/Lindholm Split: Personal Rivalries and Anti-Capitalist Rhetoric

The year 1933 witnessed two important developments inside the miniscule movement: the split between Lindholm and Furugård in January and Furugård's ousting by his own party branch in Gothenburg in October.

Behind these moves there were both personal rivalries and ideological conflicts mutually reinforcing each other. In its ideological form this struggle is reminiscent of the factional strife inside the NSDAP prior to and the year after the seizure of power. The question was: who were the enemies? How sincerely anti-capitalist should the movement be? To Lindholm the main enemy of the fascists was the industrial right. In the fall of 1931 Lindholm hoped the party would be banned. This, he argued, would drive the remaining 'bourgeois' elements out of the movement and leave the true heroic National Socialists to carry on the struggle. Both Lindholm and Furugård agreed that their national socialism should not be identified with any of the non-socialist parties. At the same time they maintained that both social democracy and the communists were instruments of big capital. Only their party advocated a *national* socialism.

Ever since the inclusion of the 'New Swedish' Gothenburg wing these disagreements had been present, albeit in suppressed form. This «New Swedish» group resented the socialist colorings of Lindholm's political views. Most of them were small entrepreneurs, or otherwise uninterested in leftist politics. They saw the salvation of Sweden in a strong, authoritarian government, the eradication of class struggle and unrelenting warfare against Jews. Lindholm's view of the non-socialist parties as being insensitive to the plight of the common people were of course anathema to this group, a Marxist poisoning of national socialism, although they all were agreed on the need to abolish parliamentarism. These ideological controversies were exacerbated by personal rivalries, particularly between Lindholm and Furugård, conflicts which in turn reflected the underlying issue of the 'plebeian' vs. upper class character of the movement. Lindholm lashed out against Furugård's personal habits, his alleged misuse of alcohol and choice of friends on the right. These were people who disliked Lindholm's advocacy of industrial peace through what he termed the 'nationalization' of labor. Accusing Furugård of accepting money from these circles, Lindholm was finally excluded and formed his own party *Nationalsocialistiska Arbetarpartiet* (The National Socialist Labor Party – NSAP). The new party published *Den svenske Nationalsocialisten* (The Swedish National Socialist) and hired Per Dahlberg, a leading theoretician, as its editor.

There is no trace of official German financial support at this time, but the party received contributions from Swedes sympathetic to National Socialism who lived in Germany. Lindholm himself has stated that an unsolicited offer from Himmler in 1934

728

was politely refused. When, shortly after, the Lindholm party convened its first convention in Gothenburg, about 500 delegates from all over Sweden attended. The convention decided to establish a youth organization *Nordisk Ungdom* (Nordic Youth). The NU imitated Hitler Jugend, used the swastika as its symbol and aimed at the 12–19 year olds. It was not the only youth organization on the fascist fringe in this period. In the summer of 1937 the Nordic School Youth Association was formed (*Nordiska Skolungdomsförbundet*). Along with the *Blå Garder* (the Blue Guards) and *Det unga Sverige* (Young Sweden), two similar attempts to organize young people, these organizations were active in demanding an end to Swedish membership in the League of Nations.[28]

The October split when Furugård found himself excluded by his own followers in Gothenburg only acquires interest because it can be seen as a move towards unifying the diverse fascist groups in a more respectable organization. This organization was to be The National Socialist Bloc *(Nationalsocialistiska Blocket)* under the leadership of Colonel Martin Ekström. Furugård maintained that despite the treason in his own ranks, he commanded the loyalty of 90 per cent of the party's members. When the general elections in 1936 showed this estimate to be wrong – Furugård got only 3,025 votes as compared with Lindholm's 17,483 – he conceded defeat and urged his followers to join Lindholm. Furugård dissolved his party on November 13, 1936. The last remnants of his movement were submerged in the fascist organization *Svensk Opposition* (Swedish Opposition) in Malmö in 1943. This group was under the leadership of Per Engdahl. Furugård's role in Swedish ultra-right politics had thus come to an ignominious end.

Lindholm, the NSAP and the Turn Against the German Connection

Faithful to his resistance to alignments with the traditional Right, Lindholm in his new program devoted particular attention to the plight of the small retailer, repeating his demand for control over the chain stores. Otherwise it was a repetition of previous programs, though with a clearer anti-capitalist bent. It urged nationalization of the commercial banks, the organization of the economy in corporations, profit-sharing between employees and employers and the safe-guarding of workers' rights through representation on the board. The program also called for stiffer penalties for economic crimes, bribes, embezzlement, etc. The government should be independent of economic interests, informed by professional people and guided by an advisory assembly based on the corporations. Jews were to be treated as aliens. Sweden's valuable human material and her resources made it possible to gain self-sufficiency in most areas, the program stated. The crucial point was to wrestle control away from 'moveable capital', the moneylenders. These capitalists had to be barred from dominating the country's productive capacity. In 1937, in an attempt to launch in embryo the future corporations, the NSAP founded its own trade union federation. But this organization remained utterly defunct: In 1939 it had only between 10 and 12 local chapters.[29]

External developments proved rather unhelpful to Lindholm. Under the impact of increasing brutality towards the Jews in Germany and Hitler's foreign policy ventures, any association with Nazism across the Baltic Sea became a burden. In 1938, «in order to salvage the ideas», Lindholm decided to shift his emphasis away from symbols associated with the German brand of National Socialism. The name of the party was changed to *Svensk Socialistisk Samling* (Swedish Socialist Unity) and the

Hitler greeting abolished. Furugård's party had used both the swastika and the Vasa sheaf *(Vasakärven)* as symbols for the party. Now with the ideological change the Vasa sheaf was pushed more in the foreground as the emblem of the organization. The Vasa sheaf was the royal coat of arms used by King Gustav Vasa (1523–1560) and the symbol of unitary, absolutist royal power which in Sweden lasted from 1536 until 1818 (the death of the last Vasa). The Sieg Heil greeting was replaced by the less foreign battle cry: «We Want Sweden for the Swedes». On the whole, however, this shift was cosmetic in nature: the animosity to democracy was retained though in a more 'Swedish' form. The change at least reflects a general feature of European fascism: the primacy of one's own nation. As Juan Linz has argued in his contribution to this volume, the internationalism of the communist parties in the thirties was of a more binding nature, with Moscow as the unquestioned locus of power. To the fascists, doctrinal loyalty to Berlin and Rome (this partition is in itself significant) counted very little if such an association impeded progress at home. It should be added that in the minds of collaborators there is no necessary contradiction between collaboration with an invader and this commitment to one's own nation. Quisling's collaboration in neighboring Norway for example was always couched in terms of Norway's interests.

Colonel Ekström and the National Socialist Bloc

Among the attempts to unify the «nationals» and the divergent fascist and Nazi movements in Sweden, the most significant was the National Socialist Bloc *(National-socialistiska Blocket)* headed by Colonel Martin Ekström. Like Sigurd Furugård and Vidkun Quisling, he had also a background in the east. As a soldier in the Finnish army he served on the White side in the Civil War (1917–18) and participated in the siege of Viborg, the stronghold of the Red faction. Thereafter he went on to Estonia as a volunteer. Having organized the police in Lithuania, he returned to Sweden as head of a military garrison. Colonel Ekström's Bloc got off to a good start: he won over the remnants of the Furugård movement in Gothenburg to his cause. As mentioned, the jettisoning by this group of its own leader was in fact the first step in this direction. He also succeeded in getting the support of small fascist groups in Skåne and in Umeå in Northern Sweden. The Stockholm chapter of the SNU signalled they would join if there was no break with the Conservatives. The SNU people wanted more stringent anti-socialist propaganda in their own organization. Lindholm soon understood, however, that Ekström's Bloc aimed at making Swedish fascism more *salonfähig,* more acceptable to the traditional right. Scornfully he rejected Ekström's offer of cooperation and warned against the dangers of right-wing influence in the fascist movement.

The program of the Bloc had much in common with the earlier attempts to import fascism to Sweden, but there were a few interesting differences. First, Ekström did not advocate outright nationalization of the banks. The state should exercise 'control' over the banks but only in extreme cases ought this control to go as far as a complete take-over. The resentment against chain stores and monopolies was as conspicuous as before, the program also expressed respect for property and supported «healthy private initiative» in the economy. The position of Sweden as a Baltic power should be defended, in accordance with «the historical purpose of the nation», as the program put it.[30] The appeal of the program was primarily directed to the lower middle class, to retailers and farmers. In no way a traditional bourgeois statement, it was nevertheless on the whole more acceptable to the non-socialist parties than Lindholm's policies.

730

The most prominent fascist elements were toned down. When Ekström tried to launch his movement in January, 1934, his appearance was a fiasco. In April, the party branch in Skåne, disgusted at such amateurism, returned to the Furugård party. The publication of the newspaper *Riksposten* (The National Gazette) from 1934 to 1938 could in no way remedy this failure: Ekström soon faded into oblivion until he reappeared in his original profession, as a soldier in the Winter War in Finland 1939–40.

Per Engdahl and the Ideology of 'New Swedishness'

We have had occasion to examine the Engdahl movement before, in connection with the skirmishes leading to the joining of forces by Lindholm and Furugård in 1930. Engdahl is important in two ways: first as a representative of the ideology of 'New Swedishness', a corporativist, anti-Semitic, anti-communist and fiercely nationalist doctrine built around a cult of the person Engdahl himself; and second, because it was the only fascist movement to survive the war.

His political ideology was a curious blend of professed ideological distance to National Socialism, admiration of Mussolini and a belief in his ideology of 'New Swedishness' as the blueprint for the unification of all anti-democratic forces in Sweden, fascist or non-fascist. As Engdahl saw it, the political parties had weakened the executive power, leaving the state to a «clique of financiers, trade union bureaucrats and party loyalists who increasingly became dependent on international capital beyond the reach of national laws.»[31]

In this insistence that the corporation should not be allowed to dominate the executive, he was influenced by Mussolini: the state was the symbol of «the common good», the regulator, set on a higher level than «changing societal interests.» His own New Swedish movement was intended to fulfil the role of a mobilizing agent for this new government. There was no room for any opposition outside this movement. Anti-Semitism remained the unifying core of the movement, until, in 1946, tougher anti-defamation laws forced him to tone down his propaganda.

The Remaining Fascist or Pseudo-Fascist Fringe

On the margin of the fascist fringe there were a variety of groups promoting activism of a racialist, authoritarian nature. A survey of Swedish fascism would be incomplete without a few notes on each.

In this welter of fascist or pseudo-fascist groups and men, C. S. Dahlin was probably the most exotic. In 1927 Dahlin, who published the magazine *Fäderneslandet* (The Fatherland) founded his *National-radikala Samlingspartiet* (The National Radical Unity Party) whose aim was nothing less than to unify not only the bourgeois parties but all existing parties. Racialism, attacks on the political parties, anti-monopoly propaganda, profit-sharing schemes in the form of shares for employees and calls for the «extirpation of politics» in the trade unions mingled with appeals for decency and moralism in the press. Dahlin advocated economic protectionism and launched a «national day for the unemployed»: an occasion when all unemployed should meet the employers and ask for work. After a few skirmishes with Furugård, Dahlin faded into oblivion as unnoticed as he had entered.

Sympathy for fascism and national socialism was also apparent in the *Sveriges Fosterländska Förbund* (The Swedish Patriotic League), which was an outgrowth of a conservative student club in Stockholm, established in 1916 to discuss prospects for unifying all rightist forces. The League regarded Hitler's seizure of power as a victory of the West against 'Asiatic Bolshevism' and published the magazine The National Democrat *(Nationaldemokraten)* from 1916 to 1924 and from 1930 to 1936.

An interesting specimen of nascent clerical fascism on Swedish soil was the Rev. Ivar Rhedin's Church People's Party *(Kyrkliga Folkpartiet)*. Founded in 1930, the party was primarily an expression of a fundamentalist reaction against secularizing trends from Stockholm in the form of changed curricula for religious instruction in the schools. It immediately singled out the class struggle, the parties, the monopolies and everything threatening to the morals of the people as its main enemies. The party was fiercely pro-monarchist, defended private property and «the freedom to work,» a slogan against trade unionism, and soon came to identify with the Lapua movement in Finland. In the spring of 1932, Rhedin participated in a big rally in Helsinki at which he attacked «liberal cosmopolitanism» and the lack of «Swedishness» in his country's cultural life. In a similar vein he deplored the passivity of the church in the struggle against 'subversive' forces, and he accepted Nazi advertisements in the church journal he edited, *Gøteborg Stiftstidning* (the Gothenburg Parish Gazette). The lay revivalist congregations in Western Sweden who wanted orthodox Lutheranism to have a greater influence in the *Riksdag,* were urged to vote for Rhedin. In the 1932 general elections his party won 9,000 votes in South and South West Sweden, but this was far from sufficient to gain representation in the national assembly.[32] Rhedin was not uncritical to Hitler: the Nazi attempts to 'aryanize' the churches caught him in a dilemma. He remained sceptical towards the Nazi attacks on the Confessing Church, but fought Swedish efforts to express support for persecuted Jews in Germany. In his paper he spread the image of the good, puritan Hitler. During World War II he participated in Nazi rallies in Gothenburg, applauding German victories in the battlefield. His political activities drew criticism from ecclesiastical authorities, and on one occasion, from a court.

Another example of the affinities between the traditional right and the anti-democratic fringe is provided by the conservative student club *Heimdal* in Uppsala. This club remained affiliated with the SNU from 1918 until 1933. It left the SNU as a protest against the abandonment of democratic ideals within that organization. The break with the SNU did not imply a thorough break with the non-democratic right, however. The club invited Engdahl to speak on «After democracy, what?», and there were several attempts to reunite traditional conservatives with adherents to the anti-democratic right, including the 'New Swedes'. In 1937 one 'New Swede' and three nationals were elected to the board of the club, a move which created a stir at the time.

In the field of propaganda, fascist sentiments found a loyal protagonist in C.S. Carlberg, an engineer by education, founder of the Manheim Society *(Samfundet Manheim)* and the publishing house Svea Rike. Carlberg was the Swedish publisher of the German pictorial «Signal». Himself a wealthy man and a renowned athlete – he was a participant in the 1912 Olympics in Stockholm – he launched the magazine *Gymn* in 1928 which soon became a spokesman for an aesthetized form of body culture under the motto «Health, Character, Beauty.» This was of course no base for fascism in itself, although worship of youth, strength and physical fitness has always been integral to fascist ideology. But from 1931 the affinities to the anti-democratic right became more and more pronounced. Influenced by Elof Eriksson, the magazine published articles on race protection, glorified the simplicity of rural life, became explicitly anti-communist and anti-Semitic and sponsored public debates on race biology. Carlberg's publishing venture was instrumental in spreading the Nazi message in Sweden before, during and shortly after the war. His Manheim Society became a clearing station for the different pro-Nazi groups in Sweden. The lecture series on Nordic culture, race biology, genetics and 'evangelical Nordic faith', as one lecture was entitled, attracted quite a few intellectuals who for the most part did not dissociate themselves from Carlberg after he had turned unequivocally Nazi. Carlberg advocated a healthy farmers' class, protection for 'loyal' Swedish private initiative and urged the elimination of the 'deceptive Marxist ideology' in the trade union movement. Carlberg also ran a film studio where he showed German films barred from Sweden by censorship. As late as 1959 he wrote a poem in honor of Hitler.

Finally, pro-German sentiments were expressed through the two more official friendship associations, the National Association Sweden-Germany (Riksföreningen Sverige-Tyskland), and Svensk-Tyska Föreningen (The Swedish-German League). The former was launched in 1937 after a public invitation by most of the prominent representatives of the pro-Nazi or 'nationalist' front. The attitude taken by the Swedish press towards Germany was labelled one-sided and anti-German, a bias the association wanted to correct. Around New Year 1938 the association had 3,025 members, increasing to 5,141 at the outbreak of war with the Soviet Union.[33] The pro-Nazi orientation of the association grew more and more prominent. Warnings against the U.S.S.R. mingled with support for Franco and Chamberlain's appeasement policy. The legitimacy of Germany's claim for a return of her colonies was seen as self-evident. Czechoslovakia was an 'artificial' state formation which implied a threat to Europe through the access it opened for the Soviet Union. The League of Nations was branded as a hypocritical alliance, its sanctions against Italy as a disgrace. Despite Sweden's lack of any disputed territorial claims, she should appreciate the reasons why Germany wanted the Anschluss. Martin Niemöller's basic fault was his inability to obey, possibly caused by war injury, the association magazine alleged. The Kristallnacht pogroms in 1938, following the murder of a German diplomat in Paris, were regarded as an expression of justified rage, etc. Sweden's position in relation to her Southerly neighbor across the sea should be determined by her exports: too much moralism would obviously carry its price. A visit to Germany in 1941 by the chairman of the association, Professor H. Odeberg, prompted him to praise the lack of coercion in the Reich: indeed, according to him the limits on freedom of expression were far stricter in other comparable countries than in Nazi Germany.[34]

Explicitly National Socialist sympathies were also expressed by the journal Klingan (The Sword or 'Cutting Edge') published by Rolf A. Nystedt in Linköping. The aim of Klingan was, in a spirit of patriotism, as it said, to rally around the people's community (Folkgemenskapen), the Swedish equivalent to the German word Volksgemeinschaft. The magazine published articles on the history of National Socialism in Sweden, the white race and modern technology, the 'soul of communism' and on the inevitable erosion of democratic systems of government. The Klingan gives examples of the whole range of Nazi beliefs, from the catharsis of war to the innate strength of the Nordic race. It became one of the clearest expressions of cultural fascism in the inter-war period.[35]

The reasons impelling communists to join fascist parties have always posed intriguing questions for any comprehensive theory of fascism. In France Jacques Doriot completed his political transformation in the uniform of the Waffen SS,[36] in Sweden the communist Nils Flyg ended as a discredited leader in the twilight of treason. His fate, tragic on the personal level, is illustrative of this rare, but interesting form of political conversion.

Flyg, who belonged to the left-wing in the Swedish labor movement, became leader of the *Socialistiska Partiet* (The Socialist Party) in 1937. This party grew out of a split within the Swedish Communist Movement in 1929 over Comintern's sharpened attacks on the social democratic parties (the third period).[37] He soon turned anti-Stalinist, branding Soviet Russia just as totalitarian as Hitler's Germany. Stalin's pact with Hitler in August 1939 he saw as a desertion from the 'peace bloc', the result of a double game with Chamberlain's representatives in Moscow. The Soviet attack on Finland intensified Flyg's anti-Soviet attitude; he doubted whether it could any longer be called a socialist state. Thus far Flyg was safely within the bounds of accepted Swedish opinion. His turn towards a more pro-Nazi attitude became apparent in the late summer of 1940 when he called the British declaration of war against Germany the year before a mistake. Flyg came to see the victory of the Allied powers as nothing but a confirmation of the rule of big capital. In 1942 Flyg had talks with Germans about support for a new government in Sweden. It should be added that in the general election in 1940 the SP lost all its representatives in the legislature, a trend which was confirmed in the municipal elections two years later. In the process the party had lost its paper, and the workers in the printing shop had struck in protest against the new policies of the party. The conversion to fascist positions was completed in the brochure «The Road of the Working Class to Socialism» in 1944.[38] In his memoirs Walter Schellenberg disclosed that Flyg had accepted money from him to bolster the economy of his newspaper. In this way Flyg had become financially dependent on German sources for the continued publication of his paper.[39]

War-Time Fascism

The war greatly enhanced the power of the fascists to influence events out of proportion to their number. The situation was precarious for Sweden, surrounded as she was by belligerent nations on all sides. The usefulness of the fascists groups as spies, *agent provocateurs* or as a fifth column was too obvious to overlook. In November 1944, 12,990 fascists were registered in the police archives in Stockholm, of whom 330 were classified as dangerous.[40] In the early phases of the war, the government had to proceed with extreme caution: actions against the indigenous fascists could easily cause diplomatic ruptures with Germany. Despite the surveillance, the activity of the fascists continued unabated. Their main issue was Swedish participation in the war against the Soviet Union. The fascists issued repeated calls for Swedish endorsement of the anti-Comintern pact. In November, 1942, Lindholm was granted an audience by King Gustav V to present to him his plans for Swedish participation in the war.[41] It is also widely believed that fascists stood behind the bombing of the editorial offices of the communist newspaper *Norrskensflamman* on March 3, 1940, which killed five people in Northern Sweden. The publishers Svea Rike issued a list of names of prominent Swedish anti-fascists, complete with address, telephone numbers, and in some cases even fingerprints.

On the organizational level, there were a few re-alignments. The year 1941 saw the emergence of a new Nazi organization, *Bruna Gardet* (the Brown Guards), an offshoot from a split in Lindholm's party in 1938. Headed by A. Engström, the guards co-operated closely with the German occupation forces in Norway, crossed the border and were trained by the Germans there. In Sweden they formed armed battalions ready for action in the event of a German invasion. The guards prepared lists of persons to be arrested after an invasion and cultivated close links with the German embassy in Stockholm. In April 1944, when the foreign policy repercussions could be more easily contained, Engström was sentenced to five years imprisonment for preparations involving high treason. Throughout the war the fascists were actively recruiting soldiers to the German army. According to their own estimates, about 800 men were recruited through the *Svensk Socialistisk Samling* party, Lindholm's organization.[42] In Norway, approximately 15,000 were recruited to the front, but only about 7,000 served in combat.[43]

Per Engdahl carried on as before and formed in October 1941 his Swedish Opposition which became a leading protagonist for Swedish participation in the war on Germany's side. By 1944, electoral support for these fringe groups had dwindled to insignificance. In 1942 the Swedish Opposition publicly announced it would side with Germany in case of war. For this proclamation, the editor was sentenced to six months imprisonment for high treason.[44]

Notes on Sweden's Immunity to Mass-Scale Fascism

Why did Sweden remain so immune to mass-scale fascism?

As in Norway's case, the country *lacked most of the requisites for a successful fascist seizure of power:* there was no protracted unification process, no simultaneous occurrence of centralization and mobilization, no clash over the religious, political and cultural definition of the nation, no disputed territorial claims (the only border problem with another country concerned the Åland island in the Baltic Sea and was solved through intervention by the League of Nations in 1921.) Nor for that matter had Sweden lost a war. Hence there was no volatile segment of ex-servicemen easily mobilizable by anti-democratic activists. True, the issue of pacifism had played a role during World War I. Sympathy for the German side in the war was widespread in Sweden. On the left wing of the Social Democratic Labor party (SAP) fears that the right would align Sweden with Germany led to a peace congress in 1916 which strongly advocated continued Swedish neutrality in the war (later this vocal peace faction, mostly from the youth league, seceded from the SAP, launching its own left wing secessionist party). But in contrast with what happened in Italy in the immediate post-war period, the Swedish socialists were not expressly disdainful of the military. And the Swedish socialists were reformists. They did not, as in Italy, combine maximalist rhetoric with rejection of participation in government. The result was that despite serious hunger demonstrations in 1917–18 which probably brought the country closer to a revolution than ever before in its history,[45] the Swedish political system was not irrevocably polarized. This absence of a failed revolution attempt which later could fuel a fascist reaction is important for grasping the limited success attained by fascist use of the socialist bogey. In the turmoil following World War I, the Social Democrats threatened to resort to extra-parliamentary acts, but the constitutional crisis was soon resolved. The extension of the franchise (1918–21) and the subsequent Social Democratic ascendancy to executive power soon dampened the political tensions. Once the Social Democrats had assumed power, neither their rhetoric nor their actions could be construed as threatening either democracy or a middle class with completely different political experiences from those of their Italian and German counterparts. The Comintern affiliation later laid the communists open to charges of national unreliability, but support for the Moscow wing of the party soon declined so sharply as to quite discredit attempts to foment political *Angst* through the bogey of a communist take-over.

Equally important, foreign territorial expansion was no issue: after her participation in European power politics in the 17th century Sweden withdrew to her mainland, i.e. the Scandinavian peninsula and Finland. The territories wrested from Denmark and Norway at the apex of her imperial power (1645–1660) were smoothly incorporated, and Finland, which was linguistically distinct, was ceded in 1809. The Baltic Sea continued to be of prime interest for Swedish security and commercial interests, but calls for a return to a heroic past by the fascists evoked only mild amusement. It is worth noting that imperial legacy, which occupied such a prominent role in the political symbolism of the fascist movements in Germany and Italy, had no impact whatsoever in Sweden at large and was on the whole not much used in the propaganda of the fascist groups. Likewise, although anti-Semitism did reach a rather large proportion of the population, at least in comparison with Norway and Denmark, it had little to thrive on as a mass movement. Despite the demonstrations against Jewish immigration, the racialist undercurrents both among the Agrarians and the Conservatives and the use of the Jew as the embodiment of all ills, anti-Semitism could not be used as a mobilizing issue the way it was in Germany and Austria. The Jews had been integrated into Swedish life a long time and were not disproportionately represented in politically sensitive institutions like banking, publishing or academic life.

In addition to these more general reasons why Sweden was less prone to anti-democratic activism of the fascist kind than the Central European and Mediterranean powers, there were also a few more specific factors. In ascending order of importance, I would argue the following:

1. The Sheer Amateurishness of the Fascist Leadership

If broader social structures gave Swedish fascists little to exploit, the opportunities which did exist were largely wasted by the low-calibre leadership in the fascist groups. Sweden had a long tradition of admiration for German culture and science; there had been a strong lobby in favor of Swedish entry on the side of Germany in World War I, and the authoritarian and racialist sentiments on the right were stronger than in her neighbors. Even so, the fascists in Sweden never succeeded in getting rid of their image as importers of a foreign doctrine. They had little to show for themselves either in the way of doctrinal innovations or in organizational skills (the only exception may be their use of the immigration issue which gave them a lever by which to reach down into popular prejudices). On the whole, Swedish fascism remained a playground for marginal men. This marginality made for continuous internal strife which further aggravated their powerlessness.

2. Highly Effective Crisis Management

The Social Democratic Minister of Finance Ernst Wigforss was one of the first to apply deficit spending (deliberately created for expansionary purposes) in order to fight the slump. In fact, in an imaginative anticipation of Keynesian thinking, Wigforss had advocated deficit budgeting as early as the 1910's [46] The compromise with the Agrarians traded a much expanded public works program to combat high unemployment with subsidies for agriculture. It provided the political foundation for a concerted attack on the depression. By showing that the democratic parties were not at a loss in handling the problems and by gradually alleviating the crisis, the anti-depression policies pre-empted political space among the agricultural producers and in the middle classes which could have left room for anti-democratic agitation. That the Agrarians were not alien to agrarian romanticism with racialist overtones has been shown above. Prolonged economic misery could have activated these sentiments. It is doubtful, however, whether the Swedish farmers could ever have furnished so fertile a recruiting ground for Nazis as the German farmers did. The Swedish farmers had not been subjected to the same prolonged Junker dominance, organizationally and ideologically, as their German brethren, nor was there any feudal remnants of the East Elbian kind in Sweden. Comparisons with Germany are instructive also with regard to the middle sector. There was no resonance in the Swedish middle classes for the *völkisch*, anti-capitalist reaction to modernity which proved so fateful in preparing the ground for Nazism in these strata in the Weimar Republic. In contrast to Germany, Sweden had a liberal middle. The liberal transitional phase was short but vigorous; it has been argued that in political innovation and originality it rivalled the subsequent Social Democratic reforms.[47] By the same token, Swedish industrialization diverged from the German pattern in several ways crucial to later propensities for régime instability: the artisan classes and the retailers were commercialized without leaving vestiges of pre-industrial, authoritarian sentiments. These branches were not artificially protected from intrusion of market forces by the state to serve as defense barriers against the political demands of the working class (as was the purpose of the policy of *Sozialprotektionismus* in the Bismarckian Reich).[48] Thus a series of structural preconditions for the preservation of a 'feudalized' social consciousness were removed. A flare-up of latent anti-democratic sentiment in times of social duress became a more distant possibility.

3. The Success of the Farmer-Worker Alliance

Without analyzing the course of Swedish political development in full,[49] the comparison with Germany can be taken one step further. A compromise between farmers and workers never came about in Germany. This fact accounts for much of the inherent instability of the Weimar period and can only be understood as the result of deep-seated ideological animosities in both camps. In Sweden, the increasingly rigid segmentation characteristic of the Weimar republic was notably absent. The political system was more open to new party configurations than in Germany. Conflict resolution through parliament worked because of this basic malleability of the alliance structure.

Inside the farmers' organizations there was a significant shift away from the traditional leadership in the period immediately preceding the deal with the Social Democrats. The established leadership, linked to the wealthy farmers in the southern part of the country, was generally conservative in outlook; tariff protection, and higher prices to the producers resulting from this measure, became the cornerstones of their agricultural policy. When they were replaced by a more liberal brand of farmers who acted more as representatives of the smallholders, the chances for a compromise with the Left increased immediately. This new leadership could identify with the plight of

737

the workers; many people on the smaller farms found themselves in the same position. The new leaders did not see themselves purely as representatives of producer's interests against consumers. Rather, they saw the solution to the crisis in a unification of all the agricultural producers, including the farm workers. Agriculture would be better able to compete on the market. What was required was rationalization, specialization and sales co-operatives. The new leadership rejected tariff protection as a means of increasing their income and thereby departed significantly from the traditional conservative agricultural policy. Compared to the importance of the tariff issue in preserving the supremacy of the Junkers' interests over those of the German peasantry, this modern attitude of the Swedish farmers is striking and shows their independence of larger landowner groups.[50] This political maneuverability was made possible by the lack of deeper tensions in Swedish society. While in Finland the bitter political memories from the Civil War were superimposed on the agricultural depression and were instrumental in the rise of the Lapua, in Sweden there was no such barrier against seeking new alliance partners.

On the socialist side co-operation was made possible by the unorthodox view on agricultural matters taken by the SAP (The Social Democratic Labor Party). In Germany, the crude adaptation of the Marxist law of concentration to agriculture had triggered fears in rural communities that land under a SPD government would be nationalized. As late as the 1920's the SPD remained largely insensitive to the problems of agriculture and were unable to make any inroads in the farmer groups in the elections.[51] The Swedish socialists, on the other hand, left this ideological luggage behind as early as around 1900; any nationalization scheme was abandoned and respect for the tiller's property proclaimed. From each side, then, the conditions were ripe: what proved impossible in Germany became an adequate crisis response in Sweden, a stabilizing political move which was indicative of the consensus on democratic procedures and which left no room for any fascist alternatives.

Bibliographic References

The literature on Swedish fascism is sparse. To my knowledge there is no professional sociological inquiry into the social composition of the diverse fascist groups, nor any extensive archive like the ones available in Norway and Denmark which would make such an analysis possible. An opportunity might present itself in the archives (referred to above), compiled by the secret police during the war, but these archives of course suffer from serious methodological shortcomings, imprecision in the use of occupational categories, unsystematic procedures for determining who would qualify for inclusion, etc.

The standard work on the subject is Eric Wärenstam, *Fascismen och nazismen i Sverige 1920–1940* (Fascism and Nazism in Sweden 1920–1940). (Stockholm: Almqvist & Wiksell 1970). A paperback edition was published in 1972 which includes a new chapter on the fascist movements during World War II. This is a controversial book, but used cautiously it provides a wealth of material. This essay is largely based on this work with added information from a survey article by Olga W. Tschernischewa, «Faschistische Strömungen und Organisationen in Schweden bis zum Ende des zweiten Weltkrieges», *Nord-Europa Studien. Wissenschaftliche Zeitschrift der Ernst Moritz Arndt-Universität*, Griefswald, DDR, 7, 1974, pp. 41–59. I am indebted to Hans Fredrik Dahl for calling my attention to this work. The lack of scholarly studies is to a certain extent compensated by an extensive journalistic literature. The most comprehensive is A. Sastamoinen, *Hitler's svenska förtrupper* (Hitler's Avantgarde), published in Stockholm in 1947. The same author published a book on Neo-Nazism in 1962 *(Nynazismen)*. A short history of the movements is found in K. Johansson, *Fascism, nazism, racism* (Malmö 1966). German efforts to influence Swedish opinion is described in Å. Thulstrup, *Med lock och pock. Tyska forsök att påverka svensk opinion 1933–45* (Stockholm 1962). (By Hook or by Crook: German Efforts to Sway Swedish Opinion 1933–45). The Swedish Communist party issued several pamphlets on inter-war fascism in Sweden: A Wretling, *Nationalsocialismen i svensk upplaga* (National Socialism – the Swedish Design) (Stockholm 1932), K. Senander, *Nationalsocialismen – arbetarklassens dödsfiende* (National Socialism – The Deadly Enemy of the Working Class) (Kristianstad 1932). Contemporary attempts to come to grips with the fascist phenomenon include N. Holmberg, *I Hitler's fotspår* (In Hitler's Footsteps) (Stockholm 1934) and A. Möller, *Svensk nazism* (Swedish Nazism), (Stockholm 1935). Another broad survey is H. Carlsson, *Nazismen i Sverige* (Nazism in Sweden) which appeared in 1942, the same year as K. Wirén, *Svensk nazism utan mask* (Swedish Nazism Unmasked). The publicist and Professor of medicine Israel Holmgren who waged an incessant war on the extreme right, published two brochures *Nazisthelvetet* (The Nazi Inferno) and *Vart syfter den svenska nazismen?* (What Are the Aims of Swedish Nazism?), published in 1941 and 1942 respectively. The Tschernischewa article gives several references to pamphlets issued by the fascists themselves. Further bibliographical aid is provided in Wärenstam's book.

As to the affinities between the traditional right and fascism, the case of the young nationals is described by Eric Wärenstam in his second treatise on the period: *Sveriges Nationella Ungdomsförbund och Högern 1928–1934* (The Swedish National Youth League and the Conservatives 1928–1934) (Stockholm 1965). The ideological developments in the Agrarian and Conservative parties have been subjected to a thorough analysis by Rolf Torstendal in his *Mellan nykonservatism och liberalism. Idébrytningar inom högern och bondepartierna 1918–1934*. (Between Neo-conservatism and Liberalism: Clashes of Ideas in the Conservative and Agrarian Parties 1918–1934) (Studia Historica Uppsaliensia XXIX. Scandinavian University Books, Uppsala 1969.)

NOTES

* Editorial assistance and helpful comments on earlier drafts by Lars Alldén, Michael J. Clark, Hans Fredrik Dahl and Jan Petter Myklebust are gratefully aknowledged.

[1] This is not to deny that fragments of the original movements have lingered on until the present day. In an article entitled «Fascism och nazism i Lund» in the Lund student magazine *Lundagård* (1974), Kenneth Winsborg has traced several fascist or pseudo-fascist organizations still in existence. They are mostly confined to the Southern Swedish towns of Lund and Malmö. A short guide to the present fascist fringe: In the general elections in 1973 a party called *Svenska Folkets Väl* («Swedish People's Welfare Party») participated with two lists of candidates in Southern Sweden. The party is a curious blend of fascist and plainly reactionary views. It advocates restrictions on immigration, racial purity, cutbacks in foreign aid, etc., but is not entirely in favor of a corporate economy. The party manifesto attacks the non-socialist parties and the Social Democrats alike. Another explicitly fascist organization working for the reorganization of the economy along corporativist lines is headed by Per Engdahl, the only remaining figure from the inter-war period still active (his activities will be discussed in a later section). Today, his movement is called *Nysvenska rörelsen* (The New Swedish Movement) and has gone

through a series of transformations, mostly in name. The paper published by this organization, *Vägen Framåt* (The Way Forward), is for the most part devoted to attacks on the democratic parties, international capital and Bolshevism. The Swedish National League *(Sveriges Nationelle Förbund)* which was quite active in the thirties is still in existence. Then the SNF could be seen as the right wing of Swedish fascism, drawing its social support from the upper classes. Today it tries to present a more popular image, describing itself as a «cultural conservative movement fighting communism even in its most specious democratic guises in order to protect Christianity, a strong state authority, and defense». The most extreme of these fringe organizations is the *Nordiska Rikspartiet* (NRP) (The Nordic Reich Party). In its program élitist attitudes mingle with a generous use of expletives to characterize the democratic organizations. The party, mostly the creation of one man, published the magazine *Nordisk Kamp* (Nordic Struggle). All these parties are of course utterly insignificant in a wider context, but fascists were active handing out leaflets in the Lund student union elections as late as 1971. With increasing tension between immigrant workers and the indigenous population in recent years there have been signs of a reactivation of Swedish fascist or Nazi groups. For a journalistic survey of the contemporary fascist scene, although with no indications of sources, see D. Eisenberg, *The Re-Emergence of Fascism*, chapter IX, pp. 221–237 (New York 1967).

[2] A. Sastamoinen, *Nynazismen* (Stockholm 1962) p. 10, and H. Carlsson, *Nazismen i Sverige* (Stockholm 1942) p. 199, ff.

[3] Olle Nyman, *Krisuppgörelsen mellan socialdemocraterna och bondeförbundet* (The Crisis Agreement Between the Social Democrats and the Agrarian League. Skrifter utg. av Statsvetenskapelige Föreningen i Uppsala, 119, 1944. Cf. also Hans Fredrik Dahl, *et al.*, «Krisen og det politiske liv», i *Kriser och krispolitik i Norden under mellankrigstiden* (Crises and Crisis-politics in the Nordic Countries in the Inter-War Period) (Uppsala 1974), pp. 71–103, esp. p. 96.

[4] O.W. Tschernischewa, 'Faschistische Strömungen und Organisationen in Schweden bis zum Ende des Zweiten Weltkrieges», *Nord-Europa Studien*, 7, 1974, p. 47.

[5] Cf. the following: Conservatism «must eradicate *(mala sønder)* the democratic ideology and replace it with its own positive concepts». (Jarl Hjalmarson). Discussing the new SNU program in 1929, Hjalmarson argued that the party should not bind itself to democracy, an ideology which he said is «completely alien» to conservatism. R. Torstendal, review of Eric Wärenstam, «Sveriges Nationella ungdomsforbund och högern,» (The SNU and the Conservatives) i *Historisk Tidskrift*, 4, 1966, p. 474.

[6] R. Torstendal, *Mellan nykonservatism och liberalism* (Between New Conservatism and Liberalism) (Uppsala 1969), p. 117. Torstendal's analysis is based on a close reading of the official Conservative party documents. In his review of the book Nils Elvander pointed out that Torstendal might face a problem of representativeness: how did Torstendal know that the documents, more than the party's newspapers, reflect the ideological line of the party? Another scholar, Donald Söderlind, using the newspapers as his source, has a different opinion from Torstendal's. Söderlind states that criticism of democracy abated in the early 20's. He interprets this as a sign of higher estimation of democracy in the party. Nils Elvander, «Högerideologier i mellankrigstid». Review of Torstendal, *Historisk Tidskrift*, 4, 1969, p. 510.

[7] Eric Wärenstam, *Fascismen och nazismen i Sverige* (Paperback edition, Stockholm 1972), p. 54 & 55, and Torstendal, *Mellan nykonservatism . . ., op.cit.*, p. 149.

[8] Torstendal, *op.cit.*, p. 214.

[9] Per Lysander, «Den akademiska fascismen», (Academic Fascism) *Ord & Bild*, 1–2, 1972, p. 86.

[10] Tschernischewa, *op.cit.*, p. 49.

[11] Wärenstam, *op.cit.*, p. 130ff.

[12] T. Karlbom, *Den svenska fackföreningsrörelsen*, (The Swedish Trade Union Movement). (Stockholm 1955), p. 280.

[13] P.-E. Back, *En klass i uppbrott. Den fackliga lantarbetarrörelsens uppkomst och utvecling*, (A Class in Transition. The Foundation of the Trade Union of Rural Workers), (Malmö 1961).

[14] J. Björgum *et al.*, «Krisen og arbeiderbevegelsen», (The Crisis and the Labor Movement) p. 261, in *Kriser och krispolitik, op.cit.*

[15] They were: Sven Hedin, the explorer and geographer, known for his pro-German attitude during World War I; Professors Bengt Lidforss and Herman Lundborg, both interested in genetic issues, but sharing relatively few other similarities with fascist ideology; Mauritz Rydgren and Barthold Lundgren who in the early decades of the century became known as fanatical anti-Semites. Lundgren published an anti-Semitic magazine in Gothenburg called *Vidi* which later influenced one of the Furugård brothers (published 1913–31). Caution should be exercised in equating these writings with fascism. Hedin never joined a fascist party, and Lidforss inspired the nascent socialist movement in Sweden. But they are all indicative of an important feature of Swedish academic life and culture in this period: the admiration for German science and scholarship. There were those whom this admiration would render susceptible to Nazi or more generally fascist sympathies.

[16] R. Kjellén, «Nationalitetsidén» (The Idea of Nationality) in *Politiska essayer* (Stockholm 1914), p. 8ff, 24ff. For a general discussion of Kjellén's political philosophy, see Walter Vogel, «Kjellén, Rudolf», *Encyclopedia of the Social Sciences,* vol. VII–VIII (New York: MacMillan Company 1932), p. 576, and Nils Elvander's extensive discussion, «Rudolf Kjellén och national-socialismen», (Rudolf Kjellén and National Socialism), *Statsvetenskaplig Tidskrift,* 1, 1966, pp. 15–41.

[17] *Politiska essayer,* II, p. 32, quoted from Elvander, *ibid,* p.21.

[18] The Quisling story is found in Sverre Hartmann, *Förer uten folk. Quisling som politisk og psykologisk problem* (Leader Without People. Quisling as a Politial and Psychological Problem), (Oslo 1959), p. 91 ff.

[19] Wärenstam, *op.cit.,* p. 64.

[20] In a private letter to Hedengren, Lindholm thought the German attack on Norway had destroyed all chances for his party in Sweden. See Wärenstam, *op.cit.,* p. 138.

[21] Wärenstam, *op.cit.,* p. 68. In 1928 one incident shed light on military uneasiness about the reforms. A sergeant who had just lost his commission physically attacked Per Albin Hansson, the Minister of Defense, in public. There is reason to believe that while the lower officers joined Lindholm's party, the higher ranks tended towards the official friendship organizations which gradually became more and more Pro-Nazi. For a discussion of these organizations, see pp. 518ff. The Swedish-German League seems to have held particular attractions for officers of higher rank. Tschernischewa writes, *op.cit.,* p. 51, that in this society there were 69 officers of higher rank, of whom several were generals and admirals. The fascist journal «Den Svenske» reported that «a significant part of the higher echelons of the Swedish armed forces were either Nazi themselves or harbored Nazi sympathies». See I. Holmgren, *Nazisthelvetet* (Stockholm 1941). There is no way to validate these claims, and in absence of more reliable data these assertions should be regarded with suspicion. In 1931 a scandal involving General Bror Munck focused on the unrest within the military. A voluntary military formation led by him had illegally received weapons from Germany. About 2,000 men were thus armed to aid the Stockholm police in fighting subversive elements. The group was not affiliated with the SFKO and its activities seem to have been rather restricted, but the knowledge of the Stockholm police chief about this private army and his acquiesence became a scandal. Even a cabinet minister seems to have known about it. The banker A. W. Högman who was actively supporting the SFKO, furnished some of the arms. Vigilante groups of this kind were outlawed in 1935. This law was used to prosecute attempts to establish uniformed protection squads for the fascist parties. In 1933 a law was passed making it illegal to wear uniforms for political purposes. Wärenstam, *op.cit.,* 84 *passim* and Tschernischewa, *op.cit.,* p. 50.

[22] Wärenstam, *op.cit.,* p. 72.

[23] *Ibid,* p.75.

[24] *Ibid,* p.81.

[25] *Ibid,* p. 98. But no further sources for these assertions are given.

[26] *Ny Dag,* Stockholm, March 16, 1933, quoted in Tschernischewa, *op.cit.,* p. 53.

[27] Wärenstam, *op.cit.,* p. 105.

[28] In May, 1938, Lindholm presented a petition signed by 26,500 people demanding Swedish withdrawal from the League of Nations. Similar efforts were initiated by the Swedish National League. Tschernischewa, *op.cit.* p. 50.

[29] Carlsson, *op.cit.*, p. 157, quoted in Tschernischewa, *op.cit.*, p. 45.

[30] Wärenstam, *op.cit.*, p. 146.

[31] *Ibid*, p. 151.

[32] *Ibid*, p. 171.

[33] *Ibid*, p. 193.

[34] *Ibid*, p. 200.

[35] Cf. Britt Hultén, «Kulturell Beredskap. 30-talet och tidsskrifterna» (Cultural Alert – The Thirties and the Periodicals) *Ord & Bild*, 7/1972, p. 378.

[36] For discussions of Doriot, see Gilbert Allardyce, «The Political Transition of Jacques Doriot», in *Journal of Contemporary History*, vol. 1, No, 1, 1966 (in book form, Harper, New York, 1966, pp. 56–75), and on his activities during the war: Pascal Ory, *Les collaborateurs 1940–1945* (Paris, 1977).

[37] A good treatment of the party's pre-collaboration history is given by Bernt Kennerstrøm, *Mellan två internationaler. Socialistiska Partiet, 1929–37* (Between two Internationals. The Socialist Party 1929–37) (Lund, 1974).

[38] *Arbetarklassens väg till socialismen* (The Working Class' Road to Socialism) (Stockholm, 1944). Se also Tschernischewa, *op.cit.*, pp. 55–56.

[39] Walter Schellenberg, *The Schellenberg Memoirs*, Foreword by Alan Bullock (London, 1956) and Wärenstam, *op.cit.*, p. 36.

[40] Mert Kubu, *Gustaf Möllers hemliga polis. En bok om spionaget i Sverige under världskriget* (Gustav Möller's Secret Police) (Stockholm, 1971), p. 38.

[41] Ture Nerman, *Sverige i beredskap* (Sweden on the Alert) (Stockholm, 1942), quoted in Tschernischewa, *op.cit.*, p. 56.

[42] A. Sastamoinen, *Hitler's svenska förtrupper, op.cit.*, p. 112.

[43] Svein Blindheim, *Nordmenn under Hitlers fane* (Norwegians under Hitler's Banner) (Oslo, 1977). About 8,000 Danes fought on the German side in Soviet Russia, of whom 4,240 were killed in action. Of the 7,000 Norwegians serving on the East front about 1,000 fell in battle.

[44] Sastamoinen, *op.cit.* p. 9.

[45] Accounts of this turbulent period are found in S. Klockare, *Svenska revolutionen 1917–1918* (Stockholm, 1967) and H. Arvidsson (ed.) *Revolutionen i Sverige 1917–1924* (The Revolution in Sweden 1917–1924) (Gothenburg, 1972).

[46] D. Winch, «The Keynesian Revolution in Sweden», in *The Journal of Political Economy* LXXIV, 2 (1966), pp. 168–76.

[47] This is the point of Douglas Verney's «The Foundations of Modern Sweden: The Swift Rise and Fall of Swedish Liberalism», in *Political Studies*, XX, no. 1, pp. 42–59. His views are challenged by Barbara G. Haskel in her discussion of the relative innovatoriness of the Liberal and Social Democratic governments: «What is Innovation? Sweden's Liberals, Social Democrats and Political Creativity», in *Political Studies*, vol. XX, no. 3, pp. 306–310.

[48] For a discussion of the role of the middle sector in Germany in historical perspectives and the policy of social protectionism, see Heinrich A. Winkler's important study, *Mittelstand, Demokratie und Nationalsozialismus. Die politische Entwicklung von Handwerk und Kleinhandel in der Weimarer Republik* (Cologne 1972).

[49] This is done admirably within the framework of Barrington Moore's models by F.G. Castles, «Barrington Moore's Thesis and Swedish Political Development» in *Government and Opposition*, volume 8, no. 3, 1973, pp. 313–331.

[50] For a discussion of the SPD agricultural policies, the tariff issue as a lever by which the Junkers forged the rye-iron alliance in the Bismarckian *Reich* and their domination of the smaller German agricultural producers, see A. Gerschenkron, *Bread and Democracy in Germany* (Los Angeles 1943).

[51] The shifting political alignments within the Swedish agricultural organizations as a precondition for the compromise with the Social Democrats is discussed by P. Thullberg, 'Bönderna blir konsumenter», (The Farmers Turn Consumers) in *Ord & Bild*, 3, 1972, pp. 144–150. See also chapter V of *Kriser och Krispolitik, op.cit.* pp. 155–204, which deals with the agricultural depression in Scandinavia in a comparative perspective.

Nazism in Iceland*

ASGEIR GUDMUNDSSON

By 1932 the Great Depression had started to make itself felt in Iceland. The economy of the country depended almost exclusively upon the export of fish products. When the world was hit by the depression and most nations insisted on trading on a quota basis, such a one-sided economy proved fatal. Prices for Icelandic export products dropped considerably and hence the whole economy suffered. In the wake of the depression came great unemployment and a disrupted labor market along with an increasingly intense class struggle.

The Icelandic Nationalist Movement

In the years that followed various people began to voice their angry discontent with the existing political parties and began to put forward their own solutions to the problems facing the country. The discontented voices considered the political parties to have failed in solving the problems of the economy and talked of establishing a new party. One of these dissatisfied people was the owner of a large farm in the North. Early in the year of 1932 he travelled to Reykjavik where he met with some people who shared his opinions. At these meetings the current political situation was discussed as was the possibility of founding a new party which would devote itself to improving the economy.[1]

The result of these talks was a pamphlet published by the farmer. In this pamphlet he expressed his opinions on the prevailing political party system which he believed to be misguided and argued instead for a party that should unite the nation. Furthermore, the pamphlet contained a draft for the platform of the new party, focusing only on the restructuring of the economy on a 'nationalist' basis.[2]

In March 1933, the attempts to form a new party made some progress. Three men offered themselves as the founding fathers: the above-mentioned prosperous farmer, a Reykjavik stamp-dealer with German business connections, and a young man who had just completed his studies in Germany. The new party which was founded in April 1933 was called the Icelandic Nationalist Movement. The 23 articles that made up the platform all started out with the words: «We demand ...»; and of these 23, five clearly showed Nazi influence. The establishment of a powerful government to maintain law and order was demanded. The race was to be kept clean from hereditary diseases. National health was to be protected and strengthened by methods of racial selection and breeding *(Rassenhygiene, Eugenik)*. The welfare of the nation was to be placed above both private and party interests. An understanding and sympathy was to be cultivated between all classes of society; and finally, a compulsory labor duty for all citizens was to be initiated.[3]

The rest of the platform, which among other things dealt with the economic situation, makes it doubtful whether the Icelandic Nationalist Movement was a

743

genuine Nazi party in a strict sense. This doubt is heightened by an examination of the motives inducing age groups to join. The movement consisted of two different age-groups. The first consisted of middle-aged men, many of whom belonged to the Independence party (the biggest political party, conservative). They found their party too weak in the struggle against communism and wanted to hoist the banner of nationalism, as well as to improve the economy. This was the old-fashioned nationalist wing. The second group, on the other hand, was made up of young men who were either in their early twenties or still teenagers; they were the enthusiasts who admired the theories and the policy of the German Nazis.

Though not institutionalized, the Nationalist Movement was closely connected with the Independence party through multiple membership affiliations: a substantial number of members of the Independence party also joined the Nationalist Movement. The main reason for the overlapping membership of the two parties was the resolute anti-communist stand which they had both taken. Accordingly, *Morgunbladid* (The Morning Paper), the largest daily newspaper and one which supported the Independence party, received the Nationalist Movement with great sympathy. The paper asserted that the aim of the Nationalist Movement was to fight against the communist and other destructive foreign ideologies.[4] The reception in the rest of the press, i. e. the party organs of the Social Democratic party, the Progressive party (a farmers' party) and the Communist party was less friendly. They did not hesitate to declare that the Nationalist Movement had an alien policy, an alien sign (the swastika), and a platform based on violence.

The Nationalist Movement announced its desire to abolish the other political parties. However, the Nationalist Movement's papers concentrated mainly on the danger of communism which in their opinion intended to overthrow the Icelandic social system with the aid of Jewish capital coming from Russia. The goal of the Nationalist Movement was the total extermination of communism.[5] In sum, the Nationalist Movement was a response both to the poor economic conditions prevailing in Iceland in the early thirties and to the Icelandic Communist party which had been founded in 1930.

The German influence on the Nationalist Movement was obvious. Its members adopted the swastika as their sign and freely expressed their admiration for Adolf Hitler, «the poor common man who rescued Germany from her enemies.»[6] The Nationalists believed that the history of Nazism was the story of the miraculous resurrection of the German people from its humiliation and disgrace. «The history of Nazism proves that when an entire nation rises up against Marxism and communism guided by the true principles and goals of nationalism, then nothing can stop it.»[7] Furthermore, the Nationalist Movement asserted that the «measures which Germany had taken against the Jews» were justified and were in fact nothing but self-defense.[8] In January 1934, the Nationalist Movement published a pamphlet containing the speech made by Adolf Hitler on the occasion of Germany's resignation from the League of Nations shortly after the Nazi seizure of power.[9]

As was mentioned earlier, the Icelandic Nationalist Movement was established in April of 1933. The new party made its first public appearance on April 23, 1933. On that day a meeting of communists interested in establishing a common front with the Social Democrats was held in Reykjavik. A group of young Nationalists wearing swastikas harassed the attending members and some fighting broke out. Later members of the Nationalist Movement marched through the streets of the town under the Icelandic flag.[10]

Still, the party did not really begin to function until the following month, when meetings were organized throughout the country and an office was opened in Reykjavik. Funds for these operations were raised by a group of contributing members. Great optimism flourished in the Nationalist camp and it was commonly believed that the movement enjoyed tremendous popularity throughout the country and would soon replace the other political parties.[11] However, this optimism later proved to be unfounded.

The supreme authority in the Nationalist Movement rested with the General Council which consisted of five men. Ironically, the first exertion of this power was the confiscation of party propaganda. In May of 1933 the movement started the publication of two papers: *Íslensk endurreisn* (Icelandic Resurrection) and *Ákæran* (The Charge). Both papers were decorated with a swastika just below their titles. The former was published by the middle-aged members of the party, while the latter was run by the young men of the marching squad which had been organized to maintain law and order at the meetings of the Nationalist Movement. The *Ákæran* proclaimed itself to be «a weapon in the hands of the Icelandic nation in its fight against Marxism, capitalism and oppression of any kind.»[12] *Ákæran* was far more extremist than *Íslensk endurreisn* and thus the difference between the two papers reflected the difference between the two age groups. The General Council was quick to react against the extremists in the movement, and in June of 1933 the 2nd edition of *Ákæran* was confiscated because the paper savagely attacked one of the leaders of the Independence party by accusing him of embezzlement. In addition to this the paper blamed the Independence party as a whole for having allowed communism to enter Icelandic society.[13]

As a result of the confiscation the relationship between the General Council and the young members of the party became rather uneasy although everything seemed calm on the surface. The showdown did not come until the end of 1933.

A municipal election was to be held in Reykjavik in January, 1934. The General Council decided to cooperate in the forthcoming election with the Independence party which held a majority in the City Council in return for the nomination of two supporters of the Nationalist Movement, who also belonged to the Independence party, to safe places on the Independence party election list.[14] A number of Nationalists, particularly the young ones, refused to comply with the decision of the council to cooperate with the Independence party during the municipal elections. They blamed the General Council for having sold out to an unrelated political party and went on to secede from the Nationalist Movement and to form a party of their own. On January 2, 1934, they established the Icelandic Nationalist party which ran a separate list in the municipal election.[15] The new party received 399 votes (2.8 per cent) and failed to get a candidate elected.

In March of 1934 the Icelandic Nationalist Movement and the Icelandic Nationalist party merged to form a single party: the Nationalist party.[16] In reality the merger meant that the Icelandic Nationalist Movement no longer existed and most of its middle-aged members went back to the Independence party, but some, among them the three above-mentioned founding fathers of the movement, dropped out of politics altogether.

The Nationalist Party

The ideology expressed by the Nationalist party was a variation of the earlier platform. Above all, the Nationalist party wanted to protect Icelandic ethnic purity by taking radical measures against degeneration, which in fact meant the sterilization of anyone suffering from a hereditary disease or of parents who were unfit to raise their children. The Nationalists who adhered to the racist theories of the German Nazis asserted that the Aryan race was one of the most perfect in the world. Accordingly, the Nationalist papers were markedly anti-Semitic. They attacked artists of Jewish descent and insinuated that various Icelandic political leaders of foreign descent had Jewish blood in their veins. The Nationalists further demanded that the interests of the nation as a whole should always have priority over the interests of individuals and classes, while the party also wanted to preserve the traditions of Icelandic agriculture and protect the farms against dilapidation, mortgage entanglements, and speculation to make sure that they stayed in the hands of independent farmers as their ancestral homes. The Nationalist party also exhibited traces of corporatism in its ideology, advocating common associations of employers and workers. Workers were to be given a share in the profit of their companies wherever this was possible. The class struggle was to be abolished.

The Nationalists demanded an end to all undeserved speculative profits and the abolition of usurious rates on loans. A compulsory labor duty was to be established in the interests of the nation as a whole: it was to improve young people's morals and feelings of responsibility, and to give them a better opportunity for education, physical exercise, and healthy habits of living.

Another part of the Nationalists' policy was to increase government support for new industries in order to create new jobs. In their opinion the government had a duty to provide everybody who wanted to work with a job and a decent standard of living. Furthermore, the state was supposed to supervise the economy, especially those parts of it which were kept going by government loans.

The Nationalists were totally opposed to parliamentarism. They wanted to see the *Allting* (the Icelandic national assembly) abolished and replaced by a corporate state based on peace and justice, where no internal disputes existed and the whole nation took care of its interests by behaving like a single individual. [17]

The Icelandic Nationalist platform can be compared to the program of its Danish counterpart as it is found in a book called *National Socialism* by Fritz Clausen, [18] leader of the Danish Nazis at that time (translated into Icelandic and published in 1936). It appears that the above-mentioned parts of the Icelandic platform by and large conform with Clausen's work on National Socialism, making the Icelandic Nationalist party a clear manifestation of the political currents of corporatism, extreme nationalism, racialism and anti-Marxism which made up the phenomenon of inter-war fascism. In addition, the Icelandic Nationalist platform contained noble platitudes about the Nationalists' desire to make people believe in their country, their own future, man's potential goodness, and finally a perfect peace and brotherhood, not only between nations, but also between individuals. The Nationalists defined their aims in the following way: «Our motto is justice, freedom and peace. That is what we stand for. Armed with this motto and the hammer of Thor which symbolizes the power of a united nation, we shall take up the fight for the best of all causes.» [19]

Various Icelandic Nationalists regarded their work as a continuation of Iceland's struggle for independence in the 19th century. Accordingly, they claimed to stand close to the *Fjølnir* (a periodical published by Icelandic intellectuals 1835–47) group and Jón Sigurdsson, the renowned leader of the 19th century fight for independence.[20]

The operations of the Nationalist party began in the spring of 1934 with the publication of *Ísland* (Iceland), the party paper. *Ísland* was soon followed by another publication of a similar kind: a periodical called *Mjølnir* (the name of Thor's hammer, meaning 'he who crushes') issued by the Nationalist Student Association. The party operations were mainly devoted to publications, meetings, and work in the local divisions. The Nationalists celebrated the 1st of May with their marching squad parading through the streets of Reykjavik led by the Icelandic flag and two swastikas. Finally the celebrations were concluded by a downtown rally.

Like the German Nazis, the Icelandic Nationalists were opposed to class struggle of any kind. For instance, their 1st of May slogan read: «The motto of today is unity and equality between the classes. Our aim is a united nation, strong and active.»[21] For the occasion the marching squad wore uniforms which consisted of a gray shirt, black trousers, a necktie, a leather strap over the shoulder and an armband with a red swastika. The participation of the marching squad in the 1st of May celebrations came to be a matter of routine in the operations of the party and did not cease until 1938.

The Icelandic Nationalist party differed from other Nazi parties in that it did not have a particular leader. During its five years of existence no less than four men served as party leaders. Furthermore, the party never made use of any violent tactics to accomplish its goals. In March 1936, the police ransacked the headquarters of the party but nothing was discovered and the case was dismissed. It was believed at the time that the police had expected to find arms in the office of the Nationalist party.[22]

In the fall of 1936, however, the Nationalists discovered quite a sensational weapon. Somehow they managed to get hold of a diary which the Icelandic Minister of Finance had kept in 1935 when travelling abroad on behalf of the government to secure foreign loans. In September of 1936 the Nationalists published bits and pieces from the diary in their party paper, although it contained information about the foreign borrowing of the government and various other items of a strictly confidential nature.[23] As a result of this, the Nationalist paper was confiscated and three members of the party were taken into custody. However, the police neither discovered the culprits nor the missing diary, and three days later the men were released. This affair turned out to be a great source of publicity for the Nationalist party which followed it up by organizing a protest meeting two days after the arrests. The Minister of Justice responded by prosecuting seven men who were accused of high treason for having published classified government papers, but eventually all seven were acquitted.[24]

The Support for Icelandic Nazism: Electoral Base and Membership Figures

The public response to the Nationalist party can be measured in two ways; in the first place by noting the number of votes which the party received in municipal and *Allting* elections, and secondly by counting the actual party members. As was mentioned earlier, in January 1934 the Nationalist party received 2.8 per cent of the total vote in the Reykjavik municipal elections. In the summer of 1934 the Nationalists decided to participate in the coming *Allting* elections, although their party paper asserted that elections were a slapstick comedy staged every four years. The party nominated candidates for 3 constituencies out of 27. In Reykjavik it received 215 votes (1.4 per cent), in the South-West 84 votes (4.4 per cent) and in the Vestmanna Islands 64 votes

(4.1 per cent). Of the total vote cast in the elections, the Nationalist party only received 0.7 per cent and had no candidate elected. The Nationalists explained the results by stating that many voters had been led to believe that the Independence party was the bulwark against Marxism and would provide a solution to their miserable condition. But these voters were badly mistaken, the Nationalists continued. Only a corporate social system could be the basis of such a remedy.[25]

In 1937, when the next *Allting* elections took place, opinions among the Nationalists were divided on whether or not to participate. Because of this disagreement, the party made a bid for only one constituency, the South-West. However, a proclamation from the party council declared that their participation in the South-West district was intended only to show the rapidly increasing support which the party enjoyed, but otherwise the Nationalist party would leave what they regarded to be an election farce to the class-system parties. At the same time party members were urged to muster strength for the municipal elections in January 1938, because that election would place the party in an influential position.[26] The party candidate for the South-West district received 118 votes or 4.9 per cent. In relation to the total number of votes cast in the elections this amounted to 0.2 per cent.

In the municipal elections in January of 1938, the Nationalist party nominated candidates for Reykjavik and the Vestmanna Islands. Furthermore, the party declared that the concepts of left and right in politics were no longer valid. The Nationalist party was the party of the future and discontented members of other parties were now pouring into it in great numbers.[27] The Nationalists hoped to get one candidate elected in Reykjavik and another in the Vestmanna Islands but their hopes were completely shattered. In Reykjavik the party got 277 votes (1.4 per cent) and thus fell short of the 1,100 votes that were needed to get a candidate elected. In the Vestmanna Islands the party got 62 votes (3.4 per cent) and no candidate was elected. The Nationalists blamed their failure in the elections on the Independence party which they accused of having used filthy tricks to snatch votes from the Nationalist party.[28] *Morgunbladid,* on the other hand, gleefully announced that the Independence party had successfully suppressed the right wing extremists.[29]

Still, the Nationalists managed to get one candidate elected for *four years in a row (1934–37)* to the University of Iceland Student Council while the left wing and the right wing were tied with four representatives each. During their third year the Nationalists lent their vote to help the right wing to obtain power within the Council; but during their fourth year they withdrew their support from the right wing representatives, because their promises were not to be trusted.[30] This was the only example of a Nationalist candidate being elected on a democratic basis.

In 1936, the best year the Nationalist party ever had, party membership rose to its highest number – approximately 300. For comparison it might be mentioned that at the same time the population of Iceland was 116,880. The great majority of the party members were between 15 and 20 years old and therefore were not eligible to vote. The Nationalists had some support from students at the University, the Reykjavik Grammar School, the School of Commerce and the Technical Training School; the headmasters of the latter two were very sympathetic toward the Nationalist cause.[31] Finally, the party was also made up of small groups of workers, seamen, craftsmen and shop-assistants.

Apart from the Reykjavik party division, Siglufjørdur, Olafsfjørdur, Akureyri, Eskifjørdur, the Vestmanna Islands, Keflavik and Hafnarfjørdur all had their separate divisions. Outside Reykjavik the biggest divisions were in Siglufjørdur, the Vestmanna Islands and Keflavik.[32] The Nationalist party had proportionally most supporters in two constituencies: the Vestmanna Islands and the South-West district (where two divisions of the party operated, one in Keflavik and one in Hafnarfjørdur). Both of the party candidates for each constituency owned a *small* fishing fleet and their main concern was government policy regarding the fishing industry, which they were particularly unhappy about. Their efforts were mainly aimed at improving the economic condition of small firms in the fishing industry as well as the earnings of seamen.[33] All this seems to indicate that most of the support which the Nationalist party got in these two constituencies came from discontented owners of fishing vessels and from seamen.

The Nationalist party raised funds for its operations with voluntary contributions from its members and membership dues. In addition, various individuals within the Independence party supported the Nationalist party with monthly contributions. This money came in handy because the party was always under financial stress. The publication of *Ísland*, for instance, was a costly operation and a considerable burden. The reason for this generosity on behalf of some I. P. members was their image of the Nationalist party as a junior division of the Independence party[34] even though no ties existed between the two, apart from their mutual opinion about other political parties – especially the Communist party and the Social Democrats.

There is no evidence to show that the Nationalist party ever received financial support from Germany. Various signs indicate that the German Nazis were not impressed with the party and its leadership, because of its inability to gain wider support. However, the Icelandic Nationalists made no attempts to conceal their admiration for the German model, but they flatly denied having ever received orders from their heroes.[35]

The material which I have discussed so far shows clearly that the Nationalist party was a tiny and a rather uninfluential organization. The party failed completely in winning support for its Nazi-oriented program among the Icelandic population, despite depression and unemployment. In Iceland the Nationalists had proportionally much less support than their Danish and Norwegian counterparts. After the municipal elections of 1938 the operations of the party gradually came to an end. The marching squad appeared for the last time on May 1st, 1938, and in that year the party paper was only published three times. The last sign of life which the party showed was a pamphlet called *The Aims of the Nationalist Party* which was published in March 1939.[36] During the winter of 1939–40 the Nationalists organized a debating club in Reykjavik. After that, cell meetings were held until 1944 when it was clear that Germany had lost the war.[37]

It is difficult to explain why the Nationalist party never obtained more support. It is possible that the lack of able leadership had something to do with it. The Icelandic population seems to have been completely immune to the panacea of National Socialism – the tiny Nationalist party never grew to be more than a strange mixture of immature youths and discontented adults.

NOTES

* English translation by Magnus Fjalldal.

[1] *Íslensk endurreisn* (Icelandic Resurrection), June 22, 1933; *Ákæran* (The Charge), January 16, 1934.

[2] Thorbergsson, J. H.: Thjódstjórnarflokkur. *Drøg ad stefnuskrá* (The Party of National Coalition. A Draft for a Platform). Reykjavik 1932.

[3] *Íslensk endurreisn*, May 11, 18, 26, June 2, 1933.

[4] *Morgunbladid* (The Morning Paper), June 2, 1933.

[5] *Íslensk endurreisn*, June 29, 1933; January 25, 1934.

[6] *Íslensk endurreisn*, September 29, 1933.

[7] *Íslensk endurreisn*, August 10, 1933.

[8] *Íslensk endurreisn*, September 15, 1933.

[9] Hitler, Adolf: Fridarrædan (The Peace Speech). Reykjavik 1934.

[10] *Morgunbladid*, April 25, 1933; *Verklýdsbladid* (The Workers Daily), April 25, 1933.

[11] *Íslensk endurreisn*, June 1, 1933; February 16, 1934.

[12] *Ákæran*, Mai 28, 1933.

[13] *Ákæran*, June 14, 1933; June 23, 1933.

[14] *Íslensk endurreisn*, January 6, 1934.

[15] *Ákæran*, January 7, 1934.

[16] *Ákæran*, March 13, 1934.

[17] *Ísland*, May 1, 1934; June 3, 1934; February 22, 1936; June 27, 1936; July 18, 1936; *Mjølnir*, Oct.–Nov. 1935; Adils, J.: *Markmid Flokks thjódernissinna* (The Aims of the Nationalist Party). Reykjavik 1939.

[18] Clausen, Fritz: *Thjódernisjafnadarstefnan* (National Socialism). Reykjavik 1936.

[19] *Ísland*, May 1, 1934.

[20] *Mjølnir*, Oct.–Nov. 1935.

[21] *Ísland*, May 1, 1934.

[22] *Ísland*, March 16, 1936.

[23] *Ísland*, September 26, 1936.

[24] *Ísland*, March 6, 1937.

[25] *Ísland*, July 23, 1934.

[26] *Ísland*, May 29, 1937.

[27] *Ísland*, January 29, 1938.

[28] *Ísland*, April 30, 1938.

[29] *Morgunbladid*, February 4, 1938.

[30] *Mjølnir*, March–April 1936; December 1937.

[31] Information supplied by Jón Th. Árnason, who was a member of the Nationalist party.

[32] Jón Th. Árnason.

[33] *Ísland*, May 29, 1937.

[34] Jón Th. Árnason.

[35] *Ísland*, July 18, 1936.

[36] Adils, J.: *Markmid Flokks thjódernissinna* (The Aims of the Nationalist Party). Reykjavik 1939.

[37] Jón Th. Árnason.

PART 7

COMPARING FASCIST MOVEMENTS

Comparing Fascist Movements

PETER H. MERKL

Identification of Fascist Movements

Fascist movements have been compared by contemporary observers, political opponents and scholars since the very beginning of the «fascist epoch» in 1919. But these comparisons have rarely been very objective or encompassing until about the last few decades. It is difficult to single out particular works[1] or a particular time, especially since there is an intimate link, as in all comparative study, between new research on one country and the advancement of comparative understanding. One of the biggest hindrances to effective comparison has always been a question dear to historians and crucial to protagonists and enemies of fascism, namely what exactly fascism is and, consequently, which particular movements deserve this label. We have left the question of definitions to the theoretical section of this book and can in any case afford to ignore it here, because comparative methods can help us to test the boundaries set by a given definiton.

As for the protagonists and antagonists of particular movements or trends, it is typically a case of politics itself threatening to engulf systematic attempts to understand politics. During the height of the «fascist epoch,» and in some settings even today, certain political leaders and groups, *incredibile dictu,* have considered it a mark of distinction to call themselves fascist or to identify with Mussolini or Hitler. There have also been some fascist leaders and movements that stoutly insisted they were not. On the other hand, people of every political persuasion, and especially socialists and communists, have tended to attach the label of fascism so freely to whoever happens to oppose them as to obscure all distinctions. There is no need to go into the motives for this tendency to mislabel opponents except to say that they range from naive single-mindedness to self-interested advocacy of all kinds of causes ranging over the political spectrum. At times the label «fascist» has served both parties to a controversy as charge and countercharge. At a more sophisticated level, but no less misleadingly, politically *engagé* social scientists or historians have sometimes lumped together in a sweeping gesture their analysis of contemporary policies of capitalistic states with historic fascism, or equated the latter with all species of contemporary repression or aggression. It goes without saying that there is little to be gained for this comparison by any of these processes of mislabelling.

The widening scope of the study of historical fascist movements in recent decades undoubtedly enriched our understanding of the fascist phenomenon, even though historians still disagree whether this or that particular group should be called fascist. Just bringing fascist movements other than those of Germany and Italy into the field of comparison was a major advance, although it also had its drawbacks. In terms of comparative method, it obviously broadened the sample, but added mostly rather dissimilar and far less successful movements to the collection. It also showed the fascist phenomenon to be far more widespread than was popularly known.

Apart from the label and definition, any attempt to compare social or political movements across geographic or time boundaries has to meet at least certain minimal requirements to command scientific respect among social scientists and historians.

752

We cannot meaningfully compare a Platonic essence called «German fascism» with another essence called «French fascism», as language would tempt us into doing. And there is no point in comparing, say, a fascist regime with «a fascist book», assuming for the sake of the argument that there is such a thing. We *can* compare fascist persons, groups, organizations, regimes, or policies, as long as we first establish some equivalency among the units of our comparison. If we are to compare the social composition of fascist movements in different countries, we have to do so at roughly equivalent stages of organizational growth. We should also take into account, as far as possible, analogous situations and forms of organization. The meaning of social composition in this context in itself requires explanation and demystification in order to make sense.

Factors Determining Growth of Fascist Movements

Preconditions of Growth

Reading the various contributions to this book, one cannot help noticing the different stages of organizational growth of the various movements. The earliest such phase, in fact, appears to be a kind of preorganizational phase comparable, perhaps, to the cultural or literary stage of modern nationalistic movements. At this stage, a «fascist mood» may be generated – a mood manifested in special discussion groups and in periodicals aimed at a special readership; but also in a one-track-minded interpretation of certain writings, e.g., those of Friedrich Nietzsche and Georges Sorel. Zeev Sternhell gives us revealing glimpses of this fascist mood in his paper, as does the literature on the German *völkisch* writers and their ideology.[2] It could also be a sudden mood of the whole country, a mood of «cultural despair», or of «social malaise», or a fear of the rising challenge posed by a socialist or syndicalist movement, or by long suppressed but now awakening ethnic minorities. The fear of the Italian bourgeoisie in the face of the «Red Week» disturbances of June 1914, the wave of sit-down strikes of the same year in the Po Valley, the Veneto, Umbria and Tuscany are good examples of such a «fascist mood» that easily could help to set the stage for fascist mobilization, even if it did not always do so. There may be a sense of recklessness, a propensity to look for scapegoats, and a cult of heroes, but at this stage there is not yet any organization.

The second stage is no longer free of fascist organization, but consists rather of isolated habitats or possibly even of several crypto-fascist developments that may later compete or coalesce with one another. The Moldavian university setting at Iasi was one such habitat, complete with a charismatic professor, the anti-Semitic nationalist A.C. Cuza, and an anti-communist workers' group. These combined to put Corneliu Codreanu and his Iron Guard on their way. It took a while before this terrorist student group spread to the other Romanian universities and even longer until Codreanu and Cuza formed a political party, the League of National Christian Defense, and won six seats in the parliamentary elections in 1926. By that time, Romanian fascist development had obviously gone beyond its original isolated habitat and its characteristic mixture of politico-religious yearnings and violent actions. Such isolated habitats are generally difficult to compare across national boundaries because of the central importance of particular cultural factors and personalities in every case. In Romania, for example, a kind of *narodnik,* anti-Western, peasant romanticism was combined with great religious fervor and anti-Semitism. The anti-Russian imperialism of the Finnish Academic Karelian Society (AKS) was another kind of prefascistic student movement. The *Camelots du Roi* of the Left Bank in 1908/1909, on the other hand, were royalists, anti-Semites, and integral nationalists who with the support of the *Action Française* soon graduated from disrupting classes in their student habitat to a broader stormtrooper role throughout France.[3]

Whether some milieu qualifies as an isolated fascist habitat is, of course, a question of degree in relation to the large nation-state concerned. Thus, university student habitats are isolated both locally and socially, but other settings may be only more dubiously isolated. A typical case in point is the story of the first years of the NSDAP/DAP in Munich which after all was one of the metropolises of the Weimar Republic. There were several unique factors present, the aftermath of the violent suppression by the Republic of Workers' and Soldiers' Councils, the accumulation of demobilized army officers' and militant veterans' organizations, and the peculiar mixture of *völkisch*, nationalist, and conservative groupings in Bavaria.[4] Early Weimar Germany is also a good example of several isolated fascist developments occurring at the same time, because there was also the stridently anti-Semitic agitation of the *Deutsch-soziale Partei* (DSP) with orators such as Julius Streicher, and countless other *völkisch* organizations – the large *Schutz-und-Trutzbund*, for example – which contained certain militant action groups.[5] There were also a number of further local settings which contributed a pronounced fascist potential such as the conflict situation between the Franco-Belgian occupation forces in the Rhineland and the local citizenry in 1923 and earlier, or the ethnic conflicts at the borders of the new Polish nation-state. Both of these conflict situations became major recruiting grounds for National Socialism and generated local militant defense groups which in time tended to join the NSDAP *en bloc*. Finally, there were isolated fascist habitats developing at various junctures among *völkisch* veterans' groups and more especially among *völkisch* youth groups throughout the duration of the Weimar Republic – not unlike a pestilence breaking out all over a body. Isolated habitats can, of course, coalesce or they may wither away each in its locality.

As the last column of table 1 shows, most of the countries under consideration had, in fact, more than one fascist movement. In some multinational states such as Czechoslovakia, Belgium, Yugoslavia, or Switzerland there were different movements for each nationality. In France, they followed each other in time and differed also in whether they had financial support from bourgeois ultraconservatives. In many cases, their social origins, their relation to veterans' groups, or their ideologies divided them. We may finally add that in some of the countries bordering on and later occupied by Nazi Germany or fascist Italy, the question of initiation and later of collaboration could also prove divisive.

The next phase after the isolated habitat is, consequently, a stage of mass settings for fascist development. One of the aspects of the end of World War I which greatly increased the potential for fascism in most European countries was the massive presence of demobilized officers and veterans, trained in violence and often with access to arms. The importance of the *arditi* (shock troops) and other military elements in the years of the struggle for power in Italy or of the Free Corps and militant veterans' organizations for the development of the German stormtroopers can hardly be overestimated. Gerhard Botz and the other contributors on Austrian fascism in this volume devote much of their attention to the *Heimwehr*, the Front Veterans, and other military components of the competing fascist movements of Austria. Veterans and officers also played major roles in Hungary, Poland, Finland, Ireland, Sweden and France. In Norway, Quisling was a major. However, it is not enough to notice the presence of veterans in many early post-war fascist movements, for there were veterans also in all the other mass movements including those of the left after the Great War. In some cases, such as in Germany and Italy, fascism tended to pit the senior officers against the junior and the latter against the men. What are important are war-related fascist attitudes among the veterans, or officers, such as the agonies of defeat or of the disintegration of empire, of feeling robbed of the fruits of victory, as deep resentment of territorial losses or nationalistic irredentism, and, of course, anti-Bolshevism related to revolution attempts by the extreme left or actual civil war.

Massive civil war experiences such as the immediate, post-World War I years in Finland, and even in Ireland, or the establishment and violent suppression of councils-of-workers-and-soldiers regimes in Hungary or in Munich and Berlin likewise tend to leave a mass setting for fascist recruitment with all the elements required for fascist development. There is the memory of violence and a thirst for getting even with the revolutionaries, or fears that they may rise again. There are heroes or leaders of the struggle and the hated leaders of the «reds» and, most important, there are the military or para-military organizations left over from the civil war which can be readily reactivated or drawn upon for further agitation or violent action. In Eastern Europe, as Peter F. Sugar has pointed out,[6] power in the successor states to the various empires first tended to fall into the hands of the old imperial élites who were immediately challenged by various ethnic and often socialist popular forces, including the new ethnic minorities created by the peace settlement. To combat their challengers, these old élites tried to create their own popular following in the form of the various fascist movements. This, too, explains the massive following among the professional soldiers and civil servants of the imperial period which flocked to the Szeged group of officers or to the Austrian fascist movements.

Rising socialist or communist strength, even without strong-arm attempts, showing itself for instance at the polls or in the form of the establishment of the Spanish republican regime, can also create a mass setting for fascist recruitment, although it may benefit conservative or liberal parties instead. The fears of the propertied bourgeoisie, farmers, and landowners about being expropriated or overwhelmed by a «Bolshevik» revolution may tend to mobilize considerable numbers and to induce them to counter the «Bolsheviks» with a pre-emptive strike. Incitement from the economic crisis of the early thirties, by other agricultural crises, or the threat of bankruptcy for small shopkeepers and independent craftsmen are other preconditions belonging to this category.

It is a truism that the Great Depression (see table 12a) had a deep impact on the fortunes of all kinds of extremist movements. The starting dates of the fascist organizations in table 1 clearly show that the early thirties were the most likely time for fascism to gain a foothold (with or without the example and encouragement of Nazi Germany) in most Northern and West European countries including the Iberian peninsula. Only Germany, Italy, Austria, France, Sweden and Eastern Europe had earlier starting dates and of these, all the countries but France and Sweden were directly involved in the collapsing empires, territorial changes, and ethnic irredentism that were the legacy of World War I. The dates of the highest pre-takeover membership or vote of the fascist movements in table 1 also tend to be in the middle of or near the peak of the depression years in each country. There were also other economic crises at work such as the impact on Irish agriculture of British economic sanctions,

Country	Name of Group	Leader	Start	Highest Membership before Takeover	Highest Membership after Takeover	Highest Percent Vote before Takeover	Other Fascist Groups
Norway	Nasjonal Samling	Quisling	1933	1936/40: 9,000	43,000 (under occupation)	1933: 2.8	No
Iceland	Iceland Nationalists		1933	1936: 300		1934: 0.7	No
Denmark	DNSAP	Clausen	1930	1939: 4–5,000	19,100 (under occupation)	1939: 1.8	Yes
Netherlands	NSB	Mussert	1931	1935: 47,000		1935: 8	Yes
Belgium	Rex	Degrelle	1936	1939: 12,500		1936: 11.5	
	Flemish Nationalists			1939: 12–13,000		1939: 8.3	Yes
Ireland	Blueshirts	O'Duffy	1932–36				No
Great Britain	British Union of Fascists	Mosley	1931	1934: 17–40,000			Yes
France	Faisceau	Valois	1925	1926: 50,000			Yes
	Jeunesse Patri-otes Legion	Taittinger		1926: 55,000			Yes
	Solidarité Française	Redier Renaud	1924 1933	1926: 10,000 1933: 15–20,000	(180–250,000 readers)		
	Francistes	Bucard	1933	1933: 10,000			
	PPF	Doriot	1936				
	RNP	Déat	1941		50–60,000		
Spain	JONS/Falange	José Antonio	1931	1936: 35,600	900,000	1936: 0.4	No
Portugal	National Syndicalists	Preto	1932	1935: 50,000			No
Switzerland	National Front		1930	1935: 10,000		1933: 27.1	Yes
Germany	NSDAP	Hitler	1919	1933: 849,000	1937: 2.5 million	1932: 37.2	Yes
Italy	PNF	Mussolini	1919	1922: 300,000	1929: 1.1 million		No
Austria	DNSAP/NSDAP		1918	1938: 177,000	1945: 523,000	1930: 3	Yes
	Heimwehr	Starhemberg	1927	1930: 150,000		1930: 6	
Hungary	Arrow Cross National Socialists	Szalasi Gömbös	1935 1919	1944: 500,000		1939: 25	Yes
	Scythe Cross	Böszörmeny	1932	1934: 20,000			
Romania	Iron Guard	Codreanu	1923	1938: 350,000		1937: 16	No
Yugoslavia	Ustasha	Pavelic	1929	1938: 40,000		1935: 30,000 (Ljotic)	Yes
	Orjuna/Zbor	Ljotic (Zbor)	1921				
CSR	DNSAP (DAP)	Henlein	1920			1938: 88 of German vote	Yes
	Slovak Peoples Party	Hlinka	1920			1920–38: 25–40	
	Czech Nationalists	Gajda	1925			1935: 2 (1931:11% i. Prague)	
Poland	Great Poland/ ONR	Dmowski	1926	1937: 26,000 (Rutkowski)			
Finland	Lapua/IKL	Kosola	1929			1933: 14 seats (of 200)	Yes
Sweden	Swedish National Socialists (diverse names)	Furugård/ Lindholm	1924	1930: 7,000 (uncertain)		1932: 0.6	Yes

the marketing problems of Icelandic fishermen, and the lingering agricultural depression among Scandinavian, Finnish, Flemish, and German farmers, at times with strong cultural overtones of a traditional way of life.

These economically-motivated fears of social decline explain why the Depression era witnessed the rise of many new fascist movements and enormous increases in the vote for existing fascist parties. Here too, the economic motive usually requires an admixture of other motives before it provides a plausible explanation of the fascist surge. It can hardly be taken for granted that a hard-pressed small businessman or farmer would expect immediate economic relief from a fascist fringe movement unless there are additional elements of nationalism, ideology, irredentism, and of course leadership that combine with the economic motivation.

There are also some other kinds of mass settings that have benefitted fascist recruitment, especially in conjunction with factors already mentioned above such as the «mood of the country» or an ideology of cultural pessimism. They are generally related to flaws and crises in the social and political development of a country, and the particular alliance structures prevalent in the early phases of democratization, such as those described above by Bernt Hagtvet and Stein Rokkan. A class structure disintegrating under the impact of war and industrialization raises status anxieties and social conflicts, and creates the «mobsters» and *declassés* often credited with fascist mobilization. Economic development may be arrested at a particular stage and stagnation or decline lead to radicalization and conflict. Major cultural change, especially as a result of war's impact, may create anxieties, frustration, and conflict, especially between the generations. The end of World War I marked in many European countries an unprecedented crisis of bourgeois values and convictions relating to liberal visions of social progress and to religious interpretations of life itself. As Joseph Baglieri explains above in the case of Italy, the cultural crisis of the liberal bourgeoisie was generally accompanied by a crisis of its political institutions and representative organizations at the very time when the organized working classes began to push against the gates of power. Worse still, this cultural agony often blinded the liberal bourgeoisie and, in a kind of psychological «double-bind», prevented it from seeing its own situation in its true light and coming to terms with its antagonists. Bourgeois youth, in particular, was alienated from the values and traditions of its elders. Skillful fascist agitators like Mussolini took advantage of the disorientation of the bourgeoisie and the crisis of the liberal state and moved into the vacuum of power left by the collapse of political liberalism, often attracting especially the formerly liberal bureaucracy, school teachers, professionals, university students, and white-collar employees. Another aspect of this social development *manqué* is presented by some instances of rural-urban migration, as in Germany, where many of the new urbanites failed to complete their cultural adjustment to city life and instead remained curiously vulnerable to the agrarian romanticism of *völkisch* ideologues. Finally, there is ample evidence that religious decline and confrontations played a role in fascist development in such countries as Belgium, Germany, Austria, Czechoslovakia, Romania, and Yugoslavia, creating a massive reservoir of confused quasi-religious fears and longings open to exploitation by fascist demagogues.

In sum, then, these mass settings of fascist recruitment are the precondition for the actual development of fascist movements. It should be noted, however, that there is no determinism in such development. Each of the factors and circumstances enumerated so far could just as well have led to very different consequences depending on the available leadership and on what Nico Passchier, in the context of electoral geography above, called «opportunity space» not yet pre-empted by well-established political parties or groups and organization. A comparison of fascist developments, therefore, has to stress most of all the progress of the fascist organizations themselves.

Phases of Growth

Any attempt to account for the success of fascist movements has to account for a variety of aspects, none of which may be in itself conclusive. There is the sheer growth of the movement in membership and supporters, especially of voters in elections. Then there is the role and growth of a para-military arm of the movement, and possibly its attempts to gain power by force at a crucial time. Finally, there are the coalitions entered with other forces and the mergers undertaken with other movements before and after the fascist takeover, if there is one. Most European fascist movements, of course, never did come to power and some did so only thanks to foreign intervention, which makes these derivative fascist régimes and their movements rather different. There was also a wide range of relationships between the occupying powers and native fascist parties.

It goes without saying that a fascist movement in power is a very different phenomenon from its pre-takeover self. Not only is there a fundamental change in its whole orientation, but there is likely to be a great onrush of the established social forces to join it and to share power with it. Once in power, moreover, it may well go through further stages of transformation, accommodation, or institutionalization, including possibly its withering away among such competing fores as the leadership, the secret police, and the army or bureaucracy. The Spanish *Falange* may be a case in point of a fascist movement that failed to conquer by itself, and, despite some fascist institutionalization under General Franco, never managed to take on the dominant function of other fascist parties in the leading fascist regimes. Perhaps it could still have done so, had the Axis powers won World War II. Finally, there are also some post-totalitarian fascist movements such as the gaggle of neo-Nazi groups in post-war Germany or the MSI *(Movimento Sociale Italiano)* in Italy, not to mention minor groups elsewhere. They all suffer from the loss of innocence after a decade or two of fascist dictatorship and war. Made up largely of old, ungenerate Nazi-fascists and their children, they tend merely to subsist on the defensive fringes of their political systems, vacillating between their popularly detested heritage and pretenses of a self-contradictory, democratic fascism.

Of these disparate aspects, the fascist membership and voting curves are the easiest to compare. The largest, longest-lived movements, in particular, offer time-series data from their origins up to their ascent to power, even if some of the information on other movements is scarce and unreliable. To be sure, there are some limitations on the degree of significance to be attached to these figures (Fig. 1). Membership figures, for example, must be viewed in relation to the degree of intensity of political activity in the system as a whole. A readily available index of such intensity, the number of people participating in political organizations, is very crude and does not measure the degree of involvement, the willingness to spend time and effort in the movement, in short, the subjective emotional attachments to parties. A mass movement amid a politically unmobilized population, or motorized, armed fascist squads against a large, organized, but poorly coordinated socialist movement, who can attach numerical values to their respective sizes? We cannot even begin to estimate the percentages of a given party membership who may have furthered their cause by demonstrating, proselytizing, or street-fighting unless we have the kind of information furnished by the Abel Collection of early Nazis. It helps, of course, to have on record the size of stormtrooper or *squadristi* units engaged in known battles or statistics of rallies or demonstrations collected by the police agencies, but essentially such criteria permit only a summary judgment made with the benefit of hindsight.

There is a strong thread of continuity which tied the German stormtroopers (SA), for example, to the shocktroops of the war and to the frequently unemployed veterans and officers of the Imperial Army. The SA originated precisely at the time the

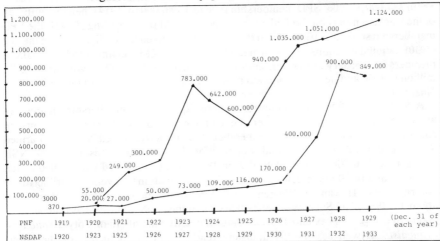

Figure 1. *Membership growth of PNF and NSDAP*

Source: The Italian figures stem from *L'Impero* of September 23, 1929, the German figures from a variety of sources. See Peter H. Merkl, *Political Violence Under the Swastika: 581 Early Nazis,* (Princeton University Press, 1975), p. 557 and Dietrich Orlow, *The History of the Nazi Party: 1919–1933,* (University of Pittsburgh Press, 1969), pp. 110–111, 236 and 239. While the sources permit only an educated guess, there was an extraordinary surge of membership following the September 30 elections, but also a rather high rate of turnover. The rapid growth of the movement during 1931/1932 ended with a downturn, but we have no reliable information on how high the membership wave went before it crested.

Reichswehr was limited to 100,000 men and the anti-revolutionary *Einwohnerwehr* was dissolved in Bavaria, an armed vigilante organization headed by the same Captain Ernst Röhm who later became the chief SA leader.[7] From numbering about 300 troopers in 1921, the SA became a sizeable revolutionary army of about 77,000 in January of 1931, at the beginning of the great influx of unemployed into the brownshirt movement. A year later, the SA had nearly quadrupled in size (291,000), and in August of 1932 there were 519,000,[8] including by then also large numbers of students, workers, and farmers who had not been veterans in World War I. The unbroken line connecting the German *Sturmbattalione* (shocktroops) of World War I – of which SA Chief Captain Ernst Röhm was an officer – with the Free Corps of 1919/1920, the SA of the fighting years, and finally the SS tank divisions of World War II, suggests speaking of «military reserve armies» of fascist development, as Marx spoke of the «industrial reserve armies» of capitalist development.[9] The Italian *squadristi* were likewise born from a bodyguard of unemployed *arditi* (shocktroops) in 1919 and the ex-officers and student elements were dominant at first.[10] Their numbers also swelled from a few hundred at the outset to 213,000 by October of 1921, to 322,000 by May of the following year, and perhaps to 500,000 at the time of the March on Rome. But who can say how large a para-military army would have been a match for the regular Italian army, or the German *Reichswehr* of 100,000? Neither Hitler nor Mussolini had any intention of letting it come to a showdown in the arena of violence.

We could, of course, attempt to compare the membership strength of these two fascist movements with their principal antagonists. The pre-war German Socialists

(SPD), for example, had experienced a similar surge of membership in just a few years. From 384,000 in 1906, SPD membership rose to 1,086,000 by 1914 when the outbreak of the war sent most able-bodied males to the front. At the beginning of 1931, the SPD membership stood at 1,037,384 and the party had received 8½ million votes in the last (1930) national elections. The German Communists (KPD) claimed to have 200,000 members in February of 1931 and another 200,000 a year later. Their vote stood at 4½ million in 1930 and nearly 5½ million in July, 1932,[11] as compared to the 13.7 million Nazi votes.

A look at the few other countries where comparable membership figures are available, shows the mass character of even the more obscure fascist movements. In Austria in 1928, 150,000 *Heimwehr* members (52,000 active) faced 90,000 well-armed *Schutzbund* members of the socialist opposition. In the Netherlands, the 47,000 NSB members and 80,000 readers of VOVA in 1935 can be compared with 84,000 Dutch Socialists and 148,000 subscribers to socialist periodicals in that year, according to the contribution of H. van der Wusten and R. Smit to this book. In France, there were about 130,000 SFIO Socialists and 29,000 Communists (PCF) in 1933 as compared to about 10,000 Francistes and 15 to 29 thousand active members of Coty's *Solidarité Française,* as well as 180–250 thousand readers and sympathizers of the latter. Colonel de La Rocque's *Croix de Feu* had 36,000 members in 1932 and an estimated 250–400 thousand by 1935.[12] Jacques Doriot's PPF, which started in 1936, soon claimed 150–250 thousand members. By that time, to be sure, another wave of socialist mobilization had given the PCF 284,000 and the SFIO almost as large a number of members. The fact remains that the fascist movements of that period were about as massive as the socialist mass movement.

Judging from the membership curves of NSDAP and PNF before the takeover, even these large and most successful fascist mass movements appear to be marked by sudden surges of membership. In between these surges, the turnover is high and the membership stagnates or declines.[12a] As we noted in the introduction to the German and Italian section, the great breakthroughs of the NSDAP were either related to mass settings for fascist recruitment, such as the ones described above, or to well-organized drives. In any case, the NSDAP seemed to be incapable of gradual sustained growth; witness the turnover rate of one to two thirds of the membership. The immediate post-war setting in Italy turned out to be rather favorable[13] to the growth of the PNF. In Germany the strength and the revolution attempts of the extreme left produced instead the counter-revolutionary *Einwohnerwehr* and Free Corps formations. These organizations may appear to have been good recruiting grounds for the Nazis, yet there was too much of a time and generational lag between them and the final Nazi surge for them to have been decisive. In 1923, the NSDAP became so deeply entangled with other militant organizations on the Right that it missed its chance of a spectacular «March on Berlin». It was only in 1929, as a pay-off from the Young Plan campaign, and later with the benefit of mass unemployment and political crisis that the Nazi membership curve achieved a steep upward turn. The sudden breakthrough owed much to the thorough organization, skillful propaganda, and most of all the missionary zeal with which the Nazi movement went out proselytizing for the cause. There is an obvious parallel here with religious, proselytizing crusades, but again, we have no way of gauging the extent of the recruitment or propaganda efforts unless we have specific behavioral information from participants or close observers.

The Italian fascists were carried into office by their first surge and undoubtedly benefited subsequently from having Mussolini as the head of the government. There is also the very large membership of the syndicalist corporations to consider, said (by *Popolo d'Italia*) to have reached 458,000 by mid-1922, and consisting mostly of agricultural (60.4 per cent), industrial, and transport workers. The 1923 drive for the «Fascists of the second hour», furthermore, reflected both the absorption of the large, bourgeois Nationalist following and the expansion of the party throughout the country. The membership drive of 1926 and after, which was accompanied by whole-sale purges, was rather comparable to the NSDAP's after the March elections in 1933, and brought in large numbers of bourgeois *fiancheggiatori*, especially public em-ployees and civil servants, analogous to the Nazis' recruitment after their takeover. For the NSDAP, as we pointed out in the introduction to the German and Italian section above, the great surge in membership after the 1930 elections tended to go mainly in the direction of older, rural or small-town, bourgeois and even upper middle-class recruits, whereas many a young unemployed worker joined the SA which could often give him shelter and food in an SA dormitory *(SA-Heim)* in exchange for his services. While the Great Depression was obviously taking its toll, we must not underestimate the extent to which the NSDAP now became «respecta-ble» by attracting prominent bourgeois establishment figures and civil servants, by its penetration of such established groups as the conservative Agrarian League *(Reichslandbund)* and the *völkisch* Retail Clerks Union *(Deutsche nationaler Hand-lungsgehilfenverband* – DHV), and by setting up its own student and professional associations amid the welter of German associational life. After Hitler's appointment as Chancellor, the party tripled in size in two years, bringing in considerable numbers of civil servants and school-teachers, thus diminishing the proportion of housewives and farmers.[14] Behind these gross figures, however, stood the effective penetration of the traditional social élites in the higher bureaucracy, industry, and the army, and their forcible accommodation with the new men in power.

Measures of Success of Fascist Movements

There are a number of ways to gauge the extent to which the fascist movements under consideration were successful in their respective countries, bearing in mind that most of them did not really succeed in gaining power. The most obvious, at least in democratic countries, is to look at their highest vote before and after the fascist takeover. Trying to pinpoint the causes for the breakdowns in the process of national territorial and political consolidation, Stein Rokkan and Bernt Hagtvet undertook such a comparison with the five most fascist countries that could be said to have had a competitive system of mass politics at the time of the arrival of fascist movements: Germany, Italy, Austria, Spain and Portugal.

But what about the others? A look at our table 1 shows that the use of electoral statistics for measuring fascist success is very problematical, to say the least. First of all, many of these countries, especially in Eastern Europe, were still relative new-comers to electoral politics. To be sure, this did not prevent the Hungarian and Romanian movements from achieving very respectable percentages at the polls, but it may well have made these elections into praetorian plebiscites of aroused new nations rather than the rational choices typical of established democratic systems. Secondly, there are a number of multi-national states such as Switzerland, Belgium, and Czechoslovakia, in which there were different fascist movements for each major ethnic group and where national election totals can be rather misleading. It is inter-esting to see also the regional strength of some fascist movements, such as the NSB or

DNSAP near the German borders. In most cases, including Italy and Spain, the electoral percentages achieved by fascists before their takeover are pitiful and would lead us to surmise that fascism was no threat at all in its time. Finally, several early fascist movements, particularly under the influence of Mussolini, chose to show their contempt for democratic procedures (and their fear of poor results) by not contesting any elections.

This brings us to the related feature of fascist pride in non-electoral methods such as violence, demonstrations, and proselytizing. While our current materials are not quite adequate to a broader comparison in tabular form, (see table 2) there would be considerable insight to be gained from comparing the forms and intensity of fascist violence from street-fighting to assassinations, terrorism and attempted coups.

Another aspect of fascist non-electoral successes are the coalitions formed by fascist movements at critical moments in their countries' histories. In a variety of cases, for example, fascist movements were the instrument and satellites of «respectable» conservative parties who used them against their socialist or other enemies while keeping their own hands unsullied with violence. This appears to have been true particularly of the Finnish *Lapua* movement and the Agrarian Union and the big business-oriented Coalition *(Kokoomus)* party which was itself a client of the white grandees of the civil war. The relationship between the Irish Blueshirts and the *Cumann na nGaedhael* party is another case in point. The first Blueshirt (ACA) leader, Col. T.F. O'Higgins, in fact, had been a leading member of the conservative mother party. In other cases, such as the Nazi stormtroopers of the early phase (1921–1923), the para-military arms (but not the party) sprang directly from the military and maintained a client relationship. In some cases, allegations of a similar relationship between other established forces, such as the church, the monarchy, or business need to be examined in detail.[15]

The word «coalition» also conjures up the range of complex arrangements by which some fascist groups came to share power, or which prevailed after they had come to power. Since the fascist parties outside of Germany did not attain power alone or rule by themselves, all of these complex relationships should be categorized and catalogued. Even in Germany, the Nazis came to power at first in coalition with the German Nationalists (DNVP), a party subsequently swallowed up along with *Stahlhelm* and other groups. In Spain, the *Falange* was forced to coalesce with the Carlists and, having lost its original leaders during the Civil War, to adapt itself under the leadership of General Franco and his generals. Finally, special emphasis should be put on the frequent impact of foreign powers in the form of financial support, as with the Austrian *Heimwehr* or the Croatian *Ustasha*. The most decisive coalition support, of course, came from the German or Italian occupation which often helped native fascist movements to take over. Future research might attempt to study the linkages between the international situations and the growth of fascism more systematically, or compare the violent behavior which frequently constituted the very identity of these movements.

While obviously challenging historians to suggest corrections in detail, we have here tried to tabulate both the degree of violent confrontation introduced by the fascist movements and the coalitions they entered (table 2).

Fascist movements, as has been pointed out before,[15] were part and parcel of an extraordinary wave of mass social mobilization involving, for example, the tenfold growth of trade union membership in Italy in the years from 1911 to 1920 but also the mobilization of the war itself and later of the Great Depression. This social mobiliza-

Table 2. *Starting Point, Profile of Violent Activities, Coups, Coalitions, and Success*

Country	Name of Group	Leader	Start	Paramilitary (name)	Youth Organization (name)	Propaganda Yes/No	Demonstrations Yes/No	Street-fighting	Coup plans	Coalitions with	Reached Power
Norway	Nasjonal Samling	Quisling	1933	Hird	Unghird	yes	yes	rural violence	Plans in '39	Germans	yes
Iceland	Icelandic Nationalists		1933	March.Squad	idem	yes	yes	some violence	none	Independent Party	no
Denmark	DNSAP	Clausen	1930	SA	yes		some	none	none	Germans	no
Netherlands	NSB	Mussert	1931		yes			none	none		yes
Belgium	Rex	Degrelle	1936	Guards		yes	yes	none		Hitler	no
	Flemish Nationalists									Hitler	no
Ireland	Blueshirts	O'Duffy	1932	idem	League of Youth	yes	yes	violent agrarian politics	none	Conservative Party	no
Great Britain	British Union of Fascists	Mosley	1931	Biff Boys		yes	yes	street violence			no
France	Faisceau	Valois	1925	Guards	Fascists University Guards	yes	yes	raids, street violence			no
	Jeunesse Patriotes	Taittinger				yes	yes				no
	Legion	Redier	1924	idem			yes	street violence		Action Française	no
	Solidarité Française	Renaud	1933					street violence		Coty Action française	no
	Francistes	Bucard	1933			yes		street violence		Germans	no
	PPF	Doriot	1936							Germans	no
	RNP	Déat	1941	MSR	Union Populaire Jeunesse	yes	yes	street violence			no
Spain	JONS/Falange	José Antonio	1931	Squads/Military	SEU	yes	yes	random terrorism	try '34	Franco	yes
Portugal	National Syndicalists	Preto	1932	Armed Militia	–	yes	yes	some violence		Union Nationale	no
Switzerland	National Front		1930	Harst/Auszug	National Jugend	yes	yes	some violence		German funds	no
Germany	NSDAP	Hitler	1919	SA/SS	Hitler Jugend	yes	yes	heavy street-fighting	'23	DNVP	yes
Italy	PNF	Mussolini	1919	Squadristi	idem	yes	yes	raids & terror	'22	German	yes
Austria	DNSAP/NSDAP		1918	SA/SS	Hitler Jugend	yes	yes	assassinations & terror	'34	German	yes
	Heimwehr	Starhemberg	1927	idem				raids & terror	'30–34	Italian	yes
Hungary	Arrow Cross	Szalasi	1935	idem		yes	yes	terrorism	'44	German	yes
	National Socialists	Gömbös	1919	Squads & vigilance		yes	–	terror, executions		Christliche Nationale Union	yes
	Scythe Cross	Böszörmeny	1932								no
Romania	Iron Guard	Codreanu	1923	Legionaries	Nests	yes	yes	assassinations & terror	40–41	German	yes
Yugoslavia	Ustasha	Pavelić	1929	Assassination Squads		yes		terror		Italian, German	yes
	Orjuna/Zbor	Ljotic	1921	Paramilitary units		yes	yes	assassinations & terror			no
CSR	DNSAP (DAP)	Henlein	1920	Volkssport Verbund	Union of Young People	yes	yes	some violence	plans 20's	Germans	yes
	Slovak Peoples Party	Hlinka	1920	Hlinka Guard	Hlinka Youth	yes	yes			Germans	yes
	Czech Nationalists		1925							Agrarian Peoples Party	no
Poland	Great Poland/ONR	Dmowski	1926	Falanga ('37)				assassinations & terror	plans	Agrarian Union & Coalition Party	no
Finland	Lapua/IKL	Kosola	1929		Blue-black Youngsters	yes	yes	terrorism	'32–37	Young Nationalist conservatives	no
Sweden	Swedish National Socialists	Furugård/Lindholm	1924	SA	Nordic Youth	yes	yes	terrorism			no

tion turned into a political mobilization at first favoring the great socialist push for power in the years 1919/1921, and again in the thirties. Then came the fascists, whose leaders and followers often sprang from the lap of pre-existing «older» socialist parties or dissident socialist groups. In fact the fascist movements can only be understood vis-à-vis the massive rise of socialist labor movements, which they proceeded to fight with all the vigor they could muster. Their anti-socialist struggle ranged from civil war or «white terror» against the «Bolshevik» movements, régimes, and coups of Eastern, Central, and Southern Europe to propaganda and political coalitions with the traditional right wing. By the same token and contrary to common belief, these fascist movements were not uniformly part of the traditional right-wing forces. To begin with, there were considerable differences in what constituted the traditional Right and how united and dominant it was in various countries, just as there were enormous differences in the size and unity of the socialist working-class movements so crucial to their success or to the political threat they may have posed to the established Right. There are obviously important differences between fascist movements in an economically underdeveloped country like Hungary and in an industrial-urban society such as Germany. In Hungary a fascist mass grew mostly from the tens of thousands of gentry-derived military men and civil servants who had to flee the lost Hungarian lands and came to serve the pre-war imperial and feudal establishment against a short-lived socialist revolutionary régime in Budapest and against the forces that had torn off two-thirds of Hungarian territory and population after the war. The motivation was obviously political and irredentist rather than economic. In Germany, the impact of the war was not absent, but more important than German irredentism was war's effect in aggravating existing social cleavages. Prussian aristocratic control over the state and the army had been greatly weakened, and the real confrontation was over issues of political economy between the highly organized working-class and the various elements of the bourgeoisie. In this situation the Nazi movement was less successful than, say, Mussolini in attracting working-class support, but it maintained a degree of autonomy from its right-wing allies that ultimately spelled its complete, authoritarian control over all elements of society, rather than its subservience to a pre-existing «ruling class». Many other fascist movements such as the *Lapua* movement of Finland or the Icelandic Nationalists, were little more than an instument for direct action of the «respectable» conservative, business, or agrarian parties and groups. Even where fascist movements started out with some autonomy, as with the Spanish *Falange*, they ended up as captives of the establishment.

Who were the Fascists?

Interpretation of Social Origins

Some of the literature on fascist movements, including many of the contributions to this volume, has focused on the relations between the movements and the social structure of the societies in question. Such an undertaking generally goes in one of the following three directions, or combines two or more of them: First, there have been studies of the social composition of the membership, leadership, or voters of fascist movements, including their age, occupation, social class, education, and ethnic or geographic origins. Another approach has raised the question of the identity of their sympathizers and supporters, (there being, perhaps, members of established élites) and, more especially, their sources of financial support. The third one relates fascism to major social or political cleavages of a pre-existing, ongoing, or temporary nature. It is important that the theories underlying these approaches be critically discussed and related to one another before we proceed to a comparison of the social origins of the movements presented in this book.

The worst social-scientific mystifications have tended to gather round studies of the social composition of the membership or leadership. This has been so not only because statistics of social composition, however incomplete or inadequate, tend to look impressively scientific to laymen and novices, but because most researchers have been singularly reticent about the true significance of their findings. Some have hinted at a relationship between their findings and our third category, major socio-political cleavages such as the class struggle between bourgeoisie and proletariat, without spelling out the precise nature of this relationship. Others have simply neglected to point out the limitations of their statistical or social-scientific expositions. To be more concrete, for example, an occupational breakdown of fascist leadership is rather limited as a tool of analysis because political leaders of any political movements tend to be from the upper strata or political élites although they may be individually marginal in this milieu. (Table 3). Demonstrating upper-class origin, in any case, is hardly sufficient to label a movement an upper-class movement. A look at the differential between German NSDAP leaders (from *Ortsgruppenleiter* on up) and followers in 1935, for example, shows the leaders to be considerably less proletarian and less artisan (including more teachers, civil servants, or white-collar employees) than the members. If we focused on the leadership from the *Kreis* (county) or *Gau* (district) level only, it would turn out to be even more heavily white-collar and civil service and less proletarian and peasant. Conspicuously less prominent at the higher level are business, handicraft, and farming for the simple reason that these professions are not as easily neglected for a political career as are white-collar or civil service positions.

If the membership at large could be shown to belong overwhelmingly to a certain class, say the «lower middle class», the link-up would undoubtedly be much more significant, but even then the problems of interpretation would only have begun. The concept of the lower middle class is notably vague and has rarely been treated with the

Table 3. *Occupations of German NSDAP Leaders and Members in 1935*

	NSDAP Members	NSDAP Office Holders	Gainfully Employed Population
	per cent	per cent	per cent
Workers	32.1	23.0	46.3
White-Collar Personnel	20.6	22.6	12.4
Civil Servants	9.6	10.5	3.9
Teachers	3.4	7.1	0.9
Professional People	3.2	2.1	1.0
Business Folk	7.5	7.3	3.9
Artisans/Craftsmen (indep.)	19.5	10.1	4.7
Farmers.....................................	10.7	14.7	10.0
Others	3.4	2.6	16.9
	100.00	100.00	100.00

Source: Wolfgang Schäfer, *NSDAP, Entwicklung und Struktur der Staatspartei des Dritten Reiches*, (Hannover: Norddeutsche Verlagsanstalt, 1957) p. 47.

kind of precision needed for constructing a convincing case. There is disagreement, for example, as to whether farmers, the lower professional military, the lower civil service, white-collar employees, or certain minor professions, belong to it or not. Given the scarcity and inadequacies of the data, moreover, most researchers use very sketchy, crude occupational information on membership to establish social class. There is rarely any information about the status or occupation of a member's father – something that is normally required for contemporary social-class research. Even less attention is paid to the presence of upward or downward mobility which in the case of the «lower middle class» Nazis of the Abel Collection, for example, showed this status to be mostly a way-station of either upwardly mobile members of farm or proletarian origins or of socially declining families.[16] To picture Nazism as the revolt of a static German lower middle class thus turns out to be largely myth and mystery.

On the level of statistical analysis, too, the interpretation of occupational break-downs often raises unanswerable questions of sampling and of coding. The sketchy data available, including «Who's Who»s such as Edoardo Savinio's *La Nazione Operante*[17] for the Italian PNF, rarely permit a solid assessment, considering also the frequency of changes in occupation and the likelihood that a life-long political functionary will indicate an occupation representing, perhaps, only his earliest years in gainful employment or his training, or, worse yet, an occupation considered «in» by his movement. The question of what percentage of a party has to be, say, lower middle class to qualify as a «lower middle class party» likewise has never been seriously tackled. To answer it, as is customary, by indicating by what percentage each occupational group exceeds or falls below the population average is not very satisfactory, for even catch-all parties never perfectly match the population. To come back to

Table 4. *Occupational Structure of the NSDAP 1923, 1930, 1933 and 1935*

	1923	1930	1933	1935
	per cent	per cent	per cent	per cent
Workers	19.7	26.3	32.5	32.1
(incl. skilled)	(8.5)			
White-Collar Personnel	12.9	24.4	20.6	20.6
Civil Servants	6.6	7.7	6.5	9.4
Teachers				3.6
Students (univ.)	4.2	1.0	1.2	
Professional People	3.1	18.9	17.3	20.2
Business	16.2			
Artisans/Craftsmen	21.3			
Farmers	10.4	13.2	12.5	10.7
Pensioners		1.9	1.6	
Women	1.1	3.6	4.1	
Others	4.5	3.4	3.5	3.4
	100.00	100.00	100.00	100.00

Sources: The 1923 column is taken from Michael H. Kater, «Zur Soziographie der frühen NSDAP», *Vierteljahreshefte für Zeitgeschichte*, XIX (1971), p.139 where the categories are subjected to sophisticated analysis. pp. 124–137. The other columns are from Schäfer, *op.cit.* pp. 19 and 38.

table 3, there is no question but that artisans, teachers, the professions, civil servants, business folk and white-collar employees, in this order, were over-represented in the NSDAP of 1935. But did they really form *one* class, perhaps including the farmers? Or did they seem united only from the point of view of the organized working-class, which, incidentally, was by that time far less under-represented than in the early days of the movement? On the other hand, the «old middle class» elements of business and independent handicraft and professions made up a larger share in 1923 than later. (Table 4). The problems of heterogeneity are compounded by the party's development over time, especially before and after the take-over.[18]

A much better documentation, if only the data were available, would be a comparison of the occupational structure of the membership or the voters of several parties or movements of the period.[19] Such a comparison, say, of the Weimar parties would very likely show that the occupational structure of the Nazi party was in some respects rather similar to that of the four or five other bourgeois parties of the Weimar Republic, the German People's Party (DVP), German Democrats (DDP), German Nationalists (DNVP), and the Economic Middle Class parties – perhaps even the Catholic Center Party – from all of whom the NSDAP stole votes and members.[20] The significance of such a finding would consist in its undermining any special claim made for the Nazis as the party of the middle class revolt. Any analysis of the social origins of leaders, members or followers should try to explain motivations for political action. Showing that the Nazi party had the same social basis as other bourgeois parties, therefore would fail to explain why the Nazis obviously had a different motivation for joining the NSDAP than the members of the bourgeois parties had for joining theirs. This realization would weaken the significance of comparing the Nazi social base to that of the Social Democrats (SPD) and the Communists (KPD). (Table 5). On the other hand, the percentage of working-class members of many fascist parties (tables 4 and 5)

Table 5. *Occupations of Austrian Nazis Compared to Socialists and Communists in 1934*

	NS	SPÖ	KPÖ
	per cent	per cent	per cent
Unsk. Workers	27.0	19.8	22.5
Skilled Workers	10.9	24.2	30.0
White-Collar Employees (priv.)	18.7	12.8	10.0
Public Employees and Civil Servants	6.6	15.2	2.5
Teachers	0.3	2.3	2.5
Professional People	2.6	2.5	2.5
Students	6.6	0.2	2.5
Businessmen & Farmers	7.3	2.0	
Craftsmen/Artisans	19.0	11.9	25.0
Pensioners	1.0	1.4	
NA		7.7	2.5
	100.00	100.00	100.00
	n=301	n=503	n=40

Source: Computed from Gerhard Jagschitz, *Vom Justizpalast zum Heldenplatz,* (Vienna, 1975) p. 150. The sample are political prisoners held at Woellersdorf in October 1934.

is not all that much lower than that of comparable socialist parties. Unlike other bourgeois parties, fascist movements had a substantial number of workers among their members. Nor can it be said that the difference lies in the inclusion mainly of skilled workers who often seem to have more in common with dependent handicraft occupations than with the unskilled proletariat. According to most accounts, European socialist movements are substantially composed of skilled workers who have long been active in the trade union movement.[21]

Generational Differences

Other important lines of interpretation, those based on age, education, ethnicity, or geographic origin are likewise essentially attempts to delineate political motivation. The significance of age-differences between memberships of political parties or between those of a fascist movement and the governmental, social, and cultural élites of a country may be very considerable but only in situations where there is a generation gap, or youth revolt in society at large. In other words, there has to be an important age-related cleavage of the kind which occurred in some European countries between the young World War I veterans and their established elders in government, business, and in the leadership of the political parties. A typical example of such a generational cleavage occurred in Hamburg after World War I, when the old trade union and SPD stalwarts in their fifties faced the competition of much younger Independent Socialists (USPD) and later Communists (KPD) for the support of vast numbers of non-unionized younger workers and war veterans.[22]

Table 6. *Ages of the German and Austrian NSDAP Compared with Socialist Parties, 1930 and 1934*

Age	Austria[1] (1934)			Age	Germany[2] (1930)		Abel-Merkl 1930	SPD 1930
	NSDAP	SPÖ	KPÖ		Popula-tion 1933	NSDAP 1933		
–18.......	1.0	–	–	18–30	31.1	42.7	41.2	18.1
19–23.....	24.8	6.1	20					
24–28	28.5	7.3	30					
29–33	14.4	14.4	15	31–40	22.0	21.2	37.5	26.5
34–38	15.0	19.5	10					
39–43	5.9	15.8	5					
44–48	5.6	15.6	15	41–50	17.1	17.2	13.9	27.3
49–53	3.3	10.5	–					
54–58.....	1.5	5.1	5	51–60	14.5	9.3	} 7.4	19.6
59–.......	–	5.7	–	61–	15.3	3.6		8.5
	100.0	100.0	100.0		100.0	100.0	100.0	100.0
	n=301	n=503	n=40					

Sources
[1] From Gerhard Jagschitz, *Vom Justizpalast zum Heldenplatz,* (Vienna, 1975) p. 150.
[2] The figures on the SPD are from Richard N. Hunt, *German Social Democracy, 1918–1933,* (New Haven, Conn.: Yale University Press, 1964.) p. 107.

Here again, the most useful information would be a comparison of different contemporary parties. Table 6 on the age distribution in the NSDAP and SPD in 1930/33 is a good example of such a comparison. It pits the Nazis with their slogan «Make way, you oldsters!» against the «old» SPD and bourgeois parties and against the whole gerontocracy of the Weimar Republic. Only the Communists could compare favorably in age with the NSDAP.

From the point of view of many younger voters, especially the veterans, the SPD was a party of established old men and its socialist doctrine an «outdated legacy» which had to be replaced with something more nationalistic, more revolutionary, or both. Here is a strong, if less intellectual, parallel to the national-syndicalist, integralist, or revolutionary-syndicalist precursors of fascism in the Latin countries.

The Austrian data in table 6, although the sample of political prisoners may be far from reliable, show the same fatal age differential between the Socialists and their National Socialist and Communist challengers. Here too, the generation gap became intensified by the socializing experiences of the war and the political and socio-economic crises following the dismemberment of the Hapsburg Empire. The majority of the Socialists had grown up politically before the war and were unable to win the support of many of the young workers and veterans. A comparison of the scant data available (table 7) shows several significant features. The youthfulness of the fascist parties of Denmark, Norway, Sweden and the United Kingdom matches that observed in Germany and Austria. The Austrian *Heimwehr* was obviously rather young and composed mostly of veterans. In Switzerland, too, the average age of National Front members appears to have been 34.[23] Throughout Eastern Europe from Romania to Finland the prominent role of veterans and students was likely to keep the average age of fascist movements very low, even if their traditionalistic sponsors may have been anything but young.[24] The Italian fascists were obviously young even though there seems to be little statistical information about their ages. The Icelandic Nationalists were said to be frequently below the voting age,[25] the Irish Blueshirts were largely army veterans, and even the Spanish Falange had a strong student element and generally a low average age,[26] as we would expect of the activists of the French radical right as well. There is abundant evidence, then, that fascist movements all over were a youth phenomenon.

A second aspect of the age statistics in table 7 relates to the passage of time with respect to any one movement. There is some evidence, at least with regard to the German and Austrian Nazis, that a considerable aging process was at work. Among the German NSDAP members of 1923, for example, the youngest groups tended to be students, apprentices, white-collar employees and skilled workers, while officers, entrepreneurs, civil servants, and the university-trained made up the older groups. In the late twenties and especially after the takeover in 1933, new recruits to the NSDAP tended to be older and older until the average age of the new members was 5–10 years higher than when the movement first gathered momentum. In other words, not only do the «fascists of the first hour» get older from year to year like everyone else, but the new recruits tend to belong largely to the same aging age-cohorts as the old fighters. The Austrian figures confirm this theory which seems to point to a rather specific Nazi generation born between about 1893 and 1912. This span of dates of birth would account for about two thirds of the known members, although it would not cover the continued recruitment of youth into the youth organizations of established Nazi régimes. The average years of birth fluctuate in the German case around 1898 to 1909,

769

Table 7. Ages of Members of Fascist Movements (in %)

| Germany | | | | | | | | Austria | | | | Denmark | | Norway | | United Kingdom | |
| 1923[1] | | 1930[2] | | 1930a[3] | | 1933[4] | | 1934[5] | | 1946[6] | | 1935[7] | | On Joining[8] | | 1930s[9] | |
Age	Per cent	Age	Per cent	Age	Per cent	Age	Per cent	Age	Per cent	Age	Per cent	Age	Per cent	Age	Per cent	Age	Per cent
–23	47	–25	37	–20	9	–28	43	–18	1	–19		–20	17	–18	10	–20	33
–23	53	26–35	31	21–23	11	29–38	27	19–23	25	20–29	5	21–25	21	19–25	22	21–30	47
		36–45	18	24–27	21	39–48	17	24–28	29	30–39	18	26–30	18	26–35	21	31–40	7
		46–55	9	28–34	29	49–58	9	29–33	14	40–49	32	31–40	19	36–50	27	41–	13
		56–	5	35–44	16	59–	3	34–38	15	50–59	28	41–	26	51–	16		
				45–51	7			39–43	6	60–	17			NA	4		
				52–	7			44–48	6								
								49–53	3								
								54–58	1								
								59–	–								
	100		100		100		100		100		100		100		100		100
n=4,800		n=129,563		n=321		n=349,000		n=301		n=108,405		n=2,740		n=54,000		n=15	

Sources:
1 Michael H. Kater, «Zur Soziographie der frühen NSAP», *Vierteljahreshefte für Zeitgeschichte.* XIX (1971), p. 155.
2 and[4] NSDAP, *Parteistatistik.* 2 vols.
3 Abel-Merkl breakdown, above p. 261.
5 G. Jagschitz, *Vom Justizpalast zum Heldenplatz*, p. 150. 6 Botz, above, p. 220.
7 Poulsen and Djusaa, above p. 710.
8 Larsen, above, p. 606.
9 John D. Brewer, above, p. 544.
n=total sample.

the first draft ages for World War I. In the Austrian case, the (less reliable) 1934 sample has an average date of 1907, and the 1946 sample of registered members one of 1899.

How do the ages of the members of fascist movements compare with those of the leaders as compiled by Juan Linz? More than half the fascist leadership was born between 1890 and 1910 and probably participated in the war or lived through it with the open eyes of an adolescent. The socialist leaders, by way of contrast, tended to have been born between 1860 and 1880, and the leaders of Christian parties such as the Geman Center or Italian Popolari between 1870 and 1890. If one had to assign an average date of birth to the leadership of the most common parties, it would be about 1893 for both the fascists (PNF and NSDAP) and the Communists (PCI and KPD), 1875 for the Socialists (PSI and SPD), and 1878 for the Christian parties.[27] The German *Reichstag* of 1930 was composed overwhelmingly of deputies between 50 and 70 years of age, with the SPD only slightly younger than the gaggle of bourgeois, regional, and Christian parties. The NSDAP and KPD, by comparison, were dominated by men in their thirties. These two extremist parties, in fact, between them had 110 of the 154 persons of that age group in the chamber.[28] It would appear that the leaders generally belong to the same generation as their followers but often to the older range of that generation.

The use of such age statistics can serve to illustrate by analogy the pitfalls of comparing social origins. Since age is a continuous variable, it is up to the researcher to delineate the precise age cohorts that are claimed to be in conflict. It will not do just to show some age differences or to engage in vague talk about a youth revolt. There is no reason to expect less precision in the definition of occupational and status groups that are said to be engaged in class conflict. At the very least we should be able to show that a majority of, say, members or leaders under 35 dominated the one movement while a majority of members over 35 dominated their antagonists, assuming for the sake of the argument that a convincing case can be made for the significance of age 35 as the borderline.

In the case of the differential between the SPD and NSDAP (table 6), the age groupings need to be brought into relation to meaningful generational experiences, such as service in World War I or exposure to the revolutionary turbulence of 1919/1920 or the right-wing upheaval of 1923. Unlike the compilers of official party statistics of NSDAP and SPD, we need to establish the prime war generation (born 1895–1901) and note, among other things, that these respondents were already 32 to 38 years old in 1933, which is not to deny that they may well have begun their process of political radicalization at a more youthful stage in their lives, or that older age-cohorts were also drafted during the last years of the war. In many of the other fascist movements the example of Mussolini's March on Rome must also be considered a major event.

To give significance to generational cohorts, we have to operate on the basis of a political socialization theory that attributes decisive impact in the formation of political attitudes to historical events at a particularly impressionable age, generally between 15 and 20, or at most 25. Thus the generations born before 1895, and certainly the ones born before 1890, are likely to have grown up in a peaceful, pre-war atmosphere, whatever other circumstances[29] may have socialized them in the direction of the NSDAP. Further analysis of the direction and intensity of the impact of the war generation is required. Once we acknowledge that our central concern is to construe political motivation, it is quite likely that those who volunteered the first enthusiasm of 1914–1915, or people who received medals or promotions, may have been affected differently from the frightened youngsters drafted in the years of disillusionment 1917–1918.

The post-war generation (born after 1901), which in the case of the 1933 Nazis amounted to about one half of the party and the vast majority of the stormtroopers, again falls into several distinctive age-cohorts. The oldest of these consists of respondents who, while being too young to be drafted, were nevertheless deeply impressed by the heroics and patriotism of the war effort (born 1902–1905). This age-cohort was likely to be further influenced by the clashes between revolutionary forces and Free Corps units of 1919/1920 and possibly by the right-wing conspiracies and agitation of the year 1923 as well. The youngest age-cohort of the 1933 NSDAP, by contrast, comes from the politicized youth of the Weimar Republic which marched under many different banners, the SA, the Communist Red Front, the republican *Reichsbanner*, the liberal *Jungdeutscher Orden*, the conservative *Stahlhelm*, and many others. The generational conflict, in a nutshell, pitted the war and post-war Nazi youth against the pre-war generations dominating the SPD and the «reactionary» conservative and liberal parties.[30] Such a thesis of generational conflict requires, of course, in every case also a documentation of the conflict attitudes to be found on both sides. The age statistics alone, like the occupational statistics by themselves, are not a sufficient proof of generational struggle.

Education and Geographical Origin

Information about other kinds of revealing indicators among the members of fascist movements is, unfortunately, almost non-existent or sketchy at best. If we had statistics on their levels of education as compared to those of their antagonists, for example, we might be able to fathom the extent to which the fascists were either underdogs against a better-bred establishment or, alternatively, relatively well-educated, upwardly mobile late-comers demanding entrance to the establishment. The latter description would fit considerable portions of the German NSDAP and the Italian PNF. (Table 8). Comparing the educational level of the NSDAP membership and élites with Linz's sample of fascist leaders is instructive, even though the Nazi leadership was probably not as well-educated as the fascist leaders of the Latin countries[31] where intellectuals have always been more accepted as the leaders of mass parties than in Germany. The *Führerlexikon* élite includes many members of the established social élites who were co-opted by that time by the Nazis. The rank and file, especially the hard core of pre-1930 members predominant in the Abel-Merkl sample, are far less educated than the leaders, although their record of secondary education compares favorably with the population average.

Data on ethnic or geographical origin, if systematically collected, might generate theories of ethnic conflict as explanations of fascism in many Eastern European countries such as Czechoslovakia, Finland, Poland and Eastern Germany, Hungary, Yugoslavia, Austria, and Northeastern Italy. The collapse of the Russian, Prussian, Austrian, and Ottoman empires and the new national minority problems of many of the successor states elevated the long-endemic ethnic conflicts of these areas to the status of major political factors.[32] Differences in the size of the community of residence are another feature that deserves further investigation. The Nazi movement, for example, started out with a majority in rural areas by 1923. In the first years after its re-establishment in 1925–1929, however, the bulk of the party became urban and, for a

Table 8. *Level of Education of Fascist Leaders, and of the NSDAP Membership*

	Abel-Merkl	Führer-lexikon	Fascist Leaders (Linz)
	per cent	per cent	per cent
Primary School only............................	22.9	5.0	2
Technical-Vocational	42.2	11.3	6
Secondary......................................	27.6	12.6	6
Specialized (Military, Teachers etc)		3.0	21
University not completed	3.8		7
University degree	3.5	68.0	38
NA..			20
	100.00	100.00	100.00

Sources: Merkl, *Political Violence Under the Swastika,* p. 724, Juan Linz, «Some Notes Toward a Comparative Study of Fascism in Sociological Historical Perspective» in: Walter Laqueur (ed.) *Fascism, A Reader's Guide,* p. 49, and Lasswell and Lerner, *op. cit.* p. 216.

while, was particularly strong in the small towns of Northern Germany. The hectic growth of the early thirties once more witnessed a return to the rural areas, but also a relative increase of membership in the metropolises of Germany at the expense of the small towns.[33] The importance of the «agrarian phase» in the growth of Italian fascism is well-known. By comparison, the fascist movements of the Netherlands, Great Britain, Sweden, and France appear to have been highly urban. The movements in the Protestant parts of Germany and in Norway, Ireland, Finland, Slovak Czechoslovakia, Romania, Hungary and Poland, together with the *Heimwehr* of Austria, had strong peasant or landowner elements, frequently with religious overtones. It is important, of course, to distinguish between a fascism of freeholder peasants and one inspired by the feudal or agrarian landed oligarchies of Eastern Europe or the Italian Po Valley. There are also other geographic patterns such as the strength of national socialist movements in North Schleswig or in the parts of Belgium near the German frontier. The larger the country, the more likely are diverse developments of rural, urban and metropolitan movements side by side.

Occupation and Social Class

With all the caveats expressed earlier, we can now return to the comparison of the sketchy occupational information on various fascist movements. As Michael H. Kater has already shown in his discussion of the «sociography» of the early Nazi movement, there are likely to be very considerable regional and rural-urban differences in the occupational structure of such a heterogeneous movement.[34] White-collar members, officers, or skilled workers for example, are far more likely to be found in metropolitan than in rural areas, and farmers almost exclusively in the countryside. The same heterogeneity seems to characterize the information in table 9. The number of fascist workers, for example, appears to have been far higher in the French PPF (57.3 per cent incl. peasants), the Spanish Falange (49.5 per cent), the Swiss National Front (32–46 per cent), or the Italian PNF (40.7 per cent) of 1921 than in the Dutch, Belgian,

Table 9. *Members' Occupations in Fascist Movements: Netherlands, Belgium, France, Norway, Spain*

	Netherlands¹				Belgium²			France³	Norway⁴		Spain⁵	Germany⁶	Italy⁷	Austria⁸
Workers:														
Skilled	20	7	–	–	8	5	10	57	7	9	10	9	16	18
Unskilled					2						39	16	24	
Agricultural									22	11				
White collar														
Employees	15	9	14	9	15	12	21	9	7	8	29	10	10	13
Public employees													5	20
Civil service					5	11	8	2	1	2		11		
Teachers													1	
Professions	25	40	8	2	6	11	18	8	7	3	10	5	7	5
& Students			54		1			3	5	4	3	1	13	
Businessmen			19	38	29	24	18	8	4	2	2	12	12	28
& Craftsmen					8	7	19	11	2	11		26		
Farmers				18		12			9			8	12	16
Others					3	15	5			9				
Officers	10			8							2			
Pensioners					16						5			
Women	20								13					
Youth		17							19	13				
No answer		21	46	4	6	3	1		13					
	100	100	100	100	100	100	100	100	100	100	100	100	100	100

Sources:
1. Estimated figures from local samples as described by Wusten and Smit, above p. 534 ff.
2. Small local samples as described by Wallef above p. 519 and Schepens above p. 515.
3. 736 PPF delegates in 1937, see Sternhell, above, p. 493. The entry for workers includes peasants.
4. 2,691 NS members before (1st. col.) and 49,437 after 1940 (2nd. col.) see Larsen above p. 611.
5. 1,103 FE members in Madrid in 1935, se Payne, above p. 425.
6. 849,000 NSDAP members in 1933, Parteistatistik.
7. 151,644 fascists in 1921, cited by Renzo de Felice, *Mussolini il fascista – La conquista del potere 1921–1925*, Torino, 1966, p.7.
8. See Botz, above p.218 f.: 541,727 registered members of the NSDAP in 1945. If we were to include pensioners, women, and students, these percentages would be somewhat lower. See Radomir Luža, *Austro-German Relations in the Anschluss Era*. Princeton University Press, 1975, p.381.

Table 10. *Class and Occupation of Members of the Swiss National Front and the Austrian Heimwehr*

	Switzerland			N.F. initiat.		Cantonal elect. candidates 1935			Austrian Heimwehr 1928*
	Schaff-hausen-Land 1935	Schaff-hausen-Stadt 1938	Sch.-Kanton 1942 (N.G.)	1934	1935	N.F.	Free p.	Soc. Dem.	
Unsk.workers ..	15.9	9.3	8.9	13.7	10.5	3.6 }	} 3.5	5.2 }	} 10.0
Skilled workers .	16.7	26.7	37.5	30.9	17.4	17.2 }		29.0 }	
White-collar empl.........	24.6	31.0	26.2	18.1	23.6	40.5	27.7	41.9	
Business folk ...	29.4	27.8	20.2	21.4	35.0	15.6	20.6	11.0	
Farmers	7.1	0.6	2.1	15.2	11.5	5.4	1.4	1.9	70.0
Upper class	6.3	4.6	5.1	0.7	2.0	17.1	46.8	11.0	20.0
	100.0	100.0	100.0	100.0	100.0	100.0	100.0	100.0	100.0

Sources: See Glaus, above p.473f. and, for the *Heimwehr, The New York Times,* Dec. 2, 1928. Other pertinent information tends to be non-quantitative. The Arrow Cross movement, for example, was composed of gentry-based officers and civil servants, artisans, small business folk and, most numerously, unorganized workers. The Iron Guard consisted of students, peasants, school teachers, public servants, workers and some entrepreneurs. In the early days, the *Heimwehr* was more of a popular defense movement against marauding soldiers of the Austro-Hungarian army: In Styria and Carinthia, they also had to fight off Yugoslav raiders. In Styria after 1927 it had a substantial workers' element from the Alpine-Montan works there. Otherwise, according to Andrew Whiteside in Weber and Rogger, *op.cit.,* p. 331, it consisted of urban middle class tradesmen, professional men, civil servants, ex-officers, small property owners, and pensioners concentrated in the provinces and mobilized by the metropolitan *Schutzbund* and events such as the 1921 veto of *Anschluss,* Mussolini's March on Rome, the 1927 Socialist uprising, and financial support from Italy and Hungary. Ustasha consisted of students (esp. seminarians), lower clergy, unorganized workers, and poor peasants (esp. from Bosnia and Herzegovina). Ljotic had the support also of students, intellectuals, and some priests, as did Orjuna. It is very instructive to compare these elements with the information cited by Burks, *op.cit.,* p. 35, for the inter-war Communist parties, bearing in mind that some Eastern European Communist parties have presented landless peasants and white collar employees along with the industrial workers as «wage workers». Burks concludes that two-thirds of the Communist voters of Poland, Czechoslovakia, and Bulgaria were small or landless peasants in this period, and that the proletarian element was minor or even absent. *Op.cit.,* pp. 40–44. There were also substantial middle class elements in the Communist parties of inter-war Eastern Europe whose motivation owed much to their belonging to persecuted ethnic minorities.
* G. Botz, *Gewalt in der Politik,* (Vienna; W. Fink Verlag) 1976, Heimwehr militants were composed of

31% Unskilled and agricultural workers
23% Skilled workers
15% White-collar employees
 8% Public service employees
23% Independents and farmers.

Militants are likely to be more lower class and younger than the rest of the movement.

Table 11. *Starting Point, Occupational Structure, and Important Components of Fascist Movements*

Country	Name of Group	Leader	Start	Occup. Structure (dominant elements)	Syndicalist organization (name)	Veterans	Important elements Farmers	Students	Church	Development index Industrial (1930s) versus agricultural employees	Self-employed versus dependent labor
Norway	Nasjonal Samling	Quisling	1933	White collar & farmers	–	–	x	x	–	27/36	28/65
Iceland	Icelandic Nationalists		1933	Seamen & shop assistants	–	–	(fish)	x	–	14/54	26/41
Denmark	DNSAP	Clausen	1930	Famers & urban middle classes	–	–	x	–	–	27/35	31/69
Netherlands	NSB	Mussert	1931	Old middle classes	Workers' Groups	–	–	x	–	38/21	19/70
Belgium	Rex	Degrelle	1936	Old and new middle classes, shop assistants	–	x	x	–	x	48/17	23/67
	Flemish Nationalists	DeClercq	1933			x		x			
Ireland	Blueshirts	O'Duffy	1932	Farmers/old middle classes	–	x	x	x	–	17/50	27/54
Great Britain	British Union of Fascists	Mosley	1931	Workers & white collar	idem	x	–	–	–	47/06	12/88
France	Faisceau	Valois	1925	Workers & white collar	Mutual Aid	x	–	x	–	33/37	42/58
	Jeunesse Patriotes	Taittinger									
	Legion	Redier	1924								
	Solidarité Française	Renaud	1933	White collar, old middle classes	–	x	–	x	–		
	Francistes	Bucard	1933	White collar workers, old middle classes	–	x	–	–	–		
	PPF	Doriot	1936	Workers & farmers	idem	x					
	RNP	Déat	1941								
Spain	JONS/Falange	José Antonio	1931	Workers, white collar & middle classes	Ledesmists	–	x	x	x	27/46	22/67
Portugal	National Syndicalists	Preto	1932	Students, young officers, workers	–	x	–	x	–	21/57	21/73
Switzerland	National Front		1930	Workers, white collar	–	–	–	x	x	44/21	22/70
Germany	NSDAP	Hitler	1919	White collar, old middle classes	NSBO	x	x	x	–	41/29	17/64
Italy	PNF	Mussolini	1919	Workers, old middle classes	Syndicalist Corporations	x	x	x	–	28/49	28/52
Austria	DNSAP/NSDAP		1918	Old & new middle classes	Workers DGB/NSBO	x	–	x	–	32/37	19/63
	Heimwehr	Starhemberg	1927	Farmers & military old middle classes	–	x	x	x	x		
Hungary	Arrow Cross	Szalasi	1935	Workers, military, civil servants	–	x	x	x	–	23/51	
	National Socialists	Gömbös	1919	Farmers, military, civil servants	–	x	x	x	–		
	Scythe Cross	Böszörmeny	1932	Poor peasants	–	x	–	–	–		
Romania	Iron Guard	Codreanu	1923	Peasants, students, bourgeoisie	Workers' Corporations	–	x	x	x	9/80	
Yugoslavia	Ustasha	Pavelic	1929	Students, workers, clergy	–	–	x	x	x	10/76	
	Orjuna/Zbor	Ljotic	1921	Students, clergy	–	x	–	x	x		
CSR	DNSAP (DAP)	Henlein	1920	Workers, old middle classes	DNAB	–	x	–	x	–	38/26	
	Slovak Peoples party	Hlinka	1920	Farmers, clergy							
	Czech Nationalists	Gajda/Str.	1925	Middle classes, students, farmers	–	x	x	–	x		
Poland	Great Poland/ONR	Dmowski	1926	Students	–	–	–	x	–	19/65	
Finland	Lapua/IKL	Kosola	1929	Farmers, students	–	x	x	· x	–	14/68	26/41
Sweden	Swedish Nat. Socialist Freedom League	Furugård/Lindholm	1924	Military officers, white collar, students	–	–	x	–	x		

Norwegian (17–30 per cent), German (27 per cent) and Austrian (17.5 per cent) movements. The Rexist movement in Belgium rates particularly low in this respect, if one can trust the sketchy information.

White-collar members and civil servants, by way of contrast, appear to be almost uniformly strong with 15–29 per cent, which is surely in excess of the share of these elements in the population of these countries.[35] Switzerland's (table 10) National Front (or National Community) also has a very high white-collar component, although here the blue-collar element was even higher. As for the old middle classes of business, handicraft and the professions, their share was very high in Belgium (25–40 per cent), the Netherlands (42–54 per cent), Germany (43.6 per cent), France (28.9 per cent), Austria (38.3 per cent), Italy (31.6 per cent), and Switzerland (20–30 per cent), in some cases even approaching a majority. Norway (9–16 per cent) and Spain (14.7 per cent) are the exceptions. The farmer element is relatively small compared with these other groupings except for the Austrian *Heimwehr*.

Table 12. *Starting Point, Triggering Events of Fascist Movements, and Development Index*

Country	Name of Group	Leader	Start	Depression (high, low)	Other economic crisis	World War 1	Civil war (red revolt)	Ethnic-Territorial conflict	1 Development index	2 Development index
Norway	Nasjonal Samling	Quisling	1933	low	Agricultural depression	-	-	-	27/36	28/65
Iceland	Icelandic Nationalists		1933	high	fishing	-	-	-	14/54	26/41
Denmark	DNSAP	Clausen	1930	low	agricultural depression	-	-	-	27/35	31/69
Netherlands	NSB	Mussert	1931	very severe	-	-	Socialist threats	-	38/21	19/70
Belgium	Rex	Degrelle	1936	severe	-	low	-	-	48/17	23/67
	Flemish Nationalists									
Ireland	Blueshirts	O'Duffy	1932	low	farm crisis	-	yes; «red» threat	-	17/50	27/54
Great Britain	British Union of Fascists	Mosley	1931	low-moderate	-	low	-	-	47/06	12/88
France	Faisceau	Valois	1925	severe	economic stagnation	medium	Popular Front	-	33/37	42/58
	Jeun. Patriotes	Taittinger								
	Legion	Redier	1924							
	Solidarité Française	Renaud	1933							
	Francistes	Bucard	1933							
	PPF	Doriot	1936							
	RNP	Déat	1941							
Spain	JONS/Falange	José Antonio	1931	very low	economic stagnation	-	«Red» threat	-	27/46	22/67
Portugal	National Syndicalists	Preto	1932	very low	economic stagnation	-	«Republican anarchy»	-	21/57	21/73
Switzerland	National Front		1930	moderate	-	-	-	-	44/21	22/70
Germany	NSDAP	Hitler	1919	very severe	agricultural depression	high	Yes; «red» threat	medium	41/29	17/64
Italy	PNF	Mussolini	1919	severe		high	Yes; «red» threat	low	28/49	28/52
Austria	DNSAP/NSDAP		1919	very severe	-	very high	Yes; Socialist uprising	high	32/37	19/63
	Heimwehr	Starhemberg	1918			very high				
Hungary	Arrow Cross National Socialists	Szalasi	1935	moderate	-	very high	Yes; Bela Kun	very high	23/51	
		Gömbös	1919							
	Scythe Cross	Böszörmeny	1932							
Romania	Iron Guard	Codreanu	1923	low	-	high	-	medium	9/80	
Yugoslavia	Ustasha	Pavelic	1929	low	-	high	-	very high	10/76	
	Orjuna		1921							
CSR	DNSAP (DAP)	Henlein	1920	severe	Sudeten business	high	-	very high	38/26	
	Slovak Peoples Party	Hlinka	1920							
	Czech Nationalists	Gajda	1925							
Poland	Great Poland ONR	Dmowski	1926	very severe	credit	high	-	high	19/65	
Finland	Lapua/IKL	Kosola	1929	low-moderate	forestry	-	Yes; «red» threat	high	14/68	26/41
Sweden	Swedish National Socialist Freedom League	Furugård/Lindholm	1924	low	agricultural depression	low	-			

Sources: Contributions to this book. For the impact of the Great Depression, see table 12a.
[1] Percentage employed in industry vs.agriculture.
[2] Self employed vs.dependent employees.

In this respect, the *Heimwehr* somewhat resembles the fascist movements of many Eastern European countries,[36] where movements such as Lapua, Hlinka, and the Iron Guard appear to have had a similarly large peasant element. On the other hand, there were strong farmer elements also in certain regions of the support of the Norwegian *Nasjonal Samling,* the German and Danish Nazis, or among land owners and laborers backing the Italian PNF. The Irish Blueshirts also enjoyed strong support among the farmers affected by the «economic war» with Great Britain. By the same token, however, looking for the countries with the highest proportion of their labor force in industry, Belgium (48 per cent), Great Britain (47 per cent), Switzerland (44 per cent),

777

Germany (41 per cent), Czechoslovakia (38 per cent), and the Netherlands (38 per cent) may not at all produce the fascist movements with the most working-class support but the fascists in these countries have sometimes been the most hostile to organized labor.

The old middle class basis of some fascist movements, likewise, is not always clearly related to unusually large numbers of self-employed in the population. Germany, for example, has one of the lowest proportions, as do Austria and the Netherlands, and yet their movements took in many a frightened small businessman or professional. Norway and Iceland, on the other hand, have high proportions of self-employed, but few of them in their fascist movements. Only Italy, France, and Belgium permit us to link the two. The recruitment of fascist parties, and perhaps of most political parties, appears to be difficult to reduce to such simple formulae. Instead it seems much more revealing to link fascist movements comparatively to the roles played by the veterans or military men, to students, to the church, or to such triggering events as the impact of World War I or subsequent civil wars or «red take-over» attempts, to the severity of the Depression, or to the presence of ethnic-territorial conflict. (Table 12)

In the case of Switzerland (table 10), there are also the two initiatives of the National Front of 1934 and 1935 which may, however, also have attracted some non-fascist voters for different reasons. Since the occupational distributions of the two lists of signatories differ considerably, they probably did not appeal to exactly the same public to begin with. Finally, there is also an occupational breakdown on cantonal candidates of the National Front and of two other competing parties. Like the earlier comparisons (table 3 and p. 764 f.), it shows both the considerable differences between the competing parties and the differential between members or voters and leaders. As to the first point, the National Front seems to have been closer to the Social Demo-

Table 12a. *Impact of the Depression: Gains and Losses in Industrial Output, 1932, and 1937 (in % of 1929)*

Country	Impact	1932 (as against 1929)	1937 (as against 1932)	1937 (as against 1929)
Sweden............	low	÷ 11	67.4	49
Norway	low	÷ 7	37.6	28
Denmark	low	÷ 9	47.2	34
Netherlands	very severe	÷ 38	46.7	÷ 9
Belgium	severe	÷ 31	36.2	÷ 6
Great Britain	low-moderate	÷ 17	49.3	.24
France	severe	÷ 31	4.3	÷ 28
Germany	very severe	÷ 42	100.0	16
Italy	severe	÷ 33	49.2	–
Austria	very severe	÷ 39	73.7	6
Hungary	moderate	÷ 23	77.9	37
Romania............	low	÷ 11	48.3	32
Yugoslavia...........	low			
Czechoslovakia.......	severe	÷ 36	50.0	÷ 4
Poland	very severe	÷ 46	57.4	÷ 15
Finland.............	low-moderate	÷ 17	79.5	49

Sources: League of Nations figures quoted by David S. Landes, *The Unbound Prometheus, Technological Change and Industrial Development in Western Europe from 1750 to the Present,* (Cambridge University Press, 1969) p. 391.

crats (including their high share of white-collar occupations) than to the Free (Liberal) party, evidently a party of old-style representation with many upper-class notables among its candidates. Nevertheless, the NF candidates were notably more white-collar and upper class than the NF members. Other leadership occupational data, especially on Belgium and Austria,[37] confirm this conclusion, and there is reason to believe that those on the Hungarian Arrow Cross candidates would do likewise, if we had more information about the membership. An occupational comparison of PNF deputies with those of the Popolari (PPI) in 1924, incidentally, yields hardly any differences except for a handful (14) of PPI working-class deputies that have no counterparts among the fascists.

What do these comparisons of occupational structures mean? We could attempt to interpret the fascist movements characterized by more working-class members (PPF, Falange, PNF, and National Front) as a «fascism of the left», the high white-collar- and civil-service elements as «fascism of the center» (Rexism, Falange, Nasjonal Samling, National Front and the German and Austrian NSDAP), and the movements with strong old middle-class and farmer components (NSB, Rexism and Verdinaso, PNF, and again the German and Austrian NSDAP) as «fascism of the right». This classification, based on rather impressionistic data, would yield a continuum from left to right about as follows:

Left: PPF (including farmers), Lindholm's brand of Swedish fascism
Left-Center: National Front, Falange
Center: Nasjonal Samling
Center-Right: Rexism, German and Austrian NSDAP
Left-Right: PNF, PPF
Right: NSB, Verdinaso

But this is not only a weakly documented and crude classification which does not take into account the shifts and realignments in the various fascist movements taking place over time. It also leaves two thirds of the movements under consideration without a label for lack of information. Worst of all, it fails to account for the greatly varying social structures of the countries, tacitly expecting from each of them the same proportions of worker, white-collar, or old middle class members.

We have tried to make up by estimates for such information as is unavailable or non-statistical (table 11). We added to this a mention of important groups, including veterans, ex-officers, or students. Finally, we also listed such major triggering events as the Depression and World War I and its political aftermath of civil wars, revolutionary upheavals of the left etc. in another table (table 12), along with an indicator of the degree of socio-economic development in the form of the percentages of the population employed in industry and agriculture. All this at times required subjective assessments which will hopefully challenge the scholarly community to offer corrections. It is obviously more important to introduce the right questions into the scholarly dialogue than to try and start out with all the right answers.

With the help of these estimates, now, we can add to the earlier left-right classifications a number of further movements:

Left: Icelandic Nationalists
Left-Center: BUF
Center-Right: Danish DNSAP, Irish Blueshirts, Solidarité Française, Francistes, Sudeten DNSAP

779

Left-Right: Faisceau, Iron Guard, Arrow-Cross
Right: *Heimwehr,* Hlinka, Lapua/IKL, Ustasha

The information is sketchiest on Eastern Europe which appears to be the most deviant sector of the fascist universe. The reason appears to lie 1. in the degree of socio-economic development, which gave little room for the presence of an industrial working class. Most of the other fascist movements sprang from the confrontation between socialist labor movements and the established bourgeois and land-owning classes, typically appealing to new bourgeois (white-collar) elements and seeking to draw workers away from the socialist movements. Eastern European fascism found its supporters more readily among the military and bureaucratic minions of the pre-war establishments of these areas, at times with pronounced clerical support.[38] This accounts for its place on the right of the continuum. 2. The Eastern European movements largely share a heritage of painful ethnic-territorial conflict from World War I which otherwise only touches the German and Austrian NSDAP, and marginally, the PNF. World War I rather than industrialization appears to have been the prime mover of Eastern European fascist mobilization, having uprooted millions and given new poignancy to ancient ethnic and social conflicts. This is another reason the veterans or military officers played such a prominent role in fascist movements in Hungary, Yugoslavia, Finland, and Poland. The officers or ex-officers are generally derived from the old ruling classes, or at least the lower gentry, and the veterans represent the peasant masses mobilized by the war and the territorial shifts of the peace settlement. In the case of Hungary, for example, tens of thousands of officers and civil servants flooded back from the ceded territories into Budapest and became a ready reservoir of nationalistic and later fascist organization. The shifts in the ethnic balance of power and privilege, moreover, were most quickly perceived by the students, who played a seminal role in most Eastern European movements, especially in the Iron Guard and Ustasha, but of course also, for cultural reasons, in Italy, France, and Spain.

If we put together the two lists of left-right classification, the geographic patterns also emerge sharply in the rest of Europe: The left and left-center patterns seem to predominate in the West and South, while centrist fascism and center-right combinations are more typical of Central and Northern Europe, including Belgium and the Netherlands.

Individual and Collective Motivations

In all these investigations, we should be careful not to forget the unexplored structures that would give more meaning to these findings. The point of identifying a fascist's occupation as we said before, is to indicate his political motivation. But it is only the first step. Data on occupation will not tell much without additional attitudinal evidence that might tie his motivation to broader, collective motivations such as nationalism, aggressive imperialism, or social pacification or restoration under a corporatist or communitarian *(Volksgemeinschaft)* label.

Lacking attitudinal information in most instances, we can try to construct a convincing case by relating occupational structure to economic crises such as the Depression or lingering agricultural decline, to cultural crises alluded to in fascist ideologies, or to the socio-political crises of the pre-war, often liberal, established order. But the evidence will remain merely circumstantial as long as it is not being fleshed out with first-person accounts of what the fascists in any one country really wanted and why.

The information on members' youthfulness presented in this essay may appear more convincing in comparison to the occupational heterogeneity and differences observed. All of the fascist movements indeed were very young as compared to their antagonists and predecessors among the parties, with the sole exception of the communists. However, here too, there has to be specific corroboration with structural (generational) and attitudinal information that often still remains to be explored. In the meantime, and pending further research, the evidence for generational revolt as the one great motivating force all these diverse fascist movements have in common appears to be strong and persuasive indeed.

NOTES

[1] Among the more notable comparisons in English are William Ebenstein's *Today's Isms,* (Englewood Cliffs, N.J., 1954), now in its sixth edition (1970); Seymour M. Lipset, «Fascism-Left, Right, and Center», in Lipset, *Political Man,* (Garden City, N.Y., Doubleday, 1959); Ernst Nolte, *Three Faces of Fascism,* (New York: Holt, Rinehart, 1966); Hans Rogger and Eugen Weber, *The European Right* (University of California Press, 1965); Weber, *The Varieties of Fascism* (Princeton: Van Nostrand, 1964); Walter Laqueur and George L. Mosse, eds., *International Fascism, 1920–1945* (New York: Harper Torchbooks, 1964); John Weiss, *The Fascist Tradition, Radical Rightwing Extremism in Modern Europe* (New York: Harper and Row, 1967); S. J. Woolf, ed., *European Fascism* and *The Nature of Fascism,* (both New York: Vintage Books, 1969); F. L. Carsten, *The Rise of Fascism,* (University of California Press, 1967); and Peter F. Sugar, ed., *Native Fascism in the Successor States, 1918–1945,* (Santa Barbara: ABC Clio Press, 1971). The literature on particular fascist movements frequently includes comparative excursions as well.

[2] See, for example, Fritz Stern, *The Politics of Cultural Despair, A Study in the Rise of the Germanic Ideology,* (University of California Press, 1961), or George L. Mosse, *The Crisis of German Ideology: Intellectual Origins of the Third Reich,* (New York: Grosset & Dunlap, 1964).

[3] Eugen Weber, *Action Française, Royalism and Reaction in 20th Century France,* (Stanford University Press, 1962), pp. 53–56.

[4] See, for example, the remarks of A. J. Nicholls in Woolf, ed., *European Fascism,* pp. 71–73, and the new historical literature on the Bavarian setting of these years.

[5] Martin Broszat lists and discusses many of these groups in *German National Socialism, 1919–1945* (Santa Barbara: ABC Clio Press, 1966), pp. 33–37, although he tends to consider them as bourgeois debating clubs rather than action-oriented predecessors of fascism.

[6] *Native Fascism in the Successor States, 1918–1945,* pp. 149–153.

[7] See esp. Andreas Werner, *SA und NSDAP,* unpublished dissertation, University of Erlangen-Nuernberg, 1964, pp. 5–49. For awhile, the early SA units were even under the command of Navy Captain Ehrhardt rather than under Hitler. Ehrhardt's naval brigade had been involved in the *Kapp Putsch* of 1920 which temporarily toppled the government.

[8] Werner, *op. cit.,* p. 544–552. The author estimates the SA and SS together at about 700,000 at the time of the appointment of Hitler.

[9] The Versailles Treaty created large numbers of unemployed military men by reducing the German army from an estimated 250,000 to 100,000 in 1920. The first major such reduction, in fact, brought on the *Kapp Putsch* of 1920 when army and navy units dislodged the Weimar republican government. The Free Corps already had a membership of some 400,000 in 1919, composed of veterans, including N.C.O.'s and officers (mainly younger ones) willing to go on fighting. See Herbert Rosinski, *The German Army,* (New York: Praeger, 1966) pp. 156–158.

[10] In 1919, about 150,000 Italian reserve officers were discharged, of whom many had come directly from a secondary school or university background. About 20,000 officers were enrolled in higher education while at their garrison posts.

[11] See Sigmund Neumann, *Die Parteien der Weimarer Republik,* (Stuttgart: Kohlhammer, 1965) pp. 120 and 136. This book appeared originally in 1932. As early as in 1930, the KPD was already ahead of the SPD in votes in several important metropolitan areas of the North and West. See also Horst Duhnke, *Die KPD von 1933 bis 1945* (Cologne, Kiepenheuer & Witsch, 1972).

[12] According to Sternhell, above, the last-mentioned figure probably doubled by 1939, and there were some three million «adherents», probably sympathizers, in 1938. These figures are likely to be rather inflated.

[12a] According to Wolfgang Schäfer more than half of the new members of the NSDAP were dropping out before 1930, and between 1930 and 1933 the rate was still one-third. *NSDAP: Entwicklung und Struktur der Staatspartei des Dritten Reiches,* (Marburg: 1957).

[13] We must be careful not to overstate the inducements. As Adrian Lyttleton points out, the PNF failed to attract «the mass of the rank and file of the ex-servicemen», even of those not committed to the Socialists or the Popolari. The sizeable ex-combatant movement of the South never turned fascist either.

[14] David Schoenbaum, *Hitler's Social Revolution,* Garden City, N.Y.: Doubleday, 1966, pp. 72–73.

[15] See the discussions, above in the introduction to the German and Italian section.

[16] See Merkl above, p. 269f. See also the sophisticated study of the Nazi *Führerlexikon* of 1934 in Harold D. Lasswell and Daniel Lerner, *World Revolutionary Élites* (Cambridge: MIT Press, 1965), where many of these problems are tackled though not always satisfactorily solved. A study of this type, of course, also is open to criticism of its sample basis, in this case the *Führerlexikon.*

[17] Milan, 1934.

[18] It would seem from table 4 that the 1919–1923 phase of the NSDAP was heavily older middle class and far less dominated by the new middle class elements: (white-collar and civil service) than the party had been in 1930 and after the take-over. At a recent German historical convention, Kater presented a paper on the changes in the NSDAP after the takeover with a table on new members which clearly shows the steep increases among civil servants, white-collar employees, skilled workers and the professions in 1933 and 1937, while the share of the older middle class was declining.

[19] The available statistics for contemporary parties are much more exhaustive, permitting, for example, a comparison of the West German party membership and voters of the SPD, CDU/CSU, and FDP. See Ossip K. Flechtheim, ed., *Die Parteien der Bundesrepublik Deutschland,* (Hamburg: Hoffmann & Campe, 1975) pp. 63, 400–406.

[20] While the Center party prided itself on being «of all classes», in other words a catch-all party, the liberal and conservative parties had their support among protestant agrarians ranging from small vintners to estate owners, the Prussian clergy and bureaucracy (DNVP), professionals and academically-trained persons, industrialists (DVP), teachers, and commercial and banking interests (DDP). Women and retail clerks also voted heavily for the DNVP. Since these parties were cadre parties rather than mass parties, however, this hardly describes their «membership».

[21] Hans Neisser, in 1930, also estimated 40% of the German SPD voters of that year to be composed of such non-labor elements as one third of all lower civil servants and one fourth each of the white-collar and the business and handicraft vote. *Die Arbeit,* vol. 10 (1930), 657–658. Hermann Weber, in his preface to the reissued *Die KPD in der Weimarer Republik* by Ossip K. Flechtheim, (Frankfurt: EVA, 1969), pp. 63–68 describes the extraordinary fluctuations among the German communists which make a comparison difficult. The KPD had always had a high share of unemployed members who by 1932 rose to 85% of the membership. There was a high turnover which meant losses nearly as high as the membership gains. In 1928, skilled workers made up 40%, the unskilled 28.2%, and agricultural laborers 2.2% of the party, which leaves 29.6% for the non-proletarian elements; the skilled workers were dominant in all party offices. See also Wienand Kaasch «Die soziale Struktur der KPD», *Kommunistische Internationale* vol. 9 (1928), p. 1050 f.

782

[22] Richard A. Comfort, *Revolutionary Hamburg*, (Stanford University Press, 1966) chaps. 4–7.

[23] See Beat Glaus, above, p. 475.

[24] See Stephen Ficher-Galati, above, p. 352 f.

[25] See Asgeir Gudmundsson, above, pp. 748.

[26] See Stanley Payne, above, pp. 423.

[27] See J. J. Linz, «Some Notes Towards a Comparative Study of Fascism in Sociological Historical Perspective» in W. Laqueur (ed.) *Fascism. A Reader's Guide* (Berkeley University of California Press) 1976 and also the remarks of Philippe Schmitter, above, pp. 443.

[28] Newmann, *op. cit.*, p. 133. The previous *Reichstag*, of 1928, had only half as many deputies of that age group. Daniel Lerner's sample from the *Führerlexikon* of 1934 also indicates averages around 40 and below for his leadership groups. Lasswell and Lerner *op. cit.*, p. 204.

[29] Among such pre-war factors, according to the Abel study, membership of the respondent or his parents in anti-Semitic organizations and class resentments of a kind of in between status between the socialist working-class and the nationalistic bourgeoisie were prominent. See Merkl above, p. 270 ff.

[30] This is not to suggest that the fighting organizations of the SPD, or of the other republican parties were much older than the SA or the Red Front. The *Reichsbanner Schwartz-Rot-Gold* which by 1932 had some 250,000 members was composed largely of veterans, but also of members of the post-war «political youth».

[31] Linz's conclusion that the fascist leaders were about as well-educated as their Christian, bourgeois, and socialist antagonists would probably not hold true in Germany except for the socialist parties. Studies of the *Gauleiter* level have shown them to be overwhelmingly lower middle class.

[32] On this subject, the breakdown given by the Stanford élite studies may be the best available, with about one third foreign contact experiences though no record of ethnic conflict. The Abel collection is rich in detail on this point, but hardly representative in numbers. Lasswell and Lerner, *op. cit.* p. 220. An outstanding example of the bearing of ethnic conflict on party formation is analyzed by R. V. Burks in *The Dynamics of Communism in Eastern Europe*, (Princeton University Press, 1961) which also contains useful comparative information on fascist parties in Eastern Europe.

[33] The *Führerlexikon* sample shows the Nazi and pro-Nazi élite to have been born in considerably more urban surroundings than the members, Lasswell and Lerner, *op. cit.*, p. 239.

[34] See the table in Kater, *op. cit.*, p. 150.

[35] Even in industrialized and urbanized Germany, the percentage of white-collar employees in 1930 was only 12.4% and of the civil service 4.8%. On the other hand, the workers amounted to 46.3% of the population.

[36] The development index in table 2 shows the extent of the agrarian element in Finland with 68%, Poland with 65%, Yugoslavia with 76% and Romania with 80% employed in agriculture; truncated Hungary with 51% comparison was closer to Ireland (50%), Iceland (54%), Portugal (57%), Italy (49%), and Spain (46%) in the percentage of its labor force employed in agriculture (and fishing).

[37] See Juan Linz, *op. cit.*, p. 57 especially the table on the Rexist candidates at the legislative provincial and municipal level or the information on Austrian Nazi candidates in Botz, above p. 204. In both cases, the old and new middle class elements among the candidates by far outnumber their equivalents among the membership.

[38] The Hungarian Arrow-Cross movement appears to be a mixture of the military-civil-servant element with a good admixture of workers, especially in public enterprises.

List of Contributors

Risto Alapuro, born 1944, Ph.D., lecturer in Sociology at the University of Helsinki, Finland. Author of *Akateeminen Karjala-Seura* (The Academic Karelia Society) (1973), and of several articles on political mobilization in Finland.

Stanislav Andreski, born 1919, Ph.D. (London), Professor and Head of Department of Sociology, University of Reading. Books: *Military Organization and Society*, London, 1954; *The Uses of Comparative Sociology*, 1965; *Parasitism and Subversion: The Case of Latin America*, 1966; *The African Predicament: a Study of Pathology of Modernisation*, 1969; *ed. Herbert Spencer: Structure, Function & Evolution*, 1971; *Social Sciences as Sorcery*, 1972; *The Prospect of a Revolution in the U.S.A.*, 1973; *ed. The Essential Comte*, 1974; *ed. Reflections on Inequality*, 1975; *Mental Pollution, forthcoming*.

Yannis Andricopoulos, born 1939. B.A., 1961; Panteios Graduate School of Political Science. Ex-President, Greek National Union of Students (EFEE). In journalism since 1964. Completing Ph. D. at London University. Publications include: *1944: Krisimi Chronia* (1944: A Critical Year), Athens: Diogenes, 1964; *Oi Rizes tou Ellinivou Fascismou* (The Roots of Greek Fascism), Athens: Diogenes 1977; *Ta Balkania Kai Oi Megales Dinameis* (The Balkans and the Great Powers), Athens: Diogenes, 1979. Presently working on a book on the Metaxas dictatorship.

Joseph Baglieri, born 1949, B.A. in Political Science and History, 1973, M.Phil. in Political Science from Yale University. He has been a Doctoral Fellow at the Johns Hopkins University in Bologna and is currently a Ph.D. candidate at Yale University.

Zevedei Barbu, born 1919 in Sibiu, Romania. D. Phil, University of Cluj, Romania, 1941; D. Phil., University of Glasgow, 1954. Professor of Sociology, University of Sussex. Main publications: «The Historical Pattern of Psycho-Analysis», *The British Journal of Sociology*, III, 1952; *Democracy and Dictatorship*, London and New York, 1956; *Problems of Historical Psychology*, London and New York, 1960; *Society, Culture and Personality*, Oxford, 1971; «Nationalism as a Source of Agression» in de Reuck et al. *eds. Ciba Foundation of Conflict in Society*, London, 1971; «Die sozialpsychologische Struktur des nationalsozialistischen Antisemitismus», in W. Mosse *(ed.) Entscheidungsjahr 1932*, Tübingen, 1965: «Violence in the Twentieth Century Literature», in D. Daiches et al. *(eds.) World History of Literature*, Vol. IV., London, 1975: 'Roumanian Fascism'», in S. Woolf *(ed.) European Fascism*, London 1969.

Jerzy Borejsza, Dosent Dr. Habil., Assistant Professor, Historical Institute of the Polish Academy of Sciences. Author of seven books and numerous articles on aspects of nineteenth and twentieth century European history, especially in the areas of European diplomacy, the history of socialism, the 19th century political emigration and most recently on the history of fascism. Major works related to the study of fascism: «L'Italia e le tendenze fasciste nei paesi baltici, 1922–1940», in: *Annali della Fondazione Luigi Einaudi*, Torino 1974, vol. VIII, pp. 279–316: «Italian Fascism and East-Central Europe 1922–1943«, in: *Poland at the 14th International Congress of Historical Sciences in San Francisco*, Wroclaw 1975, pp. 257–285: «Italiens Haltung zum Deutsch-Polnischen Krieg», in: *Sommer 1939. Die Grossmächte und der Europäische Krieg; Schriftenreihe der Vierteljahreshefte für Zeitgeschichte*, Sondernummer, Stuttgart 1979, pp. 148–194; *Mussolini byl pierwszy* (Mussolini was the First), Warsaw 1979; Rzym i wspólnota faszystowska (Rome and the Fascist Community), Warsaw 1980, Italian version: *Fascismo e l'Europa centro-orientale 1922–1943*, forthcoming.

Gerhard Botz, born 1941; Dr. phil., University of Vienna; 1968 to 1978 assistant and lecturer at the Institute of Contemporary History, in 1978 Dozent for modern and contemporary history, University of Linz; since 1980 Professor of Austrian History, University of Salzburg; Author of *Die Eingliederung Österreichs in das Deutsche Reich* (Vienna: Europaverlag 1972, 2nd ed. 1976), *Wohnungspolitik und Judendeportation in Wien 1938–1945* (Vienna: Geyer-Edition, 1975), *Gewalt in der Politik*, (Munich: W. Fink Verlag, 1976, 2nd ed. 1979), *Wien vom Anschluß zum Krieg* (Vienna: Verlag für Jugend und Volk, 1978).

John D. Brewer, born 1951, M. Phil. in Sociology, University of Birmingham, 1975.

Malene Djursaa, born 1949, Ph.D. University of Essex, 1979. Thesis: «Danish Nazism: The Membership of «Danmarks National-Socialistiske Arbejder Parti», 1930–1945». Book: *DNSAP. Danske Nazister 1930–1945,* Gyldendal, Copenhagen, forthcoming.

Renzo de Felice, born 1929, Professor of History, University of Rome. Publications include: *Storia degli ebrei italiani sotto il fascismo,* Torino, Einaudi, 1972; *Le interpretazioni del fascismo,* Bari, Laterza, 1974, (English translation by Brenda Everett, *Interpretations of Fascism,* Cambridge, Mass., 1977); *Mussolini* I (1883–1920), II (1921–1925), III (1925–1929), IV (1929–1936) . . ., Torino, Einaudi, 1969–74; *Mussolini e Hitler. I rapporti segreti 1922–1933,* Firenze, Le Monnier, 1975; *Fascism: An Informal Introduction to Its Theory and Practice,* New Brunswick, N.J., 1976.

Stephen Fischer-Galati, born 1924. B.A., M.A., Ph. D. History at Harvard University. Professor of History and Director, Center for Slavic and East European Studies at the University of Colorado. Editor of the *East European Quarterly.* Author of numerous books and articles on the history of Eastern Europe including *Ottoman Imperialism and German Protestantism,* Harvard Univ.Press, 1959: *The New Rumania,* The M.I.T. Press, 1967: *Twentieth Century Rumania,* Columbia University Press, 1970; *The Communist Parties of Eastern Europe,* Columbia University Press, 1979.

Beat Glaus, born 1935. Eidgenössische Technische Hochschule (ETH), Zürich. Head of Information and Users Service section, Main Library of ETH. Publications: *On Swiss Political Catholicism,* Schweiz, Rundschau, 1966: *The National Front,* 1969.

Asgeir Gudmundsson, born 1946. Cand.mag. History, University of Iceland 1975.

John Haag, born 1940, Associate Professor of History at the University of Georgia since 1969. Articles in *Journal of Contemporary History, Austrian History Yearbook, The Historian, Wiener Library Bulletin* and *Yearbook of the Leo Baeck Institute.*

Bernt Hagtvet, born in Oslo 1946, was educated at the universities of Oslo and Bergen and did his graduate work at Yale. He was a Research Fellow at the University of Oslo 1975–78 and spent the academic year 1975/76 at Nuffield College, Oxford. He is currently Senior Lecturer in Political Science at Oppland Regional College, Lillehammer, Norway. Current research interest: Theories of fascism; nationbuilding; intellectuals in politics.

Reijo Heinonen, Lecturer, University of Helsinki. Main Publications: *Anpassung und Identität. Theologie und Kirchenpolitik der Bremer Deutschen Christen 1933–1945.* AKIZ, Bd. 5, Göttingen: Vandenhoe & Ruprecht, 1978 *Work and Community. The Finnish Association of Ministers, 1918–1968;* Pieksämäki, 1969. (In Finnish).

Hans Hendriksen, born 1946. Cand.philol., Bergen, 1972. Contributor to R. Danielsen and S.U. Larsen *(eds.) Fra Ide til dom* (From Idea to Sentence), Bergen: Universitetsforlaget, 1976. Lecturer at Alta Regional College 1975–79.

Yeshayahu Jelínek, born in Czechoslovakia 1933, B.A. 1961, M.A. 1963, The Hebrew University of Jerusalem, Ph.D. 1966, Indiana University. Publications: *The Parish Republic: Hlinka's Slovak People's Party, 1939–1945,* Boulder, Colorado: *East European Quarterly, 1976.* «The 'Final Solution' – the Slovak Version,» *East European Quarterly,* IV, 4, July 1971; «Storm-troopers in Slovakia: the Rodobrana and the Hlinka Guard,» *Journal of Contemporary History,* VI, July 1971; «Slovakia's Internal Policy and the Third Reich, August 1940 – February 1941,» *Central European History,* IV, 3, September 1971; «Nationalism in Slovakia and the Communists, 1918–1929,» *Slavic Review,* XXXIV, 1, March 1975; «The Vatican, the Catholic Church, the Catholics, and the Persecution of the Jews During the Second World War: the Case of Slovakia,» in B. Vago and G.L. Mosse, *eds., Jews and Non-Jews in Eastern Europe, 1918–1945,* Jerusalem: Israel Universities Press, 1974; «Slovakia and Her Minorities, 1939–1945: People with and without National Protection,» *Nationalities Papers,* IV, 1, 1976; «The Slovak Right: Conservative or Radical – Reappraisal,» *East Central Europe,* IV, 1, 1977; «Nationalities and Minorities in the Independent State of Croatia,» *Nationalities Papers,* VII, 2, 1979.

Reinhard Kühnl, born 1936. Studied in Marburg and Vienna, Ph.D. (Habilitation) 1971. Since 1971 Professor of Political Science at the University of Marburg, West Germany. Publications include: *Die NS-Linke 1925–1930,* (Hain Verlag, Meisenheim 1966); *Die NPD.*

Struktur, Ideologie und Funktion einer neofaschistischen Partei, (Suhrkamp Verlag, Frankfurt/Main 1969) with R. Rilling; *Deutschland zwischen Demokratie und Faschismus,* Hanser Verlag, München 1968); *Formen bürgerlicher Herrschaft. Liberalismus und Faschismus* (Rowohlt Verlag, Reinbek 1971); *Texte zur Faschismusdiskussion I* (Ed.), (Rowohlt Verlag, Reinbek 1974); *Der Deutsche Faschismus in Quellen und Dokumenten,*(Pahl-Rugenstein Verlag, Köln 1975); (Ed.); *Faschismustheorien. Ein Leitfaden. Texte zur Faschismusdiskussion II,* (Rowohlt Verlag, Reinbek, 1979.) Articles in: *Politische Vierteljahresschrift, Vierteljahreshefte für Zeitgeschichte, Neue Politische Literatur, Das Argument,* and *Blätter für Deutsche und internationale Politik.*

Miklós Lackó, born 1921 in Budapest. Professor of History, University of Budapest since 1954. Also affiliated with the Institute of History at the Hungarian Academy of Sciences. Professor Lackó's main interests are Hungarian and Eastern European social and cultural history between the wars.

Stein Ugelvik Larsen, born 1938. M.A. in Political Science, University of Oslo, 1964. Assistant Professor, University of Bergen. Co-editor of two books on Norwegian National Socialism: *Fra Ide til dom* (From Idea to Sentence), Bergen, 1976; and *Nazismen og norsk litteratur* (National Socialism and Norwegian Literature), Bergen, 1975.

Juan J. Linz, born 1926 in Bonn, Germany. Educated at the University of Madrid and Columbia, Ph.D. in Sociology 1959. Pelatiah Professor of Sociology and Political Science at Yale. Juan J. Linz has written extensively on Spanish society and politics and on West Germany, Italy and Brazil. His main work has been in the theory of authoritarian regimes, political parties and elections, European Fascism, and the work of Robert Michels. His most recent publication is with Alfred Stepan, *The Breakdown of Democratic Regimes,* Baltimore: The Johns Hopkins University Press, 1978.

Hans-Dietrich Loock, born 1927. Dr.phil., Professor of Modern History, Free University, Berlin. Publications: *Offenbarung und Geschichte,* 1964, *Quisling, Rosenberg und Terboven* 1970, (Norwegian ed. 1972).

Maurice Manning lectures in the Department of Politics at University College, Dublin. His publications include *The Blueshirts* (Dublin & Toronto 1971); *Irish Political Parties* (Dublin 1972).

Peter H. Merkl, born 1932, Ph.D. University of California, Berkeley, 1959. Professor of Political Science since 1968, University of California, Santa Barbara. Author of *The Origin of the West German Republic* (1963); *Germany: Yesterday and Tomorrow* (1965); *Political Continuity and Change* (Rev. ed. 1972); *Modern Comparative Politics* (Rev. ed. 1977); *German Foreign Policies, West and East* (1974);*Political Violence Under the Swastika* (1975); and *The Making of Stormtroopers* (forthcoming). Editor of *Western European Party Systems: Trends and Prospects* (forthcoming) and of two series in comparative politics with Holt, Rinehart & Winston and Clio Press and Co-author of *American Democracy in World Perspective* (5th. ed. with Herman Pritchett, William Ebenstein, Henry Turner and Dean Mann) and of *Pluralist Democracies in Western Europe* (with Mattei Dogan), both forthcoming. Current research interests: German local government reform and a comparison of economic development policies in post-war Japan and West Germany.

Alan S. Milward, Ph.D., Professor of European Studies at the University of Manchester Institute of Science and Technology (UMIST). Author of *The German Economy at War; The New Order and the French Economy; The Fascist Economy in Norway; War, Economy and Society;* and joint-author of *The Economic Development of Continental Europe, 1780–1870;* and *The Development of the Economies of Continental Europe, 1850–1914.*

Jan Petter Myklebust, born 1947. Cand.polit. 1974. Norwegian Central Administration, 1975–77, UNDP Expert to Central Bureau of Statistics, Jakarta, Indonesia, 1977–78. Editor of *Indonesian Social Developmental Atlas, 1930–1978,* CBS: Jakarta, 1978.

Sten Sparre Nilson, born 1915. Associate Professor of Political Science, University of Oslo. His publications include: *Knut Hamsun und die Politik,* Ring Verlag, Villingen, 1964 and «Wahlsoziologische Probleme des Nationalsozialismus», in *Zeitschrift für die gesamte Staatswissenschaft,* Vol. 110, 1954.

Nico Passchier, born 1943, *Doctorandus* in Human Geography from the University of Amsterdam. Lecturer at the Social-Geographical Institute of this University and formerly editor of the *Tijdschrift voor Economische en Sociale Geografie.*

Bruce F. Pauley, born 1937, Professor of History, University of Central Florida. Ph. D. University of Rochester. Main Publications: *The Habsburg Legacy 1867–1939; Hahnenschwanz und Hakenkreuz: Steirischer Heimatschutz und Österreichischer Nationalsozialismus, 1918–1934.* A book on Austrian Nazism, *Hitler and the Forgotten Nazis: A History of Austrian National Socialism* will be published in 1981 by the University of North Carolina Press. Also contributions to the *Austrian History Yearbook, East European Quarterly, East Central Europe* and *Rocky Mountain Social Science Journal.*

Stanley G. Payne, born 1934. Ph.D. (History) Columbia University, 1960. Professor of History, University of Wisconsin. Books: *Falange* (1961); *Politics and the Military in Modern Spain* (1967); *Franco's Spain* (1967); *The Spanish Revolution* (1970); *A History of Spain and Portugal,* 2 vols (1973); *Basque Nationalism* (1975); (ed.) *Politics and Society in Twentieth-Century Spain* (1975); *Fascism. Comparison and Definition* (1980).

Henning Poulsen, born 1934, candidate in history 1960, dr. phil. 1970, Professor of Modern History at the University of Århus 1974. Author of: *Besættelsesmagten og de danske nazister* (1970). (The (German) Occupational Force and the Danish Nazis).

György Ránki, born 1930. Ph.D. 1957. Deputy director of the Historical Institute at the Hungarian Academy of Science since 1962 and Professor at Debrechen University since 1964. Visiting Fellow All Souls College (1972/73) Oxford, Ecole des Hautes Etudes en Sciences Sociales, Paris 1976. Main publications: *On Germany's Occupation of Hungary* (in Hungarian); *Economic Development in East Central Europe,* Columbia University Press, 1974; in Italian 1977, in Japanese, 1978; *Hundred Years of Hungarian Economy* London, 1974.

R. John Rath, born 1910. A.B., University of Kansas, 1932, M.A., University of California (Berkeley), 1934; Ph.D., Columbia University, 1941; Mary Gibbs Jones professor of History, Rice University; founder and editor, *Austrian History Yearbook;* corresponding member of the Austrian Academy of Sciences; author of *The Viennese Revolution of 1848.* (Austin, Texas: University of Texas Press, 1957) (reprinted by Greenwood Publishers, New York, 1969); *The Provisional Austrian Regime in Lombardy-Venetia, 1814–1815* (Austin, Texas, University of Texas Press, 1969); and *The Fall of the Napoleonic Kingdom of Italy* (New York: Columbia University Press, 1941) (reprinted by Octagon Books, New York, 1975).

David D. Roberts, born 1943, Ph.D., University of California, Berkeley, 1971; Assistant Professor of History, University of Virginia, 1972–1978; Associate Professor of History, University of Rochester since 1978. Publications include: *The Syndicalist Tradition and Italian Fascism,* Chapel Hill: University of North Carolina Press, 1979.

Stein Rokkan, born 1921, died 1979, Professor of Sociology, University of Bergen. Co-editor and co-author of several books: *Democracy in a World of Tensions* (with R. Mc Keon); *Comparing Nations* (with Richard Merritt); *Party Systems and Voter Alignments* (with S.M. Lipset); *Mass Politics* (with Erik Allardt); *Building States and Nations* (with S. Eisenstadt); *Quantitative Ecological Analysis* (with Mattei Dogan), co-author of *Comparative Survey Analysis* (1969). Numerous articles on comparative methods, data archives, citizen participation and nation-building. Author of *Citizens, Elections, Parties* (Oslo: Universitetsforlaget, 1970).

Luc Schepens, born 1937. Licentiate in Roman Philology, University of Gent 1961. Publications include works on Flemish emigration during the 19th century; the political situation in Belgium during the First and the Second World War and the «Royal Question». Author of *Joris van Severen. Een raadsel* (J. v. S. An Enigma), article in the Flemish review *Ons Erfdeel,* Rekkem 18th, 1975. pp. 221–239.

Philippe C. Schmitter, born 1936. Studied at Dartmouth College, the Universidad Nacional Autónoma de Mexico, the Université de Geneve and the University of California at Berkeley. (Ph.D.), Professor at University of Chicago. Selected Articles: «Still the Century of Corporatism?» In F.B. Pike and T. Stritch (eds.), *The New Corporatism,* Notre Dame University Press 1974; also in *Review Politics* (Jan. 1974).

«Corporatism and Public Policy in Authoritarian Portugal», Sage Publications, *Contemporary*

Political Sociology, No. 06–011, 1975. «Retrospective Thoughts about the Liberation of Portugal», paper presented at the Mini-Conference on Contemporary Portugal, Yale University, March 1975. Published in *Armed Forces and Society,* Fall 1975.

Carolyn W. Schum, born 1935; M.A., Southern Methodist University, 1961; associate editor, *Austrian History Yearbook;* writer, Baylor Medical School.

Ronald E. Smit, born 1948, Studied Social Geography 1967–1975 at the University of Amsterdam.

Zeev Sternhell, born 1935 in Poland. Professor of Political Science, The Hebrew University, Jerusalem. Educated at the Hebrew University of Jerusalem and the Fondation Nationale des Sciences Politiques, Paris. Author of *Maurice Barrès et la Nationalisme français* (Paris, A. Colin, 1972) and of *La Droite Révolutionnaire 1889–1914* (Paris, Editions de Seuil, 1978). Articles and contributions, related to the study published in this volume: «Irrationalism and Violence in the French Radical Right: The Case of Maurice Barrès,» in Philip P. Wiener and John Fisher (eds.), *Violence and Aggression in the History of Ideas,* New Brunswick, Rutgers University Press, 1974, pp. 79–98. «Fascist Ideology,» in Walter Laqueur (ed.), *Fascism: Analyses, Interpretations, Bibliography – A Reader's Guide,* Berkeley, University of California Press, 1976, pp. 315–376. «Le déterminisme physiologigue et racial à la base du nationalisme de Maurice Barrès et de Jules Soury,» in Pierre Guiral et Emile Témime (eds.), *L'idée de race dans la pensée politique française contemporaine,* Paris, Editions du Centre National de la Recherche Scientifique, 1977, pp. 117–138. «Paul Déroulede and the Origins of Modern French Nationalism,» *Journal of Contemporary History,* VI (1971), pp. 46–70. Reprinted in John C. Cairns (ed.), *Contemporary France: Illusion, Conflict, and Regeneration,* New York and London: Franklin Watts. 1978. «Barrès et la Gauche: de Boulangisme à La Cocarde (1889–1895)» *Le Mouvement Social,* 75 (1971), pp. 77–130. «National-Socialism and Antisemitism: The Case of Maurice Barrès,» *Journal of Contemporary History,* VIII (1973), pp. 47–66. «Anatomie d'un Mouvement Fasciste en France: le Faisceau de Georges Valois,» *Revue Française de Science Politique,* 26 (1976), pp. 5–40.

Daniéle Wallef, born 1949, *Licence* in history from Université Libre de Bruxelles, presently employed in the Belgian radio and television corporation. Publication: *Rex et les collusions politico-financières* (forthcoming).

Herman van der Wusten, born 1941. Ph.D. in Social Geography at the University of Amsterdam, 1977. Senior lecturer at the same university. Did research on political mobilisation in 19th century Ireland, on Dutch political parties and on agriculture and migration in Ireland and Morocco. Will publish a book on the NSB (together with N. Passchier) in 1980.

Friedrich Zipfel, born 1920, died 1978. Professor, Freie Universität, Berlin. Publications: *Vernichtung und Austreibung der Deutschen aus den Gebieten östlich der Oder-Neisse Linie,* Tübingen 1954; *Plötzensee,* Berlin 1960; *Gestapo und SD,* Berlin, 1960; «Krieg und Zusammenbruch», in: *Das Dritte Reich,* Hannover, 1962; *Kirchenkampf in Deutschland, Religionsverfolgung und Selbstbehauptung der Kirchen in nationalsozialistischer Zeit,* Berlin, 1965; «Hitler's Konzept einer Neuordnung Europas», in *Aus Theorie und Praxis der Historie, Festschrift für Hans Herzfeld,* Berlin, 1972.

INDEX

Due to the comprehensiveness of this volume the index has been delimited in the following way:
  Names of places, towns, regions have been omitted and only names of states will appear. However, Germany and Italy are excluded since they appear on every other page. Likewise concepts like fascism or Nazism and the names of Hitler and Mussolini are excluded for the same reasons. We have included names of all organizations, parties, institutions etc. mostly in English translation but occasionally in original language. Names of persons are included if they appear more than once.

eds.

Abel, T. 268, 282
Abel, W. 108, 259, 261, 617, 758, 766, 768, 770, 772, 773, 783
Abendroth, W. 50, 51, 116, 129
Academic Karelia Society (AKS) (Finland) 594, 681, 682, 683, 689, 690, 692, 693, 696, 698, 699, 700, 753
Ação Integralista Brasileira (Brazilian Integralism) 164, *see* A.I.B.
Acción Española 164
Action catholique de la Jeunesse belge (Catholic action of the Belgian Youth) 507
Action Française 120, 158, 164, 173, 179, 183, 185, 188, 254, 394, 479, 483, 484, 485, 487, 488, 492, 498, 499, 505, 506, 511, 515, 516, 754, 763, 781
– membership 486
Action nationale (Belgium) 504, 505
Action socialiste et révolutionnaire (Socialist and Revolutionary Action) (Belgium) 501
Adler, V. V. (Austro-Marxist leader) 160, 182
Adorno, T. 16, 106, 278
Afa association (Allgemeine freie Angestelltenbund) 87
Africa 127, 128, 453
Agrarian party (PAB) (Switzerland) 144
Agrarian party (Norway) 592
Agrarian party (Sweden) 592, 740
Agrarian People's Party (CS) 763
Agrarian Union (Finland) 679, 681, 682, 684, 688, 692, 693, 695, 762, 763
A.I.B. (Brazil) 187
Alapuro, R. 182, 185, 593, 678–86, 698, 699, 784
Albania 360, 363, 364

Alff, W. 50, 180, 181, 188, 282
Alfonsine monarchists (Renovación Española) 425
Algeria 492
Alker, H. 287, 291, 299
Allardt, E. 182, 462, 645, 684
Allardyce, G. 24, 742
Alldeutscher Verband 173, 188, 189
Allen, W. 78, 86, 100, 102, 108, 114, 115, 116, 117, 162, 183, 266, 284, 299, 620
All-Student Union (Greece) 571
Almond, G. 105, 108
America 66, 127, 128, 186, 552
Andenæs, J. 618, 656
Andreski, S. 12, 52–55, 784
Andricopoulos, Y. 422, 568–84, 784
Angola 452, 453
Angress, W. T. 112
ANI (Italy) 15
Annala, V. 690, 697, 698
Ansaldo, G. 328, 342, 347, 433
Anschluss 176, 193, 195, 201, 215, 217, 218, 220, 222, 224, 225, 226, 227, 229, 230, 231, 234, 235, 237, 245, 248, 395, 733, 774, 775
Antonesco, M. 362, 363
Antonescu, I. 179, 359, 362, 427
Antonio, J. 756, 763, 776, 777
approaches to the study of fascism, *see* theories
Aquarone, A. 336, 365
Ardelt, R. 201
arditi (shock troops) (Italy) 261, 328
Arendt, H. 12, 16, 17, 24, 33, 66, 67, 68, 71–74, 82, 85, 92, 97, 107, 161, 182
Aristotle 69, 106, 242
Army Comrades Association (ACA) 558, 559, 560, 564

A.R.P. (Anti Revolutionary Party) (Netherlands) 528
Arrow Cross Movement 22, 155, 159, 168, 352, 395–416, 756, 763, 775, 776, 777, 779, 780, 783
– election results 398–99
– election results – age 408
– election results – occupation, other parties 403–7, 410–15
– leadership – occupation 396–97
– membership – occupation 396–97
Asia 127, 128
Asia Minor 568, 569, 570
Associazione Nazionale Combattenti (war veterans) 326
Associazione Nazionalista Italiana 166, 173, 176, 183, 186, 188
Atatürk, K. 158, 357
Aune, A. 611, 618
Australia 127, 128
Austria, 21, 54, 120, 131, 132, 137, 138, 141, 143, 146, 147, 148, 155, 161, 163, 166, 168, 171, 175, 181, 182, 184, 186, 188, 191–256, 358, 363, 380, 383, 437, 640, 641, 683, 736, 755, 756, 757, 760, 761, 763, 769, 770, 772, 773, 774, 776, 777, 778, 779
Austrian Legion (in Germany) 215
Austrian Social Democratic Worker's Party 202
Austro-fascism 197, 200
Auszug (militarized part of the National Front) (Switzerland) 472, 473, 475
Avanti! (Socialist newspaper) (Italy) 327

Baden 81, 297, 468
Baglieri, J. 186, 259, 261, 318–36, 757, 784
Balbo, I. 330, 336
Banco de Angola 452
Banco de Portugal 452
Banco Nacional Ultramarino 453
Banque Ouvrière et Paysanne 492
Barber, B. 48, 49, 106, 107
Barbu, Z. 352, 379–94, 784
Barker, E. 106, 255
Barrès, M. 158, 188, 479, 481, 484, 486, 498
Bauer, O. 43, 199, 200, 205, 216, 223, 253, 255
Bavarian People's Party 81, 84
Bavarian police (BPP) 305
Bayerische Volkspartei 121
Bayerischer Bauernbund 286

BBP (Germany) 306
B.B.W.R. (Bezpartyjny Blok Współpracy z Rzadem) (Nonparty Bloc of Corporation with the Government) (Poland) 357
Beck, J. 357, 365
Beegle, J. 83, 90, 110, 112, 283, 291, 299, 638, 649
Belgium 21, 128, 137, 141, 143, 148, 155, 160, 162, 168, 171, 180, 183, 186, 192, 420, 421, 437, 501–16, 754, 757, 761, 763, 773, 774, 776, 777, 778, 779, 780
Bendix, R. 82, 110
Benedikt, H. 199, 224, 248
Benelux 182
Benewick, R. 554, 555
Bergsgård, A. 676, 677
Berlin 31, 80, 82, 109, 153, 170, 176, 266, 268, 280, 297, 302, 306, 307, 310, 361, 368, 369, 375, 584, 599, 669, 723, 727, 730, 755
Bernaschek, R. 216, 225
Berne 468, 469, 470, 476
berufständische Ordnung 97
Best, W. 308, 310, 311
Betriebszellenorganisation 222
Biétry, P. 481, 482, 498
Biff Boys (Great Britain) 763
Bismarck 46, 79, 95, 96, 103, 138, 147, 243, 302
Bjørgum, J. 677, 740
Black Hundreds 173
Blom, I. 649, 650
Blocchi Nazionali (Italy) 331
Bloch, C. 49, 130
Blue Blacks (Sinimustat) (Finland) 696, 697, 763
Blueblouses (female Blueshirts) (Ireland) 565
Blum, L. 480, 490, 497
Blå Garder (Blue Guards) (Sweden) 729
Boerenbond 503
Bonapartism 29, 46
Bonapartist theory 43, 151
Bondepartiet (agrarians) (Denmark) 707, 708
Bondepartiet (agrarians) (Norway) 161, 618, 636, 641, 644, 656, 661, 663, 667, 668, 672, 673, 674, 676
Bonsdorff, G. 685, 686
Borejsza, J. 176, 352, 353, 354–66, 619, 784
Borg, O. 698, 699, 700
Borkenau, F. 15, 24, 50, 172, 187

Bottai, G. 342, 345, 347
Botz, G. 192–225, 254, 256, 754, 770, 774, 775, 783, 784
Boudon, R. 292, 299
Boulangism 479, 481, 485, 488, 489
Bracher, K. 18, 19, 25, 29, 45, 49, 105, 109, 130, 266, 291, 299, 418
Brandstøtter, R. 200, 223, 224, 236, 237
Brazil 21
Brazilian Integralists 155, see A.I.B.
Brevig, H. 619, 620, 650, 656, 666, 674, 675, 677
Brewer, J. 542–56, 770, 784
Britain 38, 148, 233, 557, 558, 561, 563, 574, 577, 580, 773
British Fascisti (G.B.) 554, 763
British Labour Party 53
British Union of Fascists (BUF) 157, 177, 186, 187, 542–56, 644, 770, 756, 776, 777, 779
– membership 554
– membership – age, class 544, 545
– membership – occupation 546–47
Brook-Shepherd, G. 237, 238
Broszat, M. 49, 85, 111, 121, 129, 225, 376, 377, 781
Brotherhood of the Cross (Romania) 387, 389
Bruknap, D. 620, 647
Bruna Gardet (Brown Guards) (Sweden) 734
Brüning 67, 93, 286
Brzezinski, Z. 24, 33, 48
Bucard, M. 491, 494, 756, 763, 776
Buchheim, H. 249, 254, 256
Bulgaria 158, 159, 161, 169, 172, 185, 350, 352, 359, 361, 362, 363, 364, 365, 370, 383, 569, 775
Bull, E. 117, 628, 645, 676, 677
Bund der Landwirte (Germany) 89, 91
Bund Oberland (Austria) 231
Burks, R. 185, 775, 783
Burnham, W. 111, 638, 649, 657, 665, 666
Burrowes, R. 48, 107
Bygdefolkets krisehjelp (Farmers' Relief Association) (Norway) 592, 597, 607, 645, 647, 661, 662, 664, 665, 667, 675
Burån for arbets- og næringsfrihet (Bureau for Free Enterprise) (Sweden) 719
Bärnthaler, I. 237, 238, 248, 254, 255, 256
Böszörmény 395, 756, 763, 776, 777

Caetano, M. 435, 437, 459, 463, 464, 465
Caixa Geral dos Depositos (Portugal) 452
Caixa Nacional de Crédito (Portugal) 452
Camelots du Roi (shock troops) (France) 485, 486, 753
– membership 485
Cammett, J. 327, 335
Campbell, J. 556, 582
Cannistraro, P. 365, 366
C.A.P. (Cadres Actifs de Propagande or Active Propaganda Staff) (Belgium) 507
Caracciolo, A. 334, 347
Carlberg, C. 732, 733
Carlist 425, 427, 428
Carlsson, H. 739, 740, 742
Carpatho-Danubian Great Fatherland 182
Carpinelli, G. 517, 518, 523
Carsten, F. 200, 201, 223, 249, 251, 253, 254, 255, 256, 265, 350, 353, 466, 781
Cartel des Gauches (France) 484
Cassels, A. 18, 25, 422
Castle, F. 618, 742
Castronovo, V. 334, 335
Casucci, C. 187, 347
Catalonia 137, 140, 160, 182, 424
Catholic Academy of Art 369
Catholic Church 124, 137, 141, 175, 176, 184, 193, 199, 240, 324, 367, 376, 501, 511
Catholic Conservative Lager (Austria) 192, 193, 194, 196, 197, 198, 205, 214, 223
Catholic Party (Belgium) 502, 503, 504, 505, 506, 507, 508, 511, 513, 514
Catholic Party (Hungary) 407
Catholic Party (Lithuania) 180
Catholic Party (Netherlands) 534
Catholic segment/pillar (Netherlands) 525, 531, 532, 534, 538
Catholic Union (Italy) 320
Catholic Zentrum (Germany) 81, 84, 102, 638, 767, see Zentrum party (Germany)
C.A.U.R. (Comitati d'Azione per l'Universalitá di Roma) 362, 363, 366
Cecilja, V. 377, 378
Centralförbundet for arbetets frihet (Central Association for the Freedom of Work) (Sweden) 719
Centre Party (Ireland) 562, 563, 566

«centrifugal democracy» 67
«centrism of the extremists» 52
Chamberlain 733, 734
Charlemagne 138, 146
Chetnik resistance 370, 373
Chile 44
Christian-Democratic Party (Belgium) 503, 521
Christian National independent (Hungary) 413, 414, 763
Christian opposition (Hungary) 413
Christian Party (Hungary) 398, 399, 415
Christian Social Party (Austria) 192, 193, 194, 197, 201, 209, 212, 213, 223, 229, 233, 234, 416, 424
Christian theories, see fascism as the moral disease of Europe 28
Christiansen, C. 713, 714
Christliche Soziale Arbeiterpartei (Social Conservative) (Austria) 120
Christlich-National Bauern und Landvolkpartei 96
Christlich-Sozialer Volksdienst (Germany) 286
Christus Rex (Belgium) 507, 517–23
– candidates – occupation 519
– election results – regions 508–11, 517, 518
– membership 522
– representatives – occupation 520
Church of Rome 149, 150
Church People's Party (Kyrkliga Folkpartiet) (Sweden) – election results 732
Ciano, G. 362, 364
city belt 138, 142, 143, 144, 145, 146, 151
City-state Europe 137
Civil Guard organization (Finland) 683, 688
Clark, J. 104, 644, 739
Clarke, H. 111, 555
Clausen, F. 703, 706, 707, 709, 746, 750, 756, 763, 776, 777
Clemenz, M. 50, 113, 114, 250, 251, 253, 254, 255, 256
«clerical fascism» 197
CNT (the anarcho-syndicalist worker confederation) (Spain) 423
Coalition Party (Conservative Party) (Finland) 679, 681, 685, 687, 693, 694, 695, 697, 699, 762, 763
Codreanu, C. 169, 380, 383, 386, 387, 388, 389, 391, 392, 394, 433, 753, 756, 763, 776, 777

Comintern's «agent theory» 46, 640
Comité de politique nationale (National Policy Committee) (Belgium) 504
Communists (PCI) (Italy) 322, 331, 332
Communists (Switzerland) 474, 475
Communist International (Third International) 363, 590, 687, 734, 736
Communist Party (Germany) 122, 126, 301, 303, 767
Communist Party (Belgium) 502, 505, 521
Communist Party (Denmark) 592, 702
Communist Party (P.C.F.) (France) 480, 490, 491, 492, 495, 499, 500, 760
Communist Party (Greece) 571, 573
Communist Party (Iceland) 744, 749
Communist Party (Norway) 590, 591, 592, 635, 653, 656, 658
Communist Party (Sweden) 592, 739
Communist Red Front (Germany) 772
concepts of fascism, see theories
conceptual map of Europe 132, 136, 137, 147
Confederación Española de Derechas Autónomas (CEDA) 156, 180, 424, 425
Confédération Nationale des Ouvrièr du Batiment (France) 492
Confederation of German Employer's Associations (Vereinigung deutscher Arbeitgeberverbände) 79
Confédération Genérale du Travail (C.G.T.) (France) 483, 487, 488, 492, 497, 498
Confederation of National-Syndicalist Workers (France) 425
Confindustria (Italy) 264, 267
Confederazione Generale del Lavoro (C.G.d.L.) (Italy) 324
Conservative Catholics (Italy) 321, 324
Conservative Party (Sweden) 717, 718
Conservative Party (Finland) 679, 683
Conservative Party (Great Britain) 549, 551, 763
Constituent States' Political Police Headquarters (Der Politische Polizeikommandeur der Länder) 306
Constitutional-Democrats (Italy) 321
Conze, W. 105, 300
corporative Ständestaat 241
Corradini 162, 479
Corti, W. 467, 477
Coselschi, E. 362, 363

Cosgrave, W. 557, 559, 561, 562, 563, 564
Coston, H. 499, 500
Coty, F. 490, 494, 499, 763
coup d'etat by instalments 102
Coverdale, J. 179, 753
Croat Ustasha 169
Croatia 156, 158, 161, 352, 363, 370, 371, 372, 373, 374, 375, 376
Croatian Peasant Party 370, 372, 376
Croatian Ustasha Revolutionary Organization 367
Croce, B. 15, 24, 28
Croix-de-Feu (France) 485, 492, 493, 760
– membership 494, 495
Cumann na nGaedhael (Ireland) 557, 558, 559, 560, 562, 563, 564, 565, 566, 762
Cuza, A. 387, 394, 753
Czech legion 185
Czech Nationalists 756, 763, 776, 777
Czechoslovakia (CS) 54, 55, 131, 158, 161, 168, 171, 182, 185, 192, 198, 202, 203, 226, 227, 255, 351, 352, 359, 364, 366, 367, 369, 374, 375, 733, 754, 756, 757, 761, 763, 772, 773, 775, 776, 777, 778
Czermak, E. 255, 256
Czichon, E. 38, 51, 64, 114, 130

da Costa, G. 463, 465
Dahl, H. 116, 117, 619, 644, 647, 650, 677, 685, 738, 739, 740
Dahl, R. 189, 645, 649
Dahrendorf, R. 29, 41, 50, 105, 115, 247, 299
Danielsen, R. 618, 620, 640, 649, 650
Danish Boy Scouts 703
Danneberg, R. 199, 200, 211, 213, 223, 224
D'Annunzio, G. 161, 165, 182, 324, 362
Dansk samling (Danish Unity) 592
Dante Alighieri (Italy) 363
Darré, W. 91, 282
Darwin, C. 162, 174, 244, 720
DDP (Liberal Democrats) (Germany) 82, 95, 96, 102, 109, 121, 129, 272, 285, 286, 289, 767, 782
de Bruyne, A. 515, 518
Déat, M. 420, 479, 480, 484, 491, 493, 496, 497, 498, 500, 756, 763, 776
Declercq, S. 504, 505, 776

Degrelle, L. 177, 187, 506, 507, 508, 510, 512, 515, 517, 518, 519, 522, 523, 756, 776, 777
de Jong, L. 540, 541
de Jonge, A. 540, 541
de Jouvenal, B. 479, 492
de la Cierva, R. 424, 433
de La Rocque, C. 480, 494, 496, 500, 760
de Man, H. 480, 512
Demerdijs 575, 576
Demichel, A. 463
«Democratic Army» (communist-led) (Greece) 568
«Democrático» Party (PRP) 455, 458
Democrats (Italy) 321
Democrats (Switzerland) 474, 475
de Neuflize, J. 500
Denis, J. 507, 515, 519, 522
Denmark 137, 141, 142, 159, 162, 186, 519, 522, 587, 588, 589, 590, 591, 593, 600, 619, 640, 702–14, 738, 756, 763, 769, 770, 776, 777, 778
Depression movements (Finland) 680, 681, 684, 685
de Rivera, P. 154, 157, 160, 169, 189, 424, 425, 427, 433, 456
Déroulede, P. 422, 485, 486, 499
de Ruggiero, G. 340, 347
de Tocqueville 69, 77, 94
Det Unga Sverige (Young Sweden) 729
Deutsche Arbeiterpartei 173, 188, 226, 754
Deutsche Bank 59
Deutsche Bauernbund 89
Deutsche Bauernschaft (formerly Bauernbund) 89, 286
Deutsche Landwirtschaft 89
Deutsche Lebensgebiete 308
Deutsche Studentenschaft 244
Deutscher Gewerkschaftsbund für Österreich (German Trade Union Federation in Austria) 208
Deutsch-Hannoversche Partei 286
Deutsch-Nationale Volkspartei 80, 84, 112
Deutsch-Soziale Partei (DSP) 262, 754, 759
Deutschvölkischen Schutz- und Trutz-Bundes 189, 262, 754, 760
de Valera 557, 559, 560, 561, 563
DHV (Germany) 87, 94, 114
Dickinson, R. 284, 299
Diels, R. 303, 304, 305, 306, 307, 308

793

Dietschland (a state where the Dutch-speaking areas would be reunited) 182
Dietsche Militanten Orde (Dutch Militant Order) 505
Dimitrov, G. 29, 687, 697
Djursaa, M. 593, 618, 619, 644, 703–15, 785
Dmowski, R. 352, 355, 356, 756, 763, 776, 777
DNSAP (Austria)
 – candidates – occupation 204
 – candidates – sex 203
 – election results 202
 – election results – sex 203
 – election results – urbanization 223
 – membership – age 768, 770
 – membership – occupation 767, 774
 – membership – papers-sirculation 204
 – militants – age 206
 – militants – occupation 206
 – representatives – occupation 204
 – trade-union votes 209
DNSAP – Danmarks Nationalsocialistiske Arbejder Parti (Denmark's National Socialist Workers' Party) 702–14, 776, 777, 779
 – election results – regions 702–6
 – election results – urbanizations 708
 – membership 702, 712
 – membership – class 711
 – membership – drop outs/urbanization 712
 – membership – month of joining 709
 – membership – regions 708
 – membership – sex, age 710, 770
 – membership – year of joining/urbanization 713
DNVP (Germany) 15, 30, 82, 94, 95, 109, 112, 121, 123, 129, 264, 270, 285, 289, 290, 295, 297, 762, 763, 767, 782
Doblin, E. 84, 111
Dolchstosslegende 160
Dollfuss, E. 131, 197, 199, 215, 216, 226, 229, 232, 234, 237, 238, 248, 249, 250, 251, 253, 254, 255, 362
Domobranda (Home Guards, armed units) (Croatia) 370
Dopolavoro (Italy) 234
Doriot, J. 157, 177, 420, 480, 484, 491, 492, 493, 494, 496, 498, 500, 733, 742, 756, 760, 763, 776

Dreyfus 481, 483, 488, 489
Drossopoulos 577, 578
Drucker, P. 15, 24, 69, 105, 478
Duncan, D. 293, 299
Durica, M. 375, 376
Durkheim 69, 107
Dutt, R. 15, 24, 153, 179
Dúverger, M. 187, 492
DVP (National Liberals) (Germany) 82, 95, 96, 109, 121, 130, 285, 286, 289, 767, 782

Edmondson, C. 201, 236, 237
Eggen, E. 629, 645, 646, 676
Eibl, H. 240, 242, 243, 244, 245, 247
Eichholtz, D. 51, 59, 64, 130
Eichstädt, U. 237, 248
Eicke, T. 305, 310
Einsatzgruppen (Germany) 302
Einwohnerwehr (Germany) 272, 759, 760
Eisenberg, P. 555, 740
Eisenstadt, S. 47, 50, 150
Ekstrøm, M. 725, 729, 730, 731
Elvander, N. 740, 741
Emilia 167, 327, 329, 330, 331
Engdahl, P. 725, 727, 729, 731, 732, 733, 735, 739
Engels, F. 43, 51
England 21, 127, 128, 137, 138, 146, 147, 151, 153, 184, 542–56
Eriksson, E. 722, 723, 724, 726
Estado Novo (Portugal) 169, 178, 187, 421, 437, 438, 439, 446, 448, 449, 458, 459, 461, 462, 465
 – election results – regions 460
 – representatives – age 443, 447
 – representatives – occupation 440, 445, 447
 – representatives – regions 442, 447
Estat Català (the separatist semi-fascist) (Spain) 161
Estonia 133, 155, 159, 160, 169, 172, 179, 180, 187, 686, 730
Ethiopia 364, 661
Étienne, J. 514, 515, 517, 518, 519, 520, 523
«extremism of the center» 12, 29, 513, 646, 657, 665, 666

Fabian society 323
Fabry, P. 28, 45
Factory Cell Organization (NSBO) (Germany) 263

Fagopposisjonen av 1911 (Union opposition in 1911) (Norway) 590
Fachgruppe Werkzeuge 60
Faisceau 479, 484, 485, 486, 487, 489, 490, 494, 498, 499, 756, 763, 776, 777, 780
– membership – occupation 488
Falange (Spain) 55, 169, 179, 185, 422, 758, 779
Falange Española 424, 428, 762, 764, 769, 773
– militia regions 428
Falange Socialista Boliviana 181
Falconi, C. 376, 377, 378
Falter, J. 105, 110
Farinacci, R. 60, 342
Farmers' Party (Ireland) 144, 558
Farmers' Party (Bauernpartei) (Switzerland) 474, 475
Farneti, P. 260, 322, 333, 335, 336
Faró 460, 464
«Faschismus als Bündnis» 46
Fasci di Combattimento (FC) 314, 325, 327, 330, 332
– leadership – occupation 314–15
– membership – occupation 314
– membership – regions 327
«fascists as moderates» 52
«fascist epoch» 752
«fascist era» (epoch of 1919–1945) 422
Fascist International, 1928–1936 184, 363
«fascist minimum» 19, 20, 566
«fascists of the first hour» 769
«fascists of the second hour» 262, 761
fascist theories, *see* theories
Fatherland Front (Austria) 194, 233, 235, 250, 252
– membership 234
FDP (Germany) 782
FE de las JONS (Spain)
– election results 426
– membership – occupation 425–26, 433, 774
Feder, G. 61, 527, 722
Federal Social Workers' Party (Eidgenössische Soziale Arbeiter-Partei) (Switzerland) 469
Federal Union (Eidgenössische Sammlung) (Switzerland) 470
Fédéderation des Cercles Catholiques (Belgium) 507
Fédéderation International des Mineurs (France) 497

Fédération Nationale des Jaunes («Yellows») de France 481–82
Federterra (Italy) 324
Fedrelandslaget (Patriotic League (Fatherland)) (Norway) 614, 642, 644, 667, 668, 672, 674, 677
Felice, R. de 15, 18, 19, 23, 25, 44, 45, 46, 178, 181, 185, 189, 258, 259, 266, 312–17, 330, 335, 336, 337, 338, 339, 345, 346, 347, 418, 422, 774, 785
Fellner, F. 200, 249, 253
Ferrara 329, 330
Fest, J. 28, 45, 50, 265
FET Movimiento-Organización (Spain) 429, 430, 431, 432, 434
– leadership 430
– membership 429
– membership – occupation, age 431
Fetscher, I. 37, 50
Fianna Fail Party (Ireland) 557, 558, 559, 564, 566
Fine Gael (Ireland) 561, 563, 565
Finland 131, 133, 137, 141, 143, 144, 145, 159, 160, 161, 166, 172, 182, 185, 192, 361, 437, 586, 587, 588, 589, 590, 591, 592, 593, 654, 678–701, 731, 736, 738, 755, 756, 763, 764, 769, 772, 773, 776, 777, 778, 780, 783
Finnish Communist Party 590, 592, 687, 688
Finnish Socialists 696
Fischer-Galati, S. 184, 350–53, 783, 785
Fisher, F. 87, 130
FKV (Austria) 194
Flemish Catholic Party 514
Flemish Nationalist Militia 505
Flemish Nationalists 502, 503, 508, 511, 512, 513, 756, 763, 776, 777
– election results 502
Flyg, N. 716, 734
Flächenstaaten 151
Four Year Plan 59, 61
F.P. (Front Populaire or Popular Front) (Belgium) 507
FPÖ (Austria) 194
Framstegspartiet (Progress Party) (Iceland) 593
France 21, 38, 127, 128, 131, 135, 136, 137, 138, 141, 143, 144, 145, 146, 147, 148, 149, 151, 158, 160, 162, 163, 164, 168, 170, 171, 175, 183, 184, 229, 232, 233, 365, 380, 419, 420, 421, 422, 423, 454, 479–500, 502, 504, 513, 518, 522,

733, 754, 755, 756, 760, 763, 773, 774, 776, 777, 778, 780
Francistes (France) 489, 490, 494, 499, 756, 760, 763, 776, 777, 779
– membership 491
Franco 54, 55, 178, 179, 180, 361, 422, 427, 428, 432, 733, 758, 762, 763
Frauenfeld, A. 205, 232
Free Corps (Germany) 262, 270, 272, 273, 274, 281
Free Economy Union (Freiwirtschafter) (Switzerland) 475, 779
Freiheitliche Partei Österreichs (since 1955) 194
Freikorps-Epp 84, 754, 759, 760, 772, 781
French organic chemicals industry 59
French Workers Study and Mutual-Aid Group 487
Fricke, G. 376, 377
Friedrich, C. 24, 33, 34, 35, 36, 47, 48, 49, 188
Frisch, H. 237, 238
Frisinnede Folkepartiet (National Liberals) (Norway) 642, 644, 667, 668, 677
Frisinnede Venstre (Moderate Conservatives) (Norway) 618
Fromm, E. 15, 16, 31, 32, 33, 48, 105
Front Veterans' Association (Frontkämpfervereinigung) (Austria) 193, 194, 197, 200, 205, 223, 230, 231, 234, 235, 237, 754
Frontbeweging (Movement of the Front) (Belgium) 503, 505, 511
Frøland, K. 675, 676
Funder, F. 254, 255
Furre, B. 649, 677
Furugård, B. 721, 722, 723, 727, 728, 729, 730, 731, 741, 756, 776, 777
Furugård, G. 721, 724, 741
Furugård, S. 721, 722, 724, 725, 730, 741, 763
Führerprinzip 20, 169, 201, 202, 233, 235, 418, 486, 506, 643, 694, 720, 724
Föreningen Det Nya Sverige (Association «New Sweden») 725, 728, 731, 732
Föreningen för teknisk samhällshjälp (literally «The Association for Technical Societal Assistance») (Sweden) 719

Gaeta, F. 188, 334, 338, 346
Gajda 756, 763, 776, 777
Galicia 427, 428

Galkin, A. 15, 24
Galvão, H. 446, 464
Garruccio, L. 17, 188
Gasset, J. 16, 24, 69, 106
Gay, P. 105, 247
GEDAG (Gesamtverband Deutscher Angestelltenwerkschaften) 87
Gedye, G. 252, 255
Geiger, T. 29, 47, 101, 111, 116, 225, 283, 290, 299
general theories of fascism, see theories
generic category of fascism 185
«generic fascism» 14, 20, 22, 27, 45, 418, 419, 420, 423, 466
generic phenomenon 21
genesis of fascism 38
geoeconomic-geopolitical model 131–52
geo-political theories 720
German Athletes' Association (Deutscher Turnerbund) 205
German Brewer Association 262
German Christians (Deutsche Christen) 696
German Commercial and Industrial Employees' Union (Deutscher Handels- und Industrieangestelltenverband) 209
German Communists (KPD) 760
German Earth and Stone works 63
German Labour Front 57
German National Lager (Austria) 192, 193, 194, 198, 205, 208, 213, 223
German National Socialism 17, 21, 29
German National Socialist Labour Party 53, 109, 202, 226
German Peoples' Party (DVP) 94
German Social Union (Deutsch-Sozialer Verein) 210
German Sturmbattalione (shocktroops) 759
German trade unions federation (DGB) 87
German Transport Union (Deutsche Verkehrsgewerkschaft) 208
German Workers' Party (Austria) 188, 202, 226, 230
Germani, G. 189, 253
Gerschenkron, A. 113, 180, 742
Gerth, H. 92, 111, 283, 290, 291, 299
Gessner, D. 112, 113
Gestapo 179, 217, 265, 281, 301–11, 578
– occupation 304
Gewerkschaft der Angestellten (socialist) (Germany) 86

Gewerkschaftsbund der Angestellten (GdA) (Germany) 87
Gilg, P. 467, 477
Giolitti, G. 165, 176, 315, 318, 319, 320, 321, 322, 323, 325, 327, 331, 332, 334
Giolittian Liberals (Italy) 321, 322, 332, 333
Giovannini, C. 330, 335
Glaus, B. 420, 467–79, 775, 783, 785
«Gleichschaltung» 53, 60, 71, 113, 291
Goebbels 258, 362
Gonatas, 569, 570
Goodman, L. 293, 299
Gossweiler, K. 46, 51, 64, 130
Goudsblom, L. 298, 299, 540
Government Party (Hungary) 398, 399, 404, 405, 407, 408, 410, 411, 412, 413, 414, 415
Gramsci, A. 186, 320, 334, 343, 347
Grand Duchy of Luxembourg 504
Grandi, D. 330, 336, 339, 342, 345
Great Britain 141, 182, 437, 518, 542–56, 756, 763, 777, 778
Great Poland/ONR 756
Greater German People's Party (Grossdeutsche Volkspartei) 193, 194, 211, 228, 230, 234, 235, 237
Greece 44, 159, 161, 172, 183, 184, 360, 362, 364, 366, 380, 383, 421, 422, 568–84
Greek National Socialist Party 571
Green Front (Germany) 89, 95
Greenland 161, 592, 600, 640, 649
Greenstein, F. 46, 107
Gregor, A. 15, 18, 23, 24, 25, 44, 106, 182, 184, 187, 188
Greiffenhagen, M. 47, 49
Griffuelhes, V. 483, 497
Grossdeutsche Volkspartei (German Nat.) 212, 231
Groupes mobiles (later Jeunes Gardes, Young Guards) (Belgium) 505
Gruner, E. 467, 477
Gruppo Misto (Italy) 322
Grünberg, E. 47, 116
Guardias de Franco 433
Guarneri, F. 60, 65, 267
Gudmundsson, A. 593, 594, 743–50, 783, 785
Guérin, D. 15, 24, 64
Gulick, C. 200, 224, 236, 237, 238
Gummerus, H. 689, 692, 699
Günther, W. 357, 365

Gömbös, G. 226, 232, 756, 776, 777
Göring, H. 258, 303, 304, 306, 307

Haag, J. 201, 225, 237, 239–48, 254, 785
Haataja, L. 685, 686
Habicht, T. 211, 216, 217, 228, 231, 232, 235
Habsburgs 138, 146, 182, 192, 195, 202, 224, 229, 237, 238, 240, 243, 530, 769
Hagtvet, B. 12, 26–51, 66–117, 131–152, 162, 186, 259, 264, 266, 299, 593, 594, 618, 619, 621–50, 666, 675, 714–42, 757, 761, 785
Hallgren, K. 724, 726
Hamel, I. 111, 114
Hamilton, R. 31, 48, 82, 109, 110
Hanisch, E. 44, 201, 205, 254
Hansson, H. 670, 676
Hansson, P. 726, 741
Hantsch, H. 236, 254
Hardach, G. 105, 114
Harst (vanguard formations) (Switzerland) 471
Hartmann, S. 675, 676, 741
Haubenberger, L. 223, 236
Hayes, P. 466, 646, 649
Heberle, R. 90, 109, 112, 113, 266, 283, 290, 291, 297, 299, 638, 649, 665, 666
Hedengren, S. 724, 726
Hedilla, M. 432, 434
Heimatblock (Austria) 236
– election results – regions 212
– representation – occupation 196
Heimatbund (Austria) 236
Heimatschutzbewegung (Austria) 236
Heimwehr (Austria) 159, 194, 195, 197, 198, 200, 201, 205, 206, 207, 210, 211, 213, 214, 222, 223, 226, 227, 228, 229, 230, 231, 234, 235, 236, 237, 249, 250, 252, 253, 255, 630, 754, 756, 762, 769, 773, 775, 776, 777, 780
– leadership – occupation 231
– members – occupation 228
– representation – occupation 196
Heinonen, R. 594, 687–702, 785
Helsinki Finnish Socialists 694
Hendriksen, H. 593, 596, 618, 628, 631, 638, 647, 649, 651–56, 666, 785
Henlein's Sudetendeutsche Partei (CS) 168, 183, 756, 763, 776, 777
Henne, R. 468, 470, 471, 478
Hennig, E. 46, 47, 50
Hervé, G. 480, 491, 496

Heydrich, R. 304, 305, 306, 307, 308, 309, 310, 311
Hildebrand, K. 23, 25, 47, 107
Hildisch, D. 671, 677
Himmler, H. 217, 258, 266, 304, 305, 306, 307, 308, 309, 310, 376, 584, 722, 727, 728
Hindenburg 67, 93, 123
Hird (Norway) 613, 647, 654, 669, 670, 671, 763
Hirschmann, A. 639, 649
Hitler Youth (H.J.) 274, 307, 310, 602, 696, 729, 763
Hjort, J. 597, 599, 646
Hlinka, A. 183, 352, 367, 756, 763, 776, 777, 780
Hlinka Guard (Hlinková garda) 368, 374, 375, 763
Hlinka's Slovak People's Party 375
Hoare, Q. 334, 500, 583
Holland 420, see Netherlands
Holmgren, I. 739, 741
Home Ustasha (Croatia) 370, 371
Horthy, M. 169, 359, 361, 362, 427
Hory, L. 376, 377
Hubay, K. 395, 400
Huber, F. 306, 307
Hudal, A. 240, 245, 247
Hugelmann, K. 240, 244, 247
Hugenberg 92, 123, 264
Hughes, H. 44, 105, 106, 254
Hungarian national socialists 22
Hungary 21, 22, 54, 133, 137, 159, 161, 163, 167, 172, 183, 195, 210, 226, 232, 352, 359, 362, 363, 364, 370, 380, 383, 395, 755, 756, 763, 764, 772, 773, 775, 776, 777, 778, 780, 783
Hunt, R. 291, 299, 768
Huntington, S. 189, 430, 433
Huuhka, K. 685, 698
Hameenlinna 689, 700
Högern (Conservatives) (Sweden) 739
Högman, A. 726, 741
Høire (Conservatives) (Norway) 607, 618, 636, 642, 644, 650, 658, 665, 667, 674

Iceland 137, 141, 143, 144, 145, 586, 591, 593, 594, 743–50, 756, 763, 776, 777, 783
Icelandic Nationalist Movement 743, 744, 745, 746, 750, 756, 763, 764, 769, 776, 777, 779

– election results 745, 747
– membership – age, occupation, regions 748–49
Icelandic Nationalist Student Association 747
I. G. Farbenindustrie 59, 64
IKL (Fatherland movement) (Finland) 592, 594, 679, 682, 683, 685, 686, 687–702, 756, 763, 767, 777, 780
– election results – regions 691
– leadership – occupations 699
– membership 694.
Il Popolo d'Italia 263, 771
ILVA (Italy) 328
Independence Party (Iceland) 744, 745, 748, 749, 763
Independents (Ireland) 558
Independents («Landesring der Unabhängigen») (Switzerland) 469
«Independent State of Croatia» (Nezavisna Država Hrvatska, NDH) 370
Independent-Socialists (Italy) 321, 322
India 38
Ingman, L. 694, 699
Institut für Konjunkturforschung 101
Integralismo (Latin American fascist party) 169, 438
I.R.C.E. (Italy) 363
Ireland 131, 137, 143, 144, 163, 172, 418, 420, 557–67, 755, 756, 763, 773, 776, 777, 783
Ireland, Northern 557
IRI (Italy) 60
Irish Blueshirt (ACA) 420, 557–67, 756, 762, 763, 769, 776, 777, 779
Irish Free State 557–67
Irish Republican Army (IRA) 163, 557, 558, 559, 560, 561, 564, 565, 566
Iron Guard 22, 155, 157, 166, 168, 173, 179, 180, 183, 352, 353, 359, 379–84, 389, 426, 427, 433, 753, 756, 763, 775, 776, 777, 780
– election results 392
– membership – occupation, age 389

Jablonowski, W. 355, 365
Jaeckel, E. 23, 25
Jagschitz, G. 200, 205, 206, 225, 238, 767, 768

Japan 38, 39, 40, 175
Japanese fascism 39
Jaurés 482, 497
Jedlicka, L. 199, 200, 206, 223, 225, 254, 255
Jelínek, Y. 352, 367–78, 785
Jenkner, S. 47, 107
Jeunesses Communistes (France) 491, 492
Jeunesses nationales (National Youth) (Belgium) 504
Jeunesses Ouvrières Chrétiennes (France) 492
Jeunesses Patriotes – La Legion (France) 485, 486, 489, 492, 494, 499, 756, 763, 776, 777
– membership 485
Jeunesses Radicales (France) 492
Jeunesses Socialistes (France) 492
Johnsen, B. 656, 666, 676
Jones, L. 108, 115, 116
JONS (Juntas de Ofensiva Nacional-Sindicalista) (Spain) 189, 425, 427, 428, 466, 756, 763, 776, 777
– membership – occupation 423
Jonsson, T. (poet) 629, 646
Juillard 138, 139, 140, 151
Jungdeutscher Orden 772
Juva, M. 698, 700
Juventud de Acción Popular (JAP) (Spain) 180
Jääkärit (national activist liberation group) (Finland) 688

Kaila, E. 697, 700
Kaltefleiter, W. 83, 110, 113, 168, 186
Kapp Putsch 273, 781
Kares, K. 698, 700
Kater, M. 83, 111, 129, 766, 770, 773, 783
Keele, M. 111, 266
Kekkonen, U. 685, 692, 697
Kerekes, L. 237, 254, 255
King, A. 464, 465
King Alexander I 363, 370
King Boris III 359, 361
King George 569, 573, 574, 575, 577, 582
King Gustav Vasa (1523–1560) 730, 734

King Harald Fairhead 628
King Leopold III 503, 512, 513
Kirschbaum, J. 375, 378
Kitchen, M. 44, 46, 47, 107
Kjellén, R. 643, 719, 720, 721, 741
KPD (communists) (Germany) 82, 84, 92, 280, 285, 286, 687, 767, 768, 771, see Communist Party (Germany)
– election results 80
Klinge, M. 698, 699, 700
Klingenstein, G. 200, 247, 253
Klöckner family 114
Klönne, A. 37, 49
Kocka, J. 86, 87, 109, 111, 114, 116
Kohn, H. 24, 28, 45
Kondylis 569, 570, 572, 573, 574, 575, 576, 577, 582
Konservative Volkspartei (Germany) 286
Korizis 577, 581
Kornhauser, W. 12, 16, 24, 68, 69, 71, 72, 73, 75, 76, 84, 90, 91, 92, 93, 94, 97, 98, 99, 103, 108, 113, 114, 116, 299
Kosola, V. 690, 756, 763, 776, 777
Kozich, T. 224, 225
Kreissler, F. 237
Kriegel, A. 499, 500
KU (Konservativ Ungdom) (Denmark) 642
Kuhn, A. 44, 46, 151
Kulturkreis theory of cultural diffusionism 244
Kühnl, R. 12–13, 15, 26–51, 59, 105, 109, 110, 111, 114, 118–30, 182, 200, 223, 250, 254, 259, 684, 685, 785

Labour Battalions (Metaxas life-guard) (Greece) 578
Labour Party (Great Britain) 551
Labour Party (Ireland) 558, 559
Labour Party (DNA) (Norway) 161, 290, 590, 591, 592, 614, 618, 635, 636, 640, 642, 644, 652, 653, 656, 658–59, 660, 662, 667, 668, 671, 673, 674, 676, 722
Lackó, M. 352, 395–400, 786
La Conquista del Estado 423, 432
Lafferty, W. 117, 644, 645
Lagardelle, H. 480, 483, 498

Lancillo, A. 259, 342
Landbrukernes sammenslutning (Denmark) 592
Landbund (L.B.) (Austria) 194, 211, 212, 234, 235, 237, 286
Landvolk movement (Germany) 90, 286
Landwirtschaftsbund Ostpreussen 89
Lang, P. 468, 478
Lapua movement (Finland) 182, 363, 590, 591, 592, 593, 594, 654, 678, 679, 680, 681, 682, 683, 685, 688, 689, 690, 692, 693, 694, 732, 738, 756, 762, 763, 764, 767, 777, 780
Laqueur, W. 44, 45, 46, 178, 179, 181, 335, 773, 781, 783
la Rochelle, D. 157, 184, 479, 498
Larsen, S. U. 586, 621, 622, 644, 645, 647, 649, 650, 656, 770, 774, 786
Lasswell, H. 773, 782, 783
late-comer's dilemma 325
Latin America 380, 464
Latvia 155, 172, 179, 183, 359, 360
Lauwery, J. 645, 666
la Victoire group (France) 491
Lazarsfeld, P. 200, 555
League for Independence (Finland) 689
League of Loyal Swiss National-Socialist Ideology (Bund treuer Eidgenossen nationalsozialistischer Weltanschauung) 470
League of the Archangel Michael (Romania) 379, 380, 388, 391, 426
League of National Christian Defence (Romania) 388, 753
League of National Defence (Romania) 387
League of Nations 60
League of Youth (Ireland) 561, 763
Le Bon, G. 70, 107
Lebovics, H. 49, 115
Le Corbusier 505–6
Ledeen, M. 24, 182, 184, 422
Lederer, E. 12, 16, 24, 47, 68, 72, 74–76, 97, 107
Ledesma, R. 63, 424, 425, 527
Lega National Ticinese (Switzerland) 469
Legião Portuguesa (para-military) 435, 445, 446, 449

Légion nationale (Belgium) 505, 513
– membership 505, 512
Lehmann, H. 113, 676
Lehmkuhl, J. 674, 677
Lenin 188, 555, 688
León 423, 427, 428, 431
Leopold, J. 216, 217, 225, 235
Lepsius, M. 79, 105, 107, 108, 113, 115, 283, 290, 291, 299
Lerner, D. 84, 111, 773, 782, 783
Lettland 179, 187, see Lithuania
Liberal bloc segment (Netherlands) 533
Liberal Party (Belgium) 502, 503, 513
Liberal Party (Great Britain) 551
Liberal Party (Greece) 571, 572, 574, 577
Liberal Party (Netherlands) 526, 528, 532, 535, 539
Liberal Party (Romania) 183, 383
Liberals (Hungary) 398, 399, 404, 405, 406, 407, 410, 411, 412, 413, 414, 415
Lidman, A. 717, 721
Ligue Antisémite (France) 486
Ligue d'Action Française 486
Ligue de la Jeunesse nouvelle (France) (League of the New Youth) 501
Ligue de la Patrie Française 486
Ligues des Chefs de Section (France) 485
– membership 485
Ligue des Patriotes (France) 485, 486
Ligue pour la restauration de l'ordre et de l'autorité dans l'Etat (France) 501
Ligue nationale pour la défense dè l'Université de Gand et de la liberté des langues (Belgium) 504
Ligue pour l'Unité belge (League for Belgian Unity) 504
Lijphart, A. 107, 298, 299, 540
Lindholm, S. 719, 723, 724, 725, 726, 727, 729, 730, 731, 734, 735, 741, 756, 763, 776, 777, 779
Linna, L. 685
Linz, J. 12, 13, 20, 46, 107, 108, 114, 115, 153–89, 200, 215, 216, 227, 239, 259, 298, 299, 325, 333, 335, 422, 430, 431, 433, 462, 730, 771, 773, 783, 785
Lipset, S. M. 18, 25, 29, 30, 31, 47, 48, 52, 82, 83, 95, 108, 109, 110, 113, 115, 150, 186, 200, 249, 253, 254, 256, 259,

283, 290, 291, 299, 513, 636, 638, 645, 647, 649, 657, 665, 666, 781
Lithuania 155, 172, 180, 183, 359, 360, 361, 730, *see* Lettland
«Little Brothers» (Romania) 390
Ljotic, D. 352, 756, 763, 775, 776
Lohalm, U. 189, 266
Loock, H.-D. 593, 619, 666, 667–77, 786
Loomis, C. 83, 90, 110, 112, 283, 290, 291, 299, 638, 649
Lopukhov, B. 15, 24
Lorković 377, 378
Los von Rom movement (Austria) 231
L.T.S. (Lithuania)
– membership 361
Ludendorff, E. (General) 721, 723
Ludz, P. 47, 49
Lueger, K. 120, 192
Lukács 29, 45, 130
Lunde, G. 671, 676
Luther 45, 265
Luxembourg 155, 508
Luza, R. 201, 219, 225, 774
Lyons, F. 138, 566
Lyttelton, A. 46, 258, 266, 323, 334, 339, 344, 347, 781

Macedonia 159, 161, 185, 363, 569, 570, 571, 574, 581
Machine Tool Manufacturers Association 60
Machtergreifung 154, 170, 245, 283
MacRay, D. 287, 299
MacVeagh 583, 584
Mellet Frènes et Cie. Bank 500
Manheim Society (Samfundet Manheim) 732, 733
Mann, G. 28, 45
Mannerheim, C. 361, 427, 680, 685, 686, 689
Manning, M. 183, 420, 557–67, 786
Manfeld copper works 59
Mansfeld-Konzern 64
March on Berlin 760
March on Rome 14, 15, 131, 156, 165, 261, 262, 263, 264, 265, 315, 316, 355, 356, 442, 560, 688, 759, 771, 775
March on Warsaw 354, 356

Marić, T. 376, 377
Marzues, O. 443, 455, 463, 465
Marschak, J. 47, 107
Marseilles 363, 370
Martins, H. 463, 465, 466
Marx, K. 31, 35, 48, 69, 107, 149, 151, 339, 454
Marxist critiques of modern capitalism and its culture 69
Marxist theories 29, 38, 42–44, 49, 50, 170, 171
Mason, T. 15, 24, 38, 44, 49, 51, 65, 104, 117, 130, 249, 254
mass society, *see* theories
mass theory, *see* theories
Mathias, E. 105, 110, 285
Mathon, E. 487, 499
Matica Slovenskà (Slovakia) 369
Matthys 519, 522
Maurras, C. 484, 485, 486, 505, 515
Mayer, A. 47, 108, 334, 554
Mazzini, G. 339, 342, 345, 347
McGovern, W. 28, 45
McKibbin, R. 83, 110, 113, 186
Meinecke, F. 15, 24, 28, 45
Meldrum, J. 287, 299
Melograni, P. 267, 347
Meneghello-Dincic, K. 376
Menghin, O. 240, 244, 245, 247
Merkl, P. H. 182, 239, 258–82, 617, 752–83, 786
Merritt, R. 200, 299
Metaxas, I. 363, 569, 571, 572, 573, 574, 575, 576, 577, 578, 579, 580, 581, 582, 583, 584
Messerer, I. 200, 237
Mestrović, I. 377, 378
Michalopoulos 578, 581
Mechels, R. 163, 184, 483
Miguel 298, 299
Milatz, A. 110, 283, 285, 299
Military Ustasha (Croatia) 370, 371
Millerand, A. 482, 486
Milward, A. 12, 56–65, 64, 65, 259, 786
Ministero della Cultura Popolare (Italy) 362, 363, 365
Ministry of Armaments in Germany 60
Missiroli, M. 259, 336
Mocidade Portuguesa 445, 446, 449

801

modèle parisien 138
modèle peripherique 138
modèle rhenan 138
modernization theory, *see* theories
Mommsen, H. 46, 49, 64, 88, 109, 111, 114, 115, 130, 225
Moore, B. Jr. 18, 25, 29, 38, 39, 40, 41, 50, 130, 149, 150, 380, 678, 684, 685, 686
Moore, C. 189, 430, 433
Morocco 159, 162
Morsey, R. 110, 285
Mosley, O. 157, 169, 177, 187, 420, 480, 543, 544, 546, 548, 549, 550, 554, 644, 756, 763, 776, 777
Mosse, G. 47, 115, 165, 184, 185, 189, 249, 254, 376, 498, 781
Mota, I. 183, 385, 386, 387, 391, 392, 394
Mother Protection Association (Mutterschutzwerk) (Germany) 234
Movimento Sociale Italiano (MSI) 758
Movimiento Nacional (Spain) 429
Mozambique 452, 453
MSR (France) 763
Mussert, A. 526, 527, 529, 531, 534, 538, 541, 756, 763, 776, 777
Müller, J. 47, 49
Müller, H. 236, 243, 306, 307, 308, 310, 687
Myklebust, J. P. 105, 113, 593, 618, 621–50, 676, 739, 786

Napoleon, L. 138, 149
Nasjonal Samling (NS) (Norway) 157, 161, 593, 595–678, 756, 763, 776, 777, 779
– candidates – occupation 608
– election results – other parties 658, 663
– election results – precincts 658
– election results – regions 597–99
– leaders – occupation 608, 611, 671
– membership 599–601, 697
– membership – age 602, 770
– membership – age/sex 606
– membership – age/sex, year of joining 603, 604, 605
– membership – communes 627

– membership – election results/other parties, polarization 636
– membership – farm size/NS farmers 634
– membership – motivations 614
– membership – motives/occupation 616
– membership – occupation, year of joining 608, 609, 611, 612, 774
– membership – regions 625, 669–70
– membership – region, urbanization/ year of joining 622, 624
– membership – votes for other parties 638
Nationaal Socialistische Beweging (National Socialist Movement – NSB) (Netherlands) 524–41, 756, 760, 761, 774, 776, 777
– election results – gains from other parties 533
– membership 536, 537
– membership – paper circulation 528
– membership – regions 529–35
Nationaal-Socialistische Vlaamsche Arebeiderpartij (The Flemish National-Socialist Workers Party) 512
National Association Sweden-Germany (Riksföreningen Sverige-Tyskland) 733
National Bank of Greece 574, 577
National Club (Norway) 667, 670
National Corporate Party (Ireland) 563
National Democrats (Poland) 354, 355, 357, 358, 359
National Democrats (Switzerland) 475
«Nationale Gemeinschaft» organization (Switzerland) 472, 473, 775
Nationale Zadruga Faczisti (Bulgaria) 181
National Federation of Labour (LO) (Norway) 653, 654
National Federation of German Industry (Reichsverband der deutscher Industrie) 79
National Front (Hungary) 410, 413, 414
National Front (Switzerland) 467, 756, 763, 769, 773, 774, 776, 777, 778, 779
– candidates – age 475
– candidates – occupation 473, 474

- election results - regions 468
- membership - occupation 473, 474
- membership - regions 469
- petition signers - occupation/region 474, 475
National Guard (Ireland) 560, 562
National Union of Greece (EEE) 571
National Legion (Norway) 667
National Liberation Front (EAM) (Greece) 568, 581, 582
National Peasant Party (Romania) 383
National Progress Party (liberal) (Finland) 681
National-radikala Samlingspartiet (Sweden) (National Radical Unity Party) 731
National Republican Guard (Portugal) 450, 457
National Security Battalions (TEA) (Greece) 568
National Socialist Bloc (1933–34) (Sweden) 723, 725, 729, 730
National Socialist German Workers Party 56
Nationalsocialistiska Arbetarpartiet (National Socialist Workers Party) (Sweden) 725, 728, 729
National Socialist Party of Macedonia – Thrace 571
ᐧ National Socialist Society of Helsinki 694
National Socialist Swiss Workers' Party 478
National-sozialistische Beamten-Arbeitsgemeinschaft (National Socialist Work Group) (Germany) 303
National Syndicalism (Spain) 63, 169, 421
National Syndicalism (Portugal) 461, 466, 756, 763, 776, 777
National Women's League (Switzerland) 471
National Unity Movement (Nationella samlingsrörelsen) (Sweden) 723
National Youth (Nationale Jugend) (Switzerland) 471, 763
National Youth Organisation (EON) (Greece) 577, 579
- membership 578

nation-liberal Hirsch-Durker unions (Germany) 86
NCO (Greece) 571
NDH (Croatia) 371, 372, 373, 374, 375, 376, 377
Nebe, A. 303, 308, 310
Netherlands 137, 138, 141, 143, 144, 146, 147, 148, 151, 156, 159, 160, 162, 171, 183, 184, 186, 298, 437, 503, 504, 506, 515, 524–41, 756, 760, 763, 773, 774, 776, 777, 778, 780, see Holland
Neumann, F. 12, 49, 107, 117, 285
Neumann, S. 68, 71, 72, 74–76, 81, 85, 92, 99, 107, 108, 299, 781
«New authoritarian right» 23
New Front (Neue Front) (Switzerland) 467, 477, 478
«New Life» (Austria) 234
New Party (Great Britain) 177, 554
Nicholls, J. 105, 781
Nietzsche, F. 69, 753
Nilson, S. 113, 180, 290, 299, 593, 619, 644, 645, 657–66, 786
Nisbet, R. 105, 106
Nitti 327, 332, 333
Noakes, J. 84, 102, 111, 117, 266, 297, 299
Nolte, E. 18, 19, 24, 28, 29, 44, 45, 47, 50, 176, 182, 187, 188, 200, 250, 253, 254, 256, 418, 422, 466, 467, 477, 498, 566, 781
Non-Giolittian Liberals (Italy) 321
Nonn 138, 139, 140, 151
Nordic People's Movement in Norway (Nordiske folkereisning i Norge) 667, 668, 670, 671, 675
Nordic School Youth Association (Nordiska Skolungdomsförbundet) (Sweden) 729
Nordiska Rikspartiet (NRP) (Nordic Reich Party) (Sweden) 740
Nordisk Ungdom (Nordic Youth) (Sweden) 725, 729, 763
Norges Nasjonalsosialistiske Arbeiderparti (NNSAP) (National Socialist party of Norway) 667, 670
Norges Samfundshjelp (Norway's Community Relief) 641, 649
Norse Legion 614

Norway 112, 117, 137, 141, 143, 145, 159, 161, 162, 168, 290, 366, 437, 519, 522, 586, 587, 588, 589, 590, 591, 592, 593, 595–678, 717, 722, 726, 730, 738, 741, 755, 756, 763, 769, 770, 773, 774, 776, 777, 778

Norwegian Farm and Forestry Workers Union 653, 664

Norwegian Industrial Association 677

Norwegian Medical Association (Læge-foreningen) 649

Norwegian Social Democratic Party, see Labour Party DNA) 590

NSDAP (Germany)
- as agents of mobilization 94–99
- election results 79, 81, 85, 108, 118, 121, 285
- election results – class/size cities 108, 109
- election results – region/occupation 109, 112
- election results – regional differences 286–89
- election results – rural arèa 112
- election results – urbanization 94–99
- election results – vs. other parties, catholics 296
- leadership – age 84
- leadership – education 84
- leadership – occupation 84, 765
- leadership – sex 84
- membership – age 768, 770
- membership – anti-Semitism, violence 279
- membership – geographical mobility 270
- membership – life experience 280
- membership – occupation 774
- membership – war experiences 271
- membership – year of joining 759, 766
- motives 268
- occupations 83, 84, 85, 111, 121
- representation – occupation 84

NSDAP (Austria) 206, 210, 232, 233, 235, 756, 763, 776, 777, 779, 780, see DNSAP (Austria)
- election results – regions 211, 212, 213, 224, 230
- leadership – occupation 231
- membership 214, 215
- membership – age, sex 220, 261
- membership – occupation 218, 219, 220, 231, 260
- militants – occupation 217
- representation – occupation 196, 217

NS-Student Federation (Germany) 307
Nyman, O. 717, 740
Nysvenska rörelsen (New Swedish Movement) 739

Oberschall, A. 108, 299, 300
Obriegkeitsstaat 66, 114
O'Duffy, E. 559, 560, 561, 562, 563, 564, 565, 566, 756, 763, 776, 777
Oehler, H. 468, 469, 470
O'Higgins, T. 559, 762
Ohlendorf, O. 308, 310
O'Lessker, K. 82, 110, 283, 300
Omodeo, A. 340, 347
ONR (Poland) 54, 756, 763, 775–77
Opitz, R. 46, 50, 130
opportunity space 298
order of the death's head (Order unter den Totenkopf) (Romania) 310
Ordnertruppe (Austria) 204, 205
Organisation Escherish (Orgesch) (Germany) 227
Organisation Kanzler (Orka) (Germany) 227
Organski, A. 17, 24, 29, 38, 117, 188
Orjuna/Zbor (Yogoslavia) 756, 763, 775, 776, 777
Orlow, D. 111, 180, 238, 266
Orwell, G. 543, 554, 759
Ostara (Austria) 205, 214, 223, 224
Ostmärkische Sturmscharen (the Ostmark Storm Bands) (Austria) 223
O.W.P. (Obóz Wielkiej Polski – Greater Poland Grouping) 356, 358, 776, 777
O.Z.N. (Obóz Zjednoczenia Narodowego – National Unification Grouping) (Poland) 357–58

Pais, S. 443, 458
pan-Americanism 182
Pangalos (General) 569, 570, 581
Panhellenic National Front (Greece) 573
Panunzio, S. 342, 347
Papagos (General) 574, 575, 576, 581
Papadopoulos 52, 575
paradigmatic Italian fascism 21
Parming, T. 179, 187
Parsons, T. 16, 24, 106

Parti National Populaire (Popular National Party) (Belgium) 504
Parti Populaire Français (PPF) 169, 479,
480, 490, 491, 492, 493, 494, 495, 500,
756, 760, 763, 773, 776, 777, 779
– leadership – occupation 491–93
– membership 495
– membership – occupation 774
Parti Socialiste National (France) 481,
491, 496
Partito Agrario (Italy) 322, 332, 333
Partito Economico (Italy) 322
Partito Nazionale Fascista (PNF)
– leadership – occupation 330
– membership 330
– membership – age 261
– membership – occupation 260, 774
– membership – year of joining 759
– representation 332, 333
Partito Popolare 315, 324, 325, 326, 331,
333, 779, 781
Party of Hungarian Life (MPE) (Hun-
gary) 398
Party of National Unity (Hungary) 398
Passchier, N. 264, 283–300, 326, 757, 787
Passikivi, J. 694, 699
«Patriotic Action» citizen's bloc (Vater-
ländische Aktion) (Switzerland) 468
Pattee, R. 377, 378
Pauley, B. 197, 201, 224, 225, 226–38,
787
Pavelić, A. 352, 361, 369, 371, 373, 378,
756, 763, 776, 777
Payne, S. 12, 14–25, 150, 179, 200,
418–34, 463, 466, 774, 783, 787
PCE (Spain) 181
PCF (France) 760
Peasant Party (Poland) 180
Peasant Party (Romania) 180
Peasant's League (Landbund) (Ger-
many) 193, 197, 212, 230, 235, 237,
250
Peasant Union (Latvia) 360
Peball, K. 224, 225
People's Liberation Movement (Croatia)
376
People's Party (Norway) 658
Perkonkrus 155, 179
peronism 55, 187
Persche, A. 231, 237
Pétain 422, 483
Petzina, D. 38, 49, 64
Pfrimer, W. 228, 229, 231, 235, 236

Pilsudski, J. 54, 354, 355, 356, 357, 359,
365
Pinard, M. 94, 114, 116
Pinon, R. 80, 110
Plastiras (General) 569, 570, 572, 573,
581
Plessner, H. 46, 130
PNV (Partido Nacionalista Vasco (Chris-
tian democratic Party) (Spain) 163,
183
Pohly, C. 84, 111
Poincaré 489, 494
Poland 54, 63, 137, 158, 161, 172, 180,
183, 185, 305, 352, 354, 355, 356, 357,
358, 359, 360, 364, 365, 380, 426, 522,
755, 756, 763, 772, 773, 775, 776, 777,
780, 783
Polen-Partei (Germany) 286
Polish National Party 54
Polish Socialist Party (PPS) 355
Pollock, J. 83, 110
Polsby, N. 46, 107
Popolari Italiano (PPI) (Italy) 156, 166,
180, 322, 328, 329, 332
Popular Party (Greece) 571, 572
Popular League for the Independence of
Switzerland (Volksbund für die Unab-
hängigkeit der Schweiz) 468
Popolo d'Italia 761
Portugal 44, 131, 132, 137, 146, 147, 148,
150, 151, 155, 158, 159, 162, 172, 178,
184, 418, 421, 422, 435–66, 506, 679,
756, 763, 776, 777, 783
Portuguese Catholic Center 463
Portuguese Legion 444
Portuguese national syndicalists 169
Pouget, E. 483, 498
Poujadist movement 520
Poulantzas, N. 15, 24, 463, 684
Poulsen, H. 593, 619, 702–15, 770, 787
Pratt, S. 108, 109, 290, 291
Preto, R. 169, 421, 461, 756, 763, 776,
777
Preussische Geheime Staatspolizei (the
Prussian Secret State Police) 303
Pridham, G. 111, 237
pro German clerical Lager (Austria) 194
Progressive Party (Iceland) 744
Proksch, A. 224, 231, 232, 235, 237
Protestant Party (Netherlands) 526
Protestant People's Party (Evangelische
Volkspartei) (Switzerland) 475
Protestant segment/pillar (Netherlands)
525, 526, 532, 533, 539, 541

«Protocols of the Elders of Zion» 394, 470, 478
Provasi, G. 319, 334
psychological explanations, *see* theories
psychosexual explanation, *see* theories
psychosocial theories, *see* theories
Puhle, H. 112, 113
Pulzer, P. 104, 117, 183
Päts 169, 362

Quadragesimo anno 250, 251, 252, 560, 562
Quisling, V. 114, 115, 177, 363, 568, 595, 597, 599, 600, 602, 606, 613, 614, 616, 617, 618, 619, 623, 628, 639, 640, 642, 643, 644, 645, 646, 650, 657, 658, 661, 662, 663, 664, 665, 666, 667, 668, 669, 670, 674, 675, 676, 677, 721, 741, 755, 756, 763, 776, 777

Radandt, H. 59, 64
Radical Democrats (Freisinn) (Switzerland) 473, 474, 475
Radicals (Denmark) 592
Radicals (Italy) 321, 322
Ramos, R. 157, 162, 169, 180, 182, 187, 189, 423, 432
Ránki, G. 400, 401–16, 787
Rasila, V. 685, 686
Rath, R. J. 197, 200, 201, 249–56, 787
Rassemblement National Populaire (RNP) (France) 479, 491, 493, 496, 497, 500, 756, 763, 776, 777
Raupach, H. 105, 297, 300
Rauschning, H. 84, 111
Raven-Thomson, A. 546, 555
«Red Biennum» (Italy) 324
Redier, A. 486, 756, 763, 776, 777
Rego, R. 449, 465
Reich, W. 16, 31, 32, 33, 48
Reichlandsbund (RLB) 89, 91, 761
Reichsbanner 772, 783
Reichshammerbund 189
Reichserbhöfe 60
Reichsicherheitshauptamt (Reich Security Main Office) (RSHA) 301–2
Reichswehr 123, 166
Renaud, J. 490, 495, 756, 763, 776, 777
Renner, K. 100, 200, 225
Republic of Salo 59, 63, 65
Republican («Agrarian») Party (Czechoslovakia) 367
Republican Schutzbund (Socialists' paramilitary) (Austria) 232

Republicans (Italy) 321, 322, 331, 336
Retail Clerks Union (Deutsche nationaler Handlungsgehilfenverband – DHV) 761
Rex (Belgium) 180, 186, 187, 420, 502, 503, 505, 506, 507, 508, 509, 510, 511, 513, 514, 515, 756, 763, 776, 777, 779, 783, *see* Christus Rex
– candidates – occupation 515
– election results 502
– membership 512
– membership – occupation 774
Rex-Brussels 522
Rex-Flanders 518, 522
Rex-Wallma 522
Rhallys, J. 568, 572, 573, 581
Rhodesia 52
Ribbentrop, J. 282, 361
ridimensionamento 18
Ridruejo, D. 431, 434
Riehl, W. 200, 202, 203, 210, 223, 224, 226, 227, 231, 235, 236, 237
Riemer, S. 283, 290, 300
Ringer, F. 115, 242, 247
Rinnovamento (Italy) 322
Rintala, M. 685, 686, 695, 699, 700
Risorgimento 163, 165, 345
Rittberger, V. 105, 108
Ritter, G. 24, 28, 106
Roberts, D. 259, 337–47, 584, 787
Robinson, R. 180, 433
Robles, G. 156, 185, 424, 433
Rodna Zachlita («home guard») (Bulgaria) 181
Rogger, H. 180, 188, 334, 394, 515, 775, 781
Rokkan, S. 12, 46, 95, 112, 113, 115, 131–52, 162, 200, 299, 462, 635, 636, 637, 645, 647, 649, 652, 715, 757, 761, 787
Roman Catholic Church 136, 164, 192, 233, 235
Romania 21, 54, 156, 158, 160, 163, 164, 167, 168, 172, 183, 184, 350, 351, 353, 359, 362, 363, 364, 365, 366, 379–94, 437, 756, 757, 763, 769, 773, 776, 777, 778, 783
Romanian Action Group 394
Romanian Legionary 24, 28, 106
Rosar, W. 200, 225, 237, 248
Rose, R. 115, 645, 666
Rosenberg, A. 50, 99, 282, 599, 666, 675, 677
Rosenberg, B. 106, 116, 619

Rossi, E. 64, 185
Rostow, W. 38, 50
Roth, G. 75, 108
Roveri, A. 335, 346
RSHA (Germany) 281, 308, 309, 310
Russia 17, 40, 120, 128, 181, 183, 185, 188, 235, 380, 381, 555, 586, 587, 680, 683, 688, 721, 722, 734, 744
Ruutu, Y. 690, 692, 694, 696
Ryszka, F. 358, 365
Räikkönen, E. 689, 692
Röhm, E. 216, 222, 306, 723, 759

SA (Germany) 129, 130, 157, 205, 207, 215, 216, 222, 228, 266, 273, 274, 277, 301, 303, 304, 305, 306, 308, 368, 654, 702, 709, 723, 758, 759, 761, 763, 772, 781, 783
SA (Austria) 231, 235
– membership 214
Sabbatucci, G. 181, 182, 335
Saladino, S. 322, 334
Salandra Liberals (Italy) 322, 328, 332, 333
Salazar, A. 155, 178, 421, 422, 435, 437, 438, 439, 443, 446, 455, 456, 457, 458, 461, 462, 465, 579
Salvatorelli, L. 29, 47, 165, 185, 259, 315, 316, 333, 336, 337, 338, 339, 343, 344, 345, 346, 347, 366
Salvemini, G. 266, 328, 335, 347
Salzgitter steel 59
Samfunnspartiet (Social Consciousness) (Norway) 592, 658
Samlingspartiet (Finland) 686
Sanacja (Poland) 354, 355
Santarelli, E. 338, 339, 346, 347
Sarić, I. 371, 374, 377
Sarti, R. 64, 188, 267
Sas, G. 15, 24
Sastamoinen, A. 739, 740, 742
Sauer, W. 17, 18, 25, 41, 46, 49, 50, 76, 108, 347, 422, 629, 646
Scandinavia 22, 91, 113, 138, 161, 171, 180, 183, 586, 588, 639, 640, 641, 679, 719, 736, 742
Schaffhausen National Community (Nationale Gemeinschaft) (Switzerland) 470
Schaffner, J. 469, 470
Schapiro, L. 49, 107, 256
Schausberger, N. 199, 201
Schellenberg, W. 734, 742
Schepens, L. 420, 501–16, 774, 787

Schmidhauser, J. 467, 477
Schmidt, W. 240, 244
Schmitter, P. 421, 435–66, 783, 787
Schnaiberg, A. 82, 110
Schober-Block (German national) 212, 213
Schoenbaum, D. 29, 41, 49, 50, 64, 86, 111, 117, 782
Schorske, C. 241, 246
Schulz, G. 44, 49, 105, 111
Schulz group (Austria) 194
Schulz, K. 210, 228, 229
Schumann, W. 51, 59, 64
Schumpeter, J. 101, 116
Schushnigg, K. 197, 215, 216, 223, 226, 229, 231, 232, 234, 237, 238, 245, 246, 249, 251, 252, 253, 255, 256
Schutzbund (Social Democratic Republican) (Austria) 214, 215, 216, 250, 775
Schwarz, R. 201, 225
Schweitzer, A. 37, 38, 41, 49, 50, 60, 65, 130
Schäfer, W. 83, 111, 283, 290, 291, 300, 765, 766, 781
Schönerer's movement (Austria) 199, 201
Scieder, W. 47, 49, 111
Scythe-Cross movement (Hungary) 395, 756, 763, 776, 777
SD (security service) (Germany) 265, 281, 301–11, 376, 378, 584
– leadership – occupation, age, war experience 308–9
– membership – age, occupation, education 308–9
– members – social background 309
SD – Ausland (Germany) 308
Sechi, S. 335
Second Spanish Republic 105
«Security Batallions» (Greece) 568, 570
Seidel, B. 47, 107
Selvstendighetspartiet (Independence Party) (Iceland) 593
Septemberlinge (opportunists) (Germany) 269
Servicio Español de Magisterio 433
Servicio Español de Profesorado 433
Seton-Watson, C. 37, 46, 49, 249, 253, 254, 256, 334
SEU (the Falangist student syndicate) (Spain) 426, 431, 433, 763
Seyss-Inquart 201, 216, 217, 225, 237, 245, 248
SFIO (Socialists) (France) 496, 497, 760

S.F.L.O. (France) 499
Shively, P. 83, 110
Sidonismo (Portugal) 458
Sidor, K. 376, 378
Silver Shirts (USA) 187
Sima, H. 392, 433
Simojoki, E. 692, 696, 698, 699, 700
Simon, J. 255, 499
Simon, W. 211, 212, 224
Simrak, J. 371, 374
Sinn Fein (Ireland) 557
Skodvin, M 619, 620, 656
Skylakakis 580, 581
Slovakia 156, 158, 161, 163, 171, 183, 185, 352, 361, 364, 367, 368, 369, 372, 373, 374, 375, 376, 378, 773
Slovak People's Party (HSPP) 367, 368, 374, 756, 763, 776, 777
– election results 182, 367
– leadership – occupation 368
Smallholders' Party (Hungary) 398, 399
Smetona, A. 357, 359, 360, 362
Smit, R. 299, 524–41, 760,788
Småhird (Norway) 602, 606
SNU (Swedish National Youth League) 641, 642, 649, 716, 717, 718, 730, 732, 739, 740
Social Catholics (Portugal) 462
Social Christian Party (Austria) 222, 223
Social-Christians (Christlichsoziale) (Switzerland) 474, 475
Social Democratic Labor Party (SAP) (Sweden) 592, 735, 738, 740
Social Democratic Party (Germany) 100, 126, 192, 209, 212, 213, 215, 216, 222, 223, 226, 229, 291
Social Democratic Party (Hungary) 396, 397, 399, 406, 407, 409, 410, 411, 412, 414, 415
Social Democratic Party (Iceland) 593, 744, 749
Social Democratic Party (Norway), see Labour Party (DNA)
Social Democratic Party (Netherlands) 526, 527
Social Democrats (Denmark) 592
Social Democrats (Finland) 592, 680, 681, 687, 696, 697
Social Democrats (Latvia) 360
Social Democrats (Switzerland) 469, 473, 474, 475, 775, 778–79
Social Democrat segment/pillar (Netherlands) 525, 526, 532, 533, 538, 539, 541
Socialist Lager (Austria) 192, 205

Socialist Party (Belgium) 502, 503, 505, 521
Socialist Party (PSI) (Italy) 318, 320, 321, 322, 324, 325, 326, 327, 329, 330, 331, 332, 333, 340
Socialist Party (Spain) 424
Socialist Party (Socialistiska Partiet) (Sweden) 734, 742
– election results 716
Socialist Trade Union Federation (CGL) (Italy) 262
Social-Reformists (Italy) 321, 322, 332, 333
Societá Luce (Croatia) 363
Sohn-Rethel, A. 37, 49
Solé-Tura, J. 250, 254, 465
Solidarité Française (corps France) 489, 490, 491, 494, 495, 499, 760, 763, 776, 777, 779
– membership 490
Sontheimer, K. 49, 105, 185
Sorel, G. 326, 479, 482, 483, 484, 753
Sotelo, C. 153, 179
Sottosegretariato per la Stampa e Propaganda (Italy) 362
Soucy, R. 188, 498
South Africa 52
Soviet Communist Party 668
Soviet Union 36, 63, 158, 181, 182, 247, 350, 359, 361, 370, 383, 460, 561, 590, 591, 614, 626, 630, 667, 668, 671, 684, 688, 689, 695, 696, 700, 733, 734, 742, see Russia
Sozialdemokratische Arbeiterpartei Österreichs 202
Sozialistische Partei Österreichs (SPÖ) 202
Spaak, P. 508, 513
Spain 22, 44, 63, 131, 132, 137, 138, 141, 142, 143, 145, 146, 147, 148, 150, 153, 154, 156, 159, 161, 162, 163, 168, 169, 172, 178, 179, 180, 181, 182, 185, 189, 192, 358, 365, 386, 418, 420, 421, 422, 423–34, 435, 563, 577, 755, 756, 761, 762, 763, 764, 777, 780, 783
Spann, O. 201, 233, 235, 237, 242, 243, 244, 245, 247, 250, 254
SPD (Germany) 85, 91, 102, 103, 113, 129, 180, 261, 272, 280, 285, 286, 290, 638, 738, 742, 767, 768, 769, 771, 772, 781, 783
– election results 80
– Reichsbanner 102
Special Security branch (Greece) 578

Spiro, H. 25, 106
Spitzenverbände (Germany) 79, 108
SPÖ (Austria) 767, 768
squàdristi (Italy)
– membership 759
Srbik, H. 240, 244, 245, 247
SS (Germany) 63, 65, 157, 215, 216, 217,
  222, 272, 277, 281, 303, 304, 306, 307,
  310, 311, 368, 369, 370, 759, 781
– membership 304
– motivations to join 309
– NSDAP-membership 309
SS (Austria) 234
– membership 214
– occupation 207
SS Totenkopf-Standarte 305
Stadler, K. 199, 200, 201, 214, 224, 225
St. Albert Foundation 369
Stahlhelm 237, 270, 273, 762, 772
Stalin 36, 55, 480, 687, 695, 734
Stambolisky 159, 181
Starhemberg, E. 194, 229, 232, 234, 235,
  236, 237, 252, 253, 255, 256, 756, 763,
  776, 777
Stegmann, D. 46, 49, 130
Steidle, R. 228, 231, 235
Stein 468, 474
Steiner, H. 129, 225
Steirischer Heimatschutz (Austria) 194,
  201, 236, see Styrian Heimwehr
Stengers, J. 183, 515, 517, 523
Stepan, A. 105, 108, 114, 115, 182, 333
Stephan, W. 81, 110
Stepinac, A. 371, 374, 377, 378
Stern, F. 47, 105, 115
Stern, J. 45, 781
Sternhell, Z. 188, 419, 422, 479–500, 753,
  774, 781, 788
Stokes, D. 286, 300, 556
Storm-Troopers (SA) (Germany) 262
straperlo (Spain) 168
Strasbourg theses (1928) 591
Strasser, G. 722, 723, 725
Streel, J. 507, 515, 522
Streicher, J. 394, 722, 723, 754
Sturmkorps (Austria) 234
Styrian Heimwehr (Steirischer Heimat-
  schutz) (Austria) 193, 195, 232
«Stände-Staat» 129, 243
Suckert, C. 342, 345, 347
Sudetendeutsche Partei (CS) 186
Sugar, P. 200, 238, 253, 255, 755, 781
Sundstrøm, B. 690, 694, 699

Svenska Folkets Väl (Swedish People's
  Welfare Party) 739
Svenska Nationalsocialistiska Frihätsför-
  bundet (Swedish National Socialist
  Freedom League) 724, 741, 776, 777
Svensk Opposition (Swedish Opposition)
  725, 729, 735
Svensk Socialistisk Samling (SSS – Swe-
  dish Socialist Unity) 719, 725, 729, 735
– election results 715
Svensk-Tyska Föreningen (Swedish-German League) 741
– membership 733
Sveriges Fascistiska Folkparti (Swedish
  Fascist People's Party) 724
– membership – occupation 724
Sveriges Fosterländska Förbund (Swedish Patriotic League) 732
Sveriges Nationalsocialistiska Folkparti
  (Swedish National Socialist Party)
  724, 727, 728, 756, 763
– election results 715
– election results – age 727
Sveriges Nationella Förbund (SNF, Swedish National League) 718, 722, 740
– election results 716
– leadership – occupation 721
Sweden 137, 141, 143, 144, 147, 148, 155,
  162, 186, 437, 586, 587, 588, 589, 590,
  591, 592, 594, 639, 640, 641, 642, 643,
  649, 652, 653, 692, 715–42, 755, 756,
  763, 769, 773, 776, 777, 778
Swedish Fascist Combat Organization
  (SFKO) 723, 724, 726, 727, 741
– membership – occupation 726
Swedish National Protection Squads
  (Svenska Nationella Skyddskåren) 719
Swedish National Socialist Farmers' and
  Workers' Party (Svenska Nationalso-
  cialistiska Bonde- och Arbetarpartiet)
  722, 724
Swiss Radical-Democratic Party 467
Switzerland 137, 141, 143, 144, 147, 148,
  155, 162, 192, 363, 420, 437, 467–79,
  754, 756, 761, 763, 769, 775, 777
Sylos-Labini, P. 260, 334
Szálasi, F. 395, 397, 400, 756, 763, 776,
  777
Szálasi's «Hungarist» 22, 169, 182
Szymansky, A. 330, 335
Sächsischer Landvolk (Germany) 286

Taittinger, P. 485, 486, 494, 756, 763,
  776, 777

Tannenbaum, E. 336, 338, 347
Tasca, A. 49, 50, 119, 129, 327, 335
Terboven, J. 599, 614, 615, 619, 651,
656, 666, 675, 722
Thalheimer, A. 43, 46
theories:
Agent theory of fascism
– agent of capitalism, big business,
monopoly capitalism, upper classes. Instrument capitalist system
14–15, 23, 36–38, 57, 59, 122–36,
436, 683
– Comintern, communist agent theory 46, 640 (see Marxist theories)
– NSDAP as agent of political mobilization in Germany 94–99
– fascist state as the agent for capitalism 43

Agrarian fascism
– support of fascism by farmers/
rural areas 283, 290, 327–30, 335,
442, 459, 475, 520, 534, 536, 538,
564–65, · 590, 613, 626, 628–29,
634–35, 664, 671, 679–81, 682,
683, 688, 693, 705, 708, 722,
737–38, 773, 777, 779

– agrarian fascism from above: reactions to mass mobilization, actions and unrest among small farmers in rural society 290, 328,
330, 335, 564, 565, 664, 671,
679–81, 683, 773, 777, 779

– agrarian fascism from below: crisis among small farmers, mobilization of small farmers 328–29,
335, 654, 565, 630, 631, 632, 633,
634, 635, 638, 643, 653, 662, 664,
671, 680, 681, 683, 773, 777, 779

– agrarian   parties/organizations
641–42, see Catholicism and fascism, Protestantism and fascism

Alliance theories of fascism
– alliance with upper classes
(church, industrialists, bureaucracy, military) 114, 264, 316–17,
439, 449, 472, 762, 764
– temporal alliance in common interest 59
– Faschismus als Bündnis 46
– NSDAP support as a deliberate
intentional and political act of
social groups 91–93

Alternative ruling élites (authoritarian
groups/regimes without mass mobilization) 352, 400, 421, 755, 780
Aesthetic underpinnings of German
politics (utilizing national culture)
20, 47
– aesthetic appeal of symbols, style
177, 189, 273–75
Accumulation of crisis syndrome (national building) 12, 46, 117, 131–52,
640
Accumulation of social tensions thesis
172
Anti-liberalism and anti-parliamentarism (distrust, wish for totalitarianism) 249, 345, 418, 421, 455, 476,
481, 575, 717–18, 719–21, 737
Anti-modernism (revolt against modernization, process involving, industrialization, secularization etc.)
18, 28–41, 42, 50, 103, 104, 338–39,
342–44, 385, 390, 391, 627–29, 644,
646, 737
Atomization: individuals from state 73
Atomization: groups for state 76, see
segmentation
Authoritarian personality, authoritarian discipline 16, 126, 276–80, 386
Authoritarian revolutions from above
451
– right authoritarianism 15, 22–23,
see alternative ruling élites
Availability of political space as basis
for growth (problem of late-comer)
153, 155, 156, 180, 225, 226, ' 325,
485, 526, 530, 535, 640, 672, 693,'
757
Bonapartism and fascism 29, 43, 46,
149, 151, 454
Borkenau's thesis of fascism as a developmental dictatorship 172
Breakdown of parliamentary regimes,
instability of democratic institutions
105, 168
– crisis of liberalism, parliamentary
democracy 600, 643
– political crisis of the State 272,
318–36, 340–42, 436, 455, 489,
496, 521, 538, 548, 558, 600, 757
– instability of liberal, democratic
regimes as basis for fascist growth
155, 169, 180
Capitalist system and fascism

- fascism and the process of capitalist concentration 167
- fascist success due to support from capitalists (big business) 264, 315, 424, 494, 495, 496, 507, 571, 578, 579, 643, 677, 683
- fascist success only possible with fall of capitalist economy 316
- Marxist theory of fascism as a product of capitalism (critics) 29, 170–73, 187–88, 250
- Marxist analysis of fascism and capitalism 449, 454, 544, 678, 687
Catholicism and fascism 426, 504, 507, 508, 535, 638
- rural communities among farmers 423, 426
- as obstacle to fascist success 164, 184–85, 213
- NSDAP-support immunized by Catholic influence/organizations 113
- fascist susceptibility among Catholic clergy 367
Class polarization and Party polarization 329, 404, 660
- in local area 631, 635, 637, 653–54
Class structure and fascism
- fascist success dependent on class disequilibrium 29
- outgrowth of intensified class animosities 99–103
- expression of the bent up frustration of the middle classes 99–103
Communist theory of social fascism 170, 171
Conservative interpretations 28
Continuity of fascism from before 1914 480, see «Yellow socialism»
Counter-revolutionary efforts and fascism
- Europe's syndrome of counter-revolutions 29
- of big business 205, 220
- preventive counter-revolution thesis 43
- reaction against liberal, democratic, political system 340–42, see alternative élites
Cultural crisis and fascism 16, 23, 163
- cultural and moral crisis 15
- Europe's moral disease 28
- pathological cultural tradition 29

- result of neurotic or pathological psycho-social impulses 15–16
- «escape from freedom»-thesis 163
- «search for community» 163
Democratic *Führer* personality 28
Decline in support radicalizes the movement 228–29, 420, 425, 510, 512, 518, 522, 540, 563, 694, 725
Destruction of society
- fascism as response to the destruction of society 75, 249
- as response to disintegration of society 74
- as disruption to communal life 106
- concept of social strain 113
Defeat in World War I as basis for fascist success 126, 158–59, 173–76, 181, 271–73, 328, 340, 382, 418, 421, 481, 571, 617, 640, 754, 755, 779, 780
Diffusion and imitations from Italy and Germany 176–78, 189, 353, 354–66, 456, 471, 504, 508, 517, 527, 560, 562, 682, 690, 694, 702, 707, 715, 717, 726, 727, 743–44, 749
Downgrading of the party after emergence to power 429
Economic crisis and growth of fascism 126, 167–68, 186, 187, 249, 269, 312, 328, 338, 436, 489, 501, 503, 505, 548, 558, 570, 589, 590, 597, 600, 617, 628, 631, 678, 688, 689, 693, 696, 707, 708, 717, 737–38, 743, 749, 755–57, 779
- crisis of capitalism 453
- fascist success in underdeveloped areas (countryside) 399, 459
- stages of economic development 170–73, 187–90
- stages of imperialist economy 59 *see* political development
Electoral system, elections
- fascism and electoral system 168–69, 187
- fascism and the timing of elections 168–69
«Extremism of the center» 12, 29, 52, 513, 646, 657, 665, 666
- fascism between capitalism and proletariat/socialist and their organizations 333, 337–38, 339, 520, 546, 655, 661, 766
- fascist success due to status barriers (between proletariat, bour-

geoisie and their organizations)
269–70, 290, 313, 315
Genesis of fascism 38
– «generic fascism» 14, 19, 20, 22,
27, 45, 418, 419, 420, 423, 466
– generic phenomena/category 21,
185
Growth of fascist regimes and implementation of their policies were
independent of their social support
313
Immunization mechanisms 115, *see*
working class immunization
Imperial ambitions, patriotic feelings
for Empire, national frustration
127–28, 161–63, 182, 549–50
Integral nationalism/pan-nationalism
153–55, 290, 316, 345, 425, 503, 506,
511, 513–14, 549, 588, 600, 617, 640,
682, 683, 688, 690, 692, 695, 707,
717, 719, 735, 736
Internal problems of plurality of
groups and leaders in each country
and fascist growth 169–70, 183
Late-comer *see* Availability of space
Left-wing activists recruitment to fascism 480, 483, 491, 492, 493, 496,
497
Loss of hegemony over the society of
the ruling classes produced fascism
454, 489, 571, 678, 683, 684, 687
– fascist success based on the crisis
of the state, and the loss of the
monopoly of violence («legitimacy vacuum») 165–66, 185
Marginality and fascist growth
– concept of marginality 239
– intellectuals and marginality as
social group 381, 391
– marginality of people in relation
to their social group 621, 736
– marginal people of all social
groups 546, 551, 553
– the role of individuals 236–48
a) legitimate fascism
b) breaking up democratic liberalism
Marxist theory of functional alternatives to fascism 170–72, 177–78.
Middle classes
– fascist success and the middle
classes 110, 203–4, 213, 221, 222,
259, 282, 290, 390–91, 405, 416,
420, 423, 427, 473, 480, 487, 506,

508, 514, 517, 535, 538, 544, 545,
590, 597, 606, 607, 610, 643, 655,
657, 665, 679, 681–82, 683, 720,
722, 765–66, 767
– the lower middle class thesis 109
– middle class extremism, *see* Extremism of the center
– middle class thesis today 29–31
– middle class fascism as revolt, not
revolution from a heterogenous
middle class 315
– petty bourgeoisie and fascism 314,
333, 337–47, 367, 397, 520, 546,
765–66, 776, 778
– moral predisposition of the middle classes 76
– social insecurity of the middle
classes 76
– unique radicalization of the middle classes 18
– downward mobility of the middle
classes 205
– fascist success by combined
appeal to middle class and unorganized working class 416

Multidimensional stress and opportunism 657, 665
– political outsiders and opportunists 341–42

Mass theory and mass society
– conformity and passivity more likely outcome of mass conditions
106
– fascist success due to their capture
and utilizing organizational structures 290–91
– losing representation and direct
contact with highest level of the
State 339
– mass society 46, 48, 66–117, 299,
312
– NSDAP support as a result of
weakening of internal cohesion
and the external bonds 86–91
– success of fascist regimes due to
ability to mass mobilize, bring
feeling of individual contact 313,
345
– sudden centralization processes
and its importance for massification 113
– timing of crucial waves of massification 71

- two-stage theory of massification (before and after Machtergreifung) 72, 74, 77
«Neighbors» and fascism:
  - absorbation of neighboring groups, parties 289, 294–98
  - competing with neighboring and similar parties 231, 315, 533, 539, 694
Non-voters and new voters 81–83, 213, 660–61
Political, economic development and fascist growth (stages of development and nation building) 16–17, 46, 390, 586–87, 735, 757, 761, *see* economic crisis
  - geopolitical model of fascism 131–52
  - late stage of industrialization 450–51, 737
  - NSDAP support caused by the rapid industrialization and disruption of society 117
  - stages of economic development 170–77, 187–88
Political ideology of fascism on organic, universalistic («whole») society 242
Populist reaction 341–42, 346, 382, 481, 520
Primacy of politics in fascism 117
Protestant religion and fascist support 213, 231, 290–94, 467, 671, 688, 690, 694–97, 733, 773
  - fascism and protestantism in rural areas (immunization) 637–38, 651–56
Proximity to German borders 468, 509, 510, 533, 535, 538, 630, 705, 707, 762
Proximity to Soviet Union 626, 630
Psycho-historical perspective: a feeling of «estrangement» 382–85
Psychological explanations 31–33
Psychosexual explanations 16
psychosocial explanations 29
Reactions to strong movements or to revolutionary events from Communist or Socialist 273, 313, 329, 338, 340, 383, 419, 422, 424, 560–61, 562, 571, 590, 600, 617, 629, 631, 640, 679, 680, 682, 683, 735, 744, 753, 755

Recruitment to fascist parties/movements and fascist voters
  - fascist leaders not of the same age as the members, but of the «first hour» generation 771
  - fascist organization: the higher social strata in the leadership and main party, the lower in the militia 214, 220, 221
  - fascist organizations: the higher strata formed the party, the lower filled the ranks 207, 220, 261–63
  - higher status formed the party, lower status filled the ranks 437, 538, 606, 608, 609, 611, 712
  - lagged recruitment of women to the party 603, 711
  - latest mobilized to fascism: old women in the countryside 603
  - lower middle class, working class recurited to the militia 309, 351
  - occupations:
    Railway and transport 208–09, 221, 367, 397, 402, 403, 487
    Technicians and engineers 440, 448, 488, 613, 671
    War veterans 205, 222, 328, 341, 342, 343, 358, 501, 503, 520, 561, 564, 565, 571, 575, 671, 726, 754, 755, 759, 762, 780
    see middle class, immunization of workers, agrarian fascism, students
  - recruitment to fascism through the family 608, 710
  - «second hour fascists» tend to be older than «first hour fascists» 769
Segmentation in society created favorable conditions for fascism
  - degree of direct and effective representation to highest level of state, combined with internal socialization and self-contained organization prevents fascist success 291–92, 298–99
  - fascist success as a result of segmental affiliations 198, 233, 298
  - high level of participation under conditions of superimposed segmentation 104
  - integral segmentation (Verzuilung) 513, 526, 532–33, 535, 537, 539, 641

- segmentation from above 78–79
Stability of fascist éites 215, 221
- continuation of the leadership 610
Status decline (loss of social status), downward mobility 167, 239, 249, 269, 312, 317, 324, 338–39, 341, 407, 615, 629, 756, *see* middle class
Strength of Jewish population 163, 183–84, 383, 415
Strength of minorities in state 383, 753, 778, 780
Student milieus, as locally and socially isolated, breed fascism 754
Totalitarianism thesis: Fascism equal/ parallel to Communism (movements/regimes/ideology) 33–36, 47, 69, 71, 85, 106, 107, 327, 350
- manifestation of totalitarianism of 20th century 17, 29
- Marxist use of fascism to all opponents 758
- unitotalitarian bias 34
Transcendence and fascism 17, 18, 184, 385, 390, 391, 392, *see* modernization, anti-modernization
- revolt against transcendence 36
Transition of fascism from a religious to a political movement 393
Weaknesses of the left and fascist growth 126, 331, 340
Working class immunization to fascism 215, 263, 283, 291, 317, 338, 367, 397, 400, 402, 407, 416, 420, 425, 473, 475, 481, 487, 492, 493, 508, 520, 537, 545, 546, 565, 606–07, 622, 657, 671, 768, 773, *see* mechanisms of immunization
Unemployment and fascist success 81–83, 548–49, 653, 719
- mass unemployment 480
- «the myth of the unemployed» 110
Urbanization vs. ruralization (stability) and fascist growth
- fascism and urbanization: the large cities and wealthiest areas 537
- fascism as originating in rural areas and spreading to the urban (where ethnic conflicts were present) 772
- fascist success in medium sized cities 291
- higher degree of urbanization, less fascism 294

- lag of rural mobilization compared to towns 706–07, 711, 712
- recruitment-process as spreading out from capital, and time-lag in peripheral regimes 622–623
«Yellow socialism»
- continuation of national syndicalism and «yellow socialism» 482
Young people, – student-recruitment as a result of lacking intergenerational transmission of political values and partisan allegiances 420, 443, 501
the partner theory 46
the personalistic interpretation 45
the psychohistorical approach 45
Theotokis 573, 575, 581
Third International (Communist International) 15, 28, 161, 590, 591
Thrace 568, 574
«three faces of fascism» 18, 498
Thyssen, F. 93, 264
Tilly, C. 46, 150
Tilton, T. 90, 112, 113
Tiso, J. 361, 368, 369, 374, 376
Tobler, R. 467, 468, 470, 478
Torgersen, U. 643, 649, 650
Torstendal, R. 718, 739, 740
Trevor-Roper, H. 249, 254
Tsaldaris 572, 574, 576
Tschernischeva, O. 738, 740, 741, 742
Tudjman, F. 376, 377, 378
Turati 342, 345, 347
Turin Industrial League 320
Turkey 158, 159, 357, 380, 383, 568, 569
Turner, H. Jr. 15, 18, 19, 24, 25, 29, 41, 44, 45, 46, 50, 63, 105, 113, 114, 115, 117, 150, 183, 184, 188, 264, 266, 267, 628, 645
«two faces of fascism» 18, 420

United Kingdom 88, 143, 144, 158, 162, 163, 168, 171, 175, 183, 186, 464, 542–56, 769, 770
Ukraine 120, 162, 185, 667, 721
Ulmanis, K. 179, 360, 362
Unge Høire (Conservative youth organization) (Norway) 643, 650
Unghird (Norway) 763
União Nacional (Portugal) 439, 445, 446, 461
Union Nationale (Switzerland) 469, 763
Union of Russian People 173, 188
Union of Young People (Poland) 763

814

Union Populaire de la Jeunesse Française 492, 763

Unión Patriótica (Spain) 425

United Lands and the March of Hungary 182

Urwin, D. 115, 618

USA 38, 39, 79, 88, 115, 147, 151, 159, 168, 182, 577, 641, 665, 666

USPD (Independent Social Democrat (Germany) 285, 286, 768

Ustasha from abroad (Croatia) 370, 371

Ustasha («Rising») Revolutionary Organization (Croatia) 369, 370, 371, 372, 373, 374, 375, 378, 756, 762, 763, 775, 776, 780 .

Vago, B. 182, 183, 184, 376

Vajda, M. 15, 24

Vallauri, C. 188, 325, 335

Valois, G. 479, 484, 485, 486, 487, 488, 489, 490, 494, 496, 497, 498, 499, 756, 763, 776, 777

van der Wusten, H. 299, 420, 524–41, 760, 788

van Geelkerken, C. 527, 529

van Severen, J. 182, 420, 504, 505, 506, 507, 511, 515

van Zeeland, P. 508, 518

Varain, H. 108, 114

Vargas 155, 169, 178, 187

Vatican 184, 362, 368, 369, 372, 373, 374, 378

Vaugoin, C. 201, 228, 229

Vaterländische Front (Austria) 238, 248, 254, 255

VdU (Austria) 194

Vedeler, G. 670, 676

Veniselos 568, 569, 570, 572, 573, 576

Venstre (Liberals) (traditional farmers' party) (Denmark) 707

Venstre (Liberals) (Norway) 592, 618, 636, 644, 652, 658, 659, 660, 663, 665, 667, 674, 677

Verdinaso (Verband van Dietsche Natio-naal-Solidaristen) (Federation of Dutch National-Solidarists) 420, 504, 505, 506, 508, 513, 514, 515, 779
– candidates – occupation 515
– membership 512

Vereinigte Aluminiumwerke 59

Vereinigung der christlichen-deutschen Bauernvereine 89

Vermeil, E. 28, 45

verspätete Nation syndrome 157

Verzuiling (Netherlands) 198, 298, 524, 525, 535, 538

Vichy 422, 482, 491, 492, 497

Vieja Guardia (Spain) 433

Viereck, P. 29, 44, 45

Vita-Finzi, P. 326, 335

Vivarelli, R. 327, 335, 338, 346, 347

Vlaamsche Nationale Militie (Belgium)
– membership 505

Vlaamsch Nationaal Verbond (Flemish National Federation) (V.N.V.) 420, 504, 506, 511, 513, 514
– membership 512

Vlaamsche Front or Frontpartij (Party of the Front) 503, 504, 505, 506

Voegelin, E. 107, 255

Vogelsang, Baron 241, 246

Vogt, B. 675, 676

Vojtaššak, J. 368, 374, 376

Volontaires Nationaux (France) 492

Volos 569, 576

Volpe, G. 326, 363

Von der Dunck, H. 512, 513, 515, 516

von Papen 93, 264, 303

von Schönerer, G. 193, 226, 231, 244

Vos, J. 540, 541

völkisch 115, 176, 181, 185, 189, 207, 209, 210, 226, 244, 266, 272, 273, 275, 276, 737, 753, 754, 757, 761

Völkisch-sozialer Block (Austria) 211

Wabse (Estonia) 155

Wache, K. 223, 236

Waffen SS (Germany) 614, 707, 734

Wahlbäck, K. 685, 686

Waite, R. 45, 266

Wallef, D. 420, 517–23, 774, 788

Wallerstein, I. 140, 146, 148, 149, 150, 151

Wandruszka, A. 192, 199, 224, 248, 254

Waterlow (the British Minister at Athens) 574, 575, 577, 579, 582, 583, 584

Weber, A. 109, 111, 121, 129

Weber, E. 18, 21, 25, 50, 69, 151, 180, 183, 188, 334, 379, 390, 394, 422, 477, 515, 516, 554, 775, 781

Weber, M. 79, 107, 108, 110, 188, 247, 388

Weerafdeling W.A. (defense section) (Netherlands) 539

Weinzierl, E. 199, 201, 254

Weissbecker, M. 44, 51

Welk, W. 64, 65

Whiteside, A. 188, 199, 223, 236, 775
Wilson, S. 161, 498
Winkler, H. 37, 38, 47, 48, 50, 88, 100,
  111, 113, 114, 115, 116, 117, 129, 184,
  225, 266, 646, 666, 742
Winter, E. 253, 256
Winterhilfe 234
Wipperman, W. 44, 46, 187, 687, 697,
  698
Wirtschaftspartei des deutschen Mittel-
  standes 96, 108, 109, 285
Wirtschaftsgruppe Maschinen 60
Wolf, W. 467, 477
Woolf, S. 24, 37, 44, 49, 117, 188, 199,
  200, 253, 254, 335, 394, 465, 466, 554,
  781
Workers' Brigade (Romania) 392
Wyller, T. 115, 619
Württemberger Bauern- und Win-
  gärtnerbund 286
Wysocki, A. 360, 365
Wärenstam, E. 715, 738, 739, 740, 741,
  742

«Yellow» socialism 482, 654
Young Farmers (Switzerland) 475

Young Liberals (Jungfreisinnige) (Switzerland) 467
Young Plan 264
Young Nationalist (Sweden) 763
Young Socialist Guards (Belgium) 505
Yugoslavia 158, 161, 166, 172, 185, 192,
  210, 215, 227, 231, 352, 359, 360, 362,
  364, 366, 369, 370, 373, 376, 377, 630,
  754, 756, 763, 772, 776, 777, 778, 780,
  783

Zawodsky, F. 247, 555
Zeiss-Konzern 64
Zentrum party (Germany) 81, 121, 155,
  156, 180, 285, 289, 291, 295, 297, 771,
  782, see Catholic Zentrum
Zernatto, G. 234, 238, 255, 256
Zetkin, C. 15, 24
Zipfel, F. 301–11, 788
Zoberlein, K. 467, 477
Zweig, S. 240, 246

Österreichische Volkspartei 194
Österreichischer Heimatschutz 194

Date Due